THE OXFORD ENCYCLOPEDIA OF
ECONOMIC HISTORY

THE OXFORD ENCYCLOPEDIA

OF

ECONOMIC

HISTORY

Joel Mokyr

Editor in Chief

VOLUME 3

Human Capital

—

Mongolia

OXFORD

UNIVERSITY PRESS

2003

OXFORD

UNIVERSITY PRESS

Oxford New York

Auckland   Bangkok   Buenos Aires   Cape Town   Chennai
Dar es Salaam   Delhi   Hong Kong   Istanbul   Karachi   Kolkata
Kuala Lumpur   Madrid   Melbourne   Mexico City   Mumbai   Nairobi
São Paulo   Shanghai   Taipei   Tokyo   Toronto

Copyright © 2003 by Oxford University Press, Inc.

Published by Oxford University Press, Inc.
198 Madison Avenue, New York, New York 10016
www. oup.com

Library of Congress Cataloging-in-Publication Data
The Oxford encyclopedia of economic history / Joel Mokyr, editor in chief.
p. cm.
Includes bibliographical references and index.
ISBN 0-19-510507-9 (set)
ISBN 0-19-517090-3 (v. 1: alk. paper)
ISBN 0-19-517091-1 (v. 2: alk. paper)
ISBN 0-19-517092-X (v. 3: alk. paper)
ISBN 0-19-517093-8 (v. 4: alk. paper)
ISBN 0-19-517094-6 (v. 5: alk. paper)
1. Economic history–Encyclopedias. I. Title: Encyclopedia of
economic history. II. Mokyr, Joel. III. Oxford University Press.
HC15 .O94 2003
330'.03–dc21

2003008992

1 3 5 7 9 8 6 4 2
Printed in the United States of America
on acid-free paper

Common Abbreviations Used in This Work

AD	*anno Domini*, in the year of the Lord
ASEAN	Association of Southeast Asian Nations
b.	born
BCE	before the common era (= BC)
c.	*circa*, about, approximately
CE	common era (= AD)
CEO	chief executive officer
cf.	*confer*, compare
d.	died; penny (pl., pence)
diss.	dissertation
EC	European Community
ed.	editor (pl., eds), edition
EEC	European Economic Community
EU	European Union
f.	and following (pl., ff.)
FAO	Food and Agriculture Organization
FDI	foreign direct investment
fl.	*floruit*, flourished
FTA	free trade area
GATT	General Agreement on Tariffs and Trade
GDP	gross domestic product
GNP	gross national product
G-10	Group of Ten industrialized countries
IMF	International Monetary Fund
ISI	import-substitution industrialization
l.	line (pl., ll.)
LDC	less developed country (pl., LDCs)
MDC	more developed country (pl., MDCs)
MFN	most-favored nation
MITI	Ministry of International Trade and Industry (Japan)
MNC	multinational company (pl., MNCs)
n.	note
NAFTA	North American Free Trade Association
NBER	National Bureau of Economic Research
n.d.	no date
NGO	nongovernmental organization
no.	number
n.p.	no place
n.s.	new series
OECD	Organization for Economic Cooperation and Development
OEEC	Organization for European Economic Cooperation
OPEC	Organization of Petroleum Exporting Countries
p.	page (pl., pp.)
pt.	part
r.	reigned
R&D	research and development
rev.	revised
s.	shilling
SEC	Securities and Exchange Commission (United States)
ser.	series
supp.	supplement
UNESCO	United Nations Educational, Scientific, and Cultural Organization
UNRRA	United Nations Relief and Rehabilitation Administration
USD	U.S. dollar(s)
USSR	Union of Soviet Socialist Republics
vol.	volume (pl., vols.)
WHO	World Health Organization
WIPO	World Intellectual Property Organization

THE OXFORD ENCYCLOPEDIA OF
ECONOMIC HISTORY

H

(CONTINUED)

HUMAN CAPITAL. Human capital can be defined as the embodied flow of human services in the individual human agent. In this regard, a human being is comparable to machinery or to animal livestock that can provide productive services not just once but over an extended period of time. Valued as a capital asset, the price of a human being should vary according to the expected time profile of the value of labor services provided and the value of maintenance costs required to keep the person in service. This concept of the human being as embodying a flow of labor services has been evidenced, in the existence of markets for chattel slaves throughout human history. Evidence from the antebellum Southern United States indicates that the price of a slave varied according to the expected future flow of profits he or she would provide. The concept has also surfaced in Anglo-Saxon law in compensation for loss of life, in early modern attempts to estimate the contribution of labor to national income, and in the market for life insurance.

The human capital concept can also be defined in terms of the cost of the investment required to produce a productive human agent rather than in terms of the value of the services provided. Both rearing costs, as evidenced, for example in long-term trends in nutrition levels, and health investments have considerable significance for the economic history of labor as a productive agent. To provide one brief example, Dublin and Lotka (1930, pp. 128–129) estimate that the increase in mean length of life expectancy at birth in the United States for males from 47.9 years in 1901 to 57.9 years in 1927 raised the present value of lifetime earnings of a man by about 5 percent.

Biological survival is a necessary condition for obtaining the services of a worker, so obviously health and nutrition come into play in considering investment in human capital. However, the concept of human capital has been most commonly associated with investments in schooling, skill, and related means of improving the cognitive and judgmental abilities of the human agent beyond provision for basic health. The rest of this entry will focus on this aspect of human capital.

The underlying principle behind the concept of investment in human capital is that by forgoing certain earnings and consumption opportunities at one point in time, the human agent can become more productive later. Some experiences are more prone to develop skill and cognitive capabilities than others. In the presence of labor mobility, tasks involving such experiences should be able to attract labor at lower rates of compensation than tasks that do not. Hence the acquisition of skill entails sacrificing present earnings in order to gain employment in such experiences; to that degree it requires a capital investment. Other influences such as native ability and social connections certainly also affect earnings. And critics of human capital approaches to labor productivity and earnings have argued that a variety of possible institutional and incentive arrangements other than the impact of human capital investments could result in a worker's earnings profile that rises with experience. However, putting these other factors to one side, under a pure human capital framework the discounted flow of enhanced future earnings would be exactly equal to the present value of forgone past earnings differentials incurred to acquire these experiences. Thus, from a pure human capital perspective, the difference between skilled and unskilled labor reflects the extent of past earnings sacrificed in order to enhance future earnings.

Role of the Family in the Production of Human Capital. Simply as a result of trial-and-error learning stemming from experience, the human agent is likely to improve in productivity with age. However, not only are some experiences more likely to enhance future productivity than others, but survival of the human species is also enhanced through avoiding life-threatening experiences while pursuing those most likely to augment the value of future productivity. There is a pervasive tendency for adult humans as with adults in some animal species to educate their young offspring in basic survival skills and in ways of getting a living more generally. In modern hunting and gathering and subsistence agricultural societies children are given tasks and situations that cultivate skills and knowledge that will aid in survival. Activities for developing food procurement and subsistence skills in the young in hunting and gathering and low-technology agricultural societies seem commonly to be based on supervised and structured activities rather than on unsupervised trial-and-error experiences. An emphasis on tradition and custom in these societies can be accounted for by the risk to survival of trial-and-error experimentation in educating the young in subsistence skills.

One can conjecture that tradition formed the basis of education as well in prehistoric hunting and gathering and subsistence agricultural societies. The family was well situated to influence the immediate range of experiences encountered by the child and maturing adolescent and so to guide the process of learning. It could have provided protection during the time when the child was most vulnerable. The family also had incentives to develop the productive capacity of the child. These incentives stemmed not only from altruism, but also because the family might use some of the future enhanced flow of services of the child later—for example, to support elderly parents. However, poverty could weaken the willingness of parents to sacrifice current consumption for future productivity of their children; also, low life expectancy would lower the expected benefits from children's support during old age. With the advent of written legal codes, some provision seems to have been made to enforce the expectation that parents would educate their children in exchange for future support when elderly. For example, there are reports from ancient Greece of a law of Solon that exempted children who had not been trained in a trade from supporting their parents in old age.

As specialized occupations developed in ancient societies they were commonly passed on from father to son. In the Code of Hammurabi dating back to 2000 BCE in Mesopotamia, the contractual relationship between a master workman and a trainee receiving instruction was one of legal adoption. This feature of the code has been interpreted as according legal recognition to the hereditary and familial nature of the transmission of trades. In the medieval Italian apprenticeship contracts surveyed by Steven A. Epstein (1991, p. 105), a substantial proportion of apprentices were the masters' own children. And high rates of intergenerational occupational inheritance continue to be in evidence throughout the world in modern times. The phenomenon of occupational inheritance from father to son can be attributed in some degree to genetic inheritance and to passing on of an established business as a means of conveying wealth. However, the ease of transmitting the skills required in a family setting is surely also an important consideration.

Market Provision of Human Capital. With the development of occupational specialization and with changes in the composition of demand for various types of occupations, situations were likely to arise in which young people or their parents would seek to acquire skills for occupations more in demand than those of the parents. Thus, not surprisingly, there is evidence from ancient times on of a private market in skill instruction. Apprenticeship regulations in the Code of Hammurabi include the provision that if the adopting master did not teach the boy apprenticed his trade, the boy could return to his natural father's house. And Plato and Xenophon describe instruction for hire in particular crafts in ancient Greece.

For those who could not directly pay for instruction, provision was made for the trainee to work for an employer in exchange for training received. Thus, apprenticeship documents from Roman Egypt distinguish between teaching contracts in which the teacher of the craft received monetary payment for providing instruction and apprentice contracts in which the provision of instruction took the form of a quid pro quo for the use of the apprentice's labor. Work performed for which the trainee was not paid would compensate for training expenses and also provide an implied loan during periods of low productivity while receiving training. In thirteenth-century Genoese contracts studied by Steven Epstein (1998, p. 128), apprentices were often not paid in their first one or two trial years and received payment only with more experience and presumably an increase in their productivity. In thirteenth-century Paris, terms of apprenticeship for a given trade could vary with a larger initial payment on entry resulting in a shorter term of service than if a smaller payment or no payment was made on entry. For example, in the wool guild an entry fee of eighty sous required four years of apprenticeship, an entry fee of sixty sous required five years, and seven years of service was required if no entry fee was paid; see Steven Epstein (1991, p. 144).

Apprenticeship contracts were often quite vague about specifying any standard of instruction to be provided in the craft in question. Thirteenth-century Genoese contracts studied by Epstein (1991, p. 108) simply referred to teaching the apprentice "as is the custom." One printed form for apprentice indenture used in the United States in the 1830s and reprinted by the U.S. Department of Labor (1964, p. 10) specified that "the said master shall use the utmost of his endeavors to teach, or cause to be taught or instructed, the said apprentice in the trade or mystery of [blank to be filled in]...." However, one apprentice contract for a tanner quoted in the same source (p. 13) specifies tasks that the apprentice is to be allowed to attempt, including the "privilege of tanning and curring six calves skins and two large sizes only tan'd." Rappaport (1989, p. 235) cites instances of London masters who were fined or even dismissed from livery because they provided inadequate instruction for their apprentices.

Market provision of education emerged in agricultural societies as well as in the training of urban artisans. In early modern Europe, the institution of service developed in rural areas whereby adolescents would contract out for terms of work to households other than their parents, receiving support and training in exchange for the work they provided. Some accounts have suggested that service of this sort bore affinities to the institution of apprenticeship.

Informal versus Formal Methods of Human Capital Development. Apprenticeship involved explicit provision for instruction and training even if the standard of instruction was often unspecified. And tasks assigned to the apprentice tended to progress from the less skilled to the more skilled. However, workers have also commonly acquired skills on the job simply by observation and imitation of other workers, with no explicit time set aside for learning and with progression to more skilled tasks determined by the abilities of the trainee. In late Victorian England two such informal arrangements—following up and migration—were commonly distinguished from formal apprenticeship. Following up entailed assigning the trainee as an assistant to an experienced worker. While providing assistance, the trainee also had an opportunity to observe and begin to master the tasks involved in the regular occupation. This method was common in English cotton textile spinning as well as in iron and steel manufacture during the nineteenth century. Migration consisted of rotating the trainee from task to task and firm to firm in order to make the trainee familiar with the range of tasks required in a particular occupation. This method of training appears to have been common in various machine-tending occupations such as mechanized shoe and boot making, in the Birmingham metal work trades, and in railroad work.

Younger workers do appear to have been willing to accept a cut in earnings in order to acquire training informally, as is argued in H. M. Boot's study (1995, pp. 283–303). Boot compares boys who began work at age ten in a cotton mill with those who were laborers in brickyards and those who began work in a coal mine at the same age. He estimates that by the age of fifteen, a boy working in a cotton factory would have sacrificed earnings relative to that in a brickyard with a net present value of 5.2 English pounds. In compensation, at his peak earning age of thirty-five, the cotton worker would have earned 2.3 times the wage of a brickyard laborer, a premium that can be estimated at 33.8 English pounds per year.

However, in other instances youths appear to have been unwilling to sacrifice present earnings for training opportunities. In early-twentieth-century Britain, social observers raised concerns that relatively intelligent adolescents were forgoing skilled apprenticeship programs to take messenger boy and other service occupations that on entry paid higher wages but that turned into a blind alley in terms of subsequent career prospects. They attributed the choice of such blind-alley employment by relatively able youths to the unwillingness of their parents to sacrifice their children's relatively high earnings of the moment.

There has been a recurring tension in the history of training in various occupations and professions regarding whether the learner should begin with full-time instruction in basic principles of the craft or profession or whether learning should primarily be grounded in the accumulation of experience in practical activity. The history of both legal education and medical education provides striking illustrations of this tendency. In western Europe, university faculties in both law and medicine can be traced back to the Middle Ages. However, substantial components of apprenticeship to experienced practitioners have also characterized training in both professions from the Middle Ages through to the present day. The tension between theory and practice is evident in many other spheres as well. In considering the proper preparation for the skilled worker in manufacturing, employers in Victorian England were noted for emphasizing the importance of practical on-the-job experience. However, in late-nineteenth-century Germany, a system of technical secondary schools was developed to provide instruction in basic science for those aspiring to become shop-floor foremen in manufacturing firms. National differences with regard to theoretical versus practical training have also been noted in the area of managerial and business education.

Types of Human Capital: Specific Skills versus General Abilities. There is a long intellectual tradition of advocating the advantages of specialization and division of labor based on the principle that a person can do a given task more effectively by concentrating on that task and continually repeating it rather than by doing a wide range of tasks. However, how long can the task can be repeated before proficiency gains are exhausted, and how steep is the learning curve while proficiency gains are present? Boot's evidence on cotton textile spinning in early-nineteenth-century Lancashire, cited above, suggests extensive gains in proficiency over a period of years, though Boot argues that only a narrow range of skills was involved. But in other situations the proficiency gains may have been minimal and exhausted in a matter of weeks or even days.

In some settings skill can entail primarily the mastery of a diverse range of tasks related to a particular production process. The requisite for this versatility can be small-scale production in which the worker will have to perform diverse tasks to keep fully occupied. This mastery of a range of tasks may account for periods of apprenticeship of several years to master a given trade. Looking at this from the other side, the process of division of labor has often been termed de-skilling or dilution. The process of de-skilling or dilution provides a way of identifying the components of skilled mastery of a complex of tasks.

One example is in the changes made in skills and length of training expected of U.S. shipyard workers during World War II. Prior to the war, a four-year apprenticeship entailing the mastery of some forty to seventy skilled operations was common for those engaged in shipyard crafts. The increased volume of production during the war facilitated standardization of construction and the specialization of a given worker on a narrower set of operations and tasks. This specialization in turn facilitated the increased employment of women in shipyards, who could be trained in a few months or even a few weeks because of the limited range of operations each performed.

One can distinguish between the return to general workforce experience and occupation-specific experience. Eichengreen (1984, pp. 822–834) found that male workers tended to have a higher earnings premium on years of work experience of all kinds while female workers had a higher premium on experience in a given occupation. However, we can also distinguish between experience and knowledge specifically relevant to the workplace and the development of general intellectual powers, which can be applied in a diverse range of situations.

One place where the contrast between specific knowledge and general intelligence and versatility is evident is in farmer adaptation to changing circumstance. On the one hand, successful farming requires familiarity with local growing conditions, including knowledge of soils, climate, and suitable crop and livestock varieties. This can account for the tendency for farmers in the early- and mid-nineteenth-century United States to migrate primarily in an east-west direction within certain latitudinal bounds. On the other hand, studies of farmers in both the United States and developing countries in the twentieth century have commonly found that farmers with higher levels of formal (i.e., classroom) schooling are more likely to make optimal responses to changes in their economic environment. These studies have also found that increased change in economic environment such as an acceleration in technical change increased the economic returns to schooling for farmers.

Whether and why classroom schooling should cultivate general intelligence and related competencies rather than simply specific types of skills is more problematic. One view involving intangible aspects, put forward by T. W. Schultz, is that classroom work develops problem-solving abilities with general properties that contribute to the allocative and entrepreneurial performance of economic agents. Another view, put forward by Adam Smith, emphasizes that the actual skills commonly taught in classroom schooling, such as basic literacy, accounting, geometry, and mechanics, tend to be of general applicability in a range of economic settings.

Government funding of general primary education has primarily been justified on grounds that society at large benefits from a more educated populace in ways not perceived by individual parents and children, who thus make socially suboptimal choices about levels of educational investment. This motivation for human capital investment applies not only to formal schooling, however. Social assimilation benefits were also used to justify government regulation of apprenticeship in early modern England.

The social externalities would seem to be weaker with regard to vocational training. The private return to such training would seem to provide incentives for their acquisition without government subsidy. It has been argued that liquidity constraints result in underinvestment by potential trainees and require employer funding to overcome. However, a given firm should be reluctant to incur costs of providing training of general economic value to its workers because those workers may then be poached by other firms. Moreover, some advocates of vocational training argue that a structured curriculum for training that integrates on-the-job training with classroom and company instruction in vocational and technical subjects is required for the effective development of skills. Countries in which structured vocational training has been most successful, such as Germany and Japan, seem to have included extensive participation by the various stakeholders involved: firms, unions, and governments, as well as the employees receiving the training. But they seem to have roots in historically based alliances at the local level between the various groups. Establishing generally recognized standards for performance and proficiency may be key to making these standards work. In the absence of such locally based institutional support, efforts at implementing structured training schemes have foundered in the United States and Great Britain.

Challenges to Human Capital Interpretations. As noted in the introduction to this essay, critics of the human capital perspective argue that earnings rise with experience for reasons other than the impact of learning on raising productivity. In the case of guilds fees for training may have been used primarily as barriers to entry to maintain monopoly premiums in earnings as much as compensation for training actually provided. Rising age-earnings profiles in more informal training settings such as in cotton textiles during the English industrial revolution have been interpreted as providing incentives to long job tenure so that firms could obtain good work effort in the presence of monitoring problems. A positive association between earnings and training time could also reflect processes of screening and signaling for workers with higher ability rather than reflecting actual improvements in productivity from training. Both human capital forces and nonhuman capital incentive arrangements are likely to have been behind observed rising experience-earnings profiles, with their relative importance subject to considerable variation over time and space. Yet granting these reservations, experience and training have still been important forces contributing to improvements in worker productivity throughout history.

Long-Term Trends in the Accumulation of Human Capital. The family has always been an important agency

VOCATIONAL TRAINING. Trainees at the Underprivileged Childrens' Education Programme (UCEP), a non-governmental organization that works with poor children. UCEP trains children in specific areas such as garment manufacturing and mechanics, Bangladesh, 1998. (© S. Noorani/Woodfin Camp and Associates, New York)

of human capital formation. Private apprenticeship arrangements appear to have peaked in importance, at least in western Europe, during the early modern period. A remarkable development over the last two centuries has been the rising importance of formal schooling as a source of human capital formation. Some degree of confidence in the ability of classroom instruction to cultivate general intelligence would seem to underlie this trend. According to UNESCO statistics, by 1958 some 53 percent of the population over the age of twenty-five in some fifty-five countries reporting had completed six years of primary schooling. By 1979 this figure had risen to 69 percent. The percentage in the same sample countries completing secondary schooling rose from 9 percent to 23 percent, and for tertiary schooling from 2 percent to 5 percent. Comparable percentages for the period around 1800 for such a broad sample of countries are not available. However, there is little reason for doubt that schooling levels were dramatically lower then.

Whether the spread of formal schooling represents a large net increase in human capital accumulation over time depends on the learning value attached to alternative activities during childhood and adolescence. The fact that more and more societies have chosen to allocate an increasingly greater proportion of childhood and adolescence to formal school attendance indicates a perception that schooling markedly increases the human capital

stock. Rising life expectancy and falling fertility have also increased the average age of populations; given the role of experience in producing more human capital these should also have contributed to human capital stock increases. Still, as larger shares of some populations move beyond years of peak productivity, allowance should be made for net depreciation of the human capital stock as well.

Human Capital Accumulation and Economic Growth. Insofar as labor has accounted for a sizable share of output and has generally received estimated returns of at least the same order of magnitude as physical capital, considerable increases in the human capital stock should make significant contributions to economic growth. In countries such as the United States and Canada, whose labor forces have become much better educated during the last century, growth accounting estimates indicate that education can account for between 15 and 25 percent of output growth. However, for many European and Latin American countries, where the increase in educational attainment has been more modest, the share of economic growth explained by education is well under 10 percent.

This simple view of human capital accumulation contributing to economic growth by augmenting labor productivity should be modified to obtain a more realistic view. How has human capital influenced growth rates in the past? First, allowance should be made for the contribution of factors other than human capital. It is possible that sizable output growth can occur without sizable increases in the human capital stock. England, during its industrial revolution between 1780 and 1840, experienced a notable acceleration in economic growth yet displayed little evidence of improvement in the educational attainments of its workforce.

Second, one of the principal channels through which human capital is commonly thought to influence economic growth is through increasing the rate of technological advance. This mechanism in turn implies that high but unchanging levels of human capital capable of advancing technology can lead to high rates of economic growth. It also implies that high rates of technological advance can raise the contribution of human capital to economic growth even in the absence of ongoing increases in human capital investments. We should also consider which groups in an economy are most likely to influence technological advance and what specific forms their human capital investments should take. One prominent historical case concerns the claim that Victorian England's decline from technological preeminence in manufacturing was due in significant degree to the limited education of its shop-floor foremen compared with the superior technical training received by their counterparts in Germany.

A third consideration is that rather than human capital investment in specific skills, investment that influences general decision-making ability may have the greatest aggregate impact on growth rates and this may depend on how broadly the opportunity for decision making is spread. The implication is that because agriculture offers more opportunity for decision making and lack of concentration of farm management authority also spreads opportunities for decision making, general human capital investments are more important in such settings. This would explain why education played a prominent role in the spread of improvements in rice cultivation in Meiji Japan or high yielding varieties in the green revolution in India in the 1970s and 1980s. Both cases involved small-scale farming.

One pervasive area of decentralized decision making is the household. Women as household managers and mothers have a distinctive role to play in this regard. There is evidence from late-twentieth-century developing countries that women's education improved their capacity in household tasks and child rearing. For example, children of more educated mothers are likely to have lower rates of infant and child mortality. Improvements in women's human capital have thus led to substantial improvements in human development, even if they are not apparent in market-based measures of national income or in cross-country regressions of determinants of economic growth based on such measures. Improvements in medical and public health knowledge would appear to have contributed to increasing the social returns to women's education, thus supporting the principle that increasing rates of technical advance increase returns to human capital.

A fourth consideration is that the level of human capital may contribute to increasing the rate of catch-up or convergence to some international technological or productivity standard. Economies with lower levels of human capital may actually experience higher rates of economic growth during some periods because of greater catch-up opportunities. Tsarist Russia by some accounts would fall into this category. In the late nineteenth century, its level of mass education was low and its agriculture backward. However, it was able to employ foreign technological expertise to adopt advanced technologies and undergo rapid development of its manufacturing sector. In sum, history points to a variety of channels through which human capital can influence economic growth.

Human Capital and Economic History. The concept of human capital points to two recurring phenomena in economic history. First, markets have recognized that the individual worker provides a flow of services over his or working life. This has been manifested in a variety of forms, ranging from the pricing of chattel slaves in the antebellum American South to modern court awards for wrongful death cases. Second, willingness to sacrifice income at younger ages provides opportunities to enhance productivity at later ages. The nature of these opportunities has varied widely, from a daughter learning her mother's cooking secrets to obtaining an advanced degree in physics, reflecting the protean nature of human capital investments. Individual investments in human capital can have a variety of consequences for aggregate rates of economic growth. Thus human capital provides both an important underlying principle and a powerful source of diversity in the study of economic history.

[*See also* Apprenticeship; Education; Health; Labor Productivity; Literacy; *and* Mortality.]

BIBLIOGRAPHY

Anderson, C. Arnold, and Mary Jean Bowman, eds. *Education and Economic Development*. Chicago, 1965. A collection of influential papers presented at a conference on the relation between education (as well as human capital more generally) and economic development. It has the virtue of covering differing time periods and geographical areas with papers employing diverse methodological approaches.

Becker, Gary. *Human Capital: A Theoretical and Empirical Analysis, with Special Reference to Education.* 3d ed. Chicago, 1993. The seminal exposition of the human capital concept.

Blaug, Mark. *An Introduction to the Economics of Education*. London, 1970. An insightful, critical survey of both empirical and theoretical studies employing the human capital concept.

Blaug, Mark. "The Empirical Status of Human Capital Theory: A Slightly Jaundiced Survey." *Journal of Economic Literature* 14.3 (September 1976), 827–855. A lucid review and evaluation of criticisms commonly made of human capital approaches.

Bonner, Thomas. *Becoming a Physician: Medical Education in Great Britain, France, Germany, and the United States, 1750–1914.* New York, 1995. A convenient comparative overview of how the history of medical education has exhibited a recurring tension regarding the use of practical experience versus formal instruction.

Boot, H. M. "How Skilled Were Lancashire Cotton Factory Workers in 1833?" *Economic History Review* 2d series, 48.2 (1995), 283–303. Develops a cogent argument supporting a human capital interpretation of age-earnings profiles for a case of considerable significance in economic history.

Bowles, Samuel, and Herbert Gintis. *Schooling in Capitalist America: Educational Reform and the Contradictions of Economic Life.* New York, 1976. One of the most influential pieces of iconoclasm toward human capital interpretations, with extensive historical sections.

Conrad, Alfred H., and John R. Meyer. "The Economics of Slavery in the Antebellum South." *Journal of Political Economy* 66.2 (April 1958), 95–122. The economic framework that Conrad and Meyer employ for viewing the slave as a capital asset has been very influential and provides considerable insight into the more general concept of human capital.

Dublin, Louis I., and Alfred J. Lotka. *The Money Value of a Man.* New York, 1930. A useful framework from the standpoint of the life insurer for analyzing the value of capitalized earnings in the human agent; contains a number of historical examples.

Easterlin, Richard. "Why Isn't the Whole World Developed?" *Journal of Economic History* 41.1 (March 1981), 1–19. In his presidential address to the Economic History Association, Easterlin presents a cogent explication of why education has been important to long-term economic development.

Eichengreen, Barry. "Experience and the Male-Female Earnings Gap in the 1890s." *Journal of Economic History* 44.3 (September 1984), 822–834. A useful example of how to estimate the returns to different kinds of informal human capital empirically using a sample of California workers from the 1890s.

Epstein, Steven. "Labour in Thirteenth-Century Genoa," *Mediterranean Historical Review* 3.1 (June 1988): 128.

Epstein, Steven A. *Wage Labor and Guilds in Medieval Europe.* Chapel Hill, N.C., 1991. A careful account of how the acquisition of training by apprenticeship worked.

Goldin, Claudia, and Lawrence F. Katz. "The Origins of Technology-Skill Complementarity." *National Bureau of Economic Research* Working Paper no. 5657. July 1996. Goldin and Katz develop a framework for examining historical phases in the demand for skill with specific reference to nineteenth- and early-twentieth-century American manufacturing.

Hansen, Hal. "Caps and Gowns: Historical Reflections on the Institutions that Shaped Learning for and at Work in Germany and the United States, 1800–1945." Ph.D diss., University of Wisconsin, 1997. Valuable for its exposition of the factors influencing the emphasis on vocational training in Germany as against an emphasis on formal schooling in the United States.

Lane, Joan. *Apprenticeship in England, 1600–1914.* London, 1996. Useful both for its description of how apprenticeship worked in various occupations and for its account of the decline of formal apprenticeship.

Locke, Robert R. *The End of the Practical Man: Entrepreneurship and Higher Education in Germany, France, and Great Britain, 1880–1940.* Greenwich, Conn., 1984.

Locke, Robert R. *Management and Higher Education Since 1940: The Influence of America and Japan on West Germany, Great Britain, and France.* Cambridge, 1989. Locke's two studies present contrasts in national approaches to business and managerial education.

Lynch, Lisa, ed. *Training and the Private Sector.* Chicago, 1994. Studies of contrasting recent national approaches to the market failure problems that can arise with vocational training.

Mincer, Jacob. *Schooling, Experience and Earnings.* New York, 1974. Presents a widely used framework for examining the influence of on-the-job experience and formal schooling on earnings.

More, Charles. *Skill and the English Working Class, 1870–1914.* New York, 1980. A lucid exposition of the ways in which skill was acquired through both apprenticeship and more informal methods in English manufacturing.

Rappaport, Steve. *World Within Worlds: Structure of Life in Sixteenth-Century London.* Cambridge, 1989.

Sanderson, Michael. *Education and Economic Decline in Britain, 1870 to the 1990s.* Cambridge, 1999. A concise survey of contrasting views regarding whether education contributed to Britain's relative decline over the past century and provides a useful case study of how human capital can influence economic performance.

Schultz, Theodore W. "The Value of the Ability to Deal with Disequilibria." *Journal of Economic Literature* 13.3 (September 1975), 827–846. Significant for its exposition of an important mechanism through which human capital can influence economic performance.

Snell, K. D. M. "The Apprenticeship System in British History: The Fragmentation of a Cultural Institution." *History of Education* 25.4 (December 1996), 303–321. Useful both for its concise overview of the history of apprenticeship in early modern Britain and for its argument that apprenticeship was intended to be holistic, providing not just training in particular skills but experiences integrating the apprentice into society at large.

Topel, Robert. "Labor Markets and Economic Growth." *Handbook of Labor Economics,* vol. 3, edited by O. Ashenfelter and D. Card, pp. 2944–2981. Amsterdam, 1999. A careful overview of recent empirical studies of the relationship between human capital and economic growth.

Tortella, Gabriel, ed. *Education and Economic Development since the Industrial Revolution.* Valencia, Spain, 1990. Papers by economic historians applying the human capital approach to diverse geographical areas.

U.S. Department of Labor. *Apprenticeship Past and Present.* Washington, D.C., 1964.

Westermann, W. L. "Apprenticeship Contracts and the Apprenticeship System in Roman Egypt." *Classical Philology* 9.3 (July 1914), 295–315. Despite the narrow scope suggested by the title, Westermann provides wide-ranging evidence on how apprenticeship systems, and hence more generally systems for the acquisition of human capital, functioned in ancient times.

Willis, Robert. "Wage Determinants: A Survey and Reinterpretation of Human Capital Earnings Functions." In *Handbook of Labor Economics,* vol. 1, edited by O. Ashenfelter and R. Layard, pp. 525–602. Amsterdam, 1986. An overview of empirical studies based on human capital approaches as well as evidence regarding hypotheses critical of human capital explanations of earnings.

Yasuba, Yasukichi. "The Profitability and Viability of Plantation Slavery in the United States." *The Economic Studies Quarterly* 12 (September 1961), 60–68; reprinted in Robert Fogel and Stanley Engerman, eds. *The Reinterpretation of American Economic History,* pp. 362–368. New York, 1971. Yasuba develops a method for estimating trends in the expected value of the capitalized flow of future labor services provided by a slave from time series on slave prices. This paper provides an important historical application of the concept of the human agent as a capital asset.

DAVID MITCH

HUNGARY. Hungarian economic history has evolved in the context of changing state borders. From the formation of the Hungarian Kingdom in the tenth century until its "golden age" at the end of the fifteenth century, its territory increased several times. During the Ottoman conquest in the sixteenth and seventeenth centuries, the former Hungarian Kingdom was divided into three parts: the northwestern region of so-called Royal Hungary, ruled by the Habsburgs; the semi-sovereign eastern region called the Transylvanian Principality; and the middle and southern territory occupied by the Ottoman Empire. After the liberation wars at the end of the seventeenth century, the former Hungarian territories were integrated as parts of the Danubian Habsburg Empire, although the composing units of Hungary proper, Transylvania, and the southern and eastern military frontier remained under a separate administration. A sovereign kingdom was formed during the "dualization" of the Austro-Hungarian Monarchy (1867–1918) as a multinational state. After the Treaty of Trianon (1920), the territory of the Hungarian Kingdom was reduced to one-third its former size, practically to the present-day territory of the Hungarian Republic.

Early History. Hungary was an agrarian country throughout its history until World War II. From state formation onward, farming became increasingly important, along with animal husbandry. A European feudal land-owning system was adopted, in which the principal landowner was the landlord, and the serfs only used the land, in return for which they paid feudal rents. The early manorial economy of the landlords cultivated by serfs (*praedium*) disappeared by the thirteenth century, and agriculture began to be based on a system of tenures of serfs endowed with equal rights, including that of free migration. Until the end of the nineteenth century, the extension of arable land proceeded without difficulty. During the fourteenth and fifteenth centuries, the value of the forced labor duty (*robot*) decreased in the feudal rents, whereas the proportion of the rents paid in products (*nona*) and money increased. The different estimates put the population at three to four million. According to some historians, the heavy burden of taxation in the second half of the fifteenth century was a contributing factor in the recession and troubles of the following century. Increased agricultural production for the market promoted the rise of urban centers; besides thirty to thirty-five royal free towns (*civitas*), a network of agricultural market towns consisting of more than seven hundred settlements (*oppidum*) constituted the principal urban development. These agricultural market towns existed under a landlord's authority and according to the privileges he granted. The functions of urban settlements made possible the concentration of commerce and handicrafts, mostly organized in forms of medieval guilds; but an early decline in their development occurred in the western part of the country in the second half of the fifteenth century.

The economy developed in different ways in the three divided parts during the sixteenth and seventeenth centuries. As a result of permanent war preparations and efforts, the landlords of Royal Hungary tried to concentrate their revenues and the domestic consumption of their household, at the costs of the serfs, the agricultural market towns, and the royal towns as well. The rising prices of the sixteenth century, and the fluctuations of the uncertain seventeenth century (with fifteen-year, thirty-year, and liberation wars), combined with depreciation of the currency, produced upturns and downturns in agriculture. A permanent labor shortage and a growing need for military service had contradictory consequences: a general prohibition of the migration of the serfs (1514) and yearly regulation of the real practice of free movement by the noble county administration (1608) contributed to the rigidity of serfdom and at the same time to the growth of a freely migrating peasant population (with some groups, such as the hajduks, granted collective nobility). There was no significant difference in the average production yield between the newly formed manorial economy of the landlords and the peasant patches. The consequences of wars also exerted contradictory effects on the territory of Ottoman occupation. An important part of the rural population left the small settlements of the Great Hungarian Plain, with some escaping to Royal Hungary and some migrating to the market towns of the region. The most favorable conditions for agrarian development occurred in the agricultural market towns, which were under the direct administration of the sultan (*khas*, possessions). Ottoman rule caused heavy losses of population and of agricultural production forces; and with an increase of land owned (and hired) by agricultural market towns, it promoted the further rise of animal husbandry (first with gray cattle), beginning in the fifteenth century. The international activity in live cattle and wine exports, achievements of market-town peasant farming, extended to north Italy, southern Germany, and Poland.

Integration and Reunification. After the liberation wars, with losses that approximated those of the Ottoman conquest, the Danubian Habsburg Empire integrated the territories of the former Hungarian state. The total population has been estimated as barely greater than that of the end of the fifteenth century; but in the eighteenth century, owing to migration from north to south, spontaneous immigration, and the planned settlement activity of the landlords, it more than doubled. In the framework of a new Habsburg customs policy (decree of 1754), during the French wars at the turn of the nineteenth century, a prolonged upswing in grain production started, and after 1815, a boom in wool production began. During the mid-nineteenth century, a series of institutional changes—

BUDAPEST. Main food hall at the city's central market, 2000. (© Catherine Karnow/Woodfin Camp and Associates, New York)

emancipation of serfs in 1840, 1848, 1849, and 1853; customs union of the Habsburg monarchy in 1850 and 1867; dissolution of guilds in 1859 and 1872—opened the way for Hungarian industrialization, led by the food industries. Soon, due to the establishment of the Budapest Stock Exchange (important to the corn business), the long term low prices of agriculture (1878–1896), and successful technical innovations in the milling industry, Budapest became the second-largest commercial flour-milling center after Minneapolis. Instead of the dominant cattle and woolen exports that characterized the first half of the nineteenth century, Hungarian exports were led by grain and flour by the eve of World War I.

After 1920. After dissolution of the Habsburg Monarchy and the Hungarian Kingdom, peace treaties offered a new system of adjustment for the successor states; the building of new customs and currency areas by the mid-1920s was almost necessarily protected by high home tariffs and helped by foreign aid. During Hungarian financial stabilization (1924), the rate of exchange of the new currency (after 1926, *pengö*) was fixed to the overvalued pound sterling. The competitiveness of Hungarian agriculture did not really improve after the limited land reforms of the 1920s and the introduction of protectionist tariffs in neighboring states. An inflow of international capital during the second half of the 1920s also supported the development of the still deficient textile industry instead of its redundant milling capacity. After the financial crash of 1931, the Hungarian government was forced to introduce restrictions on foreign exchange (and imports). New international treaties based on the compensatory technique of the clearing system (Italian–Austrian–Hungarian and German–Hungarian treaties in 1934) once again gave preferences to exports of Hungarian raw products. The next step toward government intervention was a rearmament program, announced at Györ in 1938, clearly helping heavy industry as part of a revision of borders and war preparations.

The industrial and infrastructural capacities built up during World War II, in spite of serious losses. The burdens of the $300 million war compensation contributed to the concentration of investments into branches of heavy industry. In consequence of Soviet occupation, the establishment of a planned economy and nationalization of capital goods (1946–1950) emerged in parallel as a basis for "socialist industrialization." After radical land reform in 1945–1946, the collectivization of small-scale farms was successfully enforced as late as a second attempt, in 1958–1961. An institutional structure neglecting market relations determined the economic development of the country for the next forty years, although the organization of the economy even in the Stalinist 1950s did not reach the overcentralization and "planned anarchy" of Soviet-type state socialism. The agricultural cooperatives (after 1967 based on cooperative land ownership) were organically interwoven with the household plots of their members.

After the introduction of the so-called new economic mechanism in 1968, economic policies attempted to admit the market into the interfirm relations of the state-owned enterprises. Because of newly accumulated government debts, the establishment of a two-level banking system was postponed until 1987; and despite new types of undertakings in the 1980s, capital and labor markets did not really take off until the political transition of 1989 and the following privatization. The institutional reform then brought about a temporary decline in production, but at the turn of the twenty-first century, the Hungarian economy was making a sound recovery.

[*See also* Austria, *subentry on* Austro-Hungarian Empire.]

BIBLIOGRAPHY

Berend, T. Iván, and György Ránki. *Economic Development in East Central Europe in the Nineteenth and Twentieth Centuries*. New York and London, 1974. The first summary of the economic development of the whole region, based on a macroeconomic approach of modern growth theories.

Berend, T. Iván, and György Ránki. *Hungary: A Century of Economic Development*. New York, 1974.

Draskóczi, István, János Buza, Zoltán Kaposi, György Kövér, and János Honvári. *Magyarország gazdaságtörténete a honfoglalástól a 20. század közepéig*, edited by János Honvári. Budapest, 1996. The latest summary of the economic history of the country in Hungarian. The main chapters were written by specialists of different periods; consequently the concept has been based on eclectic points of view.

Engel, Pál. *The Realm of St. Stephen: A History of Medieval Hungary, 895–1526*. London, 2000.

Good, David F. *The Economic Rise of the Habsburg Empire, 1760–1914*. Berkeley, Los Angeles, and London, 1984.

Gunst, Péter. *Magyarország gazdaságtörténete (1914–1989)*. Budapest, 1996.

Gyimesi, Sándor. *Utunk Európába: A magyar és az európai gazdaság viszonya a honfoglalástól a 20. század elejéig*. Budapest, 1993.

Katus, László. "Economic Growth in Hungary during the Age of Dualism, 1867–1913: A Quantitative Analysis." In *Social-Economic Researches on the History of East-Central Europe*, edited. by E. Pamlényi, pp. 35–70. Budapest, 1970. The first and still the best quantitative analysis of the transition to modern economic growth of Hungary.

Komlos, John. *The Habsburg Monarchy as a Customs Union: Economic Development in Austria-Hungary in the Nineteenth Century*. Princeton, 1983.

Kontler, László. *Millennium in Central Europe: A History of Hungary*. Budapest, 1999. The most recent critical and comprehensive survey on the general history of Hungary, including important chapters on economic history.

Kövér, György. *Iparosodás agrárországban: Magyarország gazdaságtörténete, 1848–1914*. Budapest, 1982.

Paulinyi, Oszkár. "Nemesfémtermelésünk és országos gazdaságunk általános alakulása a bontakozó és a kifejlett feudalizmus korszakában (1000–1526): Gazdag fold—szegény ország." *Századok* 106. 3 (1972), 561–602.

Petö, Iván, and Sándor Szakács. *A hazai gazdaság négy évtizedének története, 1945–1985. I. Az újjáépítés és a tervutasításos irányítás időszaka*. Budapest, 1985.

Szûcs, Jenö. "The Three Historical Regions of Europe: An Outline." *Acta Historica Academiae Scientiarium Hungaricae* 29. 2–4 (1983), 131–184.

GYÖRGY KÖVÉR

HUNTING. Hunting has been an important economic activity since the time of early hominins. Chimpanzees regularly hunt and kill other primates, and their hunting becomes more frequent and successful whenever and wherever male chimpanzees forage in larger parties (Mitani and Watts, 2001). Hominins show marked gut reduction and brain expansion relative to chimpanzees beginning around 2 million years ago. At the same time, animal remains became much more common in hominin archaeological sites (Aiello, 1998). Gut reduction indicates increased reliance on nutrient-dense, low-fiber foods, and brain expansion requires an ample supply of essential fatty acids found mainly in animal foods. The coincidence of these traits in time strongly indicates an increased reliance on meat rather than plant foods in the diet of our ancestors during the period of early *Homo*.

In the late *Homo erectus* period and continuing in Neanderthals and early *Homo sapiens*, archaeological sites show tremendous quantities of animal remains from mammalian megafauna, leaving little doubt that our ancestors were highly dependent on hunted food for a long period of evolutionary history (Gaudzinski, 1999). Not until the end of the Pleistocene, with drastic climate changes and megafaunal extinctions, do we see a shift toward increased reliance on collected foods in hunter-gatherer diets.

Although early *Homo* probably hunted with hand-held weapons, clubs, or thrusting spears, by about four hundred thousand years ago, our ancestors had developed throwing spears for killing large game. Later, spear throwers provided leverage necessary to hurl spears and darts at high velocity with good accuracy. The bow and arrow may have been invented independently several times in human history, and this technology replaced spear throwers in most places where both were present. But Australian hunters never obtained bow-and-arrow technology, using spears and spear throwers up to the time of European contact. In some areas of the world, alternative hunting technology was also developed, for example, blowguns in Amazonia or harpoons used by coastal natives.

Hunter-gatherers who have been observed in modern times use a tremendous variety of methods and technologies to obtain game. Most of these fall into the categories of mobile encounter-based hunting, sit-and-wait ambush hunting, or game drives. Mobile encounter-based hunting is walking through an area suspected to be rich in game, hoping to encounter prey and stalk and kill it before it can escape. This may also include the use of game calls when there is a strong indication that a target species is near. Some prey swiftly flee long distances, but many hide in thickets, burrows, bodies of water, or climb trees. Human hunters are very opportunistic about the tactics they use to obtain such hidden prey, and a variety of special tools and techniques have been developed by hunters everywhere. Killing the prey usually means shooting projectiles, stabbing with a sharp instrument, breaking the neck, clubbing, or suffocating. Ambush hunting is hiding along game trails or near feeding and drinking areas, killing prey that come within range. Blinds are constructed by hunters to better camouflage their hiding spot. Game drives generally consist of hunters surrounding prey and spooking them toward each other, or leaving a subset of hunters in a good ambush location while others attempt to frighten prey in their direction. Many game drives include environmental modification that forces game to move through a narrow area where hunters are waiting. In most ethnographically

HUNTING. Mentawai man hunting, Siberut, Indonesia, 1990. Although the Mentawai cultivate some crops, they remain primarily hunters and gatherers. (© Lindsay Hebberd/Woodfin Camp and Associates, New York)

described cases, mobile and ambush hunting are accomplished by solitary men who sometimes leave camp as a group but split up before beginning pursuit of prey. Groups of solitary hunters sometimes cooperate to hunt social living animals after they are encountered, and in such circumstances hunters may communicate by long-distance calls and signals. The majority of well-known modern hunter-gatherers were solitary hunters (eg., Kung, Hadza, Agta, Punan, Ona, Eskimos, Australian aborigines.). A few modern groups were oriented more toward cooperative hunting (eg., Ache, BaMbuti, Hiwi, Plains Indians.)

In general, medium- to large-sized mammals are the most important prey items for human hunters around the world, with reptiles and birds being considerably less important in total biomass obtained. The largest animals hunted in recent times were whales (American N.W. Coast Indians) and elephants (BaMbuti), whereas the smallest animals hunted (not trapped) were probably small birds (everywhere), small rodents that were extracted from burrows (Ona, Shoshone), and small reptiles (desert Australia). A recent survey of all hunter-gatherer groups for whom we have quantitative dietary data suggests that from 30 percent to 80 percent of the energy in the diet of such groups comes from game animals (Kaplan, et al., 2000). Another crosscultural survey based on estimates of economic patterns shows that 73 percent of all hunter-gatherer groups probably derived more than 50 percent of their daily energy intake from animal foods (Cordain, et al., 2000).

The returns from hunting (including search time) have been measured only for groups studied in the late twentieth century. In general, the group mean for adult male hunters obtain ranges between about 0.2 kilograms (Gwi, Efe, Mbuti) to 2.5 kilogram (Hiwi) meat (live weight) per hunter hour in the bush (mean 0.63 kilograms/hour in fifteen studies), using traditional weapons among foraging societies. Variation in hunting returns between men in foraging societies can be considerable. For example, among the Ache there is more than a tenfold difference in return rate between the best and worst adult male hunter in a sample of twenty-four men observed over a long time period (Hill and Hurtado, 1996, p. 333). Mean hours hunted per day in groups without agriculture or domestic animals ranges from only 1.5 hours per day by the Hiwi of Venezuela (Hurtado and Hill, 1987, p. 177) to about 9 hours per day by Canadian Chippeweyan hunters (Irimoto, 1981) with the average about 4.9 hours per day in twenty-five studies.

One of the most notable things about hunting is the long period of learning required for attaining expertise. In many groups, men do not reach peak hunting skill until their mid-forties or later, and young men at the peak of their strength often obtain hunting returns much lower than older, more experienced men (Walker, et al., 2002). This observation, in combination with the fact that acculturated youths are often poor hunters, suggests that hunting is a complex skill requiring a long learning period. Tracking skills of hunters are reported to be astounding by those who have observed them (eg., see Bridges 1947, pp. 306, 328–330, for examples of Ona tracking skills). Likewise, the ability to know where to search for game, when to ignore unimportant signs of game, or when to follow up on promising leads, and how to extract game when it burrows, climbs, submerges, or otherwise makes itself inaccessible, seems to be a complex learned skill requiring years to master.

[*See also* Gathering.]

BIBLIOGRAPHY

Aiello, Leslie C. "The Expensive Tissue Hypothesis and the Evolution of the Human Adaptive Niche: A Study in Comparative Anatomy."

In Science in Archaeology: An Agenda for the Future, edited by J. Bayley, pp. 25–36. London, 1998.

Bridges, E. Lucas. 1949. *Uttermost Part of the Earth.* New York, 1949.

Cordain, Loren, Jennie Brand Miller, S. Byrd Eaton, Neil Mann, Sam H. A. Holt, and John D. Speth. "Plant-Animal Subsistence Ratios and Macronutrient Energy Estimations in Worldwide Hunter-Gatherer Diets." *American Journal of Clinical Nutrition* 71 (2000), 682–692.

Gaudzinski, Sabine. "The Faunal Record of the Lower and Middle Palaeolithic of Europe: Remarks on Human Interference. In *The Middle Palaeolithic Occupation of Europe,* edited by W. Robroeks and C. Gamble, pp. 215–233. Leiden, 1999.

Hill, Kim, and A. Magdalena Hurtado. *Ache Life History: The Ecology and Demography of a Foraging People.* New York, 1996.

Hurtado, A. Magdalena, and Kim Hill. "Early Dry Season Subsistence Ecology of the Cuiva Foragers of Venezuela." *Human Ecology* 15: 2 (1987), 163–187.

Irimoto, Takashi. *Chipeweyan Ecology: Group Structure and Caribou Hunting System.* Senri Ethnological Series 8. Osaka, Japan, 1981.

Kaplan, Hillard, Kim Hill, J. Lancaster, and A. Magdalena Hurtado. "The Evolution of Intelligence and the Human Life History." *Evolutionary Anthropology* 9:4 (2000), 156–184.

Mitani, John C., David P. Watts, and Martin N. Muller. "Recent Developments in the Study of Wild Chimpanzee Behavior." *Evolutionary Anthropology* 11:1 (2002), 9–25.

Walker, Robert, Kim Hill, H. Kaplan, and Garnett McMillan. "Age Dependency of Strength, Skill, and Hunting Ability Among the Ache of Paraguay." *Journal of Human Evolution.* In press, 2002.

KIM R. HILL AND A. MAGDALENA HURTADO

HYPERINFLATION. *See* Inflation and Hyperinflation.

I

ICELAND. *See* Nordic Countries.

IMMIGRATION POLICY sets out the terms and the conditions under which foreigners are admitted to a given country. The conditions include such factors as defining the annual level of arrivals, the regional or country allocation of landing visas, the occupational composition of prospective immigrants, their political background, and so on. The weight of these conditions varies across countries, and they have changed dramatically over time. For example, early legislation in such receiving countries as the United States, Australia, and Canada excluded only those immigrants who might become "wards of the state," that is, criminals, the diseased, and paupers. All others were welcome. However, as the nineteenth century drew to a close, the receiving countries gradually increased the number of excluded classes. In the 1880s, for example, specific legislation was enacted to limit, or, in some cases, exclude, the arrival of migrants from Asia (the infamous Chinese Immigration Acts). In addition, a number of countries introduced acts to prohibit the import of contract labor to work on large-scale government projects such as railroads and canals.

It was not until the twentieth century that immigrant-receiving countries passed legislation to limit both the level and the composition of immigrants. The United States, for example, the largest country of destination for European emigrants, began to debate placing restrictions on the level of immigration as early as the 1890s; but it was not until 1917 that a literacy test was imposed. Legislation setting numerical quotas first was enacted under the Emergency Quota Act of 1921. This was followed by the 1924 Immigration Act and in 1929, by the National Origins Quota Act. The overall result was to bias admissions toward traditional source countries of northern Europe. By the end of World War I, the era of mass migration had come to an end.

Canada also adopted discriminatory immigration policies toward European migrants. In 1910, the country passed its first major immigration act in over forty years. This act was designed to provide the government with greater control over the level and the composition of immigrant arrivals—that is, a policy of selective immigration.

IMMIGRATION. *The Steerage*, photograph by Alfred Stieglitz, 1907. The photograph appeared in *291* magazine in 1915. (Hervé Lewandowski/Musée d'Orsay, Paris/Réunion des Musées Nationaux/Art Resource, NY)

Under the terms of the act, explicit powers were given to the cabinet through orders-in-council provisions to prohibit or to limit the number of immigrants according to their race, occupation, lifestyles, and ability to become readily assimilated. The act left the government of the day free to admit any immigrants it thought would serve the best interests of the country, and to limit their numbers. By 1919, the act was amended to require a literacy test (a short piece to be read in the language of the immigrant's choice), and in 1924 a clause was inserted that divided the world between "preferred" immigrants, that is, those originating in Britain, the United States, the white Commonwealth countries, and, under special conditions, northern Europe, and "non-preferred" immigrants, essentially those from the rest of the world with the exception of Chinese immigrants, who continued to be admitted under a separate act. However, virtually all Canadian immigration offices were located in either Britain or the United States, so that it was difficult for immigrants from other countries to gain admission. Canada did not fix explicit quotas on admission; instead it varied the flow according to the needs of the economy.

Australian immigration policy closely paralleled that adopted in Canada although the timing was slightly different from that of Canada. For example, Australia imposed restrictions on Chinese immigrants from the early decades of the nineteenth century; and a literacy test was adopted in 1901. However, it was not until 1925 that its Immigration Act was amended to give the Governor-in-Council (the cabinet) authorization to restrict the immigration "of any specific nationality, race, class or occupation." Essentially, with this revision, Australia had adopted a "white Australia" immigration policy focused on attracting immigrants from Britain and northern Europe.

Two questions arise from this brief review of the evolution of immigration policy in the nineteenth and twentieth centuries. First, why were the main receiving countries so open to mass migration during the nineteenth century when the effect was to depress the wages of the resident population? Second, why did "free entry" virtually disappear by the early twentieth century? As these policies were introduced by governments, one may ask who the losers were from this migration.

In the nineteenth century, most governments were controlled by landowners and capitalists, and the voting franchise was fairly narrowly held. Under these conditions, when labor demand was strong enough to put upward pressure on wages, and so threaten profits and rents, it was in the interest of property owners to encourage immigration. This is seen in the receiving countries' governments adoption of such policies as free land grants and transportation subsidies to attract immigrants. However, at the turn of the twentieth century, a number of changes occurred. First, frontiers closed, and growth became concentrated in cities. Second, as the franchise was extended, the number of voters, especially among urban workers, increased; and thus governments became more widely representative of the population and more prolabor in their approach to economic policies. Finally, as the level of immigration increased, especially from the new source countries, there emerged a perceived threat to the relative earnings of unskilled native-born and resident-immigrant workers. The response of governments, now with a different mix of constituents, was gradually to restrict immigration. The form these regulations took depended on the constitutional arrangements in the different countries.

After 1945, many of the receiving countries reopened their doors to immigration following almost complete cessation of international migration during the 1930s. Unskilled workers dominated early arrivals, again threatening the livelihood of low-income workers. The response was twofold. First, regulations were changed to discourage the entry of unskilled workers (thus generating a surge of illegal immigration) while encouraging the inflow of highly skilled workers such as engineers, physicians, scientists, and so on (creating a "brain drain"). In the 1960s, when the supply of these workers became scarce, the racist policies of the pre–World War II era were replaced by a universal admission policy based on the personal characteristics of the prospective immigrant rather than on the individual's national origin. The resurgence of immigration during the last two decades of the twentieth century stimulated debate similar to that encountered during the early years of the century. Immigration policy is clearly an area where knowledge of the policy's history is crucial to an understanding of its future direction.

BIBLIOGRAPHY

Foreman-Peck, James. "A Political Economy of International Migration, 1815–1914." *Manchester School* 60.4 (December 1992), 359–376. An attempt to answer, using very straightforward economic analysis, the question of why the policy of free migration, so widely adopted by many countries in the nineteenth century, was abandoned in the twentieth century. A widely cited article.

Goldin, Claudia. "The Political Economy of Immigration Restriction in the United States, 1890 to 1921." In *The Regulated Economy: A Historical Approach to Political Economy*, edited by Claudia Goldin and Gary Libecap, pp. 223–257. Chicago, 1994. An economic analysis of why Congress, and the president, after several decades of bitter debate, finally agreed to end mass migration.

Green, Alan, and David Green. "The Economic Goals of Canada's Immigration Policy." *Canadian Public Policy* 25.4 (December 1999), 425–451. An attempt to interpret, using simple economic analysis, how Canadian immigration policy developed over the last century.

Hutchinson, Edward. P. *Legislative History of American Immigration Policy, 1798–1965.* Philadelphia, 1981. A descriptive account of the evolution of American immigration policy. The authoritative work in its field.

Knowles, Valerie. *Strangers at our Gates: Canadian Immigration and Immigration Policy, 1540–1990.* Toronto, 1992. A well-written piece, very easy to read, but lacking any in-depth analysis of events.

Roe, Michael. *Australia, Britain, and Migration, 1915–1940.* Cambridge, 1995. A detailed exploration of the social and economic forces that shaped twentieth-century immigration policy in Australia. Pays particular attention to the interaction between British and Australian views on this subject. Very readable.

Trimmer, Ashley, and Jeffrey G. Williamson. "Immigration Policy Prior to the Thirties: Labour Markets, Policy Interaction, and Globalization Backlash." *Population and Development Review* 24.4 (December 1998), 739–771. An attempt to make positive (factual) predictions about the interaction between political institutions and the marketplace over the emergence of immigration restrictions. Challenging reading, in places, for the noneconomist, which nevertheless provides a good outline of the evolution of immigration restrictions across a number of prime receiving countries.

ALAN G. GREEN

IMPERIALISM. *See* Economic Imperialism.

INCOME MAINTENANCE *[This entry contains two subentries, on transfer payments and public assistance and on social insurance.]*

Transfer Payments and Public Assistance

Until the late nineteenth century, in most societies, assistance to the poor, if it was provided at all other than by the family, was delivered through various combinations of publicly funded, poor-relief systems and nongovernmental voluntary action. Since that time, most countries with developed economies have instituted a proliferation of income-maintenance plans, designed to provide a safety net, to protect the poorest from total destitution and, if possible, to promote their independence. The plans provide for several types of need, including poverty from old age, unemployment, ill health, large family size, malnutrition, and inadequate shelter. Different forms of need have been defined and ranked in different times and places; such transactions are defined in the language of modern economists as *transfer payments*, because governmental institutions arrange for the transfer of funds to those defined as being in need from those defined otherwise. The payments are made in a variety of ways, but, in most times and places, in one of two ways: direct, from local or central taxation; or by means of social insurance systems, for which individuals make earmarked contributions when they have the capacity to do so. Such social insurance systems are usually subsidized, to varying degrees, from direct taxation. It is conventional to distinguish between "public assistance," which is wholly or primarily funded from government revenues without earmarked contributions by recipients and "social insurance," for which there is at least some personal contribution—although the distinction between them is not always clear. In general, public assistance provides funds for the poorest people, social insurance (whether unemployment insurance, health-compensation benefits, and old age/social security payments) is usually for the regularly employed.

This entry is concerned with public funding for the poor. In the United States, such public assistance is today called "welfare"; in Britain, elsewhere in Europe, and in Australasia, *welfare* is the generic term for all forms of publicly managed transfer payments. From the late nineteenth century onward, there have been gradual moves away from public, generalized or nonspecific, poor-relief systems and toward forms of public assistance targeted on specific problem groups with differing needs. Those innovations have remained in place, although they undergo constant adaptation, in response to various pressures. France led the way in introducing publicly funded payments and facilities for the health and welfare of mothers and young children, in preference to other forms of public assistance. In 1904, each French province was enabled to provide a maternity home with qualified medical attendance; in 1913, a small subsidy was also provided for poor women in the final month of pregnancy and for the first two years of the child's life; in 1914, additional means-tested assistance was given to poor large families, whether headed by a male or female. At the same time in France, tax relief for each child was provided for better-off families, as it was in Britain from 1913. These measures resulted from concern that France then had the lowest birthrate of any developed country—with supposed though unproven adverse consequences for the future supply of human resources in both economic and military endeavors. Such concerns were of central importance to government decision making in an era of intense international economic and military competition. The size and fitness of the population was believed to be essential for "national efficiency," in the language of the time; a concomitant requirement was exclusion of the supposedly inefficient, such as the aged and disabled (hence the growth of public transfer programs to disabled people and the elderly).

Birthrates fell internationally from the 1870s to the 1930s, especially after World War I, and concern intensified with the scale of wartime deaths and postwar unemployment, mainly in Europe, Australia, and New Zealand. One outcome was the demand for family allowances, since it was widely believed that falling family size was due to a widespread desire, and capacity, to maximize living standards. Larger families were recognized to be in especial risk of poverty. In France, family allowances were introduced by employers during World War I, as an alternative to the general wage increases that workers were then demanding. Family allowances provided through business firms became compulsory in France in 1932, when the birthrate reached its then lowest-ever level (primarily to boost the birthrate), and in Belgium for similar reasons in 1930. In Britain, the demand for family allowances had grown in the interwar years, driven by the women's movement, which was concerned more with the health and welfare of women than with "national efficiency." Little response came, despite the fact that Britain had the lowest fertility of any European country in the interwar years. In Britain, where the trade unions were strong, family allowances were resisted by them until 1945. Public-assistance measures were closely associated with the labor-market strategies of both employers and the national government. Wages in Britain rose during the World Wars and state allowances compensated the families of servicemen; after the wars, allowances in proportion to family size were paid to the unemployed. Tax-funded family allowances were introduced in Britain in 1945, for all but the first child in all families. By that time, the motive of the government was to hold down wage demands throughout postwar economic reconstruction.

In 1926, New Zealand had introduced the first national scheme of family allowances. It was restricted to the third and subsequent children, aged under fifteen, of poor (means-tested) families, excluding alien and illegitimate children. In most countries, public assistance has played a role in defining citizenship rights, by excluding those who are not citizens. In 1927, the Australian state of New South Wales created a similar family allowance, designed to relieve the poverty of large families, (not to boost birthrates or to curb wage inflation). New Zealand and Australia were innovators with targeted assistance schemes, because unlike most European countries and many of the U.S. states, they had no poor-relief system to assist the indigent. Universal, tax-funded family allowances were introduced in Australia in 1941 and New Zealand in 1946, by which time there was greater concern in those countries about population growth. By the beginning of World War II, New Zealand, Belgium, France, New South Wales, Italy (in 1936), Spain and Hungary (in 1938), and Norway (in 1939) had introduced family allowances of some kind. Australia, Canada, Finland, Ireland, Romania, Britain, the Soviet Union, and some Swiss cantons did so during the war years. Support for the adoption of family allowances in the United States was limited, and it was never seriously contemplated by the U.S. government.

Internationally, there was a lively and unresolved debate between proponents of family allowances and those who argued that targeted services were more effective in diminishing poverty. Targeted services were preferred in Sweden until family allowances were introduced in 1947. To make the best of the birthrates already achieved, parallel measures were devised to reduce high rates of infant mortality; there were welfare clinics, cash maternity benefits (introduced in Britain and France in the 1900s), and other sources of advice to mothers (such as the local-authority health visitors introduced in Britain and the health clinics and visiting nurses provided in the United States under the Sheppard-Towner Act from 1921 to 1929, then continued in a modified needs-based form). Such activities contributed to an international fall in infant mortality. Equally important were measures to ensure that children who survived became strong and effective, by providing free meals for poor children at school in Britain in 1906 and in other countries later.

Such assistance measures were inextricably related both to politics and to their assumed salience for economic growth, so increased expenditure on public assistance was not just associated with liberal or socialist regimes. Italy, after the fascist leader Benito Mussolini came to power in 1922, followed French government measures of the early 1920s—they introduced transfer payments from the celibate and from childless married partners to large families through increased taxation of the childless. Italy raised tax allowances, cash benefits, and services to large families, although at that time Italy had one of the highest birthrates in Europe. As in France, medals and cash bonuses were granted to "prolific mothers" and public-health services for mothers and children were improved.

The falling birthrate caused concern in Weimar Germany, where the state introduced measures to improve health and welfare—but these were cut during the economic crisis of the late 1920s. After the National Socialists (Nazis) came to power in Germany in 1933, government investment in health and welfare centers, maternity benefits, and income-tax allowances for dependent children were increased; marriage loans were introduced, which were not to be repaid after the birth of the fourth child—a measure also adopted by the left-wing Popular Front government of France in 1939. The Nazi measures, like the French and Italian, were partly funded by the "celibacy tax" transfer. The benefits of German public assistance were, however, restricted to those of "Aryan" stock (a pro-Nordic "racial" assignment). Similar assistance for large families was introduced by right-wing nationalist governments in Brazil, Spain, and Portugal in the 1930s, as well as in the Communist Soviet Union. Nowhere did they lead to a significant reversal of the birthrate, though they brought improvements in women's health and in the living standards of poor families.

An important influence on transfer payments during the early 1900s was the emergence of active women's movements; they seized the opportunity provided by economic and military concerns about birthrates to improve the conditions in which women gave birth and reared children. Such women's movements were soon suppressed by both right-wing and left-wing dictatorships. Similarly, the growing labor movements in liberal democracies demanded improved state welfare to assist workers, although they feared that some forms would be provided only in substitution for higher pay. On a political level, some countries, as in Bismarck's Germany, explicitly promoted social-assistance measures, to counter the appeal to workers of the growing labor and socialist movements. Such fears were reinforced by the Russian Revolution of 1917, which prompted legislation, as in Britain after World War I and other countries for major programs of state-subsidized housing, rent controls, and the extension of unemployment insurance and assistance to cover most of the employed. In this era, the right to vote gradually became universal in Europe, the British Commonwealth, and the Americas—for men and then for women—so both right-wing and left-wing governments competed for the support of mass electorates.

Growing concern with the physical efficiency of their citizens led in the late nineteenth century to plans for maintaining the fitness of workers—mainly men of the manual and lower white-collar workforce—by providing health care and more rarely cash benefits in times of sickness, designed to facilitate speedy return to work. Such transfer payments were introduced in a variety of forms in Germany (1883), Austria (1888), Hungary (1891), Sweden (1891), Denmark (1892), and Belgium (1894); then in Italy, Norway, Britain, Romania, Switzerland, Russia, and Serbia between 1890 and 1912, mainly in the form of social insurance. Because regularly paid workers were thought capable of contributing to their own assistance, they were mostly subsidized by various transfers from general taxation. In Denmark, for example, the "unpropertied" received similar (but noncontributory) care and cash benefits to those of insured contributors. Other systems, as in Germany and Britain, did not provide for those who not were regularly employed—overwhelmingly the young, the female, and the casual workers—despite their relatively high levels of sickness; their care was left instead to the residual poor-relief systems.

The other major international innovation in public assistance during the later nineteenth century was the unemployment benefit, in various forms, which was also taken up slowly and unevenly. This was a prime objective of labor-movement demands, to protect workers' living standards during lows in the economic cycle over which they had no control. Trade unions developed their own funds, but in 1914 unions covered only a minority of manual workers in all countries. By 1908, such funds became publicly subsidized in Belgium, the Netherlands, France, Norway, Denmark, and Italy. From the 1880s, economic theorists, notably Wichsell in Sweden, recognized the reality of involuntary unemployment, and an understanding of the labor market was increasingly refined, for example, in the work of William Beveridge in the United Kingdom. At that time, unemployment assistance was recognized as a strategy to stabilize the labor market, to reduce casual and underemployment, and to target permanent employment for the most efficient workers. To this end, national unemployment insurance, introduced in Britain in 1911, had been based on publicly funded Employment Exchanges in 1909, designed to match workers to work.

The political and economic changes precipitated by World War I facilitated the expansion of public assistance in the 1920s and 1930s despite, or in some respects because of, international economic recession and political crisis. In Germany in 1910, about 34 percent of government expenditure had gone to health, housing, education, social insurance, and assistance; by 1930, about 70 percent. For Britain, the comparable figures were 30 percent and 45 percent public expenditure. There were compara-

ble changes in Sweden and elsewhere. Publicly funded assistance was considered positive for promoting both economic and political stability. In Britain, for example, attempts to cut transfer payments at the onset of the recession (Slump) in 1922 and again after the financial crisis of 1929 to 1931 were followed by increased government spending on unemployment relief, health, welfare, and housing—for fear of the political consequences of cuts at a time when the labor movement was growing in strength.

In the political climate of the 1920s and 1930s, unemployment was a major reason for rising expenditure. After the expansion of unemployment insurance, a massive unemployment exposed the limitations of such insurance schemes—which had been designed to cover only short-term unemployment. Supplementary tax-funded assistance systems, of varying degrees of generosity, were introduced in the countries affected. Germany, which in 1927 introduced comprehensive unemployment insurance, had difficulty in paying those many who were unemployed from 1928 to 1932; the long-term unemployed were driven to poor relief, which caused a great drain on local government resources—and some came close to bankruptcy. Britain had already provided a relatively successful series of supplementary unemployment-assistance schemes for a long period of unemployment. Sweden only in 1932 adopted its first unemployment-insurance measure (subsidization of trade-union funds), during high unemployment, when the Social Democrats first came to power; they accompanied it, however, with public investment designed to create work, the first government to act on the public works proposals developed by the British economist John Maynard Keynes. In the United States, Wisconsin introduced a state-based unemployment insurance in 1932. Although discussed for some time in the United States, not until the Great Depression did the American Federation of Labor supported unemployment insurance; great obstacle at the state level was employers who feared that imposition of a payroll tax would weaken their competitiveness against employers in other states with no such tax.

In 1934, President Franklin D. Roosevelt, a longtime proponent of social insurance, established the Committee on Economic Security, to frame national social-insurance legislation. One of the most difficult issues was whether unemployment insurance should be wholly national (federal) or a shared state-federal system. The committee supported a system whereby employers in all the states were subject to a federal payroll tax, most of which was excused if they contributed to their own state's unemployment system, one that conformed to standards specified in the U.S. Social Security Act of 1935; this was extremely effective and by 1937 all the states had enacted their own unemployment-insurance legislation. The states were free to frame their own provisions concerning the amount and duration of benefits, eligibility, and, to a large extent, their own tax schedules. An exceptional feature of U.S. unemployment insurance, found almost nowhere else, is that in the great majority of the states it is financed only by an employer-payroll tax, with no employee contribution. Also, the employer tax is subject to "experience rating"—employers who experience little unemployment pay a very low (even zero) tax, whereas those with high unemployment pay a much higher tax. The intention was to provide an incentive to employers to minimize unemployment.

The Soviet Union operated a system of compulsory unemployment insurance from 1922 to 1930, when it was suspended as part of the strategy of controlling the movement of labor. Thereafter, until its collapse in 1991, the Soviet Union had no system of unemployment assistance—because, officially, there was no unemployment. The outcome was extensive "overmanning," inefficiency, and high production costs. Until the downfall of the regimes of communist Eastern Europe between 1989 and 1991, the citizens of those countries were provided with subsidized housing, food supplies, transport, health care, education, and pensions—if sometimes at very basic, and by the 1980s, diminishing levels. After the demise of the Communist regimes, the member countries of the former Soviet Union had great difficulty in constructing effective assistance systems; other former Eastern-bloc countries moved, generally more successfully, toward a variable mix of insurance and assistance, public and private systems.

World War II had transformed the international economy, as well as many national economies, political systems, and popular expectations. In the years after the war, assistance programs were expanded, and expenditure rose in all developed economies—a trend that had begun in New Zealand in1938 and in Australia in 1941. An international trend began toward providing universal access to health insurance and health care, unemployment insurance, old age and disability pensions, family allowances, and education. These replaced the previous targeting upon low-paid workers, while subsidized housing continued to be provided for those unable to find shelter through the private market. Details of the extent and form of assistance varied from nation to nation. Canada, for example, did not have cash sickness benefits until 1971; Italy and Greece did not develop national health-care services until the 1970s. The United States has never introduced a universal health-insurance system supported by public funds, although the elderly, the disabled, and the poor receive benefits from federally funded medicare, Social Security, and Medicaid, as well as some state or local public-health services for children and/or the general public. Private insurance is notionally compulsory in the United States, but the large numbers of people who were not in fact covered caused persistent concern.

Predominantly, this expansion of welfare states (a term that came into use during World War II, initially in Britain, whose immediate postwar social legislation provided a model for many countries) took the form of social insurance. Such systems required complementary means-tested and tax-funded social-assistance programs, to provide a "safety-net"—effectively a guaranteed minimum income— for those excluded from full-time labor and lack of other resources. The assumption was that the need for such assistance would diminish with postwar economic growth; that expectation was not realized, largely because social-insurance benefits rarely provided adequate incomes for the substantial numbers of people who proved unable to supplement them from other forms of savings. In 1970, both Britain and the United States were still spending 2.5 percent of gross domestic product (GDP) on public assistance; France, 2.2 percent; West Germany, 2.3 percent; Canada 4.5 percent; Australia 5.4 percent; and Japan 1.3 percent. Thereafter, expenditure rose—rather than falling as predicted, from increased unemployment. Statistics, however, disguise important differences. In Britain, the share of social-security expenditure absorbed by public assistance doubled from the late 1940s to the mid-1970s; from 1975 to 1985 (with unemployment rising), it rose from 2.5 to 6 percent. Comparable U.S. figures were 3.6 and 2.8 percent. In Germany, Austria, and Italy, it fell during that period. In France, centralized public assistance was abolished in 1966, leaving the long-term poor to a very restricted, localized, poor-relief system.

Postwar international trends were partly influenced by the fact that, for the first time, "full employment" became a policy objective of the democratic as well as the communist governments. Complementary to that was provision for those who were unable to enter the paid labor force for any reason; assistance was also designed to maximize the efficiency and security of workers. High standards of health, education, and welfare were seen, internationally, as complementary to economic growth—a justifiable object of public expenditure and necessary in view of the poor levels of health, education, and housing of substantial sections of the populations of most countries in the 1940s and in many cases beyond. Also highly influential were the postwar political imperatives of building liberal democracy (or communist regimes), in place of fascism— and the desire of each side in the growing Cold War to win popular consent for its system. The United States, under President Harry S. Truman, encouraged and subsidized (partly through the postwar Marshall Plan) the development of welfare states in war-torn Western Europe, Japan, and Korea—then considered essential for ongoing peace, stable liberal democracy, and worldwide economic growth.

Growing public expenditure upon an expanding array of transfer programs continued internationally until the early

PUBLIC ASSISTANCE. Waiting their turn at the welfare office in the courthouse in Franklin, Georgia, 1941. (Jack Delano/Prints and Photographs Division, Library of Congress)

1970s—though, as always, local and regional patterns of provision were in use. In Western Europe, the predominant form was universal and insurance based, supplemented by targeted cash benefits and services, and integrated in various countries with occupational and/or private provision. The communist regimes of Eastern Europe continued to make universal, state-funded provision. In the United States, an awareness of continuing high levels of poverty in some communities led in the 1960s to President Lyndon B. Johnson's civil-rights legislation, the War on Poverty, the introduction in 1965 of Medicare (which provided health-insurance benefits for the aged), and Medicaid (which provided grants to the states for part of the cost of medical assistance to the poor). Since they were targeted on social groups in which the incidence of ill health was relatively high, these were costly programs; most of the employed U.S. population then had employer-based, contributory health insurance. Toward the end of the twentieth century there were complaints in the United States that certain politically weak groups—notably children—were disadvantaged, in comparison with the politically strong, such as relatively wealthy older people.

The East Asian pattern was different, despite U.S. influence after World War II and their pragmatic adoption of some features of Western systems. The postwar Japanese constitution, strongly U.S. influenced during the Occupation period, stated a principled commitment to government support of public welfare—but in practice little was done. Rather, as with South Korea after the dislocations of the Korean War (1950–1953), in Taiwan (after the Chinese Communist takeover of the mainland in 1949), and in Singapore, economic growth was substituted for social welfare; provisions were made by big employers (pensions, housing, health care), and there was strong public encouragement to the family to provide for other needs, as it had traditionally. Voluntary community organizations then provided for the needy. Even during Japan's highest economic growth, from 1955 to 1975, the government kept public-welfare expenditure stable at about 2 percent of gross national product (GNP). As in Korea and Taiwan, Japan's provision of pensions centered on social insurance (coverage was least in Taiwan), economic growth, and limited public expenditure on assistance (except of a residual kind). The cost of such systems to families is unquantified, though the high levels of private savings was one of the responses to low levels of public assistance. Political activism in Japan in the 1960s brought an extension of provision for specific groups, such as maternal and child welfare, care for the mentally retarded, and free medical services for the aged. Social-welfare expenditures continued to increase modestly in Japan until the OPEC oil embargo of the mid-1970s. Then, even more severely than in Western countries, public-welfare expenditure was criticized as inimical to investment in a successful economy—so government expenditures fell while encouragements to families and community groups were reinforced. In the late 1990s, that approach was repeated during the unexpected crash of the Asian economies.

From the 1980s to the twenty-first century, there were sustained efforts, especially in the West, to reduce both total social expenditures and the number and coverage of social programs. The latter was somewhat more easily attainable than the former due to rising unemployment, above all, together with other unforeseen changes: the aging of societies, and increased marriage breakdown, marriage avoidance, and single parenthood, which generally increased the numbers of women and children with inadequate incomes. All of these changes tended to increase levels of public-assistance expenditures. Established welfare states are constrained, even if they were so inclined, from consigning significant numbers of voters to destitution or to very low living standards, in view of the steadily rising expectations of the previous centuries.

[*See also* Poor Laws *and* Poor Relief.]

BIBLIOGRAPHY

Bock, Gisela, and Pat Thane. *Maternity and Gender Policies: Women and the Rise of the European Welfare States, 1880s–1950s*. London, 1991.

Flora, P., ed. *Growth to Limits: The Western European Welfare States since World War Two*. 4 vols. New York and Berlin, 1987–1988.

Gordon, Margaret S. *Social Security Policies in Industrial Countries: A Comparative Analysis*. Cambridge, 1988.

Kaim-Caudle, P. *Comparative Social Policy and Social Security: A Ten Country Study*. London, 1973.

PATRICIA M. THANE

Social Insurance

Social insurance is the provision (or regulation) by government of the collective protection of all (or selected groups of) its citizens against a range of risks to their income, most typically old age, sickness, and unemployment. First introduced in Germany in the 1880s, it spread through western Europe to the rest of the industrialized world in the twentieth century; and because its cost and coverage appear easily quantifiable, it has become the conventional measure for comparing welfare systems. Such comparisons are dangerous, however, because social insurance is but one of a number of ways in which individual welfare can be maintained, with or without state intervention. Having been introduced and developed in response to a wide range of economic, social, and political factors, its own nature has also varied greatly over time and between countries. Indeed, one of the reasons for its ubiquity is its ability to fulfill any number of roles—from the insurance of individuals against specific risks to the redistribution of resources throughout society.

Social insurance has typically been introduced when traditional support systems have failed, the market has been unable to provide an acceptable alternative, and governments have felt compelled to act. In late-nineteenth-century western Europe, for example, migration to industrializing towns severed links with families and traditional charities. The increased longevity and mobility of existing and prospective members also undermined other independent forms of mutuality, such as friendly societies in the United Kingdom. Dependence on cash wages therefore increased, and the inherent instability of wages threatened not only to increase poverty but also to undermine the authority of the "male breadwinner" on which "patriarchal" society was based. Governments, which were already under other escalating external and domestic pressures, felt compelled to respond. Externally, the need to compete both commercially and militarily placed an increased emphasis on "national efficiency." The health and productivity of future soldiers and workers could not be jeopardized by periods of destitution. Internally, the congregation of workers in towns, their industrial and political mobilization, and their increasing enfranchisement represented a significant threat to existing elites. A rich debate has subsequently developed between those who maintain that social insurance was a deliberate strategy to legitimize existing regimes (the "Bonapartist" argument) or one conceded under duress (the "social democratic" explanation).

Governments had to act because, as later economists have confirmed, the market was unable to do so. The viability of private insurance depends, for example, on the ability to estimate the nature and likely spread of risk, and the probability of any one person incurring a given risk. Certain "social risks" that affect the whole population, such as unemployment or the rate of long-term inflation, cannot be accurately forecast. Consequently, private unemployment-insurance schemes are unviable as are inflation-proof pensions unsupported by government guarantees. Similarly, private insurance cannot succeed when the probability of an individual incurring a risk is high (as with medical insurance for the chronically ill), can be hidden (the problem of "adverse selection"), or manipulated (the problem of "moral hazard"). Government can surmount such difficulties by using its powers of coercion and taxation to "pool" risks more widely and to raise, when necessary, additional finance. Social insurance is thus the only practicable means of guaranteeing certain services that are essential to national efficiency, social harmony, and private peace of mind. In addition, social insurance can be technically more efficient than private insurance because it does not incur high transaction costs inherent in private individual contracts.

Social insurance, therefore, was introduced in western Europe to meet a given set of historical circumstances and a particular instance of market failure. Its nature, however, was not uniform and it continued to vary. In each country, a restricted range of services for selected groups evolved unevenly toward a universal and comprehensive service, designed to redistribute resources throughout society. The principal variations concerned its coverage of risks and people, its structure, and operational practice.

The range of risks covered typically expanded from industrial injury through sickness and old age to unemployment. Germany pioneered insurance against the first three in 1871, 1883, and 1889 respectively, while the first major scheme of unemployment insurance was inaugurated by the United Kingdom in 1911. The number of people covered was initially small, particularly when schemes were voluntary. When they were compulsory, key industrial workers were usually covered, while those excluded were higher earners or high-risk categories such as agricultural workers and the self-employed. Universal coverage against a specific risk was first attempted in Sweden with its 1913 pensions legislation. However, the twin ideals of universalism and comprehensiveness (signifying the coverage of all people against all risks) were not fully expressed until the 1942 Beveridge Report. These ideals were first implemented in the United Kingdom in 1948, but adoption elsewhere was slow. The coverage of different schemes continued to vary, and as late as the 1970s, under two-thirds of the western European workforce was insured against unemployment.

Structurally, there were two major divergences. The first was between schemes that were funded (with contributions calculated and set aside to meet future liabilities) and those that were "pay as you go" (with expenditure on current claimants being met by contributions from current workers). In Europe, as elsewhere, an initial attempt was made to mimic the market with funded schemes, but as the circumstances that caused market failure arose, these attempts were abandoned. The other divergence was between centrally administered funds and semiautonomous ones, dealing with different risks and occupational groups.

This latter divergence arose as the result of historical accident as well as for constitutional and political reasons. The exceptional centralization of social insurance in the United Kingdom, for example, is a consequence of the unitary nature and fiscal capacity of government in the early twentieth century. Central government lacked competition from a strong regional or local tier of government and had the ability to raise revenue both to subsidize and administer insurance. In addition, the Gladstonian legacy of fiscal probity made the government reluctant to subsidize nongovernmental bodies without strict conditions, which those bodies found unacceptable. In contrast, Bismarck wished to establish an equally centralized system in Germany as part of his strategy to construct a "social monarchy" that would tie workers' allegiance to the Reich. He was unable to do so, however, because the federal government was fiscally weak and opposition from the states and municipalities was strong. Instead, semiautonomous funds were established, which built up such loyalty and vested interests that the Allies were unable to dissolve them, as they wished, in the 1940s. Nevertheless, political choice also lay behind continuing divergences. For example, in welfare regimes classified as social democratic by Esping-Andersen (such as those in Scandinavia), a central fund is an embodiment of social solidarity and of a commitment to equality. On the other hand, in "conservative-corporatist" states (such as Germany and France), separate semiautonomous funds deliberately protect status differences and, thus, continuing inequalities.

Such political differences also help to explain divergences in operational principles and practice. One concerns the level of benefit, which may be either flat-rate (based on subsistence) or earnings related (to preserve an individual's accustomed living standard). The former was historically favored by "liberal" welfare states, such as the United Kingdom before 1959, wishing to minimize government intervention and maximize individual choice. The latter was adopted more widely on the continent and, despite its maintenance of market inequalities, was significantly endorsed by social democratic parties in Germany and Sweden during the major pension reforms of 1957–1959. These parties reasoned, as the fiscal crisis of the 1970s later proved, that the poor had most to gain from an insurance system to which the middle class was fully committed by self-interest—the "paradox of redistribution" as identified by Korpi and Palme (*American Sociological Review* [1998], pp. 661–687). Other divergences include the extent of tax subsidies, the inclusion of dependant's allowances, and terms of eligibility (such as tests to establish disability, waiting times for benefits, and duration of coverage). Each of these detailed differences, which comparative analysis frequently ignores, significantly affects the economic and social nature of each scheme and particularly its redistributory impact.

Social insurance spread spasmodically from western Europe to the rest of the world. In the United States, contributory pensions were introduced at a federal level in 1935 as part of the New Deal. However, as in Germany, the constitutional power of individual states was sufficient to prevent the introduction of further federal schemes; and the openness of the political process enabled vested interests to veto medical insurance in the 1940s and 1990s (although Medicare for the elderly was introduced in the 1960s). There was also a widespread bias against government provision, which was reinforced after the worldwide fiscal crisis of the 1970s by research purporting to show that social insurance actually reduced individual welfare.

Economic growth, it was claimed, was slowed by the discouragement of both private savings and work effort—with generous pensions and unemployment benefits, for example, encouraging early retirement and malingering. Allegedly, collective insurance also generated returns that were lower than those of private schemes. The validity of these claims was later challenged on empirical and theoretical grounds; but the assumption remained that, should government intervene, it should only be to regulate or subsidize private insurance.

Ideological and economic pressure from the United States greatly influenced the evolution of social insurance elsewhere. In Latin America, for example, the essential pillars of welfare remained the family and employment rights (such as work contracts and redundancy pay). As in western European conservative-corporatist states, however, workers in the formal sector increasingly enjoyed a measure of social insurance, organized on occupational lines. Introduced, for instance, to Argentina and Brazil in the 1920s, it expanded to countries such as Mexico in the 1940s and embraced the whole continent by the 1960s. However, rather than expanding thereafter to incorporate the informal sector (as in Europe), the coverage of even existing schemes was curtailed by a combination of economic instability created by trade liberalization and expert advice from the United States. Most notoriously, proceeds from the privatization of copper mines in Chile were used to establish a private system of funded individual accounts. These temporarily boosted savings; but high transaction costs and falling returns after the stock market collapses of the mid-1990s soon served to highlight the market failings that had originally led to the introduction of social insurance.

In Asia, social insurance generally remained less developed. Family and employment rights continued to be the main providers of welfare with government policy targeted on health and education, rather than income maintenance, in order to stimulate economic development. However, as in late-nineteenth-century Europe, social insurance has been gradually recognized as a means both to legitimize unrepresentative regimes and to accumulate "forced" savings for investment. In the highly regulated Central Provident Fund of Singapore, for example, government controls investment decisions. The fund has also been used to finance a housing policy, which has encouraged racial integration. Elsewhere, latent domestic pressure and international advocacy have encouraged other initiatives to offset economic instability. As with early experiments in Europe, they tend to be divided along occupational lines, receive little government subsidy, and exclude unemployment insurance.

The innovation of social insurance in western Europe has been described by Heidenheimer, Heclo, and Adams as "a great watershed in the history of social welfare policy" (*Comparative Public Policy*, 1990). It provided a practical solution to the failure of both traditional support systems and the market. It was also, as its subsequent history demonstrated, politically neutral. It could be used to reinforce the existing status quo. Alternatively, it could empower citizens and generate greater economic and social equality. It could facilitate economic growth as much as discourage it. In western Europe, where it has been most fully developed, it has tended to promote political change and greater equality. This does not preclude it from being adopted elsewhere purely on the grounds of economic efficiency.

BIBLIOGRAPHY

Baldwin, Peter. *The Politics of Social Solidarity*. Cambridge, 1990. The leading archival-based explanation for divergences in major western European welfare states between 1875 and 1975.

Barr, Nicholas. *The Economics of the Welfare State*. 3d ed. Oxford, 1998. A basic theoretical introduction, applied to the United Kingdom.

Classens, Jochen, ed. *Social Insurance in Europe*. Bristol, U.K., 1997. Examines the erosion of social insurance since the 1970s.

Esping-Andersen, Gosta. *The Three Worlds of Welfare Capitalism*. Cambridge, 1990. The pioneering classification of welfare states, which has provoked much debate but on which most comparative analysis is now based.

Flora, Peter, ed. *Growth to Limits: The Western European Welfare States since World War II*. 4 vols. New York, 1986–1987. Contains separate chapters on the evolution of welfare policy in each country.

Flora, Peter, and Arnold J. Heidenheimer, eds. *The Development of Welfare States in Europe and America*. New Brunswick, N.J., 1982. The classic defense based on detailed statistical research.

Goodman, Roger, Gordon White, and Huck-ju Kwon, eds. *The East Asian Welfare Model: Welfare Orientalism and the State*. London, 1998. The pioneering analysis of Japan, Singapore, South Korea, Taiwan, Hong Kong, and China.

Gough, Ian. "Globalization and Regional Welfare Regimes: The East Asian Case." *Global Social Policy* 1.2 (2001), 163–189. Updates and deepens Goodman's analysis.

Gough, Ian, and Geof Wood, eds. *Insecurity and Social Development Regimes in the Developing World*. Forthcoming. Examines Latin America, Africa, East Asia, and Bangladesh within a framework broadly informed by Esping-Andersen.

Hill, Michael, ed. *Income Maintenance Policy*. Cheltenham, U.K., 2000. A collection of classic articles.

Hills, John, John Ditch, and Howard Glennerster, eds. *Beveridge and Social Security: An International Retrospective*. Oxford, 1994. An appraisal of Beveridge and his legacy in Great Britain, continental Europe, Israel, and Australia.

International Labour Office. *Introduction to Social Security*. Geneva, 1970.

Kohler, Peter A., and Hans F. Zacher, eds. *The Evolution of Social Insurance, 1881–1981*. New York, 1982. A highly detailed, technical summary.

Social Security Administration. *Social Security Programs throughout the World*. Washington, D.C., 1999. Biennial survey of international practice.

Stiglitz, Joseph E. *Economics of the Public Sector*. 3d ed. New York, 2000. A basic theoretical introduction, applied to the United States.

RODNEY LOWE

INCOME TAX. *See* Taxation.

INDENTURE. *See* Contract Labor and the Indenture System.

INDIA *[This entry contains four subentries, on the economic history of India during the early Indian civilization, the Muslim period and Mughal Empire, the colonial period, and after independence.]*

Early Indian Civilization

Until very recently, forest environments dominated most of the Indian landmass, supporting hundreds of ethnic groups (today called tribes) that engaged in hunting and gathering or practiced varieties of slash-and-burn agriculture. On the edges of the forests, within the extensive desert areas of the northwest and semiarid expanses of central India, and in complex interactions with the peasant world, pastoralism remained the way of life for a large minority of the population. Fishing has always been the main occupation along the very long coastline. From early Indian history until the present, a main theme of Indian life has been the steady expansion of peasant farmers into the forest, the extension of arable lands, and the coordination of networks for transfer of the agrarian surplus to emerging states. Commerce and urbanization were already established in regional pockets thirty-five hundred years ago, forming the basis for long-distance linkages within wider ranges of the subcontinent, Eurasia, and Africa.

The First Urbanization. By 1500 BCE, the northwestern part of India had already experienced over ten centuries of urbanization, commonly called the Indus Valley Civilization because of the concentration of sites in modern Pakistan or the Harappan Civilization after one of its main sites. The extensive network of town sites covering much of Pakistan and northwestern India, with long-established trade connections to ancient Sumeria, rested on the cultivation of domesticated grains as well as artisan production and commerce. The remarkable similarity of material cultures over this huge area, manifested in pottery styles and standard weights and measures, indicates common value systems even if there is no suggestion of political unification. One of the most striking features of the Harappan complex is its original writing system, found almost entirely in association with icons on small square seals probably used as identification markers for trade and public affairs. Earlier archeology suggested that the Harappan complex had already declined by 1500 BCE, but more recent research has demonstrated that it continued in parts of northwest India for several more centuries. Schol-

ars have expended considerable effort trying to show that the economy of agriculture and craft production developed by the Harappans slowly spread into central India. Recent archeology has indicated, however, that by 1500 BCE many regional agricultural societies had already appeared all over the subcontinent, with no apparent connection to Harappan culture.

Discussions of Indian history typically begin with a people calling themselves the Arya, who were living in the northwest part of India as early as 1500 BCE and are known through the preservation of their religious hymns, called the Vedas. Because their language, an archaic form of Sanskrit, is closely related to older forms of languages spoken in Iran, Central Asia, and Europe, historians often have described the Arya as descendents of nomadic or seminomadic peoples who had migrated into South Asia. The Vedic hymns, composed to accompany offerings for the gods during fire sacrifices, preserve no memory of migrations, portraying instead a number of warlike groups long established in the region today called Punjab. Although the Vedic peoples worked metal, knew agriculture, and encountered walled settlements, much of their economy rested on livestock rearing and cattle raiding. They used wagons for transport and chariots in war. They were in regular contact with societies that they viewed as distinct from themselves. Seen from the perspective of the entire subcontinent, the Arya at this early stage occupied a limited geographic range and exhibited the characteristics typical of many social groups. Through a still poorly understood process, however, the language and the culture of the Arya began to spread throughout the subcontinent while the economic bases for their social organization underwent radical changes.

The Second Urbanization. Archeological research indicates that around 1000 BCE the Ganga and Yamuna rivers in northern India became the focus for a new type of agricultural expansion and urbanization. Iron tools became common in agriculture and in war. Walled cities appeared and steadily grew in size. A common ceramic style called painted grey ware came into use within a geographical area extending from modern Pakistan to Bengal and to central India. The earliest phases of this expansion are visible in the great epics of the *Ramayana* and the *Mahabharata*. In the former text, a prince from the north Indian city of Ayodhya penetrates the forests of central and southern India, forming alliances or waging war with indigenous polities. In the latter, power blocs of north-Indian city-states struggle for dominance of the region around modern Delhi. The later phases of this expansion appear in records of the fifth century BCE that describe the careers of Mahavira, the founder of Jainism, and Gautama, the founder of Buddhism, both preaching around the eastern Ganga River in the modern state of Bihar. Although the forest is always near in these texts, the leaders spend most of their time in and around cities such as Kausambi, Vaisali, Sravasti, and Rajagriha, where merchants make their fortunes coordinating artisan production and long-distance trade. People engage in hundreds of different occupations. Sophisticated courtesans interact with the rich and the powerful, troupes of entertainers travel from town to town, and educated scholars and religious mendicants produce some of the world's greatest philosophical literature. Archaeological excavations have yielded varieties of regional coinages in circulation by this time, and have demonstrated an expansion in the density of farming villages.

By the third century BCE, the north-Indian expansion culminated in political unification under the Mauryan Empire, based in the kingdom of Magadha where Mahavira and the Buddha had preached. Rock and pillar edicts left by Emperor Ashoka (c. 269–232 BCE) indicate that the polity stretched from Afghanistan to Bengal, and from the Himalaya Mountains to Karnataka in south India. Greek ambassadors described the Mauryan capital at Pataliputra (modern Patna) as the largest city on earth, the center of an extensive urban and commercial economy. One of the most important source materials for ancient Indian economy, the *Arthashastra*, or the treatise on wealth and power, originated during this period. It portrays a highly centralized, bureaucratic state, collecting tax revenues from mining, agriculture, craft production, and commerce: the state establishes agricultural colonies, where it retains land ownership rights and regulates behavior of colonists, or conducts land surveys and collects heavy taxes directly from private landowners; state officials levy tolls at borders, regulate weights and measures, conduct land surveys, and oversee the maintenance of elephant forests. Many scholars of Indian history have assumed that the prescriptions of the *Arthashastra* applied in their entirety to a Mauryan administration spread over the vast expanse marked by the several dozen surviving rock and pillar edicts. In fact, the treatise is most likely a composite text from several centuries that describes an idealized administration, and the edicts portray an administrative setup that varied regionally, with little direct impact over "forest people" who lived outside the state's authority. The sources demonstrate, however, an expansion in the scale of political and economic organization emanating from northern India, and the drive toward increasing state control over economic activities.

By the first century CE, India was a major component within an interlinked system of trade that spanned Eurasia. Central Asian peoples known in India as the Kushanas commanded an empire stretching from modern Kazakhstan to the Ganga River, pacifying trade routes that traveled toward the Parthian and Roman empires in the west

and the Han Empire of China in the east. Thus was consolidated for the first time the fabled Silk Road, with major lines extending into northern India. Buddhism, spreading originally with the Mauryans, evolved into the major religious institution in India, centered around monasteries located along trade routes and on the outskirts of major cities, supported by rulers, merchants, and artisans organized in guildlike confederations. Buddhism also traveled along with merchants on the Silk Road, eventually becoming a major cultural and economic force in East Asia. A remarkable Greek manual compiled by seamen trading along the west and east Indian coasts, the *Periplus of the Erythrean Sea*, describes the wide array of ports and goods traded within the Indian Ocean. Major hoards of Roman coins in south India, the presence of Mediterranean-style goods in coastal excavations, and the movement of ceramic types throughout the western Indian Ocean littoral give support to Latin sources that describe a thriving trade between the Roman and the Indian worlds. The Sangam literature in the Tamil language from south India portrays a series of coastal emporia and capital cities of royal dynasties that interacted with merchant empires trading in agricultural products, precious stones, and craft production. This literature views human life within five ecosystems—coast, lowland, desert, forest, and mountain—each with characteristic products, economic activities, and social organization. Along the coasts, the Yavanas (Ionians, or Greeks) arrive in ships laden with precious goods and bargain for fish with local women; in the lowlands, irrigated rice cultivation by peasant farmers is the most significant source of surplus. The texts capture for one region the variety of environments found throughout India, and a well-developed capacity to exploit them locally while feeding commodities into long-distance trading networks.

Patterns of Regional Growth. The Gupta Empire reestablished the empire of Magadha throughout northern India in the fourth and fifth centuries, but during the reigns of its later rulers there already was a marked decline in the circulation of coins and in urbanization. External factors contributed to these changes. Collapse of the four great ancient empires had disrupted the Silk Road and affected Indian Ocean trade. Invasions of the Hunas from the northwest caused political dislocations that reverberated into southern India, sweeping away many of the ancient ruling houses. A growing body of deeds, preserved on metal plates and stone, described the alienation of rights to land, taxes, or labor to ritual specialists (*brahmanas*) or temples. This may represent a broad process of shifting control of the agrarian surplus toward a multitude of localized authorities, or it may represent a process of incorporating many local lords within common systems of ritual legitimation. The overall effect was a limitation in the scale of commercial and political organization, which resembled contemporary changes in Europe. The shrinking of organizational scale does not seem to have inhibited the steady spread of farming communities into new areas; in fact, the expansion of agriculture may have pulled investment away from earlier commercial networks. While long-distance trade toward the west may have declined for some time, it seems to have picked up after the seventh century, as conquests under the Umayyad and Abbasid caliphs provided a security umbrella for traders in the Arabian Sea. This period witnessed an eastward expansion of Indian traders that exerted a profound cultural impact on Southeast Asia.

From the ninth and to the thirteenth centuries, the economy of India entered a period of sustained growth under the aegis of regional dynasties, each willing to claim the title of emperor but never able to impose its will on all the others. The Rashtrakuta dynasty of present-day Maharashtra and Karnataka (eighth to tenth centuries) achieved the most spectacular military successes throughout the subcontinent, followed by the Chola dynasty from Tamil Nadu (ninth to thirteenth centuries), which extended its influence over parts of present-day Sri Lanka and Southeast Asia. Core agricultural zones formed the hearts of these kingdoms, where private or corporate owners of land transferred a percentage of agrarian surplus to the state while retaining a percentage for their own consumption and for the cultivating and laboring classes that tilled the soil. On the edges of the core zones were the domains of subordinate lords, jostling with confederations of local leaders, bound by ritual and military allegiance to the regional kingdoms. Kings exercised the prerogative to manage, exploit, and expand the economy, constructing impressive irrigation facilities and gigantic religious monuments, such as the Chandella dynasty's temple complex at Khajuraho in north-central India. Most agricultural surplus and investment remained in the hands of local lords, mercantile groups, and religious institutions. Within these systems of complex property rights and cross-cutting political allegiances, commercial confederations such as the "Ayyavole 500" linked local markets and long-distance trade into transregional systems stretching from Cairo to Canton. Monetization and transfers of real estate steadily increased. New cities were growing around settlements of traders, religious institutions, and the capitals of the regional kingdoms. The city of Kanchipuram in Tamil Nadu, for example, was seat of the Pallava dynasty (seventh to tenth centuries), a center for textile production, and the site of shrines for Jainism, Buddhism, Vishnu, Shiva, and the goddess Kamakshi.

In the year 1000, Mahmud of Ghazni, ruler of an expansive principality in Afghanistan, began a series of raids into northwest India that culminated in the sack of the fabulously wealthy temple of Somanatha on the coast of Gujarat. These raids set in motion a train of events that led to the foundation of the Delhi Sultanate at the beginning of the thirteenth century, and the eventual installation of Turkish and Afghan military regimes throughout India. From the perspective of most regional states in India, however, the raids of Mahmud went almost unnoticed, and from an economic perspective, they had limited consequences. In fact, the dynamic of agrarian expansion combined with commercialization under the aegis of regional kingdoms and local lords proved remarkably durable, even under new overlords, lasting in South Asia and Southeast Asia well into the fifteenth century.

BIBLIOGRAPHY

Allchin, F. R. *The Archaeology of Early Historic South Asia: The Emergence of Cities and States.* Cambridge, 1995.
Chakrabarti, Dilip K. *India: An Archaeological History: Paleolithic Beginnings to Early Historic Foundations.* Oxford, 1999.
Champakalakshmi, R. *Trade, Ideology and Urbanization: South India 300 BC to AD 1300.* Oxford, 1996.
Chattopadhyaya, Brajdulal. *The Making of Early Medieval India.* Delhi, 1997.
Chaudhuri, K. N. *Trade and Civilisation in the Indian Ocean: An Economic History from the Rise of Islam until 1750.* Cambridge, 1985.
Hall, Kenneth. *Trade and Statecraft in the Age of the Colas.* New Delhi, 1980.
Jha, D. N., ed. *The Feudal Order: State, Society and Ideology in Early Medieval India.* New Delhi, 1999.
Kulke, Hermann. *The State in India, 1000–1700.* Delhi, 1995.
Liu Xinru. *Ancient India and Ancient China: Trade and Religious Exchanges, AD 1–600.* Delhi, 1994.
Ludden, David. *An Agrarian History of South Asia.* In *The New Cambridge History of India,* vol. 4. Cambridge, 1999.
McCrindle, John Watson. *The Commerce and Navigation of the Erythraean Sea.* Amsterdam, 1973.
Randhawa, M. S. *A History of Agriculture in India.* 4 vols. Delhi, 1986.
Ray, Himanshu P. *The Winds of Change: Buddhism and the Maritime Links of Early South Asia.* Delhi, 1994.
Roy, Kumkum, ed. *Women in Early Indian Societies.* New Delhi, 1999.
Sahu, Bhairabi Prasad, ed. *Land System and Rural Society in Early India.* New Delhi, 1997.
Shamasastry, R., trans. *Kautilya's Arthasastra.* 5th ed. Mysore, 1956.
Wheeler, Sir Mortimer. *Rome beyond the Imperial Frontiers.* Westport, Conn., 1971.

JAMES HEITZMAN

Muslim Period and Mughal Empire

The economy of India in the Muslim period (c. 1200–1761) was a mixed one, with agriculture, trade, finance, handicrafts, and industries overwhelmingly important and expanding throughout the subcontinent, and with a generally more patchy pastoral/nomadic sector diminishing in importance over time.

Geography and Climate. The mixed character of the Indian economy has to be understood within its ecological framework. India's enormous agricultural capacity basically derived from the presence of large alluvial river plains and deltas, such as those of the Indus and the Punjab rivers and of the Ganges-Yamuna Doab, as well as others in the peninsula. The fertility of these river plains was much higher than that of European soils, allowing for much denser populations. The alluvial plains had an almost limitless agricultural potential and could absorb more and more people by the extension of clearing operations to virgin lands. The great alluvial plain that extends from the delta of the Indus to that of the Ganges was the demographic heartland of India from early times. By the tenth century CE it already was one of the world's richest agricultural regions. As late as the thirteenth and fourteenth centuries, however, large tracts of the Gangetic plains were still under forest. By the end of the sixteenth century these lands too were almost entirely under cultivation.

India in this period appears to have had a relatively low demographic growth rate. The warm and humid conditions in the densely settled river plains were more conducive to the survival of infectious microparasites than colder and drier climates. Numerous tropical "fevers" and the endemic presence of diseases such as smallpox, bubonic plague, and cholera brought down the demographic growth rate to levels considerably lower than that of the rest of the world on average. The effects of this can be seen over many centuries. Taking into account the low demographic growth rate, and using figures of early-modern times, the total Indian population may be estimated to have risen from around 100 million in 1270 CE to perhaps 150 million in 1600 and to about 200 million in 1800. Disease rather than war was probably the most significant check on population growth. Among the early Muslim invaders of India more may well have died of diseases than on the battlefield. Entire regions were depopulated between Eşfahān and North India in the years around 1033 CE, when a major epidemic raged in the wake of several decades of Ghaznavid raids. Remarkably, however, India was the only major region of the Old World that was not devastated by the Black Death in the fourteenth century. For reasons that are not well understood it remained largely untouched by that epidemic.

Of fundamental importance for the understanding of Indian economic history is archaeological evidence that appears to indicate a truly extraordinary degree of environmental change associated with the instability of rivers, soil erosion, earthquakes, and delta formation. Because of the flatness of the alluvial landscape and the alterations of wet and dry seasons inherent in the monsoon climate, as well as seismic instability throughout the Indo–Gangetic Plain and northern mountain ranges, settlements were often disrupted, and India became a land of lost rivers and lost cities. River instability and hydrological disorder resulting from the silting-up of deepwater channels and the retreat of the sea are not unique to India, but the dramatic digressions that occur there are not paralleled in the more temperate climate zones. Throughout the Muslim period, the hydrographic map of the alluvial plains of especially North India has changed radically. All major and tributary rivers of the region have changed their courses innumerable times, often with catastrophic consequences, making it hard or impossible to identify many historical sites. This is especially true in the Ganges delta, the area now constituting Bangladesh and a wedge of eastern India, where the Ganges is joined by another great trans-Himalayan river, the Brahmaputra. The currents of water coming down from these two rivers have never cut a permanent path to the ocean. Between the twelfth and sixteenth centuries CE the entire Bengal river system shifted eastward, creating an entirely new alluvial delta, which allowed intensive wet-rice cultivation and the expansion of a society of Muslim peasants in its wake. In the Punjab, by contrast, the Indus and all its tributaries have been moving westward throughout history. Here, too, the entire hydrographic network changed quite abruptly in the early fifteenth century, owing to extensive flooding. Everywhere, archaeological evidence shows the remains of numerous abandoned cities and other settlements, and there is pervasive evidence of changes in the cultivation patterns due to changes in the courses of rivers. Navigation had to adjust itself as well; and since most seaports were at the mouths of rivers, sedimentation was a major factor in the decline of many of them. In large parts of India, too, agriculture remained a gamble on the monsoon, and there is evidence of recurrent famines in extended regions throughout the Muslim period. High-yield rice cultivation, moreover, was characteristic only of the most populous regions of the north and east. In much of the Deccan and the peninsula, rather than rice, crops such as sorghum, millet grains, and other coarse, tropical cereals were found, which were used for human food. These crops were more adaptable to unfavorable conditions but less high-yielding than rice. Even millet cultivation, however, was dependent on rainfall, which varied from place to place, from year to year, and from decade to decade.

Revenue Collection. Enough is known for historians to conclude that the main preoccupation of Indo-Muslim states was land revenue and its collection in cash through a hierarchic chain of intermediaries, including a superior class of rural landholders that, from about the fourteenth century onward, became known as zamindars. This revenue unquestionably constituted the bulk of the state's income. Flexible systems of revenue collection were designed, and appear to have been subject to frequent revision. Actual revenue accounts have survived from as far back as the mid-seventeenth century, mostly from the Deccan. Also descriptions of revenue settlements are found in historical chronicles of the reigns of various Muslim rulers from the thirteenth and fourteenth centuries onward. The

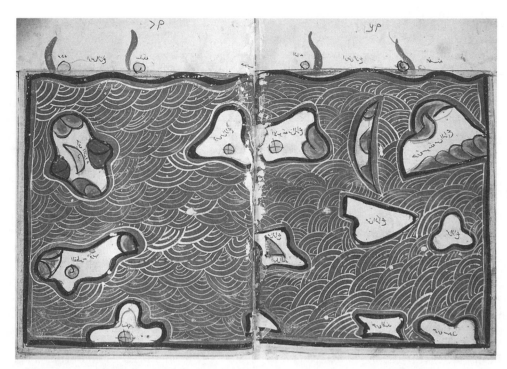

MUGHAL INDIA. Al-Idrisi's map of the Indian Ocean, eleventh to twelfth century. (National Library, Cairo/Giraudon/Art Resource, NY)

first far-reaching attempt to impose a uniform taxation system over large parts of North India was made under Al'ad-Dn Khalji (1296–1316). The foundations of the Mughal fiscal system were laid during the Afghan interregnum of Sher Shah between 1540 and 1545. It was subsequently extended by a Rajput official of the emperor Akbar, Todar Mal, in the late sixteenth century. These so-called *tankhwā* reforms occurred simultaneously with the growing importance of the silver domain, which was due to large-scale silver imports from the New World, Japan, and elsewhere. In the Deccan similar revenue reforms were executed somewhat later under the Deccan sultanates and under the Mughal governors of the Deccan, or under the Brahman ministers of the Maratha successor states.

The actual assessment rates levied by the successive Muslim governments have been the subject of some debate. Recent reinterpretations have questioned whether the earlier estimates of one-third to one-half or more are correct, thereby raising the issue of whether the Indo-Muslim state was, in fact, the crushing Leviathan that it has been made out to be. The rates of assessment, in any case, seem to have varied a great deal; and the agrarian management system was not without incentives for agricultural development. Concern for the welfare of peasants is expressed in innumerable bureaucratic memos. There was also the growth of property rights in land and a growing market in land. The idea that the demise of the Mughal Empire in the eighteenth century was simply due to overtaxation is no longer credible. Ordinary peasants are described in contemporary sources as extremely poor, but not uniformly so.

Pastoralism. The expansion of agriculture in the Indian subcontinent often occurred at the expense of the pastoral domain. Pastoralism in India, however, while becoming increasingly secondary to the agricultural economy, was not insignificant at any time during the Muslim period. The Indian subcontinent has always been an area of transition between the arid zone of Afro-Eurasia, of deserts and steppes where pastoral nomadism predominated, and the humid tropics where intensive agriculture prevailed. In this sense too the ecological situation produced a mixed economy. Important extensions of the arid zone reached from western and northwestern India into the Deccan plateau and the peninsula, and up to northern Sri Lanka. These arid and semiarid extensions provided special opportunities for the breeding of cattle, sheep, and goats. Grazing movements there were relatively short in comparison with Central Asia and the Middle East since the arid and humid areas that served as summer and winter pasturages were in close proximity to each other. Mostly, Indian pastoralists were involved in a kind of herdsman husbandry, moving up and down hills or back and forth between riverbeds. Transhumance, combining pastoralism with crop cultivation and a form of permanent settlement, has also been common in many parts of India. Exceptionally long distances were covered throughout the subcontinent by the nomadic Banjaras, bands of grain dealers with huge bullock trains that supplied armies from the twelfth century onward. Likewise, the Powindas, pastoral nomads of the northwest frontier, for many centuries undertook caravan transportation between India and Iran and Central Asia. Almost everywhere in India, however, nomads and seminomads were or came to be closely associated with sedentary agriculture and represented a form of "enclosed nomadism." Ecologically, the subcontinent was unable to sustain an autonomous or quasi-autonomous pastoral-nomadic economy. Bedouin- or Turkish- and Mongol-style nomadism was impossible because of the general lack of sufficient pastureland, particularly for horses. Moreover, the more that sedentary agriculture encroached upon the pastoralists, the more the latter were pushed into the meadows above the valleys and beyond the irrigated river basins. Genuine pastoral nomadism thus became confined largely to the frontier areas of Baluchistan, Sind, and the Afghan borderlands.

Considering the limitations on pastoral nomadism set by ecological conditions that favored sedentary agriculture, it is not surprising that the Indian subcontinent never suffered a genuine nomadic conquest. The Arabs who conquered Sind in the eighth century did not bring along nomadic pastoralists but merely brought a military occupation force. Similarly, the Turks, laying the foundations of Muslim rule in North India in the eleventh to thirteenth centuries, introduced new military techniques associated with horsemanship and new patterns of political mobilization, but did not bring pastoral nomads. India largely escaped the major Mongol attacks and devastations that occurred in the Middle East, Central Asia, China, and parts of Russia in the thirteenth century. Specifically, the situation in India was quite different from that of the Iranian plateau, where Seljuq-Turkish and, even more, Mongol conquest was followed by extensive nomadization, often leading to the destruction of agriculture. There were numerous short-range Mongol incursions, principally in the Punjab and Sind, and on the northwest frontier. Delhi was sacked by Timur in 1398. In the Punjab, the Mongols devastated some cities, and they turned some agricultural land into pasture. Sometimes agriculture did not revive there until after the fifteenth century. Still there was no lengthy Mongol occupation anywhere. Rather than being devastated by nomads, the agricultural plains of India were brought under Islamic rule, from the twelfth and thirteenth centuries onward, by Turkish invaders who often were of nomadic origin but left their nomadism behind and were not accompanied by nomadic elements with flocks and herds. The Islamic conquests were effected by relatively small, mostly professional armies; they were slow and in-cremental and did not noticeably modify the equilibrium between nomads and sedentaries. Equally significant perhaps was that India became the silver lining around the Mongol cloud as it came to accommodate large numbers of fugitives from Mongol-occupied territories to the west.

Trade. In the new commercial order of the thirteenth century, India emerged with a much greater trading capacity than it had had in late antiquity and the early medieval period. It now quickly achieved a position of economic dominance within the wider Indian Ocean world—a position it could maintain to the extent that it could escape the devastations of the Mongols and the Black Death. There being almost no domestic production of precious metals, the subcontinental propensity to attract precious metals exceeded that of any other medieval civilization. After an initial outflow during the early Muslim conquests, due to plunder removal of treasures, the revitalized economy—with its emerging tax structures, growing populations, and markets—demanded new currencies. India's products were much in demand everywhere, whereas its only imports, next to precious metals, were horses. Indian exports, both to the Middle East and Europe and to Southeast Asia and China, now included not merely luxury items but bulk commodities as well, among them textiles, metals, utensils, weapons, raw silk, foodstuffs, forest produce, oil seeds, narcotics, spices, tannins, dyes, diamonds, pearls, slaves, and others. The leading manufacture was cotton textiles, probably produced in every part of the country, for local consumption as well as for export. The return flows of gold and silver, rather than being immobilized in hoards—as an earlier interpretation had it—were used throughout the subcontinent for both monetary and nonmonetary purposes, with silver coinages preferred in the north and gold in the south. With increasing urbanization, the economy became ever more monetized. Everywhere the monetization of the economy fostered the development of an intermediary group of financiers and traders, converting land revenue into cash, extending credit, and transmitting funds and bills of exchange throughout the length and the breadth of the subcontinent. Propped up by European imports of silver from the New World, Japan, and elsewhere, Mughal imperial coinage reached unprecedented quantities and a uniformly high quality from the middle of the sixteenth to the first half of the eighteenth century. In the seventeenth century there must have been tens of millions of Mughal silver rupees in circulation.

There is evidence of significant Hindu finance and trade diasporas beyond the Indian subcontinent, particularly in East Africa, the Red Sea area, the Persian Gulf, Central Asia and Iran, and Southeast Asia. Meanwhile, much of the long-distance maritime trade in the five hundred years preceding the Portuguese discovery of the sea route to India was in the hands of Muslims. The Muslim trading communities of South India have, in effect, always been more closely connected with the Muslims of the Persian Gulf and coastal Arabia, and with those of the Malay Peninsula and Indonesia, than with the "Tatar" Muslims of the rest of the Indian subcontinent. The mestizo communities that developed here and became known as the Nāvayat of the Kanara coast, the Mappillas of Malabar, and the Ilappai of the Coromandel, all shared the same Arab/Shafi'ite orientation and functionally monopolized the trade in high-value tropical goods such as pepper, as did their Malay-Indonesian counterparts. The ethos of the South-Indian Muslims of the harbor towns was the exact opposite of the isolationism, aversion to the sea, and rural orientation of Malayali Hindu society. Among Muslims of the seaboard the hierarchy of social ranks came to be determined by their traditions of physical mobility and participation in overseas trade. The peculiar militancy that the Mappillas developed in the sixteenth century and afterward was to a large extent a reaction against the Portuguese assault on their trading monopoly in pepper and the prolonged commercial war fought along the Malabar coast between the sixteenth and the eighteenth centuries.

Portuguese, Dutch, and English expansion in India and the Indian Ocean up to about the mid-eighteenth century was essentially a commercial venture. Establishing sovereignty over the sea by the creation of fortified settlements, naval patrols, and passes, the Europeans successfully usurped large segments of the spice trade, and soon started trading in cotton textiles, silk, indigo, coffee, tea, and a wide range of other commodities. They became middlemen in a vast network of commercial activities. European traders, however, were aware that their purchases were but a fraction of the total trade of India and the Indian Ocean. The bulk of the maritime trading activity remained outside their orbit. Similarly, overland trade routes from India to Central Asia and Iran do not appear to have been much affected by the European maritime presence. There is substantial evidence that the overland caravan trade remained vigorous throughout the Muslim period. Generally, historians over the last quarter-century have considerably toned down the picture of economic decay and disintegration in the eighteenth century, when the central structure of the Mughal Empire broke up. Bengal is the most striking example of growth in this period; but other Mughal successor states, such as the Nawabis of Awadh and Hyderabad, the Afghans, Jats, Sikhs, and Marathas also show signs of continued economic vigor until late in the eighteenth century.

BIBLIOGRAPHY

Chaudhuri, K. N. *Trade and Civilisation in the Indian Ocean: An Economic History from the Rise of Islam to 1750.* Cambridge, 1985. A good introduction to the history of trade and navigation in the Indian Ocean.
Dale, S. *Islamic Society on the South Asian Frontier: The Māppilas of Malabar, 1498–1922.* Oxford, 1980. Highlights the role of Muslims in the pepper trade of Malabar, South India.
Das Gupta, A. *Malabar in Asian Trade, 1740–1800.* Cambridge, 1967. An important study of maritime South India in the eighteenth century.
Eaton, R. M. *The Rise of Islam and the Bengal Frontier, 1204–1790.* Berkeley, Los Angeles, and London, 1993. An explanation of the growth of Islam as part of a process of ecological and agrarian change in eastern India.
Habib, I. *Atlas of the Mughal Empire: Political and Economic Maps with Detailed Notes, Bibliography, and Index.* New Delhi, 1982. An indispensable work for the information it provides on all aspects of the economic history of Mughal India.
Habib, I. *The Agrarian System of Mughal India, 1556–1707.* Bombay, 1963. 2nd rev. ed., New Delhi, 1999. A classic study of the agrarian economy of Mughal India, which is, however, dated on the causes of the decline in the eighteenth century, even in the revised version.
Hinze, A. *The Mughal Empire and Its Decline: An Interpretation of the Sources of Social Power.* Brookfield, Vt., 1997. An extended discussion of new work on the decline of the Mughal empire and recent debates about the eighteenth century.
Raychaudhuri, T., and I. Habib, eds. *The Cambridge Economic History of India,* vol. I, *c. 1200–1750.* Cambridge, 1982. The most comprehensive work to date on the economy history of India in the Muslim period.
Richards, J. F., ed. *The Imperial Monetary System of Mughal India.* New Delhi, 1987. A volume of specialist studies on all major aspects of the monetary system of the Mughals.
Wink, A. *Al-Hind: The Making of the Indo-Islamic World.* 2 vols. Leiden, 1990, 1997. A work (with three more volumes forthcoming) that situates India in a wider historical context, especially that of the Islamic world from the seventh to the eighteenth century.

ANDRÉ WINK

Colonial Period

After being under British colonial rule since the 1750s, India attained independence on 15 August 1947, setting in motion the decolonization movement in both Asia and Africa. In India at the time of independence, economic development was still very limited: the average daily per capita foodgrain availability was about 400 grams; the literacy rate was 17 percent of those over the age of 10; and average life expectancy at birth was 32.5 years. As for population growth, national income, and per capita income during the last century of colonial rule, it is useful to differentiate the period before 1920 and the period of 1920 to 1947. There were different patterns; from 1860 to 1920, India's population grew by about 30 percent and per capita income also grew by at least 35 percent, or less than 0.5 percent per year. This growth performance was partly the result of the worldwide influenza epidemic of 1918, which lowered the population of the 1921 census and thereby would show a higher per capita income around that year. For the 1920 to 1947 period, most estimates suggest a stable per capita income, with an annual growth of both population and national income of perhaps 1 percent. Thus fair growth in per capita income through the last half of the nineteenth century appears to have ceased after 1920. One could take the range of per capita income estimates for India and say that for the whole century before independence, Indian growth was less than that of Japan, western Europe, or the United States. As for the industrial distribution of the workforce, the bulk of it remained employed in agriculture into the early twentieth century and remained at 70 percent or more throughout, although the contribution of the agricultural sector to national product probably declined during the period.

While India's overall aggregate rate of growth was somewhat sluggish, there were changes occurring in the Indian colonial economy. At certain times, in various sectors and regions, there was considerable growth in output associated with capital accumulation by peasants, landlords, merchants, bankers, and industrialists; there were also some investments in productivity-enhancing and profit-enhancing production processes. Some agriculturists were able to take advantage of increased world demand for such crops as jute, cotton, and peanuts (groundnuts), while Indian businessmen manufactured cotton yarn for export in the nineteenth century and a wide range of products for the domestic consumer market in the twentieth. While all the best agricultural land was probably in use by 1900, some new cultivation went on until the 1940s; the area under irrigation almost doubled between 1900 and 1939. Considerable evidence also exists for technical change in agriculture, handicrafts, and mechanized industry. The spread of new seed types and crop strains aided output growth in cotton and peanuts, while such techniques as the transplantation of rice and the ginning of cotton increased yields and marketability. Indian workmen had few difficulties acquiring the skills needed to operate modern textile machinery, while the Tata Iron and Steel Company, one of the premier industrial enterprises of colonial India, set up the successful Technical Institute in 1921 and in 1931 the Indian-staffed Research and Control Laboratory. In handicrafts during the 1920s and 1930s, fly-shuttle looms and the use of rayon and some artificial fibers broadened the technological base of handloom weaving.

Government and Administration. In government and administration, the small but enormously powerful elite cadre of Indian Civil Service (ICS) officers was seen as the "steel frame" that held the British Empire in India together. Authority and responsibility were concentrated in their hands in the districts where they acted as both heads of the administration and of the judicial institutions—maintaining law and order and collecting revenues. In 1950, the adoption of India's constitution became a new stage in the move toward representative government. This process began with the Indian Councils Act of 1861, and it continued through the Morley-Minto Reforms of 1909, the Montagu-

Chelmsford Reforms of 1919, and the Government of India Act of 1935. At each of those reforms, the participation of Indians in the central and state legislatures, as well as in the executive councils, was increased by the British Colonial Office, and the franchise was extended to ever larger numbers of people. A considerable degree of continuity existed between the Government of India Act and the Constitution of India; the features of continuity included the adoption of a federal system of government, with three legislative lists of powers to be exercised (1) exclusively by the central government, (2) exclusively by the states, or (3) concurrently. There was a combination of a considerable degree of provincial autonomy, with extensive powers left to the central government, including emergency powers—and this made it possible to convert the federal system into a unitary government. In several respects, however, the Constitution of India makes a sharp break with the British colonial past, but not with British colonial practices. First, the constitution adopts in total the Westminster form of parliamentary government, rather than the mixed parliamentary–bureaucratic authoritarian system that actually existed in India. Second, fundamental human rights were included in the constitution but not in the Government of India Act of 1935. Thirdly, the constitution introduced universal adult suffrage.

It was commonly argued by the British rulers of India that parliamentary democracy was unsuited to that society—intensely divided into various religious and other communal groupings—whose social structure was also imbued with an ideology of hierarchy, not equality. The British, operating on a set of assumptions that treated Hindus and Muslims as distinct peoples, introduced mechanisms, notably separate electorates, which served to keep them apart. Divisions among the elite and the middle-status land-controlling castes in large parts of India also existed at independence. In some parts of India, particularly in the states of Tamil Nadu and Maharashtra, movements had been launched to displace the dominant Hindu Brahmin caste from disproportionate control over jobs in the public services and other socioeconomic advantages. Before independence, the leaders of lower castes had argued that their members might not be treated fairly within a parliamentary system that elite castes could turn to their advantage—therefore they thought they might require special protections.

Colonial Rule and Economic Growth. To what extent can the limited growth of the Indian economy be attributed to British colonial rule since the 1750s? It need hardly be stressed that colonial rule is designed to promote the interests of the metropolitan (mother) country, if necessary at the expense of those of the colony. In India, the colonial episode began in 1757, with the British East India Company seizing control of the rich province of Bengal. In 1759, it

INDIAN MARKET. Women selling grains and vegetables. Painting by Shiva Dayal Lal, Patna, mid-nineteenth century. (Victoria and Albert Museum, London/Art Resource, NY)

quashed the last vestiges of the ruling Mughal influence at Surat, in Gujarat Province. After a brief rearguard action in defence of the core area of Delhi, in 1784 the Mughal emperor submitted to the protection of the greatest of the Maratha war chiefs, Mahadji Scindia. Then, in 1803, with the defeat of the Marathas by the British armies of Lord Lake, Delhi was occupied by the East India Company, and the Mughal emperor was reduced to a "tinsel sovereign." Following the Mutiny of 1857, also known as the First War of Indian Independence, in 1858 the British Crown assumed direct charge of the Indian possessions. In the Delhi Durbar of 1877, Queen Victoria was proclaimed Queen Empress.

Access to the monetized land revenues of India from 1757 to 1818 made it possible for Britain to build one of the largest European-style standing armies, thus augmenting the British land forces, which had been small and logistically backward, except for the few years of the final struggle with Napoleon. Britain's Indian army was used in large measure to hold the Indian subcontinent, but after 1790 it was increasingly employed to forward British interest in southern and eastern Asia and the Middle East.

Nationalist Critique. In second half of the nineteenth century, a spirited Indian nationalist critique began, with the British rule the fountainhead of India's miseries. The nationalist argument was put forward most forcefully by Dadabhai Naoroji, a Parsi businessman and the founder of the Indian National Congress; he was elected to the House of Commons to speak for Indian interests in the 1890s. There was also R. C. Dutt, who resigned from the Indian Civil Service to pursue his attacks on the revenue administration of Bengal; he focused on the distortions to the Indian economy brought about by British rule and the impoverishment of the mass population through the colonial "drain of wealth" from India to Britain throughout the nineteenth century. Nationalists asserted that the British had destroyed or deformed a successful and smoothly functioning precolonial Indian economy. British colonial rule was seen to have removed indigenous sources of economic growth and power, replacing them with imperial agents and networks, which deprived Indian entrepreneurs and businessmen in the "modern" sector of the opportunity to lead a process of national regeneration through economic development. The result was also severe welfare and distributional effects in India's "traditional" sector, owing to the imposition of foreign competition on handicraft workers and forced commercialization on agriculturists.

The Deindustrialization Debate. The Industrial Revolution in Britain, which started in the second half of the eighteenth century and matured during the first half of the nineteenth, had important consequences for the Indian economy. As late as the 1770s, one writer on India had commented that the demand for Bengal manufactures could never lessen because the quality of its cloth was so fine that no other nation could compete with it. Yet the invention and application of machinery to spinning and weaving had, within fifty years, undermined Bengal's position as one of the most important areas of textile production in India. By about 1830, the elimination of Indian handloom textiles from international markets was all but complete; the next stage was the emergence of Britain's Lancashire-made cotton textiles as the single most important class of foreign goods imported into the Indian subcontinent. A primary plank in India's nationalist argument regarding the negative aspects of British colonial rule was the presumed destruction of the Indian handloom sector— often described as the process of deindustrialization. There was merit in this argument; research suggests a decline of some 3.6 million jobs in the Indian nonfactory textile sector from 1850 to 1880. If this figure is subject to error—based on estimates of handspun yarn, the assumed growth of population and the per capita income, as well as the coefficient relating cloth production to full-time jobs— it conveys the order of magnitude involved. At the same time, the handloom sector adopted a range of survival strategies and, by and large, managed to hold its own. The primary strategy was the identification of specific market segments for which the sector enjoyed a clear and substantial advantage over the mill sector, both foreign and domestic. These market segments ordinarily included either the most expensive of the luxury textiles, involving a good deal of embroidery and other handwork, or the very coarse cotton varieties. Inexpensive machine-made yarns were also employed by the handloom sector. From the early years of the twentieth century onward, the sector also used new technology, as well as new institutional arrangements for raising credit and for marketing. The destabilizing influence of British competition in textile imports was thus neutralized to some extent.

The other major economic development in India was the rise of a modern industrial sector. From the 1850s, when the first major industries were started, to 1914, India had the world's largest jute-manufacturing industry, the fourth-to-fifth largest cotton-textile industry, a modern iron- and steel-manufacturing sector, and the third largest railway network. The jute industry was initiated, managed, and entirely controlled by Europeans. Every mill (except one started by an American group in 1914) was promoted by Englishmen or Scotsmen. The mills were typically initiated as rupee firms, although a few (nine of the sixty-four existing in 1914) started as sterling ventures. Rupee companies tended to be financed mainly by investors in India; sterling companies probably obtained much of their initial capital in Britain, but they also offered blocks of shares for sale in India. In all cases, most of the capital came from British investors—civil servants, other officials, and merchants. Only during the 1920s and 1930s did Indian enterprise—mainly Marwaris—enter the jute sector.

The modern cotton-textile industry began in western India about the time the jute industry was established in Bengal. Whereas the jute industry was dominated by non-Indians, the cotton industry was essentially Indian in origin, largely controlled by Indian investors, and increasingly administered by Indian managers and technicians. Given the widespread impression that India's industrial development was impossible because of implacable British hostility to Indian competition, India's cotton-mill history seems particularly paradoxical; it flourished despite competing against the most important, the most internationally aggressive and politically most powerful industry in Britain. Its rapid expansion began only after 1870, yet by 1910 the Indian industry had become one of the world's largest. Unlike the jute industry, its expansion—although certainly assisted by substantial opportunities in foreign trade—ultimately depended on its own domestic markets.

The establishment of India's modern iron- and steel-producing unit at Jamshedpur in Bihar in the early years of the twentieth century owed a great deal to the vision of J. N. Tata, probably the most creative of the first generation of Indian industrial entrepreneurs. Initially, he planned to obtain all or most of the capital for the project in London. Despite favorable reports about the quality and quantity of raw material and careful planning of the enterprise, negotiations in 1906 and early 1907 proved fruitless. The Tata concern was unable to get solid financial support for the project; a major factor seems to have been an unwillingness to yield control. London investors were not prepared to risk their capital in ventures controlled by Indian entrepreneurs, even those with the strong reputation of the Tatas. Only then did the Tatas turn to India, and the Tata Iron & Steel Company (TISCO) was registered in August 1907 with a nominal capital of 23.2 million rupees (approximately 1.6 million British pounds), and the entire amount was subscribed to the Bombay firm by some eight thousand people in three weeks. Not only was Bombay then a major commercial center, where people were prepared to take some investment risks in modern enterprises, but since 1904 the city had experienced a boom. At the same time, India was generally engulfed by an enthusiastic nationalism, to which the Tatas appealed in their prospectus. Known for their financial competence, caution, and golden successes, the Tatas were able to take advantage of this fortunate set of conditions.

India's overall industrial growth, which continued during the interwar years, should not be overstressed. When the political philosopher Karl Marx wrote in the mid-1800s, he expected that the introduction of railways and modern factories would rapidly transform the subcontinent—he was excessively optimistic. Modern industrial processes did not spread easily from region to region or sector to sector, and the total effect was not cumulative. At the time of independence, India was still largely nonindustrial and one of the world's poorest areas. Most interpretations have attributed the limited scale of modern industrial development either to British policy, which inhibited local initiative, or to the Indian value system and social structure, which diminished entrepreneurial drives. While these elements may have set parameters within which business behavior occurred, they do not explain the specific and diverse characteristics of actual entrepreneurial choices. The Indian economy in the nineteenth and twentieth centuries was essentially a private-enterprise economy, and the vast bulk of decisions about the allocation of resources was made by private businessmen. In no decade between 1872 and 1947 did the state's annual share of gross national product (GNP) average more than 10 percent; usually it was less than that.

Rise of the Modern Sector. To the extent that the expansion of modern industry depended on decisions made by private entrepreneurs, no single social or economic characteristic can explain the slowness of India's industrialization process; no single act of policy or change of behavior could have made for much more rapid progress than did occur. It is not that India was caught in a low-level equilibrium trap from which, once liberated, development would be cumulative. When the great array of evidence is considered, the image that emerges is one with a web of relationships that served to dampen the performance level and the rate of change. Expansion in a single sector, however successful, proceeded only in a limited way; it could not generate, on its own, an ever-widening chain of reactions throughout the system. Rapid and sustained industrial expansion on a broad front required not only an extensive array of basic social, political, and economic preconditions but also the development of an institutionalized mindset—one that solved the new problems that continually emerged. Despite its other virtues, the Indian system had not possessed these features at the beginning of the nineteenth century. Then, during the next 150 years, various necessary but insufficient elements of economic expansion were introduced. Most of the economic changes were not only limited in scale and scope, they also generated contradictory features that did not promote widespread economic success.

BIBLIOGRAPHY

Bayly, C. A. *Indian Society and the Making of the British Empire*. In *The New Cambridge History of India*, vol. 2.1. Cambridge, 1988.
Brass, Paul. *The Politics of India since Independence*. In *The New Cambridge History of India*, vol. 4.1. Cambridge, 1990.
Chatterji, Basudev. *Trade Tariffs and Empire: Lancashire and British Policy in India, 1919–1939*. Delhi, 1992.
Chaudhuri, K. N. "Foreign Trade and Balance of Payments 1757–1947." In *The Cambridge Economic History of India*, vol. 2, edited by Dharma Kumar and Meghnad Desai, pp. 804–877. Cambridge, 1983.
Harnetty, Peter. "'Deindustrialization' Revisited: The Handloom Weavers of the Central Provinces of India, c. 1800–1947." *Modern Asian Studies* 29 (1991), 455–510.
Heston, A. "National Income." In *The Cambridge Economic History of India*, vol. 2, edited by Dharma Kumar and Meghnad Desai, pp. 376–462. Cambridge, 1983.
Morris, Morris D. "The Growth of Large-Scale Industry to 1947." In *The Cambridge Economic History of India*, vol. 2, edited by Dharma Kumar and Meghnad Desai, pp. 553–676.
Muchie, M., O. Prakash, and H. L. Wesseling. *North-South Perspectives: Debates on Colonialism and North-South Relations*. Amsterdam, 1989.
Ray, Rajat K. *Industrialization in India: Growth and Conflict in the Private Corporate Sector, 1914–47*. Delhi, 1979.
Tomlinson, B. R. *The Economy of Modern India 1860–1970*. In *The New Cambridge History of India*, vol. 3. Cambridge, 1993.
Twomey, Michael J. "Employment in Nineteenth Century Indian Textiles." *Explorations in Economic History* 20 (1983), 37–57.
Visaria, Leela, and Praveen Visaria. "Population 1757–1947". In *The Cambridge Economic History of India*, vol. 2, edited by Dharma Kumar and Meghnad Desai, pp. 463–532. Cambridge, 1983.

OM PRAKASH

Independent India

Epitomizing the views of British classical economists on the difficulty of bringing enlightened governance to the Indian subcontinent was David Ricardo's comment to James Mill in 1818: "What a frightful obstruction to improvement does the immoral character of the people of India present!" It was later echoed by many commentators. From Gunnar Myrdal's famous portrayal in *Asian Drama* (1968) of the Indian economy trapped in a "low-level equilibrium," caused by a regressive social structure governed by a "soft state" too weak to change it, to Deepak Lal's 1984 analysis of a "Hindu equilibrium" brought about by the impact of ecological fragility and nonmaterial cultural values, an apparent unwillingness of Indian producers and consumers to compromise their social and cultural identity for the sake of increased economic productivity has baffled many analysts—especially those reared on liberal economic models of human behavior and motivation. A broad band of Marxist opinion—beginning with Karl Marx's nineteenth-century analysis of the primitive accumulation of the "Asiatic mode of production," in which the impetus of material change was vitiated by a system of predatory states and self-sufficient villages—has also concluded that the hierarchical structures within Indian culture and society formed the greatest barriers to economic change and progress in the subcontinent in modern times.

An alternative explanation for India's problems in economic development has come from those who stress the long period of exposure to British imperial control and neoimperialist influence, rather than the unique Indian system of cultural values. Here, modern dependency theory has built on the insights of the classic accounts of Indian nationalist critics about the effect of British rule, such as Dadabhai Naoroji (1901) and Romesh Chandra Dutt (1904). The result has been an analysis of a vicious circle of underdevelopment dominated by peasant production in agriculture with low returns to labor, as well as limited industrialization dependent on foreign technology and alliances with international capital. This distinctive political economy of underdevelopment is thought to have created a hierarchy of dominant classes in towns and countryside, to reward capital at the expense of labor, and to suppress collectivist models of development in favor of a dependent form of individualistic capitalism. Both neoclassical and neo-Marxist theorists have identified the Indian middle classes—especially public-sector employees and private producers who allied with state enterprises—as the main beneficiaries of limited economic growth, as well as the main impediments to allowing that growth to spread more widely through the economy in ways that might disrupt their privileged control over capital, educational opportunities, and employment. The political and administrative structures of the Indian state that emerged with independence in 1947, and that has maintained a system of authoritarian democracy since then, have often been placed at the heart of the process of "rent-seeking"—by which the owners of the scarce factors of production have been rewarded for that ownership alone, with little incentive to secure increased productivity in competitive markets.

Shaping the Planned Economy. At independence in 1947, India displayed the hallmarks of an underdeveloped economy: population had been rising at over 1.2 percent per year since the 1920s (and was to exceed 2 percent per year by the 1960s); less than 25 percent of the adult population was literate; average life expectancy was less than 35 years. For females, the low level of basic health services and other inequalities of opportunity were demonstrated by life expectancies lower for them than for males. Agriculture, which employed more than 75 percent of the labor force in 1947, produced about 60 percent of national income; the availability of food grains per capita, which had been static at best in the 1920s and 1930s, probably declined in the 1940s and early 1950s. The agricultural economy had been severely affected by the Great Depression of the 1930s, which had disrupted the supply of rural credit and had dented the profitability of the export staples of the colonial economy—notably jute, tea, wheat, and raw cotton. In the 1930s, some government support for import substitution in industry and India's participation in World War II helped to stimulate the emerging industrial sectors of western and eastern India (based around Bombay and Calcutta, respectively); yet wartime shortages and supply problems held industry back and caused severe disruptions to the internal market for consumer goods, which culminated in the Bengal Famine of 1943 that claimed more than 3 million lives. In 1947, the British Indian Empire was partitioned into the two independent countries of India and Pakistan (a Muslim country with territory to the northwest of India and to the northeast; East Pakistan broke away to become the new state of Bangladesh in 1971). Partition was followed by communal rioting, resulted in the loss of some 200,000 lives, and created 14 million refugees. It also damaged important internal economic linkages, especially within the jute industry of Bengal and the wheat-farming industry of Punjab. The uncertain and unstable international and interregional economic context of the post-war years soon increased the difficulties of food supply, export competitiveness, and the adoption of appropriate foreign-exchange regimes in the new states.

From the early 1950s to the mid 1960s, the government of India followed a classic import-substituting industrialization (ISI) strategy, based on the replacement of imported consumer and capital goods with domestic manufactures, and coordinated by a series of five-year plans that had been devised and implemented by central government. In the early 1950s, export-pessimism and economic management were understandable responses to the disturbed international and internal conditions. The planning process of the 1950s and 1960s, which was supported by the intellectual weight of many leading economists in India and abroad, rationed foreign exchange and imports of capital goods, while trying to build the public sector as the supplier of essential inputs to industry. In agriculture, land reform was not effective in the redistribution of rural social and economic power; the provision of cooperative credit and price-support mechanisms tended to benefit the largest farmers at the expense of the rest of the rural economy. While the proportion of rural families with no access to land was comparatively small, many deficit producers still needed some employment within the rural labor market (either directly or through sharecropping arrangements), to bring their household incomes up to subsistence levels. Without major investments in infrastructure and irrigation, the rural economy remained largely under the control of those who dominated the interlinked markets for agricultural land, credit, and employment.

Beyond ISI. The ISI phase of India's economy had unprecedented average annual growth rates between 1950 and 1965, of more than 5 percent for agriculture and more than 7 percent for industry despite the growing uncompetitiveness of India's exports and the increased dependence on external sources of aid and capital investment. By the late 1960s, however, that strategy could no longer be sustained because of falling agricultural output as a result of poor monsoon seasons, as well as pressure from India's aid donors (especially the United States) for fundamental changes in policy. The political interregnum that followed the 1964 death of Jawaharlal Nehru (prime minister of India since 1947) also weakened the ability of the central government to impose a firm direction on the planning process. Foreign advisors then looked to technical change

MODERN INDIA. Wheat reaping machine at work in fields near Ludhiana, Punjab, 1981. (© Marc and Evelyne Bernheim/Woodfin Camp and Associates, New York)

in agriculture to solve the pressing problems of development (especially population increases), and India was exposed to the package of technical and economic changes associated with the Western imposition of the Green Revolution in Asian agriculture. In practice, the cultivation of high yielding varieties (HYVs) of staple food grains proved difficult to organize in many parts of the subcontinent, especially for rice and millet, and the effect of the associated policies of subsidizing such capital inputs as fertilizers, pesticides, and mechanical equipment initially benefited the producers with adequate capital resources over those who depended on selling their labor to survive. Total reliance on HYVs for agricultural income in India had significant risks, and those able to avoid such risks took advantage of the opportunity. Thus the Green Revolution has often been seen as a weaker and less progressive force in India than it was in East and Southeast Asia, where it was perhaps better adapted to the prevailing social and ecological conditions.

Like many developing economies, India suffered severely from the stagflationary international environment of the early 1970s, especially from the rise in import prices for oil and oil-derivatives, on which the early models of the Green Revolution depended. State-administered purchasing and distribution systems for food grains and other essentials were slow to react to rapid, externally induced changes in the prices of both agricultural and industrial inputs, leading to widespread discontent with the ruling government. That discontent soon resulted in the imposition of a "state

of emergency," in 1975, by Prime Minister Indira Gandhi (Nehru's daughter), and led to her temporary fall from power in 1977. Despite a widespread perception of "urban bias" in development policies during this period, there were significant advances in agricultural production that resulted from the spread of mechanical power for irrigation, as well as the unbundling of the Green Revolution inputs and their adaptation to local conditions. These presented new opportunities to many farming families and led to the rise of what have been called "bullock capitalists"—peasant families with relatively small landholdings (2.5 acres), who could then produce a surplus of staple crops for sale from their own labor. One result was a significant tightening of the rural labor market, with a rise in real wages and increased interrural migration. Food production also increased significantly, with India becoming self-sufficient in food for domestic consumption by the late 1970s—although the skewed nature of India's labor markets and other mechanisms for distribution meant that many Indians still lived at or below acceptable levels of subsistence.

The Limits of Structural Reform. During the 1980s and 1990s, successive Indian governments of different political complexions and degrees of stability attempted to implement a series of structural reforms that limit the bureaucratic barriers to economic expansion and diversification in the secondary and tertiary sectors of the economy. While Indian's manufacturing industry has faced significant competition in world markets—especially in textiles—new service sectors, such as computer software and programming, have responded to these opportunities, and the public sector has acquired the technology necessary to manufacture nuclear weapons. Reforms in fiscal policy in the 1990s gave greater incentives for private and foreign capital, including investment by Indians resident abroad, which led to a significant decline in state involvement in industry and strong growth in industrial output, especially in consumer durables. The ninth five-year plan predicted an average annual growth in GDP of 6.5 percent from 1997 to 2002. By 1999 the secondary sector produced 23 percent of GNP, against 27 percent from the primary sector, although it employed a much smaller proportion of the workforce of 439 million.

It is still unclear what benefits these nodes of growth brought to rural areas, where three-quarters of the population still live, and to the mass of the deprived population which suffered from low capabilities and few opportunities.

At the end of the twentieth century, India remained home to one-sixth of the world's population (even with annual emigration), almost half of whom are at or below the World Bank's primary international poverty line (an income equivalent to U.S. $1 per day in local purchasing power), according to the latest *World Development Report* (Washington, D.C., 2000). While average life expectancy rose to 62 for males and 64 for females, adult illiteracy remained high (31 percent of males over 15; 61 percent of females), and access to public services—especially basic medical facilities—remained poor in many rural areas. Aggregate figures for that large and diverse country are misleading, since they fail to distinguish such regions as Kerala, which has rates of development of human resources as high as those in advanced areas of China, from such regions as Bihar or Uttar Pradesh, which display gender inequalities in access to life chances that are larger than those of most countries in sub-Saharan Africa. Some analysts, such as Amartya Sen (1995), have argued that the political and social activism of disadvantaged groups in the most developed areas of the country can spread to other regions, but ongoing concerns with environmental degradation in India suggest yet another set of constraints to sustainable development. Only the history of the twenty-first century will tell how far any of these problems can be overcome by enlightened policy or political activism at local, national, or global levels.

BIBLIOGRAPHY

Bagchi, Amiya Kumar. *The Political Economy of Underdevelopment*. Cambridge, 1981. A clear statement of the "dependency" analysis of India's poor development record, both before and after 1947.

Bhagwati, Jagdish, and Padma Desai. *Planning for Industrialization: India's Trade and Industrialization Policies, 1950–1966*. Oxford, 1970. An exposition and critique of import-substituting industrialization in India by two prominent Indian economists.

Drèze, Jean, and Amartya Sen. *India: Economic Development and Social Opportunity*. Delhi, 1995. A wide-ranging account of the possibilities and limitations of "sustainable human development" in India, seen in a wide comparative perspective; offers a substantial statistical appendix.

Dutt, Romesh C. *Indian in the Victorian Era: An Economic History of the People*. London, 1904. A classic attack on the costs of British rule in the nineteenth century.

Lal, Deepak. *The Hindu Equilibrium: Cultural Stability and Economic Stagnation, India, 1500 BC–1980 AD*. Oxford, 1984. A bold attempt by the most prominent neoclassical critic of Indian development policy to demonstrate the timeless and ahistorical qualities of the subcontinent's economic structures and problems.

Joshi, Vijay, and I. M. D. Little. *India's Economic Reforms, 1991–2000*. Oxford, 1996. A useful account of recent policy changes and an attack on the "rent-seeking" structures that have allegedly vitiated the benefits of economic management in India.

Myrdal, Gunnar. *Asian Drama: An Inquiry into the Poverty of Nations*, vols. 1 and 2. Harmondsworth, U.K., 1968. A classic exposition of the hopes and fears of the first wave of professional development economists, who tried to analyze the problems of engineering Indian economic growth.

Naoroji, Dadabhai. *Poverty and Un-British Rule in India*. London, 1901. A retrospective collection of the polemical writings and speeches of a prominent critic of British rule, who became the first black Member of Parliament at Westminster in 1892.

Rudolph, Lloyd I., and Susan Hoeber Rudolph. *In Pursuit of Lakshmi: The Political Economy of the Indian State*. Chicago, 1987. An account of political and economic changes in the 1970s and 1980s; identifies the emergence of a new group of peasant entrepreneurs as "bullock capitalists."

Tomlinson, B. R. *The Economy of Modern India, 1860–1970*. Cambridge, 1993. A convenient introduction to the history of the modern Indian economy and the main lines of literature about it; stresses continuities across the political changes of 1947.

B. R. TOMLINSON

INDOCHINA. Vietnam, Cambodia, and Laos are three striking exceptions in the Southeast Asian context to the rapid economic growth experienced during the second half of the twentieth century. Although these countries attempted to emulate the East Asian experience of the 1990s, a tremendous income gap remains. Recent studies in economic history indicate, first, that precolonial and colonial economic and social conditions were rather similar to those of the neighboring countries. Second, the current north-south economic divide was a permanent feature in Vietnam. Third, it is not possible to identify a single factor explaining the emergence of the economic gap. It was rather the consequence of a tragic accumulation of mismanagement under French rule (1858–1954), the disruptive impact of military conflicts (1940–1979), and the failure of Soviet-style economic development policy (1954–1989).

Before 1802. Vietnam, Cambodia, and Laos experienced significant institutional transformations and economic changes before colonization. The most important features were related to Vietnam's southward move (*nam-tien*).

Before the fifteenth century, the ethnic Vietnamese population was concentrated in present northern Vietnam (Tonkin under French rule). The present central Vietnam (Annam under French rule) was colonized between 1426 and 1794, at the expense of the Cham kingdoms. Between 1658 and 1757, it was the turn of the Khmer provinces of the Mekong Delta, present southern Vietnam (Cochin China under French rule), to be invaded and annexed. This was followed, during the early nineteenth century, by an attempt by Vietnamese rulers to occupy eastern Laos and the rest of Cambodia, in a fierce competition with Siam (Le, 1992). Around 1800, Vietnam was already a demographic power by Southeast Asian standards: 7.5 million people compared with nearly 1 million for Cambodia and Laos (Reid, 1988).

Superior techniques in hydraulic works permitted higher rice yields and rural density in Vietnam than in Cambodia, Laos, or Siam, where floating rice or dry cultivation remained the dominant technique until the twentieth century. In Vietnam's southward move, the first step was land reclamation by ethnic Vietnamese, opening lower plains and marshes to rice cultivation and other lands to cash crops. The second step was the gradual military occupation by Vietnamese rulers and the introduction of Confucian bureaucracy. The Chinese influence embodied in the administrative system provided military superiority. Vietnamese rulers were able to organize a tax system, extracting a rice surplus and financing huge permanent armies. In addition, local militias of peasant-soldiers were granted tax or corvée exemptions.

Between 1627 and 1802, Vietnam was split into two parts under rival rulers: the Trinh controlled the north, and the Nguyen ruled the affluent provinces of central Vietnam. The core of the Trinh possessions was the overcrowded areas of the Red River delta and northern Annam, affected by recurrent famines and epidemics. The Trinh had loose control over various ethnic groups living in higher regions, close to the Chinese and Lao borders. The north was virtually an autarkic economy, although there was some export to China of mining, hunting, and gathering products and some import of Chinese luxuries or cultural goods. The Nguyen of central Vietnam were deeply involved in intra-Asian and international trade, exporting cinnamon, sugar, silk, or pepper, and importing Western, Chinese, and Japanese goods (Nguyen, 1970).

With the help of immigrants from the north and some ethnic Chinese, the Nguyen expanded the rice frontier of the south. These provinces continued to export more rice from the hub of Saigon-Cholon. These twin cities had a combined population of around 100,000 inhabitants in the late eighteenth century, the estimated total population of southern Vietnam at that time being 500,000, with an important Khmer minority. This figure also included a sizable Chinese community, mostly in Cholon, the China-town close to Saigon. Other ethnic groups of the southern and central Vietnam highlands were collectively described by the Vietnamese as *moi*, or savage. They were occasionally captured and enslaved as manpower for large rice estates and cash crop plantations, along with ethnic Vietnamese bonded as slaves for debt insolvency.

By Vietnamese standards, the affluence of the Nguyen possessions was impressive. Around 1850, southern Vietnam had a yearly exportable rice surplus of about 0.4 ton per capita. Although tax rates were lower than in northern Vietnam, export revenues provided the Nguyen with the financial basis for their military supremacy. In 1802, they reunified Vietnam under a new imperial dynasty. Reviving the Chinese Confucian model, they established a centralized administration and ruled from their new capital established in Hue (central Vietnam).

The Nineteenth Century. According to Vietnamese dynastic sources, Vietnam experienced an economic recovery during the first two decades of the 1800s as a result of the reunification. But during the mid-nineteenth century, this was followed by a succession of terrible famines, epidemics, and devastating natural hazards. In 1849, a cholera epidemic killed more than 600,000 people. From 1858 to 1860, following Vietnam's refusal to accept free trade, French and Spanish troops invaded Saigon. In 1863, the court of Hue had to accept unequal treaties, to cede Cochin China to the French as a colony, and voluntarily withdraw its mandarins (high-ranking officials). With the collaboration of lower-ranking officials of the local administration, the French established direct rule (Osborne, 1969).

The extent of the lucrative rice export trade to coastal cities of southern China or to Singapore and other Southeast Asian cities explains why Cochin China had a structural trade surplus until 1945. On the import side, trade distortion favoring French equipment and luxury goods had a limited impact until the 1930s. With the rice frontier expanding rapidly to the south of the Mekong River, cultivated area and population increased tremendously in Cochin China: 0.7 million hectares and 1.7 million inhabitants around 1880, 1.2 and 2.8 million in 1900, and 2.2 and 4.4 million in 1930.

Capital, labor force, techniques, trading, and informal finance networks were mostly Asian. Colonization itself had a limited impact except in two fields of innovation: the use of modern equipment for hydraulic public works undertaken by French companies and, more important, the development of steam-machine-powered rice mills, mostly controlled by ethnic Chinese. Vietnamese landlords invested their revenues to expand their rice estates, with Vietnamese tenants or small landowners using the same technique of single cropping. Ethnic Chinese, on the other hand, held dominant positions in finance, rice milling, transportation, and international trade.

CAMPAIGN IN COCHIN CHINA. Taking of the citadel and of the upper town of Saigon by vice admiral Rigault de Genouilly, commander of the Franco-Spanish corps, on 17 February 1859. Painting by Antonie Morel-Fatio (1810–1871). (Chateaux de Versailles et de Trianon, Versailles/© Réunion des Musées Nationaux/Art Resource, NY)

The colonial administration adopted most precolonial institutional arrangements, including the traditional tax system based on land tax, poll tax, tariffs and tax farming (including some new taxes for opium, alcohol, and salt), and corvée, which was gradually abolished, at least officially. Until 1930, the monetary regime was based on a silver standard using the Mexican peso and silver coins called piastre, which were almost the same value and issued after 1873. One innovative measure adopted was the granting of a monopoly for issuing notes, and therefore the status of central bank, to the Bank of Indochina, a private French commercial bank. Despite its prosperity, the colony experienced initial difficulties in achieving a balanced public finance budget. The French central government had to transfer resources until the 1890s.

The French decision to impose a protectorate on the kingdom of Cambodia in 1863 was related to the potential for an expansion of rice cultivation and export, indicating a legacy of the Vietnamese vision of Cambodia: a rice frontier open to Vietnamese colonization. In central and northern Vietnam, no similar incentive existed since no rice export surplus existed in normal circumstances. A protectorate on Laos was also gradually imposed after 1879 but with limited impact in terms of economic activities. The colonization of southern Vietnam did not limit either internal southward migration or trade: Cochin China exchanged rice for Annam's sugar and cinnamon or Tonkin's handicrafts.

The French invasion of Annam and Tonkin was related to the role of Saigon as the commercial hub for Vietnam's international trade and also to the possibility of access to the Chinese market via northern Vietnam. It took almost two decades for the French to achieve total control over Annam and Tonkin (1882–1897) and officially establish their colonial administration under a protectorate regime (established in 1884). The north-south income gap was probably amplified by the invasion. On average, prices were lower in the north, except for rice, but wages were even lower.

Early Twentieth Century. In 1887, the colony of Cochin China and the protectorates of Tonkin, Annam, and Cambodia (and Laos in 1899) were incorporated in a new administrative and economic framework—French Indochina. It was a de facto customs union and a monetary union with the piastre as the common currency. After the reform of 1897, customs, public monopoly revenues, and some indirect taxes were transferred to the General Government of Indochina, a central government with headquarters in Hanoi. The *raison d'être* for this new framework was to facilitate the transfer of public resources from rich Cochin China to impoverished Tonkin and Annam for investing in transportation and telecommunication infrastructure.

The most important investments were in railways linking Haiphong to Hanoi and the Chinese province of Yunnan, built between 1901 and 1911, and the Hanoi to Saigon railways, initiated in 1905 and completed in 1936. Public bonds were issued in Paris in francs before 1913 and in Indochina in piastre during the 1920s and 1930s. These projects had dubious returns on investment. The trade with Yunnan never reached the level expected. Railways remained much more expensive than traditional coastal navigation between Tonkin and Cochin China.

Huge investments were also required for hydraulic works in order to limit floods in the double-cropping areas of high density in the Tonkin delta and to expand irrigated rice surfaces in Annam. As rice yields increased only marginally before the 1960s, increases in cultivated areas had to follow the pace of demographic growth, a resource constraint acknowledged with some anxiety by the colonial administration from the 1920s (Gourou, 1945). The reconstruction of Vietnam's population indicates that the natural growth rate was actually lower than indicated by colonial estimates: 14.8 million in 1890, 18.6 million in 1913, and 22.2 million in 1930 (Banens, 2000).

Export of traditional products of central and northern Vietnam either stagnated or declined under French rule. Silk production declined due to increasing Chinese competition resulting from Sino-French trade agreements. This was partly compensated by the success of diversified agricultural production during the 1910s and 1920s. These decades saw the growing export of maize, cultivated by small landowners in Tonkin and Cambodia, and the development of rubber plantations in Cochin China and Cambodia, as well as coffee plantations in Annam to some extent.

French companies, along with ethnic Chinese or Vietnamese local entrepreneurs, invested in mining and manufacturing between the early 1890s and the late 1920s, resulting in a strong increase in mining and manufacturing output. Several products, such as coal and cement, became important export items. In terms of per capita output in manufacturing and mining, Vietnam was still ahead of Korea around 1910 (Bassino, 2000). The mid-1920s saw a rush of French investment. In context with the depreciation of the French franc and the stability of Vietnam's currency, the piastre, in relation to the U.S. dollar and the British pound, Vietnam was seen as a land of opportunity and a safe haven. (The French franc was the currency of the rest of the French empire.)

The economic recession of the 1930s that hit all Asian countries was amplified in Vietnam by the impact of the franc peg policy introduced in 1930. The relative appreciation of the piastre against most Asian currencies caused a decline in exports of rice, coal, cement, and other primary and manufactured goods to Asia. In the meantime, the economic recession resulted in a contraction in income and a worsening of wealth distribution. Part of the lower class benefited from the decline in the price of rice. A drop in the share of opium and other revenue from tax farming indicates a modernization of public finance associated with an increase in public expenditures in health and education. The development of public education in Vietnam, in French and in Romanized Vietnamese, was exceptional by French colonial standards: nearly 30 percent of boys attended elementary school around 1942. The literacy rate was high in precolonial Vietnam: around 20 percent of male adults were able to read Chinese characters.

Since 1940. Between 1940 and 1945, under Japanese indirect rule, the French colonial administration introduced planning in resource allocation and established French-Japanese joint-venture companies in mining and trading. But the administration also promoted ethnic Vietnamese to higher ranks in civil administration. Between 1944 and 1945, economic conditions deteriorated. A terrible famine killed around 1 million people in the north. In March 1945, the Japanese ended French rule and formed pro-Japanese nationalist governments in Vietnam, Cambodia, and Laos. In September 1945, the Viet-Minh government, an alliance of communist and nationalist forces, headed by the Communist leader Ho Chi Minh, proclaimed the independence of Vietnam in Hanoi, with the initial support of the United States and China.

Between 1945 and 1954 during the Indochina war, Vietnam remained under French indirect rule. The gradual process of the independence of Vietnam was associated with an economic collapse of the modern sector and a gradual dissolution of the Federation of Indochina associating Vietnam, Cambodia, and Laos officially within the framework of the French Commonwealth (Union Française, created in 1946). The Viet-Minh government controlled most rural areas and established an underground administration, collecting taxes and introducing its own currency.

In 1954 at the end of French rule, Vietnam was divided into two independent political entities of almost the same size and population: North Vietnam, under Communist rule, and South Vietnam, supported by the United States. This partition was associated with the migration of 1 million people to South Vietnam. The two economies experienced steady economic recovery during the late 1950s and early 1960s. Both countries officially implemented land reforms and attempted to introduce a green revolution and industrialization, funded by foreign aid. Although income remained higher in the South than in the North, both countries were still comparable to Thailand around 1960 in terms of per capita gross domestic product.

The Indochina war and Vietnam War accelerated urbanization: in 1940 the population of Saigon-Cholon was 256,000 and in Hanoi, 149,000; by 1970, these figures were around 1.8 million and 1.4 million, respectively. It also caused an explosion of services, funded by massive military and civil foreign aid (Dacy, 1986; Nguyen, 1987). The economic stagnation and decline in living standards during the late 1960s and early 1970s was the direct consequence of war operations, especially the bombing of infrastructures and factories in the North. Despite heavy human casualties on both sides, the population growth accelerated after 1945 and began to slow down only during the 1980s and 1990s (25 million in 1945, 34 million in 1960, 48 million in 1975, and 80 million in 2000).

After 1975, the military victory of the North and the political and economic reunification was followed by the economic collapse of the South. In the three countries of Indochina, the economic context was characterized by a dramatic failure in economic development policy. This was caused mainly by bureaucratic inefficiency (Nguyen, 1982) and political repression, with severe consequences in Cambodia under the Khmer Rouge (1975–1979). The economic stagnation was also the result of wars: Vietnamese intervention in Cambodia against the Khmer Rouge, followed by the Chinese invasion of northern Vietnam in 1979, and civil war in Cambodia. In Vietnam, the adoption of significant economic reforms (*Doi-Moi*) between 1988 and 1989 marked the end of economic stagnation and the beginning of a new phase of green revolution and industrialization.

[*See also* France, *subentry on* The French Empire between 1789 and 1950.]

BIBLIOGRAPHY

Banens, Maks. "Vietnam: A Reconstruction of Its Twentieth-Century Population." In *Quantitative Economic History of Vietnam,* edited by Jean-Pascal Bassino, Jean-Dominique Giacometti, and Konosuke Odaka, pp. 1–40. Tokyo, 2000.

Bassino, Jean-Pascal. "Economic Development in Vietnam, Japan, Korea, and Taiwan between 1900 and 1945: Convergence and Divergence in the Chinese Periphery." *Journal of International Economic Studies* 14 (2000) 127–146.

Bassino, Jean-Pascal, Jean-Dominique Giacometti, and Konosuke Odaka, eds. *Quantitative Economic History of Vietnam.* Tokyo, 2000.

Brocheux, Pierre, and Daniel Hémery. *Indochine, la colonisation ambiguë, 1858–1954.* Paris, 1995.

Dacy, Douglas D. *Foreign Aid, War, and Economic Development: South, Vietnam 1955–1979.* Cambridge, 1986.

Gonjo, Yasuo. *La banque de l'Indochine, 1875–1940.* Paris, 1994.

Gourou, Pierre. *Land Utilization in French Indochina.* New York, 1945.

Le, Thanh-Khoi. *Histoire du Vietnam, des origines à 1858.* Paris, 1992.

Murray, Martin J. *The Development of Capitalism in Colonial Indochina, 1870–1940.* Berkeley, 1980.

Nguyen, Thanh Nha. *Tableau économique du Vietnam aux XVIIe et XVIIIe siècles.* Paris, 1970.

Nguyen, Tien-Hung. *Economic Development of Socialist Vietnam, 1955–1980.* New York, 1987.

Nguyen, Van-Canh, and Earle Cooper. *Vietnam under Communism, 1975–1982.* Stanford, Calif., 1982.

Osborne, Milton E. *The French Presence in Indochina and Cambodia: Rule and Response, 1859–1905.* Ithaca, N.Y., 1969.

Popkin, Samuel L. *The Rational Peasant: The Political Economy of Rural Society in Vietnam.* Berkeley, 1979.

Reid, Anthony. *Southeast Asia in the Age of Commerce,* vol. 1, *The Land below the Winds.* New Haven, 1988.

Reid, Anthony. *Southeast Asia in the Age of Commerce,* vol. 2, *Expansion and Crisis.* New Haven, 1993.

Robequain, Charles. *The Economic Development of French Indo-China.* New York, 1944.

Trinh, Van Tho. *L'école française en Indochine.* Paris, 1995.

JEAN-PASCAL BASSINO

INDONESIA. The scattered islands of what we now call the Indonesian archipelago vary enormously in terms of size, population densities, and level of economic development. Although many popular histories of Asia speak of the Dutch controlling the archipelago for three hundred years from the mid-seventeenth to the mid-twentieth centuries, the reality was rather different. The Dutch were first attracted to Eastern Indonesia, and especially to the islands comprising the present-day province of Maluku, by the highly lucrative trade in spices. By the end of the seventeenth century they had also established a presence on the island of Java, but in most other parts of the huge archipelago Dutch rule was largely indirect, if it existed at all, until the twentieth century.

Dutch Colonial Policy in the Nineteenth Century. Few regarded the sprawling collection of islands as a political, administrative, or economic entity until late in the nineteenth century, but gradually, over the last seven decades of the colonial era, the Dutch turned the "Netherlands Indies" into something much more than a loosely integrated free-trade area. A substantial administrative presence was built up on the island of Java, and increasingly also in Sumatra, the Celebes (now called Sulawesi), and the Dutch-controlled parts of the two huge islands of Borneo and New Guinea (now called Kalimantan and Papua), as well as in the chain of islands east of Java (including Bali, Lombok, Sumba, Sumbawa, Flores, and the western part of the island of Timor). Java became the hub of a vast archipelagic economy. Trade, which might naturally have been conducted through ports like Singapore, was forced to flow through the ports of Java, especially Batavia (now Jakarta) and Surabaya.

During the nineteenth century (from the 1820s to 1870), the Dutch implemented á system of compulsory cultivation of export crops, known in Dutch as the *cultuurstelsel* in Java, West Sumatra, and North Sulawesi. This system involved using indigenous officials to coerce farmers into growing such crops as coffee, sugar, and indigo for sale in the Netherlands. These exports generated substantial revenues for the Dutch budget, but the impact on the indigenous cultivators was (and continues to be) highly controversial. Some scholars have argued that it was a brutal but ultimately effective way of forcing peasant cultivators to become involved in export production. Others point out that the Dutch would have done better to encourage export crops through market incentives, which would have increased cultivator incomes and led to the establishment of a robust class of entrepreneurial farmers.

The rise of political and economic liberalism in the Netherlands in the middle decades of the nineteenth century led to mounting criticism of the coercion used to extract exportable surpluses in the colony; it was widely believed that accelerated economic development in the colony would be better achieved through the freer play of market forces. In 1870 the Dutch parliament passed legislation designed to give Western enterprises greater freedom to operate in Indonesia (especially to lease land for large-scale cultivation of agricultural exports). This year is often considered as marking the demise of the system of forced cultivations, although the system did continue in a diminished form until the early twentieth century.

In the last three decades of the nineteenth century, the economic impact of the new "liberal policy" was rather disappointing. Even though export volume growth did accelerate, growth of GDP was slow; in per-capita terms it was virtually zero. Rice production growth on Java (few data are available for other parts of the country) slowed sharply after 1880, and rice consumption per capita fell between 1880 and 1905. By the turn of the century, some Dutch in the colony and at home began to be concerned about overpopulation in Java.

Population had increased in Java more or less continually over the nineneenth century, with an acceleration in the growth rate after 1850. For the century as a whole, population growth in Java was well over 1 percent per annum. By 1900 the indigenous population was estimated to be 30.4 million. As only about 5 percent of the indigenous population lived in towns and cities, the great majority were dependent on agriculture for most of their income. The Dutch realized that the supply of arable land on the island was running out and that even with expanded irrigation, it would not be possible to accommodate the growing population in agriculture indefinitely.

The Ethical Policy and the Great Depression. In 1901, Queen Wilhemina made a famous reference in her speech from the throne to the declining welfare of her Javanese subjects. Her speech ushered in a series of changes in colonial policy, often referred to as the "ethical policy." These changes were designed to improve living standards in the colony, especially in Java, and by implication, to narrow the gap in income between colony and metropole. The Dutch placed emphasis on improving smallholder agricultural productivity through irrigation and agricultural extension. Javanese without access to land were encouraged to move to agricultural resettlement sites in Sumatra and Sulawesi. In addition, some colonial officials began to argue that the colony must diversify its economic base away from agriculture and into manufacturing in order to provide more employment. At the beginning of the century most manufacturing had centered around agricultural processing and some production of perishable foodstuffs.

The immediate effect of the ethical policy was for the government to spend more in the colony, as officials implemented a range of policies in infrastructure development, public health, and agricultural extension and resettlement. The first two decades of the twentieth century saw considerable growth in export production and an improvement in export prices. These positive signs, combined with the growth in government expenditures, accelerated GDP growth. GDP per capita grew by between 1 and 2 percent per annum between 1900 and the onset of the Depression in 1930. Population continued to increase throughout the archipelago; the 1930 census found that the total population was sixty-one million, of which almost forty-two million were on Java.

By 1930, infrastructure in Java was probably more developed than in any other part of Asia outside Japan. There was an extensive road and rail network, two large ports in Batavia and Surabaya, and more than three million hectares of irrigated land. In addition, the government had built up an extensive rural credit program embracing banks, paddy barns, and pawnshops. These achievements attracted admiring attention from both French and British colonial administrators.

Outside Java the impact of the ethical policy on infrastructure was less obvious, but substantial economic change was occurring in many parts of Sumatra, Kalimantan, and Sulawesi. Indigenous populations were certainly increasing, in many cases diversifying their sources of income away from subsistence agriculture. In particular, there was a rapid increase in the production of export crops (coffee, copra, rubber, and pepper and other spices) by smallholder producers. This growth was not the result of deliberate government policies. Rather, the smallholders responded to the challenges created by rapidly growing markets for crops like rubber in the industrialized world. During the Depression years of the 1930s, smallholders proved to be more resilient in the face of adverse world prices than the large estates.

The effect of the slump of the 1930s on Indonesia's export economy was serious, especially for the Javanese sugar industry, which lost most of its markets in the British Empire and elsewhere as a result of expanding protectionism. Between 1929 and 1934, export volume and per-capita GDP declined sharply. The plight of the export sector was aggravated by the decision of the Netherlands government to stay on the gold standard until 1936; the colonial guilder was pegged to the metropolitan currency, and appreciated sharply against most other currencies. One effect of this policy was a flood of cheap manufactured imports from Japan. The colonial authorities reacted by imposing quantitative controls, especially on textile products. This policy assisted domestic industrialization, as did the policy of actively soliciting foreign investment in the manufacturing sector. From 1934 on the economy, and especially the manufacturing sector, recovered rapidly.

Transition to Independence and the Sukarno Era. The era of Dutch colonialism was brought to an abrupt end in 1942 when the Japanese Imperial Army swept through Southeast Asia, inflicting humiliating defeats on the British, Dutch, and American colonial regimes. In Indonesia the Japanese at first were greeted as liberators, but their economic policies became increasingly exploitative over the next three years. They requisitioned substantial amounts of rice for the army, leaving the native population to survive on staples other than rice. Rubber, oil, and other raw materials were exported to feed the Japanese war machine but little was sent back in return.

In 1944–1945, Allied bombing inflicted damage on the oil installations in Sumatra and Kalimantan. On 17 August 1945, Sukarno and Hatta, two leaders of the independence struggle who had been imprisoned by the Dutch, took advantage of the power vacuum created by the Japanese surrender to declare Indonesia an independent and sovereign republic. The returning Dutch refused to negotiate with men they regarded as collaborators, and a bitter war of attrition between the republicans and the Dutch army ensued. Only after intense pressure from the United States had been brought to bear did the Dutch finally concede that a return to the prewar colonial regime was impossible. Independence was finally granted to the Republic of Indonesia in 1949.

The new government faced a daunting set of economic problems. Dutch policy had been to allow only a very small number of indigenous Indonesians access to Dutch education, and the great majority of the indigenous population in 1950 had either never been to school or had had at most a few years in a vernacular-language rural school. Although by the 1930s a significant proportion of the indigenous labor force was in nonagricultural employment, very few Indonesians were to be found in skilled trades or in professional, technical, and managerial occupations. Such jobs were taken either by European expatriates or by immigrant Chinese, of whom there were well over one million in 1930. Dutch policy had been to give the Chinese preferential access to education in their own Dutch-language schools; a significant number went on to higher education in Europe or in other parts of Asia.

The acute lack of education and skills among the Indonesians after independence meant that many Dutch citizens and immigrant Chinese continued to occupy senior positions both in the civil service and in private business.

In addition, some ethnic groups that had converted to Christianity, such as the Ambonese, the Menadonese, and the Bataks, were also overrepresented in these occupations because they had had access to superior education in mission schools. This situation was galling to the Muslim majority, which felt that even with political independence, they were still second-class citizens in their own country. Although there was some economic progress in the early 1950s, and per-capita GDP had returned to its 1942 level by 1954, the forces of economic nationalism became much stronger as the decade progressed. In 1957, President Sukarno, angered at the failure of the United Nations General Assembly to ratify a resolution calling for the Dutch to leave the western part of New Guinea, announced the takeover of all Dutch companies in Indonesia. Virtually all the remaining Dutch citizens were forced to leave, in most cases receiving no compensation for their confiscated assets.

By the early 1960s the Indonesian economy was in a parlous state. An increasing proportion of the budget was devoted to military expenditures; after the campaign to "liberate" West New Guinea was concluded a military confrontation was launched against the newly created federation of Malaysia. Infrastructure fell into disrepair and the agricultural and manufacturing sectors stagnated. Outside the oil sector there was no new foreign investment. Indeed Indonesia became a pariah state for Western investors and President Sukarno, who had abandoned parliamentary democracy, appeared to be leading the country into the Communist camp. By 1965, per-capita GDP was no higher than it had been in 1913. A very high proportion of the population was living below a very modest poverty line; in parts of Java and Eastern Indonesia near-famine conditions prevailed. Inflation accelerated, fueled by increasing budget deficits, and caused widespread hardship and economic dislocation.

The Suharto Era. A failed coup, launched in late September 1965 by a small group of officers alleged to be acting in alliance with the Communists, gave the military an excuse to intervene. By March 1966, the commander of the Army Strategic Reserve, General Suharto, together with other anti-Communist officers and civilians, wrested power from President Sukarno. Suharto subsequently became president and stayed in that office until May 1998. He realized that economic development must have top priority if his regime were to gain legitimacy, and he assembled around him a team of civilian technocrats, drawn mainly from the economics faculty at the University of Indonesia. The United States was only too willing to assist an anti-Communist regime in Southeast Asia at that time, and foreign aid and assistance, denied to Sukarno, was made available in substantial quantities. By 1969 inflation had been reduced to single digits and the economy, assisted by an improvement in the terms of trade, began to grow at unprecedently high rates. Over the three decades from 1967 to 1997, Indonesian GDP growth averaged more than 6 percent per annum.

Suharto and his technocrats steered the economy successfully through the oil-boom years of the 1970s and the difficult phase of post-oil-boom restructuring in the1980s. Living standards improved considerably, and after the disintegration of the former Soviet Union, Indonesia, with a population of close to two hundred million in 1995, became the fourth largest country in the world. By the early 1990s, export diversification had progressed to the point where, for the first time in Indonesia's history, manufactured exports accounted for more than half of total export earnings.

But the new export industries were dominated by Chinese entrepreneurs, and to an increasing extent Suharto seemed to be favoring Chinese conglomerates, as well as the business empires of his own children. Old antagonisms flared again as many Muslim Indonesians felt themselves sidelined in the race for power and riches. In addition, there was increasing anger in the resource-rich provinces outside Java at the cavalier way in which the center appropriated the profits from resource exploitation and gave little back to the producing regions, whose development lagged behind that of Java.

Matters came to a head in late 1997, after the government appeared unable to respond to the crisis triggered by the devaluation of the Thai baht in early July 1997. The rupiah depreciated rapidly in late 1997, and many highly leveraged companies were unable to maintain payments on their foreign debts. The domestic banking system collapsed under the weight of nonperforming loans. After serious urban riots in May 1998, President Suharto was forced to resign. GDP, having more than quadrupled in real per-capita terms between 1966 and 1996, contracted by more than 13 percent in 1998. Elections in 1999 brought a populist government led by Abdurrahman Wahid to power, but the new president and his cabinet demonstrated an uncertain touch in economic policymaking in the first months of their regime. Economic recovery, in early 2000, seemed likely to proceed more slowly than in other Asian economies affected by the 1997–1998 crisis.

[*See also* Low Countries, *subentry on* Dutch Empire.]

BIBLIOGRAPHY

Booth, Anne. *The Indonesian Economy in the Nineteenth and Twentieth Centuries.* London and New York, 1998.

Booth, Anne, W. J. O'Malley, and Anna Weidemann, eds. *Indonesian Economic History in the Dutch Colonial Era.* New Haven, 1990.

Creutzberg, P., and P. Boomgaard, eds. *Changing Economy of Indonesia*, vols. 1–16. Amsterdam, 1975–1996.

Eng, Pierre van der. *Agricultural Growth in Indonesia: Productivity Change and Policy Impact since 1880.* London, 1996.

Furnivall, J. S. *Netherlands India: A Study of Plural Economy.* Cambridge, 1944.

Glassburner, Bruce, ed. *The Economy of Indonesia: Selected Readings.* Ithaca, N.Y., 1971.

Hill, Hal. *The Indonesian Economy since 1966.* Cambridge, 1996.

Lindblad, J. Thomas, ed. *New Challenge in the Modern Economic History of Indonesia.* Leiden, 1993.

Lindblad, J. Thomas, ed. *The Historical Foundations of a National Economy in Indonesia, 1890s–1990s.* Amsterdam, 1996.

Maddison, Angus, and Prince Ge, eds. *Economic Growth in* Indonesia, *1820–1959.* Dordrecht, 1989.

Penders, C. L. M., ed. *Indonesia: Selected Documents on Colonialism and Nationalism.* Queensland, 1977.

Ricklefs, Merle. *A History of Modern Indonesia since c. 1300.* London, 1993.

Touwen, Jeroen. *Extremes in the Archipelago: Trade and Economic Development in the Outer Islands of Indonesia, 1900–1942.* Leiden, 2001.

Wertheim, W. F., J. H. Kraal, et al., eds. *Indonesian Economics: The Concept of Dualism in Theory and Policy.* The Hague, 1966.

ANNE BOOTH

INDUSTRIAL DISTRICTS. The notion of industrial districts was first put forth by Alfred Marshall. Throughout his career—and systematically in *Industry and Trade*, published in 1919—Marshall noted that in many industries the gradual transition to large-scale organizations predicted by mainstream economic theory had not taken place. In important cases, ranging from textile production in Lancashire to cutlery production in Sheffield, relatively small firms proved quite successful and resilient. Moreover, these firms showed a distinctive geographic concentration. In order to explain the peculiarities of these specialized local industrial systems, Marshall introduced the idea of "external economies," the advantages linked not to the technology, organization, and strategies internal to individual firms, but to the relational qualities of the system as a whole. According to Marshall, such qualities fell into several categories. First of all, there were the advantages linked to specialization and the division of labor among firms: by dividing a production process into distinct phases, agents in distinct—and yet connected—firms could take advantage of the economies of scale arising from the use of specialized means of production. Second, there were the advantages linked to the reduction of transaction costs. Especially in the case of nonstandardized goods and production processes, agents in a specialized district could rely on reiterated personal contacts to solve coordination problems. Moreover, these contacts fostered mutual knowledge and trust, which discouraged opportunistic behaviors. Third, Marshall identified a series of cognitive advantages linked to the specialization and agglomeration of firms in industrial districts. Geographic and cultural proximity created integrated and efficient labor markets for specialized skills, an arena in which learning by doing could effectively develop, and a network of contacts in which innovations could be spread and improved upon. Marshall summarized these cognitive advantages by arguing that successful districts were endowed with an "industrial atmosphere" conducive to economic growth.

In the late 1970s and early 1980s, the relevance of Marshall's insights was recognized by several Italian economists and sociologists. At the time, Italy was experiencing a second "economic miracle" led by networks of specialized small and medium-size firms located in the northeastern and central regions of the peninsula. The international success of the textile centers of Prato and Treviso, of the machine-building firms of Emilia-Romagna, and of many other local systems outstripped that of the older industrial cities of Turin, Milan, and Genoa, where many large companies were downsizing. Inspired by this contrast, economist Giacomo Becattini proposed that the industrial district, rather than the industrial sector, should be the primary unit of analysis of industrial economics.

Defined as networks of small producers in a localized area who share the benefits of external economies and solidarity ties without neglecting the efficiencies linked to competition, industrial districts are first of all historically rooted communities built on mutual trust among local agents. In the Italian context, industrial districts are characteristic of the area that sociologist Arnaldo Bagnasco has called the "Third Italy," the regions of the central and northeastern parts of the country located neither in the northwestern "industrial triangle" (Turin-Milan-Genoa) nor in the underdeveloped regions of the south. According to political scientist Robert Putnam, these are the areas most richly endowed with social capital; that is, with associations, norms, and civic traditions dating back to the Middle Ages.

Scholars have extended the idea of industrial district from post–World War II Italy to other historical and geographical contexts. One of the most important contributions for historical studies has been Charles Sabel and Jonathan Zeitlin's work on the survival of communities of small independent producers in the era of mass production. Sabel and Zeitlin challenged teleological interpretations of industrialization, which argued for the gradual convergence of preindustrial and artisanal economies toward large-scale organizations employing single-purpose machinery and unskilled labor for the production of standardized goods. Instead, wherever social and economic conditions made it possible, alternative forms of organization, founded on multipurpose technology, skilled labor, and custom-specific production, developed and thrived in many parts of the industrializing West. These alternatives to mass production, grouped under the category of flexible specialization, constitute an evolutionary bifurcation that has proved fruitful after the crisis of Fordism in the last two or three decades.

Theories of industrial district and flexible specialization (the technological principle informing the production practices of most districts) have greatly contributed to a growing revisionist movement in industrialization studies. These revisions have regarded both the localization of industrialization and its promoters. Against Gerschenkronian interpretations based on the importance of "substitutive factors" (above all the support given by the state and industrial banks to large-scale and vertically integrated companies), many scholars have shown that the emergence of industrial production was a highly diverse process assuming a wide variety of forms in different local and regional contexts. Therefore, these scholars argue, Gerschenkron's focus on the nation-state as both the main site and the promoter of modernization in the so-called latecomer countries was misplaced.

This revisionist thrust has not even spared the cradles of mass production and big business, Germany and the United States. Gary Herrigel has argued for a radical reinterpretation of German industrialization based on the coexistence of two organizational patterns or "industrial orders," both fundamentally regional. Germany's decentralized industrial order consisted of networks of specialized small-scale manufacturers (Baden-Württemberg is the most celebrated example of this pattern). The "autarkic" industrial order describes the more famous (but not more relevant) conglomerates of vertically integrated companies typical of the Ruhr basin. By the same token, Philip Scranton has shown that even in the United States the paradigm of mass production remained only one of the organizational possibilities well into the twentieth century. Even though flexibly specialized producers were not necessarily small and clustered, a variety of industrial districts, ranging from the furniture makers of Grand Rapids to the jewelers of Providence, greatly contributed to the diversity of America's industrial landscape. However, the category of industrial district—as these studies demonstrate—is more than a mere plea for the recognition of diversity. Rather, it contributes to the awareness that economic action is always embedded in dynamic networks of social, political, and cultural relations.

BIBLIOGRAPHY

Goodman, Edward, and Julia Bamford, eds. *Small Firms and Industrial Districts in Italy.* London, 1989.

Herrigel, Gary. *Industrial Constructions: The Sources of German Industrial Power.* New York, 1996.

Putnam, Robert D. *Making Democracy Work: Civic Traditions in Modern Italy.* Princeton, 1993.

Sabel, Charles, and Jonathan Zeitlin. "Historical Alternatives to Mass Production: Politics, Markets and Technology in Nineteenth-Century Industrialization." *Past and Present* 108 (1985), 133–176.

Scranton, Philip. *Endless Novelty: Specialty Production and American Industrialization, 1865–1925.* Princeton, 1997.

DARIO GAGGIO

INDUSTRIAL RELATIONS. In capitalist labor markets, workers have jobs in which they exchange their time for wages, working for capitalists who control the tools and machinery needed for production. This relationship can be harmonious when workers and employers cooperate to increase production. But there are also grounds for conflict, for example, over the division of output between wages and profits and over working conditions, including control over the work pace. Unlike slaves, unhappy wage earners can quit to seek better employment, or they can join with others to take collective action, forming political movements or labor unions.

First in England, then throughout the capitalist world, the creation of a wage-earning proletariat was followed by the development of labor unions and working-class political movements until, by the end of the nineteenth century, labor unions and labor-oriented political parties had attracted a large membership and had become major influences on wages and working conditions. In this essay, I explore the nature and development of labor unions in the capitalist world, including the United States, western Europe, and Japan, focusing especially on labor disputes and the development of modern systems of industrial relations.

Followers of Karl Marx and Friedrich Engels expected wage workers to unite against their employers by forming trade unions and socialist political parties to overthrow capitalism (Marx and Engels, 1978, pp. 480–481). This model has shaped both understanding and action. But it is problematic and one-sided. First, it is wrong to assume a simple connection between workers' grievances and collective action. Quitting a bad job, is a straightforward, simple act for an individual. But supporting collective action, such as participating in a strike or joining a labor union, is difficult because it requires that individuals commit themselves to produce "public goods" enjoyed by all. "Free riders" who contribute nothing to the group effort will receive the same benefits as do activists if the union succeeds. But if it fails, the activists suffer while those who remained outside lose nothing (Olson, 1971).

Free riding is a problem for all collective action, including Rotary Clubs, the Red Cross, and the Audubon Society. But the one-sided nature of the Marxist model becomes clear when one considers that unions are usually formed over the opposition of employers and, sometimes, state officials. Because unionization comes only after overcoming resistence, the process of forming unions is contingent not only on the workers but also on the attitudes of employers and state officials and on the relative powers of resistance of labor, capital, and the state. In any particular location, unions are formed for the following reasons: The workers wanted a union, employers and state officials did not oppose unionization, the workers were in a particularly strong bargaining position, or because employers and state officials were divided and in a particularly weak bargaining position. Focusing on workers and their grievances, the Marxist model addresses only the first circumstance. But, as I will explain, the other cases are all important as well.

Seeking to mobilize the power of a united working class, Marxists have favored inclusive unions uniting all wage workers in industries and regions on the basis of their common lack of productive property. Class-wide solidarity gives unions a broader membership and greater political leverage. But narrower unions also have fighting advantages when craft workers can use a monopoly of knowledge to restrict access to the trade. A narrow craft strategy was followed by the first successful unions throughout Europe and America, including those of printers, furniture makers, carpenters, gold beaters and jewelry makers, iron molders, engineers, machinists, and plumbers. A craft strategy offers nothing to common laborers. But it can be an attractive strategy for skilled workers who can win concessions on their own that they do not have to share with other workers.

Early Unions and Industrial Strife. Before modern labor unions, guilds united artisans and their employees, setting minimum prices and quality and regulating wages, employment, and output. Controlled by independent craftsmen—the "masters" who then employed journeymen and trained apprentices—guilds regulated industry to protect the comfort and status of the masters. Apprentices and journeymen benefited from guild restrictions only when these workers advanced to master status.

Guild power was gradually undermined in the early modern period by merchants employing semiskilled workers in factories. By the early 1800s, few could anticipate moving up to become a master artisan or to owning their own establishment. Instead, wage earners began to seek a collective regulation of their individual employment (Thompson, 1966).

Some of the first unions were formed by skilled workers to protect their interests as craftsmen with specialized training. Representing the interests of journeymen, these craft unions sought to establish a labor monopoly to balance their employers' control over the machinery of production. Other unions, including Robert Owen's General National Consolidated Trades Union of the 1830s and the American Knights of Labor United States in the 1880s, were formed on a broader basis, uniting all wage workers on the basis of their lack of property. They were part of the radical democratic movement of the early nineteenth century, upholding the worth of workers and the value of labor (Friedman, 1998; Montgomery, 1987; Thompson, 1966).

Seen in this light, the fundamental idea of the labor movement—that employees should have a voice in the management of industry—is comparable to the demand that citizens should have a voice in the management of public affairs. Of course, democratic values did not guarantee that unions would represent all workers. By reserving good jobs for their members, unions, especially craft unions, lowered wages for the unskilled, contributing to the exploitation of women and nonwhites.

Few of these early unions were able to establish a constructive working relationship with employers. Before World War I, collective bargaining was well developed only in the United Kingdom and in a few industries elsewhere. Even relatively strong unions, such as those representing Parisian construction workers, German coal miners, or American iron and steel workers, rarely negotiated contracts with management. In most industries, management barely tolerated unions and seized every opportunity to undermine them by firing union activists and locking out union members. The lack of union recognition meant that unionization was usually associated with rising levels of labor strife (see Table 1). Most of these strikes ended without collective negotiation when one side surrendered to the demands of the other.

Notwithstanding the persistence of craft unions, especially in the United States, the Marxist model appeared to explain labor militancy well into the *belle époque*. By 1914, unions had attracted a sizable membership in all capitalist economies, and a growing share of members belonged to industrial unions formed without regard for craft or skill (see Table 2). In most countries, unions were allied with growing socialist parties (see Table 3). Support from ideologically committed socialists helped many unions overcome the collective action problem; the German Social Democratic Party (or SPD), for example, promoted union organization throughout Germany. Sometimes, socialist politicians were able to shield unions from employer and state repression, as in France during the Third Republic (Friedman, 1998). Even in countries where the national union confederations were explicitly apolitical, including revolutionary syndicalist France and the United States with its more conservative unions, there was growing cooperation between socialist politicians and unions before 1914.

Unions grew by persuading whole groups to abandon individualism and throw themselves into the collective project. Rarely did unions grow incrementally. Instead, workers joined unions *en masse* in periods of great excitement, attracted by what the French sociologist Émile Durkheim labeled "collective effervescence" or the joy of participating in a common project without regard for individual interest. Growth came in spurts punctuated by major strikes such as the sit-down strikes in the United States in 1937. In thirteen countries, unions grew by more than 10 percent a year in years with the greatest strike activity but by less than 1 percent a year in years with the fewest strikers (Friedman, 1998; Shorter and Tilly, 1974). But upheaval provoked a hostile reaction from frightened employers and state officials. Rising opposition ended periods of rapid union growth, beginning a new phase of decline followed by longer periods of stagnant membership.

TABLE 1. *Strikers per 1000 Workers, Five Year Averages, 1880–1985.*

Year	Canada	United States	Austria	Denmark	France	Italy	Germany	Netherlands	Norway	Sweden	United Kingdom	Australia	Japan
1880		7.8											
1900	6.2	24.7		26.3	12.9		5.8			7.4	8.7	n.a.	0.2
1914	13.5	40.3		9.5	17.3		10.9	16.6	34.1	7.4	29.9	47.6	0.2
1928	7.0	8.8	1.2	2.4	22.8		16.1	6.5	25.3	17.6	39.1	58.2	2.0
1939	12.7	27.5	n.a.	1.9	69.7		n.a.	3.8	22.6	8.0	13.3	44.6	0.9
1947	31.9	76.1	4.8	1.8	134.7		n.a.	29.1	6.1	28.1	21.8	128.0	3.4
1950	26.1	52.9	1.2	1.8	251.3	207.8	10.8	5.3	6.2	2.3	14.7	136.4	10.8
1960	16.9	27.0	3.0	2.6	104.9	167.1	3.5	6.6	7.4	0.6	59.5	102.4	5.6
1975	76.0	26.7	6.8	6.4	105.6	694.9	6.0	5.1	6.9	4.4	49.1	202.9	5.8
1985	31.5	7.7	4.2	1.9	80.8	313.9	8.1	3.3	7.1	13.1	36.0	33.7	0.3

This table shows the average striker rate, or the number of strikers divided by the number of nonagricultural workers, in the five years centered on the year given. The 1939 rate is for the five years 1934–1939; the 1914 rate is for 1909–1914.

SOURCES: Canada: *Historical Statistics of Canada*, series E197; *Canada Year Book, 2001*, p. 262.

United States: Friedman, "The Decline of the American Labor Movement: Explanations and Implications for the United States Industrial Relations," p. 41.

Austria, Denmark, France, Germany, Italy, Netherlands, Norway, Sweden, United Kingdom: P. Flora, F. Kraus, W. Pfenning, *State, Economy, and Society in Western Europe, 1815–1975*, pp. 689–693, pp. 699–701, pp. 709–710, pp. 715–717, pp. 726–728, pp. 731–734, pp. 737–739, pp. 740–744, pp. 751–753.

Australia: *Year Book Australia, 2002*, 147.

Japan: B. R. Mitchell, *Industrial Historical Statistics: Africa, Asia, Oceania, 1750–1993*, pp. 121–123.

TABLE 2. *Union Members per 100 Nonagricultural Workers, 1880–1985: Selected Countries.*

YEAR	CANADA	UNITED STATES	AUSTRIA	DENMARK	FRANCE	ITALY	GERMANY	NETHERLANDS	NORWAY	SWEDEN	UNITED KINGDOM	AUSTRALIA	JAPAN
1880	n.a.	1.8	n.a.	n.a.	n.a.	n.a.	n.a.	n.a.	n.a.	n.a.	n.a.	n.a.	n.a.
1900	4.6	7.5	n.a.	20.8	5.0	n.a.	7.0	n.a.	3.4	4.8	12.7	n.a.	n.a.
1914	8.6	10.5	n.a.	25.1	8.1	n.a.	16.9	17.0	13.6	9.9	23.0	32.8	n.a.
1928	11.6	9.9	41.7	39.7	8.0	n.a.	32.5	26.0	17.4	32.0	25.6	46.2	6.3
1939	10.9	20.7	n.a.	51.8	22.4	n.a.	n.a.	32.5	57.0	53.6	31.6	39.2	5.3
1947	24.6	31.4	64.6	55.9	40.0	n.a.	29.1	40.4	55.1	64.6	44.5	52.9	45.3
1950	26.3	28.4	62.3	58.1	30.2	49.0	33.1	43.0	58.4	67.7	44.1	56.0	46.2
1960	28.3	30.4	63.4	64.4	20.0	29.6	37.1	41.8	61.5	73.0	44.2	54.5	32.2
1975	35.6	26.4	58.5	66.6	21.4	50.1	38.2	39.1	60.5	87.2	51.0	54.7	34.4
1985	33.7	18.9	57.8	82.2	14.5	51.0	39.3	28.6	65.3	103.0	44.2	51.5	28.9

This table shows the unionization rate, the share of nonagricultural workers belonging to unions, in different countries in different years, 1880–1985. Because union membership often includes unemployed and retired union members it may exceed the number of employed workers, giving a unionization rate of greater than 100 percent.
SOURCES: Canada *Historical Statistics of Canada*, series E176; *Directory of Labour Organizations in Canada, 1998*, p. 15.
United States: Friedman, "The Decline of the American Labor Movement: Explanations and Implications of the United States Industrial Relations," 43.
Austria, Denmark, France, Italy, Germany, Netherlands, Norway, Sweden, United Kingdom: Viser, *European Trade Unions in Figures*, pp. 19–20, pp. 41–42, pp. 70–71, pp. 95–96, p. 120, pp. 150–152, pp. 174–175, p. 196, p. 244.
Australia: Bain and Price, *Profiles of Union Growth: A Comparative Statistical Portrait of Eight Countries*, pp. 123–124; *Yearbook Australia, 2001*, p. 150.
Japan: Levine, *Industrial Relations in Postwar Japan*, p. 67; Visser, "Trends in Trade Union Membership," *OECD: Employment Outlook*, p. 110.

TABLE 3. *Socialist Voting in National Elections, 1880–1985.*

YEAR	CANADA	UNITED STATES	AUSTRIA	DENMARK	FRANCE	ITALY	GERMANY	NETHERLANDS	NORWAY	SWEDEN	UNITED KINGDOM	AUSTRALIA	JAPAN
1880	0			0	0		6.1		0	0	0	0	0
1900	0.3			17.6	10.9		27.2		0	0	1.3	18.7	0
1914	1.8			29.4	16.8		34.8	18.5	26.3	36.4	6.4	50.9	0
1928	1.5		42.4	40.6	29.3		40.5	24.5	40.8	43.4	33.6	44.6	0
1939	14.0		n.a.	45.3	35.2		n.a.	25.3	42.8	53.6	38.8	43.2	n.a.
1947	19.7		46.9	46.8	45.4		n.a	38.9	52.9	57.0	48.6	52.8	31.5
1950	17.1		44.7	44.2	42.3	31.0	34.9	33.3	51.5	52.4	46.4	47.6	23.3
1960	12.1		47.9	49.3	34.7	36.9	31.8	34.6	51.7	51.8	43.9	52.8	39.3
1975	20.5		51.6	41.2	46.4	41.9	46.1	37.4	46.5	48.9	39.9	46.9	39.4
1985	18.9		45.4	43.2	40.8	45.4	38.2	34.5	42.5	50.0	27.6	55.0	36.1

This table shows the share of the national vote going to socialist, labor, and communist parties in the national election prior to the year shown.
    These include parliamentary elections in all cases except the United States where the presidential vote is shown.
SOURCES: Canada *Historical Statistics of Canada*, series Y75-Y198; *Canadian Parliamentary Guide, 2000*, pp. 359–516.
United States: Guide to United States Elections, pp. 440–466.
Austria, Denmark, France, Italy, Germany, Netherlands, Norway, Sweden, United Kingdom: C. Cook and J. Paxton, *European Political Facts, 1848–1918*, pp. 316–318; C. Cook and J. Paxton, *European Political Facts, 1900–1996*, pp. 165–167, pp. 183–186, pp. 203–205, pp. 198–200, pp. 206–207, pp. 222–223, pp. 227–229, pp. 229–231, pp. 254–257, pp. 270–274.
Australia: T. Mackie and R. Rose, *The International Almanac of Electoral History*, pp. 6–21.
Japan: T. Mackie and R. Rose, *The International Almanac of Electoral History*, pp. 282–297.

Twentieth-Century Union Growth. War gave labor extraordinary opportunities. Low unemployment strengthened workers' bargaining positions at the same time that combatant governments rewarded pro-war labor leaders with positions in the expanded state bureaucracy and support for collective bargaining. Unions grew rapidly during and immediately after World War I. For eleven countries, membership grew by 130 percent between 1913 and 1920.

Even before the war, frustration with the slow pace of social reform had led to a shift toward the revolutionary socialist and syndicalist left in Germany, the United Kingdom, and the United States. War fanned the flames of discontent into a raging conflagration with the number of strikers rising to ten or even twenty times after the war. Inspired by the success of the Bolshevik revolution in Russia, revolutionary Communist parties were organized to promote revolution by organizing labor unions, strikes, and political protest. This was a mixed blessing for labor. The Communists included some of labor's most dedicated activists and organizers. But Communist help came at a price. Secretive, domineering, intolerant of opposition, the Communists divided unions between their dwindling allies and a growing collection of outraged opponents. More, they galvanized opposition, depriving labor of needed allies among state officials and the liberal bourgeoisie.

As with other surges in union membership, the postwar boom was self-limiting. Helped by a sharp postwar economic contraction, employers and state officials ruthlessly drove back the radical threat, purging their workforce of known union activists and easily absorbing futile strikes during a period of rising unemployment. Union membership fell by almost one-third from a 1920 peak of 28 million members in thirteen countries in 1920 to 19 million in 1924. In Austria, France, Germany, and the United States, labor unrest contributed to the election of conservative governments; in Hungary, Italy, and Poland it led to the installation of dictatorships that banned labor unions. Economic stagnation, state repression, and anti-union campaigns by employers prevented any union resurgence through the rest of the 1920s. By 1929, unions had lost another 500,000 members.

Even more than World War I, World War II promoted unions and social change. The war divided the world not only between warring countries but between those, usually on the political right, who favored fascism and those who defended democracy. The Allies' victory was a triumph that led to the entry into European governments of socialists and Communists and briefly strengthened the Japanese left. Union membership exploded. In 1947, unions had enrolled a majority of nonagricultural workers in Scandinavia, Australia, and Italy and more than 40 percent in most other countries (see Table 1). Accumulated depression and wartime grievances sparked a postwar strike wave that included over 6 million strikers in France in 1948, 4 million in Italy in 1949 and 1950, and 5 million in the United States in 1946. Leftist postwar governments nationalized industries and banks throughout Europe and established new programs for socialized health insurance and old-age pensions. In Europe and Japan, the share of national income devoted to social services jumped dramatically, as did the share of income going to the working classes.

In some countries, labor's position deteriorated quickly from this position of strength. In France, Italy, and Japan, the popular front uniting Communists, socialists, and bourgeois liberals dissolved with the onset of the Cold War.

In these countries, union membership declined after 1947, and unions remained on the defensive for more than a decade. Elsewhere in continental Europe, however, labor was strong enough to compel management and state officials to accept centralized labor movements as social partners. Stable industrial relations in these countries allowed cooperation between management and labor to raise productivity and to open new markets for national companies. Such policies could not be instituted in countries with weaker and less centralized labor movements, such as France, Italy, Japan, the United Kingdom, and the United States, because their unions were not accepted as bargaining partners by management and lacked the centralized authority to enforce income policies and productivity bargains (Alvarez, Garrett, and Lange, 1992).

It was after World War II that the United States emerged as the advanced, capitalist democracy with the weakest labor movement. America went into continued decline right after World War II. At 35 percent, the unionization rate in 1945 was the highest in American history, but it was lower than in most other advanced capitalist economies, and it has fallen steadily since. The postwar strike wave, the largest in American history, provoked a powerful reaction among employers. Unable to overcome racial divisions and private and state repression, unions drove to organize the South. But "Operation Dixie" failed dismally in 1946, leaving the South as a nonunion, low-wage domestic enclave and a bastion of anti-union politics. In 1946, a conservative majority was elected to Congress, replacing hopes for a renewed, postwar New Deal with postwar nightmares of a labor union squeezed between hostile politicians and a rising wave of employer reaction.

Union Decline. The postwar accommodation was challenged after 1973 when economic slowdown and growing international trade threatened the well-being of unionized firms. Nonetheless, union membership has been maintained, and has even increased, in Scandinavia and German-speaking Europe—countries with highly centralized union movements in which labor has considerable political power. In Germany, for example, the share of workers covered by union contracts rose from 91 percent to 92 percent between 1980 and 1994, and virtually all workers are covered by union contracts in Scandinavia, Denmark, Austria, and the Netherlands. Unions have fared as well in France and Italy, two countries with highly centralized unions, in which labor's political leverage increased in the 1980s and 1990s. Union contracts now cover nearly all French workers and a large majority of Italians.

By contrast, unions have fared much worse since the 1970s in countries with decentralized labor movements, especially where labor has had little political influence. In Japan, the United Kingdom, and the United States, union membership has fallen sharply since the mid-1970s, and it has fallen in Canada despite relatively favorable state policies. In these countries, unionized firms face growing domestic competition because union contracts cover only a minority of workers—less than one-half in the United Kingdom, one-third in Canada, and barely one-fifth in Japan and the United States. Especially in these last two countries, labor unions have nearly disappeared as an economic force. After a century of the labor movement, Japan and the United States are pioneering a different, nonunion industrial relations system.

[*See also* Bargaining, Collective; Employers' Associations; *and* Unions.]

BIBLIOGRAPHY

Alvarez, R. Michael, Geoffrey Garrett, and Peter Lange. "Government Partisanship, Labor Organization, and Macroeconomic Performance." *American Political Science Review* 85 (1992), 539–556.

Annual Report, 1990. International Labor Office. Geneva, 1990.

Bain, George Sayers, and Robert Price. *Profiles of Union Growth: A Comparative Statistical Portrait of Eight Countries.* Oxford, 1980.

Canadian Parliamentary Guide, 2000. Detroit, 2000.

Canada Year Book, 2001. Ottawa, 2001.

Cook, Chris, and John Paxton. *European Political Facts, 1848–1918.* London, 1978.

Cook, Chris, and John Paxton. *European Political Facts, 1900–1996.* London, 1998.

Directory of Labour Organizations in Canada, 1998. Ottawa, 1998.

Flora, Peter, Franz Kraus, and Winfried Pfenning. *State, Economy, and Society in Western Europe, 1815–1975.* London, 1987.

Friedman, Gerald. *State-Making and Labor Movements: France and the United States, 1876–1914.* Ithaca, N.Y., 1998.

Friedman, Gerald. "The Decline of the American Labor Movement: Explanations and Implications for the United States Industrial Relations." Unpublished manuscript, University of Massachusetts, Amherst, 2002.

Griffith, Barbara S. *The Crisis of American Labor: Operation Dixie and the Defeat of the CIO.* Philadelphia, 1988.

Guide to U.S. Elections. Congressional Quarterly. Washington, D.C., 1994.

Historical Statistics of Canada. Ottawa, Canada, 1983.

Levine, Solomon. *Industrial Relations in Postwar Japan.* Urbana, 1958.

Mackie, Thomas T., and Richard Rose. *The International Almanac of Electoral History.* Washington, D.C., 1991.

Mitchell, B. R. *International Historical Statistics, Africa, Asia, and Oceania, 1750–1993.* Oxford, 1995.

Montgomery, David. *Citizen Worker: The Experience of Workers in the United States with Democracy and the Free Market during the Nineteenth Century.* Cambridge, 1987.

Olson, Mancur. *The Logic of Collective Action: Public Goods and the Theory of Groups.* Cambridge, Mass., 1971.

Shorter, Edward, and Charles Tilly. *Strikes in France.* Cambridge, 1974.

Thompson, Edward P. *The Making of the English Working Class.* New York, 1966.

Tucker, Robert C., ed. *The Marx-Engels Reader.* New York, 1978.

Visser, Jelle. *European Trade Unions in Figures.* Boston, 1989.

Visser, Jelle. "Trends in Trade Union Membership." *OECD: Employment Outlook* (July 1991), 110.

Year Book Australia. Canberra, 2001.

GERALD FRIEDMAN

INDUSTRIAL REVOLUTION. The term *Industrial Revolution* is normally reserved for a set of events that took place in Britain roughly from 1760 to 1830. The historical events in question consisted of a set of technological, economic, and social changes that in the long run revolutionized not just the British economy but that of the rest of western Europe, North America, and eventually much of the rest of the world. The Industrial Revolution brought about a "modern" economy in which technological progress did not just happen from time to time in isolated sectors but became a sustained and continuous process, resulting eventually in unprecedented economic growth and increases in living standards in much of the world. Its effects led to a complete reorganization of production, consumption, locational patterns, international relations, demographic behavior, and almost every aspect of the human condition. Yet unlike the American and French revolutions that were contemporaneous with it, the Industrial Revolution brought economic changes that were neither dramatic nor very abrupt. There are no industrial equivalents to the Battle of Lexington or the conquest of the Bastille. Yet in the economic history of humankind, the Industrial Revolution marks a watershed. Although some other events are sometimes designed as "industrial revolutions," to say nothing of "agricultural," "demographic," and other assorted revolutions, none of them equals the Industrial Revolution in importance.

The Industrial Revolution was not the beginning of "industrialization"; much manufacturing had already been taking place in European cities and in the countryside by the middle of the eighteenth century. Nor did the Industrial Revolution increase by much the number of human hours spent on manufacturing processes; industrial output expanded greatly, but in the long run productivity increased so much that labor could be siphoned off into services. Nor was the Industrial Revolution the beginning of innovation as a force for change in the human condition; early medieval and renaissance Europe had witnessed a series of inventions that revolutionized agriculture, textiles, power use, shipping, iron making, communications, and warfare. Nor was the Industrial Revolution the absolute beginning of economic growth as such; the British economy in 1700 was clearly much richer than it had been at any point in its past, as Adam Smith had already noted. The Industrial Revolution was in some sense a change in the *degree* of change—but in economic history degree and amount are everything.

It should be emphasized nonetheless that the classic Industrial Revolution was a localized affair, one that most Britons were only dimly growing aware of. Napoleon famously referred to Britain as a nation of "shopkeepers," not "cotton spinners." Many of the most interesting developments took place in two or three loci; a number of counties around Lancashire and the town of Manchester, the Scottish Lowlands, and some smaller regions in the midlands and Wales saw almost all of the action. In the eastern parts of the country and the area south of London, there was little evidence of rapid economic change before 1830. After 1830, the structural change in the economy accelerated rather than wound down, thanks to the railroads, the telegraph, and the spreading of technological changes to new industries. The foundations of a new economy in which change was the normal condition were laid from 1760 to 1830.

Technology was at the core of everything. An anonymous schoolboy, immortalized in a classic 1948 book by T. S. Ashton, called the Industrial Revolution "a wave of gadgets" that swept Britain. Yet these inventions did not rain upon Britain like manna from heaven. Technology may have been an engine that propelled the economy forward, but it took its fuel from a society and an economy that were exceptional, not just relative to non-European nations but even in comparison to its close European competitors and enemies such as France and the United Provinces. Eighteenth-century Britain was what we may call a technologically competent society. It was teeming with engineers, mechanics, millwrights, and dexterous and imaginative tinkerers who spent their time and energy designing better pumps, pulleys, and pendulums. Even wealthy landowners and merchants displayed a fascination with technical matters. Men such as John Smeaton, often called the first modern engineer, Joseph Bramah, thought of as the originator of hydraulic power, and the prodigiously gifted engineer Richard Roberts could turn to almost any technical question and resolve it as well as could be done. Britain had an unusual number of such people. One famous quote from a Swiss visitor in Britain in 1766 declared that for a thing to be perfect it had to be invented in France and worked out in England. As it turned out, some of the great inventions of the Industrial Revolution were produced in Britain, whereas others came from the Continent. Yet in the kind of society that Britain was in these years the question of "where it came from" was not important. "Does it work?" and "Can it make money?" were what mattered.

The main technological breakthroughs of the Industrial Revolution were the famous ones listed in high school history textbooks; yet these "heroic" inventions were only the tip of the iceberg. Right below them lay a large number of important breakthroughs that solved major bottlenecks and opened the door to further improvements. A third layer contained an even larger number of small improvements, adjustments, new applications, and minor technical insights that never made it to the patent office, much less to the history of technology books; yet they, maybe more than the textbook inventions, consolidated the achievements of ingenuity and imagination in terms of productivity gains.

The most famous invention of the Industrial Revolution was the steam engine. Strictly speaking, the steam engine was the result of work carried out, mostly on the Continent, in the last third of the seventeenth century. The first steam engine prototype was built by a Frenchman named Denis Papin, but there is no question that the first useful atmospheric steam engine was built in 1712 by a Cornish mechanic named Thomas Newcomen. For half a century Britain used Newcomen engines, which, though noisy and voracious in their fuel use, served mostly as pumps. The conversion of the steam engine into a source of industrial power was the handiwork of Scottish inventor James Watt, who introduced a number of famous improvements to the steam engine, such as a separate condenser, the principle of double-acting expansion, improved gears, and regulators. Watt turned steam power from an atmospheric pump to a true steam engine. When his patent expired in 1800 after thirty-one years, a new principle in steam power, the high-pressure engine, was developed, which soon threatened the Watt engine's monopoly. High-pressure engines provided increased power from engines lighter and smaller than older counterparts, and were thus ideal for transportation; and after years of experimentation they were successfully adapted to locomotives by Robert and George Stephenson, in 1825.

Yet the steam engine, its psychological impact and technological future aside, had a relatively minor impact on the British economy before the advent of the railroad. Of about twenty-two hundred machines operating in Britain in 1800, almost half were employed in mining and quarrying, and about 40 percent in manufacturing. By 1835 Lancashire had switched over to steam, but the cotton industry in the rest of Britain still depended on water mills for about half its horsepower. The Industrial Revolution witnessed enormous progress in the utilization of waterpower, above all Smeaton's breast wheel (which combined the advantages of over- and undershot wheels), and the growing use of iron in the manufacturing of water wheels. Even more than did steam, waterpower benefited from the growing scientific understanding of its principles, especially among hydraulic engineers in France. In other nations, especially the United States, France, and Switzerland, waterpower remained of central importance.

A second industry often identified with the most dynamic aspects of the technology of this time is textiles. By the middle of the eighteenth century, cotton was a small and rather unimportant sideshow in the British textile industry, famous for its woolens. Cotton's growth during the Industrial Revolution was truly amazing. Value added in cotton went from less than half a million pounds in 1760 to around 25 million in the mid-1820s. It is no wonder that some economic historians have thought of this industry as the "leading sector" in the Industrial Revolution. The reason for this success was cotton's physical characteristics. It lent itself uniquely to mechanization and mass production and produced a good that was of even quality, attractive, and above all inexpensive.

The weaving of cotton had already gained in productivity when the flying shuttle was introduced in the 1730s and 1740s, but spinning in 1760 was still carried out by hand. As long as spinning remained a manual process, the yarn produced remained both costly and of uneven quality. This bottleneck was resolved by a string of brilliant mechanical inventions between 1765 and 1779, which led to the famous mule (so-named because it consisted of a combination of the 1765 spinning jenny and the throstle), patented in 1769. The mule became the industrial machine par excellence, and within a few years it was coupled to the steam engine, so that the first truly "modern" factory (or "mill" as it was known at the time) was born. The mule was perfected in 1825 by making it automatic through the introduction of the self-actor. An indication of the magnitude of the improvements attained is shown by the number of hours needed to spin a hundred pounds of cotton. The "old" technology employed an Indian handspinner, who took about 50,000 hours. The mule brought that number down to around 300 hours in the 1790s, and three decades later the self-actor reduced the figure to 135.

Many of the other processes used in manufacturing cotton were also mechanized to some extent, though some of the problems proved more difficult than others. Carding, the process that prepared the cotton for spinning, was mechanized early on; ginning, the removal of the seeds from the raw cotton, was mechanized in 1793. Weaving by machine turned out to be more difficult, and power looms did not become successful until after 1820, though their use then spread rapidly. Calico printing was mechanized by the invention of copper rollers that printed patterns on finished cloth. Bleaching was revolutionized by the introduction of chlorine-based bleaching agents in the 1790s. By 1830 only the extremes of the upstream and the downstream of the industry were not mechanized: raw cotton was still grown and picked by hand in American fields, largely by black slaves; and finished clothes were still sewn together by hand by apparel makers, seamstresses, and tailors.

Growth in the mechanization of textiles was not confined to cotton, but the other textiles inevitably lost a great deal of market share. Worsted (combed wool) yarns were easily adapted to the cotton spinning machinery, but the combing process itself was not mechanized successfully until the middle of the nineteenth century. In the heavy woolen industry, the labor-intensive preparation and finishing processes were successfully mechanized early on,

but spinning and weaving proved more difficult and were not fully mechanized until the 1840s. Linen, the other major textile, made from the stem of flax, was also hard to spin mechanically. A French inventor, Philippe De Girard, tempted by a large prize promised by the Emperor Napoleon, solved the problem in about 1810; and his "wet spinning" process was introduced into the flax-spinning industry in Britain in about 1825. One of the most interesting inventions of the Industrial Revolution was the loom invented by Joseph-Marie Jacquard in 1801, which automated the weaving of patterns in a piece of fabric. Used for upmarket silks and worsteds, this machine was the first to code information using a binary code; and it inspired the work of Charles Babbage, a British mathematician who pioneered the first digital calculating machine.

A third area in which the Industrial Revolution achieved major advances was iron making. One important innovation was the use of new fuels in the smelting of iron ore in blast furnaces. The replacement of charcoal by coke (purified coal) in blast furnaces remedied the costly need to access remote forest areas. Blast furnaces became bigger, hotter, and more efficient as more powerful machinery was used to blow air into the furnaces. In 1828 a Scotsman, James Neilson, discovered that by using the blast furnaces' own gases he could cut fuel usage by up to a factor of three.

The problem remained, however, to refine the end product of the blast furnace, known as pig iron, into the more malleable and usable wrought iron. After decades of experimentation and searching, a British ironmaster named Henry Cort solved the problem in 1785, through what became known as the puddling and rolling process, a truly epochal breakthrough of the Industrial Revolution. Cort's process took Britain (and soon after that, the rest of Europe) by storm. In one dramatic stroke, the bottleneck that had occupied thousands of small-time forges and smithies was resolved. Even in steelmaking, a difficult art in which specialists fiercely kept their trade secret, there was progress: Benjamin Huntsman, a Sheffield steelmaker, perfected what became known as crucible steel, a high-quality product that became famous the world over. Steel remained expensive, however, and would not be mass-produced until the second half of the nineteenth century.

These three sectors—energy, textiles, and iron—are rightly famous for their bold and pathbreaking innovations. Yet the period witnessed a large number of other industries that in some way or another modernized, either by revolutionizing the manufacturing process itself or by adopting some form of machinery. In chemicals, two major inventions stood out. The first was the manufacturing of alkalis (used in industries such as soap-boiling and glassmaking) by means of a soda-making process perfected by Nicholas LeBlanc in 1787. This process dominated

INDUSTRIAL REVOLUTION. The iron bridge at Ironbridge, Shropshire, England, circa 1900. (Prints and Photographs Division, Library of Congress)

world production until the 1860s. Even more revolutionary was the second invention, the use of a new chemical (discovered only in 1774), chlorine, for the bleaching of textiles. Long, expensive processes of bleaching were replaced, almost overnight, by a fast and reliable alternative.

Machine and instrument making also made enormous progress. John Wilkinson, a Shropshire ironmaster, patented a boring machine to be used for cannon, which he adapted to make the cylinders needed for Watt's engines. One of the most famous technological challenges in the Western world, how to measure longitude at sea, was solved by a British clock maker, John Harrison, around 1762; although it still took a few decades for such clocks to be made cheaply, the invention stands as further testimony to British ingenuity in these years. A long list of British engineers and instrument makers, including Joseph Bramah, his brilliant student Henry Maudslay, and Maudslay's gifted student Richard Roberts, redesigned every machine-making tool known; lathes, planing machines, boring machines, screw-cutting machines, and measuring tools, all looked very different in 1820 compared to 1760. These tools made it possible to build parts and machines with greater and greater accuracy and thus increased industrial efficiency.

Many of the "old" industries also were overhauled. In papermaking, a machine that produced paper in a continuous roll rather than by individual sheet, patented by a Frenchman named Nicholas Louis Robert, was introduced

around 1800. In glassmaking, pottery, flour milling, sugar refining, printing, and mining, the use of machines, whether steam-driven or not, changed the way production took place. The invention of gaslighting in the 1790s not only helped to light streets but allowed factories to work longer hours in the short winter days of northern Europe. Roadbuilding was revolutionized by John McAdam, canal building by James Brindley, and bridge construction by Thomas Telford. The iron bridge, the first of which was completed in 1779, became a symbol of the Industrial Revolution. Even before the electromagnetic telegraph, long-distance communication made a giant step forward with the introduction of the semaphore telegraph. Food canning, invented in 1795, was picked up quickly; and in 1814 the British navy and army were already being supplied with canned soups and meats. Many small but useful inventions that came into being in those years simplified daily life: matches, steel pens, lawnmowers, safety lamps for miners. Innovation was simply in the air: in 1783 for the first time in history humans flew, if only in hot air balloons; in 1796 Edward Jenner vaccinated people against smallpox. In short, the years of the Industrial Revolution were truly years of miracles.

The economywide effects of the Industrial Revolution were less than spectacular, however. Estimates about growth of income per capita for the years from 1760 to 1800 put it at 0.2 percent a year, and for the period from

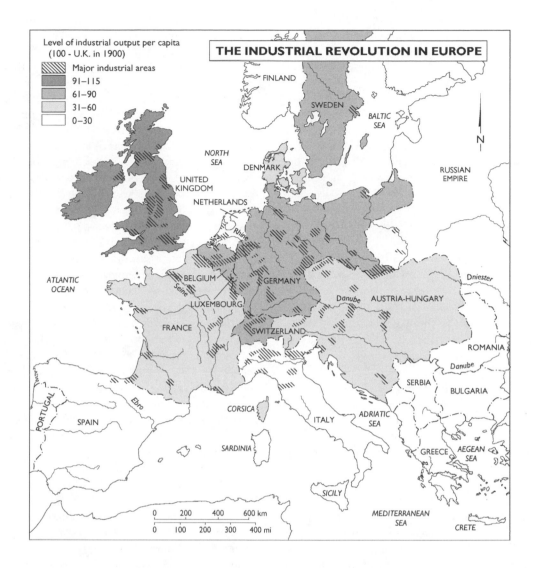

1800 to 1830 at the modest level of 0.5 percent. These modest numbers have persuaded some authors that perhaps the entire concept of Industrial Revolution is misplaced. Clearly, one should not identify the Industrial Revolution with the entire British economy for this period. The dimensions of the "modern" sector—those industries and services in which technological progress was the most marked—were quite modest in the early stages; although this sector was growing rapidly, its impact on the economy at large was limited. For the hundreds of thousands of workers employed in agriculture, construction, shipbuilding, retail trade, personal services, and other traditional occupations, the new technology as yet made little or no difference. Furthermore, the Industrial Revolution was a period of rapidly growing population, and the economy had to feed, cloth, and shelter ever-increasing numbers of people. To make things worse, Britain fought a number of expensive wars (the American independence war and the French wars) between 1756 and 1815, with only two decades of peace in be-

tween. Wars raised taxes and, because of trade disruptions, the prices of consumer goods. It is no wonder that real wages and average living standards show little trend upward until the 1840s. Those who lived through the Industrial Revolution did not enjoy its fruits.

In the process of structural transformation of the industries, a great deal of human suffering was experienced along with the obvious gains to consumers. The new technology produced cheaper and better goods that competed with those produced by home-workers, who gradually lost their desperate struggle with the machines. The plight of the handloom weaver who was gradually pushed aside by the power loom after 1815 is well known, but in many other areas in textiles and handicraft production the Industrial Revolution also meant the end of independent producers and their way of life. Moreover, work in the early factories was very difficult. Work hours were long, and the shop floors were noisy, cold, and often dangerous. The workers—many of them women and teenagers—had to submit to the discipline and regime of the factory, controlled by strangers, in which transgressions were severely penalized. The industrial novels describing the harshness of this life made a deep impression on contemporary readers, but it took a long time for effective measures to restrain child labor and factory conditions to be enforced.

To make things worse, the Industrial Revolution was accompanied by rapid urbanization. The industrial towns, such as Manchester and Glasgow, grew at unprecedented rates, attracting thousands of rural workers or their family members. Yet life in the early industrial towns was very unpleasant. The overhead capital in cities—devoted to water supply, sewage and garbage disposal—could not accommodate the sudden surge in the number of inhabitants. People lived in overcrowded, dirty, ugly, dark tenements, and poor sanitary conditions led to high mortality rates. These conditions inspired an angry literature, of which Friedrich Engels's *Condition of the Working Class in England* (1844) is the most celebrated contribution. Part of the higher wages earned by factory workers thus must be regarded as compensation for deterioration in their quality of life relative to village conditions.

Life was not easy even for the industrialists and entrepreneurs who were the driving force behind the innovation process. For every successful capitalist such as Richard Arkwright or Boulton, there were many who failed for one reason or another. Britain's legal framework was not friendly to limited-liability corporations, and many bankruptcies ensued because of complex networks of partnerships with unlimited liability. Henry Cort, for one, lost all his business because of such a partner and in the end had to be satisfied with a modest pension while others used his invention. Dr. John Roebuck, Watt's first partner, also went bankrupt, because of the troubles of one of his other partners. On the surface patent law meant protection for inventors, but with some notable exceptions it actually provided few financial safeguards. Richard Arkwright, the cotton spinner, just gave up his patent altogether rather than continue to spend time and money on litigation. Then, as now, entrepreneurial activity was a highly risky gamble, with the odds stacked against bold innovators. The historical record, by recounting the success stories, tends to obscure these risks. The people who became rich and richer during the Industrial Revolution were those who owned land, particularly urban real estate and lots with favorable physical characteristics such as mining or waterpower sites. Also merchants, shipowners, and the providers of financial services to trade generally did well. Moreover, many of the successful industrialists came from the ranks of the mercantile and landowning classes. The Industrial Revolution created a class of rich capitalists, but not all of the newly rich were industrialists and certainly not all industrialists became rich.

The most remarkable social consequence of the Industrial Revolution was the emergence of the factory. It is insufficiently realized today that before the Industrial Revolution the vast majority of people worked in their homes or in fields or attached workshops. Even workers who had lost their economic independence, such as those in the so-called putting-out industries (in which a merchant supplied them with raw materials or intermediate products that the worker then processed at a fixed piece wage), worked in their own homes. Independent artisans, shopkeepers, and farmers were domestically based, and employed members of their own households. Even those whose work required being away from home, such as masons and carters, normally operated from a home base. Colliers, soldiers and sailors, and some workers in manufacturing (in large ironworks, breweries, and shipyards) were among the few who worked under conditions that would remind one of modern labor arrangements. With the Industrial Revolution, this situation began to change. The "mill," in which production took place in a large room in coordinated fashion and under supervision, slowly spread; and although the changeover took many years to reach its full course, its roots are clearly in the fateful years of the late eighteenth century.

Karl Marx, one of the first social commentators to fully realize this, found the rise of the factory to be a deplorable development. Workers were "alienated" from the means of production, treated as machines, exploited, and often humiliated. Modern research is a bit more cautious: conditions in the mills were harsh, but the domestic manufacturing system was not less backbreaking, and the harsh discipline of factories has to be compared with the discipline to which apprentices, wives, and children were subjected in the traditional economy. In the nineteenth century, those domestic industries that remained were known significantly as "sweated trades." At first, factory masters preferred the more docile and malleable labor supplied by women and youngsters and found it difficult to manage adult males, who were often unruly and intoxicated. Over time, however, many factory owners came to realize that factory labor required male workers as well and did their best to convince these workers, by a mixture of propaganda and incentives, to conform to factory requirements of punctuality and obedience.

The new factories required more than just buildings, machinery, and lighting. With the emergence of large production units, new management problems surfaced. Some of the most successful entrepreneurs—such as Robert Owen, the cotton spinner, and Josiah Wedgwood, the pottery manufacturer—were able to overcome lack of experience and training through intuition and genius, and put together well-organized operations. But in this age most managers had little experience in cost and capital accounting, inventory control, personnel management, financial organization, and marketing. All of those functions had to be improvised and mastered through experience. A few did well, but many got it wrong and suffered the consequences. Moreover, there was no "venture capital" in this age. Banks and other financial institutions rarely risked their funds on the new technology. Much of the fixed capital in which the firms invested—the purchase of buildings and equipment—came from retained earnings, that is, the owner's own resources.

Why were factories necessary? Part of the answer must be that the minimum scale of production increased for a variety of reasons. Power was cheaper, horsepower for horsepower, in larger steam engines. Most machines had a minimum efficient scale that exceeded the small size of household labor, even if augmented by apprentices. Heating and lighting, inventory management, and, least appreciated of all, the growing requirements of engineering and technical knowledge made for economies of scale. This was not true for all industries, not even for all "new" industries; what is now known as flexible specialization held its own in many industries. Mass production required the design, construction, and maintenance of machines that could not be mass-produced themselves; but in some cases, deliberate choices were made to specialize in mass-produced factory-made goods. The custom-made products of self-employed, highly skilled specialists required less machinery and provided fewer scale economies but also avoided some of the more egregious excesses of the factories and the early industrial towns. France chose a trajectory that, compared to Britain, was along more traditional lines.

Physical economies of scale were not the only reason why factories emerged. The putting-out system could work only if its employees could be paid a piece wage, as employers could not monitor the time employees spent working. For many products this system was becoming increasingly difficult to follow because of a finer and finer division of labor or because the monitoring of the quality of the product was getting harder. As products became more sophisticated, and markets expanded, the need for standardization was felt more acutely. Manufacturers realized that direct and continuous monitoring of production workers to conform with product specifications was necessary. Furthermore, as technological changes became more and more frequent, workers had to be trained on the job, instructed in the use of new tools and equipment. The emergence of factories thus was partly due to the economics of information. However, more must have been involved because even when workers were paid a piece wage, they were often put in mills and worked under supervision. The expensive equipment owned by the master needed to be tended with care; raw materials and fuel had to be protected against pilfering. Factories, then, offered many advantages, and no single explanation will do for all cases.

Consideration of why the Industrial Revolution occurred at all needs to be split into why it happened when it did, why it happened in Britain before anywhere else, and why it took the form it did. These three questions are likely to have different answers. The timing clearly has something to do with the ability of inventors and engineers to crack technical problems that were beyond them a century earlier. It is also argued that the timing depended on the existence of a market in which the new products could be sold. Up to a point, this latter argument must take into account that the products pretty well sold themselves through lower prices and higher quality. Perhaps the really important question is not one of why did the great inventions of the 1760s and 1770s take place, but why the wave of technological progress did not peter out after 1815 or so, as it had always done in the past. As to why it happened in Britain, as opposed to some other economy, there is a large and lively literature on the "British advantages," ranging from Britain's good fortune of having large supplies of iron and coal, to its being an island, that—almost alone in Europe—saved it from the invasion of foreign armies. Above all, however, Britain had the kind of institutions that were conducive to economic development and technological progress. Its government was by no means laissez-faire, but it supported innovating entrepreneurs and inventors against the fury of artisans and domestic workers who tried to protect their turf. The British government opposed the conservative forces who petitioned Parliament for legislation to prohibit the new machines or tried to stop mechanization by breaking the new devices and threatening with violence those who intended to employ them. Britain was comparatively peaceful, it had good internal transportation, and its social institutions above all respected private property. Laws, contracts, and ownership could be and were enforced. Labor and capital were relatively free to move around and deployed wherever their return was highest. Furthermore, British culture, more than others, recognized commercial and industrial success as a legitimate source of social status, and members of its elite were often fascinated with the mundane technical details of farming, bridge building, and pumping.

The significance of the Industrial Revolution in economic history cannot be overestimated. Its immediate effect was to establish Britain as the leading economic and technological nation in the world, with all the political prestige and power that came with that, and it imposed the *Pax Britannica* on Europe for a century. Beyond that, it changed the parameters of economic change. Growth before the Industrial Revolution had been usually short-lived, a passing episode that with luck might propel an economy to a somewhat higher plateau. After 1830, it became a permanent condition of those economies that followed the British example and continually introduced new techniques into their production processes. New technology acquired increasing importance in the process of growth. Before 1750, most economic growth, when it occurred, was the result of institutional improvement that permitted trade where none had existed before, or secured better property rights that allowed people actually to enjoy the fruits of labor and patience. Technological change did occur, but its role in growth as such was probably modest. During the Industrial Revolution and after, growth became increasingly dominated by improvements in technology. As people increasingly realized, this was the one form of economic growth that did not run into diminishing returns, that did not slow down, and that could sustain itself.

Not all countries that emulated Britain followed its precise technological example. Some specialized in upmarket, high-quality products. Others relied on different sources of energy, such as water or wind, or found niches in specialized industries. The Industrial Revolution, however, was not about one technical detail or another. It was about the willingness to use a growing understanding of nature (physics, chemistry, biology) in industrial production, implemented by private enterprise, for the sake of profit. It was about the ability of capitalists to mobilize capital and labor on a large scale to introduce these new techniques. It was this feature of the Industrial Revolution that prepared the ground for modern economic growth and the unprecedented prosperity it has brought to much of humanity, a prosperity that would have been unimaginable anywhere in 1750.

[*See also* Patents *and* Technology.]

BIBLIOGRAPHY
Ashton, T. S. *The Industrial Revolution, 1760–1830.* Oxford, 1948.
Berg, Maxine. *The Age of Manufactures.* 2d rev. ed. London, 1994.
Crafts, Nicholas F. R. *British Economic Growth during the Industrial Revolution.* New York, 1985.
Hartwell, R. M. *The Industrial Revolution and Economic Growth.* London, 1971.
Hudson, Pat. *The Industrial Revolution.* London, 1992.
Jacob, Margaret. *Scientific Culture and the Making of the Industrial West.* New York, 1997.
Landes, David S. *The Unbound Prometheus: Technological Change and Industrial Development in Western Europe from 1750 to the Present.* Cambridge, 1969.
Mantoux, Paul. *The Industrial Revolution in the Eighteenth Century.* Rev. ed. New York, 1961.
Mokyr, Joel, ed. *The British Industrial Revolution: An Economic Perspective.* Boulder, 1993. Expanded and updated 2d ed. 1998.
Mokyr, Joel. "Knowledge, Technology, and Economic Growth during the Industrial Revolution." In *Productivity, Technology and Economic Growth*, edited by Bart van Ark, Simon K. Kuipers and Gerard Kuper. The Hague, 2000.
Pollard, Sidney. *The Genesis of Modern Management.* London, 1965.

JOEL MOKYR

INEQUALITY OF WEALTH AND INCOME DISTRIBUTION. Economic-historical research on the level and evolution of wealth and income inequality has been dominated by the so-called Kuznets curve. In 1955, Simon Kuznets launched the hypothesis of a systematic relationship between income inequality and the process of modern economic growth that began during the first half of the nineteenth century. According to this hypothesis, the relationship between the level of per capita gross domestic product (GDP) and the degree of income inequality can be visualized as an inverted U curve: Inequality tends to increase during the first phase of modern economic growth, but in the second phase, which appears to begin in most Western countries around the turn of the twentieth century, a marked leveling out of income differences follows. This hypothesis of an inverted U curve (or Kuznets curve) has since dominated the research on long-term development of wealth and income. The relevant literature has focused on two issues: Does the Kuznets curve exist (or are long-term changes in income and wealth inequality much more complex), and if it exits, how does one explain these systematic tendencies toward greater or smaller inequality?

The literature on the interpretation of these changes can be summarized briefly here. Kuznets related the rise in inequality during the first stages of modern economic growth to a shift of labor from a sector with low income and inequality (agriculture) to sectors with high income and inequality (i.e., industry and services). Given this income gap between traditional and modern sectors, income inequality will increase during the first phase of growth. This continues until about 50 percent of the labor force is employed outside agriculture. Beyond this point, inequality will diminish because a growing part of the population earns the higher industrial income. In short, the inverted U curve is a consequence of the transition from a traditional agrarian economy with a low income level to a modern industrial society with a high income level.

A second approach has its origins in the work of the classical economists. It accounts for variations in income inequality through changes in the functional distribution of income. According to this view, the quantitative relations between income from wages, capital, and land are decisive, and these relations are ultimately determined by the relative position and power of the various social groups—landowners, entrepreneurs, and the working class. During the first stage of industrialization, the position of laborers is relatively weak, and real-wage increases lag behind productivity growth as a result. During later stages, the rise of unions, and of the welfare state (the result of the development of democratic institutions) and the growing scarcity of labor result in a reversal of the trend toward growing inequality (Soltow and van Zanden, 1998).

SOCIAL CLASSES. A mixture of classes—the wealthy on horseback, middle-class women distributing temperance tracts, the barefoot and ill-clothed poor, and workingmen—are observed by the historian Thomas Carlyle and the Christian social theorist F. D. Maurice in *Work*, a painting by Ford Madox Brown (1821–1893). (© Manchester Art Gallery)

Increasingly, however, research has moved away from changes in the functional distribution of incomes and has concentrated on the analysis of earnings differentials. The link between earnings and the scarcities and productivities of specific skills is at the core of this approach. Williamson (1983 and 1985) has adopted this approach in his analysis of British and American inequality in the nineteenth century. His explanation of the upswing in the Kuznets curve is that demand for certain kinds of skilled labor rapidly grew during the first phase of the process of modern economic growth. As a result, the difference in pay between unskilled and skilled labor (the skill premium) increased. This rise in the skill premium explains the increase in inequality during the first half of the nineteenth century. The expansion of education and changes in the production process resulted in an increase in the supply of skills and a relative decline in the demand for skilled labor. As a result, the skill premium began to fall during the second half of the nineteenth century, and income inequality diminished over the long term.

Switching back to the debate on the actual development of income and wealth inequality, Kuznets used two kinds of evidence to support his hypothesis. He explained that cross-section data of the relationship between GDP per capita and income inequality show an inverted U curve, but a relatively weak one. Many studies have tried to verify his findings using more and better data and more sophisticated estimation techniques. Most have concluded that if an inverted U curve can be found, it appears to be rather weak and perhaps caused by other factors; for example, the countries in the middle-income regions are mainly from Latin America and have a traditionally high level of inequality, caused by unequal access to land and other resources (Deininger and Squire, 1998).

The second kind of evidence put forward by Kuznets was longitudinal data of income inequality in a number of countries. In particular, the German data showed the inverted U pattern. From 1955 onward, a great deal of research has been conducted into long-term developments

of income and wealth inequality of industrialized countries (in particular Great Britain, the United States, Sweden, Norway, Germany, and the Netherlands). A review of the literature by Kaelble and Thomas (1991) concluded that there was clear evidence for a decline in income inequality during the first seven decades of the twentieth century, but that the increase of inequality during the nineteenth century was found in only a few countries and that its timing and magnitude were still unclear. The lack of consensus on the rising leg of the Kuznets curve is related to a number of issues. First, dependent on the theoretical approach that is selected, different measures of inequality have been used. Kuznets concentrated on data on the distribution of incomes among households, but scholars who were mainly interested in the relative scarcities of skills of course focused on relative earnings, whereas others have used data on the functional distribution of income, the distribution of wealth, or even the distribution of the heights of conscripts to study trends in inequality. Different measures of inequality have led to different answers to the question whether inequality increased during the Industrial Revolution. Second, the poor quality of data and related problems about their interpretation have given rise to a number of discussions on the existence of the rising leg of Kuznets curve in Great Britain and the United States. The evidence presented by Williamson (1983 and 1985) for a rise in inequality during the first phase of modern economic growth has been the subject of some debate, and his results have been criticized.

Comparable research on nonindustrialized countries has been slow to develop. Moreover, persistent regional variations in the level of inequality appear to be more important than long-term changes. During the second half of the twentieth century, Latin America (with Gini coefficients of about 0.5) and sub-Saharan Africa (Gini's between 0.4 and 0.5) have much higher levels of inequality than the Organization for Economic Cooperation and Development (OECD) countries, South Asia, and eastern Europe (with median coefficients of 0.23 to 0.33) (Deininger and Squire, 1998). Oshima (1994) showed that in Asia there is no evidence at all for a Kuznets curve (see also van der Eng 1998 for the Indonesian case).

The debate on the Kuznets curve has also affected research on long-term change in inequality before the Industrial Revolution. Van Zanden (1995) showed that the expansion of the Dutch economy during the seventeenth century was accompanied by a strong increase in wealth and income inequality (see also Soltow and van Zanden, 1998). Hoffman, Jacks, Levin, and Lindert (2002) documented systematic trends in the development of inequality in Europe between 1500 and 1850, and in particular analyzed changes in relative prices that favored high-income groups and resulted in a relative decline of real earnings of low-income groups (i.e., food prices and rents went up much more than the prices of most luxury goods, including the wages of servants). Real-wages trends in large parts of Europe in this period also tend to show a decline of the standard of living during the early modern period, despite the (modest) increase of income per capita (van Zanden, 1999). Nineteenth century Europe's high levels of inequality, therefore, may have been the product of developments that preceded the Industrial Revolution (see also Morrison and Snyder, 2000, for eighteenth-century France).

As indicated by Kaelble and Thomas (1991), however, there is no doubt that during the middle decades of the twentieth century inequality of income declined sharply in almost all industrialized countries. Gini coefficients of income inequality between 0.50 and 0.60 had been normal in nineteenth-century Europe; during the 1960s and 1970s they had declined to about 0.30 to 0.35. Other authors have documented this leveling of wealth disparities during the twentieth century. Therefore, this "egalitarian revolution" is so for the most important change recorded in income and wealth inequality. It was, however, followed by an increase in inequality during the 1980s and 1990s, in particular in the United States and Great Britain, where the rise of income and wealth inequality has been much sharper than in the rest of the OECD countries.

[*See also* Living Standards.]

BIBLIOGRAPHY

Borodkin, L., and P. Lindert, eds. *Trends in Income Inequality during Industrialisation.* Madrid, 1998.

Deininger, Klaus, and Lyn Squire. "New Ways of Looking at Old Issues: Inequality and Growth." *Journal of Development Studies* 57 (1998), 259–287.

Eng, Pierre van der. "Industrial Growth and Inequality: The Case of Indonesia." In *Trends in Income Inequality during Industrialisation,* edited by L. Borodkin and P. Lindert, pp. 129–149. Madrid, 1998.

Feinstein, Charles H. "The Rise and Fall of the Williamson Curve." *Journal of Economic History* 48 (1988), 699–729.

Hoffman, Philip T., David Jacks, Patricia A. Levin, and Peter H. Lindert. "Prices and Real Inequality in Western Europe since 1500." *Journal of Economic History* 63 (2002).

Kaelble, Hartmut, and Mark Thomas. Introduction to *Income Distribution in Historical Perspective,* edited by Brenner, et al. Cambridge, 1991.

Kuznets, Simon. "Economic Growth and Income Inequality." *American Economic Review* 45 (1955), 1–28.

Morrison, Christian, and Wayne Snyder. "The Income Inequality of France in Historical Perspective." *European Review of Economic History* 4 (2000), 59–85.

Oshima, H. T. "The Impact of Technological Transformation on Historical Trends in Income Distribution of Asia and the West." *Developing Economics* 32 (1994), 237–255.

Soltow, Lee, and Jan Luiten van Zanden. *Income and Wealth Inequality in the Netherlands, Sixteenth–Twentieth Century.* Amsterdam, 1998.

Williamson, Jeffrey G. *American Inequality.* New York, 1983.

Williamson, Jeffrey G. *Did British Capitalism Breed Inequality?* Boston, 1985.

Zanden, Jan Luiten van. "Tracing the Beginning of the Kuznets Curve: Western Europe during the Early Modern Period." *Economic History Review* 48 (1995), 643–666.

Zanden, Jan Luiten van. "Wages and the Standard of Living in Europe, 1500–1800." *European Review of Economic History* 3 (1999), 175–198.

JAN LUITEN VAN ZANDEN

INFLATION AND HYPERINFLATION. Inflation is generally defined as a long-term sustained increase in the general level of prices, or more commonly now in the "cost of living." Although there exist a myriad of indicators of the cost of living in most countries, inflation is usually thought of in terms of a consumer price index (CPI). The CPI, however, is an imperfect measure of changes in the overall price level. In several countries, most notably the United States, there has been a concerted attempt to reduce the biases in the measurement of consumer prices arising from changes in household spending patterns, market structure, and technology, to name but three of the relevant factors contributing to such biases (see, for example, U.S. Senate, 1996). An understanding of inflation and its causes is vital since continuous increases in some indicator of the cost of living imply a concomitant fall in the purchasing power of money. In other words, a given quantity of currency is able to command fewer quantities of goods and services as prices rise.

Inflation can also be fairly said to be a phenomenon of the twentieth century and, in particular, of the post–World War II era. There also were, of course, major episodes of long-term sustained inflations in earlier European history—most notably during the "long thirteenth century" (c. 1180–c. 1320), the early modern Price Revolution era (c. 1520–c. 1640), and the Industrial Revolution era (c. 1760–1815). However, the severities of these past inflations, as measured by rates of compounded annual percentage increases in the CPI, rarely if ever matched those of the twentieth century, principally because these past inflations (with the exception of that from 1797 to 1815) occurred within predominantly commodity-money regimes, that is, of silver-based coinages (on which the money-of-account pricing systems also were based), as opposed to the predominantly fiduciary or paper-money regimes of the twentieth century, especially during its second half.

Figure 1 plots two centuries of consumer prices for the United States and the United Kingdom, countries that have a long and fairly reliable series for the CPI, dating from the late eighteenth and early nineteenth centuries. What is especially striking about this figure is that, prior to about 1945, consumer prices rose and fell over time although there does not appear to have been a persistent rise

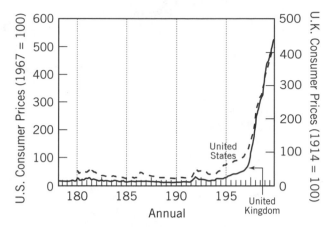

FIGURE 1. *The Evolution of Consumer Prices in the United States and the United Kingdom, 1781–1999.* SOURCE: Burdekin, R. C. K., and P. L. Siklos. "Exchange Rate Regimes and Shifts in Inflation: Does Nothing Else Matter?" *Journal of Money, Credit and Banking*, 31 (1999), 235–247. Data after 1993 updated from International Monetary Fund, *International Financial Statistics*, Washington, D.C.

in the cost of living. The period after 1945 is another matter since price levels in both countries have experienced a steep increase to the present day. Nevertheless, it could be argued that the 1970s and early 1980s are unique episodes of relatively high inflation, having occurred in peacetime (see De Long, 1997).

The post–World War II phenomenon was not, however, unique to these two countries. Indeed, as shown in Table 1, inflation in the second half of the twentieth century was a global phenomenon. Even in the so-called economies in transition—formerly referred to as centrally planned economies—inflation has been a fixture of their experience, though a combination of subsidies and artificial price fixing produced a form of repressed inflation until the transition to market began in earnest in the 1990s. (The dating of the transition is not uniform across these countries; see Fischer and Sahay, 2000). Even mainland China is not immune to the inflation disease. Table 1 masks the fact that several countries, particularly in Latin America and South America, have lived for decades with chronically high inflation (roughly 20 percent or more inflation on an annual basis). Finally, it is noteworthy that inflation continues to persist in all parts of the world with the exception of the industrial countries, where inflation dropped sharply during the 1990s. Indeed, inflation among these countries is now not much higher than during the high point of the gold standard era (1900–1913), when average annual inflation rates in the United States and the United Kingdom were, respectively, 1.23 percent and 1.22 percent. There is some evidence that having central banks with a mandate to control inflation—hence the

TABLE 1. *Post–World War II CPI Inflation in Selected Areas of the World*

Country Grouping	1969–1999	1991–1999
	(PERCENT PER ANNUM)	
Asia	8.90	8.34
Developing countries	27.49	29.30
Europe	48.35 (1971–1999)	79.84
Industrial countries	5.63	2.46
Middle Eastern countries	13.62	12.39
Western Hemisphere	80.23	92.65
Economies in transition	41.61 (1961–1989)	101.18 (1991–1998)
Mainland China	9.37 (1987–1999)	8.28

SOURCES: International Monetary Fund, *International Financial Statistics*, CD-ROM, Washington, D.C.; Sahay, R., and Végh, C. "Inflation and Stabilization in Transition Economies: An Analytical Interpretation of the Evidence," *Journal of Policy Reform*, 1 (1996), 75–108; Austrian National Bank, "Focus on Transition," 2 (1999), p. 111. The host of countries included in the groupings shown in the table are also provided in the sources. Economies in transition consist of: Bulgaria, Czech and Slovak republics, Hungary, Poland, Romania, Yugoslavia, Estonia, Latvia, Slovenia, and Russia.

designation inflation targeting—has contributed significantly to this outcome (see Bernanke et al., 1999).

Hyperinflation: Definition and Performance. Ever since Philip Cagan's (1956) seminal work on hyperinflation, academics have accepted the classification of such events as occurring whenever the inflation rate exceeds 50 percent on a monthly basis. In contrast to inflation, hyperinflation is both a pre– and post–World War II phenomenon, as shown in Table 2. The first recorded episode of hyperinflation occurred in China in the eleventh and twelfth centuries (see Lui, 1983). The most spectacular episode of hyperinflation is the second Hungarian hyperinflation of 1945–1946, when, in the final week alone, inflation stood at 158,486 percent (see Siklos, 1991).

Generally, though not exclusively, a combination of weak governments, civil disorder, and unrest produces conditions that facilitate the development of hyperinflation (Capie, 1986). Partly for this reason, episodes of hyperinflation are typically of short duration.

Theories of Inflation and Hyperinflation. Currently, the various theories of inflation and hyperinflation have one thing in common: assigning their proximate cause to movements in the money supply (Friedman, 1992, chap. 8). For cases of low or chronic inflation, changes in the money supply eventually feed into the price level, but the lags are long and variable (Friedman and Schwarz, 1982). In contrast, monetary factors almost exclusively fuel hyperinflation. Nevertheless, the vast majority of economists are generally in agreement with the view that inflation is fundamentally a monetary phenomenon. That said, the profession is nevertheless divided about the direction of causality between monetary factors and inflation and, finally, about the ultimate causes and cures for inflation.

The debate about the role of money supply changes in explaining price level movements is centuries old. Consider the following statement by Joplin (1826, p. 3): "There is no opinion better established, though it is seldom consistently maintained, than that the general scale of prices existing in every country, is determined by the amount of money which circulates in it." However, in the April 1939 issue of its *Bulletin* (p. 256), the Board of Governors of the U.S. Federal Reserve stated that "the facts show clearly that the volume of money does not control the price level." More than five decades later, Milton Friedman would once again declare the triumph of the quantity theory relationship between the money supply and the price level (see below) over others by declaring that "inflation is always and everywhere a monetary phenomenon" (reproduced in Friedman, 1992, p. xi).

Causes and Cures for Inflation. By the early 1970s, inflation was persistent and beginning to rise. Since wages represent a major component of production costs, it was natural to search for explanations of inflation in the behavior of wage setters, most notably unions. Put simply, excess demand for goods and services would lead to wage hikes (and a lower unemployment rate) and thence inflation. The resulting inverse relationship between inflation and unemployment, known as the Phillips curve, for a time led policymakers to believe that such a simple trade-off offered governments a menu from which they could select an appropriate combination of these two variables that was consistent with their political preferences. What determines the preferences of the political authorities? A large literature in political economy claims that a looming election puts pressure on elected officials to influence economic performance—higher gross domestic product (GDP) growth or lower unemployment—to enhance their

TABLE 2. *Main Episodes of Hyperinflation*

COUNTRY	YEAR ENDED	DURATION (NO. OF MONTHS)	AVERAGE MONTHLY INFLATION RATE (PERCENT)
Pre–World War II			
Austria	1922	11	47.1
Germany	1923	15	37.2
Poland	1924	13	81.1
Russia	1924	37	57.0
Hungary I	1924	28	46
Greece	1944	13	365
Hungary II	1946	12	2345×10^3
Post–World War II			
Taiwan	1949	17	30.7
Bolivia	1985	18	48.1
Peru	1989	8	48.4
Yugoslavia	1989	4	50.9
Poland	1990	4	41.2
Brazil	1990	4	68.6
Argentina	1990	11	66.0
Ukraine	1993	14	1024
Georgia	1994	13	44.1
Zaire	1994	36	665

SOURCES: Wang, J.-Y., "The Georgian Hyperinflation and Stabilization," IMF Working Paper WP/99/65, May 1999; Beaugrand, P., "Zaire's Hyperinflation, 1970–96," IMF Working Paper WP/97/50, April 1997; Siklos, P. L., ed., *Great Inflations of the 20th Century*, Aldershot, Edward Elgar, 1995; Banaian, K., *The Ukranian Economy since Independence*, Cheltenham, Edward Elgar, 1999; Siklos, P. L., *War Finance, Reconstruction, Hyperinflation and Stabilization in Hungary, 1938–48*, London, Macmillan, 1991; Cagan, P., "The Monetary Dynamics of Hyperinflation," in *Studies in the Quantity Theory of Money*, edited by M. Friedman, pp. 25–117, Chicago, University of Chicago Press, 1956; Siklos, P. L., "Interpreting a Change in Monetary Policy Regimes: A Reappraisal of the First Hungarian Hyperinflation and Stabilization, 1921–28," in *Monetary Regimes in Transition*, edited by M. D. Bordo and F. Capie, pp. 274–311, Cambridge, Cambridge University Press, 1993.

reelection prospects (see Alesina et al., 1997; Persson and Tabellini, 1994). If, in addition, economic performance can be improved by stimulating aggregate demand with positive consequences for inflation, a political inflation cycle emerges.

Alternatively, in many countries, most notably the United States, voters must choose from among the economic policies of two major parties or party blocks. A "leftist" party may consistently favor lower unemployment over inflation, whereas parties on the "right" of the political spectrum will opt for policies that place a relatively greater emphasis on lower inflation. As a result, a partisan inflation cycle emerges. Both views of the political connection between inflation and electoral outcomes are predicated on the view of an exploitable Phillips curve in the short run. Voters need not be naive, however. All that is required is uncertainty over electoral outcomes and over the actual policies elected officials will carry out during their mandate. Existing empirical evidence is slightly more favorable to the partisan view of inflation cycles.

In terms of the determinants of the Phillips curve, many economists have noted that the duration and slope of the trade-off, between either the rate of wage change or the rate of inflation and unemployment, is tied to wage earners' and consumers' *expectations* of the future. Factoring this in, one concludes that *real* wages may rise only temporarily, and that unemployment will settle at some level once the adjustment is complete. In other words, the Phillips curve shifts in time to reflect changes in expected inflation. The rate of unemployment (or output) at which the economy eventually settles is the so-called natural rate (or NAIRU, the non-accelerating inflation rate of unemployment). There has, of course, always been considerable controversy over how to measure this equilibrium rate of unemployment (see "Symposium: The Natural Rate of Unemployment," *Journal of Economic Perspectives*, vol. 11, winter 1997).

Institutional considerations and market structure play no role in the above scenario. By the later 1960s, however, a belief in the growing market power of large corporations, which presumably permitted them to set prices, and union strength, enabling wage demands to be "pushed" onto employers, led to the formulation of the cost-push theory of inflation. Institutions, therefore, were responsible, at least in part, for driving up wages and the cost of living. On a theoretical level, some economists were dissatisfied with the cost-push hypothesis because of its implication that wage demands, combined with firms' price-setting behavior, could logically lead to an unstable wage-price spiral. Second, the cost-push models ignored the role of the central bank as an institution that could influence expectations and, by implication, wage and price behavior. On an empirical level, the early studies favorable to the cost-push hypothesis were being overturned by more careful analyses of wage and price behavior. As a result, an early survey of inflation (Laidler and Parkin, 1975) concluded that one should reject the cost-push hypothesis. Nevertheless, there is a large body of evidence suggesting that even if cost-push factors are not present, there is considerable downward nominal wage rigidity. The same cannot be said, of course, to be true of real wages.

Increasingly, during the 1970s and 1980s, oil-price or supply-side shocks—the first occurring in 1973–1974, the second in 1979–1980—and policy makers' reactions to them changed the focus of research explaining inflation developments significantly, toward the policies of the monetary and later the fiscal authorities. Together with more precise and formal models of the expectations-formation process, theoretical developments led to the conclusion that, at least in the long run, monetary policy could influence only inflation and not unemployment or output. The long run is the state of affairs that exists when expectations have fully adjusted to the current policies in place. Expectations can be adaptive; that is, individuals extrapolate the future from past inflation forecasts and performance. These individuals are backward-looking. Later, expectations can be treated as rational; that is, individuals are forward-looking and generate forecasts of inflation conditioned on some information set believed to determine inflation in the future. These individuals make future plans as if generating forecasts from some model that describes the underlying structure of the economy. Short-run bursts of inflation then are possible because a politically motivated central bank persistently fools the public into making incorrect forecasts of future inflation. The driving mechanism of forecasts of future inflation is the rate of money supply growth, linked with inflation via the venerable quantity theory relationship. The bottom line then is that monetary policy is ineffective in the long run in the quest permanently to raise an economy's output.

Another category of models of inflation does not permit prices to be set each and every period; but custom, labor contracts, and transaction costs (also referred to as menu costs) prevent the market for goods and services from clearing all the time. Once again, in the long run, monetary policy is ineffective; but, in the short run, policy makers can exploit the inflation-unemployment trade-off.

Both variants of the policy ineffectiveness proposition, as this hypothesis has been called, suggest that policy makers have an interest in generating some inflation since it allows them, at least temporarily, to exploit the Phillips curve trade-off. In effect, governments choose a short-run inflation rate because the central bank, as the government's partner in implementing economic policies, has full discretion in setting money supply growth. This idea has been termed the time inconsistency problem. Kydland and Prescott (1977) originated the idea, and its policy implications were spelled out by Barro and Gordon (1983). The time inconsistency arises because policy makers choose the desired inflation rate *after* individuals have formed their expectations and made their consumption/production plans. One of the arguments then for reforming central banks to enhance their transparency and accountability is that it makes it more difficult for the central bank or the government to spring inflation surprises on the public.

By the early 1990s, as evidenced by a second major survey of inflation (McCallum, 1990), cost-push factors had disappeared entirely from the scene, and the search for causes of inflation shifted toward the institutional relationship between governments and their central banks (Alesina and Summers, 1993). Paralleling this develop-

ment was a growing recognition that three other seemingly nonmonetary factors were important ingredients in the inflationary process: fiscal deficits, the exchange rate regime, and the framework of monetary policy.

Fiscal deficits might lead to inflation since excessive borrowing threatens the ability of governments to borrow without resorting to financing via the issue of money by the central bank. An extreme manifestation of this possibility is the case of a government that has little or no recourse to generating revenues other than through seigniorage. Concern over the connection between the exchange rate regime and monetary policy has a long history that can be traced back at least to Hume's price-specie flow mechanism outlined in the eighteenth century (Hume, 1875). Also decisive in this respect was the literature outlining the Monetary Approach to the Balance of Payments (MABOP), developed around the 1950s, and reaching its zenith during the 1970s (Frenkel and Johnson, 1976). Its importance lies in the fact that, as the Bretton Woods exchange rate system took hold, balance of payments difficulties became all too common in many industrial countries. The MABOP was able to show that the external balance could be attained without inflation and, as a consequence, without changing domestic incomes or interest rates. In other words, a balance of payments deficit need not be deflationary, nor does a balance of payments surplus necessarily entail inflation. Since these are equilibrium conditions, the dynamics from one equilibrium to another become decisive and can, of course, entail change in inflation. The exchange rate regime is a potential determinant of inflation because, under a floating exchange regime, policy makers are free to choose inflation if the exchange rate consequences are ignored; in a fixed regime, inflation is determined by the value of the currency (or currencies) to which it is tied. In an open economy, the propensity to inflate is lower in part because of the adverse effects of inflation on competitiveness and trade (Romer, 1993). In the case of intermediate exchange-rate regimes, inflation is influenced by a mix of internal policy choices and external factors. Finally, the framework of monetary policy refers to an explicit decision by a government to allow the central bank to pursue a numerical inflation objective, referred to as an inflation target (Bernanke et al., 1999). An inflation target, together with more central bank autonomy, permits the monetary authorities to pursue their inflation objectives without political interference. Notice that, for all the nonmonetary factors just described, money supply growth provides the mechanism by which inflation eventually shows up in the economy. However, nonmonetary factors still may help explain why governments in different countries choose different inflation rates. Empirical evidence has tended to confirm that each of the nonmonetary elements discussed above can explain a significant portion of inflation in a wide range of countries, especially that occurring in the 1990s (Cottarelli et al., 1998). However, it was the idea that central bank autonomy could deliver lower inflation (Cukierman, 1992), at little or no economic cost, that attracted considerable attention during the 1990s. Unfortunately, there are serious flaws in the construction of indexes of central bank independence (Banaian et al., 1998), together with a belief, not shared by all, that economies suffering from low to moderate inflation do not sacrifice output growth or create additional unemployment when they reduce inflation. Bruno and Easterly (1998) offered a puzzle: why have more governments not taken advantage of the "free lunch" afforded by central bank autonomy?

As should be clear from the foregoing discussion, economists' understanding of the inflation process has grown greatly over the past four decades or so. Theories and policies toward inflation have evolved from a belief that economies could be modeled precisely and the implications of policies predicted with great accuracy, in the 1960s, through an era when aggregate-demand-type policies were viewed as ineffective, and later with contempt, until the present-day view in which inflation is seen as once again controllable if the appropriate institutional mechanisms are put into place. In other words, much more has become known about the driving forces of inflation and how monetary policy can work to influence them (see, in particular, Sargent, 1999, and Taylor, 1999).

Causes and Cures for Hyperinflation. There is little controversy about the role of monetary factors in explaining every one of the reported episodes of hyperinflation. Governments, deprived of conventional taxation as a principal source of revenues, suspend any limit on borrowing from the central bank. This leads to an almost exclusive resort to the printing press to satisfy the fiscal authorities' need for revenues. As inflation accelerates, the fiscal authorities, by now effectively in full control of the monetary authorities, must stay ahead of inflation and, more important, ahead of inflationary expectations, to ensure a steady stream of revenues. However, in this setup, it is conceivable that money supply growth begets more money supply growth in the future; for, otherwise, the government's revenue from inflation—seigniorage—would disappear. This suggests the theoretical possibility that inflation can display explosive behavior, in that past inflation leads to more future inflation in response to the government's need to print money, its only revenue source. The possibility of an ever-increasing inflation rate, an inflation bubble, is an intriguing one; but the brevity of hyperinflation episodes, combined with the historical setting in which the vast majority of hyperinflationary episodes took place, makes it doubtful that such bubbles were ever really a feature of any hyperinflation.

INFLATION. After World War I, inflation was so high in Germany that a woman starts the morning fire with banknotes. (Prints and Photographs Division, Library of Congress)

There is, similarly, little controversy in the economics profession over the cures for hyperinflation. Fiscal policy that respects a budget constraint without resort to excessive monetary expansion, together with a monetary authority that can resist financing the government's budget, can do the trick quickly and successfully as long as the public perceives the newly implemented policies to be credible ones. Although these conditions generally have been viewed as necessary to end a hyperinflation, some exceptions to the rule have been reported by Makinen and Woodward (1989), who observed an end to the Taiwanese hyperinflation without fiscal adjustment. Other examples, such as the ending of the high inflation in China in 1949–1950, as well as the Russian hyperinflation of the 1920s, also suggest that even if a sustainable fiscal policy is a necessary condition to end a hyperinflation, it is not always sufficient. In addition, there is the thorny issue of how to quantify credibility since it is not an observable phenomenon. Instead, it usually has been assumed that the reforms aimed at ending a hyperinflation must have been credible, or such episodes would not have ended abruptly.

At the theoretical level, two other controversies have emerged over the consequences of ending a hyperinflation. A successful end to a hyperinflation means price stability and usually the introduction of a new currency. Since hyperinflation effectively demonetizes an economy, the end of a hyperinflation involves remonetizing the economy. Consequently, currency in circulation rises much faster than the price level, with the implication that the purchasing power of those balances, called real balances or the real value of the money supply, also rises quickly. If so, then it would appear that the close connection between money and price-level movements predicted by the quantity theory is severed in the aftermath of a hyperinflation. According to Sargent and Wallace (1985), the quantity theory then is a special case of a more general theory of the price level in which the latter is determined by the rationally expected future path of the money supply. This view has been termed the real bills doctrine. Supporters of the quantity theory respond by pointing out that the close connection between money supply and price-level movements is a long-run proposition, and that the money-prices nexus can be nested within the quantity theory framework if output is allowed to grow quickly, or if the rate at which the money supply changes hands also changes. The latter concept is referred to as the velocity of money. Indeed, quantity theorists point out that velocity, in particular, drops rapidly following the credible end to a hyperinflation so that it is easy to explain the rise in real balances following such episodes. Episodes of inflation in U.S. colonial history were an early testing ground for the real bills versus the quantity theory positions. For example, Smith (1985), takes the view that price-level movements ultimately are determined by the real bills approach, whereas Michener (1987) instead interprets the same period as one that is consistent with the basic quantity theory propositions (also see Friedman, 1992). The debate remains unsettled in part over disagreements about how policies were carried out at the time. In another sense, however, it is also unclear whether the differences between the two camps are as meaningful as once thought. After all, both sides accept the notion that, ultimately, price-level movements are a monetary phenomenon. The real bills approach simply does not treat all money supply movements as inflationary since increases in the money supply backed, say, by future budget surpluses are not to be treated the same as injections of money into the economy that cannot be so financed. In contrast, adherents to the quantity theory point of view prefer to focus on velocity of circulation (or the demand for money) and its determinants. Velocity is not a constant, a sometime inaccurate portrayal of adherents to the crude quantity theory, but is deter-

mined by, among other factors, the interest rate, inflation expectations, and the development of the financial system. A large literature is devoted to this topic as well. See in particular Bordo and Jonung (1987) and Laidler (1993).

The second source of controversy centers around the real economic costs of terminating hyperinflation. Strictly speaking, the Phillips curve predicts that a sharp reduction in inflation should lead to a massive rise in unemployment, particularly so under hyperinflation. Siklos (1995) surveys the literature and finds that there is a mix of evidence both favorable and unfavorable for the view that the output or unemployment consequences of the end of very high inflations are great. Since the essential issues surrounding this debate are the same as the ones discussed earlier under the heading of more moderate inflations, there is nothing more to add except that the historical contexts in which the classic hyperinflations took place unfortunately limit severely the data (both in quantity and quality) required to confirm or reject either hypothesis; so the question is likely to remain unresolved.

[See also Price Revolution and Prices.]

BIBLIOGRAPHY

Alesina, Alberta, Nouriel Roubini, and Gerald D. Cohen. *Political Cycles and the Macroeconomy.* Cambridge, Mass., 1997.

Alesina, Alberta, and Lawrence H. Summers. "Central Bank Independence and Macroeconomic Performance." *Journal of Money, Credit and Banking* 25 (May 1993), 157–162.

Banaian, King, Richard C. K. Burdekin, and Thomas D. Willett. "Reconsidering the Principal Components of Central Bank Independence: The More the Merrier?" *Public Choice* 97 (October 1998), 1–12.

Barro, Robert J., and David B. Gordon. "A Positive Theory of Monetary Policy in a Natural Rate Model." *Journal of Political Economy* 91 (August 1983), 589–610.

Bernanke, Ben, Thomas Laubach, Frederic S. Mishkin, and Adam S. Posen. *Inflation Targeting.* Princeton, 1999.

Bordo, M. D., and L. Jonung. *The Long-Run Behavior of the Velocity of Circulation.* Cambridge, 1987.

Bruno, Michael, and William Easterly. "Inflation Crises and Long-Run Growth." *Journal of Monetary Economics* 41 (February 1998), 3–26.

Cagan, Philip. "The Monetary Dynamics of Hyperinflation." In *Studies in the Quantity Theory of Money,* edited by Milton Friedman, pp. 25–117. Chicago, 1956.

Capie, Forrest. "Conditions in Which Very Rapid Inflation Has Appeared." In *Carnegie-Rochester Conference Series on Public Policy,* vol. 24, pp. 115–168. Amsterdam, 1986.

Cottarelli, Carlo, Mark Griffiths, and Reza Moghadan. "The Nonmonetary Determinants of Inflation: A Panel Data Study." International Monetary Fund Working Paper 98/23. Washington, D.C., 1998.

Cukierman, Alex. *Central Bank Strategy, Credibility and Independence.* Cambridge, Mass., 1992.

De Long, J. B. "America's Peacetime Inflation: The 1970s." In *Reducing Inflation: Motivation and Strategy,* edited by Christina Romer and David Romer, pp. 247–278. Chicago, 1997.

Fischer, S., and R. Sahay. "The Transition Economies after Ten Years." International Monetary Fund Working Paper WP/00/30. Washington, D.C., 2000.

Friedman, Milton. *Money Mischief.* New York, 1992.

Friedman, Milton, and Anna J. Schwartz. *Monetary Trends in the United States and the United Kingdom.* Chicago, 1982.

Hume, David. *Essays: Moral, Political, Literary*, edited by T. H. Green and T. H. Grose. London, 1875.

Joplin, Thomas. *Views on the Subject of Corn and Currency.* London, 1826.

Kydland, Finn E., and Edward C. Prescott. "Rules Rather than Discretion: The Inconsistency of Optimal Plans." *Journal of Political Economy* 85 (June 1977): 473–491.

Laidler, David E. W. *The Demand for Money.* 4th ed. New York, 1993.

Laidler, David, and Michael Parkin. "Inflation: A Survey." *Economic Journal* 85 (December 1975), 741–809.

Lui, F. T. "Cagan's Hypothesis and the First Nationwide Inflation of Paper Money in World History." *Journal of Political Economy* 91 (December 1983), 1067–1074.

Makinen, Gail E., and G. Thomas Woodward. "The Taiwanese Hyperinflation and Stabilization of 1945–1952." *Journal of Money, Credit, and Banking* 21 (February 1989), 90–105.

McCallum, Bennett T. "Inflation: Theory and Evidence." In *Handbook of Monetary Economics*, edited by B. M. Friedman and F. H. Hahn, vol. III, pp. 964–1012. Amsterdam, 1990.

Michener, R. "Fixed Exchange Rates and the Quantity Theory in Colonial America." In *Carnegie-Rochester Conference Series on Public Policy*, edited by K. Brunner and A. H. Meltzer, vol. 27, pp. 233–308. Amsterdam, 1987.

Persson, Torsten, and Guido Tabellini. *Monetary and Fiscal Policy.* Cambridge, Mass., 1994.

Romer, David. "Openness and Inflation: Theory and Evidence." *Quarterly Journal of Economics* 108 (November 1993), 869–903.

Sargent, Thomas J. "The Ends of Four Big Inflations." In *Inflation Causes and Effects*, edited by R. H. Hall, pp. 41–97. Chicago, 1982.

Sargent, Thomas J. *The Conquest of American Inflation.* Princeton, N.J., 1999.

Sargent, Thomas J., and Neil Wallace. "Some Unpleasant Monetarist Arithmetic." *Federal Reserve Bank of Minneapolis Quarterly Review* 5 (Fall 1985), 1–17.

Siklos, P. L. *War Finance, Reconstruction, Hyperinflation and Stabilization in Hungary, 1938–48.* London, 1991.

Siklos, P. L. "Hyperinflations: Their Origins, Development and Termination." In *Great Inflations of the 20th Century*, edited by P. L. Siklos. pp. 3–34, Aldershot, U.K., 1995.

Smith, B. "Colonial Evidence on Two Theories of Money: Maryland and the Colonies." *Journal of Political Economy* 93 (December 1985), 1178–1211.

Taylor, John B., ed. *Monetary Policy Rules.* Chicago, 1999.

U.S. Senate. Committee on Finance. *Final Report on the Advisory Commission to Study the Consumer Price Index.* Washington, D.C., 1996.

PIERRE SIKLOS

INFLATION TAX. An inflation tax is a tax levied on holders of money balances and nominal monetary claims issued by the government or the central bank. The tax rate is equal to the inflation rate, and the tax base is the real stock of money balances. It is levied when the government attempts to finance its budget deficit by printing money or other nominal liabilities that cause inflation. Inflation diminishes the purchasing power of the public's stock of outstanding monetary assets and reduces its real income or wealth and subsequently its demand for goods and services that are made available for government consumption.

From an optimal taxation perspective, the marginal cost of this tax (inflation) should equal the marginal costs of other taxes. However, the advantages of an inflation tax are that its imposition does not require any legislation or consent and its collection is instant and is practically costless. These benefits have made this tax a favorite of governments in times of emergency, especially during wars and political instability. Its disadvantage lies in its short-term effectiveness, which prevents it from serving as a sustainable mode of public finance. Effectiveness is undermined in two related ways. First, inflation also taxes the government by reducing the purchasing power of the public's liabilities to the government, namely those in regular taxes. Second, the public can protect itself from its tax incidence by reducing its holding of money balances. If the budgetary crisis is not resolved, attempts by the government to increase inflation tax revenue may run the risk of causing an inflationary spiral, hyperinflation, and eventually the government's financial collapse. The dynamics of inflation tax can be described by using the well-known Laffer curve, whereby increases in the inflation rate initially increase revenues until they peak and eventually decline.

An inflation tax involves money creation and is sometimes used interchangeably with the term *seigniorage*, that is, the government's revenue from money creation. This is not necessarily accurate, because money created at a rate commensurate with increased demand for it is not in itself inflationary. However, the quantity theory of money suggests that, in long-run equilibrium, attempts by the government to finance its deficit by printing money do result in a rate of inflation equal to the rate of monetary expansion such that seigniorage revenues equal inflation tax revenues. Nevertheless, rigidities that prevent prices from immediately adjusting to the change in the money supply allow the government to collect seigniorage revenues on top of inflation tax revenues.

Inflation Tax and Historical Commodity Money Regimes. The inflation tax model was developed in the context of fiat money, whereby governments enjoyed a monopoly over the provision of monetary assets that allowed them to finance their deficits by printing money. It is perceived that in historical commodity money regimes, the government earned seigniorage from minting coins but it did not engage in inflation tax finance. However, recent research argues that governments used inflation tax even while on a commodity money regime.

First, a distinction should be made between commodity money regimes in which rulers minted coins from their treasury and those in which coins were struck from private sources of precious metals. In the former, the government did not earn seigniorage when its minted its own bullion reserves to effect its purchases (equivalent to selling foreign exchange reserves by the central bank). This situation prevailed in many centralized empires, such as the Roman Empire. The term *seigniorage* owes its origin to the latter case: the seigniorial right of medieval lords to charge a fee for using their private mints to mint coins. The fee was usually a percentage of the bullion minted. Seigniorage was charged at mints until modern times and in some states until the twentieth century.

Inflation tax is a tax on nominal money balances. Therefore it seems impossible to levy such a tax when the money supply consists of metallic coins. Yet during the reign of commodity moneys, episodes of debasement occurred whereby rulers reduced the intrinsic (metallic) value of coins while maintaining their face value. This practice prevailed under both minting arrangements. In the first case, a ruler under fiscal pressure might mint his or her stock of bullion into more coins by reducing their metallic content and trying to pass them at their previous rate. When the public became fully aware of the coinage changes, the price level normally rose, and thus some degree of inflation ensued, thereby eroding the benefits from debasement. This case is similar in most respects to modern (fiat money) inflation tax.

Assuming that coins were traded according to their intrinsic values, as so many economic historians do, relying on theoretical models of commodity money, it may appear difficult to explain the prevalence of debasement under a minting regime where merchants sold high-grade bullion to state mints in return for debased coins. Two explanations that are not mutually exclusive have been provided. The first suggests that rulers cheated those who brought their bullion to the mint. This may have been possible, if only for a while. However, since some merchants might have been able to afford an assay of the coins, they would presumably discover this fraud and stop coining at that mint.

More recently, Carlo Cipolla, in his book *The Monetary Policy of Fourteenth Century Florence* (1982), reiterated an explanation for debasements, propounded many years earlier by, inter alia, Hans Van Werveke (1949), Marc Bloch (1954), and Albert Feavearyear (1963), based on evidence that coins were usually traded at face value rather than at their intrinsic values. If coins were exchanged at face value, it was profitable for merchants to mint bullion into debased coins that would pass at the older coin's value. In this scenario, the ruler is not necessarily cheating the bearers of bullion, for he or she could actually make it profitable for them to have their metals coined during debasements. This explanation was challenged by some, most notably Harry Miskimin. In his book *Money and Power in Fifteenth Century France* (1984), Miskimin tried to prove that coins were exchanged at their metallic values, rendering debasements ineffective in raising fiscal revenues. But Miskimin did not take full account of the fact that determining the coins' metallic values was a cost-

ly and inaccurate procedure. Touchstones were used almost entirely for gold coins and were reliable only within a quarter carat. The fineness of silver coins could be assayed only by the costly and difficult cupellation process, which destroyed the coin being tested. Furthermore, most merchants did not possess accurate scales, and the nature of "hammered coinage," that individual coins were rarely identical, meant a large number had to be weighed on these scales. Therefore, only properly equipped merchants and money changers dealing in large quantities of coins could afford to assay them accurately.

More recently, a second generation of this debate was initiated by Nathan Sussman (1993), who also assumed that coins traded at face value and modeled debasement as an inflation tax. Using data from the Hundred Years' War in France, he showed that debasements were profitable for the crown and that their dynamics resembled those of modern episodes of inflation tax finance. A Laffer curve can be traced as the debasement (inflation) rate accelerated. Debasement increased the volume of minting and reminting as the public found it profitable to mint more coins per unit of precious metals and exchange them with goods as if they were not debased. The ruler therefore was able to raise more seigniorage with increased minting activity. When goods prices started to rise and inflation broke out, debasements became less profitable. This account was challenged by Arthur J. Rolnick, François R. Velde, and Warren E. Weber (1996), who argued that this explanation does not make sense if people trade coins according to their metallic values. The debate came full circle when Thomas Sargent and François Velde, in their book *The Big Problem of Small Change* (2002), developed a commodity money model based on circulation by tale.

Finally, inflation tax and debasements differ in important respects. First, under commodity money regimes, debased coins contain some precious metal alloy, limiting the inflationary process to some finite magnitude. Under fiat money there is no such limit. Second, expected stabilization under fiat money increases the demand for money and lowers the inflation rate. It has the opposite effect under commodity money. Since commodity money stabilization is carried out by recoinage, which taxes holders of debased coins, its anticipation reduces demand for money, leading to higher inflation rates and lower inflation tax revenues than in the case of fiat money.

The Political Economy of Inflation Tax. The unique features of inflation tax have important implications for economic historians. Inflation tax can be levied unilaterally and rapidly provides revenues at the expense of the state's or the ruler's reputation and the stability of the monetary system, which is seen today as a prerequisite for long-term economic growth. Thus inflation tax is used during severe crises, when long-term reputation and economic performance are sacrificed for short-term survival. Many historical accounts of debasement and inflation ascribe the demise of a regime to the economic consequences of the inflation it unleashed. Yet the same causes that made it necessary to resort to inflation tax were probably responsible for its demise. Since inflation tax finance is not sustainable in the long run, it cannot solve any of the regime's long-term or fundamental problems.

Inflation tax mainly affects holders of nominal wealth (bondholders, for example), creditors or rentiers, and wage earners, creating distributional effects that have political ramifications. Nominal wealth holders or rentiers usually belonged to the elite and were exempt from other forms of taxation. Historically, inflation taxes enabled the state to tax those who were exempt from regular taxes. Nevertheless, it risked alienating the politically and militarily powerful, who may have jeopardized the ruler's already weak position. Conversely, inflation taxes hurt the lower strata of the population by taxing their nominal wage income, making the regime vulnerable to popular revolt. One way to view the recourse to inflation tax is as a policy game in which the (weak) government needs additional revenues that no political group is willing to provide. According to Alberto Alessina and Allen Drazen (1991), the recourse to inflation tax is analogous to a war of attrition that is played out until one political group surrenders and grants taxes to the government.

Inflation Tax and Debasements in Historical Perspective. A monetary system controlled by the state is a prerequisite for recourse to inflation tax. With an eye for seigniorage and inflation tax revenues, most states sought to establish a sovereign monetary system and to control the production of money. Having secured control over the money supply, the recourse to debasement and inflation finance was just a matter of time, as sooner or later all states faced budgetary crises brought by wars and political instability. Debasement probably occurred first in ancient Persia. The biblical book of Isaiah describes the practice of debasement in the kingdoms of the Near East. The most documented debasement of ancient times occurred in Rome during both the republican and imperial regimes. The infamous debasement of the third century CE ended with Diocletian's reforms. Inflation during the third century amounted to 15,000 percent and brought about the breakdown of the Roman banking system during the reign of Galleinus (268 CE). After a brief period of reforms and stability, the fundamental fiscal problems of the Roman Empire resulted in yet more debasements.

With few exceptions, the demise of empires and dynasties from Asia to America was preceded by rampant debasements. While almost all debasement episodes tell a similar story, a few merit special attention. The first episode of fiat money inflation tax is the story of China, which started issuing fiat currency in the ninth century CE, predating Europe by eleven centuries. However, the Chinese experienced periodic inflation and hyperinflations brought about by recourse to inflation tax. Finally, following the Ming hyperinflation episode in 1448, China reverted to a commodity money regime.

France had a long history of inflation tax finance, providing a laboratory case for debasements. In the 1290s, Philip IV, needing more cash to fight wars with England and Flanders and lacking parliamentary support for taxation, resorted to debasements. In contrast, the English maintained their monetary standard and relied on taxation, consented to by Parliament. During the Hundred Years' War in the fourteenth century, domestic hostility to royal debasement policics inspired the philosopher Nicolas Oresme to produce a treatise on money that may be regarded as the first premodern theoretical discussion of the political economy of debasement. Unlike in most inflation tax finance episodes, the French crown managed to win critical battles of the Hundred Years' War with the aid of debasement, which in its late stages was unparalleled by any other with the exception of the interwar hyperinflations of the 1920s. In the course of five years (1418–1423), the nominal value of the currency rose by 3,500 percent. The success of debasement finance instilled a sense of power in French monarchs. They financed and won a war without parliamentary consent and at the same time reduced the power of the nobility and clergy, who suffered from the depreciation of their nominal rents. Therefore the French monarchy ruled without parliament, contrary to the political development of England. Some conjecture that inflation tax finance had far-reaching effects on French history.

Yet France's success in medieval times haunted it later on. Eventually, the French monarchy succumbed to the havoc of its own inflation tax policy. The John Law Bank affair and the Mississippi Bubble of the 1720s and subsequent recourse to note issue culminated in the issue of assignats, paper currency, after the revolution, and the eruption of hyperinflation brought the revolutionary regime to bankruptcy. On the other hand, Britain, with its parliamentary tradition and sound fiscal policies, used moderate levels of inflation to collect an inflation tax during the Napoleonic Wars after Parliament voted to suspend convertibility of the pound in 1797. However, mild as inflation in England had been, after a century of monetary stability this inflationary episode produced the first modern monetary treatises, which form the basis of monetarist economic analysis and policy to date. It also seems that for the first time, calculations of the incidence of inflation tax were made. *The Economist* on 28 September 1844 presented an explicit calculation of the inflation tax paid by holders of British government annuities, known as Consolidated Stock of the Nation (Consols).

The United States had its own share of inflation tax finance. Inspired perhaps by the success of the French against the English, the nascent country engaged in successful inflation tax finance during its War of Independence. During the Civil War, the North and the South both used inflation tax finance. As in all other cases, the regime that relied almost solely on this mode of finance, the financially strapped South, succumbed to its own inflation tax schemes, which ended in hyperinflation and financial ruin.

Yet the most famous episode of inflation tax finance belongs to Germany (and its former allies) in the aftermath of World War I. The financial strain of war reparations, coupled with a weak and fragmented democracy, produced history's most severe hyperinflation. At its peak in October 1923, the inflation rate was 25,900 percent a month. With Germany on the verge of financial ruin and civil disorder, the Allies stepped in and provided loan guarantees, allowing Germany to pursue policies that stabilized its currency. As in previous episodes, the financial ruin suffered by many and the deflationary measures that inflicted additional economic hardship may have cultivated the seeds for the rise of Nazi Germany and the advent of World War II.

Inflation tax is not only an integral part of history, it is a policy measure used repeatedly by states facing similar conditions to their historical predecessors. Historically, inflation tax was almost always a stopgap measure that bought only a little time for governments. More often than not, it signaled the collapse of regimes, and unless the time bought was used for fundamental policy and political changes, it accelerated their financial collapse.

BIBLIOGRAPHY

Alessina, Alberto, and Allen Drazen. "Why Are Stabilizations Delayed?" *American Economic Review* 81 (1991), 1170–1189.

Blanchard, Olivier J., and Stanley Fischer. *Lectures on Macroeconomics*. Cambridge, Mass., 1989. Theoretical background.

Bloch, Marc. *Esquisse d'une histoire monétaire de l'Europe*. Paris, 1954. Mainly medieval accounts of debasements (published posthumously).

Bordo, Michael D. "Money, Deflation, and Seigniorage in the Fifteenth Century: A Review Essay." *Journal of Monetary Economics* 18.3 (1986), 337–346.

Capie, Forrest H., ed. *Major Inflations in History*. Aldershot, U.K. 1991. Historical accounts of fiat money inflation tax.

Cipolla, Carlo. *The Monetary Policy of Fourteenth Century Florence*. Berkeley, 1982.

Feavearyear, Albert F. *The Pound Sterling: A History of English Money*. 2d rev. ed. Oxford, 1963. See especially Chapters 1–3 for the medieval period.

Gould, John D. *The Great Debasement*. Oxford, 1970.

Kindleberger, Charles P. "The Economic Crisis of 1619 to 1623." *Journal of Economic History* 51.1 (1991), 149–175.

Kleiman, Ephraim. "Inflation Tax Theory and Estimates." *History of Political Economy* 32.2 (2000), 233–266. History of inflation tax theory.

Miskimin, Harry. *Money and Power in Fifteenth Century France*. New Haven, 1984.

Motomura, Akira. "The Best and Worst of Currencies: Seigniorage and Currency Policy in Spain, 1597–1650." *Journal of Economic History* 54.1 (1994), 104–127.

Munro, John H. A. *Wool, Cloth, and Gold*. Toronto, 1972.

Pamuk, Sevket. "In the Absence of Domestic Currency: Debased European Coinage in the Seventeenth-Century Ottoman Empire." *Journal of Economic History* 57.2 (1997), 345–366.

Rolnick, Arthur J., François R. Velde, and Warren E. Weber. "The Debasement Puzzle: An Essay on Medieval Monetary History." *Journal of Economic History* 56.4 (1996), 789–808.

Rostovtzeff, Michael I. *The Social and Economic History of the Roman Empire*. 2d ed. Oxford, 1957.

Sargent, Thomas, and François Velde. *The Big Problem of Small Change*. Princeton, 2002.

Sussman, Nathan. "Debasements, Royal Revenues, and Inflation in France during the Hundred Years' War, 1415–1422." *Journal of Economic History* 53.1 (1993), 44–70.

Werveke, Hans Van. "Currency Manipulation in the Middle Ages: The Case of Louis de Male, Count of Flanders." *Transactions of the Royal Historical Society* 4th ser. 31 (1949), 115–127. Reprinted in Werveke, *Miscellanea Mediaevalia*, pp. 255–267. Ghent, 1968.

NATHAN SUSSMAN

INFORMAL CREDIT. Informal credit is usually taken to encompass small loans to households and small enterprises. The boundary between formal and informal credit is roughly that between loans made by specialist financial intermediaries (such as banks) on the one hand, and those made by individuals, households, and other enterprises on the other hand. Informal credit has been used to finance both small-scale enterprises and consumption. The scope and variety of informal credit across the globe and human history is vast.

Lending itself is ancient, but banks and other institutional intermediaries are relatively recent developments. As late as the early twentieth century, much of the world's population lived in areas not served by such institutions, and even where banks were present they usually confined their lending to firms and to relatively wealthy individuals. Others had to rely on either informal credit or less formal financial intermediaries such as ROSCAs (rotating savings and credit associations) or credit cooperatives. These institutions were far from universal, and the latter did not emerge until the mid-nineteenth century. There are at least two reasons not to equate informal credit with the lack of banks or other specialist financial institutions. In some situations, sophisticated financial markets developed without the participation of financial intermediaries. In others, a merchant or other large enterprise provided credit as part of its business operations. Lending of this sort involved variants on some of the mechanisms to be described below, but the large loans made in this way are once again not what the literature usually means by "informal." Informal credit markets often present especially stark examples of the information and enforcement problems typical of credit markets. Borrowers are often poor or lack assets that make sensible collateral, and the small scale of loans does not make legal enforcement cost-effective, so loan terms are usually structured to be self-enforcing. Informal credit is especially common in societies or circumstances where legal systems are inadequate or nonexistent. There are four categories of informal credit arrangements to consider.

Interpersonal Credit. Probably the most common but least documented form of informal credit consists of loans between individuals or households. We can never know the volume of this kind of credit in most historical societies, because most such loans were undertaken without written records, even in societies with written languages. Interpersonal loans might be for consumption or investment purposes. The indirect references to such loans suggest that they were most common among kin or neighbors, people whose repeated and complex interactions would imply a great deal of information about the borrower and the ability to use several ways to compel repayment if necessary.

Christopher Udry's study of four villages in northern Nigeria in 1988–1989 documents dense networks of interpersonal loans and highlights the connection between informal credit and insurance. An important feature of his study is what appears to be a near-absence of information and enforcement problems: that loan market dispensed with the usual mechanisms for reducing information problems and compelling repayment. In fact, Udry notes that interpersonal loans acted as a form of *ex post* insurance system. If Smith lent money to Jones, and Jones had a bad year, then Smith forgave the loan. More strikingly, if Smith had a bad year and Jones had a good year, Jones was expected to repay the loan at a higher-than-normal rate.

Moneylenders. Individuals who earn all or part of their living by lending at interest are difficult to distinguish from early banking houses, and the credit they provided has much in common with the final two categories below. Nonetheless, a long tradition (much of it polemical) treats moneylenders as a separate category. Urban moneylenders faced more serious information problems, because they were less likely to know their clientele well, and the more fluid urban environment made it easier for debtors to flee without repayment. Some moneylenders combined lending and secondhand retail business in pawnshops. Rural moneylenders tended to operate in fixed areas with more stable populations. Some relied on loan security, such as West Africa's pledging of cocoa trees. Other rural lenders relied on the more intensive information-gathering and repeated interaction with clients small villages allow, and made unsecured loans.

Specialist moneylenders operating in informal credit markets are often largely or entirely from a given ethnic or caste group. The role of ethnicity or caste works in two ways. In some circumstances (such as Deuteronomy 23:20), religious strictures allow one to charge interest to the "other" but not to members of one's own group. In other circumstances, diasporas were major sources of credit, but primarily to their own members.

Consumer Credit. Shopkeepers and other petty retailers have long provided credit to their customers. Some view the practice as the only way to sell to poor people with irregular incomes. Others see shop credit as an independent source of profit, in which case the shopkeeper is difficult to distinguish from the moneylender. Examples of this type of consumer credit can be found in many times and places. One that has been made famous by its connections to larger political questions is post-Famine Ireland's "gombeen men," merchants and publicans who provided credit to Ireland's rural poor.

Tied Credit. Informal credit arrangements often take the form of tied credit, in which transactions are bundled together. The consumer credit discussed above is a form of tied credit. More common are arrangements where a landlord provides credit or an employer provides credit as part of the bargain with a worker. One famous example of tied credit appeared among rural tenants (mostly sharecroppers) in the South after the U.S. Civil War. Landlords usually provided both land and credit to their tenants, the credit most often in the form of a line of credit at a particular rural store belonging to the landlord. This example is unusual in that the landlord/merchants themselves were tied into sophisticated financial networks, made possible by their valuable cash crop, cotton. In a West African variant on this arrangement, a borrower would provide the lender a "pawn," an individual who would provide unpaid labor services to the lender, for the duration of the loan. The pawn was at once collateral and part of the borrower's interest payments.

Interlinked transactions would seem to limit markets. If Smith has land to let and money to lend, it would seem most efficient to find the best farmer for the land and the best borrower for the money, instead of insisting that the renter and the borrower be the same person. Historians and economists have suggested several reasons for interlinked credit transactions. In some circumstances, the arrangement is a way to hide an interest payment that is forbidden by religious law. In other circumstances, the interlinks reduce information and enforcement problems. Combining the renter and borrower into one person allows Smith to reduce the costs of monitoring both his tenant and his borrower (a trip to the farmer's field would tell Smith how the land is being worked and the loan being used). A related implication is that the landlord can advance some of the loan in kind, in the form of factors of production (such as fertilizer or seed) and thus increase the chance that his land is farmed well. Interlinks provide the lender with a twofold threat: if the tenant does not repay the loan, Smith can remove the tenancy, which under some circumstances may be a more effective threat than refusing future credit.

One theme in many studies is the relationship between informal credit and the process of economic development. Informal credit may flourish in environments where the institutional and technological environment militates against formal lending by financial intermediaries. An example is the development of consumer lending in wealthier societies over the past fifty years or so; consumer credit, supported by specialist lenders and low-cost information technology, is now available at reasonable cost to most households in developed economies. The prevalence of informal credit seems inversely related to the degree of economic development, although it survives today in some very wealthy societies.

[*See also* Agricultural Credit; Gifts and Gift Giving; Pawnbroking and Personal Loan Markets; *and* Usury].

BIBLIOGRAPHY

Austin, Gareth. "Indigenous Credit Institutions in West Africa, c. 1750–c. 1960." In *Local Suppliers of Credit in the Third World, 1750–1960*, edited by Gareth Austen and Kaoru Sugihara. London, 1993. Notes that in West Africa, where ethnic groups mingle, informal credit relations are usually confined to members of the same group.

Bell, Clive. "Credit Markets and Interlinked Transactions." In *Handbook of Development Economics*, edited by Hollis Chenery and T. N. Srinivasan, vol. 1. New York, 1988. Classic study of the connection between credit markets and product and input markets in developing countries.

Coate, Stephen, and Martin Ravallion. "Reciprocity without Commitment: Characterization and Performance of Informal Insurance Arrangements." *Journal of Development Economics* 40 (1993), 1–24.

Cohen, Abner. *Custom and Politics in Urban Africa: A Study of Hausa Migrants in Yoruba Towns*. Berkeley, 1969. A study of the Hausa, West African traders whose complex credit practices help support their domination of long-distance trader networks.

Hoffman, Philip, Gilles Postel-Vinay, and Jean-Laurent Rosenthal. "What Do Notaries Do? Overcoming Asymmetric Information in Financial Markets: The Case of Paris, 1751." *Journal of Institutional and Theoretical Economics* 154.3 (September 1998), 499–530. Shows that in eighteenth-century France, for example, notaries acted as loan brokers and in so doing promoted efficient credit relations without banks.

Olney, Martha L. *Buy Now, Pay Later: Advertising, Credit, and Consumer Durables in the 1920s*. Chapel Hill, 1991.

Ransom, Roger, and Richard Sutch. *One Kind of Freedom: The Economic Consequences of Emancipation*. New York, 1977. A study of the post–Civil War U.S. South, stressing the role of credit relations in the creation of a dependent sharecropper class.

Rothenberg, Winifred B. "The Emergence of a Capital Market in Rural Massachusetts, 1730–1838." *Journal of Economic History* 45.4 (1985), 781–808. Notes that in eighteenth and early nineteenth century Massachusetts, historical sources tend to underreport informal loans, both because documents are lost and the parties to the loans have reason to fear tax or inheritance consequences.

Udry, Christopher. "Credit Markets in Northern Nigeria: Credit as Insurance in a Rural Economy." *The World Bank Economic Review* 4.3 (1990), 251–269. Classic study of the use of credit in a situation where information and enforcement problems are negligible.

TIMOTHY W. GUINNANE

INFORMATION AND COMMUNICATION TECHNOLOGY.

Since the Upper Paleolithic period (35,000–10,000 years ago), humans have developed ever more elaborate and effective means to acquire, process, store, and transmit information. By technology, we mean not only physical artifacts but also the skills and organizations that contribute to this development. Over time, the technologies of communication and information have increased in speed, in reliability, and in their ability to carry different forms of information, such as words, music, or pictures. They have not improved in the permanence or in the security of the information they carry, however.

Language. Language was the first method of communication that marked a radical departure from the communications of animals. We have no record of the origin of speech, but some daring linguists have proposed that the first language originated with the emergence of *Homo sapiens* some 100,000 years ago and later spread and diverged into the dozens of language families for which we have firm evidence. Given the propensity of all known human societies to dance and make music, dance and music must have equally ancient roots.

Speech, music, and dance, if repeated, become embedded in memory. All preliterate societies employed elaborate mnemonic devices to remember important stories and beliefs. The ancient Greeks, among others, memorized poetry, rhymes, riddles, and plays. In many African societies, griots or professional storytellers were the keepers of the group's oral history. Memorization as a form of information storage has lost prestige since the invention of writing, yet it is still retained in certain areas of our culture, such as the theater.

Writing. Writing is a means of preserving words and ideas in a physical form outside the minds of speakers and listeners. After language, it is the technique that has had the most profound impact on human history. Yet long before the creation of full-scale writing, humans devised ways to create a permanent physical record of their thoughts. Small sculptures may have been the first such medium, the oldest now known being the Lion-Human of Hohlenstein-Stadel in Germany, dated at 30,000 to 26,000 before the present. Cave painting and rock drawings are also extremely ancient techniques; the earliest, dated at 28,000 years ago, is the rock art in the Apollo-11 cave in Namibia, followed by the famous cave paintings of Pech-Merle and Lascaux, France, which are 16,000 to 13,000 years old. Notches carved on bones by Cro-Magnon people some 30,000 years ago may have constituted the first lunar calendars.

Works of art are important means of expression but have limitations as information storage techniques, for they serve primarily as reminders for those who already know their meaning; that is why archaeologists find it so difficult to decipher the meaning of ancient works. Furthermore, they could not be readily moved from place to place. Hence, humans devised numerous other forms of proto-writing that offered greater flexibility. In Mesopotamia and the Fertile Crescent, clay tokens were used to record business transactions for hundreds of years before the first cuneiform writing appeared. Both Egyptian and Mayan hieroglyphs developed out of pictures of persons, animals, and other familiar shapes. In the Andes, the Incas used quipus or knotted strings to convey messages throughout their extended empire. And in the Pacific, Polynesian sailors navigated with maps made of sticks and string that showed islands, wave formations, and other important nautical information.

Writing has two associated functions: it can be used to transmit information in the form of letters and messages, and it can serve as a repository of information in the form of inscriptions carved in stone or painted on walls, papyrus, and other surfaces. Full writing, capable of conveying any series of words, evolved in several places at different times: as cuneiform in Mesopotamia (c. 3300–3000 BCE), as hieroglyphics in Egypt (c. 2600 BCE) and Mesoamerica (c. 300 BCE), and as ideographic characters in China (c. 1500 BCE). The most widespread writing system, the alphabetical, first appeared in Egypt around 1800 BCE. Societies that developed or adopted writing used it for ceremonial inscriptions (the Rosetta Stone), to proclaim laws (the Stela of Hammurabi), to preserve epic poetry (Homer's), or to create sacred texts (the Bible and the Qur'àn). Writing was also used to record business transactions, philosophical and literary works, and ordinary correspondence.

Postal Systems. In many societies, writing was associated with the development of bureaucracies, organizations that kept records of legal cases, financial transactions, and political events. Small politics, like the Greek city-states, could handle most business orally, but large ones required not only writing but also the means of conveying messages throughout their territories. To keep control of their far-flung lands, the Persians created a postal system with relays of horses along the Royal Road that stretched from Ephesus on the Aegean Sea to Susa in western Iran. The Roman network of imperial messengers and relay posts was called the *cursus publicus*. The Chinese, Inca, Mongol, and other empires established similar networks but reserved them for official messages.

Although these postal systems served the needs of imperial governments, an ordinary person who had a message to send had to find a traveler going in the right direction and willing to deliver it. In medieval Europe, various unofficial messenger organizations, such as pilgrims, peripatetic university students, traveling cattle dealers, and merchants' associations, catered to the needs of businesses and private individuals. This situation lasted until the seventeenth century, when the royal postal networks of various countries were opened to the public to provide governments with a source of revenue and a means of surveillance.

Several innovations allowed postal systems to grow exponentially in the eighteenth and nineteenth centuries. The introduction of mail coaches in France in the 1770s and of railroads in England in the 1830s speeded up mail delivery. In 1792, the United States government made newspaper delivery almost free. And in 1840, the British Post Office introduced the one-rate "penny" postage, bringing letter writing within reach of even the poorest members of society. These innovations spread to all Western countries in the late nineteenth century and to the rest of the world in the twentieth. Inexpensive mail and newspaper delivery were important politically in fledgling democracies. They also contributed to economic growth through advertising, mail catalogs, and the reliable transmission of business correspondence.

Printing. The use of movable type to create multiple copies of a text derived from the much older technique of woodblock printing used by the Chinese to print paper money. The first example of printing with movable type is the Bible printed by Johannes Gutenberg of Mainz, Germany, in 1456. Various methods of engraving, first woodblock, then copperplate, then lithograph (engraving on stone), produced a proliferation of pictures as well as texts.

Printing revolutionized both the storage and the transmission of information. The technique was applied to pamphlets, posters, broadsides, calendars, newspapers, and other ephemera. It was also used to create permanent repositories of information, such as Bibles, encyclopedias, dictionaries, and atlases. In between were numerous semipermanent forms, such as popular periodicals, maps, novels, and playing cards. All such works were widely circulated. The *Encyclopédie*, a multivolume work published in the mid-eighteenth century, became a best-seller despite its high cost.

The printing revolution not only changed the way information was stored and transmitted, it also affected the culture, politics, and economies of the societies that adopted it. In western Europe and North America, education and literacy spread to the working class and even the peasantry and made all classes of society receptive to new ideas, from the Protestant Reformation of the sixteenth century to the revolutionary movements of the late eighteenth and early nineteenth centuries.

Optical Telegraphy. Despite revolutionary advances in other fields, communication at a distance was no easier or faster in the late eighteenth century than in ancient times. This changed with the advent of semaphore telegraphy on land and flag-signaling systems at sea.

For centuries, inventors had proposed various methods of communicating rapidly over long distances but could not find the backing to implement their ideas. Until the eighteenth century, the best that could be achieved was to transmit a prearranged message in one direction only. The first system to overcome these limitations was the one built by the Frenchman Claude Chappe in 1794, at the height of the French Revolution. It consisted of a series of towers equipped with wooden masts and articulated arms that could be moved into several positions. The positions of the arms could be repeated down the line of towers, while a codebook allowed the correspondents at each end of the line to translate the signals into words. Under Chappe's direction, the French telegraph administration built a network of lines from Paris to major provincial cities. By the end of Napoleon's reign, the network stretched as far as Venice, Amsterdam, and Mainz. Sweden, Prussia, Britain, Spain, and other countries built short lines, connecting a coastal lookout point with an inland city or the capital city with a royal palace.

At the same time, and for the same reason, namely, the necessity of warfare, several officers of the Royal Navy devised flag-signaling systems that could transmit any message in either direction between two ships at sea, the most famous being Admiral Horatio Nelson's message before the Battle of Trafalgar: "England expects that every man will do his duty" (1805). Flag signaling transformed naval tactics and was adopted by the world's merchant marines in the nineteenth century.

Electrical Telegraphy. By the 1830s, discoveries in electricity and electromagnetism led several inventors to propose ways of using electricity to transmit information. Two systems that appeared in 1837 had a lasting impact. In Britain, Charles Wheatstone and William Cooke patented a five-needle telegraph that was quickly adopted by the new railroads. At the same time, the American Samuel Morse invented a code of dots and dashes that could be used to send messages using only one wire, the earth serving as a return. Morse and his associate, Alfred Vail, built a telegraph line between Baltimore and Washington in 1843 and opened it to public traffic in 1844. The electric telegraph had a much greater capacity than its optical predecessor, for it was faster, cost less to install, and could operate even at night and in foggy weather. It spread rapidly, first throughout North America and Europe, then to India, Algeria, the Middle East, and Latin America, and by the 1870s, to China and Japan. The electric telegraph became indispensable to the operation of railroads and was widely used by such businesses as the daily press, commodities markets, financial institutions, and companies with many branches. By speeding up the flow of capital, it made capital cheaper but also more volatile.

The telegraph industry grew both technologically and organizationally. To coordinate national networks, the countries of Europe founded the International Telegraph (now Telecommunications) Union in 1865. Most American lines were absorbed into the giant Western Union Company. The invention of time-division multiplexing by Emile Baudot (1871) and quadruplexing by Thomas Alva Edison (1874) greatly increased the capacity of the world's telegraph lines. In the 1920s, telegraph organizations introduced teleprinters, which received and printed out messages automatically. Soon thereafter, switched networks such as Teletype and Telex replaced human telegraph operators.

Submarine Telegraphy. Bodies of water were an obstacle to the early electric telegraph. The first experiment to send a message through water in an insulated wire took place in Calcutta in 1838. In the 1840s, the discovery of gutta-percha, the sap of a tree that grows in Southeast Asia and forms a natural insulator, allowed inventors to manufacture submarine cables that were resistant to the effects of seawater. A submarine cable was successfully laid across the English Channel in 1851. The first cables laid across the Atlantic, the Mediterranean, and the Red Sea failed, however. In the late 1860s, new techniques of manufacturing and laying insulated cables allowed reliable deep-sea cables across the Atlantic (1866–1867) and from Britain to India (1870). British firms, which held a near-monopoly on this technology, laid cables to China, Australia, and South America during the 1870s and around Africa during the 1880s. In 1902, a cable from Canada to New Zealand completed the "All-Red" route, a globe-girdling network in British hands. Submarine telegraph cables had the same impact on intercontinental trade as land lines did on national markets. They allowed the efficient routing of cargo steamers, lowered transaction costs such as insurance, and hastened the diffusion of technology to distant countries.

Britain's predominant role incited other countries to lay their own cables. By the early twentieth century, German, French, and American-owned cables crossed the Atlantic. Elsewhere, however, the high cost of cables and the low volume of traffic made it uneconomical to compete with the British cable giant Eastern and Associated. Thus, the invention of radio aroused the interest not only of engineers and businesspeople, but of governments and the military as well.

Telephony. As the telegraph was connecting the world through wires and cables, a new technology appeared that permitted the transmission of voice. The telephone,

TRANSATLANTIC COMMUNICATION. Manufacture of the Atlantic telegraph cable at the Gutta Percha Company's works, Wharf-Road, London. *The Illustrated London News*, 14 March 1857. (Prints and Photographs Division, Library of Congress)

invented almost simultaneously by Alexander Graham Bell and Elisha Gray in 1876, was dismissed by the giant Western Union Company as a toy of little value. Telephone exchanges, installed in various cities from 1878 on, soon made the telephone an indispensable instrument for businesses and wealthier homes. A growing subscriber list threatened to overwhelm the manual exchanges needed to interconnect them, however. The Strowger automatic switch (1889) and the crossbar switch (1913) allowed subscribers to dial the numbers they wished to reach, thereby removing a major obstacle to the expansion of local networks.

Long-distance telephony lagged for decades because of the attenuation of current in the wires. The Audion, a triode or vacuum tube invented by the American Lee De Forest, was adapted to amplifying telephone signals in 1912. It permitted the construction of the first American transcontinental line, from New York to San Francisco, in 1915. By then, AT&T and its associated Bell Telephone companies practically monopolized telephone service in the United States and Canada. In most other countries, telephone service was placed under the postal and telegraph administrations of the governments.

Telephony has benefited from many recent inventions. The transistor (1947) led to the development of electronic switches (1965 on) that were compact, efficient, and reliable. The first transatlantic telephone cable, equipped with regenerators, was laid in 1956. Satellites and microwave links in the 1970s and fiber-optic cables from the 1980s dramatically reduced the cost and increased the volume of long-distance communications. Since 1990, mobile cellular telephones have proliferated worldwide and have already surpassed the number of wired telephones in several parts of the world.

Radio Telegraphy. The first person to demonstrate the practical application of electromagnetic waves to communication was the young Italian inventor Guglielmo Marconi, who brought his invention to England in 1895. The Royal Navy, the War Office, and British shipping and insurance firms showed an immediate interest in radio

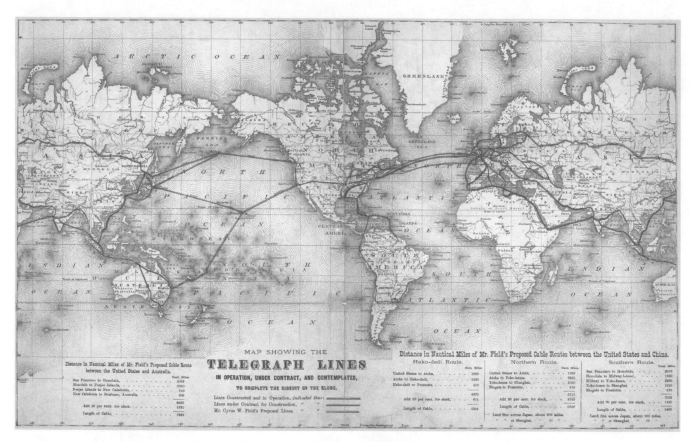

INFORMATION SYSTEMS. Map showing telegraph lines in operation, those under contract, and lines proposed, to complete the circuit of the globe, circa 1867. (The New York Public Library/Art Resource, NY)

communications, or wireless telegraphy as it was then called. By 1907, when Marconi opened a commercial wireless service between Britain and North America, his company had a monopoly on maritime communications almost as complete as that of Eastern and Associated in submarine cables. But this monopoly did not last long. In 1903, the German government founded the Telefunken company to compete with Marconi's. In the United States, inventors sought new means of generating radio waves. Lee De Forest's Audion, Cyril Elwell's arc, and Reginald Fessenden's alternator all produced continuous waves that were less prone to static and interference than Marconi's spark generator and therefore allowed the transmission of voice and music as well as dots and dashes. Because neither submarine telegraph cables nor Marconi's spark transmitters could carry voice, overseas telephony had to await the development of powerful continuous-wave transmitters. The first transatlantic voice transmission took place in 1915, and the first commercial telephone service was inaugurated in 1927 between London and New York.

Until the 1920s, radio technology concentrated on the long-wave (less than 300 kHz) part of the spectrum, where the distance a signal could travel was proportional to the power of the transmitter. Communication companies and governments therefore vied to build ever bigger, costlier, and energy-voracious transmitters in order to reach across oceans and continents. When the United States entered World War I in 1917, the government took over all commercial stations. After the war, it set up the Radio Corporation of America (RCA) to replace Marconi's firm. Likewise, every major country established one or more national radiotelegraph companies to handle its long-distance communications, thereby ending the hegemony that Britain had long exercised.

Meanwhile, amateurs were experimenting with war-surplus vacuum tubes. In the early 1920s, they discovered that short waves (2.5–22 MHz) could carry over enormous distances, albeit erratically. Experiments carried out by Marconi turned these fortuitous discoveries into a new communications technology, shortwave radio. During the 1930s, shortwave radio transmitters proliferated, putting every part of the world into communication with every other at a very low cost. This new technology threatened the very existence of submarine cables and long-wave stations, which survived mainly because they offered strategic advantages in time of war. Long-wave radio could broadcast to the entire world at once, including submarines under water, whereas cables offered secrecy and protection against enemy code breaking.

Broadcasting. The transmission of radio and later of television programs to many receivers at once played a tremendous role in the history of twentieth-century culture. Reginald Fessenden transmitted voice and music as early as 1906, but the technology was too crude and costly for commercial use. After World War I, amateurs used surplus vacuum tubes to build inexpensive transmitters and receivers. Private broadcasting began in Britain, the Netherlands, and the United States in 1919. European governments quickly moved to take over or control the new medium. The Westinghouse Company's station KDKA in Pittsburgh, Pennsylvania, inaugurated commercial radio broadcasting in the United States in 1920. By November 1922, 564 stations, supported by advertising, crowded the airwaves in the United States alone, creating an enormous demand for inexpensive receivers. After 1926, radio stations began merging into national networks like NBC and CBS in the United States and BBC in Britain. Radio technology, until then mainly concerned with point-to-point data transmission, fostered a large-scale consumer products industry.

From the very earliest days of radio, inventors sought ways to transmit images. Television, however, was much more complex than radio and required the efforts of many inventors over many decades before it became practical. Among the contributions to the development of television, we might cite A. A. Campbell Swinton's cathode-ray tube (1908) and V. K. Zworykin's iconoscope or camera tube (1923). J. L. Baird carried out the first experimental television transmission in Britain in 1926, as did Philo T. Farnsworth in the United States in 1927. By the 1930s, television had become technically feasible, though still costly and unreliable. The first public transmissions began in 1936 in Britain and Germany and in 1939 in the United States as technical demonstrations rather than as commercial products. By 1940, the United States had twenty-three television stations and a few thousand receivers. During World War II, the production of all television equipment was diverted to military use. Soon after the end of the war, television networks began offering popular entertainment to a fast-growing public of television owners. By 1960, the United States had 600 stations broadcasting to 50 million receivers. Europe and Japan lagged behind by a decade or more, but they have since caught up in the penetration of television into households and popular culture. Color television, introduced in 1954, spread rapidly in the United States in the 1960s and in Europe in the 1970s. For political as well as technical reasons, three incompatible systems were developed: NTSC in the Americas, PAL in Britain and Germany, and SECAM in France and the Soviet Union and in their client states. Broadcasting by radio and especially by television grew into industries in their own right, but more important, they provided a vehicle for advertising. As industry became more efficient, the output of goods threatened to outpace consumer demand (as it did in the Great Depression). Advertising constantly stimulated consumer demand to keep up with the output of new products.

Television broadcasting can carry only a few miles. Stations that served local audiences had to be linked by coaxial cables. Increasingly, households have also been connected to cables that can carry dozens of different programs at once. The launching of the Telstar satellite in 1962 inaugurated the first overseas transmission. Since the mid-1960s, geostationary satellites have allowed programs to be transmitted around the world. The first landings on the moon in 1969 are said to have been seen by 100 million viewers worldwide.

Recording Media. The telecommunications media are ephemeral, seldom retaining records of their transmissions. Fortunately, their development was paralleled by the creation of several new recording media. The first of these was photography, an optical and chemical means of creating a permanent image of a fleeting scene. Joseph-Nicéphore Niepce made the first permanent photographic image in France in 1823. In 1839, the Frenchman Louis Daguerre invented the daguerreotype, a means of recording a positive image on a sheet of metal, while the Englishman William Fox Talbot invented the paper negative, an image that could be used to create numerous positive copies. For decades thereafter, photographers needed heavy view cameras and glass plates that had to be prepared on the spot and developed immediately after the photograph was taken. This limited the technology to professional studios and horse-drawn darkrooms. The mass production of celluloid film and cheap portable cameras by the American George Eastman in the 1890s put photography in the hands of the general public. Experiments with color photography began in the late nineteenth century, but only reached maturity and commercial success in the 1930s. Since the 1990s, chemical photography has been challenged by images captured in digital cameras, recorded on magnetic media, and processed by computers.

Sound recording developed a half century after photography. Thomas Alva Edison made the first sound recording in 1877, using a vibrating stylus that engraved indentations on a sheet of tinfoil wrapped around a rotating cylinder. The Gramophone, a flat disk invented by Emil Berliner in 1887, not only saved space but permitted multiple copies to be produced from a negative mold. Since then, sound recording has seen many innovations that have improved the quality of the sound: 78 rpm records in 1915,

33.3 rpm "long-play" records in 1948, and stereo in 1958. Since the 1970s, records have been displaced by two new technologies.

One of these is magnetic recording. The first person to record sound magnetically was the Danish inventor Valdemar Poulsen, whose Telegraphone (1900) recorded human speech on a steel wire. Before World War II, wire recorders were used mainly for dictation. The development of audiotape by German engineers in the 1940s led to the marketing of inexpensive tape recorders in the 1950s and cassettes in the 1970s. Since the 1980s, a new competitor has challenged the dominance of audiotapes in sound recording, namely, compact discs or CDs, developed by the Japanese Sony Corporation and the Dutch firm Philips. CDs record sound in the form of tiny pits burned into a metallic surface. The pits represent sound data in digital form that can be transformed by an integrated circuit, or chip, into an analog electrical signal that can in turn generate sound.

Motion Pictures. Motion pictures consist of a series of still photographs presented to the eyes so rapidly that the brain interprets them as a continuous motion. The first series of photographs taken in rapid sequence were scientific studies by Étienne-Julcs Marey (1882) and Eadweard Muybridge (1887). In 1893, however, William Dickinson, an associate of Edison, presented the Kinetograph, the first motion picture device for popular entertainment in "penny arcades." The most important contribution to motion pictures was the cinematograph of the brothers Auguste and Louis Lumière (1895), a system that consisted of film, a camera, and a projector. By the turn of the twentieth century, movie houses were showing full-length feature films such as *The Great Train Robbery* (1903). Silent black-and-white films were superseded by films with sound in the late 1920s and by color films after 1936. The films produced in Hollywood, California, and various European centers were the most popular form of public entertainment in history, with hundreds of millions of viewers worldwide.

In 1956, Ampex, an American company, pioneered the recording of images on videotape, permitting television stations to prerecord their programs instead of broadcasting them live. By the 1970s, several Japanese manufacturers had come up with inexpensive portable videocassette players and cameras, leading to a boom in video rentals and in home movies. Music recordings and motion pictures have grown from technological marvels into giant industries whose contribution to the economies of developed countries (and even some developing ones like India) are on a par with older industries like steel, railroads, and electricity.

Data Processing. Tax and business accounting and land surveying are forms of data processing that go back to the earliest civilizations. Enumerations of men of military age and of taxable property are mentioned in the Bible and were carried out in ancient Rome and China. The first accurate censuses and other demographic statistics were collected in Sweden, Canada, and the United States in the late eighteenth century. The presentation of statistics in graphical form also began in the eighteenth century.

With the exception of the abacus, which goes back 5,000 years in China, data-processing devices are fairly recent. The French philosopher Blaise Pascal invented a mechanical adding and subtracting machine in 1642, and the German mathematician Gottfried Wilhelm Leibniz improved it so it could also multiply and divide. Yet mechanical calculators remained rare until the nineteenth century.

The French engineer Joseph-Marie Jacquard invented a method of programming a silk loom with the use of punched cards in 1804. In the 1820s, the English mathematician Charles Babbage tried to build a programmable calculator, the Difference Engine, but ran into technical and financial difficulties. These and other inventions came together in the work of Herman Hollerith, an employee of the United States Census. In 1880, faced with the seemingly impossible task of tabulating the census returns by hand, Hollerith devised a punched-card tabulator that could perform the necessary operations in a fraction of the time previously required. This device became the foundation of the International Business Machines Company, or IBM.

In the early twentieth century, engineers began searching for ways to solve complex mathematical operations electromechanically or electronically. Boolean algebra (named after the British mathematician George Boole) turned out to be ideally suited to devices that could switch electric currents on and off rapidly. During World War II, Herman Zuse in Germany and Howard Aitken in the United States designed large electronic calculators. John Mauchly and J. Prosper Eckert built the first programmable digital electronic computer, the ENIAC, at the University of Pennsylvania in 1946. By the 1960s, as transistors replaced vacuum tubes, IBM was able to manufacture business-oriented computers, the 360 series. Integrated circuits, or "chips," containing thousands of transistors and other electronic devices, allowed manufacturers to build ever smaller and more powerful computers. Large-scale integrated circuits, or microprocessors, introduced by Intel in 1974, contained most of the circuits of a computer on a single chip and led to the appearance of personal computers in the 1980s.

Magnetic media proved to be ideally suited for the storage of computer data. The computers of the 1950s stored enormous amounts of data on magnetic tapes. By the 1960s, tape storage, which slowed down data retrieval, was replaced by magnetic disks and drums, on which data could be accessed randomly and quickly. The explosion of personal computers since 1980 relies as much on ever larger and faster magnetic hard drives and removable disks as it does on more powerful microprocessors. Like the mass media before it, the computer and software business has grown into one of the largest industries in the developed countries. More important, computers have contributed to the growth of productivity in other industries, especially those that are information-dense like finance, insurance, engineering, and entertainment. They have also stimulated consumer demand by making credit cards easy to obtain and to use.

Soon after personal computers became common business and household appliances, the versatility that came from storing and processing information in digital form made possible their connection to networks for the exchange of data. The Internet, pioneered in the 1970s for military and scientific use, was opened to commercial use in the 1990s. Its audiovisual portion, the World Wide Web, has rapidly become a major form of entertainment and an industry in its own right.

As of the beginning of the twenty-first century, digital technology is bringing about the merger of all media of communication and of information processing and storage. How this will affect the economies and cultures of the world is still unclear, but most thoughtful observers are finding parallels between this information revolution and the Industrial Revolution of the eighteenth and nineteenth centuries, which created tremendous wealth but in a very unequal and unjust manner.

[*See also* Advertising; Book Industry; Computer Industry; Magazines; Newspapers; Radio and Television Industry; *and* Telephone Industry.]

BIBLIOGRAPHY

Aitchison, Jean. *The Seeds of Speech: Language Origin and Evolution.* Cambridge, 1996.

Aitken, Hugh. *Syntony and Spark: The Origins of Radio.* New York, 1976.

Aitken, Hugh. *The Continuous Wave: Technology and American Radio.* Princeton, 1985.

Campbell-Kelly, Martin, and William Aspray. *Computer: A History of the Information Machine.* New York, 1996.

Coates, Vary T., and Bernard Finn. *A Retrospective Technology Assessment: Submarine Telegraphy: The Transatlantic Cable of 1866.* San Francisco, 1979.

Eisenstein, Elizabeth L. *The Printing Press as an Agent of Change: Communications and Cultural Transformations in Early Modern Europe.* 2 vols. Cambridge, 1979.

Headrick, Daniel R. *The Invisible Weapon: Telecommunications and International Politics, 1851–1945.* New York, 1991.

Headrick, Daniel R. *When Information Came of Age: Technologies of Knowledge in the Age of Reason and Revolution, 1700–1850.* New York, 2000.

Hobart, Michael E., and Zachary S. Schiffman. *Information Ages: Literacy, Numeracy, and the Computer Revolution.* Baltimore, 1998.

Kilgour, Frederick G. *The Evolution of the Book.* New York, 1998.

Lubar, Steven. *Infoculture: The Smithsonian Book of Information Age Inventions.* Boston, 1994.

Martin, Henri-Jean. *The History and Power of Writing.* Translated by Lydia G. Cochrane. Chicago, 1994.

Millard, Andre. *America on Record: A History of Recorded Sound.* Cambridge, 1995.

Riordan, Michael, and Lilian Hoddeson. *Crystal Fire: The Birth of the Information Age.* New York, 1997.

Robinson, Andrew. *The Story of Writing: Alphabets, Hieroglyphs, and Pictographs.* New York, 1999.

DANIEL R. HEADRICK

INHERITANCE SYSTEMS. Inheritance is an important economic institution, particularly in historical times because it involves the allocation of one of the main scarce resources in preindustrial economies, namely land. The variety of inheritance traditions is vast and reflects cultural and political values, as well as the mode of economic production.

Inheritance institutions are an example of humanly devised constraints that provide structure and organization to the process of transferring property and preparing the next generation for economic activity (North, 1991). Inheritance rules and traditions serve to reduce the uncertainty regarding the intergenerational transfer of wealth and the nature of how parents should invest in their offspring. As such, the type of institution used in a society has had ramifications on its economic and cultural life, something observed in both historical and contemporary times. Inheritance rules have affected the relationships between the generations and those between siblings and in-laws. They have also influenced the degree of income inequality and life options, especially in economies in which economic growth was minimal and property was not distributed among all children. Inheritance should be given a wide interpretation to include many forms of property and transfers to heirs while the property owner is still alive (inter vivos), as well as transfers upon his or her death.

Variety of Inheritance Systems. Inheritance systems come in many varieties and differ widely across time and geography. This is also true of previous societies. This tremendous diversity is evident when examining the information on inheritance compiled for 862 different societies in Murdock's *Ethnographic Atlas.* Although this work provides a rough outline of inheritance systems used across the world in the mid-twentieth century, it can serve as a starting place for describing a world inheritance grid.

Rules of descent, kinship, and residence patterns influence which inheritance systems are used in a society. Descent groups are especially important in preindustrial societies and determine which family members belong to a particular social group. Descent groups can also be an important influence on the nature of inheritance because different lineage systems sometimes favor particular offspring over others in the intergenerational transfer of properties and rights. A descent group is made up of family members who descend from a common ancestor. Lineage or descent groups come in four main types: patrilineal, matrilineal (also referred to as *uterine*), cognatic or bilateral, and double-descent groups. Patrilineal and matrilineal descent groups are both unilineal systems and refer respectively to those societies in which families recognize membership through either a common male ancestor or a common female ancestor, but not both. Cognatic-lineal or bilateral descent groups, on the other hand, do not favor either gender and recognize family members from all lines of possible descent (Fox, 1983). Yet a third possibility, although rare, is the double-descent system, in which certain rights and duties are passed from the patrilineal side and others from the matrilineal side.

Property transmission between generations does not always take place within the descent group but may be passed more generally to kin. Each society observes certain guidelines about which family members can be recognized as kin, which leads to a concept of kinship. Relationships derive through blood ties (consanguinity) and through marriage ties (affines), such that relatives of one's father are considered one's patrilateral kin, and relatives of one's mother are thought to be matrilateral kin.

Rules about residence can also be important since they foster social relationships that can influence the distribution of property, especially if communications over distances are difficult. Most societies have abided by the patrilocal tradition, whereby the husband and his wife join the male's family. Other possibilities include matrilocal residence, neolocal residence (living apart from parents), or avunculocal residence (living near an uncle).

Rules about descent groups, kinship, and residence can all influence social traditions in a myriad of ways. The number of rule combinations regarding descent, kinship, and residence that are logically possible is vast and has the potential to generate all sorts of complicated traditions. A culture that characterizes group membership in one way may determine property transmission or other social traditions very differently. Among Jews, for instance, membership is determined matrilineally, but many aspects of Jewish culture are patrilineal in nature. Further, although the Navajo American Indians practice matrilineal descent, they recognize consanguine relatives as kin, often live in matrilocal circumstances, and practice mostly bilateral inheritance.

Nevertheless, in most societies kinship ties have mattered the most in inheritance transactions (Goody, 1976). Thus, property is rarely transmitted to friends and mostly to one's spouse, one's children, or one's sisters' children. Examples of patrilineal, matrilineal, and bilateral inheritance exist across the globe. In practice, however, the modal rule in history has been some form of patrilineal inheritance and subsequent distribution of property among the men of a family. Murdock estimated the distribution of descent groups across the world in the first part of the twentieth century to be 47 percent patrilineal, 36 percent bilateral, 14 percent matrilineal, and 3 percent double descent. This sample, however, is particular to one point in time, and the statistics generated do not reflect relative population sizes of each society or the prevalence of different inheritance traditions.

In historical times, inheritance traditions have been tied to the mode of economic production. Inheritance mattered less in hunting-and-gathering societies, in which a person's physical property consisted of tools and such that would typically be destroyed or buried with the deceased. Hunting-and-gathering groups with inheritance traditions usually adhered to bilateral inheritance practices, which some social scientists attribute to the need for social adhesion (Goody, 1976, p. 16).

The more important a deceased's property became for generating a livelihood, such as land in agricultural areas, the more likely survivors were to be concerned about its distribution to the next generation. Most societies with some type of agricultural production adopted a unilineal system at some point. With time, this evolved further. Over centuries, many societies increased the productivity of their agriculture, moving from a hoe-based cultivation to one that required animal power, a plow, and even irrigation. Such capital improvements increased the amount that farmers could harvest and expanded the ways that the land could be utilized, thus eventually creating an agricultural surplus. The subsequent increases in productivity of the land raised property values and made societies wealthier. A natural companion to economic growth is the development of social differentiation in economic status and, thus, an unequal distribution of wealth among a society's members. Families became interested in retaining or, better yet, increasing their wealth holdings and their standard of living in the transmission to the next generation. The more advanced the agricultural production systems and the more scarce land became, the more a society's kinship groups sought to control marriage behavior through endogamous practices, thus keeping the property within the family kinship group or at least within the clan.

Advanced agriculture spread easily through Eurasia, where much land existed at the same latitude. This allowed for easy adoption, from one region to another, of new ideas about cultivation and livestock, and new types of plants. In contrast, new agricultural methods did not spread widely across different latitudes in Africa and in the Americas; much of this had to do with the difficulty of transferring new ideas from one climate to another (Diamond, 1997).

Thus, inheritance practices that deviated from those of unilineal descent groups developed in Eurasia but rarely in Africa, except in northern and eastern Africa, in areas eventually observant of the Islamic faith and its guidelines. With the increase in wealth inequality, many Eurasian cultures distinguished between those with rights in land and those without them, including those with less wealth and fewer rights, such as serfs or tenants, and those with more, such as lords and landlords. Such distinctions did not exist in most African civilizations (Goody, 1976, p. 25).

African societies tended to stick with unilineal descent groups, as shown from Murdock's study of 193 different African societies (Goody, 1976, p. 12). Pastoral societies such as the Zulu and Swazi of southern Africa and the Nuer of southern Sudan, mostly used patrilineal inheritance systems. Matrilineal inheritance existed in cultures that practiced extensive hoe agriculture, especially in Central Africa (*Encyclopedia of Africa South of the Sahara*, 1997). Not all the matrilineal groups in Africa passed property down through the men. Among the Bemba of Zambia, women owned the property and passed it down to daughters and practiced either matrilocal residence or avunculocal residence. With less social differentiation and, thus, less emphasis on economic status (than Eurasians), the need to adopt alternatives to the traditional unilineal inheritance practices was weak (Goody, 1976, p. 25).

In Eurasia, the traditional practice was patrilineal inheritance. As societies became wealthier, various social strategies emerged to keep wealth within the clan. Concubines and polygyny, for instance, provided men with extramarital partners and increased the likelihood of male heirs. Families exerted more control over women and often pressured their young to make an endogamous marriage match. Thus, one can observe in the early history of Israel, Greece, and China marriages between close kin, such as cousins—in other words, unions between the children of two siblings (Goody, 1976, p. 15). Over time, with more advanced agricultural production and wealth accumulation, bilateral inheritance became a common practice through much of Eurasia. The option of women as "residual heiresses to their brothers" was also recorded in many of the main texts of Eurasia, including "Greek, Roman, the Hebrew and Chinese texts, and in Babylonian, Hindu and Buddhist law-books" (Goody, 1976, p. 21).

In some regions, religions played a large role in the evolution of inheritance systems. Eventually, bilateral inheritance was encouraged by rabbinic Judaism, Christianity, and Islam (*Jewish Encyclopedia*, 1901–1905, p. 583; Goody, 2000; *Oxford Encyclopedia of the Modern Islamic World*, 1995, p. 203). The Christian church, for example, made many inroads in abolishing various patrilineal traditions used in Europe prior to the wide adoption of Christianity.

It forbade endogamous marriages, such as marriages between siblings or cousins, which were a common practice throughout the Mediterranean. The Catholic church further discouraged second marriages and polygamy. Many of the various inheritance strategies that societies used in Europe, Asia, and in Arab societies to further their family line, including adoption, polygamy, divorce (of infertile spouses), remarriage, and endogamous marriages, became difficult or impossible in European society (Goody, 2000). These new regulations on social behavior had the effect of limiting the number of possible heirs, weakening the patrilineal family kinship groups, and strengthening women's roles within families. A similar development took place among South and Central American native societies as a result of European conquest in the fifteenth and sixteenth centuries. Within Europe, in just a matter of centuries after the adoption of Christianity, massive amounts of wealth were bequeathed to the Catholic church to make it the major landowner in many parts of Europe. Such changes especially affected the economic chances of illegitimate children by denying them legal access to their biological parents' wealth.

Families usually had two objectives: to care for all their offspring and to preserve the family estate, which was best done by favoring one child. These two objectives were not easy to achieve all at once. On top of the wishes of individual families came legal and religious guidelines. Thus, various institutions continued to evolve to handle the challenge of distributing land from one generation to the next. Differences frequently existed between de jure and de facto inheritance practices, as families did not always stick to the de jure traditions. In addition, and depending on the law of the region, parents in some areas could get around the local inheritance customs by leaving written wills expressing their designated legatees.

Not surprisingly, a wide variety of inheritance strategies arose out of the agricultural economies of Eurasia. Women's property rights were a key variable in the de facto set of inheritance practices because in many regions, women were residual heiresses or prevented from inheriting. Families could still use dowries to assist their daughters and to maintain some type of long-term clout over the family resources. Many inheritance traditions thus describe the nature of property division among sons. Some societies practiced equal division of property among sons, as was the case in England prior to the Norman Conquest of 1066, under the tradition of *Gavelkind*. This practice is still in use in some English regions, in particular the county of Kent. In China, Confucian precepts dictated that although the eldest son inherited the responsibility of carrying on the ceremonial functions of the family, property was divided among the sons in equal portions (Levy, 1968, p. 167).

MAKING A WILL. At lower left, a man makes his will; at upper left, his family gathers around his deathbed. At lower right, Saint Remigius raises the man from the dead. Flemish tapestry of the life of Saint Remigius, 1531. (Musée de Saint-Remi, Reims, France/Foto Marburg/Art Resource, NY)

Birth order, however, could also be of great importance. Thus, under some Eurasian customs, only certain males inherited. Typically, this meant that the eldest inherited all of his father's property or that property was distributed by birth order, with the oldest sons getting the most. Male primogeniture was the modus operandi during much of Japanese history. Primogeniture was also practiced across great areas of Europe, including Great Britain, parts of France, and in many regions of Germany, particularly those areas not close to the border with France. The French practice is referred to as *Borough French*, and in German the practice is referred to as *Anerbenrecht*. In England, the use of entail, a legal option that allowed property owners to restrict the number of heirs, helped preserve the estate to the detriment of noninheriting siblings. Other European countries had legal provisions similar to the English practice of entail. Judeo-Christian cultures could easily find support for special treatment of the eldest born in biblical writings: just one among several biblical citations, the book of *Deuteronomy* states that the firstborn son should receive a double portion of the existing inheritance (*Jewish Encyclopedia*). In the most recent millennium, primogeniture had been a widely used institution in Europe.

The rule of primogeniture could be flipped around, so that the youngest fared the best. Such was the case under the borough-English practice, whereby land passed to the youngest son only, also known as ultimogeniture. This custom was practiced in parts of England until its abolishment in 1925. Ultimogeniture became an oft-used method of property transmission in Ireland in the decades after the potato famine (Guinnane, 1997).

Various regions of Europe practiced partible inheritance, whereby land was distributed among all the offspring, both sons and daughters. This tradition was common, for instance, in the southwest area of Germany, in northern France prior to the French Revolution, and later in all of France with the adoption of Code Napoléon.

With industrialization and modernization, fewer individuals participate in the agricultural economy. Wage-labor activities outside the agricultural sphere have become the basis of how individuals and families provide for themselves in modern industrial economies. They invest in shaping the human capital of their offspring, and grants and gifts that occur while children are young may be more important than wealth children receive upon the death of their parents or other relatives. Investment in human capital of the young provides parents an incentive to distribute some portion of their wealth prior to their own passing. At the same time, with longer average life expectancy, parents must also accumulate as much wealth as possible in the expectation of lengthy retirement spells. For young people, however, the larger number of occupational opportunities in industrial economies helps to minimize the impact of inheritance outcomes: in modern economies, economic success depends more on individual effort and talent than it did in the past.

Implications of Inheritance Systems. The inheritance strategy used by a society affects many different economic and social outcomes, including the distribution of wealth and labor mobility. Inheritance rules can exert an exogenous effect on such economic outcomes. Endogenous change is also possible, whereby certain economic outcomes, such as population change, in turn can affect inheritance rules. Social groups and families react to economic and social change and alter their inheritance traditions to better serve their interests. They thus can change the nature of constraints that inheritance rules represent.

Distribution of resources. One of the more important economic outcomes resulting from inheritance traditions is the distribution of scarce resources, such as land. Many societies have used some type of unigeniture system, whereby one child, often the eldest, received the largest chunk of property. By favoring the productivity of only one of their children, parents and society placed great importance on the continuance of the family lineage. The trade-off was obviously the welfare of the remaining offspring and the possible opportunity cost of losing the best-suited progeny to economic endeavors outside the family business. Unigeniture inheritance systems had the potential of producing suboptimal outcomes, since the chosen heir was not necessarily the child with the best aptitude toward farming or running a business. It mattered especially where land was scarce. For centuries, scores of men and women with more ambition, drive, and talent than their sibling who inherited the family business have stepped back in the name of lineage and institutional rules in the transfer of important resources across generations.

How this has affected agricultural efficiency in history or output levels in other industries is unclear. Certainly, the development of markets increased the incentive for an improved allocation of talent within families. A further impediment to economic growth may have been the inheritance tax, still an open question among social scientists. It is one of the oldest taxes, however: Caesar Augustus instituted a tax on inheritances to provide retirement funds for the Roman military.

Economic inequality. Economic theory suggests that unigeniture systems lead to greater economic inequality (Chu, 1991). Still, such inequality is tempered where access to land is cheap, such as it was in colonial America (Shammas, Salmon, and Dahlin, 1987).

Becker's classic works on human capital and family behavior do not predict the mode of inheritance strategy a society might use, but they make predictions about the size of bequests and the degree of intergenerational mobility in modern economies. Parents care about both the quantity as well as the quality of children they raise. With increased opportunity costs of leisure in modern economies, parents choose smaller family sizes. Bequests to children are larger when the fraction of family's income spent on children is greater, when the rates of return on investments in children are greater, or when the rate of growth in incomes over time is smaller. The resulting differences in bequest outcomes easily promote increased inequality in wealth and income distributions across families (Becker, 1991, pp. 230–231). Although Becker's work has implications for economic history, certain assumptions need modification. Parents' preference on quantity, for instance, implies that parents have control over family size, less realistic in historical times.

The economic stratification that Becker's models predict can occur additionally within families in cases of unequal inheritance. In times and places where resources were scarce, the economic and social fate of noninheriting siblings depended on the options open to them. Often it has meant a decline in social and economic status. In one European region, the German principality of Hesse-Cassel, individuals were more likely to migrate from villages where one child inherited the farm than from those that practiced more equal forms of inheritance (Wegge, 1999).

Further applied work on the determinations of bequest sizes or dowries include Shammas and others (1987) on the United States, McGranahan (2000) on seventeenth-century Britain, and Botticini (1999) on Renaissance Italy. Botticini's study indicates that dowries, an inter vivos type of bequest, were positively related to a woman's age and to the degree of marrying "down."

The plight of women. In historical times and, to an extent, in contemporary times, men traditionally have had a great deal of control over resources in most societies. Even in many matrilineal cultures, property was often transferred through the uterine line from one man to another man, such as from a sister's brother to her own son. Exclusion of women from owning and managing land simplified the practice of inheritance, so that in a patrilineal system men transmitted property to their sons or to their brother's sons, and in some matrilineal systems, men bestowed property to their sisters' sons. Agarwal (1994) describes extensively the barriers to women's land ownership and control in South Asia.

When women are forbidden from owning property and thus from inheriting important economic resources, they are often dependent on male relatives, husbands, or sons for their well-being. Their plight can be particularly trying in cases where widows have no sons and the deceased husbands' family possesses rights to his property. The destitution of widows through such means is well documented among Hindus in India (Dasgupta, 1993, p. 323).

Unilineal inheritance systems operated differently if women were allowed to own land. In a patrilineal system, women could inherit land if the deceased male owner bestowed land first to his spouse or to another female relative, or alternatively if no sons existed and property went to a spouse and to daughters. Likewise, a matrilineal system with the possibility of female ownership meant that women granted other women, typically their daughters, with property, a practice observed in parts of central Africa.

Changing of Inheritance Rules across Time. Inheritance traditions evolve over time, much like other important social and economic institutions. They develop in response to changes in the nature of economic production, as well as shifts in population size. Exogenous forces—in particular, pressure from religious institutions or from the state—can greatly affect de facto rules of inheritance.

Heirship strategies in Europe and other parts of Eurasia changed in radical ways with the spread of Christianity, Islam, and rabbinic Judaism, as discussed above. These religious doctrines each paved the way for greater opportunities for land ownership by women by encouraging other social objectives, besides keeping the property within a family and within the male line.

Political revolutions can have drastic effects on the inheritance strategies a society uses. Communist revolutions in China and Russia resulted in the weakening of family life and individual property rights. Property was often taken over by the state upon the death of an individual, which discouraged the living from saving and thus capital accumulation (Goody, 2000). Dramatic changes were also witnessed in the aftermath of the French Revolution, during which the Code Napoléon was enacted. One of its new edicts was the outlaw of primogeniture and the establishment of partible inheritance, whereby all siblings would receive an equal portion of their parents' property.

Economic and demographic shifts, such as changes in the size of the relevant population, have often provoked modifications in inheritance traditions, usually in the case of providing families with appropriate incentives to alter the rules. A powerful influence on the evolution of inheritance rules has often been population pressure. This is particularly true in the most recent centuries and in agricultural societies that distributed land to more than one child. Transferring land to multiple children resulted in smaller average land holdings compared with those of the parents, unless parents were able to accumulate additional assets over their own working lives. A family working a smaller plot of land quickly experienced diminished returns to their marginal product of labor. Over time, uninterrupted division of land, along with population growth, resulted in a decrease in the average family's standard of living. Various responses to this downward shift in economic circumstances developed. Where possible, young people migrated out of their home communities to pursue economic opportunity elsewhere. Some communities switched from the tradition of partible inheritance to unigeniture to counter the effects of subdivision, as was witnessed in the case of the German principality of Hesse-Cassel in the nineteenth century (Wegge, 1999).

Population decreases can affect inheritance rules as well. One example is the experience of Irish households in the nineteenth century. Prior to the potato famine of the 1840s, Irish families with land preferred to divide up their holdings in equal portions among their children. In stark contrast, in the 1850s and thereafter, the preferred mode of inheritance strategy was unitary inheritance, seldom primogeniture but often ultimogeniture. Established emigration networks and the overall impact of the famine helped to encourage alternative family heirship strategies (Guinnane, 1997, p. 164).

Inheritance practices are a serious matter in most cultures. In those societies in which inheritance has represented one of the few methods toward a life of material happiness and social position, inheritance institutions have remained at the forefront of cultural traditions. The emotional joy and pain resulting from inheritance outcomes have found an outlet in the fiction, folklore, and fables of many cultures.

BIBLIOGRAPHY

Agarwal, Bina. *A Field of One's Own: Gender and Land Rights in South Asia*. Cambridge, 1994. Analysis of the economic, historical, legal, and ethnographic factors of inequality in land ownership in South Asia.

Becker, Gary. *A Treatise on the Family*. Cambridge, Mass., 1991. Economic theories on modern family behavior and intergenerational transfers.

Botticini, Maristella. "A Loveless Economy? Intergenerational Altruism and the Marriage Market in a Tuscan Town, 1415–1436." *Journal of Economic History* 59.1 (1999), 104–121. Applied work on characteristics of inter vivos transfers.

Chu, C. Y. Cyrus. "Primogeniture." *Journal of Political Economy* 99.1 (1991), 78–99.

Dasgupta, Partha. *An Inquiry into Well-Being and Destitution*. Oxford, 1993.

Diamond, Jared. *Guns, Germs and Steel: The Fates of Human Societies*. New York, 1997.

Esposito, John L., ed. *The Oxford Encyclopedia of the Modern Islamic World*. New York, 1995.

Fox, Robin. *Kinship and Marriage: An Anthropological Perspective*. Cambridge, 1983. One of the best works in anthropology on kinship-system theory.

Goody, Jack. *Production and Reproduction: A Comparative Study of the Domestic Domain*. Cambridge, 1976. Explains connections between economic production and inheritance systems.

Goody, Jack. *The European Family: An Historico-Anthropological Essay*. Oxford and Malden, Mass., 2000.

Guinnane, Timothy. *The Vanishing Irish: Households, Migration and the Rural Economy in Ireland, 1850–1914*. Princeton, 1997. Applied work showing connections between inheritance, economy, and family structures.

The Jewish Encyclopedia: A Descriptive Record of the History, Religion, Literature, and Customs of the Jewish People from the Earliest Times to the Present Day. New York and London, 1901–1905.

Levy, Marion J. *The Family Revolution in Modern China*. New York, 1968. Sociological study of kinship structures in China.

McGranahan, Leslie Moscow. "Charity and the Bequest Motive: Evidence from Seventeenth-Century Wills." *Journal of Political Economy* 108.6 (2000), 1270–1291. Applied work on characteristics of bequest decisions.

Middleton, John, ed. *Encyclopedia of Africa South of the Sahara*. New York, 1997.

Murdock, George P. *Ethnographic Atlas*. Pittsburgh, 1967. Data analysis of a sub-sample of Murdock's work published in the journal *Ethnology* between 1962–1980.

North, Douglass C. "Institutions." *Journal of Economic Perspectives* 5.1 (1991), 97–112.

Shammas, Carole, Marylynn Salmon, and Michel Dahlin. *Inheritance in America from Colonial Times to the Present*. New Brunswick, N.J., 1987. Applied research of bequest habits and inheritance systems.

Van den Berghe, Pierre L. *Human Family Systems: An Evolutionary View*. Prospect Heights, Ill., 1990.

Wegge, Simone A. "To Part or Not to Part: Emigration and Inheritance Institutions in Mid–Nineteenth-Century Germany." *Explorations in Economic History* 36.1 (1999), 30–55. Applied work on effect of different inheritance regimes on village economies and on migration behavior.

Simone A. Wegge

INHERITANCE TAX. *See* Taxation.

INSURANCE *[This entry contains seven subentries, a historical overview, and discussions of maritime, fire, life, health and accident, unemployement, and old age insurance.]*

Historical Overview

The origins of insurance are unclear. C. F. Trenerry's thesis (*The Origin and Early History of Insurance*, London, 1926) that insurance contracts were widely known in the ancient world has not been generally accepted by modern historians, skeptical of the lack of direct evidence. However, other forms of contracts existed that contained elements of indemnity and insurance, most notably the loan on bottomry, the earliest reference to which can be found in Babylonia's Code of Hammurabi (third millennium BCE). This was a contract whereby money or goods were lent for trading purposes at a high rate of interest, with the understanding that the borrower was freed of liability in the event of a loss. If the goods arrived at their destination, the borrower was liable to repay the loan plus interest. The margin between the bottomry interest rate and the rate charged for normal loans represented a risk premium, but this distinction, it seems, never was made. A less tenuous connection can be made between life insurance and Roman burial societies, which by the fourth century CE had moved away from their earlier cultural and religious functions toward providing a lump sum to the relatives of deceased members. This burial-insurance function can be found later among the guilds and fraternities of early medieval Europe and Tokugawa Japan, sometimes extended to include mutual insurance against a variety of other hazards such as loss of property by fire, confiscation, capture, robbery, and theft of cattle.

Early Insurance. The emergence of modern premium insurance is commonly dated to the growth of marine underwriting in fourteenth-century Italy. By 1300, the Italian city-states had come to dominate Mediterranean trade and led the expansion of commerce on the transalpine and sea routes to northern Europe. Italian merchants revived the use of the bottomry loan and also developed the basic devices of distance trade, the business partnership, the bill of exchange, the bill of lading, and the bill of insurance. The earliest surviving insurance policy covered a ship traveling from Genoa to Majorca in 1347. Merchants acted as underwriters, but notaries were employed to draw up the contracts. The Barcelona notary, Bartolomé Masons, drafted 380 policies covering 104 different ships between July 1428 and December 1429. By this date, there were several hundred notaries working in Genoa, Pisa, Florence, Marseille, and Milan. They helped to standardize practice, and by the sixteenth century the marine insurance policy had acquired the basic form that would be used in marine underwriting for the next three hundred years.

Premium life insurance developed in the fifteenth-century Mediterranean as a by-product of marine polices covering passengers or slaves on sea voyages although slave cargoes were formally indistinguishable from other objects of marine insurance. The growth of marine underwriting was also accompanied by extensive regulation. A number of ordinances issued at Barcelona between 1435 and 1484 placed maritime insurance under the Consolat de Mar and formed the basis for international commercial law in the Mediterranean area. Further insurance ordinances, largely codifying existing practices, were passed in Italy, Spain, Flanders, and England during the sixteenth and early seventeenth centuries. Their chief purposes were to prevent fraud, to reduce the costs of arbitrating disputes, and thus to improve the stability of commerce and to provide a valuable source of tax revenue (Genoa had begun to tax insurance policies as early as 1401). They helped establish the key principle of full disclosure between insurers and the insured, and they also shared a common regulatory insistence on a level of self-insurance to reduce moral hazard.

Entrepreneurs also found profit opportunities in issuing insurance contracts without any insurable interest. In particular, life insurance was commonly employed as collateral for loans in fifteenth-century Italy and Spain; and when such collateral insurances were taken on lives of public figures, they quickly mutated into speculations. Given the existing religious objections to usury and political concerns about commercial instability, this development in turn provoked stricter regulation of a wide range of these wager-type insurances. Insurance gambling and all life insurance were suppressed by the Barcelona ordinances, and this prohibition was later adopted by several other European states.

Early insurance can thus be regarded as following two distinct paths of development, which only began to converge in late-seventeenth-century Europe. First, premium insurance for profit, entrepreneurial and aleatory in nature, grew directly out of business risk—the hazards implicit in commercial ventures, particularly in transporting goods by sea. It attracted fiscal and regulatory intervention by the state. Second, non-profit-motivated mutual insurance by subscription, providing funeral expenses and reimbursing losses by fire, theft, sickness, and accident, derived from the desire to protect the property and livelihoods of members of societies and communities. It was closely related to forms of charitable relief, and was generally encouraged by religious and secular authorities. In both cases, a fundamental fear of loss—which, behavioral economists argue, compels individuals to reduce risk more than the desire to maximize utility drives them to take risks—was the likely factor behind the expansion of insurance. In neither case did the greater use of insurance necessarily reflect a declining belief in providence. Astrological and religious beliefs coexisted with underwriting for centuries before the rise of scientific rationalism and classical probability theory that occurred in the seventeenth and eighteenth centuries.

Seventeenth and Eighteenth Centuries. In his speech to the English Parliament during the debate on the insurance bill of 1601, lawyer and philosopher Francis Bacon (1561–1626) declared that insurance is "the loadstone that draws him [the merchant] on to adventure, and to stretch even the very punctilio of his credit." From the point of view of the insured, insurance may be regarded as an incentive for investment, by reducing the information, moral hazard, and adverse selection costs in commercial transactions, and the uncertainties imposed upon individuals by the existence of hazards such as fire, disease, storms, floods, earthquakes, accidents, theft, and war. Institutional economics emphasizes the role of formal rules and bodies, and of informal norms and customs, in providing incentives for, or imposing constraints upon, economic growth. Thus, modern insurance can be seen as an institutional product of changing attitudes to providence, natural hazard, and mortality during the seventeenth and eighteenth centuries. These shifts in perceptions of risk, and an increasing emphasis on the sanctity of private property associated with the growth of the commercial and professional bourgeoisie, increased the demand for insurance and encouraged the establishment of new types of institutions for supplying it. By combating fear of loss, the diffusion of fire, crop, and livestock insurance through large public and private companies helped support accumulation, investment, and innovation. By encouraging the postponement of present consumption in favor of provision for the future, early life insurance offices stimulated prudential motives for the transference of wealth between generations, even where, as in early-eighteenth-century England, speculation and gambling continued to characterize much of the industry.

From the underwriter's point of view, the organizational form of insurance adopted was dependent upon the nature of the risk. In maritime trade, each risk was relatively large, discrete, and short-term—up to eighteen months for transatlantic and African voyages after 1500. Few individual merchants could or would incur the whole of such a liability on their own. Thus, coinsurance of one risk by several merchants, each underwriting part of a ship and its cargo, became the predominant form of marine insurance. However, for entrepreneurial insurance to develop in other areas, it was necessary to underwrite large numbers of small, relatively homogenous and widely distributed risks, over the medium-to-long term—a standard duration of seven years for fire insurance policies, and usually longer for whole-term life insurance. This practice required the establishment of well-funded business organizations, with the resources to sell insurance over a large territory, to maximize income and spread liabilities and to settle claims quickly and efficiently in order to retain consumer confidence. Thus, it became a characteristic of modern insurance that marketing determined the competitive strategy, which, in turn, shaped organizational change. In fire and life insurance, hierarchical and bureaucratic companies evolved—in a remarkable variety of forms, both public and private, stock and mutual—to meet the challenge of selling, via networks of agents, mostly standardized products to great numbers of customers at a distance.

The nature of these risks also encouraged the continuous collection of data, which, eventually, would place insurance on a more scientific footing. Commencing with the work of John Graunt on the London bills of mortality in the 1660s, the interest in compiling mortality tables increased rapidly among scientists and political arithmeticians across Europe. However, it was a hundred years before these tables began to be systematically employed by English life insurance offices to calculate age-related premium rates. The delay was largely due to the unreliability of the demographic data and the persistent, but not unreasonable, belief that a fairly constant rate of mortality prevailed for most of adulthood. In other branches of insurance, the *a posteriori* calculation of premium rates based on a systematic analysis of underwriting data did not become commonplace until the nineteenth century, when the improved organization of Lloyds and the establishment of tariff associations in fire insurance facilitated the sharing of information and a greater convergence of prices. As one historian has observed, many insurers during the early nineteenth century were "like short-sighted people embarking on a walk along a cliff edge" (Borscheid, p. 65). Only chance, falling mortality rates, and lower frequencies of loss by fire, shipwreck, and piracy allowed them to survive. Thus the early growth of corporate insurance was not subject to the triumph of statistical thinking. As late as the mid-eighteenth century, marine underwriters in Barcelona paid for masses to be said for the safety of the cargoes they insured.

What was critical was the availability of capital for new, larger insurance enterprises, a regulatory and fiscal regime that encouraged insurance investors, and growth in the market, especially for all types of property insurance, that allowed liabilities to be spread and the law of large numbers to operate—conditions that had begun to appear in northwestern Europe by 1700. In most places, the volume of insurance regulation increased from the second half of the seventeenth century on. It was accompanied by a growing number of official chambers of insurance and monopoly chartered companies, while small local widows and orphans funds as well as pension, sickness, accident, and burial funds and communal fire and livestock insurance societies were encouraged by absolutist states as part of their demographic and social policies. However, insurance progressed furthest where it was least regulated, notably in Britain. There was little English case law on life insurance before the 1770s, the first major legislation being the prohibition of wagers on lives by the Gambling Act of 1774. British fire insurance developed rapidly under a light fiscal burden before 1782 with virtually no form of regulation. Marine insurance was hardly hampered by the ban on wagers passed in 1746 (insurances issued without a demonstrable insurable interest), and the chartered monopoly given to two London companies in 1720 (repealed in 1825) only ensured that this

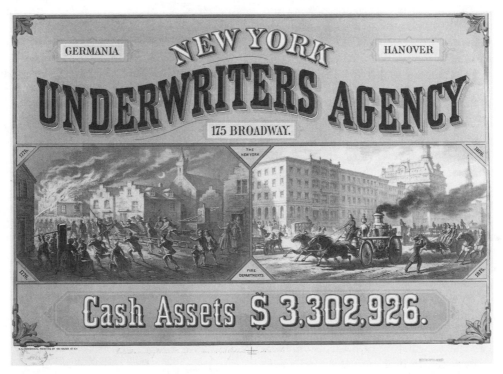

INSURANCE. Advertisement showing two firefighting scenes, New York, circa 1876. (Prints and Photographs Division, Library of Congress)

branch of insurance remained largely the preserve of individual underwriters at Lloyds rather than unchartered stock companies.

The British system was adopted initially in North America. Early American shipping was largely insured through London, but the first independent marine insurance brokers appeared in Philadelphia and Boston during the 1720s. The first American fire insurance company, Benjamin Franklin's Philadelphia Contributionship, was founded in 1752, based closely on the model of a London mutual fire office. However, American insurance, especially after the Revolution, began to acquire continental European rather than British characteristics, notably in the greater use of legal incorporation and the increasing rigor of state licensing systems. By 1806, there were already some fifty U.S. insurance companies, with a total capital of $15 million, representing some of the first modern business enterprises in the United States.

Nineteenth and Twentieth Centuries. The large corporate insurers most directly faced the challenge of the rapid technological advances and the new risks associated with economic development in the Western world during the nineteenth and twentieth centuries. The British fire insurance offices were the first to struggle with the problems of insuring steam-powered machinery and textile factories, from the 1780s on. They did not cope well, and for over half a century modes of risk assessment were constantly having to catch up with developments in manufacturing and commerce. This early experience of "newfangled" risks may explain why the big British insurance offices remained reluctant to develop new insurance products until the beginning of the twentieth century. Instead, specialist accident insurers emerged to meet the demand for protection from the hazards associated with railways, electricity, and the marriage of science to mass production. By 1880, there were already about fifteen lines of accident insurance available, such as engineering, boiler, plate glass, and railway passenger insurance. By World War I, this figure had risen to fifty, with new lines including employers' liability, bicycle, automobile, elevator, and electrical machinery insurance.

Beginning in the last third of the nineteenth century, technological change thus spawned a host of new lines of insurance, which became assimilated by giant composite offices selling multiple products over one counter, and sometimes within one policy. The new complexity of insurance required big organizations with greater levels of technical expertise in underwriting, large bodies of clerical staff processing policies and claims, and large marketing operations to spread risk as widely as possible. Branch organizations were developed to deal with the monitoring and moral-hazard problems that plagued the existing system of selling via individual agents. The trend toward globalization of business was also enhanced, with insurance one of the first areas of business to develop national and transnational competition between large firms. Fire and life insurance became internationally traded commodities from the late eighteenth century on, when several London insurance offices began to exploit their mercantile founders' overseas connections. The development of reinsurance in the nineteenth century further accelerated this process. The world wars interrupted the trend, but since 1945, and particularly during the last two decades of the twentieth century, globalization has reemerged as a major feature of the insurance industry. The nature and the immense scale of some modern risks, especially in the area of disaster insurance, have necessitated not only their diffusion around the world via reinsurance, but also the creation, through international mergers, of megacorporations able to compete on a global scale.

Since the 1980s, there has been a marked acceleration in the incidence of major catastrophic events, notably earthquakes, hurricanes, and floods, which because of the huge sums involved in losses, and because of the interconnected liabilities produced by reinsurance, have had global repercussions for the industry. The new dimension of terrorist attacks represented by the events of 11 September 2001, which cost an estimated $50 billion in property, liability, and life insurance losses, has added to this problem. These developments have placed in question the very ability of traditional insurance to provide adequate cover in the face of such events, and alternative ways of financing and managing risk are now being sought, most notably in the capital markets. Nevertheless, the extent of insurance provision around the world, though impressive when viewed historically, remains very uneven. In 1998, for example, the combined insurance premiums of China and India were less than those of Switzerland. There appears to be abundant opportunity for further development, especially given the increasing deregulation of many insurance markets around the world.

BIBLIOGRAPHY

Arps, Ludwig. *Auf sicheren Pfeilen: Deutsche Versicherungswirtschaft vor 1914*. Göttingen, 1965. Dated, but still the best general study of German insurance, erratic in its approach.

Boiteux, L. A. *La fortune de la mer, le besoin de sécurité et les débuts de l'assurance maritime*. Paris, 1968.

Borscheid, Peter. "The Establishment of the Life Insurance Business in Germany in the Nineteenth Century." *German Yearbook on Business History* (1984), 55–74.

Clark, Geoffrey. *Betting on Lives: The Culture of Life Insurance in England, 1695–1775*. Manchester, 1999. A recent, pioneering study that uncovers the diversity of early English life assurance.

Clayton, G. *British Insurance*. London, 1971.

Daston, Lorraine J. "The Domestication of Risk: Mathematical Probability and Insurance, 1650–1830." In *The Probabilistic Revolution*, vol. 1, *Ideas in History*, edited by L. Krüger, L. J. Daston, and M. Heidelberger, pp. 237–260. Cambridge, Mass., 1987.

Del Treppo, Mario. "Assicurazioni e commercio internazionale a Barcellona nel 1428–1429." *Rivista storica italiana* 69 (1957), 508–541. A good example of the ways in which early maritime insurance records have been utilized to study Mediterranean trade.

Pearson, Robin. "Towards an Historical Model of Financial Services Innovation: The Case of the Insurance Industry, 1700–1914." *Economic History Review*, 2d series, 50.2 (1997), 235–256. Charts the diffusion of new insurance products and the international growth of accident insurance before 1914, within a neo-Schumpeterian theoretical framework.

Perkins, Edwin J. *American Public Finance and Financial Services, 1700–1815*. Columbus, Ohio, 1994. Provides a good overview of early American insurance in Chapter 13.

Raynes, Harold E. *A History of British Insurance*. London, 1948.

Spooner, Frank C. *Risks at Sea: Amsterdam Insurance and Maritime Europe, 1766–1780*. Cambridge, 1983. An innovative economic study of eighteenth-century marine insurance with a focus on prices and investment.

Westall, Oliver M. "Marketing Strategy and the Competitive Structure of British General Insurance, 1720–1980." *Business History* 36.2 (1994), 20–46. Argues for the central place of marketing in determining competitive strategies and business structures in British insurance history.

Wright, Charles, and C. Ernest Fayle. *A History of Lloyd's: From the Founding of Lloyd's Coffee House to the Present Day*. London, 1928.

Zelizer, Viviana A. Rotman. *Morals and Markets: The Development of Life Insurance in the United States*. New York, 1979. A study of nineteenth-century life insurance from a sociological perspective, emphasizing the influence of cultural and ideological factors.

ROBIN PEARSON

Maritime Insurance

A well-developed insurance system is essential to any modern economy. Reducing risk by spreading losses among a greater number of parties, insurance institutions enable economic expansion and enhance security in many fields, particularly that of shipping. Present-day maritime insurance falls into five main categories: hull insurance, cargo insurance, freight insurance, marine liability or protection and indemnity (P&I), and war risks.

Maritime Insurance in the Ancient and Medieval Worlds. The oldest known form of insurance concerns the shipping and the transport of goods in China, Sumer, and Babylonia from about 3000 BCE, when merchants and traders engaged in a form of self-insurance. About 1200 BCE Phoenician merchants introduced *bottomry*, a system in which merchants borrowed funds to finance their voyages, using the ships' bottoms or hulls as collateral. The lender advanced a sum smaller than that required for repayment, the difference being in effect a premium or interest. If the vessel and cargo reached their destination unharmed, the sea loan was repaid in full, and if not the loan was canceled. This practice of maritime loans was later adopted by the merchants of Rhodes, Greece, Rome, and the Italian maritime cities. The enhanced security provided by sea loans promoted their widespread use. In 1227 CE, however, Pope Gregory IX prohibited them as usurious. But insurance itself was not in conflict with canon law, so the loan contract was separated from the undertaking to assume risk, leading to the independent contract of insurance. As marine insurance became more readily available during the fourteenth century, the demand for sea loans decreased. The development and diffusion of a system of premium-based insurance policies for maritime trade in later medieval Europe has been attributed to the Northern Italians. First Genoa and then Florence led in the creation of explicit insurance contracts, which came to be widely used by about 1400. Gradually the contracts became standardized in terms of both the risks covered and the guarantees offered by the underwriter. Storm, shipwreck, and seizure by pirates and privateers were covered. By around 1450 reinsurance was becoming increasingly common, as was the negotiability of insurance contracts. Premiums were specified in the contracts, with the calculation of rates based on distance, route, season, type of ship, and the likelihood of war or piracy.

In the fifteenth century marine insurance spread from Genoa and Florence to western Mediterranean ports, the Low Countries, and England and from Venice to eastern Mediterranean ports. The opening up of the oceans by the Portuguese and Spaniards boosted trade, so Barcelona, Bilbao, and Seville became important centers of marine insurance. In 1558 an exchange for trade and insurance was established in Hamburg (1558), followed by Rotterdam (1598) and Amsterdam (1611). The Hanseatic League adopted the Italian system of marine insurance and promoted its spread to other European countries.

Maritime Insurance in Early Modern and Modern England. Thanks to Italian commerce with England from the mid-thirteenth century, maritime insurance was well established in England certainly by the sixteenth century. In 1566 the Royal Exchange was opened in London as a marketplace for all insurance operations. But the growth of London's maritime insurance was hampered until the late seventeenth century by competition from Antwerp, Amsterdam, and Hamburg.

Lloyd's of London. With the growth of English commerce from the late seventeenth century, marine insurance developed rapidly in London. Edward Lloyd's (d. 1713) Coffee House, first mentioned in the *London Gazette* in 1688, became the central venue for individual underwriters in the marine market and a place to collect reliable shipping news. The wealthy individuals took shares of a risk, stated the amount they agreed to cover, and confirmed it with their signatures on the policy, thus introducing the term *underwriter*. Lloyd's played a seemingly unchallenged role in the marine insurance market until 1720, when the Royal Exchange Assurance Company and the London Assurance Company obtained royal charters for transacting marine insurance, thus becoming the first

MARITIME INSURANCE. Front page of *The World,* 16 April 1912, headlining the sinking of the *Titanic* (*New York World-Telegram* and the *Sun* Newspaper Photograph Collection/Prints and Photographs Division, Library of Congress)

corporate marine insurance enterprises in Europe. The formation of the two companies reduced competition in the marine insurance market in the period from 1720 to 1824, since other corporate companies were precluded from writing marine insurance. The two companies, however, took only a small share of the business. Thus the individual underwriters prospered through restrictions placed on corporate competition and the growing demand for insurance. Business morale at Lloyd's deteriorated, so by 1769 the leading underwriters and brokers had established the New Lloyd's Coffee House. By 1774 they had settled at the Royal Exchange and formed a society with fixed rules. In 1779 its members agreed on a standard form Lloyd's policy, the so-called S.G. Form of policy, in which the *S* stood for the ship and the *G* for the goods.

Some shipowners, however, were not satisfied with the terms offered by the chartered duopoly and organized their own mutual associations or clubs to offer cheaper insurance. By the end of the eighteenth century more than twenty clubs in England offered mutual insurance of their members' ships. Because many ships of questionable quality were insured, the risks became great, and many clubs had to close down. After the duopoly was abolished in 1824 and the Bubble Act was revoked in 1825, permitting the establishment of unincorporated joint-stock companies, about seventy such companies were established in the United Kingdom over the following fifty years. They offered improved rates, terms of cover, and service.

Some of the new companies established in England after 1824 threatened Lloyd's dominant position, especially after they began pooling underwriting information. In 1884 twenty of the companies established the London Institute of London Underwriters, but from the outset Lloyd's worked closely with the new organization.

In response to the competition from the companies, declining international trade, and the pressure for lower premiums for steamers, Lloyd's altered both its structure and its business practices in 1871, when Lloyd's was incorporated by act of Parliament, with its business governed by a committee of twelve elected from among its members. Deposits and guarantees were made compulsory for members, and minimum requirements were strengthened to avoid underwriting failures. Nevertheless it still remained not a company or a mutual club but an international insurance market. A large number of well-to-do individuals, as underwriting members, accepted insurance, while each member also accepted unlimited liability for his share of risks written by him or on his behalf.

After 1885 Lloyd's of London gradually became a place where almost any risk of any type could be covered. Thus Lloyd's emerged as the world center of risk insurance. It also meant that Lloyd's entered arenas whose economic consequences could not readily be foreseen. As a result the underwriters left the risk writing in the hands of a professional underwriting agent or lead underwriter, whereas they themselves became sleeping partners, often referred to as "Names." Business was organized in syndicates with a lead underwriter acting on behalf of the members of the syndicate. The sizes of the several hundred syndicates vary from a few members to more than a thousand. The modern Lloyd's survived the burdens of catastrophes like the San Francisco earthquake (1906) and the sinking of the *Titanic* (1912).

It was vital for Lloyd's to maintain its good name and protect the policyholder against any losses. In 1923 a lead underwriter informed the committee that his syndicate was insolvent. It was decided that all underwriters should contribute so the debts could be paid off. To meet similar incidents the Lloyd's Central Fund was established to serve as an ultimate safeguard to the assured in case the total wealth of all members of a syndicate proved insufficient. In 1968 Lloyd's had to announce its first overall loss of $3.9 million, caused by miscalculation of risks and premiums and of the effects of inflation, all coinciding with a series of catastrophic disasters. The existence of many syndicates was threatened; several Names faced financial ruin, and others retired. In order to replace the retiring members and their financial resources, the prestigious underwriting membership of Lloyd's, that is, being a Name, which had been restricted to male British citizens, was extended. In 1969 foreign nationals were admitted and in 1970 women.

During the late 1980s and early 1990s Lloyd's took another financial blow with a total loss of almost $10 billion. A number of members suffered financial ruin, and many situations resulted in personal tragedies. Lloyd's underwriting agents were accused of having failed to advise their clients properly of the potential risks involved. In 1996 the suing Names accepted a settlement offer of $3.2 billion from Lloyd's. It became apparent that no longer was it realistic to demand total liability of the underwriting members. In order to attract new capital, Lloyd's was forced to change policy by accepting corporate money and offering limited-liability investments. The situation was reflected in a drastic decline in the number of members and syndicates. In 1994 the first corporate members commenced underwriting. Soon the Names being the major risk takers will be history, and institutional investors will dominate the insurance market of Lloyd's. Like other marine insurers, Lloyd's experienced renewed trouble in the late 1990s and the first years of the new millennium. This continuous deterioration was caused mainly by severe competition with enormous pressure on pricing. In addition after 1997 came many multiyear contracts. Some of these contracts set fixed premium rates for up to five years without providing any review clauses. Such competition resulted in forced mergers, suspensions of business, and cooperation among former competitors.

The events of 11 September 2001 marked a watershed in the insurance business, resulting in the largest single loss ever for Lloyd's and the insurance industry as a whole. Lloyd's alone suffered a net loss of nearly $2 billion.

The Protection and Indemnity Clubs: Great Britain and Scandinavia. As noted earlier, an alternative form of insurance in England had been provided by mutual "hull" clubs, which suffered some significant decline with the proliferation of joint-stock insurance companies from 1825. But they managed to survive in a different form when, from the 1850s, their ways of organizing business and apportioning risk were adopted by a group of similar associations known as protection and indemnity (P&I) clubs. The emergence of these clubs must be viewed in the light of the growth in third-party liabilities. Worth mentioning is "Lord Campbell's Act"—the Fatal Accidents Act, 1846—which imposed stricter rules of liability for death and personal injury. The first P&I club, the Shipowners' Mutual Protection Society, was founded in London on 1 May 1855, when the United Kingdom Merchant Shipping Act (1854) came into force. Initially the P&I clubs covered liabilities for loss of life, personal injury, and collision risks, so-called protection insurance. After 1874 protection clubs began adding cover for loss of or damage to cargo carried on board. This was called indemnity insurance, whence the name P&I clubs. At the risk of oversimplification, it might be said that P&I insurance now covers everything not covered by some other insurance policy.

The number of P&I clubs has been drastically reduced by mergers and closures. Nineteen of the remaining major associations, insuring more than 90 percent of the world's oceangoing tonnage, belong to the International Group of P&I Clubs, which provides collective insurance and reinsurance to its members. With the enormous sums involved in maritime transport, especially when it comes to indemnity in connection with oil pollution, the members have pooled their larger risks under the auspices of the International Group. The United Kingdom Mutual Steam Ship Assurance Association (Bermuda) Ltd. (UK P&I Club), founded in 1869, is the largest mutual marine P&I organization in the world, and the Norwegian Gard P&I Club is the second largest. Together the two insure around two-fifths of the world fleet. In order to meet the challenge of a declining marine insurance market in the 1990s, many P&I clubs entered into strategic alliances with hull insurance associations.

In the Scandinavian countries, however, the mutual clubs continued to thrive, especially in Norway, where, because of the country's shortage of capital and an inadequate commercial banking system, shipowners were obliged to insure their vessels abroad. In 1837 the first Norwegian mutual marine insurance association was formed. Today the world's two largest mutual hull clubs are the Norwegian Hull Club and the Swedish Club. The Norwegians also emulated the British P&I clubs when in 1897 the Norwegian P&I club Skuld became the first established outside the United Kingdom.

Marine Insurance for War Risks. When the S.G. Form came into use in eighteenth-century England, marine and war risks, including many of the perils now described as war risks, were insured by the same policy. As early as 1739, however, underwriters started to exclude liability for the risks of capture and seizure in their policies. By 1863 it was common to include a free from capture, seizure, and detention clause (FC&S clause) in the policy. A clear and concise distinction between marine and war risks was adopted in 1898, when Lloyd's decided to insure war and marine risks under separate policies. The following year it was determined that, in the absence of contrary agreement, all marine policies should include FC&S clauses, which became the common practice of the London market. The clause endured, subject to revision, until 1982, when it disappeared together with the S.G. Form. The demand for separate marine war risks insurance was met by the London market. In addition some nationalities of shipowners formed mutual associations to offer war risks cover to their members. In the United Kingdom nine associations were known as the London Group of War Risk Associations. Marine war risks insurance covers a wide range of risks, from war and warlike events to terrorist attacks, riots, rebellion, and seizure in times of war. Insurance against war risks are subject to the market "current excluded areas," a list of world areas that are excluded because of a higher risk potential. Owners of ships sailing into such an arena must give prior notice to the insurer, pay an additional premium, and accept special warranties of coverage.

Before World War I the British government realized that private enterprise could not accommodate sufficient marine insurance in time of an extensive war. In cooperation with the London Group, the problem was solved. The group insured "King's Enemy Risks," whereas the government gave them 80 percent reinsurance cover. Loss or damage suffered by merchant ships in both world wars was paid for by this arrangement, primarily by the London Group, which was reinsured by the British government. Since World War II the scheme has been effective on three occasions, the Korean War (1950–1953), the Anglo-French invasion of Egypt (1956), and the Falklands War (1982).

BIBLIOGRAPHY

Andersen, Håkon With, and John Peter Collett. *Anchor and Balance: Det norske Veritas 1864–1989*. Oslo, 1989.

Brækhus, Sjur. *Handbook on P&I Insurance*. 3d ed. Arendal, Norway, 1988.

Buglass, Leslie J. *Marine Insurance and General Average in the United States: An Average Adjuster's Viewpoint*. 3d ed. Centreville, Ala. 1991.

Cockerell, H. A. L., and Edwin Green. *The British Insurance Business: A Guide to Its History and Records*. 2d ed. Sheffield, U.K., 1994.

Dover, Victor. *A Handbook to Marine Insurance*. 8th ed. London, 1975.

Flower, Raymond, and Michael Wynn Jones. *Lloyd's of London: An Illustrated History*. 3d ed. Colchester, U.K., 1991.

Gibb, D. E. W. *Lloyd's of London: A Study in Individualism*. London, 1957.

Hewer, Chris. *A Problem Shared: A History of the Institute of London Underwriters 1884–1984*. London, 1984.

Ivamy, E. R. Hardy. *Marine Insurance*. 4th ed. London, 1985.

Mantle, Jonathan. *For Whom the Bell Tolls: The Lesson of Lloyd's of London*. London, 1992.

Miller, Michael D. *Marine War Risks*. 2d ed. London, 1994.

Raphael, Adam. *Ultimate Risk: The Inside Story of the Lloyd's Catastrophe*. London, 1995.

Templeman, Frederick. *Marine Insurance, Its Principles and Practice*. 6th ed. London, 1986.

Thowsen, Atle. *The Underwriters Follow the Fleet: From Norwegian Underwriters' Agency to Scandinavian Marine Claims Office, Inc., 1897–1997*. Bergen, Norway, and Stamford, Conn., 1998.

Thowsen, Atle. *150 Years of Marine Insurance in Bergen: Bergens Skibsassuranseforening and Its Predecessors*. Bergen, Norway, 2000.

Wright, C., and C. E. Fayle. *A History of Lloyd's*. London, 1928.

ATLE THOWSEN

Fire Insurance

An awareness of fire hazards, the desire to prevent conflagrations, and an attempt to relieve their victims had long predated the emergence of modern fire insurance. Large destructive fires were not the motivators sufficient to induce insurance. Instead, fire insurance required some erosion of fatalistic and superstitious attitudes toward risk and a wide enough social distribution of wealth to enable underwriters to spread their liabilities. These were conditions that by 1700 had been fulfilled in the large cities of northwestern Europe, but not elsewhere. In contrast to the long-established marine insurance, fire insurance also required the underwriting of many small risks, mostly unknown to the insurer, and therefore difficult to value. It required a permanent organization, with a fund to cover abnormal losses in bad years and a staff to collect premiums and settle claims. Thus it required the investment and retention of large capital sums, not the already familiar short-term credit flows that lubricated commodity trade.

Corporate fire insurance took three organizational forms—public, proprietary, and mutual—which came to shape its market structures well into the twentieth century. There was a long "prehistory" of small, local cooperative insurance associations in both Europe and Asia, and many of the first permanent fire offices were also mutual "contributionships." These offices had no share capital and all policyholders were members who participated in the profits. Proprietary offices—based on a joint stock of share capital in which most policyholders had no stake—as well

as public insurance offices emerged almost simultaneously with the larger mutual offices. In 1666, the Great Fire of London, which destroyed thirteen thousand houses, gave rise to all three schemes of insurance, although the joint-stock company later became the preferred form of organization in Britain.

In many parts of Europe, beginning in Hamburg in 1676, many of the earliest fire insurance offices were either municipal- or state-owned, and there was a widespread tendency to make such insurance on buildings compulsory through these offices—while leaving owners and occupiers to insure their own house contents with the private companies. Typically, the public offices did not differentiate premiums by type or by location of risk, and they excluded large and hazardous risks (however their primary purpose was not to protect private property but to generate a secure source of public revenue; they represented a means of guaranteeing the rebuilding of taxable property without this becoming dependent on private charity).

Since the 1830s, compulsory building insurance was gradually abolished in several European states, and the private societies captured an increasing share of the markets. Public offices survived, though in smaller numbers. Belatedly, they adopted risk classifications, which allowed them to compete, for it ended their propensity to raise premium rates on better risks to compensate for losses incurred on more hazardous properties. In addition, nationalist and populist concerns from the 1870s onward—about the profiteering and unethical behavior of private insurers and the sympathy of many governments for a wholesale nationalization of the insurance industry—created a more congenial environment in which public offices could survive.

Having to make their own markets, the private offices were the first to develop assessment procedures. These were sophisticated and accurate enough to make underwriting financially viable and to sell their product widely enough, via extensive networks of agents, so as to spread the risk. In Britain by the 1720s, the basic brick/timber division of insured properties, which had been in use since 1680, was developed into a three-part classification of properties: common, hazardous, and double hazardous, with manufacturing processes rated as "special risks." In Britain, this classification was used into the mid-nineteenth century, and it was also adopted in the United States. The established London fire offices, however, were generally slow to adapt to the challenges posed by the new and complex hazards that were presented by the factories and workshops of the Industrial Revolution. From 1780 to 1820, underwriters learned by bitter experience, incurring horrendous losses on the insurance of textile mills, warehouses, and sugar refineries. Such losses were subsidized by profits made on the much larger business of insuring ordinary residential dwellings, until safety improvements like "fireproof" mills, gas lighting, and enclosed stoves reduced the level of claims on industrial properties.

Elsewhere, benefiting from the British experience, more complex and "scientific" systems of risk assessment were developed quickly. In France by 1850, buildings were classified in three major divisions, according to their construction, contents, occupants, and contiguity to other risks. By the second half of the nineteenth century it was recognized in both Britain and the United States that even such classification could not properly reflect the hazards that were becoming ever more diverse. The propensity, already visible in England in the 1820s—to subdivide risks, place separate values, and charge specific rates on different hazards within one policy—had became standard practice by 1870, helped by the presence of tariff organizations. In Britain, from the 1840s, formal collusion over tariffs in an increasing range of markets kept prices higher than they might have been, while repeated waves of corporate takeovers ensured a high attrition rate among new entrants to the market (elsewhere collusion was hampered by fragmented markets, by the opposition of state authorities, and by the public insurance offices). Everywhere there was a trend to combine, not just for price and product regulation but also for fire protection, for salvage, and for the exchange of risk information.

During the course of the nineteenth century, fire insurance became global. The pioneering exporters were British, beginning with the Phoenix—the fire office of the London sugar refiners—which established more than forty agencies in Europe, the West Indies, and the Americas between 1786 and 1815. From the early 1820s, bilateral and multilateral trade began to develop in the form of reinsurance agreements, initially involving French, German, Belgian, and British offices. After 1850, foreign markets became increasingly congested. For example, in San Francisco, California, there were 163 fire insurance offices by 1886 where there had been just twelve in 1857. The United States emerged not only as the largest insurance market in the world but also as the most crowded. By 1890, there were more than twenty-three hundred fire and marine insurance companies operating there; at any time during the decades before 1914, some one hundred foreign fire insurance companies were represented there, holding an aggregate share of the market as high as 45 percent in California.

Between 1700 and 1920, fire insurance remained the principal form of land-based property insurance, sometimes outstripping, but at other times lagging behind, the growth of industrializing economies (for reasons as yet unknown). Toward the end of the nineteenth century, a rising tide of novel insurance products, covering plate glass to automobiles and loosely collected under the heading accident insurance, encouraged brokers and new companies to specialize in these new branches of insurance. None of these products were developed by the established fire insurance offices, but by 1900 it had become clear that they could not be ignored. The belated response of the fire insurance offices was to move into accident insurance, usually by taking over existing specialists and creating composite insurance offices able to offer several lines of insurance under one roof, often in one policy. By the 1920s, fire insurance was fast disappearing as a distinct line of underwriting, to become fused with other types of property and casualty insurance.

BIBLIOGRAPHY

Cockerell, H. A. L., and Edwin Green. *The British Insurance Business: A Guide to Its History and Records*. 2d ed. Sheffield, 1994. A comprehensive listing of British insurance archives, with an excellent introductory essay on British insurance history.

Dickson, Peter G. M. *The Sun Insurance Office, 1710–1960*. London, 1960. The earliest of the three classic histories of the major British fire insurance foundations of the eighteenth century. The others are by Barry Supple (1970) on Royal Exchange and Clive Trebilcock (1985; 1998) on Phoenix (see below).

Pearson, Robin. "The Development of Reinsurance Markets in Europe during the Nineteenth Century." *Journal of European Economic History* 24.3 (1995), 557–571.

Pearson, Robin. "British and European Insurance Enterprise in American Markets, 1850–1914." *Business and Economic History* 26.2 (1997), 438–451.

Raynes, Harold E. *A History of British Insurance*. London, 1948. A dated but still valuable general history, written by an actuary man; especially strong on legal aspects of the business.

Supple, Barry. *The Royal Exchange Assurance: A History of British Insurance, 1720–1970*. Cambridge, 1970.

Trebilcock, Clive. *Phoenix Assurance and the Development of British Insurance*. vol. 1, *1782–1870*. Cambridge, 1985; vol. 2, *1870–1984*. Cambridge, 1998.

Westall, Oliver M., ed. *The Historian and the Business of Insurance*. Manchester, 1984. Includes essays on provincial insurance in early nineteenth-century England and on the British tariff organization, called the Fire Offices Committee of 1868.

ROBIN PEARSON

Life Insurance

From its beginnings in morally dubious wagers on an individual's mortality, the life insurance industry has expanded to become a central part of economic and business activity in all major economies. By 1983, life-insurance premium payments accounted for an average of 2.95 percent of gross domestic product (GDP) in the Organization for Economic Cooperation and Development (OECD) countries and 4.58 percent by 1998. In the course of this expansion, life insurance companies have been at the forefront of business innovation, developing novel ways of balancing the interests of clients, owners, and managers, and creating new products for sale into an expanding market.

European Origins. Life insurance originated in early-fifteenth-century Mediterranean trade to provide financial protection against the potential loss of slaves from shipwreck or capture. These insurance contracts were indistinguishable from general marine insurance, which indemnified owners for the price of goods and chattels lost at sea. This principle of insurance against financial loss of life was rapidly extended to provide collateral for personal loans—borrowers could take out policies on their own lives and name their creditors as beneficiaries; lenders could secure their loans by insuring the lives of their borrowers. But parties with no financial interest in an individual's life also could take out an insurance contract, which was no more than a wager on how long the individual would live. Not only were these wagers held to be incompatible with Christian ethics, but they also created incentives for unscrupulous beneficiaries to murder or to fake the death of the insured. Public authorities quickly took action to suppress this threat to propriety. In 1435, the Barcelona Ordinances established the first comprehensive code of insurance law, which included a blanket prohibition on life insurance. Similar regulations were adopted in Genoa (1494), the Low Countries (1570), Amsterdam (1598), Sweden (1666), and France (1681). It was not until the 1860s that life insurance made significant advances in European markets.

English Developments. England remained apart from these European restrictions on life insurance for two reasons. First, the precedents existing in Roman Law against treating life as a mere commodity were not sustained in the principles of English Common Law. Second, the application of Newtonian principles of scientific inquiry to all aspects of the natural world in seventeenth-century England encouraged social arithmeticians to seek regularities in the pattern of mortality. The earliest-surviving English life insurance contract dates from 1583 and was a simple twelve-month assurance on the life of one man, the premium for which was 8 percent of the sum assured. But by the early eighteenth century, a number of group-insurance schemes had been developed in which individuals pooled their resources, though there was no explicit calculation of risk or rate of return. "Scientific" life insurance, in which the premium was adjusted to reflect the age and expectation of life of the assured, did not commence until the foundation of the Equitable Assurance Society in 1762. This crucial conceptual innovation by Abraham de Moivre (1667–1754), a Huguenot refugee, drew upon the application of probability theory to the pricing of annuities. Other insurance companies rapidly adopted the principle of age-related premiums, and new companies were established: 8 between 1803 and 1808, 29 between 1815 and 1830, 56 from 1830 to 1844. The names of these life offices—Clergy Mutual (1829), Provident Clerks (1840), Architects and Builders (1847)—indicate that life insurance was being adopted by the expanding middle-class population. By the early 1850s, there were at least 150 life insurance offices in Great Britain with £150 million of insurance in force, annual premium income of £5 million, and investments of more than £50 million, figures which almost doubled by 1870.

International Expansion. By contrast, there were no more than 44 life insurance offices in the whole of continental Europe in 1852. In the United States, early-nineteenth-century attempts to launch life insurance companies met with little success, but the next three decades witnessed rapid growth. The number of companies rose from 18 in 1840 to 52 in 1851 and 135 in 1870; annual premium income rose from less than $1 million in 1845 to $4 million in 1851 and $107 million in 1870. In the last third of the nineteenth century there was considerable merger activity and business consolidation in both the U.S. and British markets, so that by 1900, 83 U.S. and 85 British life insurance companies remained active. At this date, accumulated assets stood at $1.8 billion in the United States and £246 million in the United Kingdom, and annual premium income represented 2.9 percent of U.S. and 1.5 percent of U.K. national income, figures which rose to 3.5 and 3.7 percent respectively by 1983.

British life insurance offices rapidly established agencies throughout the British Empire—for instance, in Australia in 1824 and in Canada in 1833—and their example was copied by domestic companies. These in turn looked for foreign expansion, with Canadian companies being particularly successful, gaining more than 40 percent of their business from outside of Canada by 1938. In Europe, life insurance developed slowly in the early twentieth century and was adversely affected by inflation and currency instability in many countries through to the 1950s. In Japan, the first life assurance company was established in 1887, but it was not until the 1950s that rapid growth occurred, with life insurance being a preferred form of popular saving. By 1990, Japan, with 6.38 percent of GDP devoted to the payment of life insurance premiums, was the most densely insured country in the world.

Business Organization. The paucity of mortality data until the 1860s prevented the early "scientific" life assurers from setting accurate premium levels. Most erred on the side of caution by setting high premiums, and they rapidly accumulated capital funds greater than their actuarial liabilities. Some of these companies were mutuals—that is, they were owned by the policyholders, who regularly distributed surplus funds to themselves. But in stock companies owned by shareholders, policyholders had no entitlement to surplus capital, and shareholders had an incentive to extract excessive premiums from policyholders. Henry Hansmann (1996) has argued that the inability of stock companies to make credible promises that they would not exploit policyholders accounts for the dominance of the mutual form in U.S. life assurance in the mid-nineteenth century. By the early twentieth century, the picture is less clear: In the United States, in the period from 1900 to 1936, 15 stock life insurance companies converted to mutuals, but 17 mutuals converted to stock companies. By this time, legislation to protect policyholders' interests made the organizational form less critical. In the United Kingdom, mutual and stock companies coexisted throughout the nineteenth century. But in order to compete, the stock companies paid bonuses from accumulated funds to "with-profits" policyholders. As early as 1826, two-thirds of stock insurance companies in the United Kingdom were paying bonuses, and by the 1890s many were distributing 90 percent of their profit to policyholders.

Product Innovation. Early policies provided life insurance for a fixed period, usually between one and seven years; these were known as "term insurance" policies. The Equitable pioneered the sale of "whole-life" policies, which provided insurance cover until death, and by the 1850s these dominated a market in which middle-class males wished to make financial provision for dependants in the event of their death. The late-nineteenth-century growth of life insurance depended on two key product innovations. First, in 1854 the Prudential Assurance Company in London initiated "industrial life assurance" in which low-cost policies were sold to manual workers and their families by means of small weekly payments collected door-to-door by itinerant insurance agents. The policies covered little more than funeral expenses, and more than 40 percent of contributions were expended in the cost of collection, but these policies proved to be extremely popular. By 1913, more than half of the U.K. population was covered by industrial assurance. By 1920, it was more than three-quarters. The use of collecting agents made the industrial assurance companies large-scale employers: In 1929 the Prudential, with seventeen thousand workers, was larger than most manufacturing companies and was bigger than any U.K. bank.

Second, insurance policies became popular savings devices with the development of the endowment assurance. With these policies, the sum assured was paid out at a fixed date in the future or on death if sooner. (In the United States similar results were achieved through the sale of tontine policies, in which flat-rate benefits were paid on early death, but accumulated dividends were distributed to all surviving policyholders at a fixed future date.) When endowment assurances were sold "with profits," the insurance policy effectively became a long-term saving instrument, with policyholders assigning the management of their assets to the insurance company. In Great Britain in 1890, endowments accounted for about 19 percent of insurance policies, but 62 percent by 1913. In the 1920s and

1930s, insurance companies combined their expertise in insurance and investment by developing group pension policies that they sold to employers. In the 1970s and 1980s, further expansion came through the use of endowment assurances to pay off long-term mortgage loans. Product innovation underpinned continual growth, but the sale of increasingly complex financial instruments made the business more risky, as shown by the collapse in 2000 of the world's first "scientific" mutual insurer, the Equitable, because of losses from a gamble on long-term annuity rates.

BIBLIOGRAPHY

Clark, Geoffrey. *Betting on Lives: The Culture of Life Insurance in England, 1695–1775*. Manchester, 1999.

Cockerell, H. A. L., and Edwin Green. *The British Insurance Business: A Guide to Its History and Records*. Sheffield, 1994.

Dennett, Laurie. *A Sense of Security: 150 Years of the Prudential*. Cambridge, 1998.

Hansmann, Henry. *The Ownership of Enterprise*. Cambridge, Mass., 1996.

Organisation for Economic Cooperation and Development. *Insurance Statistics Yearbook*. Paris, 1993–.

Pritchett, B. Michael. *Financing Growth: A Financial History of American Life Insurance through 1900*. Philadelphia, 1985.

Supple, Barry. *The Royal Exchange Assurance: A History of British Insurance, 1720–1970*. Cambridge, 1970.

Swiss Reinsurance Company. *Insurance Markets of the World*. Zurich, 1964.

Zelizer, Viviana. *Morals and Markets: The Development of Life Insurance in the United States*. New York, 1979.

PAUL JOHNSON

Health and Accident Insurance

State-sponsored health insurance has been aimed at extending medical treatment from a privilege of the rich to a social right—first for industrial employees and eventually for all citizens. Numerous controversies exist concerning issues of cost and appropriate structures for delivery. New medical technologies are expensive; medical professionals desire to charge fees commensurate with specialist skills; and insurance provision reputedly fosters moral hazard (collusion between patient and doctor in the provision of expensive treatments unnecessary to the improvement of a medical condition). As with unemployment insurance, a fundamental difficulty exists in defining the risk insured; initially indicative of a physical inability to work, definitions of sickness under health insurance may now embrace any condition that indicates less than perfect health. Consequently, in periods of rising demand (in Europe, notably the economic recessions of the 1930s and 1980s), arguments raged about how incapacity for work should be defined. A minor physical ailment may become transformed into a major medical complaint when a job seeker discovers that chances of work are ruined repeatedly because of it; the tighter the labor market, the more careful employers become about an applicant's state of health. In countries without universal health insurance, coverage has been made available through private policies paid by individuals, employers, or jointly by both.

Accident insurance, guaranteeing employers' compensation to workers injured in the course of their work, has been less central to the domain of public policy; in consequence, few historians have studied its operation. In many European countries before World War I, legislation guaranteed compensation for workers injured or diseased as a result of industrial employment. Only Germany and Austria-Hungary required employers to insure collectively against the risk; elsewhere, commercial insurance companies, mutual insurance associations, and other private agencies offered voluntary coverage for firms that took this option. As a result, in many European countries, private accident-insurance and public health-insurance systems provided help for sick workers, in accordance with the way the cause of the malady was understood.

Nineteenth-Century Debates. Historical studies on the emergence of working-class movements and on the origins of welfare states have fostered interest in the growth of mutual-aid societies among the urban poor, particularly since the nineteenth century. Although not insurance institutions (where actuarial calculation determined both rates of contribution and claimants' benefit rights), these mutual aid organizations are commonly viewed as forming the foundations of later health-insurance programs. The pooling of risk was attractive to households that could neither withstand prolonged loss of earnings nor afford medical fees. There was a variety of forms: some employers ran mutual-aid societies for their workers, others were run by local authorities, by ethnic groups, religious foundations, or by local physicians (to extend their practice and income). Some of the European societies dated back to medieval artisan and trade guilds, which protected their own members. Some were organized in accordance with religious or political conviction. Questions of health were not their sole concern—most also offered help to widows and orphans, and almost all organized feast days and collective conviviality (a tendency that public authorities later tried to discourage as counterproductive to the financial probity needed in efficient insurance practice). Such voluntary mutual-aid groups existed worldwide by the late nineteenth century: in Eurasia, Latin America, Australasia, Canada, and the United States.

In Europe, the introduction of the first state-sponsored schemes of compulsory insurance against ill health and accidents is commonly credited to Otto von Bismarck, chancellor of Imperial Germany from 1871 to 1890, under legislation passed in 1881 and 1883. First, in 1881, industrial employers were required to subscribe to professional organizations that insured their obligations against the consequences of accidents at work (underwriting earlier legislation on workmen's compensation). Second, in 1883, workers and their employers were required to subscribe to sickness funds, based on firms, professional organizations, mutual-aid societies, or local associations; these were run by elected representatives of employers and employed (two-thirds employee, one-third employer). The contributions and the benefits were income-related, a characteristic that was widely included in later European health-insurance schemes. Bismarck's ideas drew on Prussian precedent; in the 1850s, compulsory health and accident insurance was extended first to coal miners, later to all factory workers. The German example was imitated in Austria-Hungary, by compulsory accident insurance in 1887 and compulsory health insurance in 1888; the farm and forestry workers were excluded, and so the acts of Austria-Hungary covered a smaller proportion of the working population than in Germany.

In Britain, the earliest such legislation dates from 1793; it legitimized "friendly societies," by distinguishing them from associations of possible insurrectionary intent (after the French Revolution), through the registration of their rules and the protection of their funds. Britain's creation of a punitive poor law in 1834 helped membership in the societies and, with new friendly society legislation in 1875, the government promoted insurance principles and the introduction of actuarial science in the administration of benefits (mostly associated with health). By 1900, membership in friendly societies was 4.5 million—roughly 50 percent of the male employed workforce. Compulsion and state subsidies were introduced under the National Insurance Act of 1911, which allowed friendly societies, industrial insurance companies, and trade unions to register as administrative agencies under the state scheme.

In France, health protection followed a different pattern. With the French Revolution of 1789 came the Le Chapelier Law of 1791, which outlawed all collective organizations standing between the individual and the state, abolished the old guilds, and placed mutual-aid societies on a dubious legal footing. At the foundation of the Second Empire in 1852, Napoleon III secured mutuality by offering public subsidies to societies (*mutuelles*) recognized by the regime; governed by imperial appointees and dominated by the Roman Catholic church, for subscribing members such societies combined charity with insurance. French mutuality spread, with increasing focus on sickness and its consequences (helping widows and orphans). Through reliance on gifts, legacies, and subscriptions, the *mutuelles* were not insurance societies. Their reform in 1898 by France's Third Republic broadened their scope and democratized their governance, but (the hated Germanic) insurance was repudiated in favor of republican principles of solidarity.

Before World War I, supports for voluntary health insurance by public recognition and subsidy were also found in Belgium and Sweden. Denmark confined public subsidies to poor working-class subscribers. The protection of workers against the consequences of industrial accidents was also covered by the extension of workmen's compensation legislation in Denmark (1897), as well as in Britain (1896), France (1898), Italy (1898), and Sweden (1901). Protection proved less comprehensive in those countries than in Imperial Germany or Austria-Hungary; workers had to prove an employer's liability before being able to claim compensation (and some small employers were unable to pay). Legislation encouraged employers to insure themselves privately against future liability, extending private commercial and mutual financial-service interests in the issue. The subsequent altercations between sickness societies and private insurers, concerning the origins of specific medical conditions, encouraged an extension of employers' liability from accidents to industrial diseases.

In explaining why European governments took an interest in extending insurance against sickness and industrial accident in the late 1800s and early 1900s, historians have stressed the threat posed by the industrial working class to established conservative political elites, who tried to secure popular support by introducing "social welfare." Such explanations emphasize the counterrevolutionary politics of Napoleon III (at the demise of France's Second Republic) and Bismarck (who outlawed the German Social Democrats and the free trade unions at the time of his insurance initiatives). Others, anticipating Scandinavia's reputation as a paradigm welfare state, point to social democracy as a primary influence in the development of health insurance. The issue should be rebalanced: if social democracy was of such paramount importance, why did not the United States, or Canada, or Australia (all more democratic nations than Imperial Germany) embrace health-insurance programs at that time? It makes more sense to understand the early birth of state-sponsored health and accident insurance as the broader consequence of industrialization and urbanization, which from the start of the Industrial Revolution generated disease and raised levels of social displacement and dependency. Traditional systems of relief could not cope with these social burdens, so enthusiasm for the fruits of industrial progress made it necessary to address its costs. The various health and accident insurance programs, schemes, and plans evolved through that process.

Twentieth-Century Extensions. By the mid-twentieth century, state-sponsored health insurance was consolidated and extended to entire populations of many European countries. The transfer of Alsace-Lorraine from Germany to France at the end of World War I allowed the French government to witness the advantages of compulsory insurance. After prolonged debate, contributory health insurance was introduced in 1930 for all French industrial workers. Following the 1941 German invasion of the Netherlands, the Dutch voluntary system, first ratified in 1930, was also transformed into compulsory insurance. In the aftermath of World War II, universal compulsory health insurance was also put in place in Sweden, France, Italy, and Belgium as part of the overall reform of post-war social security. Most systems were still administered by registered societies that were ordered by profession, by locality, by employing firm, or by religious or political affiliation. In Nazi Germany in the 1930s, health insurance had been centralized and politicized; after losing the war, Bismarck's scheme was revived by West German chancellor, Konrad Adenauer and his Christian Democrat government.

Most European health-insurance systems initially excluded rural workers and the self-employed—groups to whom social security was gradually extended in the post-war decades. In Sweden in 1953, state subsidies permitted the inclusion of the rural poor under health insurance reform; there, the subsequent growth of locally organized health and social services for all citizens confined health insurance to the provision of sickness benefits (albeit one that remained income-related, as in most European states). The only European country to abolish its prewar health-insurance scheme was Britain; there, the popularity of the wartime Emergency Medical Service stimulated support for a state-owned National Health Service, introduced in 1948, and initially free for all citizens. Its advent and the administrative unification of all social insurance under the National Insurance Act of 1946 required the abolition of the National Health Insurance Scheme of 1911 and its associated "approved" societies.

In general, state-sponsored health insurance proved popular and successful in Europe, but that was not so true elsewhere. In New Zealand, health insurance had been repudiated and, in 1938, the world's first state-funded national-health service was established. In Australia, the adoption of British health (and unemployment) insurance was discussed in 1937 and 1938; there, trade-union opposition to contributions, constitutional queries over the federal government's powers to introduce the measure, the opposition of the medical profession, and the difficulties of defining employer and employee in a predominantly rural economy combined to defeat the initiative. Australia's federal government and its powers were extended during World War II, and payments to the sick were introduced on a tax-funded basis. After the war, Australia's Labour government lost power in 1948 after its failure to introduce an Australian National Health Service along British lines. With the election of the new administration in 1949, federally sponsored health insurance was introduced instead—a measure more acceptable to the powerful Australian Medical Association than the proposed health service had been.

Opposition to government sponsorship of universal national health insurance or socialized medicine has proved permanent in the United States (although Medicare and Medicaid were provided to low-income people and the elderly or disabled, respectively, by a 1965 amendment to the Social Security Act of 1935). The situation has been repeatedly complicated by constitutional constraints on federal intervention in an area considered to be the province of the states. In the nineteenth-century, United States, much as in Europe, some health protection had spread under the auspices of mutual-aid societies that continued to flourish in the 1920s and 1930s. Attempts by several of the states to introduce health insurance had failed between 1915 and 1920. The cautious support of the then newly emerging American Medical Association eventually became transformed into permanent marked hostility from a powerful medical lobby. The New Deal of the F. D. Roosevelt administration managed to pass the U.S. Social Security Act in 1935, but it was not for health insurance. During the Great Depression, as mutual-aid organizations faded, the introduction of tax concessions for employers' health contributions fostered commercial insurance packages for employees. Such arrangements were strengthened during the war years from 1941 to 1946, when wages were frozen by government fiat but fringe benefits were not. After the war, new congressional legislation (the Taft-Hartley Act of 1947) brought conditions of employment into the sphere of collective bargaining; in 1949, the U.S. Supreme Court ruled that this included all employee benefits. Thus commercial health insurance became part of industrial bargaining.

The 1947 attempt by U.S. President Harry S. Truman to introduce federally sponsored health insurance was defeated by Congress. As the Cold War commenced and developed, socialized medicine was depicted as a communist conspiracy, inimical to democratic freedoms and the American way of life. The link between industrial relations and health protection was thereby sustained. In the 1960s, legislation introduced by President Lyndon B. Johnson was passed by Congress, introducing the above-mentioned Medicare and Medicaid programs. The rising costs of U.S. medical insurance stimulated new legislation in the 1970s, to establish health maintenance organizations (HMOs); subject to state regulations, they seek to guarantee quality health care for anyone at reasonable cost and maybe billing individual plans or group, employer, or employee plans. The result is an overall system of U.S. health care that may be complex, confusing, or expensive.

Evaluation and Reform. In the late twentieth century, the rising costs of health care (the consequence of rising

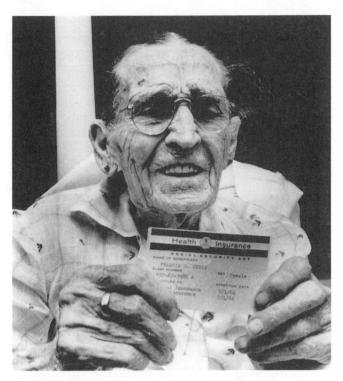

HEALTH INSURANCE. One-hundred-year-old Francis Perry with her Medicare card, 1 July 1966, the day that the health insurance plan went into operation, Dallas, Texas. (UPI Telephoto/Prints and Photographs Division, Library of Congress)

demand, aging populations, new medical technologies and treatments and, indirectly, of economic recession) have forced many governments to curtail health coverage or reduce demand. For example, in Germany, some "inessential" treatments have been excluded from state-sponsored health insurance; in France, the central government has taken direct control of hospital budgets and imposed restrictions on physicians' freedom of action. In many European countries, the issue of medical (particularly specialist) fees has come under scrutiny, and the extension of private health insurance to supplement public schemes is openly discussed.

Comparisons of performance of the various schemes depend on the values involved. State-run health services, as in Britain and Sweden, are seen as both more equitable and redistributive; however, such schemes allow state doctors to secure the advantages of monopoly providers, since there is no competition to promote service efficiency or quality of care, hence no guarantee of value for money spent by the state. Although the British system is frequently cited as one of the cheapest forms of health provision in the world, British health insurance in the interwar years held the same record (this indicates something about British willingness to pay for health rather than an inherent superiority of socialized medicine over a health-insurance scheme).

State-sponsored health insurance has offered the advantages of democratic choice and universal coverage. Although criticized as less redistributive (and offering fewer controls over possible moral hazard), French health insurance was vindicated as the best scheme of health care in the world by a World Health Organization report in 2000, in terms of patient choice, quality of care, and cost effectiveness. The private systems in the United States may provide the most sophisticated medical treatments to those with the money or the right policy, but they are widely criticized for overall expense and for only partial coverage, a disadvantage to the poor. Private health-care markets cannot guarantee equity or efficiency in the provision of a public good.

[*See also* Health Industry *and* Income Maintenance, *subentry on* Social Insurance.]

BIBLIOGRAPHY

Baldwin, Peter. *The Politics of Social Solidarity: Class Bases of the European Welfare State, 1875–1975*. Cambridge, 1990. Includes a detailed examination of the political factors underpinning the introduction and development of health (and accident) insurance schemes in Denmark, Sweden, Germany, and France.

Bouget, Denis. "The Juppe Plan and French Social Welfare." *Journal of European Social Policy* 8.2 (1998), 155–173. A summary of the principles of French social security since 1945, the problems encountered by the health-insurance scheme, and the measures adopted in the mid-1990s to correct the situation.

Flora, Peter, and Arnold J. Heidenheimer, eds. *The Development of Welfare States in Europe and America*. New Brunswick, N.J., 1990. Chapter 2 offers an overview of the main legislative developments in health and accident insurance in western Europe; chapter 3 examines North Amercia.

Gillespie, James. *The Price of Health*. Cambridge, 1991. A history of medical politics in Australia.

Hennock, E. P. *British Social Reform and German Precedents: The case of Social Insurance, 1880–1914*. Oxford, 1987. Contains the best description of the development of accident insurance in the two countries for that period.

Immergut, Ellen, M. *Health Politics, Interests and Institutions in Western Europe*. New York, 1992. An account of post–World War II developments.

Kohler, Peter A., and Hans F. Zacher, eds. *The Evolution of Social Insurance, 1881–1981: Studies of Germany, France, Great Britain, Austria and Switzerland*. London, 1982. A country-by-country account —now slightly outdated.

Ritter, Gerhard. *Social Welfare in Germany and Britain*. New York, 1986. A comparison of welfare reforms in the two countries before World War I.

Skocpol, Theda. *The Time Is Never Ripe: The Repeated Defeat of Universal Health Insurance in the Twentieth Century United States*. Dublin, 1995. A review of U.S. debates that were provoked by the William J. Clinton administration to introduce reform.

Steinmetz, George. *Regulating the Social: The Welfare State and Local Politics in Imperial Germany*. Princeton, 1993. Less on the motives behind Bismarck's innovative legislation than on the way health insurance worked there in practice: a detailed and important study.

Van der Linden, Marcel, ed. *Social Security Mutualism: The Comparative History of Mutual Benefit Societies*. Berne, Switzerland, 1996. A wideranging review of the role played by mutual-benefit societies in the development of health insurance since the mid-nineteenth century.

Weindling, Paul. *Health, Race and German Politics between National Unification and Nazism, 1870–1945*. Cambridge, 1989. Includes material on German health insurance and the debates over medical salaries.

Whiteside, Noel. "Private Provision and Public Welfare: Health Insurance between the Wars." In *Before Beveridge: Welfare before the Welfare State*, edited by David Gladstone. London, 1999. A review of the performance of British National Health Insurance before its abolition in 1946.

NOEL WHITESIDE

Unemployment Insurance

The concept and practice of providing unemployment insurance generates problems: how to identify (and protect) the genuine out-of-work claimant without fostering idleness ("benefit induced" or "voluntary" unemployment); how to fund unemployment benefits without raising labor costs and/or encouraging employers to discharge workers. Such benefits may then permit the recipients to prolong the search for a better job, this sustains high wages and may create unemployment. Unemployment insurance schemes seek to eliminate these socioeconomic risks, through regulations that distinguish the idle from the involuntarily unemployed. During economic recessions, the numbers of claimants to an unemployment fund rise as contributory income falls; the regulations then become stringently applied and politically contentious, since governments are forced to provide tax-funded subsidies to sustain the established schemes. Unemployment insurance operates most effectively in the context of full employment; some countries (e.g. Sweden, Finland, Denmark) have given greater priority to sustaining employment than to developing universal, compulsory unemployment insurance as such.

A key difficulty for providing unemployment insurance lies in defining the risk against which it is offered. At the end of the nineteenth century—when unemployment insurance was first discussed—waged work varied according to trade, season, region, and country. The ways in which unemployment was politically apprehended as a problem invariably influenced the nature of insurance (and other) schemes designed to cope with its consequences; these tried to distinguish the unemployed from the mass of indigent poor. When there were layoffs, unemployment benefits offered the means for regular workers to sustain their independence and their labor market status. (The moral element underpinning that, with its overtones of Taylorism and its prescriptive views on regular employment, can be missed by those today who take unemployment as a given and ignore the ways that sociopolitical factors shape access to benefits. This is most evident in the treatment accorded female claimants; historically, a woman's right to unemployment benefits has been circumscribed in many countries, reflecting less her previous employment record—although domestic work or part-time employment have commonly been excluded from unemployment insurance—than her marital status and family responsibilities.) Unemployment insurance is as responsive to social convention and political convenience as it is to actuarial principle. In many European countries, its close relationship to prevailing forms of employment has fostered the involvement of labor representatives in its administration, to help identify genuine claimants from the rest.

Nineteenth-Century Developments. The terms *unemployment* and the *unemployed* entered the English language in the late nineteenth century, although destitution from want of employment was already widely recognized. In Britain, poor relief (locally funded support developed from earlier church practices) had only been available under semi-punitive conditions following the reform of the Poor Laws in 1834. In reaction, some British skilled workers in shipbuilding, metalworking, engineering, construction, and artisanal trades had developed mutual protection schemes against job loss from sickness, bad trade, or industrial dispute. Early British trade unions offered benefits to members out of work or for refusing to work for an employer who ignored established trade practices. This blurred distinctions between industrial dispute and unemployment and subsequently became a source of contention under state-sponsored schemes. This method of protecting the trade had sustained both wages and union organization; the member in breach of union rules or in arrears lost benefit rights, whose level tended to rise with length of membership. To maintain the dues that sustained those schemes, high wages were essential; the employers were paying for the collective protection of skilled workers under union schemes that had integrated wage bargaining with a form of unemployment insurance. While emigrant members from Britain exported those schemes to Australia, Canada, and the United States, coverage in Britain remained limited. By 1908, British unemployment benefits were available to a minority of workers (1.8 million): the unions organizing textile workers or coal miners, for example, coped with slack trade by negotiating with their employers work-sharing schemes (short-time working and/or split-shift systems).

In Europe, artisan societies—mainly print and typographical trades—then offered unemployment protection; travel funds, which had been used to make the unemployed member search for work, were transformed into unemployment benefits by the late 1800s. In Germany and Sweden, that practice spread to the growing metalworking unions in the industrial districts, where the lack of an alternative to charity, or poor relief, reinforced the attrac-

tions of union membership. In general, such protection was considered desirable, not least by local authorities seeking to minimize local liability during slack periods. The early official initiatives promoting unemployment insurance took the form of municipal subsidies to trade-union funds. Pioneered by the Belgian cities of Liège and Ghent in 1897 and 1900, respectively, subsidies raised levels of voluntary insurance; in Ghent, municipal savings funds supplemented trade-union cover for those few who refused trade-union membership. The idea of municipal subsidies soon spread to cities in Germany, France, Northern Italy, Switzerland, Norway, and Denmark, as well as within Belgium and the Netherlands; before 1914, municipal subsidies were supplemented by national grants in France, Belgium, Denmark, and Norway. The numbers involved remained small; even in Belgium, where the voluntary schemes were the most widespread, fewer than thirty thousand workers were covered by 1912. Belgium's Ghent system was criticized for subsidizing skilled workers who possessed resources to protect themselves—arguably those workers least in need of help. The early efforts in Europe to extend protection through compulsory membership were unsuccessful. The Swiss canton of Saint Gall had tried in 1893 but the scheme collapsed, undermined by high claims from building laborers in winter and in the face of opposition from permanent workers, who resented their contributions going to subsidize irregular employees in the casual trades.

Britain alone introduced a national, compulsory unemployment insurance scheme before 1914. Focused on London's highly casual labor market, government policy aimed to promote economic efficiency and reduce the reliance on poor relief, by balancing labor supply and demand. Public labor exchanges were established to send job seekers to registered vacancies, to classify those looking for work, and to distinguish those who (for reasons of age or illness) could not work regularly from the rest. Exchanges were to exclude the idle and the incapable from the labor market, in order to help the genuinely unemployed, who were those workers with a past record of regular employment unable to secure a new job. In Britain, compulsory contributory unemployment insurance—funded by employers, workers, and the state—was introduced for five trades under Part 2 of the 1911 National Insurance Act. The act also reinforced new classifications, by admitting claims for a limited period and only from those with a record of regular contributions. For the first time, the "morality of mathematics" (in government minister Winston Churchill's words) offered actuarial soundness and a national identity for Britain's unemployed.

Even so, the policy was never implemented as originally intended, since it lacked support outside government circles. Employers and workers hated paying contributions

EMPLOYMENT EXCHANGE. Bishop Street, Derry, Ireland, early 1900s. (Magee Community Collection/University of Ulster)

and resented state intervention in labor market operations. During World War I (1914–1918), a strong union movement repudiated in 1916 the extension of unemployment insurance to war workers. After the war, in 1920, unemployment insurance was extended to the entire industrial workforce, but political pressures during the interwar recession led to a series of postwar legislative amendments. Britain's unemployment fund soon fell into deficit as benefit rights were extended to claimants without the required contributions. As a result, the label "unemployed" was extended to long-term cases, and insurance benefits were transformed into a tax-funded "dole." Official discretion identified the "genuine" claims as insurance principles were abandoned.

Widespread industrial dislocation both during and after World War I changed western European state attitudes toward voluntary unemployment insurance; during the 1920s, central subsidies assumed great significance. The International Labour Office (ILO), created by the League of Nations in 1919, extolled the virtues of the British scheme and promoted its adoption elsewhere. Imitators remained few: under the Fascist government of Benito Mussolini, Italy introduced compulsory unemployment insurance for industrial workers in 1920; Germany's Weimar Republic created a dual-funded scheme in 1927. Elsewhere in Europe, unemployment insurance policy was confined to the subsidizing of voluntary schemes along established lines.

The Great Depression. Mass unemployment after the 1929 stock-market crash and the subsequent collapse of world trade resulted in new policies for the unemployed in most Western industrialized countries. The extension of unemployment relief and job-creation programs demonstrated that governments and the public were perceiving the unemployed as victims of circumstances beyond individual control. In the United States, unemployment reached unprecedented proportions during the 1930s, complicated by a drought and the dustbowl conditions prevailing in the farm belt of the Midwest and the South. With the exception of a few company plans and trade-union benefit schemes, no protection existed for the unemployed. European-style contributory insurance had been discussed by a number of the states since World War I, but progress was impeded by opposition from U.S. labor unions and fears that the contributory burden might provoke industrial relocations. The first statewide unemployment insurance plan was Wisconsin's in 1932, which bore little resemblance to its European counterparts; it relied on employers' contributions to fund workers' benefits. Following the 1933 inauguration of President Franklin D. Roosevelt, the U.S. government adopted a more interventionist stance; the Social Security Act of 1935 introduced compulsory unemployment insurance for the forty-eight states. Constitutional constraints required each state to introduce its own plan. In addition, a federal tax on businesses with more than ten employees was offset by their contributions to state-run unemployment funds. Since the form and nature of unemployment protection was left to the state legislatures, uneven provisions resulted within the United States as a whole; some of the states provided more comprehensive benefits than other states.

In Europe, the worldwide depression resulted in crisis for voluntary and for compulsory schemes; neither had the resources to cope with soaring costs. Major firms were forced to rationalize employment and its distribution. Labor management was based on delimited job descriptions, defined in terms of both time and space; the underemployment that was characteristic of artisanal work practices was diminished—hence the unemployed became more visible, more identifiable—and systems of national relief reflected those changes. Under the Ghent system in Belgium, Denmark, France, and Holland, state subsidies became essential to the viability of any unemployment insurance scheme; most collapsed, and the rest became subject to stricter central control. Constraints on state budgets and criticism of the adverse effects of generous protection provoked benefit cuts, notably on women's claims. Compulsory systems fared little better. In Italy, the Fascist government centralized compulsory provincial schemes in 1933: workers who were not members of Fascist party trade unions and without any record of regular work lost all protection. In Germany, the crisis was met by the final governments of the Weimar Republic, which raised subsidies but cut benefits, pushing increasing numbers onto local relief rolls. After Adolf Hitler's election in 1933 as German chancellor, solutions to Germany's high unemployment (involving compulsory wage cuts, the removal of women and Jews from the labor market, and other targeted labor controls) assumed high priority. State-directed industrial reconstruction and rearmament allowed the German unemployment fund to recover its solvency; and later, its reserves funded public works and the Nazi urban projects (beloved of Albert Speer). In Britain, unemployment benefit levels were also cut, and a household means test was introduced for long-term claimants; this interrogation of personal circumstances (reminiscent of Britain's hated poor law) stimulated hunger marches and provided the support for the Beveridge Report (1942), which promised to abolish means tests.

In much of postwar Europe, the experience of the 1930s stimulated popular support for universal, comprehensive unemployment insurance as a central component of social security; yet that reaction was not universal. In Australia, hardships provoked by the Great Depression (the Slump) did not stimulate the introduction of unemployment insurance as such. In the 1930s, unemployed Australians with families eked out an existence on local relief, while many jobless received nothing and, in effect, disappeared from official view. When Australian unemployment benefits were introduced in 1944, they were means-tested and funded by general taxation, not by the contributions that had long been opposed by trade unions and the Labour

Party. In Sweden in 1934, after the election of the Social Democrats, innovative full employment policies were complemented by state-subsidized, voluntary unemployment insurance, administered by trade unions. In France, postwar social-security legislation did not include unemployment insurance; that was created by collective agreement between employers and unions in 1958 and is centrally administered by representatives of the social partners (UNEDIC). Behind apparently uniform shifts toward centralized state provision of benefits, the meaning and nature of unemployment insurance remained highly varied. The differing sociopolitical contexts continued to shape claimants' rights in a variety of ways.

Aftermath. After World War II, social security in Western Europe was reconstructed and reformed; during the 1950s and 1960s, earnings-related unemployment insurance was extended to cover not just members of the industrial workforce, but also white-collar workers, the self-employed, and agricultural sectors. By the 1970s, continental European schemes offered generous unemployment benefits, adjusted to family size and previous earnings. Representatives of employers and insured were commonly involved in administration of the schemes; the principles of social insurance attached benefit rights to previous contributions. Once benefit was exhausted, claimants resorted to social assistance (welfare) which entailed a considerable drop in income. In Scandinavia (except Norway), membership of trade-union run unemployment insurance schemes remained voluntary—although coverage was high as elsewhere. By contrast, Britain retained flat-rate, subsistence-level unemployment benefits. Although these were adjusted sporadically, the poorest claimants had to "top up" on means-tested National Assistance (welfare). Unlike other Western European states, British unemployment insurance did not involve representatives of the social partners, but relied on central state bureaucracy. This facilitated government control over the scheme. Although benefit rates were raised during the 1960s, it was relatively easy to cut them in ensuing years.

In the 1950s and 1960s, strong economic growth in Western Europe generated labor shortage not labor surplus; joblessness virtually disappeared. Faith in the ability of governments to sustain full employment (which reached its apotheosis in the Communist block countries of the Soviet Union and Eastern Europe) meant that unemployment insurance was no longer as politically important as it had once been. This changed as high levels of unemployment re-emerged in the closing decades of the twentieth century; and the costs of social dependency rose. The operation of unemployment insurance became confused as state subsidies were introduced to help jobless labor market entrants (who lacked contributions), to support training schemes or to help older workers into early retirement.

An increased reliance on tax funding and the resulting explosion of state expenditure caused some governments to reappraise the existing terms of access and levels of support in order to contain the impact of unemployment benefits on the public purse.

This reappraisal was most evident in Anglo-Saxon countries, particularly Britain, where rights to unemployment benefits based on contributions alone were repeatedly revised in the 1980s and disappeared in 1995. In open imitation of strategies pursued in the United States designed to cut welfare roles, emphasis was placed on how unemployment benefits sustained wage levels that were no longer commensurate with economic competitiveness. In the 1970s and 1980s, neo-liberal economists questioned the effects of welfare support on the unemployed: benefit payments seemed adversely to affect job search, worker mobility, labor costs and industrial relocations. According to this perspective, rising levels of long-term unemployment in the countries of continental Europe were due to high wages, labor overheads, and unemployment benefits; these discouraged investment and undermined recovery, while they divided the workforce into the securely employed and the socially excluded. In the 1990s, comparisons of unemployment rates in Europe and the United States demonstrated how limited welfare provision, flexible employment and low labor overheads fostered low U.S. unemployment, while in Europe's regulated labor markets the opposite conditions pertained and unemployment remained high.

This neo-liberal critique has not gone unchallenged; some researchers stress that institutions like social insurance sustain employment relations and foster economic prosperity by reinforcing consensus building and mutual trust. Although the risk of moral hazard has evidently exercised an important influence on unemployment policies in the United States, Australasia, and Britain, it has had far less impact in continental Europe, where levels of unemployment benefits have only been marginally curtailed since the 1980s. Within the European Union, opinion has nonetheless shifted towards a more neo-liberal point of view. Following the Luxembourg Agreement (1997) and the Amsterdam Treaty (1998), member states agreed to promote more flexible employment and higher rates of labor market participation by introducing National Action Plans for Employment. This new strategy partly reflects the influence of American 'workfare' programmes, pioneered in the 1990s to reduce social dependency (although, in Europe, as much emphasis is given to raising female labor market participation rates as to the reintegration of unemployment benefit claimants). By 2001, the previous almost unprecedented unemployment rates had started to fall in many Western European states. The possible moral hazards of unemployment insurance continue to command extensive attention and the debate between opposing opinions may never fully be resolved.

[*See also* Income Maintenance, *subentry on* Social Insurance.]

BIBLIOGRAPHY

Atkinson, A. B., and John Micklewright. "Unemployment Compensation and Labor Market Transitions: A Critical Review." *Journal of Economic Literature* 29.4 (1991), 1679–1727. A rebuttal of the argument that unemployment benefits cause unemployment.

Benjamin, D. K., and L. A. Kochin. "Searching for an Explanation of Unemployment in Interwar Britain." *Journal of Political Economy* 87 (1979). The article opening historical debates on moral hazard and unemployment benefit; the findings are extensively criticized in *Journal of Political Economy* 90 (1982).

Carroll, Eero. *Emergence and Structuring of Social Insurance Institutions: Comparative Studies on Social Policy and Unemployment Insurance*. Stockholm, 1999. A sociological study, involving eighteen countries, analyzing the relationship between types of unemployment protection and national politics.

Clasen, Jochen. *Paying the Jobless: A Comparison of Unemployment Benefit Policies in Great Britain and Germany*. Aldershot, U.K., 1994. Contrasts German efforts to sustain insurance principles with the reversion of British policy to means-tested systems since the mid-1960s.

Eichengreen, Barry, and T. J. Hatton, eds. *Interwar Unemployment in International Perspective*. Dordrecht, Netherlands, 1988. Includes a chapter that reviews the Benjamin and Kochin (1982) debate.

Esping-Andersen, Gosta, ed. *Welfare States in Transition: National Adaptations in Global Economies*. London, 1996. Chapter 3 analyzes the effects of social protection on unemployment rates in continental Europe during the 1980s.

Flora, Peter, and Arnold J. Heidenheimer. *The Development of Welfare States in Europe and America*. 4th ed. New Brunswick, N.J., 1990. A basic account that documents the introduction of social-insurance schemes, including early unemployment-insurance schemes in western Europe.

Friot, Bernard. *Puissances du salariat: Emploi et protection sociale à la française*. Paris, 1998. One of the more provocative accounts of the history of French social protection.

Garside, W. R. *British Unemployment, 1919–39: A Study in Public Policy*. Cambridge, 1990. A definitive account of unemployment (and unemployment benefits) in interwar Britain.

Harris, J. *Unemployment and Politics*. Oxford, 1972. A detailed study of the development of British unemployment policy in the years before World War I.

Keyssar, Alexander. *Out of Work: The First Century of Unemployment in Massachusetts*. New York, 1986.

King, D. *Actively Seeking Work? The Politics of Unemployment and Welfare Policy in the United States and Great Britain*. Chicago, 1995. A thorough examination of the politics behind forcing the unemployed back to work in those two countries.

Pierson, P. *Dismantling the Welfare State*. New York, 1994. A classic account of welfare retrenchment policies under the 1980s Ronald Reagan and Margaret Thatcher administrations in the United States and United Kingdom.

van der Linden, Marcel. *Social Security Mutualism: The Comparative History of Mutual Benefit Societies*. Bern, Switzerland, 1996. A wideranging review of the role played by mutuality in the provision of protection against all types of social risk—including unemployment—since the mid-nineteenth century.

Weir, M. Orloff, and T. Skocpol, eds. *The Politics of Social Policy in the United States*, Princeton, 1988. Includes an excellent chapter on the constitutional constraints circumscribing the New Deal of the Franklin D. Roosevelt administration.

Whiteside, Noel. *Bad Times: Unemployment in British Social and Political History*. London, 1991. Chapter 4 provides a brief account of the fate of British unemployment insurance in the interwar years; Chapter 6 offers a comparative evaluation of its role in sustaining political stability in the 1930s.

NOEL WHITESIDE

Old Age Insurance

National governments began to legislate for publicly funded old age insurance plans as early as the 1880s. Since that time, most developed countries have introduced such plans, though they vary considerably in structure. Some, from an even earlier date—for example, Britain and France from the mid-eighteenth century—provided pensions for aged public servants, which became increasingly systematized. Soldiers, sailors, and servants in royal households had been pensioned from much earlier times, though generally unsystematically, at the grace and favor of royal or other official authorities. Such pensions increasingly became established rights during the nineteenth century and into the twentieth. Similarly, some private employers had for centuries made provision of various kinds for the support of favored employees who had aged past the capacity for regular work. In the late nineteenth century, associated with the growth in scale and bureaucratization of business firms, occupational pension schemes were introduced, most rapidly in Britain.

The first national old age pension program was embodied in the 1889 German invalidity and old age insurance law. This covered wage earners in most occupations who then received no more than 2,000 marks (about U.S. $500) a year. Those pensions were funded by contributions from employers and workers; both contributions and pensions were related to workers' earnings and were subsidized from national taxation. Contributions were fixed at a level designed to accumulate a reserve to meet future growth in expenditure; yet it was not an insurance system, in the commercial sense, in which premiums were calculated to cover individual risk. The pensions were targeted at the lowest paid regular workers who needed support in old age but who could not afford commercial premiums. The pensions were payable after a minimum of about twenty-four years of contributions, to contributors aged seventy or older, or at earlier ages to those who became so disabled as to have lost all earning capacity. Excluded from the scheme, since it required regular weekly premiums over an extended period, were all who did not engage in regular paid work—most women and casual workers—those among whom serious poverty was especially concentrated. The scheme was not targeted at the poorest citizens, but it was designed to provide economic security for key workers, on whom the growing German economy depended. It was to assure them of the goodwill of the government, for fear, as German Chancellor Otto von Bismarck made clear, that they would become alienated supporters of socialism and trade unionism.

The next of the national plans was introduced in Denmark in 1891; it differed from Germany's plan in being targeted at the poorest citizens. It aimed to reform Denmark's poor relief system, by removing older people from it and providing them with a less punitive alternative. The pension was funded wholly from taxation, was means-tested, and was granted to native citizens aged sixty or more with records of socially acceptable behavior. The amount of the pension was locally determined, according to individual need. Similar schemes were introduced in New Zealand (1898), Australia (1908), and the United Kingdom (1908); these were nationally administered and they paid nationally uniform pension rates, though they differed in such details as pension ages. They were "noncontributory," paid from public taxation, and targeted at the poorest, hence they tended differentially to benefit women.

Thereafter, until World War II, most continental European countries (outside the Nordic countries, which initially followed the Danish model) introduced insurance pensions, broadly similar to the German model, though often initially more restrictive in coverage (often excluding domestic and agricultural workers). In Britain, in 1925, an insurance pension for skilled manual and lower white-collar workers aged sixty-five and above was added to the noncontributory system. A limited insurance ("social security") system was introduced in the United States in 1935, revised and extended in 1939 to cover about 58 percent of people sixty-five or more who had regular paid employment (and various family members); both employer and employee contributed. In some Latin American countries, restricted insurance schemes were introduced. In 1938, New Zealand was the first country to introduce a universal pension, for everyone aged sixty-five or above. It was flat-rate, small, and funded from government revenues through an earmarked tax on all adults, which was not described as an insurance contribution.

After World War II, most Western pension systems became at varying speeds universal, were paid at higher rates, and became on differing bases insurance schemes. Most, in effect, operated on a pay-as-you-go basis (annual receipts equal national estimated expenditures plus a modest reserve) far removed from commercial insurance principles. An exception was Australia, which continued to rely on means-tested pensions, except for a brief period from 1973 to 1985. Continental Europe (excluding initially the Nordic countries but including Communist-controlled Eastern Europe) preferred income-related contributions and pensions. The United Kingdom, the remainder of the English-speaking world including Ireland, Canada, and the Nordic

DE STAAT
WAARBORGT ALLE UITKEERINGEN

V.O.V.

„'N APPELTJE
VOOR DEN
DORST"

VRIJWILLIGE OUDERDOMS VERZEKERING
VRAAGT INLICHTINGEN BIJ . . . .
DE RADEN VAN ARBEID . . .
OF HUN VERTEGENWOORDIGERS

PENSION. "The state guarantees all payments" of the V.O.V. (voluntary old-age insurance program), proclaims a Dutch poster of the 1950s. (International Institute for Social History, Amsterdam)

countries initially chose the flat-rate approach, normally paying relatively low pensions supplemented by means-tested social assistance. Most had a two-tier system of social insurance, plus means-tested public assistance for the poorest. In the Nordic countries, there was growing dissatisfaction with the low level of state pensions, which led to the introduction of income-related systems in the late 1950s; these enabled greater flexibility as well as redistribution from higher to lower income earners than did the flat-rate systems. Most countries eventually introduced some income-related element (Sweden and, in a more limited way, Britain in 1959; Canada in 1965; Finland in 1961; Norway in 1966). Australia, New Zealand, and Ireland did not.

In most countries, pensions were indexed to earnings or to prices. Flat-rate pensions remained the predominant mode in Britain, where by the 1980s they were conspicuously lower than elsewhere in the European Union or in the United States (where automatic cost-of-living raises were legislated for U.S. Social Security recipients in 1972). In the 1990s, New Zealand pensions were severely cut. In 1980, the pension represented, for an aged couple, 83 percent of average earnings in Sweden, 75 percent in France, 61 percent in Japan, 66 percent in the United States, 49 percent in Canada, 47 percent in Britain—proportions that remained stable to the end of the twentieth century. An important influence on the shape of national pension systems in most advanced countries after the 1950s was a third tier of occupational (employer-provided) and private pensions, provided either by insurance companies or (diminishingly) by nonprofit mutual institutions, such as Friendly Societies. That tier grew rapidly, often encouraged and subsidized by states anxious to diminish public funding for pensions; it favored male workers and the better paid.

Asian states (including those that expanded rapidly from the 1960s) gave primacy to the family as the source of support in old age, but company-provided welfare became increasingly important in the postwar non-Communist Asian economies. Despite the introduction there of some form of income-related social insurance, beginning in the 1960s, the family and the company continued to be regarded as the primary providers. This was so even in the Peoples' Republic of China (the communist state founded in 1949), where companies were state-owned. However, by the end of the twentieth century, insurance was being introduced by the government as a substitute for the family support that was being undermined by the "one-child" family policy—imposed to help counter the vast overpopulation.

[*See also* Income Maintenance, *subentry on* Social Insurance.]

BIBLIOGRAPHY

Gordon, Margaret S. *Social Security Policies in Industrial Countries: A Comparative Analysis.* Cambridge, 1988.
Hannah, Leslie. *Inventing Retirement: The Development of Occupational Pensions in Britain.* Cambridge, 1986.
Lloyd-Sherlock, Peter, and Paul Johnson, eds. *Ageing and Social Policy: Global Comparisons.* London, 1996.

PATRICIA M. THANE

INTEGRATION *[This entry contains two subentries, on horizontal and vertical integration.]*

Horizontal Integration

Horizontal integration refers to the merger of one or more firms in the same industry, or of firms producing similar products, most often by similar techniques of production.

Vertical integration refers to the combination of one or more firms specializing in different stages or activities of a final product. Although the rationale for vertical integration is often explained by transaction costs, horizontal integration does not straightforwardly fit this mode of explanation. The simple explanation is that firms that merge horizontally are competitors, not usually cooperators; but they may be collaborators, or coordinators (so there is no gain in reducing transaction costs since no transactions take place). When firms merge horizontally, competition is apparently lessened, and the motives and outcome simply indicate a gain in market power. For an apparently exhaustive list of the motives and *raisons d'être* of horizontal integration, see Peter O. Steiner's book *Mergers: Motives, Effects, Policies* (Ann Arbor, 1975). This article offers only a few general reasons for the occurrence of horizontal integration, while focusing on the synergy and market-power motives. The historical context of horizontal integration receives special attention.

Reasons. Horizontal mergers occur for several reasons, which may be grouped under two broad categories by motive: (1) efficiency, or market power, and (2) control. The latter seems to be the generally accepted explanation, from Adam Smith to the present day. However, economists, legal experts, and others have been providing sound explanations that rely on efficiency. Each case has to be examined individually. The market-control explanation is based on a rather simple theory, which relies on the fact that firms with a greater share of the market are better able to control the industry. Consider first, however, a simple alliance of firms that contract, either explicitly or implicitly, to control market forces. Problems of collusion may arise, bringing substantial information and transaction costs; but if the transaction costs are small, the firms may align their incentives and control the market. The creation of the trust organization alleviated many of the problems of collusion. Establishment of the Standard Oil Trust in the 1880s was a stable and formidable horizontal merger of oil refineries that controlled the industry as a monopoly. Such arrangements, however, are illegal in the United States under antitrust legislation, beginning with the Sherman Act of 1890. Another way to gain market control is to merge; this method led to an increase in market power in the U.S. airline industry in the 1980s, for example. This article will not discuss of the theory of monopoly profits, but will take it for granted that greater concentration of an industry into a few powerful firms lessens competition and increases the firms' ability to raise prices above the competitive level. The focus here is on efficiency reasons for mergers, that is, economies and synergy.

The most basic and static form of economies gained by merging has to do with the efficient use of existing resources. In *The Structure of Competitive Industry* (New York, 1932), E. A. G. Robinson argued that there is a minimum efficient use of processes in a plant and that a balance of these processes will determine the minimum efficient scale of the plant. If there are two processes involved, say manufacturing and packaging, running at different rates of output (minimum efficient use), say one hundred units per hour for manufacturing and fifty units per hour for packaging, then the firm would apply the principle of the least common denominator—the plant would operate two packaging machines and one manufacturing machine. The problem becomes more complex when more processes are involved. This principle may be applied to all facets of the firm, not just the plant. A firm with excess capacity in one or more activities may gain economies when merged with another firm.

The key point is that there usually are differences among firms, even those in the same industry, and these differences may involve any capability, organizational or technological. Thus, a process that is a bottleneck in one firm may be alleviated by merger with another firm with excess capacity in that process. Two conditions must be met for this to result in greater efficiency: first, the transaction costs between the two firms working out an agreement for a market outcome (that is, exchange between the two firms) must exceed the managerial costs of one merged firm; second, the economies achieved must exceed those of effecting the merger and any consequent increase in managerial costs. Thus, the economies would have to be somewhat substantial. Also, a merger allows inefficient activities, plants, machines, and so on to be abandoned in favor of more efficient ones. When the United States Rubber Company centralized production and other activities, it learned that it could achieve economies by this method. In the company's 1896 annual report, the firm's new policy was: "to undertake to reduce the number of brands of goods manufactured, and to consolidate the manufacturing of the remaining brands in those factories which have demonstrated superior facilities for production or advantageous labor conditions. This course was for the purpose of utilizing the most efficient instruments of production and closing those that were inefficient and unprofitable." Without the merger, this course would have taken longer by selection processes in the market. The centralized firm has the ability to coordinate activities rapidly, whereas the market might take much longer for selection.

Even when there are no differences in firms, economies may still be achieved, given that the two conditions above are met. Assume there are two parallel production processes in which there are five steps each. Assume that in each of these processes the fourth step is capable of handling twice the volume of any of the other steps. If a single owner controls both processes, economies of scale can be realized by combining the two processes at this fourth step. If the two processes are separately owned, then there are three possibilities. First, the two firms jointly use the facilities for the fourth step owned by one firm and shut down the other. Second, the two firms each spin off their fourth step of operation, let the two compete, and jointly contract with the more efficient new firm; the other will not survive. Both of these possibilities involve high risk, uncertainty, and other transaction costs. More likely is the third possibility, in which the firms merge and close the less efficient of their fourth steps. This possibility normally involves the lowest transaction costs, as it is the simplest way to divide the gains from realizing the scale economies through horizontal integration. When many of the automobile firms merged in the 1950s, it was not uncommon for many plant closings to occur.

Synergy. The above analysis considers static economies and transaction costs, that is, it involves only existing resources and the short run. Efficiency may result from dynamic sources when two firms merge. This is often called synergy, a catchall term that does little justice to what actually goes on in the merged firm. This article cannot exhaustively discuss the synergy two firms can achieve by merging, but will examine some of the more important issues. Here firm differences really matter. By bringing together different capabilities, some of which complement one another or lead to crossbreeding to form new offspring, synergy can be achieved. To use an analogy, each firm contains different genes (routines or capabilities) that when wed may yield offspring with a different set of genes that gives the organism (the firm) greater chances of survival (greater efficiency and the ability to produce greater profits). The merger of several of Great Britain's chemical firms in 1926 to form Imperial Chemical Industries is a case where these economies are evident. The firms in the merger possessed various capabilities, among them research and development and commercialization. This merger enhanced the competitive strength of the British chemical industry, which had been waning in the previous years.

One type of synergy comes from entrepreneurial ability, or Schumpeterian capabilities (a term that refers to the means necessary to carry out Schumpeterian competition or innovation). Two organizations may have different approaches on, say, how to market a product and how to improve or develop it. Firm A may know a better way to market new products, and firm B may possess superior capabilities in developing new products. Dynamic cost considerations will dictate whether the firm is better off developing its own capabilities or buying them on a market. Since idiosyncratic capabilities—those capabilities that are tacit and indivisible in some sense—cannot be divorced from the organization within which they are used, a firm cannot buy many of the necessary capabilities

piecemeal. It must acquire or merge with the entire firm. Dynamic economies such as these are not easily accounted for in quantitative analyses. A case-by-case study of mergers over a long period of time would be necessary. Some analysis will undoubtedly reveal synergistic effects; other study will not. It is important to understand, first, that there are differences among firms' capabilities, which may be small or substantial; and, second, that there are some capabilities that are idiosyncratic to the firm.

Another source of synergy is the reduction of uncertainty and risk. The pooling of interests of insurance companies covering similar accidents is an obvious reason for merging in that industry. Instead of this kind of calculated risk, this discussion focuses on parametric, strategic, and structural uncertainty. By merging, firms may reduce their parametric uncertainty (the kind where the outcomes are known to some degree but their probabilities are not). The managerial costs of merging must be of little importance for this kind of merger to occur, as firms may solve their problems easily through the market since transaction or information costs can be solved through contractual modes. The more important type of uncertainty is that of a strategic or a structural kind, which is genuine uncertainty. This kind involves rearranging capabilities and activities in radical ways difficult to achieve through market mechanisms. Research and development capabilities, especially those that are idiosyncratic, are important determinants. Moreover, when structural uncertainty is present (mixed with strategic decisions), a merger may create this dynamic form of synergy.

The acquisition of American Motors (AMC) by Chrysler in 1987 illustrates to some extent the dynamic efficiency a firm can experience by merging. When Chrysler acquired ailing AMC, it had already pioneered a new type of vehicle, the minivan, which would lead to a burgeoning market for the sport utility vehicle (SUV). This acquisition represents a genuine type of uncertainty because Chrysler could hardly predict that the sales of automobiles in the United States would be more than 50 percent light trucks and SUVs by the end of the century. One division of AMC, Jeep, gave the merged firm an advantage in this new market; this AMC capability, its skill in making the prototype of the SUV, dovetailed with Chrysler's innovations in the minivan market. Chrysler was able to expand and profit from this merger, which also benefited the consumer. This was only one of thousands of twentieth-century mergers, especially in the latter half of the century, marked by such synergy.

History. Horizontal mergers were not common before the last quarter of the nineteenth century. If they occurred at all, they were usually state-sponsored monopolies. Firms in the same industry usually were able to cooperate freely in many matters and make binding agreements. Also, most firms were commercial rather than industrial firms before the nineteenth century. Most industrial firms, except those outside Great Britain (where firms were mostly in textiles), were small concerns with a limited market. Neither economies nor market control could be gained by firms merging horizontally. An iron mill in Connecticut had little or nothing to gain by merging with an iron mill in Pennsylvania in the eighteenth century; nor was it an easy task, given primitive communications and transportation. Markets outside of commerce—that is, trade—were small. A prerequisite for the formation of large industrial firms or combinations of smaller ones is a sufficient infrastructure. It is a common assertion that the developed U.S. infrastructure, which reached a proficient stage toward the end of the nineteenth century, either allowed or played a large role in determining the Great Merger Wave (hereafter, GMW).

Since the GMW in the United States was the first such large-scale movement, it receives much historical attention. Although economywide factors must have played a role in triggering the movement, which occurred among thousands of firms, the GMW could reveal much also about the individual motives involved, if the economywide factors are seen as more of a catalyst than a primary determinant. There have been several such merger waves in the United States, including most recently the mergers of the late 1990s. Merger waves of the magnitude of the U.S. ones had not occurred in foreign countries until the late 1990s. The United States has experienced about five or six merger waves, including the GMW, roughly between 1926 and 1930, some years in the 1940s and 1950s, from 1966 to 1973, from 1985 to 1989, and, most recently, from 1995 into the early 2000s. Although each wave was prompted by different circumstances, it is instructive to examine the greatest of these, that from 1898 to 1902.

The United States has seemed to lead the world in merger waves of any consequence, although Great Britain experienced a merger wave—on a much smaller scale—at approximately the time of the first U.S. merger wave. Mergers up to the end of the twentieth century were usually national events. There were of course exceptions, for example, Royal-Dutch Shell, Unilever, and British-American Tobacco. Furthermore, although mergers have occurred in consequential numbers in other countries, there do not appear to have been any waves or movements. At the turn of the twenty-first century, there appears to be an *international* merger wave, with the acquisition of Chrysler by Daimler among the new breed of truly international mergers.

The GMW in American industry occurred at the end of the nineteenth century, and many have hypothesized that the timing of the wave was not a chance event. Historical circumstances weighed heavily, so the theories go, in influencing firms' decisions to merge. The reasons for merger can be divided into a hierarchy with a fundamental basis, or ultimate cause, and more immediate motives. Several key factors include: technological changes in industry and transportation; innovations in financial markets; rapid economic growth; and institutional, especially legal, changes. Perhaps the most immediate cause was that of economic uncertainty and large business swings. At any rate, waves of any kind can be explained by movements that affect all equally (as a tidal wave may be explained by an earthquake), and historians must accept the existence of an underlying historical cause(s) of the merger wave. However, it is not necessary to approach the matter holistically. Only by examining firms individually can one get the entire picture—although this is a difficult task, since thousands of mergers occurred. Nor can the motives of just a few firms explain the other mergers that took place. Nonetheless, examples are enlightening in exposing some of the reasons for merger. The two definitive works of mergers on this period are Ralph L. Nelson's *Merger Movements in American Industry, 1895–1956.* (Princeton, 1959) and John Moody's *The Truth about Trusts* (New York, 1904).

The wave began in 1898 (although some regard the year as 1895) and peaked in 1901, with 1,028 firms disappearing altogether. The wave was short, intense, and made a lasting impact and impression on American business, government, and the public. Thenceforth, many would view big business with suspicion. Among the firms created in this period was the product of the largest merger for many years, U.S. Steel (the first billion-dollar company). Although U.S. Steel would control a leading share of the industry, its holdings did not constitute a monopoly. Another merger, although not so important as that of U.S. Steel, was that of the American Brass Company. Its history illustrates many of the motives that students of the GMW offer for its occurrence.

The American Brass Company was formed in 1899 in a consolidation of the very first U.S. brass firms. The U.S. brass industry first established itself in the Naugatuck Valley of Connecticut, and by 1855 the major firms in the industry (which numbered less than seven) included Scovill Manufacturing, the Waterbury Brass Company, Benedict and Burnham, and Holmes, Booth, and Haydens. The last three would become integral firms in the American Brass Company.

The industry began slowly, growing out of button manufacturing. Eventually a thriving industry emerged. The development of the industry closely followed what would be called today a Marshallian industrial district; such an industry is populated by many firms that rely on external economies for their growth. Innovations would often spread from firm to firm. When one of the founding fathers of the industry, Israel Holmes, wanted to expand production, rather than create a new mill, he would organize an entire new firm and endow it with a different strategic course. This created an environment where firms at once cooperated and competed. Evidently Holmes and others recognized that rapid growth of knowledge and capabilities, which were severely lacking in the United States—Birmingham in Britain already possessed a commanding lead—depended on a wide variety of approaches. This effort could best be exploited through differing frameworks of action, or organizations. To use a biological analogy, to get the most out of the resources of the earth, many different kinds of organisms are needed.

By 1853, the firms in the brass industry created one of the first price agreements in the United States. These agreements would dissolve and then re-form periodically through the end of the nineteenth century. The organization eventually created, the American Brass Association, had become untenable by the last decade of the century, and the president of the Coe Manufacturing Company began to pressure other firms in the valley to consolidate. The other firms were slow to respond because of differences about how to handle consumer products. Some of them, such as Scovill Manufacturing, made and marketed a wide variety of products for the consumer; others were heavy in the intermediate market. Their situation was in keeping with Naomi Lamoreaux's later argument (1985) that the firms most pressing for consolidations were those that made and sold undifferentiated products. The external economies that the firms once relied upon for their growth had disappeared by century's end; internal economies of scale were becoming far more important than external ones. At any rate, perhaps feeling compelled by an antitrust suit brought against them, several of the firms, excluding Scovill Manufacturing, consolidated their holdings into the American Brass Company, which would come to control about 45 percent of the market for brass in the early decades of the twentieth century. This merger by no means gave it monopoly power, but did incline it toward a leadership role, which was always difficult for it, unlike U.S. Steel, to sustain.

The firm operated first as a holding company, until 1912 when it became officially an operating company. The firms in the company conducted their business largely autonomously for their day-to-day operations, but were operated strategically by the parent company. For instance, an inefficient wire mill was closed, and operations were moved to newer facilities. Also, a new company was created, the American Brass Goods Corporation, to handle the consumer manufacturing activities of the company. The company achieved economies through its ability to coordinate and rearrange capabilities, activities, and other assets. Whether it benefited from its leadership position in the industry is debatable because the advent of World War I saw its production, capacity, and profits increase enormously. After the war, the firm experienced sharp declines in demand, as did its suppliers, the large copper companies. In 1922, the American Brass Company itself was acquired by Anaconda Copper.

There are many views on the GMW, including that of market power, which seems to be the dominant theory. Many observers even have thought that the mergers did not produce a high survival rate; but this conclusion was challenged by Livermore (1935), who considered many of the mergers to have been successful, given the large amount of time that had passed when he was writing. His use of the survival technique seems to indicate that enough of the mergers were successful that scholars should not discount the GMW as an accident of the many changes in the business environment of the late nineteenth century. The great successes include some firms that have lasted for many years, such as International Harvester, DuPont, U.S. Steel, General Electric, and many others. As to the coincidental development of antitrust laws, many argue that those laws and policy uncertainty were crucial in causing the GMW. Other writers view the development of capital and financial markets as vital to the creation of the wave. Still others point to the development of managerial and organizational skills as causative; and there is reason to believe that this was of some importance, given the fact that some firms' development of these capabilities was excessive. Firms with excess managerial capabilities will find themselves seeking to expand, either by new construction or by acquisition and merger. There is probably no single explanation that adequately fits; one must look for reasons on a case-by-case basis.

By the turn of the twenty-first century, mergers were assuming vast proportions. An infamous merger that occurred in an infamous decade, the 1980s, was that of RJR Nabisco. Nabisco itself was a product of the GMW, as the National Biscuit Company; in 1985 it was acquired by tobacco giant RJR. This consolidation may not seem to have been a horizontal merger prima facie, but it was. The recent (1999) unsuccessful attempt by WorldCom to merge with Sprint (both telecommunications firms) would have created the largest merger in U.S. history, exceeding $125 billion. Many believe it would not have produced substantial synergy or economies. The largest U.S. merger by the early 2000s, that of AOL and Time-Warner (both communications giants but with different services), has created a megalithic corporation that sees itself as delivering a universe of media services. Since the beginning of the new century, firms are seeing themselves much more broadly. Thus, AOL Time-Warner is not merely providing Internet services, but offers media services that include magazines, movies, cable television, and so on; and RJR Nabisco provides consumer nondurables.

BIBLIOGRAPHY

Bittlingmayer, George. "Did Antitrust Policy Cause the Great Merger Wave?" *Journal of Law and Economics* 28 (1985), 77–118.

Bittlingmayer, George. "Antitrust and Business Activity: The First Quarter Century." *Business History Review* 70 (1996), 363–401.

Chandler, Alfred. *Scale and Scope: The Dynamics of Industrial Capitalism.* Cambridge, Mass., 1990.

Everett, Michael. "External Economies and Inertia: The Rise and Decline of the Naugatuck Valley Brass Industry." Ph.D. diss., University of Connecticut, 1997.

Kim, E. Han, and Vinjaj Singal. "Mergers and Market Power: Evidence from the Airline Industry." *American Economic Review* 83 (1993), 549–569.

Knight, Frank H. *Risk, Uncertainty, and Profit.* Boston, 1921.

Lamoreaux, Naomi R. *The Great Merger Movement in American Business, 1895–1904.* Cambridge, Mass., 1985.

Langlois, R. N., and P. L. Robertson. *Firms, Markets and Economic Change: A Dynamic Theory of Business Institutions.* London, 1995.

Leijonhufvud, Axel. "Capitalism and the Factory System." In *Economics as a Process: Essays in the New Institutional Economics*, edited by Richard Langlois, pp. 203–223. New York, 1986.

Livemore, Shaw. "The Success of Industrial Mergers." *Quarterly Journal of Economics* 50 (1935), 68–96.

Nelson, R. Richard. "Why Do Firms Differ, and Does It Matter?" *Strategic Management Journal* 12 (1991), 61–74.

Penrose, Edith. *The Theory of the Growth of the Firm.* Oxford, 1959.

Stigler, George J. "A Theory of Oligopoly." *Journal of Political Economy* 72 (1964), 44–61.

Thorelli, Hans. *The Federal Antitrust Policy.* Baltimore, 1955.

Williamson, Oliver. "Economies as an Antitrust Defense: The Welfare Tradeoffs." *American Economic Review* 58 (1968), 18–36.

MICHAEL J. EVERETT

Vertical Integration

Vertical integration is the organization within a single firm of more than one stage of the production or distribution of a good or service. Producing any good or service involves several stages: producing (for example, growing or extracting) raw materials, processing raw materials into an intermediate and then final good, and distributing the good to wholesalers and retailers before it reaches the final consumer. Vertical integration can refer either to forward integration, in which a firm combines manufacturing with distribution of the product, or to backward integration, in which a firm combines manufacturing a product with producing the raw materials that are an input to its manufacture. Vertical integration can also refer to combining previously distinct stages of the manufacturing process, such as the prototypical case of the merger of spinning and weaving.

Vertical integration need not be an all-or-nothing decision. Firms may partially integrate as, for example, when an auto producer both manufactures an auto part, such as car seats, and purchases them from independent suppliers. A firm can be vertically integrated because it has a subsidiary that produces goods that are inputs for other subsidiaries of the firm. The extent of the true economic and engineering integration of such financially integrated but legally distinct firms varies substantially. Conversely, two independent firms can have a long-term relationship that allows their behavior to mimic that of a vertically integrated firm even though the two organizations are legally and financially distinct.

When a firm is not vertically integrated, it acquires inputs at market prices. When a firm is vertically integrated, it often uses internal "transfer" prices to value inputs. These transfer prices can be based on production costs, market prices, or other measures.

Historical Changes. Most U.S. manufacturing firms were not vertically integrated, either backward into raw materials or forward into distribution, during the first three quarters of the nineteenth century. Wholesalers specializing in a particular product or industry organized most distribution of manufactured goods. These specialized wholesalers had replaced colonial merchants, such as John Hancock, who had engaged in a general import-export-finance business, providing economic and political leadership in the colonial and early national periods (Livesay and Porter, 1971). Nineteenth-century wholesalers often had long-term, and sometimes exclusive, relationships with various manufacturers. Merchants and wholesalers often provided capital, especially working capital, to manufacturing firms with which they had long-term relationships. But the distributors and manufacturers were legally and financially distinct firms. Nineteenth-century wholesalers had specialized information and expertise necessary for distributing goods, including information about transportation, finance, and consumer preferences. They purchased goods from local manufacturers and placed those goods into growing and increasingly complex regional, national, and international distribution networks. They often provided business guidance to manufacturers, who were relatively uninformed about market opportunities. For example, even the largest U.S. manufacturing firms during the first half of the nineteenth century, the New England textile mills, sold their output through independent agents, who made critical decisions about production—such as which styles and types of cloth to manufacture—that would be considered the purview of the manufacturer today.

Within the manufacturing process itself, the early industrialization of the first half of the nineteenth century probably decreased the extent of vertical integration. During this period, substantial productivity gains were made in many areas of manufacturing as firms introduced a detailed division of labor (Sokoloff, 1984). This division of labor allowed the separation of several stages of the manufacturing process into distinct firms; that is, an increased division of labor is associated with vertical disintegration. With the introduction of new power-driven machinery, vertical reintegration of stages of manufacturing occurred in some industries. For example, Francis Cabot Lowell's textile mill, built in 1814, while not vertically integrated into distribution, was the first U.S. textile producer to vertically integrate spinning and weaving into the same mill.

While early industrialization was associated with vertical disintegration, late-nineteenth-century industrialization was associated with increasing vertical integration, both of the stages of manufacturing and of manufacturing with distribution and raw materials production. These organizational changes reflect several related but distinct changes in the national economy. First, technological changes increased the scale of manufacturing, which meant that a single firm could use sufficient distribution services to warrant specialized in-house distribution capabilities. Second, growth in firm size meant an increase in the size of the average consumer of intermediate goods. Larger customers reduced the value of the services provided by independent distributors, whose niche was providing information about diverse customers. Third, urbanization led to increased concentration of retail demand, so that individual manufacturers could profitably distribute their own goods in local markets. Fourth, the emergence of a more integrated national market increased manufacturers' incentive to invest in brand reputations. Food manufacturers such as the cereal producers of Battle Creek, Michigan, who previously sold generic goods through wholesalers and general-store retail establishments, advertised in the emerging national media. Having a brand reputation further increased firms' incentive to use their own distribution staff. McCurdy (1978) argues that this process was self-reinforcing, in that vertically integrated firms challenged interstate barriers to trade, further integrating the national market and increasing the incentive to vertically integrate.

In some industries, forward integration was driven by the introduction of new products for which existing distribution networks were unable to provide the necessary service and finance. For example, according to David Hounshell (1984), Singer Sewing Machine Company, founded in 1851, established its competitive advantage in the growing international market for sewing machines on the basis of its ability to both teach potential customers how to use the machines and service the machines after the sale.

Vertical integration permitted managers to better coordinate the flow of materials through the production process. This allowed higher utilization rates in the increasingly capital-intensive manufacturing processes adopted during the late nineteenth century, creating what Chandler (1977) called "economies of speed." Vertical integration into distribution provided manufacturers with more information about fluctuating demand so that they could better control inventories. For example, in the early 1920s, Alfred P. Sloan began using high-frequency sales data from General Motors' automobile dealers to set production levels. With vertical integration also applied to the provision of consumer credit, firms such as General Motors integrated and sped up the entire Marxian circuit of capital—production, distribution, and finance, thereby accelerating the process of accumulation and the rate of economic growth.

Measurement. There are few aggregate quantitative measures of vertical integration in the United States. Because of measurement problems, past attempts to quantify secular trends in vertical integration are not entirely convincing. One set of studies measures vertical integration by looking at the ratio of value added to total output. If a firm were entirely vertically integrated, producing all of its inputs, this ratio would be one. At the other extreme, if a firm were vertically disintegrated, purchasing most of its inputs, this ratio would be much less than one. Adelman (1955) argued that there was no change in vertical integration between 1849 and 1939 because he finds that, for the U.S. economy as a whole, the ratio of value added by manufacture to the value of total output remained constant. Using firm level data that allowed a qualitative determination of the range of activities in which each firm was engaged, Livesay and Porter (1969) find a trend toward forward integration among U.S. manufacturing firms.

Examining the mid-twentieth-century period, Adelman (1955) found that the ratio of corporate income to corporate sales in the United State remained roughly constant between 1929 and 1951. Thus he argued that the degree of vertical integration remained constant during much of the twentieth century. In contrast, Tucker and Wilder (1977) computed a more disaggregated version of the same measure, and found a slight increase in vertical integration between 1954 and 1972. These disparate results can be reconciled by recognizing that vertical integration of the manufacturing process varies substantially across industries, for both technological and economics reasons. Michael Gort (1962) found that levels of vertical integration were four times as high in the 1954 petroleum industries as in textile mill products. Food products, paper products, and machinery industries, although not as vertically integrated as the petroleum industry, were much more vertically integrated than the tobacco, electrical machinery, or transportation equipment industries.

We do not have similar measures of aggregate vertical integration for the late twentieth century, though many of the mergers of the 1990s were of vertically related firms, suggesting that integration has increased in many industries. We have observed both significant vertical disintegration, as with the spinning off of integrated automobile parts suppliers (Delphi Automotive in 1999 and Visteon in

2000) by General Motors and Ford, respectively, and significant vertical integration in the communication and media industries (for example, Viacom's 1999 purchase of CBS and Disney's 1995 purchase of ABC). The direction of vertical integration in other industries, such as telecommunications, is not clear. AT&T has recently fluctuated between pursuing vertical mergers (for example, with TCI in 1998 and Mediaone in 2000) and vertical spinoffs with dizzying rapidity.

Competition. The growth of vertical integration among manufacturing firms during the late nineteenth century disrupted preexisting formal and informal cooperative arrangements among distributors that had limited competition in some industries. For example, Livesay and Porter (1971) describe how Philadelphia drug distributors (jobbers) acted as one another's collection agents and shared information regarding the credit worthiness of customers. The benefits of such cooperation diminished distributors' incentive to engage in price competition. Levenstein (1995) argues that in some markets, distributors organized explicit cooperative agreements, setting prices, dividing up customers and regions, and limiting manufacturers' output.

Vertically integrated manufacturers displaced distributors, creating the potential for increased price competition. But, as Lazonick (1991) argues, the large fixed investments in brand reputations and in-house distribution increased the ratio of fixed to variable costs, so that firms needed to avoid intense price competition that could drive prices below average cost. Vertical integration, however, also provided the basis for new restrictions on competition. This could take two forms. First, firms with brand reputations and a sales force were able to differentiate their products in the minds of consumers. With more information about their customers, firms could even provide customer-specific products that would further tie the customer to the firm. Second, vertical integration could create barriers to entry by depriving potential competitors of access to critical inputs or distribution facilities.

Concerns that vertical integration could discourage competition led to the passage of pertinent antitrust legislation. The Federal Trade Commission and Clayton Acts of 1914 created a mechanism by which the federal government could block vertical mergers that would substantially lessen competition. At the time, Congress considered and rejected stricter limits on vertical integration. In 1950, the Celler-Kefauver Act amended the Clayton Act to extend its limitations on mergers to the acquisition of stock in other companies. In the precedent-setting cases that broke up the GM-DuPont alliance (*U.S.* v. *E. I. DuPont de Nemours & Company et al.* [1956]) and prohibited Brown Shoe's acquisition of Kinney shoe retail outlets (*Brown Shoe Company, Inc.* v. *U.S.* [1962]), the U.S. Supreme Court ruled

that mergers that substantially reduce competition in either the supply of or the market for an intermediate good are prohibited under section 7 of the Clayton Act.

Legal challenges to vertical integration were rare in the late twentieth century. Current U.S. Department of Justice guidelines for "nonhorizontal mergers" were written in 1984. (Current guidelines for "horizontal mergers" were written in 1997.) By 1984, the Reagan Justice Department had accepted the Chicago School argument that vertical integration enhanced efficiency, and rejected concerns regarding the possibly anticompetitive (or antisocial) consequences of increasing vertical integration spelled out in Supreme Court decisions such as *Brown Shoe* and *du Pont*.

U.S. antitrust law does not restrict vertical integration by internal firm growth (as opposed to merger). It does, however, restrict the way in which a firm may use such internally developed capacity, as the recent Microsoft case demonstrates. In particular, vertically integrated firms are enjoined by U.S. antitrust law from using vertical restrictions or foreclosure to monopolize an industry or to compete unfairly.

Alternative Explanations of Vertical Integration. Fluctuating judicial and policy attitudes toward vertical integration reflect different explanation of vertical integration. Sympathetic government policy toward vertical integration follows from the view that vertical integration lowers production and distribution costs and increases innovation in production, distribution, and product design. Opposition to vertical integration reflects concern that integration creates barriers to entry, competitive advantages not based on better service or price for the customer, and increased concentration of economic and political power.

The simplest justification of vertical integration is that, for technological reasons, production costs are lower when the stages of production are vertically integrated. For example, vertically integrated mills produce steel at lower cost because molten steel is transferred from blast furnaces to rolling mills without cooling and reheating. Although separate ownership of two adjacent and physically integrated mills is in principle possible, the technology is what creates the imperative for the close physical integration of the stages of production.

Ronald Coase's seminal article "The Theory of the Firm" (1937) argued that a firm will choose to integrate two vertically connected functions when the transactions cost of using the market to coordinate these activities is higher than the cost of using an authority relation within the firm. Williamson (1985) argues that asset specificity increases the transactions cost of using the market. Market mechanisms for contracting become costly if information is "impacted" (partners to the transaction cannot observe and verify one another's actions), firms behave opportunistically (are willing to lie or mislead or back out of agreements to increase profits), and there exists specificity to the relationship so that competition from outsiders does not force the participants to offer the best possible price and service. In this case, Coase and Williamson both argued, the firm may lower transactions costs by avoiding the use of the market and integrating the two stages into a single firm where managerial authority determines resource allocation, production, and distribution decisions.

Klein, Crawford, and Alchian (1978) illustrate the transactions cost approach with General Motor's 1924 acquisition of Fisher Body, the Lansing, Michigan, manufacturer from whom General Motors had been purchasing most of its car bodies. They argued that the ongoing relationship between the two firms created a bilateral monopoly that could have led to holdup or bargaining problems if the Fisher brothers had demanded a higher price for their critical input to GM's production. To prevent such problems, GM purchased the entire firm and turned itself into a more vertically integrated manufacturer. Helper (1991) challenges this interpretation of the Fisher Body acquisition. Helper argues that GM's acquisition of Fisher Body reflected a desire to bring the managerial capabilities of the Fisher organization into General Motors. Drawing on the work of Hirschman (1971), she argues that firms vertically integrate where, for strategic or technological reasons, they choose to use "voice" (that is, communication and authority) rather than the threat of "exit" to influence suppliers and distributors.

Others, however, such as Comanor (1967), argue that firms vertically integrate to foreclose competition. Vertical integration may increase the costs and decrease the availability of inputs to other producers, increase the capital required to compete, and limit access to distribution channels. For example, Alcoa maintained its monopoly position in the U.S. aluminum market in part through its backward integration into bauxite ore, controlling most of the world's known reserves before World War II. Vertical integration of different stages of production may allow a firm to squeeze out downstream competition if the firm is a monopoly producer of the upstream good. For example, in *U.S. v. the Aluminum Company of America et al.* (1945), the United States argued that Alcoa's price for processed aluminum (over which it had a monopoly) was so high that downstream producers of aluminum goods could not compete. (Judge Learned Hand's "transfer price test" argued that a firm was illegally exercising monopoly power if its own downstream producer could not profitably operate if it had to pay the price that the upstream part of the firm charged to outside producers.) Similarly, in *Brown Shoe*, the Supreme Court found that the proposed vertical integration of Brown Shoe with one of the largest shoe retailers in the United States would have cut off an important distribution channel for other shoe manufacturers, limiting their ability to compete. The control of distribution

networks may require other manufacturers to integrate into distribution as well, increasing their distribution and capital costs, and possibly foreclosing them from the market altogether. Similarly, the Court ruled in *U.S. v. DuPont* that DuPont's control of General Motors gave DuPont an unfair advantage relative to other producers of automotive finishers and fabrics. The Court ordered DuPont to divest itself of its stock ownership in GM.

Conversely, vertical integration can mitigate the effects of concentration when each stage of production is controlled by a monopoly. In such a case, there may be output restriction at each stage, and vertical integration can increase both total profits and consumer welfare by eliminating "double marginalization."

Stigler (1951) emphasizes that there is a life cycle to the extent of vertical integration. During the early stages of the production and distribution of a new good or service, the industry is likely to rely on vertically integrated firms. A competitive supply of inputs and distribution services may not be available because the industry is new and requires specialized inputs or distribution services. As the industry matures, a number of firms may enter each stage, creating a competitive supply. Bilateral monopoly, holdup, and opportunistic bargaining are no longer as likely. At this stage, Stigler argued, the benefits of vertical integration will be outweighed by the increased costs associated with managing a larger, more complex firm. Firms will choose to vertically "disintegrate," spinning off vertically distinct stages into separate firms.

A good example of this life cycle of vertical integration and then disintegration is the sewing machine industry. When the sewing machine was a novelty, it made sense for Singer to have its own, vertically integrated distribution network to provide training in the use of its machines and after-sale service of mechanical problems. A century later, Singer sold off its network of retail outlets (many of which are now operated as Joanne's Fabrics). Potential sewing machine consumers no longer needed to be assured by Singer that they would be able to find after-sale repair services. Skills in using sewing machines were widespread throughout (half of) the population.

There is an analogous case for backward integration into sources of supply. For example, when the Dow Chemical Company began producing carbon tetrachloride (for use as an industrial cleanser), it introduced a new production method that required carbon bisulphide as an input. Since there were few other industrial users of carbon bisulphide at the time, Dow was dependent on a single firm that was the sole supplier to the entire eastern half of the United States. Because that supply was irregular, Dow chose to integrate backward into bisulphide production; this was defensive integration designed to assure that its expensive carbon tetrachloride plant was not left idle for long periods of time. With the growth of the market, such defensive integration is less necessary. Whether vertical disintegration actually occurs as the industry matures, however, depends on the extent of competition at each stage. If vertical integration by first movers has led competing firms to integrate, nonintegrated firms may not be competitive even in a mature industry. Thus vertical integration at some point in an industry's history may set it on a vertically integrated path that persists long after the original economic motivation has passed.

BIBLIOGRAPHY

Adelman, Morris A. "Concept and Statistical Measurement of Vertical Integration." In *Business Concentration and Price Policy: A Conference of the Universities-National Bureau Committee for Economic Research.* Princeton, 1955, 281–330.

Chandler, Alfred D., Jr. *The Visible Hand.* Cambridge, Mass. 1977.

Coase, Ronald. "The Theory of the Firm." *Economica* 4:16 (November 1937), 386–405.

Comanor, William. "Vertical Mergers, Market Power and the Antitrust Laws." *American Economic Review* 57.2 (May 1967), 254–265.

Gort, Michael. *Diversification and Integration in American Industry.* Princeton, 1962.

Helper, Susan. "Strategy and Irreversibility in Supplier Relations." *Business History Review* 65.4 (Winter 1991), 781–824.

Hirschman, Albert. *Exit, Voice, and Loyalty: Responses to Decline of Firms, Organizations, and States.* Cambridge, Mass., 1970.

Hounshell, David. *From the American System to Mass Production.* Baltimore, 1984.

Klein, Benjamin, Robert C. Crawford, and Armen A. Alchian. "Vertical Integration, Appropriable Quasi-Rents, and Comparative Contracting Process." *Journal of Law and Economics* 21 (1978).

Lazonick, William. *Business Organization and the Myth of the Market Economy.* Cambridge, 1991.

Levenstein, Margaret C. "Mass Production Conquers the Pool: Firm Organization and the Nature of Competition in the Nineteenth Century." *Journal of Economic History* 55.3 (1995), 117–137.

Livesay, Harold C., and Glenn Porter. *Merchants and Manufacturers.* Baltimore, 1971.

Livesay, Harold C., and Patrick G. Porter. "Vertical Integration in American Manufacturing, 1899–1948." *Journal of Economic History* 29.3 (Sept. 1969) 494-500.

Marx, Karl. *Capital,* vol. 2. New York, 1947.

McCurdy, Charles. "American Law and the Marketing Structure of the Large Corporation, 1875–1890." *Journal of Economic History* 38.3 (Sept. 1978), 631–649.

Sokoloff, Kenneth. "Was the Transition from the Artisanal Shop to the Non-mechanized Factory Associated with Gains in Efficiency?" *Explorations in Economic History* 21 (1984), 351–382.

Stigler, George. "The Division of Labor Is Limited by the Extent of the Market." *Journal of Political Economy* 59.3 (June 1951), 185–193.

Tucker, Irvin B., and Ronald P. Wilder. "Trends in Vertical Integration in the U.S. Manufacturing Sector." *Journal of Industrial Economics* 26.1 (Sept. 1977), 81–94.

Williamson, Oliver E. *The Economic Institutions of Capitalism.* New York, 1985.

COURT CASES

Brown Shoe Co., Inc. v. *U.S.,* 370 U.S. 294 (1962).

U.S. v. *the Aluminum Company of America,* 148 F.2d 416 (2d Cir. 1945).

U.S. v. *E. I. DuPont de Nemours and Company,* 351 U.S. 377 (1956).

MARGARET C. LEVENSTEIN

INTEREST RATES. Interest is payment for the use of funds for a period of time, and the interest rate is the amount paid per unit of time expressed as a fraction, or percentage, of the amount of funds used. The user of funds, or borrower, pays interest to the provider of funds, or lender. Interest and interest rates are thus analogous to wages and wage rates as well as to rents and rental rates. All three are payments for the use of productive resources: wages for the use of labor, rent for the use of land, and interest for the use of financial capital. With defined property rights, those who provide productive resources temporarily to others retain ownership of them. In the case of financial capital, a borrower returns the amount of funds borrowed to the lender along with an interest payment for their use.

Despite the apparent similarities of the three resource prices, the interest rate has proved much more difficult than the other two resource prices to explain in terms of economic theory. Moreover, interest historically has always been the most controversial and regulated of the three. Although history reveals sporadic attempts to regulate levels of wages and rents, no one seriously suggested, as was true of the rate of interest for centuries in many cultures, that the only proper level was zero. Even in today's advanced economies, although few countries regard wages and rents as control variables for macroeconomic policy, interest rates are routinely varied by central banks for purposes of economic stabilization.

Theories of Interest Rates. Modern economic theory explains interest rates in two ways, namely, with nonmonetary and monetary analyses. Nonmonetary theories, best exemplified in Irving Fisher's *Theory of Interest* (New York, 1930), emphasize two determinants of the rate of interest. One is the productivity of capital: if people save now, refraining from current consumption, and invest the savings in productive assets, they can have more consumption in their future, that is, they can have a positive return on their savings and investment. The other determinant is time preference: people value consumption now more highly than they value the same amount of consumption in the future. Fisher demonstrated that a positive rate of interest would naturally arise from balancing the ability to save and invest now, and thus have more consumption in the future, with valuing consumption now more highly than consumption in the future.

Nonmonetary theories thus explain and justify a positive rate of interest. In doing so, they provide a rebuttal to the influential view of the ancient Greek philosopher Aristotle, who saw money only as a medium of exchange and therefore interest on the use of money as something unnatural. Aristotle's view was adopted by the medieval Catholic Church in its ban on usury, that is, the taking of interest; and it still survives in Islamic theology and practice. Crucial to the economic rebuttal of arguments against interest is the notion of the productivity of capital. That concept was outside the ken of ancient and medieval thinkers, who regarded loans as financing current consumption rather than productive investment, and made mostly by rich lenders to poor borrowers. Elements of ancient and medieval views survive even in modern economies that, although they normally allow interest rates to allocate financial capital, nonetheless use usury laws to set maximum allowable rates of interest, particularly on consumer loans.

Monetary theories of interest are even older than nonmonetary theories. They were discussed during the seventeenth and eighteenth centuries by mercantilist writers, who were usually involved in business and observed from their practical experiences that increases in money available for lending often tended to reduce interest rates and stimulate trade. Modern monetary theories build on the early analyses, arguing that interest rates are determined by either the demand for and supply of loanable funds or the demand for and supply of money. Since the demand for loanable funds can be thought of as a supply of claims (such as securities) to be sold for money, the two theories, despite conceptual differences, can be shown to be roughly equivalent.

Nonmonetary and monetary theories of interest rates are complements, not substitutes for each other. Nonmonetary theories emphasize fundamental, long-term factors, such as the productivity of capital and time preference, underlying the determination of interest rates. However, the demand for loanable funds or money in the monetary theories arises from desires to invest, that is, to form capital and reap a return from its productivity, or to consume more than one's income allows now, that is, time preference, or, finally, to build up money balances now to finance investment or consumption at a later time. By introducing the money supply into interest-rate determination, monetary theories of interest are more comprehensive than nonmonetary theories, and more useful because both money and interest rates are significant variables in economic history. Money stocks historically have changed, often quickly, as a result of discoveries of precious metals, changes in monetary standards, and financial innovations such as banking. Also, in modern economies, central banks and other monetary authorities deliberately manipulate money stocks and interest rates for policy reasons.

Economic theories, whether nonmonetary or monetary, discuss determinants of *the* interest rate. In reality there is a whole structure of interest rates that vary along two major dimensions, time and risk. The time dimension deals with the term structure of interest rates, that is, with rates of the same borrower or similar borrowers classified by loan maturity (the so-called yield curve). For example, the U.S. government, whose credit is impeccable, usually pays a different rate of interest when it borrows by issuing short-term Treasury bills than it pays on five-year notes, and still a different rate on thirty-year bonds. The risk dimension of interest rates recognizes that different borrowers—whether governments, business enterprises, or consumers—have different probabilities of defaulting on their loan payments, both interest and principal. Borrowers with higher perceived probabilities of default will be charged higher interest rates than those whose credit is considered impeccable. Higher-risk borrowers may also be asked to pledge collateral security for the loan; in the event of default, the lender can take over and perhaps liquidate the collateral to avoid or minimize a loss. The interest rate on any loan thus reflects a "pure" interest rate and an added risk premium to reflect a nonzero probability of default and other uncertainties.

History of Interest Rates. Interest rates are among the best documented of the fundamental prices of economic history, with recorded rates extending back to the earliest civilizations. Despite temporal and geographical gaps, the historical record of interest rates covers some five thousand years. This discussion summarizes the lowest rates, those on best credits, recorded at various times in history.

Ancient world. In the third millennium BCE, Sumer used both grain and ingots of silver as mediums of exchange; customary interest rates were 33 1/3 percent per annum for loans of grain and 20 percent per annum for loans of silver. The Babylonian Code of Hammurabi (c. 1800 BCE) made these rates legal maximums, establishing a tradition of interest-rate regulation that has lasted to the present. Customary Babylonian rates declined to 10 percent during the height of that civilization, and then rose as high as 40 percent by the fifth and fourth centuries BCE. Ancient-world loans were for purposes of consumption and commerce; there are few records of loans to rulers and governments, which probably seized whatever resources they needed instead of borrowing and repaying debts.

The Greek and Roman civilizations show a similar pattern of falling and rising rates, with the lowest rates recorded in periods considered to be the heights of those civilizations. Greek rates fell from highs of 16 to 18 percent in the sixth century BCE to lows of 6 percent in the second and third centuries BCE before rising again. Roman rates, similar to Greek rates in the fourth and fifth centuries BCE, fell to as low as 4 percent during the first century BCE and the first century CE, the last decades of the republic and the first decades of the empire. By the third and fourth centuries CE, with Rome in decline, rates on best credits rose to 12 percent. The eastern Byzantine Empire recorded its lowest rates, 6 to 8 percent per annum during the sixth and seventh centuries CE.

Medieval and Renaissance Europe. From the twelfth century on, the European record of interest rates becomes richer, with rates given for short-term commercial loans and bank deposits as well as a variety of long-term debt instruments such as annuities and mortgages. The trend of interest rates from the twelfth to the sixteenth century was down, declining from rates of 8 to 10 percent initially on best credits to levels as low as 4 percent by the sixteenth century. Throughout the period, the lowest rates were in the commercial cities and city-states of Italy, the Netherlands, and Germany. Then the centers of economic and financial development in western Europe, they introduced a number of the financial institutions, instruments, and markets that later became mainstays of modern financial systems.

A significant difference between this premodern period of European history and the modern period is that the best credits were those of merchants and other private agents, whereas political rulers were considered by lenders to be far riskier recipients of credit. The rulers fought numerous wars, their fiscal systems were primitive, and their debts often went into default, sometimes to the ruination of their creditors.

Modern world. Key developments of the modern era for interest-rate history were the formation of nation-states, representative governments with strong fiscal arrangements and public debts, and related financial-system developments including sound currencies, banking systems, central banks, and securities markets. The successive leaders of these financial developments, which not coincidentally became the leading economies of their eras, were the Dutch republic in the seventeenth and eighteenth centuries, Great Britain in the eighteenth and nineteenth centuries, and the United States from the nineteenth century to the present. Other European economies, overseas offshoots of Europe, and Japan followed the examples of the three leaders and became modern, highly developed economies. A widespread availability of credit at low interest rates was at least as important a factor in modern economic history as the technologies of the Industrial Revolution; it usually preceded the appearance of those technologies and facilitated investments in them.

The long-term trend of interest rates from the seventeenth to the mid-twentieth century was downward. Dutch long-term public securities yielded 7 to 8 percent early in the seventeenth century and 3 percent toward its end. In the eighteenth century, similar Dutch securities yielded as low as 2½ percent, and Dutch investors became active purchasers of higher-yielding securities issued by other countries such as Great Britain and the United States. Toward the end of the nineteenth century, British government debt yielded as low as 2¼ percent, and during the 1930s and 1940s, U.S. government debt reached even lower yields of just under 2 percent. Reversing the premodern pattern, these yields on public debts became the benchmark low interest rates, with private securities and loans priced to

have higher yields, reflecting the higher risks of lending to borrowers without the taxing and money-creating powers possessed by governments.

The second half of the twentieth century witnessed what seemed to be a decisive interruption of the long-term trend of history toward lower interest rates. In these decades, the lowest long-term interest rates available anywhere in the world soared to levels not seen since the Middle Ages, and the lowest short-term rates rose to levels not seen since the Napoleonic Wars or perhaps even the early Dutch republic at the start of the seventeenth century.

To a great extent the dramatic rise of interest rates after 1950, with peaks in the 1970s and early 1980s, was an illusion. Early in the twentieth century, Irving Fisher made the fundamental distinction between nominal interest rates and real interest rates, the latter being adjusted to take into account inflation, or the change in the value of money between the time a loan is made and the time it is liquidated by repayment or sale to another creditor. Fisher's distinction was of only academic interest until governments and monetary authorities irresponsibly unleashed a great inflation during the 1960s and 1970s. Sophisticated modern investors and financial markets quickly incorporated expected inflation into interest rates, making real rates far less than the observed nominal rates.

A lesson of this recent historical experience is that although the modern state possesses great power over interest rates, and can use that power responsibly for economic stabilization or irresponsibly, as did medieval kings and princes, to debase money and in effect default on debts, its power is not absolute. The state's power to manipulate interest rates for good or for ill is constrained ultimately by representative political institutions and sophisticated financial systems. These are the same institutions that gave modern economies the low interest rates and widespread use of credit that allowed them to become highly developed, a fact increasingly appreciated by less economically developed countries that lack such institutions.

[*See also* Capital Markets; Pawnbroking and Personal Loan Markets; *and* Usury.]

BIBLIOGRAPHY

Conard, Joseph W. *Introduction to the Theory of Interest.* Berkeley, 1963. Thorough discussion of the concept of interest in economic theory, as well as of nonmonetary and monetary theories of interest rates.

Ferguson, Niall. *The Cash Nexus: Money and Power in the Modern World, 1700–2000.* New York, 2001. Discussion of the relationship of interest rates and financial systems to economic and political power.

Homer, Sidney, and Richard Sylla. *A History of Interest Rates.* 3d ed., rev. New Brunswick, N.J., 1996. Comprehensive account of five thousand years of interest-rate history.

Neal, Larry. *The Rise of Financial Capitalism: International Capital Markets in the Age of Reason.* Cambridge, 1990. Discussion of the founding of modern financial systems and the integration of the Dutch and English capital markets in the eighteenth century.

Poitras, Geoffrey. *The Early History of Financial Economics, 1478–1776: From Commercial Arithmetic to Life Annuities and Joint Stocks.* Cheltenham and Northampton, Mass., 2000. Discussion of the transition from medieval to modern ways of thinking about interest rates and finance.

RICHARD SYLLA

INTERNAL MIGRATION. Migration is an essential component of many historical phenomena, among them development, urbanization, and suburbanization. It is difficult to define because it could include widely different movements. A common definition is a change of residence across an administrative border (commune, county, or city border) with no return within a year. The terms *emigration* and *internal migration* may be problematic. For example, nineteenth-century migration from Ireland to Britain is usually described as emigration and immigration, yet Britain and Ireland had been part of the same country since 1802, and, more important, by midcentury, they were part of a single goods and labor market.

Migrant Characteristics. The characteristics of migrants were first discussed systematically by Ravenstein, a British statistician writing in 1885, and most are still relevant. He observed that migrants tended to be young, short-distance moves predominated, migration streams created return flows, and the motivation was largely economic. The most universal differential, applying to most migrants in most periods, was that they were disproportionately young adults. Migration involves an investment decision, in which current income is forgone in the expectation of higher future income, benefiting the young more than the old. It often is associated with particular stages in the life cycle, such as marriage and/or leaving home for the first time. The reason why many internal migrants moved only a short distance was that migration involved psychic costs (leaving home) and economic costs (income forgone while searching for employment) that were minimized if the destination was close. Age was a particularly important differential; emigrants, for example, traveled long distances but were still relatively young. There were several reasons for reverse flows, the most important being that many migrants left with the intention of returning. Their savings benefited the home community, and, as in many third world countries, could be essential for a family's survival.

Migration Models. Rational-choice models are commonly applied. A push-and-pull model emphasizes economic conditions in the origin and the destination community. This is a relative concept, as even in pogrom or famine not everyone migrated. A superior formulation is that a migration decision depends on the difference between the expected (lifetime) income if staying and if moving, discounting the cost of moving and the uncertainties inherent in migration. (Migration does not have to be for a long period to affect a migrant's lifetime income; and income may be broadly defined to include nonmaterial benefits, although they are difficult to quantify.)

In his model, Todaro, a development economist, addressed an important paradox. Migration to third world cities in the 1960s was rising despite low urban incomes, high unemployment, and serious urban disamenities, including poor housing. By rational choice the rate of in-migration should have been falling. The Todaro model included three key variables: income differences, employment growth, and, crucially, the probability of a migrant's obtaining employment in a given period. Hence, migration could increase when unemployment was rising. The implication was that improved urban job opportunities would not reduce unemployment, and rural–urban migration was unlikely to fall without major structural change in agriculture. The Todaro model, and its later refinements, have been criticized because, implicitly, they assume that migration is affected by economic conditions but economic conditions are not affected by migration (a simultaneous-equation bias); but they were a step forward.

The effect of distance on migration rates may be represented by a simple gravity model, incorporating city size. (Naturally, the effect of distance is not linear.) The Stouffer model of intervening opportunities is a refinement. Since relatively short moves involve less risk, a migrant, for example, from a rural area would be more likely to go to the local market town than a distant larger town despite superior prospects in the latter. What is less clear historically, is whether the overall migration pattern was created by a series of systematic moves—with migrants moving stepwise, say, from village to a small town and then to a larger town—or whether the ultimate destination followed a series of random moves. (Many French historians insist on a distinction between *migration*, which was historically important, and *mobilité*, which was not, but this is a very fine distinction.)

One may ask whether rational-choice models are appropriate. There are many possible noneconomic motives for migration, including personal relationships, marriage, pregnancy, and the lure of "bright lights." Some migration has been deeply rooted in family circumstances and culture; for example, moving temporarily to the mines could be a right of passage for young southern African men. However, it has proved difficult systematically to relate such factors to migration rates from different localities. This has led some historians to emphasize information as a cause of migration. Obviously, information is a necessary condition of all migration, but some historians have argued that it is a sufficient condition, as shown by the phenomenon of chain migration, of which there are many examples, often involving considerable distances. Most of the masons in Paris in the middle of the nineteenth century came from the Limousin, and about a third of the migrants in "Zheijiang Village," south of Beijing in the 1990s, came from a single distant province, with only 15 percent from Beijing itself. Chains were important because the most reliable information (e.g., about employment and housing) came from friends and relatives who had moved or had returned. Chains also could be useful to employers looking for reliable workers, thus segmenting the labor market. Obviously chains mattered, but historians cannot tell if they were a sufficient reason for migration because chains and migration rates were interrelated—an increase in the migration rate increased information. Nor is there much evidence about individual migrants who did not move in chains.

With regard to the question of economic motives, there is insufficient evidence to determine the number of migrants affected by personal influences. However, a range of evidence, from late-nineteenth-century Britain, the United States, and many third world countries, suggests that the overall historical pattern of migration is predictable by models including economic variables, such as income differences. In other words, on average, people who left home because of personal problems also must have made a rational decision to move to places where they expected to fare better economically.

Migration and Industrialization. The effect of industrialization on migration rates is problematic. In the "mobility transition," migration rates follow an inverted-U shape over time, increasing with development but ulti-

mately declining. There is a measurement problem, however. Historical migration rates often are calculated as the residual from the changes in births and deaths in a population; so they measure only the net effect of migration, not the rate of migration itself. However, it is known that migration rates were high in preindustrial Europe. Transience was common, but there also were complicated harvest migration systems in the Po Valley, southern Russia, the North Sea coast, and the Mediterranean coast; and leading cities (London, Paris) took a disproportionately large share of the migrants, many of whom had traveled long distances. Several of these characteristics were still true of third world migration in the later twentieth century—the dominance of capital cities (Bangkok, Lima) and circular migrations from farm to city to farm in, for example, parts of Africa.

One would expect internal migration rates to have been high in Europe in the classic industrialization period. Transport improvement, particularly railway development, meant that industry became more localized and service employment grew fastest in the capital cities, both implying increased migration. In contrast to the preindustrial period, harvest migration declined; there was a new destination, the new industrial cities, usually located in the coal fields (Düsseldorf, Middlesbrough, Lille); and there was large-scale emigration, which included a new phenomenon, temporary emigration. (By the early twentieth century, a third of all European emigrants were returning.) Transience remained common, as can be told from those

MIGRANT LABOR. Digging potatoes near Homestead, Florida, circa 1939. Potatoes not worth gathering have been left to rot. (Marion Post Wolcott/Prints and Photographs Division, Library of Congress)

countries with continuous population registers. In 1881, for example, 11 percent of the urban population of Prussia left the city in which they were living, and another 14 percent entered. The total number of moves may have increased since the preindustrial period, but historians cannot be certain of that. The pattern had changed, however. There were proportionately more rural to urban and urban to urban moves and fewer rural to rural moves, in time, leading to relative depopulation of the rural areas, such as Auvergne and the Scottish Highlands. African-American migration from the American South (3.5 million, 1920–1960) was essentially rural to urban, peaking during World War II, at a time of labor shortage in Northern cities.

The industrialization period saw migration into frontier areas, the most important of which were in North America. Frontier migration was not new—earlier frontiers included the Ukraine, Siberia, the Irrawaddy delta, southern Africa, and northern China; but migration rates to nineteenth-century frontiers were higher than earlier ones. Railroads and steamships connected resource-rich, labor-scarce regions with urban markets, thus raising the returns from agricultural expansion. (The view that the causes of westward expansion in the United States were noneconomic, such as a desire for independence, has been discredited. The location of new farms, the high levels of investment, and the relatively low acquisition of (inferior) free land all imply profit maximization.) Most frontier farmers were the children of farmers, not urban workers, usually moving directly westward in order to raise the same crops that their parents grew.

In the late twentieth century, internal migration rates in developed countries were relatively low. Transience was still common but, in Europe at least, the rate, as measured by change of address, had fallen since the early twentieth century—typically 6 to 7 percent per annum in continental Europe. (This was a lower rate than in North America, but considerably higher than in India, China, or the former Soviet Union.) The primary reason for this was convergence. Regional income differentials had narrowed, reducing the economic benefits of migration. Moreover, economic activity was less tied to resources; that is, capital had become more mobile, labor less mobile. Finally, expectations had risen, with the paradoxical effect of inhibiting migration. Potential nineteenth-century migrants, for example, were much less inhibited by the supply of good schools or the price and quality of housing than these migrants. Hence, in some countries, commuting had become a substitute for migration.

Urban Population Growth. In preindustrial cities, deaths normally exceeded births. Urban population growth depended entirely on migration. By the mid-nineteenth century, most western European cities, including Paris, Berlin, and London, had a positive natural increase, but the southern and eastern European cities did not achieve this until the 1870s at the earliest, despite the relative youth of the migrants. (Late-twentieth-century third world cities were different: with mortality lower, migration only accounted for about a third of population growth.) Although commonly performed, this sort of calculation is rather crude. The effect of migration was to alter the place where the natural increase of the population occurred. In other words, unless the rate of in-migration continuously increased, migration could never have been the main cause of urban population growth, except when the city population was relatively very low.

Some years ago, Brinley Thomas and others argued that internal migration and emigration were substitutes—emigration rates were determined by the ability of the cities to absorb rural migrants. According to this view, the fall in emigration from eastern Germany after the 1880s was caused by industrialization and, particularly, the demand for labor in the Ruhr. This analysis rests on an assumption that most European internal migration was rural to urban and that most emigrants came from the rural areas. For obvious reasons, most European emigrants did come from the rural areas, but in many countries urban emigration rates exceeded rural rates. However, many emigrants from the European cities actually had been born in the rural areas; they were "stage" migrants. Historians do not know if they had made an initial decision (ultimately) to emigrate or were converted to emigration while living in the cities. In the English case, rural to urban stage migration was relatively unimportant. Using a demographic simulation, Baines was able to show that in the period from 1861 to 1900 emigration was primarily an urban phenomenon, and more important, that the great majority of the urban emigrants had been both born and brought up in a city. In other words, the industrialization of England had led to emigration from the center of economic change, not from the rural periphery. Internal migration was not a substitute for emigration.

[*See also* International Migration *and* Urbanization.]

BIBLIOGRAPHY

Anderson, Barbara. *Internal Migration during Modernization in Late Nineteenth Century Russia*. Princeton, 1980. Includes a comparison of the characteristics of rural frontier migrants and rural to urban migrants.

Baines, Dudley. *Migration in a Mature Economy: Emigration and Internal Migration in England and Wales, 1861–1900*. Cambridge, 1985. A detailed analysis of the origins of migrants, including the relation between internal migration and emigration.

Châtelain, Abel. *Les migrants temporaires en France de 1800 à 1914: Histoire économique et sociale des migrants temporaires des campagnes françaises au XIXe siècle au début du XXe siècle*. Paris, 1976. A famous analysis of migration within France, more comprehensive than its title suggests.

Davin, Delia. *Internal Migration in Contemporary China*. Basingstoke, U.K., 1999. The most recent book on this important subject.

Hochstadt, Steve. *Mobility and Modernity: Migration in Germany, 1820–1989*. Ann Arbor, 1999. Uses the Prussian continuous population registers to analyze total mobility, particularly movement into and out of the cities.

Lindsay, Beverley, ed. *African Migration and National Development*. Philadelphia, 1985.

Moch, Lesley Page. *Moving Europeans: Migration in Western Europe since 1650*. Bloomington, Ind., 1992.

Piore, Michael. *Birds of Passage: Migrant Labour in Industrial Societies*. Cambridge, 1979. A more wide-ranging book than suggested by the title. Includes several chapters on internal migration and migration differentials.

Ravenstein, Ernest. "The Laws of Migration." *Journal of the Statistical Society* 48 (1885), 167–222 and 52 (1889), 241–301. The first taxonomy. Remains very influential.

Skelton, Ronald. *Population Mobility in Developing Countries: A Reinterpretation*. New York, 1980. A very wide-ranging survey including material on historical migration patterns in Europe and elsewhere.

Stouffer, Samuel. "Intervening Opportunities: A Theory Relating Mobility and Distance." *American Sociological Review* 5 (1940), 845–867. With the paper by Todaro, a key article in the theory of migration.

Thomas, Brinley. *Migration and Economic Growth: A Study of Great Britain and the Atlantic Economy*. Cambridge, 1954. An analysis relating rural–urban migration in Europe to emigration and relating migration to changes in the direction of investment. Criticized in Baines's book.

Todaro, Michael. "A Model of Labour Mobility and Urban Unemployment in Less Developed Countries." *American Economic Review* 51 (1969), 138–148.

DUDLEY BAINES

INTERNATIONAL CAPITAL FLOWS.

Capital flows internationally whenever a transaction takes place across a national border and involves assets, whether they are involved in exchange for other assets or goods or merely flow as a transfer, factor income, or remittance. The study of such flows, their causes and consequences, extent and efficiency, is nothing less than a study of the integration of the international capital market itself, its historical evolution, economic underpinnings, and social and political milieu.

International capital markets could thus date as far back in time as long-distance trade itself. Those familiar with *The Merchant of Venice* know that finance and trade are really inseparable once exchange takes place over any substantial distance in time or space. This kind of large-scale commerce at a distance first flourished in the medieval Mediterranean world and was notably concentrated in such centers as Florence, Venice, and Genoa. Studies of the institutional bases of trade have examined how the particular problems of exchange have arisen—and to what extent they have been solved—over the course of history. The narrower purpose of this essay is to consider a broader definition of capital markets that goes beyond the above short-term "needs of trade" finance and encompasses both short- and long-term trades in debt and equity. The gains from such trade permit long-term development finance in capital-scarce regions (optimal allocation across space), intertemporal smoothing of shocks (insurance across time), and portfolio diversification (insurance across states of nature).

The first hint of international capital flows of this broader form usually dates to the creation of the centralized exchanges that evolved into today's modern financial centers of Europe, the prototypical examples being London and Amsterdam in the late seventeenth century. There was remarkable integration across these centers even at early dates, as measured by arbitrage in stocks of the banks and trading companies of each city. As now, they were sophisticated and fluid markets with derivative products and small margins. And as now they also attracted suspicion from the public and the authorities for their mysterious, and profitable, ways. Nonetheless, absent occasional interference, and some heavier controls in wartime periods, these markets evolved on a mostly laissez-faire basis into the late nineteenth century.

The Modern Era. Sophisticated as the early international markets were, they were still small in terms of their impact on overall national economic activity. Most accumulation and saving was still done at home, even within the firm or household, and home bias in portfolios was strong. For example, scholars have explored the links between the two largest markets, London and Amsterdam, to try to measure the extent to which Dutch capital inflows assisted economic growth during the British Industrial Revolution. The effects seem uncertain and the controversies in this debate still rage, but what most can agree on is that beyond this small corner of northwest Europe, the penetration of foreign capital into local economies was on a fairly small scale before around 1850.

After 1850, this picture changed drastically. In the so-called Age of High Imperialism, increasingly rich European countries with high marginal products of labor, but low marginal products of capital and abundant savings, sought to allocate their funds to more productive uses overseas in the developing countries, or "periphery," of that era. Differences in rates of return were the economic fundamentals that, despite risk, drew capital overseas. These fundamentals, in turn, reflected cross-location differences not only in technology but also in endowments.

The periphery encompassed two types of regions. There were rich land-abundant regions of new settlement, such as the United States, Canada, Australia, and Argentina, where capital and labor chased land. There were also poor labor-abundant and land-scarce regions, as in Asia, Africa, and most of the remainder of the Americas, where capital chased labor. Relatively open immigration policies in the settler economies encouraged labor inflows, at least from some sources such as continental Europe, and this in turn pulled in more capital. Transaction costs or immigration policies implied that labor in the poorer parts of the periphery was significantly less mobile, and thus capital came to chase this labor, if they met at all, rather than vice versa.

From 1870 to 1914, capital exports to the periphery took an ever larger share of savings in countries such as France, Germany, and, most notably, Great Britain. From 1900 to 1914, roughly half of British savings went overseas and half into domestic investment—an embrace of foreign investment by one nation never seen before or since. A large fraction of this capital, however, went to only a few countries, the settler economies, making them richer still. And it tended to bypass much of the third world, apart from some large flows into major imperial territories such as India. In terms of fundamentals, this is understandable given the huge differences in factor endowments such as land and resources across locations, but it implies that capital flows are not the universally pro-convergence force that the simplest models of growth suggest.

Thus, the world just prior to 1914 was an increasingly globalized economy, not just for trade in goods and in the migration of labor but also for capital. As is well known, this structure was effectively destroyed over the subsequent thirty years by two world wars, the Great Depression, and a rise in distrust among nations that fueled inward-looking economic policies and restrictions on the international movements of goods, capital, and people. This twentieth-century experience was unusual, since for centuries the world had not experienced a backward step in market integration, or certainly not one that could offset for long the powerful forces that technological change, communication, accumulation, and arbitrage had set into play.

It seemed to some observers that, when society so turned its back on market forces, a fundamental turning point had been reached, and the high-water mark of globalization achieved circa 1914 would never be seen again. Recent developments beginning in the late twentieth century cast doubt on that belief, as we now once again see increasing integration in global markets. Taking a long view, this may be viewed as an unsurprising development—a return to a deeper historical trend that was lost in the detours of the mid-twentieth century, notwithstanding the shock that globalization has prompted in some quarters. The historical parallel between then and now poses two major questions for researchers. First, why was there such a reversal in the degree of international capital mobility from circa 1914 until the 1980s, and is the explanation consistent with a reasonable theory of political economy? Second, in terms of the degree of integration, have we only just returned to where we once were, and can we establish any quantitative measure of whether today's market is more or less globalized than that of a hundred years ago?

Political Economy and the Trilemma. A convincing political economy of capital market intervention issues as a corollary from the Mundell-Fleming model, that workhorse of open-economy macroeconomics. According to this theory, policymakers confront a trilemma. They may hanker after the three goals of a fixed exchange rate (for price stability), capital mobility (for gains from trade), and an activist monetary policy (for demand management); but the triad is incompatible, and they can have only two out of the three at any one time.

An account of the evolution of global capital mobility in the modern era can be structured around this explanatory device. Under the classical gold standard before 1914, countries effectively sacrificed their monetary-policy autonomy to achieve goals one and two. In the interwar period (1914–1945), floating exchange rates dominated (except for a brief interlude), and goals two and three edged out fixed rates. In the Bretton Woods era (1946–1973), capital mobility was severely curtailed under the auspices of the International Monetary Fund (IMF) articles, and goal two was edged out in favor of one and three. Finally, under the post-1973 floating rate era, most countries have opened up capital markets to achieve goal two, while keeping goal three, and yielding on the fixed exchange rate again.

This account seems consistent with the historical record of policy choices, but a deeper question is why these particular political economy choices took hold when they did. In the interwar period, an evolution toward greater democracy in many core countries had allowed new voices, especially those of workers, to demand the use of activist macroeconomic policy, specifically to tame the business cycle. When the interwar experiment failed, the IMF architects such as Keynes and White sought a different solution to the trilemma that would restore fixed rates. But once the activist cat was out of its bag, capital controls were the only answer. Exactly whom this benefited in terms of political economy is uncertain, though it surely tied up capital in more capital-abundant regions and thus, again, distributionally assisted workers in the richer democracies. To the extent that this has reversed under the float, tensions have recently risen in developed economies over the export of capital to poorer countries. The origin of the recent float, however, has long been explained as the manifestation of an irresistible force, the inability of policymakers to make barriers to capital movements truly impermeable when necessary. When capital leakage occurs in such times, fixed rates become susceptible to speculative attacks and crises—and such was the fate of the system in the early 1970s.

This overall characterization is not equally apposite for all developed and developing countries. Periodically, some developing countries have still attempted limited capital-control solutions (for example, Chile and Malaysia in recent years), but the extent to which these controls will bind as a long-term constraint seems unclear. For the moment, most countries fall far short of total controls, leaving market forces ample scope to work on the margin. And many developing countries ostensibly float, but in practice they exhibit quite heavy-handed (and transparent) fixing of their exchange rates. Excepting the hard-core fixers and currency boarders, (for example, Argentina until recently), this schizophrenic state of affairs continues to expose many corners of the globe to ongoing crises whenever the "inconsistent trinity" comes into play.

Nonetheless, a renewed emphasis on capital mobility has allowed international capital markets to flourish once again when, for much of the twentieth century, they had languished in a state of poor integration. The evidence of these trends broadly takes two forms: first, evidence on the quantity of international transactions in stocks and flows; second, evidence on the size of price differences between markets using a variety of tests. Neither form is necessarily conclusive. Flows may increase (or decrease), and prices may converge (or diverge), due to technological or other fundamentals, even as the degree of integration remains constant. As is often the case in applied economics, auxiliary assumptions are necessary to interpret each form of evidence. But collectively, the patterns in the data seem to support conclusively the "U-shape" hypothesis: that integration was high at the beginning and end of the twentieth century but fell to much lower levels in between.

Quantity Evidence. A cursory look at the level of foreign capital penetration measured by stock data (Figure 1) delivers support for the "U-shape" hypothesis. The measure normalizes for the size of the world economy (or the sub-sample used) by dividing outstanding foreign assets (or liabilities) by the relevant aggregation of income (gross domestic product, GDP). Obviously, it is simpler to base this calculation on asset data (principally in a few core countries) than on liability data (in manifold periphery economies), since the latter peter out more quickly as we go back in time.

This measure shows a recent rise to levels not seen prior to 1914, but decomposing these gross stocks into net positions would show a different picture. Almost all the recovery in foreign capital stocks after 1980 took the form of small net, but large gross flows. The reason is surely that the large and persistent flows from developed to developing countries seen one hundred years ago, and the correspondingly large one-way stock position established by creditors like Great Britain, are simply not repeated today. Instead, there is now much exchanging of assets between countries, but small net flows. The current rebirth of globalization in capital markets reflects increased diversification rather than long-term development finance. As this

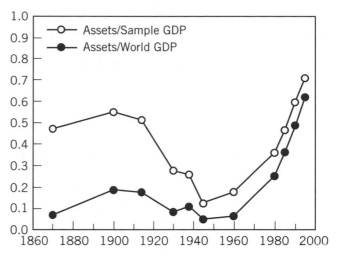

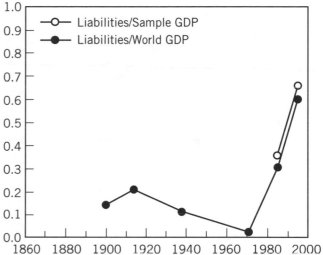

FIGURE 1. Stocks of foreign capital relative to GDP, selected countries, 1860–2000. Stock of foreign assets divided by GDP. Sample or world GDP used as specified. SOURCE: Obstfeld and Taylor, forthcoming.

suggests, "globalization" is not a single concept and takes on many different forms even in this one market.

Similar conclusions about quantity of capital flows can also be derived from an analysis of flow data, such as long-run series on capital account-to-GDP ratios for a cross section of countries. In the pre-1914 era, flows so measured were large and the cross-sectional correlation of saving and investment rates were low, suggesting a fairly strong de-linking of local saving and investment decisions in the global economy, as one would expect in a single market. For most of the subsequent years, certainly since the 1920s, the flows have been small and the correlations tight, at least until the 1980s. Again, the U-shape is seen.

Price Evidence. There are several forms of price evidence, as discussed below.

Bonds and nominal interest parity. The simplest form of price evidence in international capital markets examines interest parity conditions on bonds. The need to control for varying risk premia is the bane of this literature, and historical studies are similarly afflicted. Attention is usually centered on government bonds or prime commercial paper to minimize such problems.

A seeming "nontest" for such parity would be to examine covered interest parity (CIP) between markets, comparing forward-spot exchange-rate differentials with interest differentials. Since in today's open capital markets in developed countries, CIP is used to price forward contracts, this appears to be an identity. But such was not always the case, and even for such well-integrated markets as London and New York, there is ample evidence that in eras of high capital controls, such as the interwar years, deviations from CIP were substantial. And in periods when transaction costs might have been high, as in the early classical gold standard, high but decreasing CIP deviations are seen, based on a synthetic forward rate derived from discounts on sight versus nonsight bills of exchange. These data suggest that even looking at some of the fundamental arbitrage concepts in the capital market can be informative in regard to frictions that reflect barriers to trade.

Real interest parity and purchasing power parity. Uncovered interest parity (UIP) holds when expected exchange-rate changes match interest differentials; purchasing power parity (PPP) holds when those changes match expected inflation differentials. The common failure of tests for uncovered interest parity and purchasing power parity hypotheses hints that another hypothesis that relies on UIP and PPP, real interest parity (RIP), should be doomed to failure. But recent research on all these hypotheses suggests otherwise, at least over long horizons. RIP requires that expected real interest rate differentials match expected real exchange rate changes. Real interest rates in a sample of developed countries have shown at times fairly close coherence over the course of the twentieth century, these times being principally the early years of the gold standard and the later years of the float. Conversely, in the interwar period, bond spreads in both core and periphery exploded (Figure 2). A formal analysis of RIP, based on the standard auxiliary (Meese-Rogoff) assumption of a slowly reverting real exchange rate, reveals strong support for RIP in the bookend eras of the twentieth century, and not much in between—again confirming the stylized U-shape characterization of market integration.

Equity prices and returns. International equity markets remain a frontier for research, but perhaps deservedly so. Standard open-economy macro models usually concentrate on incomplete markets with a simplifying assumption of asset trade reduced to a riskless bond. This is an attempt to match reality, since home bias in equities has

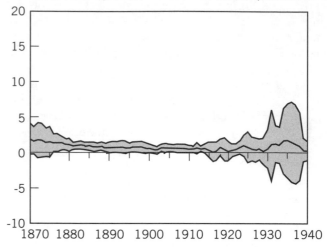

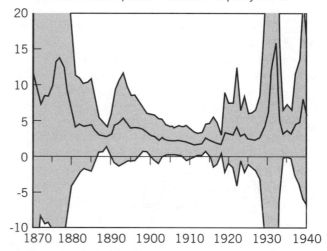

FIGURE 2. Dispersion of London bond spreads, selected countries, 1870–1940. Percentage point spread between external bond yield to maturity and yield of British consol. SOURCE: Obstfeld and Taylor, forthcoming.

been so strong historically, but even given that bias, much can be learned from the changing linkages between local equity markets, as historical conditions have changed.

Cutting-edge contemporary research demonstrates the remarkable cross-country correlation of today's equity returns, suitably measured in a common currency (or, equivalently, the strong correlation of domestic equity returns and exchange rate movements). Speculation abounds as to whether this seemingly new observation is related to globalization, but it then behooves historians to check whether such correlations have been as strong in the past. They have, such as in the 1920s, but not always, since prior to 1914 such correlations were not as high, even in a supposed era of great capital mobility.

A detailed discussion of the reasons for such patterns would likely involve a discussion of disaggregated capital flows by type, such as a portfolio versus direct and debt versus equity, that is beyond the scope of this essay. But the recent emergence of this phenomenon perhaps bespeaks again a renewed tendency to globalization in a portfolio-diversification sense (consistent with the above discussion of strong gross but weak net flows).

Real cost of capital. Lastly, we should remember that financial capital mobility is not an end in itself, but a means to use capital to achieve certain goals. One, the cross-country efficient-allocation goal, requires real marginal products of capital to be equalized across countries, but recent historical research has confirmed that this criterion can be seriously impeded by cross-country differences in capital-goods prices that reflect protection, other policies, or simply local comparative advantage in certain nontraded goods.

Countries with large price distortions (such as postwar Argentina and India) often repelled foreign capital by their high domestic prices for capital goods. In such settings, only projects with extremely high domestic returns (in output terms) could offset the investment cost (in the locally acquired capital goods). Although it is often considered a puzzle that capital does not flow to poor countries, history shows that capital is not a uniformly priced good across locations. Its high price in some poor countries has had profound negative effects on long-run development, yet it can also help explain the persistent absence of foreign capital in these same countries.

[*See also* Banking; Bills of Exchange; Bretton Woods System; Commercial and Trade Diasporas; Exchange Rates; Free Trade; Gold Standard; Great Depression; International Migration; Joint-Stock Trading Companies; Long-Distance Trade; *and* Stock Markets.]

BIBLIOGRAPHY

Bordo, Michael D., Barry Eichengreen, and Douglas A. Irwin. "Is Globalization Today Really Different Than Globalization a Hundred Years Ago?" In *Brookings Trade Forum*, edited by Susan M. Collins and Robert Z. Lawrence, pp. 58–62. Washington, D.C., 1999.

Collins, William J., and Jeffrey G. Williamson. "Capital Goods Prices and Investment, 1870–1950." *Journal of Economic History* 61 (1999), 59–94.

Davis, Lance E., and Robert A. Huttenback. *Mammon and the Pursuit of Empire: The Political Economy of British Imperialism*. Cambridge, 1986.

Davis, Lance E., and Robert E. Gallman. *Evolving Financial Markets and International Capital Flows: Britain, the Americas, and Australia, 1865–1914*. Cambridge, 2001.

Edelstein, Michael. *Overseas Investment in the Age of High Imperialism*. New York, 1982.

Eichengreen, Barry J. *Globalizing Capital: A History of the International Monetary System*. Princeton, 1996.

Feldstein, Martin, and Charles Horioka. "Domestic Saving and International Capital Flows." *Economic Journal* 90 (1980), 314–329.

Fishlow, Albert. "Lessons from the Past: Capital Markets during the 19th Century and the Interwar Periods." *International Organization* 39 (1985), 383–416.

Green, Alan, and M. C. Urquhart. "Factor and Commodity Flows in the International Economy of 1870–1914: A Multi-Country View." *Journal of Economic History* 36 (1976), 217–252.

Hall, A. R., ed. *The Export of Capital from Britain, 1870–1914*. London, 1968.

International Monetary Fund. *International Capital Markets: Developments, Prospects, and Key Policy Issues*. Washington, D.C., 1997.

James, Harold. *The End of Globalization: Lessons from The Great Depression*. Cambridge, Mass., 2001.

Jones, Charles I. "Economic Growth and the Relative Price of Capital." *Journal of Monetary Economics* 34 (1994), 359–382.

Lucas, Robert E., Jr. "Why Doesn't Capital Flow from Rich to Poor Countries?" *American Economic Review* 80 (1990), 92–96.

Neal, Larry. *The Rise of Financial Capitalism: International Capital Markets in the Age of Reason*. Cambridge, 1990.

Obstfeld, Maurice. "The Global Capital Market: Benefactor or Menace?" *Journal of Economic Perspectives* 12 (1998), 9–30.

Obstfeld, Maurice, and Alan M. Taylor. "The Great Depression as a Watershed: International Capital Mobility in the Long Run." In *The Defining Moment: The Great Depression and the American Economy in the Twentieth Century*, edited by Michael D. Bordo, Claudia D. Goldin, and Eugene N. White. Chicago, 1998.

Obstfeld, Maurice, and Alan M. Taylor. "Globalization and Capital Markets." In *Globalization in Historical Perspective*, edited by Michael D. Bordo, Alan M. Taylor, and Jeffrey G. Williamson. Chicago, forthcoming.

Obstfeld, Maurice, and Alan M. Taylor. *Global Capital Markets: Integration, Crisis, and Growth*. Cambridge, forthcoming.

Polanyi, Karl. *The Great Transformation*. New York, 1944.

Taylor, Alan M. "Argentina and the World Capital Market: Saving, Investment, and International Capital Mobility in the Twentieth Century." *Journal of Development Economics* 57 (1998), 147–184.

Taylor, Alan M. "Sources of Convergence in the Late Nineteenth Century." *European Economic Review* 43 (1999), 1621–1645.

Taylor, Alan M. "A Century of Purchasing Power Parity." *Review of Economics and Statistics* 84 (2002), 139–150.

Taylor, Alan M. "A Century of Current Account Dynamics." *Journal of International Money and Finance*. Forthcoming.

Taylor, Alan M., and Jeffrey G. Williamson. "Capital Flows to the New World as an Intergenerational Trasfer." *Journal of Political Economy* 102 (1994), 348–371.

Taylor, Alan M., and Jeffrey G. Williamson. "Convergence in the Age of Mass Migration." *European Review of Economic History* 1 (1997), 27–63.

ALAN M. TAYLOR

INTERNATIONAL CARTELS. A cartel is an agreement between independent organizations of the same branch of industry, set up with the purpose of influencing the market. Such a comprehensive definition is needed to cover government-run organizations, such as the Organization of Oil Exporting Countries (OPEC), founded in 1960, or the cartel on rubber, run by the Dutch government in the interwar period. Strategic alliances formed by enterprises of the same branch of industry are cartels by definition. Concentration in industry is contradictory to competition, and cartels are one form of such concentration. At the same time, firms and organizations forming a cartel used to compete in other fields apart from the cartelized one, for example, in innovation or rationalization in order to maximize profits. This and the fact that nearly all cartels fail after a certain length of time suggest that cartels are a less dangerous form of concentration compared with a monopoly firm. The mention of OPEC and strategic alliances points out that the problems connected with cartels are by no means only historical ones.

Cooperation and Competition. Cartels represent one form of cooperation, but the idea that cartelized firms do not compete with each other is wrong: a cartel is a temporary truce in competition in a defined field. No cartel comprehends all activities of a firm. Cartels exist on prices, on quotas, on information (e.g., patents), on access to raw material, division of markets, and a few on a combination of these. None is all comprehensive (in this case, a merger would be preferred). All cartels are defined or meant to last for a certain time (often one to three years, very few more than ten). While cooperating within the defined field, for example, in prices, firms are still able and do compete in the amount of sales. If included in the contract, they competed in the reduction of costs, also. Even when all sides want the cartel to be prolonged, the renegotiation of quotas is always competitive, which means that the partner with the highest potential of threat can achieve better conditions.

The Relationship of Swings of the Economy and Cartelization. The first book on the issue suggested that cartels are "children of need," since they are related to the downswing in the economy (Kleinwächter, 1883). However, during the deepest recession, between 1930 and 1933, more cartels failed than were formed anew. The collapsed cartels included the largest ones, such as the International Steel Cartel (ISC) and the Convention Internationale de l'Azote (CIA; nitrogenious fertilizers). Indeed, persons who were active in the cartel movement, such as Ervin Hexner, the Czech secretary of the ISC, argued against the idea that cartels are "children of need." Since the 1890s, when businessmen became aware that the tool of cartelization can be used not only in periods of recession, they increasingly applied it in the course of time. Though theoretical logic suggests the "children of need" thesis, empirical evaluation before and after 1945 found no evidence for it.

Perception over Time: Collusion or General Welfare? The United States was always very critical toward cartels, in contrast to Europe and Japan, where cooperative thinking was widespread. In Germany, cartels were recognized as private contracts since the 1890s, which meant their contents could be legally enforced. Other states followed. It was argued that cartels would give a "fair chance" to small and less-competitive firms as well, and thus help them to cope with problems of employment, a major issue

in the interwar period. Additionally, export cartels would create welfare effects in exporting countries. Consequently, governments passed laws not to fight the cartels themselves but only their abuse. For example, in Norway, Wilhelm Thagaard, president of the cartel control council, was strongly in favor of economic cooperation because in his view it represented a positive force, active for the accumulation of national wealth. When in 1929 the Norwegian canned food industry applied for a long-term cartel, Thagaard not only approved but also justified it: " . . . the usefulness [of the cartel—H.G.S.] had been revealed, which by merger and cooperation, by strict planning and economic security in production and export of canned food, was sought after." During the 1930s, several European states, such as The Netherlands, Italy, and Germany, made the cartelization of nearly the whole of their economies compulsory by law.

After 1945, the tide turned. The United States had not only shown how to win the largest war ever, but also demonstrated that the U.S. way of running a competitive economy was superior to the cooperative method used in Europe and Japan. Cartels were prohibited in countries where the United States could decide (Germany, Japan), and other countries began to outlaw cartel abuse. While the European Community for Iron and Steel in 1952 still could be interpreted in the tradition of the interwar international cartels on steel and coal, the European Economic Community in 1957 outlawed all cartels. Still, it took a whole generation to change the minds and hearts of European business administrators to understand that competition, not cooperation, was the "natural" issue in the economy. One of the most cartelized countries even after 1945, and one of the latest to decartelize, was Switzerland, a fact that earned the country the title of "world champion in cartelization."

Beneficial Cartels? Today cartels are generally understood to be detrimental to the economy. However, a certain set of cartels, for example, on norms and types, are generally beneficial. Such agreements are widespread. Firms that offer goods of different concentrations, weights, and so on have often experienced difficulties in selling their product because the customer cannot compare directly. Therefore, cartels on norms and types are rarely forbidden. This applies to services, too. Insurance companies have agreed to certain basic definitions. All major airlines have signed the International Air Transport Association (IATA) agreement, which limits the liability of the airline, defines what "dangerous goods" are, and so on. Without this cartel on the conditions of the contract, it would be impossible for the customer to compare prices.

National Differences in Cartelization. The most cooperative countries used to be the most cartelized ones. In central and northern European countries, between 50 percent and 80 percent of goods were cartelized in the interwar period. A classification was set up, which divided the most important countries into four different groups during this time:

1. Positive on cartels: Austria, Belgium, Canada, Czechoslovakia, Finland, France, Germany, the Netherlands, Norway, Sweden, Switzerland;
2. Ambivalent, state intervention: Hungary, Italy, Japan, Poland, Spain;
3. Generally ambivalent perception of cartelization: Bulgaria, Canada, Denmark, South Africa, United Kingdom;
4. General prohibition of cartels: Argentina, Australia, New Zealand, United States, Yugoslavia.

After 1945, a strong trend toward decartelization emerged, which, however, took some time to mature. A similar classification for 1950–1990 suggested three groups:

1. Decartelization: Canada, European Economic Community (European Union), Germany, Japan, United Kingdom, United States;
2. Anti-abuse, strictly applied: Denmark, Ireland, the Netherlands, Sweden;
3. Anti-abuse, co-operative tendencies: Austria, Belgium, Finland, France, Greece, Italy, Norway, Portugal, Spain, Switzerland.

Cartels and Their Relationships to Governments. Up to 1945, most governments did not interfere in cartels, since they were perceived as private businesses. However, some set up registers for cartels in order to monitor them— and offer a helping hand. Therefore, we know about twenty-five hundred cartels existed in Germany, up to two thousand in Czechoslovakia, and up to one thousand in Norway. Large cartels were helped internationally by their national diplomacy. The following illustrates the power of a cartel: in 1925, Herbert Hoover furiously announced his assault on the newly founded French-German potash cartel, because it "milked the rest of the world." Potash is a fertilizer that farmers needed, and it could be obtained only from the cartel worldwide. Hoover took the French and German cartel partners to court. The cartel was in a position of an indispensable monopoly, a fact even the U.S. government had to take into account. After several years of legal proceedings, the U.S. judges interdicted what the German and French cartel members were not doing— selling directly on the U.S. market. Their common sales organization, which had been set up in the Netherlands, was explicitly exempted from this ruling. The U.S. potash market remained cartelized, but Hoover had not lost face.

In contrast to governments, nearly all firms were in favor of cartel participation. Thus U.S. enterprises, which were legally prohibited from taking part, tried to obey the law and still play by the rules of a cartel. For example, Alcoa negotiated the international aluminium cartel, but never signed it. Its Canadian daughter firm signed it, and Alcoa itself played by the rule. Similar proceedings were observed with a cartel on explosives (DuPont, ICI, IG Farben). When questioned by the U.S. Senate, DuPont's chairman, Lammot du Pont answered: "We are guided by it, yes. We are not bound to it." The Nitrogen cartel (CIA) signed a contract in 1935 that explicitly valued its rules more than any possible government intervention. In such a case, an agreement should be hammered out by which the law could be circumvented.

After 1945, cartels were condemned because the Nazi government had used them to extend its power (Hexner, 1946; Stocking and Watkins, 1947). New research has questioned the evidence for the theory that cartels were neither more nor less instrumental than private enterprise, for example, and nobody suggested that this latter institution be abandoned.

Conditions for the Existence and for the Success of Cartels. Several economists have tried to find a measure of the success of cartels, for example, profits. In contrast, Malchup (1952) discussed an "index of depression sensivity," built on the asumption that cartelized branches master depressions better than uncartelized ones. Both measures can, but need not be useful. Some cartels simply try to reduce competition by building up barriers to entry into the industry, something not measured in prices. The success of a cartel is simply defined through the perception of its members. The international steel cartel was signed in 1926, at a time when the German industry was economically and politically weak. German firms reconstructed and later sold more than their quota. As long as they were ready to pay the fines, the cartel functioned. When payment of fines was stopped, the cartel broke down, though it never was officially terminated.

In some sectors of the economy, cartels are more easily constructed than in others. In defining these sectors, literature pointed to uniform products, such as raw materials. But that is only part of the truth. The sectors are defined by accountability. Trusted accounts can be achieved in sectors with uniform products, as well as in those characterized by oligopolies, with only a few producing firms or enterprises that command a certain know-how. Thus there have been cartels in raw materials and metals, as well as in electrotechniques and pharmaceutials. Trust was the basic precondition of all cartels.

Organizational Structures. A few simple cartels have been based on a tacit understanding of a group of men trusting each other. Apart from this exception, most cartels set up written contracts. These define not only the cartel's purpose but also the players, their fields, and the rules. It took several decades of experience to learn how watertight contracts were constructed. Chambers of commerce employed consultants on this subject. The Scandinavian cartels on paper and pulp, some of the tightest and most able organizations of their kind, were constructed with the help of German cartel specialists. Sophisticated cartels set down rules of accountance. Some cartels accumulated a "war chest" for internal or external punishment. Cartels that can count on one hegemon, defined by an unusually large quota or other abilities, used to be quite stable. In case of the international dyestuff cartel, IG Farben as the hegemon carried out all negotiations with outsiders and announced the results. International cartels often were built on top of national cartels. For example, British firms were not allowed to enter the steel cartel since there was no U.K. cartel that could be made responsible for a potential violation by a British firm. Since 1960, Saudi Arabia acted as the hegemon of OPEC.

Technical Progress and Cartelization. Economists have argued against cartelization on the asumption that because of cooperation, technical progress is slowed down. There is empirical evidence for it. Because of its guaranteed quota, the French dyestuffs industry nearly stopped its research and development. Other cartels caused the contrary, since a strong position in innovations was a good stepping stone for renegotiations. ICI and DuPont set up a (very successful) cartel to help each other in research and development. Standard Oil and IG Farben founded a cartel in order to sell their know-how on hydrogenation. In contrast, the dyestuff cartel not only excluded technological transfer but also strictly monitored this clause. Thus the issue remains contradictory.

BIBLIOGRAPHY

Barjot, Dominique. *International Cartels Revisited.* Caen, France, 1994.
Hexner, Ervin. *International Cartels.* Chapel Hill, N.C., 1946.
Jones, Geoffrey, ed. *Coalitions and Collaboration in International Business.* Aldershot, U.K., 1993.
Kleinwächter, Friedrich. *Die Kartelle: Eine Frage der Organisation der Volkswirtschaft.* Innsbruck, Austria, 1883.
Kudo, Akira, and Terushi Hara, eds. *International Cartels in Business History.* Tokyo, 1992.
Malchup, Fritz, ed. *The Political Economy of Monopoly: Business, Labor and Government Policies.* Baltimore, 1952.
Pohl, Hans, ed. *Competition and Cooperation of Enterprises on National and International Markets (Nineteenth and Twentieth Century).* Stuttgart, 1997.
Schröter, Harm G. "Cartels as a Form of Concentration in Industry: The International Dyestuffs Cartel from 1927 to 1939." *German Yearbook on Business History* (1988), 113–144.
Schröter, Harm G. "Cartelization and Decartelization in Europe, 1870–1995: Rise and Decline of an Economic Institution." *Journal of European Economic History* 251 (1996), 129–153.
Spar, Debora L. *The Cooperative Edge: The Internal Politics of International Cartels.* Ithaca, N.Y., 1995.
Stocking, George W., and Myron S. Watkins. *Cartels in Action: Case Studies in International Business Diplomacy.* New York, 1947.
Teichova, Alice. *An Economic Background to Munich.* Cambridge, 1974.

HARM G. SCHRÖTER

INTERNATIONAL MIGRATION. International migration has been a key element in the development of the Western world since the Industrial Revolution. Its most important influence has been on the peopling of the continents of North America, South America, and Australasia with emigrants of European stock and their descendants. In the century after 1820 some 55 million Europeans sought a new life in another continent, and this experience has spawned a large literature, covering a wide range of different approaches to the fundamental questions: Who migrated, when, where, and, above all, why and with what effect? Recent studies have greatly enriched historians' understanding of the characteristics of migrants, the communities they joined, and those they left. This survey seeks to place such studies in a wider context and to outline the broader causes of mass migration and its economic effects.

Patterns of Migration. Settlements of Europeans were progressively established in different parts of the New World between the sixteenth and the eighteenth centuries, but it was from the middle of the nineteenth century that mass migration gained momentum. The only comparable intercontinental migration had been that of black slaves from Africa to the Americas and the Caribbean. It was not until the 1840s that annual (free) European migration exceeded the (coerced) African migration, and it was not until the 1880s that the cumulative European migration exceeded the African (Eltis, 1983). Some coerced migrants were transported from Europe in convict chains: in the eighteenth century to America, and then in the first half of the nineteenth century to Australia.

One common form of migration was indentured servitude, which accounted for half of European immigration to the United States in the eighteenth century. Under their contracts migrants received free passage and were provided with subsistence needs in exchange for a fixed period of labor. Some of them were convicts, but many were voluntary emigrants. The supply of these indentured servants declined sharply after 1820 as the tide of free migration advanced (Grubb, 1994). Until well into the nineteenth century, the costs were too high relative to the perceived gains for many free migrants. Declining costs of passage, increasing family resources, and the growing attractiveness of New World destinations increasingly favored free migration as the century progressed.

European intercontinental emigration is plotted in Figure 1. In the first three decades after 1846, the number averaged around 300,000 per annum, doubling in the following two decades and exceeding one million per annum by the turn of the twentieth century. The source country composition also changed dramatically. In the first half of the century the dominant source of migrants was the British Isles. They were joined in midcentury by a stream of

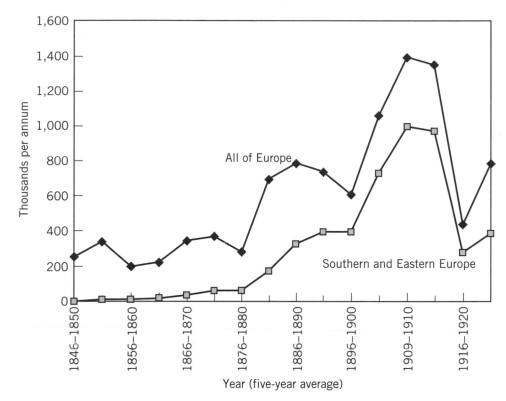

FIGURE 1. Emigration from Europe, 1846–1924. Five-year averages. SOURCE: Hatton and Williamson, 1998, p. 9.

emigrants from Germany, followed, after 1870, by a rising tide from Scandinavia and elsewhere in northwestern Europe. Emigration surged from southern and eastern Europe from the 1880s on, accounting for most of the increase in total emigration. It came first from Italy and parts of the Austro-Hungarian empire, and then from the 1890s on it included Poland, Russia, Spain, and Portugal.

The characteristics of emigrants changed over the century. The pioneer migrants of the early nineteenth century were often farmers and artisans from rural areas traveling in family groups, intending to acquire land and settle at the New World's frontier. But by midcentury emigrants from England, a country that had already undergone half a century of industrialization, were increasingly urban and unskilled (Erickson, 1994, chaps. 3, 6). Nevertheless European migrants remained largely rural in origin as the source countries changed. The mass migrants were typically young and single, and about two-thirds of them were male. More than three-fourths of the immigrants entering the United States were sixteen to forty years old, at a time when 42 percent of the U.S. population was in this age group.

The bias toward certain emigrant characteristics reflects the economic calculus underlying their migration. Although the young and the single might be the most adven-

turous and enterprising, they also had the most to gain from the move. By emigrating as young adults, they were able to reap gains over most of their working lives while minimizing the costs of earnings forgone during passage and job searches. Also by moving as single adults, they were able to minimize the direct costs of the move. Unskilled emigrants also had little technology- or country-specific human capital invested and hence stood to lose few of the economic returns from such acquired skills (except language). This characterization reinforces the premise that economic considerations were paramount, and that most emigrants moved in the expectation of a more prosperous future.

Cross-National Differences in Emigration. Emigration rates varied widely across Europe in the late nineteenth century. Table 1 presents average emigration rates per thousand of population for twelve countries. The highest rates were from Ireland, averaging thirteen per thousand between 1850 and 1913. Norway and Sweden had emigration rates averaging nearly five per thousand from 1870 to 1913, whereas those from Germany and Belgium were at or below two per thousand, and France was close to zero. These emigration rates also display different trends. Emigration from Ireland declined after the 1850s, and from Germany and Norway it declined after the 1880s.

TABLE 1. *Gross Emigration Rates from European Countries, 1850–1913 (Emigrants per 1000 population per annum, decade averages)*

	1850–1859	1860–1869	1870–1879	1880–1889	1890–1899	1900–1913
Belgium	1.90	2.22	2.03	2.18	1.96	2.32
Denmark	—	—	1.97	3.74	2.60	2.80
France	—	0.12	0.16	0.29	0.18	0.15
Germany	1.80	1.61	1.35	2.91	1.18	0.43
Great Britain	4.83	2.47	3.87	5.71	3.92	7.08
Ireland	18.99	15.16	11.28	16.04	9.70	7.93
Italy	—	—	4.29	6.09	8.65	17.97
Netherlands	0.50	1.67	2.66	4.06	4.62	5.36
Norway	—	—	4.33	10.16	4.56	7.15
Portugal	—	—	2.91	3.79	5.04	5.67
Spain	—	—	—	3.91	4.63	6.70
Sweden	0.51	2.52	2.96	8.25	5.32	2.93

SOURCE: Hatton and Williamson, 1998, p. 33.

Almost at the same time, emigration rates from Italy and Spain began a steep ascent, a trend halted only by the outbreak of World War I in Europe.

There were also significant cross-border migrations within Europe, which are included in these figures. The main receiving countries within Europe were France, Germany, and Switzerland, and the main sources were Belgium (to France), Poland (to Germany), and Italy. Such cross-border flows could be quite large, as in Italy where they accounted for 45 percent of emigration between 1876 and 1915; but for Europe as a whole they were small relative to the intercontinental movement. Moreover, these migrations were typically temporary or seasonal, and the numbers increased much more slowly than did intercontinental migration.

Various theories have been offered to explain the wide range of experience, not only across countries but across regions and over time. One typology divides these theories into four groups (Lowell, 1987, chap. 2): "structural change and response," which stresses economic modernization and the demographic transition; "economic," which stresses the relative income incentive to migrate; "innovation and diffusion," which stresses the spread of information through social networks; and "rural ecology," which stresses change in the structure of landholding and in farming methods. Although these theories are sometimes seen as competing explanations, they are not mutually exclusive: accepting one theory does not imply rejecting the others.

One recent study of emigration rates for the twelve European countries in Table 1 takes advantage of recently assembled data for internationally comparable real wage rates for unskilled workers (Hatton and Williamson 1998, chap. 3). Decade average emigration rates were explained by a number of variables, including the wage *ratios* between source and destination countries that are relevant to the migration decision. The results indicate that relative wage rates were important: a 10 percent rise in the wage ratio (destination to source country) raised the annual emigration rate in the long run by 1.3 per thousand of the population. By contrast, the share of the labor force in agriculture had a weak negative effect, suggesting that, on balance, agricultural populations were less mobile than industrial populations.

Labor force growth (as measured by natural increase twenty years earlier) had powerful effects, with emigration increasing by up to half of the excess births. This strongly supports Easterlin's (1961) argument that the demographic transition drove emigration, but it is important to note that it was not the result of a labor force boom pushing down wage rates since wage effects already were taken into account. Rather it was a direct spillover into emigration. Other important influences on decade emigration rates are the lagged emigration rate in the previous decade and the stock of previous emigrants living in destination countries. The migration literature often has stressed chain migration, sometimes called the "friends and relatives effect," as an important influence. Once established, channels of migration perpetuated themselves through earlier migrants' providing prepaid tickets for the passage, providing food and shelter, and using social networks to permit access to job opportunities. To the extent that the migrant stock captures this effect, it indicates that for each thousand previous emigrants, between twenty and one hundred more were pulled abroad each year.

One important phenomenon that theories of emigration must explain is this: during the onset of modern economic growth in Europe national emigration rates often rose gradually at first, reached a peak, and then gradually declined.

This "life cycle" of emigration has been identified for a number of European countries prior to World War I. The influences just described can help explain this pattern. Demographic growth, a declining share of the labor force in agriculture, and consequent growth in the stock of previous migrants all contributed to the upswing of the emigration life cycle. However, a narrowing wage gap, as real wages in Europe converged on those in the New World, had a countervailing influence. Eventually the peak was passed as continuing real-wage convergence overcame the weakening effects of industrialization, demographic boom, and the migrant stock.

Existing quantitative findings are largely confined to western Europe and exclude eastern European latecomers to mass migration. To encompass a broader range of experience, it sometimes is argued that the so-called poverty constraint must be taken into account. In the least developed countries and regions, despite large incentives to migrate, those who had the most to gain were simply too poor to finance the move. Thus some growth in wages and income was a precondition for participating in mass migration, a point that has been argued for countries such as Italy (Faini and Venturini, 1994). Once a migration flow became established, the help of friends and relatives who already had emigrated served to attenuate the poverty constraint. This would help explain why emigration could be high from a country such as Ireland and low (at least until the end of the nineteenth century) from the south of Italy, an equally poor region. In the Irish case, the great famine of the 1840s effectively ejected a million Irish migrants, who formed a substantial migrant stock, particularly in the United States. In the absence of the poverty constraint, emigration from Ireland declined as real wages rose. By contrast, in Italy, emigration increased as rising income and the growing migrant stock gradually eased the poverty constraint.

Local and Regional Differences in Emigration. An important challenge to any theory of emigration is to see if it can explain differences in emigration rates between regions and localities in the same country. Differences in local emigration rates were often larger than those between countries, and any convincing theory of emigration should be able to account for at least some of the variation. In Italy, for example, in 1882 rates of emigration across the sixteen Compartimenti varied from close to zero in Lazio to fifteen per thousand in Basilicata. Among the sixty-nine provinces the variation was even greater: emigration from the province of Belluno was as high as forty-six per thousand. Similar variations can be found in other countries, but despite such clear and obvious differences there has been little consensus about how they should be explained (Baines, 1994).

A number of studies have suggested that access to land, the availability of other rural employment opportunities, and population growth all interacted to produce emigration from rural areas. For Norway and Sweden, Lowell (1987, pp. 212–216) found that emigration was negatively related to local wage rates but also positively related to the number of landless laborers and the share of land occupied by large estates. In northwest Germany, proto-industrial areas where cottage industry was interlocked with agriculture (especially seasonally), had higher rates of natural increase than did other areas. They were also vulnerable to factory competition and thus had increasing difficulties absorbing young workers generated by booming birth rates two decades earlier. Thus "emigration was highest where there were many agriculturalists but little agriculture" (Kamphoefner, 1976, p. 182).

Recent econometric analyses of county-level data for Ireland confirm some of these findings. First, larger family size was associated with higher emigration. Second, emigration was strongly related to indicators of poverty—clearly the Irish were escaping poverty and were not constrained by the poverty trap. Third, the share of small-holdings in total landholding reduced emigration, suggesting that where there were opportunities to inherit (or acquire through marriage or other means) small plots of land, there was much less emigration (Hatton and Williamson, 1998, chap. 5). A similar analysis f.or Italian provinces emphasizes the emigration-increasing effects of natural increase, urbanization, and industrial development. In contrast to Ireland, the proportion of owner-occupiers and sharecroppers was positively related to emigration. The study also highlights the effects of chronic underemployment in southern agriculture, leading to emigration.

In an important article, John Gould (1980) argued for what he called the innovation and diffusion approach. He argued that emigration was often constrained in its early stages by a lack of information and knowledge about the opportunities for emigration. In the innovating (often coastal) areas, contacts with travelers and traders got a stream of emigration started. As knowledge of conditions in destination areas grew, emigration increased and began to spill over into neighboring localities and regions, producing a convergence of emigration rates. The evidence for such effects is somewhat limited because of the difficulty of measuring information flows, but the fact that a good deal of the variation between localities can be explained by economic and demographic variables indicates that such effects were not critically important once migration was well established.

In the early stages of emigration, information effects may have been important. In a study of individual villages in Hesse-Cassel (Germany) in the 1850s, Wegge (1998) was able to distinguish between migrants who emigrated as part of networks and those who did not. Emigrants who were not following in a chain had less knowledge of their

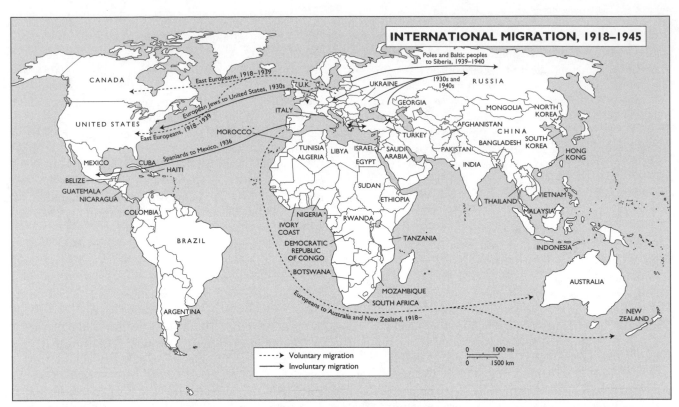

INTERNATIONAL MIGRATION, 1918–1945

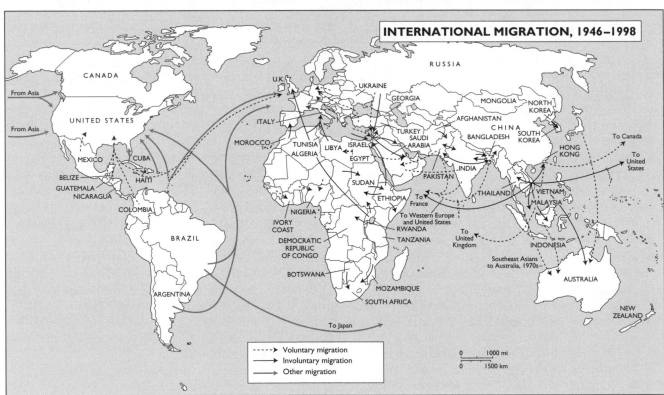

INTERNATIONAL MIGRATION, 1946–1998

destination and took more cash with them. Those who subsequently moved as part of a chain benefited from better information and less uncertainty, and thus faced lower costs of emigration. It is not so clear how far information *alone* generated increases in the migrant flow, and how much chain migration was simply a matter of reducing the costs of migration and releasing the poverty constraint.

Short-Term Fluctuations in Emigration. Emigration rates from individual countries or regions were extremely volatile. They often increased, or they fell sharply, only to recover again in a few years. Much of the quantitative literature, following Jerome (1926), has focused on whether "push" or "pull" forces were the more important determinants of emigration from a variety of different countries. The debate has often turned on the size and the statistical significance of variables representing conditions in the source versus the destination countries. A further issue has been the question of whether variations in real wage rates or differences in job opportunities (as represented by indices of production or employment) mattered more. In reviewing the literature up to the late 1970s, Gould (1979) pointed to a lack of consistency in the results of different studies. Nevertheless, emigration decisions must have been based on some comparison, however approximate, between conditions at home and at the destination. Similarly, although cyclical conditions clearly mattered in the timing of emigration, real wage ratios also must have been important, especially in the long run.

Recent studies have used an economic decision-making framework where potential emigrants compare expected future income streams at home and abroad. Following Todaro (1969), expected income depends on the wage rate and the probability that the migrant will find a job. Because migrants are risk-averse, and because greater uncertainty attaches to the probability of employment than to the wage rate, the latter has a larger "weight" in the migration function. Econometric results for emigration from the United Kingdom for the period from 1870 to 1913 provide support for this approach. They indicate that wage rates *and* unemployment rates, at home *and* abroad, help explain emigration (Hatton, 1995). Although variations in unemployment were the key determinant of short-run fluctuations, the long-run trends were determined chiefly by wage ratios, consistent with the findings for emigration rates by decade mentioned earlier. Estimates for Ireland indicate that a 17 percent fall in the wage ratio (foreign to home) between 1876 and 1880 and from 1909 to 1913 contributed four per thousand to the fall in the emigration rate (Hatton and Williamson, 1998, p. 83).

Short-run fluctuations in economic activity account for as much as half the volatility in annual emigration rates, but this itself is something of a puzzle. Given that migration decisions were based on comparing future expected lifetime earnings profiles, one might expect that short-run changes, quickly reversed, would have little effect on the long-run comparison. One reason for the surprising volatility in emigration is the so-called option value of waiting. Although it might be worth emigrating immediately, in spite of high unemployment at the destination, it would be better still to wait a year or two (retaining the option to emigrate) if conditions were expected to improve. Hence migrants timed their moves to maximize the overall life-cycle benefits.

Destination Choice and Return Migration. What determined emigrant choices among different overseas destinations is a somewhat neglected topic. Given the economic calculus revealed in other aspects of emigrants' decisions, it is difficult to believe that different destinations were not compared and treated as alternatives. Choice of destination within a receiving country, such as the United States, is associated with measures of regional income, as might have been expected, and especially with the stock of previous migrants to that state/region (Dunleavy and Gemery, 1978). However, choice among countries involves additional factors such as cultural and linguistic affinity with the country of origin. Thus emigrants from Britain and Ireland chose from among the English-speaking British Dominions and the United States. Emigrants from Italy, Spain, and Portugal revealed much stronger preferences for South American countries such as Argentina and Brazil than did other emigrants from continental Europe.

The effects of wages and living standards on the choice of destination is difficult to discern. An analysis of the choices of Italian emigrants between Argentina, Brazil, and the United States at the turn of the twentieth century suggests that the substitution effect of relative wages was relatively small (Hatton and Williamson, 1998, p. 120). Choice among these destinations seems to have been influenced more by emigration traditions favoring one country or another than by wages. As emigration from Italy grew, the prominence of the United States increased; but this shift occurred only gradually despite a substantial wage difference favoring the United States. Much of the growth in emigration came from southern Italy, where the tradition of emigrating to South America was weakest. Thus when new streams of emigration arose, economic factors carried more weight in the choice of destination than they did when emigrant streams were well established.

These preferences were sometimes reinforced by policy and/or prejudice in the receiving country—incentives to some emigrants and restrictions on others. Such incentives evidently had powerful effects in drawing immigrants. For example, in the early 1840s an increase in the number of free passages offered to British immigrants to

Australia and New Zealand increased the share going to these destinations (Erickson, 1994, p. 168). Such subsidies were likely to be particularly important early in the nineteenth century when costs of travel (including time) were high. Later in the century they continued to influence emigration, especially to the more distant destinations. Thus, during certain periods, subsidized passages were offered to British immigrants to Australia and to (northern) Italian immigrants to the state of São Paolo (Brazil). On the other hand, some groups such as the Chinese were completely excluded, as, for example, under the Chinese Exclusion Act of 1882 in the United States and under the "white Australia" policy.

Although most intercontinental migrants were permanent settlers, there were mounting flows of return migrants. By the end of the nineteenth century about a third of European migrants to the United States were returning home, usually after only a few years. Increasing destination wages and falling travel times contributed to the trend, but the upward trend in return migration owes much to the changing country composition of emigrants—particularly the growing share from southern Europe. Many of these emigrants intended to return to their country of origin and to use their accumulated savings to marry and set up homes and often to start farms and businesses. In such cases, the outward flows were more male-dominated than those where permanent settlement was the goal. Although return-migration strategies are not well understood, it is clear that differences in rates of return migration are associated more with the country of origin than with the country of destination. Thus high rates of return migration among southern Europeans at the turn of the twentieth century applied equally to those emigrating to North America and to South America.

Cultural factors may account for some of the difference in return migration across countries. The evidence suggests that, whatever the deeper reason, family and social structure and patterns of landholding lay at the heart of return migration decisions. This may be seen in the contrast between Ireland, where small-holdings were associated with lower emigration, and Italy, where small ownership and sharecropping were associated with high emigration. It is consistent with the view that for Italians, emigration was often used as a strategy for acquiring land or property back home (see Cinel, 1991). This strategy often involved migration and remigration, sometimes by several family members. It should not be interpreted as the product of overoptimistic expectations followed by disillusionment with the New World.

Immigrant Assimilation. It is sometimes argued that immigrants faced discrimination and disadvantage in the receiving countries, factors that made migration less attractive or encouraged return migration. The United States Immigration Commission, which reported in 1911, argued that many immigrants, particularly those from southern and eastern Europe, were unable or unwilling to integrate into American society, and that they lacked the skills and motivation to be successful in the labor market. Instead they crowded into ghettos and into unskilled occupations with little hope of upward mobility. Revisionist writers have argued that immigrant communities were not backward-looking and isolationist. Rather, they provided a means through which immigrants could benefit from social support networks and gain economic advancement while at the same time maintaining their ethnic identity (Bodnar, 1985).

An important question has been that of whether immigrants did suffer economic disadvantage, and whether they caught up with the native-born as they acquired knowledge, skills, and experience in the host-country labor market. Although some studies have found that the earnings disadvantage of immigrants relative to the native-born increased over the life cycle, more recent analysis suggests the opposite (Hatton and Williamson, 1998, chap. 7). On arrival in the host country, immigrants suffered a substantial earnings disadvantage; but as they accumulated host-country experience, their earnings converged on those of the native-born. Some groups of immigrants, chiefly those from northwestern Europe, eventually overtook the native-born, whereas others, often from southern and eastern Europe, did not do so. These persistent differences in the labor-market performance of immigrants by country of origin were associated with initial disadvantages in literacy, skills, and language. Such disadvantages were negligible for immigrants who arrived as children and nonexistent for second-generation immigrants.

The Labor Market Impact. In the United States and in other immigrant-receiving countries, immigrants were absorbed easily into expanding labor markets. Comparability of earnings suggests that immigrant labor was a close substitute for that of native-born workers, particularly the low-skilled. Nevertheless, immigrants were often concentrated in specific occupational groups. Thus, for example, the Italian-born accounted for 55 percent of barbers and hairdressers, 97 percent of bootblacks, and 34 percent of shoemakers in the United States in 1900. However, there is no evidence that native-born workers could not have filled these jobs. Rather, the competition of immigrants crowded out native-born workers, who then competed in other labor markets. Such influences also can be observed geographically. For example, as immigrants settled in the cities on the eastern seaboard of the United States, they helped boost the westward migration of the native-born (and previous immigrants). One estimate is that for every one hundred immigrants arriving in the northeastern states, forty of the native-born were displaced to other regions (Hatton and Williamson, 1998, p. 168).

Findings such as these imply that the effects of labor-market competition between immigrants and the native-born would be spread across the entire economy rather than being felt only in places and occupations where immigrants were located. This makes it difficult to observe and measure the effects on the earnings (of both immigrants and the native-born) arising from the immigrant labor supply. One approach is to specify a general equilibrium model of the economy where the effects of an increase in the labor force percolate though the entire economy. An exercise along these lines indicates that had there been no immigration to the United States after 1870, the labor force would have been 27 percent smaller than it actually was in 1910, and the real wage of unskilled workers 34 percent higher than otherwise (Hatton and Williamson, 1998, p. 213). Therefore, immigration, by adding to labor-force growth, tended to reduce the growth rate of real wages in the countries that received immigrants.

Similar effects were working in the source countries, but in the opposite direction. The classic example is Ireland, where, as a result of the high rates of emigration, the population fell from 6.5 million in 1851 to 4.4 million in 1911. In the absence of emigration the population in 1911 probably would have been somewhere between 6.4 million and 9.8 million. The decline in the agricultural labor force would have occurred more slowly, as would the shift in the structure of agriculture from tillage to pasture. Agricultural wages probably would have been between 15 and 30 percent lower than they actually were in 1911. In fact, real wages in Ireland relative to those in England and Wales increased from about 60 percent in 1861 to 75 percent in 1911, and most of this convergence can be attributed to emigration-induced shrinkage in the labor force (Boyer et al., 1994). Effects similar in nature but smaller in magnitude were working in other sending countries, including England and Wales.

If immigration depressed real wages in receiving countries and emigration raised them in sending countries, it could have caused a convergence in wages and incomes between the New World and the Old. In 1870 the ratio between real wages for unskilled workers in the major New World and Old World countries was 1.96; by 1910 it had fallen to 1.79. It has been estimated that, in the absence of international migration, the ratio would have increased to 2.50 in 1910. Hence the reallocation of labor toward the labor-scarce, resource-abundant New World fostered convergence rather than divergence in wage incomes. However, this was but one element in what might be called the globalization of the late-nineteenth-century international economy. Another element was international capital flows. Large flows of capital, moving in the same direction

as the migrants, raised labor productivity in the New World relative to the Old. These capital flows muted the contribution of migration to international wage convergence.

The End of the Age of Mass Migration. In the early twentieth century, as immigration reached new heights, opposition to immigrants increased, and calls for the restriction of immigration grew louder. The United States Immigration Acts of 1921 and 1924, which introduced quotas on immigrants by national origin, often are seen as putting an abrupt end to the age of mass migration. Since quotas were based on the *stock* of foreign-born in prewar censuses, they favored the countries of northwest Europe, which were in the downswing of their emigration cycle and thus would have sent fewer immigrants anyway. The quotas bit deepest into emigration from southern and eastern Europe, many of which were still in the upswing stage when emigration was halted by World War I. Added to this, the worldwide depression of the 1930s, which was particularly severe in the New World, discouraged immigrants from most European countries.

After World War II, emigration revived as prosperity returned to the world economy, but it did not reach the peaks attained before World War I. One reason for this is that migration chains, which had been an important factor in the earlier period, had been broken by thirty years of war and economic upheaval. Emigration from Europe grew over the following decades but not so fast as it had in the fifty years prior to 1914. This difference was partly due to continuing restrictions on immigration; it also reflects the renewed convergence of living standards in Europe on those of destination countries such as the United States.

[*See also* Economic Imperialism; Internal Migration; *and* Settler Economies.]

BIBLIOGRAPHY

Baines, Dudley. "European Emigration, 1815–1930: Looking at the Emigration Decision Again." *Economic History Review* 47 (1994), 525–544.

Bodnar, John. *The Transplanted: A History of Immigrants in Urban America.* Bloomington, Ind., 1985.

Boyer, George R., Timothy J. Hatton, and Kevin O'Rourke. "The Impact of Emigration on Real Wages in Ireland, 1850–1914." In *Migration and the International Labor Market, 1850–1939,* edited by T. J. Hatton and J. G. Williamson, pp. 221–239. London, 1994.

Cinel, Dino. *The National Integration of Italian Return Migration, 1870–1929.* Cambridge, 1991.

Dunleavy, J. A., and H. A. Gemery. "Economic Opportunity and the Responses of Old and New Immigrants in the United States." *Journal of Economic History* 38 (1978), 901–917.

Easterlin, Richard. "Influences in European Overseas Migration before World War I." *Economic Development and Cultural Change* 9 (1961), 33–51.

Eltis, David. "Free and Coerced Transatlantic Migrations: Some Comparisons." *American Historical Review* 88 (1983), 251–280.

Erickson, Charlotte. *Leaving England: Essays on British Emigration in the Nineteenth Century.* Ithaca, N.Y., 1994.

Faini, Ricardo, and Alessandra Venturini. "Italian Emigration in the Pre-War Period." In *Migration and the International Labor Market, 1850–1939*, edited by T. J. Hatton and J. G. Williamson, pp. 72–90. London, 1994.

Gould, John D. "European Intercontinental Emigration: Patterns and Causes." *Journal of European Economic History* 8 (1979), 593–679.

Gould, John D. "European Inter-continental Emigration: The Role of 'Diffusion' and 'Feedback.'" *Journal of European Economic History* 9 (1980), 267–315.

Grubb, Farley. "The End of European Immigrant Servitude in the United States: An Economic Analysis of Market Collapse, 1772–1835." *Journal of Economic History* 54 (1994), 794–824.

Hatton, Timothy. J. "A Model of U.K. Emigration, 1870–1913." *Review of Economics and Statistics* 77 (1995), 407–415.

Hatton, Timothy J., and Jeffrey G. Williamson. *The Age of Mass Migration: Causes and Economic Impact.* New York, 1998.

Jerome, Harry. *Migration and Business Cycles.* New York, 1926.

Kamphoefner, Walter D. "At the Crossroads of Economic Development: Background Factors Affecting Emigration from Nineteenth Century Germany." In *Migration across Time and Nations*, edited by I. A. Glazier and L. De Rosa, pp. 174–201. New York, 1976.

Lowell, Briant Lindsay. *Scandinavian Exodus: Demography and Social Development of 19th Century Rural Communities.* Boulder, 1987.

Thomas, Dorothy Swaine. *Social and Economic Aspects of Swedish Population Movements.* New York, 1976.

Todaro, Michael P. "A Model of Labor Migration and Urban Unemployment in Less Developed Countries." *American Economic Review* 59 (1969), 138–148.

Wegge, Simone A. "Chain Migration and Information Networks: Evidence from Nineteenth Century Hesse-Cassel." *Journal of Economic History* 58 (1998), 957–986.

Timothy J. Hatton

INVESTMENT AND COMMERCIAL BANKS. Commercial and industrial firms deal primarily with three main categories of financial institutions: commercial banks, investment banks, and universal banks. The first type deals primarily with the short-term financing needs of firms, the second handles underwriting and issuing of securities, and the third combines the services of the first two types.

Investment and commercial banks normally differ in their internal financial structure. For example, investment banks naturally hold fewer short-term, liquid assets than commercial banks. A typical commercial bank holds some portion of its assets in reserves, owing to either government regulation or simple prudence, whereas investment banks may hold virtually no reserves. Because of this potential asset illiquidity, investment banks primarily fund their activities from long-term liabilities—very often share capital—and rarely take significant deposits or other short-term liabilities.

Financial institutions may significantly influence the macroeconomy, but in varying ways. Deposit taking, if it attracts investors who would not otherwise invest directly in securities, mobilizes capital for use in industry. As a bank transforms its liabilities into circulating assets, such as loans or securities, it expands the money supply. Banks also help transmit government monetary policy as they pass along changes in official interest rates dictated (directly or through fluctuations in money supply) by the monetary authority. By virtue of their minimal deposit and loan business, pure investment banks mainly engage in asset transformation and multiple expansion, rather than interest rate transmission. Commercial and universal banks, in contrast, can play a significant role in policy transmission through their lending activities.

Commercial Banking. The term *commercial bank* covers a wide range of banking institutions that provide services to the commercial and industrial sectors. Having their roots in the preindustrial period, commercial banks developed gradually into their modern form. Most countries with a continuous history of large, specialized commercial banking systems are Anglophone—England and the United States, for example—or are closely related to England historically—for example, Argentina and India. Many countries, such as France and the Netherlands, have supported substantial numbers of specialized commercial banks alongside universal banks or have attempted for a period of time to force specialization in banking. Most such provisions, such as those in Belgium, Greece, and Italy, appeared during the upheaval following World War I and lasted for several decades. By the 1990s, nearly all highly developed economies had started to integrate (or reintegrate) commercial and investment banks into financial conglomerates, though the subsidiary institutions often remained largely independent of one another in their operations.

The principal activities of commercial banks include deposit taking and short-term lending. In their pure form, commercial banks historically have offered little in the way of investment-banking services, as those functions are usually performed by a distinct group of intermediaries. Reflecting the primary source of operating funds, the British commercial banks are often termed deposit banks. Early on, deposits were often taken for fixed terms and required advance notice for withdrawal. By the late nineteenth century, and expanding significantly thereafter, commercial banks developed demand or sight deposits, which could be withdrawn without notice. Nearly all highly developed economies had built national branch networks by the onset of World War I, facilitating the growth of the deposit business by making depository offices convenient to potential customers.

Commercial banks typically provided capital to firms through very short-term loans, bills of exchange, and loans and advances. In the British case, very short-term loans, termed money at call, consisted primarily of loans to stockbrokers for transactions in the London discount market or the London Stock Exchange. Commercial banks, particularly in England, also held a substantial proportion of their investments in the form of government and government-guaranteed assets.

Investment Banking. The term *investment bank* refers to a class of financial institutions primarily concerned with the intermediation of securities, such as stocks, bonds, and government debt. These banks, typically private, are the principal conduit for directing long-term capital to corporations and governments. Investment banks at least provide primary issuance and placement of securities, and many offer additional services. Pure investment houses do persist and may further specialize in either wholesale or retail placements.

Investment banks are closely associated with securities markets and, in the case of specialized investment banks, brokerage houses; they depend on both kinds of institutions to provide a market for their products. The larger the potential market for a primary security issue, the easier it is for the investment house to sell the security. Moreover, the subsequent trading of securities, from one investor to another, falls in large part within the purview of these same institutions. Even in the case of universal banking, the secondary market for many securities exists in an organized exchange. As investors know that they later may desire to sell their shares, ease of trading—in the form of a large and liquid secondary securities market—enhances the prospects for initial placements.

Investment banks place securities in two main ways. Some may purchase a complete issue from an issuer and subsequently sell off stakes to investors; others take subscriptions from investors and go forward with the issue once they have garnered sufficient participation. The choice of one method over another may significantly impact the structure of the bank and its financial relations with its customers. In particular, investment banks that use the former method may become more actively involved in both ownership and control of industrial firms than those using the latter method. Direct equity stakes can arise by design, but often result from the undersubscription of a new issue that is fully owned by an investment bank or a universal bank.

Government regulation and securities market rules vary in determining what functions investment banks may perform and how they do so. Historically, some governments or exchanges have regulated the portion of an issue that must be paid up in advance of an issue. In some countries and periods, for example, it has not been possible for new issues of stocks to be listed officially on a given exchange without the full value being paid up. Yet in other countries, stock shares have been listed with a small fraction of the capital actually paid in to the company. Particularly in the United States, the government has limited the scope of services that chartered banks legally can provide. Thus,

HOUSE OF ROTHSCHILD. Mayer Amschel Rothschild (1744–1812) founded the London-based House of Rothschild that soon became the largest banking enterprise in the world. (Prints and Photographs Division, Library of Congress)

the operations of investment banks can vary with the political and regulatory regime in place.

Specific institutional forms vary somewhat, but most countries that underwent industrialization by the turn of the twentieth century followed similar patterns of financial evolution. Investment banks emerged as a significant, distinct institution in the early nineteenth century. Before then, investment banking functions were performed mostly by merchants or other middlemen. Investment banks or bankers certainly existed prior to 1800, yet the early ones concentrated primarily on government business. The relative scarcity of true investment banks must have stemmed from legal hurdles to incorporation that naturally limited the existence of industrial equities in most countries during the first half of the nineteenth century. Thus, the real expansion of investment banks, most notably in continental Europe and the United States, followed the relaxation of incorporation laws in the 1860s and 1870s and tended to progress hand in hand with the growth of railroads and large-scale industry, both public and private.

England. Pure investment banks dominated the nineteenth-century investment banking scene in England. Securities markets appeared relatively early, as did the institutions for placing those assets. Likewise, the advanced state of railway construction provided additional need for investment banking, especially by the turn of the nineteenth century. As in most countries, however, the pool of public share companies—and therefore the business of placing industrial equities—remained constrained until later in the nineteenth century.

United States. From the start of the nineteenth century on, a range of intermediaries—merchants, incorporated commercial banks, private bankers, lotteries, auctioneers, and brokers—provided some form of investment banking services. Specialized investment banks arose in the 1850s and, responding to an immense demand for borrowing by the federal government, multiplied with the Civil War. The most famous American investment banker is undoubtedly John Pierpont Morgan. J. P. Morgan cofounded his first bank in 1860 and worked with a variety of partners over subsequent decades. Investment banks were largely specialized institutions in the United States, but some quasi-universal institutions were formed through the integration of investment subsidiaries into commercial banks. Legal restrictions on the activities of chartered commercial banks, most notably the politically motivated Glass-Steagall Act of 1933, tended to enforce the separation of investment and commercial banking until the unraveling of those provisions in the 1990s.

Universal Banks. Universal banks combine investment banking with brokerage, short-term lending, deposit taking, insurance, or other financial services. Thus, the activities described under commercial and investment banking headings apply equally to the universal banks. Although proto-universal banks existed in the form of private bankers well before the nineteenth century, large-scale joint-stock universal banks first took shape in the 1830s, with the first real wave of foundings coming in the 1850s. As with pure investment banks, the most important period of growth came with the rapid rise of stock companies in the mid- to late nineteenth century.

Along with their traditional financing activities, universal banks (and pure investment banks) may participate in the governance of nonfinancial corporations, particularly through placement of representatives on boards of directors. Representation may arise through direct ownership of equity or via proxy votes assigned to the bank. Of all banking-institution types, universal banks may gain access to company boards most easily because they issue and broker securities and then often hold them on deposit or for safekeeping for customers. Pure investment banks, because they tend not to engage in account services for small stakeholders, have a less obvious and ready source of proxy votes. Nonetheless, there are no iron-clad connections between scope of banking services and involvement in corporate governance. Not all universal banks hold significant equity stakes or board positions in nonfinancial firms, and many banks that are not universal participate in both ways.

Universal banks, since they also provide short-term commercial lending, hold liquid assets and assume outside liabilities, even sight deposits. Thus, the financial structure of this class of bank can range anywhere from that of a pure investment bank to that of a pure commercial bank, depending on the services provided and the management principles in place.

The structure of a bank's assets and liabilities affects its own profitability and riskiness. Turning deposits and capital into loans and securities, known as qualitative asset transformation (QAT), yields a return to the bank. The more a bank uses its resources to invest in working assets, the greater are the potential profits to the bank. At the same time, such QAT poses risks to the bank if the bank's resources have significantly shorter maturity or greater liquidity than its assets. Although all banks face this trade-off between profit rates and risk, universal banks contend with the additional problem of striking the optimal balance of commercial and investment services. The combination might offer economies of scope or benefits of diversification, but one can equally hypothesize diseconomies of scope, conflicts of interest (between the investment and the commercial banking functions), or excessive riskiness stemming from liquidity mismatching.

Belgium. Home to the Société Générale (S.G.) and to much heavy industry, Belgium appears to have been the first country to introduce large-scale mixed or universal banks. Founded by the king in 1822, the S.G. initially played the part of a development bank. By 1834, it had assumed the role of commercial bank as well, and it provided the blueprint for a number of similar mixed banks elsewhere in continental Europe. Other mixed banks, most notably the Banque de Belgique, arose in Belgium in the later 1830s and thereafter. In this early period of heavy industrialization, mixed banks sometimes took large direct equity positions in firms they promoted; but the practice proved risky, and some—the Banque de Belgique, in particular—were forced out of the investment side of the business. In general, however, the largest industrial banks have provided the majority of investment-banking services for Belgium since the early nineteenth century, and universality of one form or another remained the norm, except during a period of government regulation starting in the mid-1930s.

France. As in most other countries, investment-banking services first emerged in France among merchants-cum-bankers. Beginning around 1830, and expanding particularly toward the end of the July monarchy (1848), these private, family-run firms joined together into investment associations and promoted many savings banks, insurance companies, industrial firms (especially in mining and metals), and railways. The first investment bank of the Belgian type arose in the form of the famed Crédit Mobilier. Founded in 1852, the bank immediately became actively engaged in the promotion of industrial companies, particularly railroads and real estate. Indeed, its highly illiquid position in its own real estate subsidiary proved the downfall of the bank during a liquidity crunch in 1866–1867. A number of mixed or universal banks appeared in the 1860s, but the combination of investment and commercial services subsided considerably thereafter. Specialized investment banks began to operate alongside commercial and mixed banks in the 1870s.

Germany. Private banking dominated the investment services sector in Germany until the late 1840s. In 1848, the Cologne bank of A. Schaaffhausen was incorporated, and thus began the era of the joint-stock universal bank. A series of similar banks opened in the 1850s, many of which failed in the succeeding two decades. These early universal banks participated actively in the financing of the first German railroads and a number of key industrial sectors. The early 1870s brought a new wave of universal-bank creation and a corresponding period of closures during the depression that followed. Growth of the universal banking sector, particularly in joint-stock banking, accelerated with the renewed industrial growth of the mid-1990s. Joint-stock universal banks, particularly the larger ones, along with certain private banking firms, have provided the vast majority of investment-banking services for German firms and government bodies; the specialized investment bank has never played a significant role in the German economy.

Traditionally, German universal banks have been credited with offering a critical mix of financial and managerial capital to nascent industrial firms and guiding them "from cradle to grave," through all stages of development. More recent revisions of the historical accounts suggest that the universal banks' activities did not differ radically from those of any other commercial banks of the time. In particular, at least by the 1880s, these banks engaged rather conservatively in the holding of industrial equities and, over time, took on a financial structure quite similar to that of the English commercial banks.

Austria. The first Austrian universal bank, the Credit-Anstalt, was founded in 1855, apparently patterned after the French Crédit Mobilier. A small number of similar banks appeared shortly thereafter, mainly in the Austrian portion of the empire. Like many of their counterparts in other countries, the large Austrian banks initially focused on railroad financing and remained primarily engaged in the conversion of large, relatively safe firms. On the commercial side of their business, they secured their credits with the best-quality securities. Thus, the banks' investment services tended to exclude smaller, potentially riskier ventures. The universal banks developed along the lines of the German institutions, with some equity participation and board memberships. Although recent research has undermined the view of the crucial role of the universal banks in industrialization, slightly more of the traditional story seems to hold for Austria than for Germany.

Italy. Although Italy followed a pattern of financial development quite similar to that of other European countries in the early nineteenth century, its industrial and financial development proceeded more slowly than that of its northern neighbors. It followed the familiar path of private merchant banking early on; but perhaps because of its lateness in developing large-scale industry, the demand for investment banking also lagged. Italy's first investment bank, the Banca Generale (B.G.), appeared only in 1871. The B.G. and the Credito Mobiliare Italiano were the leading investment banks until the financial crisis of the early 1890s. As in other countries, the investment banks tended to concentrate on metals, mining, and engineering; but having overinvested in the building sector, these and several smaller banks failed in the face of liquidity shortages from 1891 to 1893. In the following two years, coalitions of continental European banks formed two new mixed banks, Banca Commerciale Italiana (the Comit) and Credito Italiano (the Credit), both of which closely resembled their founders. The two banks engaged actively in investment banking, yet they balanced those services with a greater proportion of commercial business than had their predecessors. The Comit and Credit, particularly the former, appear to have obtained significant numbers of board positions and, as in Germany and Austria, focused on the largest firms. Their involvement with industry, however, spanned a broad range of sectors.

BIBLIOGRAPHY

Benston, George J. *The Separation of Commercial and Investment Banking: The Glass-Steagall Act Revisited and Reconsidered.* New York, 1990.

Benston, George J. "Universal Banking." *Journal of Economic Perspectives* 8 (1994), 121–143.

Cameron, Rondo E. *Banking in the Early Stages of Industrialization: A Study in Comparative Economic History.* With the collaboration of Olga Crisp, Hugh T. Patrick, and Richard Tilly. New York, 1967.

Cameron, Rondo E., ed. *Banking and Economic Development: Some Lessons of History.* New York, 1972.

Carosso, Vincent P. *Investment Banking in America: A History.* Cambridge, Mass., 1970.

Cassis, Youssef, ed. *Finance and Financiers in European History, 1880–1960.* New York, 1992.

Cassis, Youssef, Gerald D. Feldman, and Ulf Olsson, eds. *The Evolution of Financial Institutions and Markets in Twentieth-Century Europe.* Aldershot, U.K., 1995.

Fohlin, Caroline. "Universal Banking in Pre-World War I Germany: Model or Myth?" *Explorations in Economic History* 36 (1999), 305–343.

Fohlin, Caroline. *New Perspectives on the Universal Banking System in the German Industrialization.* Forthcoming.

Goldsmith, Raymond W. *Financial Structure and Development.* New Haven, 1969.

Goodhart, Charles A. E. *The Business of Banking, 1891–1914.* London, 1972.

House of Representatives, Committee on Banking, Finance and Urban Affairs, Subcommittee on General Oversight and Investigations. *Bank Powers: Activities of Securities Subsidiaries of Bank Holding Companies: Report to the Chairman.* Washington, D.C., 1990.

Lavington, Frederick. *The English Capital Market.* London, 1921.

Lévy-Leboyer, Maurice. *Les banques européennes et l'industrialisation internationale dans la première moitié du XIX siècle.* Paris, 1964.

Pohl, Manfred, and Sabine Freitag. *Handbook on the History of European Banks.* Aldershot, U.K., 1994.

Riesser, Jacob. *The German Great Banks and their Concentration in Connection with the Economic Development of Germany.* New York, 1977.

Saunders, Anthony, and Ingo Walter, eds. *Universal Banking: Financial System Design Reconsidered.* Chicago, 1996.

Teichova, Alice, Terry Gourvish, and Agnes Pogany, eds. *Universal Banking in the Twentieth Century: Finance, Industry and State in North and Central Europe.* Aldershot, U.K., 1994.

Weber, Adolf. *Depositenbanken und Spekulationsbanken: Ein Vergleich deutschen und englischen Bankwesens.* Munich, 1915.

Whale, Philip B. *Joint Stock Banking in Germany.* London, 1930.

White, Eugene N. "Before the Glass-Steagall Act: An Analysis of the Investment Banking Activities of National Banks." *Explorations in Economic History* 23 (1986), 33–55.

CAROLINE FOHLIN

IRAN *[This entry contains three subentries, on the economic history of Iran during the ancient period, the Islamic period between 640 and 1800, and the modern period since 1800.]*

Ancient Period

In ancient times (antiquity) Iran referred to all the territories inhabited by Iranian-speaking peoples, that is, areas in Afghanistan and Pakistan, and in the Central Asian republics of Kyrgyzstan, Tajikistan, Turkmenistan, and Uzbekistan, which together encompassed a wider area than the modern state of Iran.

Iran in its present-day borders is divided into several regions with different ecological conditions; these affect the dominant forms of social and economic organization. Khuzistan (called Susiana in antiquity), adjacent to southeastern Iraq, is an alluvial plain formed by the Karkeh and Karun Rivers, which, in ancient times, led directly into the Persian Gulf. The Zagros mountain range in the west separated Iran from the lowlands of Iraq, which were formed by several valleys stretching from northwest to southeast, permitting nomadic pastoralism as well as permanent settlements of agriculturalists. Two main trade routes from the Mesopotamian lowlands to Iran crossed the Zagros: One was the Khorasan Road, leading along the Diyala River, an eastern tributary of the Tigris, to the area of present-day Hamadan; and the other went from the Susiana into the Persis (today Fars with its main urban center, Shiraz). To the east, the big Iranian deserts separated the western parts from those bordering Pakistan and Afghanistan.

Historical Outline. In historical terms one has to differentiate between six distinct periods: (1) the early or protohistoric period; (2) the period of Elamite dominion of parts of present-day Iran; (3) the period of the Persian dynasty of the Achaemenids; (4) the Macedonian-Seleucid dominion; (5) the period of the Arsacids and Sasanians; and (6) the period of Islamic rule.

The Early Periods. Most of the history of ancient Iran in the fourth millennium BCE and before is documented through archaeological data, which indicate rain-fed agriculture on the Iranian plateau, agriculture by artificial irrigation in Khuzistan by village communities, and nomadic pastoralism. At the very end of this millennium, indigenous writing systems developed on the Iranian plateau (Tepe Sialk, Shahr-i Sokhta, Tepe Yahya, Malyan/Anshan, Godin Tepe) as well as in the Susiana (Chogha Mish, Susa). As in Mesopotamia, writing was done on clay tablets. It is uncertain what language these early numerical and pictographical tablets reflect, but it is likely to be an early form of Elamite, a language evidently associated with the Proto-Dravidic languages of the Indus valley before the Vedic invasion circa 1600 BCE.

The wide diffusion of the early written records reflects the existence of several independent polities. The numerous administrative texts from Susa, which are not yet deciphered completely, attest to a political organization with a complex bureaucratic system necessary to manage an economy based—as in Mesopotamia—on large institutional households supported by irrigation agriculture.

Iran under Elamite Rule. From the twenty-third century BCE, ancient Iranian history was identical with the history of the Elamite-speaking elite that ruled Iran. The Elamite state was formed by several political entities, which united the lowlands of Khuzistan with regions in the Zagros region and the Persis. Varying forms of political and warlike interaction between the Elamite and the dominant Mesopotamian states largely determined its history until its demise in 640 BCE. At various times, Mesopotamian rulers conquered parts of Khuzistan, with its preeminent city, Susa. Political relations in the twenty-first century BCE were, on occasion, supported by political marriages. Over the centuries the Elamite rulers, on their part, tried to control the region east of the Tigris and even parts of northeastern Syria (eighteenth century BCE).

Evidently the political and socioeconomic structures, by and large, remained the same as in the earlier parts of the third millennium. They were dichotomous in nature. In Susiana, agriculture on the basis of artificial irrigation generated economic structures that are comparable to the *oikos*-economy of Mesopotamia in the third millennium. On the Iranian plateau one has presumably to reckon with a situation in which nomadic pastoralists and agriculturalists organized in village communities existed side by side

ANCIENT IRAN. Audience hall of Darius, Persepolis, circa 500 BCE. (Oriental Institute, University of Chicago)

with manorial households of the palace and the ruling elite.

Indo-Iranian People in Iran. During the late second and early first millennium BCE Iran was invaded by people speaking Iranian (i.e., Indo-European) languages, including Median and Persian. The Medes were politically organized in small territorial polities centered around fortified castles. They controlled mainly the valleys of the Zagros mountains. On the Iranian plateau in southwestern Iran, Persian clans had settled in Fars, which Greek writers called the Persis. Around 640 BCE, the Medes vanquished the Elamite state and then brought large parts of western Iran under their control. During the sixth century, the Achaemenids (550–330 BCE), a Persian dynasty named after their ancestor Achaimenes (Greek form), gained supremacy over the Median state. Subsequently the Persians conquered Mesopotamia, Asia Minor, Syria, and Palestine, as well as areas adjacent to Iran in the north (Middle Asia), to form a multiethnic empire. Eventually, under Artaxerxes and Xerxes, they conquered Egypt, although they failed to subdue Greece.

It is from this era that we know most about ancient Iran's political organization and socioeconomic conditions. The sources from which the history of these centuries is reconstructed are the numerous administrative tablets from Persepolis, written in Elamite (still the language of the administrative records), along with various Babylonian and Greek sources. The nature and structure of the economy were determined by the ecological condi-tions that permitted agriculture—either as rain-fed agriculture or as one based on artificial irrigation in the alluvial plain of the Susiana. Rain-fed agriculture on the Iranian plateau (e.g., in the Persis) was complemented by artificial irrigation using weirs or dams and bringing the groundwater from the mountain ridges in subterranean canals or ducts (qanāt) to the fields.

The Achaemenid state was organized as an oligarchy of great families that controlled the state and its economic resources. The grandees of the realm had their economic basis in large manorial estates—farmed in part or in whole by sharecroppers—within the Iranian homeland as well as in the conquered territories, as far away as Anatolia and Egypt. Along with these manorial estates, a free peasantry still existed. Its economic situation had not yet reached a point so typical for agrarian societies, in which bad harvests produced agrarian debts that eventually led to bondage and subsequent consolidation of most of the arable land in the hands of manorial lords.

For the Persis and most likely also for the Susiana and other parts of the realm, the Persepolis documents reveal a redistributive economic system in which large parts of the population were integrated as servants and administrators into the royal domains and manorial estates of the elite. They received rations according to status, rank, and function; the minimum wage for a male was about 600 grams of flour per day.

To sustain their vast empire, which was organized in provinces (satrapies) and reached from the borders of

India to the Mediterranean, the Achaemenids needed a well-equipped army and a complex administration. To support them they exacted heavy tribute from the provinces (details are reported by Herodotus) and head taxes from the population in the Persian homelands. The tribute paid by the provinces reduced the necessity for internal exchange because the regions of the empire produced more or less everything needed to sustain the needs of the empire.

Well after the "invention" of coinage, in Anatolian Lydia at the end of the seventh century, Darius I (522–486 BCE) issued the first Persian coins, initially as Lydian coins. But sometime after 515 BCE, he struck his own golden coins, which the Greeks called *Dareikos*. The Daric or "Archer" (for the royal figure with bow and arrow on the coin) weighed about one shekel (8.4 grams), the common weight unit of the region, especially in Mesopotamia, to express equivalencies in silver. A silver coin, which the Greeks called *siglos* (after the Mesopotamian shekel [*šiglu*]), was also struck. The introduction of these coins, used throughout the empire to pay the army, also had a propagandistic intent in bearing the image of the king throughout his realm.

The Macedonian-Seleucid Interlude. Greek sources about the Macedonian-Seleucid dominion over those territories that had been under Achaemenid rule provide no information about the internal economic situation from 330 to 247 BCE. Presumably the economic structures of the Achaemenid period continued, since the Seleucids had deliberately left the social fabric of the land alone, and kept the Persian nobility—which was in large parts willing to accept the new rulers—in their positions, incorporating them into their administrative system. As a consequence, presumably no changes took place in the land tenure system.

Iran under the Seleucids continued to be an intermediary in the long-distance trade network that stretched from India and China to the Mediterranean. The overland routes across Iran were now more and more paralleled by sea routes using the Persian Gulf for the voyage to India.

The Parthian (Arsacid) and Sassanian Periods. Parthian and Sassanian societies (247 BCE–651 CE) were societies of nobles with both a free and a dependent peasantry, subject to dues to the manorial lords, but also to royal head taxes and taxes on arable land and pasture. Agricultural production in Khuzistan during Sassanian times consisted of cereals (wheat, barley, rice), sesame and vegetables, dates, sugar cane, and cotton. All these were exempt from taxation because they were part of the subsistence of the peasantry. At the same time, impressive irrigation installations (canals, dams) in the alluvial plains of Mesopotamia and Khuzistan indicate a substantial engagement of the state in agricultural affairs.

During Parthian and Sassanian times, Iran continued to serve as an important intermediary between the Mediterranean world and India and China. Raw silk, silk garments, spices, perfumes, jewelry, other crafted goods, hides, and also slaves (eunuchs) and wild animals found their way into the Roman world. The oasis of Palmyra in the Syrian steppe served as a port of trade between the Parthian and the Roman empires. Moreover, merchants from Palmyra maintained trading colonies in several cities within the Parthian empire, besides those in Bahrain and the Indus delta.

For its own consumer needs, Iran imported silk, seric iron (steel), apricots, and peaches. Iran exported gold, silver vessels, linen garments, pomegranates, wine and vines, and luzerne. From the fourth to sixth centuries CE, the manufacture of silver bowls was a royal monopoly. These bowls served as prestigious gifts in a royal gift exchange system.

Iranian dynasties used their strategic position as intermediaries by imposing tolls on the luxurious Indian and Chinese merchandise that passed through their territories. Rome and Byzantium in turn tried more or less unsuccessfully to break the Iranian monopoly on trade with China by circumventing the trade routes passing through Iran; that is, by using the sea route from the Persian Gulf to India.

Coinage in Iran. With the Seleucids, the Attic coinage system was introduced into Iran; it was adopted and transformed by the succeeding Parthian and Sassanian dynasties. As far as one can see, taxes and dues under the Achaemenids were paid in kind or in gold or silver. The widespread distribution of Parthian coins probably indicates that the monetization of taxes and dues began during Parthian rule. Under the subsequent Sassanian rule, head taxes and dues on arable land were levied in coined money. In an agrarian society, taxes and dues that were paid by the rural population had to be transformed from natural products into gold, silver, or coins, which implies some form of exchange processes. We do not know to what extent this indicates a developed market exchange, since the rural population was living under subsistence conditions and the elite was gaining its livelihood from its autarchic manorial estates. The widespread distribution of Seleucid, Parthian, and Sassanian coins in Asia and Europe is a sign that coinage played some substantial role in facilitating long-distance trade.

[*See also* Iraq, *subentry on* Ancient Period.]

BIBLIOGRAPHY

Adams, Robert McC. "Agriculture and Urban Life in Early Southwestern Iran." *Science* 136 (1962), 109–122.

Carter, Elizabeth, and Matthew W. Stolper. *Elam, Surveys of Political History and Archaeology*. Berkeley, Los Angeles, London, 1984.

Dandamayev, Muhammad A., and Vladimir G. Lukonin. *The Culture and Social Institutions of Ancient Iran*. Cambridge, 1989.

Gershevitch, Ilya, ed. *The Cambridge History of Iran*, vol. 2, *The Median and Achaemenian Periods*. Cambridge, 1985.

Goebl, Robert. "Sassanian Coins." In *The Cambridge History of Iran*, vol. 3.1, *The Seleucid, Parthian and Sasanian Periods*, edited by Ehsan Yarshater, pp. 299–339. Cambridge, 1983.

Sellwood, David. "Parthian Coins." In *The Cambridge History of Iran*, vol. 3.1, *The Seleucid, Parthian and Sassanian Periods*, edited by Ehsan Yarshater, pp. 279–298. Cambridge, 1983.

Vargyas, Péter. "*Kaspu ginnu* and the Monetary Reform of Darius I." *Zeitschrift fuer Assyriologie* 89 (1999), 247–268. Contains a thorough discussion of coinage in ancient Mesopotamia and the Persian Empire at the beginning of the sixth century BCE; with extensive bibliography.

Yarshater, Ehsan, ed. *The Cambridge History of Iran*, vol. 3.1, *The Seleucid, Parthian and Sassanian Periods*. Cambridge, 1983.

Wiesehoefer, Josef. *Ancient Persia*. London, 1996. The most comprehensive survey of the history of ancient Iran from the sixth century BCE until 651 CE, the beginning of the Islamic dominion.

JOHANNES M. RENGER

Islamic Period, 651–1800

For the early Islamic and medieval periods, the geographic boundaries that can be culturally and linguistically defined as Iranic, and since the eleventh century Turco-Iranic, included present day Iran, Afghanistan, most former Soviet-block central Asian countries, and until the sixteenth century, eastern Anatolia. The administrative boundaries were fluid and changing and the sociocultural and administrative area expanded eastward beginning in the eleventh century. Theoretical studies on the economic history of the period are limited and controversial. Those pertaining to the classical Islamic period, before the eleventh century, examine the Islamic Empire at large, and those on the later period range from explaining the specific characteristics of Iran as feudal, Asiatic mode, or nomadic dynastic cycles. There is also a large body of descriptive literature on the land-tenure and revenue administration systems and other socioeconomic aspects. This article does not examine the controversies and makes no conclusive theoretical assessments about the decline and stagnation of the economy after the eleventh century. Since the significance of evolutions in the institution of property rights has been emphasized by scholars from very different ideological and methodological perspectives ranging from Karl Marx to Douglass North (1994), and since the period under study shows two distinct paths in the evolution/disruption of property rights, the subject will be examined with a focus on the developments in property rights. The period under study is divided into the early and classical Islamic, the seventh through the tenth centuries, and the subsequent Turko-Mongol nomadic dynasties, eleventh to the nineteenth centuries. The classical period is generally perceived as having experienced positive evolutions in property rights, long-term growth in agriculture, urbanization, trade, and development of production tech-

niques. In contrast, the rule of nomadic dynasties showed disruptions in the evolution of property rights, economic stagnation, and in the case of the Mongols (1220–1350), massive destruction and drastic decline in population, agriculture, and cities.

The Classical Islamic Period (651–1038). The Arab conquest of Iran (651) ended more than four hundred years of the Sassanian administrative empire. The conquest resulted in political, religious, and cultural changes, but landholding rights were not significantly disrupted. The Muslim elite came from the merchant families of Mecca, and the mercantile tradition impacted the legal theory. The early Muslims also adapted aspects of the Sassanian fiscal administration. The legal theory was thus conducive to evolution of property rights and relied on the Sassanian networks of taxation. Although instances of land grants and confiscations existed, in general the conquered lands were not subject to division among those who had fought the wars and remained in the hands of the original holders. If land was forcefully taken, it became subject to a specific tax, *khāraj*. If the inhabitants surrendered peacefully, they maintained ownership and paid a lower tax, *ushr*, similar to that of the Muslim lands. Those who did not convert to Islam paid a poll tax, *jizya*, that was removed upon conversion to Islam. But land taken forcefully remained subject to *kharāj*.

During this period most Sassanian landowners, *dehqāns*, maintained control over their lands and were tax collectors. By the tenth century most *dehqāns* in Khurasan and Turkestan came from the same families as those of the Sassanian period, there was significant development of small-scale private ownership, and land transactions were prevalent. The *dehqāns* were an influential group. During the period the underground irrigation systems, *qanats*, were expanded, many new crops were introduced and developed, and production techniques evolved. During the ninth and tenth centuries Iranian agriculture was prosperous. With the possible exception of the Ummayads (661–749), who imposed restrictions on movements, peasants were free. There is also no indication of the existence of significant nomadism in Iran. The rise of nomadism in the subsequent period was due to the incursion of nomads from central Asia.

Military victory, aided by seminomadic Arabs, mercenaries, and Turkish slaves, was the main contributor to political change. Nevertheless factors that prompted and people who brought change were diverse and complex and included quasi-class and/or anti-Arab ethnic Iranian component (conflicts) combined with religious and ideological conflicts. Often the *dehqāns* and urban professional and religious groups, *futowwa*, participated in the conflicts. The rise of Umayyads was aided by the traditional Meccan merchants. They treated Iranians as second-class citizens, *mawālī.* The subsequent rise (749) of the Abbasid caliphates, however, was supported by Iranians and the Arabs who had been excluded from power sharing under the Ummayads. As a result the influence of Iranian administrators grew and the concept of *mawālīs* disappeared. Finally, during the ninth and tenth centuries the rise of the quasi and independent dynasties in Iran included ethnic and cultural components and was partly owed to the declining central control of the caliphate. Some Iranian dynasties, for example, the Saffarians (868–903), undertook comparatively harsh military expeditions, while others, for example, the Tahirids (821–873) and the Samanids (874–999) contributed to prosperity. In general the sociolegal and administrative systems experienced continuity, innovation, and evolutionary developments. The decline of the central control of the caliphs was gradual. The Tahirids enjoyed autonomy but paid tribute. The Saffarids, Samanids, and Ghaznavids (977–1186) did not pay tribute but sent gifts and recognized the caliph's supremacy by mentioning his name in the Friday prayers. The dynastic changes did not result in disruptive structural and institutional changes. The rise of Iranian dynasties, however, was accompanied by the formal use of a new Persian language that used Arabic letters, and this new literature flourished.

With some disruptions and changes, the process of urbanization that had begun under the Sassanids continued. Major Iranian cities, such as Ray, Isfahan, Nishapur, and Samarqand, were smaller than Baghdad or Cairo. Prior to the Mongol invasion, however, they were larger than all major late medieval European cities. Communal urban life was a mixture of Arabic and Sassanian traditions of *futuwwa* (Persian *javānmardān*). The *futuwwa* came from different religious groups and all had professions, usually in crafts, but at this point they did not form specific guilds yet. These groups also exerted military power. The founder of the Saffarid dynasty owed the origin of his power to *futuwwa.* Artisans worked in small workshops with limited capital.

Trade and pilgrim routes went through Samarqand, Marv, Balkh, Nishapur, Ray, Hamadan, Shiraz, Isfahan, Ghazana, and on the Persian Gulf, Siraf. Merchants included different religious and ethnic groups from within and outside Iran, but the majority were Iranians. On land and in the Indian Ocean, from Malaysia and China to East Africa, the vocabulary of business and navigation was, even in Arabic, deeply impacted with Persian. Between the seventh and tenth centuries the legal developments were conducive to trade. The Muslim jurists who formulated the legal system were influenced by customs of the regions that had come under Islamic rule, including Sassanian traditions. They refined the borrowed rules to accommodate the needs of the merchants.

Nomadic Dynasties (1038–1800). From about the eleventh century to the nineteenth century twelve major dynasties ruled Iran. With the exception of the Safavids (1501–1722), all had nomadic central Asian origins. In contrast to the earlier dynasties that were rooted in the mercantile Islamic legal and Iranian administrative systems and were interested in maintaining status quo in property relations and in collecting orderly taxes, the nomadic dynasties had their origins in the tradition of the steppe. In this tradition property relations were undeveloped and plunder was the primary mechanism of accumulation of wealth. They viewed both land and its produce as objects of plunder and subject to division among the tribal contingencies. The fourteenth century historian Ibn khaldun, in *Muqaddimah* (Introduction to History, 1967), based his theory of dynastic cycles on nomadic military superiority due to mobility and seasonal migration. Given precapitalist methods of warfare, nomads in general have superior military abilities over sedentary people. These dynastic changes were entirely military and, in the case of the early Mongols, Chengiz (1220–1227) and Hulagu (1253–1265), were highly destructive and disruptive. From the start the Saljuqs (1038–1156) and the Timurids (1370–1453) adapted aspects of the indigenous administrative and legal systems and were less disruptive. Nomadic dynasties owed their military power to tribal confederacies. During the periods of expansion military alliances increased the possibility of victory and plunder. Once expansion came to an end, however, unity lost its central objective. Invariably the dynasties were unable to maintain central control over all of the conquered lands, and tribal uprisings, claims to independence, and anarchy ensued. This process was reminiscent of the disintegration of Germanic empires in western Europe into feudalism. In Iran, however, there were new conquests, and new nomadic empires rose, which can be explained by its proximity to central Asia.

The rise of the Safavids too was aided by seven Turkish tribes, the Qizilbash. Other factors, such as a popular Shi'ite ideology and the support of urban *futowwa,* were also important. The post-Safavid nomadic military groups were endogenous and semisedentary. The only exception is the Afghan invasion (1722–1729), which was short-lived and had no lasting impact. Thus nomadic influence was significantly eroded.

In general the conquerors viewed all forms of property as objects of plunder. Thus land, its produce, and its inhabitants were subject to arbitrary treatment. Furthermore land grants were the primary mechanism of revenue administration. Each group or conqueror viewed itself as proprietor of the conquered lands. Invariably a new dynasty resulted in massive confiscations and the rise of a new landed elite. In theory all land belonged to the monarch, who could assign it in return for service. In practice many assignments were de facto recognitions of land held by military chieftains or local influentials. Land assignment was not the only mechanism of legitimization of tenure; sales and usurpations were also prevalent. At the beginning of the eleventh century most land proprietors were of Persian descent. By the time of the Mongol invasion many were of Turkish descent. The composition of the landed elite changed drastically after the Mongol invasion. The rise of the Safavids was accompanied by a substantial increase in land held by members of their family and by the Qizilbash tribes. The rise of the Qajars (1779–1925) too was accompanied by a new landholding elite. The recurrence of nomadic dynasties thus disrupted the evolution of property rights.

Nomadic invasions, in particular the Mongol invasion, were accompanied by massive destruction of the irrigation system, turning agricultural land into wasteland and pastures. Thus the nomadic population increased substantially. With the exception of the Safavids, the period was marked by a general decline in production and stagnation in development of production techniques. Even under the Safavids agricultural production did not achieve its classical Islamic level.

Arbitrary confiscation continued throughout the life of each dynasty but on a smaller scale. With the exception of the relative success of the Safavids, specially under Abbas I (r. 1587–1629) and his successors, rulers failed to collect sufficient taxes and resorted to arbitrariness. But under an existing dynasty the composition of the ruling elite was fairly stable. The state tended to lose control, and land grants became privatized. There was also increased ownership through land reclamation and purchase. The Safavid period showed clear tendencies toward development of private property through purchase and expansion of the irrigation system. Privately owned lands, *melkī*, were an important category and enjoyed relative security. Furthermore charitable religious lands, *vaqf*, expanded, became secure, and provided an unprecedented economic autonomy for the Shi'ite clergy. Developments of the Safavid period were disrupted by the Afghan invasion and the subsequent dynastic changes. Each change subsequently contributed to arbitrariness and insecurity but on a smaller scale than in the pre-Safavid period. Some effort was made to adhere to the Safavid traditions. Despite a decline in the relative share after the Safavids, *vaqf* continued to be an important category of holdings and one of the most resistant to confiscation.

Peasants lived in village communities and shared the produce with landlords according to the Islamic rules of sharecropping, *muqāsemeh*. The landlords could be the land grantees, the private proprietors, or both. The clergy, as trustees and beneficiaries of the *vaqf*, shared the produce with the peasants. Peasants' customary rights over the land, the produce, and even their personal safety varied with the extent of political stability. Except during the Mongol rule, peasants were not tied to the land.

The most devastating impact of the Mongol invasion was depopulation. Although the numbers are probably exaggerated, sources report massacres of about one million people in each major city, such as Nishapur, Marv, and Herat, between 1220 and 1258. But other cities, such as Tabriz, escaped such devastations and in the fourteenth century became major trade centers. The Saljuqs, Mongols, and Timurids were politically close to central Asia, and Iran served as a gateway to Europe. Thus long-distance trade expanded under the Saljuqs and showed periods of recovery under the Mongols and Timurids. Expansion and recovery depended on the administrative control over the maintenance and safety of roads. Invariably trade declined during the periods of dynastic disintegration, tribal anarchy, and wars. Under the Safavids, especially after the rule of Abbas I, roads were secure, and many caravansaries were built. The Safavid capital Isfahan became the most important urban center.

During the classical Islamic period the legal system was innovative and accommodating to trade, but after the tenth century it became static. This coincided with the development of dynamic commercial laws in Europe. Until the fifteenth century Iran widely participated in maritime trade from the Persian Gulf to the Indian Ocean and beyond. By the sixteenth century, however, European superiority was evident. Shah Abbas had to rely on British assistance to recapture from the Portuguese the main port in the Persian Gulf. Because of the developments outside of Iran, the Safavids had fallen behind Europe. Under the subsequent nomadic dynasties, the gap widened.

BIBLIOGRAPHY

Barthold, Vasili V. *Turkistan*. 3d ed. London, 1968. This is a major work based on original sources that examines the property and labor relations for the period prior to the Mongol invasion.

Bosworth, Clifford E. "The Tahirids and Saffarids." In *The Cambridge History of Iran*, vol. 4, edited by R. N. Frye, pp. 90–135. Cambridge, 1975.

Cahen, Claude. "Tribes, Cities, and Social Organization." In *The Cambridge History of Iran*, vol. 4, edited by R. N. Frye, pp. 305–328. Cambridge, 1975. This and other writings by the author focus on political economy analysis as opposed to descriptive historical approaches.

Crone, Patricia. *"Mawla."* In *Encyclopaedia of Islam*, new ed., vol. 6, pp. 874–882. Netherlands, 1991.

Fragner, Bert. "Social and Internal Economic Affairs." In *The Cambridge History of Iran*, vol. 6, edited by P. Jackson and Lockhart, pp. 491–567. Cambridge, 1986.

Frye, Richard N. "The Samanids." In *The Cambridge History of Iran*, vol. 4, edited by R. N. Frye, pp. 136–161. Cambridge, 1975.

Ibn khaldun. *Muqaddimah* (Introduction to History). Translated by Franz Rosenthal, 3 vols. London, 1967. Ibrahim, Mahmood. *Merchant Capital and Islam*. Austin, 1990. This is an interesting study of the evolution of mercantile relations in Arabia prior to and during the early Islamic era. The discussions on capitalism and feudalism in the last chapter, however, are somewhat tentative.

Khazanov, Anatolii M. *Nomads and the Outside World*. Cambridge, 1984. This contains comprehensive scholarly research on nomadism and nomadic dynasties. It also includes many references to other works in Russian, English, and French.

Lambton, Ann K. S. *Landlord and Peasant in Persia*. London, 1953. This is a classic work on the land tenure and revenue administration in Iran from the Arab conquest through the mid-twentieth century. It is largely based on original Persian and Arabic sources. This and other writings by the author are cited in nearly all studies on the subject.

Moghadam, Fatemeh Etemad. "Nomadic Invasions and the Development of Productive Forces: An Historical Study of Iran, 1000–1800." *Science and Society* 52.4 (1988–1989), 389–412. See this article for an examination of the theoretical controversies on the economic history of Iran.

Moghadam, Fatemeh Etemad. *From Land Reform to Revolution*. London, 1996. This is a more detailed explanation of the period 1000–1800; for the relevant sources, see pp. 14–32.

Morony, Michael G. "Landholding in Seventh-Century Iraq: Late Sassanian and Early Islamic Patterns." In *The Islamic Middle East, 700–1900*, edited by A. L. Udovitch, pp. 139–143. Princeton, 1981.

Nomani, Farhad. "Notes on the Origins and Development of Extra-Economic Obligations of Peasants in Iran, 300–1600 AD" *Iranian Studies* 9.2–3, 121–141.

North, Douglass. "Economic Performance through Time." *American Economic Review* 84.3 (1994), 359–368.

Petrushevsky, Ilya P. "The Socio-Economic Condition of Iran under the Il-Khans." In *The Cambridge History of Iran*, vol. 5, edited by J. A. Boyle, pp. 483–537. Cambridge, 1968. This author has written other major works in Russian that have been translated into Persian.

Udovitch, Abraham L. *Partnership and Profit in Medieval Islam*. Princeton, 1970.

Watson, A. M. *Agricultural Innovation in the Early Islamic World*. Cambridge, 1983. This is an excellent account of agricultural development during the early Islamic period.

Yahya Ben Adam. *Kitab Al-kharaj* (Taxation in Islam). Translated and edited by Ben Shemesh. Leiden, 1968. This is a translation of an early Islamic document concerning property rights and treatment of conquered lands.

FATEMEH ETEMAD MOGHADAM

Modern Period, since 1800

The nineteenth century marks the beginning of the modern era in Iran whose geographic boundaries roughly correspond to those of present-day Iran. The period is marked by the penetration of western European influence, growing participation in world markets, and disintegration of nomadic dynasties. From this date economic, infrastructural, and institutional developments gave rise to new interest groups that interacted with the old and created new developments and complexities. Modern Iran has been an arena of conflict between national and foreign interests over resource control, especially oil; positive evolutions as well as insecurity and occasional disruptions in property rights in land and industrial capital; decisive disintegration of nomadic tribalism; and continual competition between secular and religious groups for political power. It marks a long, incomplete, but growing struggle to create a democratic form of government.

During the nineteenth century the main impetus of change was a gradual integration into the world economy accompanied by a slow growth of output and expansion of markets and exchange. Population nearly doubled, and the share of the population that was urban rose from 10 to 20 percent. During the first half of the century tribal wars ended, output grew in both agriculture and handicrafts, and exports increased. Although the external impetus played a role, the recovery was mainly due to the establishment of order and the ending of the tribal wars. During the second half of the century a marked improvement in the monetary and communication systems resulted in internal integration of the economy. The real volume of commodity trade, largely agricultural, quadrupled. But most handicrafts declined due to foreign competition.

During the nineteenth century property rights evolved. The share of privately held lands, *mulki*, increased, and voluntary exchange became the dominant transfer method. In addition to the landed aristocracy, merchants became an important landowning group. Charitable religious endowment lands, *vaqf*, remained an important category with security from confiscations. The *ulama* (religious leaders), as guardians of *vaqf* and as private owners, comprised a major landholding category. Nevertheless the administrative system of land grants, *tuyul*, continued, and arbitrary confiscations existed. The century was also marked by the growing penetration of European powers and the rivalry between Russia and Britain over a series of concessionary rights. Iranians perceived these concessions as the plundering of their national resources. The concessions were especially in conflict with the interests of the indigenous merchants and the *ulama*, who received religious dues from the merchants. At the beginning of the century Iran suffered two major defeats from the comparatively modern Russian army. The need to build a modern professional army became evident. Military development, however, was modest, and nomadic militancy continued to be a problem. By the end of the century, however, a small but efficient professional army was formed. The founder of the Pahlavi dynasty (1925-1979), Reza Shah rose from its rank and file. Thus the era of nomadic dynasties ended.

Constitutional Revolution. Complex factors contributed to the Constitutional Revolution (1906–1907) that formally ended the system of absolute monarchy in Iran. The weakness of the central government allowed increased autonomy for the traditional communal groups. Commercial developments resulted in the growth of indigenous merchants. Contact with the West and modern education created an intelligentsia interested in a constitutional form of government. The evolution of property

TEHRAN. City scene, 1996. (© Barry Iverson/Woodfin Camp and Associates, New York)

rights, however, was an important factor causing and shaping the revolution. Historically each dynastic change in Iran had resulted in massive confiscations. While the propertied groups wanted to challenge absolutism, they did not wish to remove the ruling Qajar dynasty. The Constitutional Law (1907) recognized private property and abolished the system of *tuyul*. Nationalism was also an important factor, resulting from the perception that the concessionary rights were due to the arbitrary nature of rule. At the beginning of the twentieth century Iran officially adopted a system of constitutional monarchy. Inadequate infrastructure and institutions, however, prevented the establishment of an effective central government. Tribal militarism claims to autonomy and other forms of anarchism ensued, and foreign pressure continued. Furthermore the modernist aspirations of the constitutionalists, secular reforms in the education and judiciary systems, and government supervision of charitable endowments, *ouqaf*, entailed serious financial threats to the *ulama*, generating opposition.

Pahlavi Dynasty. The rise of Reza Shah (r. 1925–1941) was a significant change. His military support came from a professional army, and his rise to power was based on considerable urban political and British support. He created a modern professional army and bureaucracy and suppressed tribal and other provincial autonomous groups. His rule resulted in infrastructural and economic development, modernization, and industrialization. He nationalized banking, customs, and a few other resources and institutions. Reza Shah aggressively secularized and mod-

ernized both the education and judicial systems. In 1936 he forced urban women to appear unveiled in public. He was also successful in controlling *ouqaf* but did not challenge the *ulama*'s rights as the legal beneficiaries. Instead of the constitutional ideal of democracy, however, he advocated the pre-Islamic ideal of central administration and challenged the parliament. Although to a smaller extent than the nomadic dynasties, he undertook large-scale confiscations. As a large landowner, and in cooperation with the landlord-dominated parliament, however, he helped the passage of laws that strengthened landownership. Furthermore, after his abdication in 1941, landowners enhanced their rights through parliamentary representation. Thus the first half of the twentieth century witnessed evolutions in private property rights.

An important development was the discovery and extraction (1908) of oil. The growing importance of oil and the Iranian perception that the British monopoly concession was unfavorable marked Iranian politics and relations with Britain. In 1933, under British pressure, Reza Shah signed another unpopular agreement. During the period of social uprisings (1941–1953), oil nationalization was the dominant issue. The rise and fall of the nationalist government of Mohammad Mussaddeq (1951–1953) was directly linked to oil. The uprisings, however, contained other components. After the abdication of Reza Shah, the power of the parliament increased. In addition the protests included a significant urban working-class component and the active presence of the pro-Soviet Communist Party, Tudeh. As was the case with the Constitutional Revolution, initially a segment of the *ulama* supported the Mussaddeq. Although tribal militarism previously had disintegrated significantly, unrest in the tribal areas reappeared. In 1953 a coup staged by the U.S. Central Intelligence Agency (CIA) succeeded in overthrowing Mussaddeq and reinstating Muhammad Reza Shah who had succeeded his father in 1941. The existing property relations were also a contributing factor. Once the nationalist government assumed a radical antimonarch position, the propertied groups feared a collapse of law and order and insecurity in private ownership. The fear was compounded by the active presence of the Tudeh Party and by the proximity of the Soviet Union. Even the traditional bazaar and its religious allies turned against the movement.

The subsequent Oil Consortium Agreement (1954), the establishment of the Organization of Petroleum Exporting Countries (OPEC) (1960), rising world demand, and the Arab oil embargo (1973) all contributed to sharp increases in Iranian revenues. During the 1960s on the average Iran produced 7 percent of the world's total crude oil. This share rose to 10 percent during the first half of the 1970s. The state was transformed from a relatively poor quasi-colony to a country with substantial purchasing power. During the period from 1963 to 1977, real per capita income rose from about $200 to $1,000. Industry and mines grew on average by about 14 percent in real terms, and agriculture grew by about 4 percent. The labor force composition changed from 55 percent in agriculture and 44 percent in combined industry and mines in 1963 to 32 percent and 54 percent respectively in 1977. Females accounted for 20 percent of the labor force in 1976. The number of universities rose significantly, with females comprising about a third of the students. Mass education became widespread in urban areas, attempts were made to reach out to the isolated rural areas, and the gender gap in education declined. By 1977 the population was estimated to be about four times that of the beginning of the century. By 1978 Iran's productive capacity had far outgrown its nineteenth-century and earlier twentieth-century capacity.

After 1953, in order to undermine two major categories of opponents, the landlord-dominated parliament and the left, the shah opted for implementation of a massive land reform. More than 35 percent of the total agricultural lands were redistributed. For election, landlords depended on peasant votes, and the reform undermined this relationship. It also deprived the left of a major source of propaganda. Land reform was a reversal of the earlier evolutionary trends in property rights and included the redistribution of *vaqf* lands. It ended the uneasy alliance between the landholding elite and the monarch. In 1963 a major uprising against the shah, led by Ayatollah Khomeini, was unsuccessful.

During the postreform period agricultural growth was slower than the growth of the modern sectors of the economy. To accelerate agricultural growth, the government adopted a controversial and embarrassingly unsuccessful policy of creating large-scale mechanized farms that threatened to reverse small-scale ownership. The policy was abandoned after 1976, and its impact on ownership was marginal. Despite the initial publicity for the policy, abandonment was not publicly acknowledged. The feeling of insecurity persisted in rural areas, and the monarch failed to consolidate the support of the beneficiaries of the reform.

After 1960 merchant and industrial capitals grew substantially. The shah's reform package, "the White Revolution," included a marginal attempt to make workers shareholders in private companies. This and some other measures were perceived as indications that, should the monarch find it suitable for his own purposes, he may implement more radical policies. During the 1960s and 1970s women were enfranchised, and jurisdiction over divorce was moved to a special civil court, eroding the last judicial stronghold of the clergy, that of the family. The clergy considered these and other sweeping modernization policies as serious threats.

The growing gap in employment possibilities between rural and urban areas resulted in massive migrations, more than 1.6 percent on average annually from 1956 to 1976. The population of Tehran grew from 2.7 million people in 1966 to 4.5 million in 1976, and other major cities also grew. These numbers understate the rural presence in urban areas, because seasonally migrant and commuter workers are not included. Economic growth had generated inequalities. Migrants were among the poor, who suffered from housing shortages, retained traditional and religious outlooks, and were uncomfortable in an urban and modern environment, and their participation contributed to the popularity of the religious ideology of the Islamic Revolution.

In summary, land reform ended the uneasy alliance between the monarch and the propertied groups, and modernization, secularization, and emancipation of women alienated the traditional segments of the population. Socioeconomic modernization was not accompanied by political democratization, and as a result the supporters and beneficiaries of modernization were alienated as well. Rapid growth generated income inequalities, rising expectations, and massive internal migrations bringing people who felt displaced to urban centers. Finally, despite success in increasing the revenue from oil, the shah's reign was marked by his collaboration in a CIA-staged coup. The participants in the revolution had different grievances and aspirations, but were united in their opposition to the monarch.

Islamic Revolution. A massive revolution (1978–1979) led by Ayatollah Khomeini ended the monarchy. Protest against the challenges to private property was a primary factor mobilizing the propertied groups. The secular left assumed that the revolution would open political space, and they participated. But the clergy monopolized the revolution, assumed an unprecedented constitutional power for the spiritual leader, *rahbar,* and returned the judiciary to the religious courts. After 1979 large-scale capital investments belonging to the former elite, but not those of the regime's supporters, were confiscated. A network of "revolutionary foundations," including the giant Foundation for the Oppressed, controls them. The beneficiaries are a major political support for the system. The state has oscillated between a populist anticapital and a liberal proaccumulation interpretation of Islam, keeping the private sector uneasy and in suspense. Between 1977 and 1988 per capita income declined by 50 percent but subsequently has shown signs of improvements. Between 1978 and 1996 average annual gross private investment was 60 percent of the 1977 figure. While the socioeconomic and cultural factors are far from resolved, the situation has somewhat normalized. Some social indicators, such as participation in the electoral process, achievement of universal education, and reduction of the gender gap in education, have shown positive developments. The legal changes have been a curious mixture of retrogressive and progressive adaptations. Under these competing and contradictory developments, Iran can best be described as a society in transition.

BIBLIOGRAPHY

Abrahamian, Ervand. *Iran between Two Revolutions.* Princeton, 1975.
Behdad, Sohrab. "From Populism to Economic Liberalism." In *Iran's Economy: Dilemma of an Islamic State,* edited by Parvin Alizadeh, pp. 100–141 London, 2002. This and other publications by this author, referred to in his article, provide information about the postrevolutionary structural and economic changes in Iran.
Hakimian, Hassan. "Economy in the Qajar Period." In *Encyclopaedia Iranica,* vol. 8, edited by Ehsan Yarshater, pp. 138–143. New York, 2002.
Issawi, Charles, ed. *The Economic History of Iran, 1800–1914.* Chicago, 1971. This is a pioneering collection of articles on nineteenth-century Iran.
Karshenas, Massoud. *Oil, State, and Industrialization in Iran.* Cambridge, 1990.
Katouzian, Homa. *The Political Economy of Modern Iran, 1926–1979.* New York, 1981.
Kazemi, Farhad. *Poverty and Revolution in Iran.* New York, 1980.
Lambton, Ann K. S. *Landlord and Peasant in Persia.* London, 1953.
Lambton, Ann K. S. *The Persian Land Reform.* London, 1969. This is a firsthand observation of the implementation of land reform in Iran.
Moghadam, Fatemeh. *From Land Reform to Revolution: The Political Economy of Agricultural Development in Iran, 1962–1979.* London, 1996. This book includes an extended version of the interpretations for the period prior to 1979 presented in the present article.
Pesaran, Hashem. "Economy in the Pahlavi Period." In *Encyclopaedia Iranica,* vol. 8, edited by Ehsan Yarshater, pp. 143–156. London and Boston, 1982–.

FATEMEH ETEMAD MOGHADAM

IRAQ *[This entry contains three subentries, on the economic history of Iraq during the ancient, Islamic, and modern periods.]*

Ancient Period

Ancient Mesopotamia comprised two geographically distinct regions with different climatic and ecological conditions between 4000 BCE and 630 BCE. They included the alluvial plain of southern Iraq (the area south of Baghdad to the Persian Gulf between the Euphrates and the Tigris Rivers, with a width of 50 kilometers at the maximum and a length of about 300 kilometers), called Babylonia; and the northeastern region of Iraq north of the Hamrin mountain ridge on both sides of the Tigris, called Assyria. Agriculture in the alluvial plain was possible only through artificial irrigation, while in Assyria rain-fed agriculture was complemented by artificial irrigation.

The economy of ancient Mesopotamia (ancient Iraq) was based on an agriculture integrated with animal husbandry. Manufacture and the production of crafted goods were of subsidiary importance. Most mineral and other natural resources had to be obtained through long-distance trade—in particular, metals (tin and copper for making bronze, iron, gold, and silver for prestigious purposes and for payments or exchange), lumber for construction of ostentatious public buildings (temples and palaces), semiprecious and other stones for building and art purposes. Canals were constructed as part of an extensive irrigation system that encompassed the entire alluvial plain. Also, numerous palaces and temples, city walls, and other edifices of enormous size and splendor were built. All these—and the support of a complex administration and army—were possible only because of the surplus production of agriculture and animal husbandry.

General and Theoretical Considerations. Throughout its long history, Mesopotamia's economic development was not determined by technological advances. And there are no significant signs of economic growth other than by demographic expansion, which, however, was limited by the arable land available.

Our knowledge of the processes and institutions that gave the economy of ancient Mesopotamia its structure is based on more than 100,000 published legal and administrative documents, letters, and collections of laws. The earliest administrative documents date from around 3200 BCE, and the latest to the Hellenistic period (third century BCE). In addition, archaeological artifacts permit the reconstruction of the material culture of ancient Mesopotamia and add to our perception of economic facts.

Two opposing views account for the nature of an economy like that of ancient Mesopotamia. Karl Polanyi, an American economic historian—whose theses were supported by

Sir Moses Finley, professor of ancient history at Cambridge, and by Nobel Prize winner Douglas North—has argued that there is a fundamental difference between modern economies governed by price-fixing markets and traditional, nonindustrialized economies, ancient and medieval, in which embedded social structures determined economic activities and behavior. Polanyi postulates that such differences require their own analytical approach and contends that attempts to understand premodern economies on the basis of analytical methods derived from the experiences of modern economics are quite inappropriate. Polanyi's position stands in contrast to the views of many other historians of ancient Mesopotamia who—without regarding the theoretical implications—unconsciously apply their experiences with today's market-oriented economy to ancient economies.

From *Oikos* to Tributary Economy. For the earlier parts of the fourth millennium BCE, agricultural production in the alluvial plain was based on the communal exploitation of the village arable land. This land was held in common by communities made up of nuclear-type families, who exploited it as a joint effort. Work connected with irrigation installations required cooperation and reciprocal help. Labor was divided according to sex and age groups.

The political organization, in the form of small territorial polities, centered around urban settlements characteristic for Babylonia. It first becomes visible in the archaeological record during the fourth millennium, although Assyria still remains a terra incognita for lack of archaeological and written sources. The dominant mode of production in Babylonia was determined by large urban institutional households. From around 2700 BCE, the growth of the centrally organized irrigation network led to a rather rapid integration of the rural population, most living in village communities, into the institutional households as dependent laborers. As a consequence, almost all the arable land and therefore the entire agricultural production and the majority of the population came under the direct control of these institutional households.

In a Weberian ideal-type sense, this form of economy—redistributive *oikos* economy—has two major characteristics. First, the patrimonial household (*oikos*) of the ruler was identical in institutional as well as in spatial terms with the "state." Second, being autarchic, these households produced everything that they needed themselves, except for a few strategic commodities, such as metal and prestige goods, which had to be obtained by long-distance trade. As is characteristic of the redistributive mode of production, the central authority appropriated the outputs of the collective labor in both agricultural and nonagricultural activities, and the outputs were subsequently redistributed among the producers, that is, the entire populace

of the state. Redistribution took the form of daily or monthly rations in kind, which provided for the subsistence of the populace—in other words, for its daily minimum dietary requirements. The purpose of the redistribution was to guarantee the physical reproduction of the labor force and thus the reproduction of the state in all its manifestations.

The amount of the rations depended on status and professional or labor function. For the lowest ranking male worker, the daily ration consisted of about 0.5–1.0 kilogram of barley. In addition, there was oil for anointment, wool or a piece of fabric for clothing once a year, and other gratifications and distributions on special occasions. Women, children, and elderly persons received less. Rations in kind for certain groups of the labor force and the administrative personnel were supplemented by assignment of small plots of fields. The lowest ranking members of an institutional household received an area of about 0.7 hectare (ha). These subsistence fields were granted for the entire life span of a person according to a person's membership in one of the institutional households and then passed on to the next generation, as long as the descendants fulfilled the same service. These fields, together with the rations, ensured a family's basic subsistence needs. In this type of redistributive economy, individual property on arable land did not play any decisive economic role. Private enterprise was practically nonexistent.

The Emergence of the Tributary Economy. Both external and internal factors brought about significant political and socioeconomic changes during the twentieth century BCE. These changes included the influx of tribal groups, military attacks from neighboring Elam, political rivalries, overextension of the *oikos* system, and salinization in the south of Babylonia. As a result, the household or *oikos* system of the third millennium gradually lost its predominance as a decisive economic factor. It was replaced by a system in which a large proportion of economic activities that had previously taken place within large institutional households were now assigned to individuals farming small plots of land or to entrepreneurs for other activities, as a kind of franchise; for example, for the collection of dues and taxes, storage and distribution of agricultural products, contracting of labor, or long-distance trade.

Individuals, who still remained subjects of the ruler, were given land for their sustenance in exchange for various types of corvée (labor service) or for payment of rental dues in kind. The minimum size (about 6 ha) of land allocated was enough for the subsistence needs of a typical family. From the nineteenth to seventeenth centuries BCE, some forms of private property in arable land existed in certain parts of Babylonia, along with subsistence and rental fields that the royal palace had assigned to individuals.

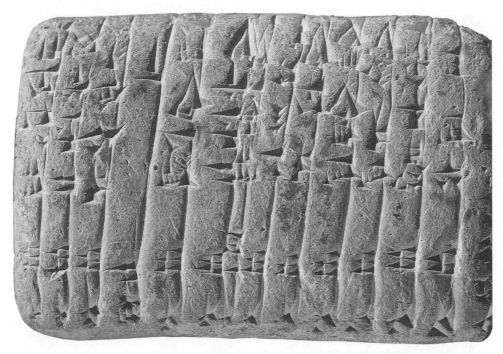

MESOPOTAMIA. Clay tablet listing, in cuneiform writing, barley rations for seventeen gardeners for one month, Third Dynasty of Ur, 2113–2006 BCE. (Dagon Agricultural Collection, Haifa, Israel/ Erich Lessing/Art Resource, NY)

There is no way to quantify the relationship between these types of land. However, the more that people satisfied their subsistence needs by individual farming—under any type of legal entitlement—the less dependent they were on rations and other allocations in kind from the palace or any other institutional household. On the other hand, people were thus more severely exposed to the risks of natural or economic disaster; they had lost the protection that the redistributive system had provided.

Second Half of the Second and First Millennium BCE. A different system of land tenure prevailed in the areas of rain-fed agriculture. For example, in Assyria, the arable land previously under the control of village communities tended to become concentrated in the hands of the urban elite because of increasing agrarian debts. The peasants and their families lived in villages or hamlets as retainers within the confines of manorial estates. The retainer families on a manorial estate had their subsistence guaranteed by being part of the estate.

The dominant tributary land tenure system of Babylonia during the eighteenth and seventeenth centuries BCE was characterized by sustenance fields and those domain fields of the palace and temple that were managed directly and through sharecroppers. There were also some privately owned fields, which again became visible during the Neo-Babylonian and Achaemenid periods (sixth to fourth centuries BCE). Entrepreneurial families (sometimes erroneously described as banking firms) who were intimately linked with the economic operations of the palace form the picture of an urban elite playing an important role in the economy during the second half of the first millennium BCE. During the fifth and fourth centuries, these family firms administered the big manorial estates of the Persian elite in Babylonia. Yet evidently these urban elites had very limited political power.

Macedonian (Seleucid), Parthian, and Sassanian Rule. After the end of Persian rule, the economy of Mesopotamia did not undergo any fundamental changes in agricultural management and land tenure patterns. The pattern of large-scale irrigation installations reconstructed on the basis of archaeological surface surveys and Landsat photographs signifies a massive involvement of the state in maintaining and even enlarging areas to be used for agricultural production. Among the novelties was rice cultivation in southern Mesopotamia. But there are no technological advances improving agricultural production.

Between 330 BCE and 630 CE, Mesopotamia was part of an extensive trade network that was sustained by a political dominion that, from Achaemenid times, encompassed territories stretching from the borders of India to the Mediterranean (Achaemenid and Seleucid periods) and up to the Euphrates (Parthian and Sassanian periods). The sea routes to India via the Persian Gulf were only accessible through southern Mesopotamia. Especially in the

Parthian and Sassanian periods, trading patterns were determined by interaction with the Roman Empire and (later) Byzantium.

Mesopotamian Agriculture. From early in the fourth millennium, agriculture attained extraordinary accomplishments not by technological advances but by highly developed managerial means and agronomic skills and an intensive use of natural advantages. Babylonian cereal agriculture was barley monoculture. Since no natural fertilizer (dung) was used, the fertility of fields was maintained by a rigid fallow system. The hazards of salinization from artificial irrigation were met by leaching and drainage. Unparalleled in antiquity was the high seed-yield ratio of 1:16 up to 1:24 and yields of approximately 750 kilograms her hectare (classical Attica 1:7; Apulia 1:10, medieval central Europe 1:3; Herodotus's report about a yield of 1:200 has to be considered as a ten-year average). Such results were achieved by using a seeder-plow by which seeds were planted about 5 centimeters apart in rows about 50 centimeters apart. Draft animals (oxen) were trained to work in teams of four and were a major factor in handling the preparation of the soil and the sowing of large tracts of fields on the institutional domains, which had an average size of between 50 to 100 hectares.

Along with cereal agriculture, date-palm cultivation was most important. (Even today, Iraq is the world's main producer of dates). But date palms also provided a sheltering shadow for smaller fruit trees growing within a date grove; between them, one grew vegetables.

Trade and Market. In the *oikos* economy of the third millennium BCE, almost the entire population was provisioned through a redistributive ration system. From the second millennium, subsistence agriculture on family-farmed plots produced everything needed. Whatever was produced on these plots was consumed by those who farmed them. In both cases, not much of a marketable surplus existed. On the other hand, there was no need to obtain one's livelihood through market exchange. Moreover, the record shows no term for "market" occasions or for physical marketplaces or installations.

Mesopotamia was devoid of natural resources, so it had to rely on trade with its neighbors to obtain strategic goods (especially metals). The scope, content, and direction of trade changed over time. In the third millennium BCE, Mesopotamia had traded with the Indus Valley civilization (carnelian, tropical woods), Oman (copper), Iran (lapis lazuli and other semiprecious stones, tin), and the Levant (timber). Later, other countries provided copper (Cyprus) or iron (Iran). Mesopotamia served as an intermediary in supplying tin and semiprecious stones from Iran and India. Its only major export good were textiles of the highest quality. From the twentieth to the eighteenth century BCE, Assyrian merchants from Assur in northern Mesopotamia

brought tin and textiles that came from Iran and Babylonia, respectively, to Anatolia, where they had established a number of permanent trading colonies. From Anatolia they brought back silver, which they exchanged in turn for tin and textiles. The Assyrian merchants were organized as family firms; their business can be traced through their extensive correspondence, contracts, memoranda, and notes over several generations.

Labor, Credit, and Money. The labor force needed by the state for its maintenance and reproduction consisted of the royal subjects—that is, the entire population. They worked in agriculture (individually, in which case they owed dues and taxes, or on large institutional domains). They were also conscripted for public work, especially in building city walls and fortifications, palaces, and administrative buildings, and in digging and maintaining canals. Slave labor was therefore not a decisive productive factor. The evidence for more than two thousand years indicates that basically slaves were employed just for domestic purposes. Only from the sixth century BCE could slaves work independently as craftsmen, although they were then obliged to pay an amount of silver annually to their masters.

Throughout Mesopotamian history, economic activities and social relations generated debt and credit transactions that are well documented by notes and contracts. Interest was usually 20 percent for silver and 30 percent for grain loans. Debts were frequently agrarian or consumption loans, reflecting the social and economic situation typical for agricultural subsistence economies. Business transactions often required loans between partners. An innovation of the sixth and fifth centuries BCE was the use of abstract debt notes (that is, without a stated purpose for the debt or credit) as negotiable instruments within a delimited social and economic circle. Entrepreneurial relations with the palace—obligations owed the palace by an entrepreneur—were usually contracted in the form of fictitious credits.

Mesopotamian merchants brought back silver from their commercial journeys to use within Mesopotamia as money—that is, as a means of payment, expressing equivalencies or prices, or of exchange, or as a form of hoarded savings.

Legal documents from the early sixth century BCE attest to the use of Persian silver coins in business transactions—apparently weighed, not counted—and called *Kasper Ginnu* ("true silver") in Babylonian. These coins were called *siglos* (shekels) by the Greeks. During the Hellenistic period, Greek (gold) coins were used in business transactions as metal-equivalent for a stipulated amount of (weighed) silver. It is possible that in the economic sphere of the Greek cities in Mesopotamia, coins were used in the way that was customary for the Mediterranean world. In

Parthian and Sassanian times, coinage gained greater importance.

BIBLIOGRAPHY

Adams, Robert McCormick. *Land behind Baghdad: A History of Settlement on the Diyala Plains*. Chicago, 1965.

Adams, Robert McCormick. *Heartland of Cities: Surveys of Ancient Settlement and Landuse in the Central Floodplain of the Euphrates*. Chicago, 1981.

Civil, Miguel. *The Farmer's Instructions: A Sumerian Agricultural Manual*. Barcelona, 1994. Edition of a Sumerian text with extensive commentary on the agronomy of ancient Mesopotamia.

Grégoire, Jean-Pierre. "Les grandes unités de transformation des céréales: L'exemple des minoteries de la Mésopotamie du Sud à la fin du IIIe millénaire avant notre ère." In *Préhistoire de l'agriculture: Nouvelles approches expérimentales et ethnographiques*, edited by Patty Ch. Anderson, pp. 321–339. Paris, 1992. Contains an outline of the structures of the *oikos* economy.

Larsen, Mogens T. *The Old Assyrian City State and Its Colonies*. Copenhagen, 1976. The most comprehensive assessment of the structures and processes of trade between the city of Assur in northern Mesopotamia and Anatolia during the twentieth to the eighteenth century BCE. The study elucidates the relationship between the societal organization of a small city-state and its economic activities.

Leemans, W. F. *Foreign Trade in the Old Babylonian Period*. Leiden, 1960. Structures and processes of trade between southern Mesopotamia and its neighbors during the nineteenth to the eighteenth century BCE.

Postgate, J. Nicholas. *Early Mesopotamia—Society and Economy at the Dawn of History*. London and New York, 1992. Has extensive bibliography.

Powell, Marvin, ed. *Labor in the Ancient Near East*. New Haven, 1987. Collection of essays on slave and nonslave labor in ancient Mesopotamia, Anatolia, Syria, and Egypt. The essays represent the current state of discussion.

Renger, Johannes. "Patterns of Non-institutional Trade and Non-commercial Exchange in Ancient Mesopotamia at the Beginning of the Second Millennium B.C." In *Circulation of Goods in Non-Palatial Context in the Ancient Near East*, edited by Alfonso Archi, pp. 31–123. Rome, 1984. Despite my critique of some of Polanyi's tenets, his general thesis of a marketless economy is supported on the basis of an extensive survey of letters and legal documents from the nineteenth to the seventeenth century BCE.

Renger, Johannes. "On Economic Structures in Ancient Mesopotamia." *Orientalia NS* 63 (1994), 157–208. This review article rejects a neoclassical interpretation of the Mesopotamian economy on factual and theoretical grounds.

Renger, Johannes. "Institutional, Communal, and Individual Ownership or Possession of Arable Land in Ancient Mesopotamia from the End of the Fourth to the End of the First Millennium B.C." *Chicago-Kent Law Review* 71 (1995), 269–319.

Skaist, Aaron. *The Old Babylonian Loan Contract—Its History and Geography*. Ramat Gan, Israel, 1994.

Stol, Marten. "Old Babylonian Corvée (*tup-ikkum*)." In *Studia historiae ardens—Ancient Near Eastern Studies Presented to Philo H. J. Houwink ten Cate*, edited by Theo P. J. Van den Hout and Johan de Roos, pp. 293–309. Leiden, 1995. Contains bibliographical references to corvée in most periods of Mesopotamian history. Supplements the volume edited by M. Powell; see Powell entry above.

Stolper, Matthew W. *Entrepreneurs and Empire: The Murašû Archive, the Murašû Firm, and Persian Rule in Babylonia*. Leiden, 1985. An outline of how a tributary economy functioned; that is, of how the economic activities of the palace and of the manorial estates of the governing elite were franchised to private entrepreneurs.

Van de Mieroop, Marc. *The Ancient Mesopotamian City*. Oxford, 1999. Discusses the role of craftsmen and traders, the role of credit in commerce and in the procurement of agricultural resources, and how Mesopotamian cities were fed.

Van de Mieroop, Marc. "Economic History." In *Cuneiform Texts and the Writing of History*, pp. 106–137. London and New York, 1999. General overview of the theoretical and practical issues concerning the Mesopotamian economy.

Van der Spek, R. J. "New Evidence on Seleucid Land Policy." In *De Agricultura: In Memoriam Pieter Willem de Neeve*, edited by R. J. Van der Spek, H. C. Teitler, and H. T. Wallinga, pp. 61–79. Amsterdam, 1993.

Vargyas, Péter. "*Kaspu ginnu* and the Monetary Reform of Darius I." *Zeitschrift fuer Assyriologie* 89 (1999), 247–268. A thorough discussion of coinage in ancient Mesopotamia and the Persian empire at the beginning of the sixth century BCE. With extensive bibliography.

Zaccagnini, Carlos. "Ideological and Procedural Paradigms in Ancient Near Eastern Long Distance Exchanges: The Case of Enmerkar and the Lord of Aratta." *Altorientalische Forschungen* 20 (1993), 34–42. Customary trading patterns and conventions in long-distance trade are exemplified by an analysis of an early Mesopotamian epic (twenty-first century BCE) and an Egyptian tale (eleventh century BCE).

JOHANNES M. RENGER

Islamic Period

The area currently known as Iraq was controlled by Persia at the time of Muhammad's death in 632 CE. Arab armies from the Arabian peninsula invaded Iraq two years later and, in a succession of battles, drove out the Persians by 638. There had been many Arabs living in Iraq before this period, and this combined with the religious conviction of the invading armies caused much of the population to convert to Islam in a short time. Military garrisons at Al-Kufa and Basra were established, and these eventually grew to cities of around a quarter of a million persons. A fiscal system was introduced, with lower taxation than the Persians, and Islamic law was imposed.

Christians and Jews were not overtly discriminated against and could remain in positions of influence, but not in public service. Initially, converts to Islam were exempt from land tax, which encouraged conversion to the new religion, although this tax exemption was removed around the turn of the eighth century. Black slaves, brought from East Africa, were used for manual labor, particularly in the southern provinces. The land was cultivated between the Tigris and Euphrates Rivers, facilitated by a complex system of canals.

Iraq was ruled by the Umayyad caliphs from Damascus and was a rebellious province, held in control by a strong military garrison in Wasit, central Iraq. During this period, the language of government changed from Persian to Arabic, and an Arabic coinage was introduced. A clear distinction was held between the nomadic tribesmen, who were confined to certain areas, and the mainly Arab population which was concentrated in the cities. The Abbasid branch of Muhammad's family succeeded in toppling the

Umayyads from power and moved the site of the Islamic caliphate from Damascus, first to Al-Kufa in 749 and later to Baghdad, when that city was founded in 762.

Much trade flowed through the region, both by sea via the Persian Gulf from India and China and by overland routes. The canal system was extended and improved, with a consequent increase in agricultural productivity in central and southern Iraq. The first few centuries of Islam in Iraq were periods of scientific advancement in the larger cities, with mathematics, medicine, astronomy, and geography prominent. It was also a time of artistic and literary composition, both religious and secular, and libraries and universities expanded.

Iraq was the border between predominantly Shīah Islam to the east in Persia and Sunnī Islam to the west. The power of the caliph tended to weaken over the following centuries, and fighting between the rival streams of Islam kept down the level of economic advancement. The Abbasid dynasty was biased in favor of urban dwellers, with high taxation on the countryside used to maintain living standards in the cities, principally Baghdad. The wealth distribution became more acute between the urban upper class and the rural and urban poor. The rural villagers were squeezed between migrating to the cities or returning to nomadic practices.

The ninth and tenth centuries saw a decline in the power of the caliph and a weakening of central government, which meant a general deterioration in the maintenance of the canal system, with a resultant drop in agricultural productivity. A trend toward greater religious orthodoxy resulted in a gradual loss of intellectual liberty in the eleventh century, which emphasized accumulation of existing knowledge rather than original thought and research. The arrival of Mongol armies in the thirteenth century and the sack of Baghdad in 1258 saw the canal system fall apart. The Mongols destroyed villages since they preferred more space for grazing their herds. Over the next few centuries, northern Iraq was desertified, and arable land became steppe, while swamp and marshland grew in southern Iraq.

The population of Iraq began a return to a nomadic form of life following the Mongol conquest, due to the threat of further invasion, an influx of Arabian bedouin, and the poorer returns of farming. When the Portuguese discovered the trade route around Africa to India and established a fort at the Strait of Hormuz, Iraq's trade routes were cut, which further hastened the decline of the cities.

Iraq was conquered by the Ottomans in 1534 and brought order, lighter taxation, and a uniform administration, with four districts—Mosul, Kirkuk, Baghdad, and Basra. However, in the seventeenth century sporadic warfare between Ottomans and Persians and a general decline of Ottoman power slowed efforts to improve the functioning of government in Iraq, which became more decentralized and corrupt. Tax farmers were used in this period to collect government revenue. In this period, land ownership became concentrated in the hands of urban (absentee) landlords and tribal sheiks, with peasants working as sharecroppers. Southern Iraq had the highest concentration of land ownership, with northern Iraq the lowest. Occupations in the cities tended to be passed on from father to son. Rural women had a more traditional role in society, and polygamy and arbitrary divorce by the man was not uncommon.

A large migration by Arab tribes into western Iraq beginning in 1640 disrupted trade routes and completed a process of nomadization of the rural areas, where the tribes grazed camels, goats, and sheep. Mamluk ascendancy in Iraq, which commenced in 1704, marked an increase in the quality and power of government, with distant provinces of Iraq brought back under the central government and most revenue kept within Iraq, rather than remitting it to Istanbul. Government policy encouraged the settlement of nomadic tribes, partly to deter revolt.

Direct European interest in Iraq commenced when Great Britain established a factory in Basra in 1643 and then a presence in Baghdad in 1766. By late in the eighteenth century, Great Britain had a hegemony on trade, which lasted until independence. The opening of the Suez Canal in 1869 enabled land use to shift from a grazing basis to one of cash crops, primarily cereals for export from the main port of Basra. The second half of this century saw the introduction of the telegraph, a postal service, secular schools, and steamship routes on the main rivers. Reforms of the civil service, legal code, and armed services, the beginnings of a railway network, and work on reconstructing a functioning canal system continued through to the early twentieth century.

In 1890, oil had been discovered in Persia and was suspected in Iraq, which resulted in the founding of the Anglo-Persian Oil Company in 1909. However, no commercial quantities were found before World War I.

BIBLIOGRAPHY

Harris, George L. *Iraq: Its People, Its Society, Its Culture*. New Haven, 1958.

International Bank for Reconstruction and Development. *The Economic Development of Iraq*. Baltimore, 1952.

Longrigg, Stephen, and Frank Stoakes. *Iraq*. London, 1958.

Marr, Phebe. *The Modern History of Iraq*. Boulder and London, 1985.

Naval Intelligence Division. *Iraq and the Persian Gulf*. N.p., 1944.

Penrose, Edith, and E. F. Penrose. *Iraq: International Relations and National Development*. London, 1978.

Simons, Geoff. *Iraq: From Sumer to Saddam*. New York, 1994.

LYNDON MOORE

Modern Iraq

Following a military occupation of the area after World War I, the British created Iraq in 1921 through the consolidation of the former Ottoman provinces of Mosul, Baghdad, and Basra; installed a monarchy; and set up a mandate rule. While some, led by Colonel Stephen Longrigg, argued that the mandate regime should back small cultivators, followers of Henry Dobbs, who later became high commissioner, deemed it impossible to maintain British rule without the support of the sheiks, traditional tribal chiefs, who were given large estates. This system maintained traditional sharecropper relations and, in some views, was an impediment to the development of agriculture and a deterrent to national growth. Many sheiks resisted the 1920 popular revolt against British rule, cementing their alliance with the mandate state. After the revolt was crushed, sheiks were given land, money, and tax exemptions and were awarded seats in the parliament, introduced in 1924. The mandate state created an agricultural development plan in hopes of accelerating commercialization and productivity through the building of canals and dams and the introduction of modern machinery, new and improved seed strains of barley and wheat, and new industrial crops, such as cotton and flax. Agricultural exports expanded under British rule, but traditional crops such as dates were still the most important, and while barley and wheat exports increased, the new varieties were unsuccessful because of their poor quality. The plan to modernize agriculture conflicted with the decision to adhere to the sharecropper system.

Independence. In 1932 the British mandate was terminated through the Iraqi-British treaty, which designated Iraq as an independent monarchy. However, Britain kept much of its power, since the treaty stated that the British could keep their military air bases intact and that Iraq had to consult with Britain in foreign policy and extend all possible assistance in times of war or threat of war. The power of the sheiks was solidified and expanded after independence through the Law of the Settlement of Land Rights in 1932. The law recognized prescriptive rights to tribal lands, which allowed chieftains to gain control over large areas of cultivable lands with tenuous evidence of prescriptive rights. The law also legalized renting of state lands, which further expanded the landholdings of sheiks, since laborers could not afford these rents. The law resulted in the concentration of two-thirds of the land in the hands of 2 percent of landowners. Grain output and exports grew in response to high demand during World War II. But rather than invest in the land to raise productivity, sheiks tended to increase production through expansion of cultivated areas, while yields remained constant. Prices rose during the war, but the increased profits went to landowners, as cultivators were forced to sell at a fixed price.

Post–World War II. Development planning began in 1950 with the founding of the Development Board, which

was given 70 percent of oil revenues to develop resources and raise the standard of living through projects in water storage, flood control, irrigation, drainage, industry, mining, and communications. However, the board ignored the most important barriers to agricultural development, such as high concentration in landownership, low productivity, and poor drainage, focusing instead on irrigation projects that ensured continuous colonization of new lands, against the advice of the International Bank for Reconstruction and Development. Wasteful use of irrigation water caused salination, making many fields useless and lowering the quality of barley, the principal crop. But since land reclamation cost landholders almost nothing, they could abandon salinated land for newly reclaimed land. There was no need to make capital investments, such as crop rotation, fertilization, or machinery, in the land. Declining productivity led to intensified exploitation of sharecroppers, many of whom received only 15 to 20 percent of the crop after paying rent and interest on accumulated debt. Deteriorating conditions in agriculture caused peasant migration to towns, and the rural population decreased from 70 percent of the country's total population in the 1930s to 58 percent in the 1950s. Most migrants came from central and southern Iraq, where sharecropping conditions were worst.

Agricultural development was fundamentally restricted by the predominance of an inefficient agrarian system, which was also a barrier to industrial development. Agriculture was labor-intensive with low productivity, which limited the proportion of the population available to provide a labor force for industry. The impoverished rural majority could not provide a market for local industry or generate savings for investment. Before World War II the industrial sector consisted of cottage industries and quasi-mechanized industries, like textiles, with a few modern factories. There was a spurt of industrial growth during the war period caused by shortages of imported goods and absence of competition, but the postwar flood of foreign industrial goods weakened this fledgling sector. In 1950 the Law for the Encouragement of Industry granted income and tax exemptions for use of local raw materials and investment in capital-intensive industries, but industrial expansion was slow because of the small domestic market and tight foreign competition. During the 1950s the rise in oil revenues erased the trade deficit of the 1940s, and the quota system was relaxed. Bureaucratic inefficiency and struggles among contending interests caused trade policy to oscillate back and forth between protection and free trade.

In 1925 and 1927 concessions for exploration and production of oil granted to British, French, and American interests had almost no impact on the domestic economy, as 90 percent of the staff was foreign until the mid-1950s and construction materials and machinery were imported. Iraq began producing oil for the market in 1934, but output was limited by the capacity of pipelines carrying oil to the Mediterranean. Oil production increased from one million barrels in 1930 to twenty million in 1940. It reached 51 million in 1950, after which production rates rapidly increased further, with 356 million barrels produced in 1960. The demands of the Iraqi government for more royalties along with the 1951 nationalization of the Iranian oil industry and profit sharing in Venezuela and Saudi Arabia led to negotiations between the Iraqi government and the foreign oil companies that culminated in the agreement of 1952, which granted Iraq half of all profits earned. The agreement launched an era of unprecedented economic growth, as oil became the leading sector of the economy in response to a worldwide increase in the demand for petroleum after World War II. The demand boom was led by the rebuilding of shattered European economies, an increase in peacetime military demand for oil, and the widespread mechanization of agriculture, growth of transportation sectors, and substitution of oil for coal. Rising oil revenues made it possible to expand social services in health and education while increasing mass consumption, which continued for the next two decades.

In July 1958 the Abdel Karim Qasim regime overthrew the monarchy and established a republican regime with the goals of establishing agrarian reforms, such as setting ceilings on landownership; creating social programs; delinking the Iraqi dinar from the British pound; establishing economic relations with the Soviet Union and Eastern Europe; and stressing industrial development. The 1958 Agrarian Reform Law limited landholdings and gave smallholdings to peasants, but the revolutionary changes in land tenure were not accompanied by agricultural investment. Only 29 percent of the allocated funds was actually spent on agricultural improvements, and Iraq changed from a food-exporting nation to a net importer. There was also no substantial change in industrial investment, though it was considered necessary to achieve economic independence. The new regime was successful in bringing about a more egalitarian distribution of land through the destruction of the political power of landlords. It also expanded social services to the poor, diversified foreign trade though relationships with the Soviet Union, and ended the last remnants of British colonialism with the delinking of the dinar from the British pound. The beginnings of the national oil sector were also established under this regime with the 1961 creation of Law #80. This law gave the government control over any lands not actually developed by the oil companies, which included 99.5 percent of the lands covered in the original concessions. The Iraq National Oil Company was founded in 1964, it but was not given

the essential legal and financial resources needed to develop the lands until 1972.

In February 1963 the regime was overthrown by an alliance, of which the military wing, under Abdel Salam Aref, ousted its civilian counterparts in November. The alliance developed a five-year plan with the goals of economic stability in the short term, a rise in living standards of at least 8 percent per year, full employment, expansion of social services, more even income distribution, Arab economic unity, and set annual growth rates for agriculture and industry. This regime was overthrown in July 1968 by the Baath Party, but the plan was allowed to run its full period, the first development plan to do so. Employment increased by 427,000 during this time, rather than the projected 262,000, but all other economic indicators failed to reach their targets by considerable margins.

National Development Plan. The Arab Baath Socialist Party, which is still the governing regime, had no coherent political, social, or economic program. Its goals were to achieve Arab unity, freedom, and socialism by removing political divisions. The National Development Plan set for 1970–1974 was the first plan to run its full course under the same political power structure, and planners were able to use the studies, planning and technical experience, and administrative competence that Iraq had attained over the previous two decades. The plan set growth rates for agriculture and industry and aimed to increase savings, investment, production, and labor productivity; modernize technology; expand and diversify exports; adopt a rational import policy to improve living standards; exploit mineral resources to reduce dependence on oil; and expand social services and employment opportunities. However, despite the regime's claim to be revolutionary, the plan continued the work of past governments. Most investment went toward completing projects that had already been started.

Iraq's oil industry was nationalized during the early years of the Baath regime. In 1972 enough resources were allocated to allow the Iraq National Oil Company to begin producing and marketing the oil from the fields denoted by Law #80. Iraq also created other facets of a well-developed oil industry, such as the training of a skilled and specialized labor force; the construction of pipelines, refineries, export facilities, and loading terminals; the acquisition of oil tankers; and the creation of marketing networks. By nationalizing oil, Iraq appropriated the entire rent of the resource. But revenues were still dependent on the supply and demand of the world market, and Iraq's economic development became increasingly dependent on one sector. Fluctuations in the world oil market reverberated through the entire economy.

The Baath National Development Plan began in an era of rising oil revenues. The Organization of Petroleum Exporting Countries (OPEC) was created in 1960 to coordinate

MOSUL, IRAQ. Downtown markets, 1999. (© Mike Yamashita/Woodfin Camp and Associates, New York)

pricing among oil-producing companies. But resolutions passed by OPEC were ignored by its members until the end of the decade, when excess capacity in oil-producing companies began to disappear and the United States emerged as the most important oil-producing company. At this point the companies agreed to OPEC–wide price negotiations, culminating in the Tehran Agreement of 1971, which stabilized taxes and prices. This was followed by the oil price explosion of 1973–1974, during which prices rose from $3 per barrel in October to $11.65 per barrel by January. While the Development Plan's official goal was to lower oil's share of Iraq's GDP to 26.4 percent, that share instead rose to 60 percent.

The 1970s were marked by unprecedented high growth rates of 11.7 percent in GDP, 10.2 percent in industry, 28.4 percent in construction, and 13.2 percent and 13.6 percent respectively in public and private consumption. Oil revenues rose from $648 million in 1972 to $5.75 billion in 1974, $10.5 billion in 1976, and $30 billion in 1980, increasing by over 46 times in less than a decade. However, the economy was wrought with deep structural problems, such as labor shortages, almost no agricultural growth, high inflation, and complete dependence on oil. The government also failed to recognize that oil demand would decline in the long run if prices remained high. A long-term development plan was created for the period from 1975 to 1995 to bring stability to the economy, but the Revolutionary Command Council (RCC), a small, nonelected group with executive power chaired by Saddam Hussein, rejected the advice of economic planners in favor of annual investment plans. In 1977 the RCC stopped publishing sectoral investments or aggregate expenditure.

Iran-Iraq War. In September 1980 Iraq attacked Iran. The Iranians retaliated by bombing Iraq's oil-exporting facilities, forcing it to suspend oil shipments from the southern fields and slashing oil exports by 72 percent. The closure of Iraq's ports to the Persian Gulf forced it to rely on overland routes, but because the transport system was not able to handle the trade reroutes, costs increased. Oil revenues decreased from $26.1 billion in 1980 to $10.4 billion in 1981, and the impact was multiplied throughout the economy. The war worsened labor shortages because of the withdrawal of foreign workers and the diversion of labor to the war front. Despite these problems, the Iraqi government sought to continue the level of civilian spending while expanding the military budget, using foreign aid from Saudi Arabia and Kuwait.

Development spending ended in 1982, and military spending absorbed one-half to two-thirds of GDP in the 1980s. The war forced the regime to create a program of economic liberalization and privatization beginning in February 1987. This included the sale of state lands, farms, and factories; competition in banking; deregulation of the labor market; incentives to private enterprise; the creation of a stock exchange; and opening the economy to foreign investment. This program exacerbated the economic crisis, evidenced by a rapid rise in prices, and forced a further decline in living standards. The Iran-Iraq War ended on 20 August 1988, and Iraq began the postwar period with the economy in ruins. Most of the major oil-exporting capacity had by this time been destroyed, blocked, or closed, and basic industries had declined. Dependence on food imports had risen, agriculture was stagnant, industrial growth was low, hyperinflation existed, and servicing foreign debt took a significant portion of the country's earnings. The entire economy had become dependent on the oil sector, whose performance left much to be desired.

Gulf War. Oil revenues reached a low of $6.9 billion in 1986, after the decline of world oil prices, but rose to $11.4 billion in 1987, following OPEC's decision to stabilize member-country output. However, Kuwait and the United Arab Emirates failed to abide by the agreement, increasing their exports and driving down prices, which Iraq considered economic warfare. Moreover Iraq and Kuwait disagreed as to whether Kuwait's assistance during the Iran-Iraq War was a loan or a grant, and Iraq accused Kuwait of drilling oil from its fields. On 2 August 1990 Iraq invaded Kuwait with the goal of a "New Iraq" with higher oil reserves and export quotas and a hope of increasing spending on development projects and imports. However, the United Nations Security Council condemned the invasion and imposed an embargo, which shut off 90 percent of Iraq's imports and 97 percent of its exports by December. On 16 January 1991 a six-week bombing campaign was initiated by coalition forces led by the United States, focusing on military targets, civilian buildings and infrastructure, power stations, oil facilities, hospitals, and industrial plants. Between 94,000 and 281,000 Iraqis died during the war and the subsequent uprising. The value of the assets destroyed totaled $232 billion, several times Iraq's 1989 GDP.

Per capita GDP in Iraq rose steadily from $654 in 1950 to $1,745 in 1970, reaching a peak of $4,219 in 1979, but it dropped to $1,479 over the next ten years (all figures in 1980 dollars). By 1993 it had fallen to $485, lower than most of the poorest nations. Fifty years of economic growth were erased by the two wars. The trade embargo remains in place, but in December 1996 Iraq was allowed to export limited amounts of oil in exchange for food, medicine, and some infrastructure spare parts through the UN's oil-for-food program. In December 1999 the UN Security Council authorized Iraq to export under the program as much oil as required to meet humanitarian needs. Living standards continued to deteriorate in the first years of the twenty-first century as a result of the economic embargo imposed on Iraq by the United Nations and the corruption and incompetence of the Baath Party government. In early 2003, an American-led invasion of the country ended the rule of the Baath Party.

BIBLIOGRAPHY

Alnasrawi, Abbas. *The Economy of Iraq: Oil, Wars, Destruction of Development and Prospects, 1950–2010.* Westport, Conn., 1994.

Haj, Samira. *The Making of Iraq, 1900–1963.* Albany, N.Y., 1997.

Issawi, Charles. *An Economic History of the Middle East and North Africa.* New York, 1982.

Longrigg, Stephen Hemsley. *Iraq, 1900–1950.* London, 1953.

IRELAND *[This entry contains three subentries, on the economic history of Ireland before 1800, from 1800 to 1922, and after 1922.]*

Ireland before 1800

Ireland, on Europe's western periphery, had never been part of the Roman empire. Its isolation had allowed it to retain a variety of distinctive features: the absence of centralized political authority and of a tradition of primogeniture, a distinctive legal code, and the vesting of landed property in the lineage group rather than the individual. However, the traditional picture of a wholly insular society characterized by a seminomadic agriculture has been discarded. Modern studies indicate a typical western European pattern of mixed farming on clearly defined holdings, trading links with Britain and northwestern Europe, and even the emergence of urban settlements on the sites of certain monasteries. Viking settlement in the ninth and tenth centuries established important port towns at Dublin, Cork, Waterford, Wexford, and Limerick, exporting hides, wool, and decorative metalwork, while importing wine, salt, and iron.

The establishment of an English colony, following an initial military intervention in 1169, was no mere armed conquest. In parts of the west, southwest, and north, Anglo-Norman lords established a precarious ascendancy over what were still predominantly Gaelic populations. But in a substantial region of the east and south there was also a significant if not precisely quantifiable inward migration of both rural tenants and town dwellers. This was part of the same great population movement, driven by demographic expansion, that brought Norman knights to England, Scotland, Wales, and the eastern Mediterranean, and carried German settlers east of the Elbe. In the areas under their control, the settlers organized agriculture along manorial lines, facilitating a more intensive exploitation of both land and labor, with clearance of woodland, more intensive tillage, and the introduction of large-scale sheep farming. Agriculture in English areas was also more commercialized, with rents paid in cash, the emergence of a network of fairs and markets, and the export of surpluses of grain and wool. Existing port towns grew in size, and new urban centers also emerged, of which the most important were Drogheda on the east coast and Galway on the west.

By the end of the thirteenth century, political fragmentation and military reverses indicated that English expansion had overreached its limits. Warfare, harvest failure, and disease, including the Black Death (1348–1349), estimated to have killed between one-third and one-half of the population, led to a decline in cultivation, a reduction in demesne farming, a loss of lands to Gaelic neighbors, and the abandonment of smaller outlying settlements. Exports also contracted, and reports of decayed buildings and wasteland within town walls indicate a degree of urban stagnation. However, the indirect evidence of extensive investment in new ecclesiastical foundations, and fragmentary trade statistics suggest a modest recovery during the mid- and late fifteenth century. The towns retained their importance as centers of networks of trade, which by this time extended into Gaelic as well as Anglo-Ireland. The Gaelic lordships also engaged directly in some overseas trade. There were even isolated instances of towns developing in wholly Gaelic areas, of which the most important was Sligo in the northwest, which flourished as a center for the export of salmon and herring. Overall, however, Gaelic Ireland remained significantly less commercialized than the English areas.

The sixteenth century initiated a period of rapid change. English government extended its effective power from an east coast enclave to the island as a whole. Fixed property titles and rents began to replace the looser Gaelic system of lordship and exactions from dependents. Plantation schemes in the midlands and Munster introduced some thousands of English settlers. However, population, held down by war, famine, and disease, grew only slowly, from around 1 million in 1500 to perhaps 1.4 million by 1600. Overseas trade continued to be dominated by the exchange of primary produce, notably fish, hides, and wool, for imported luxuries. The weakness of the commercial sector was evident both in the small size of the main urban centers and in the absence of a clear urban hierarchy. Dublin, with between 5,000 and 10,000 inhabitants in 1600, was followed by Galway (4,000), Limerick (3,000), and Cork (2,400). In the early decades of the seventeenth century, by contrast, a lengthy period of internal peace, combined with the final establishment of a uniform political and legal framework, permitted more rapid progress. Plentiful supplies of timber encouraged some iron smelting, as well as the large-scale export of staves. There were also attempts to promote tanning and cloth working (weaving, spinning, and finishing) in both linen and wool. However, all such manufacturing ventures continued to be held back by the lack of skilled workers, a shortage of capital, and poor marketing structures. Instead, the most important advances were in exports of cattle, wool, and butter. The movement of up to 40,000 English and Scottish settlers into the newly pacified northern province of Ulster promoted a more commercialized agriculture and the establishment

IRISH LINENS. Workers beetling, scutching, and hackling flax, engraving by William Hinks, circa 1790. (Prints and Photographs Division, Library of Congress)

of markets and towns in what had formerly been Ireland's most thinly populated and underdeveloped region. By 1641, immigration and natural increase had brought the population of the island to 2 million or more.

Prolonged and destructive warfare between 1641 and 1653, with famine and plague from 1649 to 1652, destroyed many of the gains of the previous forty years. A renewed recovery from the mid-1650s rested on more solid foundations: the rise of an export trade in butter, barrel beef, and, in particular, wool, aimed at new markets in continental Europe, the West Indies, and the American colonies. This expansion in trade was reflected in urban growth. By 1700, Dublin had a population of between 50,000 and 60,000. Cork, the next largest center, had about 15,000. Much of the countryside remained unenclosed, with land held under a variety of tenures in fragmented and undercapitalized holdings and pastoral farming predominant. However, agriculture was now pursued more intensively than before, within clearly defined proprietorial and tenurial boundaries, and with fixed rents in cash or kind. Living standards remained low. Sir William Petty estimated in 1672 that seven out of eight people lived in wretched cabins, and there was acute famine in 1674. Increasing use of tobacco, however, indicates a modest commercialization, and the recovery in population, from a low point of 1.3 million in 1652 to over 2 million by 1700, testifies to an overall improvement in conditions. Commercialization and population growth were encouraged by the resumption after 1660 of substantial immigration from Scotland and England into Ulster. By the early eighteenth century, more than one-quarter of the population were descendants of settlers established there since the mid-sixteenth century, a level of migration unparalleled within the boundaries of early modern Europe.

Economic growth continued in the first half of the eighteenth century. Between 1700 and 1740, exports, consisting mainly of beef, butter, and the products of a rapidly expanding linen manufacture, rose by 50 percent. Yet living standards remained low, and there were severe famines in 1721–1722, in 1728–1729, and again in 1739–1741, when an estimated 13 percent of people died of fever or starvation. The population in 1750 was probably no higher than the 2 million estimated for 1700. Contemporaries blamed Ireland's poverty on a series of British measures designed to preserve trading monopolies or cripple potential competition from Irish producers. These included the Navigation Acts, which prevented the direct importation into Ireland of colonial produce, the Cattle Acts (1663, 1671), which prohibited the import into Great Britain of Irish meat and livestock, and the Woolen Act (1699), which banned exports of Irish woolen cloth and yarn to any destination other than England, where they already faced prohibitive tariffs. Modern accounts, however, suggest that the main effect of British commercial restrictions was less to cripple economic activity than to redirect it, from wool into linen, or from British to transatlantic markets for livestock products. It can be argued that the main causes of Ireland's desperate poverty lay in the narrow basis of commercial activity, with linen and cattle products between them accounting for four-fifths of total exports, a continuing shortage of skills and capital, and inadequate external markets for the island's agricultural surplus.

Beginning in the 1740s, Ireland entered a long phase of economic expansion that was to transform economic activity, social structure, and landscape. Its westerly position made it ideally placed to benefit from the continued expansion of the Atlantic economy, by exporting growing quantities of beef and butter and other provisions to the French and British colonies in the West Indies, as well as servicing the steadily increasing volume of transatlantic shipping. By the 1790s, these Caribbean markets were increasingly supplied by North American producers. But their place was now taken by Great Britain, where a growing nonagricultural population provided an alternative outlet not only for Irish livestock products but also for growing quantities of grain. Meanwhile, Irish linen manufacture had continued to expand, eclipsing its Scottish rival; exports rose from just over 4 million yards in 1730 to 20 million yards by 1770 and to more than 35 million by 1800. Rough calculations by L. M. Cullen suggest that by 1815 the volume of Irish exports had risen sixfold since 1700 and national income fivefold since 1730. Rising agricultural prices encouraged extensive drainage, land reclamation, and enclosure, as well as improvements in transport: road building and improvement, aided by the introduction of turnpikes in the 1730s, as well as the construction of two major waterways, the royal and grant canals, linking Dublin to the midlands and west. Banking services, which had first developed in the main towns in the 1720s, expanded further. Towns grew rapidly. Dublin had 182,000 inhabitants by 1800, Cork almost 60,000. The rise of Belfast, from around 8,000 inhabitants in 1759 to 25,000 by 1800, reflected the growing importance of Ulster as the center of the linen industry. Commercialization was also evident in the spread of fairs and markets. In the 1680s, there had been 503, almost half in the eastern province of Leinster. By 1770, there were six times that number, of which only one-quarter were in Leinster.

The consequences of the increase in national wealth were most visible in the extensive rebuilding and remodeling of town centers and in the corresponding wave of building in the countryside, as the aristocracy and gentry replaced their existing modest houses, sometimes partly fortified, with Palladian and later neoclassical mansions, surrounded by elaborate demesnes. But the sustained rise in population, to around 4.4 million in 1791, indicates that some of the increased wealth was more broadly diffused. Crop failures in 1756–1757 and 1782–1784 brought hardship but no repeat of the famine experienced in 1741 and earlier. There was also growing social differentiation within what had been a largely homogeneous peasantry. A growing class of landless laborers and smallholders, heavily dependent on the potato as a staple diet and for the most part occupying marginal or poorer land, was increasingly set apart from a minority of capitalized farmers.

The prosperity of late-eighteenth-century Ireland rested on industry as well as agriculture. Linen remained by far the most dominant manufacture. Weaving was concentrated in Ulster, particularly the eastern counties, but the demand for yarn, not yet mechanized, created growing employment in the northern counties of Connacht and Leinster; there was also some spinning and weaving in the Cork region. Wool, concentrated in the towns of the south, remained significant as the main supplier to an expanding domestic market. Mechanized cotton spinning, using water power, expanded rapidly in the 1780s and 1790s, enthusiastically supported by the Irish parliament. There had also been extensive investment in flour milling, brewing, and sugar refining, and the growth of prosperity had encouraged handicraft luxury trades such as metalwork, silk weaving, and furniture and coach building.

BIBLIOGRAPHY

Aalen, Fredrick. H. A., Kevin Whelan, and Matthew Stout. *Atlas of the Irish Rural Landscape*. Cork, Ireland, 1997.

Clarke, Howard, ed. *Irish Cities*. Cork, Ireland, 1995. Popular general studies, but valuable in the absence of a detailed work on Irish urban history.

Cosgrove, Art, ed. *A New History of Ireland*, vol. 2, *Medieval Ireland, 1169–1534*. Oxford, 1987. Several substantial chapters on economy, society, and overseas trade.

Cullen, Louis M. *Anglo-Irish Trade, 1660–1800*. Manchester, 1968.

Cullen, Louis M. *An Economic History of Ireland since 1660*. London, 1972. Still the best introduction to the radical reassessment of the development of early modern Ireland initiated by this author.

Gillespie, Raymond. *The Transformation of the Irish Economy, 1550–1700*. (Studies in Irish Economic and Social History, 6.) Dundalk, Ireland, 1991. A concise overview for nonspecialist readers.

Graham, Brian J., and Lindsay J. Proudfoot. *An Historical Geography of Ireland*. London, 1993.

Truxes, Thomas M. *Irish American Trade, 1660–1783*. Cambridge, 1988.

S. J. CONNOLLY

Ireland from 1800 to 1922

Ireland was the only economy in Europe with a smaller population at the end of the nineteenth century than at its beginning. On the eve of the Great Famine (in 1845), the island contained more people than the whole of Scandinavia; by 1914, it would contain only one-third the Scandinavian population. Closer to home, when Ireland became a part of the United Kingdom of Great Britain and Ireland

in 1800, it held almost one-third of the kingdom's inhabitants; a century later it would hold only one-tenth. This is remarkable given the relatively rapid growth of the Irish population until the 1830s. Population growth decelerated thereafter, because of increasing emigration and a reduction in the birthrate. The population peaked at about 8.5 million in 1846, before the Famine reduced it to 6.55 million by 1851. High emigration and a reduction in the marriage rate caused it to fall further, to 5.2 million by 1881 and about 4.25 million by 1922. In the period from the Union to 1922, Ireland's population history is the key to its economic history.

Before the Famine, Ireland's poverty and headlong population growth struck outside commentators most. The half-century before the Famine was almost certainly an era of impoverishment for the masses, Ireland's "potato people." Their struggle for survival depended on a peculiarly Irish transaction: in return for the use of a plot of fertilized land on which they grew their own potatoes, they supplied most of the farm labor required by a highly labor-intensive agricultural system. The bargain exposed them to the risks of a poor potato harvest. Fortunately, disastrous failures of the potato crop were relatively uncommon before 1845, and the population share of those most dependent on the potato for their subsistence rose considerably in the pre-Famine decades. On the eve of the Famine, it had reached about one-third, consuming quantities of the root (four to five kilos daily per adult male equivalent) that seem incredible today. The land under potato cultivation peaked at about 2.1 million acres (or one-third of all tilled land) on the eve of the Famine. Supplemented by other vegetables such as cabbage, milk, and fish, the potato provided a monotonous but nutritious diet. Coupled with a plentiful supply of domestic fuel in the form of bog peat (or turf), it offered some compensation for poor housing and tattered clothing. As a result, the Irish poor were healthier and lived longer than poor people on similar incomes elsewhere in Europe.

Cheap labor and the tariff protection given by the Corn Laws ensured that Irish farming was more tillage-oriented in the pre-Famine era than before or since. Tillage items, mainly grain and potatoes, accounted for about two-thirds of agricultural output (compared to one-fifth in the 1920s and about one-eighth today). Irish crop yields per acre were not much lower than British, but output per worker was only about half that in Britain. Despite the dual constraint of hundreds of thousands of undercapitalized small farms and hundreds of financially embarrassed landowners, farming made some modest progress between the Union and the Famine. Improving communications, both by land and by sea, helped. The improvement was reflected in higher exports, improved livestock strains, and higher crop yields. By reducing potato yields, the potato blight reduced the effective land endowment and the attractiveness of tillage. A rise in both the wage-rental ratio and the relative price of livestock products reinforced the shift to livestock-oriented farming after 1845.

Ireland's land tenure system, a variant of the British system, was a product of colonialism: the bulk of the land was in the hands of the descendants of those who had fought against the native Irish or had professed the Protestant religion. Irish landed estates contained more farms than British, and Irish farms were much smaller; partly for that reason, landlords tended to be less involved in the running of their estates and were more likely to be absentees. Before the Famine, Irish landlords also were much more likely to be in serious financial straits than their counterparts across the Irish Sea. Investment and rationalization were unlikely on heavily mortgaged or "encumbered" estates, but the Encumbered Estates Act of 1849, by freeing up the market in encumbered land, remedied that particular problem. The 1850s and 1860s were decades of relative harmony and progress on the land. However, the agricultural downturn of the late 1870s sparked a land war between a tenantry represented by the Land League and their landlords. The "war," which began in 1879 with demands for rent reductions and fixity of tenure, culminated in the Wyndham Act of 1903 and peasant proprietorship. The verdict of recent historiography is that the switchover to owner-occupancy made little difference in output or productivity. The outcome proved that the landlords were not indispensable, but it also implied that the Land War was largely about rent-seeking. The victory of the farmers was due to their increased ability to mobilize; it reflected and contributed to democratization.

The era of the Land War presented new challenges and opportunities for farmers. Given the pastoral orientation of post-Famine Irish agriculture, the reduction in grain prices presented a smaller problem for Irish farmers than for their counterparts in the southeast of England. New opportunities were represented by the centrifugal separator and its institutional concomitant, the cooperative creamery. These innovations failed to have the same impact in Ireland that they had in Denmark, with the alleged result that Irish butter lost market share in Great Britain. However, lower cow densities and the earlier presence of a strong butter merchant interest partly account for the Irish "failure." Irish milk production was constrained by farmers' resistance to winter dairying; but the remarkable seasonality of Irish milk output, which persists today, has had less to do with the laziness of farmers than climatic conditions. Similar climatic conditions in New Zealand produce a very similar seasonality pattern. The transfer from landlord to farmer did not broach the more serious problem of too many small farms.

Industrial output and employment for the island as a whole continued to grow until the 1840s, though Ireland was losing out to Great Britain. The early promise of cotton textiles had evaporated by the 1820s, as that sector had become more regionally concentrated. Linen, which in turn became increasingly localized in east Ulster, offered some compensation. Ireland remained competitive in a range of products linked to agriculture, such as butter, bacon, whiskey, and beer. Why it failed to industrialize as its neighboring island did has been much debated; free trade, a lack of enterprise and raw materials, a high crime rate, and an anticapitalist Catholic mentality have all been mentioned. None of these explanations is entirely convincing. Geography, which placed Ireland next to the fulcrum of the Industrial Revolution but also relatively distant from the growing markets of metropolitan Britain, recently has been examined as a factor.

Meanwhile, dwelling on "deindustrialization" or blaming it on the Union ignores the fact that the northeast of Ireland went through an industrial revolution in the nineteenth century. Belfast, a small town in 1800, saw its population quintuple to 100,000 by 1850 and double again by 1880. By 1900, it contained more people than Dublin and had several other industrial towns in its hinterland. The combined population share of Antrim and Down, the two counties most transformed, doubled (from 8.8 to 16.8 percent) between 1821 and 1901. The North's industrial revolution was founded mainly on linen textiles, engineering, and shipbuilding, areas in which it became a world leader. Northern businessmen capitalized on the mechanization of linen spinning in the 1820s and weaving from midcentury on; just as cotton increasingly concentrated on southern Lancashire, Belfast and its hinterland came to be "Linenopolis." In the 1900s and 1910s, linen provided employment for 100,000 people, mainly women, while Belfast's shipyards were producing some of the biggest and most advanced ships in the world (including the ill-fated *Titanic*). The North's success was not due to its natural resource endowment; flax could grow as well in Munster as it did in Ulster, and Queen's Island, where Harland and Wolff began building ships in 1861, was an artificial creation of Belfast's harbor commissioners. Ulster's literacy and its culture helped its development, however.

As happened almost everywhere else, in Ireland the nineteenth century saw dramatic advances in communications and in banking. The Belfast-Greenock was the world's first scheduled steamship route (1818); the first railway between Dublin and Kingstown was opened in 1834, and by the early 1850s the mainline network had been established, with Dublin as its node. Before then, railway travel by coach had extended to all main roads, and Charles Bianconi managed almost nationwide service over routes extending to thirty-eight hundred miles. Bianconi reacted to the railway threat by buying railway company shares and rerouting his "bians" to provide feeder services to the mainline railway stations. The rail network continued to expand into the new century although its traffic was always light compared to that of Britain. The evolution of the Irish banking system was modeled closely on that of England, and legislation permitting joint-stock banking (1825) and restricting note issue (1845) mimicked legislation governing English banking. The joint-stock banking system that emerged in the 1820s and 1830s proved enduring. It offered stability, with the Bank of Ireland, established by charter in 1783, operating as a quasi-central bank. The Bank of Ireland exercised its function of lender of last resort competently, helping out most of the joint-stock banks at some time, but rightly allowing the Agricultural and Commercial Bank (1836), the Tipperary Bank (1857), and the Munster Bank (1885) to go under. The first of these was mismanaged; the other two were corrupt. Recent research has tended to defend the Irish banks against the traditional criticism that they were overcautious.

The Famine gave a big impetus to the mass emigration and the low marriage rate that would characterize Ireland for more than a century. Irish emigration was distinctive not only for its size but for its mainly permanent character, and for its relatively high proportion of women. Most emigrants headed for the United States, but destinations shifted in response to relative prospects. The loss in numbers brought higher living standards to those who remained; the half-century or so between the Famine and World War I was one of considerable convergence in this limited sense. Real wages, housing quality, life expectation, and literacy levels all rose. By the end of the nineteenth century, there was still much poverty, but the regional balance had shifted somewhat. Now the disease-infested slums of Dublin attracted almost as much attention as the remote west.

The nineteenth century was a time of increasing intervention in the economy. In the pre-Famine era, the introduction of free primary schooling and poor relief through the workhouse system followed public inquiries into elementary education (1834) and poverty (1835–1836). Similar inquiries into the possibilities of creating a national rail network (1838) and reforming the system of land tenure (1845) produced a smaller public response. The final decades of the nineteenth century brought a further cluster of reforms: the devolution of local government to Ireland, the creation of the Congested Districts Board and the Department of Agriculture, and, most radical of all, a shift from landlordism to peasant proprietorship. Some commentators saw these reforms as part of a plan to counter growing Irish nationalism. Meanwhile, public expenditures continued to grow, with the result that the fledgling Irish Free State would be faced with the challenge of financing a relatively large public sector. One key bequest of the Union, the noncontributory old-age pension, would account for one-eighth of all public spending in the new Ireland of the 1920s.

[*See also* Irish Famine.]

BIBLIOGRAPHY
Guinnane, Timothy M. *The Vanishing Irish: Households, Migration and the Rural Economy in Ireland 1850–1914.* Princeton, 1997.
Ó Gráda, Cormac. *Ireland: A New Economic History.* Oxford, 1994.
Vaughan, William E. *Landlords and Tenants in Mid-Victorian Ireland.* Oxford, 1994.

CORMAC Ó GRÁDA

Ireland after 1922

Today the runaway success of the Irish economy captures the headlines. In the 1990s, output and employment grew faster in the Republic of Ireland (the part of the island that seceded from the United Kingdom in 1921, often referred to as "Ireland" or "the South" or "the Republic") than in any other economy in the Organization for Economic Cooperation and Development (OECD). Yet even in the late 1980s, the case for considering the Republic a failed economic entity was a strong one, and both historiography and economic commentary concentrated on finding reasons "why Ireland had failed." Cultural explanations included the "begrudgery" (a tendency to disapprove of the success of others) highlighted by historian Joseph Lee and the "clientelism" cited by critics of Ireland's political system. Politicoeconomic explanations stressed the inward-looking focus of economic policy, as represented by restrictions on inward flows of goods and capital. The failure was evident in trends in economic well-being. In the early 1920s, on the eve of independence, living standards in Ireland, as measured by gross national product (GNP) per head, were about the same as those in northern European economies such as Norway and Finland; but thereafter Ireland slid down the European league scale. Between the early 1920s and the early 1960s, living standards and productivity in twenty-six-county Ireland did not increase much. Hundreds of thousands of Irishmen and Irishwomen "voted with their feet," and the population of the present Republic of Ireland fell from 3 million to 2.8 million.

Although it would be an exaggeration to claim that the Irish Free State was born virtually industry-free, partition in 1920–1921 nonetheless effectively divided the island into mainly industrial and agricultural parts. In 1926, the Irish Free State's first population census put employment in manufacturing at 155,000, or one in eight of those employed. In Northern Ireland in the same year, manufacturing accounted for one in three of those at work, or nearly 37 percent of the labor force. Moreover, in the north, heavy

IRELAND. Men stacking kegs at the Guinness brewery, Dublin, 1966. (John Vachon/Prints and Photographs Division, Library of Congress)

industry and textiles accounted for the bulk of manufacturing employment; in the south, construction accounted for nearly a quarter, and the food and drink sector, relatively low-tech and ancillary to agriculture, for well over two-fifths of manufacturing output.

The treaty that created the Irish Free State in 1922 led to a civil war that would influence Irish political life for several decades. The two main political parties to emerge in its wake reflected the opposing sides in the war. The economic policies pursued in the 1920s by the protreaty Cumann na nGaedheal party emphasized continuity and retrenchment. It reduced taxation, cut social welfare, maintained the link with sterling, and rejected appeals for tariff protection, preferring to dwell on Ireland's comparative advantage in agricultural produce. Its policies lacked the necessary broad political appeal, however. Antitreaty Fianna Fáil mopped up the middle ground and won power in March 1932, ruling without interruption until 1948. Fianna Fáil's more nationalist ideology led to the Economic War from 1932 to 1938, a postcolonial dispute about land annuity payments. However, there were also important socioeconomic differences between the two main parties. Fianna Fáil pursued import-substituting industrialization (ISI), subsidized tillage, and improved housing and social welfare. Both ISI and grain cultivation were intended to increase employment. In the context of worldwide trade destruction of the 1930s, Fianna Fáil's inward-looking policies were not unexceptional; indeed, at first they increased employment. Other considerations forced the

economy into semiautarky during World War II. The real economic damage was done after 1945, however, when neither Fianna Fáil nor the coalition governments that alternated with it relented on protectionism. By the late 1950s, after a decade of near stagnation and heavy emigration, there was a growing consensus that protectionism had failed. This led first to a relaxation of the controls on foreign investment and then to the liberalization of commodity trade.

For most of the period since independence, neither monetary nor fiscal policy produced much that is historically noteworthy. Linking the new Irish currency with sterling left little scope for independent monetary policy. Only during the two decades between the break with sterling in 1979 and Ireland's joining the single European currency in 1998 did monetary policy take center stage. Radical fiscal experimentation, with drastic consequences for public finances, was also a feature of the 1970s and 1980s; the slow but steady rises in public expenditures and the national debt of earlier decades, much criticized by commentators at the time, seem harmless by comparison.

Until the 1960s, the picture of a traditional, rural Ireland painted by anthropologists Conrad Arensberg and Solon Kimball in the 1930s seemed not too far off the mark. This was a society with a rural Catholic ethos, and strong, sometimes oppressive, family ties. Yet appearances concealed significant changes. The proportion of people in the Irish Free State living in cities and towns with populations of fifteen hundred or more rose from 31 percent in 1926 to

46 percent in 1961, and the percentage of the labor force relying primarily on the land fell from 51 percent to 35 percent over the same period. Although there was little enthusiasm for new contraceptive methods, marital fertility dropped by a quarter between the 1900s and the 1930s, and by another quarter between the 1930s and the 1960s. Births outside marriage still represented only 3 percent of all births in Ireland in the 1960s. The sexual revolution that began in the 1960s was reflected in an increase in the proportion of extramarital births to over a quarter and in below-replacement fertility by the end of the twentieth century.

Why, after more than a half century or so of underachievement, did the Irish economy finally find its feet? It is too soon to rank causes, but history offers some lessons. The most important explanation is the futility of the version of import-substituting industrialization pursued by a succession of administrations between the early 1930s and the late 1950s. That policy led to an initial spurt in output and employment as new firms competed for the limited home market, but to no worthwhile sustained increases thereafter. The result was a stagnant manufacturing sector populated by small plants on short production runs.

The literature on the so-called Celtic Tiger stresses the following factors: an outward-looking economic policy and direct foreign investment (DFI), funding from the European Union, relatively low taxation, an educated workforce, and a consensual-industrial-relations environment. Widely encompassing agreements between employers, workers, and the government about wages, benefits, and taxation resulted in wage moderation that saw labor's share of GNP fall significantly between the late 1980s and the late 1990s. The payoff from this social contract was lower tax rates from the government and a massive increase in capital stock in the private sector. The U.S. economic boom of the 1990s, with concomitant foreign investments by U.S. multinational corporations, was undoubtedly a factor in Ireland's growth.

The Irish economy is now one of the most open in the developed world. Foreign trade is about one and one-half times the size of the gross domestic product (GDP). The importance of the traditional U.K. market has dwindled; the U.K. share of total merchandise imports and exports has dropped from nearly nine-tenths in 1924 and three-fifths in 1960 to about one-quarter today.

In the mid-1920s, the linen textile industry still provided employment for over 100,000 workers, two-thirds of them women, in Northern Ireland. Shipbuilding provided 20,000, mainly male, jobs, whereas clothes manufacturing provided 26,000 jobs. By midcentury, employment in linen had been halved, but shipbuilder Harland and Wolff still employed 23,000 men. Three decades later, Northern Ireland was already showing signs of having become a rust-belt economy. Tellingly, linen did not even rate a mention in the official *Ulster Year Book* in 1985, which spent more space describing development policy than it did industrial production. Belfast's shipyard was kept going only through heavy subsidization by the state; by 2000, privatized and seemingly on its last legs, it employed fewer than 2,000 men.

Like the Republic, Northern Ireland tried the DFI route from the 1960s on, but its incentives were less generous and it was less fortunate in its selection of multinationals than the Republic. By the mid-1990s, the Republic had overtaken Northern Ireland in terms of GDP per head. For the first time since the Great Famine, the South's share in the island's population was rising (0.76 in 1851, 0.70 in 1926, 0.67 in 1961, 0.69 in 2001). However, Northern Ireland still maintains an edge in living standards, due almost entirely to transfers from London worth about one-quarter of personal expenditures.

In the 1990s, living standards in the Republic rose at an unprecedented rate. Full employment ensured that the benefits were widely, though unevenly, shared. By century's end, the gap between the country's richest and poorest regions was a shadow of its level eight or even four decades earlier, and the gender gap in wages had significantly narrowed.

BIBLIOGRAPHY

Arensberg, Conrad, and Solon Kimball. *Family and Community in Ireland*. 2d ed. Cambridge, Mass., 1968.

Barry, Frank, ed. *Understanding Ireland's Economic Success*. London, 1999.

Lee, J. J. *Ireland 1912–1985: Politics and Society*. Cambridge, 1991.

Ó Gráda, Cormac. *A Rocky Road: The Irish Economy since the 1920s*. Manchester, U.K., 1997.

CORMAC Ó GRÁDA

IRISH FAMINE. The Great Irish Famine (1846–1852) was not just a watershed in Irish history but was also a major event in world history, with far-reaching and enduring economic and political consequences. The Famine was a product of three factors. First, poverty made the consequences of a repeated failure of the potato crop, upon which the Irish poor depended almost exclusively for food, devastating. Second, there was an element of sheer bad luck: poor potato harvests were nothing new, but never before had there been anything like the damage wrought by the potato blight, which first struck the Irish potato in 1845. Third, public action in the wake of the potato's repeated failures after 1845 was undoubtedly inadequate. The historiography has tended to focus on the last-mentioned, perhaps because the other factors were irreversible, whereas public action was a policy variable.

The proximate cause of the famine was *Phythophtera infestans* (or potato blight), a fungus that thrives in a damp climate. The damage caused in 1845 was partial; indeed,

IRELAND.—PEASANTRY SEIZING THE POTATO CROP OF AN EVICTED TENANT, IN KERRY.

DEARTH IN IRELAND. Peasants sieze the crop of an evicted tenant, Kerry, 1886. (Prints and Photographs Division, Library of Congress)

had there been no repeat attack, there would have been no famine. However, the blight returned in 1846, about a month earlier than in the previous year, and with devastating effect. The lack of seed and counsel from some quarters against overreliance on a doomed crop reduced the potato acreage in 1847 to about one-eighth its pre-Famine norm. Nature played one of its cruel tricks on the poor in that year; there was no blight. The sense that the worst was over prompted an increase in the potato acreage in 1848, but a renewed attack of blight in that year destroyed most of the harvest. Though the introduction of new potato varieties offered some respite against blight thereafter, no reliable defense would be found against it until the 1890s. Indeed, it is still with us.

The literature on the Famine has focused disproportionately on its administrative history. The debate about relief measures in the press and in Parliament in the 1840s has a modern resonance. The authorities initially chose to rely mainly on the provision of employment through public works. At their height, in the spring of 1847, the works employed 700,000 people. They did not contain the Famine, partly because they did not target some of the most needy, and partly because they operated mainly during a period of bad weather. The publicly financed soup kitchens that succeeded them proved what was possible; they reached a maximum of three million people daily at their peak in ear-

ly July 1847, and the number of deaths seemed to fall while they operated. However, doubts remain about the effects of such a liquid diet on weak stomachs. From the summer of 1847 on, the main burden of relieving the poor was placed on the Irish Poor Law of 1838. The Famine was henceforth regarded as a manageable, local problem. The workhouse regime created under the 1838 law had not been envisaged as a means of dealing with famine conditions, however; and about one-quarter of all famine mortality occurred in the workhouses. Local histories highlight the mismanagement of some workhouses and the impossible burden placed on others; and the high overall proportion of workhouse deaths due to contagious disease is an indictment of this form of relief. The very high mortality in some workhouses in 1850 and even 1851 is evidence of the long-lasting character of the Famine in some western areas. Relief policy did not allocate the available resources in the best way, but the aggregate sum involved was also too small to reduce mortality by much.

Traditional accounts of the Famine pit the more humane policies of Sir Robert Peel's Tories against the dogmatic stance of Sir John Russell's administration, which took office in July 1846; but the contrast oversimplifies. Though Peel was more familiar with Ireland's problems and less dogmatic than some Whig ideologues, the crisis confronting him in 1845–1846 was mild compared to what would follow. Moreover, Peel broadly supported the Whig line in opposition. At the height of the crisis, the policy stance adopted by the Whigs was influenced by Malthusian providentialism, that is, the conviction that the potato blight was a divinely ordained remedy for Irish overpopulation. The fear that public generosity would mean a Malthusian lesson not learned also dictated minimal intervention.

The Famine killed about one million people, making it a major famine, relatively speaking, by world-historical standards. The death toll is approximate; in the absence of civil registration, excess mortality must be calculated as a residual. The estimate of one million does not take account of the reduction in birth due to declining fecundity and loss of libido, nor does it include Famine-related deaths in Britain and the United States. Mortality was very uneven regionally. None of Ireland's thirty-two counties was spared, but the toll ranged from one-quarter of the population of some western counties to negligible fractions in Down and Wexford, on the east coast. The incidence varied temporarily too, even in some of the worst-hit areas. In west Cork the worst was over by late 1847, but the effects of the Famine raged in Clare until 1850 or even 1851.

Like all famines, the Irish Famine produced a hierarchy of suffering. The very poor were most likely to perish; farmers found their effective land endowment reduced by the potato blight and labor more costly, and so were forced to reduce their concentration on tillage; landlords' rental income plummeted by as much as one-third. Many medical practitioners and clergymen died of infectious diseases. Pawnbrokers saw their pledges unredeemed. Least affected were those firms and their workforces who relied on foreign markets for their raw materials and their sales. It is difficult to identify any significant class of "winners," unless they were those grain merchants who grasped the opportunities offered by the trade in Indian meal when prices were still rising in the autumn of 1846 and early 1847, lawyers who benefited from the deregulation of land transfers, and pastorally oriented farmers. The elderly and the young were most likely to die; women proved marginally more resilient than men.

Living standards in Ireland were higher in the Famine's wake than on its eve. This does not mean that most survivors were significantly better off; the shift was due mainly to the disappearance of so many of the landless poor. Higher emigration was another aftershock of the Famine, as the huge outflow of the crisis years generated its own "friends and neighbors" dynamic. By reducing the domestic market, the Famine may have led to the decline of certain industries. The cultural consequences are more difficult to pin down, though they include an accelerated decline of the Irish language. The Great Famine brought the era of famines in Ireland to a brutal end. Serious failures of the potato in the early 1860s and late 1870s brought privation but no significant excess mortality.

BIBLIOGRAPHY

Bourke, Austin. *The Visitation of God? The Potato and the Great Irish Famine.* Dublin, 1993.

Grey, Peter. *The Irish Famine.* London, 1996.

Mokyr, Joel. *Why Ireland Starved: A Historical and Analytical History of the Irish Economy, 1800–1850.* 2d ed. London, 1985.

Ó Gráda, Cormac. *Black '47 and Beyond: The Great Irish Famine in History, Economy, and Memory.* Princeton, 1999.

CORMAC Ó GRÁDA

IRRIGATED FARMING. Water is essential for life, and for the growth and maturation of plants. Water flow through plants is necessary for photosynthesis, for bringing in nutrients in solution through the roots, and for temperature control. Control of that water permits us to expand what we grow, where we grow it, and how much of it we can grow. Here, *irrigation* is defined as water management on fields used to grow crops. Where crops are affected by a scarcity of water, irrigation supplies it; where crops are affected by a surfeit of water, drainage takes it away. Virtually all irrigation systems do both, but rarely simultaneously. Henceforth, *irrigation* should be read as "supply/drainage." Irrigated farming grows crops by means of irrigation technology.

Technology. If *technology* is defined as tools, processes, knowledge, and skill, then *irrigation technology* is not only the facilities in the ground (hardware) but also the knowledge and skill to build, maintain, and operate them (software). Liquid water responds to gravity, runs downhill, and is expensive (in energy) to lift. Most systems use only gravity to move water (gravity-feed), with channels dug into the earth. The system takes the water from a headgate; these vary in scale and complexity from stakes and brush in the streambed to the Aswan High Dam on the Nile River. The headgate must be above the level of the highest field to be irrigated, and it may be a distance upstream, since the streambed may be in a deep valley. A main canal leads from the headgate to the arable land; a series of smaller canals leads to the fields. Often, there are water gates in the canals—they are open for flow or shut to end it. With surface-flow systems, fields must be precisely level, so that water distributes evenly. Dry spots and wet spots cause problems for working the soil and crop growth. Excess water goes back into the canal system or into another set of drainage channels. A complete drainage system ultimately moves the water back into a natural channel.

Every irrigation system must be designed and built, with benefits from a sound and long-term knowledge of the local environment. Floods, whether infrequent or annual events, can be disastrous or helpful, so knowledge of their variability is important in design. Construction involves getting materials and laborers, then the sequencing of the construction tasks. Building the headgate may be a major construction effort, accompanied by some anxiety over its success. The main canal, feeder canals, and gates are not as dramatic to construct, but their levels must be right. With insufficient slope, water will not move fast enough, or far enough, leaving downstream users without any. If the slope is too great, water will travel too fast, causing erosion of the channels, then perhaps escaping and doing substantial damage to fields, crops, roads, houses, and more. The fields must be leveled to a proper slope to best use the water, and the drainage end must be completed so that waterlogging does not result.

Lift systems involve bringing water to the surface, then distributing it to fields. Lifting technology involves a hole dug to below the water table; a pool then accumulates at the bottom. Vertical, shallow wells are very common worldwide, can be dug with hand tools, and are usually lined (with stones, bricks, etc.) to prevent collapse; some have steps from the ground to the water. Often, a container (made of pottery, skin, metal, or wood) is lowered into the water, then raised. For domestic purposes, this may be tedious, but the amount needed is relatively small. Deep wells are an industrial phenomenon, involving drilling rigs and usually a metal pipe to line the shaft (thus called tube wells). The problem with a deep well is getting access to the water and raising it. For that, an industrial pump-and-driver is needed; these require money for purchase and a steady supply of energy (gasoline, alcohol, benzine, etc.) and spare parts to run the engine. Horizontal wells (*quanats, foggara*) are shafts dug into the side of hills, on a slightly uphill slope, to reach the ground water. Some are dozens of kilometers (miles) long. Once the ground water is tapped, it runs out with a gravity feed. Construction and maintenance are expensive, but no expense ensues for lifting water.

The vast majority of irrigation systems deliver water to the plant-root zone by gravity feed in surface ditches. If simple to construct and operate, they also tend to lose half their water to evaporation and percolation. Some water-delivery technology includes sprinklers and drip systems. With sprinklers, water is sprayed by a machine; it arrives at the sprinkler in tubes, under pressure, so little loss ensues from percolation and evaporation. Delivery efficiency approaches 90 percent, and the fields do not have to be leveled. Large energy costs run these systems—worth paying if water is a relatively scarce resource.

Drip systems have perforated hoses set underground in the plant-root zone. Water is pumped through under pressure, and it can be delivered at the push of a button; it is the most water-efficient way to irrigate, with delivery efficiency near 98 percent. Liquid fertilizers may also be added to the water. Drip systems are expensive to install, vulnerable to cuts from careless cultivation for weeds or excavation, prone to stoppage as the holes may get plugged, difficult to monitor, and expensive in terms of energy.

Operating the System. Once built, the system must be maintained. Entropy is the enemy; ditches are subject to erosion, to the accumulation of silt, and to being choked by weeds. All must be combated with regular attention, labor, and materials.

Operating the system usually requires a few knowledgeable people who are often selected for calmness, probity, and technical competence. Their job is to schedule water delivery and maintenance activities. When the system has "normal" water supply, the job is straightforward. Under conditions of drought there can be fierce competition among the farmers, so the operators have to be trusted, and calm, to keep the water moving and maintain peace. With floods, experience and talent are important in protecting the system.

Multiple-farmer irrigation systems vary in size from some 10 hectares to more than 1 million hectares. They vary in technology at the headgate from a brush weir to a modern massive dam. The costs of operation and maintenance depend on the design. Some irrigation systems serve only one purpose—irrigation—but many of the modern ones are only part of a larger enterprise, in which the headgate will store water for irrigation but will also use stored water for hydroelectricity for domestic and industrial consumption, will use the storage space for flood management, and will manage the river for transport, recreation, and the environmental management of wildlife habitat. These multiple uses may be incompatible, and often are. Large and long rivers often have several major dams on them. Activity upstream affects downstream users, so adjusting the various sections of a large system has proven a challenge, both technically and politically.

Purposes of Irrigation. The main purpose is to relieve the constraint of water scarcity for human needs, especially crop growth. Some areas are naturally too dry for the growth of some plants; an effective irrigation system allows such crops to be grown. The extreme would be a desert with no rainfall, so that no crops could be grown without irrigation. Yet even in Massachusetts, with more than 40 inches (100 centimeters) of rain a year, most farmers have supplemental irrigation, which they use to relieve water stress that may last only a few weeks.

Other uses of irrigation include temperature control. Since water has a high specific heat, it protects plants against frost; the heat in the water is extracted first, leaving the plant to be last to suffer from the frost. Irrigation water also extends the growing season, by allowing for planting before environmental moisture is sufficient for germination.

Origins. Agriculture began only at the end of the Würm (Wisconsin) glaciation, some ten thousand to fifteen thousand years ago. Water management was practiced soon thereafter in all areas of Neolithic-era agriculture: the Near East, Egypt, India, and China. Agricultural surpluses there and in the Americas led to the rise of the early civilizations, and improved forms of water control of irrigation. Water management was also important in the isolated highlands of New Guinea some five thousand years ago, as well as in North and South America, sub-Saharan Africa, Europe, and Southeast Asia, in many places where farming became the lifestyle that replaced hunting.

Economic and Political Impact. The economic effect of irrigation is the improvement of both land and labor productivity. Maintaining the system is a constant burden, but costs of maintenance relative to output, and even relative to construction, may never be known with certainty.

The political implications have been the subject of much controversy. Karl A. Wittfogel's book on the origins of irrigation and sociopolitical controls, *Oriental Despotism* (New Haven, 1957), promoted the idea of an "Asiatic" mode of production; within it, his political requirements for large-scale hydraulic systems formed the core of state governments. Such large systems, central to production, could only be overseen by a state system, he claimed; that, in turn, gave the state control over taxing the countryside and over most activity. His "Oriental despotism" has been

IRRIGATED FIELD. Filipino women planting rice, Philippines, early 1900s. (Frank and Frances Carpenter Collection/Prints and Photographs Division, Library of Congress)

called an irrigation hypothesis, which it never was, for it was as much concerned with flood protection from the major rivers (Tigris-Euphrates in Sumer, Nile in Egypt, Indus in India, and Hwanghe [Yellow River] in China) as it was with irrigation. Large-scale irrigation may not, however, "determine" the origin of the state or result in civilization.

In the late twentieth century, the Green Revolution concentrated on new and more bountiful grains for poor agricultural areas. As they were very water responsive, irrigation was a critical component wherever they were introduced. Great sums of development aid and loans from the World Bank were spent from 1950 to 2000 in constructing irrigation systems in the third world, so irrigated lands were doubled in such countries as India.

A political issue has arisen over who is in charge of the management of these systems. The irrigation systems in the industrial countries (Japan, Holland, France, United Kingdom, United States) are managed mainly by the users; yet the systems they have designed and built in their colonies and former colonies are managed by government agencies. There is controversy over the effectiveness of state management of these large systems, since farmers prefer to run them. A political choice to be made, then, is who runs these systems; an understanding of how that choice gets made, and why, is only in its infancy.

Environmental Impact. Every form of agriculture has environmental impacts, and they are both positive and negative for humans. Among the positive impacts of irrigation are the creation of large areas that will grow plants (and therefore animals) that are useful to and desired by humans, produce hydroelectricity, and prevent floods. An increased production of desired goods is one of irrigation's environmental impacts. Yet the term *environmental impact* is usually taken to mean "negative effects." Small-scale irrigation works change the distribution of water and, therefore, of vegetation; however, the force of entropy is so great that with abandonment, the irrigated area quickly returns to its pre-irrigation state.

Large storage dams have a long-term effect, both upstream and downstream of the dam. The river course is substantially changed, with often a created lake above the dam (flooded land) and consequences for animal and plant life there, down the river, along its banks, and in its estuary. Habitats are changed, and therefore flora and fauna adjust. Some fish may not be able to spawn (salmon, alewives) because the dam(s) block their progress upstream to "their" spot or because their habitat has been polluted by new human uses. The environment of the irrigated fields also changes. The increased moisture permits increased wild plant (weeds) and animal (rats, mice, birds) life—often regarded as competitors by farmers. Still, substantial changes may cause large mammals (gazelles, elephants, lions, tigers) to be uncomfortable and move away or die out as endangered species.

Two major consequences of irrigation in arid climates are waterlogging and salinity. Waterlogging occurs as groundwater rises toward the soil's surface, drowning the roots of plants. Salinization occurs when the groundwater is close to the soil's surface and the water can percolate, by capillary action, to the surface—where it evaporates and leaves mineral salts that had been in solution (most crop plants cannot tolerate high levels of soil salinity). In arid zones, careless management of irrigation water leads to both conditions. When bad enough, the soil will not grow anything of economic interest to humans, so farmland becomes wasteland. Both problems occurred in the Nile Delta in the late 1800s, but solutions were found almost immediately. Proper water management ensured that the water table remain low enough, with drains that were maintained, and that the amount of irrigation water sent to the fields was monitored. The result has been a stable system. Today, these conditions need not be permanent: if either or both occur, they can be quickly reversed with the proper application of sweet water.

The habitat changes from large-scale irrigation may lead to increased human disease conditions. For example, mosquitos may find irrigated areas for breeding, so malaria, yellow fever, or West Nile virus may be spread. Harmful bacteria and other water-borne parasites also flourish in irrigation canals and enter human digestive tracts or other organs.

Large hydraulic systems have supported many millions of people worldwide as they farm, produce, and process agricultural commodities. They have provided relatively prosperous standards of living since Neolithic times. With care, informed decisions, and conservation, they may remain dependable for centuries. Poor decisions about dams, global warming, and climate change can bring disaster to many now-arable lands. The politics of water may also result in cooperation or may lead to disputes, warfare, and ongoing terrorism as populations increase and sweet water becomes ever more scarce.

BIBLIOGRAPHY

Bromely, Daniel W. *Making the Commons Work.* San Francisco, 1992.
Hillel, Daniel. *Out of the Earth: Civilization and the Life of the Soil.* Berkeley, 1992.
Hillel, Daniel. *Rivers of Eden: The Struggle for Water and the Quest for Peace in the Middle East.* Oxford, 1994.
Hunt, Robert C. "Size and the Structure of Authority in Canal Irrigation Systems." *Journal of Anthropological Research* 44 (1988), 335–355.
Postel, Sandra. *Last Oasis: Facing Water Scarcity.* New York, 1992.
Ostrom, Elinor. *Governing the Commons.* Cambridge, 1990.
Service, Elman. *Origins of the State and Civilization: The Process of Cultural Evolution.* New York, 1975.
Uphoff, Norman, with Priti Ramamurthy and Roy Steiner. *Managing Irrigation: Analyzing and Improving the Performance of Bureaucracies.* New Delhi, 1991.
White, Gilbert F., ed. *Environmental Effects of Complex River Development.* Boulder, 1997.
Wittfogel, Karl. *Oriental Despotism.* New Haven, 1957.

ROBERT C. HUNT

IRRIGATION. *See* Water Engineering.

ISRAEL. When the State of Israel was established in May 1948 it was able to build on an economy that had developed rapidly during the British mandate, one that in structure and standards of living was similar to that of the lower-income countries of Europe. Over the next half-century, Israel's population grew from some 800,000 to more than six million. Total domestic product grew at an annual rate of 7 percent and product per capita at 3 percent. By the mid-1990s, Israel ranked thirtieth in the world in terms of per capita domestic product. In structure and level of sophisti-

cation, its economy resembled those of the more developed industrial countries.

The major factors affecting the development of the economy have been immigration (the raison d'être of the Jewish state), large capital imports, and hostilities with its Arab neighbors, particularly the war that established the state and that of 1967, as a result of which Israel occupied the West Bank and Gaza. Economic policy, starting from a strong socialist ideology, was based for many years on the belief that it was the responsibility of government to initiate and direct economic growth. There has been a gradual process of retreat from this ideology, with greater reliance on market forces and movement toward economic openness.

Immigration and Population. From May 1948 till the end of 1951, Israel's total population increased by over 70 percent, and its Jewish population doubled. An austerity program provided for the immediate needs of the immigrants, but finding permanent housing and employment were longer-term problems. Though the new immigrants had lower average levels of education and labor-force participation than the existing population, they supplied the manpower for future development.

The government financed investment and wartime expenditures by monetized debt. A depletion of foreign exchange reserves, suppressed inflation, substantial unemployment, and an inability to house properly the new immigrants combined to bring about a reassessment of policies toward the end of 1951. Efforts to encourage mass immigration were temporarily curtailed and made more selective. Though there were later periods of significant immigration posing formidable problems of absorption, particularly from the countries of the former Soviet Union in 1990–1991, annual immigration never again reached 5 percent of the existing population. However, encouragement of Jewish immigration has remained a major policy objective of all Israeli governments, and even the lower levels of annual immigration brought about a relatively high rate of population growth.

Government policy for immigrant absorption has had several strands. A major policy objective was geographic dispersion of the immigrants, encouraged in the early years by creating agricultural settlements and later by building new "development towns." Unemployment was high in the early years, declined steadily thereafter until a temporary recession from 1965 to 1967, reemerged as a problem in the 1990s, and then fluctuated close to 10 percent. Unemployment was first dealt with by make-work projects, but the main policy tool until the mid-1960s was job creation by means of investments, mainly in manufacturing financed by the government's Development Budget, itself financed with capital transfers from world Jewry, U.S. aid, and German reparations. Public housing projects helped provide employment while serving as a major source of housing for the growing population. Expansion of the education network gradually added to human capital, which was given a major boost with immigration from the former Soviet Union.

Budgetary transfer payments, first as subsidies of basic commodities and later replaced by fairly generous income transfers, have been used to decrease disparities in living standards between newer and older segments of the population. These transfers have contributed to relatively low labor-force participation, compared to other industrialized economies, particularly among the poorly educated and the ultraorthodox.

Following the 1967 war and Israeli occupation of Gaza and the West Bank, there was a significant shift in employment patterns. Whereas the earlier pattern had been gradual movement of the "Oriental" Jews into more advanced occupations and their replacement in lower-skill occupations by Israeli Arabs, now Arabs from the occupied territories took over many of the low- and middle-skill jobs, particularly in construction and agriculture. Though subject to severe curtailments in times of open hostilities and closures due to terrorist activity, the number of Arabs from the territories employed in Israel rose to about 120,000 in 1992, as much as 6.5 percent of total employment in Israel and a much higher percentage of employment in construction and agriculture. In times of restrictions on employment of workers from the occupied territories, the industries reliant on non-Israeli workers replaced the Arabs with foreign workers, particularly from Thailand and eastern Europe.

National Product: Growth, Composition, and Distribution. From 1953 until the recession of 1965, and again from after 1967 until the Yom Kippur War of 1973, total domestic product grew at an average rate of 11 to 13 percent and product per capita at 5 to 6 percent. Thereafter, rates of product growth were much lower, fluctuating between 1 and 7 percent, and per capita growth between −1 and +4 percent. Rapid growth was made possible by increased labor input, high levels of capital formation, financed mainly by inflows from abroad through public channels, and growing total factor productivity. The difference between the rapid growth rates during the first two decades and lower rates thereafter has been ascribed to an ending of the catch-up phase, and to structural change embodied in the declining growth rate of the population.

Despite early expectations that agriculture would be a major economic sector, bolstered by public finance of agricultural settlements and strong protectionist measures, its share in domestic product gradually declined from some 10 percent in the early years to less than 2 percent by the end of the century, as agricultural exports fell to less than 4 percent of total commodity exports.

The total share of manufacturing did not change much over the period, fluctuating between 18 and 24 percent, but its composition changed significantly. The major investments in manufacturing from the 1950s into the 1970s were in less sophisticated industries, primarily food production and textiles. Since the 1980s, the major developments have been in high-tech industries. By the late 1990s, the total output of sophisticated products, defined in terms of shares of high-skill labor, was about the same as that of traditional manufacturing; but their share in exports of manufactured products had grown to over 70 percent of the total excluding low value-added exports of polished diamonds, which make up close to one-fifth of total exports. The construction industry has fluctuated more than any other, owing to waves of immigration, and as in the mandatory period, has been a major cause of fluctuation in domestic product.

Israel has always had a high proportion of product concentration in services, which has been explained by the occupational structure of immigrants, the persistent import surplus—which being mainly in commodities encouraged domestic production of services—and the high demand for public services. Israel's communications, financial, and commercial services are highly developed, but road development has not been able to match the growth of private vehicles, and railroad transportation has not developed as it has in Europe.

Public civilian consumption has accounted for close to one-fifth of total product throughout the period. Defense expenditures, financed in part by U.S. aid, have always been a heavy burden. The true burden, taking into account various nonbudgetary expenditures, has exceeded budgeted amounts. The true burden fluctuated in size from less than 10 percent of domestic product between 1950 and 1965 to as high as 28 percent between 1973 and 1977, falling to 10 to 12 percent in the 1990s.

Though standards of living rose substantially for all segments of the population, so did inequality in income distribution, which had been relatively egalitarian in the early years. Most of the disparities in income distribution can be explained by differences in levels of education and length of stay in the country; but the fact that the poorer segments of the population are the Israeli Arabs and Jews of North African and Asian origin (and their descendants) has made inequality in income distribution a social and political problem. Public policy intended to decrease the inequality in income and welfare has included minimum wage laws, exemptions from income tax, and direct budgetary expenditures on education and health (in addition to housing) and transfer payments. The last, whose main components are child allowances, benefits for the aged, unemployment insurance, and income supplements, have grown in the past two decades to 13 percent of the domestic product.

MODERN ISRAEL. The shopping mall at Azreili Towers, Tel Aviv, 2000. (© Bernard Boutrit/Woodfin Camp and Associates, New York)

Thus, alongside demands of populist political parties to increase welfare transfers, there has been growing resentment that a small labor force must provide for a large, nonworking sector.

Inflationary Experience. Inflation has always been an important policy problem. A broad system of indexation of wages and savings has been used to mitigate inflation's adverse effects, but it has been accused of making the elimination of inflation more difficult. After the initial repressed inflation was unleashed by rising prices, the inflation rate dropped after 1955, ranging between 3 and 8 percent for most years until 1970. During the next few years the inflation rate rose, in several steps, to over 100 percent between 1980 and 1983 and nearly 400 percent in 1984. The stabilization program of 1985, which combined a temporary freeze in wages, monetary and fiscal restraint, and exchange rate stability, stopped the slide into hyperinflation. The inflation rate declined to under 20 percent during the rest of the 1980s, to around 10 percent during most of the 1990s, and to much lower rates toward the end of the century, as a result of decreasing budgetary deficits and restrictive monetary policy.

International Economic Relations. Being small in size and poor in natural resources, Israel has always relied heavily on foreign trade. Despite rapid export growth, imports of goods and services have exceeded exports, creating a permanent (though fluctuating) balance of payments deficit. For most years, this import surplus has added resources for domestic use equal to around one quarter of the domestic product. Israel has been fortunate in mobilizing capital inflows, unilateral transfers, and governmental loans, supplemented by large foreign private investment in the 1990s.

Exchange control was strict in the first twenty years, and then gradually reduced, first on current transactions and later on capital flows. The exchange rate was fixed, with occasional devaluations until the inflationary experience of the 1980s caused a switch to a managed float. Import substitution was encouraged by extremely high protectionism. In 1962, a liberalization policy was introduced, first replacing quantitative restrictions on industrial imports with tariff protection, then gradually lowering protection levels and the bias in favor of import substitution and against exports. The liberalization process was facilitated by and coordinated with Israel's agreements with the European Union, culminating in a free trade area (FTA) agreement on industrial products signed in 1974. An FTA agreement with the United States was signed in 1985. In 1991, a similar process of trade liberalization was undertaken on imports from countries other than those with which Israel has FTA agreements, but without completely eliminating all protection.

Israel's main trading partners have been the United States and the European Union, which together provide some two-thirds of its imports and receive two-thirds of its exports. Trade between Israel and the Palestinian territories was formalized by the Paris Protocol of 1994, which created a customs union with some exceptions similar to FTA provisions. These territories have been a growing market for Israeli exports, providing fewer imports but substantial labor services, with volumes falling in times of hostilities.

Institutional Change. The new state inherited the Labor Zionist institutions and ideology of the pre-state period, and considerable government intervention in the economy was deemed both pragmatically and ideologically suitable although Israel was never actually a socialist economy. Most government intervention instruments gave their operators considerable discretionary power, had low public visibility, and could be exploited for political ends.

Over the years there was a decrease in government intervention: in trade and foreign exchange transactions, the capital market, and public ownership of enterprises. This trend toward less public intervention and greater reliance on freer market mechanisms intensified during the 1990s, and even the Histadrut—a national federation of labor unions that had encompassed traditional union activities, ownership of enterprises, and social welfare institutions—was reorganized, giving up most of its economic enterprises and losing its virtual monopoly on health services, which was replaced by national health insurance.

Turn of the Century. Toward the end of the year 2000, many factors combined to push the economy into a severe and prolonged recession, marked by falling output and rising unemployment. A major factor was the breakout of a new and protracted Palestinian uprising and suicide bombings. Israeli retaliation, incursions, and partial occupation of some territories previously handed over to Palestine reduced trade relations and curtailed the employment of Palestinians in Israel. The Palestinian economy experienced sharp reductions in income and massive unemployment. For Israel, the new *intifada* required increased defense expenditures, brought about political and economic uncertainty that led to reductions in foreign and domestic investment, and caused the near collapse of its tourist industry. Furthermore, worldwide recession and stock market reversals, especially the decline of the high-tech industries, sharply reduced exports. The need to cut the government budget deficit led to reductions in welfare benefits, intensifying feelings of resentment and unease.

Although these problems may turn out to be short-term in nature, they underscore issues that will persist for many years. These include the economic role of government, particularly welfare policies, and how to deal with the employment and income distribution problems posed by the dualism of the new technological and traditional economic sectors. The future of the economy will depend on how and when the conflict with the Palestinians will be resolved. Israel will have to decide whether its international economic orientation is mainly regional, toward Europe, toward the United States, or not committed to a specific region.

BIBLIOGRAPHY

Bachi, Roberto. *The Population of Israel*. Jerusalem, 1974.

Ben-Bassat, Avi, ed. *Changes in the Structure of the Israeli Economy*. Cambridge, Mass., 2001.

Ben-Porat, Yoram, ed. *The Israel Economy: Maturing through Crisis*. Cambridge, Mass., 1986.

Halevi, Nadav, and Joseph Baruh. "Israel." In *Liberalizing Foreign Trade*, vol. 3, *Israel and Yugoslavia*, edited by D. Papageorgiou, M. Michaely and A. M. Choks, pp. 1–156. Cambridge, Mass., and Oxford, 1991.

Halevi, Nadav, and Ruth Klinov-Malul. *The Economic Development of Israel*. New York, 1968.

Khalidi, Raja. *The Arab Economy of Israel*. London, 1988.

Kleiman, Efraim. "The Waning of Israeli Etatisme." *Israeli Studies* 2.2 (Fall 1997), 146–171.

Patinkin, Don. *The Israel Economy: The First Decade*. Jerusalem, 1960.

Plessner, Yakir. *The Political Economy of Israel: From Ideology to Stagnation*. Albany, N.Y., 1994.

Razin, Assaf, and Efraim Sadka. *The Economy of Modern Israel*. Chicago, 1993.

NADAV HALEVI

ISTANBUL, largest city and chief port of Turkey, situated on both sides of the points of land where the Bosporus enters the Sea of Marmara, on the Golden Horn. Before 330 CE, it was called Byzantium; then, as Constantinople, it became capital of the Eastern Roman Empire, under Constantine, the first Roman emperor to accept Christianity. The Byzantine Empire was rich in goods, and its trade routes went to the Western Roman Empire and east to Central Asia, India, and China, as well as south to Egypt and sub-Saharan Africa. Conquered by the Ottoman Turks in 1453, it became İstanbul, capital of the Ottoman (Turkish) Empire until 1922. It was then capital of Turkey, until Kemel Attatürk moved the government to Ankara in 1923. The population of Istanbul grew from some 40,000 in 1453 to 500,000 by the 1550s. Muhammed II (Mehmed the Conqueror, ruled 1451–1481), took drastic measures to repopulate Istanbul, employing a method of forced transfer of population from the provinces; he also reestablished the Greek Orthodox Patriarchate there in 1454. The Ottoman sultans were Muslims; they established a theocratic state with an expansionist policy, and they assumed the caliphate of Islam for their new capital. Ottoman Istanbul developed into a typical Middle Eastern city, where Muslims and non-Muslims (mainly Christians and Jews) lived and worked, maintaining private lives in their own quarters while mingling or working in the port or the common bazaar area. Courts of law (state and local) were located in the bazaar, but the separate residential and commercial sections set the basic character of the city.

Since many of the first settlers deserted within a year of the conquest, it became apparent that the city needed a lively commercial life to attract and keep a sizeable population. Ruling over a vast empire that included Anatolia and the Balkans, the Conqueror wanted to make his new capital an imperial metropolis, as it had been for the Eastern Roman Empire. Following Islamic–Ottoman urban traditions, he established on the main thoroughfare, along the northern heights and parallel to the harbor, a commercial center with a *bedesten* or *bezzaristan*, a central domed structure for the storing and trade of valuable goods, and a grand *bazaar* (later called the Kapalı-Çarshı). Craft guilds were located in the parallel streets around the Bedestan, which included 140 shops; the Grand Bazaar grew into one with some 1,000 shops.

In Byzantine times, the overseas commerce of the harbor area belonged to the monopoly of Italian merchant

ISTANBUL. View of the city (1838–1839), by Shiviti. (The Jewish Museum, New York/Art Resource, NY)

colonies, principally those from Venice, but the town of Galata (Pera), on the northern side of the harbor, across the Golden Horn, had come under the control of merchants from Genoa. With the Ottoman conquest, the Italian states' control came to an end; they were replaced by Ottoman subjects—Muslims were favored but there were also Jews and Greeks. The Italians, however, continued their commercial activities under capitulatory guarantees in Galata. During the initial years after the conquest, commerce declined in the city, because the Italian colonies were destroyed and because Galata, put under direct Ottoman rule, lost part of its Genoese population. With the ensuing population growth, the commercial economy recovered quickly. The wharves were soon busy, each one designated for a particular product coming by sea. As in Byzantine times, the harbor area was linked with the Grand Bazaar on the hill by busy streets. The town of Galata became the principal port for Mediterranean goods and the principal location of the European communities and their embassies. On the west of Galata, the Kasimpasha district enclosed the sultan's navy and seamens' barracks; on the eastern shore, the town of Üsküdar became the terminus for caravans arriving over the Silk Road from Asia.

With endowed foundations (*waqf*) erected in various parts of Istanbul by the sultan and his viziers, as well as thriving overseas trade, the city was soon a large metropolis. It had a population of various faiths, as recorded by the census of 1477 and 1535. By the mid-1500s, Istanbul, like ancient Rome, depended on a kind of imperial economy; the state organized and controlled the trade of such necessities as wheat, meat, fats, and salt. As needed, it also prohibited the export from its provinces of such goods as wheat, cotton, hides, wool, and iron.

Istanbul's geographical location, with a vast network of sea and land routes, enabled it to become a vast metropolis, the hub of the intercontinental trade from Europe, Asia, and Africa. Not only did necessities and raw materials flow there from Egypt, the Balkans, and the Black Sea area but also from the Mediterranean and the countries

TABLE 1. *Istanbul's Population (by household)*

YEAR	MUSLIMS	CHRISTIANS	JEWS	TOTAL
1477	9,517	5,162	1,647	16,326
1535	46,635	25,295	9,070	81,000

of eastern Europe. Although Cairo, Aleppo, Beirut, Bursa, and—after the 1600s—İzmir (Smyrna) became major trade centers for the circum-Mediterranean area, the Arabian Peninsula, Iran (silk), and India, nevertheless Istanbul still remained the important middleman for goods from the Balkans, Poland, the Baltic lands, and Muscovy (Russia). Merchants based in Galata sent their agents to Bursa to obtain oriental goods, particularly Iranian silk. The Genoese, the Florentines (in the fifteenth century), and Jewish merchants competed to buy the loads of silk arriving from Tabriz. Through the Black Sea port of Caffa, valuable Russian furs and slaves, as well as wheat, flour, meat, and salted fish came to Istanbul. By 1500, Venice annually exported some one thousand casks of Cretan wine through Kilia for the Polish and Muscovite markets. During the 1500s, Istanbul also exported to the northern markets its own textile products, as well as luxury Bursa silks. The Istanbul-Dubrovnik trade route became active, during the second half of the fifteenth century, when Florentine merchants used the overland route, to avoid intervention from Venice.

The Ottoman sultans granted trade privileges, or capitulations, to friendly European countries, and they permitted Western embassies to have permanent residence in Istanbul. The capitulations, guaranteeing the safety of the persons and properties of Western merchants, enhanced trade with Europe. Every mercantilist nation in the West endeavored to obtain capitulatory privileges and wanted to establish a Levant company. Joining Venice, Genoa, and Poland, France obtained full capitulations in 1569, England in 1580 (organized in 1590 as the renowned Levant Company), and Holland in 1612. Along with the rise of the transatlantic economy of the 1500s, Ottoman trade privileges were a substantial lure for the spreading capitalist world economy. Europe's main exports to the Ottoman lands were fine woollens and silks, silver coins (from the 1580s), tin, steel and gunpowder (from the new Protestant countries). Ottoman exports were wheat, cotton, silk and cotton textiles (including coarse blue-cotton textiles from Western Anatolia shipped to Genoa—the origin of blue "jeans"), as well as hides, wool, wine, olive oil, and Iranian raw silk.

BIBLIOGRAPHY

And, M. *Istanbul in the Sixteenth Century: The City, the Palace, Daily Life*. Istanbul, 1994.
İnalcık, Halil, with D. Quataert, eds. *An Economic and Social History of the Ottoman Empire*. Cambridge, 1994.
İnalcık, Halil. "Istanbul." In *Encyclopaedia of Islam* 2d ed., vol. 4, pp. 224–248. Leiden, 1960.
Kuban, D. *Istanbul: An Urban History*. Istanbul, 1996.
Mantran, R. *Istanbul dans la seconde moitié dans XVIIe siècle*. Paris, 1962.
Mayer, R. *Byazantion, Konstantinopolis, Istanbul, ein genetische stadtgeography*. Vienna, 1943.
Müller-Wiener, W. *Bildlexicon zur Topographie Istanbuls*. Tübingen, 1977.
White, Charles. *Three Years in Constantinople, or Domestic Manners of the Turks*. 3 vols. London, 1845.

HALIL İNALCIK

ITALY *[This entry contains four subentries, on the economic history of Italy during the classical period, medieval period, early modern and modern periods, and after unification.]*

Classical Period

Italy is a hilly region that is topographically dominated by the Apennine Mountains, which form the peninsula's spine. Although this landscape contributes to the emergence of small, autonomous states, regional developments between 1000 BCE and 500 CE were driven by the growth of Roman power and the resulting unification of Italy. The economic history of Italy must be understood against the background of Roman expansion.

The transition from Bronze to Iron Age took place about 1000 BCE and was marked by developments in metallurgical and agricultural technology and the rise of Etruscan civilization in central Italy. Beginning about 750 BCE, Greek colonists settled in considerable numbers along the coastline of southern Italy and Sicily. Abundant and heavily exploited resources of copper, iron, and timber fostered a brisk trade among Etruscans, Greeks, and Carthaginians. This trade supplemented an economy that was largely agricultural and remained so throughout the Classical period. Aggressive military action by the Greek city of Syracuse and incursions by groups such as the Celts contributed to a sharp deterioration in Etruscan strength from about 500 BCE.

The decline of the Etruscans set the stage for the emergence of Rome as the dominant power in Italy. Initially no more than one of a number of towns in the Tiber River valley, Rome established its suzerainty over neighboring communities by 330 BCE. The political settlement imposed by Rome gave conquered communities local self-government while requiring regular military service. Rome relentlessly employed the sizable reserves of manpower thus put at its disposal and came to control the majority of peninsular Italy by 250 BCE.

These extensive conquests affected economic activity in a number of ways. Wealth poured into the city of Rome, which by the mid-third century BCE had a population of more than 100,000, making it one of the larger urban centers in the Mediterranean basin. This population was fed in part by the production of sizeable estates (approximately 125 to 625 hectares and up) controlled by members of the Roman elite. The practice of confiscating territory from conquered communities brought extensive tracts of Italian agricultural land under direct Roman control.

ITALY. Interior of a cloth merchant's store. Roman marble bas-relief. (Galleria degli Uffizi, Florence/Alinari/Art Resource, NY)

While some confiscated land was redistributed in small lots to individuals, much of it remained the property of the state (*ager publicus*). Roman citizens had the right to rent this land, a right wealthy families used to accumulate large tracts, over which they developed de facto ownership. Labor was provided either by slaves, available relatively cheaply due to Rome's military campaigns, or by tenants. These estates (sometimes called latifundia) were oriented to the production of such crops as wine and olive oil intended for sale in markets. Because transportation costs were critical to profitability, agricultural activity along these lines was limited to coastal and river valley sites. The economics of such estates were discussed by a number of Roman authors, such as Cato, Varro, and Columella. As Rome's interests were centered in mainland Italy, it coexisted relatively peacefully with Carthage and the Greek cities in Sicily. Carthage and Rome, for example, signed treaties that restricted Roman commercial access outside of Italy in exchange for Carthaginian guarantees of noninterference in areas under Roman control.

This delicate balance was disrupted by continued Roman expansion in the third century BCE. A series of wars between Rome and Carthage (First, Second, and Third Punic Wars) ensued, ending with Carthage's destruction in 146 BCE. The collapse of the Roman republic and its replacement by a principate (monarchy) in the first century BCE did little to slow the pace of conquest. Further military activity established Roman control over an empire stretching from Britain to North Africa to Egypt to the Black Sea by the early second century CE.

These conquests helped reshape economic activity in Italy in fundamental ways. The invasion of Italy by Hannibal during the Second Punic War wrought great destruction. Italian communities that had sided with Hannibal were punished through wholesale confiscation of territory, which in turn brought about a significant expansion in the amount of *ager publicus*. The spoils of war put huge amounts of wealth in the hands of Romans, particularly members of the elite. All of these factors contributed to a diminution in the number of small farms and an increase in the number, size, and importance of large estates. The concomitant growth in the number of slaves made the Roman economy heavily dependent upon servile labor. Much of the production of these estates continued to be sold in Rome, which grew into one of the largest cities of the preindustrial world, with a population of perhaps one million. New markets for Italian products were created by the incorporation of territories, such as Spain and Gaul, that were technologically less advanced. Archaeological evidence in the form of pottery finds and shipwrecks attests to the growth of a massive trade in goods, such as wine and fine ceramics, between Italy and these areas. This trade was also driven by the stationing of troops in frontier areas, such as Germany. The purchasing power of these troops and the need to provision them helped create and sustain long-distance exchange. The overall result was a significant increase in the size of the nonagricultural sector and in economic specialization and output, both on an aggregate and a per capita basis. This process was in part made possible by government investments in transportation infrastructure, including roads (the Romans built some 90,000 kilometers of paved roads) and harbors. Another contributory factor was the reduction in transaction costs brought about by the imposition of peace, the suppression of piracy, and the establishment of the Roman denarius as the standard currency in the entire Mediterranean basin.

A series of invasions that began around 250 CE and that continued intermittently for the next three centuries created major difficulties, including debasement of the currency and a high rate of inflation. Until the late twentieth century, it was thought that this period was marked by a sharp decline in economic activity and urban settlement. New archaeological data, however, indicate a surprisingly high degree of continuity until about 500 CE, when fundamental change becomes discernible. Relevant developments included the binding of tenant farmers to the lands they worked, a rise in the number of fortified rural sites, and increasing disintegration of the economy, with estate production increasingly oriented toward self-sufficiency. Specialized production and associated trade collapsed in Italy and adjacent areas. These developments contributed to the creation of a new social, political, and economic order, that which was characteristic of medieval Europe.

BIBLIOGRAPHY

The best single source for the political and economic history of Italy during this period is the *Cambridge Ancient History*, specifically volumes 7–14 of the second edition (Cambridge, 1982–2001). Detailed bibliographies can be found in the back of each volume. Relevant ancient literary and epigraphic sources are collected and translated in Natalie Lewis and Meyer Reinhold, *Roman Civilization*, 2 vols., 3d ed. (New York, 1990) and in Barbara Levick, *The Government of the Roman Empire: A Sourcebook*, 2d ed. (London, 2000). The latter contains material on a wider range of subjects than its title indicates and includes up-to-date bibliography. Scholars have long been divided about the importance of trade in the Roman economy. For a concise summary of the various viewpoints, see John D'Arms, *Commerce and Social Standing in Ancient Rome* (Cambridge, Mass., 1981). The view articulated here closely follows that of Keith Hopkins, which is outlined in Hopkins's introduction to *Trade in the Ancient Economy*, Peter Garnsey, K. Hopkins and C. R. Whittaker, eds. (Berkeley, 1983). On this subject, see also Moses I. Finley, *The Ancient Economy*, updated edition (Berkeley, 1999) and Peter Temin, "A Market Economy in the Early Roman Empire," *Journal of Roman Studies* 91 (2001): 169–181. A great deal of work on the Roman economy was produced in the 1980s, in part due to the availability of large amounts of new archaeological evidence. For the use of archaeological evidence in reconstructing Roman economic activity, see Kevin Greene, *The Archaeology of the Roman Economy* (Berkeley, 1986). Other recent works of some importance include Richard Duncan Jones, *Structure and Scale in the Roman Economy* (Cambridge, 1990), Kenneth Harl, *Coinage in the Roman Economy* (Baltimore, 1996), Dennis Kehoe, *Investment, Profit, and Tenancy* (Ann Arbor, 1997) and Tamara Lewit, *Agricultural Production in the Roman Economy, A.D. 200–400* (Oxford, 1991).

PAUL CHRISTESEN

Medieval Period

In its economic development, medieval Italy was a combination of diverse parts. Different traditions existed in the northern, central, and southern regions of the peninsula, conditioned by varying political, social, geographic, and climatic factors. In general, Italy experienced a dramatic, if uneven, commercial expansion in the Middle Ages, which propelled it to European-wide economic leadership. Its primacy was a result of its geographical position, which made the peninsula a natural conduit of trade between northwestern Europe and the Levant.

Conquest and Capture. The conquest of the western Roman Empire by Gothic tribes in CE 476 destroyed the political unity of Italy. It was once customary to blame the Goths for causing depopulation and economic decline, but recent research has overturned this view, stressing instead continuities with the past. The rudiments of an exchange economy persisted; commercially active towns, such as Milan and Aquileia, continued to prosper in trade and manufactures. Of far greater economic consequence were the Byzantine emperor Justinian's wars to retake Italy in the first half of the sixth century, the outbreak of plague that accompanied them, and, shortly after, a new series of invasions by a more primitive Germanic tribe, the Lombards.

The Lombards captured much of the north and central regions of Italy. Itinerant warriors, they showed little interest in trade and fiscal institutions, sustaining themselves instead by hunting and conquest. Scholars speak of the "ruralization" of Italy and of a "backward" economy characterized by barter.

Byzantium, the eastern Roman Empire, retained control over much of the Italian coast, along the Adriatic Sea and on the Tyrrhenian Sea below Rome. The cities of Venice, Ravenna, Bari, Amalfi, Naples, and Gaeta grew relatively prosperous from commercial ties with Byzantium's wealthy capital city, Constantinople. Amalfi, one of the most successful southern ports, maintained a triangular trade of wood and slaves from north and eastern Europe; gold, ivory, and precious stones from north Africa; and silks and spices from Syria and Constantinople. Local artisans produced textiles, as did their counterparts in Naples, Bari, and Gaeta.

The island of Sicily, prosperous in Roman times, also profited from its association with Byzantium. Efficiently managed estates (*latifundia*) produced high-grade wheat for export. When the Muslims took the island in 827 CE, they stimulated trade by planting such crops as sugar cane, a valuable commodity in Europe at a time when honey was the traditional sweetener. The Muslims also built up of the city of Palermo, developing a shipbuilding industry and a modest manufacturing sector that produced silk, cotton, and linen.

The Carolingians, a Germanic tribe from modern-day France and Germany, swept into Italy in the eighth century (774 CE) and defeated the Lombards. Though more advanced intellectually and culturally, the Carolingians did not significantly alter the Lombard economic system, which remained rural and dependent on war to sustain itself. In his famous and much-debated "thesis," historian Henri Pirenne (1862–1935) claimed that the advent of the Carolingians coincided with the closing of the Mediterranean by Muslim fleets, thus cutting off long-distance trade and forcing Christian civilization in on itself. This may or may not have been true. But the Carolingian period undeniably witnessed an increasing concentration of lands in the hands of powerful warlord nobles and the virtual elimination of gold coinage, the means of exchange of the more commercially sophisticated eastern Mediterranean and coastal Italy. The growth of large estates hastened the development of a feudal system, which gained additional impetus from the pressure of foreign invaders in the ninth century. The most notable fiscal innovation associated with the Carolingians was the reform of the currency undertaken by their greatest ruler, Charlemagne (742–814). Charlemagne minted a penny (*denarius*) of almost pure silver and established a list of values and weights that was used in Europe until the modern era. Charlemagne's monetary system was based solely on silver.

Economic Revival. The turning point in the economic development of Italy occurred as a result of the demographic explosion of the High Middle Ages (1000–1350). The boom brought a "commercial revolution." Italy experienced profound growth, particularly in the urban sector. Milan, Genoa, Florence, and Venice all became major cities, ranking among the largest in Europe. Even heretofore small towns, such as Pistoia in Tuscany and Piacenza in Lombardy, reached population levels they would not regain until the modern era. The urban revival was supported by expansion in the agricultural sector. Population pressure led to the breakup of large estates into smaller, more intensively exploited units. Slavery, a vestige of Roman times, disappeared and land prices rose. In the Po Valley, labor was put to use clearing lands, draining marshes, and building embankments, irrigation canals, and dykes. This set the stage for a strong agrarian sector in the region for centuries to come. There was, particularly in north and central Italy, a strong give and take between town and countryside, as urban merchants invested in rural lands and country folk migrated into the city. This characteristic

was unique to Italy and distinguished it from much of the rest of Europe.

The foci of the economic revival were the coastal cities. On the Tyrrhenian, Genoa and Pisa, freed from Lombard subjugation, grew into commercial giants. On the Adriatic, Venice became the hub of a vast international trade that ran east-west as far as China and south-north to the Baltic. All three cities benefited greatly from the Crusades (1095–1291), which brought northern Christian armies to the Middle East to fight the Muslims. The mass movement of men provided opportunities for trade and for earnings as middlemen in transport.

Genoa was perhaps the most precocious. Having established itself in the western Mediterranean by the late tenth century, the Genoese exploited the Crusades to gain access to the east and eventually set up trading posts on the Black and Caspian Seas and in Syria and Palestine. Emblematic of Genoese commercial initiative were the activities of the great thirteenth-century merchant Benedetto Zaccaria (died c. 1307). A pirate and bon vivant, Zaccaria discovered a rich vein of alum in Asia Minor. He spent the rest of his life establishing a monopoly over this valuable commodity, which was used in the cloth business as a mordant for certain dyes.

The development of Pisa paralleled that of Genoa. Located on the Tyrrhenian Sea and the Arno River, the city served as a center of imports and exports for all of Tuscany. Pisan merchants traveled to southern Italy, southern France, North Africa, and, after the Crusades, established trading posts on the Black Sea and in the Middle East. They exploited the mineral riches of the nearby island of Elba and set up a monopoly there. The close geographical proximity of Pisa and Genoa led to an intense rivalry. Genoa defeated Pisa at the battle of Meloria in 1284 and destroyed its fleet. Pisa never fully recovered.

Venice became the greatest city of them all. In antiquity, it had been a sparsely populated city of fishermen, boatmen, and salt workers. But the Lombard invasion of Italy helped push more people toward the lagoons, and by the eight and ninth century Venice was already moving aggressively to eliminate trade rivals along the Adriatic and Istrian coast. Venetian merchants profited from especially close ties with Byzantium, and, though possessed of few natural resources, initially established trade in lumber, salt—the most valuable commodity—and fish. Taking advantage of its eastern connections, its access to the Po River, and proximity to the Alps, Venice developed into Italy's premier middleman, taking in goods from all over the Mediterranean and Asia and re-exporting them elsewhere. The city became the staple for the northern Adriatic and the chief European market of silver.

Venice's success inevitably led to rivalry and conflict with the Genoese. The two fought a series of wars culminating in

MEDIEVAL ITALY. *Month of April*, anonymous fresco, fifteenth century (Castello del Buonconsiglio, Trent, Italy/Scala/Art Resource, NY)

the bitter War of Chioggia (1378–1381). Both sides were damaged, but Venice ultimately emerged the victor.

Further inland, the towns of Lombardy and Tuscany experienced vigorous economic development. Particularly favored were towns situated on such major waterways as the Po River and on important roads and pilgrim routes. In the twelfth century, merchants from Cremona, Piacenza, Milan, Lucca, and Siena exploited these advantages and became mainstays at trade fairs in southern France, Paris, and Champagne, and eventually in London and Bruges.

Much of their initial business involved purchasing woolen cloth from the booming textile businesses of Flanders and marketing it elsewhere. Several towns, among them Verona, Padua, Milan, and Florence, developed their own woolen cloth businesses. Cremona established a suc-

cessful fustian industry, while Lucca became the European leader in the production of high-priced silks. Milan exploited its nearby metal-bearing hills to develop a vibrant arms industry. Venice and Genoa established substantial shipbuilding industries.

A measure of the revival of Italian trade was the minting of gold coins for the first time since the early Middle Ages. Both Florence and Genoa introduced a gold coin in 1252, each weighing approximately 3.54 grams and consisting of almost solid gold. The Venetians followed suit in 1284. Thenceforth, the Italian monetary system was bimetallic. Florence's florin and Venice's ducat became preferred means of exchange in international markets.

The situation in southern Italy was very different. Despite the early success of some of its coastal cities, southern Italy's commercial development was blunted by intense political and factional conflicts and foreign intervention. The French house of Anjou took control of the region in the middle of the thirteenth century. The French rulers relied heavily on assistance from Florence to effect their conquest, and once firmly established, repaid their debt by allowing the Florentine merchants to dominate the local economy. Florentines collected local taxes and, most important, managed the region's lucrative grain trade. Thus southern Italy played a subsidiary role in the broader Italian economy. Although several local towns developed manufacturing sectors, notably in woolen cloth, production was relatively minor in scale.

Trade and Banking. Trade constituted the bedrock of Italian economic supremacy in Europe. A merchant manual (*Pratica della mercatura*) written in the first half of the fourteenth century by the Florentine Francesco Pegolotti (1315–1340), described a far-flung international network. Italian merchants traveled throughout the Mediterranean—to the Black Sea, to Armenia, Persia, the northern German coast, to the Baltic and Poland, to Mongolia and China. The Venetian merchant Marco Polo (1254–1324) traversed the Mongol Empire in the thirteenth century and left a famous description of his exploits. To facilitate their overseas activities, Italian states developed technologies, legal institutions, and, above all, innovative business techniques. Double-entry bookkeeping was invented in Italy, perhaps as early as the twelfth century. The new accounting method allowed for more rational reckoning of profits and losses. Italian states also made considerable advances in the field of public finances. They developed sophisticated fiscal machineries that were capable of imposing a wide array of taxes, both direct and indirect, from citizens. The Venetians and Florentines instituted successful public debts, which helped weld private wealth to public interest.

One of the most important economic developments on the peninsula was the establishment of a banking industry. This was the consequence of long-distance trade. Early on, northern Italian merchants from Asti, Piacenza, and Cremona coupled their trading activities with banking activities at international fairs. They served as pawnbrokers, issuing petty loans on small security, and performing petty exchange of coins. The bankers from Asti plied their trade in France, Burgundy, and England. North of the Alps, the term *Lombard*, a reference to the region in northern Italy, became synonymous with "banker."

Banks also developed in Genoa and Venice. These were essentially local enterprises, intended to facilitate the commercial activities of the multitude of merchants who visited the cities. In Venice, the firms, known locally as *banche di giro*, were located on the Rialto bridge, where merchants tended to congregate. They performed manual exchange of coins, both local and foreign, accepted deposits, and made payments via transfer. In the fourteenth century, the Venetians began allowing payment through book transfer rather than coin. This allowed bankers to leave only a portion of their deposits on reserve, freeing them to invest in commercial ventures. The effect was to create "bank money" and thereby increase the money supply, a basic feature of modern banks.

The largest and most sophisticated banks grew in Tuscany. These engaged aggressively in international commerce and, unlike their Geneose and Venetian counterparts, consisted of networks of correspondents and branches in various cities throughout Europe. The banks mobilized capital and extended credit across national borders. The early leaders in the field were bankers from Lucca and Siena. They gained their primacy from their connection to papal finance. The papacy, one of the richest entities in Europe, required a sophisticated network to collect its revenue from all over Europe. By the middle of the thirteenth century, the Sienese were the most important of the pope's bankers. The greatest of the Sienese firms, the Buonsignori, possessed an operating capital in excess of 35,000 florins and have been called "the Rothschilds of the thirteenth century." The business proved precarious. At the end of the century, it experienced a spectacular crash, which damaged the overall Sienese economy.

In the wake of the Buonsignori collapse, the Florentines emerged as the leaders in papal finance. The capture of the pope's accounts, added to their control of the southern grain trade, allowed Florentine banks to grow to unprecedented sizes. The largest of these, the Bardi, Peruzzi, and Acciaiuoli firms, have been dubbed "super" companies by modern scholars. In their own era, they were known as the "pillars of Christendom," a reference to the fact that their activities touched virtually all corners of Europe. The largest of the super companies, the Bardi bank, had branches across Europe, northern Africa, and the Levant and possessed assets totaling 875,000 florins in 1381, a figure dwarfing the annual revenue of most Italian states. A series of ill-advised loans to the English King Edward III (r. 1327–1377) and the collapse of the grain market from bad harvests brought down the super companies. All three were gone by 1345, sending shock waves throughout the European economy. Organizational weaknesses, particularly unlimited liability and an overly centralized structure, hastened their decline and caused them to fall like dominoes. A new generation of Florentine banks followed, organized in smaller, independent units intended to make them less susceptible to sudden collapse. The most well known of the banks of the new era were those run by Francesco di Marco Datini (c. 1335–1410), the famed merchant of Prato, and by the Medici family. At the peak of its prosperity, the Medici bank had nine branches throughout Europe. More than half their profits came from the papal branch.

The Florentines coupled their success in banking with development of the peninsula's leading textile industry. The Florentines gained entree into the business by "finishing" imported Flemish woolen cloth, adding expensive dyes and brocades. They then exported the cloths to foreign markets. Soon after, local entrepreneurs developed a native woolen cloth industry, which, by the middle of the fourteenth century, rivaled and exceeded that of Flanders, the traditional European leader. The Florentine business depended on the import of raw English wool, which was in turn facilitated by its banking connection in that country.

Crises Bring Change. The Black Death in 1348 brought an end to the demographic growth that had fueled Italy's economic development. Economic historians continue to debate the effects of the crisis: whether it produced "hard times" or per capita growth. The issue is complicated by the fact that the era was also one of intensified warfare, repeated crop failure, and, subsequently from the 1380s, according to monetary theorists, a general bullion famine.

Despite the crises, Italy did not lose its position as economic leader of Europe. Italians maintained their hegemony in trade and banking. Local manufacturers compensated for the decrease in demand by moving into the production of luxury goods, which remained in relatively high demand. Florence shifted into the manufacture of silks, as did Bologna, Venice, Milan, and Genoa. The Genoese found new financial opportunities in the sixteenth century as the managers of the fortune in silver that the Spanish extracted from their American colonies. The rural economy also adjusted. In Lombardy, such new cash crops as woad were introduced. The system of land tenure was reorganized, with increasing recourse to sharecropping. Agrarian conditions in the south, however, grew decidedly worse. Shrinking grain markets hurt local producers, as did increased competition from German producers. Sicily continued to make reasonable profits from the production of sugar and molasses.

In general, larger, more commercially sophisticated states appear to have sustained themselves the best during the "crises" of the fourteenth and fifteenth centuries. Milan, Florence, and Venice all emerged more strongly with respect to their neighbors. They ensured their economic survival by subjugating weaker towns and carving out territorial states.

By the late fifteenth century, there were ominous portents for Italy's economic future. The Portuguese, under their aggressive ruler Henry the Navigator (1394–1460), had opened new markets for gold and slaves along the African coast and were embarking on journeys around the tip of Africa that would ultimately gain for them direct access to the Indies and to the trade in valuable spices that had been so long dominated by Italian merchants. The English, heretofore minor players in the European economy, moved forcefully into the woolen cloth industry, producing finished goods rather than supplying raw materials. They took a large share of the Italian market. Meanwhile, the French invasion of Italy in 1494 set off a series of destructive wars, which lasted until the middle of the next century. The wars severely hurt all Italian businesses, and by the late sixteenth century, Italian economic hegemony was largely lost. The peninsula hereafter played a minor role in the European economy dominated by the emerging northern nation-states.

BIBLIOGRAPHY

Abulafia, David. *Italy, Sicily, and the Mediterranean*. London, 1987.
Cipolla, Carlo M. *Before the Industrial Revolution*. New York, 1993.
Epstein, Stephan R. *Freedom and Growth: The Rise of Markets in Europe, 1300–1750*. London and New York, 2000.
Hunt, Edwin S., and James M. Murray. *A History of Business in Medieval Europe*. Cambridge, 1999.
Lane, Frederic C. *Venice and History*. Baltimore, 1966.
Lopez, Robert S. *The Commercial Revolution of the Middle Ages, 950–1350*. Cambridge, 1976.
Luzzatto, Gino. *An Economic History of Italy*. London, 1961.
Waley, Daniel. *Italian City-States*. London, 1988.

WILLIAM CAFERRO

Early Modern and Modern Periods (to 1861)

From the beginning of the thirteenth century to the end of the sixteenth, the north and the central Italian regions were the most technologically and economically advanced in Europe. Their wool and silk luxury textiles had gained high reputations in the major European cities; their bankers dominated international finance; their merchants and ships were known throughout Europe, the Middle East, and North Africa. During the seventeenth century, Italian merchant and trade houses were overtaken by the Netherlands and Britain. By the eighteenth century, Italian subjection to foreign wars and foreign rule—by the Spanish Bourbons and Austrian Habsburgs—was complete. Then the Napoleonic Wars of the early 1800s and the re-

sulting Italian nationalism eventually led to the unification of Italy in 1861. The economic gap between northern Europe and Italy widened in the nineteenth century, but it narrowed again at the end of the century, with the start of modern commerce and agricultural growth in Italy.

Urban Structure. The Italian peninsula had many large cities from the time of the Romans and the Middle Ages. In the early 1500s, almost 2 million people (21.9 percent of the population of 9 million) lived in 156 cities with more than 5,000 inhabitants; 14.9 percent (1.3 million) lived in the 51 cities with more than 10,000 inhabitants. In the rest of Europe, only Flanders (Belgium) had such high rates of urbanization. Since the late Middle Ages, the increase in Italian urban population had occurred on the strength of a rising urban production of industrial goods and the provision of commercial services for distant markets. The cities of Milan, Como, Cremona, Padua, Venice, Florence, Lucca, and Bologna were the source of fine textiles; Venice and Genoa were Europe's leading Mediterranean seaports; Florence and Genoa had bankers who were among the strongest of Europe's financiers.

About 1570, exported cloth production from the Italian north and central regions was worth some 85 million Florentine *lire*: that is, 7 percent of the regional gross product. The openness of their economies to international exchange was particularly great; if the value of the construction sector and the industrial production for internal markets are added, it is 20 percent; with services, 37 percent. In the Italian south, the industrial and commercial sectors were weaker than in the north but were usually dominated by northern merchants. In the late Middle Ages, dynamic city life resulted in a strong rise in the wealth of urban populations, especially of merchants and noble families; with that came the unequal distribution of income between the cities and the countryside. The consequence was the urban demand for luxury articles, art products, palaces, and churches. Another important effect of Italian urbanization was the ongoing political contests. Rich and powerful cities tried to widen their spheres of influence and found the opposition of other cities, which formed alliances to check the expansion of their neighbor. In the Italian north, the political scene remained fragmented, with many small regional states, while in other European areas, large national states were forming, capable of developing wider and more aggressive economic policies.

Imports. Since the late Middle Ages, increasing external demand had been the strong spur in the growth of the Italian north and central economies. Investments in the leading sectors and the urban consumption that derived from industrial and commercial profits increased urban incomes. Rising incomes, in turn, increased immigration into the cities. Consequently, the demand for imports—raw materials, cereals, fuels—to feed urban expansion also grew.

While the demand for fuel was not a problem, because of the relatively mild Mediterranean climate, raw materials and cereals constrained urban growth possibilities. Northern and central industries needed cotton imports from the Middle East, wool from Africa, southern France, and England, and silk from the Near East. Southern Italy played an important role in those trades; its exports of silk thread, wool, and other raw materials, were complemented by northern finished products—particularly cloths—and by commercial services.

The grain supply was, more than anything else, the limiting factor in urban expansion. Much of the Italian Peninsula and its islands were not cultivable, with mountains, hills, and many lakes. Until the nineteenth century, there were also extensive marshes. Woods, meadows, and fallow soils comprised almost 50 percent of the land in the late 1500s. Thus, arable lands were less than 25 percent of the entire Italian territory. Then, too, the relatively dry soils of Italy were not very fertile. Yield ratios were low until the late 1800s. On such poor soils, population was among the densest in Europe. In the late 1500s, while Europe's average density (Russia excluded) was lower than 18 inhabitants per square kilometer, in Italy the average was 43. It was highest (48) in the central and northern urbanized regions, lowest in the south and the Islands (36).

The carrying capacity of the Italian arable lands was 12.5 to 13.5 million inhabitants. That level was reached at the beginning of the 1300s and again at the end of the 1500s; during the 1700s, it was exceeded. The possibility of widening the arable lands at the expense of woodlands and intensifying cultivation did exist, but it was not practical, using the existing agricultural techniques for the crops then grown. Imports of grain were relatively limited, given the high transport costs. Internal grain trades were more important—from the south, with its smaller populations and smaller cities, toward the Italian center and north, with their denser populations and bigger cities. Epidemics of bubonic plague, frequent during the three centuries from 1347 to 1657, contributed greatly to the balance between population and resources.

Long-term Movement. The long period from the 1450s to the 1800s and the advent of Italian industrialization was an age of slow growth if aggregate product is considered but one of decline if the per capita product is considered. Gross product did increase with the rise of population but at a lower rate, at least until 1820. Living conditions worsened in the long run.

In the industrial and commercial sectors, that era's increasing competition from northern Europe in textile production—England and Flanders in wool and France in silk, especially from the late 1500s—greatly reduced Italian penetration of new external markets. A strong decline took place in Italian wool production that was balanced later by the rise in silk production and particularly silk thread manufacture in the Italian north. Silk threads were then the main Italian export until the late 1800s. More difficult for Italy to counter was the competition of the new maritime powers, England and the Netherlands, both trading on a much wider scale than they had during the late Middle Ages. (From the 1600s, their colonial and state-sponsored trading companies dominated the East and West Indies.) Even in the Mediterranean, their ships had become frequent in trade ports as early as the late 1500s.

More important than trade competition in the trend of the Italian economy was the relationship between resources and population growth and movement. From the 1450s onward, the Italian population of 7.5 million began to grow, and its growth was interrupted only by plagues—from 1575 to 1580 (north), from 1629 to 1630 (north and center), and from 1656 to 1657 (south). With the end of the plague, after 1657 the population grew from 10.7 million in 1660 to 18.1 million in 1800. This demographic challenge was partly met through deforestation and the planting of rice and maize, both more productive than wheat in terms of calories per acre and thus able to feed more people. Even these innovations were, in the long run, unable to feed an ever-increasing population, so a reduction in living standards occurred, especially from 1750 to 1820, when real wages declined some 40 to 50 percent. Only after 1820 did per capita income begin to rise. By 1861 and the unification of Italy, the per capita product was still 10 to 20 percent lower than it was in the early 1400s.

BIBLIOGRAPHY

Beloch, Karl Julius. *Bevölkerungsgeschichte Italiens.* Berlin and Leipzig, 1937–1961.

Cipolla, Carlo M. *Contro un nemico invisibile: Epidemie e strutture sanitarie nell'Italia del Rinascimento.* Bologna, 1986.

Del Panta, L., M. Livi Bacci, G. Pinto, and E. Sonnino. *La popolazione italiana dal medioevo a oggi.* Rome and Bari, 1996.

Felloni, Giuseppe. *Italy.* In *An Introduction to the Sources of European Economic History 1500–1800,* vol. 1, *Western Europe,* edited by C. Wilson and G. Parker, pp. 1–36. London, 1977.

Goldthwaite, Richard A. *Wealth and the Demand for Art in Italy, 1300–1600.* Baltimore and London, 1993.

Malanima, Paolo. *La fine del primato: Crisi e riconversione nell'Italia del Seicento.* Milan, 1998.

Malanima, Paolo. "Risorse, popolazioni, redditi: 1300–1861." In *Storia economica d'Italia,* edited by P. Ciocca and G. Toniolo, pp. 43–124. Rome and Bari, 1999.

Romano, Ruggiero. *Tra due crisi: L'Italia del Rinascimento.* Turin, 1971.

Romano, Ruggiero, ed. *Storia dell'economia italiana,* vol. 2, *L'età moderna: Verso la crisi.* Turin, 1991.

Sella, Domenico. *Crisis and Continuity: The Economy of Spanish Lombardy in the Seventeenth Century.* Bologna, 1979.

Vigo, G. "Real Wages of the Working Class in Italy: Building Workers' Wages (14th to 18th Century)." *Journal of European Economic History* 3 (1974), 378–399.

PAOLO MALANIMA

United Italy

Italy, a peninsula lying at the center of the Mediterranean Sea, became a politically unified state only in 1861 (a few of its regions were added later: Venetia in 1866, Latium with Rome in 1870, Trentino and Alto Adige in 1918). The area had seen several great eras, including those of the Roman Empire and the Renaissance, but had undergone a period of relative decline in the seventeenth and eighteenth centuries. At unification the legacy of this complex and protracted history was contradictory: on the one hand, Italy was highly urbanized, had ancient and glorious universities that continued to produce elites sharing the most advanced European culture of the time, and had strong and sophisticated artisanal traditions; on the other hand, it was lagging behind in the provision of mass education, had a rather backward agriculture, though with great differentiation across the country, and above all had not been able to develop modern industry. The only established manufacturing process was for raw silk; Italian production in the first half of the nineteenth century covered two-thirds of the world exports of silk (Federico, 1997) and was of high quality, becoming increasingly concentrated in the north, particularly in Lombardy.

The new kingdom was geographically quite small (301,180 square kilometers in its present boundaries) but highly differentiated, comprising large mountainous areas, with the highest mountains in Europe, volcanoes, lakes, islands, and as much as 7,420 kilometers of sea coast; plains made up about 20 percent of the area. The population density was high, except in the mountains, and the climate generally temperate, tending to dryness in summer in the south and very cold in winter in the mountains. This lack of geographical homogeneity and the physical barriers of mountains and seawater nurtured pronounced local differences in cultures, economic contexts, and political developments, differences that have marked the life of the united Italian state to this day.

At unification, the differences were particularly pronounced in mass education, infrastructures, banking, and agriculture:

- *Literacy*: Although the northwestern regions had a literacy rate of about 50 percent, the level declined steadily across the northeastern and central regions, being as low as 10 percent in the south and main islands.
- *Infrastructures*: Roads, ports, and railways were better developed in the northwest and showed the same gradient as one moved to the south as found for literacy.
- *Banks*: Joint-stock banks and nonprofit savings banks were numerous in the north-central part of the country but entirely missing in the south.
- *Agriculture*: Types of agriculture differed greatly.

Agricultural conditions were examined by O'Brien and Toniolo (1991). Italy developed five basic types of agriculture, in the Po Valley, mountainous, hilly, southern coastal, and southern internal regions. The agricultural activity in the mountains was extremely poor, and many people migrated elsewhere until recent times, when tourism developed there, making the areas prosperous and attractive. The agriculture of the largest Italian valley, that of the river Po (lying in the north and cutting across Piedmont, Lombardy, Emilia, and Venetia) was an advanced, capitalist, continental type of agriculture, allowing substantial capital accumulation. The hilly agriculture, typical of central Italy but also found in part of the north, produced mainly grapes, silk cocoons, olives, fruits, and vegetables, with mixed farming under sharecropping arrangements, a type of contract recently subject to much study because of its adaptability to crop conditions very different from continental agriculture (Galassi and Cohen, 1994). The south of Italy had a highly productive but very limited coastal agriculture devoted to olives, citrus fruits, vineyards, and nuts; and in the interior cereals were cultivated at very low productivity levels in latifundia, with large herds of destitute daily laborers employed for only a few months per year.

The deep regional disequilibrium found in Italy's economic development to the present day is rooted in these historical differences, and in particular in the variable impact that the different types of agriculture had on capital accumulation, both physical and human, and on market connections.

Economic Policies of the Unified State and Industrial Takeoff. The elite that unified the country belonged to the northern areas and placed the new state firmly within the most advanced European legal framework. The country started its life as a new state by adopting the gold standard in 1861 and free trade in 1863, reorganizing state finances with the introduction of the income tax in 1864, and aiming at balancing the budget (which was achieved in 1875). A new comprehensive system of education was conceived as early as 1859, envisaging free compulsory elementary education for both boys and girls, technical schools at all levels, and formal education for teachers. A central bank was not put in place, under local pressures to maintain the previous banks of issue then in operation; so Italy tried to live with six banks of issue. These economic policies, although largely orthodox and acceptable, were not capable of engineering an industrial takeoff. The country suffered for lack of coal (Bardini, 1997), and too many members of the Italian elite still were convinced that its future would lie in agriculture, where two-thirds of the labor force was employed. Beside silk (Fenoaltea, 1988), such textiles as cotton, wool, linen, and hemp were manufactured in Italy, but in small amounts, and a few industrial concerns were represented in the metals, engineering, and chemical sectors. Everything else was done by artisans (Toniolo, 1990).

It took some time for conditions to change, both domestically and internationally. The 1880s saw the beginnings of the electrical and metal industry in Italy, as well as the introduction of protectionism in 1887. There is wide disagreement among scholars about the effects of this protectionism. Fenoaltea (1993) maintains that it was a failure, Federico (1998) that it was a measure incoherently administered and in the end irrelevant, and the present writer that it was the necessary condition for a change of approach to the economic development of the country (Zamagni, 1993). Be it as it may, the country underwent a major financial and balance of payments crisis at the beginning of the 1890s, which was solved with the creation of the Bank of Italy in 1893, absorbing four of the previous six banks of issue and becoming the dominant one of the three remaining. This was accompanied by departure from the gold standard in 1894, which made monetary policy more flexible but still closely connected to gold-standard rules, and by adoption of German-type universal banks, the best-known of which are the Banca commerciale Italiana, known as Comit, founded in 1894; the Credito italiano, founded in 1895; and the Banco di Roma, founded in 1898 (Hertner, 1998). The year 1896 marked a turnabout of the Italian economy and started a sustained growth of industrial production until 1908, at a yearly rate of 7 to 8 percent, which slowed to little more than 2 percent in the years 1908 to 1913. Cotton, steel, machinery, means of transport, electricity, and fertilizers took off; and two-thirds of this advanced industry was located in what has become known as the industrial triangle, namely, the regions of northwest Italy (Piedmont, with Turin as the automaking center; Liguria, with the port of Genoa; and Lombardy, with Milan as the main financial center), increasing the gap between this developing area and the rest of the country.

The Impact of World War I and Fascism. Having been allied with Germany since the 1890s, at the last minute Italy decided to enter World War I on the side of France and Britain, and thus enjoyed plentiful raw materials and foodstuffs from the United States, which permitted continuation of the country's industrialization during the war and the growth of its steel and engineering firms—but not without major drawbacks in terms of disequilibrium of state budgets, banking practices, and markets. The postwar effort to recover and reach new equilibria was made more difficult by inflation, bankruptcies, and an outburst of trade-union militancy from 1919 to 1920 (the "red biennium"), bred by the revolutionary aims of the extreme wing of the socialist party (forming the new communist party in January 1921). The Italian democratic governments were unable to meet this challenge (Forsyth, 1993),

and the discontent of vast sectors of the elite and the middle-class was channeled by the new fascist party into support of an authoritarian solution, which was put in place by the king in late 1922 through the granting of government responsibility to the leader of the fascist party, Benito Mussolini, who waived democracy entirely in 1925.

Mussolini remained in power up to the summer 1943. Under his twenty-year rule (Toniolo, 1980), it cannot be said that the Italian economy stagnated or that he favored agriculture over industry in exchange for the warm support he received from landowners; but he did launch a large program for agriculture, the so-called integral land reclamation, which pumped state money into improving productivity. Italy continued to industrialize under fascism, but its comparative performance was not outstanding, even taking into account the negative effects of the international crisis (Rossi and Toniolo, 1992). The only two remarkable new developments taking place in these years were the creation of a chemical industry in the 1920s and the rise of new industrial firms in some northeastern areas of Venetia and Emilia-Romagna, previously almost untouched by industrialization. But the most long-lasting effects of fascism on the Italian economy were institutional, in the banking and industrial sectors. As for the former, during the 1920s and the world crisis, a series of measures were taken in the banking sector that first weakened the universal banking system through the establishment of several public long-term investment banks and then abolished it altogether with the 1936 banking bill, which reintroduced specialization of credit to Italy; the Bank of Italy became the only bank of issue (1926), waiving relations with the nonbank private clientele in 1936.

An even more radical change took place in the property structure of Italian joint-stock companies as a result of the bailing out of the three major Italian universal banks. These banks, as a consequence of their large credit exposure during World War I, which worsened during the troubled 1920s and even more so in the years of the worldwide crisis, essentially had become majority shareholders of many of the large Italian joint-stock companies. The bailout, engineered by the man whom Mussolini entrusted with the task of intervening, Alberto Beneduce, tended to greatly enlarge the grips of the state on the Italian economy. Beneduce, who had been responsible in the 1920s for the creation of the public long-term financial institutes, in January 1933 established an enormous public holding company, IRI (Istituto per la Ricostruzione Industriale), which owned 21.5 percent of the capital of all existing Italian joint-stock companies but controlled 42 percent of such capital. In this way the three former mixed banks were rescued and put under IRI as public retail banks. Ultimately, about 80 percent of Italian banks were state-owned or nonprofit banks. This structure for the Italian

UNITED ITALY. Men working in Pompeian Olive Oil Company, early 1900s. (W. J. Groeninger/National Photo Company Collection/Prints and Photographs Division, Library of Congress)

banking sector, as well as Italy's large corporations, endured until the 1990s, when the process of privatization started.

One final comment about the policy of militarization of the economy carried out by the fascist regime between 1935 and 1943: there is little doubt that the policy favored the heavy-industry sector, particularly engineering and chemicals, enlarging its capacity in a substantial way. However, the results in terms of Italy's fighting power were disappointing, for lack of adequate military and industrial coordination as well as a lack of raw materials, especially coal and oil (Zamagni, 1998).

Reconstruction and the Economic Miracle. In the early years of reconstruction, Italy regained a democratic system and switched from a monarchy to a republic with a wide range of parties, including a large and powerful communist party allied with a strong socialist party. The presence of Americans—who had taken Italy from German control as the Italo-German alliance ended in the summer of 1943, with the splitting of the country into two parts—signaled that Italy was internationally regarded as part of the Western area of American influence; but internal political competition between pro-Western and the pro-Soviet supporters was decided only with the 18 April 1948 elections, which gave the center party of the Democrazia Cristiana the majority of the votes. Italy then could take full advantage of the Marshall Plan and develop diplomacy designed to put the country in all negotiations leading to cooperative agreements in western Europe, starting with the European Coal and Steel Community (1951) and the European Payments Union (1950). The reconstruction period, which conventionally ended in 1952, saw industrial production 40 percent above the 1938 level. These developments confronted Italy with the most advanced economic systems of the world and unleashed all the imitative forces the country could muster. Agriculture still employed 44 percent of the labor force in 1951; but the already more industrialized northwest took the lead, and spectacular industrial expansion, based on the Americanization of Italian industry, took place between 1952 and 1963, with growth rates of industrial production around 9 percent per year, comparable to the German rates and only less spectacular than the Japanese. Engineering, chemicals, steel, the oil and methane gas industry, electricity, telecommunications, and infrastructures drove this "economic miracle," which greatly enlarged the industrial capacity of the country and allowed Italian exports to climb from 2 percent of world exports in 1951 to 3.4 percent in 1960 (4.6 percent in 1970, and 5 percent by the end of the 1980s). The standard of living of the Italian population began to improve and to catch up with that of the more advanced countries of the world. This achievement was permitted by the comparatively low level of Italian wages and by the talent shown by many of the owners of the established corporations, as well as by the founders of newly created ones, in manufacturing products that, though not very sophisticated, had an attractive design and acceptable performance. Italian industry remained mostly in the hands of families or the state (Amatori, 1997), but both were quite ready to invest and enlarge capacity. IRI was not dismantled, and other public holdings were formed, among them the oil company ENI (1953), which became large and substantial under the early leadership of Enrico Mattei and is today, after privatization, one of the biggest oil companies in the world.

A public agency intended to develop the south, the Cassa per il Mezzogiorno, was put in place in 1951; and in spite of major shortcomings the south started some industrialization, keeping pace with the development of the rest of the country, but without ever closing the initial gap. Tourism too had a boom, especially in the sea resorts and the artistic towns, making of Italy one of the most attractive countries of the world.

A Niche Capitalism. Such phenomenal growth did not last beyond 1963. Conflicts over income distribution, peaking in the "hot autumn" of 1969 with widespread and even violent worker protests, coupled with increased international instability and unwise government policies leading to high inflation, cut the growth rates of the Italian economy in half. However, economic conditions had become difficult for all of the advanced world, and comparatively Italy continued to perform slightly better than most European countries, including Germany, continuing its convergence process. The main reason for the ability to face domestic and international instability could be found

in the unexpected flourishing of small firms. In fact, all the major Italian corporations slipped into deep crisis in the 1970s and slimmed down considerably. However, a new wave of small and medium-size firms came into being or was greatly strengthened, as they bunched together in specialized "industrial districts" (Pyke et al., 1990), where everybody was working on the same type of production in hundreds of separately owned but cooperating firms. This development took place mainly in the northeast and the center of the country and became known as the NEC (Northeast Center) model of development: from shoes to spectacles, from tiles to blouses, from wool cloth to jewelry, from packaging machinery to furniture, hundreds of industrial districts mushroomed and provided both employment and exports. Results were so remarkable that some of the NEC regions became the top Italian areas in terms of income per capita; but the others too improved enormously, producing a strong process of economic convergence within Italy. A large body of literature now exists on the mechanisms of trust and cooperation that enabled such results, as well as on the idea that the roots of the family work organization typical of the industrial districts can be found in sharecropping. Quite a number of these medium-size firms have become world leaders in the production of spare parts or niche consumer products, giving Italian capitalism for the first time a peculiar distinction—that it is no longer simply an imitative capitalism but now is a niche capitalism.

In the 1980s there was also some recovery of the large private corporations; but state-owned enterprises and public finance suffered considerably from worsening corruption in Italian politics, which became intolerable in the very years that saw the decision by part of the European Union to move to a common currency. Italy with high government deficits, climbing public debt, and excessive inflation, ran the risk of falling away from the European Union. This event was avoided by the demise of the ruling political class and its substitution with new leaders capable of getting state finances and inflation under control (Zamagni, 1999).

At the dawning of a new millennium, Italy is firmly situated among the advanced countries of Europe, having reached a per capita income slightly higher than the average for the European Union. The north-south gap has not disappeared; but the south is no longer entirely underdeveloped, and the northern regions are among the most advanced areas in Europe. Differentiation and the small size of enterprises are still distinctive features of the Italian economy and society, but in the age of the Internet this character might be turned into an asset, besides offering a generally high quality of life.

BIBLIOGRAPHY

Amatori, Franco. "Italy: The Tormented Rise of Organizational Capabilities between Government and Families." In *Big Business and the*

Wealth of Nations, edited by A. Chandler, F. Amatori, and T. Hikino, pp. 246–276. Cambridge, 1997.

Amatori, F., D. Bigazzi, R. Giannetti, and L. Segreto, eds. *L'Industria*. Turin, 1999. The most up-to-date and detailed account of Italian industry.

Bardini, C. "Without Coal in the Age of Steam: A Factor Endowment Explanation of the Italian Industrial Lag before World War I." *Journal of Economic History* 57 (1997), 633–653.

Federico, Giovanni, ed. *The Economic Development of Italy since 1870*. Aldershot, U.K., 1994. A collection of classic essays.

Federico, Giovanni. "Italy: a Little Known Success Story." *Economic History Review* 49 (1996), 764–786. An excellent survey of the most recent literature.

Federico, Giovanni. *An Economic History of the Silk Industry*. Cambridge, 1997.

Federico, Giovanni, and A. Tena. "Was Italy a Protectionist Country?" *European Review of Economic History* 2 (1998), 73–97.

Fenoaltea, S. "The Growth of Italy's Silk Industry 1861–1913: A Statistical Reconstruction." *Rivista di Storia Economica* 5 (1988), 275–318.

Fenoaltea, S. "Politica doganale, sviluppo industriale, emigrazione: verso una riconsiderazione del dazio sul grano." *Rivista di Storia Economica* 10 (1993), 65–77.

Forsyth, Douglas J. *The Crisis of Liberal Italy*. Cambridge, 1993.

Galassi, F., and J. Cohen. "The Economics of Tenancy in Early Twentieth Century Italy." *Economic History Review* 47 (1994), 585–600.

Hertner, P. "Central Banking and German Style Mixed Banking in Italy 1893–5/1914: From Coexistence to Cooperation." In *The State, the Financial System and Modernization*, edited by R. Sylla, R. Tilly, and G. Tortella, pp. 182–209. Cambridge, 1998.

O'Brien, P., and G. Toniolo. "The Poverty of Italy and the Backwardness of Its Agriculture before 1914." In *Land, Labour, and Livestock: Historical Studies in European Agricultural Productivity*, edited by G. Overton, pp. 385–409. Manchester, 1991.

Pike, F., G. Becattini, and W. Sengenberger, eds. *Industrial Districts and Interfirm Cooperation in Italy*. Geneva, 1990.

Rossi, N., and G. Toniolo. "Catching Up or Falling Behind? Italy's Economic Growth 1895–1947." *Economic History Review* 51 (1992), 537–563.

Toniolo, Gianni. *L'economia dell'Italia fascista*. Bari, 1980.

Toniolo, Gianni. *An Economic History of Liberal Italy*. London, 1990.

Zamagni, Vera. *The Economic History of Italy 1860–1990*. Oxford, 1993.

Zamagni, Vera. "How to Lose the War and Win the Peace." In *The Economics of World War II. Six Great Powers in International Comparison*, edited by M. Harrison, pp. 177–223. Cambridge, 1998.

Zamagni, Vera. "Italy." In *Western Europe: Economic and Social Change since 1945*, edited by M. S. Schulze, pp. 321–335. London, 1999.

Vera Zamagni

J

JACQUARD, JOSEPH-MARIE (1752–1834). French inventor.

Son of a Lyonnaise weaver and a weaver himself, he invented a new type of loom for *façonnées* (patterned) silk cloth. These were fashionable, up-marked silk products, and the traditional specialty of Lyon. The traditional hand looms were operated by the weaver, with up to four assistants. They raised the weft threads and let the shuttle carrying the warp thread pass, according to a set, and very complex, order. In the Jacquard loom, the warp thread to be raised was selected automatically according to a pattern set in a punched card. The new loom could thus dispose of all the assistants and save labor (as Kay's "flying shuttle" did). It also enabled even a relatively inexperienced weaver to produce highly complex patterns.

Many people before Jacquard (most notably Jacques Vaucanson) had attacked this problem, and arguably all the basic pieces of the Jacquard machine had already been invented. Jacquard conceived a way to have all the apparatus moved by the weaver himself. He exposed a first prototype of his machine at the Industrial Exhibition of 1801, and in the same year he applied for the first patent. However, the loom needed to be improved. The first working looms were installed toward the end of the decade, in spite of the hostility of workers, who feared the loss of the assistant jobs. In 1809, the Fabrique Lyonnaise used about seven hundred Jacquard looms (less than 5 percent of the total), and the figure rose to almost nine thousand twenty years later. In the first half of the nineteenth century, the Jacquard loom was adopted throughout Europe for the production of patterned silk cloths. However, no other weaving center could challenge Lyon's superiority in that business. The Jacquard mechanism was later applied to power looms, and the whole idea of prepunched cards was to have a brilliant future. In 1806, Jacquard was given a pension and a sum for each loom built, and thus died a rich man.

The idea of coding information, embodied in the Jacquard loom, inspired the Cambridge mathematician Charles Babbage in the design of his famous analytical engine. A woven-silk picture of Jacquard hung in Babbage's office. A Jacquard-type control mechanism was also used by the British engineer Richard Roberts in the design of a

JOSEPH-MARIE JACQUARD. Reproduction by Didier Petit & Cie of engraving by C. Benneford, 1839. (Prints and Photographs Division, Library of Congress)

machine for drilling rivet holes in the wrought-iron plates used on the *Britannia* tubular bridge.

[*See also* Silk Industry].

GIOVANNI FEDERICO

JAMAICA. In 1834, the population of Jamaica was 371,100, of which 83.9 percent were slaves, 10.8 percent were people of mixed ancestry, 4 percent were white, and 1.3 percent were free blacks (Eisner, 1961, p. 153). The whites were the British colonizers who ran the slave economy, whose main product was sugar. In this plantation economy, "a typical sugar estate employed about 200 to 300 slaves in unskilled or semi-skilled work, supervised by a white staff numbering about five or six" (Eisner, 1961, p. 189). The profitability of sugar made Jamaica a most valuable British colony in the eighteenth century.

The foundation of this profitability was severely undermined in the nineteenth century by a number of developments. The abolition of the slave trade in 1808 triggered a decline in the slave-labor force and in sugar output. The abolition of slavery in 1838 further reduced the supply of labor to the sugar industry because many freed slaves were unwilling to work for low plantation wages. Instead, they moved into the Jamaican hinterland to engage in small farming. In response to this artificial shortage of labor, the planters persuaded the colonial government to import indentured workers from India.

Falling Sugar Prices. In the postemancipation period, sugar prices declined sharply because of overproduction by better-capitalized producers in countries where slavery had not yet been abolished and by an increase in beet sugar production in Europe. And British planters were forced into direct competition with more efficient producers by the Sugar Duties Act of 1846, which reduced the tariff on sugar until this tariff from all sources was equalized by 1854. This signaled the end to mercantilism. The resulting decline in profitability caused many sugar estates to fail. This, in turn, led to rising unemployment as the Jamaican population more than doubled from 377,433 to 831,383 between 1844 and 1911 (Eisner, 1961, pp. 45–70). These conditions set the stage for significant postemancipation population emigration.

Between 1853 and 1914, large numbers of Jamaicans and other West Indians were recruited to work on the Panama Canal and to build railways on the sugar plantations of Central America and Cuba. But by the 1920s, the completion of the Panama Canal and the railroad projects in Central America and Cuba and the fall of sugar prices in the depression of 1921 forced the repatriation of a large number of immigrants. Between 1920 and 1934, a net of twenty-eight thousand immigrants returned to Jamaica, where no new agricultural land was available to absorb them (Eisner, 1961, p. 147). The restrictive United States Immigration Act of 1924 precluded the possibility of another large-scale migration, and the Great Depression of the 1930s sharply reduced the value of the island's sugar exports.

Declining Economy. In 1938, dissatisfied sugar workers at Frome Sugar Estates in western Jamaica touched off riots that spread to dockworkers in Kingston. Out of these disturbances arose two labor leaders—Alexander Bustamante and Norman Manley, who later became major figures in the political life of the country. The British government dispatched a ten-member Royal Commission headed by Lord Moyne to investigate the miserable social and economic conditions throughout the British West Indies. On the basis of the Commission's recommendations, the British government passed the first of a series of Colonial Development and Welfare Acts in 1940, which provided funds for West Indian social and economic development.

During World War II, Jamaica's exports suffered severely from wartime restrictions, and much of the island's banana cultivation was wiped out by Panama disease and leaf spot. Many Jamaicans volunteered for military service in Great Britain, and thousands were recruited for work in munitions factories and in agriculture in the United States. The construction of a U.S. military base in Jamaica also provided some employment (Palmer, 1995, p. 3). When the war ended, these sources of employment dried up, except for a token number of workers who continued to be recruited for work in the United States. As a result, unemployment in Jamaica rose sharply, to as high as 30 percent of the labor force (Palmer, 1995, p. 3).

Bauxite and Emigration. Against this background, two important events occurred in the 1950s: the discovery of bauxite and the mass migration of Jamaicans to the United Kingdom. American and Canadian investment in the bauxite industry gave a significant boost to the growth of the economy. However, this new industry created relatively few jobs because of its capital-intensive production process. The persistence of high unemployment and widespread poverty and the possession of a British passport stimulated massive migration to Great Britain in the 1950s. Between 1953 and 1962, net emigration to the United Kingdom was 162,000 (Palmer, 1995, p. 5). Beginning in 1962, this flow was severely reduced and later cut off by restrictive British immigration legislation.

Great Britain's postwar plan for her Caribbean colonies was to organize them into a political federation to ensure their viability as small societies and economies. Thus the West Indies Federation was created in 1958 with Jamaica as the largest member. This experiment failed, however, when in a 1961 referendum the people of Jamaica voted against it out of fear that migration of workers from the poorer islands of the eastern Caribbean would compete with Jamaicans for scarce jobs. In 1962, Jamaica achieved political independence and the Jamaica Labour Party (JLP) governed the country for the next ten years, initially under the leadership of Sir Alexander Bustamante and later under Sir Donald Sangster and Hugh Shearer.

By 1972, people had become disenchanted with the widening income disparity in an economy that was growing strongly. Investment in bauxite provided high wages for a few, and light manufacturing provided high profits for the few merchant capitalists who had benefited from industrial incentive laws in the 1940s and 1950s. These conditions provided fertile ground for the democratic socialism of the opposition People's National Party (PNP), which won power in 1972.

Under the leadership of Michael Manley, the government set out to redistribute wealth and to capture the "commanding heights" of the economy. The anticapitalist rhetoric reduced domestic private investment and discouraged foreign investors. And as new social programs expanded the size of the public sector, the size of the tax base in the private sector shrank, forcing the government to resort to borrowing. The resulting growth of the public debt imposed a great burden on the economy. And the worldwide recession triggered by the sharp increase in oil in 1973 reduced export revenues. In response, the government, unable to reach an agreement with the bauxite companies, legislated a substantial increase in the levy on bauxite production to meet the higher cost of oil imports. But the balance of payments continued to worsen, forcing the government to seek assistance from the International Monetary Fund (IMF). The austerity conditions of IMF assistance intensified economic hardship.

A Stagnant Economy. In the 1970s, an escape valve opened. Between 1971 and 1980, 142,000 Jamaicans emigrated to the United States in response to the liberalization of United States immigration policy in the late 1960s.

Under the leadership of Edward Seaga, the JLP won the elections in 1980. His free-market philosophy attracted large amounts of economic aid from the United States government, along with tariff concessions under the Caribbean Basin Economic Recovery Act of 1983 and Section 807 of the U.S. Tariff Code. Despite United States support, the Jamaican economy grew by less than 1 percent. The Seaga government nevertheless returned to power in 1983 when the opposition refused to participate in the elections. The economy continued to be stagnant and the devastation wrought by Hurricane Gilbert in 1988 made things worse.

In 1989, the PNP was voted back into power under the leadership of Michael Manley, who by then had discarded the democratic socialism rhetoric of the 1970s and embraced the proprivate sector free-market development strategy of the Jamaica Labour Party. But the new Manley regime printed money to finance public sector deficits, causing an acceleration of the rate of inflation to more than 40 percent per year. As a result, the value of the Jamaican dollar declined sharply from J $6.5:U.S. $1 at the end of 1989 to J $10.1:U.S. $1 in mid-1991 and plunged to J $21.5:U.S. $1 later that year when exchange controls were removed. The government's attempt to arrest the decline of the currency by tightening the money supply caused lending rates to rise in excess of 65 percent.

The inflow of short-term capital into the country to take advantage of the high interest rates encouraged the rapid expansion of the largely unregulated financial sector. Speculation in the stock market was rife. The collapse of stock prices in 1993 caused many financial institutions to fail, forcing the PNP government, now under the leadership of P. J. Patterson, to acquire them through the newly created Financial Sector Adjustment Company (FINSAC) in order to protect the deposits of the general public.

During the last three decades of the twentieth century, economic policy was unable to propel the foreign-trade-dependent Jamaican economy into sustained growth. To meet this challenge in the twenty-first century, attention turned toward nontraditional industries, particularly information services.

[*See also* Caribbean Region *and* Great Britain, *subentry on* British Empire.]

BIBLIOGRAPHY

Ayearst, Morley. *The British West Indies: The Search for Self Government.* New York, 1960. An examination of West Indian politics and government up to the founding of the Federation of the West Indies in 1958.

Ayub, Mahmoud Ali. *Made in Jamaica: The Development of the Manufacturing Sector.* Washington, D.C., 1981. A study of the evolution of manufacturing in Jamaica and the impact of government policy.

Beachey, R. W. *The British West Indies Sugar Industry in the Late 19th Century.* Oxford, 1957. A valuable study of the cane sugar industry in the British Caribbean between 1865 and 1903.

Beckford, George, and Michael Witter. *Small Garden, Bitter Weed: Struggle and Change in Jamaica.* Morant Bay, Jamaica, 1980. This brief volume examines the political underdevelopment in Jamaica with a critical view of the country's capitalist development strategy.

Commonwealth Economic Committee. *Commonwealth Development and Its Financing: Jamaica.* London, 1964. A study of the financing of economic development in Jamaica between 1952 and 1962.

Economist Intelligence Unit. *Country Profile: Jamaica, 1998–1999.* New York, 2000. An up-to-date assessment of the performance of the Jamaican Economy.

Eisner, Gisela. *Jamaica, 1830–1930: A Study in Economic Growth.* Manchester, 1961. An excellent study using national income accounting to explain the economic growth of Jamaica between 1830 and 1930.

Holzberg, Carol S. *Minorities and Power in a Black Society: The Jewish Community of Jamaica.* Lanham, Md., 1987. A detailed examination of the role of the Jewish community as merchant capitalists in the Jamaican economy.

International Monetary Fund. *Staff Country Report: Jamaica.* Washington, D.C. 2000. Provides a contemporary profile of the Jamaican economy.

Jefferson, Owen. *The Post-War Economic Development of Jamaica.* Kingston, Jamaica, 1972. An examination of the factors affecting the economic development of Jamaica between 1950 and 1969.

Palmer, Ransford W. *The Jamaican Economy.* New York, 1968. A sector-by-sector examination of the post-World War II economic development of Jamaica.

Palmer, Ransford W. *Caribbean Dependence on the United States Economy.* New York, 1979. A study of the nature of Caribbean economic dependence on the United States with emphasis on trade, capital flows, and population movements.

Palmer, Ransford W. *Pilgrims from the Sun: West Indian Migration to America.* New York, 1995. A succinct and well-documented study of the social, historical, and economic dimensions of West Indian migration to the United States.

Stone, Carl, and Aggrey Brown, eds. *Perspectives on Jamaica in the Seventies.* Kingston, Jamaica, 1981. A collection of papers examining the weaknesses and contradictions of the socialist development strategy of the 1970s.

World Bank. *The Economic Development of Jamaica.* Baltimore, 1952. A report of a World Bank mission to study the development requirements of Jamaica.

RANSFORD W. PALMER

JAPAN *[This entry contains four subentries, on the economic history of Japan during the ancient and medieval, early modern, and modern periods, and during the Japanese Empire.]*

Ancient and Medieval Periods

Most archeologists agree that human settlement in Japan predated 28,000 BCE, and there is inconclusive evidence for human habitation before 100,000 BCE. Paleolithic people were hunter-gatherers but did use fire.

Jōmon Era (12,000 BCE–300 BCE). Fired pottery appeared in Japan in 12,000 BCE. Food storage supported more sedentary communities, and housing was semipermanent. Neolithic people were primarily hunter-gatherers, but they also grew some dry-field crops, such as barley and millet. They fished with fishhooks and hunted game with bows and arrows. Artifacts include cooking and serving vessels and a wide variety of human and animal figurines. Social stratification was low, and wealth seems to have corresponded with shamanistic power. Communities were largely self-sufficient, and there is no evidence of broad trade patterns.

Yayoi Era (300 BCE–250 CE). Around 300 BCE wet rice agriculture began to transform Japanese economy and society. The irrigated paddy fields required a higher level of social organization than swidden agriculture but also produced a greater surplus. This surplus in turn supported a greater degree of social stratification and more complex political organizations. Several small kingdoms emerged, and some were organized well enough to send tribute to China in return for gifts and political recognition. The dispatch of slaves as tribute suggests extensive unfree labor. Rulers continued to rely on shamanistic, sacerdotal power but increased their ability to mobilize labor. Farm communities consisted of pit dwellings with hearths clustered around irrigated fields and granaries. Artisans worked metal and probably made iron farm tools. There is some evidence of local trade networks.

Yamato Period (250 CE–645 CE). Japanese rulers began to consolidate their authority around 200 CE. Elite clans, which based their authority on their decent from deities, began to mobilize labor on an unprecedented scale. They constructed enormous tombs, the largest over fifteen hundred feet in length. The ruling clans built granaries to tax agriculture. They mobilized artisans and later agricultural labor through communities of workers organized by religious and familial ties to a particular noble house. Labor was increasingly specialized, but the economy was still unmonetized. The ruling clans relied heavily on continental civilization for technology, but the quality of Japanese metalwork steadily improved.

In the fourth or fifth century the Yamato house, a clan that claimed descent from the sun goddess, emerged as the dominant noble line. This clan, later known as the imperial house, began to consolidate its authority by investing other clan chieftains with titles in a central political structure. The state drew increasingly on Chinese thought for its political system and began to codify some laws and administrative practices.

Late Yamato (645–710), Nara (710–794), and Heian (794–1185) Periods. In the mid-seventh century the imperial state began to assert direct authority over the Japanese economy. The state replaced regional tribute networks with a national system of law, taxation, and administration. The system is commonly known as the *ritsuryō* system for its penal (*ritsu*) and administrative (*ryō*) codes. Under the *ritsuryō* system the state claimed ownership of all arable land. Most fields were allocated to farm families: men received roughly twenty-three hundred square meters, while women received two-thirds as much. Slaves, less than 10 percent of the population, received smaller parcels. Allocated land, called *kubunden*, was redistributed every six years to account for changes in family composition. Each tiller owed a range of taxes, including rice, cloth, labor service, and specialized local products, such as sesame oil, flax, dye, and iron. Males were also subject to military conscription. The government exempted some parcels from reallocation: certain government officials, temples, and shrines were granted fields that they could rent to cultivators.

To facilitate administration and tax collection, the state established provincial capitals, each with government offices, a treasury, and a Buddhist temple. The state minted coins and encouraged their use, but rice and cloth remained important currencies of exchange. Commercial activity increased, but national trade remained extremely limited.

The *ritsuryō* system helped the imperial state secure its authority, but the land allocation system was seriously flawed. Parcels were too small, and the administrative costs of the system were enormous. Periodic reallocation also discouraged both the development of new paddy land and the reclamation of land lost to abandonment and natural disaster. Beginning in the 720s the state allowed exemptions from the *kubunden* system for newly reclaimed land. Nobles or institutions that reclaimed land were granted title in perpetuity and were exempted from taxes for three generations. Powerful aristocratic families seized this opportunity to expand their holdings by forcing farmers to clear land. They also systematically expanded the scope of their tax immunities. By the end of the tenth century some landholders had claimed the right to bar state officials from inspecting or even entering their holdings. Such exempt holdings, known as *shō* or *shōen*, became a central institution of the Japanese economy.

Landholders sustained these dubious exemptions in networks of patronage, through which they shared rent revenues with aristocrats in the capital. Buddhist temples used a similar strategy and secured *shōen* holdings by converting their parishioners' holdings. Initially the imperial house sought to block the growth of *shōen* through legal challenges, but this proved a losing battle. By the eleventh century the imperial house itself ranked as one of the largest *shōen* holders. Even land not claimed as *shōen* was gradually privatized. Powerful local families established hereditary claims to important provincial offices, and they invested lower-level officials with fiefs on what was nominally public land.

The privatization of the state's military paralleled the deterioration of its revenue system. Conscription was an enormous burden on farmers, and although the army proved effective in pacifying Japan's northern border, it was less useful in combating rural banditry. Beginning in 792 the state employed private groups of soldiers led by mounted warriors. These contract warriors eventually replaced the *risuryō* state's standing army. The coincident growth of private military and private economic power became the basis for samurai rule. Although temples and nonwarrior aristocrats developed the earliest *shōen*, by the twelfth century many *shōen* employed local warriors to maintain order.

Kamakura (1185–1338) and Ashikaga (1338–1467) Periods. In the mid-twelfth century rival factions of court aristocrats enlisted support from provincial warrior houses to settle an imperial succession dispute. The resultant warfare helped create a new form of government, the shogunate. As part of wartime mobilization, Minamoto Yoritomo, who later became the first shogun, promised to confirm the *shōen* claims of all warriors who rallied to his cause. This compact became the basis of shogunal rule, a vow of loyalty in exchange for a confirmation of rights to income from landholdings. The shogun established a new capital in Kamakura distinct from the *ritsuryō* capital in Kyoto. The new government initially limited its authority to warrior land claims and shared power with the government in Kyoto, but aristocratic power steadily declined.

Under warrior rule the *shōen* became the dominant mode of production. It was a highly stratified institution. Higher-ranking farmers (*myōshu*) had independent land claims and could complain to the *shōen* proprietor about the conduct of the local warrior (*jitō*) or civil administration. Lower-ranking farmers had no legal standing with the *shōen* and paid rent to both higher-ranking farmers and to the *shōen* (proprietor). Rents commonly included rice, commodities, and labor service, but the cash conversion of rents increased in the 1300s and 1400s.

The first shogunate was weakened by the Mongol invasions (1274 and 1281) and collapsed in the 1330s in fighting stemming from an imperial succession dispute. Ashikaga Takauji, a powerful warlord, founded a second shogunate in 1338, but the Ashikaga shogunate never matched the national authority of the Kamakura regime. Under the Ashikaga power devolved increasingly to the countryside, and local warriors sought confirmation of their landholdings from the shogun's military governors rather than the shogunate itself.

Warring States (1467–1568) and Unification (1568–1600) Periods. In 1467 a dispute between two military governors erupted into a civil war that lasted a century and destroyed the Ashikaga shogunate. In the absence of central control by either the shogunate or the *ritsuryō* state, regional warlords assumed vast civil authority. They drafted their own civil and military law codes, independently determined weights and measures, and regulated markets and currency. Despite continued warfare, trade expanded and merchant and artisan guilds (*za*) sought the protection of warlords. Reflecting the collapse of *ritsuryō* institutions, local warriors began to describe their holdings as fiefs rather than *shōen* parcels.

The weakening of central authority coincided with economic growth. Technological innovations (including better farm tools and irrigation systems), increased use of draft animals, and new crops (including soybeans and tea) increased the value, range, and profitability of agriculture. National trade increased, although much of the currency consisted of Chinese coins. International trade expanded greatly. Initially Japan exported only raw materials, especially precious metals, but by the late 1400s exports included commodities such as swords, fans, and scrolls. Imports, largely from China, included coins, medicines, silk, and books.

Beginning in 1568 three powerful warlords reestablished central authority. They subordinated regional warlords and used standardized systems of value to measure their investitures. They dismantled regional toll barriers, dissolved the *za*, and minted new coins. They began the first nationwide land survey since the eighth century. These developments paved the way for national rule by the Tokugawa shogunate after 1600.

BIBLIOGRAPHY

Farris, William Wayne. *Population, Disease, and Land in Early Japan, 645–900.* Cambridge, Mass., 1985.

Farris, William Wayne. "Trade, Money, and Merchants in Nara Japan." *Monumenta Nipponica* 53.3 (1998), 303–334.

Friday, Karl F. *Hired Swords: The Rise of Private Warrior Power in Early Japan.* Stanford, Calif., 1992.

Kidder, J. Edward. "The Earliest Societies in Japan." In *Cambridge History of Japan*, vol. 1, *Ancient Japan*, edited by Delmer M. Brown, pp. 48–107. Cambridge, 1993.

Kudo, Keiichi. "Shoen." *Acta Asiatica* 44 (1983), 1–27.

Nagahara, Keiji. "The Decline of the *Shoen* System." Translated by Michael P. Birt. In *The Cambridge History of Japan*, vol. 3, *Medieval Japan*, edited by Kozo Yamamura, pp. 260–300. Cambridge, 1990.

Tonomura, Hitomi. *Community and Commerce in Late Medieval Japan: The Corporate Villages of Tokuchin-ho.* Stanford, Calif., 1992.

Yamamura, Kozo. "From Coins to Rice: Hypotheses on the *kandaka* and *kokudaka* Systems." *Journal of Japanese Studies* 14.2 (1988), 341–367.

Yamamura, Kozo. "The Growth of Commerce in Medieval Japan." In *The Cambridge History of Japan*, vol. 3, *Medieval Japan*, edited by Kozo Yamamura, pp. 344–395. Cambridge, 1990.

MARK J. RAVINA

Early Modern Period

Japan in the sixteenth century had an agrarian economy based on wet rice agriculture, with much of the labor force semifree or dependent on large landholders. Markets existed in the limited number of cities and towns; farmers traded in markets held every five to ten days in the countryside; and copper coins were the principal medium of exchange, but rents and taxes were paid mostly in kind. Three centuries later, 80 percent of the Japanese were still agriculturists, but the population had doubled from somewhere between twelve and eighteen million—scholars disagree— to around thirty million, and at least 12 percent lived in cities of more than ten thousand. By the 1820s, Japan's well-developed economic institutions included large money exchangers (premodern banks) and the world's first futures market (for rice). Even villages were fully monetized, and the infrastructure had been developed to the point that Japan had the base for rapidly industrializing once it imported Western technology from the 1880s on. How did this transformation occur in a society seemingly under a feudal regime and closed to world markets and influences?

Unification and the Tokugawa Period. The answer lies in the sixteenth century, a time of intermittent civil war at the end of which Japan was unified under Tokugawa Ieyasu (1542–1616), who became the founding shogun of the Tokugawa period (1600–1868). Originally farmer-warriors, the samurai gradually gave control of agriculture to the cultivators in order to concentrate on warfare and governance, which created the incentives and opportunities for the cultivators to increase their output. At the same time, those daimyo ("overlords") most successful at enlarging their territories provided law and order, which lowered the costs of enforcing contracts, and invested in an infrastructure that would raise the productivity and output of their land. This combination of a stable government and a legal structure that reduced transaction costs, an augmented infrastructure, and incentives to commoners was provided to all after unification in 1600 and led to continuing economic growth during the Tokugawa period.

In addition to establishing law and order, unification had other important "peace dividends." To guarantee the loyalty of the daimyo, Tokugawa Ieyasu and his successors adopted a number of control measures that unintentionally stimulated the economy. A general ban on foreign trade and ocean-going vessels to prevent foreign influence resulted in the loss of gains from foreign trade and a slowing of technological progress, but it forced the economy to become autarchically self-sufficient, promoting interregional trade based on local specialization. The restriction of one castle per domain forced each daimyo to quarter his samurai in one place, creating castle towns, which grew over time to urbanize the countryside. Most important was the *sankin kōtai* system, which mandated that all daimyo spend approximately half their time in the shogunal capital of Edo.

This system transformed Japan. The quartering of the daimyo, their families, and their retinues in Edo resulted in the rapid creation of a metropolis that grew from a small group of fishing villages in 1590, when Ieyasu made it his headquarters, to a city of more than a million by 1700, probably the largest city in the world with the exception of Beijing. Osaka grew into a prosperous commercial city of three to four hundred thousand inhabitants, serving as an entrepôt to supply Edo and as the center of money exchangers. Because travel by daimyo and their retinues required the establishment of safe and well-maintained travel routes with post towns and porter services, it accelerated economic growth along the main highways throughout Japan. This travel by elites, and by commoners who could use the same roads, led to increased information about the variety of goods and relative prices, promoting regional specialization in the production of such goods as medicine from Toyama on the Sea of Japan, cotton from Okayama on the Inland Sea, and sugar from Satsuma in Kyūshū. Increased specialization meant increased efficiency of production as well as improved quality.

Equally important for economic growth was the political philosophy of the shogun and daimyo: samurai were to provide benevolent government but not to meddle either in the day-to-day administration of the farm villages or to handle economic affairs themselves. Rather, government provided predictability in the form of laws, regulations, and the standardization of weights and measures across regions. When it did intervene in economic matters, such as to ban the free cutting of much of the woodlands, it was often to the economic and ecological benefit of the country. Although the tax burden to maintain this system of government and provide incomes to the samurai (5 to 12 percent of the population, depending on the domain) was heavy, it was lightened in the eighteenth century when the system was changed from one based on an annual assessment of the harvest to a decadal assessment enabling cultivators to keep all of the increases in output between surveys.

The daimyo did invest in the economic infrastructure from the sixteenth century on, first in order to provide the economic base needed to wage war and increase their territories, and after unification to support their domains. They mandated civil engineering projects, such as building and maintaining roads and bridges, large-scale reclamation, flood control, and irrigation. They regulated commerce, including the chartering of trade associations (*kabu nakama*), but they also permitted the growth of trade in the countryside in the second half of the period, which resulted in a rising living standard.

In addition to good government and investment in the infrastructure, a third cause of Tokugawa economic growth was the incentives commoners were given to increase their wealth and income. Farming that relied on semifree servants with problems of shirking, landholders bearing all the risks, and lack of flexibility gave way during the seventeenth century to the creation of small plots cultivated by tenants or independent farmers, who in exhange for their freedom now had to share risks but gained the freedom to make farm decisions and to marry. The most efficient farm unit in most of the country became the family with two adult laborers. The demand for cash crops, such as cotton and silk, enabled farmers to produce for the market and pay land taxes in cash, with the excess used to purchase fertilizers. Farmers in the southern parts of the country could now plant two or three crops per year; those in other areas engaged in by-employments, such as weaving, in the off season. Changes in labor arrangements led to both a rise in agricultural productivity and population growth.

Technology also played an important role in Tokugawa economic growth. In the late sixteenth century, various technologies were imported from China by the warring daimyo to better wage war. In the seventeenth century, these advanced techniques in mining, smelting, refining, and civil engineering were put to peaceful purposes. Cotton, originally introduced to be used for sails, uniforms, and fuses, became the preferred material for clothing during the Tokugawa period. Warm and washable, cotton is thought to have lengthened life expectancy as well as raised the quality of life. Tools and methods used to build castles were now transferred to building houses, and it is from the mid- to late seventeenth century that houses became sturdy enough to pass down to descendants. But owing to self-imposed isolation, scientific methods and technology lagged. There were innovations in farm tools and methods, both widely disseminated through manuals and word of mouth, but these did not involve technological inventions.

Scholars now agree that all the tremendous economic and population growth in the seventeenth century slowed by the eighteenth. By 1700, land that could be easily reclaimed under existing technology was already under cultivation, and people began to limit population growth through controlling who married; later marriages; and birth control within marriage, first by infanticide and later by abortion as well. Village data from prosperous areas indicate that people were limiting family size to maintain or increase family wealth and social standing, not just because of dire economic circumstances. This led to a rate of economic growth that was faster than population growth, effectively raising the standard of living.

Growth Despite Crises. Three major famines or mortality crises also slowed growth at fifty-year intervals in the eighteenth and nineteenth centuries. Bad weather—unseasonable cold and rainy—was a factor in all three, but leafhoppers played a major role in the famine in the southwest from 1732 to 1733, and ash from the 1783 eruption of Mount Asama, north of Edo, caused widespread crop failure and death. Both of these crises prompted governmental reform, with little effect on the worsening finances of the daimyo and shogunate. The nationwide crop failures in the 1830s, following a decade of prosperity, prompted yet another attempt at fiscal reform and an effort to limit the power of the guilds, but these proved futile because of the steadily growing commercialization of the economy. This economic crisis is arguably the start of the problems that brought down the shogunate.

Despite these crises, the domestic national product continued to increase, albeit at a slower pace than in the seventeenth century. But few scholars now dispute that the standard of living rose for commoners throughout the Tokugowa period. Evidence comes from a variety of sources: rising wages, difficulty in finding labor for low-paying jobs, increase in the number of daily goods for sale in rural areas, widespread improvements in housing, and a booming urban popular culture. Although the Japanese in the Tokugawa period did not achieve the standard of living found in western Europe, they had a similar level of physical well-being. In villages for which we have detailed population records, people who lived to adulthood lived on into their seventies, in both central Japan and even in the northeast, which has been long noted for economic backwardness and hardship.

Government and the Decline of the Shogunate. The one group in Japan that did not benefit from the economic growth was the samurai class. With its emphasis on an agrarian tax base and noninvolvement in the economy, government found itself unable to tax the growing commerce and nonagricultural activities. Samurai in the service of the shogunate had stable incomes over time, but with incomes rising for other classes, many were unable to maintain servants or the level of consumption mandated by their status. Many even pawned or sold their swords, the symbol of their status. With the cost of maintaining residence in Edo increasing and faced with inadequate tax income, the daimyo were deeply in debt, and the incomes of their samurai actually fell.

By the mid-nineteenth century, despite its lack of industrial technology, Japan had many features that Western observers admired: a water-supply system in Edo that was judged to have higher-quality water than London's, a banking system that was much sounder than the American counterpart of the period, and a level of rice output that was not reached in any other part of Asia until after World War II. Mid-twentieth-century scholars, Japanese and Western alike, stressed the economic backwardness of the late Tokugawa period compared to the industrializing economies of the West, but despite the lack of industrial technology and a lower standard of living, the Japanese had a level of literacy—upwards of 40 percent—similar to England and France in the mid-nineteenth century and a life expectancy—in the 40s—that was the same as Europe's in midcentury, according to United Nations estimates.

But if the economic base developed during the Tokugawa period can be credited with the speed with which Japan industrialized from the 1880s on, it was the economic problems of government that were instrumental in bringing about the downfall of the regime. For example, the crop failures of the 1830s led to widespread death by epidemics in the 1840s, and a further loss of tax revenues to the daimyo and the shogunate, who were already in debt. The old Confucian-based reforms and development of the currency helped little, and the abolition of key institutions, such as the guilds, in an effort to alleviate economic problems resulted in confusion and only worsened the problems. The trade associations were officially disbanded in the early 1840s, resulting in even greater inflation, and were reestablished in weakened form in 1851. In 1862, the *sankin kōtai* system was abandoned, emptying Edo of samurai and causing hardship for the merchant class. The shogunate had few funds with which to fend off the demands of foreigners, and in 1853 Commodore Perry of the U.S. Navy successfully breached Japan's seclusion policy, leading to the end of the Tokugawa regime and paving the way for the industrialization of Japan.

BIBLIOGRAPHY

Crawcour, E. S., and Kozo Yamamura. "The Tokugawa Monetary System: 1787–1868." *Economic Development and Cultural Change* 18.4 (1970), 489–518.

Hall, John W., and Marius B. Jansen, eds. *Studies in the Institutional History of Early Modern Japan*. Princeton, 1968.

Hall, John Whitney, Nagahara Keiji, and Kozo Yamamura. *Japan before Tokugawa: Political Consolidation and Economic Growth, 1500–1650*. Princeton, 1981.

Hanley, Susan B., and Kozo Yamamura. *Economic and Demographic Change in Preindustrial Japan, 1600–1868*. Princeton, 1977.

Hanley, Susan B. *Everyday Things in Premodern Japan: The Hidden Legacy of Material Culture*. Berkeley, 1997.

Keiji, Nagahara, and Kozo Yamamura. "Shaping the Process of Unification: Technological Progress in Sixteenth- and Seventeenth-Century Japan." *The Journal of Japanese Studies* 14.1 (1988), 77–109.

Roberts, Luke. *Mercantilism in a Japanese Domain: The Merchant Origins of Economic Nationalism in 18th-century Tosa*. Cambridge, 1998.

Smith, Thomas C. *The Agrarian Origins of Modern Japan*. Stanford, Calif., 1959.

Smith, Thomas C. *Native Sources of Japanese Industrialization, 1750–1920*. Berkeley, 1988.

Totman, Conrad. *Early Modern Japan*. Berkeley, 1993.

Wigen, Kären. *The Making of a Japanese Periphery, 1750–1920*. Berkeley, 1995.

Yamamura, Kozo. *A Study of Samurai Income and Entrepreneurship: Quantitative Analyses of Economic and Social Aspects of the Samurai in Tokugawa and Meiji Japan*. Cambridge, Mass., 1974.

SUSAN B. HANLEY

Modern Period

In 1850, Japan was commercially isolated from the rest of the world, yet it had a per capita gross domestic product well above that of China and India and rather similar to what might have been found in a resource-rich country in Southeast Asia, such as Thailand. Japan's success in raising its level of productivity, despite the pressure of its people on resources, rested on almost 250 years of institutional adaptation. The Japan of 1850 had well-developed commercial enterprises operating throughout the length and breadth of the land and muscular networks of market-sensitive, small-scale manufacturers and farmers operating at the frontiers of their pre-Industrial Revolution knowledge base.

Japan's Opening to International Trade. In such an environment, it is hardly surprising that so many of Japan's economic actors were capable of responding positively to the many opportunities presented them when Japan was opened to international trade in 1858. These new opportunities were just more dramatic examples of the kinds of opportunities thrown up by Japan's economy as it grew and developed during the Tokugawa period.

This is not to suggest that Japan's integration into the global economy occurred smoothly. The price structure in the Japan of 1850 differed dramatically from that prevailing on global markets. To cite just one vivid example, on global markets an ounce of gold was worth fifteen ounces of silver, but in Japan it was worth only five ounces. Japan's opening to international trade created many opportunities

JAPANESE SHIPPING INDUSTRY. Western traders transporting merchandise, Yokohama, 1861. Woodblock print polyptych. (Arthur M. Sackler Gallery of Art, Smithsonian Institution, Washington, D.C.: Gift of Ambassador and Mrs. William Leonhard, S1998.55a-e)

for the profitable exploitation of such price differences. Relatively cheap products, such as gold, but also silk and tea, were exported even as relatively expensive products, such as silver, cotton yarn and cloth, and woolens, were imported.

Because Japan was a relatively small economy in the mid-nineteenth century, it is hardly surprising that international trade quickly aligned domestic prices with those prevailing on global markets. This price adjustment had dramatic consequences for the distribution of income and wealth in Japan. Owners of physical and human assets used in Japan's new export industries benefited, even while those with a stake in Japan's import-competing industries lost out. Some of the most significant short-term changes were in commercial services. Osaka merchants, whose accounts receivable had long been disproportionately denominated in silver but whose accounts payable were disproportionately denominated in gold, were gravely weakened by Japan's integration into the global economy. In contrast, the position of Tokyo merchants, whose receivables and payables were the mirror images of their Osaka counterparts, was strengthened.

The new price structure confronting Japanese merchants, handicraft producers, peasants and day laborers did not always result in rapid structural adjustment. The movement of resources from one industry to another, from one region to another and from one crop to another, in some instances, occurred only over many years. Too often old livelihoods were destroyed before new livelihoods could be created. Small wonder that the opening of Japan to international trade led to significant unemployed resources, inflation, and enormous short-term economic turmoil that helped undermine a Tokugawa Shogunate, still considered even today—if success is measured by stability and longevity—the most successful political system in Japanese history.

Government Policy and Economic Growth in the Meiji Period. The new government that came to power in 1868, ruling in the name of the emperor Meiji, moved quickly to centralize political control. The *daimyo*, Japan's hereditary provincial rulers, were induced to cede their *fiefs* (land) to the Meiji government in Tokyo. This change in the locus of political authority allowed the Meiji government to monopolize the power to tax, the power to maintain armed forces, and the power to regulate the money supply.

The Meiji government quickly recognized that there was an intimate, mutually re-enforcing link between national security and economic prosperity. The successful imposition of a nationwide land tax, and the ending of stipends for the unproductive samurai class, allowed the government the means to establish armed forces organized and equipped on nineteenth-century-European models. These armed forces, while protecting Japan from foreign encroachment, also insured that any attempt at armed rebellion within Japan would fail. The political stability, which had been the hallmark of the Tokugawa era and which was an important factor in encouraging economic progress during those years, was restored by the Meiji government. Later in the Meiji period, however, military expenditures grew beyond what was needed for national security, crowding out a significant amount of private investment even as it created the domestic interests that would ultimately lead Japan into disastrous overseas military adventures.

Despite the role price inflation had played in bringing an end to the Tokugawa Shogunate, achieving price stability was not a high priority for the Meiji government in its early years. Indeed, in its eagerness to promote a system of U.S.-style nationally chartered banks, using as capital the government bonds the samurai had been given in lieu of their stipends, the Meiji government permitted the issuing and circulation of bank notes on exceptionally liberal terms. The ensuing doubling of prices between 1877 and 1881, and attendant concerns about the possibility of hyperinflation finally led to a dramatic change in government policy. In 1882, the Bank of Japan, a European-style central bank, was established, and, under the leadership of Masayoshi Matsukata, the Minister of Finance, a policy of fiscal and monetary restraint was pursued with the goal of making the yen convertible, first into silver and later into gold. The policy proved successful, and Japan joined the silver standard in 1886. A little more than a decade later, it was finally on the gold standard, accepting all the financial discipline that participation required.

The same tax revenues that allowed the Meiji government to create a powerful army also permitted the development of an ambitious national educational program. While as much as 50 percent of the adult male population was functionally literate in late Tokugawa Japan, the Meiji government promoted universal compulsory primary school education. This program proved highly successful. By the second decade of the twentieth century, Japan's male and female workers already had two-thirds as many years of formal education as American workers, even while working with no more than one-fifteenth of the physical capital. As a result of Meiji government policies, compared with its level of per capita gross domestic product, Japan's human capital became abundant.

The impact of the government policies was not limited to primary education. In the mid-Meiji period, Japanese with advanced formal education were absorbed as teachers and administrators within a rapidly expanding educational system and in newly created positions within the Meiji government. By the time of World War I, however, the science and engineering graduates of the higher educational institutions promoted by the Meiji government became so numerous that they became employed in manufacturing in large numbers, having a significant direct effect on productivity. This new infusion of personnel with advanced formal training raised the ability of these industries to absorb new technologies, lowering the cost of imitating ideas and approaches that were developed both outside and inside Japan.

Not all the Meiji government's initiatives were successful. During the 1870s and the early 1880s, the Meiji government pursued a very active policy of import substitution and export promotion. At one time or another during these years, government subsidies, direct technical assistance, and/or model factories were used to promote the manufacture of products as diverse as silk reeling, cotton spinning, woolen spinning and weaving, textile machinery, glass, cement, brick, cod liver oil, beer, wine, iron smelting, mining, water wheels, fish fertilizer, canned fish, fishing nets, refined sugar, sodium carbonate, soy sauce, and ships. The scale of this government activity was so large in the mid-

1870s that expenditures on it were fully two-thirds of what was being spent on Japan's armed forces. Despite this massive government effort, Meiji-period industrial policy was a failure. The model factories that the government set up were not the models successful private sector entrepreneurs chose to follow. In industry after industry, the government had too little expertise to know how to evaluate foreign advice and how to advise would-be Japanese manufacturers in ways to sensibly adapt technology developed elsewhere to local circumstances. When the Japanese government finally abandoned its role of directly promoting industrial development, ceased subsidizing almost all private enterprise, and sold off what publicly owned enterprises remained, the technological foundations had not yet been laid for subsequent successful industrial development.

Rather than growth directed from above, Japan's economic progress for much of the Meiji period rested on the same foundations as Tokugawa-period economic growth. Growth continued to be led by rurally based artisans and craftsmen, small-scale manufacturers, as well as innovative farmers. To the extent that there was an acceleration in Japan's Meiji-period economic growth before 1900, it was the result of a spurt in economic activity in sectors that already existed in the Tokugawa period and made use of technology that was largely derivative from what was already known to Japan before its opening to overseas contact in the 1850s.

While the government was of little help in advising Japanese manufacturers how to use and adapt foreign technologies, the manufacturers themselves, through careful observation of successful foreign firms, through the skillful choice of foreign advisers, and through much trial-and-error, ultimately achieved great success. Characteristically, as in the cotton spinning industry, this meant adapting production processes imported from abroad to take better advantage of Japan's abundant labor force, even while economizing on extremely scarce capital. Unlike what was the norm in western Europe and North America, factories in Japan using modern machine manufacturing techniques were powered and staffed in the late nineteenth century and the early decades of the twentieth century in ways that allowed them to be operated with high rates of capital productivity at any given time, even as they were running 168 hours a week throughout the entire year with time off only for a handful of national holidays.

Japan's Institutional Adaptation. Late Meiji Japan's excellent growth performance continued, wartime excepted, for much of the twentieth century. Between 1885 and 1939, Japan's per capita gross domestic product average annual growth rate was 2.3 percent. During Japan's golden age of economic growth between 1955 and 1973, average annual growth accelerated to 7.8 percent, only to fall back

JAPAN'S MACHINE TOOLS INDUSTRY. Interior of Mitsubishi plant, Kobe, circa 1925. (Prints and Photographs Division, Library of Congress)

to 2.7 percent in the following quarter-century. In each of these periods, Japan's performance was superior to that of the prosperous western European and North American economies.

Rapid growth continued even as Japan's economic institutions changed markedly. Perhaps the most extreme example of institutional adaptation can be seen in the evolution of Japan's labor markets. In the Meiji period, and in the early decades of the twentieth century, rapid economic growth in Japan coexisted with very high labor turnover and the elaborate supervision of production workers, even while widespread use was made of piece-rate systems of compensation. Just a few decades later, following changes in Japanese labor legislation, permanent employment became characteristic of most large Japanese firms, with pay closely related to the number of years of employment. The market for experienced managers, engineers, and workers that had been active earlier in the century withered. While permanent employment practices meant that Japanese firms lost the ability to respond to short-term macroeconomic shocks by laying off workers, they gained by being able to recoup costs they might incur from investing in the training of their workforce. Until the end of the twentieth century, this was viewed as a trade-off that was to Japan's advantage.

Dramatic change in Japanese economic institutions was not confined to labor markets. The Japanese economy grew relatively rapidly, both with largely unregulated and with heavily regulated financial systems. During the early decades of the twentieth century, there was virtually free entry into Japan's banking sector. Despite the presence of a small number of banks that were affiliated with the elaborate interlocking corporate networks known as *zaibatsu* (for example, Mitsui, Mitsubishi, and Sumitomo), there was stiff competition among a large number of smaller financial institutions. In the late 1920s, the Ministry of

Finance successfully promoted regulations designed to foster concentration in banking, but it was only after wartime policies explicitly linked firms with banks that the now-familiar main-bank system emerged. Under the financial system of the 1950s, 1960s, and 1970s, a relatively small number of banks used the market power conferred on them by the Ministry of Finance to transfer the savings of their household depositors at less than competitive rates of interest to the rapidly growing finance-short corporations with whom they had developed long-term relationships. Bank finance replaced the direct financing that had dominated earlier in the twentieth century.

The increasing regulation of the financial system in the mid-1920s went hand-in-hand with a renewed interest on the part of the government in shaping Japan's industrial structure. This interest matured a decade later when, under the pressure of increasing military involvement over the Chinese mainland, comprehensive national economic planning emerged in Japan. In the 1950s, 1960s, and 1970s, the Japanese government's role in shaping the economy's structure came to resemble neither its wartime role nor the more limited approach it had played earlier in the twentieth century. Comprehensive national economic planning remained as a wartime legacy, but the Japanese government's approach was indicative and market driven. The major policy instruments the government retained to implement sectoral policy included:

1. the preferential allocation of foreign exchange and import licenses,
2. discriminatory tax-subsidy provisions and import tariffs, and
3. subsidized loans from government financial institutions and implicit influence on the allocation of loans by the heavily regulated private financial sector.

Japan's Distinctive Postwar Economic System. The economic institutions that characterized Japan in the 1950s, 1960s, and 1970s are generally regarded as less similar to Western economic institutions than the economic institutions prevalent is Japan earlier in the twentieth century. Japan's postwar institutions can be thought of as mutually reinforcing. The concentration of financial power in Japan's banking system, so long the goal of the Ministry of Finance, greatly facilitated (but also made necessary) an active, indicative, sectoral policy on the part of the Japanese government. Without countervailing government pressure, in the absence of market discipline, the complicated pressures of intragroup politics might well have skewed resource allocation in the direction of established mature industries (for example, textiles and shipbuilding in the 1950s). At the same time, with a group of powerful banks that maintained long-term relationships with the firms who borrowed from them absent, it is unlikely that many Japanese firms would have been willing to risk the financial inflexibility associated with a permanent employment system.

Much has been claimed on behalf of the Japanese economic system as it operated during the 1950s, 1960s, and 1970s. Bank-centered capital allocation and permanent employment, among other Japanese economic institutions, have been said to be unusually effective in overcoming the problems of adverse selection and moral hazard endemic in virtually all economic systems. Likewise, the Japanese government's role in the economy has been thought to have raised the share of resources being devoted to capital formation even as it played an implicit coordinating role in overcoming the market failures that inhibit structural transformation.

Such claims about postwar Japan's economic system have fared better at the theoretical than at the empirical level. Japan's economic growth in the 1950s, 1960s, and 1970s was substantially faster than that of other advanced industrialized countries. At the same time, even though Japanese economic growth in the latter decades of the nineteenth century and the early decades of the twentieth century was much slower than postwar growth, it too was superior to the growth of other advanced industrialized countries and to much the same degree as its postwar growth.

Quite apart from this aggregate evidence, systematic statistical investigations done at a less-aggregated level argue against any special positive role for Japan's distinctive economic institutions. For example, careful statistical studies suggest that the net impact of Japan's postwar industrial policies may have been little more than the support of declining industries without much impact at all on productivity. Japan's industrial structure changed dramatically during these years. Successively, steel, consumer electronic products, automobiles, and electrical machinery, to name just a few, each became world-class industries. Each emerged, however, without government aid playing a decisive role. Just as with the government's industrial policies, there are also several careful statistical studies that find main banks altering the behavior of the firms that were their long-term borrowers without necessarily improving their performance.

Systemic Evolution and Japan's Economic Distress. Inevitably, much of the analysis of the distinctive economic institutions characterizing Japan's era of high economic growth between 1955 and 1973 occurred after 1973 when these institutions were already undergoing significant transformation. High leverage with diversification and bank monitoring may well be a good recipe to force corporate managers to perform efficiently, but it may have had little to do with the Japan of the 1980s and 1990s. The deregulation of Japanese financial markets, which began in the late 1970s, changed the structure and operation of the Japanese economy. Slower growth and the freedom to raise funds directly in international (and later in domestic) markets meant a significant loosening of the relationship between many of Japan's best-known and best-run corporations and their banks and a correspondingly greater role for equity financing for such firms.

The same financial deregulation that allowed Japanese firms to draw on far more diverse sources of finance changed the role the Japanese government played in the economy. In the 1980s, Japanese firms seeking to promote new industries rarely needed the Japanese government as an ally to force a bank to turn on its financial spigot. The same deregulation that removed the need for the government to intervene also removed the means by which the government might intervene. The Japanese banking system, forced to compete with many other sources of finance, both at home and abroad, ceased to be an effective instrument with which to shape Japan's industrial structure.

While Japanese economic institutions have changed in significant ways since the early postwar decades, the prolonged downturn of the 1990s, triggered in the first instance by speculative excess in Japan's equity and land markets in the late 1980s, and later exacerbated by high real-interest rates that persisted even in the presence of zero nominal interest rates and high levels of government debt undermining consumer confidence, engendered the widespread belief that further adaptation is necessary if Japan is to return to the superior performance so long the hallmark of its economy. Most attention continues to be focussed on Japan's financial system. Twenty years of financial deregulation made it significantly easier for the bank's traditional customers to find new sources of finance without making it easier for banks to maintain the quality of their loan portfolios. By way of compensation, until recently, banks were protected by the Ministry of Finance from the consequences of this asymmetric deregulation. This created an environment where moral hazard thrived and Japanese banks came to maintain an extraordinary amount of nonperforming loans on their balance sheets. To remove the source of the banking sector's problem, in the mid-1990s, the Japanese government accelerated the pace of financial deregulation making it easier for banks to enter markets traditionally reserved for nonbank financial institutions even as it eased the way for these institutions to enter the markets traditionally reserved for banks. The increased securitization of Japanese finance and new information disclosure requirements are now beginning to work to increase the transparency of the operations of Japanese firms. With better information, Japanese financial markets, in principle, should be better able to concentrate large, much-needed resources in new areas of development.

Deregulation may be changing the character of Japanese capital and product markets, but demography is altering Japanese labor markets even as it creates enormous uncertainty about the future of the robust savings rates that have marked Japan's last fifty years. Increasing labor scarcity brought on by the aging of the Japanese population allow employees more say in their terms of employment (for example, flexibility in working hours and age of retirement) than has been true in the past. Whether permanent employment remains, in the face of Japan's uncertain future macroeconomic environment, is quite another matter.

Even though the productivity of the Japanese economy remains inferior to the global standard in many areas, by comparison with even the recent past, Japan is close enough to the technological frontier that determining the technological trajectory that a firm will follow is far more complicated than had been the case earlier in Japan's economic history. In this situation, with future human resource needs difficult to predict, Japanese firms of the future may well prefer to have their labor force bear both more of the risks associated with acquiring specialized training and the risks associated with secular and cyclical demand shocks. Such steps will require a change in the way in which training is provided and changes in the Japanese government's educational and social policies.

Japan began the twenty-first century with new economic institutions increasingly unlike those institutions associated with Japan's superior economic performance in the last half of the twentieth century. If the past 150 years provide cause for optimism, new economic arrangements, now only dimly visible among firms, labor, finance, and government and between the Japanese economy and the global economy, will work to mitigate the consequences of the changed demographic and technological environment.

BIBLIOGRAPHY

Aoki, Masahiko, and Gary Saxonhouse, eds. *Finance, Competition, and Governance in Japan*. Oxford, 2000.

Flath, David. *The Japanese Economy*. Oxford, 2000.

Francks, Penelope. *Japanese Economic Development*. London, 1999.

Hayami, Yujiro, and Saburo Yamada. *The Agricultural Development of Japan*. Tokyo, 1991.

Hoshi, Takeo, and Anil Kashyap. *Corporate Financing and Governance in Japan*. Cambridge, Mass., 2001.

Howe, Christopher R. *The Origins of Japanese Trade Supremacy*. Chicago, 1996.

Ishi, Hiromitsu. *The Japanese Tax System*. Oxford, 2001.

Ito, Takatoshi. *The Japanese Economy*. Cambridge, Mass., 1992.

Ohkawa, Kazushi, and Henry Rosovsky. *Japanese Economic Growth*. Stanford, Calif., 1973.

Ohkawa, Kazushi, and Miyohu Shinohara, eds. *Patterns of Japanese Economic Development*. New Haven, 1979.

Patrick, Hugh, ed. *Japanese Industrialization and its Social Consequences*. Berkeley, 1976.

Ramseyer, J. Mark, and Minoru Nakazato. *Japanese Law: An Economic Approach*. Chicago, 1999.

GARY R. SAXONHOUSE

Japanese Empire

By 1920, Japan's empire included formal colonies (Taiwan, Korea, and Karafuto [southern Sakhalin]), territorial lease-holds in China (Kwantung Leased Territory [Liaodong peninsula] and the South Manchuria Railway Zone), and island mandates in Micronesia. Compared to most other colonial empires, it was exceptionally compact, which made migration from the metropole relatively easy.

In the 1920s and 1930s, many Japanese Marxist historians, influenced by the Leninist theory of imperialism, argued that the driving force behind Japanese colonial expansion was the rise of "monopoly capitalism" seeking outlets for "surplus capital." Others countered that when Japan became a colonial power, in the 1890s, it was still at an early stage of capitalist development. The 1932 Comintern (international organization of Communist parties) thesis on Japan, for example, stressed the importance of "feudalistic" and "militaristic" elements in Japanese imperialism. In that view, expansion was based on a class alliance between "Asiatic feudalistic exploiters" and "capitalist investors" seeking quite different goals.

By the late 1990s, the consensus among most Western historians was that the main motive behind Japanese imperialism was concern over national security. In 1890, for example, Yamagata Aritomo, a key senior statesman and military leader, urged the acquisition of an outward "cordon of interest" (i.e., colonial possessions) to protect the country's inner "cordon of sovereignty" (i.e., the home islands). A quick look at a map of Japan's pre–World War II overseas territories reveals that the empire constituted precisely such a defensive buffer zone.

To be sure, Japan's political leaders realized that a colonial empire could serve national economic interest as well as strategic interest, but they seldom touted that as a motive for expansion. The country's economic situation nevertheless shaped the character of its colonialism. When Japan's expansion began in the 1890s, the economy was in the early stages of industrialization. A modern light-industry sector, based on cotton spinning, had taken off, but the country continued to depend on the advanced Western economies for producer durables, semimanufactures, and even modern naval vessels and other armaments. The Japanese could not have built their empire without the tacit economic or overt diplomatic support of the Western imperialist powers, especially Great Britain, with which it formed an alliance in 1902. Still, despite its backwardness vis-à-vis the Western economies, by the 1890s Japan was the only country in East Asia to have modernized institutionally, economically, and technologically. That relative advantage with respect to their East Asian neighbors enabled the Japanese to win victories in the Sino-Japanese War (1894–1895) and the Russo-Japanese War (1904–1905) and to use their victories to acquire their new colonial territories.

As colonizers the Japanese were unusually attentive to the economic development of their colonies, especially Taiwan, Korea, and the leaseholds in China. Having engineered their own economic modernization, Japanese political and business leaders had considerable experience in building the material and institutional infrastructure to sustain long-term modern economic growth. The initial goal of their colonial policy was to develop Korea and Taiwan as agricultural colonies that provided the home country with foodstuffs and industrial crops and served as a market for Japan's manufactured consumer goods. After widespread domestic popular rioting over the inflation of rice prices in 1918, the metropolitan government devoted particular attention to increasing rice production in Korea and Taiwan so as to supplement domestic supplies.

In all the colonial territories, the authorities carried out land surveys and land registration to clarify ownership rights and provide accurate assessments for new land tax systems. While some Japanese colonial settlers and metropolitan corporations acquired agricultural land in Korea and Taiwan, most of it remained under indigenous ownership. Clear-cut property rights provided incentives for both Japanese and indigenous landowners to invest in improved technology (high-yield seed stocks, commercial fertilizers, improved flood control, and irrigation systems), which was promoted by the colonial authorities. The area under cultivation did not expand greatly but agricultural output grew steadily in all parts of the empire, though slower in Korea than in Taiwan. Interestingly, the Japanese colonial authorities made no attempt to change the scale of production by introducing a plantation system or by adding new industrial crops to the crop mix. As in Japan, the basic agricultural production unit remained the small farm household, and the crops exported to Japan (rice, sugar, and soybeans) were already widely cultivated in the colonial territories.

At first, Japanese political and business leaders had no desire to encourage the growth of manufacturing enterprises in the colonies that might compete with Japanese manufactured goods. By the early 1930s, partly in response to pressure from the Japanese colonial resident community, colonial authorities worked to promote new large-scale capital-intensive mining and manufacturing enterprises in the colonies, particularly in Taiwan and Korea. They offered large metropolitan firms subsidies to encourage their investment in hydroelectric power, chemicals, metallurgy, and mineral extraction.

By the late 1930s, an increasing number of domestic firms seeking cheap labor, cheap electric power, and less government regulation built factories, particularly in Korea, which was becoming a logistical base for new expansion into Manchuria and other parts of northern China. The growth of a colonial-manufacturing sector was not broad based. It was dominated by a relatively small number of Japanese-owned and -managed firms that exported to the metropolitan market. Indigenous manufacturing for the colonial market remained in the hands of undercapitalized small or medium-size firms that relied on traditional technology.

Today, historians debate whether the colonial populations benefited from Japanese developmental policies. On the one hand, some argue that Japanese policies improved colonial economic and social conditions in the aggregate and laid the basis for postcolonial economic development. Clearly, the Japanese invested substantially in infrastructure—railroads, harbors, communication networks, roads, and the like—and statistics show measurable growth in all sectors of the colonial economies. On the other hand, many historians argue that colonial economic growth was "growth without development" or "modernization without development"; that the main beneficiaries of colonial development were the Japanese and a handful of indigenous colonial capitalists; and that most of the profits generated by development were repatriated to Japan. By contrast, the indigenous colonial populations faced systematic discrimination in the colonial capital and labor markets, and the presence of the colonial regime smothered indigenous economic initiatives. Even after colonial domination was ended with Japan's unconditional surrender to the Allies at the end of World War II in 1945—these historians argue that the psychic effects of enforced social and economic subordination distorted postcolonial growth.

BIBLIOGRAPHY

Asada, Sadao, ed. *Japan and the World, 1853–1952: A Bibliographic Guide to Japanese Scholarship in Foreign Relations*. New York, 1987.

Beasley, W. G. *Japanese Imperialism, 1894–1945*. Oxford, 1987.

Duus, Peter. *The Abacus and the Sword: The Japanese Penetration of Korea, 1895–1910*. Berkeley, 1995.

Duus, Peter, Ramon H. Myers, and Mark R. Peattie, eds. *The Japanese Informal Empire in China, 1895–1937*. Princeton, 1989.

Duus, Peter, Ramon H. Myers, and Mark R. Peattie, eds. *The Japanese Wartime Empire, 1931–1945*. Princeton, 1996.

Myers, Ramon H., and Mark R. Peattie, eds. *The Japanese Colonial Empire, 1895–1945*. Princeton, 1984.

Peattie, Mark R. *Nan'yo: The Rise and Fall of the Japanese in Micronesia, 1885–1945*. Honolulu, 1988.

Young, Louise. *Japan's Total Empire: Manchuria and the Culture of Wartime Imperialism*. Berkeley, 1998.

PETER DUUS

JEWELRY INDUSTRY. Adornment of the body is almost as old as humankind. Bones and teeth strung in pendants have been found in Europe dating back to 30,000 BCE, and beads remain one of the most common artifacts found at excavations in early settlements. The next stage in the production and development of jewelry is closely associated with goldsmithing and is influenced by two major factors: access to raw materials and the technology of gold's retrieval and processing, and the techniques employed to fashion jewelry. Its history is dominated by precious metals—principally gold—and precious gemstones, tying its manufacture and sale to the economy. Trade routes facilitated the use of a diversity of materials and the transmission of styles. The evolution of production techniques and style can be divided between jewelry made for those at the apex of society, where it was integral to status, and which, until the mid-nineteenth century, was the center of innovation, and that made by and for the rest of society. The cost of the raw materials and the high level of skills required to work jewelry have meant that its manufacture has been concentrated in cities, and that its organization has been closely regulated, both in terms of the quality of materials and workmanship and in control of the work force. Based on access to materials, levels of technological achievement and invention, and development of the market, regions taking the lead in jewelry manufacture differed over time.

The Beginnings. As early the third millennium BCE in Egypt, at Ur in southern Mesopotamia, at Troy in northern Turkey, and in Crete, gold was gathered from alluvial deposits, hammered into thin sheets, and embossed with simple patterns using bronze punches. The Egyptians incorporated stones, colored glass, and faience to achieve a vivid polychromy. They also practiced lost wax casting. By the second millennium, quartz rock was being crushed to extract the gold, and the Romans developed open-cast and tunnel mining, although the recycling of existing ware by melting was a major source of the metal. The Etruscans (700–500 BCE) refined the art of granulation for intricate surface texturing. During the Hellenistic period (330–27 BCE), gold was freely available from mines in Thrace and Persian loot and was combined with cut panels of glass, stone, and enamel. The most important constructional and decorative techniques of manufacture were thus achieved at an early date. Under imperial rule (from 27 BCE), Roman goldsmiths flourished, inventing *opus interrasile* and niello work, as gold and silver were released from military use. The goldsmiths organized into guilds, and major cities like Rome, Alexandria, and Antioch became the main centers of production, their work circulating throughout the Empire.

The Byzantine Empire saw a peak in the production of jewelry in terms of scale and complexity. It was well supplied with gold from the western Balkans, Asia Minor, and Greece, which formed the basis of trade within the empire, and it was a center for trade between east and west, circulating ivory, stones, and pearls from India, Persia, and the Persian Gulf. Production was concentrated in Alexandria and Antioch, and the Codex of Justinian (529) carefully controlled the industry. The finest materials were only available to the workshops within the palace, and a hereditary caste of skilled craftsmen worked for the emperor, his family, and the court. Fine cloisonné enamel work made Byzantine jewelry distinctve between the ninth and thirteenth centuries, although enameling technology was further developed in 1290 with *baisse-taille*, and in the 1360s with *émail en ronde bosse*.

Middle Ages and the Renaissance. In Europe, monasteries were a major source of patronage; in the period up to the early thirteenth century, many goldsmiths and jewelers were monks. For example, Theophilus wrote a treatise, *De diversis artibus*, in about 1120 that included material on precious metalworking. It is the first European writing that includes realistic detail on a wide range of technical processes. In the eleventh and twelfth centuries, as a result of urban growth, the number of secular goldsmiths grew. Workshops congregated in specific major thoroughfares like Cheapside in London, the Grand-pont in Paris, and the Ponte Vecchio in Florence to catch passing trade and to control the trade. There was a further increase in trade and urban expansion in the late thirteenth and early fourteenth centuries. It created a need to regulate both the quality of the materials and the activities of craftsmen, which resulted in the formation and control of guilds, embodied in documentation like the *Livre des métiers* drawn up in Paris in about 1268.

In the early fourteenth century, India and Persia established gem-cutting techniques that were soon acquired by European lapidaries. By 1465, Bruge had become the main center of the diamond trade. A mid-fifteenth-century painting of Saint Eloi, the patron saint of goldsmiths and jewelers, in his shop reveals a range of rings in stock as well as commissioned hollowware for sale. During the Middle Ages, Paris became the pivotal area for the most fashionable jewelry, although Venice, Cologne, and later Nuremberg offered competition. Venice and Genoa were the focal points for the importation of gems and pearls from the East. The discovery of the New World in 1492 by Columbus opened up the South American gold and silver mines to Europe, while da Gama's discovery of a sea passage to India via the Cape of Good Hope in 1498 increased the supply of diamonds. In the sixteenth century, Paris and Antwerp, and later Amsterdam, cornered most of the market for cutting and polishing diamonds. The early seventeenth century saw development in the industry focused on the cutting of stones, with the introduction of the rose cut, and at the end of the century the brilliant cut, which gave increasing fire to the stone.

Merchant bankers, especially the Fuggers in Augsberg, were a growing class that realized the lucrative combination of money making and dealing in precious stones and pearls. The names of individual jewelers from the Renaissance period survive today. They combined designing for the fine and decorative arts, supplying all manner of luxuries to the wealthy. Italians like Donatello (1386?–1466), Andrea del Verrocchio (c. 1435–1488), Sandro Botticelli (1444/5–1510), Domenico Ghirlandaio (1449–1494), and Benvenuto Cellini (1500–1571) worked for the southern Renaissance courts, while in the north the influence of Albrecht Dürer (1471–1528) and Hans Holbein (1497?–1543) were felt. Their work was quickly disseminated across Europe via the growing flood of engraved pattern books.

The seventeenth and eighteenth centuries in Europe, and particularly in France and England, saw a boom in the development of imitative materials, cheaper than their precious counterparts and ingenious in their construction. In the early part of the seventeenth century, Jaquin patented a process for making imitation pearls from blown glass painted with ground fish-scale paste and filled with wax. George Ravenscroft's new hard-lead glass, invented in the 1670s, could be faceted, and George-Frédéric Strass (1701–1773) went on to develop this into a hard-paste imitation of the diamond. Paris became the hub for imitative French paste jewelry. In the late seventeenth century, polished cut steel jewelry was introduced. It was first associated with the tourist industry around Blenheim and Woodstock, but by the 1760s had spread to London, Birmingham, and Wolverhampton. In 1732, the London toyman Christopher Pinchbeck introduced a copper and brass alloy that became a popular and cheap alternative to gold.

Specialization and Standardization. The eighteenth century offers evidence for the development of specialization within the trade, and England appears to have been at the forefront. André Rouquet in 1755 observed that "English jewelers are very expert in their profession; and the best come from abroad. Much of the trade is in the hands of specialists who supply the retailers." R. Campbell in his *The London Tradesman* (1747), an advice book to parents on the trades, remarked that the jeweler must be a judge of all manner of precious stones, must make his own molds, and forge all the metal part of his work. "He ought to be an elegant Designer, and have a quick Invention for new Patterns, not only to range the Stones in such manner as to give Lustre to one another, but to create Trade; . . . He that can furnish them [the Ladies] oftenest with the newest Whim has the best Chance for their Custom." At the same time, Birmingham began to challenge London manufacturers. Birmingham had a high subdivision of labor and high quality and could manufacture cheap jewelry under the same conditions.

The introduction of machinery, such as flatting mills in the 1720s to produce standard gauge sheet silver, fly-presses, and eventually steam power, did not affect design, but did cause a radical increase in volume and greatly reduced costs. E. H. Robinson's characterization of the late-eighteenth and early-nineteenth-century British jewelry industry as "standardisation, mass production and cheapness of production" is misleading; much was still left to hand work and the skill of trained artisans. This flexible and specialized method of manufacture adapted easily to changes in fashion and seasonal demands and was suited to the small workshops that made up the independent network of the Birmingham jewelry quarter.

Mechanization. It was in the production of chain, wire, and findings that mechanization led to the use of steam, gas, and then electrically powered single-purpose machinery, producing long runs of standardized goods. It had taken a day to link eighty-five links producing seventeen inches of chain. By machine, fifty feet of the same chain could be produced in an hour. Designs became more complex as the potential of the machine was realized. Here it was economically advantageous to invest in large machines, and large new premises were built for the purpose. The period of most rapid growth in the British jewelry trade was between 1849 and 1859 and was principally due to the discovery of gold in California in 1849 and in Australia in 1851. Silver, which had previously been imported from South America, was found in Nevada in 1865, leading to a greater use of the metal in the 1860s and 1870s. The influx of precious metals was accompanied by further development in new materials, processes, and protection of designs. In 1840, Elkington's began electrogilding, which replaced the hazardous mercury gilding. New copyright laws introduced in Britain in 1842 provided protection for new patterns and technological processes. In the 1850s, aluminum was for a short time a desirable, expensive, and prestigious new material, and following the patent of parkesine, a moldable cellulose nitrate, in 1860, plastic jewelry began to appear.

During the severe depression of 1885–1886, the British analyzed German and American competition and the trade realized the value of design in leading fashion rather than following it. Manufacturers like the Unger Brothers in New Jersey, the Gorham Corporation in Providence, Rhode Island, and manufacturers in Philadelphia ignored the path of their British counterparts and created their own fashions in advance of production. At its peak, Newark was the home to 144 manufacturing firms. An 1882 booklet for Enos Richardson and Company noted a staff of more than four hundred, housed in a seventy- by hundred-foot building. Fashion jewelry appeared at about the same time as the department store, where clothes and jewelry were sold together. A new mode of selling, not the invention of new technology, resulted in the emergence of fashion jewelry, although the jewelry did embrace new materials, like plastics. Fine and imitation jewelry continued to be manufactured in the old way, but fashion jewelry was produced in large factories, employing predominantly female labor on heavy machines, on the outskirts of the older manufacturing areas.

The Craft Reaction. Parallel to the development of mass-produced jewelry came a reaction to it, via a craft ideal based on individual and independent workshops, exploring cheaper materials like silver and semiprecious stones rather than gold and diamonds. Workmanship was valued more than the cost of materials. One of the most influential members of this movement, both at home and abroad, was the architect C. R. Ashbee (1863–1942), who set up the Guild of Handicraft in 1888, first in London, then transferring to Gloucestershire in 1902, where young men were trained to design and make individual pieces of jewelry and metalwork. Liberty's exploited the popularity of this work and further popularized it by retailing machine-made versions. In Munich the Darmstadt colony, founded in 1899, offered purpose-built houses for artisans and their families, but designers like Peter Behrens (1869–1940) and Josef Olbrich (1867–1908) created mass-produced as well as unique pieces. At the same time in Germany, *Jugendstil* was commercial from the start, adapted to limited production. Machine-made components were assembled in already existing factories at Pfozheim, Frankfurt, Schwabish Gmund, and Hanau. The products were small, unlike French and Belgian work, light, unlike British and Danish pieces, and anonymous, unlike any other country's. Naum Slutsky (1894–1965) explored design for machine production within the Bauhaus for jewelry in chromium-plated brass and silver.

World War II had an effect on the jewelry trade when craftsmen were conscripted and factories bombed, and materials were scarce because trade was disrupted and materials diverted to the armament industry. American manufacturers were less affected and developed more swiftly as a result. By the 1950s, fashion or costume jewelry had its own trade magazines, and had separated itself from the influence of high-quality jewelry. It had an independent market, where fashion overrode the problems of seasonal fluctuation in trade. The most recent development in jewelry design is the result of training rather than issues connected with materials and the economy. The 1960s witnessed an accelerated polarization between craft and commercial jewelry. A new generation of confident art-school-trained designers challenged the very idea of what jewelry is, crossing the boundaries between sculpture, clothing, and performance art, even reclaiming rubbish to turn it into jewelry. Their work is displayed in galleries like Electrum, opened in London in 1971, and Gallery Ra, opened in Amsterdam in 1976. These works exist alongside the traditional conservative designs sold in the high-end retail stores.

BIBLIOGRAPHY

Bury, Shirley. *Jewellery, 1789–1910: The International Era*. Woodbridge, 1991.

Cherry, John. *Medieval Craftsmen: Goldsmiths*. London, 1992.

Clifford, Anne. *Cut Steel and Berlin Iron Jewellery*. London, 1971.

Dietz, U. G., et al. *The Glitter and the Gold: Fashioning America's Jewels*. Newark, 1997.

Dormer P., and R. Turner. *The New Jewelry Trends and Traditions*. London, 1985.

Fales, Martha Gandy. *Jewelry in America, 1600–1900*. Woodbridge, N.J., 1995.

Gere, Charlotte. *European and American Jewellery, 1830–1914*. London, 1975.

Hughes, Graham. *Modern Jewelry: An International Survey, 1890–1963*. London, 1963.

Ogden, J., et al. *Jewellery, Makers, Motifs, History, Technology*. London, 1989.

Ogden, J. *Jewellery of the Ancient World*. London, 1982.

Phillips, Clare. *Jewelry, From Antiquity to the Present*. London, 1996.

Scarisbrick, Diana. *Jewellery in Britain, 1066–1837: A Documentary, Social, Literary, and Artistic Survey*. Norwich, 1994.

Wilson, Shelagh. *Art into Industry: the Birmingham Experiment: The Attempt to Unify Art with Manufacturing in the Birmingham Jewellery Trade, 1860–1914*. Birmingham, 1991.

HELEN CLIFFORD

JEWISH DIASPORA. Jewish Diaspora refers to the geographical dispersion of the Jews when, between 597 and 586 BCE, the Assyrian king Nebuchadrezzar conquered the kingdom of Judah, destroyed Solomon's Temple in Jerusalem, and deported many Jews to Babylon. Another group of Jews fled to Egypt, where they settled in the Nile Delta. Thus from 597 BCE onward there were three distinct groups of Hebrews: a group in Babylon and other parts of the Middle East, a group in Judaea, and another group in Egypt. The Persian conqueror Cyrus the Great permitted the Jews to return to their homeland in 538 BCE. Some Jews returned to Judaea, whereas part of the Jewish community voluntarily remained in Babylon.

The other major dispersion of Jews occurred after the revolts against the Roman Empire in the first and second centuries CE. The Great Revolt of 66–70 CE culminated in 70 CE with the destruction of the Second Temple in Jerusalem. About sixty years later another major revolt (the Bar Kokhba Revolt) broke out first in Palestine and then in Egypt. The outcome of these revolts was the end of Jewish political authority in Israel until 1948. After the revolts Jewish history coincides with the history of the Diaspora as the Jews spread over Africa, Asia, Europe, and later the Americas. Nowadays Jewish Diaspora refers to all the Jewish communities scattered in the world outside present-day Israel.

Despite the unique characteristics each Jewish community has displayed across space and time, two economic and demographic features represent the distinctive marks of the entire Jewish Diaspora. First, Jews have been a minority in almost any of the places in which they have lived. Second, since the Middle Ages, Jews have been engaged mainly in urban, skilled occupations, such as crafts, trade, finance, and the medical profession.

Population. The Jewish population, which grew from the biblical period (about 1.5 million people) to the classical period (about 4.5 million people), decreased significantly in both absolute and relative terms starting from the later centuries of the Roman Empire. Of the 4.5 million Jews living in the classical period, half were probably Jews by descent, and the rest were converted pagans. Conversions to Judaism occurred in the first century CE and then stopped at the end of the second century, when Christianity started emerging as the dominant religion. For the Jews in the Roman Empire, the key events were the two rebellions against Rome described above. The rebellions and subsequent repressions caused the deaths of thousands of Jews in both Palestine and Egypt.

The world Jewish population greatly decreased from 2.5 million in the third century to about 1–1.5 million on the verge of the Arab expansion. Jews became few, spread all around the former Roman Empire, and migrated eastward to the Persian Empire and especially to Babylon. The center in Egypt vanished, and Jews became a minority in Palestine also. The third and fourth centuries witnessed the economic decline of Palestine and the emergence of Babylon under the Sassanian regime as the main economic and religious center for Jews.

The Arab expansion in the seventh century led Babylonian Jews to migrate to Palestine, northern Africa, and southern Europe. In the ninth and tenth centuries the decline of the Baghdad caliphate and the revival of urban centers in Europe increased the stream of Jews from the Near and Middle East to western Europe. Also from the fourth century to the tenth century Jews migrated from Italy and southern France and established the first group of Ashkenazic Jewry in Northeast France and Northwest Germany. During the Muslim expansion until the Middle Ages, the Jewish population remained at the level attained during the era of the Talmud (fourth to sixth centuries). Describing his travels, the writer Benjamin of Tudela reported that in the twelfth century the world Jewish population was about 1.2 million. More than 70 percent of the world Jewry still lived in Mesopotamia and Persia. The movement to the West and Europe accelerated in the next centuries.

The declining trend of the Jewish population continued during the Middle Ages and early modern times. In the fifteenth century there were fewer than 300,000 Jews in Europe (mainly in Spain and some in Italy), and fewer than 1 million in the rest of the world. From the eleventh century to the sixteenth century Ashkenazic Jews moved from western to eastern Europe. Around 1550 there was no Jew

JEWISH DIASPORA. Group of Jewish children with a teacher in Samarkand, Uzbekistan, early 1900s. (Sergei Mikhailovich Prokudin-Gorskii Collection/Prints and Photographs Division, Library of Congress)

lawfully resident in England or France, the Netherlands, Spain, Portugal, and the Scandinavian countries. At this time most European Jews lived in Poland and some in Italy. Even considering the large settlements under Muslim rule, the total number of Jews was rapidly declining to the lowest level of the history of the Diaspora.

In 1650, when the population of Europe was 100 million (one-fifth of the world population), there were 650,000 Jews in Europe. Most of them lived in eastern Europe (especially in Poland), while there were only a few thousand concentrated in western Europe (some German cities, Austria, Bohemia, Northern and central Italy, Avignon and Provence, and Holland). There were 250,000 Jews in Turkey and Egypt and 250,000 in the rest of the world. At the end of the eighteenth century Jews numbered between 2 and 2.5 million. After 1848 the size of the Jewish population increased substantially. Compared to a world population of more than a billion, there were about 32 million Jews in the world. The increasing trend was brought to a sudden and dramatic end with the massacres during the Holocaust in World War II. Of the estimated 14 million Jews in the world today, about 4 million reside in Israel, about 4.5 million in the United States, and about 2.2 million in Russia, Ukraine, and other republics formerly of the Soviet Union.

Occupations. The second half of the first millennium CE is the period when the Jews moved away from agricultural into urban occupations. Throughout the first millennium most of the world population lived in villages and were engaged in agriculture. In biblical times and during the classical period, Jews like the rest of the population were mainly farmers. Although in Jerusalem, Rome, Alexandria, and Babylon some Jews held nonagricultural occupations, up to the time when the Mishnah was compiled around the beginning of the third century, the occupation of almost all Jews in both Palestine (where they were a majority) and in the Diaspora (where they were a minority) remained farming.

The transition of Jews from agriculture to crafts, trade, and moneylending started in the Talmudic period. Agriculture remained the main occupation of Jews living in numerous countries. Yet in Palestine and Babylonia agriculture became less and less important as a source of income and wealth for Jews after 200 CE. Most Jews abandoning agriculture moved into the towns and became small shopkeepers and artisans in the tanning, linen, silk, and dyeing industries; glassware making; and moneylending. Some Jews became wealthy traders and merchants. For example, in Alexandria, which was the center of trade between the Far East and the Western world, Jewish traders became organized in a powerful guild that obtained privileges from the Christian emperors.

The key period of urbanization occurred in Islam during the Abassides rulers from the eighth century to the tenth century. Many cities developed, and Baghdad became the main center. A small proportion of the Jewish population remained engaged in farming in both Babylon and Palestine. Urbanization in the Muslim Empire led Jews to migrate from country to country and from small villages to cities. At the end of the eighth century the Jewish population in the Muslim regions was almost entirely urban.

The movement of the Jews to the cities brought to a full-fledged stage their transition away from agriculture into urban and skilled occupations. Jews were attracted to many occupations within the cities, including handicrafts, tanning, dying, shipbuilding, corn and cattle dealing, bookselling, and tax farming. Jews were also engaged in long-distance trade. In the ninth century a Muslim writer mentioned Jewish traders who, from southern France, traveled to Islamic lands and then went to India and China. Jews were also involved in moneylending and became bankers to the rulers.

By the time Benjamin of Tudela wrote in the twelfth century, the transition of Jews away from agriculture into urban occupations was almost complete. Almost all Jews were farmers in the first century CE. Ten centuries later almost all Jews were urban dwellers with skilled occupations, whereas the rest of the population remained engaged mainly in agriculture. The selection of Jews into high-skill urban occupations continued and became stronger in the Middle Ages and in later centuries. In many western and, later, eastern European countries, Jews became engaged in moneylending, the diamond industry, trade, and the medical profession. These urban, skilled occupations remained the distinctive marks of the Jews throughout history.

In those countries with the largest Jewish communities in the nineteenth and twentieth centuries (the United States, the Soviet Union, eastern Europe, and Israel), independently of the proportion of Jews to the local population, a negligible percentage of Jews was employed in agriculture; most Jews were engaged in trade and finance and next in industry and handicrafts. For example, in Poland in 1931, 96 percent of the Jews was engaged in nonagricultural occupations, whereas the percentage dropped to 47 for non-Jews.

Different explanations have been proposed to account for the occupational specialization of the Jews in the Diaspora into urban, skilled occupations, such as crafts, trade, and finance. A common view among scholars, prominently advanced by Cecil Roth (1938), maintains that the occupational choice of the Jews was mainly the outcome of

restrictions and prohibitions. According to this argument, from the Middle Ages until modern times Jews did not engage in agricultural occupations because they were prohibited from owning land. Moreover guilds' regulations excluded nonmembers, such as Jews, from the occupations regulated by the guilds. Moneylending, the medical profession, and the diamond industry were the few occupations in which Jews were allowed to engage.

Consistent with the argument based on prohibitions and persecutions but with a different twist, other scholars, such as Werner Sombart (1913) and Reuven Brenner and Nicholas M. Kiefer (1981), have maintained that the Jews, like the members of other persecuted diasporas, preferred to invest in human rather than physical capital because the former is portable and cannot be expropriated. Thus the selection of the Jews into trade and finance was the outcome of the investment in human capital made by the Jews as members of a diaspora.

Salo Wittmayer Baron, Haim Hillel Ben-Sasson, and Moshe Gil advanced two explanations for the occupational selection of Jews into urban, skilled occupations. First, high taxes in agriculture and declining yields had already made agriculture unprofitable in the late Roman Empire. Later the new Arab and Muslim rulers ruined the agriculture of Babylonia by taxing according to area, instead of yield, and by neglecting the irrigation network during the early years of the conquest. Moreover the land tax levied on non-Muslim peasants weighed heavily on Jewish farmers. The outcome was the abandonment by Jews of rural areas and the movement into urban occupations. Second, increasing urbanization occurring during the Islamic period led Jews to move to the newly established cities.

A different theory—the economics of small minorities—has been proposed by the economist Simon Kuznets (1960). Starting from the assumption that for noneconomic reasons (that is, religious identity) a minority group has distinctive cultural characteristics within a larger population, Kuznets argues that the noneconomic goal of maintaining cohesion and group identity can lead minority members to prefer to be concentrated in selected industries and selected occupations, with the consequence of ending up living in cities where these occupations are available. Before Kuznets, Max Weber (1952) had claimed that the Jews voluntarily chose to segregate and to become an urban population in order to maintain their ritualistic correctness, dietary prescriptions, and Sabbath rules, which would have been impossible to follow in rural areas.

Avner Greif (1989) has linked the successful economic performance of the Jewish Diaspora in trade and commercial activities to the mutual pooling of resources, common linguistic skills, and the network of personal and family relations combined with the use of community sanctions, which reduced transaction costs. His study focuses on the

Maghribi traders, the Jewish merchants engaged in long-distance trade in the Mediterranean in the High Middle Ages. According to Greif's argument, these Jewish traders succeeded because, as a small but distinctive minority, they could reduce opportunistic behavior by fellow members by effectively excluding or ostracizing members who deviated from mutually agreed norms of economic behavior or abused the trust of other members of the Diaspora. Once trust existed among members of a small group and once cooperative norms have been established, members of the Jewish Diaspora were well equipped to take over long-distance trade because they could find kinspeople at long distances who they knew would not behave opportunistically.

BIBLIOGRAPHY

Ayal, Eliezer B., and Barry R. Chiswick. "The Economics of the Diaspora Revisted." *Economic Development and Cultural Change* 31 (1983), 861–875.

Baer, Yitzhak. *A History of the Jews in Christian Spain*. 2 vols. Philadelphia, 1966.

Baron, Salo Wittmayer. *A Social and Religious History of the Jews*. 2d ed. New York, 1952. A fundamental work on Jewish history with an impressive bibliography. The first edition, 1937, is also helpful.

Benjamin of Tudela. *Sefer Massa 'ot* (c. 1170) (The Itinerary of Benjamin of Tudela). Edited by M. N. Adler. London, 1907.

Ben-Sasson, Haim Hillel, ed. *A History of the Jewish People*. Cambridge, Mass., 1976. An excellent collection of contributions by Haim Hillel Ben-Sasson, Abraham Malamat, Shmuel Safrai, and Hayim Tadmor.

Brenner, Reuven, and Nicholas M. Kiefer. "The Economics of the Diaspora: Discrimination and Occupational Structure."*Economic Development and Cultural Change* 29 (April 1981), 517–534.

Chiswick, Carmel Ullman. "The Economics of Jewish Continuity." *Contemporary Jewry* 20 (1999), 30–56.

Cohen, Shaye J. D., and Ernest S. Frerichs, eds. *Diasporas in Antiquity*. Atlanta, 1993.

DellaPergola, Sergio. "Some Fundamentals of Jewish Demographic History." In *Papers in Jewish Demography 1997, Jewish Population Studies* 29, edited by Sergio DellaPergola and Judith Even, pp. 11–33. Jerusalem, 2001. An article by one of the leading Jewish demographers who presents the latest information on the demographic history of the Jews across two millennia.

Epstein, Mark Alan. *The Ottoman Jewish Communities*. Freiburg, 1980.

Finkelstein, Louis, ed. *The Jews: Their History, Culture, and Religion*. 2 vols. Philadelphia, 1960. An excellent collection of contributions on various aspects of Jewish economic, social, and religious history by Itzhak Ben-Zvi, Uriah Zevi Engleman, Judah Goldin, Simon Greenberg, Israel Halpern, Simon Kuznets, Julius B. Maller, and Nathan Reich.

Fuchs, Daniel, and Harold A. Sevener. *From Bondage to Freedom: A Survey of Jewish History from the Babylonian Captivity to the Coming of the Messiah*. Neptune, N.J., 1995.

Gampel, Benjamin, ed. *Crisis and Creativity in the Sephardic World: 1391–1648*. New York, 1997.

Gil, Moshe. *A History of Palestine, 634–1099*. Cambridge, 1992. A fundamental work on Jewish history based on an impressive set of primary sources.

Goitein, Shlomo D. *A Mediterranean Society: The Jewish Communities of the Arab World as Portrayed in the Documents of the Cairo Geniza*. Berkeley, 1967–1983. A fundamental work on Jewish history based on an impressive set of primary sources.

Goodman, Martin. *Jews in a Graeco-Roman World*. Oxford, 1998.

Grayzel, Solomon. *A History of the Jews: From the Babylonian Exile to the Establishment of Israel*. Philadelphia, 1965.

Greif, Avner. "Reputation and Coalitions in Medieval Trade: Evidence on the Maghribi Traders." *Journal of Economic History* 49.4 (December 1989), 857–882.

Gross, Nachum, ed. *Economic History of the Jews*. New York, 1975.

Johnson, Paul. *A History of the Jews*. New York, 1987.

Katz, Jacob. *Exclusiveness and Tolerance: Studies in Jewish-Gentile Relations in Medieval and Modern Times*. Westport, Conn., 1980.

Katz, Jacob. *Tradition and Crisis: Jewish Society at the End of the Middle Ages*. New York, 1993.

Katz, Steven T. *Holocaust in Historical Context*. Oxford, 1994.

Kuznets, Simon. "Economic Structure and Life of the Jews." In *The Jews: Their History, Culture, and Religion*, edited by Louis Finkelstein, vol. 2, pp. 1597–1666. New York, 1960. His work documents the economic characteristics of the Jewish Diaspora in the late nineteenth century and the early twentieth century.

Lestschinsky, Jacob. "Economic and Social Development of the Jewish People." In *The Jewish People, Past and Present*, vol. 1. New York, 1946.

Lewis, Bernard. *Studies in Classical and Ottoman Islam, 7th–16th Centuries*. London, 1976.

Mann, Jacob. *The Jews in Egypt and in Palestine under the Fatimid Caliphs*. New York, 1970.

Neusner, Jacob. *A History of the Jews in Babylonia*. 5 vols. Leiden, 1965–1970.

Neusner, Jacob, ed. *Origins of Judaism*, vol. 7, *History of the Jews in the Second Century of the Common Era*. New York and London, 1990.

Neusner, Jacob, ed. *Origins of Judaism*, vol. 8, *History of the Jews in the Second through Seventh Centuries of the Common Era*. New York and London, 1990.

Raphael, Chaim. *The Road from Babylon: The Story of Sephardi and Oriental Jews*. New York, 1985.

Roth, Cecil. *The Jewish Contribution to Civilisation*. London, 1938. A classical work by one of the most prominent scholars of Jewish history.

Roth, Cecil. *A History of the Marranos*. New York, 1975.

Safrai, Shmuel, and Menahem Stern, eds. *The Jewish People in the First Century: Historical Geography, Political History, Social, Cultural, and Religious Life and Institutions*. 2 vols. Assen, 1974–1976. Contains excellent contributions by Shimon Applebaum, Shmuel Safrai, and Menahem Stern.

Safrai, Ze'ev. *The Economy of Roman Palestine*. London and New York, 1994.

Shatzmiller, Joseph. *Shylock Reconsidered: Jews, Money Lending, and Medieval Society*. Berkeley, 1990.

Shmuelevitz, Aryeh. *The Jews of the Ottoman Empire in the Late Fifteenth and the Sixteenth Centuries: Administrative, Economic, Legal, and Social Relations as Reflected in the Responsa*. Leiden, 1984.

Sombart, Werner. *The Jews and Modern Capitalism*. Glencoe, Ill., 1913. First edition 1911.

Stow, Kenneth R. *Alienated Minority: The Jews of Medieval Latin Europe*. Cambridge, 1992.

Weber, Max. *Ancient Judaism*. Translated and edited by Hans H. Gerth and Don Martindale. Glencoe, Ill. 1952. First edition in German in 1917.

MARISTELLA BOTTICINI

JOINT-STOCK TRADING COMPANIES. One of the features of the growth of seventeenth-century overseas trade was the range of institutional experimentation in how to organize such trade. Institutional form included regulated companies, franchising arrangements, private traders, and joint-stock chartered companies. By the end of the seventeenth century the joint-stock trading company had emerged as a major institutional arrangement for the conduct of long-distance trade. The most noted of these companies were the British and Dutch East India Companies, but such companies emerged in most European countries to conduct trade across the globe. As chartered companies, these firms often have been seen as inefficient, rent-seeking institutions, but they also have been hailed as efficient institutional arrangements for the conduct of long-distance trade.

Evolution of Business Form. Joint-stock trading companies emerged as a unique business form in the middle of the sixteenth century, although not until the last quarter of the seventeenth did they achieve their mature form. In looking at the joint-stock company as a business arrangement, it is possible to trace elements from the medieval *commenda* and *societas* and from the medieval guilds. From the *commenda* and *societas* comes the concept of distribution of shares among parties involved in overseas trade; from the medieval guilds comes the concept of perpetual succession or perpetual life for an organization itself.

These ideas of course evolved and changed in the intervening centuries. The basic problem, however, remains the same, that is, how to conduct overseas trade if the owner cannot travel with his or her goods. One way to handle the problem was the regulated company, of which the Staplers and the Merchant Adventures are classic examples. In this instance the company had a perpetual life and provided corporate governance. Merchants belonged to the company, and the company set the rules on how the merchants would conduct their business, ideas that carry over from the guild structure. The regulated company gained capital through the payment of levies and fees by individual merchants. Yet within this structure each member operated his or her business independently of the other members and remained a member as long as he or she observed the company's rules. In effect these regulated companies provided a range of shipping and infrastructure services in the foreign locations. As many of the trading locations were in close geographical proximity to the home ports, the system worked well in reducing the overhead costs for member merchants.

As trade moved to more distant areas, the organization of the regulated company arrangement proved less useful. More distant trade meant longer voyage time, larger ships, and overall greater commitment of capital. Indeed distance alone meant an individual merchant's capital in trade goods could be tied up for years or the costs of conducting such a trade could be significantly greater than available personal capital. The resolution was the joint-stock trading company. As in the regulated company, the trading company itself had a perpetual life and a governance form. However, rather than each merchant placing his or her own cargo in the company's vessel, as would be the case in a regulated company, each merchant now owned a share in the company. In essence the merchant could diversify his or her capital across a number of such investments and so minimize the personal costs or risks of long-distance trade.

From the middle of the sixteenth century to the end of the seventeenth century, there is an evolution in terms of the nature of the shares individuals held, in the governance structure of the company and voting rights, and in the generation of limited liability. In the earliest joint-stock trading companies, such as the Russia Company, merchants owned shares in a particular voyage. Once the ship returned and the cargo sold, the profits were disbursed among the shareholders in that voyage. So now merchants jointly owned the cargo rather than each having a share of cargo space as in the regulated company. While such a system worked well to reduce an individual's risk for that voyage, such a system provided no capital for the ongoing life of the company. To provide ongoing capital required a further development, and in the course of the seventeenth century shares came to be vested in the company itself rather than the voyage. With this step profits could be reinvested in the company or distributed as dividends.

Although conceptually simple, the general idea of a share and of the capitalized value of the company changed over time. When the British East India Company was chartered in 1600, rather than the number of shares being determinate and the amount paid per person indeterminate, the nominal value of a share was fixed and the amount of total capital paid indeterminate. Fifty years later the United Joint-Stock East India Company charter generated the form now recognized, in which the size of capitalization and the nominal value of the shares are given.

The preamble of the 1650 East India constitution specifies voting rights in terms of shareholding. In this charter arrangement, one vote was awarded for each £500 of stock held, where stock was denominated in £100 units. In its charter of 1672 the Royal African Company specified one vote for each £100 share. By 1714, with increases in the size of the capital stock, the voting rights were such that each £500 of stock commanded one vote to a maximum of five votes. For the Hudson's Bay Company, chartered in 1670, the voting rights started at £100 of stock per vote. In each of these companies shareholders had to hold specified larger blocks of shares to be elected to the governing committees. As the capitalization of these companies increased, so too did the value of the shareholdings required for voting and for election to company office.

Relationship with the Government. Important for the history of these companies and for those individuals who wanted to invest in these long-distance trades is the issue of liability. In the regulated company the merchant's liability was limited to the size of the cargo he or she placed in the company vessel, which he or she could ensure. With joint-stock companies, where the shareholders owned the company, the issue of liability became more pressing. When a company experienced losses, the question arose as to who or how those losses would be covered. In 1662 Parliament passed 14 Car. II c 24, which created a form of limited liability for incorporated joint-stock companies in favor of shareholders. In effect, in the event of bankruptcy of the company, a shareholder was only liable for the unpaid amount on his or her shares. Thus by the last quarter of the seventeenth century England arrived at the modern form of the joint-stock company—limited liability, share ownership, voting rights, and well-defined governance structures. As a result these shares became viable assets in their own right, liquid and easily transferable, giving rise to a capital market in joint-stock trading company shares.

The Dutch joint-stock companies achieved these same features by a somewhat different route. When the Dutch East India Company was formed in 1602, both the number and the nominal value of its shares were fixed. But the company's initial charter foresaw a general liquidation after twenty-one years. Well before that date it became clear to the company directors that its capital should be permanent and that shareholders desiring to withdraw their capital should sell their shares on the stock exchange. When the Dutch West India Company was organized in 1621, both Dutch companies were fully developed joint-stock companies.

Seventeenth-century joint-stock companies were organized to initiate trade into new and distant markets for European traders. The capital requirements necessary for such an uncertain trade and the need for ongoing investment was conducive to the emergence of the joint-stock structure. Yet most of these companies received charters from their respective governments. In England companies could receive a charter from either the monarchy or Parliament. A charter gave the company defined rights over the trade, such as being the sole English or French or Dutch company to trade in the region or rights to sell the product in the respective company. One strand of the literature sees these charters as making joint-stock companies monopolies with all the inherent issues. Another strand in the literature sees these charters as equivalent to patents, wherein the new branch of foreign trade was akin to an invention and as such was entitled to some monopoly control for a number of years to encourage exploration and the opening of trade. Discussion of both views of the charter stem back to contemporary debates. While a government could grant a charter to a domestic joint-stock company giving it sole rights of trade, for example, along the west coast of Africa, in India, or in Hudson Bay, that company faced competition in the foreign market from other chartered companies and smugglers from all nations. In the domestic market the exact level of monopoly-pricing control generated by these charters is also unclear. Commodities were sold by auction, by the candle. The Hudson's Bay Company was required to sell its furs in small lots and was not allowed to sell between auctions at a price lower than the lowest prevailing auction price. While companies could withhold goods from sale, these companies had to pay import tariffs on all goods brought into the country. Thus goods purchased in Africa, India, or Hudson Bay were unlikely to be left sitting in warehouses in London, Amsterdam, or La Rochelle.

History of Various Companies. Through the seventeenth century and into the eighteenth century joint-stock trading companies dominated most European trade with non-European regions. While the Dutch and British East India Companies come to mind most immediately, such companies were set up in all European countries involved in these trades.

In England the most notable were the Muscovy or Russia Company, chartered in 1555 and disbanded in 1746; the East India Company, chartered initially in 1600, chartered again in 1650, chartered with the amalgamation of the old and new East India Companies in 1709, and wound up in 1858; the Hudson's Bay Company, chartered in 1670 and still in operation today; the Royal African company, chartered in 1672 and dissolved in 1757. The Dutch East India Company or Vereenigde Oost-Indische Compagnie (VOC) was formed in 1602 by the States General, and the Dutch West India Company or West-Indische Compagnie (WIC), was formed in 1621. The WIC charter was renewed every thirty years. Its market share was decisively curtailed with the renewal of its charter in 1730, although it went through two more renewal cycles. The French organized long-distance trade through the Compagnie des Indes Occidental from 1664 to 1674; the Compagnie des Indes Orientales, which after 1720 became known as La Compagnie Française des Indes (1664–1761); and the Compagnie de Senegale, founded in 1672, the same year as the English Royal African Company. Denmark organized a succession of East India Companies beginning in 1616, and the first expedition of the Swedish East India Company took place in 1732.

These companies traded to virtually every known corner of the globe, including Russia, India, Indonesia, Japan, Africa, the West Indies, South America, and the subarctic and Arctic regions of Canada. In many cases the trade conducted was a barter trade. Commodities purchased in Europe were carried to Russia, Africa, Canada, India, or

JOINT-STOCK COMPANIES. Seals used by the Dutch East India Company (VOC) between 1602 and 1799. (© Rijksmuseum-Stichting Amsterdam)

Indonesia, where they were exchanged for commodities that were then sold to European consumers. In the Russian, African, and Canadian trade, the companies purchased manufactured goods in Europe to exchange for primary products in the respective areas. Although cloth was the most important item traded by the Russia Company, it also exchanged a large number of other commodities, such as tin, pewter, lead, copper, wine, spices, sugar, and fruits. In exchange the company brought cordage, fish, hemp, tallow, tar, and train oil back to England for resale.

The Hudson's Bay Company also carried a wide range of European commodities, such as files, flints, guns, hatchets, powder, shot, twine, beads, blankets, brandy, kettles, baize, buttons, lace, hats, needles, and tobacco, to its posts on Hudson Bay. These commodities were exchanged for pelts and furs, such as beaver, musquash, fox, lynx, bear, and squirrel, which were sold by auction in London. The Royal African Company carried textiles, iron and copper bars, East India Company textiles and cowry shells, and pewter to the west coast of Africa, where they were sold. The company purchased primary products, such as ivory, gold, malaguetta, and redwood, which were then sold by auction in London. The company also purchased slaves, although in the seventeenth century slaves made up less than 40 percent of the trade. The slaves were transported to the West Indies, where they were sold and the Royal African Company was paid in bullion, bills of exchange, or sugar.

In contrast to companies trading to Africa, Russia, or the Americas, the East India Companies conducted their trade in a region where they formed only a small part of an already existing large trade. The most important item carried by these companies from Europe to the East Indies was silver bullion purchased either in Amsterdam, Cadiz, or Seville. In India and Indonesia these companies purchased textiles, spices, chinaware, tea, and cowry shells, which were then sold in Europe. The trip from Europe to Indonesia and back could take upward of two years.

By the end of the seventeenth century, because of the activities of the joint-stock trading companies, most regions of the globe were connected through interdependent patterns of trade. The beads purchased by Native Americans came from Venice and China, while the tobacco came from Brazil. The pelts purchased in Canada were transformed into hats that were sold as far afield as South America. In the African trade the cowry shells that served as local currency for some regions were purchased in London at the East India Company sales. The bullion used in the East India trade came from the Americas. The manufactured goods carried to these regions came from all over Europe. Because commodities were carried between regions, consumers in all parts of the world took part in the consumer revolution of the eighteenth century.

As with any sector, industry, or organizational form, some joint-stock trading companies were more successful than others. If success is measured by survivorship, the Hudson's Bay Company, still in existence today, has experienced success. The British East India Company operated for over 250 years. Indeed one could argue that many of the agency houses that came into existence after 1858 were the direct descendants of the East India Company branch offices. In the African trade, once the trade routes were established and the goods for the trade were defined, the joint-stock companies were superceded by independent private traders, and the monopoly rights of the African companies were extinguished.

BIBLIOGRAPHY

Blusse, Leonard, and Femme Gaastra, eds. *Companies and Trade: Essays on Overseas Trading Companies during the Ancien Régime.* Hingham, Mass., 1981.

Bowen, H. V. *Elites, Enterprise and the Making of British Overseas Empire, 1688–1775.* New York, 1996.

Carlos, Ann M., and Jamie Kruse. "The Decline of the Royal African Company: Fringe Firms and the Role of the Charter." *Economic History Review* 49.2 (1996), 295–317.

Carlos, Ann M., and Stephen Nicholas. "Giants of an Earlier Capitalism: The Early Chartered Companies as an Analogue of the Modern Multinational." *Business History Review* 26.3 (1988), 398–419.

Carlos, Ann M., and Stephen Nicholas. "Agency Problems in Early Chartered Companies: The Case of the Hudson's Bay Company." *Journal of Economic History* 50.4 (1990), 853–875.

Carlos, Ann M., and Stephen Nicholas. "Theory and History: Seventeenth Century Joint-Stock Chartered Trading Companies." *Journal of Economic History* 56.4 (1996), 916–924.

Carlos, Ann M., Jennifer Key, and Jill Dupree. "Learning and the Creation of Stock-Market Institutions: Evidence from the Hudson's Bay and Royal African Companies, 1670–1700." *Journal of Economic History* 58.2 (1998), 318–344.

Chaudhuri, K. *The Trading World of Asia and the English East India Company, 1660–1760.* New York, 1978.

Davies, K. G. *The Royal African Company.* London, 1957.

Eltis, D. "The Relative Importance of Slaves in the Atlantic Trade of Seventeenth Century Africa." *Journal of African History* 35 (1994), 337–349.

Glamann, K. *Dutch-Asiatic Trade, 1620–1740.* Hague, 1982.

Jones, S. R. H., and Simon P. Ville. "Efficient Transactors or Rent-Seeking Monopolists? The Rationale for Early Chartered Trading Companies." *Journal of Economic History* 56.4 (1996), 898–915.

Prakash, O. *The Dutch East India Company and the Economy of Bengal, 1630–1720.* Princeton, 1985.

Rich, E. E. *Hudson's Bay Company, 1670–1870.* 3 vols. New York, 1960.

Scott, Robert William. *The Constitution and Finance of English, Scottish and Irish Joint-Stock Companies to 1720.* 3 vols. New York, 1951.

Willan, T. S. *The Early History of the Russia Company.* New York, 1956.

ANN CARLOS

JOURNEYMEN. The first references to the journeyman (French *compagnon*, German *Gesell*, Italian *lavorante*) as a skilled laborer employed by a master craftsman by the day (Fr. *journée*) appear in European towns in the late thirteenth and early fourteenth centuries, as a by-product of the rapid increase in craft specialization during the period preceding the Black Death (1348–1350). Despite their importance to the everyday functioning of craft-based economies, however, journeymen are barely mentioned in craft legislation and emerge from the shadows chiefly at times of conflict with craft masters. Although

journeymen were not restricted to legally incorporated crafts, most action occurred within craft guilds because corporate status gave journeymen a legal basis for defending their interests.

By the fourteenth century, most journeymen would have concluded a formal apprenticeship that gave them the right to become full-time masters. In practice, however, most journeymen remained so all their lives, but not because of restrictions of access to corporations and the mastership (via entry fees and exams), as most premodern crafts were quite open to outside recruitment. Rather, craft occupations requiring major capital investments offered journeymen little prospect of becoming independent masters except on the periphery of the trade, living off subcontracting work under poorly paid and inflexible conditions. The later-medieval development of a segmented labor market, divided between a core of sedentary, married men, who were taught the innermost secrets of the trade, and a periphery of young, unmarried, mobile journeymen, who moved between shops, towns, and even occupations, placed additional restrictions on their social and economic mobility.

Although some journeymen associations began as religious confraternities, and others overcame restrictions on formal organization by posing as mutual aid societies, mutual financial aid was seldom their main function, as reflected by the fact that most countries outlawed worker associations as "confederacies and conspiracies" (see the 1563 English Statute of Artificers) against craft masters. Acting through strikes, the withdrawal of labor, and sometimes violence, journeymen based their claims upon their "property of skill," defined as a capacity to coordinate complex activities in the workplace that allowed them to emphasize the collective and cooperative nature of their work. The main sources of friction with masters were attempts to reduce piece rates, by not keeping them in step with living costs or in response to falling demand; the use of cheap apprentice labor; and the introduction of technology that reduced employment or devalued the journeymen's human capital. Concerns about deskilling and about the use of cheaper, less skilled labor often were shared by the poorer small masters, an overlap in interests that gave rise to alliances between the small masters and the journeymen against the larger, wealthier craftsmen. Whereas the journeymen's desire to control access to the labor market became a formal issue mainly during trade downturns, at other times more informal closed-shop arrangements might apply, based on the masters' need to hold on to a core of skilled labor through cyclical downturns.

Although collective action by journeymen was endemic to premodern crafts, historians' propensity to view journeymen associations as precursors of modern trade unions should be resisted; for rather than bargaining and class struggle, their most salient function seems to have been to organize and coordinate journeyman tramping. Itinerant journeymen moving from towns to town in search of work became a common feature in the period of labor scarcity that followed the Black Death, and the practice continued to expand in several European countries when populations recovered. During the sixteenth century, journeyman tramping became partially institutionalized, most notably in German-speaking lands, where it was known as *Gesellenwanderung* or *Wanderzwang*, and to a lesser extent in France, where the eighteenth-century *compagnonnages* created a considerable political stir despite not being numerically very significant. In England, independent journeyman organizations arose only after the national dominance of the London livery companies began to wane during the late seventeenth and early eighteenth centuries. Elsewhere in premodern Europe, formal organizations of journeymen were poorly developed or nonexistent because many towns and states took strongly repressive actions against them, and because their services were less needed in the more densely urbanized regions, such as northern Italy and the Low Countries. The development and the workings of markets in skilled labor have nevertheless received little attention. The effects of journeyman mobility on technological progress and on the persistence for centuries of skills-intensive "industrial districts" across Europe are equally unexplored.

[*See also* Apprenticeship *and* Craft Guilds.]

BIBLIOGRAPHY

Amelang, James S. *The Flight of Icarus: Artisan Autobiography in Early Modern Europe.* Stanford, 1998. A fascinating study of premodern craftsmen's lives, which includes details of journeyman tramping.

Epstein, Stephan R. "Labor Mobility, Journeyman Organisations, and Markets in Skilled Labour Europe, 14th–18th centuries." In *Pratiques historiques de l'innovation, historicité de l'économie des savoirs (12e B 19e siècles)*, edited by Liliane Hilaire-Perez and Anne-Marie Garçon. Paris, 2002. A discussion of why journeymen did or did not set up formal organizations, and the technological consequences of journeyman mobility.

Lis, Catharina, and Hugo Soly. "'An Irresistible Phalanx': Journeymen Associations in Western Europe, 1300–1800." *International Review of Social History* 39 Suppl. 2 (1994), 11–52. A fundamental discussion of the literature on journeymen and their struggles, with references.

Rule, John. "The Property of Skill in the Period of Manufacture." In *The Historical Meanings of Work*, edited by Patrick Joyce, pp. 99–118. Cambridge, 1987. A seminal study of the journeymen's main source of identity and bargaining power.

S. R. Epstein

JUTE INDUSTRY. Until the development of cheap synthetic substitutes, jute was second only to cotton as a textile fiber. In 1960, jute accounted for a quarter of world textile fiber production. Jute is used for yarn or as a durable coarse fabric. Most of the world's supply of jute is grown in Bengal, on the Indian subcontinent, which has the requisite hot, humid climate. The fiber comes from annual plants and is extracted by "retting" their stems in slowly running water.

For a long time, jute had been used in India for making cloth, but the fiber was first exported in 1796 by the British East India Company, which sent some to a twine factory in Abingdon, in Berkshire, England. The major export market for jute fiber, however, became Dundee, Scotland. In the early nineteenth century, Dundee had a diversified industrial structure, including a linen industry, based by then on flax imported from the Baltic. A little jute was brought to Dundee in 1823, but the fiber proved difficult to spin. By the early 1830s, persistent experiments had solved the major problems of adapting flax spinning and weaving processes to jute. Significant jute production developed in Dundee through a combination of factors. The supply of rival fibers was affected: there was uncertainty about Russian flax supplies, which were threatened by the Crimean War (1854–1856); and there was a world shortage of cotton as a result of the American Civil War (1861–1865). The demand for cheap cloth rose exceptionally because of these and other wars of the 1850s and 1860s (jute was used for sandbags) and because of the opening up of the American West.

Imports of jute into Dundee therefore rose markedly, as shown in Table 1, and peaked in the 1890s.

The impact on Dundee was striking. The city's population nearly doubled between 1851 and 1881 (from 78,931 to 142,154), and by 1881 half the city's population was employed in jute processing. Dundee had turned into "Juteopolis." Calcutta, too, benefited from the trade with port improvements, and production of the fiber was important to the income of small farmers in Bengal.

As jute products became familiar, processing capacity was established elsewhere in the world. There was some jute manufacturing in continental Europe, but the

TABLE 1. *Annual Imports of Jute into Dundee*

DECADE	AVERAGE IMPORTS PER YEAR (THOUSAND TONS)
1830–1839	1
1840–1849	6
1850–1859	23
1860–1869	60
1870–1879	116
1880–1889	172
1890–1899	335

SOURCE: Adapted from Lenman, Lythe, and Gauldie, (1969), p. 105.

significant threat to Dundee's domination of the market came from the most obvious location—India, where manufacturing minimized transportation costs and could be based on cheap labor. The initial introduction of power looms in India in the 1850s simply displaced local handloom production; but by the mid-1870s, India was becoming an exporter of jute cloth, and by 1905 there were more power looms in Calcutta than in Dundee. Ironically, much of the capital, technology, and managerial skill that developed the Indian jute spinning and weaving production came from Dundee, as Dundee entrepreneurs realized the opportunities in India. They sought to differentiate Dundee products by a move of Dundee production into finer quality and more specialized (for example, broadloom) cloths.

World War I (1914–1918) increased demand for coarse jute products. The interwar period saw severe depression in the Dundee industry—Dundee producers could not compete on most international markets, and they were losing out even in home markets to imported sacking. Import duties, which protected some U.K. industries, were not applicable to jute because of Imperial Preference. At the same time, with violent vicissitudes, the Indian industry continued to grow: there were about 2.5 times as many power looms in operation in Calcutta in 1939 as in 1907. World War II (1939–1945) gave Dundee jute a temporary boost (and curbed the growth of capacity in India), but again the demand was for coarse products, in which Dundee could in normal times no longer be competitive.

From 1945 to 1963, the Dundee jute industry was to some extent protected from foreign competition by government policy, but the removal of this protection led eventually to the almost complete extinction of jute processing in Dundee. Jute production in India received a stimulus in 1947 from the partition of the subcontinent. The main jute-growing area, East Bengal, became part of East Pakistan (Bangladesh from 1971), but about three-quarters of the manufacturing capacity was in West Bengal, which became part of India. Partition gave Pakistan the impetus to develop new productive capacity (in both East and West Pakistan), while India devoted more land to jute cultivation.

From the late 1950s, the world jute market suffered significant competition from new products and new methods of handling raw materials. Some products (for example, grain) started to be transported by bulk-handling processes, which obviated the need for bagging. In bagging, competition came from paper sacks and then, much more significantly, from synthetic fibers, especially polypropylene, which also replaced jute in many carpet backings. Polypropylene, a by-product of the petroleum industry, was produced on a commercial scale from the early 1960s. Jute has retained some of the bagging market—it has advantages in durability and "breathability"—and is still used in manufacturing, notably for quality carpet backing. Since the mid-1970s, however, world consumption of jute has been falling—a fall of about 4 percent per annum in developed countries, only partly counterbalanced by a rise of about 1.3 percent per annum in developing countries. Jute spinning is now almost confined to Bangladesh and India. Two-thirds of the world production of jute is consumed domestically—mainly in India, where government controls protect the share of jute in packaging. Bangladesh is the dominant exporter of jute fiber and products. Organizations such as the International Jute Organisation (set up by United Nations Conference on Trade and Development [UNCTAD] in 1984 to try to safeguard the future of the jute industry) have failed to arrest its steady decline. Even in Bangladesh, jute is now of limited significance: in 1971 it accounted for 95 percent of the country's export earnings, but now only 10 percent, and in 1997, earnings from jute fiber production represented under 7 percent of farming household income.

[*See also* Fiber Crops.]

BIBLIOGRAPHY

Atkinson, Ronald R. *Jute: Fibre to Yarn.* London, 1964.

Food and Agriculture Organization of the United Nations Committee on Commodity Problems. *Food Security Implications of Earnings from Production and Exports of Jute in Bangladesh.* Rome, 1998.

Howe, W. Stewart. *The Dundee Textiles Industry, 1960–1977.* Aberdeen, 1982.

Jackson, J. M., ed. *The City of Dundee: Third Statistical Account of Scotland.* Edinburgh, 1979.

Lenman, Bruce, Charlotte Lythe, and Enid Gauldie. *Dundee and Its Textile Industry, 1850–1914.* Dundee, 1969.

Official Website of the Office of the Jute Commissioner, Calcutta. <http://www.jutecomm.com>

Rothermund, Dietmar. *An Economic History of India: From Pre-Colonial Times to 1991.* 2d ed. London, 1993.

United Nations Conference on Trade and Development/Food and Agriculture Organization of the United Nations. *Recent, Current, and Prospective Developments in the World Jute Economy.* Geneva, 1999.

CHARLOTTE M. LYTHE

K

KAUTSKY, KARL (1854–1938), Prague-born German Marxist theorist.

Kautsky was the most prominent Marxist in the world from the death of Friedrich Engels in 1895 to the outbreak of World War I in 1914. His extensive writings on Marxist theory, historiography, and politics influenced all Marxists of his time. Kautsky had a close, though often strained, relationship with Engels and was one of Engels's literary executors, in which capacity he edited volume 4 of *Capital*. Aided by Engels, Kautsky wrote much of the Erfurt program adopted by the German Social Democratic Party (SPD) in 1890. Lenin frequently recognized Kautsky as one of the most important influences in the development of his own theories and later wrote a scathing attack of the master as a betrayer of the cause, *The Proletarian Revolution and the Renegade Kautsky* (1919). One of Kautsky's early works, *The Economic Doctrines of Karl Marx* (1887), was the first full-length study of Marx translated into Chinese (1911). For more than thirty years, Kautsky was a significant figure in the SPD, then the largest socialist movement in the world, primarily because of his role as editor of the party's official theoretical journal, *Die Neue Zeit*, and his close political alliance with party leader August Bebel. He also made important contributions to virtually all theoretical disputes of the Second International, and *Die Neue Zeit* served as a forum for Marxists and socialists from all over the world.

Heavily influenced by Darwin and Engels's positivistic interpretation of Marx, Kautsky was primarily a popularizer and an explicator rather than an innovator. In theoretical debates within the party and the Second International, he was a defender of Marxian orthodoxy against attacks from more moderate forces on the right (especially Eduard Bernstein's revisionism) and more aggressive and activist forces on the left (including Rosa Luxemburg and, later, V. I. Lenin). Although never explicitly rejecting violent revolution as part of the transition from capitalism to socialism, he tended to emphasize the historical inevitability of the process while downplaying the role of an elite, activist party. It was largely disagreement on this matter that led to Lenin's rejection of Kautsky's orthodoxy.

In numerous works and extensive correspondence, Kautsky contributed to the popularization of Marxism by

KARL KAUTSKY. Caricature (1919) by Otto von Kursell (1884–1967). (Prints and Photographs Division, Library of Congress)

explaining concepts such as the labor theory of value, socially necessary labor, and others, and by applying Marxian economic analysis to past events (for example, in his studies of Thomas More and Thomas Münzter) and to current affairs, including imperialism, class politics, and the impact of social-welfare reforms. The Bolshevik victory in Russia and the rise of Lenin's communism to prominence meant that Kautsky's theoretical positions were superseded by the pressing concerns of making a socialist society. When he died in 1938, in Amsterdam, having fled the German occupation of Austria, Kautsky was no longer an honored figure in the Marxian pantheon.

BIBLIOGRAPHY

Blumenberg, Werner. *Karl Kautskys literarisches Werk*. The Hague, 1960.

Gilcher-Holtey, Ingrid. *Das Mandat des Intellektuellen: Karl Kautsky und die Sozialdemokratie*. Berlin, 1986.

Hünlich, Reinhold. *Karl Kautsky und der Marxismus der II: Internationale*. Marburg, Germany, 1981.

Salvadori, Massimo. *Karl Kautsky and the Socialist Revolution.* London, 1981.

Steenson, Gary. *Karl Kautsky, 1854–1938: Marxism in the Classical Years.* Pittsburgh, 1978.

GARY P. STEENSON

KAZAKHSTAN. *See* Central Asia *and* Russia, *subentry on* Russian Empire.

KEIRETSU. The Japanese word *keiretsu* combines two Chinese characters: *kei*, which means "lineage," and *retsu*, meaning "arranged, or arrangement, in order." In practice, the term is used in postwar Japan to describe diversified groups of firms connected with one other through intergroup borrowing, transfer of personnel (or capital goods), and purchase of goods or services. The Japanese literature usually distinguishes three types of *keiretsu*: horizontal (*yoko*) groups, also called financial groups because the main alliances holding the parties together involve financial transfers; vertical (*tate*) groups, also known as industrial groups because the principal alliances revolve around subcontracting arrangements, with subcontractors supplying components and intermediary inputs to their affiliated parent companies; and *kombinato* groups, in which affiliated firms cluster next to each other geographically in order exploit by-products generated by the other firms in the group (*kombinato* are mainly limited to the petrochemical and iron and steel chemical subsectors, whose gaseous emissions are not easily transported over long distances). At the center of most financial *keiretsu* are large financial enterprises and general trading companies (*sogo shosha*). An individual firm may be part of both a vertical and a horizontal *keiretsu*. Consider Toyota, the automobile manufacturer. It belongs to the Mitsui financial *keiretsu* that clusters around Mitsui Trust and Banking, the Sakura Bank, and Mitsui and Co. (the trading company); and it is the parent company for a broad subcontracting empire. Horizontal *keiretsu* are held together through regular meetings of the chief executives of the affiliated companies (presidents' clubs), bank borrowing, and cross-shareholding of stock. Typically, main banks and other financial enterprises within a *keiretsu* own significant shares of the stock issued by the enterprises within the group.

The major horizontal *keiretsu* in postwar Japan are: the four former zaibatsu groups reassembled after 1949 as *keiretsu* groups, Mitsubishi, Mitsui, Sumitomo, and Fuyo (the former Yasuda zaibatsu); and other financial groups centered around important banks, namely, the Dai-ichi Kangyo group, the Industrial Bank of Japan group, the Tokai group, and the Sanwa group. Outstanding vertical *keiretsu* are Nissan and Toyota, the automobile manufacturers; and the consumer electronics giants, Hitachi, Matsushita, and Toshiba.

The literature concerning the *keiretsu* clusters around two main themes: the "one set-ism" hypothesis or overinvestment theory; and the notion that implicit contracts are strongly developed in, and are a source of efficiency and flexibility for, Japanese manufacturing. According to the one set-ism theory, *keiretsu* groups compete against one another. If any one *keiretsu* enters a new market, the others tend to follow its lead. Thus each and every sector penetrated by *keiretsu* tend to be dominated by large oligopolies affiliated with *keiretsu*. Since entry into new activities requires plant and equipment investment, overinvestment occurs, with a potential for overproduction and gluts. Thus, *keiretsu* must seek out foreign markets. This is the dark view of the *keiretsu*.

There is a more benign interpretation. Because of cultural homogeneity, a highly centralized compulsory educational system, and an emphasis on group activities within Japanese culture, it is relatively easy for Japanese individuals, and for Japanese firms, to enter into unwritten contracts based on mutual trust, known as implicit contracts. If it is easy to formulate implicit contracts, firms can benefit from the resulting alliances so forged. For instance, giant Japanese enterprises that typically extend permanent employment guarantees to their employees seek stability. Being able to borrow from an affiliated bank in times of crisis reduces their risk. Moreover, main banks within *keiretsu* carry out the monitoring and screening functions that security analysts, auditing, and credit-rating institutions in other countries perform. Sharing information about new technology and market developments benefits firms in different industries that are jointly affected by a particular set of innovations. Indeed, both trading companies and main banks engage in extensive information gathering, playing the role of venture capitalist. Thus, spreading out risk and generating scale economies in securing and disseminating information are two advantages of *keiretsu* that economists have heavily emphasized.

Certain questions remain. How thoroughgoing is the "*keiretsu*-ization" of the Japanese economy? Estimates for the 1970s, 1980s, and 1990s suggest that sales of *keiretsu* accounted for about three quarters of Japanese company sales. Have deregulation of retail stemming from foreign pressure intent on prying open Japan's markets and the restructuring of banking due to the crisis in Japan's financial sector flowing from the collapse of its bubble economy in the early 1990s weakened *keiretsu*-ization? Recent studies suggest that deregulation and restructuring have had, at best, a modest impact.

In sum, *keiretsu* have played a crucial role in the expansion of manufacturing in postwar Japan. Whether the chief significance of the *keiretsu* lies in the oligopoly structure and potential for excess competition or overinvestment that may result from their existence, or whether it lies in the efficiency advantages of implicit contracting is debatable. However, the great importance of the *keiretsu* in the postwar development of the Japanese economy is unquestionable.

BIBLIOGRAPHY

Caves, Richard E., and Masu Uekusa. *Industrial Organization in Japan*. Washington, D.C., 1976. The approach centers around the implications of Japanese enterprises organizing themselves into *keiretsu* groups for the industrial organization of the Japanese economy, especially in manufacturing. Using a variety of quantitative measures of concentration—in sales and shipments, and in corporate capital—for Japan and the United States, the authors examine the question of how competitive the Japanese economy is ("competitive" conceived of in terms of ease of entry into industries). They conclude that, compared to the United States, relatively low barriers to new entry of firms characterized Japanese manufacturing during the 1950s and 1960s. They attribute this to the rapid growth and the dramatic structural change of the Japanese economy between 1955 and 1970.

Gerlach, Michael L. *Alliance Capitalism: The Social Organization of Japanese Business*. Berkeley and Los Angeles, 1992. Employing a large-scale data base for Japanese and American firms involving shareholding, membership on boards of directors, and company borrowing practices, the author provides a sociological interpretation of the existence of alliance structures in *keiretsu* groups. He emphasizes the importance of constant and ongoing networking and transactions between allied companies within *keiretsu* groups, and stresses that because large Japanese companies extend permanent employment guarantees to their workers, they are especially interested in securing a stable niche within their industry. *Keiretsu* ties help ensure firms against instability, and therefore help firms meet their obligations to their stakeholder workers.

Kester, W. Carl. *Japanese Takeovers: The Global Contest for Corporate Control*. Boston, 1991. This study looks at both horizontal (financial) and vertical (production) *keiretsu* from the viewpoint of a business-school specialist interested in corporate strategy and organization. It stresses the paramount importance of growth for Japanese managers, and it examines how both ties within *keiretsu* involving the transfer of information and the diffuse nature of stakeholder claims to Japanese enterprises (workers, providers of bank credit, and equity holders all laying claim to the fruits of the enterprise) contribute to this growth orientation.

Kojima, Kiyoshi, and Terutomo Ozawa. *Japan's General Trading Companies: Merchants of Economic Development*. Paris, 1984. This study examines how general trading companies (*sogo shosha*) operate and stresses their importance as venture capitalists financing the import and export activities of their client firms. Most postwar *keiretsu* groups revolve around both a financial core (a main bank plus trust and insurance companies) and a general trading company.

Miyashita, Kenichi, and David W. Russell. *Keiretsu: Inside the Hidden Japanese Conglomerates*. New York, 1994. This study provides a good descriptive introduction to the world of *keiretsu*. The authors also discuss various economic arguments used to explain why the *keiretsu* structure exists: it spreads out risk among a variety of associated firms, thereby minimizing the possibility of bankruptcy; affiliated enterprises can take advantage of scale economies in the gathering of information by pooling their search for new organizational and technological advances; and the main banks of *keiretsu* monitor the activities of their affiliated *keiretsu* firms, performing the services of auditing and screening usually carried out by credit-rating and securities houses in other countries.

Miyazaki, Yoshikazu. "Excessive Competition and the Formation of Keiretsu." In *Industry and Business in Japan*, edited by Kazuo Sato, pp. 53–73. White Plains, N.Y., 1980. This study advances the argument that competition between *keiretsu* in postwar Japan has given rise to a competitive oligopoly system. In this system overinvestment takes place since each *keiretsu* mimics what the other *keiretsu* do. This is known as one set-ism or set control because each *keiretsu* matches the set of industries that other *keiretsu* have chosen to enter. Overinvestment may give rise to overproduction, putting pressure on manufacturers to export their output to foreign markets.

CARL MOSK

KENYA. *See* East Africa.

KETTERING, CHARLES (1876–1958), American inventor.

Kettering is considered one of the leading inventors of his time. Co-founder of Dayton Engineering Laboratories Company (DELCO), he invented dozens of important devices but is best known for his contributions to the automobile industry, most notably his improved ignition system and the first electric self-starter. Nevertheless, many of his ideas extended beyond this industry and found application in railroad diesel locomotives, in aviation, and in medicine research.

Born in an Ohio farmhouse, Kettering became a teacher in a country school soon after graduating from high school and then worked as a foreman on a telephone line crew. After severe eye problems forced him twice to drop out, Kettering finally graduated from Ohio State University in 1904 as a mechanical engineer in electrical engineering. After graduation, Kettering joined the invention staff of the National Cash Register Company (NCR). His major contributions there were the O.K. credit approval system for department stores, a low-cost printing register, an electric motor for cash registers, and an accounting machine that could both add and subtract. In 1909, Kettering set up (with Edward A. Deeds) the Dayton Engineering Laboratories Company (DELCO), which changed the automobile industry in a fundamental way. Working in Deeds's barn, Kettering and the "barn gang" invented the electric automobile self-starter first incorporated in the 1912 Cadillac. Replacing the old and dangerous hand cranks that required a great deal of physical strength, the first starter brought about the spectacular growth of the U.S. auto industry and empowered women drivers. During the DELCO years, "Boss Ket," as he was nicknamed by the "barn gang," also developed the ignition and lighting system for automobiles and the engine-driven generator, named DELCO, that upgraded life in hundreds of thousands of rural farms. In 1916, DELCO was sold to the General Motors Corporation (GM) and Kettering became the head of research and later the vice president of GM. He stayed there until his retirement in 1947. Under his supervision, the GM research lab developed a flexible lightweight diesel engine and the diesel locomotive, Freon for refrigerators and air condi-tioners, four-wheel brakes, safety glass, and quick-drying paint for automobiles, among other devices.

Kettering's research contributed to various fields. His study of the phenomenon of "knock" in gasoline engines that led in 1923 to the development of tetraethyl lead con-tributed to advances in aviation. He also pioneered the de-velopment of high-compression engines and improved fu-els that increased aircraft engine horsepower and flight safety. His medical research resulted in a device for the treatment of venereal disease as well as an incubator for premature infants. He was also a pioneer in the applica-tion of magnetism to medical diagnostic techniques. Along with Alfred Sloan, Kettering established the Sloan-Ketter-ing Institute for Cancer Research (1945). Activating his be-lief in practical education, a combination of theoretical knowledge with experience, Kettering established the Flint Institute of Technology (1919) and General Motors Insti-tute (1926), now Kettering University. As holder of numer-ous patents, Kettering received many honors and hon-orary doctorates for his ideas.

BIBLIOGRAPHY

Bernstein, Mark. "A Self-Starter That Gave Us the Self Starter." *Smith-sonian* 19.4 (July 1988), 125.

Boyd, Thomas A. *Professional Amateur: The Biography of Charles Franklin Kettering.* New York, 1957.

Leslie, Stuart W. *Boss Kettering.* New York, 1983.

National Aviation Hall of Fame. "Kettering, Charles Franklin—1979," *NAHF Inductee,* <http://www.nationalaviation.org/enshrinee/keter-ing.html>.

Scharchburg, Richard P. "Charles F. Kettering: Doing the Right Thing at the Right Time," *Biography of Charles F. Kettering,* <http://www.kettering.edu/ketternu/kettbio.htm>.

RAN ABRAMITZKY

KEYNES, JOHN MAYNARD (1883–1946), economist.

Maynard Keynes ("it rhymes with 'brains' and . . . there is no harm in that" [JMK to Don von Eisner, 26 March 1942] was the first son of John Neville Keynes (1852–1949), the Cambridge philosopher/economist, and Flo-rence Ada Brown (1861–1958), Cambridge's first female mayor. Educated locally and at Eton, he went to King's College, Cambridge, to read mathematics and graduated Twelfth Wrangler in 1905. While preparing for the civil service examinations in 1905–1906, Keynes read some economics and wrote essays for Alfred Marshall (1842–1924). During his two years in the India Office, he also worked on a fellowship dissertation for King's, later pub-lished as *A Treatise of Probability* (1921), which he submit-ted unsuccessfully in December 1907. Undeterred, he re-turned to Cambridge in 1908 at the invitation of Marshall to assist in the recently founded Economics Tripos. He be-came a fellow of King's in 1909 and Girdlers' Lecturer in Economics in the University in 1911. The same year he

was elected editor of the *Economic Journal,* a post he held until 1945.

Keynes's first book, *Indian Currency and Finance* (1913), an exposition and defense of the gold exchange standard, was coincident with his appointment to the Royal Com-mission on Indian Finance and Currency, where he suc-cessfully developed a proposal for an central bank. Briefly in the British Treasury at the outbreak of World War I in August 1914, Keynes became a temporary civil servant in January 1915. By May 1915, he was in the finance division, and, in January 1917, he became head of a division respon-sible for Britain's external financial relations. In this posi-tion he went to the Paris Peace Conference in January 1919, where much of the day-to-day responsibility for British policy fell on his shoulders. He played an impor-tant part in drafting the reparations articles of the Peace Treaty, but he was unsuccessful in keeping the total of the reparations down or in selling to the Americans an ambi-tious scheme for European reconstruction.

Depressed by the failure of his scheme and horrified by the full implications of the Peace Treaty, Keynes resigned his position on 19 May. He left Paris on 7 June and almost immediately began writing a denunciation of the treaty, *The Economic Consequences of the Peace,* which appeared in England in December 1919. That book, which has shaped all subsequent discussion of the subject, and exten-sive journalism (much of it collected in *A Revision of the Treaty,* 1922, and *Essays in Persuasion,* 1931) made him a household name. Along with financial speculation and positions in the City of London, his writing made him wealthy enough to become a supernumerary fellow of King's and resign his university lectureship.

In the summer of 1924, Keynes began work on what be-came the two-volume *Treatise on Money* (1930). Later con-vinced that the analysis of the *Treatise* was flawed, in De-cember 1931 he began revising it. The fundamental ideas of the revision were in place by early 1933, but it took three years to refine them into *The General Theory of Employ-ment, Interest and Money,* the foundation of modern macroeconomics, published in February 1936. Under-standing, interpreting, and applying the ideas of that book became a major industry among economists. Keynes took some part in these discussions, despite a severe, incurable heart condition from May 1937 that greatly restricted his activities, if not the fertility of his mind. On the outbreak of World War II, he was fit enough to mount a major cam-paign on the principles of war finance in *How to Pay for the War* (1940), and to reenter the British Treasury. Although his influence never matched the power of his pen, he played an important part in war finance and postwar planning, both domestically and internationally. There he became a founder of the International Monetary Fund and the Inter-national Bank for Reconstruction and Development.

A keen student of history, Keynes spent several years of the 1920s on a history of ancient currencies. As editor of the *Economic Journal*, he edited its annual economic history supplement between 1925 and the outbreak of war in 1939. Both the *Treatise*, with its "Historical Illustrations" of the theory, and the *General Theory*, with its attempts to rehabilitate certain forebears such as the mercantilists, were stimuli to subsequent economic historians. His major influence came through the *General Theory* and its associated statistical revolution, which provided the analytical framework for a reinterpretation of the past that itself became the object or reinterpretation three decades later.

BIBLIOGRAPHY

Harrod, Roy F. *The Life of John Maynard Keynes*. London, 1951.

Johnson, Elizabeth, and Donald Moggridge, eds. *The Collected Writings of John Maynard Keynes*. 30 vols. London, 1971 1989.

Moggridge, Donald E. *Maynard Keynes: An Economist's Biography*. London, 1992.

Skidelsky, Robert. *John Maynard Keynes*. 3 vols. London, 1983–2000.

D. E. MOGGRIDGE

KINDLEBERGER, CHARLES P. (1910–), economic historian.

Charles P. Kindleberger came to economic history after distinguished careers in public service and teaching international trade. He entered the field with his book Economic Growth in France and Britain, 1851–1950, in which he surveyed the extensive literature on these two countries and concluded that there was no single convincing explanation for the differences between them. He ended the book with these famous words: "Economic history, like all history, is absorbing, beguiling, great fun. But, for scientific problems, can it be taken seriously?"

This ironic comment set the tone for Kindleberger's future work in economic history. His books and papers are distinguished by his command of the previous literature. His reasoning is informed by an intelligent, if skeptical, use of economic theory. His prose is sprightly; his conclusions are clear, forcefully presented, and always worth debating. Many of his essays have been reprinted in two recent collections.

Kindleberger's impact on economic history comes primarily from two books published in the 1970s. The first, *The World in Depression, 1929–1939*, provided a comprehensive narrative of the Great Depression from an international perspective. Instead of seeing the Depression as a succession of national stories, Kindleberger argued persuasively that it was the result of a failure of the international economic system. The economic structure built around the gold standard had allowed the prewar industrial economies to weather various economic shocks in the late nineteenth and early twentieth centuries, but it proved unable to contain or offset the shocks arising in the period after the Great War. Kindleberger argued that the interwar economy lacked a hegemon, a dominant leader. The hegemonic power in the prewar period was England, more specifically the Bank of England, which acted to contain crises wherever they started. However, England was exhausted by the effort to defeat Germany in the Great War, and the Bank of England was in no shape to continue this role. Although the United States was the obvious candidate to pick up the baton, Americans were isolationist after their wartime efforts, and the United States declined to act. Without a hegemon, the shocks to the world economy in the late 1920s were allowed to drag the world into the Great Depression.

Kindleberger generalized this argument in *Manias, Panics, and Crashes*, surveying financial crises in the past two centuries that were important enough to have macroeconomic effects. He described the various irrationalities that preceded crises and synthesized a vast literature in a small and engaging book. He concluded that stability was promoted when a world lender of last resort existed and followed the recommendations of Walter Bagehot a century earlier to lend freely at punitive rates during a crisis. This is what a hegemonic power should have done in the 1930s in Kindleberger's view; it is what the International Monetary Fund should do today.

BIBLIOGRAPHY

Kindleberger, Charles P. *Economic Growth in France and Britain, 1851–1950*. Cambridge, Mass., 1964.

Kindleberger, Charles P. *The World in Depression, 1929–1939*. London, 1973. Rev. ed., Berkeley, 1986.

Kindleberger, Charles P. *Manias, Panics, and Crashes: A History of Financial Crises*. New York, 1978. 4th ed., New York, 2000.

Kindleberger, Charles P. *Essays in History*. Ann Arbor, 1999.

Kindleberger, Charles P. *Comparative Political Economy*. Cambridge, Mass., 2000.

PETER TEMIN

KOLA. One of the most important stimulants in Africa, was initially restricted to royalty and the elite because of scarcity and high price, but it gradually became available and affordable. Kola, the ripe seed of *Sterculia acuminata*, is the size of a walnut or a chestnut and contains roughly as much caffeine per 100 grams (3.5 fluid ounces) of coffee and as much theobromine per 100 grams (3.5 fluid ounces) of tea. It contains kolanin (a heart stimulant), strychnine, theine, and tannin. The alkaloids caffeine and theobromine are found in a mass of cells under the epiderm of the nut.

The genus *Cola* is of tropical African origin, and over forty species grow in the region between Sierra Leone and the Congo, but *Cola nitida* and *acuminata* are the most important. Outside the continent, kola spread to the Seychelles, Sri Lanka, Guyana, Dominica, Mauritius, Venezuela, Martinique, Guadeloupe, Jamaica, and Brazil.

Kola was propagated from the seed. In the past, farmers relied on seedlings under mature kola trees for planting. Over time, kola was propagated vegetatively through cuttings, grafting of shoots on rootstocks, budding, and marcotting. The tree grows well in forest soils and in savanna areas of forest outliers with adequate moisture in the rooting zone. It bears fruit in the fourth or fifth year and matures by the tenth. A full-grown kola tree produces about two crops a year, and the fruits are harvested (when the bright green coats turn pale green or light brown) with a long picking knife on a pole. Alternatively, the fruit is allowed to drop from the tree. The harvesting season opens in October and tapers off in December. A small midseason crop is harvested in late May and June. The nuts are carefully picked, and healthy ones are stored in large baskets made from the raffia palm and lined with *bal* leaves. Kola production was and is bedeviled by weevil infestation, leaf blight, and root diseases.

The kola trade has a long history. Portuguese explorers encountered the trade between Senegambia and the Upper Niger in the sixteenth century. From the late eighteenth century, the Gold Coast and Sierra Leone supplied northern Nigeria and central Sudan. From 1867 onward, kola export reached Europe (first England, and then France and Germany), and later the United States. In the 1870s, kola was mixed with sugar and vanilla as a tonic for invalids in Europe, and in 1886, John S. Pemberton, an Atlanta druggist, invented Coca-Cola using coca and kola extracts. At the same time, kola was used as the caffeine base in some pharmaceutical products in Europe and the United States.

In African societies, it was a mark of hospitality to serve kola to a friend. Chinua Achebe captures the cultural essence of this function when he observed that "He who brings kola brings life." The kola nut also served as a mild stimulant; a hunger suppressant; an antidote for certain diseases; a gift to royalty; a present to friends, acquaintances, and in-laws; and even as part of a bride's dowry. Kola also featured prominently in child naming and funerary rites. Furthermore, it was used as a token of peace or war, as a distinctive dye for decorating cloth, and a means of sustenance for families and communities that sold the nuts to Hausa kola traders who bought kola in Ghana to sell back in Nigeria and central Sudan. Due to its alkaloidal properties, kola was chewed fresh or eaten as dry powder as a remedy for dysentery and other intestinal disorders. It was also reputed to have aphrodisiac properties and was considered as one of the many cures for impotency.

[*See also* Alkaloids.]

BIBLIOGRAPHY

Abaka, Edmund. "Eating Kola: The Pharmacological and Therapeutic Significance of Kola Nuts." *Ghana Studies* 1 (1998), 1–10.

Abaka, Edmund. "Kola Nut Production in Ghana (Gold Coast and Asante), 1865–1920." Ph.D. diss., York University, 1998.

Abaka, Edmund. "Kola Nut." In *The Cambridge World History of Food*, edited by Kenneth F. Kiple and Kriemhild Coneè Ornelas, vol. 1, pp. 684–692. Cambridge, 2000.

Agiri, Babtunde. "Kola Production in Western Nigeria, 1850–1950: A History of the Cultivation of Cola Nitida in Egba-Owode, Ijebu-Remo, Iwo, and Ota Areas." Ph.D. diss., University of Wisconsin, 1972.

Ayensu, Edward S. *Medicinal Plants of the West Indies*. Algonac, Mich. 1981.

Brooks, George E. *Kola Trade and State Building: Upper Guinea Coast and Senegambia, 15th–17th centuries*. Working paper no. 38, African Studies Center. Boston, 1980.

Cohen, Abner. "The Politics of the Kola Trade." *Africa* 36 (1966), 18–35.

Goodman, Jordan, Paul E. Lovejoy, and Andrew Sherrat. *Consuming Habits: Drugs in History and Anthrapology*. London and New York, 1995.

Lovejoy, Paul E. *Caravans of Kola: The Hausa Kola Trade, 1700–1900*. London and Zaria, Nigeria, 1980.

EDMUND ABAKA

KOREA [*This entry contains three subentries, on the economic history of Korea before 1945, and on North and South Korea.*]

Korea before 1945

Korea had suffered a long history of stagnation before Japan colonized and began to modernize the country in 1910—so concluded the Japanese scholars who, during the colonial era (1910–1945), pioneered modern research into Korea's economic past. Denouncing this picture as a misrepresentation intended to defend colonial rule, postcolonial historians in both South and North Korea presented the more optimistic view that "sprouts of capitalism" emerged in Korea during the eighteenth and nineteenth centuries. Accumulating evidence on living standards indicates that neither of the two assertions is entirely correct. The standard of living fell in Korea for at least a century before improving from around 1900 on. This article addresses the long swing in Korean living standards.

The Pre-1900 Downswing. A convenient and customary starting point for an account of Korea's transition to modern economic growth is the wars with Japan (1592–1598) and China (1627 and 1636) that destroyed a huge amount of historical data as well as a large number of people. Demographic recovery from the disaster continued until about 1800, and a century of stagnating population followed. Population growth ground to a halt in the nineteenth century as mortality rose with deteriorating living standards. During that century, real wages and rents trended downward, the rate of peasant rebellion rose, poor people began to outmigrate to northern China, and fiscal crises recurred and worsened. The parallel decline in the two key factor incomes in the predominantly agrarian Korea suggests falling total factor productivity. Falling paddy land prices (as measured by the amount of rice) indicates that negative productivity shocks occurred in the rice-farming sector. In contrast, dry-farm prices (as expressed by the amount of dry-farm products) rose, and peasants converted paddy lands into dry farms during the century of regression. Although causes of the productivity decline await further research, one likely source was Korea's increasing vulnerability to droughts and floods. Rivers became shallower, as they were not properly dredged after floods, so that the likelihood of further flooding increased. The number of working reservoirs declined as they were left unrepaired after flood damage, rendering farmers less able to resist droughts.

The deterioration in water control had its origins in population growth during the eighteenth century, which caused deforestation, increasing the risks of flooding. Malthusian degeneration could develop quickly because landless peasants could readily obtain farmland by burning off forests, with property rights normally remaining poorly defined. Another institutional basis for the water control problem was a disintegrating system of government. The wars with Japan and China dealt a serious blow to Korea's primitive form of command economy of the prewar period, when the bureaucracy could mobilize labor to build and repair damaged roads, bridges, and reservoirs. Although the bureaucratic structure was restored somewhat during the eighteenth century, the following century saw different landowning families taking turns to assume command under minor or ailing kings. This decentralization of power encouraged rent-seeking activities to thrive to such an extent that provincial officials connived in the damage to irrigation that landlords and peasants caused by farming on the rich soil inside reservoirs.

One response of peasants to the decline in irrigation was to develop rice seed varieties that could better resist droughts. The new types of seeds may well have improved the peasants' chances of survival by dampening agricultural fluctuations, but the average yield per acre fell, further compressing factor incomes. Peasants also countered by building waterways linking paddy fields with rivers, but this did not fully compensate for the decaying reservoirs. Building waterways in upstream villages meant less water in downstream villages, and the spillover effects caused numerous "water disputes," which the corrupt bureaucracy could not settle efficiently. Also hampering the investment in waterways was the absence of a legal framework defining the rights different contributors could exercise over the use of completed waterways. Typically, waterways were built with peasants' labor and landlords' capital. Not infrequently, local officials took a keen interest in mobilizing resources to build waterways as a source of private income. Disputes erupted over the charges landlords or officials collected from peasants for their use of the waterways. One such incident was a nationwide rebellion in 1894, which the premodern state was able to suppress only by calling in armed forces from neighboring countries. This uprising provoked the Sino-Japanese war, with Japan emerging victorious and consolidating its control over Korea.

In contrast to rice farming, handicrafts, commerce, and dry-field farming flourished during the eighteenth and nineteenth centuries. The initial impetus for diversification away from rice farming was the "emergency conversion" from a command to a market economy dictated by the wars with Japan and China. Before the wars, the government collected taxes in the form of a wide variety of products, and mobilized labor to procure the handicrafts and services it needed. Having been badly damaged and thus compelled to resort to markets to get what it needed, after the wars the government began to collect taxes in the form of the money commodity and rice (1608), to mint copper coins (1678), and later it lifted restrictions on commerce (1791). Labor markets emerged to replace the system of forced labor. Postcolonial historians optimistically interpreted the expansion of commercial farming, the handicrafts industry, and trade as evidence of budding capitalism. However, this characterization hardly is consistent with the worsening standard of living. More plausibly, this structural change represented an exodus of productive factors out of rice farming, where rewards deteriorated. Despite commercialization and "proto-industrialization," urbanization in late dynastic Korea lagged behind Q'ing China, not to mention Tokugawa Japan.

The Upswing after 1900. Japan forced Korea open to international trade in 1876, and in the following decades agricultural exports and manufacturing imports boomed. As the terms of trade improved during the port-opening period (1876–1910), rice and corn production expanded, while the traditional cotton-textile industry declined. The agricultural exports boom triggered the diffusion of high-yield rice seed varieties from Japan. Although the use of new types of rice seed was widespread as early as in the late 1890s in the main rice-growing regions of southern Korea, the technological transfer accelerated after Japan virtually secured Korea as one of its colonies by defeating Russia in 1905. The victory drew Japanese landlords and peasants into Korea, who made efforts to repair and expand irrigation, in addition to speeding up the dissemination of new rice seed varieties. Such investment and technological advances in rice farming did much to halt the nineteenth century's downswing.

The other important consequence of the transition to an open economy was the introduction of modern medicine

KOREA. Shoe market, Seoul, early 1900s. (Frank and Frances Carpenter Collection/Prints and Photographs Division, Library of Congress)

and an improvement in public hygiene, which appeared largely responsible for a decline in mortality and a population increase, beginning in the last decades of the nineteenth century. This mortality transition and population growth substantially accelerated with the beginning of colonial rule in 1910, when the colonial government, a developmental state modeled on the Meiji government, launched an extensive health campaign. The first modern census, in 1925, counted more than eighteen million residents, and subsequent censuses show population growth of 1.4 percent per year during the last two decades of the colonial period due to falling mortality.

In addition to the health campaign, the colonial government implemented an ambitious set of policy measures to modernize the Korean economy and institutions. It expanded railway lines and the telephone and telegraph network and built roads and harbors, which led to the integration of goods and labor markets. Modern educational institutions quickly replaced traditional schools (teaching Chinese classics), as seen in the rise in the primary school enrollment ratio from 1 percent to 47 percent from 1910 to 1943. The cadastral survey (1910–1918) established a modern system of land ownership. When the Rice Riots erupted in Japan in 1918, the imperial government launched the Rice Production Development Program (1920–1933) to expand the rice supply from within the empire. In colonial Korea, the Rice Program provided subsidies for irrigation projects and established institutions to reduce information, negotiation, and enforcement costs involved in building new waterways and reservoirs. The irrigation ratio improved during the colonial period, accelerating the introduction of improved types of rice seeds sensitive to the water supply. Increased use of chemical fertilizer following the construction of a fertilizer factory in 1927 further boosted the yields from the new rice varieties.

The institutional changes, technological advances, and accumulation of human and physical capital under Japanese rule terminated the Malthusian regression and initiated modern economic growth in Korea. Toshiyuki Mizoguchi's estimate of interwar Korean national product indicates that per capita output rose 1.4 percent per year from 1918/1920 to 1935/1937, with population expanding at a similar rate. The estimate's reliability has been questioned, and it is being revised, but one of Mizoguchi's main findings—rising per capita output—is consistent with rising wages and rents in colonial Korea. Rents rose much faster than wages as the land/labor ratio fell in the course of rapid population growth.

Growth accounting results indicate that the colonial transition to modern economic growth was driven chiefly by capital accumulation, which was particularly important for nonagricultural growth. Capital formation was financed primarily by public rather than private savings. The colonial state consistently raised tax ratios and introduced new taxes, which could pay for only about half of its ambitious investment projects. The colonial government was thus led to raise funds from the capital market in Japan and to rely on transfers from the Japanese government. Foreign savings financed about two-fifths of capital formation in interwar Korea.

Although per capita output increased, per capita grain consumption fell during the transition to modern economic growth, creating another example of the "food puzzle," as noted by Gregory Clark, Michael Huberman, and Peter Lindert ("A British Food Puzzle," *Economic History Review* 48 (1995), 215–237). As a result, Koreans became shorter, at least in the final two decades of colonial rule. Postcolonial historians in Korea labeled this phenomenon "starvation exports" of rice, suggesting that the colonial state seized and sent more rice out of the colony to Japan than the output increase under the Rice Production Development Program. Buttressing this view is an image of colonial Korea as a huge plantation run and exploited by the colonial government. However, this is a gross misrepresentation, at least for the period before the beginning of the Sino-Japanese war in 1937. Goods and factor markets evolved rapidly, and government intervention was probably less extensive in the pre-1937 colonial years than during the postcolonial decades in South, not to mention North, Korea.

In the late 1920s in Korea, Japan, and China, there did not exist a significant difference in stature among male mean heights in the three countries, which hovered above 160 centimeters. Life expectancy at birth differed considerably, however, with the 37.5 years in Korea an estimated several years longer than that in China and almost ten years shorter than that in Japan. Mizoguchi's estimate of Korean per capita gross domestic expenditure at current prices from 1925 to 1929 is 36 percent that of Japan and 58 percent that of Taiwan, where Japanese colonial rule started fifteen years earlier than in Korea. According to Angus Maddison, Chinese per capita gross domestic product in the interwar period was about one-half of that of Taiwan (*The World Economy: A Millenial Perspective*. Paris, 2001, p. 215). Actual differences in living standards are likely to have been smaller than these numbers suggest because costs of living tends to be lower in poorer countries.

Industrialization and World War II. Korea remained an agrarian economy until the early 1930s, when manufacturing started to expand rapidly. This first phase of industrialization had several causes, including an investment boom during the early recovery of the Japanese economy from the Great Depression, cheap labor and natural resources in Korea, and the beginning of economic control in Japan as a response to the Depression. The slide into World War II from 1937 on gave further momentum to industrialization, as Japan began to develop Korea as a military supply base for the invasion of China. This was part of a broader strategy to erect a system of wide-ranging

control over the Japanese empire, which was to have lasting impact in postcolonial economic development in the two Koreas. The war economy provided not only the base for the North Korean system of central planning, but also many of the tools for government intervention in South Korea.

BIBLIOGRAPHY

Cha, Myung Soo. "Imperial Policy or World Price Shocks? Explaining Interwar Korean Consumption Trend." *Journal of Economic History* 58.3 (1998), 731–754. Analyzes the impact of key shocks on the living standards in interwar Korea.

Cha, Myung Soo. "The Colonial Origins of Korea's Market Economy." In *Asia-Pacific Dynamism, 1550–2000*, edited by A. J. H. Latham and H. Kawakatsu, pp. 86–103. London, 2000. Shows that commodity and labor market integration occurred during the colonial period.

Eckert, Carter J. *Offspring of Empire: The Koch'ang Kims and the Colonial Origins of Korean Capitalism, 1876–1945*. Seattle, 1991. Argues that the colonial government assisted (rather than stifled, as many previously believed) the growth of firms owned and run by Koreans.

Gill, Insong. "Stature, Consumption, and the Standard of Living in Colonial Korea." In *The Biological Standard of Living in Comparative Perspective*, edited by John Komlos and Joerg Baten, pp. 122–138. Stuttgart, 1998. Argues that Koreans became shorter during the latter half of the colonial period.

Gragert, Edwin H. *Landownership under Cololonial Rule: Korea's Japanese Experience, 1900–1935*. Honolulu, 1994. Shows the cadastral survey confirmed existing landownership, rather than forcing a large transfer of land from Korean peasants to the colonial government or Japanese immigrants, as has been asserted repeatedly.

Kimura, Mitsuhiko. "Standards of Living in Colonial Korea: Did the Masses Become Worse Off or Better Off under Japanese Rule?" *Journal of Economic History* 53.3 (1993), 629–652. Describes the shifts in different indices of living standards in colonial Korea.

Kwon, Tae Hwan. *Demography of Korea: Population Change and its Components, 1925–1966*. Seoul, 1977. A definitive study on demographic change after the first national census of 1925.

Mizoguchi, Toshiyuki, and Mataji Umemura, eds. *Kyu Nihon Shokuminchi Keizai Tokei* (Economic Statistics of Former Japanese Colonies, 1895–1945). Tokyo, 1988. A statistical volume (with English explanations), including aggregate data for colonial Korea. The time series are currently under revision, and the results are being made available on the web site of the Institute of Economic Research of Hitotsubashi University, <http://www.ier.hit-u.ac.jp/COE>.

Myers, Ramon H, and Mark R. Peattie, eds. *The Japanese Colonial Empire*. Princeton, 1984. A collection of articles on different regions and aspects of the Japanese empire.

Palais, James B. *Politics and Policy in Traditional Korea*. Cambridge, Mass., 1975. A readable introduction to political, social, and economic institutions in eighteenth- and nineteenth-century Korea.

MYUNG SOO CHA

North Korea

The North Korean economy emerged by inheriting and at the same time demolishing the legacy of the Japanese colonial rule. The founders of North Korea took over the human and physical capital accumulated during the colonial period (1910–1945) but tore down existing institutions, such as markets and property rights, to consolidate a system of central control and planning, which had evolved as a part of the Japanese war economy. One cannot place much confidence in the economic statistics concerning this secretive regime, but different estimates agree on a broad outline of its aggregate performance over the past half-century. After recovering from the Korean War (1950–1953), political elites took the country upon a growth path driven largely by capital accumulation. Economic plans in the late 1950s and 1960s promoted capital-goods industries at the expense of consumer-goods industries and agriculture, contradicting the country's factor endowment. Ever higher investment ratios achieved at the expense of consumption helped the country not only to grow faster, but also to enjoy higher living standards than South Korea until the mid-1960s when growth started to falter.

The initial growth spurts followed by slowdown (a phenomenon commonly observed in centrally planned economies) can be explained by the country's system of highly centralized control and its closed nature. Managers and workers in collective farms or state enterprises lacked incentives to improve productivity. Efficiency in resource allocation became increasingly difficult for the planning agency to achieve with rising computational complexity entailed by economic growth. Matters were made worse by the despotic and whimsical rule, which not only wasted resources but also disturbed the consistency of planning. The self-imposed exclusion from the world market caused excessive diversification in production, limited access to the world capital market, and finally minimized the rate of technological diffusion.

The stagnation prompted two different types of policy response: institutional reform and attracting foreign capital. Since the late 1960s, central planners made several attempts to decentralize, which included the introduction of material incentives and independent accounting of the state enterprises. The ruling elites, however, could not push the decentralization far enough for it to have any significant productivity impact, as it would destabilize the political regime.

The détente in the early 1970s helped North Korea attract loans from Western banks and thereby boost growth briefly. Much of the imported capital was used for military purposes and hardly contributed to export growth, causing the country to default on its external debts in 1975. The rescheduled debts were reneged on repeatedly, and as an alternative, the country introduced—with little success—a series of laws from 1984 on to encourage foreign direct investment.

The collapse of centrally planned economies in Europe in the late 1980s accelerated the decline by practically ending energy and capital goods imports at concessionary prices. Climatic shocks in the 1990s hit agricultural production, which was made worse by deforestation previously promoted to expand acreage. North Korea continues to muddle through the consequent subsistence crisis with concessions extracted by brinkmanship diplomacy and humanitarian aid from the rest of the world.

BIBLIOGRAPHY

Hwang, Eui-gak. *The Korean Economies: A Comparison of North and South.* Oxford, 1993. A comparison of the two Korean economies, using aggregate data of varying reliability.

Kimura, Mitsuhiko. "From Fascism to Communism: Continuity and Development of Collectivist Economic Policy in North Korea." *Economic History Review* 52.1 (1999), 69–86. Traces the origin of the North Korean command economy to the Japanese war economy.

Noland, Marcus. *Avoiding The Apocalypse: The Future of the Two Koreas.* Washington, D.C., 2000. Chapter three is an excellent starting point for studying the North Korean economic history.

MYUNG SOO CHA

South Korea

Since its liberation from Japanese colonial rule in 1945, South Korea underwent a rapid transformation from a war-torn rural society to a highly industrialized, technology-driven economy. Its remarkable record of poverty reduction and rapid economic growth, combined with low-income inequality, has sparked an important debate on the reasons for its success and, in particular, on the appropriate role of government in development. The purpose of this article is to present a broad overview of South Korea's economic history since 1945 and to touch upon some of the key factors behind its transformation.

The legacy of the Japanese colonial period (1910–1945) and division of the Korean peninsula at the end of World War II had both an immediate and long-term impact on South Korea's development. Japan's plan for incorporating Korea into its empire created a highly integrated but dual economy, with agriculture residing mainly in the South and heavy industry in the North. As a result of the division, the South was left with nearly two-thirds of the population and much of the arable land, while the North, with its abundant supply of hydroelectric power and minerals, kept most of the industrial and more than 90 percent of the electricity production. The political chaos that followed liberation, the sudden interruption of trade with Japan, and the complete cutoff from its main power supply in the North were a tremendous shock to the South Korean economy and contributed to the sharp decline in food and manufacturing production during the period leading up to internal war.

The Korean War (1950–1953) had both a destructive and equalizing effect upon the economy. The war is estimated to have killed 1.5 million people, destroyed a quarter of South Korea's fixed capital, and set back industrial production fifteen years. However, the war also helped to undo some of the oppressive elements of Korea's colonial legacy and to set the foundation for future growth. After the war, the government implemented a comprehensive land reform program that reversed the concentration of land ownership that took place under colonial rule. Land reform not only created a new class of owner-farmers, but, combined with the destruction from the war, also had the unintended consequence of starting South Korea with one of the most equitable distributions of income in the developing world.

Following the war, foreign aid, much of it from the United States, played a large role in South Korea's reconstruction. Between 1946 and 1976, South Korea received economic and military assistance of around $15 billion from both bilateral and multilateral sources, making it one of the largest recipients of foreign assistance in the world. Foreign assistance not only helped to finance much of the country's imports (around 70 percent) and to rebuild infrastructure destroyed during the war, but it also helped stabilize the economy, which was suffering from high inflation and shortages of basic needs.

During this period up to 1962, development policy was mainly inward looking. The government used an overvalued exchange rate and high-trade barriers to encourage import substitution, particularly for consumer goods, in order to preserve much-needed foreign exchange. Export growth was minor and only a secondary consideration. However, despite the massive assistance, economic growth was modest, inflation remained high, and the fiscal position was weakening. The bleak outlook, combined with the communist threat from the North, prompted the government to seek out a new growth strategy.

Following the military takeover by General Park Chung Hee in 1961, economic policy shifted away from reconstruction and import substitution toward aggressive export promotion. With its limited natural resource base and diminishing prospects for economic assistance, South Korea had little choice but to adopt an outward-oriented strategy that gave priority to exports, particularly of manufactured goods, as the engine for growth. The government used a number of instruments to promote exports, including preferential credits, tax breaks, and import liberalization of those intermediate and capital goods that industry needed. The government also devalued the exchange rate several times and introduced a unified floating rate in 1965 to maintain export competitiveness. Such promotion policies created an opportunity for any company with the capacity to export to do so and remain competitive in the world market.

The result was a rapid expansion in exports and one of the world's fastest-growing economies. Exports rose from $33 million in 1960 to $835 million ten years later—an annual growth rate of about 40 percent in value terms. The composition of exports also changed significantly. Exports

in the 1950s and early 1960s were mainly primary products (tungsten ore, raw silk, and fish) with manufacturing exports accounting for less than 1 percent of the total. However, by the mid-1970s, manufactured goods included clothing, electrical machinery, textiles, and footwear and made up almost 90 percent of total exports. Rapid export expansion also helped push economic growth higher than 9 percent per year.

Rapid industrialization also produced important structural changes in South Korea's economy and society. South Korea's economy was transformed within a relatively short period of time from a rural, relatively closed economy to one based upon capital-intensive industry and exports. Its population also underwent a remarkable demographic transition led by the sharp decline in death rate and a jump in the birthrate following the war. The resulting population boom, combined with the migration of farm labor seeking industrial employment, led to the creation of several large cities and put South Korea's urbanization rate on a par with the developed world. The demographic transition also helped to drive up savings rates, which in the 1980s were one of the highest in the world. High domestic savings helped the economy to maintain its rapid investment rate and reduce its dependence upon foreign capital. Industrialization also boosted employment, raised real wages, and created a demand for skilled labor. The government's program of heavy investment in education achieved near universal primary education for both sexes by the early 1970s and had immediate payoffs for both growth and income equality.

Under President Park's direction, South Korea entered a new phase in 1973 with the launch of an ambitious investment drive to develop its heavy and chemical industries (HCI). The objective was to shift production away from light manufacturing, which relied heavily upon imports of intermediate goods, to more capital-intensive exports in order to strengthen the country's self-defense and improve its balance-of-payments position. Six key sectors—chemicals, electronics, machinery, nonferrous metals, iron, and steel—were targeted for preferential credit, tax incentives, and public spending on technical training and research and development. Individual *chaebol*, the Korean version of the Japanese zaibatsu, or large conglomerates, were given the task of implementing specific projects with the heavy investment financed mainly by loans from government-controlled banks. Although the plan was successful in boosting HCI investment and in shifting the composition of output and exports, it also created severe bottlenecks, which, combined with the oil shocks of 1974 and 1979 and the turmoil surrounding President Park's assassination in October 1979, had a devastating impact upon the economy. The HCI drive also burdened the banking system with large nonperforming loans and moral hazard problems that would play a role in the financial crisis of the late 1990s. Due to its partial success, South Korea's industrial policy of "picking winners" was controversial and sparked an important debate on the role of government and the markets in formulating development policy.

Recognizing the growing problems created by the HCI drive, the government scaled back its industrial promotion policy and shifted to a more market-friendly stance. With the change in leadership in late 1979, the government embarked upon a systematic program to liberalize key sectors of the economy, including trade, the financial system, and the capital markets, but progress was slow. Trade liberalization gained momentum during this period, but heavy protection of agriculture and other infant industries remained. Starting in 1981, the government privatized some commercial banks and deregulated interest rates, but financial liberalization was hampered by the need to support banks that had been weakened by the HCI drive. Of all the sectors, progress was the slowest in the liberalization of the capital account, mainly due to concerns over foreign takeover of Korean assets. Foreign direct and portfolio investment jumped in the 1980s from very low levels as restrictions were gradually loosened, but still represented a minor share of overall investment, with much of the foreign capital coming in the form of debt financing.

In late 1997, the problems in the corporate and financial sector came to surface as South Korea was hit by a financial crisis that required one of the largest financial bailouts in history. The Asian crisis, which began with the devaluation of Thai currency in July 1997, quickly spread through the region, hitting South Korea in November. With its international reserves virtually depleted and its exchange rate in a freefall, South Korea was forced to turn to the International Monetary Fund (IMF) and the international community for a $58-billion financial package, the largest of its kind at the time. Despite the sound macroeconomic fundamentals prior to the crisis, the rapid buildup in short-term external debt, a highly leveraged corporate sector, and a financial system weakened by a legacy of government intervention left the country vulnerable to financial contagion. South Korea, however, rebounded quickly from the crisis, faster than the other Asian crisis countries, and regained its precrisis output level within a year and a half. While its external position has improved, further reform of its financial and corporate sectors are needed for South Korea to successfully take the next leap in its economic development.

[*See also* Chaebol *and* Zaibatsu.]

The opinions expressed in this paper are those of the author and do not necessarily reflect the views of the IMF.

BIBLIOGRAPHY

Amsden, Alice H. *Asia's Next Giant: South Korea and Late Industrialization.* New York, 1989.

Cha, Dong-Se, Kwang Suk Kim, and Dwight H. Perkins, eds. *The Korean Economy 1945–1995: Performance and Vision for the Twenty-first Century.* Seoul, 1997.

Lane, Timothy, et al. "IMF-Supported Programs in Indonesia, Korea, and Thailand: A Preliminary Assessment." *IMF Occasional Paper 178.* Washington, D.C., 1999.

Mason, Edward S., et al. *The Economic and Social Modernization of the Republic of Korea.* Cambridge, 1980.

Song, Byung-Nak. *The Rise of the Korean Economy.* 2d ed. Oxford, 1990.

World Bank. *The East Asian Miracle: Economic Growth and Public Policy.* Oxford, 1993.

KENNETH KANG

KRUPP FAMILY. The Krupp Family of German iron, steel, and weapons makers (1787–1968) personified the rise and fall of German heavy industry and its close relationship with the course of German expansionism in the nineteenth and twentieth centuries. Starting with the career of Friedrich Krupp (1787–1826), who cofounded a cast-iron foundry in Essen in 1811 and then took over exclusive leadership of the enterprise in 1816, the family's patriarchs displayed from the outset a single-minded, hands-on dedication to their firm's development. This resulted not only in rapid and imposing growth but also in recurrent rounds of financial overextension, one of which finally put an end to the identity of family and firm in 1968.

The characteristic Krupp style of personal and paternalistic management was set during the supremacy of Alfred Krupp (1812–1887), who inherited the already heavily indebted foundry while still a teenager. He turned the firm's fortunes around by concentrating on making presses for tableware, then conquered the international market for rolled pipe and moved into the production of specialty steels and alloys, seamless steel locomotive wheels and axles, and rifle barrels and cannon. By the 1870s, having meanwhile diversified his operations both vertically and horizontally through the acquisition of coal mines and a shipping firm, Alfred had established Krupp as the largest maker of artillery and the most advanced mass producer of steel in the world. He had also made it a model of the German style of quasi-feudal industrial organization, in which the owner demanded absolute loyalty, obedience, and discipline from the workers, and took care of them in return through such measures as co-paid health and life insurance, a pension plan, hiring preferences for their relatives and offspring, and the provision of subsidized meals, housing, and stores. When his technological and managerial innovations brought him to the brink of insolvency during the economic crisis of that decade, however, Alfred's absolute authority over the firm was curtailed by the

KRUPP FAMILY. Gustav Krupp von Bohlen und Halbach, his wife Bertha Krupp von Bohlen und Halbach, their oldest son Alfried, and his siblings. Portrait, oil on canvas, by George Simon Harcourt, twentieth century. (Villa Huegel, Essen, Germany/Erich Lessing/Art Resource, NY)

appointment of a financial overseer responsible to the Prussian State Bank. He sought to withdraw thereafter to the massive palace he had built above Essen, the Villa Hügel, and to delegate decision making to his subordinates; but he could not resist increasingly quarrelsome interference in their decisions.

This brief and rocky period of divided rule ended in 1887 with the accession of Alfred's son, the most tragic figure in an increasingly gloomy family history, though also one of the most outwardly successful. Friedrich Alfred Krupp (1854–1902), both a product of and a partner in a loveless marriage, may well have ended a suicide. Before he died, however, he extended Krupp's military production into armor plate and warships, routinized its practice of recruiting upper management from the higher ranks of the German civil service, and solidified its standing as the nation's flagship private enterprise, symbolized by his membership in the German parliament from 1893 to 1898 and his personal friendship with Kaiser Wilhelm II. Under Friedrich Alfred, the firm's annual sales and total workforce approximately doubled, to 91 million Reichsmarks and forty thousand employees, respectively.

Since Friedrich Alfred left no male heir, ownership passed to his eldest daughter Bertha (1886–1957), though as the principal shareholder in a stock corporation, rather than in her own right. A board of directors ran the company until she married Gustav von Bohlen und Halbach (1870–1950), an aloof and unbending former lawyer and diplomat of German-American descent, who then led the enterprise from 1906 to 1943. The kaiser attended their wedding, which led to eight children (six sons and two daughters), granted the groom the right to incorporate Krupp into his and his principal heirs' name, and forcefully impressed upon Gustav the obligation to serve as trustee of the great fortune he had obtained. During World War I, Krupp was by far Germany's leading arms producer (85 percent of its output went to war production) and experienced enormous growth. Vilified abroad as the prototypical "Merchant of Death," Gustav was named a war criminal by the victorious Allies but never brought to trial. Not until the French briefly occupied Germany's Ruhr region in 1923 was he hauled before a court, this time on charges of sabotage. Sentenced to seven years in prison, he served seven months. The outcome forecast, in kind if not degree, his son's experience with another attempt at "victors' justice" after World War II.

Under the largely disarmed Weimar Republic (1919–1933), Krupp downsized and reorganized itself around the production of rails, locomotives, farm implements, heavy machinery, cash registers, medical instruments, and other specialty products. In 1925–1926, the firm stood apart from the formation of the massive United Steel Trust, then sustained its independence with loans from the United States and a consortium of banks and with government aid. However, the Depression struck Krupp hard: by 1933, its assets had dropped to less than 80 percent of their 1914 level, and its workforce decreased by 40 percent between 1927 and 1932. Gustav's very traditionalism and caution ensured that he was not stampeded into the arms of the Nazis by these developments. Although he shared their hostility to unions and much of Weimar's social legislation, as well as their distaste for parliamentary rule, their determination to blame outsiders for Germany's problems, and their nationalist fervor, he mistrusted their inclinations to *dirigisme*, protectionism, autarky, and deficit spending. After being elected head of the National Association of German Industry in 1931, Krupp supported the various cabinets appointed by President von Hindenburg in preference to Hitler's movement.

Following Hitler's appointment as chancellor of Germany in early 1933, however, Krupp played a pusillanimous role. He caved in immediately to Nazi demands for a purge of liberals and Jews on the association's staff and quickly abandoned any effort to express misgivings about particular policies. Declaring that "primacy always belongs to politics," he began paying literal tribute to the new regime in the form of donations to party organizations and fund-raising drives, and he let his firm become the armory of the nation once more. Between 1933–1934 and the outbreak of war in 1939, employment at Krupp more than doubled to over 101,000 workers, and sales to the military rose fourfold to almost 85 million Reichsmarks. Increasingly ill and mentally infirm, Gustav retreated from active management at the beginning of the war, much of which he spent at the family castle in Austria.

Informally at first, then officially in 1943, Gustav was succeeded by his son Alfried Krupp von Bohlen und Halbach (1907–1967), who combined the advantages of university training in metallurgy with those of good political connections. He had joined the Nazi Party in 1938, and five years later it returned the favor when Hitler decreed that Krupp would revert from being a stock corporation to become the personal property of the family. During World War II, the firm's dedication to the German war effort led to the exploitation of more than 150,000 prisoners of war, concentration camp inmates, and citizens of occupied countries as forced laborers. Tens of thousands of them died from brutality, starvation, and neglect at installations such as Krupp's short-lived factory at Auschwitz and its new Berthawerke near Breslau.

Indicted as a war criminal after the war, Alfried was sentenced to twelve years' imprisonment and stripped of his personal and corporate property, much of which was initially scheduled for dismantling; but both he and the enterprise benefited from the increasing American interest in reconstructing Germany as the Cold War intensified. In 1951, John McCloy, the U.S. high commissioner in Germany, pardoned Alfried and returned his assets with the understanding that he would divest himself of the coal and steel holdings. After drawing this process out until the Americans lost both interest in and influence over it, Alfried returned to an expansionist course, making Krupp, by 1960, the leading steel producer in Europe and the apex of a diversified industrial empire with a workforce of over 100,000 people and annual sales of over $1 billion. Overextension during the following decade, however, brought Alfried to the brink of ruin, from which he was rescued by the German government in 1967, contingent upon restructuring the firm into a publicly owned corporation. When he died that same year the Krupp family's direct involvement in the firm came to an end. His estranged son Arndt von Bohlen und Halbach had renounced his inheritance rights, and Alfred had bequeathed his fortune to a newly founded Krupp foundation. Refounded in 1968, the firm became an ever-smaller portion of the ever-shrinking entities into which the coal and steel industries of the Ruhr consolidated during the final third of the twentieth century.

BIBLIOGRAPHY

Feldman, Gerald. *Iron and Steel in the German Inflation, 1916–1923*. Princeton, 1977.

Manchester, William. *The Arms of Krupp, 1587–1968*. New York, 1970.

Overy, R. J. "'Primacy Always Belongs to Politics': Gustav Krupp and the Third Reich." In *War and Economy in the Third Reich*, edited by R. J. Overy, pp. 119–143. Oxford, 1994.

Turner, Henry Ashby, Jr. *German Big Business and the Rise of Hitler*. New York, 1985.

PETER HAYES

L

LABOR. Condemned as Adam's curse, labor is fundamental to the human condition. People provide for their subsistence by combining their labor, or work, with natural materials and tools. However, labor is more than a dismal but necessary burden. Work creates material pleasures and luxuries, as well as civilization's artistic and religious expressions. Work is an essential part of the human experience; people labor for the intrinsic satisfaction of creation. Through work, people define themselves.

Labor and the Market. Work is social because people work together and because they exchange their products. The social organization of work has two dimensions: the distribution of labor's product and the organization of the production process. Products can be distributed either as commodities exchanged in a market or by command. At work, workers may assume particular tasks because they are hired for them in a market, or because they are assigned to them. Examined in these dimensions, labor has four different social configurations (see Table 1).

Some form of nonmarket allocation has been found throughout history. By substituting the legitimate use of force for voluntary exchange in a labor market, slavery allows owners to allocate their slaves' labor with little regard for the slaves' own wishes. Family labor has usually been organized outside the market. Self-sufficient farmers and artisans decide what to produce and how to organize production within households according to an intrafamily allocation process that may pay little respect to the willingness of outsiders to pay for their products. Caring tasks, such as providing for children, the ill, and the needy elderly, are apportioned to family members, often with little regard for the cost or the value of such services in the marketplace or for the family provider's opportunity costs; here burdens often are borne by mothers without regard for their long-term interests in the labor market.

Compared with slave and household labor, markets can be empowering and liberating. The market empowers consumers, allowing them to influence production decisions and labor allocation across products within market-oriented firms. Market allocation also can be liberating for workers. Freed from the domination of slave drivers and household patriarchs, they can strike, refusing work that they believe to be too onerous or too poorly compensated.

The market's liberating influence should not be exaggerated. The market does little to empower less affluent consumers who spend too little to influence market firms significantly. Similarly, the right to quit is often of limited value to workers; when a select few individuals control the means of production, the right to say no to the employers can mean the right to starve. Indeed, early social theorists distinguished between social classes not according to market involvement but according to ownership of the means of production necessary for economic independence. This approach bound John Locke and Karl Marx with freed slaves in the nineteenth-century American South, in urging that distribution of land was necessary to complete the work of emancipation. Without wide distribution of productive property, they argued, commodity and labor markets cause production to be an area of command, where workers labor under employers' supervision and control.

Nor has spreading marketization ensured that all workers will be valued without regard to ascribed status. Persistent social norms backed by legal restraints and the lasting impact of past practice have maintained discriminatory treatment of lower-caste workers in India, Koreans in Japan, nonwhites in South Africa, workers of African descent in the Americas, and others. Restricted from many employments, these workers have been crowded into relatively few jobs with low wages and very poor working conditions. Throughout the world, the most common form of labor market discrimination is against women. To ensure their availability to labor for their husbands and fathers, social conventions and government policy have widely

TABLE 1. *The Social Allocation of Labor and its Product*

		ALLOCATING LABOR WITHIN PRODUCTION PROCESS	
		NONMARKET	MARKET
Allocating Products	Nonmarket	Family/home production	Slavery
	Market	Self-employment	Capital/wage labor

restricted their employment outside households. Despite progress toward more egalitarian standards, women's work continues to be devalued, and their opportunities remain circumscribed.

Revolutions in Labor Markets. Markets and authority have been combined to allocate labor and products in different ways throughout history. The Roman Empire relied on its authority over slave labor for production of commodities that were exchanged in markets. The Empire's collapse led to European feudalism. Under feudalism, lords controlled access to land and exercised personal authority over serfs, who were required to provide products for the lords' consumption. By combining family production with limited commodity exchange, feudalism maintained a central conflict between the lords' legal authority against the serfs' practical control of the land and their own labor. Conflicts over the serfs' autonomy and the allocation of products culminated in fourteenth-century peasant revolts and the collapse of western European feudalism. Independent peasant farming replaced feudalism in France; capitalist farming employing wage labor to produce market commodities replaced feudalism in Britain. Feudalism's collapse gave western European males new rights over their persons without ending the use of coerced labor. European women remained under the authority of their fathers and husbands. Paradoxically, capitalist growth in western Europe created a market for tropical commodities just when Europe's growing military prowess gave it the power to compel ten million Africans to labor as slaves in the New World.

For centuries after the collapse of feudalism, free wage labor prospered in western Europe alongside New World chattel slavery. Serious opposition to slavery began only in the eighteenth century, joining a disparate coalition of Protestant evangelicals with bourgeois and working-class radicals. The Northern states of the new United States of America were the first to ban slavery, soon joined by the new French republic, born of the revolutions of 1789 and 1793, as well as Haiti in the 1790s and the United Kingdom in 1832. However, the pivotal change in the United States came in 1865 after a bloody Civil War; the emancipation of four million slaves in the Southern states cost the remaining slave states their main ally. Brazil and Cuba soon fell into line, ending New World chattel slavery.

As effected in the United States and elsewhere, emancipation was starkly limited to freeing the male slaves' persons without regard for their household relations or labor market opportunities. Males assumed a dominant position over their freed wives and children, controlling their labor as effectively as had their former masters. Freed from chattel slavery, the women were expected to serve and to obey their husbands; the right to contract freely, to refuse work, and to change employers were market rights, which did not extend to families and home production and thus were largely restricted to males. For their part, male slaves were freed in a paradoxical double sense: freed from their former owners' domination but also freed from claim to the land or to the means of production. In Haiti and parts of Jamaica, freedmen were able to withdraw from markets by establishing independent farms away from commercial plantations. Unable to gain direct access to productive land, most of the freedmen in the United States were forced to seek employment. Thrown onto the labor market, the new freedmen in the American South constituted a created proletariat (i.e., laboring class).

America's freedmen entered the labor market just when capitalist wage labor was displacing other types of production. As industrial establishments and firms grew larger, and labor moved out agriculture, independent producers were transformed into proletarians. Outside the United States, manufacturing establishments were smaller than their U.S. counterparts, and artisanal production by independent crafts workers survived well into the twentieth century. After World War II, however, European establishments quickly approached the American scale, and artisanal production in Europe was increasingly displaced by capitalist enterprises employing wage labor. By the later-twentieth century, this process extended to trade and services when chain stores replaced owner-managed restaurants and shops. From this perspective, the most important economic change since the mid-nineteenth century was not the end of slavery but the worldwide decline in independent production. No longer working on their own account and selling the products of their labor, producers sold their labor itself, their time, and their work for other masters.

The proletariat has also been inflated by the increasing provision of caring labor through the market, by substituting the commodities (e.g., food and cleaning services and child care) produced by wage labor for what was produced at home by family labor. When families purchase such caring services through the market with income earned through the market labor of wives and mothers working outside the home, the number of wage earners increases without any change in the quantity of goods and services produced.

Marketization has dramatically transformed the class structure. Its impact can be seen in the United States from the early nineteenth century on. Including both the formal labor force counted in government statistics (mostly nonfamily labor: slaves, employers, and employees) and as the informal sector involved in home production, three of four social categories had declined significantly in size by the end of the twentieth century. In addition to the slave labor force, eliminated by emancipation, marketization and the movement of women into the paid labor force had more

TABLE 2. *Class Distribution of U.S. Workforce*

SOCIAL CATEGORY	EARLY 1800s	END OF 1900s
Slaves	18%	0%
Home workers	41	16
Employers and self-employed	25	6
Proletarians	16	77

SOURCE: U.S. Census Bureau.

than halved the number of home workers. Further, the share of employers and the self-employed had declined by three-fourths as the share of proletarians had grown dramatically, increasing from 16 percent of the workforce to 77 percent (see Table 2).

Changing Work. Throughout history, most workers have produced food and provided caring services in homes; but in advanced capitalist economies, labor has moved steadily from these activities into manufacturing and to business and professional caring services. Demand for some goods, notably foodstuffs, increases slowly with increasing affluence, whereas some services, notably education and medical services, experience more rapidly rising demand. However, labor force changes also reflect increasing specialization. New categories of workers have been created, with accountants, engineers, clerical workers, and sales agents performing jobs formerly done by owner-entrepreneurs and production workers. Marketization of home production also has created new categories of child care and restaurant employees. Moreover, specialization has become global. Declining goods production in advanced capitalist economies reflects an international division of labor where poorer countries produce goods that they exchange for business and professional services that require training and a sophisticated infrastructure available only in advanced economies.

Labor-Force Participation. In the pure neoclassical model, producers allocate their time between leisure and producing goods and services for others, subject to wealth and productivity constraints. Increasing wealth leads producers to take more leisure and produce less, whereas higher returns to work encourage more labor. This approach may help explain labor decisions by independent producers, who control the timing and pace of their work; but it can be misleading in the new world of wage labor. Employers offer wage workers a bundled bargain: no work and no income or a determined number of hours of work at a specified wage and work pace. The exchange of labor time for wages gives employees different incentives from those of the self-employed, who receive the full value of their product. Paid a fixed wage, workers have no incentive to work hard or productively; they may even mask

productivity enhancements to retain control over the work pace. Employers counter this behavior with a hierarchy of otherwise-unproductive supervisors to monitor the work process, including nearly 15 percent of the North American workforce today and between 3 percent and 6 percent of the workforce in most other advanced economies. Since the "scientific management" movement of the early twentieth-century, management has sought to raise labor productivity by reducing on-the-job leisure, including casual drinking, chronic absenteeism, and haphazard work efforts. It is unclear whether modern management has increased the work effort, and the aggregate work intensity may have declined in some advanced economies with the shift out of machine-paced manufacturing work. There may be evidence of increasing work intensity in the rising the rates of some occupational injuries found in many countries, especially those associated with repetitive motions; but, overall, occupational mortality rates remain well below the rates of the nineteenth and early twentieth centuries; they have fallen in the United States, for example, by 80 percent since 1960.

Increasing wealth has led workers in advanced capitalist economies to work less, but some of the reduction has been concealed by the increasing marketization of home production. Many women have left home for market work, raising the officially measured labor force participation rate but without increasing the amount of labor performed. At the same time, male workers have responded to rising wealth by substituting leisure for work. The most spectacular increase in leisure has been the decline in the number of hours of paid employment per week, which went from nearly seventy for workers in the United States in the early 1830s down to fifty by 1915, before leveling off around forty hours since the 1930s. Workers also take more holidays. Nearly 90 percent of American workers receive paid vacations, usually for two weeks, whereas European workers have vacations of four or five weeks. The age at which children begin work has drifted up steadily, from the early teens to the early twenties. Many postpone market work until their mid- or late twenties, after they have completed college and graduate education. Increasing wealth and longevity have created a new life-stage. Retiring from market work in their early sixties or even earlier, Japanese, European, and North American men can anticipate more than a decade of postretirement leisure; retiring younger and living longer, women can anticipate twenty years of retirement.

Productivity. Improvements in management and increasing work intensity may have contributed to the remarkable rise in labor productivity of the past two centuries. Increases in output per hour worked have allowed income to grow faster than the population, even with less of the population working. Between 1840 and 1990, output

LABOR. Cadillac Motor and Fleetwood strikers, Detroit, 18 January 1937. (Walter P. Reuther Library, Wayne State University)

in the United States rose fiftyfold, far beyond the eightfold increase in the U.S. labor force and the twentyfold increase in the quantity of machinery and structures available to U.S. workers. Before 1945, productivity grew faster in the United States than in most of Europe or in the Pacific Rim countries; but American productivity growth accelerated only slightly after World War II, as productivity growth rates doubled or tripled in Japan and in continental Europe, allowing these countries to close the gap between their productivity and that of the United States.

Beginning in the 1970s, productivity growth slowed dramatically in most of the world. Scholars have been able to attribute some of the earlier growth and some of the post–World War II slowdown to identifiable factors, including increased training and human capital formation, economies of scale, the availability of inanimate energy, including electricity, and the movement of labor out of less-productive industries, notably agriculture, into more productive ones, such as manufacturing. However, much of the variation in productivity growth remains "unexplained," attributed variously to exogenous technology or to labor intensity.

In most advanced countries, wages generally have risen with productivity. For more than a century (until the 1970s), wages rose by over 2 percent a year in the United States; and they have grown faster since World War II in

many other countries, along with increased productivity growth. Recently, however, wages and productivity have not moved together. In the United States, there has been little increase in wages since 1970 despite a 30 percent increase in productivity. The recent separation of productivity and wages has dramatically widened the gap between rich and poor Americans. Most of the increase in income in the United States since 1970 has been received by the wealthiest households. Income gaps have widened in other countries, notably English-speaking countries such as the United Kingdom and New Zealand; but in no advanced-capitalist economy has the gap between rich and poor widened as much as it has in the United States.

Labor, the State, and the Socialist Movement. Following Karl Marx, social critics predicted that the new proletarians would transform society. Beginning with collective strikes and labor unions, they would build a movement to create a socialist society without commodity markets, where goods would be distributed according to need. In many countries, labor unions have grown to encompass over half the total labor force. Strong unions have won some collective worker control over the pace of work and working conditions, and have narrowed wage differentials among workers and between wage and salaried workers. Labor unions have fueled socialist political movements that have won government programs to

TABLE 3. *Industrial Distribution of U.S. Labor Force, 1820–1998*

YEAR	AGRICULTURE, FOREST, FISHING	CONSTRUCTION, MANUFACTURING, MINING	TRADE, TRANSPORT, FINANCE, INSURANCE, REAL ESTATE	SERVICES
1820	71.9	12.2	16.0	
1850	64.0	17.5	5.5	12.2
1900	37.6	30.1	16.7	14.3
1940	17.1	31.1	24.2	21.4
1960	4.4	33.1	30.9	31.6
1998	2.6	22.7	34.3	40.4

SOURCE: U.S. Census Bureau.

cushion the impact of unemployment and to provide training and wage subsidies to workers, health insurance and generous public pensions, family allowances, and other benifits.

The United States has challenged Marxists' predictions about revolutionary labor. Site of the most advanced capitalist economy, it has lacked a powerful labor movement, and its government has provided fewer welfare benefits than have other advanced capitalist economies. Debate about "American Exceptionalism" has been central to the development of labor economics and labor history, and has pivoted between emphasizing circumstances unique to the United States and arguments that the weakness of American socialism augurs a future decline of labor movements throughout the world.

BIBLIOGRAPHY

Davis, David Brion. *The Problem of Slavery in the Age of Revolution, 1770–1823.* Ithaca, N.Y., 1975.

Duby, Georges. *The Three Orders: Feudal Society Imagined,* translated by Arthur Goldhammer. Chicago, 1980.

Esping-Andersen, Gosta. *The Three Worlds of Welfare Capitalism.* Princeton, 1990.

Finley, Moses I. *The Ancient Economy.* Berkeley, 1973.

Fogel, Robert. *Without Consent or Contract: The Rise and Fall of American Slavery.* New York, 1989.

Folbre, Nancy. *Who Pays for the Kids? Gender and the Structure of Constraint.* London, 1994.

Freeman, Richard, ed. *Working under Different Rules.* New York, 1994.

Freeman, Richard, and James Medoff. *What Do Unions Do?* New York, 1984.

Friedman, Gerald. *State-Making and Labor Movements: France and the United States, 1876–1914.* Ithaca, N.Y., 1999.

Goldin, Claudia. *Understanding the Gender Gap: An Economic History of American Women.* New York, 1990.

Hilton, Rodney, ed. *The Transition from Feudalism to Capitalism.* London, 1976.

Hopkins, Keith. *Conquerors and Slaves.* Cambridge, 1978.

Lopez, Robert S. *The Commercial Revolution of the Middle Ages, 950–1350.* Cambridge, 1976.

Maddison, Angus. *Dynamic Forces in Capitalist Development: A Long-Run Comparative View.* New York, 1991.

North, Douglass C., and Robert P. Thomas. *The Rise of the Western World: A New Economic History.* Cambridge, 1973.

Perlman, Selig. *A Theory of the Labor Movement.* New York, 1928.

Stanley, Amy Dru. *From Bondage to Contract: Wage Labor, Marriage, and the Market in the Age of Slave Emancipation.* Cambridge, 1998.

Tilly, Louise, and Joan Scott. *Women, Work, and Family.* New York, 1978.

GERALD FRIEDMAN

LABOR CONDITIONS AND JOB SAFETY. Labor conditions and safety at work have been regulated for centuries by central and local governments, though it was only in the mid-nineteenth century that modern legislation that protected the health and safety of employees at work was developed. The hours and wages of apprentices in England and Wales were controlled by Elizabethan statute, and the first factory legislation in Great Britain in 1802 dealt with the health and morals of apprentices. The conditions of labor and the promotion of safety in the history of the capitalist workplace have been largely determined by three kinds of activity: first, the growth of scientific and technical expertise in relation to the conditions of work and the injuries of workers; second, the legal development of labor contracts and the statutory provision for liability and compensation, including insurance provisions to protect employers with liability for health and safety; and third, the spread of collective bargaining and the campaigns of trade unions to secure improvements in workplace safety and compensation for those who were injured as well as advances in wages and working conditions in general. The scope of health and safety provisions has altered and widened over the nineteenth and twentieth centuries as public agencies have become more sensitive to the environmental impact of economic activity as well as the mental or emotional strain that employees experience. Most arrangements for workplace safety have remained in the hands of nation states, although there have been important initiatives by international agencies to secure better standards of health and safety as well as to protect workers (for example, those working outside the territorial waters of particular states) who were not readily protected by individual governments. This article is primarily concerned with the

JOB SAFETY. Sign outside a paper mill showing the number of accident-free days at the mill, Erving, Massachusetts, 1978. (Henry Babson, United Automobile Workers/Walter P. Reuther Library, Wayne State University)

economic and social history of the United Kingdom, though references are made to the growth of safety provisions in other countries wherever possible.

Growth of Medical, Scientific, and Technical Expertise. The modern regulation of injury and safety at the industrial workplace dates mainly from the 1830s. Before this period, the safety of labor and the hazards that people faced in their working lives were rarely regarded as appropriate subjects for legislative or legal intervention. Medical understanding of ill health at work was first documented by Bernardino Ramazzini in a seminal text published at the beginning of the eighteenth century and republished in London in 1746 as *Diseases of Tradesmen* by Dr. Robert James. Ramazzini provided a useful summary of established knowledge on a wide range of occupational illnesses and emphasized the importance of a well-ventilated working environment, though his text provided little scientific or medical detail (Ramazzini, 1700). He noted both the poverty of the work people and their reluctance to seek treatment until their illness was well advanced. Ramazzini noted of potters that, "With regard to the treatment of workers of this class, it is hardly ever possible to give them any remedies that would completely restore their health. For they do not ask for a helping hand from the doctor until their feet and hands are totally crippled and their internal organs have become very hard; and they suffer from yet another drawback, I mean that they are very poor and prescribe remedies that will at least mitigate the disease; but first of all they must be warned to give up their trade" (Ramazzini, 1700).

There were important advances in the understanding of toxic poisoning from lead, mercury, sulphur, carbon, and other industrial substances during the eighteenth and early nineteenth centuries. Charles Thakrah and other physicians documented workers' illnesses in industrial districts, and the mortality tables assembled from census returns provided some insights into workplace hazards; but there is little evidence that medical knowledge had a significant impact on rates of occupational injury and disease or on legislation introduced in Great Britain to protect laboring children and females.

The most important source of information on health and safety at work during the nineteenth century was the inspectorate created by different states to monitor the hazards posed by factories, mines, and workshops. The Health and Morals of Apprentices Act of 1802 was the first modern statute that attempted to regulate hours of work for young persons. Although largely ineffective, the measure did identify the vulnerability of those who were seen as not capable of reaching their own bargain. This principle of limited agency was embodied in the 1833 Factory Act, which restricted the use of child and female labor in textiles factories and introduced the ten-hour day for young persons aged thirteen to eighteen years. Within a decade, the Mines Regulation Act of 1842 forbade the employment of women and children underground, enforced by a mines inspectorate in addition to the factory inspectors introduced in 1833. By 1848, the long campaign of the factory reformers had led to legislation for ten hours of work per day for children and females. In the 1860s, there were important extensions to the factory legislation; and in 1878, an important act consolidated earlier measures, creating a Chief Inspector and clarifying the role of certifying surgeons, who had been introduced in 1833. In 1891, the "dangerous trades" legislation provided for the regulation of specific industries by the Home Office, and in 1898 the first Medical Inspector of Factories, Thomas Legge (1863–1932), was appointed to the Factory Department of the Home Office. These appointments were arguably as important to the progress of occupational health reform as the parallel growth of statistical expertise within the Board of Trade was to the regulation of labor markets and provisions for unemployment.

The expertise accumulated by Legge and his contemporaries provided for a vital period of growth in the first three decades of the twentieth century when the British state introduced measures not only to limit the hazards of serious injury but also the threat posed by occupational diseases caused by substances ranging from asbestos to wool textiles. The Factory Department of the Home Office and the Mines Department in Great Britain were assisted by the increased understanding of toxic substances and the hazards of dust and dirt at the workplace, though it was the two world wars that provided a greater impetus to government action.

The interwar years saw the beginnings of international cooperation via the International Labor Office and the League of Nations, but important initiatives to control anthrax and other diseases failed to secure support in the years of depressed trade and mass unemployment. South Africa led the way in the investigation and treatment of dust-related illnesses among miners with its mass X-ray program in the Rand gold fields. It was only in the 1940s that medical research in Great Britain reached a consensus on the hazards presented by coal dust and identified the problems faced by agricultural labor.

Legislation to protect farmworkers finally came in 1952 and 1956, together with a Mines and Quarries Act for the nationalized coal fields in 1954. During the decade, Richard Doll and others revealed the carcinogenic properties of asbestos and paved the way for the gradual restriction of asbestos production in Europe and the United States, though the mineral continued to be extensively mined in southern Africa. The great reforming years of the factory inspectorate had long passed, and in 1972 the Robens Report proposed a radical overhaul of the machinery with the introduction of a Health and Safety Executive. In the late twentieth century, the hazards faced by office workers and the general impact of stress on the health of the working population attracted more sustained and serious research.

Health and Safety under the Law. Ramazzini's celebrated writings at the beginning of the eighteenth century indicated that medical men in Europe were well aware of the dangers posed by different kinds of work, including the burdens carried by female domestic labor and the strain on the eyesight caused by the use of tools in precise and fine tasks. Philanthropists, as well as doctors, were active in publicizing the fatalities caused by the use of child labor in chimney sweeping, and Percival Potts exposed the risks of scrotal cancer among sweeps. Sweeps in Germany wore protective clothing and suffered fewer cases of disease, though there was little European or non-European legislation to regulate work with poisonous substances until the 1870s. There was little redress for those injured at work, even after the passage of limited preventive measures in the mid-nineteenth century.

It was the demand for accident compensation that provided a more important impetus for the investigation of the causes of accidents and ill health and compelled legislators of different countries to improve access to the courts by the end of the century. The first recorded action under English common law by an injured employee took place in 1837, though the responsibility of the employer was not clarified under the Employers' Liability legislation of 1880. The costs of litigation and the scope that the 1880 act gave firms to require their workers to contract out of its provisions severely reduced the value of the measure, and few employees who were not supported by substantial trade unions or friendly societies could contemplate legal action. It was not until the passage of the Workmen's Compensation Acts of 1897 and 1906 that injured, disabled, and diseased workers or their dependents could secure financial support in the courts.

The explanation for the relatively slow development of compensation provision can be traced to the larger problem of liability for hazards at work. Figlio has noted that the growth of modern ideas of an accident depended on the growth of fresh concepts of employment law in the nineteenth century, which replaced earlier notions of masters and servants (Figlio, 1988). It was not until the passing of artisan activities and the growth of modern capitalist labor relations that the distinction of the duties of the employer and the employee allowed a more legalistic approach to the concept of injury at work and responsibility for injury. Although Figlio's work lacks precision, he does point out the growth of legal relationships and the concept of employee as related to the notion of an accident, as that which is foreseeable as an aspect of labor but not always preventable. Legal thinking lagged behind the transformation of preindustrial artisan labor and the growth of capitalist management; though by the late nineteenth century, it was broadly accepted that the manager or supervisor was the agent of the firm rather than another employee. Similarly, it was agreed that the making of a voluntary contract by the employee did not imply that he understood and accepted the hazards of employment. Nor did the payment of higher wages as a risk premium absolve the employer from responsibility for injury under the workmen's compensation laws introduced by most states, even if the accident arose from circumstances beyond the control of the employer or even as a result of safety rules being breached by his subordinates. The responsibilities of managers and supervisors for the maintenance of health and safety at work were codified in Germany and other European countries during the nineteenth century, and in Great Britain the important Mines Act of 1911 specified the safety training that mine management must undertake.

There were also important differences in the compensation provisions of Great Britain, Germany, and many of the American states during the Progressive Era. In Germany, the employers and workers were required to contribute to a compulsory state system of insurance, while in Great Britain and many parts of the United States, government schemes of national sickness and unemployment insurance were not integrated into a unitary system of risk protection. This remained true even though it was widely recognized that in many cases of injury and illness, the specific causes of accident or disease could not be demonstrated beyond dispute; and by the early twentieth century, legislation usually specified that an employee must clearly demonstrate employment at a particular works in the period of assumed injury.

Germany introduced legislation to regulate accidental injury before Great Britain but was more reluctant to compensate industrial disease. After the passage of the British compensation law of 1897, there were legal as well as medical arguments about the definition of an accident and whether industrial diseases and such infections as anthrax qualified for compensation. The consequence was the inclusion of a limited number of "scheduled" diseases under the 1906 Workmen's Compensation Act, sufferers being eligible for compensation on the same basis as though they had been injured at work, providing they could demonstrate that they were employed at the time of their illness or their condition could be traced to a particular period of work and a specific trade. The Imperial insurance authorities in Germany resisted the classification of such diseases as accidents until the Weimar Republic, and in the United States it was often necessary for a claimant to trace an illness to a particular employer as well as a specific moment in his or her working career.

One consequence of the growing awareness of hazards at the workplace was the spread of mutual and commercial insurance schemes, which were designed to protect the employer as much as the workers against the financial costs of injury and illness. British employers complained that the introduction of compensation legislation led to a marked increase in malingering as employees readily claimed sick leave and injury payments when they suffered trivial discomfort. Scholars have more generally discussed the importance of the rise in actuarial assessments of industrial injury and illness. The creation of "risk biographies" was an essential component of Germany's move to recognize occupational disease in the early twentieth century. Milles notes that diseases were excluded from compensation provisions until the Occupational Disease Ordinance of 1925 precisely because they were seen as neither accidental nor as a social phenomenon. The Imperial Insurance Court had specifically ruled in 1888 that industrial diseases were "the common and foreseeable drawbacks of an inherently unhealthy industry which must be taken into account by everyone participating in that industry" (Milles, 1993). The detailed information on injury risks gathered from friendly societies, as well as compensation returns, offered governments and industrial employers a useful tool in estimating their exposure to poor health and hazard claims. Institutional preferences and political contests also played an important part in shaping the statutory and commercial responses to the incidence of mortality and morbidity at the workplace.

Collective Bargaining, Free Agency, and the Battle for Health and Safety. The development of health and safety at the workplace has been influenced by the growth of collective bargaining and the unionization of the workforce in different countries. Considerable discussion remains as to how workers value safety versus income and, more particularly, if they value monetary compensation for injury above prevention of accidents. There have been several attempts to assess the extent to which employees were (and are) paid higher wages to offset the risks that they faced in hazardous industries and the impact of unionization on the levels of wages paid in such sectors. Research suggests that American labor markets provided compensating differentials for workers who faced the risks of fatal and nonfatal injury, though inequalities based on gender and age persist in similar periods and places (Fishback, 1992; Fishback and Kantor, 1991; Kim and Fishback, 1993).

The evidence from the late twentieth century suggests that if hazards had been historically associated with higher wages, accident and injury rates fell in those sectors where wages rose most rapidly and that the lower-paid jobs did not see such improvements, thereby increasing the unequal experience of wage labor. In other countries and sectors, such as coal mining in India, risks persisted because the perceived costs of reducing or removing the dangers was seen as uneconomical (Hamermesh, 1998; Mukhopadhyay, 2001).

Within the British context, there has also been some discussion as to whether trade unions have historically neglected the cause of industrial safety and also tended to privilege campaigns for compensation over those dealing with the prevention of hazards (Bartrip and Burman, 1983; Bartrip, 1983; Wikeley, 1993; Weindling, 1986). The evidence appears to indicate a larger range of influences and agencies in determining workers' attitudes to risk and also a more complex set of cultural and institutional preferences being displayed by union members.

The impact of bargaining and trade unionism is also a complex question. The history of labor relations in Great Britain is often characterized as voluntary and permissive, but the voluntary contract between capital and labor masked the absolute authority that the employer enjoyed in the eyes of the law (Clegg, 1983). The individual contract of employment, based on master and servant principles, remained the basis of British labor law before 1968. The various immunities granted to unions after 1875 and the measures protecting the health and safety of workers were never codified into any general labor law. The trade unions bargained for only a minority of male workers, women and young persons being virtually unrepresented in most sectors of the economy, during the nineteenth and early twentieth centuries.

The historical responsibility assumed by the British state for the protection of women and children in the workplace and the predisposition of the unions to bargain directly with employers rather than to rely on labor courts or government conciliation may have deterred some male-dominated unions from pressing for greater regulation of health and safety. It would be wrong to ignore the benefits to male workers from such measures as the regulation of toxic substances in such dangerous trades as match-making where the majority of sufferers were male, though female disfigurement from the facial disease known as "phossy jaw" gained much public attention. Similarly, the campaign to regulate anthrax and other industrial illnesses indicates that even in weakly organized trades, such as wool textiles, male workers were ready to pursue vigorous campaigns to improve safety as well as secure monetary compensation for the workforce at the end of the nineteenth century (Mortimer and Melling, 2000). It may be argued that health and safety provisions were advanced more rapidly during the two world wars, when the British state (and many other governments) imposed compulsory direction of labor and extended safety provisions to cater to the large influx of female workers. Yet such measures were actively supported by the trade unions and were widely perceived as a political reward for the unions' acceptance of legal compulsion in the labor market.

There is no clear evidence for the case that British and other trade unions put greater emphasis on securing monetary compensation for injury above steps to prevent accident and illness. Campaigns to improve health and safety were certainly more vigorous during the two world wars than they were during the intervening years of mass unemployment. It may be that unions opted to protect employment at the expense of safety issues, but there is significant evidence that unions supported both compensation and improved safety standards. It was the unions, during the 1940s, that pressed for recognition of the lung disease pneumoconiosis as an industrial disease.

Conclusions. It has been suggested that the three main influences in the history of health and safety at work have been the growth of medical and administrative expertise, the evolution and interpretation of contract law and such measures as workmen's compensation, and the spread of trade unionism and collective bargaining in capitalist societies. Economic progress and rising living standards may have contributed to placing a greater value on human life and capacity, though it is noticeable that less-industrialized regions, such as Australasia, were early pioneers of safety reforms as well as labor laws and that the major industrial nations continued to exhibit important differences in their approach to risks and hazards at work throughout the nineteenth and much of the twentieth centuries.

The medical understanding of work-related injuries and illnesses has remained a factor in the regulation of production, though the creation of state bureaucracies and government advisors with specific responsibility for the protection of the workforce appears to have been more significant in the reform process. Legislative and legal advances provided an early corrective to the freedom of labor markets, more particularly in protecting children and females against excessive hours and physical brutality. Males were also covered by the control of toxic substances and the inspection of dangerous trades, though in practice these were restricted to industries where known hazardous substances were in use rather than the accident-prone jobs on the waterfront, in the shipyards, and on building sites.

An important innovation came with the acknowledgment of industrial diseases and workplace injuries, prompting the growth of large-scale insurance schemes to shield firms from the costs of accidents and disease. The impact of trade unionism and collective bargaining on the health and safety of workers remains a subject of some debate. It is possible to read some data as evidence that hazardous occupations attracted a wage premium at particular moments, though a wide range of other influences impinged on the returns to labor. There are numerous examples of dangerous lower-paid jobs that unionization appears to have usually associated over the longer term with rising safety standards as well as wages and accident compensation. Among the most difficult areas to regulate included those beyond the reach of nation states, as firms often moved their more hazardous operations to poorly regulated regions, where the costs of health and safety were less burdensome.

BIBLIOGRAPHY

Bartrip, Peter W. J. *Workmen's Compensation in the Twentieth Century: Law, History, and Social Policy.* Avebury, England, 1983.

Bartrip, Peter W. J., and S. B. Burman. *The Wounded Soldiers of Industry: Industrial Compensation Policy, 1833–1897.* Oxford, 1983.

Clegg, H. A. "Otto Kahn-Freund and British Industrial Relations." In *Labour Law and Industrial Relations: Building on Kahn-Freund*, edited by K. Wedderburn, R. Lewis, and J. Clark, pp. 16–17. New York, 1983.

Cooter, Roger, and Bill Luckin, eds. *Accidents in History: Injuries, Fatalities, and Social Relations.* Amsterdam, 1997.

Figlio, K. "What Is an Accident?" In *The Social History of Occupational Health*, edited by P. Weindling, pp. 183–186, 197. London and Dover, N.H., 1988.

Fishback, P. V. *Soft Coal, Hard Choices: The Economic Welfare of Bituminous Coal Miners, 1890–1930.* New York, 1992.

Fishback, P. V., and S. Kantor. "The Good, the Bad, and the Paycheck: Compensating Differentials in Labor Markets, 1884–1902." University of Arizona working paper 91, July 1991.

Hamermesh, D. S. "Changing Inequality in Markets for Workplace Amenities." National Bureau of Economic Research working paper 6515, 1998.

James, Robert. *Diseases of Tradesmen.* London, 1946.

Kim, S. W., and Fishback, P. V. "Institutional Change, Compensating Differentials, and Accident Risk in American Railroading." *Journal of Economic History* 53.4 (1993), 796–823.

Milles, D. "Industrial Disease." *Dynamis* 13 (1993), 139–153.

Mortimer, I., and J. Mellling. " 'The Contest between Commerce and Trade, on the One Side, and Human Life on the Other': British Government Policies for the Regulation of Anthrax Infection and the Wool Textiles Industries, 1880–1939." *Textile History* 31.2 (2000), 223–237.

Mukhopadhyay, A. "Risk, Labor, and Capital: Concern for Safety in Colonial and Post-Colonial Mining." *Indian Journal of Labour Economics* 44.1 (2001), 63–73.

Ramazzini, Bernardino. *De morbis artificum.* Modena, Italy, 1700.

Sellers, Christopher C. *Hazards of the Job: From Industrial Disease to Environmental Health Science.* Chapel Hill, N. C., 1997.

Weindling, Paul, ed. *The Social History of Occupational Health.* London, and Dover, N.H., 1985.

Wikeley, N. J. *Compensation for Industrial Disease.* Aldershot, U.K., 1993.

Wright, W. C. "Introduction." *Diseases of Workers.* Chicago, 1940.

JOSEPH MELLING

LABOR MARKETS *[This entry contains three subentries, a historical overview, and discussions of segmentation and discrimination and integration and wage convergence in labor markets.]*

Historical Overview

The labor market is a place where labor is traded, as well as a concept by which the relationship between demand and supply of labor is analyzed. In the former context, labor actually is exchanged whether as a commodity or as a physical person, an idea that emerged with early market economies in the first millennium BCE. The concept appeared as such in the work of economists in the mid-nineteenth century, and since then it has been extensively elaborated and often cast in mathematical models to explain unemployment and the level and disparity of wages.

Studies of Labor Markets. Neoclassical economics, flourishing from the 1870s up to the 1920s and enjoying significant academic status since then, conceived of the labor market as a free space where the law of supply and demand regulates the price and the quantity of labor. The model implies an equilibrium: in a perfect situation unemployment would not exist (unless voluntarily), and wages would be fair for both employer and employee. The German theorist Karl Marx (1818–1883) proposed the theory of a reserve army of wage laborers who are forced to sell work at low price during cyclical bursts of the economy. This type of labor continuously exerts a downward pressure on all wages, and unemployment is structural. In the 1930s, the Cambridge economist John Maynard Keynes (1883–1946) objected to the neoclassical concept of the labor market, arguing that demand for labor is a function of production and, ultimately, of consumption. Hence, the demand for goods regulates employment and wage levels. The institutionalist approach, applying various lines of thought, among which Marx's, Keynes's, and the French *Régulation* (1980s), paid attention to formal and informal power relations of labor markets, such as custom and contracts. In the 1950s sociologists and labor economists suggested the structural existence of a multitude of submarkets, each using particular labor and often having important barriers that account for social exclusion of all kinds. Such a view stresses education, regulations, policy, information networks, and employment intermediaries. Far from superseding each other through time, these theories coexist, and adopt or confront one another.

None of these theories has been swiftly applied to writing history. Labor history was long the field of historians of the labor movement, with economic history limiting itself largely to empirical study of the demand for labor in industry. Apart from exceptional, implicit use, the concept of the labor market came to the fore in economic and social historiography in the early 1970s. Two approaches appeared: one putting market forces at the center and often leaning on mathematical models, the other paying much attention to institutions and custom, and taking empirical-sociological views. The two approaches may still be detected today, but in practice "economists" do not neglect institutional factors, and "institutionalists" do consider market factors.

Studies of past labor markets were the focus of many important debates. Suffice it to mention two here. One refers to proletarianization from the eighteenth century onward, addressing the emergence of markets for industrial wage labor. The thesis, originating in Marx's transition from "primitive accumulation" to the "capitalist mode of production," held that large parts of rural populations in

Europe were impoverished and were forced to sell their labor to industrial entrepreneurs who were seeking low production cost; the laborers inevitably tumbled into misery. The thesis led to debate about the nature of labor and laborers, the notion of proto-industrialization (or intermediating and complex forms of production, particularly industrial cottage labor), agricultural structure, demographic implications, urbanization, social policy, survival strategies of households, and the standard of living. A second debate refers to migration and its causes and consequences, addressing the expansion of markets for wage labor in the nineteenth and twentieth centuries. Central is the question of why people migrated. Initially, the debate was about a simple push-pull controversy: was it the prospect of high-paid employment in a new area, or was it unemployment and poor wages in the old area that made people move? Employment and income, friends-and-family information networks, chain migration (one exploring, others following), the characteristics of labor and migrants, the experiences of the new labor market, year-to-year fluctuation of migration, and the nature of migration in terms of time and space (temporary or permanent; local, international, or intercontinental) were discussed at length.

Economic Systems and the Development of Labor Markets. The above theories and debates deal with the industrialization process, and suggest that markets for wage labor made their appearance in the eighteenth century and continued from then on. However, such markets existed long before the eighteenth century, and nonmarket labor relationships continue into the twenty-first century. With regard to the latter, many forms of labor operated and still operate outside a market, such as forced labor, command labor, serfdom, artisan work within guilds, and self-employment.

It is impossible to draw a worldwide chronology of the development of labor markets because in many economies diverse forms of labor have existed next to one another, and there is no clear linear development. For example, in fascist and communist states of the twentieth century, wage labor existed alongside large-scale command labor for specific goals (such as road construction), and there were forced-labor camps. For internationally operating labor markets, the following crude chronology has been proposed: early colonization of America (fifteenth to seventeenth centuries, forced recruitment of indigenous people by Europeans), slavery (eighteenth to nineteenth centuries, transatlantic slave trade from Africa to the Americas), coolie labor (nineteenth to twentieth centuries, transcontinental indentured labor from Asia), colonial forced labor (twentieth century, labor in work camps), and capitalist labor (nineteenth to twentieth centuries, free wage labor moving to spearhead economies of the West).

Following classical economists, the concept of the labor market has been primarily associated with free wage labor. This labor is sold by people who are physically unconstrained and legally free and thus unlike slaves, for whom the owners have obligations beyond labor. The relation between buyer and seller of wage labor is strictly limited to labor time, and, formally, work conditions and wages are negotiated freely. Marxists, particularly, stress that this relationship is very unequal because of the laborers' need of income, their precarious position when demand for labor is low, and the employers' ownership of tools, raw material, machinery, and market expertise. On a global level, free wage labor probably became the dominant type of work in the second quarter of the twentieth century.

Wage labor of some magnitude existed in Athens in the fifth century BCE, and may be found in various times and places, as in ancient Rome or medieval Arabia. Its importance fluctuated over the centuries, but it was never dominant. From the fourteenth century onward the demand for wage labor grew modestly but continuously in market-oriented and expanding economies, particularly in Europe. In profit-driven sectors in Italy or the Low Countries, the demand for urban and rural labor rose strongly in the sixteenth century owing to increasing differentiation and specialization of the economy. This demand continued to grow steadily thereafter, and wage labor became the dominant work form in some European towns by the late eighteenth century. The so-called Industrial Revolution during the same period extensively used free wage labor all over Europe and the United States. This labor expanded in all parts of the world at the end of the nineteenth century, but industrialization did not automatically entail free wage labor. The Japanese nineteenth-century textile industry, for example, made use of young women, poorly paid and lodged in dormitories, who had year-long contracts to pay off the debt incurred by their families, which had accepted payment in advance.

Under the great pressure of capitalism (intensification of investment, technology, productivity, international trade, government services, and consumption), employment shifted from agriculture to industry and, gradually, from industry to services in the twentieth century. Such change occurred particularly in so-called economic core regions. Ongoing industrialization and the growing importance of services altered nature of employment, although demand for poorly skilled, casual labor remained present from ancient Greece until today (with brief, on-site training and low pay). Skilled and highly trained labor was needed in artisan industries for many centuries (with a year-long apprenticeship and good pay). Then, with the mechanization of production, increasingly there was a need for semiskilled labor (with technical education and payment linked to output). Lately, highly specialized labor has been sought (with lengthy education and monthly payment). In large companies and institutions the search for reliable expertise led to the notion of an internal labor market, or the hiring of people at low levels and their promotion from within the organization's ranks, thus minimizing hiring costs.

One crucial advantage of wage labor over other forms of work is its flexibility: laborers can be fired or replaced easily, and production can be promptly adapted to market conditions. In agriculture, in most industrial sectors, and in some services seasonal work dominated, and crises occurred regularly in modern industry. Both situations led to unemployment (with short-duration work and layoffs). Moreover, according to employers' needs, men and especially women could be hired on a part-time basis—an arrangement that has been widely used throughout the world since the 1980s. Another advantage was the generally low cost of wage labor compared to labor provided through guilds, serfdom, or slavery.

The increasing use of wage labor was made possible by its growing supply. The world's population has grown irregularly but gradually since prehistory, but at a faster pace from the fifteenth century on. Agricultural changes and international trade permitted mouths to be fed and, despite regularly occurring subsistence crises, labor could be directed toward industry and services. More wage laborers appeared in cities as well as in the countryside from the sixteenth century on. Urban workers (pauperized masters, unskilled workers, and migrants) offered their labor time outside the guild and municipal regulations. Rural labor was not restricted and, above all, was cheap. Particularly in the eighteenth century, the combination of rural and industrial wage labor increased in cottages, workshops, and factories. Moreover, wage labor became legally free. In large parts of Europe, the French Revolution (1789) and subsequent territory annexations abolished labor restrictions, although at the same time control over workers was introduced (for example, the ban on workers' coalitions). The English Poor Law Amendment of 1834 exposed workers for the first time to the "full" market forces of labor markets, by doing away with outdoor relief.

In all parts of the world and in most times, wage labor has been offered by men, women and children. From ancient Greece until today, the need to earn an income for subsistence, and, later, more diversified consumption, has been the driving force for most people to sell their labor. Diverse sources of income (including charity or unemployment compensation), gifts, work on the land, the cost of living, and preferences influence the decision to perform wage labor. Overall, this decision is based on the household and linked to its life cycle, that is, its formation, extension, aging, and dissolving. In many economies there has been a direct connection between the income of the man, the wage labor of the woman, and the income of children or other household members. Whether (married) women worked

for a wage or not was also greatly influenced by ideology. In large parts of the Arab world, women have not been allowed to work outside the home. In many mid-nineteenth century European countries, the idea of the male breadwinner, or that the man's wage should suffice to maintain a family, had some success. In fact, that concept mirrored a century-old view on gender-segregation in labor markets. Despite such ideologies, the labor force participation of women of all ages generally rose worldwide in the twentieth century. The gradual, and recently rapid, rise of women's supply of paid labor is also linked to women's emancipation and education, changes in family structure (smaller units), job opportunities, and organization of better public child care. Overall, after World War II participation rates of women rose, as those of men declined.

The supply of wage labor increasingly has been influenced by institutional and legal factors. In the early modern period, wage labor was in principle "free" since it developed outside guild and municipal regulations. However, local authorities could influence the supply of (cheap) labor through social policy, such as poor relief, the establishment of workhouses, and legislation (for example, coercion for all able-bodied people to work and prohibition of migration). Restrictions of a different type appeared in many Western countries during the nineteenth century, when the labor of children and women was legally limited. In the course of the twentieth century, and particularly through the International Labor Office (Geneva) after 1919, child labor was prohibited in many nations of the world, and there were laws about working time, maternity protection and, later, gender equality (e.g., equal pay). Furthermore, compulsory school attendance was introduced in many countries around 1900. Restriction at the other end of the age spectrum appeared with the launching of pension schemes in the course of the twentieth century. Legal constraints thus limited participation in the labor market. Control over the labor supply was also at stake in direct struggles between employers and employees. In the nineteenth century, highly skilled workers, such as printers, wished to organize all local workers of their profession in an attempt to restrict entrance into the trade and, eventually, to maintain wage levels. At moments of shrinking labor demand, these unions financed members' journeys to find work elsewhere. In the twentieth century, such actions stopped, as some modern unions functioned as employment and reeducation agencies. Also, in economic sectors undergoing difficulties, unions may barter job security for wages or working time.

Supply and demand of wage labor have met directly in various ways. With regard to the trade of physical persons, there were actual markets for labor where people were inspected, valued, and bought. With regard to the trade of a free labor force, most labor was hired through news

LABOR MARKET. Hiring fair in progress at the Diamond, Derry, Ireland, c. 1924. (Magee Community Collection/University of Ulster)

networks, locally as well as nationally and internationally, which operated primarily by means of relatives and friends who knew about jobs. In many countries, well-informed people (clergymen, officeholders) operated as go-betweens. Of course, employers actively searched for workers. Some visited workers' houses to take on employees, a primitive form of today's so-called headhunters. In many nineteenth-century industrial centers, large notice boards announcing vacancies were put up next to the factory gate. In the twentieth century, job advertisements appeared massively in newspapers and other communication media. In big companies and public services, internal labor markets operated. Formal encounters of supply and demand of labor force existed in medieval Europe (in so-called hiring halls), and in early modern times part of the harbor labor was organized via daily selection from a pool of casual workers. In seventeenth-century France, there were proposals to create a national registration service to allocate labor.

Formal organization to bring together supply and demand of wage labor appeared in the nineteenth century. After the economic depression of the 1880s, private and, primarily, public initiatives set up labor exchange offices in cities to deal with different types of labor. Generally, since 1945 institutional meetings of labor supply and demand have multiplied. Here intermediaries play a growing role in the formation, allocation, and transformation of labor, leading present-day economic theory and historiography to search for a subtle balance between market and institutional forces in analyzing the functioning of labor markets.

BIBLIOGRAPHY

Castells, Manuel. *The Information Age: Economy, Society and Culture.* 3 vols. Oxford, 1996–1998.

Duplessis, Robert. *Transitions to Capitalism in Early Modern Europe.* Cambridge, 1997.

Ehrenberg, Ronald, and Robert Smith. *Modern Labor Economics.* London, 1985.

Fallon, Peter, and Donald Verry. *The Economics of Labour Markets.* Oxford, 1988.

Grantham, George, and Mary MacKinnon, eds. *Labour Market Evolution: The Economic History of Market Integration: Wage Flexibility and the Employment Relation.* London and New York, 1994.

Hatton, Timothy, and Jeffrey Williamson, eds. *Migration and the International Labor Market, 1850–1939.* London and New York, 1994.

Leclercq, Eric. *Les théories du marché du travail.* Paris, 1999.

Pierenkemper, Toni, and Richard Tilly, eds. *Historische Arbeitsmarktforschung: Entstehung, Entwicklung und Probleme der Vermarktung von Arbeitskraft.* Göttingen, 1982.

Potts, Lydia. *The World Labour Market. A History of Migration.* London, 1990.

Strath, Bo. *The Organisation of Labour Markets: Modernity, Culture, and Governance in Germany, Sweden, Britain, and Japan.* London and New York, 1997.

Tilly, Chris, and Charles Tilly. *Work under Capitalism.* Boulder, 1998.

PETER SCHOLLIERS

Segmentation and Discrimination

Throughout history the same patterns recur: women earn less than men; oppressed racial, ethnic, and religious groups earn less than those in power; disadvantaged groups are concentrated in the least desirable jobs. These deprivations are only part of a larger pattern of social, legal, and economic discrimination; but they are important to the economist because they call into question the assumption that labor markets are efficient.

Unfortunately it is sometimes hard to distinguish labor-market discrimination (lower wages for equivalent work or limited access to jobs) from discrimination outside the labor market. For example, many groups have faced limited access to credit or limited legal rights—in the extreme, slaves were stripped of all their rights; under English law, married women were denied access to the courts. Although all forms of discrimination are important and will affect labor-market outcomes, this article focuses on labor-market discrimination.

Theories of Discrimination. The most important economic models of discrimination are the wage discrimination and the crowding models. The wage discrimination model was developed by Gary Becker (1971), who suggested that minority workers are paid lower wages than other equally productive workers because of a "taste for discrimination" on the part of the employer, fellow employees, or customers. In the crowding model, developed by Barbara Bergmann (1971), minority workers are totally prevented from entering certain occupations; and if the constraints are widespread relative to the number of minority workers, and if diminishing marginal productivity of labor exists within each occupation, then minority workers will be crowded into a limited number of jobs and thus earn lower wages than nonminority workers. Efficiency, as well as minority wages, could be improved by moving some of the minority workers into the nonminority occupations.

Gender Differences. Throughout history women have earned lower wages than men. Hebrew scriptures put the value of a woman at 60 percent of the value of a man (*Lv.* 27.3–4), which is not a bad description of relative female wages throughout history.

Relative female wages have risen over the course of U.S. history. Initially, women in the Northeast worked in agriculture and domestic industry, where they earned about 29 percent of male wages in 1815. Industrialization brought jobs in factories and higher wages; women's wages grew to 44 percent of male wages in 1832 and 50 percent around 1850. Thereafter, women's relative wages rose more slowly, and were still only 60 percent of male wages in 1980. Since then a more rapid increase has brought this wage ratio to 75 percent.

Women's relative wages have not always followed an upward path. In British agriculture, women earned 50 percent to 75 percent of male wages in the seventeenth century, but their relative wages went down rather than up by the nineteenth century. Parliamentary surveys suggest that women earned 40 percent as much as men in both 1833 and 1861. These wages were low, not only relative to earlier time periods, but also relative to other countries. In the 1830s, French women working in agriculture earned 65 percent as much as men.

With the British Industrial Revolution (1760–1830), some women, most of them in their teens, entered factories. Boys and girls earned approximately the same wages for factory work until age eighteen, when male wages jumped sharply upward. Few adult men worked in textile factories, but those who did so earned almost three times as much as the adult women. As in agriculture, British women seem to have fared worse than French women, who earned at least half the male wage in textile factories, and as much as 60 percent of the male wage weaving cotton.

Similar relative wages are found elsewhere in the world. Indian women working in agriculture earned two-thirds of the male wage in 1800 and in the 1950s. In Japan in 1900, female agricultural laborers earned 53 percent as much as male laborers, and female weavers earned 60 percent as much as male weavers. In 1930, Chinese women working in industry fared better, earning 78 percent as much as men.

Although all societies tend to sort occupations into "men's work" and "women's work," societies do not always place the same occupations in the same categories, and the categories do not remain fixed over time. In early-modern Florence and Bologne, silk weaving was women's work, whereas in Lyons, Genoa, and Venice it was primarily men's work. In the United States, clerical work switched from men's work to women's work between 1870 and 1930. Even obstetrics changed hands; although female midwives had assisted women in childbirth for centuries, by the nineteenth century they largely had been replaced by male doctors.

Racial Differences. Most African Americans did not have the opportunity to work for wages until after the Civil War. With little education, few trade skills, and no wealth, newly freed slaves earned low wages. The relative wages of black workers have risen gradually since the Civil War but remain lower than white wages. Black men earned 45 percent as much as white men in 1900; this figure rose to 61 percent by 1960 and 78 percent today. In the United States, blacks seem to have suffered mainly from occupational crowding since wage differences within occupations been relatively small. At the turn of the century, black agricultural workers earned on average only 8 percent less than white workers, and some 61 percent of Virginia farms paid the same wages to blacks and whites in the same occupations. Small wage differences within occupations have led to large differences in average wages because blacks have been concentrated in low-wage occupations.

Blacks have earned even less in South Africa, where in the 1930s they earned only 12 percent as much as whites. Apartheid laws passed in the 1950s reduced their earnings from 25 percent of white earnings in 1946 to 18 percent in 1960. In 1997, six years after the repeal of apartheid, blacks still earned only 37 percent as much as whites.

Interpreting Wage Differences. Historians often view wages as customary, which means they may depend on community perceptions of what certain groups should earn. For example, the expectation that a man had to support a family but a woman did not might have led to higher wages for men. Some claim that the nineteenth century saw the rise of the "male breadwinner" ideology and the idea, if not the reality, of an entire family supported by the man's wage.

Economists, in contrast to historians, generally assume that wages are determined by the market, and that wage gaps between groups result from productivity differences. When he defined wages discrimination as the difference in wages between two groups, Gary Becker assumed that these groups were equally valuable to the employer. This assumption does not always hold, and differences in wages that simply reflect productivity differences are not wage discrimination.

At least part of the observed gender wage gap is due to differences in productivity. Men and women are not always equally productive. In U.S. manufacturing around the turn of the twentieth century, men's earnings at piece-rate work were 25 percent higher than women's earnings; since both sexes received the same piece rate for each unit of output, this difference indicates that men produced 25 percent more than women. Sometimes differences in earnings occurred because women, with more family responsibilities, worked fewer hours than men. Some of the difference was also due to lower output per unit of time. Working the same amount of time as a man, a woman, on average, could reap two-thirds as many acres, and could weave 90 percent as much cloth. These differences in productivity have resulted from women's limited opportunities to acquire skills, as well as biology, which makes most men physically stronger than most women.

There is no evidence for biological differences in productivity by race or ethnicity, but often members of a minority group come to the labor market with fewer skills than other workers. This situation is called premarket discrimination because it occurs before the worker arrives in the labor market. An important type of premarket discrimination is a result of limited educational opportunities. Before 1954, U.S. blacks often could not attend the same schools as whites, and blacks' schools were generally of lower quality than those for whites. Even after *Brown* v. *Board of Education*, segregational differences in school quality persisted.

Given that differences in productivity may explain differences in wages, identifying wage discrimination is a difficult task. A common strategy is to see how much of the wage gap is explained by individual characteristics, such as age and education, and to interpret the remaining unexplained wage gap as wage discrimination. Some historical studies have taken this approach. In the 1850s, there was no wage discrimination against ethnic minorities in the American whaling industry; a worker's "lay" (percentage of the ship's catch) depended on age and occupation, not on the worker's race or ethnic origin. Among Southern schoolteachers in the early twentieth century, however, individual characteristics that affect productivity explained only 20 percent of the wage gap between blacks and whites. Women faced little wage discrimination in U.S. manufacturing around 1900; about 80 percent of the wage gap could be explained by individual characteristics such as work experience. However, wage discrimination grew in the early twentieth century; by 1940, individual characteristics accounted for only about 45 percent of the wage gap in clerical work. Although this strategy for identifying discrimination is common, it is limited because it will accurately identify wage discrimination only if investigators have information on all the relevant individual characteristics. Because there are many things the researcher does not know about the workers, it is likely that such studies underestimate the portion of the wage gap due to productivity differences.

An alternative method of measuring wage discrimination is to try to measure productivity directly, and see if it matches wages. Studies that adopt this approach find no evidence of wage discrimination. Estimates of female-to-male productivity ratios in French manufacturing match the observed wage ratios, suggesting no wage discrimination in the 1840s. In the United States, women were 60 percent as productive as men in Northern agriculture, and half as productive as men in Northern manufacturing in 1860. Since women at this time were earning about half as much as men in manufacturing, there appears to have been no wage discrimination.

Occupational Constraints. Even if there was no wage discrimination, members of minority groups could have suffered from labor-market discrimination if they were prevented from entering the occupations with the best wages. Sometimes employers refused to hire certain groups. Before the Civil Rights Act of 1964, employment advertisements in U.S. newspapers commonly specified the gender, race, and age of the desired worker. Employers in the early twentieth century instituted a "marriage bar," which excluded married women from employment. Employers, however, have a financial incentive to hire cheap labor, and have not always refused to hire minority-group members. In fact, in some cases employers have fought for the right to hire minority workers; in 1821, a Glasgow mill owner was shot by cotton spinners who opposed the employment of women in his mill.

Although employers lose profits from rules prohibiting minority hiring, nonminority workers gain because the restrictions reduce the labor supply and increase wages. Potential co-workers often try to prevent minority workers from entering their occupations. In early modern Europe, guilds held monopolies over many trades, and an apprenticeship requirement often effectively excluded minority workers. Later, labor unions enforced rules against employing members of certain groups. English unions excluded women and the Irish. American unions excluded blacks from membership and used work stoppages to prevent employers from hiring them. Between 1880 and 1914, there were fifty recorded strikes to prevent the employment of black workers.

Governments also have placed occupational restrictions on members of religious and racial groups and on women. European governments periodically evicted their Jewish citizens, having been influenced by the Catholic church, which excluded Jews from many professions and forbade them to employ Christian servants. South African law, beginning in 1911 and expanding in the 1950s, excluded blacks from many occupations, prevented them from owning businesses, and, in permitted occupations, restricted the number of blacks who could be hired. British laws limiting hours of work for women have been blamed for keeping women out of the compositing trade.

However, not all occupational differences are due to constraints. Generally people choose the occupations best suited to their skills. If groups have different average skills, then there may be occupational differences between the groups even if there is no discrimination. Women, for example, usually have less physical strength than men, so would not be expected to enter the steel industry or the building trades. In eighteenth-century England, the occupation of spinning was monopolized by women, while only men plowed. Women can plow but they are generally less productive than men. Consequently, the most efficient outcome was for the women to spin and the men to plow.

Competitive Markets. Gary Becker emphasized the economic costs of discriminating against members of a minority group, and claimed that employers who discriminate will have lower profits. If so, discrimination will not be viable in competitive markets, where any firm with lower profits will be driven out of business. This idea leads to the hypothesis that competitive markets must exhibit less discrimination than monopolized markets, which has been a topic of debate among economists. Some evidence suggests that Becker is right. In the American South in 1940, blacks were more likely to be employed in competitive industries than in monopolistic industries. In London, women gained access to the tailoring trade in the 1830s, when de-skilling broke the power of the male union and opened the occupation to competition. The implication is that free markets are good for minorities, and that to reduce discrimination increased competition rather than greater regulation should be encouraged. Milton Friedman, in *Capitalism and Freedom* (Chicago, 1962), suggests that free-market economies are less oppressive than other types of societies.

[*See also* Child Labor *and* Women in the Labor Force.]

BIBLIOGRAPHY

Becker, Gary. *The Economics of Discrimination*. 2d ed. Chicago, 1971. Sets forth the economic theory of wage discrimination.

Bergmann, Barbara. "The Effect on White Incomes of Discrimination on Employment." *Journal of Political Economy* 79 (1971), 294–313. Sets forth the crowding model of discrimination.

Burnette, Joyce. "Testing for Occupational Crowding in Eighteenth-Century British Agriculture." *Explorations in Economic History* 33 (1995), 319–345. Concludes there was no occupational crowding in British agriculture.

Burnette, Joyce. "An Investigation of the Female-Male Wage Gap during the Industrial Revolution in Britain." *Economic History Review* 50 (1997), 257–281. Concludes that most often the wage gap reflected differences in productivity.

Cox, Donald, and John Vincent Nye. "Male-Female Wage Discrimination in Nineteenth-Century France." *Journal of Economic History* 49 (1989), 903–920. Measures the productivity of male and female workers. Concludes that there was no wage discrimination in the 1840s, though there might have been in the 1860s.

Craig, Lee A., and Robert M. Fearn. "Wage Discrimination and Occupational Crowding in a Competitive Industry: Evidence from the American Whaling Industry." *Journal of Economic History* 53 (1993), 123–138. Examines ethnic differences among seamen; concludes that there was no wage discrimination, but there was occupational crowding.

Craig, Lee A., and Elizabeth B. Field-Hendrey. "Industrialization and the Earnings Gap: Regional and Sectoral Tests of the Goldin-Sokoloff Hypothesis." *Explorations in Economic History* 30 (1993), 60–80. Measures the productivity of male and female workers in agriculture and manufacturing in the American North and South in 1860.

Goldin, Claudia. *Understanding the Gender Gap: An Economic History of American Women*. Oxford, 1990. Comprehensive study of women in the U.S. labor market.

Higgs, Robert. *Competition and Coercion: Blacks in the American Economy, 1865–1914*. Chicago, 1977.

Horrell, Sara, and Jane Humphries. "Women's Labour Force Participation and the Transition to the Male-Breadwinner Family, 1790–1865." *Economic History Review* 48 (1995), 89–117. Concludes that women's declining labor-force participation was due to increasing institutional and ideological obstacles.

Hutt, W. H. *The Economics of the Colour Bar: A Study of the Economic Origins and Consequences of Racial Segregation in South Africa.* London, 1964. The perspective of a classical liberal on racial discrimination in South Africa.

Margo, Robert A. *Race and Schooling in the South, 1880–1950.* Chicago, 1990

Tilly, Louise. *Industrialization and Gender Inequality*, Washington, D.C., 1993. A review of the literature on gender inequality in England, France, Germany, the United States, Japan, and China.

JOYCE BURNETTE

Integration and Wage Convergence

Human labor is the central source of every society. This was already stated by Adam Smith (1723–1790), founder of modern economics, in his *Wealth of Nations* (1776). There he emphasized that labor is the real source of social wealth. This characterization has validity in every form of society, independent of the respective organization of their labor potentials: in ancient slave-owning societies, in medieval feudalism, in outmoded centrally planned economies, and in modern capitalist market economies, which seems to be the most widespread worldwide form. The latter is—among other things—mainly characterized by the fact that labor is in general organized as employment that is mediated through labor markets.

Genesis and Development of Labor Markets. The evolution of this modern form of employment occurred over a few hundred years. In the late eighteenth century, the majority of the population of western Europe and the United States were first, in conjunction with industrialization and strengthened economic growth, included in this kind of organization of societal labor. Starting then and until today, the whole world was included. Karl Polanyi (1866–1964) analyzed this process in his work *The Great Transformation* (1944). Today, in most areas of the world, the standard of living of most people is determined by market economy–based relations, that is, through labor markets. Employees are paid remuneration, in general with wages, in order to shape their way of living.

Markets are put in concrete forms through quantities and prices. Here certain definable economic goods are bartered at a uniform price. At labor markets, the good "labor" is, according to the common wording, paid with the prevailing wage rate. In practice and especially in history, the determination of quantities and prices on the labor market is not that simple. The reason for this is that on the one hand, there is the fact that labor is a heterogeneous good; and on the other hand, there exist various forms of remuneration in labor markets. In addition, the quantity of the available labor is quite variable and by no means defined only by the extent of the existing population. Institutional arrangements and social constructions exclude parts of the population from the working potentials (through age, prohibition of child labor, standards on the apprenticeship of adolescents, employment or nonemployment of women). The rules for such exclusions are variable. If one compares the numbers of employees with the total population, it can be said that the number of employed male persons is decreasing, but this is compensated by an increase in the employment of women. As a result, the proportion of employment is surprisingly constant during the last hundred years or so.

The historical genesis and development of labor markets can be differentiated according to a splitting up of the market development into a component concerning the quantity and one concerning the quality: there are on the one hand extent and structure of the exchanged numbers of work and on the other hand their prices and the development of wages. The implementation of market-relationships, especially in the allocation of human labor, which could be observed at first during the industrialization of the western states, was from the very beginning connected with a remarkable change in the structure of employment. Early modern societies were mainly characterized through agriculture, which even until the twentieth century in modern "industrial societies" provided most workplaces. At first in the course of the twentieth century, the number of employees in the secondary sector exceeded the quantity of employees in the agricultural sector. Since that time it has been possible to speak of "industrial societies," a term spread mainly by John Kenneth Galbraith (1908–), U.S. economist and Nobel Prize winner. Though in the middle of the twentieth century the tertiary sector became more and more important, a change toward a "service society" was suggested. At the turn of the twenty-first century, the Western societies already partly fulfilled this transition, and the majority of employees worked in the tertiary sector. To better characterize of this structural change, it is necessary to focus more on the decisive qualities of labor than on the sectors. In this case, it would be necessary to stress the transition from an "industrial" to a "knowledge society."

It is easy to find empirical evidence in developed "industrial societies" for this structural change in the distribution of employees in the three sectors, even if it seems that some societies skipped the stage of the "industrial society" (Kaelble, 1989). If one looks at the extent of the added value of the economic main sectors on the national product instead of the numbers of employees, the result is not as unambiguous as it seems. In this case, the dominant industrial sector maintains its standing and the presumed transition to a "service society" emerges in many cases only as a way into a "self-service society," as the British social researcher Jonathan Gershuny (1949–) has said.

In any case, the evident statistical structural change from the "agricultural" over the "industrial" to the "service society" soon caused formulation of a general sectoral theory of economic development. The founders of this theory were the New Zealander A. G. B. Fisher (1895–1976), the French Jean Fourastié (1907–1990), and the Australian Colin Grant Clark (1905–1989). The reasons given by these authors for the stated inevitable structural change in the system of employment were either the difference in labor productivity in the several sectors, which bound different numbers of employees with increasing production, or the different elasticities of demand, which allow (with growing wealth) a lesser dynamic increase at first of agricultural and then of industrial goods, whereas the demand for services seems to be extended without limits.

This long-term structural change in the system of employment was connected to an extraordinary increase in incomes. The price of the commodity "labor" on labor markets multiplied in the last two hundred years, and thereby improved the living conditions in modern industrial states. Over hundreds of years, there existed a precarious equilibrium between the two central sources of social production: land on the one hand and on the other the number of persons. Already a slight alteration in the proportion of these factors lead to times of hunger or phases of relative wealth. The German agricultural historian Wilhelm Abel (1904–1985) impressively proved this for central Europe. With industrialization, the people were liberated from these natural barriers of wealth, and a secular economic growth began, which built the basis for an until then unknown expansion of wealth.

The Move toward Industrial Relations. It was obvious at the beginning of the twenty-first century that the enormous increase in the standard of living was part of industrialization. Wage development seemed to be less obvious in relation to such other economic figures as the development of prices of other goods (real income) or the cost of other factors of production, such as land and capital (distribution of income). The rules that determine the distribution of income, wages, profit, and rents have been the center of economic analyses ever since the time of David Ricardo (1772–1823), the second founding father of modern economy. The distribution of income is said to be the most important factor for the dynamic development of the economy.

In this tradition of economics, this idea of modern societies as a system of "independent," self-regulating labor markets, where the allocation of human work should be decided, asserted itself in economic theory, even though critical countersystems had also been developed, such as that of the German philosopher, sociologist, and agitator Karl Marx (1818–1883). Marx saw nothing more than "a delusive semblance of a harmonic association of conditions" in market exchange, which only hid this peculiar general contradiction between capital and labor and the

exploitation of labor force. And it is, of course, proven through the modern labor market that commodity labor has a number of significant characteristics that distinguish it from other goods.

In modern labor markets, workers feel a certain underlying pressure for the following reasons: they are forced to sell their labor because quality, quantity, place, and time of job offers are only able to change to a very narrow extent, especially because human labor is not storable. If labor is not used to its fullest extent, it remains unused and "expires." For this very reason, workers are forced to sell their labor. It can only be a source of subsistence if it is sold and used to secure their income. There is hardly any alternative source for receiving an income to ensure the subsistence of workers in modern society. Therefore, both of these characteristics of labor form an asymmetrical structure of the labor market where the workers, offering their labor, underlie coercion of supply and disposition, and where the employers obviously do not suffer from coercion of that kind, making use of their advantage.

This potential inferiority of the workers was a major reason for the development of the labor movement in the nineteenth century. Even though they went in completely different directions in various Western countries, they all had one main goal. The labor movements wanted to collect the workers—in the sense of merging the offers—to resolve the structural disadvantage in the labor market, or at least fight against it in order to get better conditions for the workers with regard to better wages, better services, working hours, and working conditions. The obviously favorable results, achieved very soon by the labor movement, led to countermeasures from the employers. Numerous initiatives and employers' associations were founded in Western states in the late nineteenth century. One major aim was to prevent the outbreak of strikes and to shape the situation in the labor market.

It did not take long before the state entered the market as a third factor. The state intervened by social policy laws and contributed to the formation of the system that in modern times is known as "industrial relations."

Wages as Indicators. Modern theories of economics find it difficult to model such a high complexity as can be found in labor markets. Therefore, it is rather difficult to take up these selective, and at times very abstract, fragments of modern labor market-theories within economic history. As a result, historical research studies on labor markets usually orient themselves along the general pattern of the market as a first step in which special attention is paid to the fixing of quantity and price.

It is not surprising then that the economic historians also focused, from an early stage on, on the development of wages in the labor market (Bowley and Wood, 1899–1909; Kuczynski, 1913). Hereby, a number of problems occurred concerning the statistics. Which wages statistics are representative? In which way might they have to be corrected in terms of price development? To what extent should non-monetary and qualitative elements be considered, and what role do working hours, times of underemployment, and unemployment play? To what level does the height of wages, besides the economic significance, give information about the living standards of the workers (Scholliers, 1989)?

A short look at the international wage statistics shows that in the nineteenth century the interest in wages was more or less upheld by a firm belief in the functioning of the labor markets. Apologetics and critics of the capitalist system saw in it, depending on their point of view, a more-or-less-reliable indicator either for the progress or the decline of the system. It was a general opinion that the development of wages reflected the activities on the "independent" labor market in an unadulterated way.

During the interwar years, the focus shifted within the research. The standard of wages began to be an extra factor within the explanations for the arising economic crises—no matter if it was because of institutional rigorousness concerning the collective forming of wages or because wage levels were too high as a result of the political situation. The former reason was stated by John Maynard Keynes (1883–1946), founder of an alternative school of economic thinking. The latter was often named as a reason for the decline of the European economy between the two world wars (for an introduction, see von Kruedener, 1990). An "independent" labor market such as existed in the "good old times" before 1914 did not seem to work after 1918. To some extent, a reconstruction of a functioning "independent" labor market was achieved after 1945. The wage statistics, though, started concentrating more and more on the heterogeneity of the labor market, its segments and differences. New theoretical approaches made more specific studies and collections of dates necessary and gave way to a broad upswing of labor market research. This also influenced approaches of economic history, which improved them (Lindert and Williamson, 1983; Crafts, 1985).

Conclusion. A look back at the history of early modern times shows that the concept of the labor market can also be used positively for that time, even though the German Historical School of Economics at the end of the nineteenth century did quite a lot to create legends, such as the myth that in the industrial economy of premodern times the principle of nutriment prevailed the principle of usefulness in terms of the allocation of labor (Bücher, 1922; Sombart, 1921–1924). More recent research has shown that also in these times highly effective, integral professional parts of labor markets dominated the scene (Reith, 1999). Forms of wages, for example piece rates, already broadly existed in the late middle ages, whereas representatives of the Historical School thought them to be new achievements of the factory systems in the late nineteenth century.

These remarks that go beyond the industrial time illustrate how far labor markets, that is, how far mechanisms of human labor, have already been in preindustrial times. There are good reasons for this because the surplus of welfare, which could be achieved in a society with such allocation forms as these, was just too obvious. The enormous growth of the modern national economies and the possible increase of wealth in broad parts of society are especially caused by a more effective use of the economic central source, "labor." Apart from that, more effective labor markets enable increasing progress and change. They enable social adjustment processes and can diminish critical developments, and in that way contribute a good deal for stabilizing society. Adjustment processes such as these surely cause social costs, but these costs can be redistributed because of the highly increased standard of welfare. According to this, labor markets can be seen altogether as a brilliant invention of creative genius.

BIBLIOGRAPHY

Abel, Wilhelm. *Massenarmut und Hungerskrisen im vorindustriellen Europa: Versuch einer Synopsis.* Hamburg, 1974.

Bowley, A. L., and G. Wood. "Statistics of Wages in the United Kingdom during the Last Hundred Years." *Journal of the Royal Statistical Society* (1899–1909).

Bücher, Karl. *Die Entstehung der Volkswirtschaft.* In *Vorträge und Aufsätze*, vol. 1, 83–160. Tübingen, Germany, 1919–1920.

Clark, Colin. *The Conditions of Economic Progress*, London, 1940.

Crafts, Nick. "English Workers' Real Wages during the Industrial Revolution: Some Remaining Problems." *Journal of Economic History* 1 (1985), 129–144.

Fischer, A. G. B. "Production: Primary, Secondary, Tertiary." *Economic Record* 15 (1939), 24–38.

Fourastié, Jean. *Le grand espoir du XXe siècle: Progrès technique, progrès économique, progrès social.* Paris, 1949.

Galbraith, John Kenneth. *The New Industrial State: The Emerging Self-Service Economy.* Boston, 1967.

Gershuny, Jonathan. *After Industrial Society?* London, 1978.

Kaelble, Hartmut. "Was Prometheus Most Unbound in Europe? The Labour Force in Europe during the Late Nineteenth and Twentieth Centuries." *Journal of European Economic History* (1989), 65–104.

Keynes, John Maynard. *The General Theory of Employment, Interest, and Money.* London, 1936.

Kruedener, Jürgen von, ed. *Economic Crisis and Political Collapse: The Weimar Republic, 1924–1933.* New York, 1990.

Kuczynski, Robert René. *Arbeitslohn und Arbeitszeit in Europa und Amerika, 1870–1913.* Berlin, 1913.

Lindert, Peter, and Jeffrey Williamson. "English Workers' Living Standards during the Industrial Revolution: A New Look." *Economic History Review* (1983), 1–25.

Marx, Karl. *Das Kapital: Kritik der politischen Ökonomie.* 3 vols. Hamburg and New York, 1867, 1885, 1893.

Polanyi, Karl. *The Great Transformation: The Political and Economic Origins of Our Time.* New York, 1944.

Reith, Reinhold. *Lohn und Leistung: Lohnformen im Gewerbe 1450–1900.* Stuttgart, 1999.

Ricardo, David. *On the Principles of Political Economy and Taxation*. London, 1817.

Scholliers, Peter. "Comparing Real Wages in the Nineteenth and Twentieth Centuries." In *Real Wages in Nineteenth and Twentieth Century Europe: Historical and Comparative Perspectives*, edited by Peter Scholliers. New York, 1989.

Smith, Adam. *An Inquiry into the Nature and Causes of the Wealth of Nations*. London, 1776.

Sombart, Werner. *Der moderne Kapitalismus: Historisch-systematische Darstellung des gesamteuropäischen Wirtschaftslebens von den Anfängen bis zur Gegenwart*, vol. 1. Munich, 1921–1924.

TONI PIERENKEMPER

LABOR MOBILITY. Labor mobility consists of changes in the location of workers both across physical space (geographic mobility) and across a set of jobs (occupational mobility). Geographic mobility can be further subdivided into short-distance and long-distance moves and into voluntary and coerced migration. Occupational mobility can be lateral (within a broad class of jobs similar in socioeconomic status) or vertical (from one job to a better or worse job). The availability of nationally representative longitudinal surveys in the late twentieth century has made it possible to measure the extent of mobility in all these dimensions and how they are related in several developed economies. Understanding the extent of historical labor mobility has improved since the 1970s with studies in which the careers of individual workers are reconstructed by locating them in censuses and censuslike enumerations (city directories, tax lists, population registers) at successive dates.

At the aggregate level labor mobility conveys important economic benefits. The reallocation of workers across regions permits the exploitation of resources as they are discovered in new places, while reallocation across sectors makes possible the growth of new technologies and industries. At the individual level mobility allows improvements in the economic circumstances of those whose skills or aspirations are a poor match for their current jobs or locations.

The impact of labor mobility extends well beyond these economic considerations, however. The ability of fluid U.S. labor markets to deter labor radicalization has been recognized by Karl Marx, Selig Perlman, and Stephan Thernstrom. Since the work of Frederick Jackson Turner more than a century ago, scholars have debated the role of the frontier in forging a specifically American political economy. Sociologists have examined the impact of mobility on the operation of communities and interpersonal relationships, and political scientists have considered how mobility affects political participation and coalition formation.

Labor Mobility in Europe. Information on the occupational mobility of labor in Europe is rare before the nineteenth century. Parish records and civilian population registers, however, provide a glimpse of labor's geographic mobility. High rates of geographic mobility can be seen well before the advent of modern industrial economies. In Britain throughout the seventeenth and eighteenth centuries young workers in agriculture were employed off the family farm as farm servants, moving to different farms at the end of each year. On the Continent gangs of workers followed the harvest across national borders and returned to their home villages after months at a time on the road. Though much of this movement was only temporary, more permanent movement to villages and towns was essential to the growth of cottage industry. Several transnational migrations (the Irish into Britain, Belgians into France, Poles into Germany) were prominent features of European industrial and urban growth.

Recent research on labor mobility in Britain has produced more detailed conclusions. The British populace of the nineteenth century was highly mobile. England, Wales, and Scotland were virtually free of institutional barriers to geographic mobility. Though the Poor Law's provision of economic security created some disincentive to mobility, it was small compared to the effects of large-scale social welfare programs of the twentieth century. Nineteenth-century Britain saw both high rates of internal mobility and overseas emigration. These long-distance movers tended to be young, single, and male. Internal migration within England, Wales, and Scotland was a different phenomenon. Between 1851 and 1881 approximately one in four people changed their county of residence; more than half moved from one town to another. Like overseas migrants, internal movers tended to be young. Unlike overseas migrants, more females moved within the country than did males, and single people were no more likely to move than were married people.

Most strikingly internal moves tended to cover short distances. Between 1851 and 1881 the average internal migrant moved only thirty-five miles; one-quarter moved less than five miles. There was no clear regional pattern to nineteenth-century internal migration, unlike the steady flow of westward migrants in the United States at the time. One of the most distinctive patterns of British internal migration was the prevalence of rural-to-urban moves. Virtually all of Britain's nineteenth-century population growth accrued to the cities, which expanded both by natural increase and by population influx from rural areas. In the mid-1800s more than one out of every three rural residents of Great Britain left for an urban area. Most left for the nearest city, though London drew migrants from all over the country, as it had since the seventeenth century. The industrialized urban areas of Lancashire and Yorkshire also drew many rural migrants.

Overseas emigrants and internal migrants moved for many reasons, but chief among them was the search for economic gain. Wage gaps and the chance for upward occupational mobility drew migrants to the United States and to the cities. The British labor market did not exhibit as much occupational mobility, either between or within generations, as it did geographic. Nineteenth-century marriage registries indicate that well over half of all sons worked in jobs of similar socioeconomic status to those of their fathers. Following males across censuses reveals a similar pattern over individual career histories. More than half of all males did not change socioeconomic status over their careers. The socioeconomic status and occupation of the father exerted a strong influence on the socioeconomic status of the son, however, opportunities did exist to achieve upward occupational mobility. Foremost among the opportunities were education and migration to an urban area.

Labor Mobility in the United States. The most important forms of labor mobility in the first century of European settlement of North America were voluntary immigration from Europe by whites and coerced immigration from Africa by blacks. In the absence of immigration, many of the initial settlements would not have survived, given the high mortality rates and low rates of natural increase. Three-quarters of the white arrivals may have been indentured servants who agreed to work for four to seven years to repay their passage fare. By the 1680s black slaves were imported to work in southern tobacco and rice cultivation.

Since the start of the seventeenth century Americans have experienced high rates of labor mobility within the colonies and later within the United States. This stems from the propensity of those who have migrated once (like transatlantic immigrants) to make subsequent moves. Even among the native-born, mobility was frequent because of both the availability of largely unsettled land through the end of the nineteenth century and the relative absence of restrictions on movement across locations or across jobs. The absence of strong craft guilds and organized labor through the 1880s made occupational mobility similarly free from restrictions. Before 1900 American workers were employed largely through spot markets, in which job attachment was weak and turnover rates were high. By the 1920s, as more formal systems of recruitment and labor monitoring evolved, job tenure increased, though it remained substantially below levels observed in other developed counties throughout the twentieth century.

Measurement of labor mobility requires examination of sources that either record an individual's location or occupation at two or more points in time or allow inferences regarding how the locations or occupations of a particular group of individuals have changed over time. For the colonial period only a few generalizations are possible.

Through the 1660s indentured servants in the South had good success in improving their socioeconomic status after their terms of service ended but were apparently less successful later. As land prices rose in the late-seventeenth-century tobacco boom, more found it necessary to migrate to another colony to find success. Colonial army muster rolls show high rates of geographic mobility by the Revolutionary War.

For the middle of the nineteenth century it is possible to measure labor mobility directly by following individuals from one census to another. Between 1850 and 1860 roughly two-thirds of adult males moved from one county to another, with higher migration rates among less-skilled workers. Migrants experienced more occupational mobility (both upward and downward) than otherwise similar nonmigrants. Turner and other historians examined the importance of the frontier as a place where workers could improve their circumstances. More recent research validates this view of the frontier. Workers who went there indeed did better than they would have done at their places of origin. Beginning in the 1840s workers also migrated in large numbers from farms to cities. Many were young women and children employed in New England textile mills and the younger sons of farm households whose prospects were unfavorable in the farm sector.

The available evidence on wages in the first half of the nineteenth century demonstrates that the movement of workers to the West was successful in eliminating interregional wage differences within both the northern and the southern tiers of states (though pronounced North-South differentials remained). Movement of workers from farms to towns eliminated any substantial wage gap between farm and urban workers after adjusting for cost-of-living differences.

Among those who remained in agriculture, both geographic and occupational mobility is seen throughout the nineteenth century and the early twentieth century. Farmers migrated in large numbers from the Middle Atlantic and South Atlantic states to regions farther west, generally moving along lines of latitude both to economize on the direct cost of migration and to take better advantage of latitude-specific farming skills. As farm-making costs and the prices of existing farms increased, some individuals found it difficult to purchase farms early in their careers. Tenancy rose to account for perhaps a quarter of the nation's farms by 1900, but tenancy remained only a stage in the eventual transition to ownership.

Throughout the second half of the nineteenth century and into the 1920s, voluntary immigration from Europe provided millions of new workers for the economy. Most eventually were able to enter better jobs than they had possessed in Europe. Beginning in the 1910s an additional form of labor mobility is seen. Large numbers of black farm workers migrated voluntarily to northern cities and took up urban employment.

Few sources make possible long-run comparisons of labor mobility in different eras. In the 1850s migration across county boundaries was more common than in the 1970s. Upward occupational mobility was also somewhat more common in the 1850s than in the 1970s both in comparisons of fathers' and sons' occupations and in comparisons of individuals' first and last occupations.

[*See also* Labor Markets *and* Internal Migration.]

BIBLIOGRAPHY

Commons, John R., et al. *History of Labour in the United States*. New York, 1926–1935.

Ferrie, Joseph P. *Yankeys Now: Immigrants in the Antebellum United States, 1840–1860*. New York, 1999.

Long, Jason L. "Labor Mobility in Victorian Britain." Ph.D. diss., Northwestern University, 2002.

Margo, Robert A. *Wages and Labor Markets in the United States, 1820–1860*. Chicago, 2000.

Moch, Leslie Page. "The European Perspective: Changing Conditions and Multiple Migrations, 1750–1914." In *European Migrants: Global and Local Perspectives*, edited by Dirk Hoerder and Leslie Page Moch. Boston, 1996.

JASON LONG AND JOSEPH P. FERRIE

LABOR PRODUCTIVITY is most simply defined as output per unit of labor input, and the term has been widely used by economic historians to assess the performance of an economy or sector. Like other concepts of productivity, it has commonly been measured on a rate-of-change basis. However, unlike other concepts of productivity, it also has often been measured on a levels basis. Thus, for example, international comparisons of labor productivity performance often compare levels of labor productivity between countries as well as growth rates of labor productivity.

In practice, difficulties often arise in the measurement of both the numerator and the denominator. In measuring output, there can be difficulties in combining different products or in accounting for quality differences between units of the same product. These difficulties are often seen as being particularly severe in nonmarket services, although they arise to a limited extent in all sectors of the economy. In measuring the labor input, the most widely used definition is the number of workers, although hours worked is also commonly used, and attempts have sometimes been made to measure quality-adjusted hours of labor input, allowing for factors such as the level of education and training of the labor force.

Capital Intensity. One way of explaining labor productivity growth is through capital accumulation. Indeed, the positive relationship between the growth of capital per worker and the growth of output per worker has long been noted by economists and economic historians. However, if one assumes a conventional production function, with output determined by capital and labor and with the weights on capital and labor reflecting their shares of income (and hence their relative importance in the production process), increasing capital intensity can usually explain only a small part of labor productivity growth. The residual, known as total factor productivity (TFP) growth, is often more important than the growth of capital intensity.

Labor Productivity and the Convergence Hypothesis. In addition to comparing growth rates of labor productivity across countries, it is possible to compare levels of labor productivity. The observation of a negative relationship between the level of labor productivity in a country and the subsequent rate of labor productivity growth in that country has given rise to the convergence hypothesis. This idea, popularized by William J. Baumol and Moses Abramovitz during the 1980s, suggests that a country that is close to the frontier cannot grow as rapidly as a country that is a long way behind the leader. This is either because the marginal product of capital is assumed to be lower when capital intensity is higher (i.e., diminishing returns to capital set in) or because innovation at the frontier is assumed to be harder than imitation. Earlier work in this vein by Alexander Gerschenkron and Thorstein Veblen, however, emphasized that simply lagging behind was not sufficient to ensure rapid productivity growth, and that attention needs to be paid to incentives, organization, and technology.

Technology and Organization. These complex issues can be discussed only briefly. The approach taken here is to mention several strands of the literature, which can be followed up in a number of other entries. First, Kazushi Ohkawa and Henry Rosovsky coined the phrase "social capabilities" to describe the technological and organizational factors that make it possible for a backward country to begin the process of catching up rather than falling further behind. They singled out education for special attention in the case of Japan, but also emphasized factors such as the legal system, business practices, and the wider social system. Second, Mancur Olson emphasized the power of interest groups to block the changes necessary for economic growth. He noted the difficulties of getting interest groups organized in the first place because of free-rider problems in addition to the power of such groups to persist once formed. He thus argued that countries that experienced long periods without major social or political upheaval would accumulate more and more interest groups and hence find it even more difficult to grow rapidly. One implication of this is that winning a war may lead to "losing the peace" if social and political stability leads to stagnation among the victors and the shakeout of interest groups leads to more rapid growth among the defeated nations.

Structural Change. Many studies of labor productivity work in terms of aggregate economic activity. And yet, it is clear that the concept can be applied equally to sectors of the economy, such as agriculture, industry, and services—a reminder that structural change can have an impact on aggregate labor productivity, since value added per employee differs across sectors. Economic historians and development economists have long noted that an important factor in achieving high aggregate labor productivity has been to move resources out of low productivity sectors. From a historical perspective, the most important shift out of a low productivity sector has been the movement away from agriculture. Indeed, one of the best predictors of a country's level of per capita income and aggregate labor productivity level is the percentage of the labor force in agriculture.

The Industrial Revolution and the Industrious Revolution. As noted previously, labor input can be defined in terms of the number of workers or the number of hours worked. In the period of the British Industrial Revolution, the measure chosen can have quite an impact on the rate of labor productivity growth. In Table 1, we see that during the period 1760 to 1800, aggregate output in Great Britain grew at an annual rate of 1.0 percent, using the widely accepted figures of Nicholas Crafts and Knick Harley. With employment assumed to grow in line with population at 0.8 percent per annum, this yields an annual growth rate of 0.2 percent for output per worker. However, recent work by Hans-Joachim Voth suggests that the number of hours worked per year by the average worker also increased substantially during this period, particularly through a decline in the observance of "St. Monday," when many workers failed to show up for work after the excesses of the weekend. With hours per worker growing at a rate of 0.4 percent per annum, the positive labor productivity growth as measured by output per worker turns into negative labor productivity growth as measured by output per hour worked. This suggests that the higher output of the early Industrial Revolution period, at least, owed more to an increase in work effort than was previously thought. Using the terminology of Jan de Vries, output growth before 1800 was largely driven by an "Industrious Revolution."

Labor Force Quality and Productivity Growth in Great Britain, 1856–1973. The study of British economic growth during the period 1856 to 1973 by Robin Matthews, Charles Feinstein, and John Odling-Smee illustrates the importance of changes in the quality of the labor force. In Table 2, we see that with gross domestic product (GDP) growing at an annual rate of 1.9 percent and the number of hours worked growing at 0.2 percent, GDP per hour worked grew at the rate of 1.7 percent. Allowing for the increasing education of the labor force, the shifting gender balance, and the increasing intensity of work as the number of hours per worker declined, GDP per quality-adjusted hour worked grew at a substantially slower rate of 0.7 percent per annum. The quality adjustment can be thought of as one way of capturing the social capabilities of the nation, particularly in the form of education, and hence as a source of the growth in output per hour worked.

Labor Productivity and the Convergence Hypothesis, 1870–1970. I shall now consider levels of labor productivity and their relationship to productivity growth rates. Table 3 sets out the levels of GDP per hour worked between 1870 and 1992 for a sample of sixteen industrialized countries, with the United States as the numeraire country, taking a value of 100 in all years. The narrowing dispersion over time has been interpreted as confirmation of the hypothesis of convergence of labor productivity and living standards over time. This in turn implies a negative relationship between the initial level of labor productivity relative to the leader and the subsequent growth rate of labor productivity. Thus, for example, Japan had the lowest level of labor productivity in 1870 and the highest subsequent growth rate, while Australia had the highest level of labor productivity in 1870 and the lowest subsequent growth rate.

However, as Bradford de Long has pointed out, care must be taken before seeing convergence as a global

TABLE 1. *Labor Productivity Growth in Great Britain, 1760–1800*

	GROWTH RATE (% PER ANNUM)
Output	1.0
Employment	0.8
Output per worker	0.2
Hours per worker	0.4
Output per hour worked	−0.2

SOURCE: Voth, 1998, p. 55.

TABLE 2. *Quality-Adjusted Labor Productivity Growth in Great Britain, 1856–1973*

	GROWTH RATE (% PER ANNUM)
GDP	1.9
Hours worked	0.2
Quality adjustment per hour worked	1.0
GDP per hour worked	1.7
GDP per quality-adjusted hour worked	0.7

SOURCE: Matthews, Feinstein, and Odling-Smee, 1982, pp. 65, 498, 503.

TABLE 3. *Comparative Levels of GDP per Hour Worked*

	1870	1913	1929	1938	1950	1973	1992
Austria	62	57	44	39	32	65	83
Belgium	94	70	64	61	48	70	98
Denmark	67	66	68	61	46	68	75
Finland	37	35	34	36	32	57	70
France	60	56	55	62	45	76	102
Germany	70	68	58	56	35	71	95
Italy	46	41	38	44	34	66	85
Netherlands	103	78	84	72	51	81	99
Norway	48	43	45	50	43	60	88
Sweden	54	50	44	49	56	77	79
Switzerland	77	63	72	68	69	78	87
United Kingdom	115	86	74	69	62	68	82
Australia	147	103	86	83	69	72	78
Canada	71	82	69	61	77	81	87
United States	100	100	100	100	100	100	100
Japan	20	20	24	25	16	48	69

United States = 100.
SOURCE: Maddison, 1995, p. 47.

process, since the sample of countries is biased. The sample of sixteen countries included in the initial Baumol study is an *ex post* sample of countries that are now rich and have developed successfully. It excludes nations that were relatively rich in 1870 but have not developed successfully since and are now relatively poor. Hence, convergence is all but guaranteed in this sample, but it tells us little about the forces making for convergence among the *ex ante* sample of nations that in 1870 seemed likely to converge. Subsequent work has tended to make the weaker claim of conditional convergence, or convergence conditioned on other factors such as education or research and development. So although there is a negative relationship between the level of development and subsequent growth, this force for convergence may be offset by other forces making for divergence, such as underinvestment in education by poor countries.

Note that this data set exhibits the type of postwar growth pattern noted by Olson, particularly after World War II, with the victors growing more slowly than the defeated nations. Olson stressed the shakeout of interest groups in countries such as Germany and Japan, and the stability of the sociopolitical system in countries such as Great Britain and the United States. However, the more rapid postwar growth of the defeated countries must also be seen to some extent as simply reflecting the greater wartime disruption, so that the level of GDP per hour worked was abnormally low in the defeated nations immediately after the war. The convergence framework thus goes some way toward explaining postwar growth differentials between countries without appealing to the impact

of the war on interest groups in different countries. However, the fact that Germany not only caught up with Britain, but also forged ahead, suggests that convergence is not the full story.

Sectoral Aspects of Comparative Labor Productivity Performance, 1870–1990. Most analyses of comparative labor productivity performance among the developed countries since the late nineteenth century focus on aggregate GDP per unit of labor input. However, examining comparative productivity trends in the main sectors—agriculture, industry, and services—throws interesting light on the growth process. Stephen Broadberry shows that the United States and Germany both overtook Great Britain largely as a result of improving their labor productivity performance in services and by shifting resources out of agriculture, rather than by improving their comparative productivity performance in industry. The data for the U.S./U.K. case are shown in Table 4. Notice that in industry, the U.S. labor productivity lead was roughly the same in 1890 as in 1990. Although the U.S. labor productivity performance in agriculture improved over time, the share of the U.S. labor force in agriculture declined from approximately 50 percent in 1870 to less than 3 percent in 1990. Since agriculture is a low value-added sector and since it was already much smaller in Great Britain by the mid-nineteenth century, the subsequent shift of resources out of agriculture in both countries helped to boost aggregate labor productivity in the United States relative to Great Britain. Note, finally, that comparative labor productivity in services most closely mirrored the development of comparative labor productivity in the aggregate economy. Furthermore, this is not simply a statistical artifact due to the difficulties of measuring output in the service sector. Although output in the nonmarket service sector is to some extent measured by the labor input (e.g., medical

TABLE 4. *Comparative U.S./U.K. Labor Productivity Levels by Sector, 1870–1990*

	AGRICULTURE	INDUSTRY	SERVICES	AGGREGATE ECONOMY
1870	86.9	153.6	85.8	89.8
1890	102.1	164.5	84.2	94.1
1910	103.2	193.5	107.3	117.7
1920	128.0	198.2	119.0	133.3
1929	109.7	222.9	121.2	139.4
1937	103.3	190.6	120.0	132.6
1950	126.0	243.9	140.8	166.9
1973	131.2	215.1	137.3	152.3
1990	151.1	163.0	129.6	133.0

United Kingdom = 100.
SOURCE: Broadberry, 1998, pp. 375–407.

TABLE 5. *Output per Worker in Agriculture, 1300–1800*

	1300	1400	1500	1600	1700	1750	1800
England	80	92	100	76	115	154	143
Germany		85	74	57	54	56	67
Spain		102	89	76	87	80	70
Italy	72	89	80	83	81	70	57
France		76	83	72	74	80	83
Poland		102	93	78	94	93	107
Belgium		146	139	126	120	122	111
Netherlands			107	106	124	148	144
Austria		100	91	57	74	91	81

England in 1500 = 100.
SOURCE: Allen, 2000, p. 20.

services measured by the number of doctors and nurses), similar trends exist in market services such as transport, communications, distribution, and finance, where output is measured independently of input.

Labor Productivity in European Agriculture, 1300–1800. Finally, I will examine a recent attempt to measure labor productivity in agriculture in medieval and early modern Europe. Robert Allen's study begins with estimates of population and its division into agricultural, rural nonagricultural, and urban components. Data on real wages and agricultural prices are then used to derive estimates of agricultural consumption, and these are adjusted for international trade to arrive at agricultural production. Putting the agricultural production data together with the agricultural labor force data yields the estimates of agricultural labor productivity that are presented in Table 5, which sets the level of agricultural output per worker in England in 1500 equal to 100. The estimates are clearly subject to a wide margin of error. Nevertheless, the broad picture looks plausible, with output per worker in agriculture declining in Italy and Spain after 1500 and with England and the Netherlands showing a dramatic improvement.

[*See also* Total Factor Productivity.]

BIBLIOGRAPHY

Abramovitz, Moses. "Catching Up, Forging Ahead, and Falling Behind." *Journal of Economic History* 46.2 (1986), 385–406.

Allen, Robert C. "Economic Structure and Agricultural Productivity in Europe, 1300–1800." *European Review of Economic History* 4.1 (2000), 1–26.

Baumol, William J. "Productivity Growth, Convergence, and Welfare: What the Long Run Data Show." *American Economic Review* 76.5 (1986), 1072–1085.

Broadberry, Stephen N. "How Did the United States and Germany Overtake Britain? A Sectoral Analysis of Comparative Productivity Levels, 1870–1990." *Journal of Economic History* 58.2 (1998), 375–407.

Crafts, Nicholas F. R., and C. Knick Harley. "Output Growth and the Industrial Revolution: A Restatement of the Crafts-Harley View." *Economic History Review* 45.4 (1992), 703–730.

De Long, J. Bradford. "Productivity Growth, Convergence, and Welfare: Comment." *American Economic Review* 78.5 (1998), 1138–1154.

Gerschenkron, Alexander. *Economic Backwardness in Historical Perspective.* Cambridge, Mass., 1962.

Maddison, Angus. *Monitoring the World Economy, 1820–1992.* Paris, 1995.

Matthews, Robin C. O., Charles H. Feinstein, and John C. Odling-Smee. *British Economic Growth, 1856–1973.* Oxford, 1982.

Ohkawa, Kasushi, and Henry Rosovsky. *Japanese Economic Growth: Trend Acceleration in the Twentieth Century.* Stanford, Calif., 1973.

Olson, Mancur, Jr. *The Rise and Decline of Nations: Economic Growth, Stagflation and Social Rigidities.* New Haven, 1982.

Veblen, Thorstein. *Imperial Germany and the Industrial Revolution.* New York, 1915.

Voth, Hans-Joachim. "Time and Work in Eighteenth-Century London." *Journal of Economic History* 58.1 (1998), 29–58.

Vries, Jan de. "The Industrial Revolution and the Industrious Revolution." *Journal of Economic History* 54.2 (1994), 249–270.

STEPHEN N. BROADBERRY

LABOR SURPLUS MODELS. A labor surplus model is a class of model for analyzing developing countries as dual economies with a modern capitalist sector and a traditional precapitalist sector. The precapitalist sector is seen as having a large pool ("unlimited supplies") of labor from which the capitalist sector may draw at constant cost. While these models are often described as finding their inspiration in the old classical economists and Karl Marx (1818–1883), the Lewis model (1954) and its extensions are technically more neoclassical than truly classical.

The model developed by Sir W. Arthur Lewis (1915–1991) was elaborated upon and formalized by many others, most notably John Fei and Gustav Ranis (1964), with important theoretical contributions from Amartya Sen (1966) and Stephen Marglin (1976). Questions have been raised as to the historical relevance of the neoclassical labor surplus models (Arrighi, 1973; Williamson, 1985). Alternative models of a more truly "classical" and Marxian flavor may be more helpful in understanding issues of surplus labor in capitalist and precapitalist economies.

In the Lewis model, the economy is divided into two sectors, a traditional precapitalist sector and a modern capitalist sector. Lewis emphasized that this sectoral distinction is not identical to that between manufacturing and agriculture, as there may be both traditional (craft) manufactures and capitalist agriculture. The traditional sector is characterized by a large pool of labor, available to the modern sector at a constant (subsistence) wage. The wage is exogenous and above the marginal product of labor in the traditional sector. Thus the labor supply in the modern sector is infinitely elastic. Lewis stated that the marginal product of labor in the traditional sector could be small, zero, or even negative; but whereas he also emphasized that this was not an assumption of fundamental importance, later developers and critics of the model devoted considerable attention to this assumption.

For Lewis, the supply of labor is considered "unlimited" as long as the labor supply exceeds labor demand at the subsistence wage rate. The demand for labor in the modern sector is determined by the stock of capital. Under such conditions, labor shortage is never a constraint on the expansion of the modern sector. As demand is also not a constraint on expansion in the Lewis model, the modern sector hires labor out of the traditional sector, and output increases. Profits in the modern sector rise and are reinvested, fueling capital accumulation. This is how successful "development" is defined. Eventually, the marginal product of labor and the wage will become equal in both the traditional and modern sector, and dualism comes to an end. With the equalization of the wage in the two sectors, the presumption is that the wage will now be "neoclassically," that is, "market" determined.

A number of criticisms have been made of the Lewis model (see, e.g., Leeson, 1979; Bharadwaj, 1979). First, it has been argued that the model assumes that employment transfer proceeds at the same rate as capital accumulation in the modern sector, and that this will not be the case if there is labor-saving technological change in that sector. Lewis did recognize that there are two forces working in opposite directions—capital accumulation increasing employment and technical advance, which may reduce employment—though he rejected the argument that the latter would outweigh the former on empirical grounds in his original article. Second, a number of critics have asserted that the situation in many developing countries is precisely the opposite of what Lewis assumed: There is significant unemployment and underemployment in urban areas and full employment in rural areas. A defense of Lewis might point out that the traditional/modern distinction is not the same as the rural/urban distinction, and that what appears as full employment in some areas is disguised unemployment—people are working, but their transfer from the traditional to the modern sector will not reduce output in the traditional sector, or will only reduce output there by the amount that the individual is consuming. Third, it has been noted that Lewis assumes away the problem of the creation of a capitalist or entrepreneurial class in developing countries, whereas in fact this is one of the main obstacles to development. Fourth, critics have argued that real and nominal wages in the modern sector do not appear to behave in the way they are pictured in the Lewis model—both are able to rise quite rapidly—and the relationship of wages and employment also differs in that rates rise even in an atmosphere of significant unemployment. Fifth, Lewis's assumption that the sectors are homogeneous has been criticized with arguments developed that each sector can be quite heterogeneous, generating conflicts that af-

fect the accumulation process. Finally, the assumption that "perfect competition" holds in the capitalist sector has been attacked both for ignoring the way in which monopoly characteristics had been inherited from the colonial era and for the neoclassical implications for the analysis of investment, allocation, and factor payments.

The Lewis model has also been criticized on historical grounds. Jeffrey Williamson argues that the early British experience does not confirm the model, while Giovanni Arrighi has attacked the argument that the model applies to southern Africa. One of the primary challenges of colonial capitalism was getting the indigenous populations to work as wage laborers or grow cash crops when they still had possession of means of production for producing the means of subsistence. In addition to forced labor and land alienation, the requirement that taxes be paid in colonial currency was one of the most important means of pressuring Africans to work on plantations and in mines or to grow cash crops.

[*See also* Economic Development.]

BIBLIOGRAPHY

Arrighi, Giovanni. "Labor Supplies in Historical Perspective." In *Essays on the Political Economy of Africa*, edited by G. Arrighi and J. S. Saul. New York, 1973.
Bharadwaj, Krishna. "Towards a Macroeconomic Framework for a Developing Economy: The Indian Case." *The Manchester School* vol. 47, no. 3, pp. 270–302. Oxford, 1979.
Fei, John C. H., and Gustav Ranis. *Development of the Labor Surplus Economy*. Homewood, Ill., 1964.
Leeson, P. F. "The Lewis Model and Development Theory." *The Manchester School*, vol. 47, no. 3, pp. 196–210. Oxford, 1979.
Lewis, W. Arthur. "Economic Development with Unlimited Supplies of Labour." *The Manchester School*, vol. 22, no. 2, pp. 139–191. Oxford, 1954.
Marglin, Stephen A. *Value and Price in the Labour-Surplus Economy*. Oxford, 1976.
Sen, Amartya K. "Peasants and Dualism with or without Surplus Labor." *Journal of Political Economy* 74.5 (October, 1966), 425–450.
Williamson, Jeffrey G. "The Historical Content of the Classical Labor Surplus Model." *Population and Development Review* 11.2 (June 1985), 171–191.

MATHEW FORSTATER

LABOR TIME. Labor time typically refers only to those hours of work performed in exchange for pay or profit (in the case of the self-employed). The very substantial number of hours of household work, for example, and of work for charity tend to be ignored. Three factors determine the length of the working year: the number of hours worked per day, the number of working days per week, and the length of vacations. Over the very long run, working hours followed an inverse U-shape, rising to a peak in the middle of the nineteenth century before declining sharply over the last 150 years.

It is widely believed that the earliest human communities of hunter-gatherers required fewer hours of work for subsistence than agricultural societies. Societies studied today by anthropologists show stark differences. !Kung bushmen in the Kalahari and the Kayapo of northern Brazil work only two to four hours a day, whereas those communities that engage in mixed agriculture (a combination of slash-and-burn cultivation and hunting), such as the Bemba in Rhodesia and the Kikuyu in Kenya, tend to record four to nine hours. Fully sedentary agriculture, as practiced by the Kali Loro in Java and the Muhero in Rwanda, involves yet longer hours—ten to eleven on average.

Marshall Sahlins (1972) referred to hunter-gatherers as "the original affluent society" because of the apparent ease with which they secured a living and the abundance of free time. It is, however, questionable if the average working hours of hunter-gatherer tribes encountered today are representative of those that existed hundreds of thousands of years ago, unusually favorable environmental conditions may have caused the continuation of hunting and gathering as the primary mode of production. Nevertheless, skeletal remains from the period of transition to sedentary agriculture clearly show the detrimental effects of higher workloads on men, women, and children. It is therefore likely that the switch to agricultural cultivation in prehistorical times caused annual hours worked to rise considerably.

Working Trends in the Middle Ages and Later. The working year was probably relatively short during the late Middle Ages. Much of the available evidence refers to the period after the Black Death, when wages were unusually high and labor input was probably low. Wage books were often available for builders and, in England, for some agricultural estates. In Xanten, Germany, in 1356, builders worked a mere 250 days per year, but variation over time and between different individuals was pronounced. Whereas, a master of the works at Vale Royal Abbey between 1279 and 1281 rested on only four feast days, builders at Eton celebrated forty-two holy days. Additional vacations could increase the total to over fifty days. Tenants at Tewkesbury, Gloucestershire, stopped work for fifty-eight days in 1337. If Sundays are added to this, a maximum of 246 days could be devoted to work. The basis of this calculation is that the normal working week had six days. This was not necessarily the case: in the manors of Tewkesbury and Fayreford in 1337, and on the manor of Oxynden in 1338, everyone worked for five days per week. In many other trades, work stopped at noon on Saturday.

An important factor behind the relatively short working year during the Middle Ages was the large number of saints' days and other religious festivals. Their number varied by country and region and generally increased over time. Scholars such as Nicolas de Clemanges (1360–1437), in his *De novis celebritatibus non instituendis* (Why new feast days should not be introduced), argued that a large number of festivals did more to undermine true religiosity than to deepen it. The issue of feast days became central during the Reformation. Martin Luther appealed to the nobility of the German nation in 1520 to honor only Sundays. The "Hundred Grievances of the German Nation," presented to Charles V at the Diet of Nuremberg in 1522–1523, claimed that farmers could hardly find enough time to harvest and store their crops. Lobbying in favor of few holy days also occurred in England prior to the Act of Abolition in 1536, which reduced the festive calendar by a maximum of forty-nine holy days.

Protestant countries generally curtailed the number of holy days in the calendar. However, the Lutheran Church implemented reforms in far less dramatic a way than did the Calvinists. The feasts of the apostles, of Mary the Virgin, as well as some saints' days remained in force. In contrast, Calvinist towns and territories resorted to more stringent measures. In the Palatinate, for example, only Sunday as well as two days at Christmas, Easter and Whitsun, plus Ascension, were recognized as holy days. Early modern states attempted to regulate labor time and working days in a number of ways. In England, an act of 1514 is one of the most famous documents in this context. It continues the long line of acts since 1368 that regulated labor conditions. In addition to the limits on wages contained in the earlier acts, it stipulated that from March to September, work was to begin at 5:00 A.M. and to end at 7:00 or 8:00 P.M. It also allowed a half hour for breakfast and an hour and a half for lunch. During the winter, the hours of daylight determined the hours of starting and stopping; the time for meals was to be reduced somewhat.

Central control was relinquished partly with the Statute of Artificers from 1562, perhaps the best-known example of early modern government regulation of work practices. It repeats some of the rules of the act from 1514 and alters others. Hours during the summer remained the same, but greater flexibility in taking meals was allowed. There is provision for "drinking" and a half hour of sleep after dinner. All breaks combined were not to exceed two and a half hours during the summer. During the winter, the hours appointed in 1514 also remained in force, and only dinner and breakfast (taking no more than an hour and a half) were allowed.

Catholic territories began to follow the Protestant example of abolishing holy days relatively quickly. Already after the Council of Trent, two papal decrees limited the number of feasts. In 1642, Pope Urban VIII diminished their number to thirty-four. From the seventeenth century onward, reforming rulers of Catholic states pursued reductions in holy days. In 1727, the Holy See granted the abolition of some holy days for parts of Spain and Italy. Empress Maria

Theresa of Austria reduced the festive calendar by twenty-four holy days in 1754, whereas France, under Colbert, abolished some ninety holidays (including some half-holidays).

Enforcement of early modern labor regulations was probably uneven and is hard to ascertain. Maria Theresa felt the need to stipulate that the former holidays should be regarded as normal working days and that they could be used to fulfill labor obligations to the landlord. Wage books are less common during the early modern period than during the Middle Ages, and the decline of demesnes in late medieval England deprives historians of a reliable source. In more ways than one, the period from 1500 to 1850 is the true "dark age" for the history of labor time. Reliable data on working hours tend to be available again from the dawn of the factory age—the same regimented mode of production that increased output per worker also produced the records detailing patterns of labor and leisure.

Labor and the Industrial Revolution. The extent to which hours increased during industrialization is controversial. Some scholars (Jan de Vries, 1994, most prominently among them) have argued that an "industrious revolution" preceded the industrial revolution. Evidence from probate inventories suggests that, after 1700, wealth for large parts of the population of Holland and England rose at a rate that cannot be explained by the trend in wages.

Longer hours, as well as work on more days of the year, are likely to explain this puzzle. The most famous analysis of changes in working time during industrialization is E. P. Thompson's seminal article "Time, Work-Discipline, and Industrial Capitalism" (1967). He drew on a wealth of literary and other sources to argue that the lax labor regime of "merry old England" was gradually replaced by the iron discipline of the "dark satanic mills." Before industrialization, according to Thompson, work was highly irregular and often interrupted by play. Workers in cottage industries, for example, would work little during the earlier part of the week. Often, no work was performed on the first day of the week, a practice known as "Saint Monday." As the agreed day for the delivery of finished goods (normally Friday or Saturday) drew closer, hours would lengthen and intensity would rise, reaching a feverish pitch in the last day or two. Factory work, in contrast, was highly regular and left workers with few choices as to the pace or timing of work. In Thompson's view, factory time—symbolized by the clocks installed by manufacturers—and increasing discipline were conquering force that deprived workers of their earlier autonomy.

Thompson's study sparked a whole body of research on time use in England before the Industrial Revolution. Although his literary sources are suggestive, actual patterns of labor and leisure is hard to infer. Some scholars have turned to the timing of riots and weddings, for example, to trace the decline of "Saint Monday," and others have examined the records of attendance at municipal gardens. Firm conclusions are hard to come by, and a high degree of regional and sector-specific heterogeneity complicates general conclusions.

Recently, witnesses' accounts in court records have been used to analyze patterns of labor and leisure. These have the advantage of offering a glimpse into the working lives of ordinary citizens and of being available in relatively large numbers over an extended period. They suggest that "Saint Monday" was relatively common in London and in parts of northern England during the middle of the eighteenth century. Also, a surprising number of old religious festivals appear to have been observed. In the period 1760–1830, most of these feast days fell into disuse, and Monday largely became an ordinary working day. Daily hours, on the other hand, remained broadly unchanged. In most professions, work began between 6:00 and 8:00 A.M. and did not stop until twelve hours later except for breakfast and lunch. These findings suggest that, over the last 250 years, a five-day week (with work from Tuesday to Saturday) first gave way to a six-day week, before returning to a norm of five days per week (Monday to Friday) in the second half of the twentieth century.

The evidence from court records suggests that hours in the eighteenth century were indeed shorter than in the nineteenth century. At the same time, Thompson's image of a "merry old England" where hours were short and work highly irregular is probably incorrect. Annual labor input may have been as high as 2,500 hours—similar to labor input in the third world today. From this base, it increased by some 25 to 35 percent over the following century. By 1850, hours in industrializing Europe and North America were long—very long by the standards of human history and of developing countries today. Sixty-five to seventy hours per week, or 3,400 to 3,700 hours per year, were not uncommon in nineteenth-century cotton mills and other factories.

Today, countries at a similar level of development rarely record hours in excess of forty-five to forty-eight per week in manufacturing. The sheer length of the working day, combined with the widespread use of female and child labor, came to be seen as a prime symbol of capitalist exploitation—a consequence of excessive power in the hands of employers at a time of general laissez-faire. Research by Gregory Clark (1994) has called the interpretation based on the monopsony power of employers into question. Alternative modes of production—such as workshops where workers paid "rent" for machinery used and where hours were generally much shorter—existed, but eventually lost out against the factory system.

In parallel with the rise of factory employment, governments began to regulate labor time and to enforce these regulations rigorously. Maximum-hours legislation was generally first applied to children and women, and later to the entire workforce. There are three hallmarks of labor legislation in England: the Cotton Factories Regulation Act of 1819 (prohibiting child labor under the age of nine and a maximum of twelve hours of work per day), the Regulation of Child Labor Law of 1833 (which provided for state inspections to ensure enforcement), and the Ten Hours Bill of 1847, which limited daily hours to no more than ten for women and children.

Causes of the Decline in Working Hours. Hours generally began to decline after the middle of the nineteenth century. The rise of organized labor was an important contributor to declining hours, as were changing attitudes of employers and state intervention. The history of labor time since 1850 has been shaped by agitation in favor of first the ten-hour day (for men), then for the eight-hour day, the forty-hour week, and the thirty-five-hour week. During the second half of the nineteenth century, the ten-hour day eventually became the norm. The U.S. manufacturing census in 1880 showed that the ten-hour day was typical. In the 1890s, half of all men and 30 percent of all employed women worked exactly ten hours per day. It is often asserted that output does not rise above a certain number of hours per week and that reductions in the workweek from, say, sixty-five to fifty-five hours entailed no reduction in production.

The willingness of employers to accept shorter workweeks since the middle of the nineteenth century can probably also be rationalized in response to the greater skill requirements within industry. Where attention to detail, concentration, and initiative became relatively more important than sheer physical presence, reductions in the total number of hours worked could more readily be compensated by greater productivity. Hours legislation gradually became more common in the second half of the nineteenth century. Just as in Britain, U.S. labor laws first applied to women and children (with New Hampshire the first state to introduce such a law in 1847). By 1910, 58 percent of U.S. states had some kind of hours legislation, covering 7 percent of all employees.

One possible interpretation of the secular decline in hours since the middle of the nineteenth century stresses the rise of union influence, as well as the desire to negotiate "durable" improvements in working conditions at a time when price increases often eroded nominal wage increases (Bienefeld, 1972). An alternative interpretation, emphasized by Gary Becker (1965), argues that the length of the working day is partly determined by the trade-off between leisure and income, and the importance of time-intensive versus goods-intensive forms of leisure. The very large increases in "free time" over the last 150 years would then be the result of a strong preference for time-intensive leisure activities, with increases in income resulting in disproportionately higher demands for time off.

In contrast to increases in wage rates, changes in labor time have been highly discontinuous. Working hours often stayed constant for decades, only to be reduced more or less simultaneously and by the same amount in a large number of sectors. The beneficial effects of individuals working at the same time for productivity are often cited as a main cause. Strikingly, almost 80 percent of full-time workers in the United States start between 7:00 and 9:00 A.M. and finish between 3:00 and 6:00 P.M.

The eight-hour day was largely achieved as a result of the improved bargaining role of labor during World War I. By 1919, the eight-hour day (six working days per week) was the norm in Europe and the United States. However, employers worked hard to "roll back" this achievement of organized labor, with some successes in countries that experienced severe contractions in the 1920s. The Great Depression, in contrast, saw a general tendency to shorten hours. Governments encouraged "work sharing," either in the form of a general reduction in hours or by rotating the workforce into and out of employment on a fixed schedule (known as the Krümper system in Germany, OXO in Britain). The latter had the advantage of using unemployment benefits while retaining a large workforce for the time when recovery began. In the United States, average hours per week fell from forty-eight to forty-nine in 1929 to thirty-four to forty-one in 1934, with figures in manufacturing mostly in the lower part of this range. The 1930s saw a gradual increase in hours in most countries; yet it was not before World War II that the average workweek again surpassed the forty-hour mark.

In the postwar period, working hours in Japan and the United States, on the one hand, and in Western Europe, on the other, began to diverge considerably. Instead of shorter hours per day, reductions in the number of days worked per week as well as longer holidays became the principal instruments used for reducing labor input. Agitation in favor of the five-day week began in the 1920s, after the eight-hour day had become the norm. Henry Ford adopted the five-day week in 1926, yet it did not become universal until the 1960s. The United States saw the introduction of the five-day week in the period after World War II. Overtime payments (equivalent to 150 percent of normal wages) for work in excess of forty hours per week were set under the Fair Labor Standards Act of 1938, with the express purpose to provide incentives for employers to reduce hours.

Although the trend toward shorter hours continued in Europe after World War II (where levels were initially higher), it largely came to a standstill in the United States. Populist writing emphasized the "overworked American" as a sign of economic and social failure. Juliet Schor (1993) claimed that hours for most Americans increased

LABOR TIME. Chevrolet Gear and Axle employees clocking in on the first day after the 1945–1946 General Motors strike, 28 March 1946. (Walter P. Reuther Library, Wayne State University)

substantially between the 1960s and the 1990s. This claim, based on self-reported hours and disputable adjustments to official data, did not stand up to scrutiny.

Hours for most Americans did not rise in the last quarter of the twentieth century, whereas they generally fell in most other developed countries. The modal worker (male or female) in the United States worked eight hours in 1991, exactly the same as in 1973. Two factors account for the difference in annual hours worked: by the 1990s, Europeans tended to work less than forty hours per week, and vacations were substantially longer. The difference in annual hours between the United States and Europe for full-time employees is now approximately 20 percent (the gap is wider for Germany and the Scandinavian countries, and smaller for Switzerland, Spain, Portugal, and Great Britain).

One important factor influencing hours worked in the last half century has been the rise of part-time work. Historically, most women stayed at home after getting married. Today, partial employment (working between a quarter and three-quarters of a normal workweek) has become increasingly common. Average hours for women in employment have therefore often fallen, while actually rising in total and over the life cycle. Participation rates for women have increased sharply in most developed countries over the last twenty-five years, in line with average

education. There has been some suggestion that stagnant real wages for men were partly responsible for the rapid rise in female employment. The cross-sectional evidence, where available, speaks against this: female hours of labor have increased most sharply for those women whose spouses suffered the smallest deterioration in real wages.

One further important discontinuity is the decline of working hours among the elderly, analyzed for the United States by Dora Costa (2000). Whereas 68 percent of U.S. men age sixty-five and older worked in the 1890s, only 20 percent do so today. The figure for women has stayed remarkably constant—8 percent of older women worked in the late nineteenth century, and somewhat more than 8 percent did so in the 1990s. In Europe, early retirement has increased sharply in the last two decades, encouraged by generous state pensions and special incentives designed to reduce unemployment. One final factor that has curtailed lifetime hours of work is the spread of mass education. Later entry into the labor force has contributed to a sharp decline in the number of hours worked before retirement.

The welfare implications of reductions in working time can be more complex than appears at first sight. The increase in leisure over the last 150 years has undoubtedly contributed to the quality of life. Nonetheless, hours are rarely chosen, but imposed as part of collective bargaining agreements or, in some countries, via legislation reducing hours. Unions and governments have often pursued working time reductions (such as the thirty-five-hour week) vigorously in an attempt to reduce unemployment. Whether workers would have opted for these reductions in hours is not easy to assess.

In a 2002 referendum in Switzerland, the union-led initiative to reduce standard hours to thirty-six was roundly defeated. Research based on questionnaire responses among southern U.S. textile workers suggests that wages are often higher than the marginal rate of substitution between leisure and labor time, which implies that workers would prefer longer hours (Dunn, 1979). Despite being intended as a means of cutting unemployment, there is little evidence that shorter hours have had a positive effect on employment; on balance, it appears more likely that working time reductions have created yet more unemployment.

Hours no longer vary with qualifications and wages in the way they did in the past. In the nineteenth century, the best-paid employees also often worked the shortest hours. Today, the opposite is more common: those receiving the highest wage per hour also work much longer hours. This is especially true among self-employed members of the professions such as doctors and lawyers. In many sectors, such as investment banking, medicine, and management consulting, the sheer amount of time devoted to work has become an important signal of commitment, and is consequently used as a criterion for promotion. Changes in the distribution of working hours by income group have implications for recent trends in inequality—whereas in the past, the shorter hours among the well-paid counterbalanced their earnings advantage, a substantial part of the rise in earnings differences over the last century can be attributed to longer hours for the better-paid. The underlying reason appears to be that, although backward-bending labor supply curves were probably a feature of the past, they are no longer detectable in current data (with the exception of employees with extremely high incomes).

It is difficult to predict if the general decline in hours since 1850 has come to an end in developed countries. For individual subgroups, this appears to be the case, and employees show some preference for higher earnings instead of additional leisure. Governments and unions continue to pursue working time reductions as a policy to check unemployment. Further reductions in the standard workweek, combined with longer vacations, may well resurface as a major issue in labor relations.

BIBLIOGRAPHY

Atack, Jeremy, and Fred Bateman. "How Long Was the Workday in 1880?" *Journal of Economic History* 52 (1992), 129–160.
Becker, Gary S. "A Theory of the Allocation of Time." *Economic Journal* 75 (1965), 493–517.
Bienefeld, M. A. *Working Hours in British Industry: An Economic History*. London, 1972.
Clark, Gregory. "Factory Discipline." *Journal of Economic History* 54 (1994), 128–163.
Coleman, Mary, and John Pencavel. "Trends in Work Hours of Male Employees, 1940–1988." *Industrial and Labor Relations Review* 46 (1992), 262–283.
Costa, Dora. "The Wage and the Length of the Working Day." *Journal of Labor Economics* 18 (2000), 156–181.
Dunn, Lucia. "Measurement of Internal Income-Leisure Tradeoffs." *Quarterly Journal of Economics* 93 (1979), 373–393.
Hunt, Jennifer. "Has Work-Sharing Worked in Germany? *Quarterly Journal of Economics* 114 (1999), 117–148.
Reid, Douglas. "Weddings, Weekdays, Work, and Leisure in Urban England, 1791–1911." *Past and Present* 153 (1996), 135–163.
Rogers, Thorold E. A *History of Prices and Wages*. London, 1884.
Thompson, E. P. "Time, Work-Discipline, and Industrial Capitalism." *Past and Present* 38 (1967), 56–97.
Sahlins, M. *Stone Age Economics*. Chicago, 1972.
Schor, Juliet. *The Overworked American: The Unexpected Decline of Leisure*. New York, 1993.
Voth, Hans-Joachim. *Time and Work in England, 1760–1830*. Oxford, 2001.
Vries, Jan de. "The Industrial Revolution and the Industrious Revolution." *Journal of Economic History* 54 (1994), 249–270.
Whaples, Robert. "Winning the Eight-Hour Day, 1909–1919." *Journal of Economic History* 50 (1990), 393–406.

HANS-JOACHIM KLR VOTH

LAGOS, port city on several islands and the adjacent shore, in the Bight of Benin, West Africa; former capital of Nigeria. Inhabited by several million people, Lagos began centuries ago as an island crossroad of trade along a network of creeks and lagoons; it linked the Atlantic coast (Gulf of Guinea) with Africa's interior, between the Volta River in the west and the Niger Delta in the east. The area had been settled by Awori, the southernmost of the Yoruba-speaking peoples, who founded a small state there.

In the sixteenth century, the polity's strategic location led to attack and military encampment by the powerful and sophisticated Kingdom of Benin, which introduced a new ruling dynasty that is still represented in Lagos today. During the last, largely illegal, phase of the Atlantic slave trade of the early 1800s, Lagos became the leading slave port north of the equator. In the short term, the slave trade increased the wealth and power of the local *oba* (king) and his chiefs. In the longer term, the slave trade led to the small kingdom's conquest by Great Britain in 1851 and its annexation in 1861.

With British conquest came the abolition of the slave trade there and the growth of important new commerce with Europe, first in palm produce and later in cocoa. British colonialism in Nigeria encouraged the return immigration of freed African slaves from Brazil, Sierra Leone, and elsewhere, as well as Christian missionary activity, which stimulated conversions and the pursuit of Western education. By the late 1800s, there was a local educated elite of merchants, professionals, and colonial servants,

LAGOS. Scene at an outdoor market, 1961. (Douglas Jones/Prints and Photographs Division, Library of Congress)

which had developed alongside the much larger population of uneducated local crafts manufacturers. Following Britain's annexation in 1861, private ownership of land was developed to coexist with the indigenous system of land tenure. The slow growth of the colonial state was basic to such changes but did not direct them. The practice of local slavery was also gradually ended, although work for wages did not become a dominant means of organizing labor within the community until well into the twentieth century.

Within the British colony, Lagos grew rapidly as a major international port and regional commercial capital—the colonial administrative headquarters of a unified Nigeria after 1914. These developments attracted migration from many parts of Nigeria and West Africa, which increased the size and cultural heterogeneity of the city, a process that continues. Following Nigeria's independence in 1960, Lagos was the federal capital, which made the city the gateway to political and economic opportunity within the nation—especially after the 1970s development of the oil industry. Political and social pressures then relocated the seat of national government inland to the created capital territory of Abuja in 1991, but Lagos continues as the region's main port and Nigeria's commercial, financial, and industrial capital. The majority of the several millions who now live in the city support themselves through small-scale trade and informal sector activities, yet some find salaried employment with the government or with private firms, and a few make fortunes as entrepreneurs, too often through corrupt practices.

In today's Lagos, existing side by side, are great wealth and abject poverty; respect for the history and culture of the past and greed for what is new and changing in the present; as well as crumbling infrastructure, inadequate social services, and boundless human dynamism and creativity.

BIBLIOGRAPHY

Adefuye, Ade, Babatunde Agiri, and Jide Osuntokun, eds. *History of the Peoples of Lagos State.* Ikeja, Nigeria, 1987.

Aderibigbe, A. B., ed. *Lagos: The Development of an African City.* Ikeja, Nigeria, 1975.

Barnes, Sandra T. *Patrons and Power: Creating a Political Community in Metropolitan Lagos.* Bloomington, Ind. 1986.

Hopkins, A. G. "Economic Imperialism in Lagos, 1880–1914." *Economic History Review* 21 (1968), 580–606.

Hopkins, A. G. "Property Rights and Empire Building: Britain's Annexation of Lagos, 1861." *Journal of Economic History* 40 (1980), 777–798.

Mann, Kristin. *Marrying Well: Marriage, Status, and Social Change among the Educated Elite in Colonial Lagos.* Cambridge, 1985.

Peil, Margaret. *Lagos: The City and Its People.* Boston, 1991.

Smith, Robert S. *The Lagos Consulate, 1851–1861.* Berkeley, 1979.

KRISTIN MANN

LANCASHIRE. In northwestern England, the southern half of the county of Lancashire, has a strong claim to world historical significance as the crucible in which the Industrial Revolution was forged. Efforts to rehabilitate that concept in recent years, after econometricians used national-level measures to emphasize steady growth rather than sharp discontinuity between the late eighteenth and the mid-nineteenth century, have focused on regional transformations; and Lancashire has provided ample data. Its southeastern corner, within a radius of thirty miles from Manchester (which spills over into adjoining counties), hosted the dramatic rise of cotton manufacturing from the 1770s onward. This industry grew out of the domestic manufacture of cotton-linen mixtures, which spread through an inhospitable countryside, pulled small farmers into manufacturing for distant markets, accumulated small capital resources with few alternative outlets, and encouraged accelerating population growth and the proliferation of manufacturing-dependant smallholdings and cottages (households). These developments look recognizably "proto-industrial"; but, here, the transition to a modern industrial economy was swift and almost unremitting.

The key to Lancashire's industrialization was its experience with cotton as a raw material and its ability to exploit the fabric's versatility and popularity in world markets. On the west side of Lancashire county, Liverpool—as Britain's fastest growing port—linked the Manchester region into the Atlantic trade economy by importing raw cotton from Asia and the American colonies, as well as distributing manufactured cloth to distant markets. (The slave trade's part in this was more through opening out mercantile connections and insurance arrangements than the direct investment of capital in manufacturing industry.) A spate of innovations were responses to the new opportunities of the later 1700s, as supply bottlenecks were broken on the spinning side of the industry. Of the three famous inventions—spinning jenny (a multiple-spindle machine for spinning wool or cotton), water-frame (a machine that draws, twists, and winds yarn), and mule (a machine for drawing and twisting fiber into thread or yarn and winding it into a spool)—the first remained largely compatible with domestic production, the second dispersed factories across a wide area in search of appropriate water-powered sites, and the adaptability of the third to steam power generated factory-led urbanization on a new scale across the coalfield, supplied by the new canals, beginning in the 1790s. This became the dominant model for the nineteenth century, and a new urban middle class came to power locally as part of this process.

The weaving of cotton was mechanized more slowly, with the power loom's invention in the 1830s and 1840s, which inspired a new burst of urbanization in northeast Lancashire. As the proud and independent hand-loom weavers came under increasing pressure after the Napoleonic Wars, a popular politics of radical democracy and a fitfully powerful trade union movement, extending across the spectrum of trades, came to a peak in the Chartist movement: but the situation stabilized after mid-century and economic growth and urbanization proceed-

ed steadily until World War I. The southwest of Lancashire county industrialized on a different model, led by coal and chemicals rather than cotton, and with Liverpool as its metropolis, while development further north was more localized and intermittent. The cotton industry, which depended increasingly on exports to India, peaked just before World War I, and the subsequent falling sales, unemployment, contested decline, and remaking of the industry was instructive but less distinctive.

Lancashire's moment on the world historical stage came through its pioneering role in factory industry, which generated novel problems (including those associated with the work of children and later of married women outside the home). It was brought from obscurity to become the cynosure of foreign commentators. In retrospect, it seems astounding that a cotton industry could ever have flourished there, so far from raw materials and markets; consequently, efforts to explain the county's pioneering status continue to engage economic historians.

BIBLIOGRAPHY

Rose, Mary B., ed. *The Lancashire Cotton Industry: A History since 1700.* Preston, U.K., 1996.

Timmins, Geoffrey. *Made in Lancashire.* Manchester, 1998.

Walton, John K. *Lancashire: A Social History, 1558–1939.* Manchester, 1987.

JOHN K. WALTON

LAND INHERITANCE PATTERNS. When land is abundant, as was true in most of sub-Saharan Africa until recently and is still true in important areas of the African continent, corporate ownership of land assets is the rule. This means that land is the property of the whole lineage that cleared the bush to set up the village and to open agricultural fields. The representatives of the lineage hold the village or community land in custody and ensure that all members hold a sufficient portion of it to make a decent living. Rights in land are typically contingent upon its continued use, so access to land is dependent on the ability to cultivate it as well as on subsistence needs.

Tenure Rights. When population grows and land becomes scarce, however, the system of land relations evolves toward increased individualization of tenure rights. In a celebrated passage, Ester Boserup has cogently described the mechanism through which individualized rights are gradually established:

Virtually all the systems of land tenure found to exist before the emergence of private property in land seem to have this one feature in common: certain families are recognized as having cultivation rights within a given area of land. . . . As long as a tribe of forest-fallow cultivators has abundant land at its disposal, a family would have no particular interest in returning to precisely that plot which it cultivated on an earlier occasion. Under these conditions a family which needed to shift to a new plot would simply find a suitable plot, or have it allocated by the chief of the tribe, with no regard to the question of who had formerly cultivated particular plots. But the situation is apt to change with increasing population, as good plots become somewhat scarce. The cultivators may then wish to begin to recultivate a given plot before the normal period of fallow has elapsed. Under such conditions, a family is likely to become more attached to the plots they have been cultivating on earlier occasions, because it is becoming difficult to find better plots elsewhere which are not already taken up by another family. In other words, the members of the tribe would tend to become more conscious and jealous about their special right to the old plots, and they may hasten to recultivate them lest the cultivation right be forfeited by desuetude. . . . Thus, the attachment of individual families to particular plots becomes more and more important with the gradual shortening of the period of fallow and the reduction of the part of the territory which is not used in the rotation. By the same token, the general right for the members of the tribe to clear a new plot becomes less valuable. . . . As more and more land is subject to specific cultivation rights little land will be available for redistribution by the chief, and valuable land for redistribution will become available mainly when a family dies out or leaves the territory. . . . Redistribution of land thus becomes a less important and less frequently exerted function of the chief, and in the end it disappears altogether. (Boserup, 1965, pp. 79–81)

As is evident from the above, individualization of land rights reflects a shift in control over the land away from kinship and tribal groups toward the household. It does not manifest itself only through the increased assertion of the right to recultivate the same plot of land even before the normal period of fallow has elapsed, the right to plant trees and to bring other improvements to the land, or the right to use the land to the exclusion of other customary claimants (such as herders) who traditionally held subsidiary or overlapping rights. It also makes its way through an evolution of the rules of inheritance toward a more direct transmission of land from parents to children and possibly through a shift from matrilineal to patrilineal inheritance patterns. Rather than the land reverting upon the death of the landholder to the community pool to be reallocated to some member in need, it may now be bequeathed directly to the children of the deceased person (see, for example, Yudelman, 1964; Noronha, 1985; Downs and Reyna, 1988; and Bassett and Crummey, 1993).

The right to bequeath land directly to children thus seems to evolve endogenously as a response to the increasing need to intensify agricultural practices because of growing pressure on land resources. As a matter of fact, such practices can be successfully developed only if the required investments in the land are carried out, which necessitates in turn that proper investment incentives are provided. These incentives cannot exist if the farmer is not assured that he or she can reap the gains of his or her (long-term) invest-

ments. For that to be possible, he or she must have secure rights over the land he or she cultivates, meaning he or she has the right or ability to maintain long-term use of it. The right to bequeath the land is obviously part and parcel of tenure security since it guarantees that even future generations may benefit from the present efforts of farmers, thus enhancing the return on long-term land improvements and conservation measures.

Upon this reading, one should expect the prevalence of inheritance practices to be positively correlated with the extent of land pressure and the related importance of intensive agricultural techniques, and this is precisely what one systematically observes. In particular, the contrast between the age-old system of land inheritance rights in European and Asian agriculture, on the one hand, and the communal system of land tenure in many parts of sub-Saharan Africa until recent times, on the other hand, can be largely explained in terms of differences in population densities between these two parts of the world. Within sub-Saharan Africa itself, variations in the incidence of inheritance rights can be essentially traced back to differences in land pressure and population density, as illustrated by the long-established prevalence of individualized rights of inheritance in Rwanda and Burundi and contrasted with their prolonged absence in areas dominated by shifting agriculture, such as Guinea Bissau and Gabon.

Also noteworthy is the proliferation of inter vivos gifts conceived as anticipated inheritance when children assert an increasing willingness to emancipate from the parents' tutelage upon marriage or even upon their reaching adulthood. Rather than maintaining tense relations with children who have low incentives to work on the family land, parents prefer to give in to these requests, and they then reserve for themselves the land needed for their own subsistence and for the younger children still to be married. Difficult situations may ensue if land given to the eldest children has to be redistributed upon the death of a parent to ensure equitable sharing of the family property among all the surviving children. As a matter of fact, the exact number of claimants is difficult to predict, especially in polygamous systems under which a man may decide to take a new wife rather late in life (Peters, 1994; André and Platteau, 1998; Platteau and Baland, 2001).

Female Inheritance. Whether or not daughters inherit land like their brothers is an issue that cannot be resolved unless one looks at the pattern of marriage obtaining in the particular society considered. When virilocality is the prescribed rule, it is a general principle that women do not inherit the land of their fathers. This makes good sense given the high transaction costs women's inheritance would involve. In societies governed by the practice of virilocality, indeed equal inheritance of land between brothers and sisters automatically implies that women do not live close to their land property and are therefore not in a position to monitor its use effectively. One obvious solution is for a woman to rent her land parcel to a farmer who lives in her parental village. Yet as the economic theory of agrarian contracts demonstrates, such a solution is plagued by incentive problems that are hard to overcome given the pervasive presence of market imperfections in the rural areas of developing countries.

Of course in the specific instance of land inherited by daughters, one would expect the brothers to claim a privileged access to the land owned by their sisters. And the latter should be willing to oblige out of a sense of family solidarity and also because the land ought to be better managed by a close relative than by a more distant lessor. The point remains, however, that even brothers may cheat their sisters by exploiting their informational advantage and, for example, overreporting cultivation expenditures and underreporting output. Also, the investment incentive of lessors (including brothers) is blurred if they expect the land may be taken away from them and with no reliable method of assessing land improvements or enforcing the payment of the required indemnities.

Since rental contracts are fraught with problems arising from informational asymmetries and rural market imperfections, land disposal through sale transactions may apparently provide the most satisfactory solution to the problem posed by equal inheritance between sons and daughters and the principle of virilocal marriage. More precisely, a woman could sell her inherited portion of the family land, and with the proceeds she could buy a new parcel located in her husband's village. If all women were willing to thus exchange land portions through sales and purchases, an active land market would inevitably arise in the countryside. The obvious limitation of such a solution, however, is that it is bound to entail considerable transaction costs owing to indivisibility problems. Indeed, land sale transactions of the kind envisaged here unavoidably break the continuity of family land portions. As a result, a man will never find equal inheritance between brothers and sisters equivalent to the system under which only sons are entitled to inherit the father's land.

One could conceivably argue that the objective of compactness of land property could be achieved if each woman sold her portion of family land to a brother. This would nevertheless require that one brother's marriage coincide with her own marriage so purchasing power comes timely into the hands of the preferred buyer. Alternatively, if not yet married to a woman with the necessary dowry, a brother could admittedly take a loan toward the purpose of buying his sister's share of the family property. It is nevertheless evident that no lender will agree to give a loan on the promise of an uncertain marriage and an uncertain dowry payment.

The above explanation is actually supported by evidence that, when women marry men from their own communities and therefore keep on living in their native villages, as often occurs in Indian communities of the Peruvian Highlands, for example, they do inherit family land. This is in contrast to the most typical situation observed in sub-Saharan Africa, where women leave their native communities upon marriage and are not entitled to inherit land. Note that the latter is true even in Muslim areas, such as the Senegal River valley, where Islamic law provides that a daughter should inherit half of the portion of the parent's land that accrues to a brother. Here is a striking illustration of the fact that formal laws that do not suit economic and environmental circumstances are bound to be violated by the people concerned.

Primogeniture. When the pressure on land becomes high, the question of whether the family land ought to remain whole in the hands of a single child or be divided equally among all the children at the cost of extreme fragmentation of the family property becomes pertinent. Evidence from western Europe and other continents consistently shows that primogeniture—the land goes to the eldest child—has been almost systematically (with the glaring exception of Russia during the last five centuries) applied among the aristocratic classes. This is because the integrity of the land and mansion was the physical symbol of the unity and indivisibility of the political and military functions associated with the lord's estate (Bloch, 1965; Betzig, 1993; and Platteau and Baland, 2001).

Among lower social classes, primogeniture was the exception rather than the rule. Throughout western Europe, the exceptions were important, though, as attested by the prevalence of exclusive inheritance practices in large parts of England, France, Belgium, and Germany. How to account for these significant exceptions is a thorny issue that is not well understood (see Homans, 1941; Mendels, 1970; Goody, Thirsk, and Thompson, 1976; Goody, 1983; and Platteau and Baland, 2001). Yet there is solid ground to believe that areas of primogeniture tend to be characterized by either a long-established manorial tradition or strong community organizations. In the former case, the lords have usually prevented land fragmentation among the peasantry in order to benefit from scale economies in tax collection and to minimize the risk of tax defaulting. In the latter case, communities have prevented land subdivision in order to reap coordination gains (under complex land rotation systems) or to limit pressure on common-property resources through membership rules restricting the formation of new households. The prevalence of a patriarchal mode of family authority also ensures that everything is done to maintain the family property whole under the command of a single successor. The case of southern France easily comes to mind here.

Modern Practices. Variations among European countries still exist in patterns of land inheritance and succession. Thus, three such patterns are common in the European Union: equal shares and breakup of the farm, equal shares and preservation of the holding as a single unit, and unequal shares together with maintenance of the holding as a single unit (Ravenscroft, Gibbard, and Markwell, 1999). The first system largely prevails in Mediterranean countries (Greece, Italy, Spain, and Portugal), where land fragmentation over the last thirty years has hastened rural depopulation among younger people given the difficulty of assembling a viable farming unit upon inheritance. This outcome is avoided, however, when collective ownership and management of the family land is adopted or when land can be easily purchased to complement the inherited farm.

The second system is found in France, Denmark, and Belgium, where forms of "preferential allotment" have modified the civil code to allow inheritance of the family holding by one heir with a cash settlement to the others. The need to thus compensate noninheriting heirs, however, can burden existing farms with high levels of debt and lead to their decapitalization. Finally, in common law countries, such as England and Wales, but also in Ireland, the Netherlands, and Germany, there is no need to divide capital among heirs, and preservation of peasant holdings is the norm. Note that it is only in common law countries that the inheriting heir has no obligation to his or her siblings. In Ireland, the committment is to take care of the remaining parents, while in Germany and the Netherlands, the coheirs are entitled to a share of the proceeds from the sale of the family farm if it is sold.

In developing countries, on the other hand, equal sharing of family land among the sons is a general rule, and it typically results in a considerable extent of land subdivision. Adherence to it seems to be especially strong in areas where nonagricultural income opportunities are rare and in areas where labor markets are highly uncertain or are perceived as such (so sons with nonagricultural jobs fear they may lose their employment).

[*See also* Inheritance Systems.]

BIBLIOGRAPHY
André, Catherine, and Jean-Philippe Platteau. "Land Relations under Unbearable Stress: Rwanda Caught in the Malthusian Trap." *Journal of Economic Behavior and Organization* 34.1 (1998), pp. 1–47.
Bassett, Tom J., and Donald E. Crummey, eds. *Land in African Agrarian Systems.* Madison, Wis., 1993.
Betzig, Laurent. "Sex, Succession, and Stratification in the First Six Civilizations." In *Social Stratification and Socioeconomic Inequality*, edited by L. Ellis, pp. 33–74, New York, 1993.
Bloch, Marc. *Feudal Society*, vol. 1, *The Growth of Ties of Dependence*, vol. 2, *Social Classes and Political Organization.* London and New York, 1965.
Boserup, Ester. *The Conditions of Agricultural Growth: The Economics of Agrarian Change under Population Pressure.* London, 1965.
Downs, R. E., and Stephen P. Reyna, eds. *Land and Society in Contemporary Africa.* Hanover and London, 1988.
Goody, Jack. *The Development of the Family and Marriage in Europe.* Cambridge, 1983.
Goody, Jack, Joan Thirsk, and Ewen P. Thompson, eds. *Family and Inheritance: Rural Society in Western Europe, 1200–1800.* Cambridge, 1976.
Homans, George C. *English Villagers of the Thirteenth Century.* Cambridge, Mass., 1941.
Mendels, F. F. "Industry and Marriages in Flanders before the Industrial Revolution." In *Population and Economics: Proceedings of Section V of the IV Congress of the International Economic History Association*, edited by P. Deprez, pp. 81–93. Winnipeg, Canada, 1970.
Noronha, R. "A Review of the Literature on Land Tenure Systems in Sub-Saharan Africa." Working paper no. 43, Research Unit of the Agriculture and Rural Development Department, World Bank, Washington, D.C.
Peters, Pauline E. *Dividing the Commons: Politics, Policy, and Culture in Botswana.* Charlottesville, Va., and London, 1994.
Platteau, Jean-Philippe, and Jean-Marie Baland. "Impartible Inheritance versus Equal Division: A Comparative Perspective Centered on Europe and Subsaharan Africa." In *Access to Land, Rural Poverty, and Public Action*, edited by A. de Janvry, G. Gordillo, J. P. Platteau, and E. Sadoulet. Oxford, 2001.
Ravenscroft, N., R. Gibbard, and S. Markwell. "Private Sector Agricultural Tenancy Arrangements in Europe: Themes and Dimensions—A Critical Review of Current Literature." Working paper no. 28, Land Tenure Center, University of Wisconsin, Madison, 1999.
Yudelman, M. *Africans on the Land.* Cambridge, Mass., 1964.

JEAN-PHILIPPE PLATTEAU

LANDLORDISM. The concept, if not the term itself, is widely used, especially by sociologists and anthropologists, but it is quite difficult to define precisely. Seven main characteristics prominent in discussions of landlord-dominated agriculture are as follows:

1. The distribution of rights to land and, usually, to agricultural capital is very unequal. The land is divided into large estates (haciendas, latifundia, and so on), belonging to few individuals. The majority of workers have little or no land at all.

2. The cultivation is rather extensive. The overall land/labor and land/capital ratios are high; a sizable portion of the land may be left under fallow, permanent pasture, or woodland; the output consists mainly of cereals and livestock products.

3. The workers have no guarantee of permanent or quasi-permanent employment on the estate. They are either hired as day laborers or with short-term tenancy contracts. In some cases, they live on the estate; in others, they dwell in villages and go every morning to work on the estate that hires them.

4. The landlord is only marginally involved in the management of the estate and often lives elsewhere (e.g., in the capital city). The day-to-day management is entrusted

to his agents or to large-scale tenants, who rent the whole estate and then run it.

5. The relations between the landlord and the peasants are highly unbalanced, even if the landlord's power is seldom based on legal discrimination. Peasants are legally free to enter whatever contract they want or quit. However, the landless laborers have no other employment opportunity and thus must accept the terms of employment set by the landlord. The conditions are no better for those peasants with some resources of their own (e.g., land or tools), as these are by definition too small to allow them to live. Furthermore, the landlord is usually the only or main source of credit, and the cost of it may be so high as to make full repayment almost impossible. Workers could end up permanently tied to the landlord (debt peonage).

6. Part of the output may be retained by the landlord for his household consumption, given to workers as part of their salary, or sold to them. However, most of the production is sold on the market. If the local urban markets are underdeveloped, the products are exported.

7. The landlords as a group wield considerable power at a national level.

In principle, a landlord estate differs not only from the family farm but also from two other types of large-scale agricultural enterprises. It differs from the slave or feudal estates, where the workers are legally bound to the owner or to the land. It differs also from the capitalistic estate (or plantation, as it is often called in the literature about less-developed countries), which is cultivated with capital-intensive techniques.

As often happens, no actual historical case fits the definition perfectly, although many include some or most of the characteristics listed but not all. It may be even difficult to assess whether a feature exists (what does "considerable power" exactly mean?). Thus, the use of landlordism to describe any given situation may be controversial. The underlying effect seems to be a negative connotation of the term. A landlord economy is plagued by slow agricultural growth and unsatisfactory social and political development, and the agrarian structure is one of the main causes for this. Arguably, most of the conditions set forth above did hold in the United Kingdom until World War I, but no one considers it a landlord economy. On the other hand, Kang Chao (*Man and Land in Chinese Economic History*, 1986) uses the term *landlordism* for China, where the size of farms was small and the cultivation highly intensive.

Origins and Diffusion. The uncertainty of the definition makes it difficult to map the diffusion of landlordism. The category is most often employed to describe the situation that existed in Latin America and in some agriculturally backward areas in southern and eastern Europe. In

both cases, the concentration of land ownership, the easiest measure of landlordism, was high. In Mexico, before the 1910 revolution, 1 percent of families owned more than 95 percent of the land, and as late as 1960 less than 2 percent of families owned between 40 and 80 percent of the land in Argentina, Brazil, and other Latin American countries (Russel King, *Land Reform*, 1977).

In most cases, the system has evolved from a previous feudal structure. In many European countries in the late eighteenth and early nineteenth century, the abolition of serfdom left the aristocrats with a substantial share of their feudal domains as private property. In 1806, the Prussian aristocrats (or Junkers) received about half of the land and a substantial financial compensation for the rest. The deal was so good that this type of evolution is often christened as the "Junker road to capitalistic development." In not all cases, however, did the abolition of serfdom result in the development of landlordism. For instance, the 1861 reform in Russia assigned most of the land to village communities, and in the long run, peasant cultivation prevailed. In Latin America, the evolution has been more complex. Many Mexican haciendas evolved from the encomiendas, granted by the Spanish crown, to conquistadores, but many others were created or expanded later with the expropriation of village communities. In underpopulated countries such as Argentina, labor, not land, was at first the scarce resource. Viable estates could be established only when population growth and, more importantly, immigration had increased the number of potential workers.

Consequences. Landlordism had important and usually negative social and political implications. By definition, a landlord-dominated society is not a democratic one. It is often argued that it hindered economic growth as well. The critics quote at least five (not mutually exclusive) negative consequences on the agricultural growth and economic development at large.

1. Extensive cultivation was less efficient than small-scale cultivation, and thus wasted valuable resources. Albert Berry and William Cline (*Agrarian Structure and Productivity in Developing Countries*, 1979) have demonstrated that in less-developed countries in the 1960s, small farms produced more per unit of land than large ones. However, the gap may have been a product of a more intensive use of labor in family farms. The evidence on differences in total productivity (a measure that takes into account the use of all input) is much less clear-cut.

2. Landlordism hindered technical progress. Given their status, landlords should have promoted technical progress and the diffusion of innovation, but they did not deliver. Most of them were simply absentee: they

preferred living in cities and simply neglected their land as long as it provided the necessary income. Others might even have actively discouraged technical progress in their estates if they feared that it might have jeopardized their social and political status.

3. The dominance of landlords stifled entrepreneurship and social mobility, wasting valuable human resources. Peasants had no real option to prove their worth. They could not get land as the estates were usually not for sale, and when so they were sold in bulk. No other jobs were available outside the estate, and also those within the estate (e.g., supervisor) were strictly under the control of the landowner.

4. The distribution of income was very unequal. By definition, most or all the income from land and capital accrued to a small elite, and landlords could further exploit peasants—for instance, charging interest rates or company-store prices that were higher than the market ones. An unequal distribution of income is allegedly harmful for development as it reduces the market for domestic industry manufactures.

If landlordism had these negative consequences, it was necessary to get rid of it. Some authors have argued that it had to die a natural death and that traditional large estates had to transform into progressive capitalistic farms. But in historical reality, its demise has been hastened by a wave of land reform, which has sometimes been extended to all large estates. Nowadays, there are few if any cases of landlordism, and nowhere do landlords enjoy the social and political clout they used to have.

In retrospect, the economic case against landlordism is much less clear-cut than it might have appeared some years ago. Many economists beg to differ with the traditional wholesale condemnation of latifundia, stressing economic rationality instead of social relations or power as the main cause of their existence. From this perspective, landlordism was a consequence, not a cause, of backwardness. Latifundia are seen as an adaptation to environmental constraints (e.g., the lack of irrigation facilities), factor endowments (the abundance of land and the shortage of labor), and the imperfection of markets. In this view, the large estates were not inefficient, unresponsive to market opportunities, or necessarily technically backward. Many innovations were not adopted simply because they were unsuitable to the environment or to the factor endowment. The landlord provided credit because other sources were not available, and the terms were not necessarily exploitative.

[See also Latifundia.]

BIBLIOGRAPHY

Adelman, Jeremy. Frontier Development: Land, Labour, and Capital on the Wheatlands of Argentina and Canada, 1890–1914. Oxford, 1994. A comparative overview of two different paths of development of extensive agriculture.

De Janvry, Alain. The Agrarian Question and Reformism in Latin America. Baltimore, 1981. The most ambitious attempt to deal with the issue of agrarian structure from a radical (Marxist) point of view.

Edelman, Marc. The Logic of the Latifundio. Stanford, Calif., 1992. A case study on large estates in northern Costa Rica with a substantial introduction on the literature.

Feder, Ernest. The Rape of the Peasantry. New York, 1971. A typical, scathing indictment of the traditional agrarian structure.

Mayer, Arno. The Persistence of the Old Regime: Europe to the Great War. New York, 1981. A classic and highly controversial book on the power of landed elites even in the most advanced countries of western Europe.

Petrusewicz, Martha. Latifundium: Moral Economy and Material life in a European Periphery. Ann Arbor, 1996. A case study of a large estate in southern Italy from a rather sympathetic point of view.

Taylor, Alan. "Latifundia as Malefactor in Economic Development? Scale, Tenancy and Agriculture on the Pampas." Research in Economic History 17 (1997), 261–300. A case study from the revisionist point of view.

GIOVANNI FEDERICO

LAND MARKETS. The market for land, a primary factor of production in all of human history, is best understood as the sale and rental of cultivable terrain. Although land transfers through diplomacy, conquest, and government grants as well as markets for urban land, water rights, and subsoil rights (such as mineral rights) have been important at various times, these will not be considered here. Instead, of concern here are the institutions governing the trade in and arrangement of ownership and usage rights in agricultural land.

Land markets have traditionally been thin because land is a uniquely localized and indestructible asset. Its perpetuity grants security, which owners are loath to give up because prices seldom compensate for the high risks of selling such a secure asset. Owners are more hesitant to sell when alternatives, such as mortgages and leasing, are available, and thin trade reinforces this reluctance because it makes repurchasing difficult. Hence low turnover persists. Land sales therefore are undertaken primarily when shocks occur under conditions of imperfect credit and rental markets. One such shock was the introduction of tax changes. Traditional landowners in eastern India after the imposition of the British land revenue system and peasant proprietors in France of the mid-sixteenth century and the seventeenth century were forced to sell their properties as dramatically higher tax burdens impoverished many. Regular sales were comparatively few and involved owners selling parcels in less-convenient locations to procure nearby ones. Distress sales were also present in the late Roman Empire and in early modern England, where landed families that owned substantial rural territory often had adequate savings and could survive trade fluctuations, while capital-strapped peasant proprietors could not and had to sell out.

Laws on inheritance also influenced the amount of land in circulation. The seventeenth-century common law of strict settlement and resettlement limited the number of land transfers by restricting the discretion of English landowners and their heirs to sell estate property outside the family. In contrast, the Chinese practice of partible inheritance dividing property equally among sons increased transactions in the land market as heirs bought and sold parcels to achieve viable farms and to strike a balance between their landholdings and household labor.

In a land market where total supply is fixed and transactions are free, prices are determined only by demand and reflect the discounted stream of expected future net rental income. Real prices therefore may rise with higher demand from better land quality, fewer investment alternatives, population increases, transportation and farming improvements, or institutional changes. Land demand and prices can also increase in cases where food supplies are erratic or scarce and where labor has few off-farm employment opportunities. In markets where supply elasticity is greater, demand pressure tend to be met with expansion in farm acreage. India was a case in point. Demographic, technological, and institutional changes from 1600 led to more land coming under cultivation in the following three hundred years than in the previous eleven centuries. The state also plays an important role in influencing prices and supply through sales or zoning regulations. For instance, the U.S. Congress modified prices and minimum acreages of its plots released to the public throughout the nineteenth century in reaction to weak sales.

To what degree did prices reflect the economic returns from land? Historians have debated if land prices in early modern England were influenced by noneconomic factors, such as social prestige. The difficulty lies in separating the social premium, which buyers were willing to pay for the status that land holdings bestowed, from the premium paid for owning land that was relatively more secure than other forms of wealth. Moreover, as tenants have to bear higher costs of coordinating inputs than owner-occupants, one important but neglected determinant of the premium in land prices was the organizational cost saving that ownership provided. Another issue of the same ilk centers on the role of land speculation. While it was true that wealthy individuals sometimes accumulated land for speculative purposes without making productive use of their asset, it was also true that in some cases speculators played a crucial role in financial intermediation. For instance, speculation in the United States was traditionally regarded as a parasitic activity, but it facilitated the movement of capital from the eastern states to the West. Moreover, since the activity was inherently risky, it was not especially remunerative on average, after accounting for the costs of ownership and administration.

Land Law and Property Rights. The historical evolution of land markets was closely related to developments in land law that had generally, over centuries, involved the greater clarification of property rights as well as the creation of rules to protect investments. Overall, these legal changes had the benefit of raising agricultural productivity through encouraging investments and allocating land to its highest value or most efficient use, but often at the cost of increasing social inequality as well.

For much of history the right to hold land was intimately tied up with an individual's social status and defined his or her obligations and privileges within the community (for example, landowning qualifications were attached to senatorial positions in the Roman Empire and to voting rights in many societies); hence it was subject to much negotiation and contestation. Land rights were often separate and hierarchical. A plot could be cultivated by one party, held by another, and ultimately owned by a third. The distinction between usage and ownership rights is an important one. Although groups of people were at various times in history excluded from formal landownership, it does not necessarily follow that they were denied access to land and returns from agriculture. According to research on early Mesopotamian tablets, the right of exclusive usage, although informal, was accepted widely enough to enable land exchanges as early as 2700 BCE. Land trade was conducted even though ownership rights were blurred or rested with third parties, such as representatives of deities (for example, temple bureaucracies in Mesopotamia, caliphs under early medieval Islamic practice) and secular rulers from the time of Hammurabi to kings and lords in feudal Europe.

Greater clarification of rights came with the codification of the concept of *dominion* (the right to alienate property) during the early Roman Empire (c. 500 BCE), although there is some surviving evidence that contract laws and notary systems were already regulating land exchanges in ancient Egypt. Rome's codification undoubtedly aided the development of a relatively free market in land, which had speculation and arbitrage activities as well as roughly uniform prices within regions.

Although dominion rights were destroyed with the fall of the Roman Empire in the fifth century, they were resuscitated when population pressures again made land scarce in twelfth-century western Europe. In England certain institutional changes (for example, commutation of labor services into money, development of freeholds and copyholds, as well as the right to alienate land) marked a movement from "status" to "contract" in land rights. Of greatest importance was the passage of Quia Emptores in 1290, which mandated that a peasant buyer of land be directly obligated to the manorial lord instead of through the seller. Thus the law shortened and clarified the chain of obligations and reduced transaction costs in peasant land exchanges. The effect of such legal innovations was the rise of an active market that transferred land to peasants who could put it to efficient use. Similarly in China during the late Ming (c. 1400–1644) and Qing (1644–1911) dynasties, a dynamic land market developed after restrictions on land transfers were swept away, which partly accounted for the strong productivity performances in the southern region thereafter.

While clearer land rights can facilitate better transferability of property through the market, there is also a need to temper market dynamism in order to encourage specific and longer-term investments. Hence property rights that protect farming capital are also important for agricultural development, as they give farmers the incentive to invest in assets specific to the terrain in question, such as human knowledge and environmental improvements. In large parts of western Europe until the sixteenth century, the continuity of landholdings within families was protected by inheritance customs, such as strict primogeniture, under which only firstborn sons could be heirs to estate property. In the United States many states in the first half of the nineteenth century adopted legislation to protect the value of improvements by allowing the investor to recover his or her assets in cases of dispossession. Although the English common law of waste provided no similar statutory cover, the costs and uncertainties of replacing tenants often meant that landlords usually renewed leases, and turnover was low. Similar protection of farm investments was present in Qing China, where tenants on reclaimed land could acquire permanent tenancy on topsoil, as well as the right to alienate it, after investing heavily in working capital. Anglo-American case law on the use of property had a similar effect. As early as the mid-nineteenth century courts in England and Massachusetts recognized that free transfers of property could create negative externalities for third parties and intervened to prevent landowners from devaluing their neighbors' holdings.

Increased activity in land markets led in many cases to estate consolidation, increased social inequality, and the rise of new groups of landowners. This was because not everyone could exploit the improvements in land rights to participate in the market owing to obstacles such as the lack of political freedom and imperfect credit and labor markets. In the English case, alienation rights were a double-edged sword. Although they permitted freeholders and leaseholders to transfer their properties, from the eighteenth century they became the basis for forcible enclosures by parliamentary acts, which led to higher land concentration and greater inequality. Where previously

tenants could appeal to equity courts to enforce leases and compel contractual performance, parliamentary enclosures were engineered by large landlords appealing to their right as owners to alienate their properties. However, the more active land market also permitted the entry of merchants, professionals, and industrialists into the English landowning class. In Ming China the freedom to trade in land also led to large domains, which were once rare, as well as the rise of a new class of commoner landowners who were neither officials nor gentry. Likewise the Indian land market created in the first half of the nineteenth century after the introduction of colonial rule and greater monetization resulted in land control passing from traditional rural owners to merchants and moneylenders. It, however, also saw the breaking up of some large estates during the initial twenty-year adjustment period after the British imposed land taxes in the 1790s.

Land concentration may be detrimental to agricultural productivity if the inverse relationship between farm size and productivity holds under conditions of labor, credit, and rental market imperfections. However, although small farms have a comparative advantage in lower supervision costs, they have poorer access to capital, and such a disadvantage may work to the favor of larger farms. Research on the efficiency implications of parliamentary enclosures in Britain (c. 1750–1850) has shown that bigger farms, as the result of changes in property rights, were as productive as their small owner-occupied predecessors. This seems to imply that larger farms' higher costs of supervision were perfectly offset by other advantages, but that remains to be proven.

Tenure Arrangements. In theory the productivity problems of a high concentration of landownership and large farm sizes can be overcome by a well-functioning rental market, which has historically been more active than the market in land sales. Farmland was arranged according to an "agricultural ladder," with owner-occupants (or yeomen) at the top and wage laborers at the bottom. In between were tenants who paid fixed rents and bore the risks of output fluctuations or who sharecropped and divided risk and output with their landlords according to a predetermined formula.

Land leases have played a crucial role in the organization of agriculture as well as in the stability of rural societies. History indicates that landowners chose to rent parcels instead of hiring farm labor when there were cost savings and when they were confident of retaining ultimate control even in their absence. In the late Roman Empire, where a stable flow of tax revenue depended on a permanent agricultural workforce, laws were passed granting slaves and workers tenancies with the aim of reducing their mobility and extracting military services. At the same time the right to fix farm sizes and tenure durations as well as the legal prerogative to evict meant that dominion rights remained with the landlords. Likewise medieval lords in France, the Low Countries, and western Germany routinely retained their rights to change rents and tenants after issuing leases to serfs working on remote lands when high monitoring, labor, and management costs made running them as estates prohibitively costly. Peasant farmers, on the other hand, have used tenancies and other methods to balance inputs of land and labor when they did not own adequate terrain. Historians have found that land-poor households in China would rent land, hire out family labor, and adjust the type and quantity of crops to market in order to maximize returns from their resource endowments.

In cases where landowners were undermined by the advancement of tenants' rights, leases were either extended to other groups or were canceled. One example was medieval Italy, where landowners sought to increase competition for leases by suppressing local customs that excluded foreigners from holding village land after the Black Death reduced demand for tenancies. Another was the Indian land reforms of 1952. Tenants given rights to land that they cultivated were instead evicted or had their leases converted into wage or sharecropping contracts that did not provide similar privileges.

Besides political and legal considerations, landowners choosing among types of leases within the rental market were influenced by the incidence of risk too. Contracts were often highly varied even within a locale and depended in part on the nature of crops and environmental variables. For instance, in early twentieth-century southern Italy it was not uncommon for a farmer to lease grain land but sharecrop grapevines and olive trees. Although agricultural risk was and is an important consideration for rural income, farmers and landlords did not rely solely on tenure arrangements to disperse it. Other means included stipulating acceptable cultivation practices and mixing imperfectly correlated crops (as was done in the postbellum South, the Midwest, and colonial Massachusetts) as well as diversifying into livestock and off-farm employment. The use of sharecropping contracts to distribute risks became more important when these other means of risk diversification were not available or when information was poor. For example, in newly settled areas in the United States, where crop fluctuations were unknown and off-farm employment rare, share contracts were used extensively.

Tenure contracts were also explicitly employed to overcome incentive problems and promote gainful cooperation between landlords and lessees, especially in cases of factor market failures. Landlords, with their comparative advantage in credit access, have stronger incentives to provide capital in share contracts than in fixed-rent tenancies. Indeed an analysis of the 1920 U.S. census indicates that

absentee landlords were more likely to use rent contracts, while resident landlords were more likely to use sharecropping agreements. The same was true in Qing China. In the north, where tenants were more reliant on capital (for example, oxen, plows, and seeds) provided by landlords, share contracts (and capitalist farms) were more prevalent than in the south, where greater ownership of capital by tenants was accompanied by more fixed-rent tenancies.

Although theory places fixed-rent and share contracts in strict categories of the different risk incidences borne by each party, history often indicates a mixed picture. For instance, although English farms never practiced sharecropping, they did develop numerous ways to distribute output risks between landlords and tenants in times of poor harvests, such as rent discounts, rent in arrears, and other credit extensions. It was also not uncommon for contracts to change or for farmers to become yeomen as they grew older. In the United States farmers did move up the agricultural ladder over the nineteenth century, although some experienced downward mobility during times of financial hardship.

One way tenure contracts may affect efficiency is through the pace of technological adoption. Some theorists have argued that sharecropping prevents the utilization of productivity-enhancing innovations as the reduction of risk blunts incentives, but the few empirical studies on this subject have indicated that the type of contract made little difference to the pace of adopting new technologies. In Asia, for example, new rice varieties were taken up by sharecroppers and rent tenants at about the same pace during the Green Revolution of the 1960s and 1970s. There is a paucity of comparative historical work in this area, which is unfortunate, because establishing a link, if any, between contractual choice and technological advancement should shed much light on why some countries experienced agricultural revolutions while others did not.

BIBLIOGRAPHY

Allen, Robert. "The Price of Freehold Land and the Interest Rate in the Seventeenth and Eighteenth Centuries." *Economic History Review* 41.1 (1988), 33–50.

Atack, J., F. Bateman, and W. N. Parker. "Northern Agriculture and the Westward Movement." In *The Cambridge Economic History of the United States*, vol. 2, edited by S. L. Engerman and R. E. Gallman, pp. 285–328. Cambridge, 2000.

Basu, K. "The Market for Land: An Analysis of Interim Transactions." *Journal of Development Economics* 20 (1986), 163–177.

Beckett, R. V. "Landownership and Estate Management." In *The Agrarian History of England and Wales*, vol. 6, *1750–1850*, edited by G. E. Mingay, pp. 545–641. Cambridge, 1989.

Bogue, Allan, and Margaret B. Bogue. "'Profits' and the Frontier Land Speculator." *Journal of Economic History* 17.1 (1957), 1–24.

Brandt, Loren. *Commercialization and Agricultural Development: Central and Eastern China, 1870–1937*. Cambridge, 1989.

Chaudhuri, B. "The Land Market in Eastern India, 1793–1940," pt. 1, "The Movement of Land Prices." *Indian Economic and Social History Review* 12.1 (1975), 1–42.

Clay, C. "Landlords and Estate Management in England." In *The Agrarian History of England and Wales*, vol. 5, *1640–1750*, pt. 2, edited by J. Thirsk, pp. 119–251. Cambridge, 1985.

Hoffman, P. "Taxes and Agrarian Life in Early Modern France: Land Sales, 1550–1730." *Journal of Economic History* 46.1 (1986), 37–55.

Jones, A. H. M. "The Land." In *The Later Roman Empire*, vol. 2., pp. 284–602. Oxford, 1964.

Lavely, W., and R. B. Wong. "Family Division and Mobility in North China." *Comparative Studies in Society and History* 34.3 (1992), 439–463.

Ludden, D. *An Agrarian History of South Asia*, vol. 4, pt. 4 of *The New Cambridge History of India*. Cambridge, 1999.

Offer, Avner. "Farm Tenure and Land Values in England, c. 1750–1950." *Economic History Review* 44.1 (1991), 1–20.

Powelson, John. *The Story of Land*. Cambridge, Mass., 1988. A comprehensive overview of land tenure and agrarian reform in world history.

Shi, Q., and Z. Fang. "Capitalism in Agriculture in the Early and Middle Qing Dynasty." In *Chinese Capitalism, 1522–1840*, edited by D. Xu and C. Wu, pp. 113–162. New York, 2000.

Simpson, A. W. B. *An Introduction to the History of Land Law*. Oxford, 1976. A classic, highly accessible work on English land law.

Stevens, C. E. "Agriculture and Rural Life in the Later Roman Empire." In *Cambridge Economic History of Europe*, vol. 1, *Agrarian Life of the Middle Ages*, edited by M. M. Postan, pp. 92–125. Cambridge, 1966.

Swierenga, Robert. *Pioneers and Profits: Land Speculation on the Iowa Frontier*. Ames, Iowa, 1968.

Tomlinson, B. R. *The Economy of Modern India, 1860–1970*, vol. 3, pt. 3 of *The New Cambridge History of India*. Cambridge, 1993.

ELAINE S. TAN

LAND ORDINANCES. As European influence extended across the oceans, all regions of recent settlement faced the challenge of devising means for distributing, by sale, lease, or grant, lands originally held or used by aboriginal populations, and at the same time defining the political relationship between the frontier and the existing states. One of the most sweeping instances of legislation addressing this issue took place in the early years of the United States where, in exchange for the cession of claims on western lands by the original thirteen states, the federal government under the Articles of Confederation agreed to convert the public domain into private holdings as quickly as possible.

The Land Ordinances of 1785 and 1787 had lasting influences because they set the stage for the orderly distribution of western lands and provided procedures for the admission of new states to the federal Union on an equal footing with those already constituted. Their consequences were thus both political and economic—insuring that the original thirteen states would not develop an imperial relationship with western colonies, and that once title to new land was granted, the United States would step out of the picture with regard to legal claims on it, providing local and territorial governments with a foundation for their tax base.

Both ordinances reflected the handiwork of Thomas Jefferson, who had chaired a Congressional Committee appointed in 1783, and made its report in March 1784. Prior to the 1785 legislation, there had been two basic systems for the distribution of government land. Under the Southern system, a buyer simply indicated the land he wanted and then had the county surveyor mark it in the record office in terms of metes and bounds. The New England system did not permit land to be acquired until first surveyed, and thus opened new rectangular townships on a systematic basis. Development proceeded in an orderly fashion, without owned parcels leapfrogging over large intervening and oddly shaped pieces of unowned or undeveloped land.

The Land Ordinance of 1785 reflected Jefferson's preference for the New England system. The Ordinance required that lands be scientifically surveyed before sale and that the moneys collected be a one-time source of revenue for the national government but that subsequent to the sale, property would be held by the territory or future state, rather than the national government. The ordinance embraced the New England pattern of six-mile-square townships, each divided into thirty-six sections of one square mile, a section thus comprising approximately 640 acres, and to be the minimum unit of sale. In 1800, sales of half sections (320 acres) were permitted, and in 1804 minimum parcel size dropped to a quarter section (160 acres), declining finally in 1832 to 40 acres. An 1841 Preemption Act provided for marking down land unsold for ten years or more, and in 1862, as a result of the Homestead Act, the remaining public domain became available at no direct cost to settlers in exchange for occupation and improvement. A similar act was passed in Canada in 1879.

The lasting political effect of the 1787 legislation (Northwest Ordinance) was that it established conditions under which new states could be admitted to the Union on an equal footing with those existing. The legislation begins with a lengthy section specifying how property is to pass in the territory in the case of those dying interstate, and specifying how realty and personalty may legally be conveyed within it. Resolving such issues is an essential precondition for economic development to proceed within the context of a private enterprise system.

The Ordinance then proceeds to specify governance procedures in both the short and the long run. Initially, a new territory would be run by a governor and judges appointed by Congress. When population grew to include five thousand male inhabitants, a territorial legislature would be elected and a nonvoting representative sent to Congress in Washington. And upon attaining a population of sixty thousand, the territory could be admitted to the Union. Not less than three nor more than five states were to be formed out of the territory, and slavery was prohibited. Jefferson's committee had originally proposed ten states, but

Monroe objected, fearing that in the context of continued divisiveness over the slavery issue, this would be ill advised.

Ultimately, thirty-one out of the fifty American states were admitted to the United States under provisions established under this Ordinance. Far from being politically disadvantaged relative to the original seaboard colonies, many of the newly admitted states were actually advantaged, since they were sparsely populated but guaranteed two senators and a minimum of one representative. Thus did the American Republic avoid replicating the core-periphery relationship existing between England and the original colonies that had ultimately led to the Revolution. On the other hand, Jefferson's original report had included a broader provision banning slavery after 1800 in all territories west of the Appalachian Mountains. That provision was rejected in Congress in 1784 by a single vote.

BIBLIOGRAPHY

Hughes, Jonathan, and Louis P. Cain. *American Economic History*. 5th ed. Reading, Mass., 1998.

Yale Law School. "Northwest Ordinance; July 13, 1787," <http:/ www. yale.edu/lawweb/avalon/nworder.htm>.

ALEXANDER J. FIELD

LAND REFORM AND CONFISCATIONS.

The term *land reform* has been used to describe a wide range of changes in the pattern of entitlement to land use. Historically and until fairly recently, it referred to a government attempt to achieve a fairer distribution of rights to land and of the associated benefits and responsibilities. It was a response to the need to reconcile competing claims on land. Land reform, so defined, is often contrasted with the broader concept of "agrarian reform," which includes steps considered complementary to a reallocation of land rights, such as provision of credit and technical assistance to small farmers. The preferred type of reform reflects government theory on how to promote economic growth, ranging from that of the centrally planned states to that of economic liberals.

The main variant, historically, has been a redistribution of private land to benefit the small farmer or the landless agricultural worker, the two groups at the bottom of the agrarian pecking order. In a usually less contentious process, significant amounts of land have also been transferred from the public domain to private individuals or groups in many countries. Changes in the pattern of ownership are not the sole objective of reforms; the regulations guiding rental (e.g., the shares of output going to the two parties in a sharecropping arrangement) are also central in many cases.

Genesis of Land Reform. Reform designed to benefit the lower agrarian groups is usually pursued by govern-

ments to resolve or avoid a social or political crisis. Over long periods of time settled agrarian societies have tended to go through periods of land concentration that eventually produce a crisis of poverty and insecurity; this, in turn, under propitious conditions (e.g., a bad crop, an effective leader, and a feeling of being squeezed too much and too often by the landlord) may generate a peasant uprising, which if successful may lead to a significant redistribution of land. Governments sometimes undertake reforms on their own initiative in the absence of such crisis, and sometimes a degree of external pressure or assistance will make them act.

The probability of land reform reflects not only the relative power of the direct gainers and direct losers but also the perceived interests of other groups. By the time an industrial bourgeoisie has developed some strength, and is contending for power with the traditional agricultural elite, it may provide powerful support for reform, either as a weapon in the class conflict with that elite and/or on the grounds that the elite is impeding social and economic advance. Frequently this new middle class feels that reform is necessary to improve the economic performance of agriculture and through it the economy as a whole, because the old structure is judged to be inefficient (the structuralist view in Latin America, for example) or because political unrest is seen as a threat to economic performance.

Whatever the pressures and arguments for land reform under conditions of highly unequal access to land, they usually confront a basic political impediment—the power of the landed elite. Where that elite is still strong, reform has often been followed by a period of reaction, which may reverse the effects of the reform in rather short order. In other cases the reversal occurs more slowly, and takes the form of gradual reconcentration of land (perhaps in the hands of the more successful of the reform beneficiaries, as with the creation of the middle-class peasantry in early-twentieth-century Russia), rather than the recovery of lands confiscated or otherwise transferred during the reform.

Where and When. Land reforms date back as far as recorded agrarian history; early examples come from biblical times, judging by Old Testament reference to redistribution of land every fiftieth year. Land reform of some sort has been one aspect of most of the fundamental social changes in history, including the fall of the Roman Empire and the American, French, Russian, and Chinese revolutions. Until the onset of the Industrial Revolution in Europe most episodes were part of the long cycles of concentration-deconcentration that characterized many parts of the world. The French reform and several of those that followed in Europe were elements of a more general process of transition from feudalism toward modern industrial society. In the first half of the twentieth century the international Communist movement brought a new type of reform to Russia and later China, Indochina, North Korea, and Cuba and provided a powerful stimulus to preventive reforms based on private small farms, as in Taiwan and South Korea, and to the more token programs pursued in various countries of Latin America and elsewhere.

The second half of that century saw some continuation of these trends but was more notable for the relative infrequency of significant reforms than for their prevalence. The context for reform has been significantly altered by the presumption of growth that has come with the rapid economic advance in most of the developing world during the twentieth century. It is now known that the economic weight of agriculture will diminish quickly in any successfully growing country, and with it, eventually, the number of people engaged in agriculture. On the one hand, this makes land reform a more obvious option today than before, since an equalizing redistribution may provide a permanent solution to the problem of inequality (especially if reconcentration in agriculture is blocked by a ceiling on farm size), as well as being a source of dynamism helping to put the economy on a path toward healthy industrialization. On the other, it increases the likelihood that a country might survive the tensions of a period of growing land concentration by creating enough employment opportunities outside the sector.

Settings ripe for reform have arisen frequently in the twentieth century. But in many situations the advance of available forms of mechanization has made labor a less necessary input and given large landholders the option of substituting away from its intensive use. Mechanization weakens both the "land to the tiller" argument for reform and the position that smaller farms are necessary to meet the agricultural output needs of the country.

The experiences of the Greco-Roman era illustrate both the alternation between concentration and reform and the fragile political support for reform when it does occur. The setting for the reforms of Solon and Pisistratus in sixth century BCE. Athens evolved out of the frequent borrowing by poorer peasants from richer ones, leading to concentration of land and former owners working their former land as virtual slaves. Solon's attempt to reconcile the interest of the upper classes—restoration of peace in the face of an impending revolutionary threat—with that of the debtors—cancellation of debts and a redistribution of land—was, not surprisingly, partially unsatisfactory to both groups. His program and that of Pisistratus later were built on a transitory power base; much of the legislation appears to have been repealed when opponents overthrew their successors.

In a pattern similar to many twentieth-century experiences, the concentration of land in the Roman Empire by the second century BCE was the result of nobility usurping public lands. Reforms were introduced by the Gracchi brothers, but the ceilings and allotments were such that huge gaps remained between the largeholders and the beneficiaries. Ultimately the constellation of power was little affected.

Cyclical patterns of land concentration and associated conflicts are a central feature of China's agrarian history. As far back as the late Chun Qiu period (several centuries BCE) there was a shift away from feudalism, under which the peasants had been subjects of their lords, toward individual proprietorship under centralized monarchies. Over a millennium later, the emperor Shen Tsung (1068–1085) attempted major reforms on behalf of the peasantry. In so doing he generated much bitter opposition from large landowners, big merchants, and moneylenders, and his reforms were fairly soon undone. A final buildup of peasant dissatisfaction manifested itself in the victory of the Communist Revolution just after World War II.

The French Revolution brought about the first big land reforms of modern times; they set the pattern for most of the later ones. European feudalism was increasingly anachronistic; the agrarian system based on an almost total control of land and labor by an exploitative rural oligarchy conflicted with the evolving enlightenment ideals of freedom and equality. That system was also proving incapable of expanding production to satisfy increasing demand. The reforms abolished feudal relations, created an independent propertied peasantry, and secularized clerical property and sold it to the public. Though their impact on thinking and attitudes was greater than the actual economic effects, these reforms were historically important because, as well as freeing the peasantry, they institutionalized the idealized family farm.

The wave of European reforms following those in France included a number of variants. In England feudalism was replaced more by tenancy than by small ownership as in France. Elsewhere in northwest Europe the English pattern was the more common. In Russia the uneconomical nature of serfdom and its resulting hindrance to development were fairly widely recognized by the middle of the nineteenth century. Tsar Alexander II worked for years to achieve a reform, the Emancipation Act of 1861, but it was not radical enough to provide a serious remedy for the land problems. Although it freed the serfs from their labor obligations to the lord, in practice they had to pay indemnity to achieve that freedom, and they were still part of a commune, to which they had obligations. The Stolypin reforms of 1906–1911 freed the peasants from the communes and strengthened private property, but they also led to sharper differentiation between peasant classes and to growing landlessness. Their failure to relieve the tensions and problems of the agrarian sector contributed to the Revolution of 1917.

In Japan, as in Russia, the formal "abolition" of feudalism here by the Meiji government (from 1868), failed to provide a lasting cure for agrarian inequality. The land was declared to be the property of the peasants, but usurpation by the rich and by moneylenders created classes of perpetual tenants and absentee owners. This situation set the stage, first for widespread conflict between landlords and tenants, and ultimately for the postwar reform.

The Mexican land reform that grew out of the revolution of the 1910s can be thought of as the prototype nontoken reform that, without being reversed, was responsible for only modest benefits in terms of either income distribution or agricultural growth. A significant amount of land changed hands and this reform dispossessed a traditional agrarian elite, but power remained in the hands of a narrow, wealthy group. This elite proceeded to use public policy and finance to subsidize a new large-scale agriculture, while leaving the reform beneficiaries short on the sort of technical support they needed to achieve continuing productivity increases.

The important Iranian reform (begun 1962) was facilitated by oil revenues. These revenues consolidated bureaucratic control over all classes, and reform would not have been possible on anything like the actual scale without them. Its immediate political purpose was to ward off a Communist revolution, in a country where a class of extremely wealthy landowners still virtually controlled the lives of the vast majority of landless peasants. This reform created the bases for both small and large capitalist farming in the country.

The Egyptian reform of 1952 is the most comprehensive of the twentieth century outside the Communist countries. It had a positive impact on the morale of the peasants as well as on their income and status. But total output was not much affected since agriculture was already operated intensively. Even after the resulting one-shot increase in productivity incomes remained low. Without a strong small-farm support policy and an industrial takeoff soon afterward, the benefits of the reform were destined to be offset by rising population.

Nearly all of the other postwar reforms have fallen short of potential. Most of those undertaken in Latin America, famous for the degree of inequality in the distribution both of land and of income, have been small (relative to the size of the problem), designed to create "middle-class" capitalized farmers, and hence of little direct value to the rural poor. The socialist reforms of China, and earlier of Russia, were built partly on the assumption that economies of scale are important in agriculture. Their collective nature was generally an obstacle to productivity increases, though their equalizing impact was undeniable.

The Process. Land reform processes vary widely from case to case. Whether the process is orderly or chaotic depends on the politics of the moment. And whether there is a major structural reorganization of the sector depends not only on the size of the transfer, but on the type of reform. Where its essence is to provide ownership to former tenants (as in post-Revolutionary France), the operating conditions of agriculture may not be much affected; nor will the size structure of operating units. Where large farms previously operated as units are being transferred, a more significant change must occur, either to some sort of collective or to smaller family farms.

The design of reforms involves rules and guidelines on (1) how much and what sort of land may be retained by former owners and the compensation they receive for what they must give up; (2) the size of parcels the beneficiaries receive and the conditions of payment; (3) the role of the government, as administrator of the process of transition, as subsidizer (where the former owners receive more in compensation than the new beneficiaries pay for the land), and as provider of a support system for the new farms; and (4) the timing and sequencing of the reform.

The allowable retention by former owners and the amount and form of compensation can range from no retention and no compensation to high retention and compensation at market value. High compensation is usually only feasible if the reform is on a small scale relative to the size of the economy, as in the case of current market-based reforms being undertaken in Colombia and Brazil, or (partly the same thing) if the level of resources available is high, as in the case of oil countries like Iran and Venezuela.

Where the pressure for reform is strong, expropriation is more likely to be total and compensation little or nothing, as in Bolivia's 1953 reform and in China's revolutionary process. In many cases, especially in former colonies like Algeria and Tunisia, foreign-owned land is singled out for expropriation without compensation and is assigned free to the indigenous population. In others, the land of members of minority groups is the target, as currently in Zimbabwe. Usually, expropriation is above a ceiling and there is some compensation.

Where a reform cannot be carried out in one fell swoop it may in the first instance be restricted to some regions (Italy), the ceiling retainable by former owners may gradually be lowered (Cuba and Egypt), or the phasing may be qualitative, as in Taiwan, where tenancy regulation was undertaken first, then land redistribution. Such phasing allows mistakes to be corrected, but creates uncertainty. Sometimes the payment to the former owners is supposed to come from the beneficiaries, sometimes from the government, and frequently from both. Often it is less than promised, as when it takes the form of government bonds whose value disappears through high inflation (Japan's postwar reform). The Philippines experimented with compensation in terms of rights to exploitable frontier land, another way of economizing on the direct fiscal costs of reform.

The historical record confirms that the most successful reforms have created small private farms. Two conditions appear to be central to success. First, the great majority of the beneficiaries must be left in conditions that minimize the chance that they will lose their land; second, a general ceiling is needed to prevent reconcentration. In a number of cases state farms or cooperatives of one sort or another have been created, reflecting a belief in the existence of economies of scale or an ideological preference for such units rather than small private farms. Both forms have tended to perform badly or at best modestly well.

Impacts. Most land reforms have as their immediate objective to raise the economic status of groups with inadequate access to land. The quantitative record indicates that well-designed and well-executed reforms (e.g., those of Japan, Taiwan, and Korea) do achieve this goal. The short- to medium-term output impact of most land reforms appears to have been positive or at worst neutral, except when the surrounding chaos led to a running down of capital stock and/or heightened uncertainty (Russia) and/or when needed complementary support was not present (Mexico, Egypt).

The longer-run growth implications of land redistribution have received less empirical assessment. The impact on savings is unclear. When the landlords were essentially a rentier class they may not have saved much, but when they show entrepreneurial qualities they may save and invest more than the smaller farmers who replace them. Under favorable conditions, however, it is well established that small farm families can achieve high savings rates; when those savings are invested in local nonagricultural activities the overall benefits of the reforms may be maximized, as amply illustrated by the experience of Taiwan from the 1950s on. The reform itself, by leaving more income in the hands of the smallholders, raises the demand for locally produced labor-intensive consumer goods (e.g., low-cost clothing, furniture, building materials) and thus creates a favorable setting for investment in small enterprises to produce those items. In the cases of Japan and Taiwan, especially, this development is credited as one factor contributing to the successful small-scale labor-intensive industrialization path followed by those countries. In general, there is no reason to doubt that the shorter-run benefits of an equalizing land reform can be extended to the longer run, but it is also clear from experiences like those of Mexico in the twentieth century and Haiti in the nineteenth that these provide no guarantee of output increases. Land reform can make an important contribution to, but is by no means always an automatic condition of, economic development.

BIBLIOGRAPHY

Berry, R. Albert, and William R. Cline. *Agrarian Structure and Productivity in Developing Countries.* Baltimore, 1979.

De Janvry, Alain. *The Agrarian Question and Reformism in Latin America.* Baltimore, 1981.

Dorner, Peter. *Latin American Land Reforms in Theory and Practice.* Madison, Wis., 1992.

King, Russell. *Land Reform: A World Survey.* London, 1977.

Lehmann, David. *Agrarian Reform and Agrarian Reformism: Studies of Peru, Chile, China and India.* London, 1973.

Lipton, Michael. "Land Reform as Unfinished Business: The Evidence Against Stopping." *World Development* 21.4 (1993), 641–658.

Tuma, Elias H. *Twenty-Six Centuries of Agrarian Reform: A Comparative Analysis.* Berkeley, 1965.

Warriner, Doreen. *Land Reform in Principle and Practice.* Oxford, 1965.

R. ALBERT BERRY

LAND TENURE. Land tenure refers to the bundle of rights and responsibilities under which land is held, used, transferred, and succeeded. The meaning of the term varies with context. It is used to refer to land tenure prescribed by statutory or common law, customary land tenure, and observed land tenure practices in a particular historical context. Land tenure arrangements vary enormously across urban and rural areas primarily because of the use of land for agriculture in rural areas and for residences and businesses in urban areas. Economic historians have focused on analyzing tenure systems on agricultural lands, as until the twentieth century the majority of people in most societies earned their livelihoods by cultivating the land, accumulated wealth by improving the land, and transferred wealth to the next generation by bequeathing the land.

Land tenure can be categorized along three essential dimensions: (1) the presence or absence of formal land title, defined as registration of ownership rights with a government authority; (2) the extent of landowner and landholder rights to contract voluntarily for use of the land; and (3) the spectrum of private-communal property rights to the land. At one end of the spectrum is the independent farmer owning land with freehold (or fee-simple) title. Freehold title is perpetual, inheritable by a successor designated at will, freely alienable, often registered with a central authority that has undertaken a survey of the land (sometimes called a cadastral survey), and characterized by fixed annual obligations. At the other end of the spectrum, bound laborers work on parcels of land temporarily assigned to them by authorities in a communal land system.

Changes in land tenure are induced by a wide variety of factors, including relative prices of inputs and outputs, transaction costs, government policies, preferences of farmers and landlords, and technology. To illustrate how forms of land tenure emerge, function, and change, six forms of land tenure are analyzed below.

Owner Cultivation of Small, Private Lands. Owner cultivation of small, private land parcels was a major form of land tenure in the Roman Republic, as soldiers were granted small parcels from lands taken from conquered peoples. Despite its early emergence, owner operation of small farms is relatively recent, emerging in Europe and Asia as feudal institutions were dismantled; in North America from the beginning of colonial settlement; in Japan after land reforms were implemented in the late nineteenth century and after World War II; in Taiwan in the early 1950s; in the former British colonies of India, Canada, Australia, South Africa, and New Zealand in the nineteenth and twentieth centuries; and in South America in the second half of the twentieth century. Owner-cultivated farms have been praised as ideal arrangements to foster and encourage democratic institutions and for the incentives offered to small farmers to properly manage their lands and to adapt to changing circumstances. Wage laborers on farms often set a goal of moving up the "agricultural ladder" from wage laborers to share tenants to owner operators.

Family-managed farms, however, may not always be the most efficient forms of agricultural organization. Families may have inadequate managerial skills to manage the farm, may not have sufficient family labor, and may not reap full economies of scale on their small land parcel, among other things.

Squatting on Public or Private Lands. Some citizens of the Roman Republic received grants from the government to occupy conquered lands, while others—squatters—occupied and farmed these public lands without first obtaining a formal lease or land grant. Squatting is observed on privately owned lands and in run-down sections of urban areas in developed countries, on public lands near or at the frontier of settlement, and in the urban areas of poor, developing countries. It was prevalent throughout the Americas from the beginning of European colonization through the nineteenth century and is still a major form of land tenure in South and Central America, particularly in Costa Rica, Brazil, and Colombia. Sheep and cattle herders in the Cape Colony in the eighteenth century and in Australia from the 1820s to the 1840s squatted on frontier lands at and beyond official boundaries.

The impact of squatting on economic development has been much debated. Squatting has been criticized as encouraging disorderly settlement; bringing settlers to regions without churches, schools, or proper infrastructure; and encouraging violence between competing claimants to lands. It has also been praised as facilitating development by superseding overly restrictive government land policies of settlement at the frontier. In urban areas in many developing countries, squatting on public and private lands has emerged as a response to large-scale immigration and growth of populations living in poverty. It has been criticized as impeding growth in these same urban areas by forsaking the use of land for collateral, by restricting transfers of parcels, and by reducing the value of land in intergenerational wealth transfers.

Large Estates or Latifundia. In the second century BCE, wealthy Roman families received leases of newly conquered lands and were able to consolidate lands of some farmers serving in the army into ranches and large farms known as latifundia. Centered around a central villa, these lands were typically worked by slaves from conquered territories or by tenants at will. With the establishment of the Pax Romana in the first century CE, supplies of slaves from conquered territories declined, and latifundia managers responded by dividing the latifundia into smaller parcels and leasing them to small holders (*coloni*). In other instances, small landowners commended themselves and their land to latifundia in exchange for protection against central government exactions and invading tribes.

Similar landholding arrangements emerged in other societies in which governments leased or granted large tracts of land to wealthy families or in which smallholders at the frontier commended their lands to a patron. In South America, the Spanish crown granted lands and the rights to the labor of their indigenous people to a small number of families in the sixteenth and seventeenth centuries. Some economists have argued that land laws in South America were heavily influenced by this initial allocation of lands and were structured to enhance the position of the large property owners to the detriment of small, independent farmers. As landowners in South America gradually lost their rights to indigenous labor in the seventeenth century, they secured a new supply of labor by requiring peasants to provide labor services in order to gain access to land. Large estates with patron-client labor arrangements—latifundia—persisted throughout much of Latin America until the mid-twentieth century.

Feudal Tenures with Bound and Unbound Labor. With the fall of the western Roman Empire in the fifth century CE and the consequent decline in law and order came the rise of the manorial system in Europe. The system had many variations across time and place, thus the following description is a stylized account. A king owning all lands kept some lands (demesne) and granted others to lay and ecclesiastic lords in exchange for military service and loyalty. Some lords assigned their lands to followers in exchange for services and loyalty, a process known as subinfeudation. Peasants commended themselves to a lord in exchange for protection, provision of justice, and a plot of land, in the process becoming bound to the land. These peasants (serfs) held land subject to servitudes of work and produce as well as approval of marriage, inheritance, and migration. Production was partially organized by the village, with individuals typically cooperating on plowing the land and allowing communal grazing on stubble left after harvest. During the growing and harvest seasons, each serf tended individual parcels, which were often scattered in small strips throughout the manor lands. Serfs were obligated to work on the lord's demesne for a fixed number of days.

In the manorial system, individual rights to rent, transfer, succeed, and use land were limited because of communal property rights over the land. Attenuated individual property rights required that the manorial system adopt elaborate rules to structure production and distribution of agricultural output. These rules prevented participants from shirking or claiming a disproportionately large share of output.

The growth of markets and population in western Europe between the eleventh and thirteenth centuries induced changes in the feudal system. Labor dues were commuted into money payments, the demesne was leased for money rents, and tenant lands became increasingly alienable. The Statute Quia Emptores (1290) formally abolished the feudal system in England, although many of its habits and institutions lingered for centuries. While the Black Death crisis of the fourteenth century made labor more scarce and led to attempts to reimpose feudal obligations on tenants, the dismantling of traditional land tenures continued in western Europe, as exemplified by the English enclosure movements of the sixteenth and eighteenth centuries. Land enclosures were the result of a legal process that converted the common rights of villagers on specified wastelands, arable lands, and meadowlands to private titles and consolidated existing private holdings in land.

Feudalism's decline in western Europe was mirrored by its rise in eastern Europe as relatively free laborers became bound to the land during the fifteenth and sixteenth centuries. Feudalism did not decline in eastern Europe until the eighteenth and nineteenth centuries. Serfdom was partially reformed in Russia in 1861—the workers remained bound to the commune—and finally was ended by the Stolypin Reforms (1906–1911), which freed Russian laborers from bondage to the commune, established private titles, and consolidated peasant holdings. In Japan, bound labor was still predominant in the early Tokugawa period, and tenancy only emerged in the eighteenth and nineteenth centuries. In the 1870s, the Meiji government abolished feudal tenures and established private property in land in conjunction with its reform of agricultural taxation.

Communal Tenures. Communal land tenures have been prevalent in the Pacific Islands and Africa and were the norm in North America, South America, and parts of Asia until the European conquests; they are still used in many indigenous communities. Details of communal tenures differ across societies, so the following is a stylized description of communal tenure in a Pacific Island village. A common area is used for future land development and can be used with certain limits for gathering by villagers. Families carry out cultivation on scattered plots, and plots are redistributed by chiefs or village elders as family size and land fertility change. For lands requiring extensive improvement, tenure of particular households and their heirs may be longer. Rights to continued use of village land by a household persist as long as the household continues to cultivate its assigned lands.

Historians have often interpreted communal land systems as efficient responses to social and economic environments with significant environmental risks, high information costs, and poorly developed input, output, and insurance markets. Their flexibility has frequently enabled adaptations to changing demographic, ecological, and social conditions. In the nineteenth and twentieth centuries, however, economists sometimes have viewed communal land systems as impeding the growth of a modern market economy.

Communal land systems were established by central governments in China and Russia in the twentieth century after communist revolutions. After the 1917 Russian revolution, the Soviet government under Vladimir Lenin abolished private property rights in land but in the early 1920s promulgated a pragmatic system of agricultural production ("New Economic Policy") that retained many features of smallholder-owner production. Beginning in the late 1920s, Joseph Stalin began forced collectivization of peasant landholdings and established central government ownership of farmlands and control of agricultural production.

A similar process took place in China after the 1949 communist revolution, when lands were initially redistributed to tenants. By the late 1950s, peasant farmers had lost their lands and were forced into collective farming institutions (communes) controlled by the central government. In 1978, the Chinese government initiated land reforms providing households with individual parcels of village land. The "Household Responsibility System" allowed farmers to choose crops, methods of production, hours of work, and capital and labor inputs and made them residual claimants. Ownership of land, however, continued to reside with the village as a collective entity that periodically reallocated these lands among households. Agricultural output and productivity rose significantly in the decade after its introduction.

Smallholder Leasing from Private Landowners. Contracts between owners of agricultural lands and farm labor have varied enormously across time and place. Different market structures in labor, capital, resources, and land markets; government regulations; and geographic constraints often have produced a variety of smallholder leasing arrangements that coexist alongside one another. Economic historians have paid close attention to three contractual provisions exhibiting wide variation over time and across locations: the landowner's role in farm management, the type of land rent, and contract duration. Small landowners often choose to manage their lands themselves, using family and wage labor in production. In other instances, small and large landowners have better opportunities on other lands or in other occupations, and they lease some lands to tenant farmers. Only a few crops exhibit substantial economies of scale in production, leaving large landowners with incentives to lease parcels of land to smallholders. Some leases allow tenants to manage the farm themselves, while others provide limited roles for landowners in farm management. They make crop choices, arrange for credit, and procure various inputs, such as fertilizers, pesticides, and farm animals, leaving tenants to manage day-to-day production and to monitor farm labor.

Tenancy often coexists with self-managed farms. In the United States, numerous farmers were tenants even when new land was available at the frontier. U.S. census data show that mobility up the "agricultural ladder" was common, with workers often starting as landless laborers, becoming tenant farmers, and finally becoming owner-occupiers. Such mobility was lacking in India throughout the twentieth century, as social sanctions often stopped lower castes from owning or leasing land. In the Tamil Nadu province of India, sharecropping predominated in 1916, was partially replaced by fixed rent tenancy in 1937 as landlords moved to cities, and declined further with the "land-to-the-tiller" land reform in 1959.

Controversy reigns over the incentive and efficiency effects of different types of smallholder leasing. In his comparison of agriculture in France and England in the late eighteenth century, Arthur Young argued that sharecropping was responsible for the relatively poor state of French agriculture. Alfred Marshall argued that sharecropping implicitly imposed a tax on the labor input of tenant farmers and would reduce farm productivity unless landlords carefully monitored tenant inputs. Some economists have argued that sharecropping exists because of the willingness of risk-averse sharecroppers to pay a premium to reduce their income variability. Some empirical studies of share tenancy in India in the 1950s and 1960s show that output is lower under sharecropping. Other economists have argued that sharecropping reduces incentives for tenants to overuse ("mine") valuable land and provides vital incentives for landlords to provide managerial services. Empirical studies of African-American sharecroppers in the postbellum U.S. South and of farmers in the U.S. Midwest during the 1970s lend support to efficiency theories.

Does the type of land tenure affect the adoption of new technologies? Only a few studies exist, and they generally show that new technologies are adopted at about the same rate by sharecroppers and other types of tenants. For example, studies of the adoption of new rice varieties in the 1960s and 1970s generally show that sharecroppers adopted the new technologies at about the same rate as other landholders. Technological change, however, has often induced changes in the choice of land tenure. For example, the introduction of the tractor after 1910 and the mechanical cotton picker after World War II were major factors in reducing the incidence of sharecropping throughout the U.S. South during the twentieth century.

[*See also* Collective Agriculture and Collectivization; Cooperative Agriculture and Farmer Cooperatives; Latifundia; Property Rights in Land; State Farms; *and* Tenant Farming.]

BIBLIOGRAPHY

Alston, Lee J., and Joseph P. Ferrie. *Southern Paternalism and the American Welfare State: Economics, Politics, and Institutions in the South, 1865–1965.* New York, 1998.

Alston, Lee J., Gary D. Libecap, and Bernardo Mueller. *Titles, Conflict, and Land Use: The Development of Property Rights and Land Reform on the Brazilian Amazon Frontier.* Ann Arbor, 1999.

Cheung, Steven N. S. *The Theory of Share Tenancy.* Chicago, 1969.

De Soto, Hernando. *The Mystery of Capital: Why Capitalism Triumphs in the West and Fails Everywhere Else.* New York, 2000.

Hayami, Yujiro, and Keijiro Otsuka. *The Economics of Contract Choice: An Agrarian Perspective.* Oxford, 1993.

Hayami, Yujiro, and Vernon W. Ruttan. *Agricultural Development: An International Perspective.* Rev. ed. Baltimore, 1985.

Marshall, Alfred. *Principles of Economics.* 9th ed. London and New York, 1961.

Powelson, John P. *The Story of Land: A World History of Land Tenure and Agrarian Reform.* Cambridge, Mass., 1988.

Roumasset, James. *Rice and Risk: Decision Making among Low Income Farmers.* Amsterdam, 1976.

Sokoloff, Kenneth, and Stanley Engerman. "Institutions, Factor Endowments, and Paths of Development in the New World." *Journal of Economic Perspectives* 14. 3 (Summer 2000), 217–232.

Tuma, Elias. *Twenty-six Centuries of Agrarian Reform.* Berkeley and Los Angeles, 1965.

Young, Arthur. *Travels during the Years 1787, 1788, and 1789, Undertaken More Particularly with a View of Ascertaining the Cultivation, Wealth, Resources, and National Prosperity of the Kingdom of France.* London, 1808–1814.

SUMNER LA CROIX

LANE, FREDERIC CHAPIN (1900–1984), American historian who earned his doctorate at Harvard University under Abbott Payson Usher in 1930 and was professor of history at the Johns Hopkins University until his retirement in 1966.

Lane's primary research interest was the economic and social history of medieval and early modern Venice. He began his career with a book on the Venetian arsenal,

Venetian Ships and Shipbuilders of the Renaissance (Baltimore, 1934; in French, 1965), and he ended it with one dedicated to the history of medieval Venetian monies, *Money and Banking in Medieval and Renaissance Venice*, volume 1, *Coins and Moneys of Account* (Baltimore, 1985, with R. C. Mueller).

Lane's second monograph was the biography of a fifteenth-century Venetian merchant *Andrea Barbarigo, Merchant of Venice, 1418–1449* (Baltimore, 1944), a study based on the several extant account books and a letter book of this middling businessman. A case study of the "sedentary merchant," that figure of the "medieval commercial revolution," it reflects the influence of the Business History Group at Harvard, led by N. S. B. Gras.

Lane's interest in theory and economic historiography revolved largely around such figures as Arthur Spiethoff, Gustav Schmoller, Walther Eucken, and Karl Bücher. His work on the German Historical School was incorporated into a book that he edited on behalf of the Economic History Association, *Enterprise and Secular Change: Readings in Economic History*, with J. C. Riemersma (Homewood, Ill., 1954). His own formulation of a concept useful to economic historiography came out of his meditations during World War II about the costs of protection or organized violence and their influence on profits. Beginning with the examples of Venice and the Age of Discovery, Lane developed a theory of "protection rents"—the profits accruing to operations with lower protection costs than those for competitors. At the instigation of Immanuel Wallerstein, Lane subsequently republished his essays on that theme, along with some others, one of which was the fruit of his role as president of the International Economic History Association (1965–1968), when he sought to define "capitalism" in ways that would facilitate a more productive dialogue between and among economic historians of the East and the West. This volume, *Profits from Power: Readings in Protection Rents and Violence-Controlling Enterprises* (Albany, N.Y., 1979), also contains an important introduction on stage theories of growth.

Lane's interests in the sea brought him to consider the economic consequences, for example, of the invention of the compass, which permitted Venetian cargo ships (cogs) in the Mediterranean to make two trips to the Levant per year instead of one. He reexamined the theme to imagine the economic advantages accruing to advances in nautical technology and ship design, as well as the relationship of crew size to tonnage; in this case, he was more doubtful about the possibility of calculating the savings actually realized. Qualitative rather than quantitative analysis was in the forefront of Lane's concern, whether it be the proletarianization of seamen (as a result of increased specialization in the use of arms), the calories in a seaman's fare, or the reactions of individuals and crowds to economic crises.

Even when he was challenged by the most intricate monetary calculations, Lane's aim was to render comprehensible the divergent ways in which the powerful and the weak made and received payment for obligations due them.

Lane was editor of the *Journal of Economic History* for ten years (1942–1951); head of the historical section of the Federal Maritime Commission, with the task of writing a history of the construction of Liberty Ships during World War II, *Ships for Victory: A History of Shipbuilding under the U.S. Maritime Commission in World War II* (Baltimore, 1951); assistant director for social sciences at the Rockefeller Foundation (1951–1953); president of the Economic History Association in 1958, of the International Economic History Association from 1965 to 1968, and of the American Historical Association in 1964. Most of his work was translated into Italian; his historical overview, *Venice, a Maritime Republic* (Baltimore, 1973), was also translated into French and German. Lane's bibliography to 1966 can be found in *Venice and History: The Collected Papers of Frederic C. Lane* (Baltimore, 1966); that following 1966 is available in his *Studies in Venetian Social and Economic History*, edited by B. G. Kohl and R. C. Mueller (London, 1987).

BIBLIOGRAPHY
Gemelli, Giuliana. *Fernand Braudel.* Paris, 1995.

REINHOLD C. MUELLER

LATIFUNDIA. The large farm or estate has been an important and deeply rooted structural feature of most settled societies. Though most agrarian systems have a wide range of farm sizes (and also a variety of tenure arrangements), the degree of concentration of land ownership in large units is often striking. In premodern settled societies in which agriculture is the dominant economic sector, this concentration and the corresponding importance of large holdings are a (or the) major manifestation of socioeconomic inequality, since land is the main form of wealth.

Concentration of control over land, as reflected in the presence of large ownership units, is thus a starting point toward understanding the agrarian systems of many countries. Various economic forces contribute to that concentration, among them the greater savings capacity of wealthier people than of low-income people. Economies of scale in production are sometimes a factor, though usually not a very important one. More often there appear to be diseconomies of scale at the operating level in many types of agriculture, due among other things to a tendency to shirk or a lack of dedication to effective decision-making on the part of nonfamily workers. In many settings this produces some form of tenancy arrangement or rental, which combines concentration of land ownership with dispersion of land operation into smaller units. When this arrangement also suffers from inefficiency (e.g., through a lack of incentive to invest in improvements), the dominance of large owned units will tend to be lessened, with smaller farms competing with them more successfully. A more universal force for concentration involves the natural fluctuations of income in the low-income agricultural family; these often lead to distress sales that push small farmers into the ranks of the landless, from which it is difficult to reemerge. Land is also not only the main productive asset but one of relatively stable value, and thus desirable as a store of wealth in conditions of inflation or other economic fluctuations.

Along with these basically economic considerations, some social and political processes tend to favor concentration. Large amounts of land are attractive to the rich even if not particularly productive because in an agrarian class society, land gives status. Powerful political figures are often in a position to allocate public land to themselves or their friends and relatives. The wealthy often accumulate land on the agricultural frontier for speculative purposes. Land conflicts tend to be settled in favor of the larger (and hence more powerful) of contending parties, through the biased involvement of bureaucrats, police, and other relevant groups. Fears of peasant unrest or revolution can work in the opposite direction.

Types of Large Estates. Since their success depends on both land and labor inputs, large farms must concern themselves, individually and sometimes collectively, with ensuring an adequate supply of labor, preferably at low cost. Over the course of history many different arrangements have emerged to achieve this goal, including slavery, serfdom, free paid labor, tenancy, and several in-between categories. Changing circumstances, including the supply of labor, the available technologies, and social constraints on which arrangements are permissible (e.g., constraints against slavery), affect which form is most advantageous to the largeholders. The most modern type of large farm, best exemplified in the United States, uses relatively little labor; machines have largely taken the place of that factor of production. In the case of tenancy it is necessary to distinguish between the owned and the operated unit—the former is large but the latter small.

In settled preindustrial societies with high levels of inequality the large farm is a centerpiece of the socioeconomic system. The form of labor attachment affects the modus operandi of the farm. At one end of the spectrum are variants of the feudal system under which land and, to a lesser extent, other sources of income are held in fief by vassals from lords with whom they are bound by personal loyalty and to whom they owe labor and other (e.g., military) obligations. This form flourishes especially in closed agricultural economies. Feudalism provided the setting for the large farm during part of the history of most major civilizations, including those of western Europe, Russia, China, and India. At the other end of the spectrum is the profit-motivated farm that hires labor for a wage or rents the land to smallholders. The extent of the farm's focus on profits is related not only to the character of the society but also to the specific motivations of the owner; where land is held partly for its value as an inflation hedge or for the social status conferred, the largeholders may not spend much time in its management and productivity may be correspondingly low.

Classical fifth-century BCE Greece was the site of large farms cultivated for profit based on the scientific principles available at the time. By the Hellenistic period (from 323 BCE) very large estates were held by rulers, ministers, and other rich people, and by some great temples. Such estates were the scene of a wide range of activities and an extensive division of labor among workers, some of whom were slaves and some free. In ancient Rome (from which the word latifundium comes) the large estates originated from the allocation of land Rome confiscated from certain conquered communities, beginning in the early second century BCE; this pattern has been repeated many times since then.

Upper-class Romans who owned latifundia had enough capital to improve their cattle and crops, putting small peasant holders at a disadvantage, and eventually supplanting the small independent farm as the regular agricultural unit in Italy and the provinces. In the latter days of the Empire, slave labor became more expensive and tended to be replaced by tenant farmers (coloni) who cultivated small plots. As the empire declined and disappeared in the West, the latifundia assumed great importance not only as economic but also as local political and cultural centers.

The latifundia system, with large feudal or semifeudal estates, has been a common feature in many less developed countries (LDCs), especially in Latin America (the hacienda in Spanish-speaking countries and the facienda in Brazil), parts of southern Europe, and the Middle East. Land is concentrated in a few hands, there are many landless workers, and tenancy arrangements are insecure. In Latin America, for example, generally 3 to 4 percent of the owners have 60 to 80 percent of the agricultural land.

The transition from feudalism to capitalism saw the erosion of the system of social obligations surrounding the large estate and an increasing focus on profits. The largely self-sufficient economy built around the estate gave way to increasing trade with the rest of the economy. Specialization increased and many large estates eventually focused on the production of export items. These trends notwithstanding, many agrarian systems are still characterized by linkages across factor markets (land, labor, and capital) in what may be seen as a vestige of the feudal arrangements and a continuation of the underlying benefits of such interlinkages when factor markets are imperfect.

Over the last century and a half mechanization has been a major feature of agricultural change in an increasing number of countries, and has driven changes in the landowner-worker relationship. Although in a few countries some largeholders retain significant numbers of tenants as before, mechanization has generally led to the replacement of such labor-intensive arrangements. The large (in acreage) modern capitalistic farm is now prevalent in many developing countries, especially those at the middle-income ranges, as well as, of course, in developed countries. What distinguishes it from other large operating units is that it does not have a large labor force, and thereby avoids one of the frequent impediments to the efficiency of large units—the weaker incentive of the labor force.

The character of large farms has thus varied over time in each society. It also varies by type of agricultural activity. Livestock production usually requires large areas but relatively less detailed supervision and decision-making than crop farming, making it attractive to wealthy people who prefer to dedicate less than full time to the activity. Because of the large spaces and the high or prohibitive cost of fencing them, individual livestock producers or their formal or informal associations have often come into conflict with crop farmers, who normally operate on a much smaller scale. Whatever their profitability, these large operations tend to be less productive from a social than a private point of view because they keep land out of the hands of smaller farmers and generate negative externalities on the crop sector that does exist.

In Castile members of the powerful Mesta (sheepowners guild) drove their flocks over hundreds of miles from summer to winter pastures and back, spoiling much cultivated land in the process. Despite the violent hostility of the cultivators, the government backed Mesta, which paid for these privileges generously. The damage to crops helped to keep the peasants poor. Some historians blame the Mesta for Spain's underdevelopment relative to the rest of Europe. Many features of this system were exported to Latin America, where a similar criticism has been made. In the United States the conflict between ranchers and crop farmers was legendary.

The sixteenth- and eighteenth-century enclosure movements in England, by which common rights were replaced by individual property ownership, were a step in the consolidation of large private estates. At both times the process was opposed by the small and medium peasant farmers, only a small minority of whom emerged from the enclosures as landowners; the rest became proletariat, emigrated to the towns, or rented in if they had the wherewithal to do so. One interpretation of the sixteenth-century movement is that sheep farming had become more profitable for the landlord and was inconsistent with the formerly prevailing open field system. A common defense of the eighteenth-century movement was that it was needed to raise the overall efficiency of agriculture; this view is contested, however, by such experts as Doreen Warriner (1965).

Plantations are another type of large-scale operating unit associated with crops produced under conditions of economies of scale. They tend to be run on principles similar to those of a factory, with one main product and relatively routine and straightforward labor activities that do not require the workers to make many decisions. They usually attain high productivity levels.

Although crop production has generally not been characterized by important economies of scale above the family farm size, large farms continue to appear on occasion. One example was the "bonanza" corn and wheat farms in the American Midwest (especially North Dakota and Minnesota) in the 1870s and 1880s. The huge farms, in the tens of thousands of acres each, were built on the basis of exchange of railroad securities or other routes to land monopolization, availability of new machinery, wholesale purchase of inputs, and the use of migratory harvest labor. They reflected the spirit of bigness that pervaded the great transportation and industrial corporations of the East. The belief was that the principles of management applied in those other sectors could render agriculture equally profitable on this scale, while the owners typically lived elsewhere. For a few years, with good weather and high wheat prices, these farms did well. By the 1890s they found it hard to compete with the smaller farmers, who diversified their production and cultivated their land more intensively. Many disintegrated, but the best lands, instead of being subdivided into freeholdings, were broken down for sublet to tenants.

Impact. When large farms occupy the bulk of the land in any country or region, that fact normally signifies an unequal distribution of income and is in turn usually associated with social and political inequality as well. The impact of such a structure on output and on agricultural growth is less obvious and more variable. In many instances the large farms appear to have curtailed overall agricultural productivity, judging by a low land productivity that shows up in the frequently observed inverse relationship between size of plot and land productivity. Factors contributing to that relationship include the greater labor intensity of small farms due to the lower opportunity cost of that factor, and higher productivity because the owners of small farms had a greater incentive to work hard. Large farms, however, usually have the benefit of easier access to credit and to technical information; one result of the latter advantage has been that they usually adopt new, higher-yielding varieties of crops earlier and frequently achieve higher yields for specific crops.

The overall impact of the presence of large farms depends on how much size of farm and dedication to farming affect current productivity, and on how agrarian structure affects the rate of technological improvement, either directly or indirectly, through the way agricultural interests influence government investment in infrastructure, research, and so on. In many parts of the world the large (nonplantation) farm has come in for a good deal of criticism on the grounds of inefficiency, as in late-eighteenth-century France, the still substantially feudal system in Russia until at least the Emancipation Act of 1861, the hacienda system in Latin America, some of the Roman estates of the second century BCE, and the agrarian structure in many contemporary developing countries. The rising industrial bourgeoisie frequently blames the landed elite for the sluggish performance of agriculture and pushes for some sort of reform.

The economic performance of the large estate is often related to its social role. Because the landed elite are also the political and social elite, they tend not to live on their estates (they are absentee owners). This practice under many circumstances limits the productivity of their land (because of lack of attention, lack of presence to make day-to-day decisions, and so on) and inclines the use of the land toward activities requiring less attention and generally simpler to manage from a distance.

When the workers are tenants who make production-related decisions the loss of output potential is often less, though the operator still has less incentive (if any) to invest in the land. In other cases the unequal distribution of landownership may have little effect on output because the operating unit remained small. In some systems where large farms appear generally to have been inefficient, as commonly argued for much of Latin America (based on absenteeism, etc.) some large farms did play an important role in technological change, because they had the resources and other requisites to test new strains, etc.

Perhaps the broadest lesson from history is that agricultural growth can be satisfactory both in systems dominated by large farms, as many have been, and in those with few such farms. What differs greatly between them is the distribution of income, both during the agricultural phase of growth and later.

[*See also* Plantation System.]

BIBLIOGRAPHY
King, Russell. *Land Reform: A World Survey.* London, 1977.
Shannon, Fred A. *The Farmer's Last Frontier: Agriculture, 1860–1897.* New York, 1961.
Warriner, Doreen. *Land Reform in Principle and Practice.* Oxford, 1965.

R. ALBERT BERRY

LATVIA. *See* Baltic States.

LEATHER INDUSTRY [*This entry contains two subentries, on shoe and boot industries and tanning.*]

Shoe and Boot Industries

The shoe industry has been an organized sector, making and selling shoes, boots, sandals, and slippers to large shares of the population since the medieval period in the West. From a handicraft producing for custom markets, shoemaking has developed into a mechanized, capitalistic industry targeting world markets. This continuous history of commodity production, punctuated by transformations in markets, organization, techniques, and location makes shoemaking a classic case of industrial evolution.

The Shoemaking Craft. Shoemaking extends back more than five thousand years in Egypt. From the second millennium BCE, specialized workers made shoes and many other leather products in Europe, North Africa, and the Middle East. Yet there is little evidence of widespread commodity production until medieval times. By the twelfth or thirteenth century, shoemaking was a well-established trade across most of Europe. Medieval techniques, markets, and organization would be familiar in the nineteenth century. Leather was the predominant material, augmented by wood and cloth. Shoemakers cut tanned leather and stitched upper and sole pieces together using needles, awls, and waxed thread. Most medieval footwear were relatively light turn shoes, made by attaching the upper with the flesh side out to a wooden last in the shape of a foot, sewing the upper to the sole, and then turning the shoe inside out. By 1500, the heavier welted shoe had originated, formed by stitching the upper, now right-side out, to an inner sole and a thin strip of leather called a welt, and then sewing the welt to the heavier outer sole. Heels came into use about the same time.

In towns shoe markets took a typical form by the thirteenth century. Shoes for sale comprised an unknown but significant share of all shoes in western and central Europe. Shoemaking was usually conducted on a custom basis, beginning with measuring the customer's feet, so shoemakers typically were located near their customers. Where population and wealth were concentrated, such as in Florence, Paris, and London, shoemakers specialized further by shoe quality or into makers and repairers. Generic leatherworkers made earlier shoes, but medieval shoemakers were specialists, purchasing tanned leather and leaving other leather working to glovers, saddlers, and others. Some long-distance trade from areas with plentiful hides or superior leathers, including Spain, England, and Russia, supplemented local leathermaking.

Shoemaking developed an artisanal organization. Guilds dominated in larger towns, beginning with leather workers in eleventh-century Paris and Florence. By the

EGYPTIAN SHOE MAKING. Craftsmen making shoe soles, laces, and buckles. Detail of a wall painting in the tomb of Rekhmere, vizier to the pharaohs Thutmose III and Amenhotpe II, Eighteenth Dynasty (c. 1569–1315 BCE). Tomb of Rekhmere, Sheikh Abd el-Qurna, West Thebes, Thebes, Egypt. (Erich Lessing/Art Resource, NY)

thirteenth century, shoemaking guilds existed in many towns in Italy, France, England, Germany, and the Low Countries, but were less common in Spain and eastern Europe. Guild masters had the right to sell in their shops, employed and at times housed journeymen, and trained and housed apprentices for a fee. Shoemakers were in the middle of the guild hierarchy, unable to monopolize a key input, as the goldsmiths and butchers did, or a lucrative wholesale trade, as the drapers did. Capital costs were modest, consisting mostly of materials. Shops were small, with a master, a few journeymen and apprentices, and some family labor. Both apprenticeship fees and journeymen's wages were relatively low. Guilds typically received charters from towns until the sixteenth century, but especially in Germany workers traditionally "tramped" among towns and villages. Like other guilds, shoemakers regulated the quality of goods, but they had limited effectiveness in regulating supply because they never controlled townsmen outside municipal jurisdiction, peddlers selling in fairs, or village shoemakers.

The leather trades were far more important in preindustrial Europe and North America than they are today. Leather making and leather working trades often made up 20 percent of the urban workforce in sixteenth- and seven-teenth-century England, and shoemaking was the largest leather working craft. Employment in the English leather trades only lagged behind textiles and perhaps the building trades. By 1770, only woolen textiles had greater value added than the leather trades. In the nineteenth century, when textiles had become a factory industry, shoemaking was the largest artisanal trade in many parts of Britain, Germany, Spain, and France. In the United States in 1850, shoemaking employed more workers than any manufacturing industry.

Evolution of the Craft System. Craft shoemaking was hardly static. Changes in fashion and technique, such as the rise of welted and heeled shoes, were accommodated within the system. The decline of guilds, broadening of markets, and reorganization of production were more transformational. Guild regulatory powers declined in the seventeenth and eighteenth centuries. Nonguild employment emerged from conflicts within the guilds when masters employed nonapprenticed workers and when journeymen, blocked from becoming masters, produced outside guild control. Regional shoe markets began to arise in late-seventeenth-century England. Military demand stimulated shoemaking around Northampton, which supplied the New Model Army and then armies in Ireland. More important in the long run were ready-made shoes for "sale shops," which were common in mid-eighteenth-century London.

Following the pattern of textiles and metalworking, which from the fourteenth century sold regionally and internationally, shoemaking developed a putting-out (or proto-industrial) system. In it, merchant-employers, often spawned from shoemaking or leather crafts, purchased materials, employed workers laboring in their own homes in towns or the countryside, and then sold the product. Putting out did occur in custom shoemaking but was more prevalent in ready-made production. Putting out commonly divided labor between leather cutters, closers or fitters (who sewed upper pieces), and makers (who lasted and sewed uppers to soles). Costs fell because wages were lower for closers—typically women and children—and makers—often journeymen untrained in cutting. Lower costs in turn supported the expansion of wholesale markets. Proto-industrialization also grew in Germany and other continental centers.

No longer constrained by guild norms limiting employment, some protoindustrial employers grew large. By 1738, London and Northampton masters employed as many as 160 workers. According to the 1851 census returns for 17,700 master shoemakers in England and Wales, thirty one employed more than one hundred workers and about seven hundred employed ten or more. The industry concentrated around Northampton, Stafford, and Yorkshire; Northampton had five times as many shoemakers per capita as the national average. Small shops still predominated, but pre-factory capitalist employers were ascending.

The United States developed a particularly strong putting-out system. By the mid-eighteenth century, wholesale merchants employed shoemakers making the whole shoe. Around 1820, Massachusetts firms introduced central shops, which cut upper leather, put it out to women fitters, and then put out uppers and soles to makers. The central-shop system spread quickly in Massachusetts, benefiting from lower labor costs, employable labor in declining agricultural areas, the development of cheaper pegged shoes (which united soles and uppers with wooden pegs) and the establishment of standard sizes. Protoindustrial firms expanded; in Lynn, the center of women's shoes, one-fifth employed one hundred or more workers in 1832, and four-fifths employed at least ten. Massachusetts shoe firms averaged thirty seven employees in 1850—four times the U.S. average. Growing specialization in Massachusetts shoe towns increased the share of women and girls in total employment from 26 percent in 1832 to 41 percent in 1837. The central-shop system localized shoemaking in Massachusetts, which in 1850 employed almost half of the nation's shoe workers, twelve times as many per capita as the country as a whole.

Mechanization and Factory Production. Shoe machinery eliminated the hand laboring common to guild and putting-out systems. Mechanization was largely an American process. England had developed a boot-sewing machine in 1790 and shoe-nailing machinery during the Napoleonic Wars, but both were abandoned. The shoe factory originated when two kinds of sewing machines were introduced into the Massachusetts central-shop system. The upper sewing machine, first used in 1852, multiplied productivity severalfold in factories and subcontractors' shops; by 1860 it was used widely. The most revolutionary machine, the McKay bottom stitcher, united uppers and soles. Perfected while executing Civil War military orders, by 1871 it sewed two-fifths of U.S. shoes, largely in integrated factories that employed machine operatives and some hand labor to make the whole shoe.

Mechanization occurred so quickly because of a conjunction of factors inside and outside U.S. shoemaking. Potential machine demand depended on industry characteristics, including its size, rapid growth, and the presence of protoindustrial firms large enough to finance and utilize factories. The potential to supply machines rested on the technology and institutions of the machinery sector. The shoe-sewing machine evolved from Elias Howe's 1846 cloth-sewing invention, which applied his machinist's skill and knowledge of textile machines. By 1854 Isaac Singer and other mechanics developed it to practicality and sold it through company agencies. Massachusetts shoe manufacturers adapted it to upper-sewing and Boston machinists to heavier, waxed-thread stitching. The McKay machine developed when Gordon McKay, an inventor and superintendent in a textile machinery firm, developed the patent of Lyman Blake, a shoe manufacturer trained on waxed-thread machines. McKay diffused machines through leases at per-pair royalty charges. Adapting the machinery sector's technological, production, and marketing practices, capital-goods firms sold machines widely and fostered invention through the geographically localized learning accompanying these sales.

By 1870, U.S. shoe mechanization was ongoing, organized around machinery sales and usage. Shoe patents quadrupled from 1860 to 1900, and 85 percent of the patents taken out by inventors with known occupations were issued to machinists, professional inventors, and shoemakers. Patentees whose inventions were used received three times as many patents as others. Invention spread from simpler McKay shoes to more complex Goodyear welted shoes and among shoemaking operations, culminating in adequate lasting machines by 1900. Machinery firms grew, diversified to form systems of complementary machinery, and in 1899 merged to form United Shoe Machinery, which monopolized shoe machinery production.

In 1900 factories accounted for 83 percent of the industry's value added and averaged seventy one workers. They incorporated virtually all shoemaking operations and specialized by product type. Though optimal plant size remained modest, some firms grew by integrating into retailing and building several plants. Production remained localized in Massachusetts, where the major shoe machinery firms, many input firms, and two-fifths of industry workers resided. Invention reinforced this concentration; Massachusetts inventors received two-thirds of the shoe patents issued from 1882 through 1901.

Factories were slower to develop in Europe. Singer, McKay, and later United Shoe Machinery became transnational firms that sold machinery, invested, patented, and trained workers abroad. European shoe machinery firms provided little competition. England was the most important recipient. Upper-sewing machines spread most easily; diffusion of McKay and Goodyear bottoming machines was slowed by trade union opposition, not resolved until the strike of 1895, and by firms' diversity of products and short production runs. In 1891 British production costs were one-third above America's, even though wages were considerably lower. Threatened by the American export "invasion" in the 1890s and enabled by the availability of integrated systems of machinery and union agreements on mechanization, shoe firms rapidly mechanized through 1914. Outwork, still common in the 1890s, fell commensurately. Northampton remained a center, though production spread to Leicester and elsewhere.

By World War I other European centers began to industrialize, though along different paths. With virtually no factory production in 1882, Germany developed rapidly by using U.S. machines and, more than other countries, indigenous adaptations, some of which it exported. France and Austria depended more on imported U.S. machinery but retained substantial outworking and craft production. Some developed large, relatively isolated firms, including Switzerland's C. F. Bally, whose nine factories exported extensively, and Austria's (later Czechoslovakia's) Tomas Bata, which made six thousand pairs of shoes daily in 1913. Others lagged, including Italy, where incipient factories and putting out simultaneously expanded.

Twentieth-Century Directions. After World War I the shoe industry grew more slowly and stabilized its technology, yet changed its products, location, and organization. Per-capita leather-shoe consumption in the United States was unchanged between 1900 and 1987 and in Europe rose slightly after 1960. As a result, output growth slowed, and shoemaking declined in comparison with other industries. Still the eighth largest U.S. industry in 1920, employing more workers than the automobile industry, its share of manufacturing employment had fallen by one-third by 1954.

When the factory had diffused, the industry's technology stabilized. Average employment in U.S. factories grew to 130 workers in 1954, but the industry remained labor-intensive with modest capital requirements. While some firms grew large—Bata had ninety factories, 85,000 workers and 6,300 retail outlets in 1990—most remained small. Some new mechanical techniques spread widely, such as cementing rather than stitching soles to uppers. But many post-1950 changes, including computer-aided design, numerical control, injection molding, and laser cutting, spread slowly and partially. The heterogeneity of leather limited automation, and small firms, short production runs, and radically new skill requirements slowed other innovations.

The source of innovations also changed; many were more science-based. The revolution in materials was a product of the rubber and chemical industries. Rubber and synthetics are used so extensively in soles and heels that leather shoes now are defined as footwear with leather uppers. New materials gave rise to new products. Around 1900 athletic shoes were introduced by rubber firms, including U.S. Rubber, Goodrich, and Converse, whose Keds, P.F. Flyers, and All-Stars became well-known brand names. Bata and others improved manufacturing processes. Athletic shoes grew to one-quarter of U.S. shoe sales in 1962, and nonleather footwear of all types formed 55 percent of world output in 1987. Led by firms such as Nike, with sales of five billion dollars in 1996, these new products cut into leather-shoe output.

As production technologies matured, global markets arose, and production relocated. Through 1950 leading capitalist countries dominated shoe production and consumption. In 1955 the United States, Britain, and Germany produced 54 percent of the world's leather shoes (measured by pairs) and imported little. Shoemaking moved within countries—Massachusetts fell to 19 percent of U.S. employment in 1954—but not outside. Such national self-sufficiency no longer exists. Exports of leather footwear have increased from 6 percent of world output between 1961 and 1965 to 28 percent between 1985 and 1987 and 40 percent in 1995. Export growth was associated with declining production by earlier leaders. In 1995, the United States, Britain, and Germany had fallen to 5 percent of world leather-shoe production and imported 83 percent of their domestically consumed shoes.

Production moved in two directions. From the 1960s, leather-shoe production surged in southern Europe, especially in Italy, which generated 43 percent of world exports in 1970. Ultimately more important, developing countries increased their share of world output from 22 percent between 1961 and 1965 to 40 percent between 1985 and 1987 and 72 percent in 1995; their share of world exports rose from 8 to 41 to 66 percent over these years. They were even more dominant in athletic shoes. Third-world production was propelled by reduced labor costs in a context of falling trade barriers and a standard, labor-intensive technology that was readily transferred by multinational shoe machinery firms, shoe firms (including Bata, with plants in sixty eight countries), and especially by subcontracting, joint ventures, and start-ups by indigenous firms.

The growth of global markets was accelerated by the spread of subcontracting and outwork, a phenomenon that strikingly parallels the rise of putting out when national markets grew two centuries earlier. While U.S. shoe factories grew over time, the opposite occurred in Italy; average firm size decreased from 21.5 workers in 1951 to 9.3 in 1991. Operations performed within the traditional U.S. firm—including making models, cutting and stitching leather, and making soles and heels—were subcontracted, leaving only design, bottoming, and finishing within the firm. This decentralization has been interpreted as an advantage of Italian industrial districts because networks of producers, contractors, suppliers, and skilled labor led to quick turnover, responsiveness to consumer needs, high product quality, and rising wages. Italy's success was supported by its ascendance in shoe machinery, in which it now leads the world.

Developing countries followed a different path. They also rely on subcontracting, but much less on industrial districts with extensive cooperation. Instead, assemblers, component manufacturers, and machinery firms commonly are located in different parts of the world. Third-world expansion is based not only on far lower wages but also on long hours, nonunion settings, child labor, and lack of regulation, social security, and workers' rights. With these advantages South Korea became the leading third-world exporter by 1985. As Korean wages rose, China took the lead and in 1995 made one-third of the world's leather shoes. Though Italy remains competitive in high-quality shoes, the third world has come to dominate global shoemaking.

BIBLIOGRAPHY

Blim, Michael L. *Made in Italy: Small-Scale Industrialization and Its Consequences*. New York, 1990. Integrates shoemaking with the economic history of the region.

Cherry, John. "Leather." In *English Medieval Industries*, edited by John Blair and Nigel Ramsey, pp. 295–318. London, 1991.

Church, R. A. "The Effect of the American Export Invasion on the British Boot and Shoe Industry, 1885–1914." *Journal of Economic History* 28 (June 1968), 223–254.

Clapham, J. H. *An Economic History of Modern Britain*, 3 vols. Cambridge, 1938.

Clarkson, L. A. "The Leather Crafts in Tudor and Stuart England." *Agricultural History Review* 14 (1966), 25–39.

Clarkson, L. A. *The Pre-Industrial Economy in England, 1500–1750*. New York, 1972.

Dawley, Alan. *Class and Community: The Industrial Revolution in Lynn*. Cambridge, Mass., 1976. A history of class organization in relation to economic development.

Food and Agriculture Organization of the United Nations. *World Statistical Compendium for Raw Hides and Skins, Leather, and Leather Footwear*. Rome, 1983, 1998. The best source on production, imports, and exports by country since 1961.

George, M. Dorothy. *London Life in the Eighteenth Century*. New York, 1965.

Hazard, Blanche Evans. *The Organization of the Boot and Shoe Industry in Massachusetts before 1875*. Cambridge, Mass., 1921. Contains a classic periodization of the industry.

Hobsbawm, Eric. "Political Shoemakers." In *Workers: Worlds of Labor*. New York, 1984.

Rabellotti, Roberta. *External Economies and Cooperation in Industrial Districts: A Comparison of Italy and Mexico*. New York, 1997.

Thomson, Ross. *The Path to Mechanized Shoe Production in the United States*. Chapel Hill, N.C., 1989.

Thrupp, Sylvia L. "The Gilds." In *The Cambridge Economic History of Europe*, edited by M. M. Postan, E. E. Rich, and Edward Miller, vol. 3, pp. 230–280. Cambridge, 1963.

Tripartite Technical Meeting for the Leather and Footwear Industry. *Recent Developments in the Leather and Footwear Industry*. Geneva, 1992.

Unwin, George. *The Gilds and Companies of London*. New York, 1964.

ROSS THOMSON

Tanning

Tanning is the process by which animal hides or skins are converted into leather through their immersion in tannic acid extracted from oak bark. This process has existed since ancient times; however, it was only during the fifteenth century that tanning spread all over Europe. Cordoba, in the south of Spain, was until the nineteenth century the primary European center of leather production. In medieval and early modern times, leather was used in the production of a wide range of products, such as suede goods, shoes, belts, gloves, saddles, luggage, purses, buckets, cases, and book covers. The production of leather and manufacture of leather goods were represented by a large number of guilds that included cordwainers (shoemakers), curriers, girdlers (belt makers), homers (bottle makers), leather sellers, saddlers and harness makers, skinners, pursers, and tanners.

During the seventeenth and eighteenth centuries, leather production was one of the most important sectors of the British economy, and still in the 1830s it was behind only cotton, wool, and iron. Tanning and leather production were considered important areas for state regulation. The supply of a wide range of consumer goods was determined by the constant production of leather. Laws were created to control not only the import and export of raw leather and finished leather goods but also the relationship among the number of cattle slaughtered, the quantity of meat produced, and the number of available hides.

Tanning and leather production have been located for many centuries in rural regions not far from oak supplies or near slaughtering houses that provided a constant stock of skins. Tanning and curing were forbidden by law to be located in inner-city areas. Until the early nineteenth century, there were few technological changes in the sector, confining production to a small-scale basis. Between 1768 and 1770, the Irishman David MacBride and the Englishman John Johnson invented new methods for rapid tanning of leather using vitriol. Chrome tanning was first introduced in the 1830s but became widely used (with the so-called Heinzerling process) only in the 1870s and after 1884 through the Schultz chrome tanning process. Today, 80 percent of leather is tanned with chromium chemicals. Such chemically oriented innovations were accompanied by the use of new machinery, such as the hand-operated knife (to split skins) invented by William Powers in 1768, the endless band-knife machine (to split hides) invented by William Newberry in 1808, and the spiral-bladed cylinder knives invented by John Baring in 1828.

Technical change contributed not only to the decline of rural leather production but also to the increase in the scale of production in semiurban areas. As early as 1858, tanneries such as Nickols's Joppa in Leeds, United Kingdom, used steam engines and more than five hundred tanning pits. By the end of the nineteenth century, tanning assumed an industrial dimension in Phillipsburg, Pennsylvania, in the United States and Acton, Ontario, in Canada. In the twentieth century, the widespread use of synthetic materials, such as plastic, relegated leather production to niche markets, such as Italian leather goods and French luxury luggage production.

BIBLIOGRAPHY

Church, Roy A. "The British Leather Industry and Foreign Competition, 1870–1914." In *The Development of British Industry and Foreign Competition, 1875–1914: Studies in Industrial Enterprise*, edited by D. H. Aldcroft, pp. 543–568. London, 1968. Focuses on international trade and competition.

Clarkson, Lesley A. "The Manufacture of Leather." In *The Agrarian History of England and Wales, c. 1750–1850*, edited by G. E. Mingay, pp. 466–483. Cambridge, 1989. A broad overview of the post-1750 period.

Clarkson, Lesley A. "The Development of Tanning Methods during the Post-Medieval Period (1500–1850)." In *Leather Manufacture through the Ages: Proceedings of the Twenty-Seventh East Midlands Industrial Archaeology Conference*, edited by S. Thomas, L. A. Clarkson, and R. Thomson, pp. 11–21. 1993. Covers the preindustrial period.

Stern, Walter B. "Control versus Freedom in Leather Production from the Early Seventeenth to the Early Nineteenth Century." *Guildhall Miscellany* 2 (1968), 438–442. Also covers the preindustrial period.

GIORGIO RIELLO

LEBANON. *See* Levant, *subentry on* Modern Lebanon.

LEGAL PROFESSION. Lawyers (together with doctors and priests) have long been the butt of writers, artists, and popular culture, quick to seize upon the disjunction between their lofty claims and their debased reality. Indeed, lawyers were often portrayed as the devil in person. So caricatured, the lawyer is self-serving, propagating litigation and increasing the complexity and expense of the law.

Paradoxically, while criticism of lawyers is a long-standing feature of many societies, lawyers proved indispensable to their clients. Both locally and nationally, they played a vital role in facilitating and shaping economic and political change and helping to construct the larger framework of legal regulation.

The past thirty years have witnessed a sizable aggregation of both quantitative and qualitative work on the histories of lawyers, including histories of individual law firms. Much more is now known about the history of lawyers from its earliest phases in Australia, Canada, continental Europe, England, and the United States, including their numbers, social and educational background, gender, work patterns, and governance. This newer research has shown the special affiliation between professionalization and nineteenth-century capitalist society to be problematic. For instance, in terms of numbers of lawyers and their professional organization and education, the English legal profession of the 1880s looks strikingly similar to that of the 1680s, although a major decline in numbers, professional organization, and education had occurred during the intervening period. This realization has challenged linear notions of professionalization and two-class, patrician-plebeian models of society, and takes more seriously the ideologies, institutions, and practices of the middle classes.

Evolution of a Profession. Until well into the nineteenth century, the provision of legal services was not highly institutionalized. Most lawyers (at least in the common-law world) had no standardized training or formal qualifications. Neither did they make a full-time working commitment to the profession. Thus, until the late nineteenth century, lawyers were incredibly heterodox and variegated—wearing several occupational hats at once—rather than professing a single calling.

Economic forces had a significant impact on the evolution of the legal profession. In the eighteenth century, the transfer of land started to become an important source of income, status, and influence for lawyers. The central role of lawyers in the buying and selling of land, as well as in marriage settlements, crafting trusts and wills, and obtaining and lending of money for their more prosperous clients, ensured that lawyers became confidential and indispensable counselors.

The emergence of the railroad industry provided abundant new work for lawyers, who were often crucial to securing the necessary authority to create and enlarge railways. Moreover, the railways created many new legal problems in such areas as accident compensation and commercial law.

Although partnerships could be and frequently were created without the help of lawyers, lawyers nonetheless played an important role in rationalizing business organization through their innovative use of partnership and later the limited liability company. Corporate lawyers played an important role naturalizing and sanctifying the limited liability company.

Areas of facilitative law (such as contract, corporate, property, and family law) afforded the parties concerned—often aided and mediated by their lawyers—the opportunity to make their own law (private lawmaking), and even the opportunity, on occasions, to bypass or attenuate the law established by legislatures or the courts. Thus, lawyers both greased the wheels of capitalism and helped shape the content of the law.

Conflicts of Interest. As lawyers began to take on a more important role in business concerns, conflicts of interest became more apparent. Lawyers were entrusted with their client's monies and had access to inside information and opportunities not generally available to the public. Many lawyers transformed this information into opportunities for themselves and their clients that, in turn, gave rise to new information, new opportunities, and new clients. As many lawyers saw it, they were entitled to profit from possible conflicts of interest. Scandals were commonplace, and bankrupt lawyers aroused considerable disquiet.

Although businesses might find lawyers useful, they also found them expensive, technical, and time-consuming. In some quarters of the economy, there was a strong preference for forms of regulation and dispute resolution that circumvented lawyers and that relied instead on the conventions of the business community, guild, or trade association concerned.

By the beginning of the twentieth century, lawyers began to take on more important public and political roles. They were spokespersons on behalf of their clients in public arenas. Those lawyers who acted for major government institutions played a special role in economic development. For example, Freshfields, the Bank of England's solicitors, assisted the bank in its efforts to reorganize British industry in the 1930s.

Lawyers also exercised important public roles through those associations that represented the legal profession. In essence, such associations made lawyers an essential and intrinsic component in the formulation of state policy. Lawyers often had a large constituency in local and national legislatures and in government. The close involvement of lawyers and their professional bodies in the formulation of legislation, law reform, and legal practice suggests that they exercised an important influence on the available normative languages and therefore the presuppositions of the legislative and decision-making processes.

LEGAL PROFESSION. *Men of Justice,* lithograph by Honoré Daumier (1808–1879), showing the lawyer Chapotard reading in a legal newspaper his encomium of himself. (Art Resource, NY)

Expansion. As they began to take on multiple roles, lawyers found many new arenas of struggle open to them. This afforded new opportunities to be key players in many spheres—often straddling private practice, public office, and politics—that significantly added to lawyers' value to business and to their consequent influence and power. For example, James Freshfield was solicitor to the Bank of England. He also acted for Sir Robert Peel and other politicians and was a Peelite and member of Parliament who was appointed High Sheriff of Surrey. Additionally, he was a member of the Carlton and Atheneum Clubs and Royal Society. He was also the chairman of Divorce Commissioners and a director of the Globe Insurance Company.

Some historians have sought to understand the legal profession in terms of a struggle for cultural authority as well as for immediate financial rewards. Under this optic, the elite lawyers of the common-law world were cultural attachés, sharing and constituting a common language, worldview, and history. Investigation of these issues illuminates the efforts of the profession to translate economic power into moral and cultural authority, which, in turn, were dependent on the profession's claim to being independent.

A related issue is the role of the legal profession in sustaining the middle class, its values, and its importance within local communities, constituting a counterweight against the despotic elements in society. Lawyers have been important producers of the political discourse, rights talk, conceptions of polity, and so on that are deep-rooted in the institutional structure of many societies. They also have been important retailers of ideology, fitting their clients' projects into an overall ordering of social life. The importance of law talk is an empirical question rather than something that can be taken for granted. Moreover, the languages of the law have coexisted alongside other equally important discourses such as religion, the natural sciences, history, and political economy.

The divisions within the legal profession (geographical, social, and so on) also have mediated the influence of lawyers as a pressure group. Indeed, the nature and scope of legal professionalization have been continually contested. Were lawyers independent of particular interests or dependent on them, gentlemen or in business, scientists or practitioners, guardians of public or private interest, aristocratic and anticommercial or contractual and self-interested, officers of the court or the hired hands of the client? The power and legitimacy of the profession have depended, in part, on how these contradictory images are synthesized and delineated, both within the profession and in its relation to society.

The legal professions had and continue to have immense opportunities to use their professional roles and standing as springboards to business and political endeavors, generating for some (but by no means all) great personal wealth and influence. Lawyers are the creators and transmitters of specialist discourses, some of which are our most important political languages. Lawyers also are institution builders, constituting markets, states, civil societies, communities, and colonial empires. Indeed, the construction and legitimization of the liberal state and society, as well as the globalization of liberal politics, probably owe much to lawyers. Consequently, the history of the legal profession undermines that tenet of legal formalism that only those distinctly "legal" tasks, separate from "society," "business," and "politics," are what lawyering is really about. This is not only to assert that the private and public roles of the legal profession coalesced, but also to see how the legal profession was constituted by a double discourse that both claimed that the public and private are separate and that the public and private cannot be separated.

BIBLIOGRAPHY

Abel-Smith, Brian, and Robert Stevens. *Lawyers and the Courts: A Sociological Study of the English Legal System, 1750–1965*. London, 1967.

Auerbach, Jerold S. *Unequal Justice: Lawyers and Social Change in Modern America*. New York, 1974.

Baker, John H. *The Legal Profession and the Common Law: Historical Essays*. London, 1986.

Beattie, J. M. "Scales of Justice: Defence Counsel and the English Criminal Trial in the Eighteenth and Nineteenth Centuries." *Law and History Review* 9.2 (1991), 221–267.

Bell, David. *Lawyers and Citizens: The Making of a Political Elite in Old Regime France*. Oxford, 1994.

Bouwsma, William J. "Lawyers and Early Modern Culture." *American History Review* 73 (1973), 303–327.

Brand, Paul. *The Origins of the English Legal Profession*. Oxford, 1992.

Brooks, Christopher W. *Pettyfoggers and Vipers of the Commonwealth: The "Lower Branch" of the Legal Profession in Early Modern England*. Cambridge, 1986.

Brooks, Christopher W. *Lawyers, Litigation, and English Society since 1450*. London, 1998.

Gawalt, Gerard W., ed. *The New High Priests: Lawyers in Post–Civil War America*. Westport, Conn., 1984.

Gordon, Robert W. "Legal Thought and Legal Practice in the Age of the American Enterprise, 1870–1920." In *Professions and Professional Ideologies in America*, edited by G. Geison. Chapel Hill, N.C., 1983.

Halliday, Terence C., and Lucien Karpik, eds. *Lawyers and the Rise of Western Political Liberalism*. Oxford, 1997.

Halperin, Jean-Louis, ed. *Avocats et notaires en Europe: Les professions judiciaires et juridiques dans l'histoire contemporaine, droit et société*. Vol. 19. Paris, 1996.

Kagan, Richard L. *Lawyers and Litigants in Castile, 1500–1700*. Chapel Hill, N.C., 1980.

Karpik, Lucien. *French Lawyers: A Study of Collective Action, 1274–1994*. Oxford, 1999.

Kirk, Harry. *Portrait of a Profession: A History of the Solicitors Profession, 1100 to the Present Day*. London, 1976.

Kostal, Rande. *Law and English Railway Capitalism, 1825–1875*. Oxford, 1994.

Krause, Elliott A. *Death of the Guilds: Professions, States, and the Advance of Capitalism, 1930 to the Present*. New Haven, 1999.

Langbein, John H. "Criminal Trial before the Lawyers." *University of Chicago Law Review* 45 (1978), 263–316.

Langbein, John H. "The Prosecutorial Origins of Defence Counsel in the Eighteenth Century: The Appearance of Solicitors." *Cambridge Law Journal* 58 (1999), 314.

Ledford, Kenneth. *From General Estate to Special Interest: German Lawyers, 1878–1933*. Cambridge, 1996.

Lemmings, David. *Professors of the Law: Barristers and English Legal Culture in the Eighteenth Century*. Oxford, 2000.

Martines, Lauro. *Lawyers and Statecraft in Renaissance Florence*. Princeton, 1968.

Mathias, Peter. "The Lawyer as Businessman in Eighteenth-Century England." In *Enterprise and History: Essays in Honour of Charles Wilson*, edited by D. C. Coleman and Peter Mathias. Cambridge, 1984.

McQueen, Robert, and W. Wesley Pue, eds. "Misplaced Traditions: The Legal Profession and the British Empire." *Law in Context* 16.1 (1999).

Prest, Wilfrid, ed. *Lawyers in Early Modern Europe and America*. London, 1981.

Prest, Wilfrid. *The Rise of the Barristers: A Social History of the English Bar, 1590–1640*. Oxford, 1986.

Pue, W. Wesley, and David Sugarman, eds. *Lawyers and Vampires: Cultural Histories of Lawyers*. Oxford, 2002.

Rueschemeyer, Dietrich. *Lawyers and Their Society: A Comparative Study of the Legal Profession in Germany and the United States*. Cambridge, Mass., 1973.

Sugarman, David. "Bourgeois Collectivism, Professional Power and the Boundaries of the State: The Private and Public Life of the Law Society, 1825–1914." *International Journal of the Legal Profession* 3 (1996), 81–135.

Wilton, Carol, ed. *Beyond the Law: Lawyers and Business in Canada, 1830 to 1930.* Toronto, 1990.

DAVID SUGARMAN

LEGUMES AND PULSES. Pulses are a major source of protein in diets around the world. In ancient cultures, cereals and pulses developed as traditional companions. Such combinations as beans and tortillas or dal and nan bread still provide the basis of delicious meals evocative of the cultures from which they come. Pulses are plants from the legume family grown for human consumption and include beans, chickpeas, lentils, peas, and lupins. Because pulses have an association with beneficial soil bacteria that "fix" nitrogen from the air, they are high in protein and thus nutritious to eat. They also improve the soil in which they are grown.

Origins of Pulses in Agriculture. Long before the Industrial Revolution, the Neolithic Revolution of human civilization brought the transition from hunters and gatherers to agriculture, allowing development of diverse human talents and necessitating social evolution. Abundant wild relatives of the cereals wheat and barley permitted settlement in the ancient Near East and thus encouraged plant cultivation. Cultivating wheat and barley for food began about 8500 BCE in the Fertile Crescent. Within a millenium, peas, lentils, and chickpeas had been added to the repetoire.

Farming developed independently in Latin America and Asia with a similar outcome being the combination of cereals and pulses. Beans were cultivated in Mexico and Peru by about 6000 BCE, and beans and corn are still the mainstay of the diet of much of Latin America. In China, millet predated rice as the first main crop, and soybeans were grown by about 3000 BCE.

Legume Legends. There are numerous examples that illustrate the importance of pulses in early history. Pulses played a role in some of the religious observances of the ancient Egyptians. Beans (probably *Vicia faba*) were offered to the dead during earlier dynasties, and lentils were sacred to Harpocrates, the Egyptian personification of silence. The Greek historian Herodotus reported that builders of the pyramids at Giza ate lentils, perhaps aware of their benefit (from high protein) for such arduous labor; Athenians celebrated a Feast of Beans, the Kyampsia, in honor of Apollo. A well-known ancient reference to pulses is the Biblical pottage of red lentils, which Jacob used to buy his brother Esau's birthright. The importance of the chickpea and lentil on the Indian subcontinent is intertwined with the vegetarian principle required initially by Jainism, encouraged by Buddhism, and then taken up by brahmin priests of Hinduism.

Pulse Food. Pulses have obviously been traded widely, as evidenced by the use of the many beans that originated in the Americas in traditional foods in Europe and Africa and the dominance of chickpeas and lentils, which originated in the ancient Near East in the traditional diet of the Indian subcontinent. Peas, which originated in the ancient Near East, are found in traditional foods around the world, even reaching the heights of the Himalayas. Ancient people may have noticed that eating combinations of pulses and cereals resulted in improved vitality because the combination provides an excellent supply of "complete" protein. As with many things, the scientific explanation—that pulses are deficient in the sulphur-containing amino acids methionine and cysteine but have good lysine levels, while cereals are conversely short of lysine but rich in methionine—came much later. Varied and exotic images come to mind when we think of combinations of pulses and cereals, such as hummus (chickpea) and pita bread, beans and tortillas, tempeh (soybean) and rice, lentil dal and nan bread, chickpeas and pasta, pease pudding and rye bread, and even baked beans on toast.

Pulses in Crop Rotations. The association between legumes and the bacteria that colonize legume roots is mutually beneficial. Enzymes from the bacteria break apart nitrogen atoms of nitrogen gas (N_2), which makes up about 80 percent of the earth's atmosphere and "fix" that nitrogen for the legume plant. This benefits not only the legume plant but also other plants that grow in that soil after the legume plant dies and decomposes. Without this association, plant productivity would be extremely low, and life on our planet would be very different. The scientific explanation of this special role of legumes and their associated bacteria came relatively recently from the German scientist Hermann Hellriegel (1839–1895) in a report in 1888, which was rapidly confirmed by other European and North American scientists. However, the value of legumes for improved growth of other crops has been known at least two millenia.

Green manuring of legumes, where the legume is plowed into the soil to enrich it for the next crop, was a practice reported by Ts'i Min Yao Shu, a Chinese writer of the fifth century BCE. The Greeks also practiced green manuring; Theophrastus (c. 372–c. 287 BCE) reported plowing beans under in Thessaly and Macedonia. Roman writers have left a substantial written record of their agricultural practices, and the Roman agriculturalists and writers who extolled the virtues of legumes in crop rotations included Cato, Varro, Columella, Pliny, and Virgil. In his *Georgica* (30 BCE), Virgil recommended "where you have reaped the legume with shaking pod, the vetch and lupine, sow your wheat. . . ." With the decline of Rome came a lull in the recognition of the benefits of legumes in crop rotations, but in Charlemagne's empire in the Middle Ages (800–814 CE), legume rotations were reportedly introduced to the farming system and society became "more forceful" (Tannahill, 1988), probably because of increased protein in the diet. In modern times, the legume soybean is one of the major crops grown and traded in the world. In North America, it is grown in crop rotations but not for its nitrogen-fixing ability. Instead, soybeans are generously fertilized with industrially fixed nitrogen fertilizer. Of the developed countries where agriculture is an important part of the economy, Australia stands out for its reliance on nitrogen fixed by legume crops (pulses) and pastures.

Health Benefits of Pulse Consumption. Undoubtedly, one reason for the historical importance of pulses in human diets has been their high protein content (mostly 20 to 25 percent but 36 percent for soybeans, compared with 10 percent or less for most cereals). Pulses are also high in fiber and carbohydrates and low in fat (except soybeans). They have no cholesterol or gluten, a low glycemic index, high amounts of such nutrients as iron, calcium, magnesium, potassium, and trace elements of copper, zinc, selenium, and manganese, as well as such vitamins as the B group, thiamine, niacin, and folate. They also contain phytonutrients, including antioxidants and compounds with oestrogenic activity thought to help in prevention of such hormone-related cancers as breast and prostate and to reduce problems related to menopause, such as osteoporosis. Some of the health benefits of pulses are supported by clinical or epidemiological data, but many are anecdotal or extrapolated from other observations.

Because of their high protein, pulses have been considered "poor man's meat" and are still important dietary components for people who are vegetarian for philosophical or economic reasons. Because of other characteristics, pulses are credited with additional health benefits in developed countries where protein deficit is rarely a problem. Because of the delicious combinations available from this diverse group of plants, they remain popular on menus around the world.

BIBLIOGRAPHY

Diamond, Jared. *Guns, Germs, and Steel: A Short History of Everybody for the Last 13,000 Years.* Random House, 1997.

Fred, Edwin Broun, Ira Lawrence Baldwin, and Elizabeth McCoy. *Root Nodule Bacteria and Leguminous Plants.* Madison, Wis., 1932.

Harlan, Jack. *Crops and Man.* Madison, Wis., 1992.

Harris, David R., and Gordon C. Hillman. *Foraging and Farming: The Evolution of Plant Exploitation.* London, 1989.

Longnecker, Nancy. *Passion for Pulses: A Feast of Beans, Peas, and Lentils from Around the World.* Nedlands, Western Australia, 1999.

Smartt, J. *Grain Legumes: Evolution and Genetic Resources.* Cambridge, 1990.

Tannahill, Reay. *Food in History.* London and New York, 1988.

Zohary, D., and M. Hopf. *Domestication of Plants in the Old World.* Oxford, 1988.

NANCY LONGNECKER

LEISURE INDUSTRY *[This entry contains three subentries, a historical overview, and discussions of travel and tourist industries and the hobbies industry.]*

Historical Overview

Economic historians have only recently begun to study leisure, the world of production rather than consumption having been the key focus of their research. For Adam Smith, for example, what was critical was the productive power of labor and how that might be increased, although Smith did allow that the measure of whether a man was rich or poor was in part the degree to which he could afford to enjoy the "amusements" of life. Work was, for Karl Marx and others, the "essence of man," and Joffre Dumazedier (1967) has argued that the equation of leisure with idleness held sway well into the twentieth century. Today, access to and participation in leisure are birthrights of citizens in the modern industrial and urban world. Poverty, inter alia, is defined as exclusion from, or an inability to access, leisure, such as an inability to have an annual vacation. It was Thorstein Veblen, in *The Theory of the Leisure Class*, which was published in 1925, who first saw the emergence of a leisure class as a mark of the transition in society and economy from primitive barbarism to something higher. But his leisure class was a privileged group—of warriors and priests—set free from normal work by the labors of others.

That leisure, organized and provided, has become a complex of industries—in which all levels of society can participate rather than just a privileged elite—is a relatively new phenomenon of the developed economy. Leisure has now become a central rather than a subordinate concern, of considerable complexity, not merely a rest from work but a dynamic. In a moral sense, leisure has always been approved when it is the fruit of work, a reward that has been earned, and the provision of leisure activities has been used by employers and the state to encourage the work force. The leisure pursuits of a sybaritic elite, empowered by position or inheritance, in contrast, have always attracted understandable hostility. However empowered, the ranks of the consumers have been greatly augmented, and provision for them has become more and more diverse. Leisure activities and leisure industries are rather different: the first are those things that merely occupy time more or less pleasurably when there is nothing better or more pressing to do— the enforced and unchosen "idleness" of the off-seasons in the agricultural year, for example, or industrial depression. The latter are systematic activities organized for profit or at least to use time in a shaped context with defined outcomes, both economic and social.

Elements of Leisure as an Industry. What complicates any consideration of leisure as an industry is that it covers a range of activities, from tourism to sports to hobbies; each of these, in turn, is an umbrella term for a spectrum of activities, which has widened over time. The product is highly differentiated, as is demand: how "free" time is used is a key element in human experience, but one, however, that has been subject to the influence of a range of variables. People's preferences have always varied and continue to vary by age, gender, class, and income; they are also shaped by contemporary norms, context, and geography. Some are essentially solitary activities, others paired or group, yet others tribal or communal. They can be contemplative, or competitive, occasional or obsessively central. Leisure can be productive and educational, or quite the opposite; supportive of the status quo or subversive. What defines "productive" or acceptable is an open question; religious mores have circumscribed both what is legitimate (at one time or another in a particular culture sports, the theater, and gambling all have been under prohibition) and when it may be enjoyed (for example, the strict observance of Sunday as a day of rest). The state has also had its say in favoring some forms of leisure over others. In 1457, the Scottish crown issued a decree that "the golfc and futeball be utterly cried down" (that is, prohibited); according to the Scottish government, too much time was spent on these sports to the neglect of military arts such as archery. Additionally, what is central to one group—foxhunting, bearbaiting—may become anathema to a succeeding generation as moral perspectives shift.

Although it has always existed, the demand for leisure has clearly deepened and widened with economic growth. In response, the provision of leisure has become big business, as significant in terms of investment and employment as manufacturing. Indeed, it can be argued that the more advanced an economy is, the wider and more complex is its range of leisure industries. The provision of leisure has itself become big business and a major source of employment with wide linkages. There are the construction and staffing phases, the erection and operation of hotels, vacation complexes, sporting stadiums, casinos, places of entertainment, fitness centers, and other attractions. Behind them come a range of related and dependent activities: transport services, sporting equipment and clothing stores, souvenir shops, and the specialist press, to name a few, all of whose prosperity is tied to leisure as the leading sector. There are connections to both the legitimate and the illicit economy, given that gambling and betting are closely linked to many sports, through, for example, off-track betting and football pools. The provision of recreational drugs has become an industry that links some of the most backward economies in the world with the most developed. For some regions and localities, leisure has become the main prop of the economy, a kind of monoculture, and, as such, promotion and continuing

prosperity are key concerns. Should there be any downturn, the consequences are severe.

Roots and Expansion of Leisure Industries. The roots of commercial leisure lie in the classical world, in the provision of entertainment for the ruling elites and increasingly for the general populace. The games of Rome stand out as an early example; Christians and animals alike had to be supplied. The medieval period saw the proliferation of fairs and holy days. With the development of a modern economy, most traditional sports and activities either became commercialized or extinct, and the provision was shaped by the level of economic return.

The transformation of a traditional activity is illustrated in the reshaping of hunting. In premodern societies and in less developed societies, as Adam Smith observed, hunting was a central activity necessary to survival, or at least an important supplement to the diet. Although the community rejoiced in the success of the hunters, it generally did not spectate. Later, however, the hunting of game or of some prized animals became a high-status sport, the preserve of the elite, with the rights reserved to the privileged few. The royal deer park and the state reserve were their playgrounds, a pattern to be found in both feudal and totalitarian societies. But the access widened in the nineteenth century: increasingly, what mattered was the ability to pay for sporting rights, and an industry developed, packaged, serviced, and sold. Landowners, as suppliers, wanted the income, middlemen emerged to bring buyers into the market, and soon American millionaires and European industrialists alike, regardless of their social origins, could shoot and fish where they liked—at a price. Economic standing—or its proxy, political office—governed which niche market was accessed. For the rich, there was deer hunting and salmon fishing; for the masses, rat netting and coarse (as opposed to game) fishing.

A number of factors, acting in concert and feeding off each other, can be seen as significant in the expansion of leisure industries. Fundamental, of course, has been the expansion of demand, a function both of rising disposable income and of time available outside the workplace, which allowed an increasing participation by all levels of society, not just the moneyed and leisured elite. This was a general phenomenon in Western economies, with the pattern of change broadly similar.

For the working classes in Great Britain, it was perhaps less the restrictions on the length of the working day that were significant than the arrival of half-day work on Saturday and a less restrictive view of Sunday. Bank holidays helped, as did the extension by legislation of paid holidays in the late 1930s. Improvements in transportation and communication were also critical, allowing the emergence of national and regional activities, opening up new areas, and breaking down regional isolation. The transformation of tourism from an elite experience enjoyed by only the privileged few to a mass movement began in the early nineteenth century with the growth of steamship lines, accelerated with the development of railroads, and was confirmed by the charter flights of the early 1960s. The range of British tourists widened, the better-off ranging farther afield to more exotic and select destinations. Their grandparents had gone to Blackpool or Scarborough; they sought the Costa del Sol.

Sports in Great Britain equally benefited, breaking out from regional to countrywide interest as players and their supporters alike could travel much greater distances. The movement by railway of horses, jockeys, and owners—every major course in Great Britain and Ireland had its own halt or special siding—transformed racing in Britain into a national sport. Travel by air allowed car racing, soccer, and cricket alike to become international sports; in the field of tourism, distant destinations, which once could only have been reached by a long sea cruise, now could be fitted into a much tighter and more intense schedule. And with the teams went their supporters in increasing numbers on package tours.

Changes in technology played their part in the expansion of leisure, by, for example, making access to forms of leisure cheaper, as in the case of golf. The game of golf could trace its history for centuries in Scotland and was played not just by the nobility but also by fishwives. What allowed it to become much more popular was the invention in the 1840s of the gutta-percha ball, which was cheaper than the feathery. In similar fashion, the advent of the box camera changed photography The replacement of the muzzle loader by the breech-loading shotgun and the safety cartridge, which allowed faster and more reliable loading, had an equal impact on sport hunting. Model trains gripped generations of boys (and their fathers); by the late twentieth century, that hobby had scaled up to the rescue and operation of preserved steam locomotives, an important aspect of heritage tourism.

Sometimes developments in technology have been important, none more so than radio and television, which fanned interest in sports for both the traveling and the armchair audience. New technologies have also revolutionized old games: the mechanical arcade has given way to the computer game, and driving and flight simulators have both a commerical and a leisure application. Organizational changes have helped to standardize sports, for example, the Queensberry rules in boxing and the handicapping system in golf. An important innovation has been the development of supporters' organizations and of the companies that feed off their loyalty.

Common to all aspects of commercialized leisure has been the role of marketing and promotion. Advertising has played a major role in the growth of the leisure industry

and in shaping and manipulating consumer desire. Allied to this has been the role of entrepreneurs; the contribution of Thomas Cook to tourism is a familiar example, as well as that of the showman Phineas T. Barnum and his circus tours through the United States and Walt Disney in the movie and amusement park business. Their success is measured in attendance figures and financial returns. Other ventures, in which the state or even local business played a leading role, such as museums and libraries, have had philanthropic and educational objectives in mind, though recently, consumerism, rather than conservation, has become the main emphasis; the museum shop rather than the art gallery is what matters.

No modern economy can be understood without due consideration of the place and importance of leisure and the many industries that directly and indirectly draw on it. Although vulnerable to changes both in the domestic and the world economy, what seems to be a constant is the priority given within household budgets to leisure: the growing importance of the vacation and time set aside for a hobby. Work is now for many only a means to leisure.

BIBLIOGRAPHY

Bailey, Peter. *Leisure and Class in Victorian England: Rational Recreation and the Contest for Control, 1830–1885*. London, 1978.

Briggs, Asa. *Victorian Things*. London, 1988. Wide ranging and great fun either to read, or just to dip into.

Clapson, Mark. *A Bit of a Flutter: Popular Gambling and Victorian Society, c. 1823–1961*. Manchester, 1992.

Dumazedier, Joffre. *Towards a Society of Leisure*. London and New York, 1967. An important foreword by David Rieseman.

Haywood, Les, et al. *Understanding Leisure*. Cheltenham, U.K., 1989. A systematic contemporary introduction to the study of leisure.

Jarvie, Grant, and J. Maguire. *Sport and Leisure in Social Thought*. London, 1994. A review of thinking about leisure from Enlightenment writers onward.

Jones, Stephen G. *Workers at Play: An Economic and Social History of Leisure, 1918–1939*. London, 1986. Looks at developments in the provision of leisure and how, for example, severe unemployment affected demand.

Veblen, Thorstein. *The Theory of the Leisure Class*. London, 1925. A classic still worth attention.

ALASTAIR J. DURIE

Travel and Tourist Industries

Tourism has become one of the world's major economic activities, second perhaps only to oil, the mainstay of some regional economies in the first world and national economies in the third. Any change in tourism—from civil unrest, terrorism, or natural disasters—can and does have the most serious economic consequences, and the foreign tourist has become an unwitting pawn in political affairs. Some countries are elite destinations, others have become mass destinations; a few both receive and send tourists. In some areas, tourism is seasonal, whether at the beach resorts of North Germany or the ski centers of the Alps or

Colorado; in others, a serious attempt has been made to promote year-round travel. Tourism has generated considerable employment and investment through travel agencies, the provision of hotels, recreational, and other facilities. An industry with a wide range of products, some countries are rich in heritage, from stately homes to steam railways; others offer the experience of sun, sea, snow, or scenery.

The history of tourism has a number of problems, not least that of definition. What is tourism? Strictly, a working definition is that it is any form of travel that does not have a commercial focus. The businessman or businesswoman attending a conference abroad is not a tourist (though often claimed by the industry and incorporated in their statistics), but should he or she take time off to play golf or rent a car to look at the local scenery, then business travelers do become tourists. A related problem is that tourism is an umbrella term to cover a wide range of experiences: they may be differentiated by time, activity, and motive—from the eco-tourist in search of whales through an educational cruise to the wine tour, the seaside lounger, or graveyard enthusiast. It can be a group experience, programmed to the minute, or a loose one of hiking, biking, or canoeing. It can be a person alone, a couple, a family, or a focused or unfocused group of strangers. There is, for some reason, a frustrating absence for the economic historian of much coherent long-term quantitative data about the scale, direction, and nature of tourism. Even the recent statistical material is treated with a good deal of suspicion.

History. The roots of tourism go back to the premodern period, an integral part of many religious traditions, whether to Benares for Hindus, Jerusalem for Jews, or Mecca for Muslims. So an early Christian form was the pilgrimage to the Holy Land; a popular French guidebook was translated into English as *The Travels of Sir John Mandeville* (1375), and several other European languages to whet travelers' appetites and inform their itinerary. In the late 1400s, the government of Venice assigned two galleys to take pilgrims east to Palestine. Shrines and healing waters throughout Europe attracted growing numbers, and spa treatment—itself with classical origins—bridged the gap into the post-Reformation world. Although in Europe the Roman Catholic "cure" tradition was continued (and even revived, notably at Lourdes in France from the 1860s), cures became "scientific" rather than miraculous, usually under the direction of physicians rather than priests. The treatments took time, which meant that spa resorts had to provide accommodations for both invalids and their companions. A program of entertainment, as at Bath in England, with reading rooms and theaters, were soon added to the pools and pump rooms in the 1700s. The business of health was to remain an important component in tourism. Resorts such as Vichy in France, Baden-Baden in Germany, Saratoga Springs in the United States, and Buxton in Britain catered to invalids and convalescents, and they often specialized in the treatment of particular conditions. The Riviera became popular as a winter retreat for consumptives. Some health resorts were inland and at high altitude, but from the late 1700s onward, the growing fascination in Europe was with the seaside, from which were to evolve mass resorts, such as Blackpool and Scarborough. Saltwater dipping, rather than swimming, as endorsed by the Prince Regent at Brighton, was regarded as both fashionable and healthy. The beach became a source of entertainment and amusement for all ages.

Not all tourists were sickly; some traveled for sport. The Highlands of Scotland—with grouse, deer and salmon—became a hunters' playground for the rich or those well-connected. Big-game hunting in India or Africa attracted safari enthusiasts, though most followed their exploits in print, from the safety of an armchair. A much larger constituency were those interested in the scenic, who set out in search of the picturesque in nature or ancient ruins, fascinated by history, literature, architecture and antiquities, especially those of ancient Egypt and the classical world. The Grand Tour of the Continent, primarily of France and Italy, developed during the 1700s as an essential part of the education of young men who could afford it. Under the supervision of a tutor, the tour might last months or longer and might include study at a university. A Scottish banker, Robert Herries, pioneered the creation of a network of agencies, from the Channel ports to the Mediterranean, where travelers' bank notes could be cashed for local currency.

Tourism, which had been until then the preserve of the monied and leisured, changed radically during the 1800s. An important shift occurred when the Napoleonic Wars, by closing off travel in the rest of Europe, turned the British toward the discovery of their own country. Romanticism converted remote locales into places of fascination rather than fear, and Romantic literature peopled them with embellished or invented heroes and ruffians. New forms of transport allowed greater numbers of tourists to travel at lower cost with more predictable schedules than previously, thus reinforcing existing destinations and penetrating new areas. Grand *chaussées* made travel in France by private coach or public diligence quite tolerable, as did the turnpikes in Britain. The paddle-steamer, which made its appearance in the Clyde and on the Thames from about 1812, made possible and popular the river or estuary "pleasure excursion." The steamboat, whether for business, pleasure, or gambling (as on the Mississippi), was to continue to be a major influence on travel in North America, but in most countries it was the railroad that took tourism to new levels. There were the upper-class passengers who traveled first class, with their servants and extensive luggage, to a select resort; professional families from the larger cities, who migrated to the seaside for the summer (often with father returning during the week to his work); even working-class day trippers, who were sometimes rowdy and liable to ruffle "social" convention, with lack of respect for separate-sex bathing, the Sabbath, or sobriety. Excursions, whether organized by industry or Sunday schools, charitable or political groups, became part of summer life for many. Transport change and tourism have always been closely intertwined: the coming of bicycles, motor transport, and air services also exercised profound effects on the direction, scale, and degree of tourism—sometimes at the expense of domestic resorts. The charter flights of the 1960s led to an exodus of British and German holidaymakers to Mediterranean resorts, where the sun could be guaranteed. The flow of American students and tourists to Europe, which the steamboats had began in the later 1800s, was equally greatly increased; history and culture drew them, as did, if they were of European stock, an interest in their ethnic origins.

As the tourist industry grew and diversified, the level of competition increased, unrestrained by any cartel arrangements or price collusion, as was common in other industries. There were those resorts and localities that remained "select," which could count on a steady clientele, loyal from year to year. Literary tourism—to the Land of Scott, the Home of Burns, or Shakespeare's Birthplace—was anchored and relatively durable. Elsewhere, the provision of facilities, tailored to the tastes and incomes of visitors, became of increasing importance or a resort might slip out of favor. There had to be good hotels and clean lodgings with bathrooms, not grubby inns; visitors wanted museums, aquariums, theaters, bookshops, and concert halls; also casinos and racetracks; piers and promenades; golf courses, tennis courts, and swimming pools, as well as clean beaches and en-suite facilities. The continental resorts tended to be noticeably different from the British in their provision—culturally relaxed rather than carefully respectable. Private capital put up most of the necessary finance, but development was piecemeal. Some incomers designed comprehensive schemes, but not always successfully: the attempt in the early 1860s by the speculator Leopold Lewis to create a "Brighton of Ireland" at Youghal, which he had bought from the duke of Devonshire, served only to push him into spectacular business failure. Local administrations in the tourist resorts became increasingly involved in the shaping of the development, although often they were caught between the pressure of those enthusiastic for growth, such as local hoteliers and shopkeepers, and those, especially retired newcomers, who disliked the cost and disturbance.

The extent of national governments' interest and involvement varied, but in Britain the attitude was one of almost complete disinterest—not until 1929 did the treasury provide even a modest subsidy to the Travel Association of Great Britain. By contrast, in Germany, the State Kraft durch Freude handled more than 9 million holidaymakers in 1937. In Italy, from 1931, there was the Commissariat for Tourism; in Switzerland, a National Association for the Promotion of Tourist Traffic; and in Canada, a state-funded Travel Bureau was created in 1934 to coordinate the promotion of tourism at both the provincial and the national level. Japan set up a network of agencies, including a Publicity Association and a Board of Tourist Industry. There was eventually to be a radical reappraisal in Britain of the state's role after World War II, though amidst many other demands, spending on the renovation of tourist attractions did not receive much priority despite the desperate need for American dollars. In the late 1960s, comprehensive legislation brought into being the British Tourist Authority, which was given responsibility for the marketing of tourism in Britain. The balance of responsibility for tourism, between private and state initiative, and national or regional effort, varied from country to country, and over time. In the United States, the national park system advertised for campers and many of the states opened their own tourist bureaus—offering maps, brochures, and discounts for restaurants, shops, museums, and local attractions.

In the nineteenth century, the promotion of resorts and localities was left to the resort administrations themselves through their advertising committees or to the railway and steamship companies that served them, who commissioned an increasing range of attractive guidebooks and posters. Publishers such as Murrays and Baedeckers offered handbooks that both reflected and shaped tourist flows, supplemented by private travelogues and journals. Travel firms soon produced their own literature; Thomas Cook was described in 1865 by Lydia Fowler, who had travelled with one of his tours, as the "King and Father of excursions." The particular niche that Cook exploited with consummate success was the provision of supervised tours run to a very tight schedule, costed exactly—matters of real concern to those for whom holiday travel was a new experience, whose time and income alike were limited. Cook's first tour, in July 1841, was a temperance group's daytrip. He was soon ranging farther afield—to Wales and the Lake District, to Scotland with his Tartan Tours, to the Continent, and eventually Palestine and Egypt, where his firm operated a fleet of tourist steamers on the Nile River. Cook and his son had an eye on the growing American market; a partnership with an American (who was a fellow temperance enthusiast) foundered, but the firm continued.

The flow of Americans to Europe was of gathering significance in the late 1800s. The wealthy traveled first class on the great transatlantic oceanliners, but the steamship

TRAVEL FOR PLEASURE. Passengers sunbathing on the deck of a Carnival cruise ship, 1988. (© Jacques Chenet/Woodfin Camp and Associates, New York)

companies found ever increasing numbers willing to cross in less luxurious conditions, in second class, or in steerage (later renamed "tourist" class). In 1913, some 250,000 American tourists, many of whom were women, crossed the Atlantic (as against 50,000 in 1880) "doing Europe" for educational and cultural purposes. U.S. colleges organized study tours, and ethnic "societies" or "clubs" of Norwegians or Scots, returned to explore the land from which they and their families had emigrated. This flow was brought to an abrupt end by the outbreak of war in August 1914, which stranded thousands of tourists in Europe and for whom emergency rescue operations were mounted. Not until 1919, did transatlantic tourism resume. There were serious effects. There was some limited compensation in the form of battlefield tours, but longer distance tourism in the interwar years was buffeted by the economic context of difficulty, depression, and exchange rates. Domestic tourism in Britain held up well: the established resorts attracted large numbers—Blackpool 7 million visitors a year—and new forms such as caravaning and holiday camps become popular. The passing in 1937 of the Holidays with Pay Act should have been beneficial in Britain, but it appears that many of those benefited were too poor to convert time off.

World War II ended tourism in Europe from 1939 to 1946. Since the war, tourism—for all its problems of unpredictable fluctuation and seasonality—has risen high on the agenda of many nations as a good source of local income and employment. It does not go unchallenged: there is increasing criticism of its environmental and cultural impact. Two key policy objectives of developed countries have been both to persuade more people to explore their own country and to attract foreign visitors, since air travel has brought so many destinations into reach. The balance between public and private finance has varied from place to place, and country to country, but travel firms have done much to develop the industry and package tours through specific programs. A few traditional forms of tourism have held their popularity, such as golfing holidays; others have enjoyed a revival—luxury cruising or spa treatments, to name but two. There is a life cycle to tourism: countries, regions, resorts, and activities rise. But for a variety of reasons they can and do fall, and nothing is more difficult to reverse than the decay of a once-popular destination.

BIBLIOGRAPHY

Black, Jeremy. *The British Abroad: The Grand Tour in the Eighteenth Century*. Stroud, 1992. A comprehensive account that deals with all aspects of the tour, including numbers, routes, and transport.

Booker, John. *Travellers' Money*. Stroud, 1994. An examination of the mechanisms of money supply for tourists and other travelers.

Cooper, C., et al. *Tourism: Principles and Practice*. London, 1993. A comprehensive textbook that provides a clear review of key themes and concepts.

Durie, Alastair J. *Scotland for the Holidays? A History of Tourism in Scotland, 1780–1939*. East Linton, 2000. Looks at the development of tourism of all types—scenic, literary, sporting, and for health—in Scotland.

Inglis, Andrea. *Beside the Seaside: Victorian Resorts in the Nineteenth Century*. Melbourne, 1999. An Australian perspective on the development of resorts in the Melbourne area.

Levenstein, Harvey. *Seductive Journey: American Tourists in France from Jefferson to the Jazz Age.* Chicago, 1998. A splendid account that blends a knowledge of broad trends and patterns with a wide use of contemporary evidence.

Lockwood, Allison. *Passionate Pilgrims: The American Traveler in Britain, 1800–1914.* New York, 1981. Uses an extraordinary range of diaries and travel accounts to give a picture of the experience of travel on the Atlantic crossing and once arrived.

Mandler, Peter. *The Fall and Rise of the Stately Home.* New Haven and London, 1997. Shows why, when, and for whose benefit the British great houses became tourist attractions.

Morgan, N. J., and A. Pritchard. *Power and Politics at the Seaside.* Exeter, 1999. An important study and examination of how the popular resorts of Devon, England, responded to the challenges of the twentieth century.

Sillitoe, Alan. *Leading the Blind: A Century of Guide Book Travel, 1815–1914.* London, 1995. A review of what guides provided in advice and warning for travelers in Europe.

Walton, J. K. *The English Seaside Resort: A Social History, 1780–1939.* Leicester, 1983. Explores the rise of English resorts, both mass and select.

Withey, Lynne. *Grand Tours and Cook's Tours: A History of Leisure Travel, 1750 to 1915.* New York, 1997. Makes good use of Thomas Cook archival material, emphasizes the work of other entrepreneurs, and relates the rise of destinations outside Europe.

ALASTAIR DURIE

Hobbies Industry

Among leisure activities, hobbies are conventionally defined as individual pursuits, usually unconnected with one's main income-generating occupation, and carried out primarily at home, although they may also be developed through various organized associations. Hobbies are generally classified into the three groups of growing/nurturing, collecting, and making. Such activities have generally failed to spawn producers of sufficient size or distinction to warrant separate identification in schemes of industrial classification. Accordingly, studies of the sector have tended to concentrate on consumption rather than on production.

For the most part, industries catering to hobbies are a product of nineteenth-century modernization. Before the Industrial Revolution, only the relatively wealthy few had either the means or the time to indulge a practical interest in nature; to gather collections of books, paintings, furniture, fossils, antiquities, and other artifacts; or to engage personally in carpentry or needlework. Those who serviced this very restricted market did so either within a framework of individual patronage, as was frequently the case with artists, or more commonly as an activity marginal to the principal means of earning a living. In this latter group might be included the Swiss and French clockmakers who also produced complex and expensive automata for adult collectors, as well as the British printers, who in the course of the eighteenth century, began to produce both board games and jigsaw puzzles.

Industrialization was a major stimulus to hobby activities; it significantly raised the number of potential consumers by increasing disposable income and freed time through the gradual reduction of work hours. Consequently, the market for leisure activities of most kinds, including sports, tourism, and popular entertainment, became wider, deeper, and increasingly commercialized, especially in the industrializing nations of western Europe and the United States. Furthermore, the process opened up new hobby possibilities through the development of innovative technologies, such as electricity and photography, or the improvement of existing ones like printing. Indirectly, too, industrialization also served to extend the knowledge base for, and consequent interest in, the collection of artifacts—both ancient and modern—the breeding of small animals and plants, and the pursuit of various home crafts. The increasing range of goods associated with modernization soon provided additional collectables. Philately (stamp collecting) was well established in Britain by the 1860s, beginning only a few years after the introduction of the penny post in 1840. Numismatists (coin collectors) had been collecting from the time of the Renaissance, but their numbers increased greatly in the nineteenth century, with specialist journals available in Britain, the United States, and Germany. By the end of that century, hobby enthusiasts in Britain, arguably the most advanced industrial nation of the time, had at their disposal a burgeoning press and numerous clubs for gardeners, cat and dog owners, pigeon fanciers, cage-bird breeders, model builders, woodworkers, stamp collectors, and amateur photographers. Even children's toys attracted adult collectors, such as Bassett Lowke's model trains, Frank Hornby's Meccano sets, and various toy soldiers from Germany (Heyde), France (Mignot), and Britain (William Britain)—all finding ready international markets before World War I. Similar enthusiasms were developing in most industrial societies, and even Japan, a relatively late developer, had sufficient stamp collectors to support a specialist magazine, published in Yokohama, from 1913 onward.

During the twentieth century, hobby activity became much more universal as levels of prosperity in industrial nations continued to rise and as industrialization spread. Hobby activities evolved in response to fashion and technological advances. Thus the development of radio (wireless) provided a new and relatively inexpensive interest for amateur enthusiasts, while photography was made easier by the ever-increasing simplification and sophistication of smaller, lighter cameras and rolls of film (instead of glass plates). Model-making (especially of ships and airplanes) was enhanced by the development of new sources of power and simplified by the advent of new plastics amenable to injection or extrusion moulding. A British firm, Airfix, led the way in this field, although by the late twentieth century it faced growing international competition from Revell, ERTL, and Tamiya. If the collecting of coins, stamps, and fine china retained their popularity, such other items as film, music, and sports programs, photographs, and posters; matchbooks and matchbox labels; bottles; model and full-size "classic" vehicles, and memorabilia of all types—from kitchen wares to fabrics to household machines—attracted collectors. There was, as well, an upsurge of interest in decorating with and collecting antiques (which are defined as at least one hundred years old). Transport improvements, particularly in the second half of the century, allowed those with interests in horticulture or wildlife to acquire ever more exotic species of plants, as well as birds and fish—both stuffed and live. Similarly, the Japanese art of *bonsai*, familiar in the West since the time of the Meiji Restoration period, became a popular hobby pursuit from the early 1950s onward—as did gardens full of "Old Roses."

Despite both a widening range of activities and an increasing number of devotees, specialist hobby industries were slow to emerge. Demand for recreational products was always relatively small and elastic, so hobbyists usually had to rely on industries whose main output was directed elsewhere. The first national occupational census of Britain, in 1831, included few classifications pertinent to leisure and none relating to hobbies, save perhaps antique dealing. By 1914, the only hobby clearly linked to a significant industry in Britain was photography, brought within everyone's grasp after the 1888 marketing by the U.S. inventor George Eastman of the simple Kodak camera. His success, first in the large and relatively wealthy U.S. market, then in Britain and worldwide, made him (through the Eastman Kodak Company of New York) the first tycoon to build a business empire based—at least in part—on the hobby sector. By the end of the twentieth century, other large concerns had emerged, for example in horticulture (seeds and landscape gardening, as well as a small but thriving *bonsai* industry in California) and in the manufacture of pet food, needlework, and artists' materials, although most firms' main activities were directed toward the commercial, rather than the leisure, market. Generally, the specialist industries that did appear were small in scale and highly specialized. Arguably, therefore, the most significant developments were in distribution rather than in manufacturing.

By 2001, most of the world's main industrial cities could boast one or two specialist hobby shops, while the best-known international auction houses were able to specialize in antiques and collectibles, both locally and from the 1990s online. Web-sites for all these goods, and others, have become commonplace on the Internet, and e-commerce provides hobbyists, collectors, and enthusiasts a new way to interact globally. Computer use has also created a new form of hobbyist, not to be confused with "hackers." Symbolically, perhaps, the oldest and most widely known name associated with any hobby—the stamp dealer Stanley Gibbons (founded 1856)—remains essentially a distributor and publisher.

BIBLIOGRAPHY

British Toy and Hobby Association. *The Toy Industry in the United Kingdom*. London, 1992. Covers the hobby sector despite its title.

McKibbin, Ross. "Work and Hobbies in Britain, 1880–1950." In *The Working Class in British History*, edited by J. Winter. Cambridge, 1983.

Owen, John D. *The Price of Leisure*. Montreal, 1970. Includes discussion of U.S. hobby industries.

Walton, John, and James Walvin. *Leisure in Britain, 1700–1939*. Manchester, 1983. Good on the context in which hobbies developed.

Ward, Arthur. *Airfix*. London, 1999. A popular but informative history of a major world hobby firm.

KENNETH D. BROWN

LENIN, VLADIMIR ILICH (1870–1924), Russian revolutionary.

Lenin was one of the most influential figures of the twentieth century. He was a Russian revolutionary leader, a communist, and a political theorist. A militant and dogmatic interpreter of the philosopher Karl Marx and the creator of the new Marxist-Leninist ideology, Lenin led the October Revolution that brought into existence the world's first socialist state. His communist archetype of a one-party state based on common beliefs, discipline, and centralism survived for more than seven decades and spread within a generation to eastern Europe and other parts of the world.

Vladimir Ilich Ulyanov was born in 1870 in Simbirsk to a close family. His father was a school inspector and later a director of a public school, and his mother was a self-educated woman who was devoted to her children. Lenin, as Ulyanov later became known, was a lively, energetic, self-confident, and impatient young man and an exemplary student. After his expulsion from Kazan University for revolutionary activities, Lenin began to read European revolutionary literature and was especially influenced by Nikolai Chernyshevsky. In 1893, two years after becoming a lawyer, Lenin moved to St. Petersburg, where he joined an illegal group propagating Marxism among workers; he soon became its leader. One of the founders of the League of Struggle for the Emancipation of the Working Class in St. Petersburg, Lenin was arrested, then sentenced to exile in Siberia until 1900. While in Siberia, he continued to study the works of Marx and Friedrich Engels, wrote books and pamphlets, and married N. K. Krupskaya, whom he had met a few years earlier in St. Petersburg. In 1900, he left for Zurich, then for Munich, where he set the revolutionary newspaper *Iskra* (The Spark). Lenin lived in western Europe until 1917 except for a period of two

V. I. LENIN. "A specter is haunting Europe—the specter of communism." Lenin at the tribune quotes the opening sentence of Marx and Engel's *Communist Manifesto*. Russian poster, 1920. (Central Revolutionary Museum, Moscow, Russia/Snark/Art Resource, NY)

years in the 1905 revolution, during which he returned to Russia.

Lenin held that the rise of capitalism is a necessary condition both for economic growth and for a subsequent revolution. On the one hand, he favored capitalist farming to communal ownership of land and believed that capitalist large-scale machine industry brought about technical progress and development. He thought that the move toward capitalist farming created markets for manufactured goods, food, and clothing and sparked economic growth. On the other hand, he predicted that technical progress and capitalist relationships would result in a decrease in wages in cities and frustration in rural areas, which would, in turn, spark a revolution aiming to destroy capitalism. In 1902, Lenin published his controversial book *What Is to Be Done?* in which he preached a disciplined party based on common ideology and secretive political activities and pushed for a revolution led by the intellectual elite, who would lead the working masses to a victory over czarism.

His hard line of a militant and centralized party with active membership caused a split in the Russian Social Democratic Labor Party in 1903 into Lenin's Bolsheviks (Majority) and Mensheviks (Minority), and the two struggled until World War I. In 1905, after czarist troops killed a group of workers in a peaceful procession in St. Petersburg in what came to be known as Bloody Sunday, the working-class masses went on violent strikes, indicating the beginning of the 1905 revolution. The revolution lasted more than two years, but it eventually failed.

When World War I erupted, Lenin opposed it and claimed it was imperialist and bourgeois. In 1916, he wrote *Imperialism: The Highest Stage of Capitalism*, in which he pointed out imperialism's tendency to create monopolies that overpowered resources in order to overcome its self-destruction, which led to the exploitation of underdeveloped countries by a few imperialist ones. According to Lenin, the less developed countries would start a revolution to overcome the exploitation. In March 1917, in a response to bad economic conditions, some two hundred thousand workers went on strike, causing the resignation of the czar. In April of that year, Lenin wrote *April Theses*, in which he forged a strategy that would allow the Bolsheviks to seize power.

In October 1917, Lenin led the October Revolution and became the head of the new Soviet government. He nationalized banks, large factories, and later land and talked about forming a dictatorship of the proletariat. At first, he promised to bring land and peace to Russian peasants, workers, and soldiers. He abolished all private land ownership, gave peasants the right to take over land, issued a decree that allowed workers in enterprises to supervise their managers, and called on all governments to end hostility. In 1918, he signed the Brest-Litovsk peace treaty with Germany and withdrew Russia from the war. But Lenin, believing that a dictator was above the law, was not reluctant to impose his will and to crush those who were not in agreement with him. Following the treaty, the Russian economy entered a period of crisis, and Lenin called for a central and disciplined party that would be the only one to set policies and to implement them. The civil war of 1918–1920 destroyed the country's resources, and the threat of starvation in Russian cities emerged. Lenin and his party began a policy of "war communism," which entailed food confiscation (farmers were forced to deliver grain to towns). In 1919, the Comintern, or Socialist International, was established. It was based on disciplined and inflexible beliefs and soon served as a tool for the Soviet government's foreign policy.

By 1921, Lenin had realized that the regime might be in danger unless a change occurred. The oppressive policies created disincentives for agricultural production, and much of the grain-growing land was out of production. Moreover, 1921 saw a severe drought in southern Russia. Lenin introduced the New Economic Policy (NEP), which was a semiprivatization of agricultural production. The NEP was designed to encourage peasants to sell their products by allowing them, after paying a tax-in-kind, to trade in local markets. Although the NEP seemed inconsistent with Marxist ideas, it is believed to have revived the Russian economy and to have saved the new regime from collapse and the country from famine.

History remembers Lenin as the founder of the Soviet Union, a ruthless leader of Russia, and an important Marxist theorist.

BIBLIOGRAPHY

Allen, Robert C. *Farm to Factory: A Reinterpretation of the Soviet Industrial Revolution*. Unpublished ms.

Desai, Meghnad, ed. *Lenin's Economic Writings*. London, 1989.

Lenin, Vladimir I. *The Development of Capitalism in Russia*. Moscow, 1899.

Lenin, Vladimir I. *What Is to Be Done?* (1902). Translated by S. V. Utechin and Patricia Utechin. Oxford, 1963.

Lenin, Vladimir I. *Imperialism: The Highest Stage of Capitalism*. Moscow, 1975.

Lenin, Vladimir I. *April Theses*. Moscow, 1917.

Service, Robert. *Lenin: A Political Life*. 3 vols. Bloomington, Ind., 1985–1995.

Service, Robert. *Lenin: A Biography*. Cambridge, Mass., 2000.

Theen, Rolf H. W. *Lenin: Genesis and Development of a Revolutionary*. Philadelphia, 1973.

RAN ABRAMITZKY

LE ROY LADURIE, EMMANUEL (born 1929), French historian who has contributed to many fields of history, including economic history.

Ladurie is one of the most influential members of the so-called *Annales* school, the group of historians associated with the French journal *Annales*. Like other members of this school, Ladurie has focused on late-medieval and early-modern France; but his work has had an impact on many other fields because of his creative use of historical evidence.

The work that first established Ladurie's reputation was his two-volume study of peasants in southern France, *Les paysans de Languedoc* (Paris, 1966). It made innovative use of a variety of historical documents, especially local land registers that had been compiled to help assess taxes. Thanks to these land registers, Ladurie traced changes in population and the size of landholding, which he then combined with data about agricultural output derived from tithe records. Once all this evidence was assembled, it told a Malthusian story, a story of diminishing returns as rising population pressed against barriers to increases in agricultural output. The barriers included: technological rigidities, oppressive taxes, and shortages of capital; hidebound peasant mentalities and the lack of an entrepreneurial spirit; and, finally, a population growth that, combined with partible inheritance, reduced farms to an inefficient size. According to Ladurie, these barriers remained unyielding until the middle of the eighteenth century.

Ladurie extended the same Malthusian story to the rest of France in a set of collective studies of tithe records. Once again, he innovated, this time by using tithe records to study the evolution of agricultural production for all of France from the end of the Middle Ages to the late-eighteenth century. This work has been criticized (notably, by the historian Michel Morineau) because the tithe records are not always reliable, and because they often omit new crops and output from livestock. Still, the Mal-

thusian story became a staple of French and European social and economic history, particularly because Ladurie retold it convincingly in two synthetic works on the French peasantry. It has remained important despite attacks from the Marxist historian Robert Brenner, who argued that population growth in itself could never have the explanatory power that the Malthusian story implied.

Ladurie has been an innovator with other evidence as well. He was one of the first historians to study the effect of climate on preindustrial agriculture, employing evidence about wine harvests as a proxy for weather conditions. He initiated historical anthropometrics (the study of changes of stature as a measure of well-being) with a study of French army recruits. In his international bestseller, *Montaillou, village occitan de 1294 à 1324* (Paris, 1975), he managed to re-create the life of an entire medieval village, by bringing an anthropologist's eye to inquisition records. Other scholars had read these same inquisition documents, but unlike Ladurie, none of them had realized that they could be used to reconstruct a world that had been lost for seven centuries, a real mark of his skill as a historian.

BIBLIOGRAPHY

Aron, Jean-Paul, Paul Dumont, and Emmanuel Le Roy Ladurie. *Anthropologie du conscrit français*. Paris, 1972.

Le Roy Ladurie, Emmanuel. *Times of Feast, Times of Famine: A History of the Climate since the Year 1000*, translated by Barbara Bray. New York, 1971. English edition of *Histoire du climat depuis l'an mil* (Paris, 1967).

Le Roy Ladurie, Emmanuel. *The Peasants of Languedoc*, translated by John Day. Urbana, 1974. Abridged English edition of French work published in 1966.

Le Roy Ladurie, Emmanuel. *Montaillou: The Promised Land of Error*, translated by Barbara Bray. New York, 1978. English edition of French work published in 1975.

Le Roy Ladurie, Emmanuel. *The Territory of the Historian*, translated by Ben Reynolds and Sian Reynolds. Chicago, 1979. English edition of *Le territoire de l'historien*, 2 vols. (Paris, 1973–1978).

PHILIP T. HOFFMAN

LEVANT *[This entry contains seven subentries, an overview; discussions of the economic history of the Levant during the ancient period, Roman and Byzantine periods, and Islamic rule; and the economic history of modern Lebanon, of Palestine during the English mandate, and of modern Syria.]*

General Overview

The term *Levant* has been used to describe, at the greatest extent, the coasts of modern Turkey, Cyprus, Syria, Lebanon, Israel, and Egypt as well as the Greek Islands of the Aegean Sea. It was used in this sense by Wilhelm Heyd, a nineteenth-century pioneer in the study of the medieval Levant trade. A more restricted use of the term *Levant trade* concentrates on the commerce of the shores from

Antioch (Antakya) to Alexandria and is often applied by historians of the medieval and early modern periods, such as Eliyahu Ashtor. Generally the term refers to the trade in this region of Western merchants mainly from Venice, Genoa, Pisa, and Barcelona in the medieval period, trade that did not penetrate far inland (Aleppo was the principal inland center of Italian trade within northern Syria). In the early modern period Italian merchants were joined by Dutch, English, and other North European merchants as the Mediterranean became more closely tied to navigation in the oceans beyond.

The Levant trade had long antecedents. In the Bronze Age, Phoenician merchants, natives of the area that corresponds fairly closely with modern Lebanon, sailed from Tyre and Sidon across the Mediterranean and even as far as southern England in search of tin to use with copper from Cyprus in bronze wares. They set up bases in Carthage (Qart-Hadasht, "the New City") and other centers along the coasts of Sicily, Sardinia, and Spain, and were the first Levant traders whose activities are known in detail. Links to the Etruscans ensured that choice ivories and other luxuries were exchanged for base metals from the western Mediterranean. In many ways this established the character of exchanges for millennia. Luxury items from the East were in demand in less-sophisticated Western societies, and the inhabitants of the Levant for their part were short of raw materials for their industries.

In the Roman period the Levant trade also was characterized by the massive exportation of wheat from Egypt. But this traffic declined greatly by the twelfth century, when the inhabitants of Crusades Palestine often received wheat from the Norman kingdom of Sicily instead. By the late Middle Ages, Europe took the industrial lead, supplying various textiles to Levantine markets.

Following its foundation in the fourth century BCE, Alexandria maintained a dominant role in the Levant trade. During the Middle Ages it was the principal port of transshipment for spices from the Indian Ocean carried through the Red Sea for transfer to western Europe. Acre (modern Akko, Israel) was a rival in the period of the Crusades, as was Beirut under the Egyptian Mamluks. However, in the sixteenth century the role of the Levant trade changed with the opening of the Portuguese route to the Indies, which enabled European merchants to bypass Alexandria. Later still the opening of the Suez Canal in the late nineteenth century reaffirmed the strategic role of Egypt as a link between the Mediterranean and the Indian Ocean and tied that country to a buildup of French and British political and commercial interests in the region.

BIBLIOGRAPHY

Ashtor, Eliyahu. *Levant Trade in the Later Middle Ages*. Princeton, 1983.
Culican, William. *The First Merchant Venturers: The Ancient Levant in History and Commerce*. London, 1966.
Heyd, Wilhelm. *Histoire du commerce du Levant*. Translated by Furcy Raynaud, 2 vols. Leipzig, Germany, 1923.

DAVID ABULAFIA

Ancient Period

The Levant in a narrow geographical sense comprises the coastal regions of present-day Israel, Lebanon, and Syria. But this area is closely linked politically and economically with its hinterland, extending east to the borders of the Syrian-Arabian steppe. The history of the ancient Levant, which extends from the fourth millennium until the end of Achaemenid rule in 330 BCE, is well documented for most of the third millennium, at least, in archaeological sources. From the twenty-fourth century, BCE they are complemented by written sources from several localities. The texts were written in different languages and writing systems: those from twenty-fourth-century Ebla, in an Old West-Semitic dialect; those from Alalakh, from the eighteenth to the fourteenth century, and from Ugarit, from the fourteenth and thirteenth centuries, are in Akkadian, the oldest known Semitic language used in Mesopotamia. All were written in cuneiform; but some of the texts from Ugarit used an alphabet based on the cuneiform writing system. The Aramaic, Phoenician, and Hebrew texts of the first millennium BCE were written in the early Semitic alphabet. Only the palace archives from Ebla, Alalakh, and Ugarit contain substantial numbers of administrative and legal texts as well as letters that reflect directly on economic affairs.

Historical Geography. Throughout its long history, the ancient Levant consisted of several smaller or larger palace-centered states that often encompassed only the territory of an urban settlement and its immediate hinterland. Such political fragmentation was due to the landscape, which was characterized by a coastal region and adjacent mountainous and hilly areas or mountain ranges interspersed by pockets of flatlands or elevated plains of varying size.

The backbone of Levantine economy was rain-fed agriculture and animal husbandry. The chief products were cereals; others were fruit, wine, olive oil, and wool. The pattern of economic organization was dimorphic, with two distinct economic spheres, rural and urban. The rural sphere with its village communities—independent or integrated in the palace households—represented a peasant economy that produced cash crops, beyond mere subsistence needs; and it interacted with the urban sphere of the elites, who depended on dues from the rural hinterland for their consumptive needs.

The exorbitant wealth of Levantine cities was based on their role as intermediaries in long-distance trade and their export of the region's processed natural products.

The substantial profits from long-distance trade (between 100 and 200 percent or more) resulted from a demand-and-supply pattern between different regions of the Aegean and the Near East in which specific goods and materials were not available.

Roads and Routes. The Levant is situated on the crossroads of the main overland trading routes from Mesopotamia and beyond in the east, from Anatolia in the north, from Egypt and the Arabian peninsula in the south, and the maritime routes from the Aegean in the west. A northern route extended from Assyria (northeastern Iraq) on a path south, of the Taurus range that separates the Anatolian plateau from Syria. In crossing the Euphrates near Carchemish it branched off into two routes: one leading into Anatolia, and the other continuing to Aleppo, ancient Halab, and Ebla. From Aleppo it led to Ugarit on the shores of the Mediterranean. This major east-west route was followed not only by traders but also by conquering armies from Mesopotamia, invading northern Syria in the east, from the late twenty-fourth and early twenty-third centuries up to the advent of Assyrian and Babylonian rulers during the first millennium BCE. Later the "King's Road" of the Achaemenid Empire followed the same course, in part, linking the capital cities of the realm—that is, Sardis in western Anatolia with Susa and Persepolis in Iran. Finally, en route to India, Alexander the Great used the routes through Assyria and Babylonia, as did medieval traders and then the railroad tracks at the beginning of the twentieth century CE. An alternate route from Babylonia to northern Syria followed the course of the Euphrates, branching off at the river bend near present-day Meskene (ancient Emar) into two routes: one following the river up to Carchemish and from there into Anatolia; the other, leading to Aleppo.

The southbound route from Aleppo avoided the coastal areas because the mountains often extended directly to the shores of the Mediterranean, making overland travel extremely difficult. Thus it followed an inland path via Hama on the Orontes, Qatna, and the Beq'a Valley between Lebanon and Antilebanon to Hazor in northern Palestine and then to the coastal plain of Palestine and Egypt. At Qatna another branch continued to Damascus and from there east of the Jordan River through Transjordania to the Gulf of Aqaba. In the Hebrew Bible this stretch is also called "King's Road." During the first millennium this route, known as the "Frankincense Road," extended southward along the west coast of the Arabian peninsula.

Another major route from the middle Euphrates region traversed the Syrian steppe to continue, via the oasis Tadmur (later Palmyra), either to Damascus or Qatna and from there to the coast north of Byblos. Palmyra, Qatna, and Damascus occupied strategic positions in the trade network of middle and southern Syria, thus making them rich and powerful in different periods of Syrian history.

Byblos. In Byblos, the earliest occupational remains date to around 5000 BCE. Trade relations between the Levant and Egypt, first attested to in the twenty-seventh century BCE, were concentrated in Byblos for nearly two millennia. Trade with Mesopotamia is first documented in the twenty-second or twenty-first century BCE.

Ebla. The palace archives of Ebla (40 km south of Aleppo), with more than 15,000 administrative texts, permit us to reconstruct the history and economy of a territorial state in northern Syria controlling the plain of Aleppo in the twenty-third century. The economy of Ebla was organized as a complex palace or *oikos* economy, indicated by a highly developed bookkeeping system. The palace controlled all human and material resources within the state. The self-sustaining and independent village communities, which had been an earlier form of societal and economic organization, had become integrated into the patriarchal state as dependent units of production. The basis of the Eblaite economy was agriculture and animal husbandry. Bountiful cereal harvest and the outputs of fruit and olive trees sustained a population of about 20,000 people. In addition, the documents from the palace archives show that Ebla was the center of a far-reaching exchange network that extended northward into Anatolia toward middle Syria in the south, and eastward to the upper Habul River and to Emar (near present-day Meskene) on the Euphrates and beyond to the city of Mari on the border with Iraq. In the twenty-third century BCE Ebla was destroyed by the Mesopotamian ruler Naramsin.

Yamkhad. Because of a scarcity of written sources, our knowledge of northern Syria is limited to what can be gleaned from the texts from Mari (between 1780 and 1765 BCE). By now Halab/Aleppo, capital of the state of Yamkhad, had established itself as the hub for overland trade in northern Syria. Yamkhad controlled most of northern Syria up to the middle Euphrates, including the city of Emar. Halab was conquered by the Hittite king Mursili I around 1590 BCE; but under the name Aleppo it continued to play a major role in this region's economy throughout the Middle Ages until modern times.

Alalakh. The city of Alalakh (32 km east of Antakya, Turkey) in the Amuq plain on the upper Orontes flourished during the late eighteenth century and again in the fourteenth century BCE as the center of a highly productive and stable agricultural area that used natural precipitation as well as the waters of the Orontes for additional irrigation. Mural paintings in Cretan style in the eighteenth-century palace offer evidence of close relations with the Aegean world. Alalakh was destroyed by the so-called "Sea People" at the end of the thirteenth century BCE.

Ugarit. Ugarit (near present-day Lataqiyah)—whose earliest settlement took place during the sixth millennium BCE—was one of the important trading centers on the

Levantine coast, certainly from the eighteenth century until its destruction by the Sea People at the end of the thirteenth century. The palace archives indicate trading relations with other coastal towns as well as with the Hittite kingdom in Anatolia and with Egypt. Intensive trade relations with the Aegean, especially with Cyprus, are attested by texts and Minoan pottery found in Ugarit. From the sixteenth century BCE Ugarit found itself at the interface between the spheres of influence of Egypt and the Hittite kingdom. In particular, its kings tried to take advantage of their position in controlling trade with Cyprus; but during the fourteenth and thirteenth centuries, Ugarit's commercial relations changed considerably, when it became a vassal state of the Hittite kingdom.

Syria and the Levant after 1200 BCE. The end of the Bronze Age, around 1200 BCE, brought a fundamental change in the political organization of the Aegean, Anatolia, and the Levant, which in turn had severe effects on trade and trading patterns. The Minoan civilizations in Cyprus, Crete, and the Greek mainland all came to an end, as did the Hittite kingdom. Ugarit and Alalakh were also destroyed, never to recover. Most historians assume that the Sea People, whose ethnic affiliation and geographical origins remain unknown, were in part responsible for these changes. Some of them, called Philistines in the Hebrew Bible, settled in the coastal plain of southern Palestine, and thereby ended Egyptian control over this region. The palace-centered city states of the Bronze Age were replaced by "ethnic" states established by Aramaic tribal groups from the Syrian steppe who settled the area from northern Syria to Palestine (Israel, Judah) and Transjordania (Ammon, Edom, Moab). On the coast, the Phoenician cities of Arados, Byblos, Sidon, and Tyre re-established themselves. They now functioned as ports of trade or emporia, linking the Levantine hinterland with its "ethnic" states and Mesopotamia on the one side and the Mediterranean world on the other.

During this same era, the Assyrian Empire flourished. One of its most prominent rulers, Tiglath-Pileser I (1114–1076 BCE) extended Assyria's influence to the Levant, receiving tribute from Byblos, Sidon, and Arados. After an interruption of about two hundred years, the Assyrians again reached the Levant; and during the reign of Assurnasirpal II (883–859 BCE), Arados, Byblos, Sidon, and Tyre submitted to their rule. The fortified towns of Sidon and Tyre, however, retained their independence for a time, when the Assyrians again invaded the Levant during the eighth century BCE. Having been spared because they were the only gateways for maritime trade with the Aegean, they were finally conquered to become Assyrian vassals. The consequent interruption in trade relations with the Aegean world apparently proved to be more harmful to the Assyrians than to the Phoenicians. Soon

after the fall of the Assyrian Empire in 625 BCE, the latter regained their previous position, together with the rest of the Levant, in serving as an important commercial link between Mesopotamia and the Mediterranean world, especially Greece. Thus, earlier relations that the Phoenicians had established were revived. One of the first consequences of those renewed relations was the Greek adaptation of the Phoenician alphabet.

The economy of Palestine under the rule of the kings of Judah and Israel (c. 1000–595 BCE) was characterized by an agricultural regime of subsistence farming. The Judean and Israelite peasantry, a formerly nomadic people, had settled in Palestine from the thirteenth to eleventh centuries. They were soon struggling with the local Canaanite population, especially with the large landowners. In a gradual process of land consolidation, these landowners had absorbed earlier Canaanite village communities and then followed the same path with the Judean and Israelite peasantry. The ensuing social imbalance was severely criticized by the Hebrew prophets Hosea, Amos, and Mikha (Micah).

The Hebrew Bible refers to the trade relations of King Solomon (tenth century BCE) with the South Arabian kingdom of Saba and to his trading ventures and those of King Hiram I of Tyre with southern Arabia, which had become an important trading partner for other Near Eastern countries. One of the major products of this region was (besides gold) frankincense. To a large degree, it evidently replaced other fragrant substances (resins from various trees). As indicated earlier, the so-called "Frankincense Road" along the west coast of Arabia into Transjordania was one of the most important trade routes in the first millennium BCE.

Means of Transportation. Seafaring in the Mediterranean was generally restricted to seasons of good weather, especially the summer. Nevertheless, even the summer season could provide dangers to seafarers in gusty winds and storms. Thus, the shipping routes were always close to the coastline. Crossing the sea to Cyprus was common; however, the route to Crete was the more dangerous.

The only waterway leading to Babylonia was the Euphrates. River barges were used for general merchandise, while lumber from Syria and Lebanon was transported to Babylonia by float. Until the end of the second millennium BCE, overland traders used donkeys, which were able to travel about 30 km per day. Only after that period did camels (dromedaries) become the main cargo animals. Because of their higher speed and superior endurance, they were able to cross desert and steppe much more easily, revolutionizing overland trade through much greater efficiency.

Trading Patterns. Long-distance trade in the Levant was usually organized by the palaces, whose main purpose was to obtain rare and prestigious goods for ostentatious purposes. Temples played no significant economic role in general or in trade in particular. Merchants, serving as agents of the palace, were entrusted with whatever region they had to offer. Possibly these merchants were able to conduct business on their own along with their official commissions.

Because long-distance trade was concentrated in the royal palaces, official documents often described it in ideological phraseology as gift exchange or tribute, while stressing power, prestige, and status. It appears that a form of circuitous exchange of gifts consisting of silver, crafted silver objects, and valuable textiles was the basis of the exchange relations documented in the Ebla texts from the twenty-third century BCE. Well documented in the correspondence of the Egyptian kings Amenophis III (1403–1365) and Amenophis IV (also known as Akhnaton) (1365–1347) with their Near Eastern counterparts is the exchange of gifts following established rules of reciprocity. Rulers sent official missions to their partners with valuable goods and objects, hoping for reciprocal exchanges. Yet often such "gifts" were actually demanded, constituting a breach of the required customs of courtesy.

The exchange of goods between Ugarit and the Hittites was replaced or at least supplemented by tribute to the Hittite king. But it was based on mutual benefits. The exchange of goods from the Levant with the East, especially with Assyria, came to an end after the Assyrian conquest of much of the Levant and its hinterland during the eighth and seventh centuries BCE. Goods previously traded now became part of the heavy tribute, which changed direction in the flow of goods and thus impaired established trade relations. The tributary practice of the Assyrians did not contain any kind of equivalents. It was a pure and brutal exploitation that led to a gradual impoverishment of the tributaries.

Risk and Transaction Costs. Long-distance trade was risky and therefore costly. Merchants had to assume the costs of loss of their merchandise along their journey—by robbery, piracy, and murder, or by shipwreck. They also had to pay dues along their way and pay for guides or escorts. Unexpected circumstances—such as delays by sickness, injury, or bad weather—added to the transaction costs. Merchants had several methods of limiting the burden of these transaction costs. One was to follow the trajectory principle by which they brought their merchandise only from place A to place B. From place B native traders would continue with merchandise they had accumulated from various sources to place C. Thus the traders from point A had to deal with only one local ruler and his demands for tolls and other dues. A second method—perhaps supplementing the former—was to negotiate treaties between the rulers of different polities by which the traders of both were mutually protected. These rulers often provided armed escorts through their territory. A third

way was to establish trading posts within foreign territories, which was well attested throughout the ancient Near East from the third millennium BCE. These trading posts were also granted certain privileges by treaties between rulers.

A fourth method was to specialize, with the goal of monopolizing trade between certain Levantine cities and their trading partners; these monopolies helped ensure profit maximization. Thus, from the twenty-seventh to the twenty-second century BCE, trade with Egypt was concentrated in Byblos. Ugarit was the gateway to Cyprus until the end of the thirteenth century. Subsequently, during the first millennium, trade with the Mediterranean concentrated on the Phoenician cities of Byblos, Sidon, and Tyre.

Phoenician merchants usually joined together in temporary associations in order to accumulate capital for building and outfitting fleets of several ships that would sail to Egypt under the protection of a powerful ruler in an attempt to avoid the hazards of piracy. Overland trade may have been organized in a similar manner.

Merchants also minimized their transaction costs by, for example, selling their pack animals after having disposed of the bulky merchandise that they were carrying. On the return trip only a few animals were needed to transport the silver and other valuable proceeds of their commercial transactions. The same may have been the case with ships going from the Levant to Egypt.

Traders drew up legal contracts before starting a trading venture to safeguard against later unjustified claims from (silent) partners. A special legal instrument designed to minimize the risks of maritime trade was the "bottomry loan"—where money was borrowed and the ship pledged as security against the payment of the debt—which had been developed in Ugarit.

The profits of trading ventures were invested in landed property, a phenomenon known in other regions of the ancient world and early medieval Europe. The fields acquired were often of manorial size, farmed either by the personnel of the merchant-landowner or leased to sharecroppers. In both cases they provided not only status but also additional sources of income, limiting the entrepreneurial risks inherent in long-distance trade. To what degree they reinvested such income into trading ventures is unknown.

Levantine Exports. The Levant was the source of cedar wood for ostentatious buildings in Egypt and Mesopotamia. The difficulties of obtaining cedar trees are reflected in epical texts from twenty-first century Mesopotamia. According to a twelfth-century Egyptian account, cedars needed for a ceremonial boat apparently were felled only on demand and after prepayment. Because of its easy access to timber, Byblos was the most famous shipbuilding center.

From the middle of the second millennium BCE, textiles dyed with so-called Imperial purple, extracted from the mucous glands of various Mediterranean whelk mollusks (*Murex brandaris, Murex trunculus, Purpura haemastoma*), became a major trading good of the Levant; they were first documented in Ugarit, in the fourteenth and thirteenth centuries BCE. Producing these purple dyes was a very cumbersome and costly process. To produce one pound (453 grams), just enough to dye a single garment, took some 60,000 mollusks. Thus, the price of Imperial purple garments, one of the most prestigious textiles in the ancient and early medieval worlds (and of the Byzantine Empire), was exceedingly high. Indeed, subsequently, during the reign of Diocletian (301 CE), one Roman pound (327.5 grams) of wool dyed in purple was worth one pound of refined gold. During the first millennium BCE, the traditional centers that monopolized the production of this purple were Sidon and Tyre.

Craftsmanship was a significant part of the Levantine economy and of its trade relations with distant regions throughout the ancient Near East and the Mediterranean. Those artifacts made of metal, glass, wood, semiprecious stones, and ivory that have survived provide witness to the high quality of Levantine or Phoenician craftsmanship.

Lapis lazuli and carnelian (a chalcedony), originating in eastern Iran and in India, respectively, were very highly regarded semiprecious stones. Those found in workshops excavated in Ugarit provide evidence of trade relations with the East via Mesopotamia. Both stones were evidently used as applications for sumptuous garments that were sold to foreign rulers. Utensils carved from boxwood that originated in nearby mountains provided other consumer goods in Ugarit. During the first millennium BCE, the Levant was also famous for its ivory carvings—in particular, various utensils and applications for furniture, which were exported from Phoenicia. In the tenth century, metalworkers from Tyre were reputedly engaged in outfitting King Solomon's temple in Jerusalem.

Following the Assyrian military expansion into Syria and the Levant, Phoenician craftsmen were deported to Assyria. They sculpted the bas-reliefs of Assyrian palaces or were employed in ivory carving. These deportations undermined the Phoenician monopoly on ivory carving and had a negative effect on the productive capacities of Levantine craftsmen, which were so important for their trade.

Agricultural products—olive oil, wine, and figs—played an equally important role in Levantine exports, though grains did not. Wheat, barley, and other cereals were traded along the Levantine coast by boat, but only to a very limited degree, because overland transport, whether by oxen or by donkeys, to seaports was costly; most of the grain was usually consumed within the vicinity of its production. Overland grain transport was an option only during times of extreme shortages. When a famine of catastrophic dimensions hit the Hittite kingdom, grain was shipped from Ugarit via Ura in Cilicia; but the documents do not specify how far into Anatolia these shipments went. Fish were preserved by drying or salting and thus were fit to be sold in the more distant hinterland, like Damascus or Jerusalem.

Despite the drastic changes in this region's political composition and in the different forms of state organization, the main trading goods of the Levant and its immediate environs, including those transported through this region, remained more or less the same as in the second millennium.

Imports. The most important trading goods and merchandise imported into the Levant, in exchange for exports to the Aegean Sea region, Anatolia, and Egypt, were gold, silver, copper, and tin. During the first part of the eighteenth century BCE, tin was imported from Susa, itself an intermediary, via Babylonia. Copper came from southeastern Anatolia, but also from Cyprus. The main gateway for this strategic metal was Ugarit; some of the copper was then sent on to Mesopotamia.

Currency, Money, and Coinage. In Near Eastern antiquity, silver was the most important of the precious metals; and Anatolia was one of its main sources. The Levant obtained this metal in exchange for its trading goods, and its craftsmen used it to make precious objects for the palaces and temples, and for export. Silver was also the primary monetary metal of this era. It was used as a means of payment, including tribute from vassals to overlords, and it also served as a means to measure value, that is, to express equivalencies or prices. It was measured by weight, and was hoarded in the treasuries of palaces and temples. Only in a few instances was gold used as a monetary instrument. Evidently, during the middle of the second millennium, the Near Eastern gold supply was a monopoly of Egypt, which controlled the gold mines in Nubia. During the first millennium, Ophir and Punt (in Southwest Arabia and Somalia) replaced Egypt as a source for gold.

Coinage arrived in the Levant rather late. Not until long after coins were "invented," reputedly by Croesus of Lydia in the seventh century BCE, did they become a universally accepted standard for payments. For a long time coinage was gold coinage. The Persian golden dareikos introduced by Darius I (522–486) weighed one shekel (about 8.4 grams).

BIBLIOGRAPHY

Ben-Tor, Ammon. "The Trade Relations of Palestine in the Early Bronze Age." *Journal of the Economic and Social History of the Orient* 29 (1986), 1–27.

Collett, Serge. "Halientica Phoenicia I. Contribution à l'étude de la place des activités halientiques dans la culture phénicienne: Point de vue d'un non-archéologue." *Information sur les Sciences Sociales* 34 (1995), 107–173.

Elat, Moshe. "Phoenician Overland Trade within the Mesopotamian Empires." In *Ah, Assyria*, edited by Mordechai Cogan and Israel Eph'al, pp. 21–35. Jerusalem, 1991.

Finkelstein, Israel. "Arabian Trade and Socio-political Conditions in the Negev in the Twelfth–Eleventh Centuries BCE." *Journal of Near Eastern Studies* 47 (1988), 241–252.

Grégoire, Jean-Pierre, and Johannes Renger. "Die Interdependenz der wirtschaftlichen und gesellschaftlich-politischen Strukturen von Ebla." In *Heidelberger Studien zum Alten Orient*, vol. 2, *Wirtschaft und Gesellschaft von Ebla*, edited by Harald Hauptmann and Hartmut Waetzoldt, pp. 211–224. Heidelberg, 1988. Outline of the *oikos* economy in northern Syria in the twenty-third century BCE.

Heltzer, Michael. "The Economy of Ugarit." In *Handbook of Ugaritic Studies*, edited by Wilfred G. E. Watson and Nicolas Wyatt, pp. 423–454. Leiden, Boston, Cologne, 1999.

Katzenstein, H. Jacob. *The History of Tyre*. Jerusalem, 1973.

Klengel, Horst. "Near Eastern Trade and the Emergence of Interaction with Crete in the Third Millennium." *Studi Micenei ed Egeo-Anatolici* 24 (1984), 7–31.

Klengel, Horst. *Syria 3000 to 300 B.C.: A Handbook of Political History*. Berlin, 1992.

Liverani, Mario. *Prestige and Interest: International Relations in the Near East, ca. 16000–1100 B.C.* Padua, Italy, 1990. Important for its discussion of the theoretical issues concerning trade relations; describes how trade relations are phrased in terms of tribute and submission or as interstate gift exchange expressed in traditional forms of courtesy and reciprocity.

Muhly, James D. *Copper and Tin: The Distribution of Mineral Resources and the Nature of Metals Trade in the Bronze Age*. New Haven, 1973. The standard study on the two major strategic metals of the Bronze Age.

Muhly, James D. "Phoenicia and the Phoenicians." In *Biblical Archaeology Today*. Jerusalem, 1985.

Schloen, J. David. *The House of the Father as Fact and Symbol: Patrimonialism in Ugarit and the Ancient Near East*. Winona Lake, Ind., 2001.

Vargyas, Peter. "Aspects of Ceremonial Exchange in the Near East during the Late Second Millennium B.C." In *Centre and Periphery in the Ancient World*, edited by M. Rowlands, M. Larsen, and K. Kristansen, pp. 57–65. Cambridge, 1987.

Vita, Juan-Pablo. "The Society of Ugarit." In *Handbook of Ugaritic Studies*, edited by Wilfred G. E. Watson and Nicolas Wyatt, pp. 455–498. Leiden, Boston, Cologne, 1999.

Ward, William A., and Marta Sh. Joukowsky, eds. *The Crisis Years: The 12th Century B.C. from Beyond the Danube to the Tigris*. Dubuque, Iowa, 1992.

Zaccagnini, Carlos. "Ideological and Procedural Paradigms in Ancient Near Eastern Long Distance Exchanges: The Case of Enmerkar and the Lord of Aratta." *Altorientalische Forschungen* 20 (1993), 34–42. Customary trading patterns and conventions in long-distance trade are exemplified by an analysis of an early Mesopotamian epic (twenty-first century BCE) and an Egyptian tale (eleventh century BCE) reflecting the Egyptian trade with Phoenicia.

JOHANNES M. RENGER

Roman and Byzantine Periods

The region known as the Levant is traditionally understood as the coast and hinterland of the eastern Mediterranean. In the contemporary world, this means the regions of Israel, Lebanon, Syria, Jordan, and Cyprus. These areas are among the oldest on the planet to be urbanized and to have developed a sophisticated and complex economic structure.

The Levant in the Greco-Roman and Byzantine Periods (330 BCE–630 CE). The invasion of the region in 332 BCE by the Macedonian conqueror, Alexander the Great, had little immediate effect. He did not alter the Persian administrative arrangements by which the Levant consisted of a single province (satrapy), but instead appointed his own official, Menes, to oversee the region. Local rulers were maintained in power except in Tyre, which had refused to accept Alexander's authority and had to be reduced after a long siege. Alexander did insist on one change of considerable significance: the Levantine trading cities had long minted their own coinage on a distinct standard, but Alexander required that they cease this practice and instead mint Macedonian royal coinage. This established an effective currency union everywhere that Alexander ruled. A confusion of differing local weights and measures was eliminated, and a single standard for precious-metal coinage imposed.

The Hellenistic Levant (330–64 BCE). The most significant change was wrought after Alexander's death (323 BCE), when the Levant was divided between two competing dynasties of Hellenistic warlords. In the south, the Ptolemies, based in Egypt, ruled Palestine (Coele-Syria) and Cyprus; in the north, rulers of the Seleucid family controlled Syria. The Hellenistic kings tended to regard their realms as bases for military competition with one another. They sought to maximize their revenues and protect domestic production in order to guarantee a supply of food, manpower, and materiel in time of war.

In addition, they had a considerable source of wealth to call upon. The Persian predecessors of the Hellenistic kings had hoarded an immense amount of bullion in central and regional treasuries. This money was now released, initially as gifts to Alexander's followers and payments to his soldiers and subsequently as payments to mercenaries by Hellenistic warlords, and in lavish expenditures to maintain regal lifestyles.

The economic policies pursued by the Hellenistic rulers have been variously characterized as the imposition of a command economy, replete with state monopolies, or as the pursuit of autarky, in order to ensure self-sufficiency in time of conflict. The former is an overstatement, but it is certainly true that state monopolies were established in some industries, notably mining, lumber, and the production of purple dye. Others, in particular the grain industry, were subject to strict regulation. States also derived revenues from imposts on goods such as wine. In each of these cases, revenues were indirectly derived through the farming out of state contracts to collect them. Private contractors tendered for the right to gather taxes or administer monopolies on the state's behalf.

The Hellenistic rulers of the Levant sought, in imposing their rule, to disrupt traditional structures and social relations as little as possible. They found a region that they understood well: highly urbanized and aristocratic. Where there were few cities, they founded them: in northwest Syria, the great royal cities of Antioch, Seleucia-Pieria, and Apamea are notable examples; others included Ptolemais-Akko in Coele-Syria, and the cities of the Decapolis in the hinterland. Most of these cities were founded as military colonies. Their initial populations were former Macedonian or Greek soldiers, who might be expected to take up arms again. In order to support themselves, they were granted houses and land (*kleroi*).

Such colonists brought new industries with them, in particular viticulture, which flourished in the fertile valleys of northern Syria, and a taste for imported Attic pottery. The conditions created by new political conditions created a long economic boom. The ubiquity of coinage in silver and gold underpinned and strengthened an ancient economy that had been well prepared for this innovation through centuries of long-distance trade. A greatly enriched Greek world carried on a vigorous trade with the merchant cities of the Levant, which generated a prosperity that was enjoyed by those independent of the rule of Greek dynasts. The Nabataeans of the southeast Levant had long derived their wealth from the trade in frankincense and spices that passed through their lands from southern Arabia en route to the Mediterranean. From the early Hellenistic period on, the Nabataeans began to develop a monumental material culture and a sophisticated monarchy, in a clear expression of the affluence brought by the new demand in the Mediterranean region for the goods carried through their lands. One significant development occurred in Palestine, where agriculture traditionally had been practiced by relatively large kin groups. In the Ptolemaic period, this structure was gradually transformed into holdings farmed by individual families.

Political tussles over the strategic lands of the Levant had little effect on the economies of the region. There is no evidence of substantial disruption of either trade or production. Rather, the southern Levant seems to have passed easily from the hands of the Ptolemies to those of the Seleucids after the battle of Panion (200 BCE). The effect of this was to link the economies of Palestine, Transjordan, and Phoenecia with that of northern Syria rather than Egypt, as had been the case. Cyprus remained, at least notionally, in Ptolemaic hands until taken over by the Romans. What did affect the trading economy to a considerable extent was the growth of seaborne piracy in the eastern Mediterranean. The long-term defense against piracy had always been the presence of a dominant naval power in the region. In the Persian period, the Phoenecian cities had maintained strong fleets, and in the Hellenistic period, naval leadership (thalassocracy) was exercised successively by the Antigonid and Ptolemaic dynasties. The decline in Ptolemaic power in the second century BCE, particularly after the loss of Coele-Syria, led to a decline in the state and the efficiency of the Ptolemaic fleet. Other fleets, notably the Rhodian, strove successfully to suppress piracy in the Aegean; but in the eastern Mediterranean, it was slyly encouraged by the Ptolemies, who, no longer possessing the resources to suppress the pirates, encouraged them instead to prey upon the seaborne commerce of their Seleucid rivals.

Pirates did not merely prey upon commerce; they also raided settled coastal communities in order to abduct their populations and sell them as slaves. Although Hellenic and Levantine economies employed slavery, they were not heavily dependent upon slaves as a source of labor; the Romans, on the other hand, were. The Roman agricultural preference for large slave-worked plantations, together with the rapidly burgeoning wealth of the Romans themselves, led to a massive increase in the demand for slaves in the western Mediterranean.

Roman affluence also meant an increased demand for the luxury goods manufactured in, or brought through, the Levant: purple dyes (*Murex brandaris*, *Purpura haemastoma*, glass, silk, spices, and incense). A Roman economic presence was rapidly followed by a political one. Roman diplomats interfered in the political rivalry between the Ptolemies and Seleucids at the end of the third century BCE, and soon afterward Rome defeated the Seleucids in a major war. In the second century, as the Seleucid realm fragmented, and the Ptolemies became increasingly enervated by dynastic imbecility, the Romans became more directly involved with the political and economic life of the eastern Mediterranean.

The Roman Levant (64 BCE–324 CE). The pirates were eliminated, and Roman hegemony in the Levant was finally established by Pompey the Great (Roman general and politician, 102–47 BCE) in the middle of the first century BCE. From that time onward, the cities of the Levant were linked more directly with those of the western Mediterranean. New markets for luxury exports were developed as a result of the Roman promotion of local elites throughout their empire. Not only did this encourage the long-distance trade in items such as silk and spices that passed through Syria from China, India, and the Arabian peninsula, but it also encouraged the growth of domestic industries. Syrian artisans developed the art of glassblowing in the first century BCE. The Levantine cities greatly benefited from this increase in long-distance trade. Early in the second century BCE, the Seleucids had lost control of Asia Minor, a change that led to the exclusive direction of caravan routes to the ports of the Levant; so by the first century BCE, this trade was almost entirely dominated by the merchants of Phoenecia. They were not the only beneficiaries, however; the caravan cities of the hinterland, Palmyra in particular, began their climb to wealth and affluence at this time.

One region of the Levant remained problematic and unstable. In the middle of the second century BCE, Judaea had broken away from Seleucid control and established its own, Hasmonean, monarchy. The independent state became a Roman protectorate after a protracted period of civil war in the following century. Roman involvement did nothing to ease political tensions, but Roman sponsorship of the Herodian family led to an unprecedented period of building and development of the region. The port of Caesarea Maritima was founded, and agriculture was developed. This period of prosperity can be directly linked to the rule of Herod the Great. After his death in 4 BCE, instability reasserted itself with a succession of rulers and protectorates until the Jewish War of 66 CE resulted in the final annexation of the region by Rome.

Roman rule in the first and second centuries CE was rarely challenged. Within the Roman Levant, protracted peace resulted in an extraordinary prosperity. The Romans added enormously to local infrastructure by the construction of a road network all through the Levant. Syria became proverbial in the Roman world for its luxury, and Antioch came to be regarded as the third city of the empire. The caravan cities of the desert fringe, and Palmyra in particular, continued to grow in wealth and influence. In the early second century CE, the Sinai peninsula and the Transjordan were added to the empire by Emperor Trajan (c. 53–117 CE). A Roman garrison was placed in the new province, and a major road, the via Nova Traiana, was constructed, linking the port of Aelam on the Red Sea with Nabataean centers and the cities of the Decapolis.

The principal beneficiaries of this prosperity were the urban elites of the great Levantine cities. Aristocratic families became members of the Roman senate. Avidius Cassius (c. 130–175 CE), a Roman governor, of local origins, felt secure enough in his power base to challenge the emperor himself. Although Cassius's challenge failed, a number of the emperors of the third century were of Syrian origin. One of these, Caracalla (188–217 CE), was responsible for an edict that gave Roman citizenship to all free inhabitants of the empire. This had the effect of simplifying administrative complexities as well as increasing tax revenue.

Caracalla's reform was necessary to finance increased public expenditure on the army. In the latter part of the second century CE, a major epidemic had reduced the population of the empire by as much as 10 percent. This pestilence had been brought into the Empire by troops returning from a victorious campaign in Mesopotamia, so that the Roman east was hit disproportionately hard. Recession led to stagflation. Government revenue was also raised through the expedient of reducing the silver content in the coinage, the effect of which was to increase prices. Since there is no evidence that the tax assessments of the provinces were reassessed to take account of this declining tax base, there must have been an increasing burden of taxation borne by rural smallholders, who were, in the Levant, the real engine of the wider economy. Constant warfare also disrupted trade. In the Levant the Romans found themselves in political competition with the Sassanid kings of Persia.

Some coped well with this. Regional archaeological surveys in the Golan and Samaria display uninterrupted prosperity. Palmyrene trade continued to flourish, perhaps owing to the far-flung trade diaspora of Palmyrene traders. Decades of war between Rome and Persia, however, left other cities sacked and local economies ruined. Economic uncertainties are reflected in political reaction. A variety of local claimants to the empire sprang up in the middle of the third century, each exercising a degree of local power. This culminated in the brief assumption by Zenobia of Palmyra of the overlordship of the entire Levant and Egypt. Her defeat by the emperor Aurelian (c. 216–275 CE) led to the complete destruction of Palmyra.

Rome's defeat of Palmyra led to the commencement of a major Roman reinvestment in the region, linked in particular with the work of the Roman emperor Diocletian (c. 238–313 CE). Diocletian came to power in 284 CE and, over the period of his rule (284–305 CE), instituted a series of reforms that reorganized administration, taxation, the currency, trade, and defense. In the Levant, a major system of roads was constructed along the frontier zone from the Red Sea to the Euphrates, provincial units were made smaller, and imperial monopolies—particularly in minerals and purple dye—were strictly enforced. Cyprus was brought directly under the administration of a senior official resident at Antioch, which city itself was used as a major imperial residence and was a major recipient of imperial generosity. Trade was encouraged through the security of the new road network, and an attempt was made to control inflation. The twofold strategy of coinage reform and rigid legislative control over all prices did not succeed, principally because of the emperor's naive belief that he could inspire economic confidence simply by commanding it. Diocletian's major reform lay in his determination that the tax structure should be made fair and flexible through regular assessments of a region's ability to pay tax. That led to the imposition of a cycle of tax censuses (indictions). In terms of historical change, the commencement of this system marks the end of the economic conditions that pertained during the Roman period, and the beginning of the Byzantine Levant.

The Byzantine Levant (324–630 CE). The Byzantine period formally begins with the reign of the Emperor

Constantine (c. 270–337 CE), who commenced the process of the Christianization of the Roman Empire. Constantine continued Diocletian's policies, reversing centuries of laissez-faire economics. Now the state directly intervened in the economic life of the empire, through enforcement of state monopolies, establishment of new state industries (particularly in arms and textiles), and regulation of professions through official guilds (*collegia*). Although this was not a command economy, it was deliberately geared to support the military capacity of the state. Constantine also continued Diocletian's monetary reforms, effectively abandoning the old silver standard and replacing it with an entirely new precious-metal coinage in gold (the *solidus aureus*).

In the Levant, state intervention meant the establishment of arms factories and increased scrutiny by the bureaucracy. Literary evidence suggests that the new imperial structure resulted in a downturn in a once flourishing economy; but the origins of such evidence, from the wealthy tax-avoiding elite of the empire, invites suspicion. Archaeological surveys largely provide a different picture. A long period of growth commenced at the beginning of the fourth century. Evidence of growth is apparent both in cities such as Antioch, Scythopolis, Gerasa (Jerash), and Caesarea Maritima and in the countryside. The rural hinterlands of the cities were, if possible, even more prosperous. There is evidence of economic growth as reflected in an increasing population. Archaeological surveys of the hinterlands of Antioch and Apamea in Syria and the coastal plain and hill country of Palestine in the south disclose a consistent pattern of affluence in villages and rural villas through the fourth and fifth centuries CE. In Syria, there is also evidence of real growth in oleoculture and manufacture of olive oil. Moreover, even marginal agricultural land in arid regions such as the Negev was exploited.

An important indicator of private wealth is church construction. At the beginning of the period, there were no public church buildings in the Levant; but by the fifth century CE, there were major cathedrals even in minor cities such as Gerasa and Hierapolis. The pilgrim trade also brought a new source of wealth to what was now seen as "the Holy Land." The economic consequences of this ancient equivalent of tourism cannot be underestimated. Bethlehem and Jerusalem both became major centers, and shrines were constructed in Galilee. The region also continued to benefit from the long-distance trade routes in silk and spices that had their termini in its Mediterranean ports. This trade was further developed by the new trading diaspora of schismatic Christians, especially Nestorians, who fled the boundaries of the empire seeking religious tolerance. Nestorian and Manichaean communities can be identified all along the silk routes between Syria and China, and all contributed to the long-distance movement of merchandise.

One reason for this protracted period of growth was that the region was largely at peace. After the constant conflict of the third century, the military victories and political reforms accomplished by Diocletian brought a return to stability and certainty. The focus of this wealth was the countryside rather than the cities, which has led some scholars to identify an urban decline in this period. It is perhaps more accurate to note that the decline was only relative—the rural sector grew more swiftly than the urban.

The peace that underpinned this period of growth was broken during the sixth century CE in a series of conflicts between Rome and Persia. Natural occurrences also took a toll. Antioch was devastated by a fire and a series of earthquakes between 524 and 528 CE. In 541 CE, an epidemic broke out in Egypt, which quickly spread to Palestine, Syria, and thence throughout the empire. This plague had a high mortality rate, so much so that many scholars have seen it as the most significant factor in the decline that ensued. Certainly the region remained wealthy enough to sustain a number of Persian assaults, and to seek to recover from them, although in some areas inscriptions cease altogether in c. 540 CE. Conflict persisted with Persia, sapping the strength of both powers. In 610 CE, the Levant was occupied by a Persian force, which stayed for nearly two decades. Its withdrawal was forced by the Byzantines, who defeated Persia in a ruinous counterattack. Military exhaustion made both empires vulnerable to the nascent power of the Islamic Arabs. Much of the Levant passed under their rule after the battle of the Yarmuk in 637 CE , and a whole new era commenced.

BIBLIOGRAPHY

Ball, Warwick. *Rome in the East: The Transformation of an Empire.* London and New York, 2000.

Billows, Richard A. *Kings and Colonists: Aspects of Macedonian Imperialism.* Leiden, 1995.

Bowersock, Glen. *Roman Arabia.* Cambridge, Mass., 1983.

Foss, Clive. "Syria in Transition: An Archaeological Approach." *Dumbarton Oaks Papers* 51 (1997), 189–269.

Green, Peter. *From Alexander to Actium: The Historical Evolution of the Hellenistic Age.* Berkeley, 1990.

Hirschfeld, Yizhar. "Farms and Villages in Byzantine Palestine." *Dumbarton Oaks Papers* 51 (1997), 33–71.

Isaac, Ben. *The Near East under Roman Rule.* Leiden, 1998.

Jones, Arnold H. M. *The Later Roman Empire, 284–602.* Oxford, 1964.

Jones, Arnold H. M. *Cities of the Eastern Roman Provinces.* Rev. ed. Oxford, 1971.

Kennedy, Hugh. "The Last Century of Byzantine Syria: A Reinterpretation." *Byzantinische Forschungen* 10 (1985), 141–184.

McClellen, Murray C. "The Economy of Hellenistic Egypt and Syria: An Archaeological Perspective." In *Ancient Economic Thought*, edited by B. B. Price, pp. 172–187. London, 1997.

Millar, Fergus. *The Roman Near East, 31 BC–AD 337.* Cambridge, Mass., 1993.

Rostovzeff, Michael. *Social and Economic History of the Hellenistic World.* 3 vols. Oxford, 1941.

Rostovzeff, Michael. *The Social and Economic History of the Roman Empire.* 2nd ed., revised by P. M. Fraser. Oxford, 1957.

Safrai, Ze'ev. *The Economy of Roman Palestine*. London and New York, 1994.

Sainte Croix, Geoffrey E. M. de. *The Class Struggle in the Ancient Greek World*. London, 1983.

Whittow, Mark. "Ruling the Late Roman and Early Byzantine City: A Continuous History. *Past and Present* 129 (1990), 3–29.

BILL LEADBETTER

Islamic Rule

Within a few decades after the emergence of Islam around 610 CE, much of the Levant was under Islamic rule, and the economic practices and institutions now recognized as "Islamic" were taking hold throughout the region. Known also as the Middle East or the Near East, this region would display remarkable institutional creativity over the next few centuries, thus maintaining its position as one of the world's most advanced economic centers. That this economic dominance withered away forms a major puzzle of economic history.

No great civilization has built its economic institutions from scratch, and Islam was no exception. Many of the economic rules and regulations that came to be associated with Islam grew out of the region's preexisting institutions, most importantly those of the Romans, Persians, and the pagan, Jewish, and Christian tribes of Arabia. Through the emerging synthesis, which successive generations of Muslims were to refine and develop, the region sustained the world's largest cities outside of China, remained a major player in global commerce, pioneered many new technologies, and afforded its residents a standard of living comparable, and in some respects superior, to that found in the most advanced parts of western Europe. At the same time, the Islamic synthesis carried within it the seeds of institutional rigidities that gradually reduced the Levant's competitiveness and led, by the nineteenth century, to the region's economic domination by the West.

To explain the early economic successes of Islam, scholars have conventionally pointed, on the one hand, to the generally uncontested view that the Prophet Muhammad, the religion's founder, was a merchant and, on the other, to the commercial prominence of Mecca, the city where the Prophet began spreading his message in the early seventh century. According to recent research, Mecca's commercial importance on the eve of Islam's emergence has been exaggerated; and the Prophet's professional background mattered less for the region's economic evolution than the fact that after his death the leading commercial families of Arabia gained enough power to eliminate obstacles to personal enrichment. By virtue of the ascendancy of these families, over the next few centuries the economic content of Islamic law was shaped and reshaped largely by jurists sympathetic to the concerns of merchants and financiers.

Among the most significant achievements of these jurists is the law of Islamic commercial partnerships. Known as *mudāraba*, an Islamic commercial partnership typically joins a sedentary investor with a traveling merchant; the two split profits according to a predetermined ratio. The *mudāraba* resembles various ancient arrangements used to finance and conduct trade before the birth of Islam; it is similar also to arrangements that non-Muslims, including western Europeans, used throughout the Middle Ages. The *mudāraba* stands out, however, as an unusually flexible instrument, in that it allowed the profit shares of the partners to depend on such factors as the riskiness of the intended venture and the merchant's reputation. These flexibilities were so advantageous that non-Muslim traders and investors of the Islamic world, though under no compulsion to follow Islamic law, commonly opted to do so anyway. Dating mostly from the eleventh to thirteenth centuries, the "Geniza documents"—so called because they were discovered in the Geniza (storeroom) of an Egyptian synagogue—indicate that Jewish merchants of the medieval Mediterranean often formed Islamic commercial partnerships and resolved their disputes before Islamic courts.

At least for the politically dominant Muslim majority, the most important commercial event of the year was the annual pilgrimage to Mecca (*hajj*), which the Qur'ān requires every Muslim to perform at least once, provided he or she can afford it. From the rise of Islam to modern times, this pilgrimage was also an occasion for international trade both in Mecca and on the road. Caravans to and from Egypt, Iraq, Syria, Turkey, and other far-flung corners of the Islamic world could take months each way, with every stop presenting commercial opportunities. Many pilgrims financed their expenses entirely through trade, and some returned richer than when they left. Precisely because of its enormous commercial importance, the pilgrimage also had a negative effect on economic development: the reduction of incentives to establish nonreligious commercial fairs. Perhaps as a consequence of the fairs associated with the pilgrimage, the Islamic world developed no secular fairs as important as the Champagne fairs of medieval northern Europe.

The Ban on Interest. An element of Islamic law generally considered to have hindered the Levant's development is its ban on interest, although "Islamic economics"—the modern doctrine that aims to restructure economies according to Islamic criteria—holds that this ban actually contributed to early Islam's economic successes. Neither view takes account of the finding that the interest prohibition, insofar as Muslims accepted it, was frequently honored only in the breach. As in the West, where Christian theologians condemned interest on the basis of arguments similar to those put forth by Muslim moralists, the circumvention was facilitated by widely approved stratagems. One common stratagem was the double-sale: Person A buys a certain object from B for a price of P payable immediately, then sells the same object back to B for $P+r$ payable in a year's time. The material outcome of this double sale is equivalent to that of a single loan contract whereby A lends P to B in return for an interest payment of r. The Geniza documents, along with other medieval sources, indicate that through one device or another the subjects of all premodern Muslim states routinely formed debt contracts based on interest. Moreover, in certain times and places, Islamic courts readily enforced arrangements based openly on interest, provided the rate was below a generally recognized ceiling.

The ultimate justification for the Islamic interest ban is the Qur'ānic prohibition of *ribā*, the ancient Arabian practice of doubling the debt of a defaulter. Although the pre-Islamic loans that involved this practice were almost invariably taken to meet immediate consumption needs, the designers of Islamic law generally considered the prohibition of *ribā* to subsume all forms of interest, including surcharges on commercial loans. That methods were devised for circumventing the ban does not mean, however, that it was inconsequential. First of all, the ban raised the cost of certain financial transactions. Second, by blocking honest public discussion of commercial, financial, and monetary matters, it hindered the development of the capitalist mentality. Finally, because organizations cannot conceal interest charges as easily as individuals might, the ban kept the Middle East's flourishing moneylending sector from evolving into a modern banking system.

The interest ban was never construed as a major requirement of Islam. There are five such requirements, only one of which has an explicitly economic objective. This is the duty, incumbent on all adult Muslims except the poorest, to pay the tithe known as *zakat*. According to the Qur'ān, the Muslim community's *zakat* revenue must be used partly for the benefit of the poor. Yet *zakat*'s purpose is not solely to redistribute wealth or to alleviate poverty; there are seven additional mandated expenditure categories, including the advancement of Islam. This multiplicity of objectives allowed early Islamic leaders to use *zakat* collections as they saw fit, even to benefit the rich.

Zakat payments are generally considered a wealth tax, which appears to have been consistent with the practice during the Prophet's lifetime. But soon after his death, before the seventh century was over, the granting of broad exemptions turned the *zakat* obligation into a tax almost exclusively on livestock and agricultural output. Rates then came to vary across both time and space, as did the scope of collections and the identity of collectors. Equally important, the lack of standardization permitted rulers to introduce new taxes at will. Within a couple of generations,

therefore, the tax policies of the Islamic Middle East had only the most tenuous links to practices that had prevailed under the Prophet.

An early tax policy that did establish a potent precedent was the requirement that non-Muslim subjects pay, in addition to a poll tax in return for protection (*jizya*), a special land tax (*kharāj*) that was to be higher than that payed by Muslims under the rubric of either *zakat* or *'ushr*. Both taxes raised the material advantages of religious conversion, and the latter also encouraged land sales to Muslims. Because these developments threatened state revenues, as early as the late seventh century, officials in Iraq, Syria, and elsewhere took steps to discourage conversions. They also ruled that land left to non-Muslims at the time of the Islamic conquest would have to remain "*kharāj*-land" in perpetuity.

By establishing further precedents for tampering with the tax code to suit the state's needs of the moment, these rulings helped to keep property rights weak. However, the greatest threat to these rights was not the variability of taxation but the ease with which rulers were able to expropriate. In principle, rulers governing under Islamic law recognized private property rights, even as they paid lip service to the principle that all material wealth ultimately belongs to God. In practice, however, they had little trouble finding justifications for confiscating private wealth. To give an example from the early fifteenth century, whenever emergency taxation failed to yield the targeted revenue, the sultans of Mamluk Egypt financed their military campaigns through expropriations.

Partly because such episodes were common throughout medieval Eurasia, at the time the Islamic world was not yet showing the characteristic symptoms of economic underdevelopment—low productivity, technological retardation, intellectual poverty, and feeble government. In fact, right up to the seventeenth century one may find indicators of Middle Eastern economic superiority vis-à-vis the other major civilizations of the time. In the sixteenth century, grain yields in Egypt, Syria, and Turkey exceeded those in most Western countries. Perhaps as a consequence, the diet of the Ottoman army appears to have been nutritionally superior to that of its major European adversaries. In the same century, Cairo had far more inhabitants than Paris or London; and Istanbul, with its estimated 400,000 to 700,000 people, was an urban giant. Stepping back to the thirteenth century, Arab scientists were at the forefront of advances in mathematics, astronomy, medicine, and optics. The region's intellectual vitality is evident also in the splendor of its public and private libraries; each of the largest contained around one hundred thousand volumes—a number that no library anywhere else in the world came close to matching. These various accomplishments are due in no small measure to the fluidity of early

PALESTINE. Map of Palestine and Lake Tiberias (Sea of Galilee), fourteenth century. (Archivio di Stato, Florence/Scala/Art Resource, NY)

Islamic civilization and its openness to outside influences. As a case in point, the scientific leadership of the medieval Arabs rested partly on their willingness to learn from the great Hellenic thinkers of antiquity.

Development of *Waqf* System. Another critical determinant of the various successes lay in the economic institutions of Islamic civilization. The most important of these has no basis at all in the Qur'ān. It emerged, and then achieved identification with Islamic civilization, after the first Islamic century. This later-developing institution is the *waqf*, or pious foundation, whose earliest example goes back to the start of the second Islamic century, when the Arab-Islamic Empire was governed from Damascus. A *waqf* consists of property immobilized for the purpose of financing a selected religious or charitable mission in perpetuity; it is established through a personal act by the individual owner of the property. Within the limits of Islamic law, the choice of any given *waqf*'s mission is entirely up to its founder. Accordingly, from the eighth century to modern times, a bewildering array of social services has been provided through the *waqf* system. To name a few of varying economic significance, *waqf*s have been founded to build and maintain mosques, to support caravanserais on trade routes, to pay the taxes of designated neighborhoods, to run hospitals, to feed the poor, to operate schools, to

subsidize picnics for artisans and their families, to maintain public flower gardens, and even to feed the storks passing through selected towns. In the great cities of the medieval Middle East, *waqf*s supplied most of the urban services now provided almost exclusively by municipalities. *Waqf*s also formed a major instrument of poverty alleviation. Every major settlement had *waqf*-financed public shelters and soup kitchens that served poor people who could not have survived on the meager handouts they received through the *zakat* system.

In theory and to a large extent also in practice, the *waqf* system of the Islamic world emerged through the uncoordinated decisions of individual property holders. However, states endeavored, with some success, to influence the most significant investments made through the *waqf* system. A dignitary planning to establish a major *waqf* would typically receive some suggestions. He might be advised, for instance, that the main square of a certain strategically important Syrian town needs a new water fountain. This sort of advice, which was usually taken seriously, served to limit coordination failures.

The enormous economic significance of the Islamic *waqf* system, it is often suggested, stems from widespread adherence to a norm of selfless piety. This view overlooks the role that *waqf*s played as wealth shelters. A founder could make himself his *waqf*'s trustee for life, decide to compensate himself for his services, choose the *waqf*'s employees from among his relatives, and bequeath all his self-conferred privileges to his descendants. To be sure, *waqf* assets were sometimes confiscated, usually under the pretext that their founders had acquired them illegally. But at least until the eighteenth century, such confiscations were far less common than those of private property, because officials were reluctant to appear impious. So the wealth-sheltering function of the *waqf* contributed enormously to its popularity, all the more so in times of political instability, when private property generally became less secure.

Though typically free of direct state control, a *waqf* is not a corporation; once chartered, not even its founder can amend its by-laws or its mission. This imposed rigidity limited the *waqf* system's contributions to the growth of civil society. Moreover, insofar as modern capitalism requires strong "intermediate" organizations situated between the individual and the state, this rigidity ultimately retarded economic modernization. To an extent, the obstacles to strengthening civil society lay deeper, in the absence of even the concept of a corporation within the broader corpus of Islamic law. Yet Islamic law might have evolved differently had the *waqf* system, which gave property owners broad freedoms to determine the future uses and beneficiaries of their assets, also provided a modicum of autonomy to the *waqf*s themselves. If the Western experience offers any guidance, *waqf* autonomy might have stimulated a self-reinforcing movement for increasingly expansive organizational rights throughout the social system. In the West, the emergence of greater and lesser corporate bodies in the early Middle Ages gave rise, over subsequent centuries, to new laws that gradually strengthened civil society.

Lack of incorporation is also a striking feature of other social structures of the premodern Middle East. Not even the region's world-class cities were chartered as corporations, and not until the 1850s did any boast a municipality. Although certain urban craft guilds exercised considerable autonomy in their internal affairs, the state reserved the right to control their activities whenever it considered this necessary. For yet another example, colleges were not free to alter their curricula as educational needs changed; generally chartered as *waqf*s, they were required, in principle but sometimes also in practice, to teach precisely what their founders had stipulated.

Each of these rigidities reinforced the others by depriving the Islamic world of a corporate model. Limiting organizational development, they thus prevented the Middle East from maintaining the economic leadership that it once enjoyed. Had even one of these rigidities somehow been overcome, the established precedent might have stimulated organizational creativity elsewhere in the social system.

Islamic Partnerships. A possible starting point of an evolutionary path to broad-based incorporation was the institution of Islamic commercial partnerships. Yet, right up to the nineteenth century these partnerships consisted mostly of two-person enterprises. Moreover, their forms barely changed even as the typical European partnership expanded in size and gained complexity. The factors that accounted for the stagnation of Islamic partnership law are matters of ongoing investigation. A likely factor involves the Islamic inheritance system, which requires two-thirds of any estate to be divided among members of the deceased person's extended family according to standard rules. Judges sometimes looked the other way as families circumvented the rules of inheritance, but the system still raised the cost of keeping wealth intact across generations. Because adding members to a partnership increased the likelihood that it would have to be dissolved before the completion of its chosen mission, the Islamic inheritance system also discouraged the formation of large partnerships. The consequent failure to make the transition to large commercial partnerships had a critical consequence for the Middle East's economic evolution. The local merchant community did not see any reason to pressure local courts to create fundamentally new laws or to reinterpret the existing legal code, so the region produced nothing akin to the autocatalytic process that in the West led, first, to increasingly complex partnerships and, then in the nineteenth century, to a mushrooming of commercial and financial corporations.

By leaving Muslim merchants increasingly inefficient relative to their Western competitors, this institutional inertia reduced Muslim participation in Mediterranean trade. The governments of the Levant unwittingly contributed to this retreat by granting increasingly generous privileges to European traders. Known as capitulations (from *capitulum*, "chapters" in Latin), these privileges entailed lower customs duties for their beneficiaries. More important in the long run, they gave Westerners on business in the Middle East the right to be tried in courts of their own, initially only in cases involving no Muslims, but by the eighteenth century in all cases involving at least one European. By this time, Westerners doing business with the Middle East were also paying lower taxes than their local rivals.

As late as the nineteenth century, Muslims continued to dominate certain sectors of the Middle East's internal commerce, along with some of its trade with Central Asia and sub-Saharan Africa. But from the seventeenth century onward, the most lucrative components of the region's internal trade fell increasingly into the hands of local religious minorities. And the dominance of these minorities only expanded after tens of thousands of non-Muslim merchants obtained the right to become the protégés of a

Western power. By undergoing this change in political status, minorities gained exemptions from various charges imposed on locals. Much more critical, they earned the right to operate under Western laws.

If the Christian and Jewish subjects of the Middle Eastern states developed a preference for doing business under European legal systems, the reason is that these systems had gained sophistication during more than a half millennium when Islamic commercial and financial laws remained essentially stagnant. Unlike the Islamic courts, those of the West now recognized juristic personalities, gave enterprises the right to legal representation, accommodated insurance contracts, and accepted documentary evidence even in the absence of corroborating oral testimony. Such differences gave Western protégés a practically insurmountable competitive advantage over their local rivals who continued to operate under the region's traditional legal system. Up to the seventeenth century, the ancestors of these protégés had tended to operate under Islamic law for exactly the same reason, namely, to gain a competitive advantage.

In trying to make sense of the trade concessions made by Arab, Turkish, and Persian rulers, historians usually observe that these served as instruments to split western Europe, fount of the enormously destructive Crusades, by sustaining alliances between Middle Eastern powers and friendly Christian states. This interpretation leaves unexplained why Middle Eastern sovereigns did not pursue their geopolitical agendas by bringing the subjects of favored Christian states under the protective umbrella of the Islamic court system. In the early centuries, the decision to offer Westerners extraterritorial legal privileges had reflected, at least in part, a desire to secure the right to operate Islamic courts on territories under Christian control. However, after the eclipse of Muslim participation in Mediterranean trade, such a desire was no longer a major consideration. In the latter period, a more important factor was that Middle Eastern statesmen considered Western merchants more effective and more reliable, even though it took until the eighteenth century for the institutional sources of the Western advantages to begin gaining recognition. Revealingly, no unilateral trade concessions were offered to the trading nations of Asia or Africa. Such steps were unnecessary because the legal systems of these other non-Western nations did not place Middle Easterners at a disadvantage.

Economic Reforms. In the late-eighteenth century, Muslim merchants and financiers began demanding the exclusion of commercial and financial matters from the jurisdiction of the Islamic courts. Their efforts bore fruit in the mid-nineteenth century with the establishment of secular commercial courts in Istanbul, Cairo, and Alexandria. This path-breaking development was followed by further legal reforms that continued to transform the institutional foundation of the region's economies. By the end of World War I, all the principal states carved out of the defeated Ottoman Empire had made huge strides in modernizing the economically critical components of their legal systems. Some of the reforms entailed the adoption of Western legal codes; but there were also efforts to achieve legal modernization through the reinterpretation of traditional Islamic law. The most important economic component of Islamic law that successive modernization campaigns left more or less intact was the traditional inheritance system.

The economic reforms that set the Middle East on the road to modern economic growth were launched at a time when its economies were falling under European control and the leading governments of the region—Iran, Ottoman Turkey, semiautonomous Egypt—were all approaching bankruptcy. To stay afloat, these governments had tried, over the previous three centuries, to raise new revenues through tax reforms. But their capacity for direct taxation remained limited, and, in the absence of indigenous banks, none could borrow efficiently from its own subjects. So, before turning to foreign sources, they sought to borrow against their future domestic revenues, for example, by extending the terms of the tax-farming arrangements through which they had traditionally collected taxes indirectly. Another revenue-raising measure that gained significance in this period was the takeover of major *waqf* assets. Many of these nationalized assets came to be managed centrally, which made the revenues that they produced effectively fungible. This transformation thus turned out to be a step toward economic centralization. Beginning in the nineteenth century and continuing in the twentieth century, social services that the *waqf* system had long provided in a decentralized manner became government responsibilities.

As governments assumed new economic functions, they also took steps to strengthen private property rights. Starting in the 1830s, they began pledging to avoid arbitrary expropriations. The pledges became easier to enforce as jurisdiction over property transfers moved from religious courts to secular courts, for the newly adopted laws removed ambiguities concerning the definition of ownership.

The period of feverish reform also saw campaigns to overhaul the region's traditional educational systems and improve the skills of its workers. Schools with modern curricula were established in all major centers of the region, sometimes at the initiative of Europeans who also supplied funds, personnel, and know-how. By 1920, when the region's political map was being redrawn, every emerging state had a growing, if still small, class of highly educated people. And each had established the foundations of mass education. Meanwhile, new industrial technologies were spreading throughout the region. Although the Middle

East remained part of the underdeveloped world, it was now poised for an economic recovery.

Relative to the economies of the West, those of the Middle East still looked primitive. Yet the distance the region had traveled in barely a century was impressive considering how late it had started to experience the technological and institutional transformations associated with modern economic life. Two striking examples must suffice. Not until 1727 did Ottoman Turkey, and not until 1822 did Egypt, set up its first printing press—almost three centuries after the Gutenberg press went into operation in the former case, almost four centuries in the latter. And as late as the 1920s, nowhere in the region did there exist a single indigenous insurance company.

[*See also* Ottoman Empire.]

BIBLIOGRAPHY

Abu-Lughod, Janet L. *Before European Hegemony: The World-System A.D. 1250–1350*. New York, 1989. Documents the achievements of the Middle Eastern peoples in both local and long-distance commerce.

Al-Hassan, Ahmad Y., and Donald R. Hill. *Islamic Technology: An Illustrated History*. Paris, 1986. Reviews the contributions of medieval Muslims to the natural sciences, engineering, shipping, agriculture, mining, and metallurgy.

Ashtor, Eliyahu. *A Social and Economic History of the Near East in the Middle Ages*. London, 1976. Replete with facts, but analysis is minimal.

Barnes, John Robert. *An Introduction to Religious Foundations in the Ottoman Empire*. Leiden, 1987. Also covers the pre-Ottoman history of the *waqf*.

Çizakça, Murat. *A Comparative Evolution of Business Partnerships: The Islamic World and Europe with Special Reference to the Ottoman Archives*. Leiden, 1996. Highly informative empirical investigation of the evolution of Islamic partnerships.

Crone, Patricia. *Meccan Trade and the Rise of Islam*. Princeton, 1987. Controversial work that questions the importance of pre-Islamic Mecca to eastern Mediterranean commerce.

Goitein, S. D. *A Mediterranean Society: An Abridgement in One Volume*. Revised and edited by Jacob Lassner. Berkeley, 1999. Most readable interpretation of the Geniza documents.

Goldberg, Jan. "On the Origins of *Majālis al-Tujjār* in Mid-Nineteenth Century Egypt." *Islamic Law and Society* 6.2 (1999), 193–223. Shows that Muslim merchants played a key role in the Middle East's legal modernization.

Huff, Toby E. *The Rise of Early Modern Science: Islam, China, and the West*. New York, 1993. Contains many insights into the religious and institutional factors that fueled the early advances and subsequent stagnation of science within Islamic civilization.

Ibn Khaldun. *The Muqaddimah: An Introduction to History*. 3 vols. Edited by Franz Rosenthal. New York, 1958. Original Arabic edition, 1379. Features stunning insights into the political economy of the Islamic world, especially that of its Arab heartland.

Ibrahim, Mahmood. *Merchant Capital and Islam*. Austin, 1990. Maintains that merchants dominated the first Islamic state and that this domination facilitated Islam's rapid expansion.

İnalcık, Halil, with Donald Quataert, ed. *An Economic and Social History of the Ottoman Empire, 1300–1914*. Cambridge, 1994. Four chronological sections that focus on population, trade, transport, manufacturing, and land tenure.

Issawi, Charles. *An Economic History of the Middle East and North Africa*. New York, 1982. Thematic account covering the period after 1800.

Kuran, Timur. "Islam and Underdevelopment: An Old Puzzle Revisited." *Journal of Institutional and Theoretical Economics* 153.1 (1997), 41–71. Critiques, synthesizes, and extends the leading explanations put forth to account for the Middle East's economic retreat.

Kuran, Timur. "The Provision of Public Goods under Islamic Law-Origins, Impact, and Limitations of the Waqf System." *Law and Society Review* 35.4 (2001), 301–357. Explores causes of the *waqf*'s inflexibility and of its lack of corporate status.

Løkkegaard, Frede. *Islamic Taxation in the Classic Period, with Special Reference to Circumstances in Iraq*. Copenhagen, 1950. Offers much evidence on the fiscal policies of early Islamic regimes.

Masters, Bruce. *The Origins of Western Economic Dominance in the Middle East: Mercantilism and the Islamic Economy in Aleppo, 1600–1750*. New York, 1988. Provides many empirical details on Middle Eastern trade and handicrafts on the eve of Europe's Industrial Revolution.

Owen, Roger. *The Middle East in the World Economy, 1800–1914*. London, 1981. Focuses on the economic forces that transformed the whole region.

Rodinson, Maxime. *Islam and Capitalism*. Translated from the French by Brian Pearce. New York, 1973. Original French edition, 1966. Argues that Islam neither helped nor hindered early Islamic economic development.

Udovitch, Abraham L. *Partnership and Profit in Medieval Islam*. Princeton, 1970. Drawing on the legal literature, identifies the factors that made Islamic partnerships popular across the Mediterranean.

TIMUR KURAN

Modern Lebanon

Modern Lebanon was created on 1 September 1920 as a state under French control that comprised the area of Mount Lebanon, the port cities of Tripoli, Beirut, Tyre, and Sidon, the Bekaa Valley, and the southern regions bordering what was then Palestine. The country was formed from the remains of the Ottoman Empire, divided between France and Britain following World War I. The country, newly separated from Syria, remained economically linked in a customs and monetary union. It was and remains a heterogeneous country of Maronite Christians, mainly in the Mount Lebanon area, mixed with Sunni, Shi'ite, and Druze Muslims. The Christians were generally better educated, and around 40 percent were employed directly in silkworm breeding for the French export market, which was by far the largest economic activity. They comprised a large share of the public-sector workforce and received favorable tax treatment over Muslim citizens. They also tended to have commercial and service-sector employment, while the Muslims were primarily farmers in the northern and southern parts of the country and blue-collar workers in the cities. The Muslim farmers tended to be in feudal-type relationships with large landowners, in contrast to the independent farmers of Mount Lebanon. Almost two-thirds of employment was in the agricultural

MODERN LEBANON. Alcatel technician installs a digital telephone exchange, Beirut, 1994. (© Barry Iverson/Woodfin Camp and Associates, New York)

sector, with between 10 and 25 percent in the industrial sector and the remainder in commerce and services.

A continuing decline in the demand for silk and other agricultural products caused widespread economic hardship and caused many people to emigrate from Lebanon in the 1920s and 1930s. There was also much internal migration from the countryside to the coast, in particular to Beirut. Domestic and foreign banking (primarily French) expanded in Beirut and the larger cities, while in the rural areas moneylending and more primitive means of finance continued. Manufacturing industry grew on a large scale during the 1930s, often facilitated by émigrés returning from abroad. The budgetary system was an ad hoc scheme of indirect taxes and fees, which were increased whenever the French High Commission could not balance its budget. Excise duties and customs taxes were the most prevalent, accounting for four-fifths of the total tax take. The service sector of the economy was devoted to trade, with Beirut increasingly becoming a major port for transshipment to the Middle East. The major Lebanese exports were food, textiles, and leather goods, and major imports were manufactured consumption and capital goods. The major trading partners were Syria, Palestine, and France. The period before World War II saw an expansion of the road network and the port of Beirut plus improved communication facilities.

Lebanon came under Vichy French control in 1940, and this period was devoted to promoting economic self-sufficiency and setting up manufactured enterprises.

These policies were continued after the Allied occupation of 1941 in response to wartime scarcity and the general breakdown of trade throughout the region. Owners of industrial and trading enterprises tended to do well out of the increased demand caused by the war, at the expense of workers in agriculture. The war saw electricity production almost double, with the construction of hydroelectric and geothermal power plants along the Litani River. Following liberation by the Free French forces, Lebanon became independent in 1943. It had the highest per capita income in the Middle East, the most-educated workforce, and the best-developed infrastructure. Lebanon remained tied to France by a monetary agreement that kept it within the franc zone of countries, with its foreign reserves held in Paris. It was not until 1949 that it set up its own currency, the Lebanese lira. The customs union with Syria was maintained until 1950, when it broke down acrimoniously. Efforts were then made to expand the trade base to other countries in the Middle East.

In the postindependence period the Lebanese economy opened up to market forces with the removal of most forms of regulation and the repeal of tariff protection in the late 1940s. The period from 1950 until 1974 was one of sustained progress, with estimates of annual growth of 7 percent per year, which translated into 3 to 4 percent in per capita terms. Agriculture continued to decline in importance, while trade and finance expanded in its place. Financial controls were successively dropped, and Beirut became the financial center of the Middle East with an expansion in the number of banks from nine in 1945 to ninety-three in 1966. Much of the oil wealth of the Middle East passed through the Lebanese banking system, and Arab tourism expanded strongly. Farming became more capital intensive, and with a greater reliance on seasonal workers, migration from the interior to the coast and the outskirts of Beirut continued. The government's fiscal policy was primarily aimed at achieving small budget surpluses, with expansionary fiscal policy rarely used. The government primarily spent on infrastructure improvements, but even then modestly. Industry roughly maintained its share of national output during this period but, as it was relatively capital intensive, did not employ much of the labor force. As policy shifted toward export orientation, Lebanese industry focused on producing goods for the Middle East market rather than the traditional home and Syrian markets.

The late 1960s and early 1970s saw a widening of income inequality in Lebanon. The merchant class prospered, while rural workers were pushed off their farms to the outskirts of Beirut, where they searched for work. The early 1970s saw a large increase in inflation, which also caused a deterioration in the conditions of rural workers. Popular insurrection and dissatisfaction with life combined with ethnic and religious clashes led to the civil war of 1975–1976, and fighting continued sporadically until the mid-1980s. The principal economic effects of this were much migration abroad and destruction of property. Between 1975 and 1980 there was a net loss of half a million inhabitants in a nation of under 3 million. Remittances of Lebanese employed overseas increased to U.S. $600 per person per year by 1980. To finance the civil war, there was a drastic change in agricultural production from food toward hashish, with estimates that three-quarters of agricultural land in some regions was devoted to this. The hostilities, which were concentrated in Beirut, had the effect of wholly or partly damaging over half the existing infrastructure by 1985. A side effect of the fighting was the movement of population and industry to the smaller coastal cities of Sidon and Tripoli. By the mid-1980s, following the Israeli invasion of 1982, around half the population was unemployed, and inflation skyrocketed again.

The necessity of borrowing and relying on foreign aid to rebuild the country has meant the growing indebtedness of Lebanon. Currently the debt to GDP ratio stands at more than 140 percent, and debt servicing takes up around half of the budget, which has been pushed into a structural deficit by the reconstruction issue. No official census has been undertaken since 1932, but unofficial estimates have Muslims comprising 70 percent of the population and Christians the remainder. The population is 95 percent ethnically Arabic.

Growth resumed in the country in the 1990s, mainly in the finance, building, and tourism sectors. Programs to widen the tax base and reduce corruption have not been fully implemented. The state has been privatizing state enterprises and has maintained its commitment to a laissez-faire, open economy. Inflation has been brought down from 120 percent in 1992 to almost zero currently, while no official figures are available, estimates of per capita income range from $4,000 to $5,000. A recent influx of workers from Syria and East Asia have contributed to an estimated unemployment rate of 30 percent.

BIBLIOGRAPHY

Barakat, Halim, ed. *Toward a Viable Lebanon*. Washington, D.C., 1988.

Gates, Carolyn L. *The Merchant Republic of Lebanon*. London, 1998.

Gemayel, Amine. *Rebuilding Lebanon*. Lanham, Md., 1992.

Gilmour, David. *Lebanon: The Fractured Country*. New York, 1983.

Makdisi, Samir A. *Financial Policy and Economic Growth: The Lebanese Experience*. New York, 1979.

Petran, Tabitha. *The Struggle over Lebanon*. New York, 1987.

Shafik, Nemat, ed. *Economic Challenges Facing Middle Eastern and North African Countries*. Basingstoke, U.K., 1998.

LYNDON MOORE

Palestine during the British Mandate

In October 1918, British forces, fighting the Ottomans on the World War I southeastern front, effected the capture of Palestine. On 25 April 1920, Britain was given a mandate to rule Palestine on behalf of the League of Nations, and a civil government headed by a high commissioner replaced the military administration. On 24 July 1922, the League of Nations approved the text of the mandate, which incorporated the obligation of the mandatory to secure the establishment of a Jewish national home in Palestine while safeguarding the civil and religious rights of all the country's inhabitants. Soon thereafter, Transjordan was separated from Palestine; and in 1923, the boundaries of Palestine as an administratively unified territorial polity west of the Jordan River were finally shaped. On 14 May 1948, Britain terminated the mandate, and on the same day the state of Israel was created by self-proclaimed Jewish independence (based on the UN partition resolution of 29 November 1947), marking the beginning of a new era in Palestinian history.

Although failing to achieve the politically impossible task of satisfying both Arabs and Jews, Britain succeeded in providing Palestine with a well-functioning modern government. A domestic currency was introduced in 1927, with a specially designated currency board in London issuing Palestine pounds at a 1:1 conversion rate against its sterling reserves (generated by the excess of Palestine's capital inflows over its import surplus). This scheme permitted, until World War II, free sterling convertibility, making Palestine's money supply endogenously determined.

On the budgetary front, a self-contained fiscal apparatus, relying primarily (75 percent) on custom duties and other indirect taxes, was established. Public expenditures (averaging 18 percent of Palestine's output) were, as in other colonial economies, heavily concentrated in administration and public safety (60 percent), with another 27 percent being allocated to infrastructure construction in transportation and public utilities and to agricultural extension services and other economic outlays. The remaining 13 percent went mainly to education and health, which, in view of the Jews' own public expenditures, were directed mainly toward the Arab community. On the whole, the government maintained a rather low profile in the domestic economy (except for attempting to restrict Jewish purchases of land inhabited by Arab peasants); and within the institutional and legal framework that it provided, Arabs and Jews freely conducted their separate (though mutually interactive), and developmentally disparate economic lives.

The era's main demographic and economic (as well as political) development was based on the extremely rapid population increase of the Jewish community—largely self-governed by the officially recognized executive of the Zionist organization—and its extraordinary economic growth. The Jewish population, no more than 57,000 (9 percent of Palestine's total population) in mid-1919, grew more than elevenfold to 630,000 (32 percent of total population) by the end of 1947, with immigration providing 73 percent of the increase. The immigrants, concentrated in the working ages (80 percent were aged fifteen to sixty-four years) and well endowed with educational capital, raised even further the Jewish community's high level of schooling, and were instrumental in an enormous rise in its productive capacity.

Jewish production from 1922 to 1947 grew 13.2 percent annually (raising its share of Palestine's output from 17 percent to 57 percent), and Jewish per capita income grew 4.8 percent annually. The major factor fostering this remarkable growth, while the Jewish population was increasing 8.5 percent annually, was massive investments (averaging 31 percent of Jewish gross national product—GNP) that allowed capital stock to rise even faster, 11.6 percent annually. Productivity rose appreciably as well (3.5 percent annually), accounting for about a quarter of the total output growth.

The prime source of Jewish investment funds was the huge, albeit fluctuating, inflow of imported capital, averaging 64 percent of Jewish, and 22 percent of all of Palestine's, output. About two-thirds of this influx was private (unilateral transfers by immigrants and private investments), and the rest consisted of donations made by Diaspora Jewry to Zionist institutions. The quasi-governmental Zionist executive used about 73 percent of the latter to finance public outlays in the Jewish community, half of it allocated to immigration and settlement, 40 percent to

social services (mostly education), and the rest to administration. The Zionist land-buying organs (primarily the Jewish National Fund—JNF) used the remaining 27 percent of these donations to purchase land, typically from Arab landowners. Land acquired by the JNF remained national property and was leased, mostly for communal and cooperative agricultural settlements (*kibbutzim* and *moshavim*), to Jewish lessees only.

National-collective ownership of land was regarded in Zionism as both a necessary precondition for the implementation of Jewish territorial self-determination in Palestine and as a substitute for its lack under the mandate. In 1947, Jews possessed 11 percent of Palestine's land (compared to 3 percent in 1922), with half of these holdings owned by the JNF.

Another component of the autonomous Jewish public sector was the General Federation of Jewish Labor (*histadrut*). In addition to its trade union and employment services, it developed an elaborate system of health care and other social and cultural services and an array of productive establishments (collectively owned by its membership). These ventures enabled the *histadrut* to complement the Zionist executive in assuming responsibility for a significant portion of Jewish collective action in the social and economic arena.

Although most of the Zionist institutional efforts were aimed at leading immigrants into spatially dispersed agricultural settlements and other manual pursuits, Palestine's Jewish community remained primarily urban (74 percent), with 51 percent of the labor force on average engaged in services. Manufacturing and construction employed another 31 percent, and only 19 percent tilled the land.

The Arabs' socioeconomic profile was substantially different from the Jews', largely shaped by a traditional rural society, encompassing 65 to 70 percent of the fast-, mostly naturally growing Arab population (2.8 percent annually, from 594,000 in 1919 to 1,340,000 in 1947). The rural population lived in villages whose hierarchical organization was based on lineage-descent groups (*hamulot*), and partly still on communally possessed and periodically redistributed land (*musha'a*). In 1922, about 64 percent of Arab workers were engaged in (mainly extensive) husbandry as landowning peasants, tenants, and wage earners. Notwithstanding a gradual exodus from domestic agriculture (due to population pressure on the land, attractive earning opportunities outside the village, and possibly also tenant displacement caused by Jewish land purchases), 55 percent of the Arab labor force remained in the agricultural industry by the end of the mandate. Another 11 to 13 percent were employed in manufacturing and construction, and the rest in commerce, transportation, and other services. The latter included employment by the government and—up to the Arab revolt of 1936–1939 against the

PALESTINE. Workers picking olives from trees and off the ground, early 1900s. (Frank and Frances Carpenter Collection/ Prints and Photographs Division, Library of Congress)

British mandate and the Jewish buildup that it allowed, and again in the 1940s—by Jews.

On the whole, the Arab community was very poor, with income per capita about two and one-half times lower than in the Jewish community. Similar discrepancies are observed in indicators of human development. On the eve of World War II, the Arab infant mortality rate was one hundred and forty per thousand born, and life expectancy at birth was forty-eight years, versus sixty-five per thousand born and sixty-three years, respectively, among Jews. Likewise, only 25 percent of Arabs aged five to nineteen years attended school in 1940, whereas Jewish attendance reached 77 percent.

Poor as it may have been, the Arab economy was far from stagnant. Its growth performance (for 1922–1947, a 6.5 percent annual income increase overall, or 3.6 percent per capita), although eclipsed by the Jewish record, was impressive. Modest investments in reproducible capital (11 percent of GNP on average), which were facilitated by capital imports and domestic savings, allowed for an annual increase in capital per worker of 1.4 percent. However, at least half of output growth was due to productivity,

which increased at 3 to 3.5 percent annually. The Arabs managed to intensify the utilization of their productive resources and gainfully reallocate them in response to export opportunities and Jewish demand. In addition, the rise in productivity certainly reflected the effects of government investments in infrastructure and farm-supporting technical programs, as well as technological spillovers from the Jewish sector.

Intercommunal trade—with Arabs selling to Jews, apart from land, farm produce, building materials, and services of dwelling and manual labor, in return for manufactured products and various services—was beneficial enough to overcome all political obstacles prior to 1936. In 1935, land transactions constituted 37 percent of Arab sales to Jews, and the proportions of (net of land) goods and services destined for the Jewish market were 56 percent and 14 percent of Arab exports and output, respectively. The analogous proportions of Jewish sales to Arabs, though much smaller, still reached 7 percent of Jewish production and 27 percent of Jewish exports in 1935.

Palestine's foreign trade was marked by a sharp rise and a substantial upward divergence from the shrinking volume of world trade in the depressioned 1930s. Facilitated by huge capital inflows, an import surplus of no less than 32 percent of GNP was maintained through most of the period. Imports were increasing steeply in the first half of the 1930s, signaling a Palestine-specific economic upturn, enhanced by the acceleration of Jewish immigration and capital inflows from troubled eastern and central Europe at the time. It was only during Palestine's severe economic downturn, from 1936 to 1939 that imports declined somewhat.

Exports, on the other hand, which in the interwar years were dominated by citrus products (accounting for 54 percent of Palestine's merchandise exports in the 1920s and 77 percent in the 1930s), rose continuously until 1939, thanks to the expansion of groves, which allowed for rising sales abroad, albeit at declining prices. Close to two-thirds of the interwar investment in the citrus industry was undertaken by Jews, and the rest by Arabs. In 1940, war-induced closure of European markets caused the citrus industry to collapse. However, by becoming a major supply center for the Allied forces in the eastern Mediterranean, Palestine was saved from the possible economic devastation of the citrus-market destruction and enjoyed material prosperity that would last through the few remaining years of the mandate.

[*See also* Israel.]

BIBLIOGRAPHY

Bachi, Roberto. *The Population of Israel*. Jerusalem, 1977. A comprehensive quantitative account of the demographic history of Palestine and Israel through the ages. Contains the best available estimates of the composition and the change of population during the Mandate.

Gross, Nachum T. "The Development of Agricultural Techniques in the Jewish Economy in Mandatory Palestine." In *The Development of*

Agricultural Technology in the 19th and 20th Centuries, edited by Heral Winkel and Klaus Herrmann, pp. 157–168. Ostfildern, 1984.

Gross, Nachum T. "The Economic Policy of the Mandatory Government in Palestine." *Research in Economic History* 9 (1984), 143–185.

Gross, Nachum T., and Jacob Metzer. "Palestine in World War Two: Some Economic Aspects." In *The Sinews of War*, edited by Geofrey T. Mills and Hugh Rockoff, pp. 59–82. Iowa City, 1993.

Kamen, Charles S. *Little Common Ground: Arab Agriculture and Jewish Settlement in Palestine 1920–1948*. Pittsburgh, 1991. A data-rich study of the Arab farm sector as it coexisted with a fast-growing Jewish modern economy, and of the government policies and extension programs affecting it.

McCarthy, Justin. *The Population of Palestine: Population History and Statistics of the Late Ottoman Period and the Mandate*. New York, 1990. A useful compilation of official demographic statistics, with an insightful introduction discussing their merits and offering some revisions to overcome their shortcomings.

Metzer, Jacob. *The Divided Economy of Mandatory Palestine*. Cambridge, 1998. A comprehensive account of Palestine's economy under British rule, dealing comparatively with its Arab and Jewish sectors. A quantitative appendix puts together updated demographic data and national-income figures for Arabs and Jews on an annual basis.

Michaelis, Dolf. "One Hundred Years of Banking and Currency in Palestine." *Research in Economic History* 10 (1986), 155–197.

Migdal, Joel S., et al. *Palestinian Society and Politics*. Princeton, 1980. Contains a number of enlightening monographic studies of important subjects in the political economy of mandatory Palestine: "The Office and Functions of the Village *Mukhtar*" by Gabriel Baer; "Administrative Policy in Rural Palestine: The Impact of British Norms on Arab Community Life, 1920–1948" by Ylana Miller; "Legal Protection and Circumvention of Rights for Cultivators in Mandatory Palestine" by Kenneth Stein; "Peasants into Workmen: Internal Labor Migration and the Arab Village Community under the Mandate" by Rachelle Taqqu.

Owen, Roger, ed. *Studies in the Economic and Social History of Palestine, 1918–1948*. London and Oxford, 1982. An illuminating compilation of specialized studies concentrating on Palestine's economic development in the second half of the nineteenth century (by Alexander Scholch) and on various socioeconomic aspects of the Arab community and its evolution during the mandate (by Sarah Graham-Brown, Salim Tamari, and Avi Plascov). An editor's introduction discusses the broader context and issues involving study of the economic and social history of modern Palestine.

Owen, Roger. *The Middle East in the World Economy*. 2d ed. London and New York, 1993. A detailed survey of the Middle Eastern economies between the Crimean War and World War I. Provides a very useful historical background for the study of Palestine's economy under the British mandate.

Plessner, Yakir. *The Political Economy of Israel: From Ideology to Stagnation*. Albany, N.Y., 1994. A highly opinionated but thought-provoking, study of Israel's political economy, attributing the origins of governmental interventionism in the Israeli economy to the requirements of nation-building and to the market-mistrusting ideologies of Labor-Zionism during the mandate.

Smith, Barbara J. *The Roots of Separatism in Palestine: British Economic Policy 1920–1929*. Syracuse, N.Y., 1993. A well-documented investigation, arguing that the economic policies of the government paved the way for the development of a Jewish industrial enclave in Palestine and thus for a persistent economic wedge and separatism between Arabs and Jews. Although the part of the argument that rests on the tariff structure remains unverified, the general claim that government attitudes and policies facilitated (or at least did not hinder) the development of an ethno-nationally divided economy in mandatory Palestine is well taken.

Sussman, Zvi. "The Determinants of Wages for Unskilled Labor in the Advance Sector of the Dual Economy of Mandatory Palestine." *Economic Development and Cultural Change* 1 (1973), 95–113. A careful examination of the segmented labor market in mandatory Palestine, suggesting that the supply of Arab labor had a negative effect on the wages of Jewish unskilled workers.

Jacob Metzer

Modern Syria

Economic Growth and Structure. Little is known about the economic development of the Syrian region as a whole prior to the establishment of the French Mandate in 1920 because, under Ottoman rule (1517–1917), Syria, within its current borders, never had a unified government. During the Mandatory period (1920–1946), the agricultural sector was the primary source of rapid economic growth, with approximately 70 percent of the total population deriving their livelihood directly from agriculture. The total

MODERN SYRIA. Market scene, Damascus, 1990. (© Barry Iverson/Woodfin Camp and Associates, New York)

cultivated area increased from 700,000 hectares in 1920 to 2.3 million in 1945. However, several territorial changes during this period harmed the Syrian economy: the French cession to Turkey of the economically valuable region of Alexandretta in 1939; the French partition of Syria into six separately administered territories; and the establishment of borders and customs duty between the "Franc areas" and the "Sterling areas" in the Middle East, which obstructed the free passage of both goods and people. To these impediments, one should add the negative effects of the Great Depression of the early 1930s and World War II.

Following independence in 1946, the agricultural sector continued to lead Syria's economy, as the industrial sector remained on the fringe, contributing only 9 percent to the gross domestic product (GDP) in 1963. Political instability, including many *coup d'états* and frequent cabinet shifts, hindered Syria's economic growth from independence until the ascendancy of the Ba'th party in March 1963. However, owing to a lack of reliable data, it is difficult to assess the economic growth rates during that period.

Although Hafiz al-Asad's regime (November 1970–June 2000) brought about political stability, overwhelming governmental involvement in the economy and unwillingness of the regime to adopt more liberal measures constituted major barriers to economic growth in this period. The major characteristic of the Syrian economy during these years was fluctuation between high growth and severe recession, caused by increasing reliance on three *rental* income sources: (1) Oil production increased from just under 200,000 barrels/day (b/d) in 1986 to a peak of 610,000 b/d in 1995, with a slight decline to 535,000 b/d in 1999; and oil exports represented more than half of total Syrian exports and approximately 60 percent of the governmental revenues in the late 1990s. (2) There were remittances from Syrian temporary workers abroad, mainly in Lebanon (until 1975 and following the Ta'if Agreement of 1989), and in the Arabian gulf oil-states and in Jordan (following the October 1973 "oil boom"). (3) Grants came from the gulf oil-states, peaking at almost $2 billion in 1980–1981, and later declining to an average of $500 million annually during the second half of the 1980s. Thus, although the annual average GDP growth rate was 8.8 percent for the years 1970–1982, it hardly reached an annual average of 1 percent in the second half of the 1980s. This economic recession was a result of a sharp decline in oil prices—which led to a decrease in revenues from oil exports, workers' remittances, and grants from the gulf oil-states—combined with the adoption of a "strategic balance policy" vis-à-vis Israel, which consumed more than half of the governmental budget by the mid-1980s.

During the first half of the 1990s, the Syrian economy was characterized by rapid growth, averaging 7 percent per year, driven by a sharp increase in oil production,

grants from the gulf oil-states (due to Syrian participation in the anti-Iraqi coalition during the 1990–1991 Gulf Crisis), good harvests, and increasing private investments. However, during the second half of the 1990s, economic development once again slowed, with the GDP growth rate falling considerably lower than the population growth rate, mainly because of low oil prices (until early 1999), several years of severe drought, a reduction in private investments, cutbacks in grants from the gulf oil-states, and suspension of Syrian-Israeli peace negotiations.

Socioeconomic Policies and Income Distribution. During the Mandatory period and the first decade following independence, a laissez-faire approach ruled the Syrian economy, leading to an ever-widening gap in income between the upper class, comprised mainly of landlords and urban merchants, and the lower class, made up of peasants and the lower urban strata. A retreat from this capitalist approach began during Syria's union with Egypt (February 1958–September 1961), the most decisive moves in this direction being the September 1958 Land Reform Law and the July 1961 Socialist Decrees. This trend was accelerated following the ascendancy of the Ba'th party, in line with its basic socialist ideology. However, beginning in the mid-1980s, owing to disappointment in the performance of the public sector, the authorities gradually adopted some liberal economic measures, the most prominent of which was the May 1991 Investment Law No. 10, later updated in June 2000. Despite these liberal measures, private banking and stock exchange still are not permitted, and the public sector continues to be the largest employer.

Population Growth and Demography. Syria's population includes 70 percent Sunni Muslims; but, since February 1966, political power has been held by the 'Alawi minority sect, constituting 12 to 13 percent of the total population. During the twentieth century, particularly from the 1960s on, Syria's population increased rapidly,

TABLE 1. *Composition of Syria's GDP, 1963–1999 (in percentages)**

SECTOR	1963	1970	1980	1990	1999
Agriculture	44	33	32	30	27
Mining and manufacturing	9	10	7	13	19
Building and construction	4	5	8	4	4
Wholesale and retail trade	24	26	26	25	21
Transport and communication	8	9	7	10	13
Finance and insurance	4	5	5	4	5
Social and personal services	2	3	3	2	3
Government services	5	9	12	12	8
Total	100	100	100	100	100

* Constant prices of 1995.
SOURCE: Syrian Arab Republic, Office of Prime Minister, Central Bureau of Statistics (CBS). *Statistical Abstract, 2000.* Damascus, 2001.

TABLE 2. *Syria's Major Social Characteristics, 1947–1998*

CHARACTERISTICS	1947	1960	1970	1980	1990	1998
Total population (millions)	3.043	4.565	6.305	8.704	12.116	15.597
Crude birth rate (per 1,000)	—	48	48	46	44	30
Crude death rate (per 1,000)	—	18	14	8	7	5
Natural increase (%)	—	3.0	3.4	3.8	3.7	2.5
Infant mortality rate (per 1,000 live births)	—	132	99	67	43	26
Life expectancy at birth (years) (both sexes)	—	50	55	65	66	69
Percentage of under-20 population	—	54	59	60[a]	59	56
Average number of persons per hospital bed	1,986[b]	930	1,005	863[c]	887	832
Percentage of urban population	32	37	44	47	50	60
Literacy rate (10 years and over)	—	34	47	58	64	70[d]
University students (per 100,000 people)	86[e]	315	682	1,610	1,740	1,559[f]
Total labor force (millions)	—	1.0	1.4	2.1	3.1	4.4
Female labor force (% of total)	—	11.2	12.0	14.6	17.3	16.6

Dash indicates no data available.   [a]Related to 1981.   [b]Related to 1949.   [c]Related to 1982.   [d]Related to 1995.   [e]Related to 1950. [f]Related to 1994.
SOURCES: Syria, CBS, *Statistical Abstract*; UN, *Demographic Yearbook*; UNESCO, *Statistical Yearbook*; ECWA/ESCWA, *Demographic and Related Socio-economic Data Sheets for Countries of the Economic (and Social) Commission for Western Asia and Statistical Abstract of the ECWA/ESCWA Region*; UNICEF, *The State of the World's Children*; The World Bank, *World Tables and World Development Report*; ILO, *World Employment Report and Yearbook of Labour Statistics*.

from 1.3 million in 1922 to 16.1 million by mid-1999. This rapid growth is attributable to rising natural increase rates, which increased from a 2.3 percent yearly average in the late Mandatory period (1938–1947) to a peak of 4 percent in the early 1980s, as a result of decreasing crude death rates that paralleled continuing high fertility rates. Since then, the natural increase rate has steadily declined, owing to lower fertility rates, and was estimated to be 2.5 percent in the late 1990s.

Negative consequences of the rapid population growth included low crude economically active rates of economic activity, particularly among women; increasing governmental expenditures on public services and subsidies for basic foodstuffs; and a sharp decline in per capita cultivated land. These consequences led the Syrian government to withdraw in the late 1980s from its pro-natalist policy, which had been in force since 1949, and to advocate some anti-natalist measures. Nevertheless, because of its wide-based age pyramid, Syria's population will continue to grow rapidly, with forecasts predicting 24.6 million people by 2020, and 34.5 million in 2050.

Living Conditions and the Spatial Distribution of the Population. The Mandatory regime did little to improve social services in Syria, particularly in the countryside. After independence, and even more following the ascendancy of the Ba'th, the living conditions in Syria, particularly in the countryside and the provincial towns, had largely im-

proved, with the spread of electricity, safe water systems, communication systems, education and health services, and sanitation systems throughout the country. This led to a slowing of the urbanization process and to concentration of the rural migrants mainly in the provincial towns, rather than in the largest two cities of Damascus and Aleppo.

In sum, as indicated in Tables 1 and 2, although living conditions sharply improved during the second half of the twentieth century, the structural changes in the Syrian economy were minor, with agriculture still comprising about one-third of the GDP, as compared to only 7 percent for the manufacturing sector (without mining). By 1999, Syria's per capita GDP, estimated at U.S. $1,300, was one of the lowest in the entire Middle East region, and considerably lower than that of two decades earlier, at the peak of the "oil boom."

BIBLIOGRAPHY
Allan, J. N., ed. *Politics and the Economy in Syria*. London, 1987.
Asfour, Edmund Y. *Syria: Development and Monetary Policy*. Harvard Middle Eastern Monograph Series. Cambridge, 1959.
Batatu, Hanna. *Syria's Peasantry, the Descendants of Its Lesser Rural Notables, and Their Politics*. Princeton, 1999.
Economist Intelligence Unit (EIU). *Country Profile—Syria* (annual) and *Country Report* (quarterly).
Hansen, Bent. *Economic Development in Syria*. Berkeley, 1969.
Himadeh, Said B., ed. *Economic Organization of Syria*. Beirut, 1936.
Hinnebusch, Raymond A. *Peasant and Bureaucracy in Ba'thist Syria: The Political Economy of Rural Development*. Boulder, 1989.

Hinnebusch, Raymond A. *Syria: Revolution from Above*. London and New York, 2001.

Hopfinger, Hans, and Raslan Khadour, eds. *Economic Development and Investment in Syria*. Neustadt an der aisch, 1998.

International Bank for Reconstruction and Development (IBRD). *The Economic Development of Syria*. Baltimore, 1955.

Khoury, Philip S. *Syria and the French Mandate: The Politics of Arab Nationalism, 1920–1945*. Princeton, 1987.

Kienle, Eberhard, ed. *Contemporary Syria: Liberalisation between Cold War and Cold Peace*. London, 1994.

Perthes, Volker. *The Political Economy of Syria under Asad*. London and New York, 1995.

Podeh, Elie. *The Decline of Arab Unity: The Rise and Fall of the United Arab Republic*. Brighton and Portland, 1999.

Rabo, Annika. *Change on the Euphrates: Villages, Townsmen, and Employees in Northeast Syria*. Stockholm, 1986.

Seal, Patrick. *Asad of Syria: The Struggle for the Middle East*. London, 1988.

Winckler, Onn. *Demographic Developments and Population Policies in Ba'thist Syria*. Brighton and Portland, 1999.

ONN WINCKLER

LEVER, WILLIAM HESKETH (1851–1925), British industrialist.

William Lever built one of the largest industrial empires in the world. By the time of his death, Lever Brothers Limited had over eighty thousand employees producing over 400,000 metric tons of soap per year. The company was founded in 1885 by William and his brother James Darcy Lever (1853–1910), about whom little is known. The company's initial product, Sunlight Soap, was the best-selling soap in the United Kingdom by late 1887, and sales continued to soar well into the twentieth century. Sunlight's success was largely due to careful management of its brand image. William Lever was among the first industrialists to understand the importance of consistency and brand image in advertising.

Soap consumption grew rapidly in the United Kingdom throughout the nineteenth century, with several factors contributing to this rise. A new emphasis on hygiene, increasing wages, newly created public water supply systems, and dirty factory and mine work combined to increase demand. Technological innovations and reduced government regulation increased supply.

Prior to 1885, soap in Britain was sold in bulk to local grocers, who would then chisel off pieces of soap and sell them to consumers. One type of soap would be used by a grocer's customers for all of their washing, from personal hygiene to floors to laundry. The Levers' father, James Lever (1809–1897), was one such grocer. In 1867, sixteen-year-old William entered his father's business in Bolton, England. Seventeen years later, William decided to give the name Sunlight to the soap sold in his father's store. He registered the trademark although the soap itself was made by various manufacturers and not the Levers.

William Lever advertised that he sold only the best soaps of the manufacturers under the name Sunlight. One of these soaps was a vegetable-oil soap that soon would become the only soap sold under the Sunlight brand name. This soap needed to be wrapped individually so that it would not become rancid, and William Lever decided to put a brightly colored Sunlight logo on each wrapper. The packaged soap became a huge success and soon began to be sold in additional stores. When suppliers raised their prices in late 1885, William decided to build his own factory at Warrington, which would produce only this oil-based soap. By 1886, William and his brother had moved out of the grocery business altogether and dedicated themselves full time to selling Sunlight. William ran the company, Lever Brothers Limited, with James Darcy serving as a company director and William's closest adviser.

The success of Sunlight soap cannot be explained by the general increase in soap use or by the heavy advertising campaigns that William Lever conducted. Other soap companies benefited from the increased use of soap and heavy advertising, yet they did not share the Levers' success. What Sunlight soap had was a distinct brand image that was consistent with the actual properties of the product. In his advertising, William emphasized that Sunlight soap was easy to use. Unlike most of his rivals, who focused on the cleaning power of the soap, Lever sold Sunlight as a friend of the working-class woman. Sunlight alone would help her to do her work more easily and efficiently.

This image was based on the actual characteristics of the product. Because it was vegetable-based, Sunlight was softer and lathered more easily than its mostly animal-based rivals. Unlike most other soaps, Sunlight did not need scalding water to be effective. By 1888, many other British soap manufacturers had begun making vegetable-based soaps of their own; however, none of them was seen as a friend of the housewife.

The most prevalent, and perhaps most effective, of Sunlight's advertisements asked the question, "Why does a woman look old sooner than a man?" The answer, according to the advertisements, was the scalding water used in washing. William Lever's use of advertisements such as this one allowed him to build a national brand that people would trust without the recommendation of a local grocer. William Lever thus was among the first business people to understand the importance of creating a distinct brand image for a product.

The brand image of Sunlight as a friend of the working woman permeated all aspects of the Lever Brothers organization. In addition to emphasizing this image in advertising, Lever Brothers Limited treated its workers in a manner consistent with Sunlight's brand image. The factory town of Port Sunlight near Liverpool was a model industrial village when it opened in 1888. The English press praised William Lever because the workers at Port Sunlight were given pleasant, roomy homes, clean streets, and attentive doctors. Although today such a policy might be viewed in the negative light of paternalism, at the time such care significantly improved the living conditions of the working class. Lever Brothers Limited's innovative treatment of workers not only made the workers more productive, but it was consistent with Sunlight's brand image. In addition to being a friend of the working-class woman, Lever Brothers Limited was seen as a friend to its own workers and their families.

William Lever also played an important role in the British war effort during World War I. Glycerin, a by-product of soap making, is an important ingredient in making explosives, and Lever Brothers Limited sold large quantities of it to the government during the war. For his contributions to the war effort, William was raised to the peerage as a baron in 1917. He became a viscount in 1922, and he took the name Leverhulme, a combination of his own name and his wife's maiden name, Hulme. Lever's philanthropic endeavors include the Leverhulme Trust and the school of tropical medicine at Liverpool University.

William Hesketh Lever died in 1925, four years before Lever Brothers Limited merged with the Dutch company Margerine Unie to become Unilever. Today Unilever is one of Britain's (and Holland's) largest companies with annual revenues in excess of £29 billion.

BIBLIOGRAPHY

Edwards, H. R. *Competition and Monopoly in the British Soap Industry*. Oxford, 1962. A history of competitive practices in the British soap industry.

Leverhulme, Viscount. *Viscount Leverhulme by His Son*. London, 1927. A biography of William Hesketh Lever written by his son. Emphasizes his personality, political actions, and charitable donations.

Nevett, Terrence R. *Advertising in Britain: A History*. London, 1982.

Wilson, Charles. *The History of Unilever: A Study in Economic Growth and Social Change*. 2 vols. London, 1954. The definitive work on the history of Lever Brothers, Margerine Unie, and Unilever.

AVI GOLDFARB

LEWIS, JOHN L. (1880–1969), labor organizer.

Lewis is considered one of the most powerful, active, effective, and controversial leaders in American labor organization's history. He was the president of the United Mine Workers of America (UMW) for forty years, between 1920 and 1960, and was one of the founders of the Committee for Industrial Organization (CIO) in the mid-1930s. Some admire him as a labor leader and a talented public speaker, while others regard him as an opportunist and a demagogue. He was often accused of using dictatorial power in running the UMW, but for the miners he was a hero, a defender, and a spokesperson. Whatever his faults, Lewis was a colorful unionist who fought vigorously for workers' right to organize, shorter working hours, and improved benefits and safety for miners. Founder of the UMW Welfare and Retirement Fund designed to improve conditions in mines and to help the sick and the aged, he received the Freedom Medal from President Lyndon Johnson in 1964.

Born in Iowa to a Welsh immigrant coal miner, Lewis entered the mines and then became a trade unionist. In 1911, he was appointed as a special organizer for the American Federation of Labor (AFL), and he retained this position for six years. A talented public speaker, Lewis was elected vice president of the UMW before he became president in 1920. By then, the coal industry had grown dramatically, and the UMW, with 400,000 members and union contracts, was the nation's largest trade union. Lewis and his union appeared successful and had more influence in politics than ever before. However, the 1920s were years of depression in the soft coal industry in terms of both production and labor force. The economywide depression that started in 1929 made things even worse, and from 1929 until 1932 the UMW could not effectively protect its members. Between 1920 and 1932, membership fell to 150,000, and life worsened for soft coal miners as hourly earnings declined to fifty cents. Lewis supported Franklin D. Roosevelt for the presidency in 1933 and 1936 and welcomed the New Deal, claiming that only federal intervention could revive the soft coal industry. Under Roosevelt and with the lobbying of Lewis, Section 7a of the National Industrial Recovery Act (NIRA), which secured the right of workers to organize unions, was passed in 1933. A year later, miners, led by Lewis, were guaranteed a seven-hour day, five days a week. Also, they were given higher daily wages, a minimum wage of $5 in the northern districts and $4.60 in the South, and child labor was outlawed. Desiring to organize the millions of mass-production workers, Lewis set up the CIO in 1935 first as a bloc inside the AFL and later as an independent union. The CIO's success in organizing workers in the auto and steel industries in 1937 led to an increase in membership by nearly 100 percent, making it an influential force in politics and economics and a union larger than the AFL. Lewis stopped supporting Roosevelt in the election of 1940 and even resigned as president of the CIO when Roosevelt was reelected, since he thought the United States should not intervene in the European conflict.

In the next decade, Lewis led a series of strikes demanding wage increases and mine safety. The strikes during the war period resulted in public hostility toward Lewis, who was often accused of damaging the nation's war effort, and he became unpopular. In 1947, an explosion in Centralia, Illinois, killed 111 miners, and the union went on strike for six days as a response. Speaking before Congress, Lewis blamed its members for the tragedy and defended the coal miners' strike. Lewis failed to comply with a court order to

JOHN LEWIS. Seated at right, talking over the coal situation with Representative John I. Nolan, Chairman of the Labor Committee of the House of Representatives, 3 April 1922. (National Photo Company Collection/Prints and Photographs Division, Library of Congress)

resume negotiations with mine operators in 1948, which resulted in a $1.5 million fine on the UMW and a $20,000 fine on Lewis personally. Despite these setbacks, the late 1940s were rewarding for Lewis and brought one of his greatest achievements, the establishment of the Welfare and Retirement Fund. The fund was designed to help the sick and the aged and to improve working conditions for miners. By 1956, a medical and hospitalization program had enabled more than half a million patients to receive proper treatment. Programs such as rehabilitation aid, cash benefits and aid to widows allowed more than seventy-five thousand retired miners to receive pensions and tens of thousands of widows and orphans to get aid. In January 1960, Lewis retired as president of the UMW, but he remained the chairman of the Welfare and Retirement Fund until his death.

BIBLIOGRAPHY

Alinsky, Saul. *John L. Lewis: An Unauthorized Biography.* New York, 1949.

Dubofsky, Melvyn, and Warren Van Tine. *John L. Lewis: A Biography.* Urbana and Chicago, 1986.

Karsh, Bernard, and Jack London. "The Coal Miners: A Study of Union Control." *Quarterly Journal of Economics* 68.3 (1954), 415–436.

Leab, Daniel J. "Fame is Fleeting." *Labor History* 40.4 (November 1999), 481.

RAN ABRAMITZKY

LEWIS, W. ARTHUR (1915–1991), British development economist and economic historian.

Born on Saint Lucia, of African-Caribbean ancestry, Lewis taught at the London School of Economics, the University of Manchester, and Princeton University, and became United Nations adviser to the Prime Minister of Ghana, deputy managing director of the United Nations Special Fund, vice chancellor of the University of the West Indies, and president of the Caribbean Development Bank. He was a joint winner of the Alfred Nobel Memorial Prize in Economic Sciences in 1979.

Lewis's "Economic Development with Unlimited Supplies of Labour" (*The Manchester School*, 1954) originated the dual-economy approach to economic development, a two-sector general-equilibrium dynamic model of a poor economy. One sector, variously termed agricultural, rural, or traditional, interacts with a second sector, comprising the industrial, urban, or modern parts of the economy. The first sector supplies labor at a constant real wage to the second sector, providing his definition of unlimited labor. In the second sector, capitalists employ this labor to generate profits, which they save and invest there. The capital stock rises, increasing the proportion of total income produced in the second sector, which, in turn, increases the proportion of profits and savings in national income. The proportion of the labor force in agriculture falls, a basic accompaniment of development.

Economic historians have used the Lewis model, with its specific predictions of constant real wages and an increasing savings rate during initial growth, to interpret the British Industrial Revolution and Japan's early industrialization. It is also a standard tool used by development economists. The specifics of unlimited labor are not universally accepted; but Lewis established the general approach of two-sector models in a fundamental integrative view of development, with roles for the intersectoral allocation of factors of production, sectoral demands, and, concomitantly, the intersectoral terms of trade, as well as for factor accumulation and technological change. The durability and versatility of this article's general approach are proved by its centrality for understanding subsequent questions about, for example, urban unemployment, income distribution, and the Green Revolution.

The 1954 article also modeled the international terms of trade between poor and rich countries, based on the productivity of each in food production, the commodity both produce. Technological progress in the primary-product exporting sectors of poor countries leads to deterioration in their international terms of trade, transferring the benefits of progress abroad, an early example of immiserizing growth. The key to raising incomes in these countries is to increase their efficiency in food production.

Lewis elaborated both models of the 1954 article in subsequent papers. He also wrote on other aspects of development: trade, exchange rates, planning and benefit-cost analysis, public finance, education, income distribution, and the politics of development, including (disapprovingly and presciently) the African one-party state.

Although nearly all Lewis's analyses are empirically grounded, he also wrote extensively and influentially on two dimensions of economic history. His *Economic Survey, 1919–39* (London, 1949) and *Growth and Fluctuations, 1870–1913* (London, 1978) analyzed world economic history and interdependence, and other work focused on the economic history of the tropics.

BIBLIOGRAPHY

Bhagwati, Jagdish N. "W. Arthur Lewis: an Appreciation." In *The Theory and Experience of Economic Development: Essays in Honor of Sir W. Arthur Lewis*, edited by M. Gersovitz, C. F. Diaz-Alejandro, G. Ranis, and M. R. Rosenzweig, pp. 15–28. London, 1982.

Findlay, Ronald. "On W. Arthur Lewis's Contributions to Economics." In *The Theory and Experience of Economic Development: Essays in Honor of Sir W. Arthur Lewis*, edited by M. Gersovitz, C. F. Diaz-Alejandro, G. Ranis, and M. R. Rosenzweig, pp. 1–14. London, 1982.

Gersovitz, Mark, ed. *Selected Economic Writings of W. Arthur Lewis.* New York, 1983.

Lewis, W. Arthur. "Development Economics in the 1950s." In *Pioneers in Development*, edited by G. M. Meier and D. Seers, pp. 121–137. New York, 1984.

Lewis, W. Arthur. "W. Arthur Lewis." In *Lives of the Laureates*, edited by W. Breit and R. W. Spencer, pp.1–20. 3d ed. Cambridge, Mass., 1997.

MARK GERSOVITZ

LIBERIA AND SIERRA LEONE. Small, adjoining countries in West Africa, Liberia and Sierra Leone have a similar, even shared, economic history because of such factors as ecology, location in the larger region, and position in the modern global political economy. Employing rich indigenous knowledge, farmers plant many varieties of the staple rice in different cycles, with intercropping, as appropriate to microenvironments. Historically, upland planting predominated, using shifting cultivation; but since the nineteenth century, farmers have adapted rice to riverine, tidal, and inland swamps, yielding higher outputs without the environmental deterioration of dryland farming. In southwestern Liberia, cassava has been the staple. Life also has centered on the palm tree, whose varieties fill food, lighting, roofing, and other needs. Women have played a large, and increasing, role in food production.

For many centuries, people in the Sierra Leone–Liberia region exchanged kola, salt, and imports for commodities of the drier inlands such as cattle, sheep, and goats; gold, cloths, and many other goods also were traded. Beginning in the eighteenth century, professional traders assumed a greater role, and interregional routes were improved, particularly in northern Sierra Leone. After 1850, commerce expanded significantly. Caravans often numbered in the hundreds, typically led by Mande- and Pular-speakers. Their passage and trade were facilitated by hosts who housed and fed them, translated, and assisted in sales. Although marketplaces existed in some towns, much exchange was done in households or business shops.

Atlantic commerce began in the late 1400s. Early European traders sought a variety of commodities, including pepper, gold, woods, dyes, and ivory. Sierra Leone and western Liberia were particularly affected by the Atlantic slave trade. Whereas European and Eurafrican slavers established forts and barracoons in such places as the Sierra Leone River and Gallinas, a coasting "ship" trade typified eastern Liberia. African and Eurafrican rulers and trading families played intermediary roles. The slave trade began to expand in the later seventeenth century and rose greatly in the eighteenth. For an area including present-day Guinea, estimates suggest that from 1700 to 1709 nearly 35,000 enslaved people were exported, and that between 1760 and 1769 their numbers exceeded 178,000. The total for 1700–1809 was perhaps 725,000 people. It is difficult to assess the economic impact of this exodus; but many skilled people were lost, and slaving was connected with new forms of internal stratification and power. Once Britain began its antislaving patrols in 1808, slave exporting ceased around Freetown; but it continued elsewhere for several more decades.

Starting with camwood, timber, and peanuts, residents have for two centuries grown or extracted a wide range of commodities for the industrialized world: palm oil and kernels, wild rubber, ginger, sesame, piassava, coffee, cocoa, and others. Much of the production has been in the hands of small-scale farmers. After Britain established the Sierra Leone Protectorate in 1896, it promoted exports through rail, road, and port building, to the neglect of food crops. Liberia followed this pattern to a lesser degree. Producers sought income as a buffer against food shortages and other crises and to meet debts, obtain imports, pay taxes, and provide for children's education.

During the 1800s, repatriated Africans in Sierra Leone, their Krio descendants, and Americo-Liberians built Atlantic-oriented businesses through their links with suppliers and consumers, knowledge of English, and overseas credit connections. Beginning in the late 1800s large foreign firms increasingly took over import-export commerce. Lebanese and Indians gained the middle rungs as Africans were pushed down the economic ladder or out of business. In the indigenous sectors, cattle, kola, and food traders, including many women, depended on networks of suppliers and an acute sense of market outlets, including government contracting. Those who accumulated wealth invested in urban real estate, transport, and other businesses.

Plantation-grown rubber dominated the Liberian economy for three decades. Following a 1923 government grant, Firestone Rubber devoted about 300,000 acres to rubber; and other foreign companies and Liberians also gained sizable rubber holdings. Rubber eventually employed one-third of all wage workers, mostly unskilled and low-paid. Iron mining revolutionized the economy, and by the mid-1970s iron accounted for over 70 percent of total exports by value.

Since the 1930s gold boom, Sierra Leone has been shaped by mining. At its peak diamonds represented about two-thirds of the value of all exports, and independent small-scale digging began to draw from thirty thousand to sixty thousand or more laborers to the alluvial fields annually. This loss of labor added to the decline in food farming. Iron was extracted at Marampa from 1933 to 1978, when the mines were shut down; at this industry, employed over four thousand people.

In the nineteenth and early twentieth centuries, enslaved people, youths, and wives migrated to Freetown and elsewhere to escape rural labor demands; and slave resistance helped bring about slavery's abolition in 1928. Freetown workers joined urban uprisings in 1919 and 1926. In successive decades, a more militant and sustained labor movement developed in Freetown, along the rails, and in the mines. Workers engaged in day-to-day workplace resistance, mounted dramatic strikes in the 1930s and early 1950s, and led general strikes in Freetown in 1955 and 1981. After independence in 1961, Sierra Leone trade unionists attacked problems of inflation, unemployment, corruption, and mismanagement by politi-

cians. Although less militant than the Sierra Leone workers, Liberian workers also organized unions in agricultural, clerical, mining, and other sectors, and engaged in strikes.

In the 1960s and early to mid-1970s, both countries experienced new investment; but thereafter both economies were marked by declining export prices, rising oil costs, a worsening balance of payments, increased foreign debt, and declining real incomes. International Monetary Fund (IMF) and World Bank devaluations and conditionalities, including deep cuts in public employment and programs, took place. Along with poor leadership, severe economic decline contributed to civil wars that commenced in Liberia in 1989 and Sierra Leone in 1991. War further stunted the economies as farm output dropped, formal sector employment nearly ceased, and refugees numbered in the hundreds of thousands. Warlords sold resources, particularly diamonds, abroad to obtain weapons and hold their clients and troops. In 1973, Liberia, Sierra Leone, and Guinea created the Mano River Union with a goal of regional economic integration through common tariffs, joint projects, and other steps. Violence stymied such efforts, but a future cooperation may evolve from the common past.

BIBLIOGRAPHY

Abdullah, Ibrahim. "Profit versus Social Reproduction: Labor Protests in the Sierra Leonean Iron-Ore Mines, 1933–1938." *African Studies Review* 35.3 (1992), 1–29.

Dorjahn, Vernon R., and Barry L. Isaacs, eds. *Essays on the Economic Anthropology of Liberia and Sierra Leone*. Philadelphia, 1979.

Howard, Allen M. "The Relevance of Spatial Analysis for African Economic History: The Sierra Leone–Guinea System." *Journal of African History* 17.3 (1976), 365–388.

Jalloh, Alusine. *African Entrepreneurship: Muslim Fula Merchants in Sierra Leone*. Athens, Ohio, 1999.

Rashid, Ismail. "'Do Dady Nor Lef Me Make Dem Carry Me': Slave Resistance and Emancipation in Sierra Leone, 1894–1928." *Slavery and Abolition* 19.2 (1998), 208–231.

Reno, William. *Warlord Politics and African States*. Boulder, 1998.

Richards, Paul. *Indigenous Agricultural Revolution: Ecology and Food Production in West Africa*. London and Boulder, 1985.

Richardson, David. "Slave Exports from West and West-Central Africa, 1700–1810: New Estimates of Volume and Distribution." *Journal of African History* 30.1 (1989), 23–44.

Sawyer, Amos. *The Emergence of Autocracy in Liberia: Tragedy and Challenge*. San Francisco, 1992.

ALLEN M. HOWARD

LIBYA. *See* North Africa.

LIEBKNECHTS, THE. Wilhelm Liebknecht, cofounder of the German Social Democratic Party (SPD), was born 29 March 1826. He practiced law in Switzerland but was expelled from Geneva due to his influence among Swiss program was adopted in 1891, at which point the party became known as the German Social Democratic Party. Liebknecht remained one of the party's leading spokesmen and theorists of socialism and a writer for *Vorwärts*, the party's most prominent newspaper, until his death on 7 August 1900.

Liebknecht's son Karl, born 13 August 1871, followed in his father's footsteps as a lawyer and German Social Democrat. In 1904, his defense of members of the illegal Russian Social Democratic Workers' Party, accused of infiltrating socialist propaganda from East Prussia into tsarist Russia, resulted in the charges being dropped. He played a principal role in the establishment of the International Union of Socialist Youth Organizations in Stuttgart. His campaign against militarism led to his eighteen-month imprisonment for treason after the publication of his book *Militarismus* in 1907. While in prison, he won a seat in the Prussian Landtag and entered the Reichstag in 1912.

During World War I, Karl Liebknecht became a leading figure in the antiwar campaign, which brought him into closer contact with Rosa Luxemburg and her circle of party intellectuals, known as the Gruppe Internationale. He and Luxemburg circulated pamphlets warning the German proletariat not to believe government statements about the war. These pamphlets, signed Spartakus, gave the group the name *Spartakusbund*, a Berlin underground group that became the Communist Party of Germany. He was arrested after a protest demonstration on May Day 1916, and was sentenced to four years' imprisonment and six years' loss of civil rights.

In October 1918, he was granted an early release by Germany's first parliamentary government, as the political situation in Germany had changed greatly because of its failure to achieve a rapid victory in the war. Liebknecht believed that the new government, under Friedrich Ebert, was not pursuing socialist policies. He played a leading role in the formation of the German Communist Party, which tried unsuccessfully to organize the groups on the left of the political spectrum. Despite Liebknecht's opposition to the use of force, he declared it necessary to overthrow Ebert's government. On 15 January 1919, he and Rosa Luxemburg were shot to death on the pretext of attempted escape while under arrest.

BIBLIOGRAPHY

Dominick, Raymond H. *Wilhelm Liebknecht and the Founding of the German Social Democratic Party*. Chapel Hill, N.C., 1982.

Meyer, Karl W. *Liebknecht: A Man without a Country*. Washington, D.C., 1957.

Trotnow, Helmut. *Karl Liebknecht: A Political Biography*. Hamden, Conn., 1984.

LIMITED LIABILITY CORPORATION. *See* Firm.

KARL LIEBKNECHT. Portrait by Käthe Kollwitz (1867–1945). (Snark/Art Resource, NY)

workers. He emigrated to England, where he joined the Communist League, working with Karl Marx and Friedrich Engels. He returned to Berlin in 1862, becoming a prominent socialist, but was expelled from Prussia in 1865 by the prime minister, Otto von Bismarck, who resented his influence among the working classes.

After moving to Leipzig, Liebknecht joined the General German Worker's Association, founded by Ferdinand Lassalle, and formed a friendship with August Bebel. In 1867, he was elected to the North German Reichstag, where he opposed the view held by Lassalle's followers that the state should actively assist workers. Two years later, he and Bebel organized the German Social Democratic Party. Liebknecht's writings against the Franco-German War resulted in his conviction for treasonable intentions in 1872, and he and Bebel were sentenced to two years' imprisonment.

In 1875 at Gotha, because of Bismarck's attempts to repress the socialists, the followers of Lassalle and Liebknecht merged their parties into the *Sozialistische Arbeiterpartei Deutschlands* (Socialist Labor Party), which was criticized by Marx for its support of government-aided productive organizations. Bismarck was successful in limiting the socialists in 1878, when the Reichstag passed the Anti-Socialist Law. The law expired in 1890, and a Marxist

LINEN INDUSTRY *[This entry contains two subentries, a historical overview and a discussion of technological change.]*

Overview

Linum usitatissimum is a domesticated variety of the flax plant cultivated in the Mediterranean and in the temperate zones and steppe regions of the Northern Hemisphere. It is usually grown in small, dense stands in rotation with other crops. Harvesting, scutching, and retting the fibers are labor-intensive tasks. For these reasons flax has traditionally been cultivated as a side crop on small peasant holdings.

The domestication and working of flax can be traced to the Neolithic period in the Middle East and Egypt. It was cultivated around 3000 BCE by the Swiss lake dwellers, who developed advanced techniques of weaving patterned cloth. The rapid spread of the plant in the Mediterranean basin and temperate Europe in the classical period helped establish flax as the principal vegetable fiber used in the textile production of that region through the late eighteenth century. The characteristics of linen, such as durability, tensile strength, luster, and resistance to moisture, made it a preferred choice for apparel and household goods.

Ancient Linen. The widespread fame of Egyptian linens in the ancient world rested upon sophisticated techniques and the accumulated skills of a coordinated labor force of both genders working under the supervision of royal and temple administrators. Fine fabrics from Egypt and other linen-making centers in Anatolia and Syria were imported into Greece, as were yarn and flax to be worked up by female slaves using European traditions associated with the distaff, the drop spindle, and the warp-weighted loom.

Under the Roman Empire a flourishing trade in linen goods developed in the eastern Mediterranean. The export capacity of the industry is evidenced by the detailed list of specialized linen fabrics in Diocletian's Edict of Prices of 301 CE. Production of linen for export can also be attested in the cities of the Po Valley and Spain. Linen workers, organized into guilds, were subject to oversight by municipal officials. Following the barbarian invasions in the West, urban craftspeople continued to produce linen goods in the eastern provinces of the Roman Empire under regulations imposed by the imperial bureaucracy.

Medieval Linen. In the Germanic successor states of early medieval Europe, the demand for fine linens among aristocratic and ecclesiastical elites was satisfied by wares imported from the Levant by itinerant Oriental and Jewish merchants. Linens were also woven on royal, aristocratic, and ecclesiastical estates. The various stages of production from the seeding and harvesting of flax to the final bleaching and dyeing of fabrics were entrusted to highly skilled servile women, who worked in large domestic workshops (*gynaecea*) in the lord's household. Flax, yarn, and strips of cloth also formed part of the dues of many peasant households. Surplus goods entered the channels of local and regional exchange.

The expansion of Islam in the eighth and ninth centuries facilitated the convergence of existing craft traditions from Central Asia, Persia, Byzantium, and India, which opened a highly creative period in the history of textile technology. New designs and inventions carried by relocated artisans were disseminated through royal *tiraz* manufactories to numerous privately owned urban workshops in the flax-growing regions of the Maghreb, Egypt, Syria, and Palestine. There was a high degree of specialization among weavers, dyers, block printers, and embroiderers of linen cloth.

Contacts with Islam in the tenth and eleventh centuries led to Europe's reception of advanced know-how and improved implements, including the horizontal treadle loom. Gains in productivity and quality improvements in the finished product helped attract male artisans to the linen craft. By 1100 CE an increase in demand occasioned by rapid population growth, urbanization, and commercial expansion led to the emergence of regional centers of linen weaving.

The Champagne fairs gave an impetus to weaving in the towns of northern France, which were located in prime flax-growing areas. The luxury linens and sheer veiling of towns such as Reims were highly prized. A second area of industrial development was South Germany, where linen weaving rivaled woolen production in numerous towns in the thirteenth century. Finally, the cities of the Po Valley, where the cultivation of flax went back to Roman times, witnessed a notable increase in the output of yarn and linen cloth. Goods from these areas entered Mediterranean trade through the ports of Genoa, Venice, and Pisa.

While the finest fabrics were produced by full-time craftspeople in the towns, flax spinning and weaving continued to play an important part in the economic strategies pursued by owners of large ecclesiastical and secular estates with access to urban centers of consumption. In areas where more flexible terms of tenure promoted the direct participation of peasant producers in the marketplace, peasants sold their surplus yarn and unbleached cloth to village dealers operating through a network of local fairs. As rural linen production expanded, urban officials claimed jurisdiction over this branch of production. In towns connected to the linen trade, inspection of the products of rural looms was assumed by guilds of weavers and linen merchants who affixed the city seal to goods coming from districts outside the walls. Finishing processes, such as bleaching, dyeing, and printing, were the monopoly of specialized urban craftspeople working as subcontractors for linen drapers.

While linen producers faced increasing competition from fustians (cotton-linen mixtures) in the late Middle Ages, the industry continued to expand in a growing market for lower-priced cloth. In addition to finer fabrics for apparel and household goods, ordinary varieties of linen were utilized for military uniforms, clothing for servants, and a myriad of utilitarian purposes. There was a steady demand for canvas to be fashioned into sailcloth, tents, awnings, and sacks. Fine linen thread was used for embroidery and, by the fifteenth century, for lace making. Even linen rags were recycled in the papermaking process. As the consumption of linen fabrics and thread expanded within Europe, commercial spinning and weaving spread across rural districts in Flanders, Holland, France, Switzerland, northern Germany, and Austria. A steady stream of exports was directed toward the Mediterranean region, which was the principal external market for European linens up to 1700.

Attempts by the Dutch and English East India Companies to develop new outlets for Western linens in Asian commerce met with limited success because of the intense competition from indigenous textile producers. The major stimulus to European linen manufacturing came from the opening of overseas markets in the transatlantic trader, giving rise to an international commerce in flax and yarn and increased regional specialization in rural linen production geared to the global economy.

The expansion of a proto-industrial labor force producing linen cloth for export markets followed different regional trajectories. Local variations in political institutions and in agrarian social structures influenced the degree of control that landlords, merchant companies, and urban guilds exercised over rural enterprises. Estate production based on coerced labor was prevalent in some flax-growing areas of east-central Europe. Artisanal modes of organization in which the various gender-specific stages of processing were encapsulated within single farming households, persisted in many proto-industrial districts, where domestic linen output was targeted to regional and subregional markets. As the radius of trade expanded, putting-out systems took hold in advanced areas of quality linen production linked to long-distance trade. In the latter case, a division of labor developed among households specialized in a single process, such as spinning or weaving. Efficiencies realized by the replacement of the distaff and spindle with the faster, flyer-equipped flax wheel made it profitable to put out imported flax to female hand spinners working in their own domiciles for wages at or below subsistence levels.

Colonial Linen. In the sixteenth century a putting-out system in the weaving of linen and canvas developed in prime flax-growing zones of France in Normandy, Brittany, Maine, Anjou, and Poitou plus some areas of the Southeast (notably in Lyonnais, Beaujolais, Forez, and parts of Dauphiné). Brand-name fabrics, plain and dyed, from France and Belgium were in high demand in Europe and in the Ottoman Empire, where they gradually displaced Egyptian fabrics. In the seventeenth and eighteenth centuries French linens were favored by discriminating consumers in the Iberian Peninsula and by European elites in Spanish colonial America and Brazil, as well as New France. The range of products included fine lawns and cambrics for apparel and high-grade canvas for sailcloth. Bleached shirting served for naval and military uniforms, while household needs were satisfied by various sheeting materials.

A resurgence of linen production after the Thirty Years' War occurred in northern Switzerland and parts of Southwest Germany. The superior linens of St. Gall, Switzerland, were shipped through North Sea ports and figured in the English reexport trade to colonial America. Fine Swiss fabrics were also purchased by affluent urban dwellers in southern Europe.

Holland's skilled linen workers employed domestic flax in the production of damasks and other fine linens for European and foreign markets. Holland was also a major distribution center for Baltic flax and for continental linens finished in the famous Haarlem bleaching fields. Linens from Leiden and Haarlem figured prominently in the Dutch Atlantic trade.

Middling to lower grades of plain white, unbleached, dyed, striped, or checked fabrics used for sailors' and slaves' clothing and as utilitarian cloth and canvas came primarily from three leading proto-industrial regions in Germany. Linen weaving by peasant households was carried on successfully in Saxony. It was an important source of supplementary employment for landless agricultural laborers in Silesia. A cottage-based linen industry was also well established in Westphalia around Minden, Bielefeld, and Ravensberg.

Merchants from Hamburg, Lübeck, and Bremen controlled exports of yarn and coarse linen cloth that were collected as rents in kind from servile peasants on feudal estates in Bohemia and Moravia. Foreign merchants likewise provided a stimulus to linen production in the Mühlviertel region of Upper Austria, which was organized under the putting-out system. Large quantities of German, Bohemian, and Austrian linens of diverse grades and colors, including hallmark brands such as Osnaburgs (named for Osnabrück) and Dowlas, were exported to Holland, France, Italy, and Spain. They were an important component of cargoes leaving Cadiz bound for Spanish colonial America. After about 1700 a primary destination was England, from where German fabrics were transhipped to Africa, the West Indies, and British North America.

The protected North American market, with its growing population and high per capita income, presented a lucrative opportunity to British exporters seeking to satisfy a virtually insatiable demand for linen cloth. In British colonial America imported grades of domesticated seed led to the cultivation of flax on small plots that formed parts of family farms. Yarn spun at home was woven within the household or was sent out to professional weavers. However, mercantilist regulations, the high cost of labor, and a low labor-to-land ratio inhibited the development of a rural textile industry in the British colonies.

Even after the American Revolutionary War the nation's basic requirements for apparel, household goods, slave clothing, military and naval uniforms, sailcloth, and canvas tenting materials were met by imported linens. The unreliable supply and uneven quality of American flax and the competition with cotton militated against the successful establishment of mechanized linen weaving in the United States. Despite these obstacles, in the nineteenth century Thomas Barbour and other Scottish and Irish entrepreneurs made investments in spinning mills in Paterson, New Jersey, for the production of heavy grades of yarn and sewing thread from imported flax.

Irish and Scottish Linen. The dramatic rise of the Scottish and Irish linen industries in the eighteenth century is an example of export-led growth under the stimulus of British economic policies administered by state-sponsored Linen Boards. Incentives in the form of export subsidies or bounties were designed to encourage an expansion of linen production in Northern Ireland, based on domestic supplies of flax. Male farmer-weavers on small tenements in East Ulster were dependent upon scores of domestic female spinners in flax-producing rural districts, who sold yarn or paid it as rent to landlords. Local elites, such as landlords, master weavers, linen dealers, drapers, and operators of bleach fields, employed wage laborers and invested in improvements in infrastructure. However, the final value-added steps of printing and dyeing remained a monopoly of English firms. Irish linens met the needs of the domestic English market, the navy, and the merchant fleet. They were a principal article of exchange in the American colonial trade.

By contrast, the Scottish industry was dependent on imported raw materials. Russian and Baltic ports became primary suppliers of raw and spun flax of various qualities en route to new proto-industrial zones of linen weaving in Scotland and parts of England around Yorkshire, Manchester, and Somerset. While most English linen was sold in the home market, the bulk of Scottish linen exports consisted of coarser grades, including imitations of the cheap German Osnaburgs, which were destined for the English market and the colonial trade. Scottish merchant-entrepreneurs put out foreign flax to spinners and distributed the yarn to weavers working in individual households or small workshops. The British Linen Company provided credit and set standards for the various grades of cloth that were sold on consignment to factors in London. It also played a role in encouraging innovations and quality improvements. As output increased, Scottish and Irish linens captured a rising share of the British and colonial markets, to the detriment of continental linens.

Beginning in the late eighteenth century the rapid mechanization of cotton manufacturing altered the traditional alignments among the various sectors of the textile industry. The high profit margins of cotton manufacturing, with its cost advantages in materials and processing, attracted substantial capital investments. The successful launching of low-cost cotton goods into international trade led to a secular shift in demand for linen cloth, for which cotton was a viable substitute. However, in the short term the challenge of cheap cottons stimulated linen producers to improve their products while cutting costs.

While the mechanization of the linen industry lagged behind that of cotton, the capital-intensive structure of the Scottish and English industries eased the transition to factory flax spinning based on the wet-spinning process in the 1820s. Consolidation within the spinning sector led to the emergence of highly capitalized firms, such as Marshalls of Leeds. The introduction of power loom weaving in the 1830s contributed to a dramatic spurt in factory-based production. In other regions wage structures, institutional inertia, and slower rates of capital accumulation delayed structural changes within the industry for a decade or more. As mechanized spinning and weaving gained acceptance for finer yarns, spinning mills financed by joint stock companies were introduced in Belgium and France in the 1830s. Power looms for linen weaving took hold after 1840.

In Ireland a surplus of cheap female domestic labor retarded the reception of mechanical spinning until the 1830s, when spinning mills employing female wage earners became heavily concentrated in East Ulster. The availability of mill-spun yarn and a shrinking pool of male hand-loom weavers during the Great Famine of the mid-1840s facilitated the entry of women, including many displaced spinsters, into the ranks of domestic hand-loom weavers working within the putting-out system. The demand for alternatives to cotton during the American Civil War accelerated the adoption of power looms, which were first introduced in the late 1850s for coarser grades of cloth. Hand weaving of the finest fabrics on looms

LINEN INDUSTRY. Processes at mills of the Willimantic Linen ▶ Company, cover of *Scientific American*, 6 December 1879. (Snark/ Art Resource, NY)

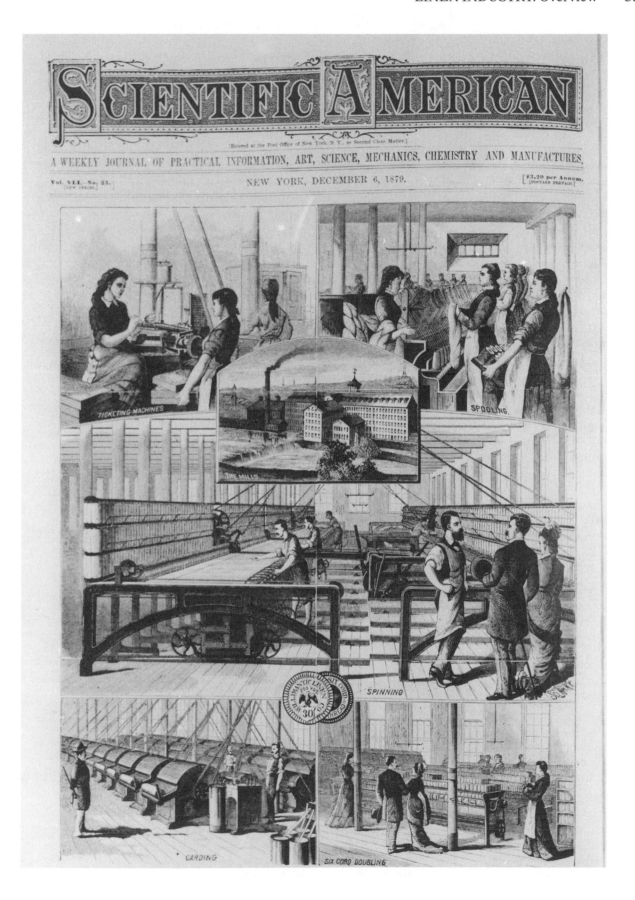

equipped with the flying shuttle persisted until the 1880s, when the remaining weavers were absorbed into a factory-based labor force that was comprised predominantly of women and children. In former proto-industrial regions the loss of supplemental household income was reflected in widespread poverty, demographic decline, and out-migration.

Industrialization. Following the lifting of the continental blockade in 1815, the intense competition of English linens and cottons in European markets adversely affected many continental linen-weaving districts. Although Belgium was famous for its Courtrai (Kortrijk) flax and innovations in retting, high wage levels caused its linen cloth to lose ground to higher quality, lower-priced imports from the British Isles. The English threat to French linens on the home market was met by higher tariff barriers against foreign cloth, which ultimately impacted Belgian goods as well. The loss of the all-important French market was correlated with a decline in flax cultivation and a noticeable contraction in Belgian linen exports after 1850. A smaller, mechanized industry failed to provide new employment opportunities for displaced Flemish rural linen workers.

The severance of the traditional handicraft occupations of flax spinning and weaving from farming was an uneven process marked by complex complementarities and disjunctures. Deindustrialization and reagrarianization occurred in many former proto-industrial zones in Württemberg, Westphalia (with the exception of Ravensberg), and Upper Austria. A successful transition to industrialization, involving a shift from linen to cotton, took place in Switzerland, Saxony, Silesia, Bohemia, and Moravia. However, even in these areas, it is difficult to posit a direct continuity between dispersed domestic units of proto-industry and centralized factory production. Both forms of organization coexisted at an early stage of industrialization.

The declining fortunes of continental linen manufacturers were reflected in diminished flax acreage in western Europe after a temporary expansion in response to a "cotton famine" during the American Civil War. As the low-cost producer, Russia came to dominate world markets for flax, grown according to improved agricultural methods, by the end of the nineteenth century. On the eve of World War I, the Russian heartland supplied the basic raw materials for the remaining linen factories in France, Belgium, Germany, and Austria.

Cotton's continuous advances in global markets put increasing pressure on linen producers. Even in advanced industrialized regions, the role of linen in the economy suffered an irreversible downturn. Despite early mechanization, by the late 1800s the United Kingdom's linen industry had entered a stage of relative decline, slipping to third place below the cotton and woolen sectors by 1914. While linen production continued in east-central Scot-land, factories in Dundee and other cities turned increasingly to jute fiber. In the same period the linen industry in England witnessed a severe drop in the number of active spindles and looms.

Despite a contraction in domestic flax acreage in the twentieth century and a greater reliance on fine Belgian and Dutch flax, the Ulster linen industry survived as a dominant player within an increasingly marginalized industrial sector. While vertically integrated firms grew up in the Belfast area, the linen industry remained undercapitalized and technologically backward because of its reliance on labor-intensive factory production and low-wage female and child workers. Workers remained vulnerable to downturns in demand during periods of economic recession. Low profit margins and the absence of linkages to other sectors of the economy relegated linen to the status of a peripheral activity, with limited potential for long-term growth.

[*See also* Clothing Trades *and* Textiles.]

BIBLIOGRAPHY

Cohen, Marilyn. *Linen, Family, and Community in Tullyish, County Down, 1690–1914.* Dublin, 1997.

Cohen, Marilyn, ed. *The Warp of Ulster's Past.* New York, 1997.

Crawford, William H. *Domestic Industry in Ireland: The Experience of the Linen Industry.* Dublin, 1972.

Ditt, Karl, and Sidney Pollard, eds. *Von der Heimarbeit in die Fabrik: Industrialisierung und Arbeiterschaft in Leinen-und Baumwollregionen Westeuropas während des 18. Und 19. Jahrhuderts.* Paderborn, 1992.

Durie, Alastair J. *The Scottish Linen Industry in the Eighteenth Century.* Edinburgh, 1979.

Durie, Alastair J., ed. *The British Linen Company, 1745–1775.* Edinburgh, l996.

Forbes, Robert J. *Studies in Ancient Technology* 2d ed. 9 vols. Leiden, 1964.

Frank, Tenney. *An Economic Survey of Ancient Rome.* 5 vols. Baltimore, 1933–1940.

Gill, Conrad. *The Rise of the Irish Linen Industry.* Oxford, 1925.

Green, Edward R. R. "Thomas Barbour and the American Linen Thread Industry." In *Irish Population, Economy, and Society, Essays in Honour of the late K. H. Connell,* edited by J. M. Goldstrom and L. A. Clarkson. Oxford, 1981.

Harte, Negley B. "The Rise of Protection and the English Linen Trade, 1690–1790." In *Textile History and Economic History,* edited by N. B. Harte and K. G. Ponting, pp. 75–112. Manchester, 1973.

Heitz, Gerhard. *Ländliche Leinenproduktion in Sachsen 1470–1555.* Berlin, 1961.

Heller, Henry. *Labour, Science, and Technology in France, 1500–1620.* Cambridge, 1996.

Horner, John. *The Linen Trade of Europe during the Spinning-Wheel Period.* Belfast, Ireland, 1920.

Mokyr, Joel. *Industrialization in the Low Countries, 1795–1850.* New Haven and London, 1976.

Ogilvie, Sheilagh C., and Markus Cerman. *European Proto-Industrialization.* Cambridge, 1996.

Peyer, Hans Conrad. *Leinwandgewerbe und Fernhandel der Stadt St. Gallen von den Anfängen bis 1520.* St. Gall, 1959–1960.

Rimmer, William Gordon. *Marshalls of Leeds Flax Spinners, 1788–1886.* Cambridge, 1960.

Schmitz, Edith. *Leinengewerbe und Leinehandel in Nordwestdeutschland (1650–1850)*. Cologne, 1967.

Vogelsang-Eastwood, Gillian. *The Production of Linen in Pharaonic Egypt*. Leiden, 1992.

Warden, Alexander J. *The Linen Trade*. London, 1967.

MAUREEN FENNELL MAZZAOUI

Technological Change

Technological change in the linen industry is largely a story of how techniques devised for other fibers were adapted to working flax. There were very often substantial lags because the irregularity of the flax fiber and its lack of elasticity made mechanized production more complicated.

Flax requires considerable processing before it can be spun. The seeds must be removed either by crushing or by combing (rippling). The fibers are then separated from the outer skin and the inner woody core of the plant in three steps: First, retting moistens the stems to break down the gum that holds together the different components; second, breaking crushes the woody core; and third, scutching beats the outer skin and the broken bits of woody core away from the fibers. These operations were typically done either by the cultivators or by specialist processors in the countryside. After scutching, the flax fibers must be sorted, cleaned, and aligned by further combing (hackling), and drawn out in preparation for spinning. These operations were usually done by the spinner, either in households or the spinning mill. During scutching and hackling, the flax is separated into line and tow (long and short fibers).

The basic techniques of deseeding, retting, breaking, and scutching changed little until the eighteenth century. As metal was substituted for wood, combs and mallets became more durable and precise, but many nineteenth-century commentators noted that the tools still used in backward areas of Europe were similar to those pictured in ancient Egyptian wall paintings. The first operations to change were breaking and scutching. Scutching machines with multiple blades, first driven by hand, then by horses, water, or wind, were developed in Ireland and Scotland from the early eighteenth century. In the late eighteenth century, rollers for breaking were added to these mills. By the mid-nineteenth century, scutch mills processed most of the flax in the British Isles and had begun to spread to continental Europe, though in Russia, the world's leading producer, much flax was still broken and scutched by hand in the early twentieth century. From the mid-nineteenth century, many, largely unsuccessful, attempts were made to speed up retting, which had been carried out by soaking the flax in rivers or pools or by exposing it to dew. From the 1920s, the use of warm water in concrete tanks became common but was abandoned from the 1960s because of high labor and energy costs. Rippling machines for deseeding and new methods of scutching were also introduced in the 1920s.

Careful hackling is important for producing the best mix of yarns from the raw material. In the early spinning mills, hackling was performed by large numbers of well-paid male workers. Hackling machines, first introduced in Leeds in the 1810s and much-improved in subsequent decades, thus generated major cost savings. Since the tow removed in hackling was carded much like cotton or wool, carding machines were quickly adapted to flax from the 1790s.

The introduction of gill frames in the 1820s transformed the preparation of flax and tow for spinning. The early mills had used rollers, as in the cotton industry, but could make only very coarse yarn because of the unequal lengths of the raw material and its lack of adhesiveness. Gill frames used a series of combs to imitate the action of fingers in handspinning, which made possible the preparation of finer and more regular rovings. The Frenchman Philippe de Girard is often credited with the invention of the gill around 1814. The screw-and-faller mechanism, invented about the same time by Lawson & Westley of Leeds, provided an effective way of propelling the gills. These inventions defined the flax drawing frame until well into the twentieth century.

The techniques of hand spinning changed only very slowly. The simplest, known to the Egyptians, was the spindle and distaff. From the late Middle Ages, spinning wheels, first powered by hand then by treadles (the Saxony Wheel, with flyer) made it possible to twist and wind on the yarn simultaneously. In the eighteenth century some wheels began to be equipped with double flyers, permitting the skilled to spin with two hands. All of these methods were still being used in the nineteenth century, though the wheel was more common for coarser yarns and where commercial production was paramount.

Mechanized spinning of flax and tow developed in two distinct forms. Dry spinning was clearly adapted from cotton spinning, but it took a decade before the Englishmen John Kendrew and Thomas Porthouse, in 1787, devised a system of rollers capable of exerting sufficient tension to draw out the flax fiber. Dry spinning predominated until the 1820s and continued to be used into the twentieth century to spin coarse yarns from flax, tow, and jute. Wet spinning, pioneered in the late 1820s in Leeds and Belfast, made it possible to produce medium and fine grades of flax and tow yarn. Earlier, Philippe de Girard had tried wetting flax before spinning but did not use enough water to loosen the small "ultimate" fibers of the flax. In 1825, the Englishman James Kay proposed macerating rovings in cold water for several hours. Shortly after, it was found that a briefer passage through hot water just before spinning was sufficient. Kay also recognized that the rollers of the spinning machine had to be set close together to correspond to the short length of the ultimate fibers. More than a century later, the machinery for preparing and spinning that been developed by the early 1830s remained essentially the same, though better metals and greater precision in metalworking meant that machines were more durable and could be run faster. Only after 1945 did high-speed frames on the ring-and-traveler principle begin to be substituted. From the mid-nineteenth century, most machines for hackling, preparing, and spinning flax and jute were made by specialist firms, mainly located in Leeds, Belfast, and Dundee.

The basic technology of linen weaving is similar to that for other fibers. The major difference is that the inelasticity of the flax fiber means that the warp must be kept under greater and more even tension. Hand looms were consequently more substantial and more expensive than those for wool or cotton. Linen power looms, first tried in the mid-1810s but only widely adopted in Scotland from the 1830s, were also more substantial and initially could make only heavy cloth. From the 1850s, with the addition of vibrating rollers to maintain more even tension and the use of special dressings to protect the warp, it became possible to weave finer cloths; and over the next thirty years, power looms made substantial inroads on hand-loom weaving. Power looms for coarse linen and jute cloth were made by specialist manufacturers in Scotland. Power looms for lighter cloth were generally made by manufacturers of cotton machinery.

Linen was more often bleached than dyed or printed. Bleaching involved soaking the cloth in repeated sequences of baths containing water, alkali, and acid, interspersed with long periods during which it was laid out to be exposed to wind and sun. When bleached, the cloth was also beaten or rolled to give it an even finish. Washing and finishing, to which water power was increasingly applied from the early eighteenth century, were the first operations in the linen industry to be mechanized. The late eighteenth and early nineteenth centuries saw major changes in the chemicals used in bleaching as the acid, buttermilk, was replaced by sulfuric acid from the 1760s; and as the alkali, lime or ashes made from seaweed, was replaced by potash, then soda ash (from the 1820s), and chlorine was added to alkali from the 1790s. Mechanization and more effective chemicals both speeded up the bleaching process and led to a large increase in the average size of bleaching works.

BIBLIOGRAPHY

Baines, Patricia. *Linen Hand Weaving and Spinning*. London, 1989. Though for hobbyists, this work contains valuable and clearly explained historical sections.

Dewilde, Bert. *Flax in Flanders throughout the Centuries*. Tielt, Belgium, 1987. Well-illustrated and detailed discussion of the techniques of flax cultivation and preparation.

Durie, Alastair. *The Scottish Linen Industry in the Eighteenth Century*. Edinburgh, 1979. Contains useful discussions of technical change, especially in bleaching.

"Lincojute." "The Evolution of Flax, Hemp, and Jute Machinery." *Fibres and Fabrics Journal* 8 (1942), 134–135, 190–191, 226–227; 9 (1942–1943), 35–37, 94–97. Valuable discussion of technical developments during the late nineteenth and twentieth centuries.

Linke, Wolfgang. *Altes Hauswerk und Handwerk auf dem Lande*, Part 1, *Die Flachsverarbeitung*. Münster, 1982. Well-illustrated guide to hand technology in Germany.

Montaigne, Jean-Marc. *Images du lin textile*. Rouen, France, 1997. Well-illustrated introduction to techniques in France.

Rimmer, W. G. *Marshall's of Leeds: Flax-Spinners 1788–1886*. Cambridge, 1960. Classic study of one of the technical pioneers in flax spinning.

Ure, Andrew. *Dictionary of Arts, Manufactures, and Mines*. London, 1839. Detailed discussions of machinery and factory organization; changes can be gleaned by consulting various editions.

Warden, A. J. *The Linen Trade Ancient and Modern*. London, 1864, reprinted, 1967. Indispensable compendium of information on the linen and jute industries.

PETER M. SOLAR

LIST, GEORG FRIEDRICH (1789–1846), the chief propagandist of German economic nationalism, responsible for making economic nationalism an integral element of German nationalism; the intellectual instigator of the Zollverein, an early advocate of German railroads; and an important catalyst of Germany's spurt to economic growth in the nineteenth century.

List began his propagandist activity in 1819 as the president of the Association of German Merchants and Manufacturers, arguing for the abolition of customs barriers between various German states and the establishment of a "universal German system [based] on the principle of retaliation against foreign states," specifically the economically dominant Britain. The views of German territorial rulers at the time being opposed to this agenda, List, elected to the Wuertemberg Diet, was expelled and sentenced to ten months' imprisonment "for demagoguery," fled, returned, was imprisoned, and obtained his release only on the condition of the immediate renunciation of his citizenship. Forced to emigrate to the United States, he was befriended there by local opponents of free trade, motivated by anti-British sentiment, and became a theorist of American protectionism, which, under the name of "the American system," informed economic policy in the United States until well into the twentieth century. Rewarded for his services to the American economy by appointment as U.S. consul to Leipzig, List returned to Germany in 1830 and resumed his activity on behalf of the German customs union, railroads, and industrial growth—work that soon began to bear fruit. His economic views were articulated in the 1841 book *The National System of Political Economy*, a paradigmatic statement of economic nationalism. Its appearance coincided with a surge of national sentiment across Germany, and it was published to great acclaim.

The book was framed as a refutation of Adam Smith's economic liberalism, which, in List's view, served Britain's national interests to the detriment of that country's trading partners. The root interest of every nation was an interest in self-realization, which could be obstructed by the efforts or a lack of cooperation of other nations, each set on its independent course by the same desire to realize its own potential. This created a state of permanent competition. With respect to the economy, Germany was at a competitive disadvantage vis-à-vis Britain, to a large extent owing to Britain's insistence on a policy of free trade, which, under the prevailing conditions, maintained it in its position as unrivaled exporter of manufactured goods. List opposed freedom of trade under these conditions and advocated protective tariffs. At the same time, he favored unbridled competition within Germany, arguing that it promoted the development of the national economy as a whole, even if it were deleterious to certain sectors of the population. What mattered was the economic strength of the nation as a whole, not the well-being of any of its parts.

Though List was a publicist rather than a scholar, his views became the foundation of a brand of economic theory especially influential in Germany and later in Japan, where it was taught in business schools alongside theories of English classical economists but had greater appeal than those theories. List's theory later found advocates among economists affiliated with such different ideological positions as fascism in Italy and the New Deal and the Great Society in America. In the late 1980s and early 1990s, List was rediscovered in the United States as the theorist behind the practices presumed to account for the strength of the Japanese economy.

BIBLIOGRAPHY

Greenfeld, Liah. *The Spirit of Capitalism: Nationalism and Economic Growth*. Cambridge, Mass., 2001.
Henderson, William O. *Friedrich List: Economist and Visionary, 1789–1846*. London, 1983.
List, Friedrich. *The National System of Political Economy*. London, 1922.

LIAH GREENFELD

LITERACY is significant in economic history because it represents a central aspect of the development of mass education, acts as an indicator of human development, and provides a technology for conveying information and recording transactions. The very development of systems of writing in ancient times has been attributed to the needs of the state to maintain accounts. Such fundamental economic institutions as taxation, credit, law, and money have all been associated with the development of literacy. The last five hundred years have seen the advent of widespread literacy, approaching universality in adult populations in many countries. Literacy, in turn, has often been seen as a key ingredient in the onset of modern economic development.

Literacy and the Development of Accounting. Keeping written accounts is of value because it can extend the human memory considerably and provide external verification of transactions between economic agents. The earliest use of accounts mentioned by most sources occurred around 3000 BCE as part of the administration of the resources collected by the empires in Egypt and Mesopotamia. Imperial administrations in China and India also seem to have made use of written records at a relatively early date. Keeping written accounts allowed officials at a given level of the tax and resource collection hierarchy to verify the consistency and hence reliability of the accounts for the resources sent along by officials at lower levels in the hierarchy. Administrators in Egypt, Mesopotamia, China, India, and Japan kept records of individual land ownership and yields for individual plots of land for past years to determine if a taxpayer in a given year was reporting a suspiciously meager crop.

Alternatives to writing have been developed throughout history for keeping accounts. Various physical objects were used in place of a formal written accounting system using writing and numbering, such as counters in the form of round objects in ancient times and tally sticks with notches cut in them in medieval and early modern Europe. Despite the existence of these possible alternatives to the use of written accounts, it is not surprising that as the scale and complexity of business transactions increased, the advantage and hence pervasiveness of written accounts over alternatives increased as well.

Other important consequences often associated with the rise of literacy include the formulation of written legal codes and enhanced ability to transmit technological improvements. Such wide possible ramifications of literacy, though indirect and difficult to isolate, are a primary reason for ongoing interest by economic historians.

The Advent of Mass Literacy. The role of literacy in accounting just described entailed primarily what has been termed restricted literacy, involving fairly sophisticated ability in reading and writing among relatively elite segments of society. However, the last few centuries have seen the advent of mass literacy. In common usage, literacy refers to basic fluency in reading and writing, and many would also include mastery of basic arithmetic. Each of these skills is subject to wide variations in mastery; the level of competence commonly expected advanced as literacy became more pervasive. This has been reflected in changing standards for what has been termed functional literacy: the mastery of reading, writing, and numerate skills required for daily life. Further complicating the definition of

LITERACY. Group of women learning to read at an adult literacy class, Ayesha Abed Foundation, Manikganj, Bangladesh, 1998. (© S. Noorani/Woodfin Camp and Associates, New York)

North America appears to have had majority adult literacy since European settlement in the seventeenth century. In western Europe, the advent of almost universal mass literacy occurred in the nineteenth century, but even earlier the majority of Germans and Scandinavians had mastered basic literacy skills. Literacy trends in southern and eastern Europe and Asia tended to lag behind, with majority literacy coming only in the twentieth century, and in much of Africa, only in the last few decades of that century. Within these general contours, some major patterns should be noted. First, female literacy has commonly lagged behind male literacy, although exceptions have occurred and the degree of any gender gap has been subject to considerable spatial variation. For 1995, UNESCO statistics indicate a world literacy rate for males over age fourteen of 84 percent compared with 71 percent for females.

Second, within a given country, identifiable minority groups have often had literacy rates well below the average. At the time of emancipation in the 1860s, the literacy rate for U.S. slaves has been estimated at under 10 percent compared with estimates of over 90 percent for free whites. Linguistic minorities, such as Gaelic speakers in nineteenth-century Britain and Ireland, the Flemish in nineteenth-century Belgium, the Basques in the Pyrenees, and Provençal speakers in southern France have commonly had literacy rates well below prevailing levels in their regions. This gap has been attributed to the difficulties of receiving instruction in school in a language different from that spoken at home.

Prior to 1500, it is a matter of controversy whether in any society the majority of adults were ever literate. Some historians have claimed that in centers of civilization like the Renaissance Italian city states, Augustan Rome, and Periclean Athens the overwhelming majority of adults were literate. But there is not enough evidence to reach a firm conclusion on the issue, and by any account these examples are exceptional. The rise of mass literacy would thus appear to be primarily a phenomenon of the past few centuries.

Causes and Consequences of the Rise of Mass Literacy. In interpreting the significance of the rise of mass literacy using a basic economic framework, one can distinguish between the acquisition of literacy with its associated costs on the one hand and the benefits or demand for being literate on the other. On the acquisition side of the equation, the most obvious early impetus to the promotion of popular literacy came from the Protestant Reformation. The Reformation encouraged widespread access to instruction in basic reading and writing skills as a way of cultivating orthodox religious practice, often with the long arm of the state mediated through local clergy. Protestantism in particular has been used to account for the high early literacy rates observed in Lutheran and related Protestant faiths in

literacy has been the linkage of its beneficial characteristics with those of elementary schooling, the means by which it has been increasingly acquired. Some have argued that over and beyond facilitating communication, acquisition of literacy has led to changed mental habits with shifts away from custom and tradition to rational practices and consequent greater openness to change. However, the empirical validity of this claim has been subject to debate.

In 1995, according to United Nations Educational, Scientific, and Cultural Organization (UNESCO) estimates, the world literacy rate for adults over the age of fourteen was 77 percent. By these estimates the world as a whole was still a considerable distance from universal adult literacy on the eve of the twenty-first century. Literacy varied considerably across major regions in these 1995 estimates, ranging from a low of 56 percent in Africa to a high of 98.5 percent in Europe.

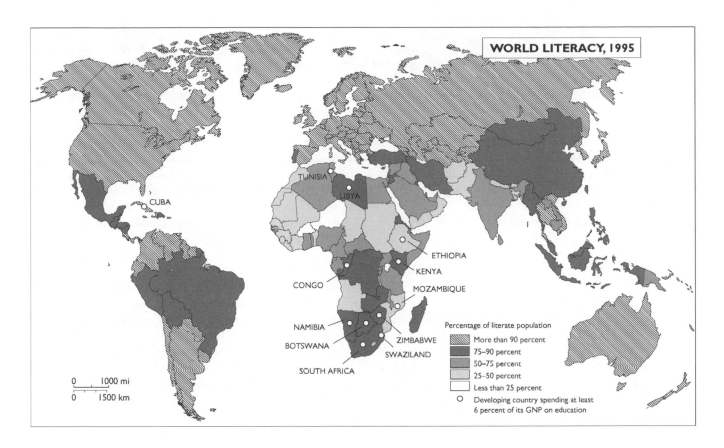

WORLD LITERACY, 1995

Percentage of literate population
- More than 90 percent
- 75–90 percent
- 50–75 percent
- 25–50 percent
- Less than 25 percent
- ○ Developing country spending at least 6 percent of its GNP on education

Scandinavia and many regions of modern-day Germany. The impact of Protestantism through individual piety appears to have been far less pervasive.

Prior to the advent of universal mass elementary schooling in the nineteenth century, it appears to have been quite common for literacy skills to be acquired informally, whether by self-instruction or tutoring by relatives, by friends, or by tutors for hire. The evidence is that literacy rates tended to rise with age through adolescence. Unfortunately, there is also evidence of depreciation or loss of literacy through lack of use. Whether literacy would be truly mastered and retained until the advent of enforced compulsory schooling legislation in the later nineteenth century would seem to depend critically on the strength of the motives for using it—in other words, the benefit side of the equation.

The strength of the pecuniary motive for acquiring literacy appears to have varied considerably over time and space. The presumption for developed societies that illiterates would be at an earnings disadvantage compared with literates does not necessarily appear to have held in early periods and for less developed societies. Evidence about immigrants to the United States in the late-nineteenth- and early-twentieth-century does indicate that literates tended to earn more than illiterates. There is also reason to think that farmers and merchants derived benefits from literacy because of its advantages in facilitating transactions. However, in many skilled and relatively well-compensated jobs in the past there is little evidence that literacy provided an advantage in securing or retaining employment or that it was of any functional use on the job. The most notable documentation is for English textile workers during the Industrial Revolution, but it also appears to have been true for English miners in the nineteenth century. Still, studies of indentured servants for eighteenth-century North America have found that literate servants tended to have shorter contracts than illiterate servants, again suggesting a positive market valuation placed on literacy.

On average, literate workers tended to be in occupations of higher compensation and higher prestige than illiterates. Nevertheless, family background was often a more powerful influence on occupation than literacy per se. It has been common to note a clear hierarchy of occupations according to literacy in early modern Europe, with gentlemen, professional men, merchants, and larger farmers all exhibiting quite high literacy rates. They were followed in the literacy hierarchy by skilled craftsmen and then lesser skilled craftsmen, with husbandmen, miners, and laborers exhibiting the lowest levels of literacy. The obvious interpretation of this hierarchy is that it corresponds to differences in the functional value of literacy in the occupations concerned. However, this hierarchy also appears to have reflected the influence of family background on literacy. The magnitude of the difference in literacy rates between categories was obviously subject to substantial collapse as economies moved toward universal adult literacy during the nineteenth century and the rank ordering across adjacent categories could also switch over time.

Aside from its functional use in particular occupations, literacy could conceivably have facilitated arbitrage to superior opportunities whether within or across occupations, both by lowering the cost of acquiring information about such opportunities and by cultivating a general mental openness to pursuing such opportunities. Along these lines, one would expect that literacy would promote migration. But in fact evidence indicates that migration could be selective both for literate people in some instances and for illiterates in situations in which migration was driven by push factors.

Literacy had obvious consumption benefits in terms of the advantages of being able to read and write in everyday life, ranging from reading newspapers and novels to writing letters. In each of these cases, surrogates, possibly for hire, could provide the services in question and their prices provide a way of placing a market value on these nonpecuniary benefits. Given that many literate people appear to have ended up in unskilled occupations making no direct call for reading and writing, these consumption uses of literacy may have provided the primary incentive to learn to read and write during much of the rise of popular literacy.

Furthermore, there were perceived external benefits to society from widespread popular literacy, ranging from less propensity to crime and rioting to more informed voting behavior. Thus, government was motivated to help provide literacy. The church and religion were also important, both demanding reading and writing ability as a way of mastering religious doctrine and wanting to engage in providing schooling as a way of conveying this doctrine. It should be noted that under some circumstances states and ruling elites have actually been opposed to the cultivation of popular literacy, viewing it as a destabilizing influence on the social order. And governments have also at times attempted to restrict access to reading material by imposing prohibitive levels of taxation, like the paper and newspaper taxes in England in the eighteenth and early nineteenth centuries.

Some spheres of interaction between supply and demand should be noted. Perhaps most fundamental is the role of the family as both supplier and demander of literacy. If parents had mastered basic reading and writing skills, it was easier to transfer these skills to their children. And having acquired basic literacy and having become familiar with its use, parents would have been more likely to want to transmit literacy to their children. Thus children of literate parents were far more likely to be literate than children of illiterate parents, a phenomenon that can be attributed to both supply and demand factors.

This tendency also implies an element of momentum to the spread of literacy. Once literacy spread among one generation, it was more likely to spread among subsequent generations. The family would also have commonly mediated the influence of poverty and income levels on the likelihood of acquiring literacy. The evidence on the strength of this influence is mixed. On the one hand, literacy was positively associated with the social status of one's father's occupation. Furthermore, some studies have reported a positive correlation between height and literacy. This has been interpreted as reflecting the underlying influence of parental resources on both nutrition and provision for a child's education. However, there also appear to have been relatively well-paid industrial occupations such as mining and cotton spinning in early Victorian England that were notorious for their low literacy rates; fathers in such occupations seem to have placed little value on their children's education.

Urbanization is commonly viewed as having a positive association with literacy levels. When cities were primarily centers for commerce, learning, and administration, they would have attracted those most likely to have received at least a basic education in letters. Higher population densities in cities would also provide larger pools of both students and possible financial support for establishing and sustaining schools and tutors than rural areas. Of particular interest is whether cities provided more general stimulus and opportunity for reading and writing because of the presence of signs, the ready availability of written and printed matter, and the greater cultivation of a more cosmopolitan attitude. Accounts of preindustrial literacy do point to higher literacy rates in cities. However, in the early stages of industrialization, rapid population growth in cities could overwhelm the ability of charity and philanthropy to subsidize schools more than in rural areas.

At the same time, urbanization could be associated with the creation of factory employment, which made no call for educated workers but which employed children and adolescents and thus raised the opportunity cost of attending school. This was notably the case in Lancashire during the British Industrial Revolution. Workers in cotton textile factories appeared to have relatively low literacy levels, and literacy levels in general went into decline. These conflicting forces are reflected in the relatively low correlation in mid-nineteenth-century England and Wales between urbanization measures and literacy.

Literacy and Economic Growth. Widespread literacy has been viewed as a prerequisite for modern economic growth. One influential formulation of this view is based on the finding of Anderson and Bowman (1965) that countries with a 1955 per-capita income of three hundred dollars had adult literacy rates of at least 40 percent. Other studies have found a positive correlation between literacy levels and per-capita incomes for various combinations of European countries in the second half of the nineteenth century and across regions of Spain for the late nineteenth and early twentieth centuries. Results have been mixed, however, on whether literacy had an effect on income or rather vice versa.

Further reflection about the conceptual foundations of the relationship between literacy and economic growth suggests grounds for skepticism about its strength. Literacy is but one level of education and it is not obvious that the specific skills involved with literacy should play that dominant a role in economic growth. Many other factors could contribute to economic growth and the expertise required for technological advance could be acquired by a small segment of the population without widespread mass literacy. Widespread literacy could instill greater responsiveness to opportunities for improvement, but the importance of this effect remains open to question.

This skepticism is supported both by late-twentieth-century evidence and by evidence from the British Industrial Revolution. In a recent influential study of human capital and economic growth, Benhabib and Spiegel (1994, pp. 143–173) find that neither does the change in literacy rates have a significant impact on economic growth (indeed, the reported coefficient on literacy was actually negative) nor does the level of literacy have a significant impact on levels of per-capita income. One striking finding for England during its Industrial Revolution between 1780 and 1830 was that literacy levels were stagnant during this period; they actually appeared to decline in Lancashire, one of the regions of greatest industrial growth during this period. Literacy may have played a more prominent role in areas of agricultural change. In particular, it may have facilitated adoption of new agricultural technologies and the enclosure of common property, as reported in Nilsson, Pettersson, and Svensson (1999, pp. 79–86).

Literacy and Human Development. Literacy has not been a categorical prerequisite for individual advancement or for aggregate economic growth. But there is reason to believe that it has contributed to both. And literacy has figured prominently both as a communications and transactions technology and as a central component of mass education. Its rise can be seen as indicative of a more general commitment to long-term human development. It can thus be seen as pointing to a number of fundamental channels through which economic progress has occurred.

[*See also* Education *and* Human Capital.]

BIBLIOGRAPHY

Anderson, C. Arnold, and Mary Jean Bowman, eds. *Education and Economic Development*. Chicago, 1965. This collection contains a number of influential papers dealing with the role of literacy in long-run economic development.

Arnove, Robert F., and Harvey J. Graff, eds. *National Literacy Campaigns: Historical and Comparative Perspectives*. New York, 1987. This volume contains useful studies of important episodes in the promotion of mass literacy both in recent times and in the more distant past.

Benhabib, Jess, and Mark Spiegel. "The Role of Human Capital in Economic Development. Evidence from Aggregate Cross-Country Data." *Journal of Monetary Economics* 34 (1994), 143–173.

Cipolla, Carlo. *Literacy and Development in the West*. Harmondsworth, England, 1969. Cipolla provides a compilation of statistics on literacy trends for a variety of Western countries for the nineteenth and early twentieth centuries.

Clanchy, Michael. *From Memory to Written Record: England, 1066–1307*, 2d ed. Oxford, 1993. Clanchy provides an account of a transition to increased use of writing in social transactions from some of its feasible alternatives.

Cressy, David. *Literacy and the Social Order: Reading and Writing in Tudor and Stuart England*. Cambridge, 1980. Cressy provides useful quantitative evidence on literacy in early modern England.

Goody, Jack. *The Logic of Writing and the Organization of Society*. Cambridge, 1986. Goody considers the early emergence of writing in association with economic affairs.

Graff, Harvey. *The Labyrinths of Literacy: Reflections on Literacy Past and Present*, rev. and expanded ed. Pittsburgh, 1995. This volume provides a collection of Graff's surveys of both historical and current issues related to literacy.

Graff, Harvey. *Legacies of Literacy*: Bloomington, 1986. Graff provides a comprehensive survey of historical material on literacy through its date of publication. It provides an indispensable starting point for any systematic study of the subject.

Graff, Harvey. *The Literacy Myth: Literacy and Social Structure in the Nineteenth-Century City*. New York, 1979. This is an influential piece of iconoclasm regarding the importance of literacy.

Harris, William V. *Ancient Literacy*. Cambridge, Mass., 1989. A useful overview of what is known about literacy levels in the ancient world.

Houston, Rab. "Literacy and Society in the West." *Social History* 8.3 (October 1983), 269–293.

Houston, Rab. *Literacy in Early Modern Europe: Culture and Education, 1500–1800*. London, 1988. Houston's two pieces provide rich and wide-ranging surveys of the early modern period.

Lockridge, Kenneth. *Literacy in Colonial New England: An Inquiry into the Social Context of Literacy in the Early Modern West*. New York, 1974. Lockridge documents the high levels of literacy in colonial New England from the start of settlement and emphasizes the influence of Protestantism.

Mitch, David. "The Role of Education and Skill in the British Industrial Revolution," in *The British Industrial Revolution: An Economic Perspective*, 2d ed., edited by Joel Mokyr, pp. 241–279. Boulder, Colo., 1999. Contains a survey of the literature on the limited contribution of literacy to economic growth during the British Industrial Revolution.

Nilsson, Anders, Lars Pettersson, and Patrick Svensson. "Agrarian Transition and Literacy: The Case of Nineteenth-Century Sweden." *European Review of Economic History* 1.1 (April 1999), 79–86.

Resnick, Daniel, and Lauren Resnick. "The Nature of Literacy: An Historical Exploration." *Harvard Educational Review* 47.3 (August 1977), 370–385. An influential article articulating the distinction between restricted and mass literacy.

Sanderson, Michael. "Literacy and Social Mobility in the Industrial Revolution in England." *Past and Present* 56 (1972), 75–104. Sanderson documents the role that literacy played in the major textile region of Lancashire during the English Industrial Revolution.

Sanderson, Michael. *Education, Economic Change, and Society in England, 1780–1870*, 2d ed. Cambridge, 1995. A concise yet thorough survey.

Schofield, Roger. "Dimensions of Illiteracy, 1750–1850." *Explorations in Economic History* 10 (1973), 437–454. An important study documenting the stagnation of literacy in England during the Industrial Revolution.

Schofield, Roger. "The Measurement of Literacy in Pre-Industrial England." In *Literacy in Traditional Societies*, edited by Jack Goody. Cambridge, 1968. Schofield provides a valuable formulation of the basic issues in trying to measure literacy.

Soltow, Lee, and Edward Stevens. *The Rise of Literacy and the Common School in the United States: A Socioeconomic Analysis to 1870.* Chicago, 1981.

Vincent, David. *The Rise of Mass Literacy: Reading and Writing in Modern Europe.* Malden, Mass., 2000. A wide-ranging survey of the last few centuries.

DAVID MITCH

LITHUANIA. *See* Baltic States.

LIVESTOCK LEASES. The terms upon which the usufruct of pastoral lands was granted were primarily determined by resource availability. In northern Europe during the so-called Dark Ages (c. 400–1100 CE) and thereafter in western Europe from 1370 to 1520, in central Europe until about 1500, and in the eastern lands of the Trans-Pontine and Asiatic steppe until the eighteenth century, contemporaries regarded supplies of pastoral land as limitless. The peripatetic inhabitants of these lands depended upon riverine systems to achieve their sense of "territoriality," a concept different from that of post-1100 medieval and early modern western Europe. In western Europe, rivers were considered one of the elements used to define the boundaries of specific bundles of property rights, forming part of a perimeter within which economic activity took place. Where pastoral lands were abundant, the indigenous populations considered rivers differently. For them, rivers provided the sinews of "territories" that lacked peripheral delineation. The settlements that they located constituted their winter residences; and these hovels were used to provide shelter for their numerous flocks in the river valleys, incised deep into the extensive wood- and grasslands. Along the course of these valleys they migrated in the spring, traversing riverbanks and crossing tributary streams to summer grazing. During the passage, the stock were fed on the adjacent grasslands. The duration of both the stops and the migration depended on how far the animals could wander from the river before the grass cover became too sparse, a function of the intensity of the summer heat and the amount of water from the river available to encourage grass growth and impede scorching. Arriving at their summer pastures, the animals could feed on rich grasslands where temporary "shieldings" might be built. The herders even could sow cereal crops in these remote places, neglecting further cultivation over the summer, until harvest time when the crop was gathered before the nomads returned homeward. Rivers thus conditioned the nature of agrarian activities and the length and spatial extent of perceived "territories," with the waterways forming a fixed element within grazing, which lacked a peripheral delineation. The allocation of pastoral resources within "territories" eschewed any concept of spatial delineation and was confined to grants of usufruct, allowing the recipient to graze a specific number and kind of animal, subject only to restrictions related to other uses of the land such as hunting.

When population pressure led to an extension of arable activity at the expense of pastoral reserves, across northwestern and southern Europe (c. 1100–1370 and after 1520), these pastoral lands had new economic value. Both arable farmers and their pastoral counterparts assumed a functional division and spatial delineation between these activities. Across Europe, once seemingly limitless upland and marshland reserves of pastoral land were for the first time (1100–1370) subject to spatial delineation and jurisdictional definition. Such lands, enhanced in value, were divided up between lords and peasants, who became functionally differentiated from their counterparts in the plain. The latter had the resources only to maintain but not to rear the necessary stock for their arable holdings. To optimize the arable–pasture balance and ensure an adequate supply of manure to maintain the fertility of the land in tillage, rights of usufruct ("stints") in the scarce pastoral resources (common pasture, hayfields, and postharvest stubble) of the new villages were attached, under customary law, to the peasant holdings.

Within each settlement, the relative availability of component pastoral elements determined the prevailing agrarian system. A relative local abundance of common grazing-hay fields was manifested in the use of continuous-cropping or three-course arable regimes. A relative scarcity of such pastoral reserves necessitated the deployment of a two-course rotational system to increase the amount of feed available for stock within the confines of the "open fields." To supplement meager pastoral resources, however, villagers also bought such resources from their lords, entering into a series of contracts for the acquisition of supplementary animal feed and bedding. "Loppings and croppings"—the branches and leaves from cut- or windfall trees—were bought to supplement supplies of straw from the fields to provide bedding. Holly could be cut, *in extremis*, for feed. Lords also sold the fruit of the oak-acorns/mast, as "pannage" for the feeding of swine. Finally, they leased to the peasants the right to graze over the arden and fielden lands that they possessed either by assigning a given area of grassland—"herbage"—or by charging a fee per head of stock utilizing their grassland—"agistment."

Peasants of post-1100 medieval and early-modern Europe thus could secure sufficient animal feed, by both contractual and customary arrangements, to maintain stocking at a high-enough level to satisfy their consumption requirements, producing meat, milk, hides, coarse wool, and draught-power and manure. The cash yielded by such activity allowed them to pass on the task of rearing this stock to those who occupied those upland and marshland reserves of pastoral land, which were subject to a process of spatial delineation and jurisdictional definition.

Such systems for the rearing and maintenance of animals continued in peasant society throughout western and central Europe until well into the nineteenth century, displaced only when and where a system of "convertible" husbandry—*Köppelwirtschaft* or "up-and-down" husbandry—was introduced into the northwestern part of the continent. On these new farms the medieval distinction between pasture and arable ceased to exist. Grassland, whether held in severalty or subject to common grazing rights, was broken up by the plow. All the new farms' lands were in tillage. Grass, like other crops, was sown to provide temporary rotational leys. Specific livestock leases became redundant within this new system. Residual common grazing, normally confined to sparse upland grassland, was attached to the property-rights packages of the new farms.

From the nineteenth century on, the extensive animal-husbandry systems described above were diffused across an increasingly integrated international economy—to Australia, New Zealand, and the Americas (Argentina, Brazil, Mexico, and the United States). The transition between the legal systems, by which the usufruct of pastoral lands was granted, was temporally telescoped. Extensive aboriginal systems of hunting–herding were rapidly displaced. Land grants, embracing rights in severalty and common, were superimposed on extensive wood- and grasslands, increasing stocking levels and gradually shifting the balance from the latter to the former form of ownership to create the stations, ranches, and farms of the contemporary world.

BIBLIOGRAPHY

Gonner, Edward C. K., *Common Land and Inclosure.* London, 1912.
Gray, Charles M., *Copyhold, Equity, and Common Law.* Cambridge, Mass., 1963.
Jones, Glanville R. J. "Multiple Estates and Early Settlement." In *English Medieval Settlement* edited by Peter H. Sawyer, pp. 15–40. London, 1979.
Kerridge, Eric. *Agrarian Problems in the Sixteenth Century and After.* London and New York, 1969.
McNiell, William H. *Europe's Steppe Frontier, 1500–1800.* Chicago, 1964.

IAN BLANCHARD

LIVING STANDARDS. By many measures, a revolution in living standards is sweeping the world. Most people today are better fed, clothed, and housed than their predecessors two centuries ago. They are healthier, live longer, and are better educated. Women's lives are less centered on reproduction, and political democracy has gained a foothold. Although western Europe and its offshoots have been the leaders of this advance, most of the less-developed countries have joined since the middle of the twentieth century, with the newly emerging nations of sub-Saharan Africa the latest to participate. The picture is not one of universal progress, but it is the greatest advance in the condition of the world's population ever achieved in such a brief span of time.

Concept. The standard of living is the composite of the various sources of well-being of a nation's population. It corresponds to the economists' idea of a utility function, in which well-being depends on a wide variety of circumstances, pecuniary and nonpecuniary. Early in the post–World War II period, the standard of living was typically conceived in purely material terms—the goods and services at one's disposal—called here the *level* of living. This conception led naturally to measuring living standards in terms of a country's total real output expressed in per capita terms. Critics expressed concern that such a measure—technically, gross domestic product (GDP) per capita—failed to reflect a number of important aspects of human welfare. They pointed to some notable disparities in the ranking of countries based on GDP per capita compared with other sources of well-being, such as length of life and education. Many of these critics feared that if policymakers focused on GDP per capita, they would be unduly biased toward economic growth as a policy objective, rather than striving for balanced human development. A social-indicators movement developed from the 1950s onward that led finally to publication by the United Nations of a human development index (HDI), reported on an annual basis since 1990. The HDI combines GDP per capita, life expectancy at birth, and a composite measure of education based on literacy and school enrollment into an overall index number. Some experimental work also seeks to include human rights in this broad measure of human development.

In another phase of the social-indicators movement, some economic historians and anthropologists, following the lead of Nobel laureate Robert W. Fogel's work on physical stature, have proposed a measure of the "biological standard of living." In this work, a measure such as height is taken to mirror living standards. As seen below, this measure trends much like life expectancy and hence is considerably less comprehensive than its advocates imply.

The definition used here reflects the movement toward a broader concept of living standards. It is influenced also by what people themselves say about their sources of well-being. In the early 1960s, social psychologist Hadley Cantril carried out an intensive survey in twelve countries, developed and less developed, asking open-ended questions about what people want out of life—what they would need to be completely happy. In every country, material circumstances, especially level of living, are mentioned most often, being named, on average, by about three-fourths of the population. Next are family concerns—cited by about half—such as a happy family life and good relationships with children and relatives. These are followed by concerns about one's personal or family health, which typically are named by about one-third of the people. After this, and about equal in importance, at around one-fifth of the population, are matters relating to one's work (a good job) and to personal character (emotional stability, personal worth, self-discipline, and so on). Perhaps surprisingly, concerns about broad international or domestic issues, such as war, political or civil liberty, and social equality, are not often mentioned, being named, on average, by less than one person in twenty. Abrupt changes in the latter circumstances do affect people's sense of well-being at the time they occur, but ordinarily they are taken as given. Instead, it is the things that occupy most people's everyday life, and are somewhat within their control, that are typically in the forefront of personal concerns—making a living, marriage and family circumstances, and the health of oneself and one's family. Education—one of the principal components of the United Nations' HDI—is not often men-tioned, no doubt because it is largely a thing of the past for most adults, but it does show up in connection with aspirations for one's children.

In what follows, indicators are assembled of various dimensions of the standard of living broadly conceived. The measures are not combined into a single index, for lack of consensus on how they should be weighted. Moreover, a single index obscures the fact that different dimensions of living standards often trend differently. Countries are grouped according to the United Nations' classification—developed areas include Europe, North America, Japan, Australia, and New Zealand; less developed, all others. World and regional averages are population-weighted means of country values, to approximate better the condition of people generally in various regions of the world. Turning points in historical time series are dated by visual inspection. The various measures used here are far from exhaustive, but they are sufficient to suggest some of the immense changes in people's lives that have taken place in the course of the past two centuries.

Long-Term Trends. In many dimensions of the standard of living, the past two centuries in the more-developed countries have seen a marked break with past experience—a sharp increase in the rate of advance. Typically, the timing of this break is different from one measure to another, suggesting that the measures are responding to different rather than the same causes.

Level of living. The quantity of goods consumed by the average person has multiplied in countries experiencing rapid economic growth at a rate never before known. The break with prior experience is evident in historical time series of real GDP per capita (Table 1). Although lack of annual data makes precise dating impossible, there is clearly a transition in the first half of the nineteenth century in

TABLE 1. *Growth Rate of Real GDP per Capita in the Half-Century before and after Its Turning Point in Seven Countries*

COUNTRY	APPROXIMATE TURNING POINT	GDP PER CAPITA AT TURNING POINT (1990 DOLLARS)	GROWTH RATE IN HALF-CENTURY	
			BEFORE TURNING POINT	AFTER TURNING POINT
			(PERCENT PER YEAR)	
United Kingdom	1820	1,756	0.4	1.3
France	1820	1,218	0.3	0.9
United States	1830	1,443	0.6	1.5
Sweden	1850	1,289	0.2[a]	1.3
Japan	1870	741	0.1	1.7
Brazil	1900	737	0.1	1.7
India	1945	663	0.1	1.7

[a] 1820–50.
SOURCE: Easterlin, 2000, p. 10.

TABLE 2. *School Enrollment around 1830 and Adult Literacy Rate around 1850 and 1950, Specified Country*

COUNTRY	PERCENTAGE OF SCHOOL-AGE POPULATION ENROLLED IN PRIMARY SCHOOL, AROUND 1830	PERCENTAGE LITERATE, POPULATION 15 AND OVER	
		AROUND 1850	AROUND 1950
Germany	77	80	98
Scandinavia	66	90	98
United States	56	77	97
England	41	68	98
France	39	58	96
Japan	30	26	98
Italy	14	22	88
Russia	4	8	93
Brazil	4	—	49
India	4	6	19

SOURCE: Easterlin, 2000, pp. 19–20.

western Europe and the United States from slow to rapid growth in living levels. The average post-transition rate of change could not have prevailed earlier—for it to have done so would imply, for example, that the United Kingdom's living level in 1670, at the time of the Scientific Revolution, was below that prevailing in Ethiopia in the 1990s. The gradual worldwide spread of economic growth is suggested by the marked rise in growth rates in the twentieth century in Brazil and India.

The rate of improvement in living levels has risen noticeably over time. In the last half of the twentieth century, the annual growth rate in the developed countries averaged 2.7 percent, a rate about double that in the half-century preceding World War I. One way of appreciating the rapidity of change is to note how it drives a wedge between the experience of successive generations. An annual growth rate of 2.7 percent means that a parent would, on average, have less than half of what her child has at the same point in the life cycle; a grandparent, less than a fifth of what her grandchild has. Considering differences like these, one can readily appreciate that serious intergenerational frictions may accompany modern economic growth.

The transformation of living levels has been qualitative as well as quantitative. By comparison with the conveniences and comforts widely available in developed economies at the end of the twentieth century, everyday life two centuries ago was most akin to what we know today as "camping out." In the late-eighteenth-century United States, for example (which even then was a relatively rich society), among the rural population, which comprised 95 percent of the total, housing typically consisted of one-story houses with one or two rooms and an attic under the rafters. Frequently there was no flooring except the hard earth. A fireplace with a chimney provided heating and cooking. Toilet facilities consisted of outdoor privies. Water and wood had to be fetched. Transportation consisted of a horse and wagon. The qualitative change from that world to the United States' current panoply of consumer goods—cars and planes, electrical appliances and running water, telecommunications and computers, pharmaceuticals and health care, and the phenomenal array of food and clothes—is literally incredible.

School enrollment and literacy. It is rarely appreciated that among the leaders in economic growth, advances in other important dimensions of the standard of living sometimes *preceded* the onset of rapid economic growth. This is notably true of the establishment of formal schooling. In the first half of the nineteenth century, school enrollment and literacy rates in northern and western Europe and the United States were already high on a worldwide scale (Table 2). Although developments prior to that time are difficult to quantify, the relatively high level of education in these areas is known to be the product of trends that reach as far back as the sixteenth century, well before the onset of modern economic growth. The picture of leadership in educational improvement is somewhat different from that for economic growth, with the United Kingdom slipping down in ranking and Germany and Scandinavia moving to the top. Clearly, if one were to tell a story of human development in terms of education, it would be somewhat different from the economic historians' tale of the onset and spread of industrialization.

It would be a mistake, of course, to read the nineteenth-century enrollment and literacy figures in the light of education today. In the nineteenth century, school years and school days were shorter. Numeracy probably lagged behind literacy. Most important, there has been a change in the schooling curriculum as systematic knowledge of the world about us has improved. As with economic growth, the quantitative measures fail to reflect immense qualitative change.

Political democracy. The extent of democracy is assessed here on the basis of the structure and functioning of a country's legislative and executive institutions. The legislative measure indicates whether a legislature exists and how important it is in political decision making. The executive branch measure reflects the openness of recruitment to the office of chief executive and the extent to which there are limits on the chief executive. Such limits might arise from a legislature, but they could also be due to a political party or parties not wholly controlled by the nation's leader or to some other groups, such as the church or military. Each measure varies from zero to one and is based on the judgments of scholars with specialized knowledge of the political histories of the individual countries. These two measures have the advantage of being readily available for most countries over the last two centuries, but they are not comprehensive—they fail to reflect, for example, the gradual expansion of the right to political participation to more and more groups within the population.

As in the case of education, there is evidence of progress in western Europe and the United States toward establishing democratic institutions prior to the onset of rapid economic growth, especially with regard to an effective legislature (Table 3). This does not mean that there existed broad-based political democracy of the type known today

TABLE 3. *Indicators of Democratic Institutions, 1820–1829 and 1950–1959 (from Minimum of 0 to Maximum of 1.0)*

BRANCH OF GOVERNMENT AND COUNTRY	1820–1829	1950–1959
A. Legislative branch		
United Kingdom	1.0	1.0
France	0.7	1.0
United States	1.0	1.0
Sweden	0.7	1.0
Japan	0	1.0
Brazil	0.3	1.0
India	(0)[a]	1.0
B. Executive branch		
United Kingdom	0.3	1.0
France	0	0.9
United States	0.9	1.0
Sweden	0	1.0
Japan	0	1.0
Brazil	0	0.6
India	(0)[a]	0.9

[a]Colony of United Kingdom.
SOURCE: Easterlin, 2000, p. 22.

in Western democracies, but the long-term trend, though far from linear in all countries, was in this direction, as the table reveals. In these countries, the rise of living standards broadly conceived has thus encompassed important advances in political rights. This is true also of Brazil and India, but, as shall be seen, has not been generally the case throughout the less-developed world.

Length of life, health, and stature. Life expectancy at birth, like GDP per capita, is typically marked by a sharp increase in the rate of improvement. In contrast to indicators of education and political democracy, turning points in life expectancy, and, more generally, measures of fertility as well as mortality, occur substantially later than those in GDP per capita among the leaders in economic growth, the countries of western Europe and the United States. In these countries, a period of mild initial gains in life expectancy is followed in the latter part of the nineteenth century by very rapid advance (Table 4). The timing of the turning points for the seven countries in the table, as well as more systematic examination, suggests that although rapid improvement in life expectancy started later than modern economic growth, it spread more rapidly.

In the 1960s, some experts came to adopt a "stationary state" expectation about the future of life expectancy in more developed countries, in which the average length of life had risen to about seventy years. The reason was that historically—as also in the less-developed countries in the late twentieth century—the great declines in mortality were due to reductions in infectious disease, which benefited especially those at younger ages. The possibility of further declines was seen as foundering on the hard rock of the degenerative diseases of older age, especially heart disease and cancer. As reasonable as this view seemed, it was very shortly undercut by events. In the late 1960s, a new decline in United States mortality set in at a pace not much different from that prevailing from 1900 to 1964, as marked gains began to be made in reducing older-age mortality due to heart disease. Similar declines in mortality rates occurred in other countries leading in life expectancy. The current improvement in life expectancy in the developed countries reflects chiefly progress on diseases previously viewed as the inevitable result of aging, especially cardiovascular disease.

There can be little doubt that health status improved in parallel with the advance of life expectancy as infectious disease was brought under control, because the same techniques that lowered deaths due to infectious disease also reduced the incidence and prevalence of such disease, and thereby the extent of sickness in the population. Comprehensive evidence of the improvement in health is hard to come by, because of insufficient morbidity data, but the advance is clearly suggested by the dwindling (and often disappearing) number of cases in the United States in the

TABLE 4. *Life Expectancy Improvement in the Half-Century before and after Its Turning Point in Seven Countries*

COUNTRY	APPROXIMATE TURNING POINT	LIFE EXPECNY AT TURNING POINT (YEARS)	CHANGE IN HALF-CENTURY	
			BEFORE TURNING POINT	AFTER TURNING POINT
England and Wales	1871	41.0	3.0	12.0
Sweden	1875	45.4	4.6	17.2
United States	1890	43.0	3.3[a]	19.9
France[b]	1893	44.9	3.4	20.3
Japan	1923	42.6	5.8	30.8
Brazil	1940	36.7	8.0	28.9
India	1945	32.1	8.3	28.3

[a]Change for 1860–1890 converted to half-century rate.   [b]Data are for females.
SOURCE: Easterlin, 2000, p. 13.

twentieth century of such reportable diseases as typhoid fever, malaria, diphtheria, whooping cough, and smallpox.

The limited evidence available suggests also that long-term trends in stature paralleled those in life expectancy and health. In six European countries (Great Britain, France, Norway, Sweden, Denmark, and Hungary) the average improvement in male stature in the nineteenth century was 1.1 centimeters; in the subsequent century—the period when health and life expectancy improved so rapidly—stature increased by 7.7 centimeters. This similarity in timing points to the powerful influence on trends in stature of changing health status.

Family circumstances. A major decline in rates of childbearing among women is indicative of a significant change in family life and women's roles, because it means that women are no longer tied to childbearing and child-rearing during most of the reproductive ages.

The onset of rapid fertility decline starts in the late nineteenth century in a number of western European countries; and in most, the timing of the onset of the decline in fertility is close to that in mortality (Table 5). Writing in the 1950s, demographers, generalizing chiefly from European experience, termed this "the demographic transition," a shift from initially high to eventually low levels of mortality and fertility. They saw the fertility decline as typically lagging the mortality decline. By the end of the twentieth century, fertility rates in a number of developed countries had declined so far that they were below two children per woman, raising concerns about the eventual onset of population decline.

There has been qualitative as well as quantitative change in childbearing behavior—a shift in the nature of fertility control. In the past, levels of infant and child mortality were so high that only one out of two children survived to

TABLE 5. *Decline in Total Fertility Rate in Three Decades before and after Its Turning Point in Seven Countries (Births per Woman)*

COUNTRY	APPROXIMATE TURNING POINT	TOTAL FERTILITY RATE AT TURNING POINT	DECLINE IN 30 YEARS	
			BEFORE TURNING POINT	AFTER TURNING POINT
United States	1830	6.6	0.5	1.3
England and Wales	1881	4.6	(0.3)[a]	1.7
France	1881	3.4	0.1	0.9
Sweden	1885	4.3	0.0	1.2
Japan	1950	4.7	0.6	3.0
Brazil	1962	6.2	0.4	3.6
India	1967	5.7	0.7	2.6

[a] Increase.
SOURCE: Easterlin, 2000, p. 17.

adulthood, and most parents (other than members of some elites) consequently made little deliberate effort to restrict childbearing. The great reduction of fertility in the twentieth century was accomplished by the adoption of intentional family size limitation by parents through the use of contraception or induced abortion. In the historical experience of European countries, the contraceptive methods chiefly employed to limit family size deliberately were abstinence, withdrawal, and the use of condoms. In today's less-developed countries, the fertility decline has benefited from new techniques of contraception that have appeared since the 1960s—the oral pill, the intrauterine device, implants, and sterilization. These developments in the nature of fertility control imply a significant shift in the way of life. No longer do most parents have as many children as they can. Rather, they deliberately limit their family size by adopting practices that were previously either nonexistent or, if known, were rarely used intentionally to reduce the number of offspring.

Distribution of gains. The growth in living standards so far described is based on averages for the population as a whole. It is obvious that participation in this rise need not be the same throughout the population and that participation may differ from one dimension of living standards to another, as well as over time for any given dimension. Unfortunately, generalization about trends in distributive aspects of living standards is frustrated by a lack of both historical data and thorough scholarly study.

With regard to living levels, it appears that in the twentieth century inequality has, on balance, lessened in the more-developed countries, implying a more equal sharing of gains. There have, however, been significant interruptions or reversals of this trend, the most recent occurring in the last two decades of the twentieth century. The long-term trend toward greater equality is suggested both by fragmentary observations on the distribution of income by size of income, and scattered data on income-per-worker differentials by industry, occupation, and region. This downtrend in inequality may have been preceded in the nineteenth century by a phase of rising inequality, but the evidence on this is even scarcer and limited to a few countries, at best.

Educational differentials within the population have probably trended downward over the long term with the legal establishment of first, universal primary schooling, and then—largely in the course of the twentieth century—universal secondary schooling. It seems reasonable to infer, too, that political rights have become more equally diffused as property, race, gender, and other restrictions on the franchise have been gradually removed over the past two centuries. Finally, it is fairly certain that differentials by socioeconomic status in mortality and child-bearing lessened in the course of the twentieth century. Thus, overall, the ad-

vances along various dimensions of living standards in the now-developed countries appear, on balance, typically to have become more equally shared in the twentieth century.

The British standard-of-living controversy. A much-debated issue is what happened to living standards in the course of the British Industrial Revolution. Did they go up or down in the period, say, from 1780 to 1850?

The search for answers to this question has paralleled in limited fashion the broadening of the concept of standard of living described above. Initially, the focus was on the economic dimension, the level of living. Although no consensus was reached, the conclusion tended to be that there were modest gains, but that inequality may have increased. In the 1980s and 1990s, research turned to so-called biological indicators—life expectancy, health, and, particularly, stature. Scholars focusing on these measures suggested that there was little improvement in living standards, and perhaps even deterioration.

It is possible that both schools of thought are correct, because each is concerned with a different dimension of living standards. Living levels, as reflected in income and wage measures, may have trended upward, while health and life expectancy, as reflected in measures of height, may have been unchanged or deteriorated. An adverse change in health would have been possible as the British population became increasingly urbanized and more exposed to contagious disease. Not until the latter part of the nineteenth century did the advance of knowledge extend to the control of contagious disease, and, as has been seen, measures like life expectancy and stature turn sharply upward. Some of the controversy about the trend in the standard of living thus appears attributable to confusion on the part of those who think that health measures should move in step with measures of income or wages.

Viewed broadly, the British standard-of-living controversy may appear somewhat provincial. Although it is of interest to inquire about the course of living standards in the first country to experience the Industrial Revolution, a much more general concern is the progress of living standards as the Industrial Revolution spread worldwide. On this there can be little mistake—the onset of modern economic growth has brought with it an unprecedented advance in living levels in country after country. And, as the technology of disease control has grown and spread throughout the world since the late nineteenth century, life expectancy, health, and stature have joined the advance. It is clear, however, that historically these great advances in the different dimensions of living standards did not go hand in hand.

Trends in the Less-Developed World since 1950. The immense improvement in living standards that has been occurring in western Europe and the United States since 1800 or earlier is spreading throughout the world. Some of today's less-developed countries—most notably in Latin America—began to share in the advance in the first half of the twentieth century, but since World War II, the advance in the less-developed world has been explosive, far exceeding that in the historical experience of the leaders, as the following figures attest.

1. Since the early 1950s, the material living level of the average person in today's less-developed countries (LDCs), which collectively account for four-fifths of the world's population, has multiplied by threefold. The rate at which improvement has been occurring, as indexed by the annual growth rate of GDP per capita from 1952 to 1995, is 2.5 percent, about twice as large as that of the more developed countries (MDCs) in the nineteenth century, when they were at a similar early stage of rapid economic growth.

2. Life expectancy at birth in the less-developed world has risen by twenty-one years, from an average of forty-one years in the early 1950s to more than sixty-two today. In some less-developed countries, life expectancy today is similar to that in the developed world. As in the case of GDP per capita, the rate of improvement in LDCs has been much more rapid than in the historical experience of the West.

3. The high level of fertility that previously prevailed in the less-developed countries has been cut by almost half, from an average of more than six births per woman in the early 1950s to close to three at the beginning of the twenty-first century. Again the rapidity of change in LDCs far exceeds that of the MDCs at a comparable stage. Declining fertility rates in LDCs have brought population growth rates down, and population growth in LDCs is projected by 2025 to be less than 1 percent,

about the same as in the MDCs in the 1970s. The so-called "population explosion" in LDCs is clearly a transient phenomenon, as implied by the demographers' concept of the demographic transition.

4. In 1950, about four adults out of ten in the less-developed world were literate; today the corresponding figure is more than seven out of ten. This is a much more rapid rate of advance in literacy than took place in the developed countries in the past.

Although the picture varies from one place to another, all major regions of the world have participated significantly in this advance. Asia, which accounts for about six-tenths of the world population, has had the most notable rates of improvement (Table 6, lines 1–3). Within Asia, India is something of a laggard, but India has nevertheless improved at about the world average on all measures used here. Only in sub-Saharan Africa, which accounts for about a tenth of the world population, is the picture mixed. Economic advance has been small—living levels in the 1990s were only about one-fifth greater than in the 1950s. However, life expectancy has improved by about twelve years since 1950, a substantial increase (Table 6, line 6). This gain is projected by the United Nations to be largely sustained, despite the serious problem of human immunodeficiency virus (HIV) in some countries there, before a marked upward trend resumes around 2010. Important strides have also been made in sub-Saharan Africa with regard to the reduction of illiteracy, and there are signs, too, of incipient fertility decline.

These advances in living standards in LDCs have, on average, been fairly evenly shared or are even more equally distributed than they were a half century ago. For forty-five countries for which income distribution data are available

TABLE 6. *Major Less-Developed Regions: Share of World Population in 2000 and Indicators of Change in Economic and Social Conditions, 1950s to 1990s*

Geographic Area[a]	Percentage Share of World Population in 2000	GDP per Capita in 1995 as Percent of 1952	Increase in Life Expectancy, Years	Decline in Fertility Rate, Births per Woman	Increase in Adult Literacy Rate, Percentage Points
			c. 1950 to c. 1995		
1. China	21	5.0	27.6	4.3	34
2. Asia other than China and India	21	4.6	22.6	2.7	48
3. India	17	2.5	21.6	2.4	33
4. Northern Africa	2	2.4	20.4	2.8	41
5. Latin America	9	1.9	16.7	2.9	29
6. Sub-Saharan Africa	11	1.2	11.7	0.6	39

[a] Ranked by growth rate of GDP per capita 1952–1995, as in second column.
SOURCE: Easterlin, 2000, pp. 11, 13, 17, 20.

back to the 1960s, there has been little change in average inequality. If there is a phase of rising inequality in the early stages of modern economic growth, it is not apparent in the recent historical experience of today's LDCs. Moreover, poverty—measured in terms of the proportion living below some absolute level of subsistence—has been considerably reduced. Education differences within national populations have also declined in most LDCs, as have differences in life expectancy. Although there are exceptions, the typical pattern in the less-developed world is one of improving living conditions throughout the population.

Although the rate of advance in economic and social conditions in today's LDCs has, on average, been greater than in the MDCs when they were at a comparable stage, the picture is somewhat different if one compares LDCs' with MDCs' performance since the 1950s. With regard to GDP per capita, the MDCs' annual growth rate of 2.7 percent since 1950 has slightly exceeded the 2.5 percent of the LDCs, and the income gap—the ratio of MDC to LDC GDP per capita—has consequently grown from 5.1 to 5.5 (Table 7, line 1). On the other hand, the gaps with regard to life expectancy, fertility, and literacy have narrowed (lines 2–4). Thus, while the gap in economic conditions has widened a little, that in social conditions has noticeably lessened.

If one turns to political conditions, the picture is less positive. The shift from colonial rule to independence in a number of LDCs must be recognized as an important advance in the political realm. But if one considers the prevalence of political democracy in LDCs, there is little evidence of improvement over the last half century (Table 8, line 2). Most striking, perhaps, is the achievement of sustained democracy in India (line 2b). Against the background of limited political democracy in most of the less-developed world today, India stands out as a sharp exception. The contrast with China is notable. When human rights are added to the human development comparison, China's relative success in economic growth, health, and fertility reduction (Table 6, lines 1 and 3) must be weighted against

India's remarkable record of political democracy. India's feat has been accomplished with a population much more heterogeneous linguistically than in most countries, and with income and literacy levels markedly lower than those of the United Kingdom and the United States in the first half of the nineteenth century, when those countries' democratic attainment was less than India's today.

Subjective Welfare. The description of living standards to this point has been based on so-called objective indicators—external observations on various aspects of the conditions of life of people in various times and places. A quite different type of measure that has come into use since World War II is based on survey data in which respondents report how they feel about their lives—how happy, satisfied, or content they are. A rather different picture emerges from these subjective measures than that given heretofore. By and large, the great advance in many objective indicators is not accompanied by a corresponding improvement in measures of subjective well-being.

Surveys of happiness are the most plentiful indicators of subjective well-being, although other questions relating to feelings of well-being give quite similar patterns. Since World War II, a large number of representative national surveys have been conducted in various countries, in which respondents are asked a simple question about how happy they are—very happy, fairly happy, or not very happy. In these surveys, each person is free to define happiness in his or her own terms. Hence, one might suppose that no useful comparisons could be made. As has been seen, however, the factors affecting happiness are fairly similar for most persons—happiness everywhere is governed by the things that take up most of one's personal everyday life: making a living, and raising and maintaining a healthy family. Hence, scholars studying these data have concluded that meaningful comparisons can, in fact, be made among sizeable groups of people. This inference is supported by regularities found in the responses.

In every survey ever conducted, the rich are, on average, happier than the poor. (This does not mean that every rich person is happy, and every poor person, unhappy—the comparison is between averages of the two groups.) This finding of a positive point-of-time relationship between happiness and income would lead one to expect that the vastly higher levels of real income that economic growth brings would lead to advances in happiness in the same—positive—direction. There is growing evidence, however, that over time, happiness does not rise with income, even with very large increases in income:

1. In the United States since World War II, real per capita income has more than doubled, but the average level of happiness was the same in the 1990s as in the late 1940s.

TABLE 7. *Gap between More-Developed Countries (MDCs) and Less-Developed Countries (LDCs), Various Indicators of Economic and Social Conditions, c. 1950 and c. 1995*

	c. 1950	c. 1995
1. Real GDP per capita: Ratio of MDCs to LDCs	5.1	5.5
2. Years of life expectancy at birth: MDCs minus LDCs	15.7	12.2
3. Total fertility rate: LDCs minus MDCs	3.4	1.6
4. Percentage of adults literate: MDCs minus LDCs	53	28

SOURCE: Easterlin, 2000, pp. 11, 13, 17, 20.

TABLE 8. *Indicators of Political Democracy, Major Areas of the World, 1950–1959 and 1990–1994 (from Minimum of 0 to Maximum of 1.0)*

	EXECUTIVE BRANCH			LEGISLATIVE BRANCH		
	1950–1959[a]	1990–1994	CHANGE, (2)–(1)	1950–1959[a]	1990–1994	CHANGE, (5)–(4)
1. More-developed areas	0.7	0.9	0.20	0.8	0.8	0
2. Less-developed areas	0.3	0.3	0	0.5	0.5	0
a. China	0	0	0	0.2	0.3	0.1
b. India	0.9	0.8	−0.1	1.0	1.0	0
c. Rest of Asia	0.3	0.3	0	0.5	0.5	0
d. Latin America	0.3	0.7	0.4	0.7	0.7	0
e. Northern Africa	0.1	0.1	0	0.3	0.3	0
f. Sub-Saharan Africa	0.2	0.1	−0.1	0.5	0.4	−0.1

[a]For Northern and sub-Saharan Africa, 1960–1969 or years in that decade for which a country's data are available.
SOURCE: Easterlin, 2000, p. 23.

2. There are nine European countries for which happiness-type measures go back at least two decades. Between the 1970s and 1990s, real income per capita rises substantially in all of these countries by amounts ranging from 25 to 50 percent. In five of the nine countries, happiness is unchanged; in two it goes up, and in two it goes down. The net change in happiness for all nine countries is zero.

3. Happiness data for Japan go back to the late 1950s, when Japan had an income level below that of many LDCs in the 1990s. Between the 1950s and late 1980s, Japan had the most phenomenal economic growth ever witnessed—in only three decades real income per capita multiplied by an incredible fivefold. But happiness remained unchanged during this period of unparalleled income growth.

4. If one follows an American birth cohort or generation over his or her adult life cycle, one finds that average income rises steadily and substantially throughout the working years and then levels off. But for the typical cohort, happiness is remarkably stable throughout the entire adult life cycle.

Thus, even though happiness is positively related to material living levels at a point in time, there is no relationship over time. The explanation of the surprising flatness of the time series trend in subjective welfare, despite a positive point-of-time relationship between happiness and income, centers on people's aspirations. Judgments of well-being are made by comparing one's objective situation with a subjective (or internalized) living-level norm. At any given time, there is a fair similarity in aspirations among broad groups of the population. Because those who have higher income can come closer to attaining their aspirations, they are happier, on average, than those with lower income. Over time, however, as living standards rise in a society, so too do people's aspirations generally. Hence, widespread growth in incomes does not raise happiness because subjective living-level norms—how people feel they ought to live—rise commensurately with income. The result is that while income growth makes it possible for people better to attain their aspirations, they are not happier because their aspirations, too, have risen. In consequence, the advances in living standards evidenced by objective indicators are not reflected in feelings of subjective well-being.

[*See also* Anthropometric History; Economic Convergence and Divergence; Economic Development; Economic Growth; *and* Inequality of Wealth and Income Distribution.]

BIBLIOGRAPHY

Banks, Arthur S. *Cross-National Time Series Data Archive*. Binghamton, N.Y., 1992, updated 1995.
Birdsall, Nancy. "Why Inequality Matters: The Developing and Transitional Economies." Unpublished paper.
Cantril, Hadley. *The Pattern of Human Concerns*. New Brunswick, N.Y., 1965.
Cipolla, Carlo M. *Literacy and Development in the West*. Baltimore, 1969.
Dasgupta, Partha. *An Inquiry into Well-Being and Destitution*. Oxford, 1993.
Easterlin, Richard A. "Why Isn't the Whole World Developed?" *Journal of Economic History* 41.1 (1981), 1–19.
Easterlin, Richard A. *Growth Triumphant: The Twenty-first Century in Historical Perspective*. Ann Arbor, 1996.
Easterlin, Richard A. "The Worldwide Standard of Living since 1800." *Journal of Economic Perspectives* 14.1 (2000), 7–26.
Jaggers, Keith, and Ted Robert Gurr. *Polity III: Regime Change and Political Authority, 1800–1994*, Boulder, 1996.
Keyfitz, Nathan, and Wilhelm Flieger. *World Population*. Chicago, 1968.
Komlos, John, ed. *The Biological Standard of Living on Three Continents*. Boulder, 1995.

Lebergott, Stanley. *Pursuing Happiness*. Princeton, 1993.

Maddison, Angus. *Monitoring the World Economy, 1820–1992*. Paris, 1995.

Mokyr, Joel, ed. *The British Industrial Revolution: An Economic Perspective*. Boulder, 1993.

O'Brien, Patrick, and Roland Quinalt, eds. *The Industrial Revolution and British Society*. New York, 1993.

Steckel, Richard H., and Roderick Floud, eds. *Health and Welfare during Industrialization*. Chicago, 1997.

United Nations. *World Population Prospects: The 1998 Revision*, vol. 1, *Comprehensive Tables*. New York, 1998.

United Nations Development Program. *Human Development Report 1999*. New York, 1999.

UNESCO. *World Illiteracy at Mid-Century*. Paris, 1957.

World Bank. *World Development Report 1998/99: Knowledge for Development*. New York, 1999.

RICHARD A. EASTERLIN

LOCAL BANKS. Relatively small, unsophisticated depository institutions whose activities are generally limited to a modest geographical area or single community, local banks fall at one extreme of a continuum that ranges from international financial behemoths (World Bank, Deutsche Bank, J. P. Morgan Chase), to central banks (Bank of Japan, U.S. Federal Reserve, European Central Bank), to large commercial banks with a nationwide or regional presence (Wells Fargo, Bank of America, First Union), to small depository institutions that operate almost exclusively in a small geographical area or market niche (Abington Bank, Nittany Financial Corporation, University of Virginia Community Credit Union). Banks of the last type are considered here. What local banks lack in scale, scope, and technological sophistication they traditionally compensate for with outstanding customer service and superior ability to reduce the information barriers (adverse selection and moral hazard) that plague financial markets.

The film classic *It's a Wonderful Life* provides an excellent introduction to local banking. The story pits quintessential local banker George Bailey against Mr. Potter, an archetype of the cold, unfeeling, extralocal financier. Bailey and Potter both head financial intermediaries. In other words, they borrow cash from noteholders, depositors, bondholders, and stockholders at relatively low rates of interest, pool the money, then rationally invest it at higher rates of return in bonds, stocks, and loans. Their gross profits arise from the difference or "spread" between the cost of their liabilities and the return on their assets.

Bailey out-competes Potter for the savings of the citizens of Bedford Falls. In retaliation, Potter steals cash from Bailey's hapless clerk. Under investigation for embezzlement, Bailey contemplates suicide. Bailey's guardian angel appears, however, and shows Bailey how awful life in Bedford Falls would be without his little bank. With the angel's help, Bailey learns that without the aid of his bank's reasonable and timely loans, the town's citizens are forced to become servants of iniquity. Rather than owning substantial homes outright, they must rent shacks in Potter's ghetto.

In the movie's famous closing scene, the citizens, who clearly realize the bank's value to the community, show their gratitude by giving Bailey the money that Potter stole. The closing scene is convincing because of its setup in an earlier poignant scene set in the depths of the Great Depression. Bailey's bank almost falls victim to a "run," the queuing of depositors eager to retrieve their investments due to uncertainty about the bank's financial solidity. Armed with his cash honeymoon fund and a lucid speech about the importance of his bank to the community, Bailey stops the run by convincing depositors that Potter's offer to buy their deposits for fifty cents on the dollar is a ploy to take over and close the bank. He also reminds his depositors that the bank's assets are not primarily held as cash but as mortgages on their homes and small businesses. By running on the bank, the depositors are injuring themselves and their neighbors.

Bailey's building and loan was fictional and somewhat stereotyped, but overall it was a fairly accurate depiction of the strengths and weaknesses of small financial institutions. Local banks are as old as financial intermediation itself, which arose with the first human civilizations—Babylon, China, Egypt, Greece, and Rome—if not earlier. Early local banks were usually sole proprietorships, family affairs, or small partnerships that safeguarded grains and other valuables, changed one form of money into another, and made highly collateralized loans at interest rates that ran into the double and sometimes triple digits. Unfortunately, little is known about banks before the Roman period. The sophistication and variety of the Roman institutions suggest, however, that banking was well understood even earlier in antiquity.

Scholars' knowledge of banking after about 1200 CE increases considerably because deposit banking based on Roman precedents began to revive in western Europe about that time. Historians bestow most of their attention, however, on international banking houses like the Medici bank of Northern Italy, the Fugger bank of Augsburg, Islamic merchant bankers, and public banks like Genoa's Bank of Saint George (established 1408). Discussion of local banking occurs mostly within the context of money changers, essentially foreign exchange and denomination specialists and pawnbrokers, small-scale lenders who took physical possession of valuable objects—jewelry, watches, clothes, linens—to collateralize short-term, high-interest loans. Such petty financiers, typified by Shylock in Shakespeare's *Merchant of Venice*, did not enjoy favorable reputations. In an age when a bewildering profusion of coins found circulation and one could be imprisoned for debt, however, they did provide valuable exchange and liquidity services for their clients.

Considerably more attention is paid to local banks after they begin to associate or formally incorporate beginning in the eighteenth century. Indeed, the sheer numbers of local financial institutions, especially in financially advanced economies like Great Britain and the United States, make them difficult to ignore. Typically, local banks known as savings banks organized as mutuals. Control of mutuals was vested in trustees; depositors owned a pro rata share of the bank's assets and net profits. Local banks known as commercial banks generally organized as joint-stock associations. Whether formally incorporated or not, the bank was owned by stockholders with claims on a pro rata share of the bank's assets and profits and with rights to vote for a board of directors.

In the United States and elsewhere, local commercial banks issued a form of bearer liability, known as a bank note, that composed a significant percentage of the money stock in the first six decades or so of the nation's existence. The notes, nonlegal tender IOUs, were redeemable in specie only at the bank of issue. In order to compensate the holder for the time and travel costs of redemption, notes were exchanged at a discount (i.e., a fraction of their face value) the farther they traveled from the issuing bank. Though notes sometimes achieved a wide circulation, market forces, personified by professional note brokers, continually remitted notes toward the issuing bank.

The monetary role of local banks, however, was generally not nearly as important as their role as financial intermediaries, linking savers to entrepreneurs. Local banks have assumed a variety of names—country banks (England and the United States); credit unions, savings and loans, building and loans (the United States); municipal banks (Germany); credit cooperatives (Russia); provincial, district, and native banks (China); ordinary, private, and quasi banks (Japan); *susu* (Caribbean); *adashi* (Nigeria); pawnbrokers, microlenders, and savings banks (universal)—and have tapped a wide variety of niches—clan networks, homeowners, Muslim women, small retailers, local governments, even prostitutes. Regardless of their names, locations, epochs, or markets, local banks help entrepreneurs—from "micro" proprietorships worth a few dollars to "small" corporations worth "only" a few hundred million dollars—increase their profits by helping them to manage their short-term cash flows and to obtain long-term capital.

Business revenue often comes in fits and starts, but overhead costs must be met punctually. Local banks help businesses to smooth out their cash flows. For instance, a local bank might lend money to a retailer in July in anticipation of the store's holiday season receipts. Banks will also finance farmers and manufacturers by advancing them cash for seeds or raw materials on collateral of the crops or goods in production. Such loans run from a few days to as long as a year.

Sometimes, entrepreneurs and consumers need loans to help fund large, long-term projects. Local banks make such loans, called mortgages, by placing a lien on the borrower's physical assets (e.g., a farm, factory, store, or home). They also sometimes make loans indirectly by purchasing the negotiable bonds of businesses or governments.

In other words, local banks provide the same basic services as larger, extralocal financial institutions. Some analysts have confidently predicted the demise of local banks because they believe that larger institutions enjoy economies of scale that will allow them to force smaller local institutions into mergers or out of business altogether. (In short, it costs almost as much administratively to make $1 million worth of loans as it does to make $1 billion worth.)

Others, however, note that local banks tend to provide superior customer service. Perhaps more important, some studies suggest that local banks understand their local markets much better than large lenders do. They are, in short, better at picking good credit risks from bad. Local banks, like credit unions, often show great leniency on defaulted loans. A surprisingly large percentage of those overdue loans are eventually repaid, suggesting that local lenders know their borrowers well and that borrowers feel a relatively strong moral obligation to repay their local banks.

In addition, local residents may trust their local banks more than national institutions because they can observe all of their activities much more easily. It is true that some local banks that were long protected by regulatory barriers to entry, like restrictions against branching, grew inefficient. It is also true, however, that since deregulation many local banks have increased efficiency and competed successfully against much larger institutions—so far, that is.

BIBLIOGRAPHY

Bodenhorn, Howard. *A History of Banking in Antebellum America.* New York, 2000. In this thin but densely researched volume, Bodenhorn shows that before the introduction of effective financial intermediation, wealth-producing ideas regularly perished for want of funds. Due to information asymmetries (adverse selection, moral hazard, and the principal-agent problem) and large fixed costs, individual savers hoarded their wealth rather than loaned it to businesses. Entrepreneurs were nipped in the bud, and economic development proceeded slowly. After the proliferation of local banks, entrepreneurs with good ideas gained financing, implemented their ideas, and increased per capita aggregate output.

Cameron, Rondo, et al. *Banking in the Early Stages of Industrialization: A Study in Comparative Economic History.* New York, 1967. This somewhat disjointed volume, which covers England, Scotland, France, Belgium, Germany, Russia, and Japan from 1750 to 1914, is still the bible for those interested in the role of banking in economic development.

Cameron, Rondo, ed. *Banking and Economic Development: Some Lessons of History.* New York, 1971. This follow-up volume to Cameron's *Banking in the Early Stages of Industrialization* contains important essays by George Green (Louisiana, 1804–1861),

Richard Sylla (United States, 1863–1913), Gabriel Tortella (Spain, 1829–1874), Kozo Yamamura (Japan, 1868–1930), and other top bank historians.

The Dawn of Modern Banking. New Haven, 1979. This book is the product of a scholarly conference sponsored by the Center for Medieval and Renaissance Studies at the University of California, Los Angeles. Despite its origin, it is quite readable and surprisingly available. Included are essays by leading historians, including Jacques Le Goff on usury and John H. Munro on the development of bills of exchange in England.

Douglass, Elisha. *The Coming of Age of American Business: Three Centuries of Enterprise, 1600–1900*. Chapel Hill, N.C., 1971. This classic comprehensive survey of business in America contains information about banking, especially in chapters 4 and 23, in addition to background information about general business practices.

Homer, Sidney, and Richard E. Sylla. *A History of Interest Rates*. 3d ed., rev. New Brunswick, N.J., 1996. This classic is still the leader in its field, the history of interest rates from ancient times to the 1990s. The book centers on interest rates in the West, but the earlier and later periods include global coverage.

Hunt, Edwin, and James Murray. *A History of Business in Medieval Europe, 1200–1550*. New York, 1999. It is too early to discern the impact of this recent survey of business practices in medieval Europe. It is clear, however, that the book is lucidly written and widely accessible. See chapters 8 and 9 for specific information on banks and the entire volume for background on borrowers.

Lamoreaux, Naomi. *Insider Lending: Banks, Personal Connections, and Economic Development in Industrial New England*. New York, 1994. The author clearly demonstrates that local banks helped to finance the Industrial Revolution in New England. Her conclusion that many banks were essentially captives of entrepreneurs is true for the industrial region of eastern New England in the few decades on either side of the Civil War (1861–1865) but does not necessarily hold for the earlier period, commercial centers, agricultural regions, or the Middle Atlantic region (New York, New Jersey, Pennsylvania, Maryland, northern Virginia).

Orsingher, Roger. *Banks of the World*. Translated by D. S. Ault. New York, 1967. This brief, readable treatment describes the banks of the ancient world and the history of banking in most of the major nations of Europe and North America. Japan receives coverage but China, India, Africa, and South America are ignored.

Sargent, Thomas, and Francois R. Velde. *The Big Problem of Small Change*. Princeton, 2002. The authors explain how monetary authorities came, over the course of centuries, to abandon the awkward medieval coinage system and to adopt the "standard formula"—the government's policy of exchanging all denominations with each other at fixed rates. In so doing, the authors develop a brilliant mathematical model of demand for coins of different metal compositions and denominations. More impressively still, they apply the model to eight centuries worth of monetary history and theory. The result is an impressive, interdisciplinary, consilient synthesis almost certain to direct monetary history research for years to come.

Usher, Abbott Payson. "The Origins of Banking: The Primitive Bank of Deposit, 1200–1600." *Economic History Review* 4 (1934), 399–428.

Vogel, Frank, and Samuel Hayes. *Islamic Law and Finance: Religion, Risk, and Return*. London, 1998. Contrary to common belief, Islam does allow for certain types of credit transactions. The form of the contract is of the utmost concern to devout Muslims. This book is an accessible entrée to the world of Islamic finance, a subject that has taken on increased importance since the events of 11 September 2001.

Wright, Robert E. "Caribbean-Type Savings Helps Build Businesses." *Wall Street Journal*, 18 October 2000. Explains Susu.

Wright, Robert E. "Matan Bariki, 'Women of the Barracks,' Muslim Hausa Women in an Urban Neighbourhood in Northern Nigeria." *Africa: Journal of the International African Institute*, 1 January 2002.

ROBERT E. WRIGHT

LOCAL PUBLIC GOODS. The term *local public goods* was introduced into the economics literature by Charles Tiebout (1956). Before Tiebout changed the focus, public goods were conceived of simply as goods that, if available to one person, were available to all. Richard Musgrave's (1969) characterization of such goods as exhibiting "nonrivalness" in consumption and "nonexcludability" from consumption has remained in the literature. The nonexcludability of public goods has an important consequence, namely, that a decentralized mechanism to achieve their optimal provision cannot be found; that is, it is not generally possible to find a way to get individuals to reveal their true valuation for public goods (Samuelson, 1954).

The Tiebout Hypothesis. Tiebout noted there was a class of public goods, local public goods, for which a decentralized mechanism for achieving optimal allocations existed. Many public goods provided by local governments are subject to congestion. A stretch of roadway, a fire department, a sewer system, and similar public services are available to everyone in the community. For any given level of infrastructure, however, the more people who use the facility, the more crowded it becomes, and the less it is available or useful to others. Using Musgrave's terminology, local public goods exhibit nonexcludability but not nonrivalness; they are partially nonrival because the space in which they can be enjoyed is limited.

Tiebout argued that local communities provide a mix of public goods. Residents receive the benefits of those goods and pay for them through taxes. The key mechanism is the assumed mobility of people who will move to the community in which the mix of services and taxes provides them with the greatest net benefit. Congestion leads each community to reach an optimal size where the benefit of sharing the infrastructure costs with another taxpayer will be just equal to the crowding cost imposed by the new person. Similar results can be derived from the theory of clubs introduced by James Buchanan (1965). The logic of the Tiebout-Buchanan argument leads to relatively small jurisdictions, like suburbs, but many believe that larger jurisdictions, like cities, make more sense politically, economically, and historically. The Tiebout hypothesis assumes that people will move to where they find the optimal mix of local public goods, but that assumption is only now being tested in a systematic way (see Rhode and Strumpf, 2002).

How many local public goods are supplied often depends on whether there are significant economies of scale or externalities associated with their production. Basic police, fire, and refuse collection services are best provided at the municipal level, as there are no significant economies of scale or externalities associated with them. On the other hand, special police services (e.g., a crime lab), a water supply to fight fires, refuse disposal, and public transit are best provided at the metropolitan level, as there are significant scale economies and externalities associated with them. In what follows, many, but by no means all, of these services will be discussed individually.

It should be noted that, at one time or another, most of these services were (and sometimes still are) supplied privately. They later became publicly provided because of objections to private provision (for example, private water companies may not have laid mains in the poorer parts of town) or because it was believed that public provision of these services was more efficient.

Police and Fire. In 7 BCE, Caesar Augustus divided Rome first into fourteen regions, then into precincts, which were overseen by magistrates responsible for fire protection, among other duties. Shortly thereafter, police responsibilities were added. Police, at least from the time of Babylon, were organizations that evolved either from the personal guards of rulers or from citizens' groups interested in mutual protection. State police to keep public order and enforce political mandates were present in prerevolutionary France, where the police system was the personal political police of the king, financed and controlled by government.

In Saxon England, the frankpledge system held sway until the middle of the nineteenth century. Under this system, all the adult males in a community had an obligation for good conduct; all citizens had an obligation, if they witnessed a crime, to raise an alarm and to pursue the offenders. Crime was an offense against society, and all society, no exclusions, were to help combat crime. Norman England added constables to oversee the night watchmen, whose primary duties were to guard a city's gates and watch for fire. There was no public body responsible for solving crime. In the absence of witnesses, victims alone were responsible, and they would offer rewards or hire "thief takers" (bounty hunters) to help recover stolen property. Ultimately, communities began to pay private citizens a set fee for apprehending and convicting wrongdoers, and a "stipendiary" police system evolved. As Britain colonized North America, Australia, and elsewhere, this system was replicated. Its inefficiency and, often, its corruption became apparent with industrialization and urbanization, but there was considerable opposition to a standing police force, as this involved an expansion of taxes and government, and the possible politicization of the force. Nonetheless, by the middle of the nineteenth century, conditions had deteriorated to where both London (1829) and New York (1844) created police departments. Others soon followed suit.

The Roman system of watching for fire remained for several centuries, especially in the nighttime hours. This was especially important in the first cities, which were built of wood. The buildings were close together, and fire was a constant threat. Beginning in the eighteenth century, less flammable building materials such as brick, stone, and tile began to replace timber and thatch in Europe, but wood persisted in North America and Asia because of its lower relative price. Events such as the Chicago Fire of 1871 accelerated the acceptance of "fireproof" construction. Other nineteenth-century improvements such as municipal water supplies, the substitution of professional for volunteer fire departments, and technological improvements in both alarm systems and fire fighting reduced the risk of devastating urban fires. Shortly after World War I, attention began to be paid to fire prevention; prior to that, most urban fire departments concentrated on fire extinguishing.

Street Lighting. What little lighting existed at night before the early seventeenth century was intended to prevent crime and to aid in fighting fire. Night light sources were few and irregular; in many cities (e.g., Rome c. 200 CE), citizens were required to hang candle lanterns outside their houses as an extension of the night watch. As late as 1660, no European city had permanently illuminated its streets, and many cities had evening curfews for the protection of their respectable citizens.

European public street lighting was an innovation of the seventeenth century. The new lighting not only promoted law and order, but it also beautified a city and encouraged respectable traffic after dark. The first steps were taken in Amsterdam by painter and inventor Jan van der Heyden, who experimented with oil lamps in glass-paned lanterns during the 1660s. A system based on van der Heyden's invention was installed in Amsterdam in 1669. Two years earlier, Paris had installed street lighting using large candle lanterns maintained at public expense. In Amsterdam and Hamburg (1673), the municipality paid for the lighting, but this was the exception. Elsewhere, citizens paid for lighting either to the monarch or to a private company that had contracted with the Crown or the municipality. With the development of effective street lighting, many activities shifted into the evening hours, reflecting a willingness to reorder daily time.

In the United States, relatively few people lived in cities. Oil-burning lamps were in use in a few cities; candles were expensive and inefficient. Illuminating gas developed in the late eighteenth century by heating coal and drawing off the volatile compounds. Gaslight first appeared in Newport, Rhode Island, in 1812, but the first American city to have a gas-lighting system (and the third in the world) was Baltimore, Maryland, in 1817. The invention spread quickly. Natural gas was first used in Fredonia, New York, in 1821, but it was not until 1858 that a natural gas company was formed. America's first electric street lights were carbon arc lights erected in Cleveland in 1877, but demonstrations took place in several cities before then, and it was the "Great White Way" at Chicago's World Columbian Exposition in 1893 that stimulated electric street lighting throughout the country and the world.

Sanitation. Municipalities have tapped groundwater and rivers for water supplies for many millennia. Waste disposal (including sewage) via covered drains began as early as 2500 BCE in small cities in the Indus Valley. Thus, water was available and waste removed for the benefit of all citizens. The Greeks were the first to provide central water supplies to a large number of cities, but Rome was the first large city to install both centralized water supply and sewers. Rome's system of aqueducts brought freshwater into the city for private and public purposes (especially fire fighting). With the fall of the Roman Empire, water supplies became increasingly local. Pumps, driven by waterwheels beginning in the sixteenth century, and by steam engines beginning in the nineteenth century, increased the capacity of public water supplies. The latter made it possible to tap distant sources for freshwater, which was important for rapidly growing cities located adjacent to saltwater.

Rome's Cloaca Maxima was the main enclosed collector for a network of underground sewers that reached into most neighborhoods by the first century BCE. The demands on urban sewers increased with the increased availability of water. In the early part of the nineteenth century, the flush toilet was developed. Its adoption required abundant low-priced water. Yet sewerage was not the only technology for removing waste. Beginning in sixteenth-century Japan, where arable land was scarce, a system was developed where human and household waste from the cities was collected, composted, and ultimately used as fertilizer. At the turn of the twentieth century, European and North American cities confronted their solid waste problem with systems that hauled trash out of the city as well as to incinerators and sanitary landfills.

Effective water supplies, sewage disposal, and refuse collection and disposal systems were in place in developed countries by the early twentieth century, when water and sewage treatment works were added. Chlorination took place in almost every city, fluoridation was adopted in many, but much of the rest of the world lacked such facilities.

Public Transit. The Assyrians had a road engineering corps by 1100 BCE; they built roads to connect lands they had conquered. A similar pattern existed in most parts of the ancient world, including China and India. The Romans were renowned for their roads; their road system reached a maximum of 80,000 kilometers (49,600 miles) around 200 CE. With the fall of Rome, the need for an avenue of egress diminished, while the fear of invaders using it as an avenue of ingress increased. Road construction was relatively ignored until Philip the Bold began paving Paris' streets in the late fourteenth century; road maintenance became a feudal obligation. Standards for road construction emerged in the mid-seventeenth century, and attempts to regulate road congestion by licensing hackneys were adopted about the same time. Roads could be built privately, and some toll roads were, but most proved unprofitable as travelers sought nonexcludable alternatives.

Until the twentieth century, most urban residents traveled by foot. The use of hackneys and horse and ox carts was restricted by the poor quality of the roads. The first horse omnibus went into use in Nantes in 1825, and within a few years the innovation was copied in many of the bigger cities of Europe and North America. Tracks were then laid in the streets to accommodate larger cars and greater traffic, but the use of horses limited capacity. The introduction of steam engines to urban transportation required that they be removed from the streets. London adopted a subway in 1863, and New York opted for an elevated in 1868. By the end of the century, electrical power had replaced steam. At the same time, motor buses and taxis made their appearance. These transport modes are still seen as essential, but the growing use of private automobiles for urban travel has placed a financial strain on public transit, especially in North America.

In our modern world, determining the optimal mix of local public goods is likely to involve a complex calculation with many tradeoffs, even if one only considers the goods discussed above. Municipalities customarily supply some goods that do not meet the strict definition of local public goods. In addition to those discussed above, schools, hospitals, libraries, zoos, and a variety of other services have been supplied privately as well as publicly. Public provision may be desirable, but it is not essential. It should be clear that this listing of publicly provided goods is not exhaustive and that it is growing. Our concern for sanitation has expanded to include pollution. The local provision of air, noise, and water pollution abatement has become important because our knowledge of the harm caused by pollution and the technology to abate that pollution have evolved. Because the benefits of abatement accrue to all, pollution control has become a local public good.

[*See also* Book Industry, *subentry on* Libraries and Bookstores; Education; Fire Control; Health Industry, *subentry on* Hospitals; Insurance; Public Goods; Public Utilities, *subentry on* Mass Transit; Road Transportation; *and* Sanitation.]

BIBLIOGRAPHY

Armstrong, Ellis L, ed. *History of Public Works in the United States: 1776–1976*. Chicago, 1976.

Buchanan, James M. "An Economic Theory of Clubs." *Economica* 32 (1965), 1–14.

Koslofsky, Craig. "Court Culture and Street Lighting in Seventeenth-Century Europe." *Journal of Urban History* 28 (2002), 743–768.

Monkkonen, Eric H. *Police in Urban America, 1860 to 1920*. New York, 1981.

Mosse, George L., ed. *Police Forces in History*. London, 1975.

Musgrave, Richard A. "Provision for Social Goods." In *Public Economics*, edited by J. Margolis and H. Guitton, pp. 124–144. London, 1969.

Rhode, Paul, and Koleman Strumpf. "Assessing the Importance of Tiebout Sorting: Local Heterogeneity from 1850 to 1990." Working paper, University of North Carolina, 2002.

Samuelson, Paul A. "The Pure Theory of Public Expenditure." *Review of Economics and Statistics* 36 (1954), 387–389.

Tiebout, Charles M. "A Pure Theory of Local Expenditures." *Journal of Political Economy* 64 (October 1956), 416–424.

LOMBARDY. Historians use the term *Lombardy* to describe a larger area than the modern Regione Lombarda, which consists only of the eastern parts of a region that stretches across the Po Valley and encompasses a high proportion of the major cities (and industrial centers) in Italy in what are now Veneto and northern Emilia. Its highly urbanized character originated in the pre-Roman period, when a number of Etruscan towns emerged in the Po Valley, notably Mantua and Piacenza. Later known as Gallia Cisalpina, Lombardy was the meeting point between Italy and continental Europe, and Mediolanum, literally "the place in the middle," acted as the effective capital of the western Roman Empire in the fourth century CE.

Germanic invaders (Ostrogoths and Lombards) did not permanently change the urban character of the region, and by the tenth century CE recovery was evident in such centers as Pavia, which was visited by Venetian and South Italian merchants. The creation of the strong German Empire that included Lombardy encouraged the opening of transalpine routes, benefiting Milan, Verona, and other towns. Milan developed as the center of the metal and cloth industries and became a leading city in the Lombard Leagues, which sought to restrict imperial power in Northern Italy (and thus rights to tax city wealth) during the twelfth and thirteenth centuries. Milan created a network of canals linking it to the Lombard river system. The architects of the network, which was still under construction in the fifteenth century, included Leonardo da Vinci.

Along with Venetian trade, Genoese commerce also passed through Lombard towns, offering banking facilities. In the fifteenth century determined state building by the Visconti and Sforza of Milan stimulated trade and industry. The period does not appear to be one of decline, especially in comparison with contemporary Tuscany. Particular strengths were the cotton-based fustian and linen cloth industries, which by the fifteenth century were accompanied by significant growth in silk production, including the planting of mulberry groves. Rice was also cultivated in the region by 1500, and it remained a significant

crop along with American maize (corn). Both had significant impacts on the diet as risotto and polenta.

During the late sixteenth century and the seventeenth century, this region experienced some degree of economic crisis, as did other parts of western Europe. The Spanish government in western Lombardy and the Venetian government in the eastern part were unable to arrest the sustained decline in the cloth industries. Although rural cloth industries expanded, it is doubtful they compensated for the decline in the urban industries. The effects of both the Thirty Years' War and a new round of plague were felt severely; population fell after a period of recovery either side of 1500.

Only after Italian unification did the area recover its position as the economic powerhouse of Italy, aided by massive immigration from Sicily and the South. The Lombard cities became major centers of the automobile industry, and Milan became the prime banking center in Italy. Milan's role in the textile industry was spectacularly reaffirmed with the rise of the Italian fashion houses chiefly based there.

BIBLIOGRAPHY

De Maddalena, Aldo. *Dalla città al borgo: Avvio di una metamorfosi economica e sociale nella Lombardia spagnola*. Milan, 1982.

Mazzaoui, Maureen F. *The Italian Cotton Industry in the Later Middle Ages*. Cambridge, 1981.

Sella, Domenico. *Crisis and Continuity: The Economy of Spanish Lombardy in the Seventeenth Century*, chaps. 2–4. Cambridge, Mass., 1979.

Vigo, Giovanni. *Uno stato nell'impero: La difficile transizione al moderno nello Milano di età spagnola*. Milan, 1996.

DAVID ABULAFIA

LONDON. The development of London parallels and in many respects leads the process of English urbanization. From Roman times on, London was the dominant city in England, the largest town, the largest port, and the largest manufacturing city. It far surpassed any other town in England. In 1300, its population was at least three times larger than that of its nearest English competitor, Norwich; by the later seventeenth century, Norwich remained its closest rival, but London was now twenty times larger. In 1801, the competitor was Manchester, with less than one-fifteenth of London's population, which grew to be one-sixth of it by 1841. From the sixteenth century on, about a tenth of the English population were living in London at any one time. Many others lived in London for some part of their lives. London's dominance of the English urban system peaked between 1550 and 1700. By 1600, London was the third largest city in Europe after Naples and Paris. It overtook Naples by 1650 and Paris by 1700, becoming one of the largest cities in the world. London kept its international prominence; its national dominance has never been shaken—even though it declined during the

LONDON. Opening of the Great Industrial Exhibition of All Nations, 1 May 1851. Engraving by George M. Cruikshank (1792–1878). (Prints and Photographs Division, Library of Congress)

Industrial Revolution, which, from London's point of view, can be regarded as a process of provincial economic and urban development, underpinned by services that London provided. From the late nineteenth century on, London regained some of its earlier position, but it could no longer claim to be the only town in England that was of serious international consequence.

London's population for 1100–1981 is given in Table 1. These figures depend heavily on the boundaries chosen. As London grew, its immediate hinterland inevitably grew with it; by the eighteenth century, it was difficult for contemporaries to define London's boundaries. It is helpful to think in terms of a built-up area within a heavily urbanized region; and from 1801 on, when the census provides reliable statistics for this region, the precise figure depends very much on definitions of built-up area. The most rapid periods of growth, from about 1100 to 1300, 1500 to 1650, and 1750 to 1850, reflect rapid national population growth. The forces for growth were strong. Over two millennia, only three major events have seriously reduced the population of London: the contraction of the Roman Empire, the Viking invasions (ninth century), and the Black Death (1348–1349). Other disasters, such as the Great

Fire (1666), which destroyed some thirteen thousand houses, forty-four company halls, and eighty-seven parish churches, and caused destruction valued at some £10 million, did not have significant long-term impacts on population growth. Epidemics and mortality crises were common; but, except for the Black Death, London's population recovered rapidly from them. However, until

TABLE 1. *London's Population, 1100–1981*

1100	c. 20,000
1300	80,000–100,000
1400	40,000–50,000
1550	75,000
1600	200,000
1650	400,000
1700	575,000
1801	900,000
1851	2,400,000
1881	4,770,000
1901	6,586,000
1931	8,216,000
1951	8,348,000
1981	7,678,000

the later eighteenth century, the capital's death rate was greater than the birth rate, and without rural immigration London's population would have fallen. This situation changed during the last quarter of the eighteenth century, and thereafter London's natural population surplus was slowly rising, although immigration remained vital.

A capital city as multifaceted as London can be analyzed in an almost infinite number of ways. This discussion concentrates on these aspects: London as a port, as a regional capital, as a national capital, as a center for services and finance, and as a manufacturing town.

Well-situated for a port, London became important in Roman times and remained so in the Middle Ages. By the 1530s, London was producing over 80 percent of the nation's cloth exports and receiving 70 percent of its wine imports. It maintained this degree of dominance until the eighteenth century when the west coast ports grew, but it continued to dominate the North Sea trade.

London assumed the roles of a capital gradually. Royal governments could never take it for granted. The city was sufficiently important to negotiate terms with William the Conqueror, being allowed to keep its privileges, and by the thirteenth century (and probably much earlier), London was too important for kings to ignore. From about the tenth century on, with an increasingly integrated kingdom and royal government, London played an expanding role, attracting a growing number of the permanent institutions of government. However, until the seventeenth century, the city generally tended to attract the court rather than the reverse. For much of its history, the city and Westminster were connected only by a few roads passing through fields. Satisfyingly to the historian, the area between the two was thoroughly built up between about 1690 and 1720, the period of the financial revolution, when the longstanding relationship between the city and the royal government began to take on a perceptibly modern shape.

It is difficult and perhaps pointless to distinguish London's role as the dominant town in southern England from its role as the dominant town in Britain. The importance of London is a reflection of the national importance of its wider region. Its immediate dominance was always broad; in the Middle Ages there was little urban competition closer to it than sixty miles. When London's population was about 100,000, as it was in the early fourteenth century before the Black Death and by the later sixteenth century, the regions that supplied it with food and goods extended over much of southern England. The capital's influence was felt everywhere; for instance, by the seventeenth century its demand for fuel was largely responsible for shaping the specialized coal industry of the northeast.

In discussing London's economic functions, it is convenient to separate services and finance from manufacturing. From medieval times on, London has been noted as a center for services and finance. Lawyers and doctors have always been disproportionately present. Merchants were involved with finance early on, and were lending to governments, a function that was forever changing its forms and finally took on a recognizably "modern" appearance with the creation of the Bank of England (1694) and the financial revolution of subsequent years. This influence grew until the term City of London became synonymous with finance, a gradual development that was achieved in popular opinion by the later nineteenth century and in reality in the twentieth century. As a combination port and capital, London had a large service sector with relatively high costs of both land and labor. The attractions of London as a market meant that, in addition to having an enormous mass of unskilled labor as was customary in most towns and particularly ports, London also had the most skilled labor force in the country. This resource in turn affected the nature of manufacturing in London, continually pressuring it to produce high-value-added, upmarket goods in relatively small premises. As a result, manufacturing did not tend to concentrate on the preliminary stages of production but operated "downstream" in the finishing trades. The advantages of proximity to such a large market gave London its share of large-scale works, but the overhead for such works was high. Historians disagree about their importance within the metropolitan economy. They certainly needed to be specialized, having to add a great deal of value to be viable. Specialized machine-building establishments fall into this category. The distinctive style of London's manufacturing has been in the nature of small-scale domestic production, often carried out in specialized neighborhoods. As technology has developed, London's manufacturing has constantly adapted to it, but the principles of downstream and upmarket have lasted from the Middle Ages to the present day. London has always been the largest manufacturing town in England and one of the largest in Europe, but its manufacturing has always been subordinated to its service sector.

BIBLIOGRAPHY

Beier, A. L., and Roger Finlay, eds. London, 1500–1700: The Making of the Metropolis. London, 1986. Contains essays on London's population, economy, and society during this period.

Clark, Peter, ed. The Cambridge Urban History of Britain. 3 vols. Cambridge, 2000. Has specific chapters on London and many references to London in its other chapters.

Creaton, Heather. Bibliography of Printed Works on London History to 1939. London, 1994. An outstanding bibliography.

Kynaston, David. The City of London. 3 vols. London, 1994–2000. As its title implies, concentrates on the world of finance.

Porter, Roy. London: A Social History. Cambridge, Mass., 1995. Provides a general and readable overview of London's development. The balance of the book is from the seventeenth century onward, and, as the title implies, is not particularly economic although there is an awareness of economic factors.

Schwarz, L. D. *London in the Age of Industrialisation*. Cambridge, 1992. Examines the impact of the Industrial Revolution on London and has references to other material for the eighteenth and nineteenth centuries.

LEONARD D. SCHWARZ

LONG-DISTANCE TRADE *[This entry contains four subentries, on long-distance trade before 1500, between 1500 and 1750, between 1750 and 1914, and since 1914.]*

Long-Distance Trade before 1500

For more than three decades, views of the Greek and Roman economies have been dominated by the arguments of Sir Moses Finley (1912–1986). In the seminal book *The Ancient Economy* (1973), he painted a historical picture of general stagnation, backward technology, and a lack of capitalistic spirit. More recent research, however, using the archaeological evidence largely dismissed by Finley, stressed the spread of technological innovations, inter alia in transport and communication. Together with political stability and monetary unification, these improvements were seen to favor long-distance trade in the Roman world itself but also between the empire and the world outside the fortified frontier or *limes*. This trade was not confined to luxury goods, although it remains difficult to assess its importance in the gross domestic product of the different regions. When Roman political structures gradually disappeared in the fourth and fifth centuries, long-distance trade was severely reduced. The famous Belgian scholar Henri Pirenne (1862–1935) nevertheless believed that international trade survived the Germanic invasions and the consequent fall of the empire. According to Pirenne, international trade collapsed only from the eighth century as a direct consequence of the Arab conquest of the Mediterranean, which disrupted commercial links between northwest Europe and the south. As trade disappeared, towns ceased to be commercial centers and at the best survived as fortified military places or administrative and ecclesiastical residences. Though brilliant and erudite in its construction, the Pirenne thesis is too simplistic and ignores almost completely the further and continuous expansion of towns and trade in Scandinavia (Birka, Haithabu), the Meuse valley (Maastricht, Huy), the Rhine-Meuse-Scheldt delta (Dorestad, Domburg), and the North Sea coast (Quentovic, Brugge). Frisian merchants and the Vikings developed a flourishing long-distance trade not only between these emporiums, or trading places, but also with the Rhine, Loire, Rhone, and Saône valleys; England; and northern Italy.

Nonetheless, Pirenne was quite right in assuming that from the eleventh century, long-distance trade received new impulses, directly associated with the rise and gradual spread of new towns and markets all over Europe. According to Carlo Cipolla, the rise of cities in this period "marked a turning point in the history of the West—and, for that matter, of the whole world" (1976, p. 139). Commercialization and urbanization went hand in hand all over Europe. Towns provided merchants and tradespeople with military and judicial protection, such as fortified walls and towers, courts, special privileges, property rights. In towns, they not only found a well-organized commercial infrastructure but also a qualified labor force, which came to be organized in craft associations. Towns offered extended administrative services (with aldermen's benches, chanceries, notaries) and represented financial (with deposit banks and money markets) and monetary (with mint workshops, money changers) centers, where merchants could buy and sell, lend and borrow, meet partners, and exchange information on fellow participants in the trade process, on the general political and economic situation, and on the vicissitudes of business.

But other elements were of crucial importance for the rise and growth of long-distance trade. When, for example, agricultural production and productivity increased more rapidly than did the growth of population (as was the case in the eleventh, twelfth, and thirteenth centuries), surpluses could be traded on the local markets for both domestic and foreign commodities. Demand itself was influenced by so-called demonstration effects. The Crusades (from 1096) failed in their religious and political goals but brought people of north and northwest Europe into direct contact with goods from the Middle East and northern Africa, products they had never seen before. Trade could prosper only in periods of political security. War was never far away in medieval society, but clearly in some periods regional and international warfare was less pronounced and less frequent.

Finally, technological and organizational progress had some influence, though it should not be overestimated for the medieval era. To be sure, better wagons were introduced, better equipment was invented to harness the horses, and new types of larger vessels appeared, such as the elegant Venetian three-masted galley, the bulky Hanseatic cog, and especially in the fifteenth century, the carrack, combining the cargo capacity of the cog with the maneuverability of the Arab-influenced caravel. But these technological improvements were limited in number and probably even less important than the organizational progress (for example, trade associations such as guilds and hanses, well-organized convoys, and in the fifteenth century, even special transport firms). One thing that is now known for certain is that medieval merchants, contrary to a widespread belief, did not use Roman roads or their remnants. Medieval people and goods circulated on roads and bridges constructed in the Middle Ages.

An Era of Expansion. All of these factors helped create a real commercial upswing in the eleventh century but especially during the twelfth and thirteenth centuries. The most striking and most powerful trade expansion took place overland between the north and the south. New routes linked the two economically most advanced areas, the most densely populated and most highly urbanized regions of medieval Europe, the Low Countries with the Rhine-Meuse-Scheldt delta and the commercial growth poles in northern Italy. A great axis was created, in fact, a few arterial roads went through the Swiss Alps, crossed central France, and came together at the four famous Champagne Fairs in northeastern France. There merchants from all parts of Europe could buy and sell, bargain and trade in luxury goods and industrial products, mainly a great variety of textiles, but they also could exchange letters of credit (such as the *lettres de foire*). So the Champagne Fairs, apart from being "the great trading emporium north of the Alps, also became the major money market and clearing center of Western Europe" (De Roover, 1963, p. 3). Later in the thirteenth century, an east-west axis was added to the great north-south overland routes, linking Kiev in the Ukraine with Cracow, Vienna, Prague, Breslau, Regensburg, Nuremberg, Erfurt, Augsburg, Frankfurt, Mainz, Metz, and the Champagne Fairs. Along with those main continental trade routes, a whole network of secondary and smaller roads was created, promoting smaller towns to dynamic export centers, and even stimulating the development of inland cities located on the new trade routes. Since the volume of trade increased both in quantitative and qualitative terms, commerce now required means of payment of greater value. Therefore, larger silver pieces—the famous *grossi* or groats—were issued from the beginning of the thirteenth century, soon followed by a gold coinage. Gold coins were first struck by Florence and Genoa in 1252, France in 1266, and Flanders and Brabant after 1326.

Maritime trade too expanded in the eleventh, twelfth, and thirteenth centuries but in a less spectacular fashion, chiefly confined to the periphery of the European continent. The most striking maritime expansion indeed took place in the Mediterranean and in the Black Sea and was principally the success story of the colonization policy by Genoa, Pisa, and Venice in that area. For centuries the town at the head of the Adriatic Sea had been a small satellite of Constantinople, but in the eleventh century it became the major rival for the former Greek colony at the Bosporus. Using its excellent geography, its military power, and its diplomatic talents, but also assisted by the presence of crusaders, Venice founded hundreds of colonies in the eastern Mediterreanean and on the Black Sea coasts.

Changes and Contrasts. Long-distance trade overland and the Champagne Fairs reached their apogee in the middle of the thirteenth century and declined shortly afterward. While overland trade and inland fairs contracted, maritime trade continued to expand. Many economic historians therefore have assigned the disappearance of the Champagne Fairs and the subsequent prolonged contraction of overland trade to the rise of new, alternative maritime routes. Indeed, as early as 1274, Genoese galleys were seen in the North Sea, the beginning of what some decades later developed into a regular and direct sea connection between Italian maritime republics and the important ports in northern Europe. Although such a causal association between two different phenomena might appear logical at first sight, the expansion of maritime long-distance trade was not the prime cause of the disappearance of the Champagne Fairs and transcontinental trade. As suggested earlier, the first signs of a commercial weakening in the strategic position of the fairs already were visible in the third quarter of the thirteenth century, while the sea routes between northern Italy and the North Sea only became more or less regular after 1306. John Munro has offered a more convincing explanation. According to him, the decline of the Champagne Fairs was not caused by competition from the new sea routes but rather by other factors, in particular, the spread of chronic warfare from the late thirteenth century, which so adversely raised transport and transaction costs along the traditional overland routes. Such insecurity and rising costs thus forced the Italians to seek other ways to reach their markets in northwest Europe.

Obviously, many who were engaged in overseas trade were able to take advantage of the decline of the old overland routes. Apart from the presence of Italian galleys in the North Sea, maritime trade in the fourteenth and fifteenth centuries was based principally on the commercial success of the German Hansa in both the Baltic Sea and the North Sea. The Hansa started in the twelfth century as a commercial fellowship of individual merchants, but around 1370 it was transformed into a confederation of some seventy German towns, to which a limited number of towns in Scandinavia, England, and the Low Countries was added. Hanseatic trade included chiefly bulk and low-valued cargoes, such as grains, timber, beer, and salt, with only a few luxury products (furs, amber). These products were traded between numerous factories—of which Bergen, London, Novgorod, and Brugge were the most important—established in towns where the Hanseatic merchants enjoyed extended privileges. Despite a rigid protectionism, the Hansa already at the moment of its formal creation was faced with a double threat. Sharp competition indeed arose, coming from English merchant ships exporting English cloth to the Continent, and from the commercial advance of Holland, foreshadowing the later triumphs of the Dutch.

One of the direct consequences of generalized warfare during the late Middle Ages was a profound change in the organization of European long-distance trade. Many more merchants ceased to be itinerant traders and became sedentary partners or agents in merchant-banking houses, often interlocking holding companies with branches in every town where an important money market had been established. Following this transition from itinerant to residential trade came a change in social status, to a much more respected place in late medieval society.

Outside Europe. Medieval long-distance trade was far from a European monopoly. Elsewhere, during the centuries before 1500, impressive empires or kingdoms developed a real network of long-distance trade within their vast territories much earlier, often with more sophistication, often with more advanced technology, and always on a wider scale than in Europe. China experienced the growth of many cities—with special areas where the merchant class also traded with nomadic neighbors—as early as the late Chou period (500 BCE). From about 100 BCE, caravans traveled to the West with silk in particular. For India, evidence indicates that a cotton cloth trade between the Harappan cities flourished well before 2000 BCE. But notorious exceptions existed, too. Even though the Inca civilization in Peru, covering a realm from Ecuador to Chile, possessed a network of more than ten thousand miles of roads and bridges and an elaborate communications system, commerce was unknown throughout the Andean world.

Commercial exchange between those civilizations and the European continent was limited and occurred only through privileged "mediators" or transmitters. As already suggested, during the Middle Ages, Constantinople, by virtue of its favorable location, dominated the transit trade in luxury goods (silk, spices, tapestries, perfumes, ivory, pearls, gems) between the Middle East, Asia Minor, the North African coast and Europe. However, its advantageous position was by no means guaranteed and depended heavily on the oscillations of growth and decline in Byzantine military and political power. This explains why, in the course of the seventh century, Arab merchants, following the Islamic conquests, challenged Constantinople's commercial sphere of influence in the area between Gibraltar in the West and the Indus in the East. With the military assistance of the powerful Italian sea republics Genoa and especially Venice, Constantinople could counter Arab competition in the eastern Mediterranean and around the Black Sea. In return, however, Constantinople was forced to grant extended commercial privileges, thus consolidating Italian commercial expansion in its own backyard. Moreover, the importance of these Arabs in long-distance trade soon exceeded the role ever played by Constantinople. Arab influence not only covered the Near East, northern Africa, Central Asia, and India but, thanks to the conversion of the Mongols in the thirteenth century, ultimately reached China. During the so-called Pax Mongolica, in what constituted the greatest political conglomerate the world has ever seen, caravan trade was protected by the khans against attacks by nomads and bandits. Different land routes from China through India and Persia to the Crimea and Trebizond (Trabzon) toward the eastern end of the Black Sea became important for the transport of silk and spices westward. This trade suffered from the death of Kublai Khan in 1294 and the subsequent disintegration of the Mongol Empire during the fourteenth century. Although such overland contacts never completely disappeared, the future of the commercial exchange between Europe and the Far East lay elsewhere.

Well before the fall of Constantinople (1453), the Portuguese explored the western coast of Africa after their conquest of Ceuta in 1415. By 1488, they had discovered the Cape of Good Hope and thus the routes to East Africa and the Indian Ocean. The subsequent Portuguese discoveries linked the new sea road directly with the European trade in the Mediterranean and even integrated it into the commercial revival that started in northwest Europe shortly before 1450. In 1501, the Portuguese crown established its official staple in the now rapidly expanding Antwerp market, chiefly because there its merchants could acquire the massive amounts of south German copper and silver and the banking facilities that allowed them to obtain African gold and slaves and Asian spices. A direct commercial axis was established between Antwerp and Lisbon. All of this happened, of course, at the expense of Venice, traditionally the leading center in the lucrative spice trade between Europe and the East and in the mid-fifteenth century, therefore, still the wealthiest city in Europe.

Significance. A whole generation of economic historians believed that long-distance trade was no more than a marginal phenomenon in a rather backward and predominantly agricultural economy, where production and technology barely were touched by progress and where the daily life of an overwhelming part of the population was overshadowed by the grim reality of mere survival. A more optimistic vision, however, accepts that things did change and develop in the medieval society, forcing acknowledgement that this economic growth was "fueled principally by international trade" (Munro, 1999, p. 1). This bold assertion is sustained by the simple fact that eras of pronounced and prolonged economic development, such as the twelfth and thirteenth centuries, coincided with periods of strong commercial expansion. Especially, transcontinental trade seems to have acted as a prime mover to the economy. Overland trade flourished in these centuries and undoubtedly contributed to the relative wealth and prosperity of

Europe's medieval "High Noon" (Genicot, 1983). The opposite was true, also. A sharp decay of the main overland routes during the fourteenth century and first decades of the fifteenth century was accompanied by economic stagnation and even recession in many parts of Europe.

Long-distance trade allowed people in and outside Europe to specialize, that is, to abandon time-consuming or costly activities and to focus on production or manufacturing processes that for some reason—thanks to the presence of traditional skills, the availability of raw materials, a favorable location—guaranteed a higher productivity. Merchants restlessly exploring new horizons created a new supply by integrating into the economic circuit resources previously not utilized or underutilized (for example, Bohemian silver, Baltic grain, north German hops). They also stimulated demand, since traveling from town to fair they needed food and drink, housing, tools, and all kinds of services. This new supply and demand increased aggregate income, consumption, and investments not only for those directly involved in the world of trade but also for other large groups of society (for example, bakers, brewers, blacksmiths, innkeepers). Bearing all this in mind, it seems difficult to overestimate the formidable contribution of long-distance trade to economic development and social welfare.

[*See also* Road Transportation *and* Water Transportation.]

BIBLIOGRAPHY

Allsen, Thomas T. *Commodity and Exchange in the Mongol Empire: A Cultural History of Islamic Textiles.* Cambridge Studies in Islamic Civilisation. Cambridge, 1997.

Cambridge Economic History of Europe, vol. 2, *Trade and Industry in the Middle Ages.* 2d ed. Cambridge, 1987.

Day, John. *The Medieval Market Economy.* London, 1987.

De Roover, Raymond. "The Organization of Trade." In *Cambridge Economic History of Europe*, vol. 3, pp. 42–118. Cambridge, 1963.

Favier, Jean. *Gold and Spices: The Rise of Commerce in the Middle Ages.* London and New York, 1998.

Finley, Moses I. *The Ancient Economy.* London, 1985. Reprint, with introduction by I. Morris, 1999.

Fleet, Kate. *European and Islamic Trade in the Early Ottoman State: The Merchants of Genoa and Turkey.* Cambridge, 1999.

Friedman, John B., and Kristen M. Figg, eds. *Trade, Travel, and Exploration in the Middle Ages: An Encyclopedia.* New York and London, 2000.

Greene, Kevin. "Technological Innovation and Economic Progress in the Ancient World: M. I. Finley Re-Considered."*Economic History Review*, 2d s., 53.1 (2000), 29–59.

Hodges, R. *Dark Age Economics. The Origins of Towns and Trade, AD 600–1000.* London, 1982.

Hodges, Richard, and David Whitehouse. *Mohammed, Charlemagne, and the Origins of Europe: Archaeology and the Pirenne Thesis.* London, 1983. 2d ed. 1989.

Kedar, Benjamin. *Merchants in Crisis: Genoese and Venetian Men of Affairs in the Fourteenth Century Depression.* New Haven and London, 1976.

Lebecq, Stéphan. *Marchands et navigateurs frisons du haut moyen âge.* 2 vols. Lille, France, 1983.

McCormick, Michael. *Origins of the European Economy: Communications and Commerce AD 300–900.* Cambridge, 2001.

Munro, John. "Patterns of Trade, Money and Credit." In *Handbook of European History 1400–1600: Late Middle Ages, Renaissance, and Reformation*, vol. 1, edited by T. A. Brady, Jr., H. A. Oberman, and J. D. Tracy, pp. 147–195. Leiden, New York, and Cologne, 1994.

Munro, John. "The Low Countries' Export Trade in Textiles with the Mediterranean Basin, 1200–1600: A Cost-Benefit Analysis of Comparative Advantages in Overland and Maritime Trade Routes." *International Journal of Maritime History* 11.2 (1999), 1–30.

Postan, Michael M. *Medieval Trade and Finance.* Cambridge, 1973.

Van der Wee, Herman. "Un modèle dynamique de croissance interséculaire du commerce mondial, XIIᵉ–XVIIIᵉ siècles." *Annales: Economies, Sociétés, Civilisations* 25.1 (1970), 100–126.

Van der Wee, Herman. "Structural Changes in European Long-Distance Trade, and Particularly in the Re-Export Trade from South to North, 1350–1750." In *The Rise of Merchant Empires: Long-Distance Trade in the Early Modern World 1350–1750*, edited by J. D. Tracy, pp. 14–33. Cambridge, 1990.

Verhulst, Adriaan. *The Rise of Cities in North-West Europe.* Themes in International Urban History, vol. 4. Cambridge, 1999.

ERIK AERTS

Long-Distance Trade between 1500 and 1750

Long-distance trade is sometimes synonymous with international trade of all kinds; sometimes the term is reserved to refer to intercontinental trade. For the period under discussion here, we prefer to define it as "intercultural" trade: trade that bridges cultures, languages, religions, legal institutions, monetary systems, and other phenomena that add significant difficulty and cost to the ordinary transaction costs that adhere to trade in general. Defined in this way, the period from 1500 to 1750, the early modern era, witnessed a revolution in the scope and volume of long-distance trade: for the first time, a global network of trade connected the continents. It also witnessed a revolution in the institutional forms used to address the problems associated with intercultural trade: a complex network of relays, intermediaries, and transshipment points that had existed since ancient times gave way to new intercontinental trading organizations controlled by European merchants and nations.

Established Routes. Toward the end of the fifteenth century, European long-distance trade was focused on the eastern Mediterranean and Black Seas and the eastern Baltic. The Venetians and Genoese dominated trade with the Levantine ports, while the Hanse, a German merchant guild, sought to monopolize trade between Novgorod in the east and Bruges and London in the west. These traders, established in international trading cities as "nations," negotiated with their host governments for protection and with traders from farther east for goods. From the Middle East, Arab traders dominated trade along the east coast of Africa, and via the Red Sea and Persian Gulf to South Asia. There, Gujarati and other South Asian merchant communities dominated the Indian Ocean routes to Malacca. Once one passed through the Straits of Malacca into the South China Sea, Chinese merchants dominated.

In general, whether goods flowed overland via the caravan routes of central Asia and trans-Saharan Africa or via the coastal shipping routes of Eurasia, they passed through trading centers that prevented the passage of merchants according to ethnicity, nationality, or religion. Consequently, goods progressed via repeated transactions at these obligatory "break in bulk" points. The system was complex and flexible, which was needed to accommodate the numerous disruptions to trade caused by political policies and warfare. The Mongol domination of central Asia and related displacements constituted a particularly severe disruption to Eurasian trade in the fifteenth century.

In the sixteenth century, this form of long-distance trade was challenged and subordinated—but not entirely displaced—as the Iberian states established a series of new maritime trade routes and reinforced them with political and technological innovations that placed intercultural trade on a new footing.

The Cape Route and Other Maritime Connections. In 1492, the voyages of Christopher Columbus established the first regular contact with the Western Hemisphere, and Vasco da Gama made direct contact with the Indian subcontinent via the Cape route in 1497. These explorations set off a sequence of political and economic developments that were rounded out by the Spanish inauguration of regular transpacific navigation, between Acapulco and Manila, in 1571. A skeletal global network of direct trade and communication was in place.

In the course of the sixteenth century, the Cape route came to dominate trade between Europe and Asia. It was first monopolized by the Carreira da India, the shipping fleets controlled by the Portuguese Crown, which established its political and commercial center at Goa. By the first decades of the following century, the English East India Company (founded in 1600) and the Dutch East India Company (founded in 1602) displaced Portugal as the dominant traders in Asia. These state-chartered joint stock companies were later joined by several others: a French East India Company, founded by Colbert in 1664, reorganized in 1684, and succeeded by the Compagnie des Indes, which lasted from 1719 to 1769; a succession of Danish companies beginning in 1616; the Oostende Company (1723–1732); and the Swedish East India Company, founded in 1731.

The Portuguese discovery of the Cape route to Asia, together with Spain's simultaneous conquest of large parts of the New World, established in short order a set of maritime trade routes that encompassed the world. For the first time in human history, regular commercial contact connected the world's continents directly, rather than by elaborate chains of intermediaries. In the case of the Western Hemisphere, of course, no regular contact of any kind had preceded Spain's intervention, nor did Europeans encounter intra-American trading networks upon which they could rely. The construction of the Spanish Empire in the Americas also entailed the construction of a trading system, controlled by the Casa de Contratación, the guild of Seville merchants who monopolized colonial trade. Throughout the early modern period, this trade was dominated by silver. Thus, the integration of the New World into intercontinental trade both established its global reach and added a trade good with monetary uses that introduced new commercial possibilities to the other major trade routes as well.

Silver flowed from its production centers in Mexico and Potosí in modern Bolivia, where it was cheap, to Seville and, via Acapulco, to Manila, where it was more highly valued, and paid for imported European manufactures, state services, and Chinese silk. Little of this silver remained for long in Spain, which used it to import goods and support an ambitious military program in Europe. Thus, silver found its way to the Baltic, to pay for grain and forest products, to the eastern Mediterranean, and, increasingly, to Asia via the Cape route, to acquire pepper and spices and, in the seventeenth century, cotton textiles, silk, and porcelain, and, in the eighteenth century, tea and coffee. Meanwhile, a transpacific exchange of silver for silk and Japan's export of its own large silver production for Asian manufactures (until the 1670s) completed a global flow of silver from its production centers toward Asia (where it consistently commanded the highest purchasing power) and a counterflow of tropical commodities and manufactures.

The Atlantic Trade. By the seventeenth century, European settlers in the New World began to add agricultural products and raw materials to transatlantic trade, and this process was greatly intensified by the development of plantation agriculture. Africa's trade with Eurasia, which had long supplied gold and ivory, and slaves to Arabia, was now more firmly integrated into the developing Atlantic trading system, as the plantation economies provided an ever-expanding market for slave labor. First the Portuguese, followed by the English, Dutch, and French, traded a variety of manufactures at outposts along the west African coast for slaves, who were transported to Brazil and Caribbean trading centers for sale to plantation owners. Slave shipments grew at the long-term rate of 2.1 percent per year over the entire period 1525–1790, by which time some ten million Africans had been sold to European traders. Approximately 85 percent of these slaves survived the "middle passage" to augment the New World's labor force; this, in turn, played an important role in the growth of New World exports.

PORTUGUESE TRADE IN INDIA. Fleet of Pedro Mascarenha and the shipwreck of one of the vessels, 1554. From a manuscript of the *Lives of the Portuguese Viceroys in India*, 1558. (Pierpont Morgan Library, New York/Art Resource, NY)

The development of the Atlantic trade can be divided into two periods. The sixteenth-century Spanish-American trade tonnage (dominated by silver and European goods) grew at an annual average rate of 2.6 percent until the 1590s. Thereafter it declined through much of the seventeenth century. Beginning in the 1640s, the northern Europeans laid the foundations for a new Atlantic economy. The total volume of sugar shipments to Europe grew at 2.2 percent per year over the period 1663–1669 to 1751–1760; Chesapeake tobacco exports grew at 5.1 percent per year from 1622 to 1775; and the total value of Iberian, English, French, and Dutch New World imports (excluding precious metals) grew by 2.0 percent per year in the period 1701–1705 to 1781–1785. Overall, with the probable exception of the period 1600–1650, the Atlantic trades grew by well over 2 percent per year by volume. The value of New World imports to Europe certainly grew more slowly than the volume, because all major commodities experienced a large price reduction as the volume of trade rose.

Diversification of Trade. The establishment of the Cape route connecting Europe and Asia represented a technological and institutional revolution, but its initial impact on long-distance trade was only to divert a long-established trade from one route to another. The Portuguese, Dutch, and English did not confine themselves to the importation of Asian goods to Europe; they all participated in the intra-Asian trades. The Dutch East India Company maintained routes from its headquarters at Batavia (Jakarta) to the Persian Gulf in the west and to Japan in the east. At times, it kept nearly as many vessels in Asian waters as it had sailing to and from the Dutch Republic. These complex trading systems caused a substantial diversification of trade. Most Asian commodities were luxuries facing a limited European demand. The overall growth of trade depended on the addition of new commodities that could both absorb the high cost of transportation and enjoy an elastic demand. By the early eighteenth century, Indian calicoes and Chinese tea were reaching a substantially broader European market than the spices and fine silks of the sixteenth century. Overall, the Cape route trades of all European traders combined grew at an annual rate of 1.1 percent from its inception to the 1790s. The growth of this trade was remarkably steady, but even after nearly three centuries of growth, the volume of Asian goods entering Europe was still not truly large. The eighty or so ships that sailed from Asia to Europe annually in the late eighteenth century had a collective capacity of about 50,000 tons, which today could be carried by one modern container ship.

Overall, the Atlantic trades grew at least twice as fast as European trade with Asia. By the 1770s, the Atlantic trades accounted for approximately 30 percent of the value of English, Dutch, and French imports, while the value of their combined imports from Asia accounted for about 10 percent.

Advances and Limitations. Long-distance trade in the early modern era presents an intriguing picture of achievement and limitation. The joint stock companies represented a novel solution to the principal-agent problems that always characterized trade over large distances and across cultures. In place of the family ties and bonds of religion that characterized merchant diasporas of Jews, Armenians, Scots, Chinese, Arabs, and so on, the companies established formal ties of employment, which structured compensation in ways designed to secure loyal service. They also replaced a dependence on the sufferance of foreign rulers with quasi-state powers that allowed them to internalize protection costs. In addition, they systematically gathered and analyzed information to guide commercial policy and investment decisions. Both their time horizons and geographical horizons far exceeded those of the peddlers and merchant families with whom they competed.

These advances had their limits, however, and they often turned into liabilities. Company employees did not always find that their own interests converged with those of their employers, and private trading often undermined the profits of the companies; the military investments of the companies (they have been called "armed merchant diasporas") placed a large overhead cost on their trade, which it often could not bear; the information they gathered at considerable expense could not always be put to timely use, or kept private. In general, the company model worked well only when the cost of entry to potential rivals was high and monopoly rights could be enforced. This was long the case in Asia, although eroding in the eighteenth century. In the Atlantic world, company monopolies were challenged from an early date by both rival nations and rival merchants in the same country. In the eighteenth century, private trade dominated in the Atlantic, and joint stock companies were either restricted to limited functions (the Dutch West India Company) or restricted to remote trading regions (Hudson's Bay Company).

Long-distance trade grew very substantially over the early modern era. The rapid growth of the sixteenth century was interrupted in the period 1620–1650, reflecting what is often called the "crisis of the seventeenth century." The Baltic trade did not recover its 1618 levels until the eighteenth century, and the Spanish fleets to and from the New World shrank in size. The crisis may have had a global dimension, for the demise of the Ming and its replacement by the Ch'ing Empire disrupted trade throughout East and Southeast Asia. But in most areas, these setbacks yielded to a "long eighteenth century" of trade expansion, centered on the Atlantic world and on a demographically expansive China. From a European perspective, long-distance trade almost certainly grew relative to per capita national income, as trade with Asia grew over 1 percent annually and trade with the Americas grew at over 2 percent, while population rates between 1500 and 1750 grew by less than 0.3 percent per year. The growth of European national income in this period can still only be guessed at, but the consensus opinion at present remains close to zero. Thus, Europe's economies, especially its Atlantic economies, became significantly more trade-intensive.

Reasons for Increased Trade. What stands behind this increasing trade intensiveness? The dramatic sixteenth-century reorganization of long-distance trade tempts one to answer that trade grew as a result of falling transaction costs. Technological advances in shipbuilding and navigation (including the discovery of the trade winds and ocean currents) and institutional advances in business organization reduced the cost of acquiring goods and selling them again in distant markets. The diversion of trade into the hands of European merchants may be taken as validation of this position, but the reduction of transaction costs was neither great nor continuous. Shipping technologies in 1750 were not significantly better than in 1600, and the slow growth of the Cape route trades relative to the Atlantic trades confirms the technological limits of early modern trade.

Indeed, the economic historian must be careful not to mistake the removal of political barriers for technological improvement. European traders entered non-Western ports as both economic agents and military powers. Whether by peaceful or warlike means, they sought to reduce the political barriers to trade: tariffs, prohibitions, tribute payments, and confiscations. This may account for as much of the growth of trade as technological change. But, in the New World, rival European empires sought to enforce mercantilist measures against one another, creating political barriers where none had existed. In Asia, the European trading companies also battled each other, but, in addition, they faced Asian polities that long retained a considerable ability to tax and control their foreign trade.

Reduced transaction costs and lowered political barriers should bring about price convergence: a reduction of price differences for the same good in distant markets. O'Rourke and Williamson (2002) argue that there is little evidence of price convergence and, consequently, that the growth of trade cannot have been driven by these two factors. The fact that most goods entering into long-distance trade were "noncompeting"—tropical commodities and "oriental luxuries" that were not produced in Europe—complicates the analysis of price convergence, but it remains likely that these forces were weaker than long had been thought.

Even absent price convergence, trade intensification could still occur for two reasons: a rise of incomes, increasing the consumption of imported goods, and a decline in the price at which suppliers offer export goods, perhaps as a result of technological change or increased competition in the export economies. Little is known about the latter possibility in Asia, although it is likely that growth of the plantation economies drove down the prices of sugar, tobacco, coffee, and other commodities. The possibility that a rise of European incomes, at least in certain social classes, drove the expansion of long-distance trade in the early modern era remains as an intriguing possible explanation. Non-European goods figured very prominently in the consumption aspirations of Europeans from the mid-seventeenth century onward. Indian calicoes appealed to a broad market that eventually led to European imitations that laid the foundation of the British cotton textile industry. Chinese porcelain led the Dutch faience industry to develop delftware and many European nations to master the techniques of porcelain production. Tea, coffee, and sugar fundamentally changed the diets and social customs of western Europeans, and not only of the elites. Some combination of income and substitution effects stood behind this renovation of Europe's material culture, and income may have been the more important.

Impact on Global Economy. What was the impact of this growth of trade on the other centers of the early modern global economy? In the Americas, the outflow of precious metals and plantation commodities was matched by an inflow of mainly European manufactures, reexported Asian goods, and slaves. The important role of slaves in the Atlantic economy obviously complicates an analysis of the motivation to engage in international trade. However, the free settlers, as well as many Native Americans engaged in the fur trade, appear to have shared with Europeans a lively interest in the developing material world made possible by long-distance trade. In Asia, matters were fundamentally different. No consequential demand for European manufactures or raw materials developed, or, perhaps, could develop. Silver, in bar or coined form, was by far the most important import. In 1500, the relative value of silver was higher in Asia, especially China, than elsewhere in the world, and this remained the case in 1750, after centuries of steady growth in the volume of Asia-bound silver shipments.

The absence of price convergence in the intercontinental silver market has long stood as a puzzle. Hoarding and decorative demand are one possibility, but they are now thought to be, at best, a secondary factor to China's enormous demand for silver as its economy was monetized on a silver standard. The rate at which Europeans supplied silver to Asia (growing about 1 percent per year) never sufficed to bring the desired and existing stocks of silver into equilibrium. Indeed, after the 1650s, it barely exceeded the rapid growth of China's population. The two ends of Eurasia were connected by a steadily growing volume of trade, but they remained in this era two very distinct economic worlds, with their own dynamics.

The early modern era was the first to possess a global trading system, but can it be called the first age of globalization? The answer is yes if, with Flynn and Giráldez (2002) and many historians, we define globalization as a condition in which all important areas of the world exchange products continuously, and on a scale sufficient to have deep and lasting effects on the trading partners. If, following O'Rourke and Williamson (2002), we take globalization to mean the full integration of international commodity markets, with the test of this integration being commodity price convergence, the answer must be a provisional no. A degree of convergence did occur within Europe, and probably between Europe and the New World, but the scope of trade remained insufficient to integrate the vast Asian markets with each other, let alone with markets farther afield.

[*See also* Road Transportation *and* Water Transportation.]

BIBLIOGRAPHY

Chaudhuri, K. N. *The Trading World of Asia and the English East India Company, 1660–1760.* Cambridge, 1978.

Curtin, Philip. *The Atlantic Slave Trade: A Census.* Madison, Wisc., 1969.

Curtin, Philip. *Cross-Cultural Trade in World History.* Cambridge, 1984.

Fischer, Wolfram, R. Marvin McInnis, and Jürgen Schneider, eds. *The Emergence of a World Economy, 1500–1914*, pt. 1. Wiesbaden, Germany, 1986.

Flynn, Dennis O., and Aruro Giráldez. "Cycles of Silver: Global Economic Unity through the Mid-eighteenth Century." *Journal of World History* 13 (2002), 1–16.

McCusker, John J., and Kenneth Morgan, eds. *The Early Modern Atlantic Economy.* Cambridge, 2000.

O'Rourke, Kevin, and Jeffrey G. Williamson. "After Columbus: Explaining Europe's Overseas Trade Boom, 1550–1800." *Journal of Economic History* 62 (2002), 417–455.

Prakash, Om. *New Cambridge History of India*, vol. 2.5, *European Commercial Enterprise in Pre-Colonial India.* Cambridge, 1998.

Steensgaard, Niels. *The Asian Trade Revolution of the Seventeenth Century: The East India Companies and the Decline of the Caravan Trade.* Chicago, 1974.

Tracy, James D., ed. *The Rise of Merchant Empires: Long-Distance Trade in the Early Modern World, 1350–1750.* Cambridge, 1990.

Tracy, James D., ed. *The Political Economy of Merchant Empires: State Power and World Trade, 1350–1750.* Cambridge, 1991.

Vries, Jan de. "Connecting Europe and Asia: A Quantitative Analysis of the Cape Route Trade, 1497–1795." In *Global Connections and Monetary History, 1470–1800*, edited by Dennis O. Flynn, Aruro Giráldez, and Richard von Glahn. Aldershot, U.K., 2003.

JAN DE VRIES

Long-Distance Trade between 1750 and 1914

By the late eighteenth century, the world economy had developed a well-defined network of trading relationships that connected Europe, Asia, the Americas, and Africa. Asia still exported traditional commodities such as spices and silk to Europe, but the role of other traditional exports such as pepper had declined over time, with Indian cotton textiles, tea, and coffee growing in importance. For example, textiles accounted for more than half of the East India Company's exports from Asia to Europe in the 1750s. Meanwhile, intercontinental trade involving the Americas largely reflected that area's abundance of natural resources, including agricultural land. The Americas accounted for 90 percent of the world's silver production in the eighteenth century and 85 percent of its gold production. As much as two-thirds of the silver was shipped to Europe, from where a substantial proportion was sent on to Asia; smaller amounts were shipped directly to Asia via the Philippines. By the late eighteenth century, however, these bullion flows no longer played the central economic role that they had done in previous centuries; rather, American exports of "colonial" goods, such as sugar and tobacco, were becoming increasingly important, serving as inputs into European industrial production. These commodities required the application of capital and labor to the abundant land of the New World, and this in turn fueled the growth of Africa's most important export during the period, namely, slaves. About two-thirds of the nine million to ten million persons transferred over the course of the Atlantic slave trade were shipped to the Americas during the eighteenth century. The last two decades of the century in particular saw a surge in slave imports in response to the cotton boom triggered by the onset of the Industrial Revolution in Britain. Meanwhile, advanced European economies such as Britain were paying for their imports largely by exporting (or reexporting) manufactured goods.

These intercontinental flows were important, but they were dwarfed by trade flows within continents. For example, 77 percent of English exports went to other European destinations in 1750–1751; similarly, Asia's trade with Europe was insignificant compared to trade between various Asian countries. Intercontinental flows would be much more economically important a century later.

Three factors combined to disrupt this late-eighteenth century pattern of intercontinental trade. The first was the British Industrial Revolution. As already mentioned, this led to a drastic increase in raw cotton imports, to the point where they had displaced sugar as Britain's most important import item by the 1820s. It also led to a surge in African slave exports. The Industrial Revolution coincided with a reorientation away from Europe in Britain's exports, with the Americas emerging as a particularly important market for British manufactured goods. This coincidence has led to a vigorous debate concerning the links between the Industrial Revolution and overseas trade. Some scholars maintain that the Industrial Revolution was purely homegrown and that the expansion in trade was its consequence (as evidenced by the decline in the relative price of Britain's export goods); others argue that the existence of overseas markets, along with the elastic supply of raw materials that New World land and slavery gave rise to, helped ensure that British growth was not choked off by an excessive deterioration in its terms of trade.

The second factor was the French and Napoleonic Wars, which lasted almost uninterrupted from 1793 to 1815. This led to widespread disruption of the transatlantic trade, as well as of intra-European trade, which had a number of permanent effects. In particular, Continental European industry's traditional Atlantic orientation was replaced by a much more inward-looking focus on import-substituting activities. Similarly, the wars facilitated the development of import-substituting industry in the United States, which in turn spurred the development of a northern protectionist lobby.

The third factor was the most important: the dramatic and worldwide decline in transportation costs in the nineteenth century, associated above all with the development of steamships, which linked the continents more closely than ever before, and the railroad, which penetrated their interiors. In addition, the opening of the Suez Canal on 17 November 1869 made it possible for steamships to compete on Asian routes, in addition to halving the distance from London to Bombay. The result was a precipitous decline in transportation costs. One broadly based index of British ocean freight rates shows relative stability between 1740 and 1840, followed by a 70 percent decline between 1840 and 1910. These declines in ocean freight rates were matched by equally dramatic decreases in the cost of land transportation. Thus, it cost 6 shillings, 11 pence to ship a quarter of wheat by boat and rail from Chicago to New York in 1868. The cost using rail alone was 10 shillings, 2 pence. The cost of shipping a quarter of wheat from New York to Liverpool by steamer was 4 shillings, 7½ pence. In 1902, these costs had fallen to 1 shilling, 11 pence (Chicago to New York, boat and rail), 2 shillings, 11 pence (Chicago to New York rail), and 11½ pence (New York to Liverpool).

These developments were not limited to the Atlantic economy. For example, the declines in freight rates between 1870 and 1914 were just as impressive on routes involving Black Sea and Egyptian ports as on those involving Atlantic ports, and perhaps even more so. Meanwhile, the tramp charter rate for shipping rice from Rangoon to Europe fell from 73.8 to 18.1 percent of the Rangoon (present-day Yangon, Myanmar) price between 1882 and 1914; the freight rate on coal (relative to its export price) between Nagasaki, Japan, and Shanghai fell by 76 percent between 1880 and 1910; and total factor productivity on Japan's tramp freighter routes serving Asia advanced at 2.5 percent a year in the thirty years between 1879 and 1909.

These transport cost declines were to some extent offset by defensive tariffs, protecting European agriculture and New World industry, but nonetheless their effect was to dramatically increase the integration of the world economy, making the period from 1815 to 1913, in particular, from 1870 onward, the canonical episode of trade expansion and commodity market integration. Recent tentative estimates suggest that world trade grew at a little over 1 percent per year between 1500 and 1800, but it has grown at around 3.5 percent a year since 1820, with the nineteenth- and twentieth-century growth rates being roughly equal. However, the nineteenth-century growth rate was more impressive than the twentieth, in the sense that world gross domestic product (GDP) growth was twice as high since 1913 as it was between 1820 and 1913: the implication is that trade ratios (e.g., the ratio of merchandise exports to GDP) grew more rapidly during the nineteenth century than they did during the twentieth. The export to GDP ratio grew more than eightfold worldwide between 1820 and 1913, when merchandise exports accounted for

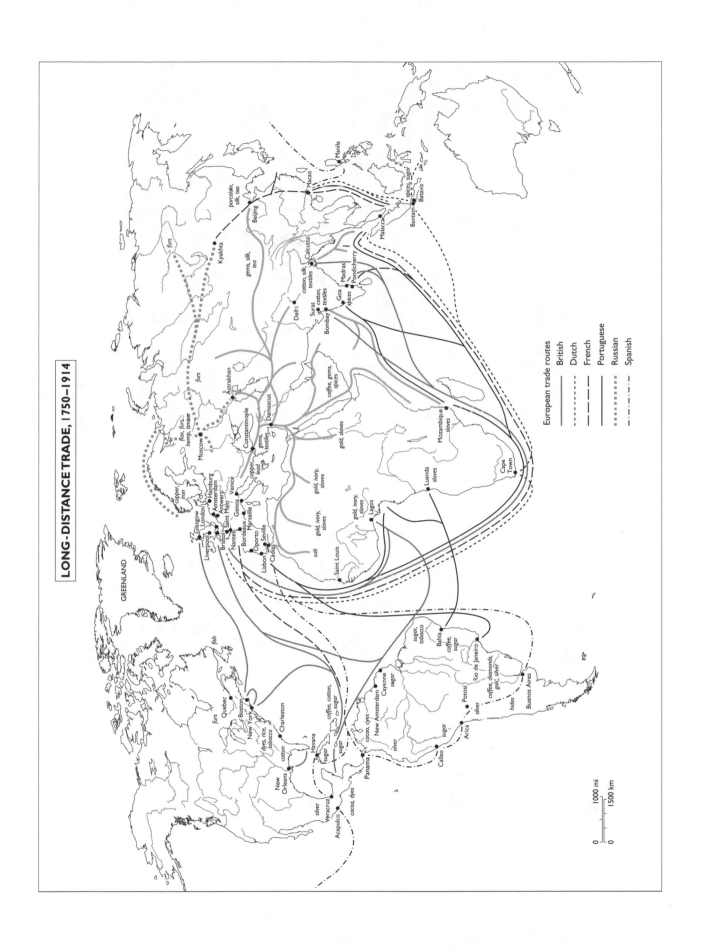

LONG-DISTANCE TRADE, 1750–1914

GREENLAND

European trade routes
British
Dutch
French
Portuguese
Russian
Spanish

furs

porcelain, silk, tea

Manila

Macao

Beijing

Kyakhta

gems, silk, tea

Batavia

Bantam, spices, sugar

Malacca

Calcutta

cotton, silk, textiles

Madras

Pondicherry

Delhi

Surat

Goa

Bombay

cotton, textiles

spices

coffee, gems, spices

furs

Astrakhan

Moscow

flax, furs, hemp, timber

copper, iron

Damascus

Constantinople

gems, textiles

gold, slaves

Mozambique

slaves

Glasgow

London

Hamburg

Amsterdam

Antwerp

Venice

Genoa

copper, lead

Liverpool

Bristol

Saint Malo

Nantes

Bordeaux

Marseille

Lisbon

Oporto

Seville

Cadiz

Cape Town

Luanda

slaves

gold, ivory, slaves

Lagos

gold, ivory, slaves

salt

Saint Louis

fish

Quebec

Boston

New York

Charleston

furs

cotton

New Orleans

dyes, rice, tobacco

Havana

sugar

coffee, cotton, sugar

sugar

New Amsterdam

Cayenne

sugar

cocoa, dyes

silver

Panama

Arica

silver

Callao

sugar

Potosi

silver

Bahia

sugar, tobacco

coffee, sugar

Rio de Janeiro

coffee, diamonds, gold, silver

hides

Buenos Aires

Veracruz

silver

Acapulco

cocoa, dyes

1000 mi

1500 km

0

0

TRADE. Public room at Merchants' Exchange, New York, circa 1830, engraving by Charles Burton. (Collection of the New-York Historical Society)

more than 8 percent of world GDP, and more than 16 percent of western European GDP.

The most direct measure of commodity market integration involves obtaining price information for identical commodities in different locations: commodity market integration will show up as a decline in price gaps between markets. It is difficult to find evidence of such commodity price convergence between continents prior to 1800, although there was certainly price convergence within continents; but there is abundant evidence of intercontinental price convergence during the nineteenth century. For example, there was little or no Dutch-Asian price convergence for cloves, pepper, and coffee prior to the nineteenth century, but substantial convergence was seen after the Napoleonic Wars. To take another example, Liverpool wheat prices exceeded Chicago prices by 57.6 percent in 1870, by 17.8 percent in 1895, and by only 15.6 percent in 1913. Anglo-American commodity price convergence can also be documented for bacon, cotton textiles, iron bars, pig iron, copper, hides, wool, coal, tin, and coffee. Meanwhile, in Asia, trade policy strengthened the impact of technological developments. The cotton price spread between Liverpool and Bombay (present-day Mumbai) fell from 57 percent in 1873 to 20 percent in 1913, and there was also substantial price convergence for jute between London and Calcutta, as well as for rice between London and Rangoon. Substantial price convergence has also been documented for cotton between London and Alexandria, Egypt, and for many other goods and pairs of markets. Commodity market integration in the late nineteenth century was both impressive in scale and global in scope.

The implications for trade volumes and aggregate trade ratios have already been mentioned, but there were other, more subtle implications as well. The nature of the commodities being traded between continents changed dramatically during the nineteenth century: transport costs fell enough that it was now economical to transport bulk commodities such as wheat, iron, and rice across the oceans of the world. Prior to the nineteenth century, intercontinental trade had been largely (but by no means entirely) in commodities such as spices, tobacco, and bullion, which had no domestic substitutes in the markets to which they were sold, or in goods such as sugar and raw cotton, which were only imperfect substitutes for European commodities such as honey or wool. By the late nineteenth century, trade in bulk commodities led to farmers and industrialists facing far more direct competition from producers in other continents. In turn, this implied that intercontinental trade was now capable of having important, economy-wide effects on income distribution.

TABLE 1. *World Trade, 1876–1880 and 1913*

	PRIMARY PRODUCTS (IN MILLIONS OF U.S. $)					
	1876–1880			1913		
REGION	EXPORTS	IMPORTS	BALANCE	EXPORTS	IMPORTS	BALANCE
United States and Canada	600	330	270	2,101	1,542	559
United Kingdom	117	1,362	– 1,245	760	2,596	– 1,836
Northwestern Europe	840	1,800	– 960	3,064	5,894	– 2,830
Other Europe	750	515	235	1,793	1,689	104
Oceania	1,413	575	838	455	129	326
Latin America				1,531	595	936
Africa				680	307	373
Asia				1,792	949	843
Total	3,720	4,582	– 862	12,176	13,701	– 1,525

	MANUFACTURED GOODS					
	1876–1880			1913		
REGION	EXPORTS	IMPORTS	BALANCE	EXPORTS	IMPORTS	BALANCE
United States and Canada	100	190	– 90	734	891	– 157
United Kingdom	865	225	640	1,751	601	1,150
Northwestern Europe	1,080	450	630	3,318	1,795	1,523
Other Europe	210	330	– 120	578	1,133	– 555
Oceania	35	1,285	– 1,250	9	370	– 361
Latin America				51	879	– 828
Africa				26	451	– 425
Asia				461	1,247	– 786
Total	2,290	2,480	– 190	6,928	7,367	– 439

SOURCE: Yates, P. Lamartine. *Forty Years of Foreign Trade*. New York, 1959.

The link between intercontinental trade and income distribution was, broadly speaking, as predicted by the Heckscher-Ohlin theory of international trade. The theory maintains that land-abundant regions should export land-intensive products such as food and raw materials, whereas labor-abundant regions should export labor-intensive goods such as manufactured goods. In turn, these trade patterns should lend to the ratio of wages to land rents falling in land-abundant areas, as agricultural exports boost the returns to owning agricultural land, whereas the wage-rental ratio should decline in labor-abundant regions, as agriculture comes under pressure from foreign imports. This is precisely what happened in the late nineteenth century, with wage-rental ratios falling in land-abundant regions such as the Americas, Burma (Myanmar), and Siam (Thailand), and wage-rental ratios rising in land-scarce regions such as Europe, Japan, Korea, and Taiwan.

The fact that intercontinental trade now had profound effects on economy-wide factor prices had important po-litical implications. Intercontinental trade had a large impact on domestic politics in several countries during the nineteenth century, and the divisions to which it gave rise can largely be understood by the Heckscher-Ohlin theory, as Ronald Rogowski's *Commerce and Coalitions* (1989) has shown. Thus, free-trading slave and land owners in the cotton South opposed capitalists in the industrial North in the antebellum United States, free-trading labor and capital opposed protectionist landowners in mid-century Britain, and protectionist coalitions of land and capital opposed labor in Germany after 1879. The fact that trade policy frequently gave rise to major political debates, and that those debates seemed to evolve along class lines, is in itself powerful evidence of significant nineteenth-century globalization.

By 1913, international commodity markets were vastly more integrated than they had been in 1750; world trade accounted for a far higher share of world output; and a far broader range of goods, including commodities with a high bulk to value ratio, were being transported between continents. There was a stark distinction between industrial and primary producing economies. According to the available figures (given in Table 1), primary products accounted for between 62 and 64 percent of total world exports in the late nineteenth century: in 1913, food accounted for 27 percent of world exports, agricultural raw materials for 22.7 percent and minerals for 14 percent. The United Kingdom and northwestern Europe were net importers of primary products and net exporters of manufactured goods. North America still exported primary products, but rapid industrialization there was leading to a more balanced trade in manufactured goods over time. Meanwhile, Oceania, Latin America, and Africa exported virtually no manufactured goods, and Asian exports were overwhelmingly composed of primary products; for example, primary products accounted for more than three-quarters of India's exports in 1913. The contrast with the importance of Indian textile exports in 1750 indicates the impact that European industrialization and intercontinental trade had on the worldwide division of labor between those two dates. The effect of this development on growth in core and periphery would become a major subject of economic debate in the twentieth century.

[*See also* Air Transportation; Railroads; Road Transportation; *and* Water Transportation.]

BIBLIOGRAPHY

Barrett, Ward. "World Bullion Flows, 1450–1800." In *The Rise of Merchant Empires: Long-Distance Trade in the Early Modern World, 1350–1750*, edited by James D. Tracy, pp. 224–254. Cambridge, 1990.

Engerman, Stanley L., ed. *Trade and the Industrial Revolution, 1700–1850*. Cheltenham, U.K., 1996.

Findlay, Ronald. "The 'Triangular Trade' and the Atlantic Economy of the Eighteenth Century: A Simply General-Equilibrium Model." In *Princeton Essays in International Finance*, no. 177. Princeton, 1990.

Findlay, Ronald, and Kevin H. O'Rourke. "Commodity Market Integration, 1500–2000." In *Globalization in Historical Perspective*, edited by Michael D. Bordo, Alan M. Taylor, and Jeffrey G. Williamson. Chicago, 2002.

Harley, C. Knick. "Ocean Freight Rates and Productivity, 1740–1913: The Primacy of Mechanical Invention Reaffirmed." *Journal of Economic History* 48.4 (1988), 851–876.

Harley, C. Knick, ed. *The Integration of the World Economy, 1850–1914*. Cheltenham, U.K., 1996.

Kenwood, A. G., and A. L. Lougheed. *The Growth of the International Economy, 1820-2000 : An Introductory Text*. 4th ed. London, 1999.

Maddison, Angus. *The World Economy: A Millennial Perspective*. Paris, 2001.

O'Brien, Patrick K., and Stanley L. Engerman. "Exports and the Growth of the British Economy from the Glorious Revolution to the Peace of Amiens." In *Slavery and the Rise of the Atlantic System*, edited by Barbara L. Solow, pp. 177–209. Cambridge, 1991.

O'Rourke, Kevin H., and Jeffrey G. Williamson. *Globalization and History: The Evolution of a Nineteenth Century Atlantic Economy*. Cambridge, Mass., 1999.

Williamson, Jeffrey G. "Land, Labor and Globalization in the Third World 1870–1940." *Journal of Economic History* 62.1 (2002), 55–85.

KEVIN O'ROURKE

Long-Distance Trade since 1914

Long-distance trade for hundreds of years stemmed primarily from differences in climate. The greatest reaches were achieved by ships sailing between temperate-zone Europe and tropical or subtropical regions. Western Europe supplied manufactures in exchange for "colonial goods"—Chinese tea, Brazilian coffee, Caribbean sugar, southern U.S. tobacco, and East Indian spices. British free-trade policy and reduced transport cost superimposed another pattern by 1914; Canadian, Australian, and Argentinian wheat, wool, and beef substituted for domestic British food supplies as Great Britain's own agriculture sector was run down, Thai rice was exported for Malayan plantations workers, and Australian food was exported for South African miners. Most remarkable among the trade consequences of industrialization was strong demand for a semitropical raw material—cotton, primarily from the United States—that was worked up into textile products in Lancashire and exported, often again to different continents.

On the eve of World War I, world trade in primary products was almost double that in manufactures. Food accounted for just under half of primary products; next in importance came agricultural raw materials (such as cotton, wool, silk, timber, and rubber), with minerals, including fuel, representing less than one-fifth (Figure 1a). The steam engine, powering ships, railways, and factories, ensured that the world's principal fossil fuel in 1913 was coal, ranking third in the volume of commodity trade behind cotton and wheat. Coal was most readily available—partly for reasons of geology and partly because of economic development—in the United States, Germany, and Great Britain. Although the United States mined more coal and burned more per person than any other country, it was much smaller Great Britain that dominated world exports. A higher proportion of coal production in the other two countries was devoted to manufacture and transport, reflecting their greater industrial competitiveness. British coal supplied Brazil and Argentina as well as Scandinavia and Italy. Asian coal production was one-tenth of North America's. Belgium mined more than Japan, the largest Asian exporter.

Commodity Patterns at the End of the Twentieth Century. By the end of the twentieth century, economic development had transformed the balance between primary commodity and manufactures trade; Asia and North America were vastly more important traders, while coal's strategic role had been entirely usurped by oil. Manufactures now amounted to almost four-fifths of commodity trade exports (Figure 1b). Office and telecommunications equipment, miniscule in 1914, was the largest identifiable manufactures group (Figure 1c). The end-of-century trade

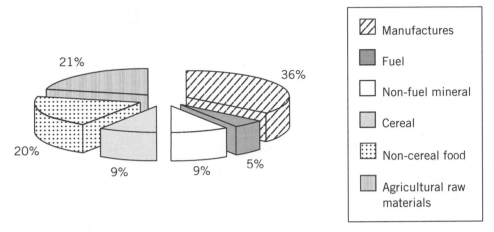

FIGURE 1a. Commodity composition of world exports, 1913. SOURCE: Maddison, 1995.

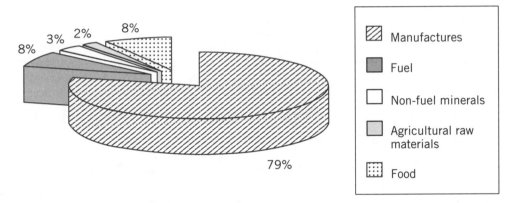

FIGURE 1b. Commodity composition of world exports, 1999. SOURCE: Maddison, 1995.

was based on new technology and new products, especially computers, semiconductors, and mobile phones—the hardware component of the information technology revolution. Asia dominated the supply of these products, accounting for nearly one-half of world exports. The sector was highly specialized and internationally integrated; developing Asian countries supplied one-third of the world's exports of office and telecom equipment and, at the same time, bought one-quarter of world imports. North America took one-quarter of world imports, but this still left western Europe as the greatest importer.

The second-largest commodity trade category, based upon a more mature technology, showed a remarkable turnaround between 1914, when the Model T Ford was conquering the world, and the end of the twentieth century. North America became the biggest net importer of motor vehicles and components, with Asia the largest net exporter. Western Europe in both periods was the largest exporting and importing region, with balance still tipped slightly toward exports, though the volume of trade was much greater in the year 2000.

Asia also dominated the much smaller world-clothing exports, supplying just under one-half. But products from China, Korea, Hong Kong, and Taiwan were being displaced in the North American market by Latin American clothing exports. Exports of the "transition economies," formerly members of the Soviet Union, with a comparable dependence on the western Europe clothing market, were making similar progress.

Trade in services was probably proportionately greater at the end of the twentieth century but nonetheless reached only one-third of the value of trade in manufactures. In 1914 international tourism was an elite pursuit from which only Switzerland earned substantial sums. From the 1960s, cheaper passenger air travel ensured that poorer countries could take advantage of mass tourism as a service export. Spain developed a huge tourist industry for northwestern Europe. In the 1990s, Egypt, Morocco, Tunisia, Mauritius, Cuba, and the Dominican Republic increasingly tapped the demand created by cheap long-haul flight charges and rising affluence in industrialized countries.

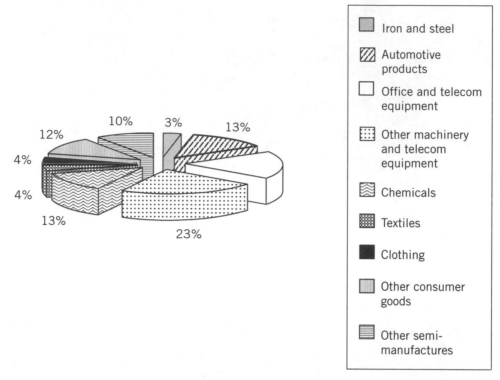

FIGURE 1c. Commodity composition of world manufactures exports, 1999. SOURCE: Maddison, 1995.

Trade in fuel became primarily trade in oil. Technological change replaced the coal-fired steam engine with the internal combustion engine and oil-fired steam turbines. Oil not only became essential for transport and industrial power but also substituted for coal as the fundamental raw material of the chemical industry. Most oil was extracted in the United States—also a major user—but the Middle East and the successor states to the Soviet Union had far larger proven reserves. Around one-quarter of the world's total was in Saudi Arabia during the last decade of the century. Since the entire population of the country was only about 15 million, Saudi Arabia was almost bound to export massive quantities of oil to more populous industrial regions. The Middle East as a whole supplied nearly 30 percent of the world fuel trade. Venezuela and Mexico were also major oil exporters.

Agricultural trade was left behind in the great boom, accounting for a mere 10 percent of world commodity exports at the century's close. Opportunities for economies specializing in agriculture were less apparent than in manufactures. Of the thirty-three countries dependent on agricultural products for more than half their total merchandise exports, twenty-eight were in Latin America or Africa. Moreover, developing countries tended to concentrate in the slowly expanding primary, rather than value-added, agricultural exports.

Reasons for These Patterns. The explanations for these patterns of long-distance trade are found in market forces, policy, technological change, and economic development. Market forces in the case of "colonial goods" were practicable long-distance transport technology, tastes for a varied diet and stimulants, and a sufficiently productive economic system that allowed substantial numbers of people to indulge their tastes. Within Europe, climate guaranteed that wine could be readily manufactured in the south, but not in the north. Vines could be cultivated in northern European heated greenhouses, but far more expensively than relying on southern sun. On the other hand, the gray skies and rain of the north allowed the growth of abundant grass for wool-bearing sheep, creating the basis for cloth exports. Even if the south could produce woolen cloth better than the north, it was still advantageous for both regions if the south exported wine to northern Europe in exchange for imports of wool. Both regions could consume more wine and cloth if they specialized in supplying the product in which they possessed a comparative advantage (as long as transport costs were low enough to make trade feasible). The south held a comparative advantage in wine because the southern sun ensured that resources in wine production yielded more, relative to wool production, than in northern Europe.

The trade pattern of 1914 reflected not only climate and mineral endowments but also land abundance. European

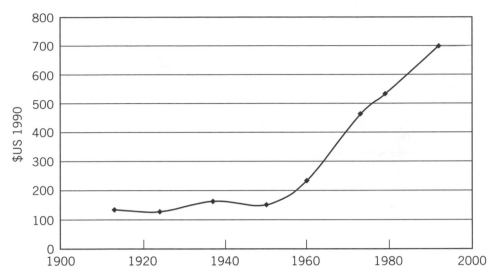

FIGURE 2. World exports per head. SOURCE: Maddison, 1995.

settlement of the New World created the land-abundant, labor-scarce production zones of the prairies and pampas, ideally suited for land-intensive agriculture.

The great expansion of international transactions in the second half of the twentieth century was different, based upon neither land availability nor climate, but on skills, innovation, and scale economies. Supplying world, instead of national, markets for manufactures supported longer, higher-volume production runs. With greater output, the fixed costs of specialized equipment and services could be spread more widely, so that unit costs fell. Moreover, the prospects of tapping a global market encouraged the direction of more resources to research and innovation than would have been worthwhile in a purely national or regional economy. Economies of scale explain why a high proportion of international trade entailed transactions between subsidiaries of the same multinational company (intrafirm trade). One-third of U.S. merchandise trade was within the firm. They also explain the exchanges of manufactured goods between national economies, but in the same industry (intra-industry trade). Greater specialization meant that the number of "industries" increased so that more two-way trade was recorded at a given level of product classification. Intra-industry exchange accounted for 60 percent of manufactures trade in six west European countries toward the end of the twentieth century.

New manufactured goods were likely to be created close to their market, and the largest market for innovative products was usually located near high-income and high-productivity users or consumers. Once a product is accepted, it can be standardized, and proximity to the market for the purposes of judging acceptability is no longer necessary. Larger-scale production can be based in regions where costs are lowest. So most of the world's televisions, for instance, were made in the United States during the 1950s, but subsequently manufacture migrated to Hong Kong, Taiwan, and elsewhere in Asia. The locations of car production and components for information technology have shown a somewhat similar evolution during the twentieth century.

Volume of Trade. World trade growth reflected increasing prosperity (because economic development typically involves more specialization in a finer division of labor), technical progress, and national trade policies. Two world wars and the Great Depression in the first half of the twentieth century (Figure 2) were the biggest blows to economic growth; between 1913 and 1950, trade per head stagnated.

Western Europe accounted for more than half of world trade in 1913 (Figure 3a). Second came "Neo-Europe," (here defined narrowly as the United States, Canada, Australia, and New Zealand). Though containing most of the world's population, Asia accounted for only one-tenth of world trade, mirroring low productivity and incomes. Latin America came behind Asia, but the most dynamic Latin American economies were those more correctly classified as "Neo-European"—Argentina and Uruguay. The entire continent of Africa contributed only 3 percent of world exports in 1913.

Regional trade patterns revealed the geographical destruction of war. In the aftermath of the World War II, Neo-Europe and Latin America attained their largest shares of world trade, while war-torn Asia and Europe achieved their smallest (Figure 3b).

In the remainder of the century, while population boomed, exports per head almost quadrupled. "Globalization" accelerated under the influence of falling man-made trade barriers and lower transport and communication

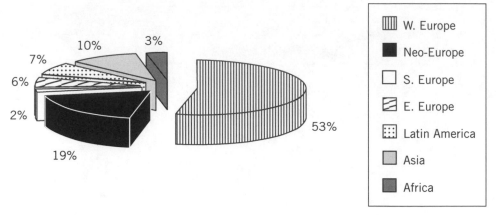

FIGURE 3a. Regional contribution to world exports, 1913. SOURCE: Maddison, 1995.

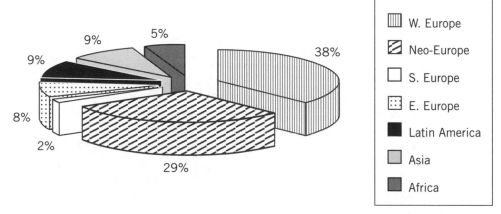

FIGURE 3b. Regional contribution to world exports, 1950. SOURCE: Maddison, 1995.

costs. Whereas earlier, much trade had increased the variety of consumption, complementing domestic products, in this great expansion of the second half of the twentieth century, multinational American-originating brands and products—Coca-Cola, McDonald's, Levi's, and the Hollywood film industry—sometimes appeared to be homogenizing the tastes of consumers across the world by providing substitutes for domestic products.

In 1950, the trade-output ratio was approximately 7 percent; by the end of the century, it had risen to around 22.5 percent. Between the two dates, a slowdown in the rate of the rise of the ratio during the decade after 1974 may be traced to the Organization of Petroleum Exporting Countries' contraction of the oil trade and also to the resulting price rises and unemployment. These ten years saw two bouts of double-digit inflation and three years of stagnant or declining output. Greater stability returned in the following decades, and growth in the trade-output ratio resumed.

By the end of the twentieth century, the greatest transformation in the pattern of world trade since 1914 was the expansion of Asia. Asia's globalization record, on the export side, was particularly rapid. But Japan's import/GDP (gross domestic product) share remained virtually unchanged over twenty years at 9 percent, whereas the export share rose from 8 to 12 percent in the early 1980s. First Japan after 1950, then the four "little dragons" (South Korea, Taiwan, Singapore, Hong Kong), followed by Malaysia and Thailand in particular, demonstrate the continent's altered position in international economic relations. As their relatively poor economic performances foreshadowed, the trade shares of Africa, eastern Europe, and Latin America contracted.

Trade Intensity. Strong economies tended to be economies open to trade, both because they pursued liberal trade policies and because their innovativeness and high productivity created great scope for international specialization. Trade intensity depended also on size. Small countries such as the Netherlands, with over half of GDP entering international trade in the 1990s, were likely to be more open than large economies such as the United States, with an export/GDP ratio of 8 percent. As already pointed out,

TABLE 1. *Trade Intensity, Size, and Output of Major Economies, 1913 and 1992*

	EXPORT/GDP 1913	EXPORT/GDP 1992	POPULATION 1913	POPULATION 1992	GDP PER CAPITA 1913	GDP PER CAPITA 1992
France	8.2	22.9	39.8	57.4	3,452	17,959
Germany	15.6	32.6	67.0	80.6	3,648	16,860
Netherlands	17.8	55.3	6.2	15.2	3,950	16,898
United Kingdom	17.7	21.4	45.6	57.8	4,878	15,738
Italy	4.9	18.9	36.2	57.9	3,021	16,229
Spain	8.1	13.4	20.3	39.1	2,255	12,498
Russia	2.9	5.1	154.0	149.4	1,488	5,367
Australia	12.8	16.9	4.8	17.5	5,505	16,237
Canada	12.2	27.2	7.6	28.4	4,213	18,159
United States	3.7	8.2	97.2	255.6	5,307	21,558
Argentina	6.8	4.3	7.6	33.0	3,797	7,616
Brazil	9.5	4.7	23.7	156.0	839	4,637
Mexico	10.8	6.4	15.0	89.52	1,467	5,112
China	1.4	2.3	437.1	1,167.0	688	3,098
India	4.7	1.7	303.7	881.2	663	1,348
Indonesia	2.2	7.4	49.9	185.9	917	2,749
Japan	2.4	12.4	51.7	124.3	1,334	19,425
Korea	1.0	17.8	15.5	43.6	948	10,010
Taiwan	2.5	34.4	3.5	20.6	794	11,590
Thailand	6.7	11.4	8.7	57.6	846	4,694

SOURCE: Maddison, A. *Monitoring the World Economy, 1820–1992*, pp. 23–24, 38, and Table A3a.

the explanation is the differential opportunities within their borders. But since 1913, when the Dutch trade ratio was 17 percent and the United States 3 percent, both economies have become more trade intensive.

Other things being equal, technical progress in transport and communications over the period should have raised trade/GNP (gross national product) ratios. In the opposite direction, trade policies encourage import substitution and domestic self-sufficiency, against the pull of the market. Working with the grain of the market means that countries that have become more open to trade will more likely also grow more prosperous. The sample of nineteen major economies in 1913 and 1992 supports this view (Table 1); only India and the three Latin American countries (Brazil, Argentina, Mexico) were less open (had a lower share of exports in GDP) in 1992 than in 1913. These are among the lowest-income countries in the sample, although it is true that China, Thailand, and Indonesia are also in the same broad income group. (There are no African countries in this sample.) Russian openness increased, but the 1992 boundaries of Russia are more circumscribed than those of 1913. Simply on these grounds, more openness would be expected.

Though trade and specialization raises world well-being, there are often losers. Widening wage differentials between the skilled and the unskilled workers in North America during the 1980s, as well as higher unemployment among the unskilled in western Europe, has been blamed on international competition from rapidly industrializing Asian economies. Countries in the developing south increased their production of labor-intensive manufactures and their imports of skill-intensive goods, raising their demand for unskilled but literate labor relative to more skilled labor (Wood, 1995). In the industrialized north, trade reversed the skill composition of labor demand. (Biased technical progress is an alternative explanation to trade for the wage and unemployment patterns).

The rise of China as an international trading power and the country's admission to the World Trade Organization are likely to increase these concerns about shifts in labor demands. Chinese exports of manufactures grew by more than one-third in current values between 1995 and 1999. The 1999 total amounted to 4 percent of world manufactured exports, and that share is expected to increase.

Even though the winners from globalization might be able to compensate those displaced by foreign competition (and remain better off), they rarely do. In the nature of political life, the losers are likely to complain, but those who have found new, profitable niches or employment options will stay silent. When assessing the overall effect of increasing trade intensity, this asymmetry should be borne in mind.

Policy as an Influence on Trade Patterns and Volumes. Most national trade policies have been reactive, a response to demands of the politically influential for insulation from globalization forces. But such policies usually damage interests in other countries. To prevent mutually

SHIPPING. Cargo vessel in the Lower Columbia River, Oregon, 1999. (© G. Braasch/Woodfin Camp and Associates, New York)

harmful trade policy wars between sovereign states, various international institutions have been created. Their success in the second half of the twentieth century is apparent in the burgeoning of trade.

The larger continental European countries, France, Germany, and Spain, declined to follow Great Britain's free trade policy, with the shrunken agricultural sector that implied. Instead, to offset falling transport costs, they raised tariff barriers against imports that could also be produced at home. As later industrializers, these countries' agriculturalists retained sufficient political power to resist the flood of produce from the regions newly settled by migrants from Europe. Established interests would have lost out—or believed they would have—from greater openness to trade. Prussian Junkers and French peasants envisaged the prices of their farm produce falling, the former suffering declining rent rolls and the latter being forced to migrate to the cities in search of alternative work, and did not relish the prospects.

The international political legacy of World War I was instability. The Austro-Hungarian, Turkish, and Russian Empires were dismembered, and the 1919 Versailles treaty exacerbated currency volatility and international distrust. These sources of instability were reflected in more aggressive and uncooperative trade-reducing policies, compared with the generally mild protectionism before World War I.

The unconditional most-favored nation (MFN) clause in commercial treaties exemplified cooperative international economic relations. The contracting parties were bound to accord each other the same treatment as given or might be given to the nation that was most favorably treated by all. Already, the introduction of maximum and minimum tariffs and finer classifications of traded products were undermining the effectiveness of the clause as a liberalizing device. Then in 1918, France renounced all treaties containing MFN clauses and instituted the principle of reciprocity in 1919 for all future treaties. The United States declared that its own tariffs were autonomous while demanding MFN status with other countries: the United States would make no tariff-reduction concessions but expected to be granted those negotiated between other nations. In short, the United States, by now matching Great Britain's share of world trade, tried to gain a free ride on the liberal economic order.

This stance contributed to stagnation of trade and to the difficulties of export industries between the wars. Under the aegis of the League of Nations (which the United States declined to join), the World Economic Conference of 1927 achieved a detailed multilateral trade agreement signed by the principal trading nations, in many respects a precursor of the 1947 General Agreement on Tariffs and Trade (GATT). But any prospect of a beneficial impact was soon destroyed by the world Depression that began in 1929. Failure of multilateralism was finally acknowledged with the abandonment of the 1933 World Economic Conference.

As a consequence, during the 1930s preferential trading blocs flourished—the British Commonwealth, the French Empire, and German informal empire in central and southeastern Europe. The missing ingredient, present in the later 1940s, was U.S. willingness to adopt the role appropriate to its economic strength. Trade policies in the second half of the century differed, because after the Soviet blockade of Berlin in 1947, the United States assumed leadership of the non-Communist world and pressed for a multilateral liberal trading regime.

The fruits of this leadership was the GATT, designed to prevent trade conflicts and promote freer trade. Two major principles underpinned the agreement: the most-favored nation clause and bilateral bargaining over trade-barrier reductions in a series of "rounds." Before negotiations started, each member passed to all others a preliminary list of tariff-reduction concessions that each nation proposed to request. When negotiations began, they were to present a corresponding list of concessions they were prepared to grant. Negotiations would then take place between two or more countries.

U.S. leadership and the scope for reducing the high U.S. tariffs at first provided the drive for progress. By the mid-1950s, it was estimated that a net reduction in U.S. duties of 50 percent had been achieved since 1934 by tariff concessions alone, the greater part of which having been accomplished in the period after 1945.

The Kennedy Round of 1964–1967 reduced tariffs on industrial products by an average of 35 percent. The Tokyo Round, which concluded in 1979, adopted further gradual tariff reductions. But for the most part, it did not successfully attempt to address the trade consequences of industrial subsidies by permitting countervailing duties. The most ambitious attempt at multilateral trade liberalization, the eighth GATT round, began in Uruguay in 1986. The negotiations included services, agriculture, and the Multi-Fibre Arrangements (imposing quantitative restrictions on textile imports from newly industrializing countries). However, more players than ever before, in addition to complex linkages, reduced the chances of success.

In 1995, the newly formed World Trade Organization (WTO) took over the functions of the GATT, but now covered services and intellectual property as well. Members of this trade club agreed to abide by its rules or pay penalties. Much of the WTO's activities were concerned with avoiding the mutual damage that trade disputes cause by adjudication of these rules. One hundred ninety complaints had been notified since January 1995, thirty-two had been settled or were inactive, and twenty-two cases were active in March 2000.

International Cartels. The international trade regime established in 1947 tolerated transnational cartels and free trade areas or customs unions. A cartel can exploit monopoly power, even prohibiting supply, to achieve political ends, as well as to boost profits. Fuels in the short term are difficult to substitute. An economy entirely dependent on foreign sources for fuel imports is potentially vulnerable to political pressure if suppliers are sufficiently unified. Italy might have discovered this in 1935 when League of Nations oil sanctions were briefly considered to counter the invasion of Abyssinia, but it did not since oil sanctions were rejected.

In 1973, matters were different. The Organization of Petroleum Exporting Countries (OPEC) was founded in Baghdad in 1960 to unify and coordinate members' petroleum policies. OPEC's hour struck when the Arab-Israeli war of 1973 triggered a display of unity and determination to sever Western support for Israel by threatening an oil export embargo. Crude oil prices quadrupled, almost all oil-importing countries were obliged to transfer huge additional sums to oil exporters, which, for most importers, meant marked reductions in purchasing power.

A second oil shock in 1979, with the withdrawal of Iranian oil from international markets caused by the overthrow of the Shah, was less disruptive. The recently created International Energy Authority quelled the panic buying that had been so damaging during the first shock. Since then, higher oil prices have encouraged the development of higher cost fields, such as those in the North Sea, and more energy-efficient production and consumption technologies.

Customs Unions and Regional Trading Blocs. Free-trade areas and customs unions are forms of discrimination between members and nonmembers, and thus appear to contradict the MFN principle. They were nonetheless accepted as consistent with a cooperative international trade regime because they could be seen as moves in the direction of liberalization. This is more obvious for a free-trade area (FTA), such as the Latin American Free Trade Area, established in 1960, or the North American Free Trade Area (United States, Canada, and Mexico), which went into effect on 1 January 1994. An FTA is intended to reduce barriers between members and does not require members to standardize barriers against the rest of the world.

By contrast, a customs union, such as the European Union, is a group of countries among which there is free trade and a common tariff with the rest of the world. Harmonization of the external tariff can raise barriers higher against certain nonparticipants. Members of the European Union, descended from the Common Market of France, Germany, Italy, Belgium, the Netherlands, and Luxembourg formed in 1958, delegated their international economic relations to the union in Brussels. By the end of the century, the union included Greece and all of western Europe except Switzerland.

FTAs and customs unions have two opposed effects. The first is trade creation, whereby a country begins importing a good previously produced at home. This is benign as far as world resource utilization is concerned, implying that expensive domestic supplies have been replaced with cheaper partner-country imports. The second is trade diversion, whereby a country begins to import from a partner country goods or services that have a higher resource cost than those previously imported from the outside world. New Zealand dairy exports, after British entry to the European Community (EC) in 1973, were such a case; they were displaced in favor of higher resource-cost continental European imports.

An FTA or a customs union could therefore bring about an inefficient use of world resources if trade creation was less than trade diversion. In fact, EC trade creation was as much as four times greater than diversion. The stance of the 1947 international regime was warranted in this instance by the conventional cost-benefit analysis criterion; the gainers from trade creation could have compensated the losers from trade diversion and still have been better off. In this sense, society was better off.

[*See also* Air Transportation; Railroads; Road Transportation; *and* Water Transportation.]

BIBLIOGRAPHY

Foreman-Peck, James S. *A History of the World Economy International Economic Relations since 1850.* Hemel Hempstead, U.K., 1995.

Lindert, Peter H. "U.S. Foreign Trade and Trade Policy in the Twentieth Century." In *The Cambridge Economic History of the United States*, edited by Stanley L. Engerman and Robert E. Gallman, vol. 3. Cambridge, 2001.

Maddison, Angus. *Monitoring the World Economy, 1820–1992.* Paris, 1995.

Ohlin, Bertil. *Interregional and International Trade.* Rev. ed. Cambridge, Mass., 1933.

Wood, Adrian. *North-South Trade, Employment, and Inequality: Changing Fortunes in a Skill-Driven World.* Oxford, 1995.

JAMES FOREMAN-PECK

LOTTERIES. As a contest in which winning (or losing) tokens are drawn randomly from among those of all participants, a lottery involves pure chance. Games based on lotteries have long existed worldwide, providing entertainment for players and revenue for sponsors. Participation in lotteries has been just as controversial since ancient times. The Old Testament relates Moses' use of a lottery to allocate land. Jewish law permitted gambling but did not sanction the collection of gambling debts. Muslim law prohibits its adherents from gambling. The American Puritan minister Cotton Mather cited biblical references to the use of lots for determining God's will as evidence that using chance to determine the outcome of games would usurp the Lord's authority. Despite such injunctions, throughout much of human history, governments seeking resources have often sponsored lotteries. The Romans frequently used lotteries to fund public construction. In China, around 100 BCE, the Hun Dynasty developed Keno, a gambling game that combines lottery with bingo, and used the proceeds to finance such defense expenditures as the construction of the Great Wall. By the middle of the fifteenth century, private and public lotteries were being used in Europe to dispose of property and to fund the construction of such facilities as churches, ports, canals, chapels, and almshouses. By the second half of the sixteenth century, Florence, France, the Habsburg Netherlands, and England were all using lotteries to finance public obligations.

Lotteries in U.S. History. Early-seventeenth-century English lotteries financed settlements in colonial North America, beginning with the venture at Jamestown. Colonials soon used unregulated lotteries extensively. Inevitably, fraud accompanied this trend, forcing colonial governments to prohibt unauthorized lotteries. Harvard, Yale, Columbia, and Princeton Universities successfully sought legislative permission for lotteries to fund the construction of dormitories and other campus buildings, as did many other institutions. The unpopularity of taxes and the difficulty of collecting them also made voluntary lotteries an attractive alternative vehicle for colonial and other governments. During the American Revolution, states used lotteries to fund militias and to pay debts. After the war, growing interest in internal improvements led companies and governments to use lotteries to raise money for constructing such improvements. These lotteries typically were privately run, though legislatively chartered. Both private and public funds were raised, but usually the fundraising was for a worthy public goal. Typically, the lottery also raised money for a particular use and not for ongoing operating funds. Between 1790 and 1860, twenty-four states financed improvements with lottery revenues.

By 1820, recurrent fraud had reduced the popularity of lotteries. In 1823, the organizers of a Washington, D.C., lottery decamped with the proceeds before paying the winners; the Supreme Court found the District government responsible for paying the winner. Continued unease about activities deemed sinful by some reinforced discomfort with all forms of gambling. This concern has arisen throughout the history of gaming. Should the state regulate individual behavior deemed unhealthy for the society as a whole? What about behavior that had no ill consequences for the rest of society beyond harming the individual who undertook that behavior?

In societies with clear class distinctions, behavior that was acceptable for the upper classes could be unacceptable for the lower classes, either because the latter were deemed less able to police themselves or because their imitation of the upper classes threatened the social hierarchy. Gambling fell into both categories in many societies. Gambling could threaten the livelihood of the gambler's family

VENETIAN LOTTERY. *The Public Lottery*, painting by Gabriele Bella (1730–1799). (Galleria Querini Stampalia, Venice/Scala/Art Resource, NY)

and could turn entire families into paupers. The belief in hard work and saving as the best means of getting ahead financially was eroded when working men and women could gamble with their earnings; luck and not thrift might seem the best way to financial rewards. English common law did not prohibit gaming and gambling, but it did restrict such activities when they created social problems. In the United States, all but two states had prohibited gambling through lotteries by 1860.

At the end of Civil War, the defeated Confederate states faced extensive physical damage and few sources of public finance. Louisiana turned with spectacular success to a lottery after the state legislature authorized a private group to establish and run one that would be played regularly. Known as the Serpent, the Louisiana lottery attracted players from across the country, many of them subscribing through the U.S. mail. This lottery continued

until its charter expired in 1890. Although the charter was renewed, the financial inducements granted to the state legislators for renewal drew considerable unfavorable publicity. The federal government forbade the sale of lottery tickets by mail in 1895, effectively killing the Louisiana lottery. More than fifty years of state prohibition on gambling in general, except in Nevada, and lotteries in particular followed. The prohibition was not complete: betting on horse racing soon became legal in those states with large racing interests. A subset of the population continued to participate in illegal lotteries in the form of numbers games.

Modern Lotteries. In 1964, after a long era without legal numbers games, New Hampshire introduced a state lottery. Similar to the Louisiana Serpent in that it was an on-going game with weekly (later daily) drawings, this lottery differed from earlier state participation in that the state not only permitted the lottery and shared in its revenue, but also directly ran the game. The success of the New Hampshire lottery invited imitation. By 2001, thirty-eight states, the District of Columbia, Puerto Rico, and the Virgin Islands had established lotteries. Most earmarked proceeds from lotteries for specific activities. New Hampshire targeted education and education remains the most frequent beneficiary of state lotteries. Pennsylvania uses lottery funds for care of the elderly, another popular objective; parks, conservation, and the environment are frequent other stipulated uses for lottery funds. Selecting popular social causes to receive lottery proceeds muted objections from those who disapproved of state sponsored gambling; nevertheless, some states still put lottery revenues in their general funds.

The first modern U.S. state lotteries featured a simple numbers game, in which winners of a fixed prize are drawn by lots or tokens. Technology soon permitted, and the states' desire to increase revenue flow encouraged, the development of more interesting games. Lotto and scratch-off/instant-win varieties have been the most successful. Under lotto's parimutuel betting, the winners of the game share the total amount that is bet. To entice more play, lotto games typically turnover the jackpot if there is no winner; large jackpots and very low probabilities of winning typify lotto games. Administrative costs absorb about 10 percent of revenues and include commissions to retail outlets that sell lottery tickets, general administrative expenses, and advertising costs of 1 to 2 percent of revenues. The payout ratio to winners typically amounts to less than 50 percent of proceeds, leaving the typical state with about 40 percent of sales for its coffers.

In a major 1977 U.S. Department of Justice study of gambling, its authors surveyed more than seventeen hundred persons to determine the demographic characteristics of gamblers. Since then, household survey and other data have been used to profile lottery players, who are typically male, middle-aged, less well educated than nonplayers, and with a wide range of income; and low-income players usually spend a larger percent of income on lottery tickets than do higher-income persons. Only 10 percent of players account for roughly 50 percent of lottery revenues. These data led to concern that lotteries provide a regressive source of revenue funds to finance state expenditures. Per capita lottery sales in 2001 equaled $157, but ranged from $34 in Montana to more than $932 in Rhode Island. Net lottery income of $38.9 billion in fiscal 2001 amounted to about 1 percent of state revenues.

Government sponsorship of gambling is popular worldwide; and in 1998, lottery sales exceeded 126 billion USD. Mexico has a national lottery and all Canadian provinces do as well. About a hundred other countries, on all inhabited continents, sponsor lotteries. Spain continues the longest-running and largest government lottery, the annual *El Gordo*, and sponsors several other lotteries as well. Countries as varied as Albania and Australia, Indonesia and Poland sponsor lotteries. Sixty-three belong to the International Association of State Lotteries.

Economic and Social Issues. From a policy perspective, state lotteries raise public finance questions. Are lotteries an effective way to raise funds? Will revenues grow sufficiently to fund expanding needs, or has the market matured? Are the right people paying for state finance, or are lotteries more regressive than alternative forms of taxation? Lotteries also raise microeconomic welfare concerns. If such games of chance are primarily about entertainment, should governments have a (near) monopoly upon their provision? Do extensive economies of scale or scope imply greater efficiency with a single provider? If so, should the single provider be the state rather than a regulated private firm? If substantial externalities exist with gambling, does government provision more effectively internalize those external benefits and costs than a regulated private agency?

Whatever society's response to these concerns, state involvement in lotteries has generated major spillover benefits for economists in the data about who plays. These data allow empirical investigation of human behavior under risk. The limited results now available give pause to the assumption that humans seek to maximize the expected value of future income, suggesting that economists should continue to revise their microeconomic models.

[*See also* Gambling and Gambling Industry *and* Taxation, *subentry on* Taxation and Public Revenue.]

BIBLIOGRAPHY

Borg, Mary O., Paul M. Mason, and Stephen L. Shapiro. *The Economic Consequences of State Lotteries.* Westport, Conn., 1991.

Clotfelter, Charles T., and Philip J. Cook. *Selling Hope: State Lotteries in America.* Cambridge, Mass., 1989.

Clotfelter, Charles T., and Philip J. Cook. "On the Economics of State Lotteries." *Journal of Economic Perspectives* 4.4 (1990), 105–119.

Cook, Philip J., and Charles T. Clotfelter. "The Peculiar Scale Economies of Lotto." *The American Economic Review* 83.3 (1993), 634–643.

McGowan, Richard A. *State Lotteries and Legalized Gambling: Painless Revenue or Painful Mirage.* Westport, Conn., 1994.

McGowan, Richard A. *Government and the Transformation of the Gaming Industry.* Cheltenham, U.K., 2001.

United States Department of Justice, National Institute of Law Enforcement and Criminal Justice, Law Enforcement Assistance Administration. *The Development of the Law of Gambling: 1776–1976.* Washington, D.C., 1977.

ANN HARPER FENDER

LOW COUNTRIES [*This entry contains five subentries, on the economic history of the Low Countries before 1568, northern Netherlands between 1568 and 1815, northern*

Netherlands after 1815, the Dutch Empire, and southern Netherlands between 1585 and 1830.]

The Low Countries before 1568

The Low Countries, or Netherlands, were a cluster of principalities comprising the current-day territories of the kingdoms of the actual Netherlands and Belgium, the Grand Duchy of Luxembourg, and northern parts of the Republic of France.

Early Development. The economic advantages of their location near the North Sea and along the great rivers of the Rhine, Meuse (Maas), and Schelde (Escaut) had become evident as early as the Merovingian and Carolingian eras, from the seventh to the tenth centuries. During this period, the Frisians, inhabiting the coastal area between the Schelde and Weser rivers, were navigating to and trading with England and Scandinavia. In continental regions to the south, particularly in the Frankish towns of Paris, Trier (Treves), and Strasbourg, they were also selling eastern goods and luxuries that the Varangians had brought to the Baltic, particularly slaves; and they also traded in such local commodities as Rhenish wines, salt, grain, and Frisian or possibly Flemish cloths. The coastal town of Dorestad (now Wijk-bij-Duurstede, near Utrecht) was their most important port of trade, where even gold coins were minted.

During the latter part of this period, only a few of the Frisian seaports survived a series of disasters: a rise in sea level, the almost incessant Viking raids, and the dissolution of the Frankish empire. Some trading posts with better inland locations revived or emerged at the end of the ninth century: Tiel, Utrecht, Deventer, Staveren, and others along the Meuse river and the Flemish coast. Agricultural revival provided a complementary stimulus. Better tools and organization and, from the end of the tenth century, land reclamation by clearing and diking enabled production and population to grow (to more than thirty-five per square kilometer around 900 CE in northern France) and consequently allowed artisanal specialization. From Roman times, Flemish textiles had been famous. The adoption of the new foot-treadle horizontal loom during the eleventh century converted cloth weaving into a remunerative full-time job for men. Because of the contraction of sheep raising on the coastal plains, which had earlier been recovered from the sea for agriculture and human occupation, the Flemish increasingly sought to obtain wool from England. The excellent quality of many English wools and the superb dyeing of the fabrics (with kermes and brasilwood from the Mediterranean, and woad from Thuringia and Picardy), combined with technical and organizational skills, made Flemish and Artesian cloth a very highly esteemed commodity, which was sold all over the known world, certainly by 1200. From their markets abroad, the cloth merchants brought home needed raw materials, foodstuffs, and wine, which they eventually sold to foreign customers. Before 1300, towns in the neighboring duchy of Brabant succeeded in Flanders's wake in developing their own cloth export industry. During the late thirteenth and early fourteenth centuries, their international breakthrough was facilitated by recurrent political frictions between Flanders and England and particularly with France. Subsequently, during the fourteenth century, some new cloth industries developed in the towns of the Meuse region and in Hainaut and Holland.

In their search for Flemish cloths, foreign merchants flocked to Bruges and its outpost Damme, later Sluis. The goods that they conveyed to Bruges were more for regional consumption than for international trade. On the other hand, the trade conducted by Flemish merchants abroad was often hindered by legal measures there. However, the towns around the Zuider Zee and on the branches of the lower Rhine remained active in navigation and trade with northern and western Germany. Dinant continued to export its brass work to England, bringing back tin, and to Germany, where its merchants fetched copper ore. The traffic to and from Flanders along the waterways of Holland and land roads through Brabant animated the commerce of a string of towns in those regions. In particular, the towns of Dordrecht, dominating the estuaries of the Meuse and the Rhine and the access to the waterways of Holland, and Antwerp, on the Schelde estuary, controlling access to the North Sea, were incapable of weakening the commercial primacy of Bruges, not withstanding their sovereigns' support.

Most towns in the Low Countries had developed spontaneously, even though their lords had sought to foster their growth with various privileges. During the thirteenth century, for political and fiscal motives, lords great and small had tried to turn mere villages and newly created settlements into urban centers. At the same time, they also felt compelled to reduce the financial and juridical burdens on the peasants, or else risk seeing them depart. In return for more freedom, the peasants paid an all-inclusive indemnity or an annual quit-rent. As the bonds between peasants and land loosened, landowners found it more attractive to lease or farm their possessions on a temporary basis, partly for cash. Hence they could adapt the rents to rising prices and replace the fixed deliveries in kind from tenants with diversified purchases acquired from urban markets. The peasants, on the other hand, were driven toward a commercialized agriculture with industrial and other cash crops. By 1300, such a progressive agriculture, which often ignored the traditional three-course rotations (i.e., with multiple rotations, to reduce the fallow), was operative around the larger towns in Artois, Flanders, and Brabant.

Intensive husbandry was the more imperative since the dimensions of most farms were modest, as a result of liberalized inheritance laws and a freer market for land. Supplementary manure was furnished by trash collected in the towns and by dung from cattle breeding, in which a farmer and an investor were often the participants. Many small farmers also sought an additional income by spinning for urban clothmakers or by working with home-grown flax.

Economic integration between towns and countryside occurred fully, however, only around the estuaries of the great rivers. The core lands of Flanders, Brabant, Zeeland, Holland, and, to a lesser degree, Hainaut, were densely populated (forty to seventy-eight persons per square kilometer), with several big cities, about half of which were active in cloth manufacturing. The regions in the periphery, less populated and with fewer and smaller towns, lived by a more traditional agricultural economy, with cattle breeding.

Changes in the Cloth Industry. During the later Middle Ages, cloth manufacturing, the economic pillar of the Low Countries, suffered several severe setbacks. New producers within and without the Low Countries competed for a shrinking market, with depopulation in Europe and changes in fashion. From the 1290s on, ubiquitous wars increased transaction costs of international trade in cheap, light textiles to Mediterranean markets, thereby favoring local producers, while forcing producers in the Low Countries to specialize more and more in very high-quality, expensive woolens, which could literally "bear the freight" of rising transport and transactions costs. But such woolens were necessarily made exclusively from the very fine, short-stapled English wools. The growing demand for English wool made that raw material relatively more scarce and expensive, all the more so when, at the outset of the Hundred Years' War in the 1330s, the English Crown began to burden wool exports with increasingly heavy export taxes (from 33 percent, finally rising to almost 50 percent), and then, from 1363 on, subjected the wool trade to the cartel of the Calais Staple Company, in order to pass the tax incidence more fully onto foreign buyers. At the same time, the Crown imposed (from 1347 on) only very light duties on exports of domestically produced woolens (about 2 percent), thus giving English clothiers an unintended export advantage. In the Low Countries, the tax-burdened English wools were accounting for as much as 70 percent of manufacturing costs by the later fourteenth century.

Reducing the value-added production costs was a difficult task in the traditional cloth-making towns because the craft guilds, following their triumph over the merchant-dominated town governments, at the Battle of Kortrijk in 1302, had imposed even more stringent manufacturing regulations. To be sure, such regulations could be justified as measures needed to maintain the confidence of their European customers in the certified quality of their woolens. However, their increasingly elaborated stipulations for standardized-quality products inhibited the adoption of labor-saving innovations and a simplification of the production process. Of course, the craft guilds also resisted any reduction of wages; and in any event, the prevailing monetary stability from the 1390s on eliminated any prior gains from wage stickiness during inflationary periods. So the old cloth towns had no option but to concentrate more and more exclusively on very expensive woolens designed for markets composed of the wealthy few, with very inelastic demand, woolens whose high quality was attested by civic inspectors who affixed the requisite lead seals.

Smaller and younger centers were less burdened by such industrial structures, regulations, high wages, and taxes. Initially, in Flanders, after their victory at Kortrijk, the craft guilds used their power in the governments of the larger towns in attempts to prevent competition from small-town and village draperies, especially those that sought to imitate their high-quality woolens. However, when the counts and then the Burgundian dukes refrained from so willingly supporting the economic imperialism of the large towns, the smaller "nouvelles draperies" began to thrive, and for a while succeeded in resisting the competition from both the large towns and the English cloth trade by producing cheaper cloths of reasonably good quality. Woven from much cheaper English and Scottish wools, and finally, by the early fifteenth century, from Spanish merino or mixed Spanish and English wools, these cloths were designed to be sold in chiefly middle-class markets, at home and abroad. From the 1430s, however, when the Crown subjected English wool exports to even harsher fiscal exactions at Calais, the cost advantages of English cloth production and then conflicts with England and the German Hanse hit both the old and new draperies badly. Dutch cloth making (especially in Leiden) survived much longer, into the 1520s, thanks especially to the aggressive Dutch merchant marine, which displaced much of the Hanseatic commerce in the Baltic by the late fifteenth century.

During the fourteenth century, some other villages in Flanders and Brabant were either compelled or were content to restrict their industrial activities to the production of worsteds, made from very coarse, long stapled wools, or mixed woolen-worsted fabrics, known as says or serges. From the mid- to late fifteenth century, when international market conditions once again favored a long-distance trade in cheap, light textiles, these rural *sayetteries* began to expand. Enjoying advantages of low taxes, low-cost rural labor, simple production techniques, and cheaper capital, they evidently also benefited from the plight of the once-prominent woolen draperies by attracting away commercial capital. Furthermore, they took advantage of the rapid growth of the Brabant fairs (Antwerp), from the 1460s, to have large volumes of their cheap says and serges marketed to Italy and other Mediterranean regions. Nevertheless, during the sixteenth century (at least to the outbreak of revolt, in 1568) none was as successful as the Flemish hamlet of Hondschoote, which had also been the leading say-exporter to similar markets in the thirteenth century.

Cloth manufacturing towns in the Low Countries never really turned to linen weaving, though many villages did engage in linen production, if only for local consumption. By 1400, the linens of Hainaut and somewhat later those of Flanders did become a fairly important export commodity. Nearby towns functioned as regional markets, centers of bleaching, and producers of finer linens. The linen industry, however, was a poor substitute for cloth making, because linen was so much cheaper a commodity than woolen cloth. Thus tapestry work flowered in Arras and Lille, during the fourteenth century, and soon thereafter in many Flemish and Brabantine towns. In the following centuries, the districts around Enghien and Oudenaarde produced a less sophisticated sort of work, the so-called verdures. Much greater success was achieved, once more, in producing other, much higher-valued fabrics. Tapestry, other artistic products, and fashionable mercery for internal consumption and for the international markets of Bruges and the fairs of Antwerp and Bergen-op-Zoom set to work many skilled craftsmen in the towns. The Brabant fairs also welcomed the English woolens that had long been banned from Flanders (since at least c. 1360); and most of them were dyed, shorn, and finished at Antwerp itself, to be resold to German merchants, who purchased them with silver and copper, the products of the central European mining boom, from the 1460s. In turn, the Portuguese, having established their staple in East Indian spices at Antwerp in 1501, sought these metals to conduct their trade with both Africa and Asia.

Further Growth and Integration. The high standard of living in the great towns spurred agriculture and cattle breeding so that Wüstungen (deserted villages) were practically unknown. The wars with France and the revolts of Flanders and Brabant in the late fifteenth century led to a general crisis and ensured the final decline of Bruges. Antwerp, which had remained neutral during the revolts, now fully established itself as a permanent international market. Its merchants and its capital were actively involved in several industrial sectors over the whole of the southern Netherlands. At the same time, however, economies of scale in both industry and commerce, along with other financial advantages of this burgeoning metropolis, did injure the economies of many minor urban centers.

The economic growth of the northern provinces had not been so affected by the political crises of the late fifteenth century. The Dutch herring fisheries, aided by the adoption of onboard salt curing, around 1400, had suffered much less from the French conflicts. Well before 1500, Dutch ships were carrying North Sea herring into the Baltic, whereas German exports of Scania (Swedish) herring had stagnated, certainly by the 1430s. In their Baltic commerce, the Dutch towns enjoyed favorable terms of trade, importing relatively cheap grain and exporting more highly valued meat, dairy, fish, and woolen textiles. Lower wages and the growth of their merchant marine allowed the towns of Holland and Zeeland to become predominant in the carrying trades along the western European coast, especially in bulk goods, and strengthened the bargaining position of the Dutch traders on the Baltic markets. In their return cargoes from the Baltic, grains soon gained ascendancy because the growing western European population in the inflationary sixteenth century was switching from French wheat to Prussian-Polish rye. Amsterdam became the main market for this grain trade, exporting much of it abroad.

By about 1550, the Netherlands had achieved one of the most highly developed European economies, integrated both internally and internationally. The per capita value of its imports was almost five times greater than in France or England. Almost half were in foodstuffs; a quarter in raw materials; and about 30 percent in textiles. About a quarter of the exports consisted of native fabrics, mostly textiles; most of the rest were foreign commodities in transit. Furthermore, the role of the industrial sector was enhanced by its "value-added" processing of imports—the most notable example being cloth finishing in Antwerp. Profits from Antwerp loans abroad and from Dutch shipping services compensated for the negative balance of trade in the commodities account.

BIBLIOGRAPHY

Blockmans, Wim. "The Economic Expansion of Holland and Zeeland in the Fourteenth-Sixteenth Centuries." In *Studia Historica Oeconomica: Liber Amicorum Herman van der Wee*, edited by Erik Aerts et al., pp. 41–58. Louvain, 1993.

Brulez, Wilfried. "The Balance of Trade of the Netherlands in the Middle of the Sixteenth Century." *Acta Historiae Neerlandica* 4 (1970), 20–48.

Brulez, Wilfried. "Brugge en Antwerpen in de 15de en 16de eeuw: Een tegenstelling?" *Tijdschrift voor Geschiedenis* 83 (1970), 15–37.

De Vries, Jan. *The Dutch Rural Economy in the Golden Age, 1500–1700.* New Haven, 1974.

De Vries, Jan, and Ad van der Woude. *The First Modern Economy: Success, Failure and Perseverance of the Dutch Economy, 1500–1815.* Cambridge, 1997.

Jappe Alberts, Wybe, and Hubertus P. H. Jansen. *Welvaart in Wording: Sociaal-economische geschiedenis van Nederland van de vroegste tijden tot het einde van de Middeleeuwen.* The Hague, 1975.

Munro, John H. *Textiles, Towns and Trade: Essays in the Economic History of Late-Medieval England and the Low Countries.* Variorum Collected Studies Series: CS 442. Aldershot, U.K., 1994.

Van der Wee, Herman. *The Growth of the Antwerp Market and the European Economy (Fourteenth–Sixteenth Centuries).* 3 vols. Louvain and The Hague, 1963.

Van Houtte, Jan A. *An Economic History of the Low Countries, 800–1800.* London, 1977.

Van Uytven, Raymond. *Production and Consumption in the Low Countries, Thirteenth–Sixteenth Centuries.* Variorum Collected Studies Series: CS 714. Aldershot, U.K., 2001.

Verhulst, Adriaan. *Rural and Urban Aspects of Early Medieval Northwest Europe.* Variorum Collected Studies Series: CS 385. Aldershot, U.K., 1992.

RAYMOND VAN UYTVEN

Northern Netherlands between 1568 and 1815

To a large degree the economic history of the early modern northern Netherlands was in line with that of northwestern Europe in general. Like its immediate neighbors, the Dutch Republic (1579–1795) was commercialized and monetized with an advanced agricultural sector and a high level of urbanization. Yet during the first three-quarters of the seventeenth century, the new republic's economic characteristics came to exceed regional levels. This period is commonly labeled the Dutch Golden Age. After a rapid economic growth (c. 1580–1620), the northern Netherlands even developed into the center of seventeenth-century world trade. A relative decline set in during the last decades of the seventeenth century, and its eighteenth-century economic performance lost much of its former exceptionalism. However, around 1800 the Dutch still enjoyed a remarkably high income per capita. In that respect only rapidly industrializing Britain was its equal.

The Economic Miracle of the Seventeenth Century. The Dutch Republic's rapid economic growth in the early seventeenth century is generally acknowledged as exceptional. Within a few decades, with hardly any mineral resources at hand and despite its restricted territory and population (about 25,000 square kilometers and about 2 million inhabitants), the northern Netherlands developed into one of the world's leading economies. Because the growth occurred in several economic sectors simultaneously, while several powerful internal backward and forward linkages existed, the northern Netherlands were even labeled "the first modern economy" by Jan de Vries and Ad van der Woude (1997). In explaining this economic miracle, external and internal factors emerge. External factors were, above all, the international state system, the influx of refugees from the southern Netherlands, and new opportunities in foreign trade. Political independence was achieved after the Holland and Zealand towns revolted against the Spanish Empire in the 1570s. Following a long and costly war (1568–1648), the free territory of the United Provinces was finally recognized as part of the international state system. In the course of this era of protracted warfare, large numbers of skilled and wealthy refugees from the southern Netherlands came to settle in the north. As the Flemish and Brabantine economy was highly advanced in the sixteenth century, this migration undoubtedly added to the Dutch economic successes in the early seventeenth century. Another external factor that gave the new republic exceptional opportunities was structural change in European international trade. During the sixteenth century more and more goods were shipped by sea instead of overland. The northern Netherlands were favorably located in among the main trade routes along the coasts of Europe. Moreover with the growing demand in the Mediterranean for grain, the Dutch reaped rich profits from their extended fleet and advanced shipping based on their strong tradition in fisheries and their existing commercial dominance in the Baltic.

Yet no full explanation of the rapid growth of the republic can focus on external aspects alone. Internal factors also contributed. Political independence was one thing, but the construction of a state apparatus that proved extremely favorable to economic growth was another. Refugees could choose to go to London or Hamburg, yet Amsterdam and Middelburg were more appealing. The geographical location entailed a strong internal element as well. The general trend in commercialization in the region of northwestern Europe, which dated from the High Middle Ages, had also pulled the northern Netherlands along. The economic networks of Flemish or Brabant towns like Bruges, Ghent, and Antwerp, next to those of the North German Hansa, had fostered a prospering agriculture and trade connections at both sides of the Channel. Along the Rhine and Meuse Rivers, links existed with the (German) territories inland, stretching up to Northern Italy and the Mediterranean. Dutch towns were thus able to reap from these regional stimuli, the more so as many had access to waterborne transportation, which lowered the costs of transportation.

Much of the land was marshy, and mineral resources were few indeed. Yet the material conditions were less poor, as one would expect at first glance. While much of the land was unsuitable for arable farming, this condition forced farmers to specialize (above all in dairies and horticulture) and to engage in seasonal occupations in shipping and industry, which raised the level of productivity significantly. Second, the flat landscape ensured the availability of a cheap energy source, wind. This allowed a wide application of windmills and sailing vessels inland. Third, the marshy grounds yielded another cheap source of energy, peat. Even though the exploitation of turf may have been less spectacular than some calculations assumed, the fact remains that Dutch households, breweries, distilleries, salt refineries, dye works, and bakeries profited greatly from this abundant heating source. Finally, the numerous rivers and canals created an outstanding distribution network not only for agricultural and industrial goods but also for peat and seasonal labor forces.

Another geographical factor that favored commercialization was the existence of numerous towns. Around 1600 the northern Netherlands undoubtedly were among the most urbanized areas in the world. About 35 to 40 percent of the population lived in towns. The demand exerted by these urban dwellers contributed significantly to the general level of specialization, both in industry and in agriculture. The overall level of literacy was impressive, which stimulated, among other things, the application of the newest technologies. The spread of "useful knowledge" was furthered by the fact that the northern Netherlands became a leading production and distribution center of books, pamphlets, and newspapers. Numerous skilled refugees from the south raised the level of applied technologies, too.

Throughout the seventeenth century, the northern Netherlands remained a net immigration country. Dutch wages were high by comparison with neighboring countries. As many arrived in their prime, these migrants raised the general standards of productivity again. Although the costs of living were quite elevated, not least because of the many excise taxes on necessities, the overall standard of living was impressive and in fact unequaled in the early modern period. Subsistence crises, common in most of Europe, had only a limited influence in the Dutch Republic. The wide economic opportunities and the regular grain shipments from the Baltic undoubtedly added to the general level of prosperity. All along most towns extended their numbers during the Golden Age, in particular in the area now known as the Randstad (including Amsterdam, Rotterdam, the Hague, and Utrecht). The urbanization accounted for another characteristic trait of the Dutch Republic. As political power was dispersed among numerous municipal elites, a fragmented state structure emerged. The federation allowed the flowering of several economic systems next to each other, one dominated by artisans and guilds, another favoring large-scale capitalist structures, a cottage economy with peasants, and polders with market-oriented farmers. In this typical merchant capitalist setting, urban governments had the opportunity to support those industrial systems they thought most appropriate.

With its relative freedom of religious worship, this fragmented setting favored the settlement of several refugee entrepreneurs (Calvinists, Portuguese Jews, and Huguenots). The political independence of the Dutch Republic, however, had its costs, including an enormous burden of war, high taxes, and a rising public debt. Yet most of the actual warfare was confined to the republic's borderlands, whereas the financial incidence of war rested ultimately upon the most commercialized and urbanized regions. A fiscal regime that emphasized taxes on consumption and trade secured a steady stream of public revenue, and this in turn supported a large and carefully managed public debt. A multitude of bonds provided a safe and favored opportunity to invest savings. As a result the interest rates on public loans descended to a mere 4 and 3.5 percent. All in all, as direct taxes were restricted and duties on international trade were low, the interests of Dutch merchants and entrepreneurs were safeguarded. Although the juridical system remained based in large part on customary law, it offered effective protection to property rights. In addition the currency was stabilized, and a full-fledged patent system was developed. This resulted in auspicious conditions for enterprising individuals, in particular in comparison with the more homogeneous and absolutist regimes of some neighboring countries.

Building on the established overseas trade of the Holland, Zealand, and Friesian shippers (who had specialized in the transport of bulky goods like herring, wood, salt, beer, and grain), the merchants of the new republic extended the networks to include international trade in luxuries and colonial goods. Above all the Dutch East India Company, established in 1602, proved an enormous success. Within two decades the company managed to drive both the Portuguese and the English from several trading posts in the Far East. The Dutch-Asian venture (the first permanent joint-stock enterprise in history) established a monopsony in fine spices and developed a highly rewarding trade within the East Asian seas that stretched from Persia to Japan.

The republic's growing overseas trade developed many strong links to domestic industrial production. Existing trade-oriented branches were boosted, for example, ship wharves, salt refineries, and the production of ropes, sails, casks, and barrels. New industries sprang up as well, sugar, dye works, and silk, to mention a few. Technologies and capital goods were exported, like ribbon mills, sawing machines, and sugar refineries. The arts (paintings, engravings, books, and furniture) profited from the rise of a mass market in luxuries. The accumulated funds were used in some large-scale operations, like canal construction and polders, which stimulated the farming sector.

All these links between producers and consumers, both foreign and domestic, were supported by a rather efficient service sector. These networks concentrated in the larger towns, especially in Amsterdam. There the Bank of Amsterdam (1609) constituted a platform for clearances among the major merchants. The Bourse, dating from 1611, profited from the existence of printed price lists and numerous newspapers. Shipping and insurance companies bloomed. Next to the more reliable trade in grain and beer, the rise of colonial enterprises, the exploitation of new peateries in the peripheral provinces, and the reclaiming

DELFT. View from across the Rotterdam Canal, painting by Jan Vermeer (1632–1675). (Mauritshuis, The Hague/Scala/Art Resource, NY)

of lands (particularly from the manifold peat lakes in the west) offered prospects of spectacular profits. All in all the Amsterdam community offered the merchant a great variety of options and the best information available as to cargoes, trade routes, markets, prices, funds, and risks.

To summarize, the exceptional performance of the seventeenth-century Dutch economy was based on a peculiar set of both external and internal factors. Each of these factors individually was not unique to the Dutch case. In fact not all Dutch institutions were the most "modern" of their kind. Some industries in Northern Italy were more advanced in technological respects, while Antwerp's achievements in banking were still unparalleled. Yet the combination and concentration of several favorable elements were peculiar for the seventeenth century in a Dutch Republic relatively free from (civil) war disturbances, while a most fertile soil had been prepared in a previous process of commercialization and urbanization.

The Languishing Economy in the Eighteenth Century. Yet like all economic miracles, this one stagnated and

halted. As foreign economic competition matured and Dutch exports declined, the home market of the northern Netherlands on its own was unable to sustain the productivity growth of the seventeenth century. Over time important parts of the international trade found they could dispense with the services of the Amsterdam trading network. In the maritime provinces, a process of deurbanization was noted as the percentage of the population living in towns fell. The number of people on poor relief increased. A new class arose, mainly consisting of middlemen in banking and trade whose main interests concentrated on foreign investments and on living as rentiers. Unlike in Great Britain, the available capital was not applied toward the development of new industries and technologies. The northern Netherlands achieved the status of an industrialized nation only by the end of the nineteenth century, much later than most of its neighbors.

In debating the slow transition to industrialization, historians have stressed the absence of mineral resources, the insipid mentality of Dutch capital owners, the increasing gap between science and industry, the decline of the distribution network (in particular, the canal system connecting the main cities), and the higher costs of energy (as the nearby "low-peat" areas were exhausted, the more distant

◀ NETHERLANDS. Engraving by Jodocus Hondius, 1611. (Geography and Maps Division, Library of Congress)

"high-peat" regions required more investments, and imports of coal were more expensive). The political institutions were quite restrictive for economic development as well. During the seventeenth century the decentralized state profited from the political turmoil elsewhere and from the weaknesses of its competitors. Above all the low tariffs boosted Dutch international trade. Yet in the eighteenth century, the northern Netherlands failed to adapt its policies to the powerful mercantilist and protectionist policies of the centralized monarchies. Although the Dutch public debt was still managed well, the fragmented and petrified political system prevented an effective reorganization of the navy and fiscal and tariff reform.

Still, the decline was more relative than absolute. Some sectors of the Dutch economy proved remarkably resilient. While much of the maritime Netherlands suffered from the decline of the urban trade networks, the economy inland showed an upward trend. Even though the international decline in grain prices beginning in the 1660s hurt Dutch farmers severely, agriculture recuperated. By the end of the eighteenth century, stimulated by a growing foreign demand, this sector yielded extraordinary outputs, rendering the northern Netherlands a net exporter of agricultural produce. And while much of the overseas trade was taken over by foreign competitors, the demand in the German territories increased, which caused the Rotterdam distribution sector to grow. Colonial trade emerged to drive the republic's eighteenth-century commercial sector. Imports and reexports of coffee, tea, tobacco, sugar, and cacao increased. In the Far East, the British surpassed the Dutch only after the 1780s. Furthermore, the Amsterdam financial market continued to enjoy a strong international reputation up to the last decades of the eighteenth century.

In the industrial sector, while many breweries and urban textiles languished, cotton printing, faience, and the pipe industry made fresh and successful starts. Much industry continued in windmills, in particular in the Zaanstreek (the region north of Amsterdam). In the inland countryside, rural textiles and paper mills flourished. Differing from the industrial development in Great Britain, though, Dutch industry remained essentially small-scale, as no steam power was applied.

Most distressing were the war years following the French invasion of 1795, which replaced the Dutch Republic with a succession of political regimes dependent on France. The ensuing economic blockades, in particular after 1806, brought numerous branches in fisheries, trade, and industry to a complete standstill. Agriculture managed to continue with its prosperous development, yet all colonial connections were broken. In some towns the number of persons on poor relief increased to 30 percent. However, by 1815, when a newly established centralized monarchy restored the independence of the Netherlands,

the Dutch were still counted among the wealthiest people of the world. Despite the economic crisis during the period of French occupation, several typical early modern characteristics endured. The extended service sector, a stable currency, the economic predominance of the Randstad region, a highly variegated production, high taxes, and a high per capita income continued at least to the twentieth century.

[*See also* Amsterdam.]

BIBLIOGRAPHY

Davids, Karel, and Jan Lucassen, eds. *A Miracle Mirrored: The Dutch Republic in European Perspective*. Cambridge, 1995.

Davids, Karel, and Leo Noordegraaf, eds. *The Dutch Economy in the Golden Age*. Amsterdam, 1993.

Israel, J. I. *Dutch Primacy in World Trade, 1585–1740*. Oxford, 1989.

Riley, J. C. *International Government Finance and the Amsterdam Capital Market, 1740–1815*. Cambridge, 1980.

'T Hart, Marjolein, Joost Jonker, and Jan Luiten van Zanden, eds. *A Financial History of the Netherlands*. Cambridge, 1997.

Van Zanden, Jan Luiten. *The Rise and Decline of Holland's Economy: Merchant Capitalism and the Labour Market*. Manchester, 1993.

Vries, Jan de, and Ad van der Woude. *The First Modern Economy: Success, Failure, and Perseverance of the Dutch Economy, 1500–1815*. Cambridge, 1997.

MARJOLEIN 'T HART

Northern Netherlands after 1815

The retarded industrialization of the northern Netherlands has long been the focus of much of the literature on economic history after 1815. Why did this highly developed, urban market economy adopt the new techniques of the British Industrial Revolution so slowly that it was surpassed economically by its neighbors? Recent research confirms that modern industrialization was launched no earlier than the 1860s. In the 1820s and 1830s, economic growth was rather satisfactory although mainly founded on the performance of agriculture (exports to Britain), international services (based on the exploitation of Java), and a narrow range of related industries (Van Zanden and Van Riel, 2000). High levels of wages, indirect taxes, prices of consumer goods, and labor productivity in agriculture have been identified as major sources of the retarded industrialization (Mokyr, 1976; Griffiths, 1979). A more recent interpretation in the tradition of Mancur Olson stresses that it was the result of the slow transformation of the Dutch institutional structure, which had become fossilized during the eighteenth century and was unable to modernize quickly during the first half of the nineteenth century. In addition, the misguided economic and financial policies of King William I played a role (Van Zanden and Van Riel, 2000). Before 1860, the structure of the economy remained more or less the same (that is, the share of agriculture in the GDP even rose relative to the share of industry), urbanization stagnated, and real wages were at best constant (Smits et al., 2000).

After a number of changes in the country's political economy during the 1840s and 1850s, the economy, especially the industrial sector, accelerated during the 1860s and 1870s. The features of this moderate spurt were the sharp rise of the use of steam engines combined with the spread of the factory system, notably in textiles (Lintsen et al., 1992). After 1875, the agricultural sector was confronted with falling prices and went into a sharp depression. Both forces triggered a renewed process of structural transformation of the economy. Urbanization revived, and nominal and real wages started to rise for the first time since the seventeenth century. The 1880s and 1890s saw a further renewal of the economic structure. For example, new companies, such as Philips in electronics and Royal Dutch Petroleum, profited from the new technologies of the "Second Industrial Revolution." At the same time, the agricultural sector was thoroughly reorganized. Better education facilities and research stations were established, and extension services and cooperatives improved the marketing system and the capital market on the countryside. Also, the links of industry and finance with the main colony, Indonesia, were strengthened as a result of the growth of private investment in the colony's plantation sector and mining industry (Lindblad, 1996).

The structural renewal of the economy in the final decades of the nineteenth century and the first decades of the twentieth century formed the basis for more rapid economic growth after 1913. Between 1815 and 1913, GDP per capita increased by almost 1 percent annually. Between 1913 and 1998, it rose to almost 2 percent in spite of sharp contractions during the 1930s, World War II, and a slowdown of growth after 1973. The Netherlands profited from its neutrality during World War I, but the real acceleration of growth occurred during the 1920s (Van Ark and De Jong, 1996). Industrial exports had been small during the nineteenth century, when they were dominated by agricultural products and international services. In the 1920s, industrial exports began to take off, although they were confronted increasingly by protectionist tendencies elsewhere. International protectionism intensified during the 1930s, explaining why the Netherlands was so heavily affected by the Great Depression. Another contributor to the depression's severity was the government's resolve to defend the gold standard, which made Dutch exports relatively expensive and forced the government to carry out measures aimed at lowering the budget deficit and the internal price level. As a result, recovery from the depression did not begin until September 1936, when the government finally decided to devalue (Van Zanden, 1996). During World War II and the German occupation, the economy was hit hard, although recent studies show that the decline during these years was probably less than the official statistics show (Klemann, 2000).

After 1945, the government was forced to cope with an economy that had contracted sharply and a money supply that had expanded enormously as a result of German extractions but also with the loss of its most valuable colony, Indonesia (whose independence was proclaimed in 1945 but was not recognized until 1949). Yet the reconstruction of the economy was rapid. In 1949, the prewar levels of GDP per capita were surpassed. This high growth regime continued after reconstruction was complete. Exports expanded rapidly, supported by the gradual liberalization of international (and especially intra-European) trade and by domestic policies to monitor wage increases. Investment boomed, and unemployment, which had been a persistent problem during the 1930s, quickly disappeared. During the 1960s, after the liberalization of wage policies, the economy became overheated. Real wages grew more than labor productivity, profits and real share prices fell, and at the same time, responding to forces of a political nature, welfare spending and related taxation exploded. A sharply rising inflation (up to more than 10 percent in the early 1970s) was another feature of this process of overshooting (Van Ark, De Haan, and De Jong, 1996; Van Zanden, 2000).

An economy weakened by these developments (which, for example, resulted in unfavorable changes in the financial structures of industry and the government), was confronted in the early 1970s with the disintegration of the international monetary system (which led to the rise of its real effective exchange rate) and a sudden change in expectations following the oil price hike of 1973. Between 1973 and the mid-1980s, unemployment increased enormously (but policy-induced changes in definitions make it difficult to quantify this exactly), mainly as a result of the decline of employment in the industrial sector, which had generated most of the new employment during the 1950s and the early 1960s. A financial crisis resulted, as expenditure on social transfers continued to grow and the tax base eroded (the generous incomes from natural gas were unable to compensate). After 1982, effective policies were developed to deal with both the budget deficit and high unemployment. Wage restraint, based on cooperation between unions and employers' organizations, again played a role in the attempt to make the Dutch economy more competitive internationally. Stringent budget cuts slowly started a gradual decline in the real public debt. After 1985, the economy began to do well again, based almost entirely on a rapid expansion of employment in services and fueled by the growing participation of women in the labor market, previously low. Agriculture, with less than 5 percent of employment, continued to make a major contribution to exports. In 1998, the government budget showed a surplus for the first time in decades, and unemployment, according to the official figures, was down to about 4 percent.

BIBLIOGRAPHY

Griffiths, Richard T. *Industrial Retardation in the Netherlands, 1830–1850*. Den Haag, The Netherlands, 1979.

Klemann, H. A. M. *Nederland, 1938–1948*. Amsterdam, 2002.

Lindblad, J. Thomas. "The Economic Relationship between the Netherlands and Colonial Indonesia, 1870–1940." In *The Economic Development of the Netherlands since 1870*, edited by Jan Luiten van Zanden, pp. 109–119. Cheltenham, U.K., 1996.

Lintsen, Harry W., et al., eds. *Geschiedenis van de techniek in Nederland*. Zutphen, Netherlands, 1992.

Mokyr, Joel. *Industrialization in the Low Countries, 1795–1850*. New Haven, 1976.

Smits, Jan-Pieter, Edwin Horlings, and Jan Luiten van Zanden. *Dutch GNP and Its Components, 1800–1913*. Groningen, Netherlands, 2002.

Van Ark, Bart, and Herman de Jong. "Accounting for Economic Growth in the Netherlands since 1913." *Economic and Social History in the Netherlands* 7 (1996), 199–242.

Van Ark, Bart, Henk de Haan, and Herman de Jong. "Characteristics of Economic Growth in the Netherlands during the Postwar Period." In *Economic Growth in Europe since 1945*, edited by N. Crafts and G. Toniolo, pp. 290–328. Cambridge, 1996.

Van Zanden, Jan Luiten. "The Dance Round the Gold Standard: Economic Policy during the Depression of the 1930s." In *The Economic Development of the Netherlands since 1870*, pp. 120–137. Cheltenham, U.K., 1996.

Van Zanden, Jan Luiten. *The Economic History of the Netherlands, 1914–1995*. London, 1998.

Van Zanden, Jan Luiten. "Post-War European Economic Development as an Out of Equilibrium Growth Path: The Case of the Netherlands." *Economist* 148 (2000), 539–555.

Van Zanden, Jan Luiten, and Arthur van Riel. *Nederland 1780–1914: Staat, instituties en economische ontwikkeling*. Amsterdam, 2000.

JAN LUITEN VAN ZANDEN

Dutch Empire

The origins of the Dutch maritime expansion beyond Europe were not economic but political. After the 1580s, the Dutch struggled to establish themselves as a republic—free from the domination of their Habsburg monarch, the king of Spain and, from 1580 to 1640, of Portugal. After 1590, the war of independence from Spain had reached a stalemate in Europe and was transferred to non-European areas, where Dutch merchants hoped to gain from privateering. By 1600, the Dutch were sending thirteen to twenty ships per year to Asia and as many as eighty per year to destinations in the Atlantic, beyond Europe, manned by about four thousand sailors. The Dutch merchant and fishing fleets then operating in European waters had more than fifteen hundred ships, with some thirty thousand men.

To limit the risks of long-distance voyages, most ships sailing to Africa, Asia, and the New World were owned and equipped by consortia and companies of merchants. In Asia, none was making much of a profit, so in 1602 the government of the Dutch Republic intervened, chartering a joint stock company, the Vereenigde Oost-Indische Compagnie (VOC), the United Dutch East India Company. The new company, whose eighteen hundred investors had endowed it with 6.4 million *guilders* of capital, exercised the exclusive rights to send ships to Asia, to trade in Asian waters, and to conclude treaties with Asian rulers.

Trade, 1621–1800. The Dutch expansion in Asia from 1621 to 1800 was of greater economic importance to the metropole (home country) than the expansion into and across the Atlantic; that made the Dutch unique in Europe, and the key to Dutch success was the East India Company. The company made a successful transition from a privateering to an intercontinental and intra-Asian trading enterprise. It became the world's largest company, then employing more than 25 percent of Dutch shipping and 13 percent of the value of all Dutch foreign trade, with offices and wharves in six Dutch cities. Despite its size, it had few innovative branches and made most of its profits by trading in Asia. At times, the trade between the Netherlands and Asia operated at a loss. Corruption was a serious problem; each year the high-ranking staff sent home to the Netherlands more money than any possible savings from their salaries would allow. The company's impact on the Dutch labor market was considerable. From 1600 to 1800, the company sent about 1 million men to Asia, of whom less than half returned alive. Without the company, these young boys and men—half of whom came from Germany and Scandinavia—would have been available for employment at home or might have been settlers in the New World colonies or South Africa. Although the company's financial impact was positive in the early decades, the returns were modest after the 1680s; during the 1700s, the Dutch money market was affected, and losses forced the company to obtain loans. After absorbing substantial amounts of money to continue its increasingly uncompetitive activities, it was declared bankrupt in 1795.

In the Atlantic, the creation of the Dutch West India Company, modeled after the East India Company, was not a success. Soon after its foundation in 1621, it got involved in a prolonged war with Portugal over boundaries in northeastern Brazil. Soon its financial basis crumbled, and the first West India Company went bankrupt in 1672, after having lost its colonies to the Portuguese in Brazil (1654) and to the British in North America (1667), especially New Amsterdam, which became New York.

The second Dutch West India Company was founded in 1674. It soon was forced to relinquish its trade with Caribbean planters in the rapidly expanding economies of the British and French colonies there. It could not rely on force, since its naval power was inferior to those of the British and the French, thus it concentrated on illegal trade with Spanish America and on selling slaves to the remaining Dutch plantation colonies on the South American

DUTCH EMPIRE. Ships of the Dutch East India Company, painting by Ludolf Backhuyzen (1631–1708). (Gérard Blot/Musée du Louvre, Paris/Réunion des Musées Nationaux/Art Resource, NY)

mainland. The Dutch share in the Atlantic slave trade was about 5 percent, and the Dutch plantation colonies had produced a similar percentage of the New World tropical cash crops, since they provided only about half of the sugar and coffee imported into the Netherlands; the remainder came from the French Caribbean.

From 1650 to 1800, the average annual value of all Dutch exports was estimated at 100 million *guilders*, 5 to 8 million of which went to non-European destinations. Dutch imports averaged about 140 million *guilders*, of which 16 million (1650) to 63 million (1770) were colonial goods. Despite their declining profitability, non-European trade and production increased in importance as the Dutch lost business in Europe.

Colonization, 1800–1945. After the Napoleonic Wars, the Dutch Empire was in a state of crisis. In the West Indies, the most rapidly growing plantation colonies—Essequibo, Demerara, and Berbice (later to become British Guiana)—were not returned by Britain; neither was the Cape Colony (in South Africa) or Ceylon (now Sri Lanka). The Dutch West and East India Companies had gone bankrupt, and the newly founded Kingdom of the Netherlands had thus been forced to assume financial responsibility for the administration and the defense of the overseas possessions, causing an economic crisis. The crisis was solved by the introduction of an unusual colonial taxation scheme for Java. From 1830 to 1870, the compulsory production of cash crops was forced upon the Javanese villages, in addition to existing taxes. The villages were ordered to use part of their arable land for the production of coffee, sugar, and indigo, for which they were paid a nominal fee; thus

with minimal investments, large revenues were generated, which were transferred to the Netherlands. At times these revenue transfers constituted as much as one-third of the total income of the metropolitan's treasury. To date, the effects of the "cultivation system" on Java are still disputed in the literature. Did the system cause or did it, at least, contribute to some major famines—or would these have occurred anyway? Did the system only add to the existing tax burden or did it stimulate Javanese peasants to increase productivity, in addition to modernizing the economy by introducing money?

The effects of the cultivation system on the Netherlands metropolitan economy are easier to establish. Javanese colonial revenues allowed the Dutch government to increase its expenditure on the construction of waterways and railways and to reduce the national debt. Some of the money was used to compensate Dutch West Indian slave owners after slavery was outlawed in 1863. Private business was profited, as more than half of Dutch international trade consisted of tropical cash crops; around 1850, the Dutch East Indies generated about 60 percent of the value added in maritime shipping. The Javanese revenues even enabled the postponement of an income tax.

Yet these windfall profits retarded the modernization of the Dutch economy. By excluding foreign competitors, Dutch shippers and traders were neither forced to modernize nor to reduce costs. Only after the "cultivation system" had been abolished in 1863 did the Dutch economy increase its competitiveness. In time, the Dutch East Indies found markets outside the Netherlands for its exports, mainly elsewhere in Asia and in the United States. In 1870, almost 70 percent of Indonesia's exports went to the Netherlands; in 1939, only 18 percent. In 1870, 10 percent of all Dutch imports came from Indonesia; in 1939, only 5.4 percent. For Dutch investors, the capital markets in Europe, the United States, and Russia became far more important than the Dutch East Indies.

Paradoxically, the Dutch political and military involvement in its colonies increased during the last period of Dutch rule, despite the growing economic rift. From 1873 to 1913, extensive military campaigns were undertaken to bring the whole Indonesian archipelago under Dutch political control and, in the 1920s and 1930s, government expenditure on defense, education, and public health was greatly increased.

Decolonization, 1945 to Present. During World War II, Japan occupied the Dutch East Indies. In 1945, the Dutch East Indies were in a constant state of war with the Dutch Colonial administration, as it tried to reestablish rule in the face of fierce opposition by Indonesian nationalists. The United States, by threatening to halt postwar Marshall Aid to the Netherlands, pressured the Dutch government into surrendering sovereignty over Indonesia in 1949. To forget this painful episode, the Dutch turned to the West Indian colonies and inundated them with aid, allowing internal self-government. In 1975, Suriname (population about 350,000) opted for independence. In an attempt to improve on the badly managed transfer of power in Indonesia, the Dutch promised to pay about 1.75 billion U.S. dollars in aid. Payment was suspended in 1982, when a military dictator came to power, who had had fifteen of his opponents murdered. The Dutch Antilles (population about 200,000) resisted attempts at full decolonization, since each islander receives in annual aid about 500 U.S. dollars.

Decolonization seems not to have impeded the continued growth of the Dutch economy but, immediately after World War II, estimates of the colonial contribution to the Dutch national income averaged only 10 percent per year. The rapid growth of both the Dutch and Indonesian economies since then indicates that the economic ties between both countries had high opportunity costs. Only the extremely small economy of Suriname has shown stagnation since the suspension of Dutch aid.

BIBLIOGRAPHY

Boogaart, Ernst van den, Pieter C. Emmer, Peter Klein, and Kees Zandvliet. *La expansion holandesa en el Atlantico*. Madrid, 1992.
Bruijn, J. R., F. S. Gaastra, and I. Schöffer. *Dutch-Asiatic Shipping in the Seventeenth and Eighteenth Centuries*. 3 vols. The Hague, 1979–1987.
Emmer, Pieter C. *The Dutch in the Atlantic Economy, 1580–1880*. Aldershot, U.K., 1998.
Emmer, Pieter C. "The Economic Impact of the Dutch Expansion Overseas, 1570–1870." *Revista de Historia Economica* 16.1 (1998), 157–176.
Eng, Pierre van der. "Exploring Exploitation: The Netherlands and Colonial Indonesia 1870–1940." *Revista de Historia Economica* 16.1 (1998), 291–321.
Vries, Jan de, and Ad van der Woude. *The First Modern Economy: Success, Failure, and Perseverance of the Dutch Economy, 1500–1815*. Cambridge, 1997.

P. C. EMMER

Southern Netherlands between 1585 and 1830

It was not until the arrival of the Archdukes Albrecht and Isabella in 1598 that the Southern Netherlands started to recover from the years of chaos and anarchy. The turmoil of the Eighty Years' War had triggered an economic crisis. Not only the Southern Netherlands suffered from the "diaspora" of Antwerp merchants, artisans, and industrial workers looking for an economic base and/or religious safety abroad. The countryside and agricultural sector suffered heavily under repeated pillaging and burning by Spanish and Dutch troops alike. With commerce and industry in the doldrums, captured by the so-called "closure of the river Scheldt," prospects for economic recovery looked very gloomy. And yet, in the first half of the seventeenth century, the Southern Netherlands experienced a truly "silver age." How was this economic comeback accomplished?

Economic Crisis to Silver Age. The foundations for this comeback, no doubt, were laid by a renewed thriving husbandry. When peace set in during the Twelve Years' Truce (1609–1621), production of cereals already surpassed the levels attained before the Revolt in 1568. A flourishing countryside also supported a renewal of population growth between 1625 and 1650, a phenomenon that boosted a new round of urbanization. The Southern Netherlands, especially Flanders and Brabant, already were among the most urbanized regions of northwestern Europe, with the total population living in towns with ten thousand or more inhabitants growing still further during this period, with urbanization percentages stabilizing at a high level. Approximately 40 percent of the inhabitants of Brabant, for example, lived in settlements with five thousand or more inhabitants. With the expansion of cities and countryside, it is hardly surprising that the price rises of the sixteenth century took off again. This especially benefited the incomes of independent peasants and craftsman, landed gentry and merchants. Many wealthy merchants now profited from the land they had acquired at giveaway prices during the crisis of the 1580s and 1590s. At the demand side, they made up the backbone for a restructured and revitalized supply of luxury industries in the Southern Netherlands. Many industries—silk, tapestry weaving, painting, furniture making, embroidery, and others—were at the core of this process, which was largely supported by strong corporatist organization. Regionally speaking, Antwerp and Brussels especially became a point in case, but other cities, such as Ghent, shared in the renewed luxury production by producing fine linen. At the demand side, apart from rising incomes (both in agriculture, as well as in commerce and industry), broader political and cultural tendencies strongly supported the radical shift in urban industries. First, the infamous "closure" of the river Scheldt by the Dutch republic generated higher costs of transaction and transportation and was indirectly a stimulus to the commerce in luxury products (such as tapestry, diamonds, or paintings). This happened at the expense of the cheaper bulk carrying and processing of these cargo-related trades. Second, the *reconquista* of the Southern Netherlands by the Spanish troops also implied the victory of Roman faith and Spanish absolutism and hence a propensity to consume luxury commodities, promoting the Catholic renewal and reinforcing the splendor and wealth of the court of Brussels. Famous painters, such as Peter Paul Rubens (1577–1640), creating masterpieces for mighty patrons (both in church and court) act as symbols of this age.

Decline to Crisis. With the peace treaty of Münster in 1648, the Eighty Years' War finally ended. Unfortunately, wartime was not over for the Southern Netherlands. After Spain's dismal defeat by the French in 1659 (Treaty of the Pyrenees), the Southern Netherlands lost their intense military, financial, and diplomatic Spanish backing. Between 1667 and 1715, the Southern Low Countries became the cockpit of Europe, surrendered as it was to a warlike Louis XIV. The ongoing wars, combined with a much harsher international economy, proved too much. After a period of marked decline in the late seventeenth century, a new economic crisis ravaged the Southern Netherlands in the first half of the eighteenth century.

For the first time in the seventeenth century, after 1660 the rural population ceased to increase. Confronted with renewed sacking and burning of farmland, many peasants left their grounds abandoned, seeking shelter from rampaging troops in the cities. It is therefore telling that during this period of rural decline, the total population of towns with ten thousand or more inhabitants was still expanding. But agricultural prices soon began to decline, foreshadowing an absolute crisis at the turn of the century. The slackening of the countryside aggravated the situation of many income groups, a phenomenon that in itself undermined the "domestic" demand, which increasingly had become a decisive economic factor in the seventeenth century. Therefore, the rising purchasing power of workers' daily wages did not generate new incomes. On the contrary, growing unemployment worsened the income situation of urban wage earners and middling groups. The urban and rural export industries of, for example, Ghent were severely hit by mercantilist policies of protectionism

and import substitution developed by the neighboring countries, the so-called emerging nation-states, such as France and England. The Southern Netherlands, driven into the political periphery of Europe, also moved out of the center of fashion shaping and taste creation. Formerly tasteful luxury items increasingly were perceived as "old fashioned," especially after the 1670 French culture conquered the European leisure classes. This coincided with a slowing down of the inspiring impetus given by the Catholic renewal. Around 1650, Roman faith was more or less safely restored, hence all means no longer were required to propagate "true" Catholicism in the Southern Netherlands. This led to a sharp decline in the demand for artistic craftsmanship. Against the background of agriculture and luxury industries in decline, commercial activities did surprisingly well in the late seventeenth century. The trade of Antwerp with Spain and Holland is said to have expanded still further during the second half of the century. However, from a macroeconomic viewpoint, trade with Holland benefited only the latter. As a consequence of the continued "closure" of the river Scheldt, the Southern Netherlands was in no position to equal the massive imports of Dutch products and the dominance of the Dutch in providing shipping services. The unfair balance of trade with the Dutch drained money, people, and wealth from the Southern Netherlands.

When the Austrian Empire acquired the Southern Netherlands after the War of Spanish Succession (1701–1713), government initially proved incapable of turning the tide. Measures aimed at import substitution and protectionist policies supporting industry became only an option after the Peace of Aachen (1748). Successful colonial activities—for example, the founding of the Compagnie d'Ostende by Emperor Charles VI in 1722—were blocked by England and the Dutch republic. Confronted with widespread deindustrialization, the total population of urban settlements started to decline dramatically. In Flanders, for instance, the total population living in towns above the 10,000-inhabitants ceiling dropped from 113,000 in 1700 to 91,000 around 1750.

Age of Revolutions. At the dawn of the nineteenth century, the Southern Netherlands experienced, as did all surrounding countries, a highly unstable political period. Infuriated by their own revolutionary ideals, French *sans-culottes* repeatedly overran the Southern Netherlands. The country was a part of the large Napoleonic Empire until Bonaparte overplayed his cards in 1815. At the Congress of Vienna (1814–1815), it was decided that the Southern and Northern Netherlands should be reunited under Willem I, acting as a kind of buffer state against the highly volatile French. This political constellation lasted until the Belgian revolution began. The Revolution of 1830 and its aftermath gave rise to the so-called "modern Belgium."

In the midst of this political instability, the Southern Netherlands succeeded in partially modernizing their industrial complex. The "industrial revolution" in the Southern Netherlands was firmly rooted in its revitalization during the second half of the eighteenth century. Already in the first half of the eighteenth century, rural population had started to grow again. The introduction of the potato in 1710 no doubt set the pace for a renewed and sustained demographic expansion, though the blessings of long-wanted peacetime cannot be overlooked (only interrupted by the Austrian Succession Wars of 1744–1748). Thanks to the growing population, agricultural prices in turn took off again. Around 1750, husbandry was flourishing as never before. During the second half of the eighteenth century, the Southern Netherlands succeeded in exporting 7 to 8 percent of its annual grain production. Population, however, did not stop growing after 1750, and this kept marginal returns increasingly low, though the expansion continued to support urban growth and local luxury demand. The threat of rural overpopulation was partially compensated, both by expanding rural industries and through rising migration to the cities, employing masses of unskilled and semi-skilled laborers in the reviving textile industries. Urban entrepreneurs could easily contract masses of cheap labor to carry through their lucrative industrial investments, but in the long run, this prevented them from investing in labor-saving capital investments. With a new expansion of colonial trade after 1750, the international demand for cheap, standardized goods (especially cottons and mixed textiles) boomed. In addition, several pieces of evidence indicate that local luxury demand was vigorously growing.

The period from 1770 to 1800 was a crucial era in transforming the economy of the Southern Netherlands. Under the apprenticeship of Lieven Bauwens (1769–1822), a Flemish entrepreneur, Ghent succeeded in mechanizing its cotton production at the turn of the century. In Verviers, William Cockerill (1759–1832), an English-born industrialist, took the same pioneering role in restructuring the wool industry. Mechanization also spurred the iron industries in Liège, and with the growing use of steam engines in Europe, the annual production of the coal mines of Charleroi and Mons accelerated. Cotton, iron, and coal gave way to innumerable backward and forward linkages of which the building of the railroads around 1830 was probably the most important example. Yet the achievements of this industrialization should not be exaggerated. In these early stages, the Belgian industrial revolution was primarily a regional phenomenon. Elsewhere, for example, on the Flemish countryside, where proto-industrial structures triumphed, cheap and abundant labor supply deprived entrepreneurs of an important incentive to modernize. Not surprisingly, these regions fell victim to a devastating poverty around the middle of the nineteenth century.

Finally, the role of the state authorities should not be overlooked. Already under the Austrian government, important paved roads were completed and canals were being built by mediation of the government, stimulating provincial and local authorities to invest in transportation infrastructure. In so doing, the government favored a policy to attract lucrative transit trades and to stimulate inland transportation. The French interplay demolished some remainders of ancien régime society, while William I partially financed the industrial expansion of the South. It was, however, the new Belgian government that—with the backing of the Belgian "haute finance" and massive support of railroad construction—consolidated the future industrial success of Belgium.

[*See also* Belgium.]

BIBLIOGRAPHY

Blondé, Bruno. "Domestic Demand and Urbanisation in the Eighteenth Century: Demographic and Functional Evidence for Small Towns of Brabant." In *Small Towns in Early Modern Europe*, edited by Peter Clark, pp. 229–449. Cambridge, 1995.

Klep, Paul. "Population Estimates of Belgium by Province, 1375–1831." In *Historiens et populations. Liber Amicorum Étienne Hélin.* Louvain, 1991.

Klep, Paul. "Religious War in the Low Countries: Some Observations on Long-Term Effects of Boundary Drawing, Sixteenth–Seventeenth Centuries." In *Historia y humanismo: Estudios en honor del profesor Dr. D. Valentin Vázquez de Prada*, edited by J. M. Usunáriz Garayoa, vol. 1, pp. 131–146. Pamplona, 2000.

Lis, Catharina, and Hugo Soly. "Entrepreneurs, corporations et autorités publiques au Brabant et en Flandre à la fin de l'ancien régime." *Revue de Nord* 76 (1994), 725–744.

Van der Wee, Herman, ed. *The Rise and Decline of Urban Industries in Italy and in the Low Countries: Late Middle Ages to Early Modern Times.* Louvain, 1988.

Van der Wee, Herman. *The Low Countries in the Early Modern World.* Cambridge, 1993.

Van Houtte, J. A. *An Economic History of the Low Countries, 800–1800.* London, 1977.

Verhulst, A. *Précis d'histoire rurale de la Belgique.* Brussels, 1990.

IILJA VAN DAMME
BRUNO BLONDÉ

LÜBECK. Located in Schleswig-Holstein, Germany, Lübeck is a seaport situated on the Trave River, roughly fourteen kilometres from the Baltic Sea. Founded in a newly occupied Slavonic region in 1143, it continued the mercantile tradition of a nearby Slavonic princely settlement and trading center that was destroyed in 1138. As its prosperity waxed, Henry the Lion, duke of Saxony, forced the founder, Count Adolf II of Holstein, to transfer the township to him in 1159. In 1160, Henry transferred the bishopric of Oldenburg to Lübeck. Subjected to the king of Denmark from 1201 until 1225, Lübeck finally became a free imperial city in 1226 and retained its independence until 1937.

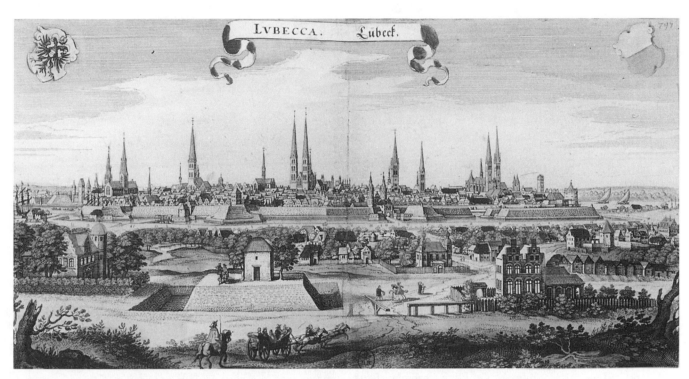

LÜBECK. View of the city. (Giraudon/Art Resource, NY)

Because of its geographical location, Lübeck's economic importance was based on the east-west long-distance trade from the Baltic and Scandinavia to the North Sea region and vice versa. Located near the end of the land route on the Lübeck-Hamburg axis, it was also a transshipment port for goods traveling via the Danish sound, probably from the beginning of the thirteenth century. Lübeck's economy was based on intermediary trade, of which herring, salt (from the town of Lüneburg), and grain were the most important commodities in late medieval times. Little is known about crafts, but there are hints of industries that finished (processed) Baltic commodities, such as furs, leather, iron, and copper.

Because of its central position in the North European trade system and its relative independence as a free imperial city, Lübeck played a leading role in the German Hansa. It was situated in the middle of the area covered by Hanseatic trade and diplomacy so most of the Hanseatic Diets were held in Lübeck. At the end of the fourteenth century, it tried to transform this trade organization into a political confederation, but it never succeeded in doing so. Nevertheless, until the last Hanseatic Diet, which met in Lübeck in 1669, the city remained *caput hanze*.

When the structure of European trade changed in the second half of the fourteenth century, the direct shipment between the North Sea and the Baltic Sea increased, and Lübeck, counting roughly twenty thousand inhabitants, lost its central position and played a less-important role in the increasing east-west trade in bulk goods. Consequent-

ly, the value of Lübeck's seaborne trade in the second half of the fourteenth century decreased considerably, and the output of silver coins shrank dramatically, too. Its importance for the east-west trade in high-valued commodities and transportation of goods from the Baltic region to central and South Germany remained constant for another century. Lübeck kept its position as a port of transshipment of high-value goods until the nineteenth century.

In the late fifteenth century, Lübeck lost its leading position even in Baltic trade, when in 1470, the Dutch began to buy grain in Prussia (because the French king prevented the Dutch from buying grain in France) and, won control of the carrying trade from the Baltic to the west. Second, South German and Italian merchants invaded the markets in middle and northeastern Europe hitherto held by Hanseatic, mainly Lübeck, merchants. Third in western Europe the commercial center shifted from Bruges and Flanders, where Lübeck had a strong position, to Antwerp, and Lübeck withdrew almost entirely from the trade with England. Additionally, its political position was weakened when it lost a war against Denmark in the 1530s, which made clear that the formerly powerful city no longer rivaled the military power of a monarchy.

In the face of these setbacks, Lübeck developed new, albeit more modestly, commercial functions. Its merchants developed new markets in Spain, Portugal, and Italy until the 1670s and benefited from the Thirty Years' War. From then on, Lübeck's shipment and trade were primarily restricted to the Baltic Sea. Of its former important trade connections with western Europe, only the one to France remained.

Lübeck's economy suffered a long depression until the middle of the eighteenth century. Its population fell from thirty-five thousand to twenty thousand inhabitants. The subsequent recovery was cut short by the continental blockade and seizure of the city by Napoleonic troops. Nearly one-third of Lübeck's merchant firms went bankrupt between 1810 and 1813. Not before the middle of the nineteenth century did Lübeck recover from this blow.

With the opening in 1895 of the Nord-Ostsee canal connecting the North Sea and the Baltic Sea, Lübeck lost its function as a port of transshipment for high-valued goods, a function already diminishing as steamships with screw propellers made direct shipping from the North Sea to the Baltic easier. The Elbe-Lübeck canal (1900), intended to answer these challenges, succeeded only in part but did become important for supplying Lübeck's industries. Industrialization in a broad manner began in the last quarter of the nineteenth century, and at the beginning of the twentieth century Lübeck transformed into a center of trade and industry, including shipbuilding, ore manufacturing, and food industries, especially canned foods, with116,000 inhabitants. As in the Middle Ages, Lübeck profited from the worldwide increase in population and the required food supply, especially preserved fish and canned vegetables.

After World War II, Lübeck lost its economic hinterland, which then belonged to the German Democratic Republic and to the Soviet Union, but integrated many refugees to count 236,000 inhabitants. Its situation as a border city to the eastern block hampered its economic development and made the transition from industries to services a severe problem. Nevertheless, Lübeck strengthened its traditional function as the Baltic harbor of (western) Germany and became the largest ferry harbor in Europe. It remains so, though rivaled by the port of Rostock (land of Mecklenburg) since the reunion of Germany in 1990. Lübeck's main connections are to Finland (paper, cellulose) and Sweden. In 2000, it had 215,000 inhabitants, and services were the most important part of the city's economy. Other major employers, besides the port, are medical equipment, optics, as metalwork, and food processing. Tourism has become important, and in 1987 the historic town of Lübeck was inscribed into the UNESCO world heritage list.

BIBLIOGRAPHY

Grassmann, Antjekathrin, ed. *Lübeckische Geschichte*. 3d ed. Lübeck, Germany, 1997.

Hammel-Kiesow, Rolf. "Lübeck—Grundlinien der Wirtschaftsgeschichte der Stadt." *Mitteilungen der Geographischen Gesellschaft zu Lübeck* 59 (1999), 5–34.

Hammel-Kiesow, Rolf. "Von Tuch und Hering zu Wein und Holz. Der Handel Lübecker Kaufleute von der Mitte des 12. bis zum Ende des 19. Jahrhunderts." In *Der Lübecker Kaufmann. Aspekte seiner Lebens—und Arbeitswelt vom Mittelalter bis zum 19. Jahrhundert*, edited by G. Gerkens and A. Grassmann, pp. 13–33. Lübeck, Germany, 1993.

Hammel-Kiesow, Rolf. "Lübeck and the Baltic Trade in Bulk Goods for the North Sea Region, 1150–1400." In *Cogs, Cargoes, and Commerce: Maritime Bulk Trade in Northern Europe, 1150–1400*, edited by Lars Berggren, Nils Berggren, and Annette Larden, pp. 55–93, Toronto, 2002.

Jenks, Stuart. "A Capital without a State: Lübeck *caput tocius hanze* (to 1474)." *Bulletin of the Institute of Historical Research* 65 (1992), 134–149.

Klinsmann, Luise. *Die Industrialisierung Lübecks*. Lübeck, Germany, 1984.

ROLF HAMMEL-KIESOW

LUDDISM AND SOCIAL PROTEST. From March 1811 until April 1812, the eastern midland and northern manufacturing counties of England were the backdrop to the most intense and prolonged outbreaks of machine breaking of the Industrial Revolution. Commencing in Nottinghamshire, where machine breaking continued to erupt for the better part of eight months, the disturbances spread into Yorkshire in January 1812 and then across the Pennines into Lancashire. From the start, these machine-breakers took their name from the apocryphal apprentice framework knitter Ned Ludd, who, when ordered to "square his needles," (that is, to adjust the tolerances on his stocking frame), had taken a hammer and flattened the entire assembly. The Luddites, or the followers of General Ludd, took Ned's example to heart. Damage to employers' property across the three regions ran into tens of thousands of pounds, but the impact of the Luddites was not merely financial. Luddism also alarmed government in a way no previous provincial disorders had since 1745.

The background to Luddism was one of rapidly rising living costs, with the price of wheat reaching an unprecedented peak of 112 shillings a quarter in the early months of 1812, and acute economic dislocation and depression, the result of the disastrous Orders in Council, which disrupted trade and occasioned a short-lived war with the United States, a major market for British textiles. However, while Luddism exhibited elements of earlier forms of social protest typical of economic distress—food riots, conflicts over apprenticeship, and wage disputes—the defining leitmotif of Luddism was hostility to machinery, reflecting a deepening crisis over the threat that new technology posed to the trades of skilled and semiskilled labor groups.

In Nottinghamshire, Luddism was centered upon the hosiery industry. Here, framework knitters produced stockings and other knitted textiles, working in their own homes or in small shops upon stocking frames, complex and expensive looms rented from master hosiers or merchants whose capital dominated the industry. Conflict between stockingers and hosiers had been growing in the years before 1811 over piece rates, frame rent, and the dilution of the trade through the employment of "illegal" workers, men who had not served the full apprenticeship term. In 1811, all these abuses of custom were present and helped fuel conflict, but the key stimulus came from the growing use of "wide frames" and the manufacture of "cut ups." Whereas "full wrought hose" was produced in the form of a tube, some merchant hosiers were switching to stockings made from widths of knitted cloth, woven as a sheet and then cut and sewn to shape. Cheaper, because they required less skill, and much less durable, the cut ups and the wide frames on which they were made had long been resisted by the stockingers. Moreover, they believed that cut ups were illegal since a charter granted to the trade by King Charles II explicitly prohibited all engines that fabricate articles "in a deceitful manner."

In Yorkshire, cloth dressers, or croppers, in the woolen industry found their trade threatened not merely with debasement but with complete destruction by the introduction of the gig mill and shearing frame. Here, the battle with machinery had been running since the late 1790s when, in common with their fellow dressers in the West of England, the croppers had sought to utilize their powerful trade union strength to deter innovators from introducing the machines. In 1802, this had culminated in the Wiltshire Outrages, extensive disorders that presaged Luddism ten years later. The Wiltshire dressers, like the framework knitters, argued that their trade was protected by the statute 5&6 Edward VI c. 22, "an act for the putting down of gig mills," which condemned products of this machine as "deceitfully made." However, the dressers' attempt to utilize this legislation, alongside a concerted campaign by the west-country weavers to prosecute the growing number of nonapprenticed workers in their trade, prompted clothiers there to ally with the cloth merchants and innovating factory-owning clothiers in Yorkshire to petition Parliament to repeal all the old statutes that regulated the industry and, they argued, hindered economic expansion. The issues were examined by two select committees in 1803 and 1806, before Parliament swept away all controls in 1809. Employers in Yorkshire were slow to take advantage of their new freedom, fearful of reprisals, but in late 1811, with trade severely depressed, some of the largest employers began to install the machinery in new factories. This in turn put pressure upon the smaller employers, the master dressers, who employed the great majority of the croppers in their workshops, to follow suit or risk losing their trade.

In Lancashire, Luddism was much less clearly industrially focused, encompassing extensive food rioting and violent political protests, but at its core was the growing impoverishment of the cotton handloom weavers. Their efforts to protect their trade had been continuing since the late 1790s, when the rapid growth of the cotton industry had seen thousands flooding into the trade. Attempts at securing regulation of piece rates through Parliament and quarter sessions had been frustrated by the hostility of the cotton masters and magistracy and by an increasing unwillingness of the government to intervene. Extensive strikes secured short-lived improvements, but the depression of early 1812 further undermined the weavers' conditions. However, it was the threat to their trade from the newly invented power loom that triggered industrial conflict in 1812. Housed in new large factories, the power looms betokened a new age of production in which domestic weavers would have no place.

The nature of Luddite attacks differed county by county. In Nottinghamshire, the hosiers' wide frames that were the Luddites' targets were found in the houses and small shops of the stockingers who worked them. Impossible to defend even by constant patrolling, many hundreds were destroyed before Luddism came to an end. In Yorkshire, the shearing frames housed in the workshops of master dressers presented an easy target for the groups of blackened-faced men armed with sledgehammers who attacked in the night. Here, however, the new factories at Horbury, Rawfolds, and Otiwells proved to be much more formidable objectives. Heavily fortified, even armed mass attacks could be bloodily beaten off, as the notorious assault on the Rawfolds mill showed. The large weaving factories in Lancashire proved just as strong, as attacks on the mills at Stockport, Tintwhistle, Middleton, and Westhaughton showed. At the latter, however, luck aided the rioters, for, after two failures, the Westhoughton mill was destroyed on 24 April 1812, when the troops guarding it were foolishly withdrawn for a short period.

Recourse to machine breaking in 1811–1812 should not be seen as evidence of an inability to effect more "orderly" forms of negotiation. The croppers had one of the most powerful combinations of any nonmetropolitan trade and had used their industrial muscle effectively in the past to secure high wages and deter the take-up of machinery. The stockingers had in 1811 revived the Framework Knitters' Company, ostensibly to petition Parliament, but it clearly acted as a trade union. And the Lancashire weavers had maintained a countywide weavers' association since 1799. Both groups had shown the capacity to conduct effective negotiations with their employers in the past. The problem for all in 1811–1812 was not that they lacked the means of peaceful negotiation. It was that the innovating employers in all regions had no intention of listening. In Yorkshire, attempts were made to secure a phased introduction of dressing machinery, but after the protracted struggle to secure the repeal of the old regulatory legislation, the large employers had no time for compromise. The same was true of the Lancashire cotton manufacturers. In Nottinghamshire, there is evidence that the less-wealthy hosiers were ready to reach agreement, but the large-scale hosiers had no intention of backing down.

The main reason for such pugnacity on the part of the large capitalists was the fact that the government made clear from the first its determination to suppress Luddism. Troops were poured into the troubled districts, not merely to patrol and tackle bands of Luddites if they could engage them but principally to act as protectors of the employers' property. Frames were brought into Nottingham itself, where they could be guarded. In Yorkshire and Lancashire, soldiers were stationed inside the new factory-fortresses. No quarter was given. Parliament showed its hostility to the disturbances by the speedy passage of a bill to make frame breaking a capital offense and by the Watch and Ward Act, which in effect put the Yorkshire administrative unit of West Riding under martial law.

The reasons for the state's overt and determined siding with the forces of capital were two-fold. One lay in the transformation of the attitudes of government toward industrial regulation. The years between 1800, when the Cotton Arbitration Act was passed, and 1812 had seen a hardening of opinion behind the ideology of laissez-faire, epitomized in the report of the Select Committee into the Woollen Trade in 1806 and in the debate on the cotton weavers' petition in 1811. Capital was to be given "freedom" to act in its own best interests, and protection of labor was denounced as restrictive. This sea change from the older paternalist tradition had been proceeding gradually for more than quarter of a century. However, the context of the French Revolution, war, and, above all, fears of political radicalism and republicanism sharpened the focus. Thus, more soldiers were committed to harrying Luddites than were sent with Wellesley to engage the French in Spain.

The government was shocked by the solid support for the Luddites from within the working community. Men unconnected with the disputing trades took part in Luddite attacks, as those wounded at Rawfolds showed, and no evidence could be procured to unmask the rioters in any county. In Yorkshire, it was only after the murder of William Horsfall, owner of Otiwells mill, that this mood changed. Nor did the respectable classes evince uniform hostility to the machine breakers. Master dressers in Yorkshire, smaller hosiers and cotton manufacturers in Nottinghamshire and Lancashire alike were suspected of covert support, reflecting their deep distrust of the market power of the mechanizing capitalists and its implications for their own businesses. Even magistrates in some districts were slow, or unwilling, to act. In this, we can discern an underpinning of Luddism much more widespread than merely the wish of those threatened by machinery to pro-

tect their employment. Behind Luddism lay an older reading of political economy, based on an essentially mercantilist view of trade that deeply distrusted the new ethos of laissez-faire. The machine-owning innovators were viewed as would be monopolists, on a par with the forestallers and regraters condemned by old marketing legislation. Allowing them to ride roughshod over customary rights would drive out smaller employers and result in large-scale unemployment and an underconsumptionist economic crisis, not the prosperity predicted by the innovators. This view was shared widely among the respectable rate-paying classes, who saw themselves picking up the real costs of the introduction of machinery.

The government's fears of Luddism as a dangerous insurrectionary movement became almost self-fulfilling. In Yorkshire, Luddism, defeated by the continued defiance of the large factories, turned from machine breaking toward arms gathering and insurrectionary plotting. In Lancashire, where radicalism had even deeper roots, insurrectionary organization and Luddite organization became, if anything, even more deeply entwined. It was only at this stage that evidence was forthcoming and arrests were made. Horsfall's murderers aside, most of those tried in Yorkshire proved to be not croppers but men from other trades such as John Baines, the radical hatter from Halifax, who was "twisting-in" (administering illegal oaths to men who joined) men into a shadowy insurrectionary society that grew out of the croppers' defeat. The same was true in Lancashire, where radicals such as John Knight of Oldham were prosecuted, unsuccessfully, for the same activity. This transition to radical politics remains the least understood and most hotly debated aspect of Luddism. But it reflected a shift from economic to political alienation, which some historians see reflected in the extraordinary take-up of radical politics in all three regions once war eventually ended in 1815.

Historiography of Luddism. The major accounts of Luddism are: J. L. and B. Hammond, *The Skilled Labourer* (London, 1919, 1979 edn.), E. P. Thompson, *The Making of the English Working Class* (Harmondsworth, 1968) and M. I. Thomis, *The Luddites* (Newton Abbot, 1970). They have very different views about the nature of the disturbances in 1811/12. the Hammonds' work has been described by John Rule as the "the essential starting point for the student of Luddism" (*Skilled Labourer*, p. xx). Fabian socialists, they are keen to emphasise the disruption which machinery entailed for workers in the three trades but are reluctant to condone industrial violence and clear that it was distinct from "constitutionalist" trade unionism. They see no link between Luddism and political radicalism. Thompson, however, places Luddism at the centre of his interpretation of the development of a working class, seeing it as a general movement which linked the three regions and developed strong ties with ultra-radicalism: Luddism, he writes, "teetered on the brink of ulterior revolutionary ambitions" (pp. 603, 604). Thomis, critical of the moral judgements which he sees as characterising both earlier volumes and of Thompson's Marxist approach, takes a much more compartmentalist approadh. "True" Luddism was distinct from trade unionism and had no political dimension. Luddites were simply trying to preserve jobs, had no inter-regional links and had little real understanding of the economic forces which were sweeping the country. Dinwiddy, "Luddism and politics in the northern counties," *Social History*, 1979, while critical of some of Thomson's claims, largely supports his contention that Luddism developed a strong political dimension in both Yorkshire and Lancashire, a view endorsed by Calhoun, *The Question of Class Struggle* (London, 1982), who, however, sees this politics as "reactionary radicalism" and not as indicating a new sense of class. Randall, *Before the Luddites* (Cambridge, 1991), examines the background of resistance to machinery in the woollen industry, arguing that industrial protest was intimately linked with trade union action and also that machine breakers shared a clear political economy which derived from older mercantilist and paternalist models. These views are developed in M. Bauer, ed., *Resistance to New Technology* (Cambridge, 1995), alongside wider theoretical and comparative discussions of current and historical resistance to new technology. K. Sale, *Rebels against the Future: The Luddites and Their War on the Industrial Revolution; Lessons for the Computer Age* (Reading, Mass., 1995) takes the parallels between the Luddites and modern "neo-Luddites" still further.

BIBLIOGRAPHY

Bauer, Martin, ed. *Resistance to New Technology: Nuclear Power, Information Technology, and Biotechnology*. Cambridge, 1995.

Berg, Maxine. "Workers and Machinery in Eighteenth-Century England." In *British Trade Unionism: The Formative Years*, edited by John Rule. London, 1988.

Bythell, Duncan. *The Handloom Weavers*. Cambridge, 1969.

Calhoun, Craig. *The Question of Class Struggle*. London, 1982. Sees Luddism as developing a political dimension but argues this constituted a "reactionary radicalism" and not a new sense of class consciousness.

Charlesworth, Andrew, et al. *An Atlas of Industrial Protest*. Basingstoke, U.K., 1996.

Darvall, Frank O. *Popular Disturbances and Public Order in Regency England*. Oxford, 1969.

Dinwiddy, John. "Luddism and Politics in the Northern Counties." *Social History* 41 (1979), 3–64. Dinwiddy, while critical of some of Thompson's claims, largely supports his contention that Luddism developed a strong political dimension in both Yorkshire and Lancashire.

Hammond, John L., and B. Hammond. *The Skilled Labourer*. London, 1919, 1979 edn. Described by John Rule as "the essential starting point for the student of Luddism" (*Skilled Labourer*, p. xx). Fabian socialists, the authors are keen to emphasize the disruption that machinery caused for workers in the three trades but are reluctant to condone industrial violence and clear that it was distinct from "constitutionalist" trade unionism. They see no link between Luddism and political radicalism.

Randall, Adrain J. *Before the Luddites: Custom, Community, and Machinery in the English Woollen Industry, 1776–1809*. Cambridge, 1991. Examines the background of resistance to machinery in the woolen industry, arguing that industrial protest was intimately linked with trade union action and also that machine breakers shared a clear political economy, which derived from older mercantilist and paternalist models.

Rule, John. *The Labouring Classes in Early Industrial England*. London, 1986.

Sale, Kirkpatrick. *Rebels against the Future: The Luddites and Their War on the Industrial Revolution; Lessons for the Computer Age*. Reading, Mass., 1995. Develops parallels between the Luddites and modern "neo-Luddites."

Stevenson, John. *Popular Disturbances in England*. London, 1992 ed.

Thomis, Malcolm I. *The Luddites*. Newton Abbot, U.K., 1970. Critical of the moral judgments that he sees as characterizing both earlier volumes and of Thompson's Marxist approach, Thomis takes a much more compartmentalist approach. "True" Luddism was distinct from trade unionism and had no political dimension. Luddites were simply trying to preserve jobs, had no interregional links, and had little real understanding of the economic forces that were sweeping the country.

Thompson, Edward P. *The Making of the English Working Class*. Harmondsworth, 1968. One of the most influential books ever written on the period, Thompson places Luddism at the center of his interpretation of the development of a working class, seeing it as a general movement that linked the three regions and developed strong ties with ultraradicalism: Luddism, he writes, "teetered on the brink of ulterior revolutionary ambitions" (pp. 603–604).

ADRIAN RANDALL

LUXEMBURG, ROSA (1870–1919), Marxist intellectual and revolutionary.

Born in Russian Poland, the daughter of Jewish merchants, on 5 March 1870, Rosa Luxemburg studied at Zürich University, where she wrote her thesis on the industrial development of Poland. In 1898 she moved to Germany, where she became active in the intellectual debates of the German Social Democratic Party and defended Marxism against the criticism of Eduard Bernstein and the revisionists. Her whole intellectual output was dedicated to the necessity of socialist revolution. Against the feminists, she argued that women could be liberated only after socialists had seized power and transformed economic and social relations. Against those Polish socialists who advocated Polish independence, she claimed that ideas of national independence were essentially bourgeois under capitalism and diverted energy from the crucial class struggle to create a socialist society. According to Luxemburg, influenced by conditions in imperial Germany, class relations were becoming increasingly polarized, and the bourgeoisie was becoming increasingly reactionary, as the industrial proletariat organized and grew in strength. Liberalism was in retreat, and the European middle classes were making peace with traditional landowning and

Роза Люксембургъ

ROSA LUXEMBURG. (Prints and Photographs Division, Library of Congress)

reactionary forces. Indeed, an intensification of class conflict was central to the age of imperialism.

For Luxemburg, imperialism denoted not only European expansion overseas but also the growth of international reaction within Europe itself, though both developments were linked to the growing socialist threat and to the structural inability of capitalism to reproduce itself. Her *Accumulation of Capital*, published in 1913, claimed, on the basis of a rather garbled reading of Marx's *Capital* and very mechanically, that capitalism required an ever-expanding market for goods as a stimulus to investment, and so capitalism needed the existence of precapitalist economies to survive. However, such economies changed the minute they were penetrated by capitalism; and there would come a day when such places no longer existed. At this stage, claimed Luxemburg, the collapse of capitalism was a logical necessity.

It is important to realize that Luxemburg did not equate the collapse of capitalism with the final triumph of socialism. The latter required the active intervention of the working classes, who would gain revolutionary conscious-ness less through socialist organization and education prior to the emergence of a revolutionary situation, as most leading Social Democrats believed, than through and in the course of action itself, in particular through participation in mass strikes, as they had in the Russian Revolution of 1905–1906. Luxemburg was dismissive of the strategy of both orthodox Marxists such as Karl Kautsky, who cautiously waited for the revolution to arrive, and Lenin, who invested revolutionary potential in a tightly disciplined party of professional revolutionaries. It was this rediscovery of praxis, which criticized both reformist caution and Leninism and stressed workers' self-liberation, that constituted Luxemburg's most important contribution to Marxist thought. Moreover, it was a contribution for which she died, in Berlin on the night of 15–16 January 1919, murdered by counterrevolutionaries.

BIBLIOGRAPHY

Abraham, Richard. *Rosa Luxemburg: A Life for the International*. Oxford, 1989.

Basso, Lelio. *Rosa Luxemburg: A Reappraisal*. London, 1975.

Dunayevskaya, Raya. *Rosa Luxemburg, Women's Liberation and Marx's Philosophy*. Atlantic Highlands, N.J., 1982. An interesting exploration of a particular aspect of Luxemburg's thought.

Fröhlich, Paul. *Rosa Luxemburg: Her Life and Work*. New York, 1972. A sympathetic study by a revolutionary contemporary.

Geary, Dick. *Karl Kautsky*. Machester, 1987. A work positing a closer relationship between Luxemburg and Kautsky than Nettl's study.

Geras, Norman. *The Legacy of Rosa Luxemburg*. London, 1976. An especially perceptive study of Luxemburg's thought.

Howard, Dick, ed. *The Political Writings of Rosa Luxemburg*. New York, 1971. A very useful collection.

Luxemburg, Rosa. *Social Reform or Revolution?* London, 1902. Reprint. New York, 1971.

Luxemburg, Rosa. *Leninism or Marxism*. Glasglow, 1904. Reprint, edited by Betram D. Wolfe. Ann Arbor, 1961.

Luxemburg, Rosa. *The Accumulation of Capital*. New York, 1913. Reprint. London, 1951.

Luxemburg, Rosa. *The Junius Pamphlet*. 1915. Reprint. London, 1971.

Nettl, J. P. *Rosa Luxemburg*. 2 vols. London, 1966. The classic biography.

DICK GEARY

LUXURY TRADES. Luxury goods have only rarely been accorded great significance by economic historians. Defined by economists as goods whose income elasticities are greater than one, they have been considered by economic historians only in relation to elite consumption, a subject that also falls outside the central concerns of the field. Luxury has been variously defined in terms of rarity or conspicuous consumption, but any definition must focus on the "relativity" of luxury; a luxury to one may be a necessity to another. In modern commercial usage, it refers to goods that are widely desired because they are not yet widely consumed, but luxury also refers to qualitative attributes of particular goods; that is, they are "pleasing," and provide a refinement on some more generic need

(Berry, 1994). Luxury, however, has entered into mainstream discourses on consumption, trade, and social structure at various cycles in history. One of these is the current centrality of consumer society. Since the 1990s, consumer aspirations have been increasingly associated with luxury and designer goods, and with lifestyle choices of affluence associated with distinction, diversity, and individuality. Luxury and branded goods rely on global production and marketing frameworks, and consumer choice has become a key marker of social inclusion and exclusion (Frank, 1999).

Luxury Goods from Ancient Society to the Renaissance. Luxury goods have played a central social and cultural role in Eastern and Western societies, and from the ancient world to the present. Their definition has always been relative to perceptions of necessities and of surplus expenditure. They have been seen by anthropologists as "social valuables" characterized by highly specific powers of acquisition, controls on distribution, patron-client relations of production and trade, and the protection and reproduction of status systems. Cultural critics have preferred defining luxury goods in terms of "incarnated signs"; they had symbolic meanings, such as pepper in cuisine, silk in dress, jewels in adornment, and relics in worship. They also had a high degree of linkage to the body, the person, and the personality. But definitions of luxury goods were always historical, shaped by public structures of meaning and private experience.

A common element in luxury goods is their association with exotic and foreign goods and their traders. Archaeologists and anthropologists have traced this connection through ancient and primitive societies. Rare and precious objects were the stimulus of long-distance trade in the ancient world. Particular materials were singled out for luxury objects: obsidian and shell in stone-age societies, precious metals and rare organics in the metal age. Amber, ivory, incense, pepper, and silk were the priorities of Roman trade. The traders in these goods were also considered in primitive societies to be strangers rather than kinsmen or friends.

The elites of ancient Athens in the fifth and fourth centuries BCE displayed their wealth in gold and silver plate; their precious metal drinking vessels waned in significance beside the gold and silver beds and thrones of the Persian Empire. Lavish expenditure on silver plate continued in Rome; in the second century BCE, there was a sumptuary law controlling the amount of plate that could be used at banquets. Luxury goods in precious metals featured in representations of imperial largesse and church splendor well into the early modern period. Luxury goods were valued for the weight of the plate that could be melted down, rather than the art of the gold and silversmiths that made them (Berg and Clifford, 1999; Mitchell, 1995; Vickers and Gill, 1994).

Silver played a similar role in China: the foundation of the currency system, a rare and precious metal whose sheen was imitated in porcelain. The discovery of new sources of silver in the New World, traded from Europe, opened a new luxury trade with Asia. Silver accounted for 90 percent of imports into China from the West, and Asian manufactured luxuries acquired a high prestige in European markets. Other Chinese exotic luxuries were otherwise imported mainly from Southeast Asia, and consisted mainly of goods that were gathered rather than planted or manufactured: sharks' fin, birds' nests, pepper, pearls, incense, and rare woods (Pomeranz, 2000).

A common feature of luxury goods manufactured in the East and West was production for an external market; preferences for luxury objects produced by nonlocal industrial sources was the key to the character of premodern trade. Artifacts produced by strangers were invested with art, religion, and magical properties. The Japanese aristocracy consumed Chinese silk before the Tokugawa period, and Islamic rulers desired Chinese celadonware. Glass and porcelain were prized luxury goods (Chaudhuri, 1990; Clunas, 1991).

Specialized production of luxury goods required skill, capital, and rapid response to the tastes and preferences of consuming markets. Artisans relied on merchants to underwrite commercial risks. High levels of technical and social differentiation characterized production of luxury goods going back to the Pharaonic-Assyrian period; skills were transmitted by family or caste, and craftsmen migrated to other centers when wars threatened their livelihoods. Contrary to common belief, luxury goods were rarely individual creations of a single craftsman. The bronzes and silks of Han dynasty China and Ming porcelain were made using extensive division of labor, interchangeable parts, highly capitalized and in some cases mechanized processes and factories. Similarly, the enormous output of early modern Dutch art relied on high numbers of craftspeople, specialization and use of standardized patterns, large-scale workshops, and subcontracting.

Luxury goods were also perceived as expressions of taste and civility. Domestic settings and their furnishings, rituals of civility, such as dining or drinking, and collections provided a context for luxury objects. The ancient Greek symposia provided the context for the display and use of gold and silver drinking vessels and wine craters. In Renaissance Italy, wealthy merchants and elites conveyed their status through their taste in oriental ceramics and fine majolica, silverware, and glass. Venetian glass was prized as a luxury good, not for the value and rarity of its raw materials, but for its craftsmanship, and was an ideal vehicle for the display of private splendor in refined hospitality at table. It was delicate and fragile, its thinness and ephemeral nature represented the *vanitas* and the transitory in the material world. It fulfilled the ideals of the Renaissance arts in its emphasis on elegance of form and proportion and the goal of harmony, as well as complex skills of artisanship. Glass and ceramics were international luxury goods; as markers of taste, they displaced gold and silver dining and drinking vessels. In later seventeenth- and eighteenth-century Europe, rituals of coffee, chocolate, and tea drinking as well as dining were conducted with a display of luxury ceramic and glass tea, dinner, and dessert services, and silver vessels, apparatus, and cutlery.

Luxury silverware was once regarded for the value of its material, and its quality guaranteed through assaying and silvermarks from 1300 on. It acquired a new place as a mark of refinement from the early eighteenth century, when heavy plate was displaced by highly crafted and ornamented goods made from much lighter and thinner silver (Goldthwaite, 1993; Berg, 2002).

Glassware also had strong aesthetic and luxury appeal in most premodern Islamic societies, where there was a long tradition of glassmaking from antiquity. Damascus and other towns in Syria took the lead in exportware, and a distinctive assembly of glassware forms and shapes developed in the Muslim West. Islamic rulers paid high prices for Chinese celadonware, which was appreciated for its beauty and luster, and there was also an extensive import trade in Chinese blue-and-white porcelain (Chaudhuri, 1990).

Sumptuary Law. Many parts of the world imposed sumptuary legislation to curb conspicuous consumption, especially among the lower social orders. Sumptuary law was designed to regulate the consumption of citizens, and entailed the political assumption that it was a function of government to regulate consumption, especially of goods related to dress and appearance. The legislation was mainly concerned with maintaining social hierarchies, and it existed in the ancient world, in medieval and early modern Europe, and in early modern Asia and Africa. In the West, sumptuary law and later mercantilist legislation was directed against foreign luxury goods, especially those imported from the East (Hunt, 1996). While sumptuary law directed to controlling consumer behavior was usually unpopular and rarely effectively enforced, taxes on luxuries have been popular ways of raising government revenue. Adam Smith (1723–1790) suggested taxing mansions, an example of the "luxuries and vanities of life"; and carriages, which displayed the "indolence and vanity of the rich." Such taxes range from the ancient Roman tax on slaves or the eighteenth-century British tax on male servants, to the widespread taxes from this time to the present on carriages and hair powder, or luxury cars and perfumes. Algeria has imposed a 150 percent tax on large cars, caviar, and "precious objects"; and Australia one of 40 per-

cent on perfume, jewelry, cars, and motorcycles. The United States in 1991 imposed a levy of 10 percent on cars, boats, aircraft, furs, and jewelry above certain threshold expenditures (Frank, 1999).

By the later seventeenth century in Europe, while little of sumptuary law was enforced, an increasing world trade in luxury goods developed within the framework of the luxury debates. The display of luxury goods was part of the "theater of the great" for lay and ecclesiastic nobility. Fears of corruption and ruin from the conspicuous consumption of the "nouveaux riches," of the sexual ruin of female luxury, and of the sapping of national virtue by Eastern luxury generated a moral critique of luxury goods (Berg and Eger, 2002).

A Growing List of Luxuries. By the seventeenth century, luxury goods were increasingly associated with the exotic manufactures of the East, as well as the foods, drink, and medicinal plants of the East and the New World. Dutch and Portuguese emporia displayed collections of curiosities, spices, such medicines as rhubarb, such flowers as tulips, and foodstuffs and raw materials from sugar, chocolate, and coffee to indigo and cobalt blue and rare woods, and manufactured consumer goods from Turkish carpets and Chinese porcelain to silk and printed calicoes. An international commodities trade in luxuries generated overseas expansion, and the East and West India Companies of several European states led the scramble for world trade in eastern and western commodities (Mukerji, 1983).

The domestic European production of luxuries and other consumer goods manufactures was fostered through mercantilist policies to create prestige quality manufactures at home, through "nurseries," workshops, and regions of producer skill, from glass and fine ironware to silk weaving and goldsmithing, and through a European diaspora of engravers and designers, gold- and silversmiths, clockmakers and cabinetmakers. The trade in luxury goods provided a new positive economic image of manufacture and trade to displace the old moral corruption of earlier luxury debates.

The trade in exotic luxury manufactures also generated new domestic manufactures of imitative commodities, such as Delftware and fine earthenware, European cottons and printed calicoes, brass and copperware, lacquerware and varnishes. A whole range of domestic European commodities that imitated Asian luxuries became the basis for the rise of a major consumer goods sector in Europe, and especially in Great Britain in the course of the eighteenth century. These were not import substitutes, but new products, relying on domestic raw materials, or materials from colonial hinterlands, but products that still conveyed recognizable characteristics of the original Asian luxuries. The markets for old luxuries and new consumer goods were not necessarily dictated by wealth and taste. French

LUXURY TRADES. Shops along London's Bond Street, 1992. (© Urs Kluyver/Woodfin Camp and Associates, New York)

economist François Véron de Forbonnais (1722–1800), in 1756, compared gold and imitation gold snuff boxes. He wrote that gold snuff boxes were bought by the man of luxury who squandered where he could, while the general taste preferred "convenience" and "a good price." An aesthetics of "patina," conveying family status and antiquity, dominated definitions of luxury goods before the eighteenth century, while a fashion system and novelty took precedence after (Berg, 2002).

The production and marketing of these new luxury goods also interacted closely with the fashion system that spread from the later seventeenth century. Luxury goods in early modern Paris were sold through the *marchands merciers*, who supplied the court, residents of the city, and tourists with objects of fine craftsmanship and fashionable design. They were considered unique among the Parisian Six Corporations because they did not work with their hands; instead they played an important design role, embellishing and remounting oriental imports, and setting luxury goods in a pattern of collecting and display, especially at Versailles. Their fashionable shops by the seventeenth century drew on the concept of novelty to shape the Parisian marketplace. They were also closely linked to the silk merchants who developed the seasonal fashion cycle in the Lyon silk industry to make Paris the fashion capital of Europe by the late seventeenth century. Retailing luxury goods provided the first model for retailing new fashion goods through *marchands merciers*, gold- and silversmiths, and toymakers (Sargentson, 1996).

Marketing, Supply, and Demand. The development of markets for these luxury goods over the course of the early modern period also contributed to markets for art, which can be considered a subset of the wider trade in luxury goods. The market for art goods helped to create the conditions for the emergence of an art system. An international market in prints from the mid-sixteenth century spread a knowledge and taste for great works of art. The trade in prints, as luxury goods and later as more widely available consumer goods, gave a wider public access to the major works of art in court and aristocratic collections. The imitation of the unique work of art both made it into a consumer good accessible to a wide audience, and helped to shape taste and to set any original artwork within a system of art (Brewer, 1997; De Marchi and Goodwin, 1999; North and Ormrod, 1998).

As prestige and status goods, the value of luxury goods is in their rarity, combined with a setting making them conspicuous and thus desirable because they convey status and wealth. They can be seen as positional goods, goods with a fixed supply and high elasticity of demand, and where consumer preferences are interdependent, an uninhabited island or an exclusive golf club or gym. But the pricing of luxury goods was about more than wealth and status; it was about identifying the sources of sensory pleasure, which made the good an object of desire: silks and furs, or fine perfumes and gold jewelry worn by or associated with young beautiful women. Luxury goods, and indeed consumer goods more generally, could be seen as a bundle of characteristics. Among those characteristics might be factors eliciting pleasure, such as novelty or ingenuity, rarity or beauty, all factors that might change over time and place (Bianchi, 1998; De Marchi and Goodwin, 1999; Hirsch, 1977).

Consideration of the economics of luxury goods more broadly passed out of the central framework of economic theory and public policy in the nineteenth century as marginal utility theories of pricing and supply-side economic models came to the fore. The role of luxury goods in the economies and wider societies of Europe and America was also displaced as an issue with widespread industrialization and new focus on mass production and standardized consumption during the nineteenth century. But luxury goods were to take on a new centrality with the excess consumption and collecting of Europe's and America's new superrich bourgeois classes. Banking and industrial families marked their wealth and status by building palatial residences or refurbishing those bought from aristocrats, and engaging in the collection of antique objects through the international auction houses, or the commissioning of unique pieces. Many of Europe's and America's major collections of furnishings, ceramics, and silverware as well as pictures arise from this later-nineteenth-century, early-twentieth-century phase of luxury expenditure. *Fin-de-siècle* debates on the decline of capitalism, moral corruption, and social division once again pushed luxury goods to the center of economic and social analysis. Thorstein Veblen represented this class in America in *The Theory of the Leisure Class* (1899). Werner Sombart, in Germany, wrote *Luxury and Capitalism* (1913) to argue the far-reaching effects of the demand for luxury. The origins of the Industrial Revolution, he argued, were not based in thrift and the associated accumulation of capital, but on the imperative to satisfy the greatly expanded demand for luxury (Berg and Eger, 2002).

Luxuries in Modern-Day Society. Luxury expenditure and luxury goods are, at the end of the twentieth and beginning of the twenty-first centuries, once again to the fore. A consumer society, marked by the quest for distinction, branding, and designer labels frame social identities. A new global economy with consumer parallels to that of the early modern world is marked by extremes of social division and an unprecedented awareness of those belonging to the new advertising world of luxury goods and those socially excluded. The global dimension of this exclusion is especially marked in a north-south divide between countries mainly in the Northern Hemisphere consuming luxuries, especially designer and fashion clothing, and those in poorer parts of the Southern Hemisphere producing them. Moral and political choices are highlighted by individuals who choose to boycott certain brands associated with the exploitation of cheap, third-world labor and by large-scale political action over recent world trade summits (Frank, 1999; Klein, 2000).

[*See also* Antiques Trade; Art Markets; Ceramics; Diamond Industry; *and* Jewelry Industry.]

BIBLIOGRAPHY

Berg, Maxine. "From Imitation to Invention: Creating Commodities in Eighteenth-Century Britain." *Economic History Review* 55 (2002), 1–30.

Berg, Maxine, and Helen Clifford, eds. *Consumers and Luxury*. Manchester, 1999.

Berg, Maxine, and Elizabeth Eger, eds. *Luxury in the Eighteenth Century: Debates, Desires, and Delectable Goods*. London, 2002.

Berry, Christopher. *The Idea of Luxury*. Cambridge, 1994.

Bianchi, Marina, ed. *The Active Consumer: Novelty and Surprise in Consumer Choice*. London, 1998.

Brewer, John. *The Pleasures of the Imagination: English Culture in the Eighteenth Century*. London, 1997.

Chaudhuri, Kirti N. *Asia before Europe*. Cambridge, 1990.

Clunas, Craig. *Superfluous Things: Material Culture and Social Status in Early Modern China*. Cambridge, 1991.

De Marchi, Neil, and Craufurd D. W. Goodwin, eds. *Economic Engagements with Art*. Durham and London, 1999.

Fox, Robert, and Anthony Turner, eds. *Luxury Trades and Consumerism in Ancien Régime Paris*. Aldershot, U. K., 1998.

Frank, Robert. *Luxury Fever: Why Money Fails to Satisfy in an Era of Excess*. New York, 1999.

Goldthwaite, Richard. *Wealth and the Demand for Art in Italy, 1300–1600*. Baltimore and London, 1993.

Hirsch, Fred. *Social Limits to Growth*. London, 1977.

Hunt, Alan. *Governance of the Consuming Passions: A History of Sumptuary Law*. London, 1996.

Klein, Naomi. *No Logo*. London, 2000.

Mitchell, David, ed. *Goldsmiths, Silversmiths, and Bankers: Innovation and the Transfer of Skill, 1550–1750*. Stroud, U.K., 1995.

Mukerji, Chandra. *From Graven Images: Patterns of Modern Materialism*. New York, 1983.

North, Michael, and David Ormrod, eds. *Art Markets in Europe, 1400–1800*. Aldershot, U. K., 1998.

Pomeranz, Kenneth. *The Great Divergence: China, Europe, and the Making of the Modern World Economy*. Princeton, 2000.

Sargentson, Carolyn. *Merchants and Luxury Markets: The Marchands Merciers of Eighteenth-Century Paris*. London, 1996.

Vickers, Michael, and David Gill, eds. *Artful Crafts: Ancient Greek Silverware and Pottery*. Oxford, 1994.

MAXINE BERG

LYON. At the intersection of the Rhône and Saône rivers in France, Lyon has long enjoyed prominence in commerce, both regional and international. In Roman times, the merchants and bargemen of what was called Lugdunum, "Capital of the Three Gauls," supplied grain, oil, and wine from the surrounding region, while artisan workshops produced high-quality pottery that, through long-distance trade went to areas as distant as Roman-occupied Egypt. In medieval Lyon—which achieved economic freedom in 1206, well before its political emancipation as a "free and royal city" in 1320—trade and money changing thrived.

LYON. View of the city and of the castle of Pierre-Encise from the Saône River, drawing by William Marlow (1740–1813). (Art Resource, NY)

Lyon's greatest century was the sixteenth. Based on a flourishing long-distance international trade in high-valued commodities, such as spices and silks, Lyon became the banking center of Europe. Four annual fairs brought to the city not only foreign merchants exchanging goods but also merchant-bankers, notably Italians, who, in the days immediately following the closing of each fair, transacted the settlement of accounts in the so-called "fairs of payment," using bills of exchange (Fr., *lettres de change*) and debentures (Fr., *obligations*) as favored instruments. Lyon's capital market supplied credit to French kings and made loans available to local peasants. Then, in the seventeenth century, the shift of international trade routes away from the Mediterranean Sea and toward the Atlantic Ocean eroded Lyon's prominence. Moreover, as Italian merchant-bankers sought proximity to the French court, with capital to feed the enormous borrowing appetite of the emerging absolute monarchy, Paris replaced Lyon as the financial capital of the kingdom.

In the eighteenth century, Lyon's economy was shifted to industry and manufacturing. The Lyon silk industry achieved international renown for the quality of its products, especially its sumptuous figured fabrics. Lyon also became the leading entrepôt for European trade in high-quality raw silk. Silk manufacture was strongly regional. Silk spinning and throwing, based on the raising of silkworms in mulberry orchards, were introduced into the rural and small-town hinterlands. The weaving of silk ornaments and ribbons flourished in the secondary urban centers of Saint-Étienne and Saint-Chamond, and in the nineteenth century, silk weaving was spread from the city of Lyon to the villages and towns of the surrounding provinces. The first weaving factories recruited a largely rural and female labor force; they were set up as the sources of raw silk, and silkworm cocoons shifted from the Mediterranean region to China and Japan. (The Middle East had imported silkworms and silkworking from China centuries before—and the Ottoman Empire had supplied Europe with silks via Italy and the Mediterranean until Europeans ventured to Asia overland on the Silk Road or by sea around Africa's Cape of Good Hope.)

The liaison of industry and commerce in silk generated streams of capital for investment in local and regional enterprises in other sectors; for example, Lyon capital was invested in the mining of coal in both of the major basins to the south and was used to build the Givors Canal, which linked the nearby Rive-de-Gier Basin to the Rhône River, thereby enabling coal to reach the Lyon market. Coal facilitated industrialization throughout the region—supplying heat and energy for metallurgy, metalworking, machinery manufacture, chemicals, glassworking, railroad-part manufacture, and railway-repair facilities. Numerous public works projects and transport innovations—bridges, docks, steamboat navigation, and especially the railroad—provided markets for those sectors or otherwise enhanced possibilities for Lyon's industrial expansion. This industrial legacy continued in Lyon into the twentieth century, through such prominent manufactures as automobiles, specialized parts for electrical-power generation, and pharmaceuticals. Another kind of legacy, embodying

Lyon's long tradition of assimilating commerce and industry to finance, was the Crédit Lyonnais bank; one of France's four "grand banks," it was founded in 1863 by the son of a Lyon silk manufacturer, Henri Germain. This new venture in the world of finance aspired to provide savers of all levels of fortune the opportunity for entrepreneurial investment, and it remains a fitting testament to an economic idealism that has often appealed to even the wealthiest of Lyon's citizens.

BIBLIOGRAPHY

Bouvier, Jean. *Naissance d'une banque: Le Crédit Lyonnais*. Paris, 1968. The best study of the origins and development of this bank, from its founding in 1863 through 1882, based largely on archival sources. A comprehensive, detailed, intelligent yet nontechnical narrative account, with some fascinating particulars about leading personalities.

Cayez, Pierre. *Métiers jacquard et hauts fourneaux aux origines de l'industrie lyonnaise*. Lyon, 1978. The standard comprehensive study of the industrialization of Lyon from the late eighteenth through the mid-nineteenth century. Makes the case for several *leitmotifs* about Lyon's distinctive pattern of capital mobilization, investment, and entrepreneurial behavior, including (1) the strongly commerical orientation of investment, which resists immobilizing capital in long-term, high-risk, large-scale enterprise, and (2) the traditionalism of Lyon's greatest industry, silk manufacture, which sets the tone for investment behavior in several, though not all, other sectors as well.

Cayez, Pierre. *Crises et croissance de l'industrie lyonnaise, 1850–1900*. Paris, 1980. Continues the story of Lyon's industrialization through the end of the nineteenth century. Despite continued reluctance on the part of "commercial-financial" capital to make long-term industrial investment, emphasis is placed on significant changes of behavior, even in the highly traditionalist silk manufacture, where industrial diversification and technological innovation become more common than in the first half of the century as responses to changing economic environment.

Garden, Maurice. *Lyon et les Lyonnais au XVIIIe siècle*. Paris, 1970. A masterful empirical study of Lyon's demography, social structure, and the social and political actions of the population during the eighteenth century. Because the economy is kept constantly in view as social developments are outlined, this remains the single most important work on the city for that period. A major contribution is the delineation of the relationship between the employment needs of the silk industry and the demographic behaviors particular to the city, which included both migration and wetnursing as linking the urban to the surrounding regional economy.

Gascon, Richard. *Grand commerce et vie urbaine au XVIe siècle: Lyon et ses marchands*. Paris, 1971. The definitive study of Lyon's grand century of economic life—the sixteenth—when it served as the banking capital of Europe, as well as a leading center of international trade; focuses on the crucial agents of this role—the merchants and merchant-bankers, particularly their activities in the fairs of Lyon.

Laferrère, Michel. *Lyon: Ville industrielle*. Paris, 1960. Written by a geographer and based on meticulous study of techniques, firms, and urban landscape, this study of Lyon's industry of the nineteenth and twentieth centuries remains authoritative in many respects, including the distinctive features of industrial organization, entrepreneurial initiative, and the connection to spatial and physical environment with respect to technological change. Each of the major industrial sectors—silk manufacture, metal work, machinery manufacture, and chemical production—are discussed, as well as transitions from artisanal methods to "modern" industrial production.

Latreille, André, ed. *Histoire de Lyon et du Lyonnais*. Toulouse, 1975. General survey of the history of Lyon, from antiquity through the twentieth century, written when social and economic factors were emphasized.

GEORGE J. SHERIDAN

M

MACEDONIA. *See* Balkans.

MACHINE TOOLS INDUSTRY *[This entry contains two subentries, a historical overview and a discussion of technological change.]*

Historical Overview

Machine tools cut, reshape, or resurface metal and draw from electric, mechanical, or hydraulic power. To reduce vibration, machine tools are large and heavy, with their frames secured to walls or to the floor. The category of machine tools ordinarily excludes portable tools, tools applied to wood, or tools powered by humans or animals. Almost all have been made principally of steel or iron.

Machine tools are classic industrial capital equipment purchased for manufacturing and used for production, not for consumption. Machine tools makers form a relatively small industry that has had a major impact on the industrialization of the world's economies.

Many machine tools are built around the basic lathe, a device that rotates a workpiece of input metal at a steady rate. This turning capability, with various attachments, is the basis for most machine tools operations, such as drilling, grinding, and sanding. Milling is the operation of cutting a workpiece by pushing it into a rotating blade. Refined control of the tools and the workpiece produces a precise cut. Progress has taken the form of greater speed, greater control and precision, and improved safety.

History to 1840. Skills and technologies from several sources merged into machine tools making. Hand-powered lathes had existed for thousands of years in China and for hundreds of years in Italy, Sweden, France, and elsewhere. Makers of clocks and scientific instruments were accustomed to intricate tools. Textile spinning devices in England and in China were complex but generally were made of wood. Guns were bored in the Netherlands, Switzerland, and Germany in the early 1700s with animal or human power (Steeds, 1969, p. 5). Over the course of the 1700s many improvements in these devices were made. In most instances the designer of the machine was also its principal user, and there was no distinct industry supplying machine tools.

In the late 1700s an industry of firms making large-framed machines meant for use by other metalworkers began in Britain. A classic example machine, patented by John Wilkinson in 1774, was designed to bore out the insides of cannons. It turned out to have a more valuable application. James Watt had designed a steam engine that was much more efficient than existing steam engines, but building it required a nearly perfectly round steam piston that would allow the arm of the piston to fit inside the cylinder and move without letting steam escape. Cylinders made by hammering leaked because they were not close enough to perfectly round. Watt confronted this problem for years, until he discovered that Wilkinson's boring machine could make smoothly rounded cylinders. Many experts consider Wilkinson's machine the first general purpose machine tool, since its design was suitable for multiple applications, boring either cannons or piston cylinders. The patent-based monopolies in both boring machines and steam engines were profitable, and these machines mark the beginning of a machine tools industry.

Large ironworks were the early makers and users of machine tools. In the succeeding decades machine tools innovations were clustered around a dozen or so legendary British mechanics and engineers who trained a generation of successors. Among them were James Watt, Matthew Murray, Joseph Bramah, Henry Maudslay, and James Nasmyth. Of special interest is the work of instrument makers, such as Jesse Ramsden in Britain and Jean-Charles Borda in France, whose improved measuring and surveying instruments helped advance a variety of activities necessary for economic progress.

In 1796 Matthew Boulton and Watt completed the first known separate heavy machine shop to support their steam engine factory. In 1797 Matthew Murray's steam engine firm in Leeds may have become the first to sell machine tools as an ongoing business. In short order several firms were making machine tools both for their own use and to supply a market. Competition developed in machine tools indirectly as a side effect of competition for quality in steam engines.

Joseph Bramah invented an improved lock in 1784 and for six years made the locks by hand. He was desperate to manufacture them in quantity but could not find a way to carry out the work accurately enough by machine. In 1790 Bramah hired the talented young mechanic Henry Maudslay, who designed and built special-purpose machinery for producing the locks. Maudslay started his own shop in 1797 and over the next thirty years became the industry's preeminent figure.

Most of the major participants in machine tools developments of the time passed through Maudslay's London shop, named Maudslay and Field. Richard Roberts, for example, left Maudslay and Field to start his own shop in Manchester. Roberts's many inventions included the self-acting mule of 1825, the most advanced spinning machine of its time, giving Roberts an important part in the Industrial Revolution's growing textile industry. Another of Maudslay's associates was Joseph Whitworth, who successfully advocated standardizing the form and size of screw threads partly because of the success of this practice in Maudslay's shop.

The founders of the industry were notably dexterous, and in general they were well traveled and had experience in multiple mechanical shops. Only a few were well educated formally, and many did not serve out a full apprenticeship because they seized valuable business opportunities before finishing. The best-known mechanics ran their own shops, rather than functioning only in a research and development capacity. They varied greatly in their success as businesspeople. Several became wealthy, but Roberts, among others, ran into financial trouble. Some had business partners who managed the entrepreneurial engineering enterprises, such as Watt's partner Boulton.

A number of these mechanical shops were open to outside visitors and only occasionally defended themselves with secrecy or legal control of patents. To some extent this tradition continued in the industry. Machine tools makers survived by having niche markets and tacit knowledge of how to make and sell appropriate products into them, not through the tight control of widely applicable technological or scientific information.

Role of the Industry. Since 1840 the industry has never been highly concentrated in a single country or by firms within any country, and there have been hundreds of companies in the United Kingdom and the United States. Few firms are large. In no large country has as much as 1 percent of the workforce been in the machine tools–making business. Most firms through 1900 were partnerships named for the partners.

Machine tools producers tend to innovate around the process of making a device, not by inventing product categories. Successful new product proposals usually have come from customers. Machine tools producers have difficulty persuading customers to switch on the basis of new technology apart from a customer's perception of a need.

The inception and early growth of the industry was in Britain. In the nineteenth century American-made machine tools were notably lighter and less durable than the British standards. American machine tools builders were supported by a growing market and defended by high tariffs, and they showed some inclination to make special-purpose tools more than did the British builders. Use of special-purpose machine tools to make large numbers of interchangeable parts was later called the American system of manufactures (discussed and defined in Hounshell, 1984). The Habakkuk hypothesis (Habakkuk, 1962) argues that Americans went in this direction because skilled craft workers were scarce and expensive. Following this path, U.S. machine tools builders gradually took technological leadership in the late 1800s. Authors have written about a corresponding British decline, though it was natural that expansion and innovation would occur in other countries as they industrialized. Later the industry became more evenly divided among industrial countries.

Interchangeable Parts and Mass Production. Early advocates and implementations of a system of uniform and therefore interchangeable parts came from gun making. French armories went this direction, driven by General Jean-Baptiste de Gribeauval and the inventor and armorer Honoré Blanc. Efforts to implement this new system started gradually around 1765 and reached considerable success by the 1780s but were subsequently abandoned (Alder, 1997). The influential military engineer and author Louis de Tousard brought the approach to the United States and persuasively argued for the benefits of this form of rationalization (Hounshell, 1984).

The vision of interchangeability became central to the U.S. gun makers, both public and private, in the first decades of the nineteenth century. Gun manufacturer Simeon North made it work, and Eli Whitney was a famous advocate. Gun makers at the public U.S. armories carried the project forward. At one armory the inventor and manufacturer John H. Hall analyzed the requirements of precise manufacture and expounded the useful principle that, to reduce inaccuracy, a workpiece should be moved as little as possible, and each machine tool should hold it fixed with respect to the same bearing point on the workpiece. By about 1825 the U.S. armories made guns with interchangeable parts.

To achieve interchangeability, parts were made to fit to gauge, that is, to fit fixed measurements built into a tool. Developing a complete set of these gauges was a task associated with machine tools work that itself required design and imagination. In practice before the late 1800s, filing parts by hand was required to make parts close enough to

HALL OF MACHINES. Universal Exhibiton of 1889, Paris. (Bibliothèque Nationale de France, Paris/Snark/Art Resource, NY)

their intended size to be interchangeable (Gordon, 1988). But following from the concept of interchangeable parts was the long-standing idea that machines could mass manufacture them with little human intervention. Over the decades machine tools did larger and larger fractions of the work, reducing the time needed for filing.

Mass production of metal objects expanded to a larger scale in the 1850s, as machine tools for making pins, screws, and needles displaced workers in several skilled crafts (Rolt, 1965, pp. 57–59). Much thought went into the question of whether or not new machine tools could replace known methods of work and the workers themselves. A recurring subject of industrial and labor history is the degree to which this was feared and the degree to which it was true. Craft work on metal did decline in importance with time. Some new work appeared in the form of making, repairing, and selling machines as the machine tools industry gradually expanded. A long-lasting principle

is that general-purpose machine tools tend to require skilled operators, but special-purpose ones do not.

Mass production methods usually required specialized, single-purpose machinery. General-purpose machine tools advanced too, notably with the invention of the turret lathe, which had several tools on one spindle and jaws (called chucks) to hold the workpiece (Steeds, 1969, p. 55). Turret lathes, developed in the 1840s or 1850s in New England, dramatically improved lathe machining over time as they were improved to have preset lengths, sequences of tool operations, and stop distances. This reduced the dexterity required of the operator, reduced errors, and increased the overall speed of operation.

After 1880 cutting edges were made increasingly of steel alloys containing tungsten, chromium, nickel, vanadium, or other materials. These high-speed steels could tolerate much higher cutting speeds than previous materials while the tool still retained precision and rigidity. The transition from steam power to electric power in factories gradually obviated the need to receive power from a central source through belts. This allowed more flexibility in the design of the factories using machine tools. Adoption of these new technologies diffused over many decades and along with many associated innovations.

Demand for machine tools rose with the appearance of new manufactured products. On the leading edge of heavy use of fast tools and mass production in the late nineteenth century were manufacturers of sewing machines and bicycles. Some bicycle parts were mass produced quickly and cheaply using new stamping machines. In the early twentieth century the leading sectors included automobiles and airplanes. In automobile manufacture especially, mass production reached new levels of analysis and refinement. In the novel assembly lines of Ford Motor Company starting in the 1910s conveyor belts automatically moved workpieces between operators of specially designed machine tools that made a continuous flow of production possible. The later need to modify the assembly line product induced a trend back toward more general-purpose machine tools.

Recent Times. Since the mid-1800s there have been hundreds of machine tools establishments in each of the large industrial countries. Japanese manufacturers specialized in making high-quality, low-priced versions of the most common machine tools. The technology and industry have diffused worldwide. Lower costs in developing countries put some companies in the older industrial countries on the defensive.

Since 1950 growing numbers of machine tools have digital measures and programmable controls over lengths, angles, and distances that may be submitted to the machine on cards or tapes. This attribute is called numerical control. Numerically controlled machines give the operator access to high precision in measurement without gauges and fixtures. This reduces the time and costs required to configure them (*The Machine Tool Industry*, 1974, p. 6).

As of the late 1990s the value of worldwide production of machine tools was estimated in the range of U.S. $35 to $40 billion. The countries producing the most were, in order, Japan, Germany, the United States, and Italy. Taken together these countries received about two-thirds of machine tools industry revenues (*U.S. Industry and Trade Outlook '99*, 1999). Major customers are the manufacturers of automobiles, aircraft, household appliances, electronics, and other machine tools.

Economics of the Industry. New machine tools usually appeared as solutions to a specific problem faced by a manufacturer and evolved jointly with their users. When a machine tool became useful to a class of customers in different industries with a similar problem, the niche market for the tool often became the basis for a separate firm. The machine tools industry thereby grew and became an important path for the diffusion of new techniques, equipment, and skills among metal-using industries (Rosenberg, 1963). Machine tools have evolved jointly and in response to leading segments of industry, notably steam engines, firearms, woodworking equipment, agricultural implements, locomotives, sewing machines, bicycles, automobiles, ships, and aircraft. Industrial districts formed as machine tools makers clustered close to their customers and a workforce of skilled metalworkers populated an area.

In machine tools building, design costs tend to be high. Production work consists principally of machining the parts and then assembling them, which is not mass production work itself. Flow production is more efficient than batch production only if the volume of demand is sufficient. There are economies of scale in production of a particular machine tool product, partly because of its learning-by-doing aspects, but historically there do not seem to be substantial economies of scale or scope from having a large firm or there would be a stronger trend toward concentration (Pratten, 1971). The largest firms, such as Alfred Herbert, Ltd., in Britain around 1900, had many thousands of employees each and long-lasting success but never dominated the industry or its technical standards.

Demand for machine tools can be erratic because machine tools are such durable goods and because demand for them is heavily dependent on demand for other machines. In a boom there can be tremendous demand, but orders can completely disappear when the demand is saturated (*The Machine Tool Industry*, 1974, p. 43). Machine tools sales, like sales of other durable goods, are therefore a leading indicator of business cycles. New demand comes more from obsolescence of a previous generation of tools than from wearing out (Brown, 1957).

BIBLIOGRAPHY

Alder, Kenneth. *Engineering the Revolution: Arms, Enlightenment, and the Making of Modern France.* Princeton, 1997.

Brown, William H. "Innovation in the Machine Tool Industry." *Quarterly Journal of Economics* 71.3 (August 1957), 406–425.

Floud, Roderick. *The British Machine Tool Industry, 1850–1914.* Cambridge, 1976.

Gordon, Robert B. "Who Turned the Mechanical Ideal into Mechanical Reality?" *Technology and Culture* 29 (1988), 744–778.

Habakkuk, H. J. *American and British Technology in the Nineteenth Century.* Cambridge, 1962.

Hirsch, Werner Z. "Manufacturing Progress Functions." *Review of Economics and Statistics* 34.3 (1952), 143–155.

Hounshell, David A. *From the American System to Mass Production, 1800–1932.* Baltimore, 1984.

The Machine Tool Industry. United Nations Industrial Development Organization. New York, 1974.

Pratten, C. F. "Economies of Scale for Machine Tool Production." *Journal of Industrial Economics* 19.2 (April 1971), 148–165.

Roe, Joseph W. *English and American Tool Builders.* New Haven, Conn., 1916.

Rolt, Lester T. C. *A Short History of Machine Tools*. Cambridge, Mass., 1965.

Rosenberg, Nathan. "Technological Change in the Machine Tool Industry, 1840–1910." *Journal of Economic History* 23.4 (December 1963), 414–443.

Steeds, W. *A History of Machine Tools, 1700–1910*. Oxford, 1969.

U.S. Industry and Trade Outlook '99. U.S. Department of Commerce, International Trade Administration. Washington, D.C., 1999.

Usher, Abbott Payson. *A History of Mechanical Inventions*. Rev. ed. Mineola, N.Y., 1954.

PETER B. MEYER

Technological Change

Although production of machine tools is a small industry composed of little-known firms, since the late eighteenth century the makers of machine tools have exerted a centrally important role in animating the world's industrial economies. Machine tools are traditionally defined as "tools that shape metal by grinding or progressively cutting away chips" under the U.S. Census Bureau's Standard Industry Classification. Over the past two centuries, tools such as lathes, milling machines, and multipurpose machining centers have provided the metalworking capacity to produce the steam engines, locomotives, guns, sewing machines, bicycles, automobiles, artillery pieces, and aircraft that are icons of industrial life. Machine tools have incorporated continuous innovations since the 1770s, largely because entrepreneurs and engineers have perceived that improvements in tool design have tremendous multiplier effects, improving the quality, increasing the quantity, or bolstering the productivity of metalworking production in a host of diverse industries. Individually or collectively, those three motives have impelled all innovation in machine tools.

British Origins. The lathe became the "master tool" of any machine shop, so called because it could accomplish most machining processes needed to make other tools or machines. Lathes to turn wooden parts were common in the late Roman period. But metal lathes of industrial scale, capable of turning large iron castings to precise dimensions, date their origins to machines of the 1770s developed to bore the cylinders of James Watt's condensing steam engines. Over the next sixty years, a succession of brilliant British engineer mechanics, including Henry Maudslay (1771–1831) and Joseph Whitworth (1803–1887), improved the lathe's precision and increased its versatility.

Working in specialized industrial districts in London and Manchester, these engineers ran general jobbing machine shops that made steam engines, printing presses, and mill gearing—whatever a customer required. In building such custom mechanisms, Maudslay, Whitworth, and others developed novel tools, such as slotters, planers, and shapers. These tools to produce flat surfaces in iron parts provided huge gains in productivity and precision over earlier hand methods. But the new tools represented a huge capital expense to potential buyers, so a market for new machine tools developed only haltingly after 1820 or so, as the spread of steam power in various applications bolstered demand for metalworking capacity. Widespread exports to continental Europe after 1830 provide further evidence of the technical leadership of British machine tools. In turn, its capacities in metalworking production, provided by this first generation of machine tools, gave Britain worldwide leadership in such industries as textile machinery, marine engineering, and locomotive building.

Transatlantic Innovations in Systematic Mechanical Engineering. One clear sign of maturity in British machine tool practice was Joseph Whitworth's success in promulgating a system to standardize the threads of nuts and bolts in use across Britain (developed in 1841, generally adopted by 1860). Whitworth traveled to the United States in 1853 and later authored an influential report of his impressions of American mechanical engineering practice. The Whitworth Report pointed especially to U.S. innovations in machine tooling to produce mechanisms like Colt pistols with interchangeable parts. While Whitworth was naturally drawn to U.S. novelties and departures from British practice, many transatlantic similarities exist in the development of machine tooling. Although lagging about thirty years behind the British, the Americans by 1860 also had generalized shops engaged in making heavy machine tools for the market. Located in industrial districts that promoted collaborations with customers (in Rhode Island, the Connecticut River valley, and Philadelphia), these toolmakers included the Putnam Machine Company, Ames Manufacturing Company, William Sellers and Company, and Bement and Dougherty. As in Britain, the heavy lathes, slotters, and planers made by these firms provided the basic American industrial infrastructure: mill machinery, steam engines, line shafting and gearing, and locomotives.

The leading proprietor-engineers who ran these British and American shops shared an interest in innovations to systematize their operations. In 1864, William Sellers (1824–1905) promulgated an American standard for screw threads, with improvements on Whitworth's system, that became widely adopted by the 1870s. In both nations, machine tool proprietors pioneered dimensioned mechanical drawings, the foundational genre of engineering knowledge and practice. Design drawings extended the engineer's innovative reach, while working drawings increased managerial control and productive efficiency. In sum, their innovations in products and in systematic production methods transformed the leading British and American tool builders into the first generation of professional mechanical engineers.

Armory Practice and Interchangeable Parts. Among systemic mechanical engineering practices, U.S. engineers led the world in precision standards of metalworking to make consumer products in large quantities using interchangeable parts. Machine tools played an important if often misunderstood role in the evolution of American mass production.

Imbued with Enlightenment rationalism, French army officers of the late eighteenth century originally developed the concept of making their muskets from metal and wooden parts fashioned so precisely that they could interchange from one gun to the next. They reasoned that such a production system would curb the powers of the craft guilds that controlled gun making, boost overall output, and greatly simplify battlefield repair of weapons. The French officers never fully tested these ideas, but they spurred the U.S. Army to undertake this revolution in metalworking.

Under a directive in an 1815 act of Congress, officers in the Ordnance Department committed to achieve interchangeable production of muskets at the federal arsenals at Harpers Ferry, Virginia, and Springfield, Massachusetts. It turned out to be a hugely demanding task. Indeed, historians now know that Eli Whitney, once credited as originating the use of interchangeable parts in musket production circa 1810, never actually achieved that goal. Notwithstanding its considerable powers and ample budget, the U.S. Army required twenty-five years of effort and experimentation to achieve consistent interchangeability of parts across the production of its 1841 model rifle. Machine tools, however, played a relatively minor role in that achievement, as tooling of the era lacked the requisite precision to make parts to interchangeable standards, two-thousandths of an inch for metal components. Making guns interchangeable chiefly required a thorough subdivision of skilled hand labor, extensive use of gauges and templates to guide workers as they filed parts to finished dimensions, and exacting standards of inspection.

In one sense, historians have overplayed the U.S. armories' antebellum work in interchangeable parts. After all, the French originated the concept. An English engineer, Sir Marc Isambard Brunel, did significant work circa 1800 in volume production using special-purpose machinery of greater originality and complexity than the armories' mechanisms (to make wooden blocks or pulleys for ships). By the 1840s, American firms were making uniform designs of clocks in huge quantities, although their parts were often not interchangeable on a strict basis, as the clocks required some fitting during assembly. Indeed, looking at the practices of many industries to 1915, as David Hounshell (1984) has, it is clear that few met the test of strict interchangeability in all parts (the armories' goal), suggesting that the goal itself was more burden than benefit to manufacturers and consumers of that era.

But this early example of government-sponsored research and development did have a considerable influence on the subsequent history of the machine tool industry. Most important, it demonstrated that the mechanical ideal of interchangeable parts could become a reality. During the Civil War, government-trained artisans carried armory practice to dozens of arms-making companies that provided conscripted armies with the instruments of mass slaughter. Two tooling innovations developed in armory practice, the milling machine and the drop forging press, later played key roles in interchangeable work as general standards of precision and mensuration improved. The first influential private-sector offshoot of armory practice, the Colt Patent Fire Arms Company, used a diverse range of machine tools to manufacture pistols with interchangeable parts by 1855. Many other firms took up this challenge as the U.S. consumer society spread in the decades following the Civil War.

Machine Tools and Mass Production. Between 1865 and 1915, many American firms perfected their techniques to mass produce a range of complex consumer durables using interchangeable metal parts, proceeding in rough chronological order from sewing machines to watches, typewriters, bicycles, and automobiles. For many decades, economic historians such as H. J. Habakkuk (1962) pointed to factor endowments to explain America's lead (and Britain's lag) in interchangeable mass production. Their thinking was that, because skilled craft workers were relatively scarce in the United States and commanded higher wages than their British counterparts, U.S. entrepreneurs had a direct incentive to substitute capital for labor by investing in novel machine tools. On balance, the evidence now developed by technological historians tends to discount this thesis. They found that U.S. firms like Singer Sewing Machine and McCormick Reaper relied upon skilled if subdivided labor well into the Gilded Age; such firms lagged in achieving truly interchangeable parts, and their shift into capital-intensive production methods generally originated in the 1880s. It appears that rising demand, often resulting from national advertising campaigns, provided the key spur that forced these manufacturers to turn to the American machine tool industry for tooling and manufacturing expertise to bolster their output.

Two machine tool firms played particularly important roles in spreading interchangeable production. Founded circa 1865 in Hartford, Connecticut, Pratt and Whitney specialized for a half century in power tooling for gun making, exporting complete sets of production machinery for national armories across Europe. A Providence, Rhode Island, firm, Brown and Sharpe, moved into the machine tool industry in the 1860s, supplying automated screw-making machines and universal milling machines to wartime

TOOLS. Block making machine, from *Cyclopedia of Useful Arts, Mechinaical and Chemical,* vol. 1, by Charles Tomlinson, 1854. (Prints and Photographs Division, Library of Congress)

gun makers. After the Civil War, Brown and Sharpe's primary business shifted from making interchangeable sewing machines to producing a broad line of machine tools, including milling and grinding machines capable of precise work to interchangeable tolerances. These two New England toolmakers supplemented their lines of machine tools with precision measuring tools, including calipers and micrometers, that aided machinists worldwide in achieving higher standards of accuracy in their work.

The New England toolmakers provide the best evidence of a powerful phenomenon known as technological convergence, which accelerated the impacts of innovation in machine tools, particularly in the United States. An economic historian, Nathan Rosenberg (1963), originated this concept with his insight that a relatively narrow range of metalworking tools and techniques could and did produce a wide range of products, ranging from firearms to automobiles. Techniques converged, while products diverged. As old and new manufacturers entered a new field, such as typewriter production in the 1880s, those that specialized in the new field gained economies over competitors. But how could such specialists garner the knowledge they needed for efficient production? They turned to the machine tool industry. Tool builders adapted metalworking

tools and techniques developed for older industries, such as sewing machine production, to solve the production needs of newer industries like typewriters.

The ultimate expression of technological convergence entailed specialization by tool producers themselves. Specialized American toolmakers emerged in the 1880s, centered largely in Cincinnati, Ohio. Lodge and Davis specialized in turret lathes, Bickford made drilling machines, G. A. Gray built metal planers, and Cincinnati Milling Machine came to dominate its namesake niche. Their product lines underwent continuous innovation, as custom solutions developed for one set of customers (such as techniques to grind ball bearings for bicycle makers of the 1890s) then became stock fixtures or accessories available to all, for example, automakers of 1910. The innovative ferment of the American machine tool industry after 1860 contrasted greatly with relative stasis in Britain. Two developments circa 1900 only widened the disparity.

High-Speed Steel and Electric Drives. Until 1890, the main thrust of innovation in machine tools in Britain, the United States, and Prussia was an increase in the precision and capacity of common types of lathes, planers, milling machines, and other standard types of tools. These innovations improved throughout for tool users, raising their return on capital. The American reach for interchangeable metalworking resulted in some novel tool designs, such as automatic screw machines and precision grinders, that deskilled work. But it appears that increased output was the dominant motive in the expansion of interchangeable manufacturing. To this point, the direct needs of tool-using manufacturers drove innovations in machine tools. But after 1890, two American developments transformed the entire industry: high-speed tool steels and electric-drive motors for tools. These innovations grew from and reflected growing sophistication in the broader community of professional mechanical engineering.

A lathe or metal planer ultimately depended upon a comparatively small piece of sharpened tool steel to actually cut the work piece. In Maudslay's day, carbon steels proved adequate cutting tools, although they needed frequent regrinding to maintain a sharp cutting edge. In 1868, a British ironmaster, Robert Mushet (1811–1891), developed an improved alloy tool steel that became essential in machining tough new materials like railway axles of manganese steel. In 1900, Mushet steel was superceded by a demonstration at a Paris machine tool show of a new chrome-tungsten alloy steel developed by two American engineers, Frederick Taylor (1856–1915) and Maunsel White (1856–1912). This "high speed steel" worked best on deep and rapid cuts. Engineers visiting the Paris show stood dumbfounded at the demonstration lathe, watching as the new steel vastly increased the common productivity of a lathe even as the tool glowed to a dull cherry red from the speed and friction of its cuts. Taylor coupled his work on tool steels with rigorous studies of ideal "speeds and feeds" for operating common tools. Taylor's innovations ultimately proved two points, that machine tools could achieve vastly higher output and that all existing tool designs required complete reengineering to achieve the strength needed to follow Taylor's precepts. American and German tool builders took up that design challenge readily enough after 1900, while the more traditional British makers lagged in updating their product lines.

After 1910, electric motors to drive machine tools became increasingly common in the best machine shops and manufacturing plants. Until then, tool-using shops and manufacturers relied on a source of water power or steam power to drive overhead line shafts, which in turn drove individual tools through belts and pulleys. The new electric drives curbed frictional power losses (offering dramatic fuel savings), promoted flexibility in plant floor layouts (improving work flows), and gave superintendents greater control over cutting speeds (increasing output and precision). Switching to electric power represented a huge expense for tool users, so for decades it was far more prevalent in novel industries than in mature plants. Largely for that reason, the United States and Germany, rising indus-

trial powers, led the Britain in adopting electric power. The makers of machine tools had to adapt their products to electric drives, a process that proceeded more or less simultaneously into the 1920s with the redesigns that high-speed steel impelled.

Machine Tools and Automobile Manufacture. High-speed steel and electric drive tooling proved particularly advantageous to the major rising industry of the early twentieth century, automobile manufacture. In many regards, the auto industry was simply the latest sector of consumer products, in a line stretching back to Colt firearms, to develop with the midwifery of machine tool firms. But within a decade following 1910, the production needs of American automakers entirely reordered the U.S. machine tool industry for three fundamental reasons. New kinds of tools, such as centerless grinders, were essential to machine novel materials like the alloy steels that automakers required to make high-strength gears, axles, and crankshafts that would withstand the speed and shocks cars encountered. Unprecedented numbers of tools were required to produce autos in the quantities the market demanded. By 1915, nearly a third of U.S. machine tool production went to the auto industry. Novel kinds of special-purpose tooling accounted for an increasing share of those sales as automakers boosted output by subdividing and deskilling work. The moving assembly line exemplified the new labor regime. But routinized assembly depended upon battalions of semiskilled operatives running specially designed machines, such as cylinder head drillers, engine block tappers, and planetary gear grinders. These semiautomatic machines turned out vast quantities of parts to the precise, interchangeable tolerances required for fast assembly on the line.

The Ford Motor Company led in creating this new generation of tooling, just as it pioneered the moving assembly line to make Model T cars (1914). Indeed, Ford often designed its own special-purpose tooling in-house, leaving machine tool builders merely to execute its blueprints. Less committed to a single model, other automakers preferred more adaptable tooling. Tool builders, particularly those in Cincinnati, responded by offering standard models of milling, boring, or grinding machines, which they rendered highly adaptable to different production environments by offering semicustom attachments. While adaptable, most tools for the auto industry had skill, precision, and automation designed into the machine. To develop these products, machine tool firms worked in close collaboration with the production engineers of the major automakers. As auto sales surged ahead in the 1950s, General Motors, Chrysler, and Ford extended their mechanization into unskilled tasks, purchasing automated loaders and transfer machines that increased output and lowered labor costs. Again U.S. machine tool makers provided the expertise Detroit needed in its long-standing campaign to bolster output by substituting capital for labor.

Recent Innovations and Their Consequences. In the three decades following World War II, the American machine tool industry focused on a challenge that was at once new and old, adapting the computer to guide the processes of metal cutting and thus replace skilled machinists entirely. During the 1950s, with motivation and financing provided by the U.S. Air Force, researchers at Masschusetts Institute of Technology (MIT) developed a method to translate regular shop drawings into an abstract mathematical language that guided the cutting tool of a lathe or miller. Computers aided the programming of these numerically controlled tools, originally customized versions of standard lathes and millers. Numeric control was a new method to achieve a goal that had animated many of the pioneering British toolmakers a century earlier, to increase productivity by replacing freethinking workers with docile machines. In the mid-1950s, a Milwaukee toolmaker, Kearney and Trecker, developed a new, automated machining center that combined three traditional tools in a single unit, another technology that interacted with numerical control.

Computerized numeric control (CNC) and machining centers became dominant technologies but proved highly disruptive to the U.S. machine tool industry, notwithstanding their American origins. Japanese toolmakers rallied to a national standard language for CNC, aiding its adoption there and abroad. In the United States, different proprietary languages vied for acceptance among machine tool users, hindering the adoption of all. Machining centers at once eroded the decades of expertise that had sustained America's specialized tool builders. The new integration of computing, electromechanical controls, and novel machine forms called for high commitments to research and development and deep expertise in the engineering sciences. German tool builders proved particularly adept at that combination, leveraging their strength in apprenticeship training and their ties to technical universities. Because of these and other factors, the Japanese and German tool industries surpassed their American competitors in the value of sales worldwide during the 1980s.

As its recent history suggests, the machine tool industry remains a mainspring of industrial dynamism, even in high-wage countries. While the tools have deskilled and automated many manufacturing jobs, their design and construction call for high value-added labor, drawing deeply from engineering skill sets. Even after two hundred years of innovation, the machine tool industry provides potent productivity gains across the industrial economies of the world.

BIBLIOGRAPHY

Alder, Ken. *Engineering the Revolution: Arms and Enlightenment in France, 1763–1815*. Princeton, 1997. Detailed account of the Enlightenment origins of interchangeable arms production in revolutionary France.

Brown, John K. "When Machines Became Grey and Drawings Black and White: William Sellers and the Rationalization of Mechanical Engineering." *Journal of the Society for Industrial Archaeology* 25 (1999), 29–54. History of the leading American machine tool firm of the mid-nineteenth century, focusing particularly on innovations in its designing capacities.

Edmonson, James M. *From Mecanicien to Ingenieur: Technical Education and the Machine Building Industry in Nineteenth-Century France*. New York, 1987. One of the few English-language studies of innovation in mechanical engineering in France, with significant coverage of machine tools.

Finegold, David, et al. *The Decline of the U.S. Machine Tool Industry and Prospects for Its Sustainable Recovery*. Santa Monica, Calif., 1994. Overview of U.S., German, and Japanese machine tool industries since 1980.

Fitch, Charles H. *Report on the Manufactures of Interchangeable Mechanism: Tenth Census of the United States*. Washington, D.C., 1880. A detailed original source on the role of machine tools in interchangeable metalworking in the United States.

Floud, Roderick C. *The British Machine Tool Industry, 1850–1914*. Cambridge, 1976. Provides some consideration of British innovations in tooling.

Gordon, Robert B. "Who Turned the Mechanical Ideal into Mechanical Reality?" *Technology and Culture* 29 (1988), 744–778. Details the reliance upon skilled hand labor to achieve interchangeable production at the U.S. armories of the mid-nineteenth century.

Habakkuk, H. J. *American and British Technology in the Nineteenth Century*. Cambridge, 1962. The leading comparative interpretation of metalworking production in the context of factor endowments.

Hoke, Donald R. *Ingenious Yankees: The Rise of the American System of Manufactures in the Private Sector*. New York, 1990. Details the uses of machine tools in consumer product industries, providing alternative interpretations to Hounshell.

Hounshell, David A. *From the American System to Mass Production, 1800–1932: The Development of Manufacturing Technology in the United States*. Baltimore, 1984. The leading secondary source on the diffusion of armory practice into high-volume American manufacturing.

Roe, Joseph Wickham. *English and American Tool Builders*. New York, 1916. Provides capsule biographies of leading innovators in machine tools.

Rolt, L. T. C. *Tools for the Job: A History of Machine Tools to 1950*. London, 1965. The best comprehensive history of innovation in machine tools, well illustrated and highly accessible.

Rosenberg, Nathan. "Technological Change in the Machine Tool Industry, 1840–1910." *Journal of Economic History* 23 (1963), 414–443. Outlines the concept of technological convergence.

Rosenberg, Nathan, ed. *The American System of Manufactures*. Edinburgh, 1969. Reprint of reports by British commissioners on American manufactures circa 1853, including the Whitworth Report, with annotations.

Saul, S. B., ed. *Technological Change: The United States and Britain in the Nineteenth Century*. London, 1970. Collection of essays on transatlantic innovations in metalworking.

Scranton, Philip. *Endless Novelty: Specialty Production and American Industrialization, 1865–1925*. Princeton, 1997. The best source on Cincinnati machine tool firms among other industries.

Smith, Merritt Roe. *Harpers Ferry Armory and the New Technology: The Challenge of Change*. Ithaca, N.Y., 1977. The leading account of armory practice.

Woodbury, Robert S. *Studies in the History of Machine Tools.* Cambridge, Mass., 1972. Detailed histories of innovation in lathes, gear-cutting machines, grinders, and milling machines.

JOHN K. BROWN

MADAGASCAR. *See* East Africa.

MAGAZINES. Magazine publishing in the twenty-first century is a multibillion-dollar industry that generates substantial revenue, not only for the publisher but also for the many advertisers who rely on the medium to sell their products. Magazines also shape public opinion and change the culture through editorial content and selection.

According to the International Federation of the Periodical Press, in 2000, 65,000 magazine titles were published around the world. These included consumer titles (news, entertainment, and general interest magazines), business titles, and scholarly periodicals. The United States dominated the list with 13,313 titles, followed by the United Kingdom (8,899), China (8,275), and Germany (5,630).

A closer examination of the best-selling magazines in each publishing category is revealing in terms of popular taste and advertising interest. Not suprisingly, U.S. titles top many of the lists, and their circulations are global, not confined to the home market. The top general interest magazine is also the largest in the world: *Reader's Digest,* with a monthly circulation of 12.5 million. In second place is *National Geographic* (7.8 million), the environmental interest publication noted for its photography. Both publications have been around a long time: *Reader's Digest* was founded in 1922; *National Geographic in* 1888.

The most popular women's magazines are all American titles, although some are owned by foreign publishers: *Better Homes & Gardens* (monthly, 7.6 million) and *Family Circle* (monthly, 5 million). The most popular men's magazines are also American (and pornographic): *Playboy* (monthly, 3.2 million) and *Maxim* (monthly, 2.4 million). The top special interest magazines are Germany's automobile monthly *ADAC Motorwelt* (13.1 million) and the U.S. weekly *Sports Illustrated* (3.2 million). The top finance/business magazines are *Money* (U.S., monthly, 1.9 million) and *China Tax Policy* (China, monthly, 1.3 million).

The modern mass-market magazine is advertising-driven, increasingly specific in its content (and opinion), and aggressive in its circulation efforts. It has evolved over a century and owes its development to the Industrial Revolution (and technological progress in printing, papermaking, and methods of distribution), the growth of literacy (and, therefore, the reading public), changes in work and income (allowing more leisure time and disposable income), and the coming of the mass market (and its dependence on advertising).

Early Publications. Clearly, the magazine industry has come a long way since its humble origins in the seventeenth century. Historians identify *Erbauliche Monaths-Unterredungen* (Edifying Monthly Discussion) as the world's first magazine. Published in Hamburg, Germany, from 1663 to 1668, this learned periodical established a pattern of regular publication (but not as frequently as a newspaper) with articles of specific interest. Periodicals of this nature, crudely printed and with a limited circulation, appeared around the world, often to provoke new ideas in established regimes. For example, in 1672, *Le Mercure Galant* in France was one of the first "periodicals of amusement," containing verse, gossip, and court news. Three English publications—*The Review* (1704), *The Tatler* (1709), and *The Spectator* (1711)—contained essays and opinions on current events. In 1731, *The Gentleman's Magazine: Or, Monthly Intelligencer,* a collection of essays and articles, was launched in London and was the first to use the term *magazine.* It published continuously until 1907. In 1741, the first magazines appeared across the Atlantic in the American colonies, and both in Philadelphia: Andrew Bradford's *American Magazine* and *The General Magazine and Historical Chronicle,* published by Benjamin Franklin. In 1815, *Chinese Monthly Magazine,* published by missionaries, appeared, and, in 1821, *Australian Magazine* was launched, the first for the continent.

In the nineteenth century, the origins of the modern magazine industry, characterized by large circulation, flashy advertising, and culture-changing content, began to emerge. A number of factors encouraged publishing in general, including books, newspapers, and magazines. For one, literacy rates were rising with the promotion of free public education, which expanded the reading public. As early as the 1840s, for example, three-quarters of the working class in England and Wales were considered fully literate, or able to read. The elimination of stamp duties and favorable postal rates were an encouragement to all types of reading matter, allowing the sale of publications at a much lower price. The growth of railways and extension of the telegraph afforded better methods of distribution and communication. Increased rail travel also created a market for light reading to while away the journey. Improved methods of lighting, in the home and public areas, encouraged reading. In the 1850s, better papermaking machinery was developed, and the cost of paper was cheapened with the use of wood pulp. The invention of the rotary printing press, which printed on continuous rolls of paper, speeded production considerably and made possible larger editions.

British and U.S. Markets. Since the nineteenth century, magazine publishing has been shaped by two countries: Great Britain and the United States. Because both exported widely (Britain to the empire and commonwealth, the United States everywhere), their influence was great and helped bolster the efforts of a number of European publishing houses, especially in Germany. In both countries, maverick publishing houses emerged that dominated the magazine market, and successful titles were often imitated by rivals, with varying degrees of success.

In nineteenth-century Britain, as in the United States, there were two classes of magazines: those for the lower classes (often called "penny dreadfuls," an indication of their price and inferior subject matter) and those for a more learned audience. Penny dreadfuls included magazines issued in parts (such as *Sweeney Todd*) and crude, bloodthirsty weeklies such as *The Boys of England* (1866) with its legendary hero, Jack Harkaway. *Black Bess*, or *The Knight of the Road*, published by E. Harrison, is, at 254 weekly parts, 2,028 pages, and over 2.5 million words, the longest penny dreadful by one author on record. A changing occupational structure persuaded many publishers to develop story papers featuring characters that would appeal to certain workers, such as mill girls, shop assistants, and domestic help.

At the other end of the market, there did exist opportunities for publishing better quality magazines that reached a wider audience at a cheaper price. These included fiction magazines such as *All the Year Round* (1859), which featured Charles Dickens, and *The Strand Magazine* (1891), which published Arthur Conan Doyle's Sherlock Holmes stories. In 1842, Herbert Ingram established a new style of publication with *The Illustrated London News*, featuring lively woodcut illustrations. In the United States, a number of landmark foundations were also made: *Scientific American* (1845), which built upon a popular interest in scientific and technological developments; *Harper's Weekly* (1857), an illustrated magazine that provided graphic accounts of the Civil War; and two magazines for the home: *Ladies' Home Journal* (1883) and *Good Housekeeping* (1885), the latter known for its testing and certification of consumer goods. *Vogue*, the first of many fashion-oriented titles, was launched in 1892.

The prosperity that characterized the 1880s and 1890s on both sides of the Atlantic precipitated a veritable explosion of publishing, especially magazines. An estimated 50,000 periodicals were published in Britain by 1900. In 1881, Francis Hitchman claimed that between five and six million penny publications—weeklies and monthlies—circulated in London alone every week, in what he described as "a remarkable phenomenon of modern times." Titles catered to every audience and interest: religion, sport, women, humor, current events, children. Advertisements and the adaptation of photography made magazines more appealing. Sales and distribution of magazines included traditional street vendors and more substantial news-

stands (such as W. H. Smith and John Menzies), as well as limited mail subscriptions.

In both Britain and the United States, the magazine industry fell under increased critical scrutiny for the luridness and poor quality of many publications, especially those that circulated among the lower classes. As publishers became more dependent on advertising revenue and, therefore, circulation, improvements were made to limit criticism, and the magazine industry was reorganized and sanitized.

Leading the crusade against the penny dreadfuls in Britain was the Religious Tract Society, publishers of *The Boy's Own Paper* (1879) and *The Girl's Own Paper* (1880). The success of these papers (each achieved an initial weekly sale of 200,000, equal to the most popular of the dreadfuls) was a revelation to the industry, demonstrating both the attractions of high-quality production and the seeming size of the market for wholesome fiction and conventional morality, laced with a strong dose of patriotism. "King and Country" themes proved to be very popular, as they were in the daily newspapers.

George Newnes was the first of a new style of publishing tycoons who brought a change in style and direction to the industry. If these tycoons were sympathetic to the aims of the reformers, their primary goal, as commercial publishers, was the greatest return on investment. Their success initiated the trend toward a quasi-middle-class domination of popular publishing as well as the monopolizing of the market by a handful of large firms. In 1881, Newnes founded *Tit-Bits*, the first snippet paper, filled with easy-to-read trivia and "useless" information. The editor described the paper's intentions in the first issue: "The business of the conductors of *Tit-Bits* will be like that of the dentist—an organized system of extracting. . . . Any person who takes in *Tit-Bits* for three months will at the end of that time be an entertaining companion, as he will then have at his command a stock of smart sayings and a fund of anecdotes which will make his society agreeable." The same formula would be used by the founders of *Reader's Digest* in the United States. *Tit-Bits* was praised as a unique attempt to edify the masses and derided as the beginning of the decline of English journalism. Nonetheless, by 1888, it was selling an average of 350,000 copies per week, rating it among the first truly mass publications in Britain. Its success prompted a host of imitations: other publishing magnates, such as C. Arthur Pearson and Alfred Harmsworth (later Lord Northcliffe), achieved their initial successes with similar papers, *Pearson's Weekly* (1890) and *Answers to Correspondents* (1888).

Advertising was used to a degree not seen before as magazines were marketed like any consumer product. Publicity gimmicks and superlatives were common. Harmsworth's achievements in magazine journalism

MAGAZINES. Newsstand in Tegucigalpa, Honduras, 1989. (© Mireille Vautier/Woodfin Camp and Associates, New York)

stand beside his landmark newspaper foundations, *Daily Mail* (1896) and *Daily Mirror* (1903). By 1909, his firm, The Amalgamated Press, published nearly fifty titles that sold 8.5 million copies weekly. The Amalgamated Press founded boys' papers such as *Marvel* (1893, which introduced Sexton Blake, Detective, a poor man's Sherlock Holmes) and established a magazine market for women with such titles as *Forget-Me-Not* (1891) and *Woman's Weekly* (1911). Harmsworth's women's magazines inspired many imitations, all designed for wives and mothers with limited means who required domestic and maternal guidance, as well as wholesome entertainment.

Rising living standards and wages after World War I stimulated the growth of all leisure activities, including reading. Disposable income could now be spent on purchasing one or more magazines, which were becoming more attractive. Letterpress production of poor quality and formulaic fiction—which characterized countless weekly magazines— was soon replaced by bright, new, unorthodox titles such as Odhams Press's *Woman* (1937), the first British weekly magazine to be produced by photogravure and in color (along the lines of glossy American magazines).

Throughout the history of magazines, whatever worked well was copied endlessly. *Reader's Digest,* as noted by John Heidenry in *Theirs Was the Kingdom: Lila and DeWitt Wallace and the Story of the Reader's Digest* (New York, 1993), made its mark by going in reverse, "by finding the lowest common denominator in order to appeal to as many readers as possible, instead of breaking new literary ground

and earning the admiration of a discriminating elite." Hence, the *Digest*, since its founding in 1922, "must publish pabulum or perish." The formula was not a new one, but its appeal is timeless. At its height in the 1990s, *Reader's Digest* published forty one editions in seventeen languages with a global circulation of 30.5 million.

Time (1923) was founded by Henry Luce as a response to a flood of current events titles on the market. The original prospectus promised "a weekly news-magazine, aimed to serve the modern necessity of keeping people informed, created in a new principle of complete organization." The publishers added that, "There will be no editorial page in TIME. No article will be written to prove any special case"—quite a refreshing change of pace. *Time* was an overnight success and prompted many rivals, including *Newsweek* (1933). The Luce empire would grow to be a powerhouse in the magazine industry, and its Time, Inc. stable of more than sixty-five titles included *Fortune* (1930), *Life* (1936), *Sports Illustrated* (1954), and *Money* (1972).

The Twentieth Century and Today. The twentieth century was filled with examples of famous magazine foundations that would become prototypes. *Life*, *Picture Post* (U.K., 1938), *Oggi Illustrato* (1945, Italy), and *Paris Match* (1949, France) discovered a market in quality photography and interesting essays, bolstered by World War II and an ever-growing interest in celebrities. Hobbies' magazines were also popular on such subjects as gardening, and the influences of broadcasting, movies, and, later, television are apparent in the enduring popularity of *Radio Times*

(U.K., 1923) and *TV Guide* (U.S., 1948). *Famous Funnies* (1934) was the first distinct color comic magazine, separate from the Sunday newspapers. In 1953, *Playboy* effectively remade the magazine market for men, as did *Ms.* (U.S., 1972), which advocated the feminist viewpoint. The celebrity, or fan, magazine reached its apogee with *People* (1974), another Time, Inc. title.

Advertising remains a potent force in magazines. As advertising revenue became more important to magazine expansion, so did efforts to verify circulation. The Audit Bureau of Circulation was established in the United States in 1914 and in Great Britain in 1931 (an international federation was created in 1963). The close bond between advertising and editorial content is most evident in the women's magazines, especially those with a certain focus. The 1990s brought amalgamation and expansion to the magazine industry. In 1994, German publishers Gruner + Jahr purchased The New York Times Magazine Group, including *YM* and *Family Circle*, the second-largest women's magazine in the world. The French firm Hachette Fillipacchi owns the fourth-largest title, *Woman's Day*. In 2001, Time, Inc. purchased the IPC Group, Ltd., Britain's leading consumer magazine publisher, with more than seventy titles. Most magazines, moreover, now maintain a site on the World Wide Web, which includes space for advertising. Time, Inc., part of the media powerhouse AOL Time Warner, displays the industry's new synergy as its magazines' Web sites complement sister Web sites in the cable news and entertainment industries.

[*See also* Advertising; Information and Communication Technology; *and* Newspapers.]

BIBLIOGRAPHY

Dancyger, Irene. *A World of Women: An Illustrated History of Women's Magazines*. Dublin, 1978.

Elson, Robert T. *Time, Inc.: The Intimate History of a Publishing Enterprise*. New York, 1968.

Heidenry, John. *Theirs Was the Kingdom: Lila and DeWitt Wallace and the Story of the Reader's Digest*. New York, 1993.

Hitchman, Francis. "The Penny Press." *Macmillan's Magazine* 43 (1881), 385–398.

Hoggart, Richard. *The Uses of Literacy*. London, 1957.

Janello, Amy, and Brennon Jones. *The American Magazine*. New York, 1991.

Keating, Peter. *The Haunted Study*. London, 1989.

Kuczynski, Alex. "A Little Light Reading, Anyone? When Weighty Issues Are the Magazines Themselves." *New York Times*, 11 April 2000.

McAleer, Joseph. *Passion's Fortune: The Story of Mills & Boon*. Oxford, 1999.

McAleer, Joseph. *Popular Reading and Publishing in Britain, 1914–1950*. Oxford, 1992.

Mott, Frank Luther. *A History of American Magazines*. Cambridge, 1968.

White, Cynthia L. *Women's Magazines, 1693–1968*. London, 1970.

Wilson, Charles. *First with the News: The History of W. H. Smith, 1792–1972*. London, 1985.

JOSEPH MCALEER

MAGHRIB comprises the North African countries of Morocco, Algeria, and Tunisia; sometimes Libya is included because of long-standing cultural and economic ties with these three states. For economic history, the Maghrib's importance has always derived from its geographical position as a crossroads area. Situated where Mediterranean, Atlantic, African, European, and Asian histories intersect, the Maghrib has acted over the centuries as an economic conduit and cultural broker between adjacent civilizations and political economies. The region first came into recorded history when the Carthaginian empire was founded in the ninth century BCE by Phoenician merchants; its capital was Carthage, located near present-day Tunis. Because of proximity to Sicily, Carthage dominated central Mediterranean trade during the sixth to the third centuries through networks of trading posts established along the North African, Spanish, and Sicilian coasts. The commodities exchanged were pottery, precious dyes, and metals from Iberian mines. With Rome's expansion, a series of wars against Carthage ensued in the third and second centuries over control of Mediterranean commerce and sea lanes. In 146 BCE, Carthage was destroyed, although Julius Caesar later ordered its reconstruction; thereafter, the region comprising modern-day Tunisia and eastern Algeria were incorporated into Rome's imperium. Indeed, Carthage became the principal urban center of Roman Africa, supplying large quantities of wheat and other agricultural products to Italy, thus earning the title of "granary of Rome." During the second and third centuries, Roman colonization of Tunisia increased grain production by establishing vast agricultural estates peopled by settlers from Italy and Sicily or soldiers from the Roman army. New cities and towns appeared along the Mediterranean littoral, making Africa Proconsularis one of the most highly urbanized in the empire.

After the Muslim conquests (beginning in the late seventh century CE), the Maghrib again achieved regional dominance as an economic broker. Through the creation of a caravan economy, West African gold was funneled to North African ports. Caravans from Sijilmasa, a desert entrepôt city in Morocco, traveled south across the desert to the African kingdoms of Ghana, Takrur, and Mali, transporting gold back to the Mediterranean world. In the early 900s, Sijilmasa produced gold coins; under the Almoravid empire, centered in Morocco by 1050 CE, these coins were the basis of trade throughout the Maghrib, Europe, and the eastern end of the Mediterranean Basin until at least the fourteenth century.

Political turmoil in North Africa and the Sahara disrupted the lucrative gold trade, as did the fourteenth-century crises shaking the region, such as the Black Death and Arab bedouin incursions from the East. The centuries-long Christian *reconquista* of Spain, governed by Islamic states for centuries, also accelerated decline for North African economies dependent upon Mediterranean and Iberian trade for prosperity. New maritime powers, Spain and Portugal, controlled the western Mediterranean and began probing along the Atlantic coast south of Morocco during the fifteenth century. Finally, pastoral-nomadic peoples increasingly overran North Africa, encroaching upon the fertile tell; settled agriculture suffered, and cities and urban economies contracted. Partially offsetting the decline was massive immigration by Spanish Jews and Muslims, seeking refuge from the intolerance of the Spanish Catholic monarchs; between 1492 and 1609, hundreds of thousands settled in North African cities, bringing with them sophisticated craft, manufacturing, and banking skills.

Throughout the sixteenth century, titanic struggles for mastery over the sea and North African littoral pitted the Spanish Habsburgs against the Ottoman Turks, who ruled from Istanbul after 1453 with extensive domains in the Balkans and Middle East. By 1574, Algeria, Tunisia, and Tripolitania (as the Ottoman province in Libya was known) were formally incorporated into the Ottoman Empire. In consequence, they were integrated into patterns of commerce and trade centered in the eastern Mediterranean and introduced to cosmopolitan fiscal, administrative, and military practices. From the seventeenth century on, Algiers and Tunis expanded rapidly as soldiers and emigrants arrived from eastern Turkish lands or Christian renegades joined corsair fleets in North African port cities. Morocco, however, was never incorporated into the Ottoman Empire. Instead, it was governed by a succession of local dynasties whose capital cities were generally inland (Fez or Meknes, for example) because of threats from Christian pirates from Iberia or Mediterranean islands.

During the "golden age" of privateering in the seventeenth and eighteenth centuries, the Maghrib's economic and political clout stemmed once again from its mediating position. The corsair economy represented a Mediterranean-wide system of forced exchange and paid protection to assure the safety of ships, goods, and crews plying the sea. Among North African states, the regency of Algiers was dominant; its port, fleet, and population expanded, owing to profits earned from sales of captured ships and cargoes or ransoms paid by European states for release of prisoners taken on the high sea. Several factors, however, prevented the North African states from achieving maritime mastery or competing successfully with European navies; shortages of wood as well as certain metals for shipbuilding meant that these items had to be imported. And by the early modern period, advances in naval technology rendered European fleets dominant in the trans-Mediterranean carrying trade. From the 1750s on, epidemics and plagues brought demographic crisis to North Africa just when European populations burgeoned. After 1815, the Maghrib's corsair economy was dismantled by European military pressure. In 1830, the French army and navy invaded Algeria, which remained part of France's empire until 1962; Tunisia was taken by France in 1881, and Morocco was divided up between Spain and France in 1912. Tripolitania fell to Italy in 1912. The age of colonialism had begun, and the Maghrib's ancient role as economic broker was eclipsed.

The colonial period witnessed the progressive implantation of European settlers on the most fertile lands of North Africa with indigenous Arab or Berber peoples supplying labor on agricultural estates. Decades of military conquest by colonial armies severely disrupted village and peasant economies, particularly in Algeria, Morocco, and Libya. Industrialization was discouraged by the colonial powers since North African economies served as sources of agrarian products (wheat, olive oil, citrus) and mineral wealth (phosphates and iron ore) or as markets for goods produced in Europe. By the early twentieth century, pauperization of the native population, combined with rapidly accelerating birth rates in all four countries, produced widespread misery and, thus, political unrest, culminating in movements for national independence after World War I. During and after that war, severe labor shortages in France were offset by the importation of Algerian men to work temporarily in factories. In 1954, one of Africa's cruelest colonial wars unfolded in French Algeria; a major factor in France's unwillingness to end that war, which claimed nearly one million lives, was the discovery of petroleum in southern Algeria.

With independence in the 1950s and 1960s, both Libya and Algeria became major petroleum producers, which, paradoxically, brought grave disequilibrium to their respective economies and societies that were already suffering from the adverse effects of colonialism. Although Tunisia is only a minor producer, the country's chief export is oil, followed by phosphates; tourism ranks third in economic earnings. Morocco has no petroleum but exports superphosphates. Despite, or perhaps because of, the exploitation of petroleum, natural gas, and other minerals, another of the region's exports are its own people who immigrate, often clandestinely, to Europe or elsewhere in search of a livelihood. With 60 percent of the population under the age of sixteen and unemployment running as high as 30 percent, the Maghrib, historically a place where "worlds met," is now regarded with trepidation as Europe's unstable "southern frontier."

[*See also* North Africa.]

BIBLIOGRAPHY

Abun-Nasr, Jamil M. *A History of the Maghrib in the Islamic Period.* Cambridge, 1987.

Amin, Samir. *The Maghreb in the Modern World: Algeria, Tunisia, Morocco.* Translated by Michael Perl. Harmondsworth, 1970.

Clancy-Smith, Julia. *Rebel and Saint: Muslim Notables, Populist Protest, Colonial Encounters; Algeria and Tunisia.* Berkeley, 1994.

Clancy-Smith, Julia, ed. *North Africa, Islam, and the Mediterranean World from the Almoravids to the Algerian War.* London, 2001.

Collinson, Sarah. *Shore to Shore: The Politics of Migration in Euro-Maghreb Relations.* London, 1996.

McNeill, John R. *The Mountains of the Mediterranean World: An Environmental History.* Cambridge, 1992.

Miller, Susan Gilson, ed. *In the Shadow of the Sultan: Culture, Power, and Politics in Morocco.* Berkeley, 1999.

Murphy, Emma C. *Economic and Political Change in Tunisia: From Bourguiba to Ben Ali.* New York, 1999.

Ruedy, John. *Modern Algeria: The Origins and Development of a Nation.* Bloomington, Ind., 1992.

Vandewalle, Dirk. *Libya since Independence: Oil and State-Building.* Ithaca, N.Y., 1998.

JULIA CLANCY-SMITH

MALAYSIA, created in 1963, was an adventure in decolonization. Like other states in postcolonial Southeast Asia, it inherited colonial frontiers, but there was no colonial precedent for the constitutional links it established between the Malay peninsula and the two states in northern Borneo, Sarawak, and Sabah. All had come under the protection of the British, but, though the latter had at times talked of associating them more closely, they had done little.

For the frontiers themselves, the British, the dominant power in colonial Southeast Asia, had been largely responsible. Anxious to avoid the destruction of an independent Thai state, they had limited their challenge to its claims over the Malay states on the peninsula, finally acquiring those over the northern states by treaty in 1909 and never challenging those over the Malay state of Pattani. The British challenge to the Dutch in the archipelago was also limited. That led to another unprecedented division of the Malay world, between the peninsula and Sumatra. It also led to the division of Borneo. Even that would not have occurred but for the adventurer James Brooke, who established his own raj in Sarawak.

For the British, the peninsula itself initially offered few economic attractions. What was important was its position. It lay athwart the route between the two great centers of Asian population, India and China. That had given it its importance since the early centuries CE, when first a portage had been made across its narrowest point, then later when it had become possible to go around its tip. Establishing an empire in India in the eighteenth century and building up a trade with China, the British wanted to keep the straits out of the hands of a major rival. Penang (acquired in 1786), Melaka (acquired in 1824), and Singapore (acquired in 1819) were designed to protect the route. The "Straits Settlements" looked outward: their trade was that of entrepôts for a wider area. Of them, Singapore was the most successful.

The peninsula was then a thinly populated region, with perhaps 500,000 to 750,000 inhabitants, divided among a number of Malay states. The main product it contributed to international trade was tin, found particularly in the alluvial districts of the state of Perak on the west coast. Its main market was China, where, beaten into leaves, it was burned in sacrificial offerings. In the early nineteenth century, world demand for the product increased, further boosted after midcentury by the growth of the canning industry. The leading industrial power of the day, Great Britain, was exhausting its own supplies in Cornwall and looking elsewhere.

Intervention in Perak and its neighbors in the 1870s, and the establishment of British Residents at the Malay courts, did not result simply from the need to acquire tin. Rather, it resulted from the disorder that the expansion of the tin trade had produced and the need, as a result, to avoid the intervention of others. Malay rulers had encouraged the immigration of Chinese miners. Their own rivalries, and those of the competing Chinese secret societies, were more than the traditional governance systems could manage.

Once established, the Residents promoted development by creating infrastructure, establishing land titles, welcoming migrants, and offering subsidies. Their success helped to locate the development of rubber planting, advocated by H. N. Ridley of the Singapore Botanic Gardens after the collapse of coffee, taking off only in the early years of the twentieth century when the automobile age began. Rubber, which was suited to the poor soils of the peninsula, could be grown in any of the states, but the existence of infrastructure on the west coast focused it there.

If tin mining extended the immigration of the Chinese, the rubber industry relied largely on the immigration of Indians. Increasingly "British Malaya," particularly its western side, came to represent, perhaps more fully than Burma, the concept of the "plural society" that J. S. Furnivall, who coined the phrase, found there: communities with distinct economic functions met only in the marketplace, and there was no social cohesion.

Though it struck severe blows at so export-oriented an economy, the depression of the 1930s did not, as in Burma, lead to intercommunal strife. It was the disaster of the Japanese conquest that finally prompted a change in British policy: the Malayan Union was designed to bring the states together and to give the immigrant peoples a prospect of citizenship. The Malays, whose role in the modern economy was limited, feared the loss of their political position and protested vehemently. The British shifted from union to federation, which brought the states together but retained the rulers, and they reduced the scope of the citizenship proposals.

The outbreak of the Emergency in 1948 and the subsequent introduction of an electoral system contributed to the creation of a system of elite-led communal politics. The alliance of the leading Malay, Chinese, and Indian parties won the election of 1955, and independence followed in 1957. Once it was secured, however, the problem of sustaining an intercommunal compromise only increased, and the riots that followed the 1969 election made that evident. The government introduced the New Economic Policy (NEP), positively discriminating in favor of the Malays, the *bumiputera*.

Growth and redistribution were goals at least in potential conflict. But without the NEP, it may be argued, Malaysia would not have enjoyed the political stability that permitted the dramatic economic expansion of the following decades. That expansion was urged on by Mahathir bin Mohamad, one of the Malay Ultras in the late 1960s and prime minister from 1981. He initiated an import-substitution industrialization (ISI) program in heavy industry, drawing on public and foreign capital, and offered the vision of a modern industrialized Malaysia by 2020. In 1987, he narrowly defeated the Malay critics who preferred redistribution to growth.

The outcome of growth could assuage or attenuate intercommunal tensions, but the process also might increase them. It certainly put a tremendous strain on Malaysia's institutions. Nor, of course, was Malaysia independent of the outside world, as the economic crisis of 1997–1998 emphasized. It was a high-risk policy.

Omitted from union and federation, Singapore had been included in Malaysia in 1963. Tunku Abdul Rahman, then prime minister, had hoped to balance the inclusion of that predominantly Chinese city by the inclusion also of the Borneo territories. When Singapore was extruded in 1965, Sarawak and Sabah remained part of Malaysia.

They had been British colonies only since 1946. Sarawak had been ruled until then by the Brooke family. Out of principle but also out of concern to avoid over-mighty subjects, the Brooke rajas had opposed large-scale development. In any case, there was little scope for it. Sarawak had no great mineral riches, though it had some gold and antimony, and from 1910 its oil was exploited by a subsidiary of Royal Dutch/Shell. It was in the Malaysia phase that its timber was turned to account. Source of political power, it was quickly depleted, and reforestation rates were low.

The same was true of Sabah. Governed by the British North Borneo Company, it had never provided its shareholders with substantial dividends. It enjoyed a short-lived tobacco boom in the 1890s and had some share in the subsequent rubber boom. It was the Japanese demand for timber that brought Malaysian Sabah its boom.

BIBLIOGRAPHY

Drabble, John H. *Rubber in Malaya, 1876–1922*. Kuala Lumpur, 1973.

Drabble, John H. *An Economic History of Malaysia, c. 1800–1990: The Transition to Modern Economic Growth*. Basingstoke, U.K., 2000.

Huff, W. G. *The Economic Growth of Singapore: Trade and Development in the Twentieth Century*. Cambridge, 1994.

Kaur, Amarjit. *Economic Change in East Malaysia, Sabah, and Sarawak since 1850*. Basingstoke, U.K., 1998.

Lim, Chong-Yah. *Economic Development of Modern Malaya*. Kuala Lumpur, 1967.

NICHOLAS TARLING

MALTHUS, THOMAS (1766–1834), economist.

Thomas Robert Malthus read mathematics at Jesus College, Cambridge, where he graduated as ninth wrangler in 1788. Thereafter he took holy orders and became the perpetual curate of Okewood, Surrey, in 1793. He became a famous and controversial figure soon after the publication of his *Essay on the Principle of Population* in 1798. In 1805, he was appointed professor of general history, politics, commerce, and finance in the newly established East India College in Hertfordshire. Subsequently he substantially revised and expanded his *Essay*, which was published in six editions. His *Principles of Political Economy* was published in 1820, and a second edition was released posthumously in 1836. Malthus frequently published pamphlets and letters, and he maintained an active correspondence with many distinguished figures of his day within Britain and abroad, in particular David Ricardo.

The *Essay*, in its first edition, was written as a counterargument to William Godwin's *Enquiry Concerning Political Justice* (1793) and the radical interpretation of the science of politics as a means of social improvement, particularly those features associated with the French Revolution and the Marquis de Condorcet. Malthus was far less optimistic, maintaining that misery and vice were the inevitable result of a fundamental law of nature that was impervious to institutional and legislative changes. Malthus specified two "postulata," that food is necessary for life and that the "passion between the sexes" could be regarded as a constant. He also argued that the capacity of a society to increase its supply of food was at best restricted to a rise by arithmetic progression, while population was capable of growing geometrically. Hence an inevitable tension would arise in agrarian societies between production and reproduction, which would require adjustments by a rise in the death rate (positive checks) or by a fall in the birthrate (preventive checks).

In the second edition of the *Essay* (1803) Malthus introduced moral restraint as a third category of check, entailing prudence and foresight when marriage was delayed until a family could be supported. He thereby became more optimistic about the future of societies that were

THOMAS MALTHUS. Portrait by Fournier and John Linnell (1792–1882). (Bibliothèque Nationale de France, Paris/Giraudon/Art Resource, NY)

well educated and lacked institutions, such as the English Poor Law, that attempted to guarantee a minimum level of subsistence. Malthus, while initially hostile to manufacturing, became friendlier over time, principally because he believed industrial products served as an incentive system to moral restraint.

In *Principles of Political Economy*, Malthus showed himself less confident about the self-correcting properties of markets and more attentive to the ways demographic and economic circles created disturbances that led to long-run privation and starvation. In proposing a remedy to the depression afflicting the British economy following the Napoleonic Wars, a remedy that would give favorable treatment to those who derived their incomes from rents by boosting their purchasing power, Malthus helped foster notions that John Keynes used in his search for cures to unemployment in the 1930s. Earlier, his ideas about the tension between population and resources had been instrumental in forming Charles Darwin's ideas about the survival of the fittest in evolutionary processes. Above all, Malthus's ideas, notwithstanding Keynes's recognition of their contemporary relevance in the 1930s, are generally

thought to be of greatest relevance to an understanding of economic-demographic relationships in societies that predated the Industrial Revolution.

BIBLIOGRAPHY

Coleman, David, and Roger Schofield, eds. *The State of Population Theory: Forward from Malthus*. Oxford, 1986.

Dupâquier, Jacques, Antoinette Fauve-Chamoux, and Eugene Grebenik, eds. *Malthus, Past and Present*. London, 1986.

James, Patricia. *Population Malthus: His Life and Times*. London, 1979.

O'Brien, Denis P. *The Classical Economists*. Oxford, 1975.

Smith, Richard M. "Welfare of the Individual and the Group: Malthus and Externalities." *Proceedings of the American Philosophical Society* 147 (2001), 402–414.

Turner, Michael, ed. *Malthus and His Times*. New York, 1986.

Winch, Donald. *Malthus*. Oxford, 1987.

Winch, Donald. *Riches and Poverty: An Intellectual History of Political Economy in Britain, 1750–1834*. Cambridge, 1996.

Wrigley, Edward A., and Roger Schofield. *The Population History of England, 1541–1871: A Reconstruction*. 2d ed. Cambridge, 1989.

Wrigley, Edward A., and David Souden, eds. *The Works of Thomas Robert Malthus*. 8 vols. London, 1986.

RICHARD M. SMITH

MALTHUSIAN AND NEO-MALTHUSIAN THEORIES. Few economists have had such controversial ideas and generated a debate on such a scale as Thomas Malthus. In *An Essay on the Principle of Population*, published in 1798, the English clergyman made public his theory on population dynamics and its relationship with the availability of resources. The essay was the result of his skepticism toward positivist theorists praising the perfectibility of man and greeting the advances and diffusion of human knowledge as a source of welfare and freedom for future generations. Disagreeing with such perspectives, Malthus maintained that the development of mankind was severely limited by the pressure population growth exerted on the availability of food.

Malthus's Legacy. The foundation of Malthus's theory relies on two assumptions he views as fixed, namely that food and the passion between the sexes are both essential for human existence. Malthus believed the world's population tends to increase at a faster rate than its food supply. Whereas population grows at a geometric rate, the production capacity only grows arithmetically. To Malthus it followed necessarily that, in the absence of consistent checks on population growth, scarce resources have to be shared among an increasing number of individuals. However, Malthus also recognized the existence of checks that ease the pressure of population growth. He distinguished between two categories, the preventive check and the positive one. The preventive check consists of voluntary limitations on population growth. Individuals, before getting married and building a family, make rational decisions based on the income they expect to earn and the quality of life they anticipate to maintain in the future for themselves and their families. The positive check to population is a direct consequence of the lack of a preventive check. When society does not limit population growth voluntarily, diseases, famines, and wars reduce population size and establish the necessary balance with resources. According to Malthus, the positive check acts more intensively in lower classes, where infant mortality rates are higher and unhealthy conditions are more common. The preventive and positive checks, by controlling population growth, eventually close the mismatch between the level of population and the availability of resources, but the latter at a cost of creating misery and wickedness that cannot be avoided and are beyond the control of people. Under this perspective, technological improvements that contribute to the increase in agricultural yields only produce a temporary increase in living standards and are offset in the long run by a correspondent increase in population size that cancels the temporary relief. Migrations could alleviate the effects of the positive check, but Malthus considered this possibility unfeasible, as general conditions were too harsh in possible receiving countries.

Malthus was strongly opposed to monetary transfers from the rich to the poor. In his view increasing the welfare of the poor by giving them more money could only worsen their living conditions, as they would mistakenly be led to think that they could support a bigger family, which would in turn depress the preventive check and generate higher population growth. At the end of this process the same amount of resources has to be split among a larger population, triggering the work of the positive check to populations. Moreover, immediately after such a transfer, people can afford to buy more food, bidding its price up and decreasing real wages, which hurt poor individuals whose main income comes from their labor. For these reasons Malthus and other distinguished economists like David Ricardo (1772–1823) opposed the English Poor Laws, legislation that gave relief to poor and unemployed people, and they played a central role in reforming the laws in 1834. Malthus held that it is better for a family to foresee its lack of ability to support children before having them than to deal with subsequent diseases and infant mortality. In other words, taking for granted that checks on populations are unavoidable, it is better to use the preventive check than the positive one.

Malthus understood his model implied that real wages could not rise permanently above the subsistence level. When real wages rose above this level, population would begin to grow, inducing a decline in nominal wages as the market was flooded with labor. The larger population would result in an increase in the demand for goods, which would force prices to increase and real wages to decrease to their subsistence level. This concept was known as the Iron Law of Wages, and although it was first conceptually formalized by Ricardo in 1817, it was constantly present in Malthus's work.

Classical economists typically assumed that diminishing returns characterize agricultural production and mining activities, whereas constant returns are features of manufacturing. This hypothesis, taken together with Malthus's population principle, yields even more pessimistic scenarios for countries that base their productive structures on manufacturing. An immediate consequence is that population growth increases employment in the industrial sector more than it does in the agricultural sector and raises manufacture supply more than it does agricultural supply. Therefore, population pressure, which increases both the supply and the demand for goods, induces prices of agriculture to move up relative to those of manufacturing, impoverishing factory workers.

This perspective had important policy implications for Britain at the beginning of the nineteenth century, especially for the debate on the Corn Laws. The Corn Laws were variable tariffs and export subsidies intended to protect English agriculture. After the Napoleonic Wars, agricultural prices fell all over Europe, and British landowners demanded more protection. These issues created an enormous debate in Britain between supporters of the Corn Laws and advocates of free trade policies. Malthus strongly opposed the laws' possible repeal and defended landlords' positions for two principal reasons. First, he held that the economic system was characterized by an intrinsic lack of demand that could endanger entrepreneurs and that landowners provided the solution to this problem. Their tastes were usually biased toward purchasing luxury goods, keeping aggregate demand at satisfactory levels. Therefore, impoverishing landowners by repealing the Corn Laws would result in a decline in living standards. Second, by specializing in manufacturing, a country would become poorer, because the pressure of population would cause a deterioration in its terms of trade (the ratio of manufacturing prices to agricultural prices), a result of the different production technologies in the two sectors presented above. Malthus's support for the Corn Laws should not be interpreted as an aversion to the industrial sector. On the contrary, he maintained that the consumption of luxury goods would alleviate the population pressure by increasing the opportunity cost of having an extra child.

Malthus's ideas have had a large impact on the advance of economics, demography, and evolutionary biology. The biologist Charles Darwin (1809–1882) formulated his concepts of the evolution of species starting with the idea of the struggle for survival over scarce resources as theorized by Malthus. In Darwin's perspective only individuals whose traits were better suited to face the environment would survive and generate a lineage that would last longer.

Malthus's Influence on the History of Economic Thought. Malthus's work exerted a strong influnce on later classical economists, especially Ricardo and John Stuart Mill (1806–1873). Both Ricardo and Mill accepted Malthus's theory of population but believed free trade could generate high profits for a long period and alleviate the pressure on scarce resources. In the later years of the nineteenth century, as the predictions of constant real wages and population explosion did not materialize, Malthus's influence waned.

From the dawn of history until the time of Malthus, most societies experienced trends in population and standards of living that appear consisted with Malthus's model. That is, temporary improvements in living standards were offset by population growth, whereas a transitory decline in living standards eventually resulted in a decrease in population size through the operation of the positive check. In the very long run, population average annual growth rates were low but increased from 10,000 BCE to the 1750s. However, this population growth was not continuous but experienced oscillations, as did living standards. Birthrates increased considerably before the year 0 and remained high until the Industrial Revolution. Malthus's model was a better description of agricultural societies that characterized antiquity and the Middle Ages than it was of the post–Industrial Revolution era. By the nineteenth century, however, things had begun to change. The modern period saw a substantial decline in fertility rates in industrialized countries, and even though population growth rates increased dramatically to almost 0.6 percent in 1950 and to more than 1.8 percent in 1990 owing to an increase in life expectancy, many countries experienced a dramatic growth in agricultural and industrial production. Living standards improved permanently without a subsequent increase in population growth rates. Malthus's prediction, which sounded so logical and powerful at the time it was made, appears to be refuted by the recent experiences of large parts of the world.

Neo-Malthusians. E. A. Wrigley (1987, 1988) has supported Malthus's theory, focusing his research on British economic and population history. He has argued that Britain, before and immediately after the Industrial Revolution, displayed all the main features of a Malthusian economy, but by the end of the nineteenth century, the relationship between population and income was broken.

Wrigley defined the British economy before the Industrial Revolution as an "organic economic system" characterized by decreasing returns to scale, where population movements set standards of living to the subsistence level. The use of wood and other organic materials as sources of energy in production processes tightened decreasing returns and narrowed production possibilities.

Wrigley showed that in modern Britain from 1566 to 1871 prices and population were closely related. When population increased, for instance, from 1781 to 1806, the price index also rose. On the other hand, downturns in population corresponded to decline in prices. Moreover he pointed out that fertility rather than mortality was the main determinant of population growth during the eighteenth century and that nuptiality changes accounted almost entirely for the movements in fertility. In modern England the incidence and timing of marriages were subjected to careful economic calculus. The economic sensitivity of nuptiality made it the main mechanism relating population size with economic conditions. This Malthusian link between population and economic growth disappeared in the last quarter of the nineteenth century, when a new socioeconomic paradigm emerged. The increased production did not lead to a rise in population as Malthus would have predicted. Individuals began to adopt different forms of birth control within families, thus reducing birthrates. By the 1930s large families had become rare in England, and more than half of the couples had only one or two children.

The neo-Malthusian literature also involves comparative studies checking for Malthusian effects. Of particular interest is the comparison between the English and the French experiences. Until 1790 France was characterized by a high-pressure system, where adjustments to the Malthusian equilibrium operated through the positive check and higher death rates, whereas Britain adjusted through nuptiality and the preventive check. After the French Revolution the progressive introduction of birth controls gradually moved France to a low-pressure system. The peculiar feature of this phenomenon is that, while England created a mechanism of adjustment based on the number of weddings and nuptiality, France bypassed this procedure and directly arrived at birth controls within families.

David Weir is also among the economists who empirically tested the existence of a Malthusian pressure. Using the tax records of Rosny-Sous-Bois, a small village south of Paris, he traced a demographic history of this locality for the year 1747. His findings suggest that Rosny was a classic Malthusian microsystem. In particular, under a Malthusian perspective, age at marriage is expected to fall with a rise in income, and mortality rates are predicted to be negatively related with living standards. Indeed, Weir found that female age at marriage was lower when the income of the husband was higher and that mortality rates of children and adults were negatively related to income.

Regarding the Malthusian comparison between demographic trends in France and England, Weir estimated the elasticity of the response of birthrates and death rates to wheat price shocks in France and Britain for the period

1670–1869. If the neo-Malthusian prediction is correct, a higher response of birthrates to wheat price shocks in Britain and a higher reaction of mortality rates in France are expected as positive enters in action. Weir's results reject the Malthusian prediction in most cases. During the second half of the eighteenth century there is no significant difference between the two countries' responses of birthrates to price shocks. Even for the period after 1790, in which neo-Malthusians asserted a higher adjustment in France through marital fertility, Weir did not find any important variation from the result obtained for the previous period. In the nineteenth century the two countries displayed the same demographic behavior, despite the introduction of birth control practices in France. Regarding the positive check and mortality rates after 1740, France seems to be more sensitive to wheat price shock, but the results are less clear. The existence of a consistent positive check is shown in only one specific simulation run for the seventy years prior to 1740. In this case a doubling of the wheat price in one year yields a much higher response for the French death rate when compared to the English one.

Malthus Criticized. Malthus's argument regarding the relationship between population growth and production capacity has been subject to considerable criticism. Furthermore, economists began to look for alternative explanations, attempting to close the gap between Malthus's prediction and the new reality revealed to them. Malthus claimed that, with a fixed amount of land and a growing population, diminishing marginal productivity would result in individuals living constantly at a subsistence level. A frequently heard critique was that he ignored the possibility that technological improvements and capital accumulation are strong forces and may relax the population pressure and improve the conditions of individuals, even in the presence of a growing population.

One kind of criticism emphasized potential positive consequences of population growth in the long run ignored by Malthus. Ester Boserup, (1945), for instance, suggested that Malthusians' arguments display a reverse causation. According to Boserup, population growth is an autonomous factor that affects agricultural productivity rather than being affected by it, as suggested by the Malthusian school. Boserup, claimed that Malthus's assumption of diminishing returns to labor needs not hold in the long run, as higher population may lead to a more efficient division of labor as well as to improved agricultural practices (signaled by the frequency of cropping). She concluded that soil fertility should not be viewed as fixed and given by nature but instead can be improved by substituting agricultural technology, which is likely to be a result of an increase in population. Primitive communities with higher population growth rates are more likely to experience economic development, provided that the necessary investment in agriculture is undertaken. Julian L. Simon (1977, 2000) is another critic of Malthusian reasoning. He has emphasized the long-run benefits of population growth. While conceding that population growth has a negative effect on living standards in the short run because of diminishing returns and the temporary burden it poses on society, Simon has argued that it has positive effects on living standards in the long run because of knowledge advances and economies of scale. Employing a simulation model, Simon found that, in the long run (after thirty to one hundred years) and when compared to constant-size population, moderate population growth improves standards of living both in more-developed and in less-developed countries. Simon held that in the long run a growing population tends to advance knowledge, which in turn increases productivity and output at a higher rate than that of population growth. Nevertheless, he claimed that a country's optimal policy regarding population growth depends on the weight given to future periods relative to the present. The more weight a country gives to future generations and the more adapted a country is for the short run decline in standards of living, the better it is for that country to pursue a policy of moderate population growth.

The second kind of criticism stressed the importance of fertility decisions made by parents that were overlooked by Malthus. This view was developed after three interesting regularities were observed. First, it was found that in the modern era, the population of poor countries grew faster than that of rich ones. Low-income countries experienced annual population growth rates of more than 2 percent between 1965 and 1990, whereas high-income countries grew at a rate of less than 1 percent in the same period. Second, fertility rates are negatively correlated with income per capita. Third, life expectancy at birth is much higher for countries with higher income per capita. Motivated by these observations, economists raised the possibility that the number of children and the investment made in each child are economic decisions taken consciously by parents. Gary S. Becker and Gregg H. Lewis (1973) were the first to formalize the idea that parents may be altruistic toward their children and that, when making fertility decisions, they will take into account both the number of children and the quality of life of each of them that is reflected in consumption, education, health, and so forth. They showed that when altruism is present the Malthusian prediction does not hold and that higher living standards are consistent with lower fertility rates, as observed in the data. Becker, Kevin M. Murphy, and Robert F. Tamura (1990) pointed out that Malthus's analysis is not suited to the modern era, as it ignores the importance of education and the higher cost of raising children in industrialized countries, a result of the higher value of time in such countries. These two factors induce parents in rich countries to invest in their children's quality rather than in their quantity, which can account for lower fertility rates than the ones suggested by Malthus.

In spite of the above critiques, Malthus's theory appears to apply to many poor countries still struggling to get out of the Malthusian cycle. Even among richer countries a neo-Malthusian relationship between population growth and the environment has been argued, based on the idea of the overuse of scarce natural resources. But this problem too is more severe in poor countries, which usually depend more on their natural resources.

[*See also* Malthus, Thomas.]

BIBLIOGRAPHY

Becker, Gary S. "An Economic Analysis of Fertility." In *Demographic and Economic Change in Developing Countries*, edited by Richard Easterlin. Princeton, 1960.

Becker, Gary S. "Family Economics and Macro Behavior." *American Economic Review* 78.1 (1988), 1–13.

Becker, Gary S., and Gregg H. Lewis. "On the Intereaction between the Quantity and Quality of Children." *Journal of Political Economy* 81.2 (1973), 279–288.

Becker, Gary S., Kevin Murphy, and Robert Tamura. "Human Capital, Fertility, and Economic Growth." *Journal of Political Economy* 98.5 (1990), 12–37.

Boserup, Ester. *The Conditions of Agricultural Growth: The Economics of Agrarian Change under Population Pressure*. London, 1965.

Galor, Oded, and David N. Weil. "Population, Technology, and Growth: From Malthusin Stagnation to the Demographic Transition and Beyond." *American Economic Review* 90.4 (2000), 806–828.

Gímenez, Martha E. "The Population Issue: Marx vs. Malthus." *Den Ny Verden* 8.3 (1973), 74–88.

Kremer, Michael. "Population Growth and Technological Change: One Million BC to 1990." *Quarterly of Journal of Economics* 108.3 (1993), 681–716.

Livi Bacci, Massimo. *A Concise History of World Population*. Cambridge, Mass., 2001.

Malthus, Thomas J. *An Essay on the Principle of Population*. London, 1798.

Malthus, Thomas J. *Principle of Politcal Economy*. London, 1820.

Toye, John. *Keynes on Population*. New York, 2000.

Niehans, Jürg. *A History of Economic Thought*. Baltimore, 1990.

Razis, Assaf, and Efraim Sadka. *Population Economics*. Cambridge, Mass., 1995.

Simon, Julian L. *The Economics of Population Growth*. Princeton, 1977.

Simon, Julian L. *The Great Breakthrough and Its Cause*. Edited by Timur Kuran. Ann Arbor, 2000.

Weir, David. "Life under Pressure: France and England, 1670–1870." *Journal of Economic History* 44.1 (1984), 27–47.

Weir, David. "Family Income, Mortality, and Fertility on the Eve of the Demographic Transtition: A Case Study of Rosny-sous-Bois." *Journal of Economic History* 55.1 (1995), 1–26.

Wrigley, E. A. *People, Cities, and Wealth*. Oxford, 1987.

Wrigley, E. A. *Continuity, Chance, and Change: The Character of the Industrial Revolution in England*. New York, 1988.

RAN ABRAMITZKY AND FABIO BRAGGION

MANAGEMENT. Management is the coordination of economic activity by administrative means. As Ronald Coase observed in his classic 1937 article, "The Nature of the Firm," this form of coordination is the defining characteristic of all firms. Coase was seeking to understand why firms exist—why all economic activity was not coordinated by price signals in the market. He reasoned that some kinds of transactions were expensive to conduct in the market because they required the parties involved to write contracts that anticipated a myriad of possible contingencies. In such cases economic actors could reduce their transaction costs by entering into more general, long-term contracts that gave one of the parties discretionary (managerial) authority over the others. These contracts, Coase argued, were the essence of the entities called firms.

As Coase's analysis underscored, managerial coordination is hierarchical by definition. For this type of economic coordination to work effectively therefore, the instructions issued by the manager have to be obeyed. However, subordinates often have their own ideas about what they want to do and may follow only those orders that they perceive to be in their interests or in the interests of their part of the organization. Effective management thus typically requires that this "principal-agent" problem be solved by investing in information systems that allow superiors to monitor subordinates' behavior or incentive programs that encourage subordinates to follow instructions.

Of course these kinds of investments only became necessary as firms grew larger and more complex. During the early nineteenth century most firms were small entrepreneurial enterprises managed directly by their owners. Although the owners of the largest firms had to delegate some of their managerial responsibilities to employees, it was still typically possible for them to monitor their managers personally. For example, the textile factories in Lowell, Massachusetts, were among the largest manufacturing enterprises in the world during the 1830s. These firms were corporations whose officers (all of whom were major stockholders) typically resided in Boston. The treasurer functioned as the firm's chief executive officer and was responsible for keeping the mill supplied with raw materials, marketing its output, and (in consultation with the other officers) making strategic decisions. The factories themselves were located on waterpower sites in outlying areas and were managed by resident supervisors, but the treasurer maintained personal oversight with frequent (typically weekly) visits.

As the coordination problems that firms faced became more complex, personal supervision was no longer adequate to maintain efficiency. U.S. railroads, for example, carried a variety of different types of goods, as well as passengers, to a multitude of different destinations. In order to keep costs under control, they pioneered in developing what Alfred D. Chandler, Jr., has called the decentralized line-and-staff divisional form, in which operational authority was delegated to those in the best position to exercise it (the managers of the roads' various geographical divisions) but in which information on divisional performance flowed upward to staff executives in the central office who were responsible for setting general policy. The railroads also innovated by creating cost accounting and other information systems that provided staff executives with the data they needed to set policies effectively and also to insure that divisional managers were following their directives.

Managerial innovation of this type was also likely to occur where firms were forced by circumstances to expand their boundaries and take on more functions. For example, in Germany, markets were relatively thin during the late nineteenth century. Rather than concentrate on one product line, firms spread their risk by diversifying into a broader range of goods. Because top executives often lacked the specialized knowledge required to direct the production of all these different goods efficiently, firms evolved decentralized structures that gave the managers of the various production divisions considerable autonomy to pursue opportunities.

Industrial enterprises in the United States were generally much more specialized than German firms through the 1920s and thus tended to have more centralized managerial hierarchies. Only when they began to diversify into new product lines did they experiment with alternative organizational structures. DuPont, for example, had flourished during World War I supplying gunpowder and related war matériel to the belligerents, but after the armistice the company sought to reduce excess capacity by entering new markets, such as paints. When the company's centralized management had difficulty running these new ventures profitably, DuPont's owners developed and implemented a multidivisional form of organization, known as the M-form, in which each distinct product line was organized as a separate business, albeit one wholly owned by DuPont. The head of a division was like the chief executive of a company, accountable to the owners for divisional profit-and-loss performance. Each division controlled all the functions required to support its operations, from product development and procurement on through marketing and sales. The DuPont board controlled the amount of capital allocated to each division as well as the appointments and tenure of divisional heads. Although this change inevitably involved some loss of scale economies (functions such as procurement and marketing moved, for example, from the central office to the individual divisions), it gave divisional executives the wherewithal and the incentives to respond to changing conditions and opportunities.

Similar problems managing different product lines inspired a handful of other U.S. firms to decentralize their managerial hierarchies around the same time, but the M-form did not spread beyond that until the post–World War II period, when a wave of mergers for purposes of diversification made the new structure attractive. Around the same time this more formal type of decentralized structure diffused through Western Europe as well.

Professionalization of Management. When owners hired managers, they needed to have some way of deciding which candidates were best qualified for the job. Initially evaluating credentials was a difficult task, and owners disproportionately chose as managers people they knew well: relatives and other close personal associates or people who had long employment histories with the company. By the late nineteenth century, however, institutions of higher education were providing owners with what was in effect a credentialing service, and large firms began increasingly to staff their managerial hierarchies with men who had obtained formal university training. French enterprises tended to recruit managers from the *grandes écoles*, particularly those specializing in science and engineering but also, after World War II, the École Nationale d'Administration, German firms from engineering and law schools, and Japanese firms from the top national universities. U.S. firms initially hired engineers as managers but over time shifted toward college graduates with liberal arts degrees, particularly those who subsequently attended specialized business schools (this American innovation has gradually spread to other countries as well). British companies, on the other hand, were relatively slow to recruit professional managers from outside the firm or even outside the founding family, and to the present day their executives are on average less likely to have advanced degrees than those in the United States, Germany, France, or Japan.

Managers with formal training tended to think of themselves as professionals engaged in the common enterprise of improving industrial efficiency. As a result they flocked into associations in which they could exchange ideas with, and secure recognition from, their peers. Where the numbers of managers in a single industry was large, as in the case of railroads, industry-specific associations emerged: the American Society of Railroad Superintendents, the Society of Railroad Comptrollers Accountants and Auditors, the American Train Dispatchers Association, and a whole host of other even more narrowly focused organizations. Managers who worked for industrial enterprises tended initially to join engineering societies, such as the American Society of Mechanical Engineers, but as their numbers increased they too organized more specialized associations, such as the American Association of Industrial Management, the Society for the Promotion of Science and Management, and the Administrative Management Association.

Whether they were specific management organizations or more general engineering societies, these associations held meetings and published journals that featured papers on new ways to improve industrial efficiency. In the late-nineteenth-century United States a flurry of articles appeared that called attention to the chaotic and wasteful practices of factory management that, the authors claimed, resulted from overreliance on the skills, knowledge, and memory of individual executives. Management, they argued, should be systematized so that these vital assets resided in the organization and managers could come and go without damage to the enterprise. Procedures detailing the various stages of production and the flow of inputs and outputs through them should be recorded in handbooks. At the same time data on performance should be collected to insure that correct procedures were being followed and also to pinpoint areas for future improvement. New technologies, such as the mimeograph and filing cabinets, facilitated the requisite collection and storage of information.

Scientific management was a further development of this general call for improvement in the internal organization of firms. Its most famous proponent, Frederick Winslow Taylor, pursued essentially the same agenda as other systematizers in promoting accounting and production-control systems that gave managers better information about what was happening in their domains. He went further than anyone else, however, in extending this effort to the shop floor, conducting time and motion studies of laborers while they worked in an endeavor to find the most efficient way of performing any task and then introducing differential piece rates to encourage workers to meet what he claimed were scientifically set standards of efficiency.

Some of the earliest proponents of systematic management set themselves up as consultants to help firms improve their productivity, but it was Taylor who transformed consulting into a major business, not only advising firms himself but organizing under his leadership an entire army of consultants whose expertise he matched to the needs of the businesspeople who approached him for help. Inevitably Taylor's success attracted imitators, some of whom had worked with him for a time before setting off on their own. Among the most important were Frank and Lillian Gilbreth, Harrington Emerson, and Charles Eugène Bedaux, who spread the techniques of scientific management to Europe as well as throughout the United States. Scholars have generally concluded that the productivity gains resulting from these efforts were relatively small. On the one hand, the innovations of these consultants were often blocked by opposition both from labor and from entrenched management. On the other, competition among consultants encouraged a focus on short-run achievements rather than on reforms that would perhaps have delivered bigger benefits, but only over the long run.

Banks also provided consulting services to businesses—not only about financial matters but also about organizational structure and strategic planning. The Glass-Steagall Act of 1933 forced them to abandon this business, provid-

ing an opportunity for a second generation of management consulting firms, led by McKinsey and Company; Booz Allen Hamilton; and Cresap, McCormick and Paget, to fill the gap. Staffed more by business school graduates than by engineers, these firms after World War II helped spread the M-form of organization to firms, both in the United States and Europe, that were diversifying their product lines. By the 1960s accounting firms were also making serious inroads in this market, and the two types of businesses began to merge.

The Rise and Decline of the Managerial Enterprise. The professionalization of management typically began with the middle ranks of a firm's administrative hierarchy, owners continuing to occupy the top jobs. Over time, however, in many firms owners relinquished their executive positions, and the managerial enterprise—that is, an enterprise run completely by salaried professionals—was born. This process began earlier and affected a greater number of large firms in the United States than anywhere else. There it was accompanied as well by a more complete dispersion of stockholdings, effectively giving salaried managers unchallenged control of the enterprises they administered.

The growing separation of ownership from control set off alarm bells among scholars (most famously Adolf Berle and Gardiner Means), who worried in the 1930s that managers would pursue their own private interests rather than maximize their enterprises' profits. But the success of large American corporations during the post–World War II period belied these criticisms and instead gave rise to the idea, most fully developed in the work of Chandler, that the managerial enterprise was the ultimate stage in the evolution of business organizations. Chandler's starting point was the observation that technological change had made it possible for firms to reap substantial economies of scale in a number of key industries. In order to capture these economies, firms had to be able to maintain a high rate of throughput through their factories and hence had to insure that shortfalls in supply did not disrupt their production processes and that output did not pile up in their warehouses unsold. The best way to do this, Chandler argued, was for firms to bring these activities under their direct control by integrating backward into raw-material production and forward into distribution and by building a managerial hierarchy capable of coordinating smoothly the flow of inputs and outputs from raw material to final sale.

Chandler claimed that firms that took these steps improved upon the workings of the market and reaped enormous competitive advantages. The only firms that could compete with them head to head were those that completely duplicated their vertically integrated structures and managerial hierarchies. Because relatively few firms could raise the enormous amounts of capital required, these kinds of industries quickly took on oligopolistic structures. Moreover because large firms could exploit economies of scope as well as of scale by diversifying their operations into other industries and adopting the M-form of organization, over time larger and larger portions of the economy became subject to their managerial authority. The conglomerate movement of the late 1960s and early 1970s seemed to be the inevitable result.

Chandler argued that, in order to achieve comparable levels of success, firms in other nations had to emulate the most important features of the American managerial enterprise. By the early 1980s, however, the deteriorating performance of large U.S. firms in the face of international competition had called the superiority of this model into question. Critics argued that top executives in the firms' central offices had in fact only the most cursory knowledge of the businesses they managed. As a result their supervision consisted of little more than setting performance targets in terms of easily interpreted financial variables like revenue, profit, and return on invested capital, effectively evaluating subordinates' performance by using rate-of-return accounting to mimic market competition. Not only did this kind of direction add less and less value over time, but it could be downright harmful. For example, the accounting assumptions typically imbedded in these calculations rewarded subsidiaries for achieving long production runs that spread fixed costs over a large output, perversely encouraging managers to sacrifice quality in the interests of quantity production.

Although presumably central offices could develop better metrics to evaluate managers' performance, many critics thought the problem ran deeper, and there was a revival of interest in Berle and Means's argument about the dangers of a separation of ownership from control. Michael Jensen, an economic theorist noted for his pathbreaking work on the principal-agent problem, led the charge. Claiming that managers were diverting resources to fund perquisites and empire building, he argued that the day of the public corporation was over. Reprivatization by means of leveraged buyouts (LBOs) would give managers an ownership stake in their businesses, at the same time disciplining them by means of high debt to equity ratios. In a similar vein, other theorists argued that the interests of managers and owners in public corporations could be better aligned by using stock options to reward managers for performance.

The financial scandals that greeted the start of the twenty-first century suggest this latter solution may actually have made the situation worse rather than better. LBOs have not been similarly tainted, but because the bulk of their earnings perforce had to go to payments on their high burden of debt, their application was limited largely to older industries in which firms did not have to invest continually in new technology to stay competitive. For solutions appli-cable to more technologically progressive industries, critics of the American managerial enterprise have looked abroad for alternative models. Some have pointed out that, in European corporations, families or institutions often own a large proportion of their firms' equity. These blockholders can thus exercise disciplinary oversight over management, particularly in Germany, where the institution of the supervisory board gives them a well-defined role. Others have focused attention on the example of Japanese firms, particularly Toyota. The epitome of what is called "lean manufacturing," Toyota has reduced over-heard costs dramatically by outsourcing the production of parts and by insisting that suppliers deliver components to assembly sites "just in time." The Japanese system of production management thus shrinks the boundaries of firms and decreases the scope of the activities subject to managerial coordination. In place of the vertically integrated firm, it offers a network of long-term relationships in which suppliers must stay on the cutting edge to retain Toyota's business but in which Toyota encourages them to invest in technological innovation while promising to absorb the lion's share of their output.

Although the relative merits for long-run performance of these alternative models is as yet unknown, it is no longer possible to posit the absolute superiority of the American-style managerial enterprise. Although the separation of ownership from control that characterizes such firms undoubtedly has benefits, it also entails costs. Most importantly, the principal-agent problems that are endemic to hierarchical organizations are likely to be greatest where managerial authority is least subject to checks.

BIBLIOGRAPHY

Baker, George P., and George David Smith. *The New Financial Capitalists: Kohlberg Kravis Roberts and the Creation of Corporate Value.* New York, 1998.

Berle, Adolf A., and Gardiner C. Means. *The Modern Corporation and Private Property.* Rev. ed. New York, 1968.

Cassis, Youssef. *Big Business: The European Experience in the Twentieth Century.* Oxford, 1997.

Chandler, Alfred D., Jr. *Strategy and Structure: Chapters in the History of the American Industrial Enterprise.* Cambridge, Mass., 1962.

Chandler, Alfred D., Jr. *The Visible Hand: The Managerial Revolution in American Business.* Cambridge, Mass., 1977.

Chandler, Alfred D., Jr. *Scale and Scope: The Dynamics of Industrial Capitalism.* Cambridge, Mass., 1990.

Chandler, Alfred D., Jr., and Herman Daems, eds. *Managerial Hierarchies: Comparative Perspectives on the Rise of the Modern Industrial Enterprise.* Cambridge, Mass., 1980.

Coase, R. H. "The Nature of the Firm." *Economica* 4.16 (1937), 386–405.

Dalzell, Robert F., Jr. *Enterprising Elite: The Boston Associates and the World They Made.* Cambridge, Mass., 1987.

Hirschmeier, Johannes, and Tsunehiko Yui. *The Development of Japanese Business, 1600–1980.* 2d ed. London, 1981.

Jensen, Michael C. "Eclipse of the Public Corporation." *Harvard Business Review* 67 (1989), 61–74.

Jensen, Michael C., and William H. Meckling. "Theory of the Firm: Managerial Behavior, Agency Costs, and Ownership Structure." *Journal of Financial Economics* 3 (1976), 305–360.

Johnson, H. Thomas. "Managing by Remote Control: Recent Management Accounting Practice in Historical Perspective." In *Inside the Business Enterprise: Historical Perspectives on the Use of Information*, edited by Peter Temin, pp. 41–66. Chicago, 1991.

Kipping, Matthias. "American Management Consulting Companies in Western Europe, 1920 to 1990: Products, Reputation, and Relationships." *Business History Review* 73.2 (1999), 190–220.

Kocha, Jürgen. "Family and Bureaucracy in German Industrial Management, 1850–1914: Siemens in Comparative Perspective." *Business History Review* 45.2 (1971), 133–156.

Kocha, Jürgen. *Industrial Culture and Bourgeois Society: Business, Labor, and Bureaucracy in Modern Germany*. New York, 1999.

Lamoreaux, Naomi R., Daniel M. G. Raff, and Peter Temin. "Beyond Markets and Hierarchies: Toward a New Synthesis of American Business History." NBER Working Paper No. 9029. 2002.

Litterer, Joseph A. "Systematic Management: Design for Organizational Recoupling in American Manufacturing Firms." *Business History Review* 27.4 (1963), 369–391.

McKenna, Christopher D. "The World's Newest Profession: Management Consulting in the Twentieth Century." Ph.D. diss., Johns Hopkins University, 2000.

Morikawa, Hidemasa. "The Role of Managerial Enterprise in Post-War Japan's Economic Growth: Focus on the 1950s." In *The Origins of Japanese Industrial Power*, edited by Etsuo Abe and Robert Fitzgerald, pp. 32–43. London, 1995.

Nelson, Daniel. *Managers and Workers: Origins of the New Factory System in the United States, 1880–1920*. Madison, Wis., 1975.

Nelson, Daniel. "Industrial Engineering and the Industrial Enterprise, 1890–1940." In *Coordination and Information: Historical Perspectives on the Organization of Enterprise*, edited by Naomi R. Lamoreaux and Daniel M. G. Raff, pp. 35–53. Chicago, 1995.

Penrose, Edith Tilton. *The Theory of the Growth of the Firm*. Oxford, 1959.

Roe, Mark J. *Strong Managers, Weak Owners: The Political Roots of American Corporate Finance*. Princeton, 1994.

Segal, Harvey H. *Corporate Makeover: How American Business Is Reshaping for the Future*. New York, 1989.

Udagawa, Masaru. "The Development of Production Management at the Toyota Motor Corporation." In *The Origins of Japanese Industrial Power*, edited by Etsuo Abe and Robert Fitzgerald, pp. 107–119. London, 1995.

Whittington, Richard, and Michael Mayer. *The European Corporation: Strategy, Structure, and Social Science*. Oxford, 2000.

Womack, James P., Daniel T. Jones, and Daniel Roos. *The Machine That Changed the World*. New York, 1990.

Yates, JoAnne. *Control through Communication: The Rise of System in American Management*. Baltimore, 1989.

NAOMI LAMOREAUX

MANCHESTER, in northwestern England, is situated on the Irwell, Medlock, Irk, and Tib rivers. The Manchester Ship Canal provides access to oceangoing vessels. The center of England's most densely populated area, Manchester was the world's first industrial city. The smokestacks of the main factory district, Ancoats, defined Manchester as "Cottonopolis" and associated the city with the Industrial Revolution, based on machines, water-driven or steam-driven factories, and an industrial proletariat. Richard Arkwright (the inventor of the water-frame in 1769, a spinning machine that made tightly twisted, strong threads) allegedly constructed the first cotton factory in Manchester in the early 1780s. Following this entrepreneurial initiative, the town's manufacturing system grew, for its time, at a revolutionary pace. Despite the economic dislocation of the French Revolutionary and Napoleonic Wars (1793–1815), there were ninety cotton-factory firms in production in 1815; by 1841, the number was 128.

Manchester's industrial development had two distinct patterns. First, there was the role of the large firm. One cannot, however, assume that the "cotton lords" dominated the town's economy. In fact, in 1815 only two firms employed about one thousand workers (McConnell & Kennedy and A & G Murray); by 1833 there were only three (McConnell & Company, Birely & Kirk, and Thomas Houldsworth). In 1841, approximately 30 percent of Manchester's cotton-factory firms employed fewer than one hundred workers, and the median number employed in a cotton mill was 174. Manchester did have its giant firms: in 1815, James McConnell and John Kennedy (McConnell & Kennedy) and Adam and George Murray (A & G Murray) employed almost 20 percent of the town's factory work force. Nevertheless the industrial structure of "Cottonopolis" was characterized by large numbers of small and medium-size firms operating in a highly competitive business environment. The manufacturing system, then, became engaged in a struggle for survival and, consequently, the number of firms was volatile, shaped by many start-ups and failures. Great fortunes were made in Manchester, but for the majority of firms, survival was a prime business objective; many small firms failed during cyclical downturns, only to re-emerge during the next upturn.

In the second pattern, Manchester employed a smaller proportion of its labor force in factories than did its satellite cotton towns, such as Ashton, Bolton, Bury, and Oldham—and the trend was more pronounced as the nineteenth century progressed. Douglas Farnie (1979) estimated the number of cotton employees as a proportion of Lancashire's population to be about 37 percent in 1811; the number employed in Manchester cotton factories accounted for no more than 12 percent of the town's population at the slightly later date of 1815. Manchester was a great commercial center, the hub of a regional manufacturing system, and its commercial institutions evolved to serve a dynamic industrial conurbation. In Manchester, the warehouse and the counting house were equally as important as the factory; in fact, the dynamic interaction between these business components stimulated the development of other manufacturing sectors, such as mechanical engineering and the chemical industry. By 1871, approximately one half of Manchester's male labor force was employed in manufacturing, and almost one-third was employed directly in cotton textiles.

The growth of a mechanical-engineering industry was crucial to the development of the factory system, and such Manchester men as William Fairbairn, Thomas Hewes, and Ebeneezer Smith, among others, pioneered the manufacture of cotton machinery, steam engines and boilers, mill-gearing and transmission systems, and machine tools. Manchester became not only the center of the world's cotton industry but also of its engineering by the 1830s and 1840s. The city, as a carrier of technological innovation, also witnessed major developments in the chemical industry, particularly those associated with the finishing trades of dyeing, bleaching, and calico printing. Entrepreneurs, such as Thomas Hoyle, William Newton, William Oliver, and Thomas Whitelegg, built some of the largest chemical and finishing works in the world. All these enterprises made Manchester the citadel of industrial capitalism, when in the mid-nineteenth century Great Britain was called the "workshop of the world."

The economic and technological power of Manchester meant that by 1850 its business leaders could claim to represent the interests not only of the city but also of a socioeconomic class, which developed a distinctive political economy—one that sought to further the aims of manufacturing interests in general. This political economy became known as the "Manchester school," and its interests were defined in terms of the principles of free trade, the abolition of agricultural protection, and the promotion of the economic and moral virtue of free and open markets. These principles became deeply embedded within British industrial capitalism, and they still have a strong resonance. They were, perhaps, best represented by Richard Cobden (1804–1865), the leader of the Anti-Corn Law League, an economist, and a Manchester man of international stature as a statesman. The volatility of trade—the conjuncture of great success and wealth with the distinct possibility of business failure and financial ruin—tested the enterprise of Manchester's business community. It also made it the focal point of the free-trade movement, which business prophets, such as Cobden, argued would open new markets for the vast increase in the volume of goods that the new industrial system could produce.

In the second half of the nineteenth century, Manchester rapidly expanded its warehouse system (the finest example was the warehouse erected for Horrocks Crewdson & Company in Piccadilly in 1898) and invested in infrastructural improvements, the most notable of which was the opening of the Manchester Ship Canal in 1894. In the twentieth century, Manchester's fortunes were inevitably affected by the long-run structural decline of the cotton industry, but unlike its satellite towns, it was never overly dependent on a single economic activity. Today, Manchester is still the third most densely populated conurbation in the United Kingdom, and Greater Manchester has a population of 2.57 million people, 1.19 million of whom are economically active.

BIBLIOGRAPHY

Farnie, Douglas. *The English Cotton Industry and the World Market, 1815–1896*. Oxford, 1979.

Farnie, Douglas. "The Commercial Development of Manchester in the Later Nineteenth Century." *Manchester Review* 7 (1956).

Lloyd-Jones, Roger. "Merchant City: The Manchester Business Community, the Trade Cycle, and Commercial Policy." In *Free Trade and Its Reception, 1815–1960*, edited by Andrew Marrison. London, 1998.

Lloyd-Jones, Roger, and M. J. Lewis. *Manchester and the Age of the Factory*. London, 1988.

Lloyd-Jones, Roger, and A. A. LeRoux. "The Size of Firms in the Cotton Industry: Manchester, 1815 to 1841." *Economic History Review* 33 (1980).

Redford, A. *Manchester Merchants and Foreign Trade*, vol. 1, *1794–1857*. Manchester, 1934.

Timmins, Geoffery. *Made in Lancashire: A History of Regional Industrialization*. Manchester, 1998.

ROGER LLOYD-JONES

MANORIAL SYSTEM. *See* Feudalism, *subentry on* Manorial System.

MARKETS. The fundamental characteristic of a market is that people use the price system to allocate resources. Other characteristics of markets are determined by the underlying institutional structure, the features of what is being exchanged, information costs, and transportation costs. Markets develop when gains from trade exist. That is, individuals will exchange only if they perceive that what they get is at least as valuable as what they give.

In almost all societies throughout history, exchange has taken a variety of forms, including reciprocity, redistribution, and gift giving, as well as exchange through markets. In addition, Ronald Coase (1937) established that the firm is a substitute for a market. Nevertheless, markets are the fundamental building blocks of productive economies, and the development of well-functioning markets is the key to the wealth of nations, as Adam Smith reminded us more than two centuries ago. The evolution of markets is a central story in economic history. In what follows, I shall first explore the underlying determinants that shape the structure and efficiency of markets, then analyze the evolution of markets throughout history, and conclude by exploring markets in the modern world.

Transactions Costs and Markets. To analyze the historical development of markets, we need some tools. These tools are the beliefs people possess about the world, which determine the institutions we develop to structure human interaction; the characteristics of the good or service being exchanged; information costs; and transportation costs. These will reveal the sources of varying characteristics of markets over time.

We begin with the beliefs people possess about the world around them. Throughout history, people have held widely disparate views about the equity, efficiency, and morality of forms of exchange. Most belief systems have their origins in religion. Religions usually have strong views about the morality of various markets, including usury and insurance, as well as the time and place of exchange, the use of a monetary unit, and broadly impersonal exchange. The characteristics of markets have been circumscribed throughout history by such constraints. Even today, the immorality of impersonal markets is embedded in much of the sociology literature, such as the work of Karl Polanyi (1968). A necessary condition for the development of markets was the evolution of beliefs justifying their equity, efficiency, and morality.

Given the beliefs people possess, those in a position to structure human interaction create institutions that, in turn, provide incentives that direct societal activity. The institutions that shape human interaction are made up of formal rules, informal constraints, and their enforcement characteristics. Formal rules consist of constitutions, laws, and regulations. Informal constraints consist of conventions, norms of behavior, and self-imposed codes of conduct. Enforcement may be carried out by the first party, through self-enforcement; the second party, through retaliation; or the third party, through ostracism by other interested parties or coercive enforcement by private groups or the state.

The actual structure of any market is a complex mix of formal rules, informal rules, and enforcement strategies. The formal rules are the property-rights structure erected by the polity, but their effectiveness is a consequence of the degree to which they are complemented by informal norms of behavior and of the degree to which they are enforced. The ideal institutional framework for markets is one in which the cost of transacting is low, which requires that measurement and enforcement costs are low.

In order to have effective property rights, one must be able to measure the dimensions of the good or service being exchanged. If, as is typically the case, the good or service being exchanged has multiple valuable dimensions, then the more precisely they can be measured, the better the terms of exchange can be enforced. In general, the lower the costs of measurement and enforcement of property rights, the lower the costs of exchange and the more efficient the market (Cheung, 1969). The evolution of more sophisticated measurement technology has played a major part in enabling the specification and enforcement of property rights.

Historically, information costs have been a major source of transactions costs. Technological change, from the semaphore of Rothschild fame to the telegraph to modern electronic communication, has revolutionized information transmission in terms of the speed at which information travels across space. Yet there is more to information than its movement across space. The coordination, integration, and interpretation of information in a world in which knowledge and information are widely dispersed entails not only a price system, as Hayek (1945) reminded us, but also institutions to coordinate the flow of information and knowledge.

Finally, transportation costs, which are affected by weight, volume, and value, have historically determined the geographic limits of markets. The revolution in transportation technology has consistently expanded markets geographically.

Historical Development of Markets. Evidence of trade goes far back into prehistory. Herodotus gives us a possibly apocryphal account of trade, which is described by Karl Polanyi as follows:

> The Carthaginians indulged in a dumb barter with the natives of the African coast, exchanging their goods for gold. Caution impelled the parties to repair in turn, to a spot near the beach, leaving an amount of goods and gold, respectively. This was repeated, until the other party was satisfied with the amounts offered, both sides withdrawing then with the purchase sought, never having met their counterparts face to face (Polanyi, 1968, p. 243).

The Agora in Athens is a prime example of a marketplace in ancient Greece. It was designed in the sixth century BCE as a civic center or open space for citizens to assemble for political, legal, cultural, theatrical, and athletic activities. Although it was not initially designed with exchange in mind, economic activities began to dominate the Agora by the fifth century BCE, and there is evidence of a lively, full-scale retail market in the Agora during the fourth century BCE. The type of exchange that took place in these marketplaces probably was similar to that in modern-day farmers' markets, characterized by many small transactions between a large number of buyers and sellers and specialization on the part of the seller.

As Rome grew into an empire, daily markets replaced periodic markets. During the height of the Roman Empire, exchange took place through shops, warehouses, and bazaars on a daily basis. The development of Roman commercial law reduced transaction costs, as did the standardization of weights and measures. For example, Roman law held principals liable for the actions of their agents. The Roman bureaucracy included *aediles*, who acted as magistrates or market supervisors. They inspected weights and measures, managed the allocation of grain, prevented the price of staples from rising "too high" in times of scarcity, and oversaw the sale of slaves and animals (Frayn, 1993).

In the fourth century BCE, both Persia and Egypt engaged in long-distance trade with Greece, India, China, and each other. In addition, Persia facilitated domestic trade through a policy of decentralization—so that the state did not interfere with regional social and economic institutions—combined with the centralized provision of roads, military protection, sea routes, and a sound, unified currency (Rostovtzeff, 1941). These policies lowered transaction costs of interregional trade within Persia's borders.

Although this brief essay focuses on the evolution of markets in the Western world, the development of more efficient markets is everywhere in history connected with economic development. The great expansion of China after the seventeenth century, which produced unprecedented population growth, was made possible by the growth of more efficient factor and product markets. These, in turn, were a product of the imperial state's improved enforcement of customary law practices and contractual exchange, which reduced transaction costs (Myers, 1982).

Personal exchange dominates history. It requires personal knowledge of the other party to exchange and repeated interaction with that party in contexts other than exchange. As a result, personal exchange has low transaction costs because both parties stand to gain by honesty and integrity. On the other hand, exchange between strangers that may never be repeated poses fundamental dilemmas. How does one know the other party will live up to his or her part of the bargain? The higher the costs of measurement and enforcement, the more likely the other party will alter the quality of the good or service being offered or renege on the agreement altogether. Game theory illustrates the dilemma. It typically pays parties in a game to cooperate when there are small numbers of players, the parties know a lot about each other, and there is no end game, as in personal exchange. However, when the parties do not know each other and when the game is not repeated, as in the case of impersonal exchange, then it pays to defect.

The *suq*, a market structure that has existed in the Middle East and North Africa for millennia, illustrates the key problem of high transaction costs in impersonal markets. The basic characteristics of the *suq* are a multiplicity of small-scale enterprises; low fixed costs in terms of rent and machinery; a very fine division of labor; an enormous number of small transactions, each more or less independent of the next; face-to-face contacts; and goods that are not homogeneous. As much as 40 to 50 percent of the town's labor force is engaged in the exchange process. There are no organizations devoted to assembling and distributing market information, systems of weights and measures are intricate and incompletely standardized, and

bargaining skills are elaborately developed and are the primary determinant of who prospers in the bazaar and who does not.

The *suq* illustrates the classic problems plaguing impersonal exchange. How were they overcome? The evolution of impersonal exchange with low transaction costs is an essential stepping stone in economic development. The development of the Western world coincided with the gradual recovery of commerce and trade from the tenth century on. The development of institutions that altered the payoff between cooperation and defection was responsible for this recovery.

Before we examine the specific institutions that generated this change, we must explore the change in beliefs that made it possible. In *The Protestant Ethic and the Spirit of Capitalism*, Max Weber shows that the religious ethic embodied in Protestantism, specifically Calvinism, contained values that promoted the growth of capitalism. But which way does the causation run, and how do we know that both the values and the growth of capitalism did not stem from some other source? Weber connects religious views, values, and economic behavior, but he does not demonstrate how the consequent behavior would generate specific institutions and organizations that would lead to economic development and growth. Moreover, Counter-Reformation Catholicism may have encouraged the same individualism and sense of discipline that Weber uniquely attributes to Protestantism. These issues are far from resolved. It has been a long-standing belief of scholars that individualistic behavioral beliefs are congenial to economic growth. In *The Origins of English Individualism* (1978), Alan Macfarlane traces the sources of English individualism back to the thirteenth century or earlier. He paints a picture of fluid, individualistic attitudes toward the family, the organization of work, and the social structure of the village community. These attitudes were manifested in a set of formal rules dealing with property inheritance and the legal status of women.

More recently, Avner Greif (1994) compares Genoese traders with traders who had adopted the cultural and social attributes of Islamic society in the Mediterranean trade of the eleventh and twelfth centuries. He detects systematic differences in their organizational structures traceable to contrasting individualist versus collectivist behavioral beliefs. Traders from the Islamic world developed in-group social communication networks to enforce collective action which, while effective in relatively small homogeneous ethnic groups, did not lend themselves to the impersonal exchange that arises when markets become larger and more diverse. In contrast, the Genoese traders developed bilateral enforcement mechanisms that entailed the creation of formal legal and political organizations for monitoring and enforcing agreements. This institutional and organizational path permitted more complex trade and exchange.

Innovations that lowered transaction costs occurred at three cost margins: (1) those that improved the mobility of capital, (2) those that lowered information costs, and (3) those that converted uncertainty (in the Knightian sense) into risk. All of these innovations had their origins in earlier times; most of them were borrowed from medieval Italian city-states, Islam, or Byzantium.

The first innovations that improved capital mobility were the techniques and methods that evolved to evade usury laws. Interest was often disguised in loan contracts, which increased the cost of contracting by making contracts cumbersome to write and enforce. With the deterioration of usury laws, the costs of writing and enforcing such contracts declined.

A second set of innovations that improved capital mobility was the evolution of bills of exchange, the development of techniques and instruments that allowed for the negotiability of the bills of exchange, and the development of discounting methods. These depended on the creation of institutions and organizations that would permit the use of bills of exchange, first in such fairs as the Champagne fairs, then through banks, and finally through financial houses that could specialize in discounting. Increasing the volume of trade was a necessary precondition for the evolution of these organizations. In addition, economies of scale in the use of bills of exchange, improved contract enforcement, and the development of accounting and auditing methods and their use as evidence in debt collection and contract enforcement were important parts of the historical development of capital markets.

A third innovation affecting capital mobility arose from the problem of controlling agents involved in long-distance trade. The traditional resolution of this problem was the use of kinship and family ties to bind agents to principals in ways that provided some assurance to principals that their orders and directions were carried out. However, as the size and scope of merchant trading empires grew, the extension of discretionary behavior to agents who had no kinship ties to the principals required the development of sophisticated accounting and monitoring procedures.

The major developments in the reduction of information costs were the printing of prices of various commodities and the printing of manuals that provided information on weights, measures, customs, brokerage fees, postal systems, and exchange rates between Europe and the rest of the trading world. These developments, too, depended on the increasing volume of international trade.

The conversion of uncertainty into risk first occurred through the development of marine insurance, which evolved from sporadic individual contracts covering partial payment for losses to contracts issued by specialized firms. These firms had developed the actuarial knowledge necessary for such insurance. Business organizations that spread risk through portfolio diversification or through institutions that permitted a large number of investors to engage in risky ventures evolved from the Italian *commenda*, with its Jewish, Byzantine, and Muslim origins, to the English regulated company and finally the joint-stock company.

The mechanisms for contract enforcement appear to have had their beginnings in internal codes of conduct of fraternal orders of guild merchants, which were enforced by the threat of ostracism. These codes evolved into merchant law and spread throughout the European trading area. Common law and Roman law gradually integrated the codes of merchant law, and the state took over its enforcement.

The last point is critical. The evolution of polities that provided a framework of law and enforcement allowed the economic institutional structure to develop. Such a framework is an essential requirement for impersonal exchange. The development was a long process of some polities shifting from Mafia-like extortion to trading protection and justice for revenue. The initial impetus for this development was the desperate search for additional revenue by rulers in the face of the escalating costs of warfare.

To be successful, impersonal exchange requires well-specified and enforced property rights and norms of behavior that create widespread beliefs in honesty and integrity in exchange. In addition, impersonal exchange requires a polity that will specify the necessary property rights, provide low-cost contract enforcement through an effective judicial system, and provide the essential regulatory structure to constrain the players to compete via price and quality rather than at other margins. This is a tall order, and creating these institutions has proven to be a fundamental stumbling block for much of the world.

The economic history of the past five centuries of the Western world is as much a story of this gradual institutional evolution as it is a complementary story of the development of the revolutionary technology. Indeed, the two developments are intertwined. The growth in the size of markets, first in the Netherlands and then in England, raised the rate of return to innovation. This in turn induced further institutional and organizational innovation to realize the potential of the new technology in an ongoing process that continues to this day. While it is beyond the scope of this essay to explore key parts of this evolution, the development of the polity in the Netherlands and in England, the rise of representative government in those two countries, the Statute of Monopolies in England in 1624, and the beginnings of English patent law were institutional steps along the way that anticipated the Industrial Revolution. In turn, in the nineteenth century, the

MARKET SCENE. *Les Halles*, the central markets in Paris. Painting (1895) by Léon Lhermitte (1844–1925). (Giraudon/Art Resource, NY)

application of the steam engine to land and water transportation and the telegraph radically reduced transportation and transaction costs, which facilitated the growth of markets.

While the Industrial Revolution traditionally has been regarded as the key to modern economic growth, such a perspective ignores the fundamental institutional transformation that preceded it. The specific factors that reduced transaction costs in impersonal exchange were the evolution of beliefs reflected in the writings of John Locke, Montesquieu, Adam Smith, David Hume, and the Scottish Enlightenment in general. These beliefs were embodied in the political and economic institutions that fostered representative government, well-specified property rights in land and other factor and product markets, the elaboration and standardization of weights and measures, the development of judicial systems, and the intangible but crucial norms of behavior that helped parties live up to the spirit, as well as the letter, of terms of exchange.

Modern productivity growth is a consequence of the second economic revolution, a revolution that began in the last half of the nineteenth century and continues today. This revolution is characterized by the development of scientific disciplines and the wedding of science and technol-ogy. The fundamental change in the stock and flow of knowledge entails an equally fundamental change in the organization of human beings and the structure of societies to realize the higher productivity this revolution generates.

The development of the disciplines of physics, chemistry, biology, and genetics is the source of the growth in the stock of scientific knowledge. The systematic application of these disciplines to the basic economic problem of scarcity not only has purged the Malthusian specter of diminishing returns from our purview but also has created the vision of a potential world of plenty. To achieve that potential, however, entails a restructuring of economic, social, and political institutions and organizations in order to realize the increasing returns attributes of the technology in which this scientific knowledge is embodied.

New technology requires occupational and territorial specialization and division of labor on an unprecedented scale; and as a consequence, the number of exchanges grows exponentially. In order to realize the gains from the productive potential associated with a technology of increasing returns, one has to invest enormous resources in transacting. In the United States, for example, the labor force grew from 29 million to 80 million between 1900 and

1970; during that period, the number of production workers grew from 10 million to 29 million, while the number of white-collar workers, the majority of whom were engaged in transacting, increased from 5 million to 38 million. The transaction sector (broadly defined) in the United States in one estimate made up 45 percent of gross national product (GNP) in 1970.

If transaction costs were simply the costs of coordinating the increasingly complex interdependent parts of an economy, then they would be simply information costs or, more specifically, the costs of acquiring the information to measure the multiple dimensions of what is being exchanged. But they are also the costs of enforcing agreements and making credible commitments across time and space. Control over quality in the lengthening production chain and solutions to the problems of complex principal-agent relationships are necessary to be able to realize gains from trade in a world that is increasingly specialized. Much technology is designed to reduce transaction costs by substituting capital for labor, by reducing the degrees of freedom of workers in the production process, or by automatically measuring the quality of intermediate goods. Measuring inputs and outputs so that one can ascertain the contribution of individual factors and the output at successive stages of production is difficult. As a result, there is room for conflict over the consequent payment to factors of production.

Firms using new technology have large fixed-capital investments with long lives and frequently low alternative scrap values. As a result, the exchange process embodied in contracts has to be extended over long periods of time, which entails uncertainty about prices and costs and the possibility of opportunistic behavior on the part of one of the parties to the exchange. A number of organizational problems emerge from the use of new technology. First, increased resources are necessary to measure the quality of output or the performance of agents. Sorting, grading, labeling, licensing, trademarks, warranties, time-and-motion studies, and a variety of other techniques are all devices that attempt to measure the characteristics of goods and services and the performance of agents. Despite the existence of such devices, the dissipation of income is evident in the difficulties of measuring the quality of automobile repairs, the safety characteristics of products, the quality of medical services, or the quality of educational output. The problems of evaluating performance are even more acute in hierarchies because low-cost measurement of the multiple dimensions of an agent's performance is difficult. Second, while team production permits economies of scale to be realized, it does so at the cost of worker alienation and shirking. The discipline of the factory is a response to the control problems of coordination and shirking in team production. Third, the potential gains from

opportunistic behavior increase and lead to strategic behavior, both within the firm and between firms. Everywhere in factor and product markets, the gains from withholding services or altering the terms of agreement at strategic points offer large potential gains. Fourth, the development of large-scale hierarchies produces the familiar problems of bureaucracy. The multiplication of rules and regulations inside large organizations to control shirking and principal/agent problems results in rigidities, income dissipation, and the loss of flexibility essential to adaptive efficiency. Finally, there are external effects, such as the unpriced costs reflected in the modern environmental crises. The interdependence of a world of specialization and division of labor increases the imposition of costs on third parties.

The institutional framework and the consequent costs of transacting, which are a product of the technology employed, as well as of the institutional framework, determine how successful an economy will be in overcoming these obstacles. Well specified and enforced property rights, decentralized political and economic decision making, and competition make up the underlying institutional structure that has induced organizational changes that enable modern economies to reap the productivity gains of new technology.

Economic restructuring entails a still more fundamental restructuring of the entire society in order to create efficient economic markets. Technology and accompanying scale economies entail specialization, minute division of labor, impersonal exchange, and urban societies. All the old informal constraints built around the family, personal relationships, and repetitive individual exchanges are uprooted. Indeed, the basic traditional functions of the family, such as education, employment in the family enterprise, and insurance, are either eliminated or severely circumscribed. New formal rules, new organizations, and new roles for government replace them. However, the modern extension of the second economic revolution, the revolution in information technology, is creating a new and still only dimly understood new structure of markets. Since transaction costs are largely made up of information costs, this revolution has the potential to reduce exchange costs, but at the same time it presents new problems in contract enforcement.

Markets in the Modern World. As the foregoing paragraphs make clear, the evolution of modern markets is intricately tied up with the transformation of the modern world. Let me conclude this essay by briefly exploring market efficiency, market structures, and global markets, sovereignty, and political systems.

Economists have a specific characterization of the efficiency of markets. An allocation of resources is said to be efficient when it is not possible to make one person better off without making someone else worse off. The two fundamental theorems of welfare economics establish that in a perfectly competitive framework, (1) when people use the price mechanism to allocate resources, the resulting allocation will be efficient, and (2) any efficient allocation of resources can be supported by the price mechanism. As Debreu (1959) points out, the two welfare theorems explain the role of markets in society.

Efficiency requires the acquisition and coordination of a great deal of information. Our intuition is that the price mechanism is the most effective way of aggregating information in order to allocate resources efficiently. Yet while the two welfare theorems justify the role of the price mechanism, the underlying theory fails to explain explicitly how it works. In fact, Grossman and Stiglitz (1976, 1980) argue that in a perfectly competitive framework, if information about goods is costly or if people have different information, equilibrium may not exist, and so efficiency is unlikely. However, explicit theories of how the price mechanism works, such as those developed by Wilson (1977), Milgrom (1979, 1981), and Pesendorfer and Swinkels (2000), reveal that as markets become more competitive, they are more efficient, even when information is costly or diffuse. Indeed, Milgrom (1981) shows that the Grossman-Stiglitz paradox arises because their agents are not truly price takers, not because information is costly or diffuse.

Thus, as markets become more competitive, prices do a better job of both aggregating information and allocating resources efficiently. Even when information about the attributes of goods is costly to acquire, and when people have different information about goods, markets yield efficient allocations as long as the number of participants is large enough that any individual has a negligible effect on the prevailing market price.

Market performance reflects not only the individual characteristics of what is being exchanged but also the institutional framework that defines the way that particular exchange process works. As noted earlier, there is no reason that markets will necessarily produce the sort of idealized result that Adam Smith characterized as the source of the wealth of nations. The complex interplay between the characteristics of what is being exchanged and the institutional framework produces widely varied outcomes. Moreover, as technology, information costs, and transport costs change within a constant institutional framework, market performance will change. Therefore, we must not only explore the performance characteristics of a market at a moment of time but also explore the process of change that will occur over time. At the heart of our discussion is the understanding that a market's performance will depend on the institutional framework, which varies at a moment of time with different factor and product markets and also varies over time as these markets change. There is no such thing as laissez faire; that is a state of anarchy in which markets cannot exist. Efficient markets must be deliberately structured to provide the correct incentives. As technology, competitive conditions, and other constraints change over time, that structure will have to change as well if markets are to continue to be efficient. Recent experience with capital markets provides unremitting testimony to the dynamic nature of markets through time.

Another example of the dynamic nature of markets and institutions over time is the rapid globalization of markets in the last part of the twentieth century and the effects of globalization on national governments. That markets have become more globally integrated since World War II is perhaps without dispute, but the extent, novelty, and ramifications of this phenomenon are not clear. Bordo et al. (1999) compare late-twentieth-century and late-nineteenth-century global market integration. They find that although world commodity and factor markets were more integrated in the late nineteenth century than they were in the period between 1914 and 1950, late-twentieth-century markets surpassed the achievements of the late nineteenth century. U.S. merchandise exports as a percent of GNP are about the same now as they were a century ago. However, commodity trade is more important today because the share of trade in tradeables production is higher, there is more trade in services, and there is more production and trade by multinational firms. In addition, Irwin (1996) points out that the bulk of U.S. exports has shifted from agricultural goods to manufactured goods. Bordo et al. (1999) suggest that lower transportation costs, reduced tariff barriers, and fewer informational barriers are stimulating global commodity market integration. They also find that financial markets are more integrated because there are fewer information asymmetries from improved information technology; there are fewer contracting problems associated with geographic distance between principals and agents and reduced legal insecurity of contracts with foreigners; and there is less macroeconomic risk generated by exchange risk, unstable and uncertain monetary and fiscal policy, and political risk. They also identify a role for government in the increased integration of global markets, specifically in the development of adequate accounting standards.

Although Williamson (1996) points out that globalization, through mass migration and free trade, explains most of the convergence in real wages and output per worker-hour among current Organization for Economic Cooperation and Development (OECD) countries during the late nineteenth century, Rodrik (1997) argues that globalization brings troubles as well as benefits. Specifically, he argues that globalization leads to greater demand for social insurance provided by national governments; at the same time, globalization reduces national governments' abilities to effectively provide social insurance.

I began by defining a market to be a form of exchange that relies on the price mechanism to allocate goods and services. Yet this definition is deceptively simple. It hides the rich variety of characteristics a market may possess, depending on what is being traded, who is trading it, and when and where the trade takes place. In fact, a market is a fluid and flexible form of exchange that has changed societies, as well as being changed by them in the never-ending struggle to satisfy peoples' desires.

[*See also* Capitalism; Command Economies; *and* Polanyi, Karl.]

BIBLIOGRAPHY

Bordo, Michael D., Barry Eichengreen, and Douglas A. Irwin. "Is Globalization Today Really Different than Globalization a Hundred Years Ago?" NBER Working Paper No. 7195, 1999.

Cambridge Ancient History. 3d ed. London, 1970–1992.

Cheung, Steven N. S. "Transactions Costs, Risk Aversion, and the Choice of Contractual Arrangements." *Journal of Law and Economics* 12.1 (1969), 23–42.

Coase, Ronald. "The Nature of the Firm." *Economica* 4 (1937), 386–405.

Curtin, Philip. *Cross-Cultural Trade in World History*. Cambridge, 1984.

De Ligt, Luuk. *Fairs and Markets in the Roman Empire: Economic and Social Aspects of Periodic Trade in a Pre-Industrial Society*. Amsterdam, 1993.

Debreu, Gerard. *Theory of Value*. New York, 1959.

Frayn, Joan. *Markets and Fairs in Roman Italy*. Oxford, 1993.

Grossman, Sanford, and Joseph Stiglitz. "Information and Competitive Price Systems." *American Economic Review* 66.2 (1976), 246–253.

Grossman, Sanford, and Joseph Stiglitz. "On the Impossibility of Informationally Efficient Markets." *American Economic Review* 70.3 (1980), 393–408.

Hayek, Friedrich A. "The Use of Knowledge in Society." *American Economic Review* 35.4 (1945), 519–530.

Irwin, Douglas A. "The United States in a New Global Economy? A Century's Perspective." *American Economic Review* 86.2 (1996), 41–46.

Macfarlane, Alan. *The Origins of English Individualism*. Oxford, 1978.

McNeill, William. *The Pursuit of Power: Technology, Armed Force, and Society since A.D. 1000*. Chicago, 1982.

Michell, Humphrey. *The Economics of Ancient Greece*. New York, 1957.

Milgrom, Paul. "A Convergence Theorem for Competitive Bidding with Differential Information." *Econometrica* 47.3 (1979), 679–688.

Milgrom, Paul. "Rational Expectations, Information Acquisition, and Competitive Bidding." *Econometrica* 49.4 (1981), 921–943.

Milgrom, Paul, and Robert Weber. "A Theory of Auctions and Competitive Bidding." *Econometrica* 50.5 (1982), 1089–1122.

Myers, Ramon. "Customary Law, Markets, and Resource Transactions in Late Imperial China." In *Explorations in the New Economic History*, edited by Roger Ransom, Richard Sutch, and Gary Walton. New York, 1982.

North, Douglass C. "Markets and Other Allocations Systems in History: The Challenge of Karl Polanyi." *Journal of European Economic History* 6.3 (1977), 703–716.

Pesendorfer, Wolfgang, and Jeroen Swinkels. "The Loser's Curse and Information Aggregation in Common Value Auctions." *Econometrica* 65.6 (1997), 1247–1281.

Pesendorfer, Wolfgang, and Jeroen Swinkels. "Efficiency and Information Aggregation in Auctions." *American Economic Review* 90.3 (2000), 499–525.

Polanyi, Karl. "Ports of Trade in Early Societies." In *Primitive, Archaic, and Modern Economies: Essays of Karl Polanyi*, edited by George Dalton. New York, 1968.

Rodrik, Dani. "Trade, Social Insurance, and the Limits to Globalization." NBER Working Paper No. 5905, 1997.

Rostovtzeff, Michael. *The Social and Economic History of the Hellenistic World*. Oxford, 1941.

Smith, Adam. *An Inquiry into the Nature and Causes of the Wealth of Nations*. Edited by Edwin Cannan. Chicago, 1976.

Williamson, Jeffrey. "Globalization, Convergence, and History." *Journal of Economic History* 56.2 (1996), 277–306.

Wilson, Robert. "A Bidding Model of Perfect Competition." *Review of Economic Studies* 44 (1977), 511–518.

DOUGLASS C. NORTH

MARKET STRUCTURE *[This entry contains four subentries, an overview and discussions of competition, monopoly and natural monopoly, and oligopoly and monopolistic competition.]*

General Introduction

Industries in which goods and services are produced mainly through market activities can be classified into one of four broad categories: pure competition, monopoly, oligopoly, and monopolistic competition. Pure competition and monopoly define opposite ends of a spectrum of possibilities driven by the goal of maximizing profits. Oligopoly and monopolistic competition, significantly more common forms of market structure today, fall between the two extremes.

In pure competition, an industry consists of many small firms that produce identical outputs. Monopoly occurs when an industry consists of a single firm producing an output with no close substitutes. Oligopoly occurs when a few large firms dominate an industry and face interdependent outcomes. The industrial structure of monopolistic competition is made up of many firms that sell closely related but differentiated goods. Monopoly, oligopoly, and monopolistic competition share characteristics that separate them from pure competition and are known collectively as imperfectly competitive market structures. Their key common feature is market power, the ability to charge a price higher than their marginal cost of production. Purely competitive firms represent such a small portion of a larger market that they cannot affect the market price for their output.

Oligopoly and monopoly are also separated from monopolistic competition and pure competition by the existence of barriers to entry. These barriers maintain the small number of firms present under oligopoly or the single firm of a monopoly and provide long-run profit-making opportunities. Cost barriers to entry create economies of scale. Firms with economies of scale so large that they can produce all of the desired output at a lower cost than even two competing firms are known as natural monopolies.

Markets have existed for millennia. In the mostly rural economies of ancient, medieval, and Renaissance times, market goods generally represented a relatively small portion of a household's output and consumption. The predominance of feudal economies in Asia and Europe left little room for trade-based existence. Transaction costs, in the forms of imperfect information, imperfect risk accommodation, and high transportation expenses, also limited opportunities for market development. The first coinage probably appeared among traders in Lydia (Persia) in the seventh century BCE as a way to overcome the restrictions of barter. Other barriers fell through institutional and technological developments as the role of markets grew. Institutions ranging from government-sponsored trade, quality control, and risk mitigation to individual contractual agreements enforcing property rights or trade agreements were developed to alleviate problems of risk and information. Financial intermediaries, roads, canals, rail, and other infrastructure were developed to reduce transaction costs. Europe and then North America led in these innovations.

As competition and markets grew, so did attempts to reduce the decline in profits. Game theoretic models show that price competition between two or more firms will result in price cuts until the price is equal to the marginal cost. Private railroads in the United States and Great Britain experienced these price wars in the mid- to late 1800s. In the United States, attempts by railroad executives to reduce competition through cartelization led only to a temporary respite. Price wars continued to erupt until friendly regulation from the newly created Interstate Commerce Commission (ICC) provided a forum for price fixing.

Mercantilist European nations and industrial giants of the late nineteenth and early twentieth century alike tried vertical integration to reduce competition. Queen Elizabeth I granted patent protection, creating a monopoly for technological development, similar to what national governments do today. Firms throughout history have sought government licensure, regulatory control, and international restraints of trade to reduce competition. Internally, oligopolistic firms such as DuPont have used careful managerial control of throughput, vertical integration, or built-in excess capacity to lower the transaction costs of business. Trade and industry associations were formed in part to foster cooperation among competitors. Medieval trade guilds as well as guilds in Asia provided this function for artisans and craftsmen. Legal Japanese cartels before World War II worked to organize production in such diverse industries as textiles, construction materials, polyvinyl chloride, tires, barber services, and aluminum.

Any industry with high fixed costs, such as Japanese, German, or American steel production, or network-dependent services such as electricity, gas, or water, can keep potential rival firms from entering the industry. This allows for sustained profits across time. Many firms, including Carnegie Steel in the United States, had or have sought to increase their fixed costs to create barriers to entry.

As nineteenth-century industrialization and market development began to concentrate wealth in the hands of a few firms and individuals, the resulting frictions pushed nations in one of two directions. Russia, China, many African nations, and others sought to control competition by creating state monopolies for all goods and using government-regulated distribution systems that were loosely based on price but more often based on other types of rationing (queuing, black markets) to allocate goods. Alternatively, the United States and Canada began to regulate against anticompetitive behavior at the end of the nineteenth century. Other market economies did not follow until the 1940s or later. Many governments in Europe, Asia, and Latin America mixed market economies with significant levels of nationalized monopoly, particularly in those industries with economies of scale or those deemed in the national interest.

[*See also* Antitrust.]

BIBLIOGRAPHY
Caves, Richard E., and Masu Uekusa. *Industrial Organization in Japan.* Washington, D.C., 1976.
Chandler, Alfred D., Jr., Franco Amatori, and Takashi Hikino. *Big Business and the Wealth of Nations.* Cambridge, 1997.
Galambos, Louis. "The Triumph of Oligopoly." In *American Economic Development in Historical Perspective*, edited by Thomas Weiss and Donald Schaefer. Stanford, Calif., 1994.
Rosenbaum, David I., ed. *Market Dominance: How Firms Gain, Hold, or Lose It and the Impact on Economic Performance.* Westport, Conn., 1998.

BROOKS KAISER

Competition

Pure competition is a theoretical market structure that serves as the benchmark of economic welfare. Characteristics that define competitive markets include atomistic price-taking firms, identical goods, price and factor mobility (free entry and exit of firms), and perfect information.

In pure competition, firms (e.g., small farms) are too small to have any influence over price. These identical (homogeneous) goods cannot command any premium on the market. Apples, corn, or wheat from one farm will look much like these products from another farm. Historically, industries without much ability to differentiate products suffered relative to firms that could do so. For example, as markets moved from farm gates to town centers and as more markets appeared, competition increased for farmers.

As transactions and transportation costs fell at the end of the nineteenth century, these small farmers, with little ability to differentiate their products, found their economic position deteriorating with respect to the rising commercial and industrial portions of the economy. Just as importantly, they found growing monopsony power among the buyers of their products as those firms sought to consolidate their own industries.

Purely competitive firms are also unable to keep new firms from entering the industry; there is perfect price and factor mobility. A farmer might easily switch his crop from corn to soybeans at the start of a new growing season if expected returns are higher. If enough farmers make the switch, prices for soybeans will fall while those for corn will rise. As farmers seek the most profitable use of their factors of production, long-run profits will tend toward a normal return (zero economic profit).

In pure competition, producers and consumers also have perfect information, particularly regarding technology and prices. Private information is profitable. The Maghribi traders, Jewish traders in the Mediterranean in the eleventh century, knew this as do contemporary American technology giants such as Eastman Kodak or Microsoft Corporation. The Maghribi developed close community ties that enabled them to sanction contract violators. Game-theoretic modeling has shown that this private information enabled trade and increased profitability to traders in the group by reducing transactions costs (Greif, 1994).

Under these assumptions—in the absence of externalities, public goods, ill-defined property rights, or market power—economic welfare will be maximized. The economically efficient outcome will create a situation in which no one individual or group can be made better off without some other being made worse off.

In common parlance, competition generally has taken on a slightly different meaning: Firms strive to eliminate rivals and to create circumstances that will sustain long-run profits. Companies pursue profits through strategic choices of price, quantity, quality, and capacity. Additionally, even before any production occurs, firms vie for support from regulatory or government agents, seeking assurances of property rights, subsidies, or other economic gain.

Industries often initially exhibit characteristics of perfect competition but soon develop a less competitive market structure as firms adopt these techniques.

Role of Government within Pure Competition. When pure competition exists, the role for welfare-improving regulation comes from the presence of market failures (e.g., externalities, public goods, or imperfect information). Otherwise, intervention is likely to benefit the few at the expense of the many and reduce welfare. Indi-

viduals vie for property rights that will deliver profits, masses clamor for food, groups argue effectively for health or safety requirements, and governments respond in ways that reduce efficient market functions.

Equally challenging to government regulators, attempts to redistribute income in competitive markets often lead to lower overall welfare. For example, governments have frequently created or exacerbated shortages by setting price controls to benefit either consumers or producers. Distribution mechanisms based on fixed prices in state-controlled economies, such as the former Soviet Union after 1917 and China from 1945, have led to excess demand. Queuing or black market activities replaced price as the rationing mechanism for these goods. The long-run signals that competitive prices send regarding consumer demand were lost, and production did not match the types and quality of goods that people wanted.

During the French Revolution, the government set price controls in Paris to alleviate food shortages that resulted in even more severe shortages, as goods moved to more profitable markets outside the city. These price controls had the additional impact of decreasing the quality of the goods offered for legitimate sale, as the higher quality goods were traded only on the black market.

Governments have also created surpluses by trying to support producers. Price supports for coffee, sugar, and produce have been devastating to Latin American and African countries over the past 150 years, as international markets have been unable to support demand for these goods that constitute such large portions of the countries' outputs. In Europe over the past half century, the European Union's (EU's) Common Agricultural Policy (CAP) served as a system of significant price supports for about 90 percent of the community members' agricultural product markets.

Major reforms to restore competitive markets began in the early 1990s when, as a result of price supports and government acquisition programs, surpluses in the early 1990s were estimated to be 30 percent higher than that required for EU self-sufficiency for sugar, 21 percent higher for cereals, and 12 percent for butter. These surpluses represent a misallocation of resources that cost society more than the beneficiaries gained.

Under pure competition, incentives for innovation will be muted if firms are unable to capture any returns for research and development. Patent protection creates short-run monopoly power in the hope of spurring research and technological advances. In the long run, it is hoped that competitive markets will emerge when patents expire.

Role of Government in Restoring Pure Competition. Since pure competition eliminates the market failures associated with market power under monopoly, oligopoly, or monopolistic competition, welfare-enhancing government intervention should restore competitive markets whenever possible.

Often it also redistributes welfare away from firms to consumers. Only in the past century has the promise of economic efficiency driven governments toward formal competition policy. This has led firms to actively oppose regulations, including the U.S. Sherman Antitrust Act of 1890, the Clayton Antitrust Act of 1914, the Canadian Anti-Combine laws of the same era, and post–World War II developments in Europe and Asia. Despite this opposition, the U.S. and Canadian laws have been used for more than a century to promote competition in such diverse industries as oil, art auctions, higher education, and telephone services.

Competition from International Sources. Access to international markets should increase competitiveness. Adam Smith's and David Ricardo's arguments for free trade have slowly opened world markets to one another, reducing distortionary tariffs (increasing price competition) and quotas (increasing quantity competition). A rise in the number of firms competing in any market should reduce the market power of any one firm and may help protect or create more competitive industries.

Since shortly after World War II, the General Agreement on Tariffs and Trade (GATT), now the World Trade Organization (WTO) sought to provide a worldwide forum for reducing international barriers to competition. In 1995, the group added the authority of international law to enforce multilateral trade agreements and establish standards for international trade with the goal of increasing global competitiveness. Acting under the economic principle that competitive markets achieve efficiency, the WTO has come under great scrutiny, partly because it has the power to deny domestic market regulators the ability to distort competitive market outcomes for other purposes. Environmental groups, for example, believe that the WTO punishes economies that attempt to correct negative externalities.

Along with the growth of international trade in the past half century, the world has been creating trade unions like the European Union and the North American Free Trade Association (NAFTA). Today, the EU's goals have expanded from limited trade agreements to federal goals that will unify currency, labor market flows, electricity markets, and competitive opportunities of all types within the union's borders.

[*See also* Antitrust *and* Market Structure, *subentries on* Monopoly and Natural Monopoly *and* Oligopoly and Monopolistic Competition.]

BIBLIOGRAPHY

Averitt, Robert T. *The Dual Economy: The Dynamics of American Industry Structure*. New York, 1968.

Barnes, Ian, and Jill Preston. *Key Issues in Economics and Business: The European Community*. London, 1988.

Bianchi, Patrizio. *Industrial Policies and Economic Integration: Learning from European Experiences*. London, 1998.

Greif, Avner. "Cultural Beliefs and the Organization of Society: A Historical and Theoretical Reflection on Collectivist and Individualist Societies." *Journal of Political Economy* 102.5 (1994), 912–950.

Hirsh, Richard F. *Power Loss: The Origins of Deregulation and Restructuring in the American Electric Utility System*. Cambridge, Mass., 1999.

Krueger, Anne, ed. *The WTO as an International Organization*. Chicago, 2000.

Laidler, Harry W. *Concentration of Control in American Industry*. New York, 1931.

Lamoreaux, Naomi. *The Great Merger Movement in American Business, 1895–1904*. Cambridge, 1988.

Rosenbaum, David I., ed. *Market Dominance: How Firms Gain, Hold, or Lose It and the Impact on Economic Performance*. Westport, Conn., 1998.

BROOKS KAISER

Monopoly and Natural Monopoly

Pure monopoly occurs when a single firm produces the output of a market or industry for which there are no close substitutes. Although real-world monopolies rarely match this theoretical definition, such firms have characteristics that can best be analyzed through this theoretical model. The theory of monopoly presents an absolute limit of market power over price and output.

The word *monopoly* conjures images ranging across such diverse firms as De Beer's Consolidated Mines (diamonds), Alcoa, Standard Oil, technology-driven companies from Eastman Kodak to Microsoft, trading companies like Hudson's Bay Company and the East India Company, and private and public utilities, in addition to state-produced goods in centralized economies. Monopolies have garnered public support, particularly for nationalized production of public utilities and other goods and services with high fixed costs (airlines, rail networks). Monopolies have received government aid ranging from patent grants in privatized economies to sanctioned government monopoly production of goods and services in more centralized economies. Governments also have fought monopolies and attempted to reduce their market power through fines, firm breakups, and other restrictions on anticompetitive behavior. The growth of decentralized market economies over the past 250 years appears to have increased the conflicts inherent in government attitude toward monopoly. Firms' economic decisions have developed as a force relatively independent of government action, and current government goals must reflect a wider range of concerns.

In decentralized economies, firms seek monopoly control of an industry to achieve market power. The development of a new technology, such as the petroleum-refining technology created by John D. Rockefeller's partner Samuel Andrews, gave Standard Oil a cost advantage over other refineries. Alcoa initially gained its market power through new technology for the refining of aluminum ore. Cases like these create the opportunity for economic profits and would, under most circumstances, attract competition. Monopoly can be sustained only if there are significant barriers preventing other firms from entering the industry. Rockefeller and Alcoa both sought to protect profits by creating barriers through vertically integrating, or owning or controlling key aspects of the layered phases of production: ownership of raw materials, transportation, refining, and distribution of output.

Monopoly and Social Welfare. Efforts to maximize profits in a monopoly often lead to economic inefficiency in the form of reduced social welfare (the sum of consumer and producer surplus), lower output levels, and higher prices. In ancient times, most municipalities, including Athens in the fourth century BCE and Rome after the beginning of the Empire, prohibited landowners, merchants, or speculators from monopolizing grain supplies and hoarding them to maintain high prices and reduce social welfare. More recently, Standard Oil was declared a monopoly that practiced illegal restraints of trade. The resolution of the case required a breakup of the company into several competing interests and set precedent for American antitrust cases for the remainder of the twentieth century. In Canada, the "consumer interest" led to antitrust legislation at the same time as the United States passed the Sherman Antitrust Act.

In different times and places, monopoly power has been less eschewed. The former Soviet Union and other Communist nations created state monopolies for the production of virtually all goods. In these cases, output and prices were directly controlled in efforts to increase social welfare. During the interwar period in Great Britain, monopoly power was promoted as a method for relieving the economic distress faced by important national industries and their workers, including coal mining, iron and steel, shipbuilding, and textiles. Indeed, the perception of public interest in these industries, as well as transportation and electricity, led to nationalization and state-supported monopoly production. In Japan, monopoly power and cartelization through a limited number of family-dominated holding company systems (zaibatsu) were accepted and promoted by the government throughout industrialization. While Great Britain has now embraced competition policy and has denationalized many of the aforementioned state monopolies, Japan has moved much more slowly toward decreasing market concentration.

These competitive policies attempt to correct for violations of static economic efficiency that occur in any time period that price is above marginal cost and output is restricted below the optimal level. Long-term concerns about efficiency also arise with monopolies. Dynamic efficiency is the maximization of social welfare across more than one time period. Efforts to attain dynamic efficiency may also be affected by monopoly. Private monopoly incentives to innovate are reduced in the presence of long-run profits unless expected internal returns to capital from innovation are higher than other uses of monopoly profits or unless serious external threats from potential innovators drive monopolists to reinvest profits in research and development. Rather, monopoly profits are often invested in rent-seeking behavior, costly to society, intended to increase the barriers to entry and further protect monopoly status. Historically, the importance of this inefficiency has been growing at an increasing rate, as the rapidity of technological innovation has grown many times over and was an important aspect of the legal cases brought against Microsoft Corporation.

Monopoly power may also aid dynamic efficiency. The Japanese Ministry of International Trade and Industry (MITI) has attempted to achieve this by directing research and development into targeted industries (for example, the ministry promoted the development of the plastics and chemicals industries beginning in the 1950s). Historically, monarchs of various Pacific Islands maintained monopoly control over natural resources such as reef fish or island timber. This control alleviated overuse and exhaustion of the resources that would have undoubtedly occurred with open access.

Interestingly, monopoly profits have funded many public works throughout the world, such as the many public lands, funds for the arts, and educational foundations that have been established by nineteenth-century industrialists such as Rockefeller and Andrew Carnegie in the United States, and Savva Mamontov and Savva Morozov in Russia. These goods were unlikely to have been provided to such a large extent had this concentrated wealth been more widely distributed, at least in a privatized economy lacking a central planner.

Barriers to Entry. A firm's barriers to entry may stem from three categories: regulatory, resource-based, and strategic. Examples of firms protected by regulatory barriers include chartered companies (e.g., the East India Company, Hudson's Bay Company), patent-protected firms (e.g., new technological innovations such as Venetian glass production and mirror making in the sixteenth century, pharmaceuticals), and many utilities (e.g., gas, telephone, electricity, water). Regulatory barriers, particularly in the case of charters, may exist primarily for political reasons, but both patent protection and utility regulation have strong economic rationales.

Most government charters of the sixteenth to nineteenth centuries served to provide geographic protection of trading rights. The desire for monopoly profits to cover risks, as from the vagaries of shipping, in order to spur trade in the absence of full insurance markets may have initiated the call for such charters. National rivalries and hopes of realizing economies of scale from reduced domestic competition also counted. The Netherlands, Great Britain, and, indeed, most European nations carved up world trade through their famous chartered companies. The British, for example, had the Merchant Adventurers in Africa, the East India Company, and Hudson's Bay Company in Canada, among others. The Hudson's Bay Company began in 1670 and continues to sell retail goods to Canadians today. The British East India Company lasted more than 250 years from its grant of charter in 1600 from the queen and touched virtually all British and colonial lives through its actions. It succeeded in reducing the power of the Dutch monopoly on the ruthlessly protected spice trade with the East Indies, and turned India into a highly profitable colony and member of the British Empire. The monopoly began to unravel under its own weight after 1760, and political interests in London slowly reduced the protective legal barriers surrounding it; in 1793, certain other traders were allowed into the East. And in 1833, the company lost its exclusive rights to Chinese trade. By the Sepoy Rebellion in 1857, political support for continued protection had fully eroded and the firm folded.

Patents serve as an incentive mechanism for expensive research and development that would be much less likely to occur without the promise of monopoly profits for a given period of time, and would reduce innovation and long-term economic growth. Early European patents for technological innovations, which spread in use in the 1500s, particularly in Great Britain, include the production of Venetian glass, mirror making in Venice and France, and British mechanical inventions for dredging and draining, and furnaces and ovens.

Revenues to the state have also been a driving factor in the granting of government licenses for monopoly or limited-term patents. Inelastic demand for salt has led several nations, including China as early as the Han dynasty (202 BCE–220 CE), to regulate the salt trade in search of treasury funds. British salt monopoly patents in the early 1600s may have raised the price of salt twelvefold in the period of a few years, with much of the revenue going to the state. Great Britain and Spain had similar incentives in mind when it granted monopolies in tobacco-goods production and trade throughout its American possessions in the eighteenth century.

Resource-based barriers to entry develop when a single firm controls access to minerals or natural resources that may be either end products or inputs into final goods. Some historical examples of imports include salt (national monopolies in China, France, etc.), bauxite (Aluminum Company of America), and diamonds (De Beers). Resource-based monopolies might occur through accidental land ownership but have historically involved more strategic acquisitions. Several highly competitive firms, including De Beers, simultaneously mined the Kimberley Diamond Mines in South Africa upon their discovery in the 1860s. The rapidly increasing supply outpaced growth in demand for diamonds and prices sagged, while capital costs grew as firms found the need to switch from open-pit mining to shaft mining. These economic constraints, coupled with political maneuvering, particularly by Cecil Rhodes, led to consolidation of the firms and De Beers control of the mines by 1888, a domination of the world diamond market that continues even today (see Worger, 1987).

Strategic barriers develop when firms use their resources to create artificial barriers to entry. Options for strategic behavior include using the firms' monopoly profits, or rents, to create regulatory barriers (e.g., rent-seeking behavior as in U.S. Food Stamps (1939–1943), and mercantilist trading companies in Great Britain, France, and Spain), inflating start-up costs for new entrants (e.g., required apprenticeships for medieval guilds; advertising to build brand loyalty by cigarette manufacturers, Coca-Cola, and Chiquita Brands), developing excess capacity to present potential entrants with the threat of rapid expansion of production (e.g., Carnegie Steel, airlines), using vertical integration to control key production and distribution resources or horizontal integration to conglomerate the market (e.g., Standard Oil, Alcoa, U.S. agriculture after 1945, United Fruit Company, DuPont, Dow Chemical, General Motors), and using anticompetitive pricing schemes (e.g., dumping, predatory pricing, limit pricing by firms such as Dow Chemical).

At the turn of the twentieth century, John D. Rockefeller used vertical integration to monopolize the oil market in the United States. By purchasing or controlling oil production from the refineries through rail and pipeline transport and final sales, his company, Standard Oil, could squeeze out any potential entrants in any portion of the process, successfully protecting its market power and creating, for example, average profits on the capital stock and trust certificates of 19 percent from 1882 to 1896 (Laidler, 1931, p. 18ff). As Standard Oil was growing, so was populist sentiment against large corporations, and the passage of the Sherman Antitrust Act of 1890 and other trust-busting activities of the federal government led the firm through several restructurings. Eventually, the national company was dissolved into thirty-three geographically distinct companies in 1911 in attempts to increase competitiveness in the oil industry.

Regulators also applied this model for increased competition through geographic breakdowns to American Telephone and Telegraph (AT&T) in 1984. In both cases, the aftermath of the breakups has had mixed success at increasing competition. For example, the Rockefellers still exerted much directorial control over each of the newly created companies and expanded their market power overseas as well. However, the control of resources, particularly the pipelines (Standard Oil) and the wire network (AT&T), by a few companies or even regional monopolies has generated the strategic incentives and costs discussed under oligopoly.

Many companies maintain barriers by combining aspects of all three. For example, Alcoa's monopoly began through the regulatory power of a patent for Charles Hall's aluminum production techniques in 1888. Vertical integration from aluminum ore (bauxite) mines through the stages of production prolonged this monopoly power and ended in antitrust regulation in 1945.

Price Discrimination. When a monopolist can both distinguish the types of buyers in the market according to their demand and prevent the resale of the product, the monopolist may price discriminate, charging different prices to different consumers. Price discrimination may take many forms. American railroads in the nineteenth century were active price discriminators, filling their trains with freight from the price breaks they gave industrialists. One consequence was the farmer discontent of the late nineteenth century that gave rise to the Populist movement. Sugar mills in the Japanese colonial era (1895–1945) may have exercised monopsony, or single buyer, power to price discriminate among sugar farmers. In Spain, from 1597 to 1650, the Habsburg monarchy used price discrimination in its currency supply to two different markets to increase its revenues and fund its many wars. It discounted the locally used copper currency while maintaining the international price of its larger denomination gold and silver coins. In this way, the rulers avoided significant long-term international financial strains (see Motomura, 1994).

Government and Monopoly. Government intervention on behalf of monopoly or against it is as old as monopoly itself. Governments have used monopolies to aggrandize the state and raise revenues. Significant business enterprises from the dawn of recorded history through industrialization have elicited government sanction but have also received grants of monopoly status. Generally speaking, governments seek to intervene against monopolies when the economic environment can support higher levels of competition, and seek to regulate the monopolies when it cannot. Government intervention on behalf of monopolies aims to provide goods that would otherwise not be produced. As industry expanded and developed into big business, governments took more and more to regulating the actions of monopolistic firms in efforts to appease populist sentiments, with new antimonopoly regulations such as the U.S. Sherman Antitrust Act of 1890 and successive legislation or the Canadian anticombine legislation begun in 1889.

Natural Monopoly. Governments may also provide regulatory protection of monopolies, particularly for utilities, if they are perceived as "natural monopolies," meaning that significant economies of scale exist. In this case, the entry of additional firms would increase the average costs and reduce productive efficiency. Industries deemed valuable to the public interest became protected natural monopolies or government owned (nationalized) in order to increase production while achieving lower-cost production.

In 1812, British Parliament granted a charter to the London and Westminster Gas Light and Coke Company, and the first gas company in the world came into being as a monopoly. Natural gas, which is transported through pipelines, had economies of scale in distribution. Baltimore followed quickly with its own monopoly grant in 1816. Paris adopted gas lighting in 1820. The trend continued around the globe until electric lighting supplanted it.

When Thomas Edison first began selling electricity in New York City in 1882, customers had to be within one mile of the generation plant to receive adequate power. Unlike natural gas, the electric industry could have developed as a small scale and competitive industry. The development of AC current during the following decade, however, meant that economies of scale in distribution of electric current were large. Since that time, most electric power companies have grown into large regulated power providers or state-owned monopolies in search of lower costs of distribution. Telecommunication services, which have historically required wire transmission, followed suit.

The lower costs have not always materialized, as government regulation or ownership may reduce incentives to produce at lowest cost. Movement toward deregulation of natural monopolies, begun in the aftermath of economic slowdowns after the oil shocks of the 1970s, is occurring globally. Chile, Great Britain, and the United States began deregulation and divestiture of state ownership in electricity, natural gas, and telecommunications in the late 1970s and early 1980s. Scandinavia began to open the electric industry with a spot market for generation in Norway in 1971. Since 1999, Sweden, Norway, Finland, and western Denmark have combined their transmission and distribution grids and coordinated international competition in generation. In 1992, Argentina initiated a highly competitive market in electricity generation coupled with a regulated natural monopoly for distribution. Australia and New Zealand each began deregulation in 1993. Today, even the former state economies of eastern Europe and Russia are working to privatize these networked services.

[*See also* Cartels and Collusion, *subentry on* Price Discrimination.]

BIBLIOGRAPHY

Deans-Smith, Susan. *Bureaucrats, Planters, and Workers: The Making of the Tobacco Monopoly in Bourbon Mexico.* Austin, 1992.

Hirsh, Richard F. *Power Loss: The Origins of Deregulation and Restructuring in the American Electric Utility System.* Cambridge, Mass., 1999.

Huan, Kuan, trans. *Discourses on Salt and Iron: A Debate on State Control of Commerce and Industry in Ancient China,* Leiden, 1931.

Kwan, Man Bun. *The Salt Merchants of Tianjin: State-Making and Civil Society in Late Imperial China.* Honolulu, Hawaii, 2001.

Laidler, Harry Wellington. *Concentration of Control in American Industry.* New York, 1931.

Le Rossignol, J. E. *Monopolies Past and Present: An Introductory Study.* New York, 1901.

Levy, Hermann. *Monopoly and Competition: A Study in English Industrial Organisation.* London, 1911.

Lloyd, H. D. "Story of a Great Monopoly." *Atlantic Monthly* 47.281 (March 1881), 317–334.

Motomura, Akira. "The Best and Worst of Currencies: Seigniorage and Currency Policy in Spain, 1597–1650." *Journal of Economic History* 54.1 (1994), 104–127.

Newbery, David M. *Privatization, Restructuring, and Regulation of Network Utilities.* Cambridge, Mass., 1999.

Rosenbaum, David I. *Market Dominance: How Firms Gain, Hold, or Lose It and the Impact on Economic Performance.* New York, 1998.

Worger, William H. *South Africa's City of Diamonds: Mine Workers and Monopoly Capitalism in Kimberley, 1867–1895.* New Haven, 1987.

BROOKS KAISER

Oligopoly and Monopolistic Competition

The industrial structures of oligopoly and monopolistic competition are imperfectly competitive markets that fall between monopoly and perfect competition in the spectrum of price, quantity, and efficiency outcomes. Oligopoly refers to industries with few firms and significant barriers to entry (oil products, Major League Baseball, automobiles, tires, chemicals). Firms in a monopolistically competitive industry face many rivals and few, if any, barriers to entry, but each firm sells a differentiated product (textiles, food, and beverages). Today, monopolistic competition and oligopoly are the most prevalent forms of industrial structure in privatized economies. They also are the least capable of being broadly modeled by economists. Many explanations and models have been derived for individual cases including price or quantity competition, quality signaling, and the benefits of private information. Since oligopolistic firms face outcomes that depend on the actions of their rivals, game theory has been the best tool to model the strategic interactions of these firms. Oligopoly and monopolistic competition are industrial structures that make little sense outside the framework of a privatized economy.

Rise of Oligopoly and Monopolistic Competition. By the end of the nineteenth century, economies worldwide were becoming more capital intensive, and operations, more streamlined. Oligopoly rapidly grew in many industries, from automobiles, airlines, agriculture, and chemicals to petroleum, steel, and railroads. Countries with large markets and capital-intensive industries (e.g., the United States and Germany) became characterized as home to "big business." In contrast, Great Britain, the leading industrial economy for most of the nineteenth century, failed to expand rapidly into manufacturing and concentrated on consumer goods including food and beverages, tobacco, glass, and rayon.

During World War I, Germany's neighbors, smaller nations with limited domestic markets, found an opportunity to replace German output and develop international markets in industries with newly adopted capital-intensive technology. These international markets allowed the smaller economies to reap the benefits of economies of scale and scope that the technology promised. Saab and Volvo (Sweden) became global automobile producers. Royal Dutch Shell (Netherlands) and Petrofina (Belgium) were multinational oil sector firms. The origins of international giants Nestlé (Switzerland) and Unilever (Netherlands and Great Britain) were set in the food industry. (The Dutch origins were in food; the English origins were in soap.) The high level of competition among these large firms for the past century indicates that not all oligopolized industries result in cooperative behavior to restrict output and raise prices.

Corporate Strategies. Models of oligopoly are structured around the idea that profits of a few firms are interdependent, so that each firm must develop pricing or production strategies that consider the potential actions of the other firms in the industry. Game-theoretic models have been used to describe strategies in industries as disparate as the North American fur trade, German universal banking, the early telephone, tobacco, medieval trade in the Mediterranean, bromine and other chemical cartels, sugar, oil, French agriculture, and British coal. To build industry models in game theory, firms are described as players in games with payoffs (profits) that depend on the actions (strategies) of the other players. These models, and empirical tests of them, predict behavior in oligopolies that may fall anywhere in the price, quantity, and quality spectrum between monopoly and perfect competition.

Pricing strategies. Theories of price competition abound. As Joseph Bertrand demonstrated, with just two firms in an industry (duopoly), the purely competitive, zero-profit outcome will result as the firms compete by lowering prices to gain market share. Other models explain strategies of predatory pricing, limit pricing, price leadership, as well as the potential unresponsiveness of price to changes in costs. Predatory pricing and limit pricing seek to drive out existing competitors or prevent entry of new ones. These strategies lower present profit levels to reduce incentives for competition. In predatory pricing, the firm lowers price below marginal cost. For example, though Standard Oil was accused of predatory pricing in the early 1900s, it may have been acting only as a firm that dominated many local markets and experienced lower costs than its rivals. The dominant-firm model fits better with the notion that Standard Oil would have wished to maintain short-run profits as well as secure long-run industry control (Mariger, 1978, pp. 341–367).

Quantity strategies. Models based on quantity competition, as explained first by Auguste Cournot and refined by Heinrich Stackelberg, among others, describe firms that expect to act as a monopolist over the portion of the market remaining to them after rival firms have acted along the same principles. This leads to production levels that are higher than a monopoly or successful cartel but are lower than in a perfectly competitive market. Price and industry profits also fall between the monopolistic and competitive outcomes. A duopoly of French mineral water in the 1800s led Cournot to describe the original theoretical model.

Incentives to restrict industry-wide levels of output, control production technology, and elevate prices above marginal cost to earn profits evolved well before the rise of big business. Guilds, or organizations of craftsmen and tradesmen, provide examples of such early strategic behavior. By restricting information on technology and access to markets, setting quality standards, and controlling output, guilds protected economic rents from production for generations. Apprenticeship requirements provided the barriers to entry; generally, the guild rather than the individual artisan developed the pricing schemes for both wages and output, and determined quality restrictions. A Chinese guild still operating at the end of the nineteenth century, the Banker's Guild of Ningpo, claimed lineage back to the Chou dynasty (1122–255 BCE). Roman legend, as told by Plutarch, indicates there may have been guilds for musicians, goldsmiths, carpenters, dyers, shoemakers, tanners, braziers, and potters as early as the kingship of Numa (c. 715–673 BCE). In these years, enforcement of guild regulations (cartel restrictions) would have been a much simpler affair—an individual craftsman could much more easily be ostracized and reduced to social and economic distress than could a larger enterprise with deeper, more independent capital resources.

Some firms have generated excess capacity or even excess inventories as a strategic barrier to entry. Carnegie Steel, for one, incorporated the strategy of excess capacity with its adoption of new technology that significantly lowered average costs, and with additional benefits from vertical control of iron ore production, the firm quickly managed to consolidate the American steel industry at the dawn of the twentieth century. Following the creation of United States Steel in April 1901, the new company adopted limit pricing in conjunction with its lower average costs and vertically integrated access to iron ore to maintain profits, stabilize prices, and keep up the appearance of competition from firms that did not attain the same economies of scale.

Quality strategies. Monopolistically competitive firms strive to create real or artificial distinctions to differentiate their product from the competition. One way that firms signal quality differences to consumers is through advertising. Advertising to mass markets began in the United States and Great Britain in the mid-1800s, coinciding with the rapid product and market diversification spawned by industrialization. Advertising quickly spread worldwide.

The proliferation of product differentiation has increased industry concentration as well. In the Australian beer-brewing industry, restraints on resale price agreements and vertical integration introduced with competition policy in 1965 led to dramatic increases in product differentiation in the 1980s and 1990s. In the ten years from 1984 to 1994, Australia's major breweries introduced 76 new products, 220 changes in packaging, and almost 20 changes in the alcohol content of existing brands (Wilson and Gourvish, 1998, pp. 229–246).

Some of these changes can be accounted for by regional differences and a changing taste for lighter beers. The changes also solidified the positions of the leading breweries by creating formidable advertising barriers to entry as well as excess capacity to threaten potential entrants. Measures of the competitiveness of an industry, such as the Hirschman-Herfindahl index and the four-firm concentration ratio, indicated significant increases in industry concentration through the 1980s.

Information. A firm's control over price is also a function of information. High search costs, or the costs that individuals must pay to identify potential goods and services they wish to consume, will separate markets in the same manner as other transactions costs. In advertising, for example, ads tend to fall into two categories: those that convey information (decrease search costs) and those that create brand identification (create product differentiation). Industries that are less competitive will tend to have ads focused more on brand name creation than on information, as the higher search costs provide additional market power and the brand loyalty decreases the elasticity of demand.

Information asymmetries between producer and consumer as well as within the firm or industry structures also affect firm strategies in imperfect competition. Nobel Prize winner George Akerlof and others have argued that the most important skill for merchants to have in a developing economy is the ability to discern quality; successful identification and guaranteeing of quality can result in profits as high as the value spread between a seller and buyer (Akerlof, 1970, pp. 448–500). Licensing practices, which may serve to restrict entry into an industry and increase profits, also seek to reduce quality uncertainties and are valuable signals when imperfect information precludes pure competition.

Profit Motive and Long-Run Developments. Long-run prospects for technological change and economic equity between the two industrial structures vary. Since long-run profits under monopolistic competition are eroded by the free entry of competitors, there is a need to create new products and markets to assure that one's products are different from one's rivals. Industries such as textiles and foodstuffs and many services that did not develop high barriers to entry have learned to differentiate their products for market power under monopolistic competition. British firms controlled the cotton textile industry throughout the 1800s, providing about 80 percent of global export volume. However, international competition that developed in the late 1800s decreased that figure to only 55 percent by 1913, as Japanese firms (e.g., Naigaiwata) moved from trading textiles into local production, and German textile firms increased their international competitiveness by reaching high-end European markets with quality exports. Finished textiles from the United States satisfied so few tastes and preferences of Europeans and the international market that U.S. exports accounted for only 3 percent of the value of textile exports by 1913, though the nation consumed 22.6 percent of world volume in cotton (Brown, 1995, and Smitka, 1998, pp. 113–144).

The sustainable profits of oligopolies may create disincentives for change as firms seek to protect barriers to entry. For example, many British companies have been managed and owned by individuals or families rather than managed by professionals and owned by shareholders. Profit investments in the British case aimed at assured income rather than risky, costly new-product development. On the other hand, oligopolies may invest long-run profits into research and into the development or adoption of new production techniques. Andrew Carnegie adopted the open-hearth technology over the already successful Bessemer process of steel production in the United States at the end of the nineteenth century to take advantage of the economies of scale.

Welfare Impacts. Though monopolistically competitive firms do not generate long-run profits, they are not productively efficient because they do not produce at minimum efficient scale. When product differentiation allows consumers greater choice of goods and services, however, net social welfare may be increased. This is because the welfare generated by the consumer's consumption set will be higher due to a willingness to pay more for goods that more closely match their desires and needs. In other words, if the differentiation of products creates a real range of quality, monopolistic competition may indeed benefit consumers. The proliferation of firms and products in apparel, food and beverages, and printing and publishing as international trade has increased and markets have expanded suggests that consumers benefit from this differentiation.

The welfare effects of oligopoly depend greatly on the forms of strategic interaction practiced in the industry. Oligopolies that successfully sustain long-run profits will have welfare effects similar to monopoly. Monopolistic competitors and oligopolies in which firms engage in price competition will have welfare effects similar to pure competition. Most oligopolies will lie somewhere in the middle.

Game theorists model the evolution of welfare outcomes over time by describing strategies that rely on trigger or response mechanisms, in which a firm's failure to collude and maintain industry profits is punished by increased competition in the industry. American railroads in the 1880s serve as an example of this dynamic cycle of competition and cooperation. The industry fits a game theoretic model of cartel formation followed by price wars and attempts at new cartelization. Long-term welfare impacts on both the industry and the public from this cycling eventually led to federal regulation of the industry through the formation of the Interstate Commerce Commission (ICC) in 1887 (Porter, 1983, pp. 301–314).

Government Intervention: For and Against. Governments have also sought to control the use of profits derived from oligopolies. In Japan, the Ministry of International Trade and Industry (MITI) has provided administrative guidance to legal cartels intended to increase industry's long-run gains. South Korea's *chaebol* need government approval of expansion plans that require funds from the state-owned banking institutions.

Nations that followed Great Britain, the United States, and Germany in the industrialization process tended toward greater levels of government intervention in industrial activities. France, Italy, Spain, and Argentina had significant government support through public investment. These countries did not develop the same oligopolistic competition in industries with barriers to entry. In particular, Italy preferred industrial diversification to the domination of a single industry by a few firms. In its domestic markets, government ownership or sponsorship helped develop limited production in steel, oil, and petrochemicals industries, deemed vital to national economic growth. Without first-mover or comparative advantage in these industries, competition in international markets did not stem from these enterprises. Instead, government schemes favored the development of niche markets producing high-quality goods in smaller scale enterprises such as textiles and apparel, household goods, and personal products.

Government intervention in Japan and South Korea took a different form. Government worked closely with family-held organizations (Japanese *keiretsu*, South Korean *chaebol*) to develop international competitiveness in heavy manufacturing and chemicals in particular. This cooperation often promoted cooperation among firms as well.

Governments have also tried to increase competition through antitrust policy. The rapid concentration of industries at the end of the nineteenth century resulted in passage of the Canadian Wallace Anti-Combines Act of 1889 and the U.S. Sherman Antitrust Act of 1890, as well as significant subsequent legislation to refine and enhance these laws in both countries (e.g., the U.S. Clayton Antitrust Act of 1914). Other nations have lagged behind in developing legal tools to reduce industry concentration. Japan and Germany initiated efforts under American occupation following World War II. India's Industries Development and Regulations Act (1951), aimed at reducing industry concentration, gives the country the power to control and regulate private industries, essentially replacing private concentration with public monopoly, not competition. Australia began developing competition policy in 1965.

Monopolistic competition has rarely attracted significant regulatory attention because long-run industry profits, and the strategic operations that might preserve these profits, are unsustainable due to the free entry and exit of firms—and when entry isn't free, it is typically the result of a governmental policy, such as licensing.

Overall, enforcement actions against collusive behavior have varied significantly throughout the century and across borders. In World War I, U.S. industry had government support to act as cartels. Today, antitrust suits are brought against such diverse concerns as art auction houses and elite colleges. Other nations have been less concerned about industrial consolidation; some, like Japan, have embraced opportunities to direct and control industrial policy without formal nationalization. The nationalization of industries into monopoly or cooperative oligopolies dominated policy in most communist nations, which attempted to directly control industry output rather than rely on market forces to determine production and price levels.

[*See also* Antitrust; Cartels and Collusion; *and* Patents.]

BIBLIOGRAPHY

Akerlof, George A. "The Market for 'Lemons': Quality Uncertainty and the Market Mechanism." *Quarterly Journal of Economics* 84.3 (1970), 488–500.

Brown, John C. "Market Organization, Protection, and Vertical Integration: German Cotton Textiles before 1914." *Journal of Economic History* 52.2 (1992), 339–352.

Brown, John C. "Imperfect Competition and Anglo-German Trade Rivalry: Markets for Cotton Textiles before 1914." *Quarterly Journal of Economics* 55.3 (1995), 494–527.

Brown, Rajeswary Ampalavanar. *Chinese Big Business and the Wealth of Asian Nations*. New York, 2000.

Burgess, John Stewart. *The Guilds of Peking*. New York, 1970.

Caves, Richard E., and Masu Uekusa. *Industrial Organization in Japan*. Washington, D.C., 1976.

Chandler, Alfred D., Jr. *Scale and Scope: The Dynamics of Industrial Capitalism*. Cambridge, Mass., 1990.

Chandler, Alfred D., Jr., Franco Amatori, and Takashi Hikino. *Big Business and the Wealth of Nations*. Cambridge, 1997.

Epstein, Steven A. *Wage Labor and Guilds in Medieval Europe*. Chapel Hill, N.C., 1991.

Galambos, Louis. "The Triumph of Oligopoly." In *American Economic Development in Historical Perspective*, edited by Thomas Weiss and Donald Schaefer. Stanford, Calif., 1994.

Grief, Avner. "The Study of Organizations and Evolving Organizational Forms through History: Reflections from the Late Medieval Family Firm." In *Firms, Markets, and Hierarchies: The Transaction Cost Economics Perspective*, edited by Glenn R. Carroll and David J. Teece. Oxford, 1999.

Grief, Avner. "Economic History and Game Theory: A Survey." In *Handbook of Game Theory*, edited by Robert J. Aumann and Sergiu Hart, vol. 3. Amsterdam, 2002.

Hart, Peter E., and Richard Clarke. *Concentration in British Industry, 1935–1975: A Study of the Growth, Causes, and Effects of Concentration in British Manufacturing Industries*. Cambridge, 1980.

Kuwahara, Tetsuya. "The Establishment of Oligopoly in the Japanese Cotton-Spinning Industry and the Business Strategies of Latecomers: The Case of Naigaiwata and Co., Ltd." In *Japanese Economic History, 1600–1960*, vol. 4, *The Textile Industry and the Rise of the Japanese Economy*, edited by Michael Smitka. New York, 1998.

Laidler, Harry W. *Concentration of Control in American Industry*. New York, 1931.

Mariger, Randall. "Predatory Price Cutting: The Standard Oil of New Jersey Case Revisited." *Explorations in Economic History* 15.4 (1978), 341–367.

Morse, Hasea Ballou. *The Gilds of China: With an Account of the Gild Merchant or Co-Hong of Canton*. 2d ed. Shanghai, China, 1932.

Nakazawa, Toshiaki, and Leonard W. Weiss. "The Legal Cartels of Japan." *Antitrust and Regulation* (1992), 317–329.

Porter, Robert H. "A Study of Cartel Stability: The Joint Executive Committee, 1880–1886." *Bell Journal of Economics* 14.2 (1983), 301–314.

Unwin, George. *Industrial Organization in the Sixteenth and Seventeenth Century*. Oxford, 1904.

Wilson, R. G., and T. R. Gourvish, eds. *The Dynamics of the International Brewing Industry since 1800*. London, 1998.

Yeager, Mary. *Competition and Regulation: The Development of Oligopoly in the Meat Packing Industry*. Greenwich, Conn., 1981.

BROOKS KAISER

MARRIAGE. Marriage is generally defined as the stable, socially sanctioned union between individuals of the opposite sex. The term *marriage* (in the sense of wedding) refers also to the ceremony or ritual, prescribed by custom or law, that establishes such a union between a man and a woman. There exists a gradient of forms of unions, differing in stability, in commitment of the partners, and in the rights they confer to offspring, that range from concubinage, free union, consensual union, and common law marriage, to religious or civil marriage. The study of nuptiality covers other marital statuses than unions: individuals can be single, married, separated, divorced, or widowed. Legal and religious codes regulate the rights and duties of individuals in different marital conditions, underlining their importance for society at large as well as for individuals. The distribution of the population by marital status affects its involvement in economic activities and its patterns of residence and consumption.

Modern vital registration systems provide data on the number of marriages and divorces in any given year, but the crude marriage rate that expresses the number of marriages per thousand persons in a year is not very useful for comparative purposes, as it is highly dependent on the shape of the age distribution. Age-specific rates can be combined into nuptiality and marriage dissolution tables, but the data are rarely available to compute such tables for historical or international comparisons. Statistical analysis of nuptiality in the past, and in countries with incomplete data, relies mostly on information about the current marital status of individuals as provided in censuses. A widely used index based on the age distribution of single people is the singulate mean age at marriage.

Legal, religious, and even literary or historical sources provide qualitative information on the institutions of marriage in the past, and ethnographic studies have described how nuptiality contributes to the organization of various social systems in a wide variety of contexts. Although these sources are important for the understanding of legal systems, they do not necessarily describe the behavior of the vast majority of the population that left few records before the era of censuses and vital registration. Many of the available descriptions refer to the upper classes, and their relevance to the rest of the population cannot be ascertained.

The modalities of marriages and the ways they are contracted present considerable variety. A large proportion of the literature concerns the West, and there is a substantial debate on why Western systems differ from those elsewhere in the world. Historically, the degree of social control (by family, church, or state) over marriage has been an area of lasting conflict in Europe. Anthropologist Jack Goody, in *The Development of the Family and Marriage in Europe* (1983), argued that a crucial transformation occurred in the West beginning in the fourth century CE, when the Christian Church limited the acceptable consanguinity of matches and shaped the strategies of heirship in its favor, thus transforming itself into a property-owning organization of great power. Another important evolution occurred when eleventh-century law and jurisprudence made the freely exchanged consent of the spouses an essential component of marriage. Reforms of canon law in the Middle Ages even granted that common law unions could be contracted merely by a clear statement of intention, preferably before witnesses, sanctioned by an exchange of gifts (rings,

for example), and followed by the consummation of the union. This form has been practiced particularly among the lower classes, where little exchange of property accompanied the match. Among the propertied classes, however, there was pressure in the direction of matches among social equals, full publication of the marriage (in the form of banns read publicly), and celebration by a priest or an official of the state. Nation-states strove to control the process, as important issues of civil status and property were at stake, and as marriage became the key to the transmission of titles, estates, and kingdoms among the ruling classes. In early modern France, Germany, and England, parental consent was required below a certain age, usually twenty five for women. Marriage as a public event came to prevail as the only fully legal form. The wedding ceremony as the clinching element from which the existence of the match can be dated has dominated the Western concept of marriage at least since the Middle Ages, and it is now a feature of a majority of modern marriages through the world.

Alternative forms of union are characterized by more fluidity. The existence of stages that make marriage a process with progressive degrees of completion still characterize traditional marriages in sub-Saharan Africa. Processual aspects were present in classical Western marriages that often encompassed a period of courtship, a promise of marriage, betrothal, and both a civil and religious wedding, followed by consummation. Some form of ceremony exists in most African marriages.

The Costs and Benefits of Marriage. Most world cultures would probably subscribe to the description of the ends of marriage enunciated by Christian moral philosophers: to ensure the satisfaction of the sexual and affective needs of individuals in a socially approved manner and to provide a stable framework for producing, rearing, and educating children. Great social prestige attaches everywhere to the legitimization and recognition of stable unions. In most societies of the past, marriage heralded the transition into adulthood, although for women, it often meant only their passage from the tutelage of their father to that of their husband. Marriage enhanced the economic worth and the social position of individuals, and even improved their chances of survival, as the mortality of married persons has been consistently found to be lower than that of the single, widowed, or divorced.

There were also costs and inconveniences attached to the married state, among them the loss of the freedom inherent in celibacy, the expense of marriage payments and of wedding festivities, and, for men, the financial burden of providing for a wife and children. As a result, in some periods of history, legislation and financial incentives were deemed necessary to promote marriage, particularly among the young men of wealthy families. The laws of the Roman emperor Augustus (63 BCE–14 CE) are a well-known example.

They were promulgated to encourage the wealthy and office-seeking class to marry early and have children. The Roman elite's lack of interest in family life may be explained partly by the availability of sexual outlets among slaves of either sex, partly by Stoic ethics that frowned upon sexuality in marriage except for the purpose of procreation. We know little, however, about the effects of these laws. The Christian position that degraded marriage as only second best after celibacy was to have a long influence on European attitudes, and it fostered the existence of a large estate of celibate clergy and religious orders. Clerical marriage was an important issue in the Reformation; it was accepted in Protestant theology but not by the Catholic Church.

There are important functions of marriage that go beyond the spouses and extend to the family groups to which they belong and to society at large; the recognition of these functions has tended to limit the freedom of individual choice. Marriage creates or sanctions links of alliance between groups and plays an important role in the transmission of patrimony across generations as well as in the allocation of resources and capital to the partners and their children. In the past, the nubile youth were subordinate to the interests of their kin, and in the upper and ruling classes, they were often wedded to seal alliances or to arrange transfers of properties. There was often a conflict between the interests of individuals and those of their family, and the opportunity to marry was denied to some family members. Thus, in systems of primogeniture, to keep the family patrimony intact, only the older son was provided with sufficient resources to set up a household. In France during the modern era, younger siblings were directed to a career in the military or the clergy; in England, they were expected to secure a career on their own, for example, in commerce or in the colonies, which may have fostered entrepreneurship.

Most societies throughout the world, however, have encouraged marriage as the main system through which kinship groups recruit new members. Weddings often mark the formation of separate households, which are the social units of residence, of consumption, and of economic production. In other systems, they mark merely the time when a woman leaves her family of origin to join that of her husband. In matrilineal systems, the bride may remain in her father's or brother's household. In all instances, however, marriage creates a hierarchical structure by assigning roles and responsibilities to the spouses and their offspring and organizes systems of descent; it legitimates children and is the source of their right to the succession of their parents and to inheritance. Because most children are produced within wedlock, the age at first marriage and the proportions ever married represent important regulators of population growth.

Marriage payments. Marriage payments take various forms. The simplest consists in the reciprocal gifts that are the token of consensual unions. There are, however, two main forms of payments involving the families of the new spouses: the bride price given by the groom or his family to the parents of the bride, and the dowry or marriage portion, provided by the woman's parents toward the establishment of the couple. Both can represent impressively large sums, a fact that allows the parents to retain control over matches in the next generation. Today, bride prices are paid largely in money, and young men accumulate them ahead of marriage. Their amount is often fixed by tradition, but it tends to reflect the "value" of brides, their social class, beauty, virginity, or today even their level of education.

It has been hypothesized by Jack Goody in *Production and Reproduction* (1976) that bridewealths are a feature of societies where wives and children provide much of agricultural labor (hoe cultures), and that they compensate the brides' kin for the loss of their productive and reproductive potential. These hoe cultures are also the ones in which polygyny has been encountered most frequently, as a man may increase his control of labor, the main factor of production, by marrying multiple wives and increasing the number of his children.

In contrast, the dowry was initially characteristic of cultures where draft animals under men's steering provided the most important source of energy, and female labor outside the home was less important. Dowries have dominated in Europe since antiquity. They represent a symmetric contribution to the conjugal fund on the part of the woman and her family, and constitute an advance payment of the young woman's inheritance. As such, they were an essential aspect of intergenerational devolution among Western propertied classes. In medieval and Renaissance Italy, for example, there existed dowry funds to which the parents could contribute during the childhood years of their daughters. This represented an important form of saving for the commercial classes of the time. These funds were also supported by public charity, to allow the marriage of poor women. Dowries were a necessary part of marriage in Europe, but the amounts differed widely across social classes. For example, the marriage portion of an upper-class English woman might represent a fortune, whereas a bride at the other end of the social spectrum would receive only household goods; in addition, she would have saved toward a trousseau and brought it as her contribution to the household stock. The amount of the dowry might often determine the choice of a bride and played an important role in the future prosperity of the household, as well as the economic success of its head. It could represent capital that would allow the groom to purchase land, a trade, a charge, or a commission to support the new household. In almost all developed countries, the dowry has now disappeared, as the importance of inherited wealth has declined and the main index of financial value of an individual consists of personal skills and education.

Other costs and the "competitive marriage market." In many countries, the marriage ceremony itself entails important costs and may be an obstacle to the early conclusion of a union. A preference for endogamy (marriage among the same group, as, for example, in cross-cousin marriages) exists particularly in Islamic countries; in addition to keeping the women's property in their kinship group, it keeps down the transaction cost of marriage. In much of the world, matches are still arranged by the parents, but there exists a trend almost everywhere toward the emergence of genuine marriage markets where matches are freely contracted among financially independent pairs.

The costs and benefits of marriage to individuals have been considered by neoclassical economists focusing on present-day developed countries. Gary S. Becker, in *A Treatise on the Family* (1991), posited that the choice of a partner is made in a competitive marriage market by individuals who act rationally so as to maximize the benefits and minimize the costs that will accrue to them from the match with a particular person. As a result, if the marriage market, that is, the supply of potential spouses, is large and competitive, assortative mating will be the rule: the marital partners will select mates with roughly similar levels of benefits to offer. Gender specialization will occur to maximize the advantages of the match. Because women have an incontrovertible comparative advantage in performing the tasks of motherhood, so goes the argument, it is rational for them to specialize in all household tasks and to leave gainful employment to men. In doing so, they will liberate their husbands to participate in the wage-earning labor force more fully, thus helping the common household unit. The Becker model has been criticized by sociologists; Paula England (1992) has objected that gender specialization was largely the result of discrimination, and that the more women were limited to home labor by tradition and lower educational opportunities, the less they were able to compete successfully in the marketplace.

Marriage and Population Growth. The social and economic consequences of a person's marital state are important for both men and women, but because the large majority of children in most societies are born to married women, the impact of female nuptiality on fertility has received special attention. For purposes of measurement, it is useful to divide the population into the ever- and the never-married. The proportion of women who have reached the end of the childbearing period, conventionally age fifty, without having been married, provides an index of the intensity of female marriage, whereas the average age at first marriage measures its timing; the conjunction

of these two indices accounts for the proportions ever-married. In addition, marriage dissolutions and remarriages contribute to the proportion married at a particular time, but they are less easy to measure with available statistics, and less important in the aggregate, although there are examples of societies (such as Renaissance Florence) where most women married and the nonremarriage of widows reduced fertility substantially. Divorce and other marriage dissolutions, such as annulment of the marriage or repudiation of the wife, have existed in many societies, but the ideal of marital indissolubility has been powerful, at least before the twentieth century in Western countries, and the influence of divorce on fertility has been small.

The proportions of women married at various ages, as reported in a census, can be weighed by a standard schedule of marital fertility to measure the proportion of the reproductive potential that is used by a particular population, provided extramarital births are relatively infrequent. The American demographer Ansley J. Coale devised a widely used index of this kind, I_m, or the proportion married at the childbearing ages weighed by a noncontraceptive high marital fertility schedule. According to this index, the European national extremes in about 1900 were for Ireland, where the proportions married allowed only 32 percent of the fertility potential to be realized, and Romania, where they allowed 73 percent.

Much of our information for the past describes the practices of the upper classes, who represent a small portion of societies but have left abundant written records. In contrast, the impact of nuptiality on population growth, which has become a major focus of historical research in Europe, has been most relevant for the mass of the population for whom the basis of subsistence was income from labor and not from property. Thomas Malthus's *Essay on the Principle of Population* (1798) argued that under a system of private property, the preventive check of marital restraint would prevent the population from growing faster than the resources for its upkeep. Such a marriage pattern prevailed effectively in western Europe at the time of his writing, and it kept population growth low. Malthus was aware that in America, because land was abundant, marriages were early and the population grew rapidly.

Before the twentieth century, the main financial support of the marital unit would generally be provided by the steady income of the groom. Even in the lower classes, gender inequality was the rule; when women were involved in economic activities, it was before their marriage or as nonpaid family workers. It was assumed that men would be the breadwinners, and that women, once married, would exchange the prospect of economic security against emotional support of their husband, domestic services, and childbearing. This justified some age difference between spouses, as men tended to reach their maximum

MARRIAGE. *The Marriage of Nala and Damayanti,* from a series of gouache illustrations, Bilaspur, Punjab, eighteenth century. (Victoria and Albert Museum, London/Art Resource, NY)

attraction to a future mate after they had secured a source of income, and as young women were expected to be more adaptable to their new situation and more obedient to the will of their older husband. Thus, in Renaissance Italy, it was common for men in their thirties to take wives in their teens. This imposed a very long period of celibacy on men, and the death of older husbands resulted in a substantial number of young widows. In western Europe, in contrast, the age difference tended to be typically less than five years.

In 1965, the British demographer John Hajnal published an important essay on what came to be called the western European pattern of marriage. As of 1900, he noted, west of a line stretching from the Baltic to the Adriatic Sea, marriage was relatively late, after twenty-five years on average for women, and a proportion of the population in excess of 10 percent would remain single. East of that line, and in most of the world outside Europe, marriage tended to be early and universal. Hajnal attributed this western European exception to a social system that required a man to earn sufficient income to support a wife and children before he could marry. Consequently, a large proportion of the reproductive potential of the population went unused before the advent of birth control. The birth rate was kept relatively low, and late marriage has been called the main contraceptive weapon of Europe before the twentieth century.

Subsequent research has added nuance to Hajnal's generalizations. In parts of Asia, for example, in Thailand, the Philippines, and Indonesia, the simple conjugal unit was the traditional form of household, particularly among the common people. In Japan since the seventeenth century, the stem family household has prevailed, and young men had to wait upon inheritance until they could marry and start a family. Age at marriage was close to twenty five for women, although spinsterhood was not as common as in Europe. Apart from Japan, statistical evidence on past marriage systems is uncommon for non-Western societies.

There has been a great deal of research to establish when and why the western European pattern of marriage originated. It is characteristic of populations with moderate mortality levels; in order to be sustainable, a marriage pattern that would result in an average of five children per woman would require an expectation of life at birth close to thirty years, a level that may have prevailed in Europe but probably not in most of the world before the twentieth century. Periods of high mortality would liberate land holdings and other economic niches by killing their married occupiers, so that they could be filled by the young and the less privileged, allowing them to start families of their own. It is likely that such a process altered the manorial economy of Europe radically after the great loss of population caused by the plagues of the fourteenth century. But after a time of recuperation, subsequent population growth would make it impossible to sustain the patterns of earlier marriage and high fertility. Such a homeostatic relation between mortality and fertility through marriage prevailed in France under the Old Regime, but appears to have disappeared in England during the seventeenth century.

In peasant societies of the world, where the family rather than the individual is the basic economic unit, the main determinant of the timing of marriage is likely to be the fact that a girl reached physical maturity. The new couple may start common life in an extended parental household, and marriage is typically early. In contrast, the western European pattern characterizes populations where marriage coincides with the independent establishment of the spouses in their own household when they have gained their own means of support; nuclear households, comprising a couple and their children, are the rule.

The date when the pattern appeared is speculative. It is likely to have prevailed in various countries at various dates, but it was well established in almost every country of western and northern Europe by the eighteenth century. Alan Macfarlane (1986) linked the European pattern with early capitalism, the dominance of market forces, and the prevalence of wage labor, and he believed that these conditions were attained in England by the thirteenth century. In particular, the existence of private property rights accruing to the marrying individuals was essential for the system to work. Elsewhere in western Europe, the pattern may have appeared later.

The existence of the pattern raises the possibility of a mechanism linking marriage to economic prosperity, such that times when real wages were high would witness earlier and more frequent marriages, and times of scarcity would lead to the opposite result. A high prevalence of marriages would stimulate fertility and, through it, population growth; this in turn could exert pressure on resources and cause a decline of real wages because of an excess of labor in economies with limited room for expansion and where productivity was growing at a slow pace. In *The Population History of England, 1541–1871: A Reconstruction* (1981), historians E. A. Wrigley and Roger Schofield found evidence of a positive relationship between real wages and the proportions married. It has been hypothesized, moreover, that the creation of new jobs would stimulate population growth through the creation of new opportunities for marriage. Thus, proto-industrialization, the development of cottage industries such as textiles utilizing female labor in the European countryside, was once thought to have resulted in the lowering of the age at marriage among the lower classes. Case studies have revealed that the reality was more complex. Similarly, it was speculated that the growth of a wage-earning industrial proletariat during the nineteenth century had fostered imprudent matches and high fertility among the lower classes, a hypothesis that has also not been confirmed by research. Recent studies show that many factors influenced the contracting of unions in sometimes conflicting directions during the modern era, including the extent to which employers controlled housing, the dominant forms of wage labor (day labor vs. live-in servants), changes in agricultural technology (animal husbandry, which uses plenty of female labor, and plough labor, which does not), the substitution of cheaper female labor for male labor in textile production, poor relief, and institutional obstacles to the marriage of paupers. Finally, higher incomes may resolve themselves in opportunities of marriage, but also in higher consumption and the standard of living, so that the very prerequisites of marriage may have increased in step with economic growth. Although there was a decline in age at marriage in France and some other countries in the course of the nineteenth century, the vast expansion of the industrial labor force and the steady increase in labor's wages did not produce a commensurate increase in the proportions married before the twentieth century in most of Europe or in the more developed countries overseas.

Hajnal (1965) noted that, in promoting saving and capital accumulation, the western European pattern of marriage, may have facilitated an economic take-off. Prior to marriage, youth of both sexes typically spent a number of years as domestic servants or apprentices outside their own homes, thus establishing a market for wage labor and constituting a reserve army of workers for the growing economy. The tardiness of female marriage gave rise to a cheap labor force that could be employed in the industrial sector. Women in turn would save toward accumulating a collection of household goods that would ensure the comfort of their future home; being older and more experienced, they would be better managers of their home and better mothers. Some Asian countries with relatively late marriage, such as Japan and Korea, would use the same route to development in the nineteenth and twentieth centuries.

Recent Developments in the West. During the first half of the twentieth century, the age at marriage and the proportions single came down progressively in most European countries and in the United States, in part because of a rise in the standard of living, and in part because, with the generalization of birth control, prolonged celibacy ceased to be the main practical way to avoid a large family. Also noteworthy was a steady increase in the prevalence of divorce.

The period immediately after World War II coincided with historic lows in ages at marriage. The 1990s, on the other hand, represented historic highs in the United States, with a median age at marriage of twenty five years for women, twenty seven years for men. Ages at marriage have increased in all Western countries, although the trend is only very recent in eastern Europe. The age at which people form a durable sexual relationship has generally decreased, however.

The proportion of people who reach their fifties without having been married has also dramatically increased, particularly in Scandinavian countries. In addition, premarital cohabitation has become the normal prelude to marriage in many countries, although the proportions are still low in southern and eastern Europe. The normative sequence that existed in the past, namely, that a couple fell in love, moved together after a legally sanctioned marriage, and proceeded to have children, has ceased to dominate. During the 1990s, more than half of first marriages in the United States, and more than 90 percent in Sweden, were preceded by cohabitation.

Childbearing is increasingly occurring outside of marriage, either premaritally, a pattern that has been encouraged by the later age at marriage, or to couples who do not intend to marry. Divorce has become common in most countries, to the point where one-third of French marriages, two-fifths of English marriages, and more than half of American marriages contracted in the 1990s will eventually end in divorce. With a steady decline in mortality, however, the incidence of widowhood has greatly decreased, except among aged women. As a result of all these parallel trends, the nuclear family household, consisting of a married couple and their children, now constitutes a minority of households. There has been a true revolution in marriage patterns in Western countries during the last fifty years that has resulted in the breaking up of two of the central ideals of Western marriage: that it lasted until death and that it was the locus of legitimate sex and licit childbearing.

The neoclassical economic theory of marriage attributes the recent changes in the nuptiality pattern to an increase in the economic power of women, which has undermined the benefits of gender specialization. Most observers agree that the recent trends are concomitant with a large increase in the labor force participation of women, both married and unmarried, which has made them more financially independent. Other factors are the cultural recognition of the intellectual equality of men and women and the access of women to educational opportunities; the waning of parents' power to determine the choice of partner; and the drop of fertility and the availability of birth control, which has allowed women to establish themselves economically and professionally before they have children. Moreover, the growing risk of divorce undermines confidence in the permanence of marriage and encourages women to be less dependent. At the same time, there have been other important cultural changes: sexual behavior outside marriage has become more acceptable, and the notion that men must share in household tasks and women in breadwinning has gained wide acceptance.

Similar evidence of a break with the past can be documented in other parts of the world, either because of the diffusion of new models of behavior by the media or because of the dynamics of other changes that are gaining ground, such as the participation of women in the labor force and the widespread adoption of birth control. Thus, the age at marriage has increased in most of the developing world (although little so far in Latin America), and female-headed households are becoming a common feature of low-income countries. Nonmarried women typically do less well economically than married ones, however, and children raised by a single parent are more likely to live in poverty. It is not now possible to talk of a convergence of marriage and family forms to Western models, as sociologist William J. Goode did in his *World Revolution and Family Patterns* (1971), because various parts of the world are evolving their own forms.

[*See also* Family Structures and Kinship *and* Marriage Payments.]

BIBLIOGRAPHY

GENERAL SURVEYS

Becker, Gary S. *A Treatise on the Family*. Cambridge, Mass., 1991.

Bologne, Jean Claude. *Histoire du mariage en Occident*. Paris, 1995. Western European laws, practices, and sentiments, as revealed by legal documents and literary or historical accounts, with a focus on France.

Goode, William J. *World Revolution and Family Patterns*. 2d ed. New York, 1971.

Goody, Jack. *Production and Reproduction*. Cambridge, 1976.

Goody, Jack. *The Development of the Family and Marriage in Europe*. Cambridge, 1983.

Goody, Jack. *The Oriental, the Ancient, and the Primitive: Systems of Marriage in the Pre-Industrial Societies of Eurasia*. Cambridge, 1990. A comparative ethnographic survey of Eurasian patterns of marriage and family formation, as contrasted with those of sub-Saharan Africa; impressive and controversial.

Quale, G. Robina. *A History of Marriage Systems*. Contributions in Family Studies, 13. New York, 1988. An attempt at comprehensive coverage, with a useful bibliography, but not a succesful synthesis.

SPECIFIC TIMES AND PLACES

Brooke, Christopher. *The Medieval Idea of Marriage*. Oxford, 1989.

Coale, Ansley J., and Susan Cotts Watkins. *The Decline of Fertility in Europe*. Princeton, 1986. Covers the role of nuptiality in the nineteenth and early twentieth centuries.

Devos, Isabelle, and Liam Kennedy, eds. *Marriage and Rural Economy: Western Europe since 1400*. Ghent, 1999. A series of studies examining the impact of economic factors on the western European pattern of marriage.

Dixon, Ruth B. "Explaining Cross-Cultural Variations in Age at Marriage and Proportions Never Marrying." *Population Studies* 25 (1971), 215–233. An examination of Hajnal's assumption that the western European pattern was unique.

England, Paula. *Comparable Worth: Theories and Evidence*. New York, 1992.

Erikson, Amy Louise. *Women and Property in Early Modern England*. London, 1993. Uses probate records to investigate women of diverse social classes.

Hajnal, John. "European Marriage Patterns in Perspective." In *Population in History*, edited by D. V. Glass and D. E. C. Eversley, pp. 101–143. Chicago, 1965.

Klapisch-Zuber, Christiane. *Women, Family, and Ritual in Renaissance Italy.* Translated by Lydia G. Cochrane. Chicago, 1985. Translations of a series of studies originally published in French.

Macfarlane, Alan. *Marriage and Love in England: Modes of Reproduction, 1300–1840.* Oxford, 1986.

Malthus, Thomas R. *The Works of Thomas Robert Malthus*, edited by E. A. Wrigley and David Souden. 8 vols. London, 1986.

Smith Richard M. "Marriage Processes in the English Past: Some Continuities." In *The World We Have Gained: Histories of Population and Social Structure*, edited by Lloyd Bonfield, Richard M. Smith, and Keith Wrightson, pp. 43–99. Oxford, 1986.

Waite, Linda, ed. *The Ties that Bind: Perspectives on Marriage and Cohabitation.* New York, 2000. An American collection that reviews recent trends, with some international coverage.

Wrigley, E. A., and Roger Schofield. *The Population History of England, 1541–1871: A Reconstruction.* Cambridge, 1981.

ETIENNE VAN DE WALLE

MARRIAGE PAYMENTS. Marriage payments consist of wealth transfers between spouses (or their families) before, during, or at the termination of the marriage, and wealth transfers from parents to their children at the time when the children get married. The term *dowry* designates the wealth transfer provided by the bride's family to the bride at the time of her marriage. The dowry can be managed and used by the groom and his family, but the bride retains the ownership, and she is entitled to get her dowry back should the marriage dissolve. *Brideprice* indicates the wealth transfer from the groom's family to the bride's family; the kin of the groom transfers wealth to the kin of the bride in exchange for the bride, who joins the groom's family. *Marriage gifts* refer to gifts and wealth transfers from the groom to the bride herself. Regretably, there is no uniform taxonomy across disciplines on this topic.

Customs of Ancient Civilizations. With some exceptions, past civilizations characterized by dowries were also virilocal (the bride moved into the groom's household) and monogamous; husbands often simultaneously gave marriage gifts (or endowments) to their wives. The relative importance of dowries from parents to their daughters and marriage gifts from husbands to their wives greatly varied from time to time.

Dowries (*sheriktum*) existed in such ancient civilizations as the Sumerian, Akkadian, and Babylonian in the third and second millennia BCE. At the time of the betrothal, the groom offered a marriage gift (*terhatum*), usually in cash, to the bride's household, who in turn bestowed it to the bride herself together with the dowry: unlike the dowry, however, it was optional, and in later Babylonian times it became less frequent. If the husband died or divorced his wife, she was entitled to keep both her dowry and the marriage gift.

Dowries were also central features of marriage customs in both ancient Greece and Rome. In the Greece described in the *Iliad* and *Odyssey* (ninth to eighth centuries BCE), the groom paid a brideprice (*hèdna*) to the bride's household and offered gifts to the bride in addition to those given by the bride's father. Later, in the Greece of the city-states (eighth to fourth centuries BCE), the brideprice disappeared and the dowry (*proix*) became the prominent marriage transfer. In Rome in early times, most women married *cum manu*: dowries became part of their husbands' estates. At the marriage's dissolution, wives together with their children had the right to inherit an equal share of their husbands' property. In contrast, by the first century BCE, most marriages were *sine manu*: although the husband could manage the dowry, at the marriage's dissolution he had to return it to his wife's family or directly to his wife. Marriage gifts from husbands to wives (*donatio ante* or *propter nuptias*) became widespread in the late period of the empire in the third century CE.

Among Jews in Biblical times, the groom family paid a brideprice (*mohar*) to the bride's household, who in turn partly gave it back to the bride herself. At the same time, bride parents provided their daughter with a dowry (*chiluhim*), which consisted of her share of the inheritance from her father. Unlike the brideprice, whose value was customary, the size of the dowry varied according to the wealth of the bride's household. The biblical brideprice later disappeared. From the Mishnah and Talmudic period (200–600) onward, instead of paying a brideprice to the bride's parents, the groom provided a marriage gift directly to the bride.

Medieval Western Europe and the Muslim Empire. The pattern of marriage payments in western Europe in the second half of the first millennium looks like a patchwork reflecting the influences of Roman law, the customs of Germanic tribes, and the rules promoted by the Catholic Church in favor of monogamy and against incest. In ancient times, among Germanic tribes, grooms paid brideprices to the bride's parents at marriage. From the sixth to the tenth century, women received wealth transfers from both their paternal families and their husbands. At marriage, daughters moved into their in-laws' households and received dowries (under Roman law) or fathers' contributions (under Germanic law) from their natal families. The ancient brideprice of Germanic descent disappeared and was substituted with the marriage gift given by the groom to the bride herself. The balance between the dowry and the marriage gift gradually shifted. Around the tenth to eleventh centuries, the dowry regained prominence everywhere in western Europe, and by the thirteenth century it had become the main marriage transfer.

In the Muslim Empire, according to the norms established in the Qur'ān, transfers of wealth associated with marriage occurred in both directions. The groom offered a brideprice to the bride's family in compensation for the

MARRIAGE PAYMENT. Women carrying a bride's dowry and her belongings to the groom's home, Lendak, Czechoslovakia, 1987. (© John Eastcott/Yva Momatiuk/Woodfin Camp and Associates, New York)

loss of a daughter, and he made a promise to provide the *mahr* (dower or marriage gift) to the wife during and/or at the termination of the marriage. The bride's family also provided a dowry for their daughter at the time of her marriage. When receiving a dowry, a daughter was usually excluded from the inheritance if her brothers were alive at the father's death.

Asia. At the same time, when in Europe the dowry was reemerging as the major wealth transfer at marriage, in Song China (960–1279) dowry payments grew in importance with respect to the marriage gifts conveyed by the groom's family. During the Tang dynasty (617–907), aristocratic grooms paid substantial brideprices (in land, livestock, or silk) to bride families. Three centuries later, in Song China, the dowry from the bride's family became the major marriage payment across all social and economic groups. In contemporary China, there seems to be a divergence between urban and rural environments. In cities, both grooms and brides contribute to the constitution of a conjugal fund. In contrast, although both dowries and brideprices exist in rural communities, brideprices are much larger than dowries.

The historical origin of the dowry system in India has been traced to the Hindu marriage among high castes in North India. Until the end of the medieval period, Brahma marriage practiced by high castes involved the giving of a daughter together with a dowry from the bride's family to the groom family, whereas in the Asura marriage, common among lower castes, a brideprice was paid by the groom to marry the bride. During the colonial period, marriages with dowries became the only legally accepted form of marriage among all social groups and castes. Brideprices are common in South India among the Dravidian kinship groups.

Dowries versus Brideprices. Anthropologists, demographers, economists, and historians have advanced various theories to explain under which conditions dowries instead of brideprices are more likely to prevail. According to the economist Gary Becker, brideprices and dowries are pecuniary transfers that clear the marriage market when sex ratios are unbalanced; in a society where women (men) are less numerous, a man (woman) will pay a brideprice (dowry) in order to attract a bride (groom). Historical and demographic research has been unable to confirm or reject that hypothesis conclusively.

The anthropologist Jack Goody maintains that a dowry is a *pre-mortem* inheritance from the bride's parents to the bride; in societies with dowries, daughters receive wealth transfers from their parents through dowries at the time of the marriage, whereas sons are bequeathed the family estate. "Diverging devolution" is the term Goody coined to describe this difference in wealth transfers according to gender. Dowries are more likely to emerge in stratified societies (like the Eurasiatic ones), in which there is a significant wealth and status inequality. Parents provide their daughters with dowries to ensure that their married daughters continue to enjoy the same wealth and social status they had in their natal families. In societies such as many cultures in Africa, where there is little social and economic stratification, brideprices are more likely to emerge. Unlike dowries, which are transfers from the kin of the bride to the bride herself, brideprices are transactions from the kin of the groom to the kin of the bride in exchange for the transfer of the bride. The bride's father will then use the brideprice received from the son-in-law's kin to find brides for his sons.

Ester Boserup has suggested an alternative theory for the origin and the development of dowries and brideprices. Brideprices are more likely to emerge in economies, such as most African societies, in which agriculture is based on light tools (e.g., the hoe) and women are actively engaged in agricultural tasks. In these economies, by paying a brideprice to the bride's family, a groom acquires her labor force and her ability to bear children. In contrast, in economies like medieval Europe, in which the emergence of the heavy plow resulted in mainly men engaging in agriculture and limited the economic role of women, a bride's parents provided their daughter with a dowry as a way to compensate the groom's household for taking care of the bride.

Finally, we can note that the provision of dowries and brideprices also has the potential of altering the bargaining power of the spouses within the household. A bride with a large dowry might have a larger say in intrahousehold resource allocation than a bride with a small dowry. The provision of dowries from the bride's parents to the bride and of marriage gifts from the husband to his wife also contributes to the standard of living of a married woman in case of divorce or widowhood. This was clearly the purpose of dowries and marriage gifts in many past societies.

[*See also* Inheritance Systems *and* Marriage.]

BIBLIOGRAPHY

Burguière, André, Christiane Klapisch-Zuber, Martine Segalen, and Françoise Zonabend, eds. *A History of the Family*, vol. 1, *Distant Worlds, Ancient Worlds*; vol. 2, *The Impact of Modernity*. Cambridge, Mass., 1996. An excellent collection of papers which cover many regions and time periods.

Becker, Gary S. *A Treatise on the Family*. Cambridge, Massachusetts, 1981. This is the economist Gary Becker's famous contribution to the economics of the family.

Birge, Bettine. *Women, Property, and Confucian Reaction in Sung and Yan China (960–1368)*. Cambridge, 2002.

Boserup, Ester. *Women's Role in Economic Development*. New York, 1970.

Botticini, Maristella. "A Loveless Economy? Intergenerational Altruism and the Marriage Market in a Tuscan Town." *Journal of Economic History* 59.1 (March 1999), 104–121.

Goody, Jack. "Bridewealth and Dowry in Africa and Eurasia." In *Bridewealth and Dowry*, edited by Jack Goody and Stanley J. Tambiah, pp. 1–58. Cambridge, 1973. This is the famous article by the anthropologist Jack Goody.

Hughes, Diane Owen. "From Brideprice to Dowry in Mediterranean Europe." *Journal of Family History* 3 (1978), 262–296. An excellent study that documents marriage payments in Europe from the fall of the Roman Empire to the Middle Ages.

Quale, Robina G. *A History of Marriage Systems*. New York, 1988. A very good survey and discussion in comparative perspective.

Saller, Richard P. *Patriarchy, Property, and Death in the Roman Family*. Cambridge, 1994.

Tambiah, Stanley J. "Dowry and Bridewealth and the Property Rights of Women in South Asia." In *Bridewealth and Dowry*, edited by Jack Goody and Stanley J. Tambiah, pp. 59–160. Cambridge, 1973.

MARISTELLA BOTTICINI

MARSHALL, ALFRED (1842–1924), British economist.

Marshall was born in Bermondsey, South London, the son of William Marshall, a clerk at the Bank of England, and Rebecca Oliver. Educated at Merchant Taylors' School, he then went to Saint John's College at the University of Cambridge. He was elected to a fellowship at Saint John's, where his initial design to study physics fell victim to an interest in philosophy and ultimately in economics. In 1866, he started working through John Stuart Mill's *Principles of Political Economy* (1848). In 1868, Saint John's appointed him to a special lectureship in moral science. For the next nine years he worked to establish political economy as a serious subject at Cambridge. Among his early pupils were H. S. Foxwell, John Neville Keynes, Henry Cunynghame, and Mary Paley (with whom he published his first book *Economics of Industry* in 1879). Marriage to Mary Paley in 1877 led to the loss of his fellowship and his move to University College, Bristol, as principal and professor of political economy. Ill health made him resign as principal in 1881; then in 1883, a position became available at Balliol College, University of Oxford, as a fellow and lecturer in political economy. His Oxford career was brief: Henry Fawcett died on 7 November 1884 and, on 14 December, Marshall was elected to his post as professor of political economy at Cambridge, one he would hold until 1908.

Although Marshall's characteristic doctrines were far developed by the mid-1870s and were taking their final form by 1883, with the exception of two papers, "The Pure Theory of Foreign Trade" and "The Pure Theory of Domestic Values," which were privately printed by Henry Sidgwick in 1879, nothing substantial appeared in print after his *Economics of Industry* until his *Principles of Economics* (1890). The latter was intended to be the first of a two-volume text, but Marshall had difficulty realizing his plan. Successive revised editions of that volume (there were six before he replaced it with *An Introductory Volume* in 1910) prevented progress on the later volume(s)—or on later volumes of its simpler version *Elements of the Economics of Industry* (1892). The project also grew to five volumes. To do this, he resigned his Cambridge chair in 1908; however, except for *Industry and Trade* (1919) and *Money, Credit, and Commerce* (1923), a light reworking of materials dating from the 1870s, nothing more appeared.

Marshall's contributions to monetary economics were largely buried in evidence to official committees and commissions: most notably, the Royal Commission on the Depression of Trade and Industry (1886), the Royal Commission on the Values of Gold and Silver (1887 and 1888), and the Indian Currency Committee (1899)—collected together by John Maynard Keynes in *Official Papers* (1925).

Marshall's *Principles of Economics* gave economists the tools of partial equilibrium analysis, which later became the theoretical staple of much of the new economic history. Marshall also spent some time on what he called "the history of economic phenomena." He may once have "proposed to write a treatise on economic history, and for many years collected materials for it" (1892, p. 507)—but he was not a historian. Nonetheless, historical facts, especially "modern" ones, were important as sources of illustrations for his economics. The introductory material of the *Principles of Economics* included two chapters on "The Growth of Free Industry and Enterprise" (relegated to Appendix A from the third edition), which drew fire from William Cunningham (1892) and a reply from Marshall in the *Economic Journal* for that year. Marshall's 1919 volume *Industry and Trade* contained substantial case studies of modern industrial development in Britain, France, Germany, and the United States.

BIBLIOGRAPHY

Cunningham, William. "The Perversion of Economic History." *Economic Journal* 2.3 (1892), 491–506.

Groenewegen, Peter. *A Soaring Eagle: Alfred Marshall, 1842–1924.* Aldershot, U.K., 1995.

Keynes, J. M. "Alfred Marshall." *Economic Journal* 34.2 (1924); reprinted in *Essays in Biography* (London, 1933).

Marshall, Alfred. "A Reply." *Economic Journal* 2.3 (1892), 507–519.

D. E. MOGGRIDGE

MARSHALL PLAN. In his commencement speech at Harvard University in June 1947, U.S. secretary of state George Marshall pledged that his government would "do whatever it is able to do for the return of normal economic health in the world," meaning the free world. Within a year, the European Recovery Program (ERP) was ready. The American end was entrusted to the European Cooperation Administration (ECA), and the European end was coordinated through the Organization for European Economic Cooperation (OEEC), in which all of the major western European states except Spain were represented. Aid was in the form of the delivery of goods (not cash). Measured by any standards, the program was generous. It was equivalent to just under 2 percent of the American gross domestic

TABLE 1. *Cumulative Assistance under the ERP (in millions of dollars)*

	DECEMBER 1948	DECEMBER 1949	JUNE 1951
Allocation	4,045	6,976	11,310
Arrival	2,063	5,441	10,631

Spagnolo, C. "The Marshall Plan and the Stabilization of Western Europe." Ph.D. diss., EVI, Florence, 1998.

product (GDP) and 2.5 percent of the GDP of the recipient countries. There is some discrepancy over the exact value and timing of the aid, partly because of the time lag between the allocation of funds and the arrival of goods in Europe and partly because of the timing of the end of the program. In June 1951, the ERP was converted to a program of military assistance under the Mutual Defense Assistance Program, but some ERP goods continued to trickle through for months thereafter.

It is fair to say that few historians now support the original "heroic" accounts that ascribed much of western Europe's subsequent economic miracle to the impact of U.S. aid. It is true that the dollars saved by the program covered almost 90 percent of Europe's dollar deficit in these years. But Alan Milward, in *The Reconstruction of Western Europe* (1984), has argued that, with the exception of France and the Netherlands, the same effect could have been obtained, without damaging investment, from holding back the increase in consumption. Measured as a contribution to investment, the ERP allowed an increase on average of about 10 percent (though closer to 20 percent in 1949 in Germany, where industry was depressed). However, since investment levels were close to 20 percent of GNP, the impact cannot be described as essential to European recovery. Besides, the ERP only came onstream late in 1948. By that time, industrial output in western Europe had regained its prewar level and, if West Germany is excluded, had surpassed it by nearly 20 percent.

While downplaying the impact of the ERP on western European recovery in purely quantitative terms, historians have begun to reasses its contribution in institutional terms. For example, since the ERP was in the form of a "structural adjustment program" rather than as ad hoc sums, as previously had been the case since 1945, it allowed the extension of planning horizons. Moreover, although states theoretically could have solved the dollar problem by restricting consumption, the ERP allowed them to avoid the damage of increased labor militancy and reduced business confidence restriction might have entailed. Recently, historians of the OEEC have added an international dimension to this argument. They point to the U.S.–sponsored efforts within the OEEC to remove quotas on intra-European trade and the creation (with the backing of $350 million of ERP funds) of the European Payments Union to allow the restoration of limited convertibility on commercial transactions. These laid the foundations for the trade-led economic growth that characterized the 1950s. Since protecting these gains and seeking further trade advantages motivated the creation of the customs union, which formed the core of the European Economic Community (EEC), Marshall aid may have had implications echoing far beyond the original goals of facilitating European reconstruction.

BIBLIOGRAPHY

Eichengreen, Barry, and J. B. de Long. "The Marshall Plan: History's Most Successful Structural Adjustment Program." In *Postwar Reconstruction, 1945–1949: Implications for Eastern Europe*, edited by R. Dornbush, R. Layard, and W. Nolling. Cambridge, Mass., and London, 1991. An important article shifting the reevaluation of the Marshall Plan into the institutional area.

Hogan, Michael. *The Marshall Plan: America, Britain, and the Reconstruction of Western Europe, 1947–1952.* Cambridge, and New York, 1987. An authoritative but U.S.–centric account of the Marshall Plan.

Griffiths, Richard T., ed. *Explorations in OEEC History.* Paris, 1997. A collection of articles looking at the Marshall Plan's contribution to liberalizing Europe's trade and payments.

Milward, Alan S. *The Reconstruction of Western Europe, 1945–1951.* London, 1984. A Eurocentric account questioning the necessity of Marshall aid.

RICHARD T. GRIFFITHS

MARX, KARL (1818–1893), German philosopher.

Marx's main contribution to economic history lies in his theory of historical change. His efforts at historical research, while interesting and often insightful, were modest, limited for the most part to a few chapters in Volumes 1 and 3 of *Capital* (*Collected Works*, New York, 1967) and occasional passages in the *Grundrisse* (*Collected Works*, New York, 1973). Since his theory is very much a product of his intellectual and political development, it is useful to review the latter before turning to the former.

Born in Trier, Marx entered the University of Bonn at the age of seventeen and, a year later, transferred to the University of Berlin. It was in Berlin that he discovered the works of the great German philosopher Georg Wilhelm Friedrich Hegel and then abandoned the study of law for that of philosophy. Although he was later to jettison much of the content of Hegel's philosophical system, he remained true to its form, that is, to the notion that history proceeds dialectically and that it is purposeful, directional, and progressive.

Degree in hand, but with no prospects of a university career (he was already much too radical for the Prussian bureaucracy), Marx accepted a position as a contributor to the *Rheinische Zeitung*. He was a brilliant political journalist, equally skilled at attracting readers and antagonizing repressive regimes. Within a year, he was editor in chief; six months later, he was out work, after the paper had been shut down by government authorities. In 1843, he moved with his family to Paris, at that time the center of radical intellectual activity in Europe, to accept a position as writer for a left-wing German newspaper.

The next two years were the most critical intellectually of his entire life. As Isaiah Berlin observes in his splendid biography *Karl Marx* (London, 1995), Marx came to believe, first, that conflicts associated with the production and appropriation of the surplus were the driving forces of history; second, that the process was understandable through objective, empirical analysis; and, third, that the proletariat was to be the standard bearer of the new millennium. He had, in other words, sketched the broad outlines of his materialist conception of history. Through the Communist party of Paris he met his life-long collaborator, friend, and benefactor, Friedrich Engels. Few of Marx's ideas were original; his originality lay, instead, in the way in which he combined and articulated the ideas of others. Aside from Hegel, he drew liberally on the German materialist philosopher Ludwig Feuerbach, the French economist and philosopher Claude Henri Saint-Simon, the English classical economists, and the French communists.

In 1845, in trouble once again with the authorities, Marx fled to Brussels. In 1848, he published (with Engels) the *Manifesto of the Communist Party* (*Collected Works*, vol. 6, New York, 1976), a brilliant piece of political propaganda in which he presented for the first time his views on historical change and the nature of class conflict. The initial success of the revolutionary uprisings of that year permitted him to move freely in Europe. He returned to Paris and then went to Cologne, where he helped found the *Neue Rheinische Zeitung*. The euphoria (and the newspaper) lasted only a year. The revolutions were crushed, and, once more, Marx was on the run. Expelled from Prussia, he returned briefly to Paris, but in August 1849 moved to England. He was to remain there virtually without interruption until his death.

Convinced that the failure of the revolutions of 1848 resulted from ignorance and lack of preparation, he decided that his task now was to educate, inform, and organize. He thus set himself two related objectives: to discover the laws of motion of capitalism and to make the proletariat aware of its crucial role in the destruction of capitalism. In a limited way, he was successful at both, in spite, it should be added, of his desperate personal circumstances. He had no money, no job, few contacts, and even fewer prospects. Thanks to Engels's generosity and occasional pay for articles published in the New York *Tribune*, Marx just managed to eke out a living and support his family. In 1864, he was instrumental in creating the First Workers' International. He wrote the constitution, gave the inaugural address, and

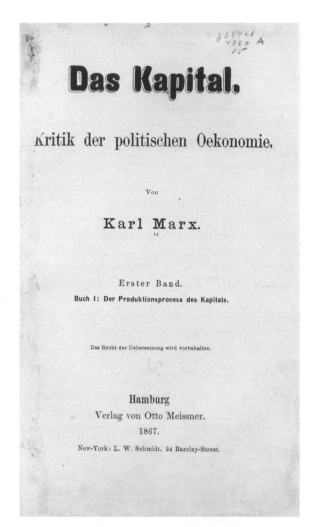

Das Kapital.

Kritik der politischen Oekonomie.

Von

Karl Marx.

Erster Band.
Buch I: Der Produktionsprocess des Kapitals.

Das Recht der Uebersetzung wird vorbehalten.

Hamburg
Verlag von Otto Meissner.
1867.

New-York: L. W. Schmidt. 24 Barclay-Street.

MARXIST THOUGHT. Cover of the first edition (1867) of *Das Kapital*. (Prints and Photographs Division, Library of Congress)

served on its board. In this and in other ways, he strove to prepare the masses for their destiny. In 1867, after a decade and a half of intense research, he published his masterpiece, the first volume of *Capital*, in which he used his fully developed model of historical change to explain the rise and fall of the capitalist system. As a result, Marx became the undisputed intellectual leader of revolutionary socialism in Europe, a role he was to play until his death.

Marx came to believe that every historical epoch could be described by a dominant mode of production; and that each was, in turn, determined by ownership or control of the means of production, the relations of individuals in the production process, and the material forces of production. All historical modes up to and including capitalism were based on an inherent contradiction: one class appropriated the surplus while another produced it and received in good times enough to ensure its own survival but no more. The key question for Marx was: what caused modes of production to evolve; that is, what were the motivating forces of historical change?

Although there is substantial controversy in the literature about Marx's answer to this question, in the preface to *A Contribution to the Critique of Political Economy* (Moscow, 1970, p. 21), he states that "at a certain stage of development the material forces of production [the economy's productive capacity] come into conflict with the existing relations of production [class or property relations]." The latter become a fetter on the former, and a period of social revolution commences; it ends with the complete transformation of the relations of production and the entire legal and political superstructure. It is, therefore, changes in productive forces that bump up against inhibiting social relations and cause the system to break apart. Although it is possible to discern in places an apparent reversed causality, that is, from relations to forces of production, Marx is fairly consistent in his view that changes in the forces of production eventually provoke changes in the mode of production. This said, class conflict is still central to his model; for, if development of the economy's productive capacity creates the conditions for change, it is the struggle between classes that makes it happen, often in complex and unanticipated ways.

According to Berlin, Marx's system is without parallel in the formulation of its questions and the rigor by which it searches for answers. "Even if all its specific conclusions were proved false, its importance in creating a wholly new attitude to social and historical questions and so opening new avenues of human knowledge would be unimpaired" (p. 116). Marx, Berlin contends, is the true father of modern economic history.

BIBLIOGRAPHY

WORKS BY MARX

Collected Works. 46 vols. New York, various dates. English translations of all the published works, manuscripts, and letters of Marx and Engels. *The German Ideology* (with F. Engels, New York, 1960) and *The Eighteenth Brumaire of Louis Napoleon* (New York, 1969) may be of particular interest to economic historians.

BIOGRAPHIES

Berlin, Isaiah. *Karl Marx*. London, 1995. The best biography of Marx, in spite of its age (the first edition was first published in 1939). In the 1995 edition, Terrell Carver provides an excellent guide to further readings.

McLennan, David. *Karl Marx: His Life and Thought*. London, 1973. Offers a comprehensive account of his life and works.

MARX'S THEORY OF HISTORICAL CHANGE

Cohen, G. A. *Karl Marx's Theory of History: A Defense*. Oxford, 1978. Makes use of analytical philosophy to build an argument in support of the primacy of forces of production.

Rigby, S. H. *Marxism and History*. Manchester, 1987. Reviews critically various interpretations of Marx's theory of history and concludes that primacy must go to relations of production.

Shaw, William H. *Marx's Theory of History*. Stanford, Calif., 1978. Champions a technological-determinist interpretation of Marx's theory of history.

MARXIST APPROACHES TO ECONOMIC HISTORY

Anderson, Perry. *Lineages of the Absolutist State*. London, 1974.

Anderson, Perry. *Passages from Antiquity to Feudalism*. London, 1974. A compelling, analytically complex account of the transition from the ancient to the feudal mode of production.

Brenner, Robert. "Agrarian Class Structure and Economic Development in Pre-Industrial Europe." *Past and Present* 70 (1976), 30–75. A provocative, highly controversial article in which class conflict acts as the motivating force and arbiter of historical development.

Cohen, Jos. S. "The Achievements of Economic History: The Marxist School." *Journal of Economic History* 38.1 (1978), 29–57. An overview of Marxian-inspired works in economic history.

Hilton, Rodney. H. *Bond Men Made Free*. London, 1973. One of many excellent works by the author in which he uses Marx's model to delineate the features of the feudal mode of production and the forces that led to its evolution.

JON S. COHEN

MARXISM AND MARXIST HISTORIOGRAPHY.

Marxism is neither a type of economics nor a particular view of history. Broader than both disciplines of study, Marxism is nevertheless inconceivable without at least a gesture toward the economic history with which all Marxists understand the class formations, political institutions, and cultural aesthetics of a given society to be associated. Central to Marxist history's origins was the radical mid-nineteenth century contention that it was the production and exchange of things necessary to the support of human life, through which wealth was created and distributed, that was the root cause both of social change and of the political revolutions of the eighteenth century. This stood much of the interpretation of the European past, so embedded in Georg Wilhelm Friedrich Hegel's (1770–1831) idealist notions of the power of "the spirit," on its head. Marxism's refinement of historical materialism as a perspective on the past that was meant not only to interpret the world but to change it fed into understandings of Revolution's past just as it would stimulate Revolution's future.

Birth of Marxism. Marxism was born at the interface of three historically evolved traditions: German philosophy, French socialism, and British political economy. Out of this cross-fertilization, Karl Marx (1818–1883) and Friedrich Engels (1820–1895) developed their understanding of the materialist and dialectical concept of history, their appreciation of the centrality of the mode of production, and their understanding of class struggle as an inevitable consequence of capitalist development and the social relations of labor and capital. From the time of its birth, Marxism would be inexplicable outside of the transformations associated with the rise of capitalism, a social formation defined by an accumulative regime driven forward by privatized property forms, the extraction of surplus associated with the wage system, and production for profit.

If there was a single, most decisive impetus to the birth of Marxism, it was perhaps Marx's and Engels's relentless drive to butt their philosophically and practically trained heads against the dismal science of early economics, in which the writings of Adam Smith (1723–1790) and David Ricardo (1772–1823) figured forcefully. It was the contribution of these Enlightenment writers to develop the notion of an autonomous, self-regulating economy, or civil society, in which commerce freed modern man of the shackles of feudal ties. Liberty was unleashed, stimulating a division of labor that, if left to the individual productive devices of humanity, supposedly promoted the collective good of all, be they nations or persons. As this conceptualization of historical progress crystallized, it nurtured understandings of social order uniquely useful to both the consolidating capitalism of the early nineteenth century and the nascent bourgeois-democratic governments that were orchestrating its development across Europe and North America. At the same point that state and economy were seemingly divorced in theory, regarded as autonomous agents advancing the material and spiritual well-being of all, they were in practice ever more interdependent. This was increasingly recognized by the perpetual thorn in the side of civil society, exploited labor. For if civil society was autonomous and beneficial, its drive forward propelled by a division of labor capable of enhancing production to the point that all would gain, then labor was the measure of all value. But this very same measure of value, labor, was also the cause or source of value that was largely reaped by those who owned the units of production, be they mills, factories, mines, or land. How could labor produce value for all society but produce that value inequitably, with the wages paid it constituting only a portion of the entire value from which capital extracted profit?

Marx utilized his grasp of Hegelian philosophy as well as his understanding of working-class socialism as it was emerging in France to channel an imaginative critique of political economy along lines that situated the Smith-Ricardo understanding of civil society historically. In this critique, Hegel was stood on his head, his rationalization of Prussian autocracy rejected, but his appreciation of the need for a transhistorical political subject reproduced in Marx's insight that labor, not a hereditary monarchy, was the foundation of a future state that would truly represent humanity. Thus Marx borrowed from the historically evolving struggle of workers for self-emancipation the notion that proletarian control over production and politics would bury the project of capitalism and all its exploitations and oppressions. In doing so, the Marxist appreciation of historical progress was premised on refusing to see capitalism as anything other than a historically limited stage in humanity's evolution. The specific contradictions of capitalism's civil society, which produced unbounded wealth and luxury for the few but left the many who produced such value wanting, would be overcome as Revolution toppled the capitalist edifice of state power and an economy commanded by bourgeois minorities, socialism leading to communism.

Marx and Engels thus used the theory of historical materialism to infuse their political project of overthrowing capitalism. They wrote articles and books, as well as propaganda pieces and programs for proletarian bodies, such as the International Workingmen's Association (1864–1876). Individual self-interest, they always argued, did not lead to collective good, but to recurring capitalist crises. As capital sought to overcome such crises, registered routinely over the course of the nineteenth century in economic depressions, it tightened the noose on working-class necks. Demanding the longer worker day, Draconian poor laws, forms of production intensified with new technologies and ever more exacting supervision, and a wider exploitation of the resources and labor of "underdeveloped" countries farther and farther afield, capital found support in the state, with its law and its capacity to suppress discontent, a la the carrot or the stick. Whenever workers rose up in opposition, they were treated to the hard lesson that the state backed capital. Civil society was proving increasingly uncivil, and economic history was riddled with the mangled bodies of injured factory children and armed laborers who had taken to ill-fated barricades.

Early Marxist economic and social histories addressed the politics of this immediate context. In his historical writings on class war in the France of the 1830s and 1840s, for instance, Marx presented scathing indictments of the personnel of bourgeois power. He exposed the contradictory nature not only of capitalist "progress," but also of those—such as Bonaparte—who would be called upon to lead its march. Engels wrote movingly of the conditions that would inevitably lead to an all-out war of "the poor against the rich" in *The Condition of the Working Class in England in 1844* (1845), a text routinely scrutinized by academic critics, but one that has held up amazingly well as an account of the urban blight associated with such first-generation factory towns as Manchester. Equally passionate were sections of Volume 1 of Marx's mature political economy, *Das Kapital*, where the ravages of capital's original accumulations (in dispossessing a landed peasantry, divorcing small artisan producers from the means of production, and pillaging new colonial conquests) and relentless appetite for surplus (manifested in extending the length of the working day, suppressing working-class collectivity, elaborating ever more intricate divisions of labor, and charting new technological innovation) were researched and presented in prose as alive with condemnation as it was with classical allusions, from Shakespeare to Dante.

KARL MARX. Karl Marx with his daughters Jenny, Eleanor, and Laura, and Friedrich Engels, circa 1860. (Civica Galleria d'Arte Moderna, Milan/Stock Montage)

Early Marxist Writers. The first generation of Marxist writers, attuned as they were to the needs of the revolutionary movement in their own locales, wrote economic history in ways that highlighted these themes, and often in order to place the accent on class struggle. Subjects such as the peasant wars of Germany (1525–1526) were broached by both Engels and the late nineteenth-century socialist, Belfort Bax (1854–1926), just as the struggle for the Paris Commune (1871), in which workers battled to take over a metropolitan capital of Europe, was treated by Marx and one of the Communards, Hippolyte Prosper Olivier Lissagaray. Karl Kautsky's (1854–1938) 1899 publication, *Agrarian Question*, explored capitalism's European and American countrysides, just as Vladimir Ilich Lenin's (1870–1924) massive 1890s study of the rural economy, *The Development of Capitalism in Russia*, attended to the combined and uneven character of the Tsarist economy. Rudolf Hilferding's (1877–1941) *Finance Capital* (1910) and Rosa Luxemburg's (1870–1919) *The Accumulation of Capital* (1913), as well as Lenin's *Imperialism* (1916) were among the pioneering attempts to extend Marxist economic history beyond the boundary of the nation state, examples of how Marxist histories were conditioned by the contemporary currents of bourgeois accumulation, bursting the confining boundaries of the nineteenth century.

As well as writing about history in this period, Marxists were also making it. The successful Bolshevik Revolution of 1917 created the first proletarian Marxist state. This momentous world-historic event was chronicled in Leon Trotsky's (1879–1940) magisterial, three-volume narrative, *History of the Russian Revolution* (1932), as well as in contemporary memoirs by the American radicals Louise Bryant (1885–1936) and John Reed (1887–1920). Soviet economists, such as Evgeny Alexeyvich Preobrazhensky (1886–1937), developed important historical arguments about the problems of industrialization and bureaucratization in the new revolutionary state, authoring such texts as *From NEP to Socialism* (1922) and *The New Economics* (1926). As with Trotsky, who would later analyze the degeneration of the revolutionary initiative under Josef Stalin (1879–1953) in *The Revolution Betrayed: What Is the Soviet Union and Where Is It Going?* (1937), Soviet commentators who dared to offer serious interpretive statements in these years ultimately faced execution or exile. Preobrazhensky was subject to a series of humiliations, expulsions from the Communist Party of the Soviet Union, and was eventually shot in prison in 1937.

Educated Writers Emerge. The luster of workers' revolution thus faded in the mid-to-late 1920s. It was swallowed up in the creation of a caste-like Stalinist bureaucracy whose governing apparatus moved from coercion and repression in the 1920s to outright terror in the 1930s. Within this unfortunate framework, the nature of Marxist writing inevitably shifted gears in the interwar years. One of the founders of the *New Left Review*, Perry Anderson, has suggested in *Considerations on Western Marxism* (1976), that this period witnessed the relinquishment of historical, economic, and political themes in Marxist intellectual production. The center of gravity of continental European Marxism, in Anderson's metaphor, turned toward metaphysical terrain. University-based Marxists replaced the likes of Lenin, Luxemburg, and the German revolutionary, Karl Liebknecht—such professors were dubbed *Kathedeersozialisten*—and class was less likely to be addressed as a combative historical process than an aesthetic possibility. From his prison cell, the Italian communist Antonio Gramsci (1891–1937) wrote his coded notebooks, while Georg Lukács (1885–1971) and Jean-Paul Sartre (1905–1980) moved Marxism into realms of literary criticism and existentialist philosophy.

Where Marxist histories continued to co-join the social and the political within a grounding in economic life, they were the product of Communist Party intellectuals, often in such countries as Great Britain or Germany. A Russian emigre turned English journalist, Theodore Rothstein, explored the evolution of the British workers' movement in *From Chartism to Labourism* (1929). Jürgen Kuczynski ranged broadly over the western European experience, offering a multivolumed set of "short histories" of labor conditions that prefigured, in their range of concerns and attention to periodization, the later approach of Eric J. Hobsbawm. Two British communist historians, Dona Torr and Maurice Dobb, were of pivotal importance in stimulating the emergence of what would be known as the British Communist Party Historians' Group. Dobb returned to the themes of volume 1 of *Das Kapital* in his *Studies in the Development of Capitalism* (1947), but he wrote extensively as well on Russian economic development in the 1920s, theories of wage systems, and other matters. Torr, a research advocate and supporter of many young left historians, would eventually publish *Tom Mann and His Times* (1956), but her importance was less in the actual publishing of Marxist economic and social history than in encouraging others and demanding a rigorous appreciation of the democratic aspirations of working-class people.

Torr, for instance, was pivotal in the encouragement of Edward (E. P.) and Dorothy Thompson, whose writings on the plebeian culture of eighteenth-century England, the working class of the 1790–1830 period, Chartism, William Blake, William Morris, women's and gender history, and varied other topics, from Indian poets to Bulgarian partisans, are perhaps the best-known examples of Marxist-inspired historical writing that placed an accent on human agency pitted against the implacable structures of ruling authorities. E. P. Thompson's *The Making of the English Working Class* (1963) became the most important and influential text in the rise of working-class history as a subject matter in the 1960s and 1970s. The Thompsons had been joined decades earlier, in the 1940s and 1950s, by an impressive, if eclectic, communist cohort of economic and social historians: Christopher Hill, Rodney Hilton, Victor Kiernan, John Saville, Eric Hobsbawm, and a precocious Raphael Samuel (future founder of the History Workshop movement and its journal). If economic history was the base, this contingent would produce a rich superstructure of social histories, and some of those in the group, such as Hill, would come to dominate entire fields of history, such as that of the seventeenth-century English Revolution.

Hobsbawm blended well the economic and the social, his synthetic abilities evident in such collections of essays as *Labouring Men* (1963) and *Workers: Worlds of Labour* (1984), as well as in broad studies of various "ages," reaching from the seventeenth to the twentieth centuries. His capacity to focus on highly significant issues of large-scale social transformation showed the potential for Marxist history to address the big picture of historical change. One of his earliest writings was an analytic *tour de force* of direct relevance to a mid-twentieth century debate over the transition from feudalism to capitalism. Hobsbawm examined the crisis of the seventeenth century, exploring why it was that the Industrial Revolution did not proceed directly from the contradictions of sixteenth-century feudalism, but stalled for a century, albeit in ways that provided the primitive accumulations necessary for capital's future expansive growth. Whereas Edward Thompson devoted his energies to understanding the ways in which the emerging disciplines of capitalism bit into the popular cultures of the time, exploring, for instance, time discipline and its erosion of task-oriented work forms, Hobsbawm and others, such as Rodney Hilton, looked more directly to the grand sweep of socioeconomic change. Marx's writing on the transition from feudalism to capitalism betrayed a specific interpretive ambivalence, stressing initially the corrosive influence of mercantile activity, and, later, the changing relations of production. Marxists pioneered a crucial discussion of these issues, drawing mainstream historiography into their frame of reference. In the first phase of this 1950s exchange, the American economist Paul Sweezy adopted the exchange focus, while Dobb stressed the importance of property/productive relations. In the pages of the United States Marxist journal, *Science & Society*, as well as in Great Britain's *Past & Present*, these statements opened a Marxist-liberal dialogue on historical development in an age of conservative hostility to radicalism of any kind.

The "transition debate," as it came to be known, was revived in the 1970s. Robert Brenner produced two highly influential articles of panache and analytic sweep. His critical approach to what he called neo-Smithian Marxism (a reaction to the demographic determinism of much non-Marxist writing that had worked its way into Marxist orientations) stimulated responses from many quarters, resulting in the publication of a book entitled *The Brenner Debate* (1987), edited by the economic historians T. S. Ashton and C. H. E. Philpin. Ironically enough, Brenner, whose account of feudalism's demise and capitalism's ascent laid stress on the class and property relations of European development, would later explore the mercantile and political side of precapitalist experience in his powerfully detailed *Merchants and Revolution: Commercial Change, Political Conflict, and London's Overseas Traders, 1550–1653* (1993).

When Marxists wrote history, then, it was often the range of their treatment of the past that was notable. However small the canvas, larger issues were never far from view. One highly influential historical event, the French Revolution, was, for much of the twentieth century, understood largely within the framework of Marxist histories. Nineteenth-century socialists, such as Jean Jaurès (1859–1914), had written histories of the economic determina-

tions of this broadly social revolution, outlining how the overthrowing of monarchical despotism and a feudal aristocracy was driven by commercial developments and the coming of capitalist social relations. With Georges Lefebvre's important, often peasant-based studies, among them *The Coming of the French Revolution* (1967) and *The Great Fear of 1789* (1973), social histories of the popular classes began to be written seriously. The urban *menu peuple* found their historian in the Marxist Albert Soboul, whose studies of the Parisian *sans-culottes* developed into a comprehensive two-volume study, *The French Revolution, 1787–1799* (1974). Well into the mid-1980s this Marxist, materialist understanding of the French Revolution as rupture with the feudal past, a bourgeois-democratic struggle that had its plebeian underside, retained interpretive hegemony. It would be displaced only as a late 1980s intellectual assault on Marxism was paralleled by the final toppling of actually existing socialism's Soviet edifice. By the 1990s, the economic interpretation of the French Revolution was often regarded as rather old hat, new analyses looking not to class formations and material developments, but to ideas and symbols and continuities with the *ancien régime*.

U.S. Marxist Writers. In the United States, where capitalism has dominated the history of a national entity most decisively and grown in ways that insure a specific global reach, Marxist histories have always been both marginal and significant. Ironically, but understandably, some of the most incisive writing in the field has been produced by scholars who, later in their careers, came to repudiate much of the Marxist project. Thus, as a young Marxist, Louis M. Hacker wrote an insightful account of capitalism's consolidation that he later, as a more conservative thinker, tried to suppress. Eugene D. Genovese, perhaps American Marxism's most creative historian of slavery, authored a number of major studies—from *The Political Economy of Slavery: Studies in the Economy and Society of the Slave South* (1965) to *Roll, Jordon, Roll: The World the Slaves Made* (1974)—before shifting intellectual and political gears and largely jettisoning his commitment to the left. As in Great Britain, such Communist Party historians as Herbert Aptheker (on slavery) and Philip Foner (on labor) contributed much, but this work never achieved the range, stylistic elegance, or imaginative heights of the British Marxist historians. With the development of New Left histories in the United States in the 1960s, such authors as William Appleman Williams, Gabriel Kolko, Gar Alperovitz, Herbert G. Gutman, Staughton Lynd, James Weinstein, and others adapted Marxism to the study of various topics: U.S. foreign policy; the misunderstood history of the American Revolution; nineteenth-century workers; and early twentieth-century socialism. With the explosive growth of working-class history in the 1970s, such Marxists as David Montgomery worked through the old liberal, institutional economists of the Wisconsin School (headed by labor specialist John R. Commons), but relied on radical understandings of political economy to develop major synthetic statements. The highpoint was two Montgomery publications of the 1980s and 1990s: *The Fall of the House of Labor: The Workplace, the State, and American Labor Activism, 1865–1925* (1987) and *Citizen Worker: The Experience of Workers in the United States with Democracy and the Free Market in the Nineteenth Century* (1993).

Marxism in Stalinist States. Not surprisingly, the ossified social formations of Stalinist states that were supposedly both the sites of socialism and environments in which Marxism should have flourished, produced little in the way of truly influential Marxist histories. Soviet and Chinese historiography in the post-World War II years was largely formulaic. Few of the interpretive breakthroughs and impassioned histories that had characterized British historiography in this period, for instance, were evident in the USSR. On the whole, Marxist historians in the post-revolutionary states produced official "Marxist-Leninist" histories that served well the orthodoxies of various Communist parties. They never quite broke out of rather mechanical modes, although there were always exceptions. Among the most useful products were anthologies of documents, such as a 1956 Soviet book, *An Anthology of Chartist Literature*. In East Germany, Andreas Dorpalen provided a rare analytic sweep across centuries of the central European past in *German History in Marxist Perspective: The East German Approach* (1985).

Marxism in the Late Twentieth Century. Marxist historiography's highwater mark was undoubtedly the third quarter of the twentieth century. Between 1950 and 1975, most of Marxism's greatest contributions emerged in social history, but in subsequent years the ground would be less fertile. As the twentieth century came to a close, Marxism as a guide to historical materialist understandings, economic history as a fruitful point of departure for all historiographic practice, and, indeed, socialism as a reality and a possibility, faced a sustained set of crises. In thought and in deed Marxism was questioned as never before.

No sooner had communism fallen in 1989, however, with Marxism proclaimed dead and history and ideology supposedly at their final, capitalist-dominated end, than Marxist ideas and movements began to reemerge out of the wastelands of Stalinist decay and bourgeois complacency. Increasing economic inequality and its manifold oppressions and destructive violence remain very much in evidence as we enter a twenty-first century in which the material divisions between countries and within nation states loom obviously large. Marxism as an analytic point

of departure will likely inform future studies of histories set in the new, global context of our times. This much has been evident in some of the best radical writing of the 1990s, where such authors as Mike Davis have pioneered new subjects of study, bringing together the economic and the ecological, the first world and the third, in such books as *Ecology of Fear: Los Angeles and the Imagination of Disaster* (1998) and *Late Victorian Holocausts: El Niño Famines and the Making of the Third World* (2000). In this they draw on old traditions and new insights, giving birth to a reinvigorated Marxism, whose histories of the past are always recast in the crises of the present and the potential of the future.

[*See also* Command Economies.]

BIBLIOGRAPHY

Anderson, Perry. *Considerations on Western Marxism*. London, 1976.

Aston, T. H. and C. H. E. Philpin eds. *The Brenner Debate: Agrarian Class Structure and Economic Development in Pre-Industrial Europe*. Cambridge, 1987.

Brenner, Robert. *Merchants and Revolution: Commercial Change, Political Conflict, and London's Overseas Traders, 1550–1653*. Cambridge, 1993.

Comninel, George C. *Rethinking the French Revolution: Marxism and the Revisionist Challenge*. London, 1987.

Davis, Mike. *Ecology of Fear: Los Angeles and the Imagination of Disaster*. New York, 1998.

Davis, Mike. *Late Victorian Holocausts: El Niño Famines and the Making of the Third World*. New York, 2000.

Dobb, Maurice. *Studies in the Development of Capitalism*. New York, 1947.

Dorpalen, Andreas. *German History in Marxist Perspective: The East German Approach*. Detroit, 1985.

Genovese, Eugene D. *The Political Economy of Slavery: Studies in the Economy and Society of the Slave South*. New York, 1965.

Genovese, Eugene D. *Roll, Jordan, Roll: The World the Slaves Made*. New York, 1974.

Hacker, Louis M. *The Triumph of American Capitalism*. New York, 1940.

Hilton, Rodney. *The Transition from Feudalism to Capitalism*. London, 1976.

Hobsbawm, Eric J. *Labouring Men: Studies in the History of Labour*. London, 1964.

Hobsbawm, Eric J. *Workers: Worlds of Labour*. New York, 1984.

Lenin, Vladimir I. *The Development of Capitalism in Russia*. Moscow, 1964 [1899].

Marx, Karl. *Capital*. 3 vols. Chicago, 1906, 1909, 1933 [1867–1884].

Marx, Karl, and Friedrich Engels. *Selected Works*. Moscow, 1968.

Montgomery, David. *The Fall of the House of Labor: The Workplace, the State, and American Labor Activism, 1865–1925*. New York, 1987.

Montgomery, David. *Citizen Worker: The Experience of Workers in the United States with Democracy and the Free Market during the Nineteenth Century*. New York, 1993.

Sassoon, Donald. *One Hundred Years of Socialism: The Western European Left in the Twentieth Century*. New York, 1996.

Thompson, Dorothy. *The Chartists: Popular Politics in the Industrial Revolution*. New York, 1984.

Thompson, Edward Palmer. *The Making of the English Working Class*. London, 1963.

Torr, Dona. *Tom Mann and His Times*, vol. 1, *1856–1890*. London, 1956.

Trotsky, Leon. *The History of the Russian Revolution.* 3 vols. New York, 1932.

Trotsky, Leon. *The Revolution Betrayed: What Is the Soviet Union and Where Is It Going?* New York, 1937.

BRYAN D. PALMER

MASS PRODUCTION. From Charlie Chaplin's *Modern Times* to Diego Rivera's murals of work in automobile plants, mass production is associated with moving assembly lines, monotony at work, the volume production of standardized goods, and life in post–World War II North America. The culmination of nearly a century of technical and social changes, the dawn of the mass-production era can be linked to the introduction of the Model T by Henry Ford in 1908. The origin of the term itself can be traced back to an article written for the *Encyclopaedia Britannica* in 1925 under Henry Ford's signature. Here it was defined as a system of production based on the principles of power, accuracy, economy, system, continuity, and speed. Social scientists have moved away from this narrow view of mass production as a series of technical changes exemplified by the moving assembly line. Today, the term *mass production* is used to describe the interrelated technical, social, and political elements that sustain a unique model of social and economic organization based on the mass consumption of standardized goods.

As a technical system, mass production involved a new model of work organization. The skilled laborer and the general-purpose machines of the first Industrial Revolution gave way to the machine-paced, unskilled worker and sequentially organized special-purpose machinery. Much of the knowledge and skill formerly supplied by skilled workers was transferred to a new class of production managers or embodied in the new machinery itself. One of the hallmarks of mass-production work organization was short job-cycle times, often measured in seconds rather than hours or days. Control over the pace of work was achieved through the use of moving assembly lines, conveyor systems, and machine pacing. In machine departments, mass producers moved away from the functional organization of machines into milling or drilling departments. Aided by the flexibility made possible by the introduction of electric motors, machinery was organized sequentially into product departments, where an entire component could be manufactured. By the 1950s, advances in automation made it possible to link these machines into a continuous flow process, thereby achieving the same level of control in machine departments that the moving assembly line had made possible in assembly areas. Many have pointed to the alienating nature of work in repetitive, machine-paced, mass-production facilities. Few deny the significant increase in the material standard of living that it made possible.

The high fixed costs associated with most mass-production factories and their integrated design made them vulnerable to slowdowns by small groups of workers and amplified the economic penalty associated with relatively small reductions in overall demand for goods. Important social changes that accompanied the new model of work organization helped to minimize these risks. On the shop floor, authority over decisions affecting output were transferred from workers to managers. The new class of managers took for themselves the responsibility for ensuring that operations ran smoothly, for planning production, and for directing the most minute details of how work was to be done. The goal was to create a specialized class of decision makers (managers) and another of instruction takers (workers). While management was never able to completely free itself of the need to rely on workers to interpret and adapt instructions, there was certainly a de-emphasis of labor inputs into shop-floor decision making. The spread of mass production was also associated with a change in consumption patterns. The high level of fixed costs made mass production facilities vulnerable to small reductions in demand. This was minimized by the rise of the "consumer" society able and willing to absorb high volumes of standardized goods. To sustain high and rising levels of consumption, employers needed to pay high and rising real wages. Male workers demanded, and mass producers often granted, the "family wage." Work in many mass-production sectors came to be associated with success and fulfillment of male social responsibilities. This in turn elevated the role of males as breadwinners and created new social norms that encouraged women to be less involved in the paid labor market and more responsible for reproduction.

At the political level, mass production's need for sustained and high levels of demand and stable relations between employers and employees opened the door for new forms of state regulation of the economy and a new interest in trade unions and collective bargaining. At the macro level, Keynesian policies of state-regulated demand management were compatible with the needs of mass producers for sustained demand. At the micro level, unions would help smooth out the demand and supply of goods by encouraging wages to rise in proportion to increases in output. Both state regulation of demand and bolstering labor purchasing power through collective bargaining were compatible with high profits under mass production as long as domestic demand was critical to the success of domestic producers. Equally important, the success of unions in tying wages to productivity gave unions a self interest in stabilizing labor relations, a factor critical to efficient production in integrated plants.

The factors behind the rise of mass production in the United States in the early twentieth century and its overall social impact continue to be debated. Most agree that mass production evolved in the United States in part because the abundance of food and shelter left the middle class with sufficient purchasing power to seed entrepreneurial interest in the volume production of consumer goods. Why satisfying this demand took the particular technical and social form it did is much more contentious. One perspective views mass production as another step in the market-driven evolution of technology toward more cost-effective processes. Here, the early-nineteenth-century craft system of production, a system that involved highly skilled workers producing nonstandardized items in small batches, was gradually transformed through the division of labor and investment in labor-saving machinery into mass production. The emergence of a large class of unskilled workers, the transfer of authority to a new class of managers, and the widespread use of machine pacing were the inevitable outcomes of this economic process. An alternative perspective sees mass production as the result of a social process shaped by employers searching for new ways to exert control over workers and maximize the rate at which purchased labor time was converted into effort and saleable commodities. The division of labor, transfer of authority to management, and machine pacing were the product of a struggle between managers and workers—a struggle that, for the most part, workers lost. Each perspective agrees that mass production resulted in a dramatic lowering of the costs of production and opened up new possibilities for consumption. But those who see mass production as the product of market-driven economic forces are more likely to emphasize the very real increases in material standards of living. Those who see social forces playing a large role are less likely to accept that mass production was the only path society could have taken in making production more efficient. They are also more likely to argue that there are significant social costs associated with mass production, including alienation at work, the standardization of tastes implicit in a mass consumer society, and, increasingly, the environmental costs of high levels of consumption.

Predecessors to Mass Production. Mass production implies more than volume production. It involves a unique way of organizing workplaces and regulating society. The roots of this system can be traced to the first Industrial Revolution and the transfer of production from home to factory. During the nineteenth century, three additional components were added. First, early-nineteenth-century armament producers perfected the techniques of interchangeable production. Second, late-nineteenth-century American meatpackers perfected the first moving assembly lines. Finally, the philosophy of managerial control gained widespread currency with the rise of *Scientific Management* and the writings of Frederick W. Taylor.

These components were brought together by turn-of-the-century American manufacturers of automobiles, electrical goods, and rubber led by Henry Ford from his Highland Park facility in Detroit.

The eighteenth-century shift to factory production gave birth to what is commonly referred to as craft production. Some work was deskilled and productivity levels rose, but the lack of standardization and relatively small batch production ensured labor would have a significant say in how work was done. The transition from craft-based production to mass production was given a significant boost by government and military interest in assembling guns from interchangeable parts. To the military mind, the key advantage of interchangeability was reducing the problems associated with battlefield repair of guns. Eighteenth- and early-nineteenth-century British and French attempts to attain interchangeability met with limited success. They were constrained by the problems associated with machining metals. Technical constraints meant metal was machined and then hardened. Hardening distorted the metal, requiring hand finishing by skilled workers. This resulted in similar, but not identical parts.

The lessons learned by the French in interchangeable production were transported to the United States by Thomas Jefferson, who brought the ideas of Honoré Blanc to the War Department. Fascinated by the potential of the new system of production, the War Department used its considerable resources to subsidize both public and private firms. At the private gun shops of Eli Whitney and Simeon North, and the federal armories at Springfield, Massachusetts, and Harpers Ferry, Virginia, a system of manufacture that came to be known as the American System of Manufactures emerged. Tentative progress was made in achieving interchangeable production by 1813 when the War Department requested Simeon North produce twenty thousand interchangeable guns. Evidence suggests that true interchangeability was only achieved in 1824, when John H. Hall began delivering breechloaders from his Harpers Ferry Armory. Interchangeability was achieved through the use of production to a standard gauge, milling machines, drop forging, and innovative fixtures for presenting material to a machine. The new techniques would soon be taken up by American watch- and clockmakers, sewing-machine and bicycle producers, agricultural equipment manufacturers, and eventually the makers of automobiles. The system received international recognition at the 1851 Crystal Palace Exhibition in London, England.

While the government armories were solving the problem of interchangeable production, it was left to nineteenth-century American meat packers to show how the division of labor and the line pacing of work could result in substantial increases in productivity and lower costs.

MASS PRODUCTION. New cars on an assembly line at the Ford Motor Company plant in Detroit, Michigan, 1949. (*New York World-Telegram* and the *Sun* Newspaper Photograph Collection/Prints and Photographs Division, Library of Congress)

Their contribution had little to do with new mechanical methods. The first meat-packing assembly line was likely introduced in Cincinnati's hog-slaughtering houses in the 1830s and paved the way for a new system of factory butchering. Within a short period of time, the all-around butcher was replaced by a killing gang of more than a hundred workers, each performing a small portion of the butchering task. As Swift and Armour replaced the butcher aristocrat with an army of low-paid common laborers, control over how to cut an animal and how many cuts each worker made per hour was transferred to management. For splitters, one of the few remaining skilled tasks in animal slaughter, the introduction of cutting lines witnessed hourly production more than double between 1884 and 1900. Management journals sang the praise of the new system of production. By bringing the work to the workers, management could ensure a steady flow of effort. Those unable to keep pace would quickly be identified and be forced to confess themselves incompetent for the job. Factory butchering also allowed a dramatic increase in the number of women in meat packing, rising from less than 2 percent of the labor force in Chicago in 1890 to 12.6 percent by 1920. The loss of control over the work pace and

the intensification of work by management pushed workers in the sector to be among the leaders in organizing industry-based trade unions.

The final step on the path to mass production was the codification of the new ethic of managerial control by Frederick Winslow Taylor under the title *Scientific Management*. Taylor argued that the existing organization of work gave workers too much say in how work was done, which allowed labor to restrict the level of output. To Taylor, this resulted in lower profits and a lower standard of living for workers. He searched for a new system of production, where the interests of labor and the interest of capital would be compatible. He sought to move the class-based conflict between employer and employee to one of mutual interest based on maximum production and improved living standards. He wrote:

> The great revolution that takes place in the mental attitude of the two parties under scientific management is that both sides take their eyes off the division of the surplus as the all-important matter, and together turn their attention toward increasing the size of the surplus until this surplus becomes so large that it is unnecessary to quarrel over how it shall be divided. (Taylor, 1947, 29–31)

The basis of this new production philosophy was laid while Taylor worked at Midvale Steel between 1883 and 1889. He conducted detailed studies of work using time-and-motion techniques. This information was systematized and provided to a "neutral" management class who would orchestrate the production process in everyone's best interest. In contrast to the craft system of production, where workers were responsible for key decisions about how work should be done, under the new system management would issue instructions. Labor would follow these instructions without questions. The workers of the day and such organizations as the American Federation of Labor were less than enthusiastic about this change. Workers regularly refused to cooperate with Taylor's time and motion people. In 1911, an attempt to implement the system at Watertown Arsenal resulted in a spontaneous strike and led to a full-scale government investigation of the system. An effective lobby against *Scientific Management* was mounted by labor, and the end result was that the system was banned in government arsenals under the instructions of the new assistant navy secretary, Franklin D. Roosevelt. The ban remained in place until 1949.

Mass Production and Henry Ford. Between 1908 and 1913, Henry Ford brought together the principles of interchangeability, machine pacing, and managerial control in the production of Model T's and launched the era of mass production. In 1908, there was little reason to suspect the world was on the edge of a social, cultural, and economic revolution. Output levels at Ford were still modest, with just over ten thousand vehicles being produced by fewer than a thousand workers. The work force was relatively skilled. Vehicles were still assembled at stationary trestles and engines were produced with general-purpose machines organized functionally rather than sequentially. Within five years, annual output of the Model T increased to nearly a quarter million, employment rose to nearly fifteen thousand workers, and the price of the Model T had fallen from $850 to $440. By 1927, when Model T production stopped, total production reached 15 million.

To meet this demand, Ford was forced to revolutionize the production process. Special-purpose machines, fitted with sophisticated jig-and-fixture systems, were introduced, allowing less-skilled workers to turn out batches of interchangeable parts. These were shipped to the assembly halls where less-skilled labor, working in teams, assembled complete vehicles. The most stunning visual change was in the assembly hall, where in 1913, the long lines of stationary assembly stands were replaced by moving assembly lines. This reduced the need to move material in the plant and, by bringing the work to the worker, rather than the other way around, managerial control of the pace of work was increased.

The system was a technical and economic success. Productivity soared. Ford was soon producing more than a thousand vehicles a day and profit levels leaped from about $1 million per year when the Model T was introduced to more than $25 million within five years. From the perspective of the workers, the new system of production was less compelling. Workers rebelled at the transfer of authority over work to management, the machine pacing, and the intense, mind-numbing nature of work. Daily absenteeism rates topped 10 percent in 1913, and annual turnover was 400 percent. Talk on the shop floor was of joining the Industrial Workers of the World, who were actively organizing local workers. For the system to succeed, Ford would have to reorganize social relations at work. In 1913, the arbitrary powers of foremen were checked and responsibility for hiring and firing was centralized. In perhaps his boldest move, Ford adopted the $5.00 day in January of 1914. Overnight, the average earnings of unskilled workers doubled. While there is some debate about who was entitled to this increase in wages, it is clear that most male workers received the enhanced wage. Women would have to wait some time before they were allowed to share in this bonanza. Ford did not stop here. The pace of work and the mind-numbing nature of work still caused trouble for male workers, who were conditioned to have some say over how work was done. Ford's solution was to reconstruct social norms of masculinity at work. It became manly to work hard and produce useful goods, even if the tasks required minimal discretion. The social engineering pioneered by the Ford sociology department had wide ramifications for American society. Men were paid a "family wage." Women were expected to stay at home and create an environment that ensured men could sustain the daily work regime. There was no place for women in the Ford production system, as this would undermine the myth Ford was creating—that only men could do Ford work, even when his engineers told him otherwise.

Ford's success until the mid-1920s was based on exploiting the economies of scale associated with producing a single utilitarian model in very large numbers. But the Ford formula contained its own contradictions. As he flooded the market with Model T's, it became increasingly difficult to attract new buyers. Each year's vehicle was more or less the same as that of the previous year, and once you purchased a Model T, there was no option of trading up to more luxurious Ford products. The solution to this dilemma was introduced by Alfred Sloan at General Motors in the 1920s. Sloan encouraged GM to produce a full range of vehicles. This would permit consumers to trade up to better cars as their economic position improved. Equally important, Sloan encouraged GM to make changes to their vehicles each year. In this way, older vehicles would become undesirable, even though they remained perfectly functional. These devices for creating demand for new vehicles soon propelled GM into the number-one position in U.S. vehicle production.

The success of mass producers in auto and in other sectors, such as electrical goods, steel, food, and clothing, was linked to the development of bureaucratic, decentralized, and impersonal corporate organizations. While Ford lagged in this regard, General Motors and Chrysler perfected the multidivision bureaucratic form of corporate organization. These new forms of corporate governance also paved the way for exploiting economies of scope, that is, the joint production or distribution of different goods within the same organization. As a result, most successful mass producers moved to become multiproduct, multinational organizations. From their offices in New York, such entrepreneurs as Chrysler managed a global organization.

The changes associated with mass production also encouraged workers to look toward new forms of collective bargaining and industrial trade unions. The formation of unions was facilitated by having a large number of workers in an establishment, most doing relatively similar work and hence having relatively similar interests. Labor's pre-1920 flirtation with unions amounted to little, and collective bargaining would emerge only with the easing of the Great Depression in the mid-1930s. By then, a new set of American labor laws sympathetic to collective bargaining had been passed, allowing unions, such as the United Automobile Workers (UAW), United Steelworkers of America (USWA), and United Electrical, Radio, and Machine Workers of America (UE) to become forces on behalf of labor. Ford had argued in 1914 that raising worker wages would help him sell cars. The same sort of logic may have

MASS PRODUCTION. Partially assembled imported cars, Oakland, California, 1985. (© George Hall/ Woodfin Camp and Associates, New York)

encouraged U.S. lawmakers to pass the Wagner Act in 1935, an act that brought collective bargaining to many workers for the first time. While the effectiveness of "efficiency wages" in raising productivity is still a matter of debate, there is little doubt that first Ford and later the UAW pushed labor markets, at least temporarily, away from the principle that the best wage was the lowest wage.

At first, the newly emerging industrial unions wanted to improve the standard of living and to regain for labor some of the control over shop-floor decision making that they had lost under mass production. Unions were more successful with the former than the latter. In a historic trade-off, unions accepted the new shop-floor power structure implicit in mass production methods in return for an improved and rising real wage. Perhaps the most famous agreement of this sort was the one hammered out by Walter Reuther and the UAW with General Motors in 1950. Reuther backed off from his demands that labor be given a greater say in "management" decisions, such as product pricing, design, and work organization. In return, GM agreed to the twin pillars of auto-sector agreements for the next forty years. A cost-of-living clause (COLA) gave workers some protection from inflation, and the annual improvement factor (AIF) provided labor with a share of productivity gains. This system brought relative peace to the auto industry and provided the model for agreements in other sectors. It created the social conditions within plants for continued productivity improvements and provided

sufficient income to ensure workers could buy the goods they were producing.

The success of mass production in the United States encouraged other sectors and other countries to adopt similar systems of production. While it was relatively easy to adopt the technical components of the new system (in fact, Ford encouraged other employers to observe what he had achieved at Highland Park), it was more difficult to implement the complementary social system critical to mass production's success. In many of the European economies that attempted the transition, the overall lack of effective demand for consumer goods, in part the result of the absence of a large middle class, and weaknesses in corporate structure and managerial skills made the system unstable. For instance, in the Soviet Union, Stalin became a big fan of the methods employed by Ford, but in the absence of a true mass market for consumer goods, and the rampant consumerism that was emerging in the United States in the post-1945 period, the system failed to lift the average standard of living of Soviet citizens to anything comparable to that enjoyed in the United States. In Britain, mergers of existing firms with the objective of creating the foundation for mass production often failed as the old owners were reluctant to hand over control of the firms to a new central management group. As important, management expressed concern that labor would not accept the regimented model of work developed by Ford and Taylor and hence remained wedded to a nineteenth-century organizational model, which demanded that wages be kept to a minimum to maintain profitability. Rather than direct control of labor through machine pacing, British automobile makers preferred incentive wages as a way of converting labor time into effort. This stunted the growth of a professional class of British managers. When capital labor ratios began to rise with the spread of automation in the 1950s and 1960s, British firms were reluctant to make the new investments in capital, fearing labor would not sustain a work pace to make the new technology profitable. Where investments were made, British managers proved themselves unable to manage the increasingly complex processes, having relied on a form of labor self-management during the incentive payment era.

The heyday of mass production was the twenty-five-year period following the end of World War II. In both Europe and North America, productivity was rising, unions were growing, wage increases were keeping pace with productivity improvements, there was a balance between consumption and demand, and corporate profits remained healthy. By the late 1970s, contradictions were beginning to emerge in the system. As global trade increased, national economies found it more difficult to manage demand in a way that ensured their mass-production plants operated at full capacity. As employers looked increasingly to offshore markets, the need to control production costs became more critical. Employers became less sympathetic to working with unions as a way of achieving stability in labor relations and even more aggressive than normal in holding wages in check. They made greater use of contracting out to low-wage nonunion firms and to suppliers from less-developed areas to avoid the high wages industrial unions had won for their members. They also resisted paying the taxes needed to fund Keynesian social welfare programs, which helped sustain domestic demand but made international competition more difficult. Of equal concern, Japanese firms were flooding markets in North America and Europe with well-designed and low-cost products. By the late 1980s, the success of the Japanese was being attributed to their moving away from the shop-floor authority structure employed by Ford and other mass producers under which management was responsible for giving orders and labor for simply implementing them. It was claimed that the Japanese producers, in what came to be know as Lean Production, had found a new formula that gave workers more say in designing their jobs and how work should be done. While most of the claims put forward by students of this new system have proven to be exaggerated, it is true that both labor and management in mass-production firms are rethinking the deal enshrined in the Treaty of Detroit, which ceded control over shop-floor decisions almost exclusively to management.

[See also Domestic Industry and Factory System.]

BIBLIOGRAPHY

Barrett, James R. *Work and Community in the Jungle: Chicago's Packinghouse Workers, 1894–1922*. Chicago, 1987.
Braverman, Harry. *Labor and Monopoly Capital: The Degradation of Work in the Twentieth Century*. New York, 1974.
Ford, Henry. "Mass Production." In *Encyclopaedia Britannica*, 23d ed., suppl. vol. 2 (1926), 821–823.
Hounshell, David. *From the American System to Mass Production 1800–1932*. Baltimore, 1984.
Lewchuk, Wayne. *American Technology and the British Vehicle Industry*. Cambridge, 1987.
Lewchuk, Wayne. "Men and Monotony: Fraternalism at the Ford Motor Company." *Journal of Economic History* 53.4 (1993), 824–857.
Meyer, Stephen, III. *The Five Dollar Day: Labor Management and Social Control in the Ford Motor Company, 1908–1921*. Albany, N.Y., 1981.
Nelson, Daniel. *Managers and Workers: Origins of the New Factory System in the United States, 1880–1920*. Madison, Wis., 1975.
Schatz, Ronald W. *The Electrical Workers: A History of Labor at General Electric and Westinghouse, 1923–60*. Urbana, 1983.
Smith, Merritt Roe. *Harpers Ferry Armory and the New Technology: The Challenge of Change*. Ithaca, N.Y., 1977.
Shiomi, H., and K. Wada. *Fordism Transformed: The Development of Production Methods in the Automobile Industry*. Oxford, 1995.
Taylor, Frederick W. *Scientific Management*. New York, 1947.

WAYNE LEWCHUK

MAURITANIA. *See* North Africa.

MAURITIUS. *See* East Africa.

McCORMICK, CYRUS (15 February 1809–13 May 1884), inventor and manufacturer.

McCormick was born on Walnut Grove farm in Rockbridge County, Virginia. He received only limited formal education, but his father, Robert, had long sought to invent new farm machinery, particularly a grain reaper, an effort to which he devoted twenty years. Cyrus soon proved mechanically adept, and in 1831 he invented and patented a hillside plow. That same year, he picked up on his father's goal of developing a reaper, approaching the challenge with a new design. In July, McCormick gave a public demonstration of an improved version.

In 1832, McCormick improved his design in several ways and exhibited the reaper on several farms around Lexington, Virginia, exhibitions that earned him his first significant media attention, including notice in several New York newspapers. In 1834, learning of the reaper Obed Hussey had invented the previous year, McCormick patented his design and warned Hussey of his claim to priority. Despite the apparent success of his reaper, McCormick spent time on other inventions, for example, perfecting and patenting a self-sharpening horizontal plow in 1833, and making iron. The panic of 1837 put his Cotopaxi ironworks into bankruptcy and left him and his father deeply in debt. He now turned his full attention to making and marketing the reaper. After trying both to manufacture it himself and to sell territorial rights to other manufacturers, McCormick had two critical insights. First, he understood that to ensure product quality and appropriate support, he had to concentrate all production under his direct control. Second, he recognized that the future marketing for grain harvesting equipment lay in the developing lands to the west, and thus resolved in 1847 to move his company to Chicago, where he soon built a factory on the north bank of the Chicago River. He then persuaded his brother Leander McCormick (8 February 1819–20 February 1900) to come to Chicago to manage the factory, a responsibility he would keep for thirty-one years. Leander had helped manufacture reapers years earlier in Virginia and had himself contributed the design for a movable seat for the driver (who had previously ridden one of the draft horses). Cyrus then recruited Leander in 1847 to go to Cincinnati to superintend construction of McCormick reapers at the A. C. Brown foundry.

Cyrus McCormick recognized the challenge of persuading farmers to buy his expensive and unproven machine, so he participated aggressively in competitions that local and state agricultural societies hosted, regularly staged exhibitions, offered a unique performance warranty to purchasers of his reaper—it would bring in more of the crop than a scythe and cradle—and sold the machines on credit, with payments made annually over two to four years. In addition to this shrewd marketing, McCormick continued to improve the machine design during the 1850s, and his firm was clearly dominant before 1860. During the Civil War, however, the McCormick Company saw a rapid decline in its market share (though not in total sales), reducing the firm essentially to a regional company with significant sales in only four Upper Midwest states. Cyrus himself spent most of the war years in Europe, leaving Leander to manage the company. With peace, Cyrus returned not to Chicago, but to New York, while Leander continued at the company headquarters in Chicago.

When the Great Chicago Fire destroyed the McCormick factory in 1871, it is uncertain whether Cyrus would have chosen to rebuild the firm. He had not only been disengaged from active management of the company for nearly a decade, but had amassed a vast fortune, of which the harvesting machine company represented perhaps only a quarter. But Nancy Fowler McCormick (8 February 1835–5 July 1923), whom he had married in 1858, went to the smoldering ruins of the factory and ordered the workers to begin rebuilding. For the next forty years, Nettie (as she preferred to be called) played a central role in the management of the McCormick Harvesting Machine Company (and later of the International Harvester Company): no major decision was made without her active involvement.

More critically, following reconstruction after the fire, she pushed for both improved machine design and a better management structure. During the 1870s, the McCormick Harvesting Machine Company restructured its marketing organization, aggressively acquired patent rights from others, and hired skilled mechanics to develop its own improvements. As a result, it soon surpassed its rivals in marketing and quickly closed in on them in product design. At the end of the decade, Cyrus Hall McCormick Jr. (16 May 1859–2 June 1936) joined the company management and quickly emerged as a highly effective business leader. But his arrival quickly brought to a head a long-simmering dispute between Leander, with his son Hall, and Cyrus McCormick Sr. As a result, Leander and Hall were soon ejected from the company.

During the 1880s, the McCormick Company, building on a sophisticated marketing organization, quality design, and aggressive selling, emerged as the dominant manufacturer of grain harvesting equipment. Before Cyrus's death in 1884, the company had also initiated foreign sales, and during the 1890s would build a large export trade, largely to Europe. By 1902, when McCormick merged with four other companies to form International Harvester, it held about 45 percent of the world market in harvesting equipment.

BIBLIOGRAPHY
The State Historical Society of Wisconsin has an enormous collection of McCormick family and business records, which contain much original correspondence from, to, and about the McCormicks and companies with which they were involved. William T. Hutchinson's massive volume two of *Cyrus Hall McCormick* (1935; reprinted 1968) offers the most comprehensive information about Cyrus Sr.'s youth and early business career. Cyrus's son, Cyrus McCormick, wrote *The Century of the Reaper* (1931), an admiring history of the McCormick Company, International Harvester, and his father. Additional material on Cyrus Sr. is available in Stella V. Roderick, *Nettie Fowler McCormick* (1956), and Gilbert A. Harrison, *A Timeless Affair: The Life of Anita McCormick Blaine* (1979). In addition, see Fred V. Carstensen, *American Enterprise in Foreign Markets* (1984), and "'. . . a dishonest man is at least prudent.' George W. Perkins and the International Harvester Steel Properties," *Business and Economic History* 9 (1981), 87–102, for a business history of McCormick/International Harvester to 1914 and the tensions arising from the merger in 1902.

FRED CARSTENSEN

MEADOWS AND WATER MEADOWS. Since late prehistoric times, meadows (prepared grasslands) have been a feature of European agriculture. Their primary function is to provide hay (dried grasses), the most important winter fodder for herd animals until the widespread adoption of turnips in the eighteenth century. Meadows are in theory different from pastures, which were natural grasslands directly grazed by livestock, a distinction reflected in most European languages: Latin *pratum* and *pascum*, French *pré* and *prairie*, German *Weise* and *Weide*. In practice, meadows were often grazed for parts of the year. In lowland regions, they were normally located in valley floors, beside streams and rivers, where moist conditions ensured good grass growth during the dry summer months. In upland regions, they were generally more widely distributed, so the line between permanent meadows and pastures was often blurred.

Strictly speaking, water meadows are those in which the growth of grass has been enhanced by hydrological management, either by controlled flooding or by "floating"—covering the grass with a moving film of water. The latter practice took two main forms. In bedwork systems, a leat (an open sluiceway) took water from a river and fed it into channels made along the tops of broad, parallel ridges. The water flowed smoothly down the sides of the channels and into drains, which returned it to the river. Simpler were catchworks, used in more undulating terrain; channels cut along the contours of a valley's sides were fed from a leat taken off the river at a high level or from nearby springs. With this gravity feed, the water flowed down the natural slope of the valley sides. Floating was a widespread practice in southern and southwestern England from the seventeenth century to the nineteenth. During the winter months, irrigation raised the ground temperature by providing an insulating blanket of water that stimulated an early growth of grass, thereby providing an "early bite"; in fact, the meadows functioned as early pasture. After the flocks had been moved to summer pastures, irrigation was recommenced, and substantial crops of hay were taken in June or July. Moist land made for good grass growth, and irrigation may have fertilized the soil with suspended nutrients.

In the north and east of England, floating was less widely practiced, largely because cold late frosts prevented successful early forcing of grass. Where it was undertaken, it was often only to enhance the summer hay crop, as was also the case in parts of Scandinavia, Poland, and the Balkans. Irrigation to extend the growing season, as described for southern England, was more a feature of regions on the Atlantic seaboard, such as Portugal and Spain. The origins of meadow irrigation are unclear. In some European upland regions, notably Switzerland, it was carried out in medieval times. Elsewhere, as in Scandinavia, it seems to have been an eighteenth- or nineteenth-century innovation. In England, floating is often said to have been invented by the Herefordshire landowner Rowland Vaughan, who published a book on the subject in 1610, but it is referred to even earlier, so it may have had medieval origins. In all districts, the practice of meadow irrigation declined steadily during the twentieth century, and today it only survives in limited areas.

[*See also* Open-Field System.]

BIBLIOGRAPHY

Bettey, J. H. "The Development of Water Meadows in Dorset during the Seventeenth Century." *Agricultural History Review* 25 (1977), 37–43.

Bettey, J. H. "The Development of Water Meadows in the Southern Counties." In *Water Management in the English Landscape: Field, Marsh, and Meadow*, edited by H. Cook and T. Williamson, pp. 179–195. Edinburgh, 1999.

Bowie, G. S. "Watermeadows in Wessex: A Re-Evaluation for the Period 1640–1850." *Agricultural History Review* 35 (1987), 151–158.

Cutting, R., and I. Cummings. "Watermeadows: Their Form, Operation, and Plant Ecology." In *Water Management in the English Landscape: Field, Marsh, and Meadow*, edited by H. Cook and T. Williamson, pp. 157–178. Edinburgh, 1999.

Emanuelsson, U., and J. Moller. "Flooding in Scania: A Method to Overcome the Deficiency of Nutrients in Agriculture in the Nineteenth Century." *Agricultural History Review* 38 (1990), 136.

Rackham, O. *The History of the Countryside*. London, 1986.

Wade Martins, S., and T. Williamson. "Floated Water-Meadows in Norfolk: A Misplaced Innovation." *Agricultural History Review* 42 (1994), 20–37.

TOM WILLIAMSON

MEATPACKING INDUSTRY. Meatpacking has been a ubiquitous activity worldwide. Its origins lay in butchering animals, especially cattle, hogs (pigs), and sheep. Butchering in rural areas developed into slaughtering and processing, either to preserve meat for domestic consumption or to send it to local markets. The majority of this packed meat was salted pork. Urban butchers initially killed animals driven from farms, and sold the majority of the edible carcass quickly before it spoiled. Small urban abattoirs or slaughterhouses also bought farm animals and transformed them into meat for sale primarily to city dwellers. Such mercantile behavior dominated the meat trade into the nineteenth century.

In those countries where supply and heavy demand were geographically separate, meatpacking matured from a small-scale, part-time activity or butcher firms into specialized operations using a disassembly line of sorts. The United States led the way. As the nation expanded across the fertile Midwest in the nineteenth century, increased urban demand for meat, both within that region and in the East, stimulated the growth of a seasonal, winter industry. Business was widely dispersed along waterways, which provided transport to markets. The growth of railroads in the 1850s changed the shape and the structure of the industry. The advantages of good rail connections, both for receiving livestock and for dispatching meat products, encouraged concentration of the industry, primarily in Chicago but also in other large cities such as Saint Louis and Milwaukee. The closure of the Mississippi River during the Civil War confirmed the dominance of rail transport and accelerated the emergence of manufacturers from the multitude of merchants.

The manufacturers took advantage of compact markets, especially those markets that initially served the Union Army, and they developed large and centralized stockyards in major cities. Simultaneously, improved technology, particularly in ice packing, and an increase of integrated packing plants favored those with capital. By 1880 the use of the refrigerated railcar facilitated the chilled beef trade and laid the foundations of the giant meatpacking industry. Internal administrative reforms and changes in marketing and distribution consolidated the big-business presence. American meatpacking became oligopolistic. The big four—Swift, Armour, Morris, and Hammond—retained their dominance into the twentieth century. In Canada, similar patterns emerged some thirty years later with the establishment of stockyards, packing plants, and oligopoly.

Labor relations and working conditions were poor, and meat products were dubious. In the reforming ethos of the Progressive years, exposés alerted the reading public and the government to major problems. Upton Sinclair's muckraking attack on the Chicago meatpacking industry, *The Jungle* (1906), made a huge impact. Though the reliability of this tract has been contested, enough powerful people read it, and it was corroborated by sufficient testimony, to ensure that regulatory legislation was passed. The Food and Drug Act of 1906 banned from interstate commerce any adulterated or mislabeled food, including drugs. The Meat Inspection Act of the same year extended and strengthened earlier requirements, but this legislation did not greatly improve the quality of meat products and did not address industrial relations.

The big packers were annoyed by the legislation, but they were more disturbed by government intervention. Their collusion over prices and territory had long been recognized, and they already had formalized arrangements through the National Packing Company (1903), more popularly referred to as "the greatest trust in the world." The federal government decided to take further action. It wanted more competition among packers and made several attempts to break up the oligopoly or what it considered was a monopoly to control meat products, livestock flows, and the production of nonmeat food products. Following the Federal Trade Commission (FTC) investigation from 1917 to 1919, the Consent Decree of 1920 formally dissolved the trust and restricted the packers' business to meat processing and distribution.

The decree, however, had little impact on the structure of the industry. Though the Packers and Stockyards Act (1921) established a federal agency to establish acceptable trade practices, packers contested the basis of the decree. The ensuing legal uncertainty meant that compliance was not obtained until 1932. Even then the Packers and Stockyards Administration rarely interfered with the packers'

dominance of the meat trade. The government was more interested in preventing monopoly in food processing and distribution than in breaking up oligopoly in the meat industry. Big business remained dominant and relatively untroubled. Nevertheless packers challenged the decree again in 1956. By then conditions in the meat industry had changed notably. The advent of road haulage and improvements to highways enabled packers and livestock producers to stop relying on railroads for shipping and on stockyards at rail terminals for markets. The geography of the industry became more flexible as truck shipments of fresh and processed refrigerated meat in smaller quantities stimulated the rise of independent packing plants near the source of materials rather than centralized in large cities. Packers also had less use for branch houses as they supplied their products directly to chain stores, supermarkets, restaurants, and hotels rather than relying on sales to smaller meat markets and local butchers or retail stores. The rise of these new wholesale and retail outlets also suggested that meat packers would be unable to dominate, let alone monopolize, food products. The government, however, remained unconvinced. The U.S. Supreme Court ruled that the threat of the monopoly in the food industry remained.

Conditions of labor in meatpacking historically were bad because of unsafe and insanitary conditions, seasonal work, and low wages. The broad-based trade union, the Knights of Labor, struggled to organize packinghouse workers in the 1880s. There were some strikes in the 1890s, but manufacturers defeated any resistance by using nonunion labor, troops, and industrial spies. As much work was unskilled, employers easily hired recent immigrants and African Americans as less troublesome employees than unionized workers. Skilled unions represented by the American Federation of Labor made little headway in organizing packinghouse workers. There were few improvements either on the shop floor or in real wages.

Some gains were made during World War I, but not until the growth of industrial unionism in the 1930s did packinghouse workers make significant breakthroughs in collective bargaining. In the early days of the New Deal, the Amalgamated Meat Cutters and Butcher Workmen of North America (AMCBW) worked with the federal government to improve conditions. The new Packing House Workers Organization Council (PWOC, 1937–1943), later the United Packinghouse Workers of America (UPWA, 1943–1968), sponsored by the Congress of Industrial Organization (CIO) and willing to use the strike as a bargaining tool, made additional progress. The two unions, aided by court decisions, gained ground during World War II, and established collective bargaining throughout the industry. Despite postwar employer and community

MEATPACKING. Stockyards, Kansas City, Missouri, 1909. (W. H. Jones/Prints and Photographs Division, Library of Congress)

resistance, unionism grew, and workers strengthened their position, securing slower production rates, higher wages, and less management control. Remarkably, UPWA was able to overcome ethnic and racial tensions. In the 1950s and 1960s, workers in both the United States and Canada were able to enjoy a relatively comfortable blue-collar existence.

Neither packinghouse workers nor the then big four American packers (Swift, Armour, Cudahy, and Wilson), nor the big three Canadian packers (Canada Packers, Burns and Company, and Swift Canadian) retained their midcentury position. New technological and organizational changes promoted further dispersion of and disruption within the industry. By the early 1970s, the major corporations were moving their operations out of the cities to new, larger-capacity plants in the rural Midwest in order to benefit from cheaper labor and proximity to supplies. Already, however, IBP (formerly Iowa Beef Packers) had pioneered new-style, cost-cutting developments. Its Dennison, Iowa, plant, located in a major cattle-raising area, had reduced the costs of transporting livestock, eliminated the middleman by buying directly from farmers, and assisted the speedup of the disassembly line with its single-story building. Its Dakota City, Nebraska, plant had introduced vacuum-packed boxed beef, which suited the retail trade and also lowered transportation costs. A move into pork packing greatly extended its product range. By the 1980s, a new-style "Super Three"—IBP, ConAgra, and Cargill—had displaced older firms such as Armour, Swift, and Oscar Meyer, and dominated beef slaughter in the United States. The American giants also moved north of the border to rationalize Canadian beef plants. Diversification into other convenience-food prod-

ucts became part of the companies' strategy of efficiency and worldwide sales.

Local and state governments in the Midwest welcomed this rural industrialization of meat and food processing because they wanted to halt rural poverty and population decline. The federal government did not intervene in the growing concentration within the meat industry because the business climate of the 1980s favored deregulation. Rural communities, however, found that higher employment in packing plants did not generate wealth. Increased automation had further deskilled work, which continued to be low-paid. Labor remained physically demanding and hazardous, and turnover rates were very high. Companies thus recruited new workers from minorities, new immigrants, and refugees, and increasingly from women. Tensions then developed between old and new residents and workers, and pressure on housing, education, health, and welfare resources grew. Companies may well have increased their profits, but the social costs faced by workers and communities stimulated another generation of muckraking exposés of the new industrial capitalism.

Other countries with less abundant agricultural lands did not witness the North American centralization of the meat industry in the nineteenth and early twentieth centuries. Their urban centers retained a closer relationship between the slaughter of animals and the consumption of meat. More recently, efforts to globalize meat production look tempting in terms of raising living standards through the consumption of animal protein. However, the wider legacy of *The Jungle* remains, given the suspicious practices of livestock raisers, the bland standard taste of products, and the less than adequate conditions of labor in producing meat.

BIBLIOGRAPHY

Aduddell, Robert M., and Louis P. Cain. "Public Policy toward 'The Greatest Trust in the World.'" *Business History Review* 55.2 (1981), 217–242.

Aduddell, Robert M., and Louis P. Cain. "The Consent Decree in the Meatpacking Industry, 1920–1956." *Business History Review* 55.3 (1981), 359–378.

Clemen, Rudolf A. *The American Livestock and Meat Industry*. New York, 1923.

Fink, Deborah. *Cutting into the Meatpacking Line: Workers and Change in the Rural Midwest*. Chapel Hill, N.C., 1998.

Halpern, Rick. *Down on the Killing Floor: Black and White Workers in Chicago's Packinghouses, 1904–1954*. Urbana, 1997.

Horowitz, Roger. "*Negro and White, Unite and Fight!": A Social History of Industrial Unionism in Meatpacking, 1930–1990*. Urbana, 1997.

MacLachlan, Ian. *Kill and Chill: Restructuring Canada's Beef Commodity Chain*. Toronto, 2001.

Perren, Richard. *The Meat Trade in Britain, 1840–1914*. London, 1978.

Skaggs, Jimmy M. *Prime Cut: Livestock Raising and Meatpacking in the United States, 1607–1983*. College Station, Tex., 1986.

Stull, Donald T., Michael J. Broadway, and David Griffith, eds. *Any Way You Cut It: Meat Processing and Small Town America*. Lawrence, Kans., 1995.

Walsh, Margaret. *The Rise of the Meatwestern Meat Packing Industry*. Lexington, Ky., 1982.

Yeager, Mary. *Competition and Regulation: The Development of Oligopoly in the Meat Packing Industry*. Greenwich, Conn., 1981.

MARGARET WALSH

MEDICI BANK. The term *bank* inadequately describes the vast range of activities in which this Florentine company was involved. The Medici's nearest modern counterparts are the Japanese zaibatsu holding companies that combined financing, industrial, and mercantile interests in large conglomerate organizations. Like most of the large companies of medieval and Renaissance Italy, the Medici housed an important banking unit (*tavola*); but it also bought and sold merchandise of all kinds, manufactured woolen and silk textiles, chartered ships, sold marine insurance, monopolized the distribution of alum for a time, and eventually operated alum and iron mines. Simply called the Medici Company by contemporaries, it is described as such here.

The participation of the Medici family in Florentine business dates back to the thirteenth century, albeit on a modest scale, as merchants and moneychangers. Of the many Medici households engaged in business, the one headed by Giovanni di Bicci de' Medici founded the great Medici Company, when in 1397 Giovanni moved the headquarters of his lucrative papal banking business from Rome to Florence. By the time of his death (1429), that flourishing company had opened branches in Geneva as well as several Italian cities. Giovanni's son Cosimo, deeply involved in politics, was unable to take charge of the enterprise until his return to Florence from exile, in 1435. A superb businessman, Cosimo, while continuing his preoccupation with affairs of state, built the company into the largest of its time, with branches in the leading commercial centers of Europe. As his death (1464), the Medici Company had reaped the benefits of nearly seven decades of first-rate leadership and had built an organization powerful enough to coast for a further thirty years on the less attentive management of Piero (died 1469) and Lorenzo il Magnifico (died 1492). The final collapse of the company occurred in 1494, when the family was expelled from Florence after the city was overwhelmed by invading French troops.

The Medici Company's longevity owed much to a well-conceived corporate structure and tightly disciplined

MEDICI PALACE. Façade of the Palazzo Medici-Riccardi, Florence. Commissioned by Cosimo de' Medici, the palace was designed by Michelozzo di Bartolommeo (1396–1472) and built in the mid-1400s. (Alinari/Art Resource, NY)

management. Like most other Florentine businesses of the period, the Medici Company was in reality a multiple partnership of unlimited liability, since the joint-stock company had not yet been conceived as a legal entity. Shares in the partnership were allocated according to each partner's investment although distribution of profit often reflected extra effort or talent contributed by certain partners. In its early years, the senior partners of the Medici Company held a majority interest in each of the branch operations, with branch managers having minority shareholdings. This structure contrasted with that of the fourteenth-century Bardi and Peruzzi super-companies, which wholly owned all their branches. The company formed by Cosimo de' Medici in 1435 added a further distinction. Cosimo and his brother, together with his general manager, Giovanni Benci, and Antonio Salutati, formed the Medici Company as an overarching equivalent to a modern holding company. Each of the branches became established as a subsidiary partnership, with the main company the majority shareholder and with branch managers and occasionally assistant managers as minority partners. The arrangement gave the branch managers an incentive to drive their

businesses forward while keeping policy and procedures firmly under the control of General Manager Benci in the head office and insulating the holding company from any deleterious actions of the local managers.

The decentralized branch structure with a centralized administration worked well under the dedicated leadership of Benci and Cosimo de' Medici. They imposed carefully considered financial and accounting controls, employing a sophisticated double-entry system that included a variety of modern-looking approaches for apportioning income and expense. They also required a regular presentation of financial statements (annually for branches within Italy and biennially for those outside the peninsula), which included a close cross-examination of the branch managers. When Benci died in 1455, the holding company was dissolved, but the decentralized structure remained intact in the pre-1435 form.

Although the Medici Company did not attain the size and the reach of the fourteenth-century super-companies, it was easily the largest and most diversified among its contemporaries, with branches in the papacy and all of the major commercial centers of Europe. The branch network enabled the company to enhance the political influence of its owners by making itself useful to the secular and ecclesiastical aristocracy in a variety of ways. Such services extended even to unearthing classical manuscripts and recruiting soprano choir boys. On a more mundane level, local branches conducted and financed trade and became bankers to local governments and their leaders. The Medici never dominated banking in these cities, but no other company of its time was so widely extended abroad, so influential, or so important as financiers of the church as the Medici was.

The banking arm of the Medici Company was powerful, efficient, and up-to-date in its application of banking techniques. However, it was in no sense an innovator. Deposit banking had long been practiced in medieval Europe, and the use of fractional reserves was severely limited by harsh laws and bitter experience (including the Medici's own experience of relending depositors' funds in Milan). The giro system still in use in Europe today is regarded as a Venetian invention. The bills of exchange arranged by the Medici would have been easily recognizable by Peruzzi Company employees of the early fourteenth century. Creating credit by discounting such bills did not occur until the early sixteenth century in the Low Countries.

In sum, modern-day banking practice owes little to the Medici Company. Its historical significance lies mainly in the uses to which the wealth it generated was put—the pursuit of political power and the acquisition of magnificent works of art by its two most famous leaders, Cosimo and Lorenzo. But the humdrum should not be overlooked; the survival of its meticulous record-keeping has enabled scholars to grasp the workings of a great multinational business five hundred years after its demise.

[*See also* Banking, *subentry on* Middle Ages and Early Modern Period; Low Countries; *and* Zaibatsu.]

BIBLIOGRAPHY

Goldthwaite, Richard A. "Local Banking in Renaissance Florence." *Journal of European Economic History* 14 (1985), 5–55. Reprinted in *Banks, Palaces, and Entrepreneurs in Renaissance Florence.* Brookfield, Vt., 1995. An analysis of the local banking scene in which the Medici operated.

Goldthwaite, Richard A. "The Medici Bank and the World of Florentine Capitalism." *Past and Present* 114 (1987), 3–31. Reprinted in *Banks, Palaces, and Entrepreneurs in Renaissance Florence.* Brookfield, Vt., 1995. An elegant article that includes a brief history of the company and presents interesting ideas on the nature of business and capital formation in Renaissance Florence.

Hunt, Edwin S., and James M. Murray. *A History of Business in Medieval Europe, 1200–1550.* Cambridge, 1999. A work touching on various aspects of the Medici and other companies in the context of evolving business in medieval Europe.

Roover, Raymond de. *The Rise and Decline of the Medici Bank, 1397–1494.* New York, 1966. A magisterial work that lucidly depicts every aspect of the company's history. Despite a few arguments now open to question, it is a must-read for anyone interested in the business and economic history of medieval and Renaissance Europe.

EDWIN S. HUNT

MEDITERRANEAN SEA AND ISLANDS. The economic history of the Mediterranean may be approached as the economic history of the lands surrounding it; as the history of its shores and of the territories it contains, islands large and small; or as the history of movement back and forth across the sea, that is, migrations, trade, and religious influences that also helped shape the economy. Here the emphasis will be on the movements across the sea, particularly commercial exchanges and the transfer of technology.

The historiography of the Mediterranean has long been dominated by the classic work of Fernand Braudel (1973), which brings together an understanding of the geographical features of the lands surrounding the Mediterranean (notably the contrast between plains and mountains) and explains the history of the sea, especially in the late sixteenth century, in the light of long-term features that barely change over time but that mold the political and economic development of the surrounding lands. Braudel's is a history "in which all change is slow, a history of constant repetition, ever-recurring cycles." This is not to say that mankind has been kind to the lands bordering the sea.

Ecological change (generally negative) is attributed to the human beings who have sawn wood for ships or sown grain for crops without thought for the longer-term consequences. More recent writers, in particular Peregrine Horden and Nicolas Purcell (2000), have emphasized instead the intense localism of Mediterranean societies and the equally intense need to exchange the specialized produce (natural or processed) of the many microcosmic societies around the Mediterranean. For them these "connectivities" did the most to mold a great panoply of different Mediterranean economies and societies in antiquity and during the Middle Ages.

Seen from this perspective, the fundamental geographical feature of the Mediterranean is the enormous complexity of the region, including jagged coasts and islands scattered across the sea (so sailors are rarely, in good weather, out of sight of land), many of them tiny islands forced to exchange goods across the sea for the population to have any hope of surviving. It is a sea with marshy coastlands, such as the Valencian *horta* famous for its rice. Yet plains and mountains are dramatically juxtaposed, feeding off one another, especially in the regular transhumance of sheep from lowlands to highlands. Human interference does less to alter the environment than is generally supposed, for as Oliver Rackham (2001) has argued, the region has an ability to recover from apparent human overexploitation.

From a more conventional angle, the importance of the Mediterranean lies in the meeting on its shores of different continents, empires, peoples, cultures, and religions. The earliest civilizations on the European flank, those of Crete and Mycenae, were heavily indebted to their neighbors across the sea in Hittite Asia Minor and pharaonic Egypt. Cyprus served as a bridge between Mycenaean and Canaanite cultures, which reached further west when the Phoenicians established trade ties to Etruscan navigators in the ninth century BCE. Rome acquired its knowledge of Greek culture after the conquest not just of Greece but of the Hellenistic world, including Syria and Egypt. The Mediterranean is the meeting place of Christianity, Judaism, and Islam; of the western Roman Empire, Byzantium, and various Islamic empires (Umayyads, Fatimids, Mamluks, and Ottomans); and of Germanic invaders, Greeks, Arabs, Jews, and Berbers. Commercial exchanges have generally continued despite the hostility between polities. Early medieval Jewish merchants could move with greater freedom than Christians or Muslims between the different religious spheres (a feature later replicated by the Portuguese Jews in the early modern era), and even the fundamentalist Almohads allowed the Genoese to trade in North Africa around 1200.

The shores of the Mediterranean were also characterized by a high degree of urbanization. Some areas that were heavily urbanized in antiquity, such as the Roman provinces in North Africa, receded in importance, possibly as local grain supplies became more difficult to maintain. Others rose to prominence, such as the Dalmatian Coast, where the Roman towns were succeeded by a host of small settlements that participated in the Venetian regional trade network of the late Middle Ages. Some of these centers, most notably Dubrovnik (Ragusa), were not originally Roman settlements. The same was true of Amalfi and Venice in Italy. Towns in rocky and marshy environments looked further afield to acquire the goods their inhabitants needed for survival, and the fortunes of early Venice were built on salt, fish, and timber rather than the pepper and silk that later became prominent. Genoa was stuck on an inhospitable coast good for producing wine and the herbs of its famous pesto, but for staple foodstuffs its people had to search across the Mediterranean.

Thus the meeting of cultures was matched by intense commercial exchanges in quite modest goods: grain, wine, oil, metals, and timber. The ecological diversity of the eastern Mediterranean led the rulers of Egypt in ancient and medieval times to look politically as well as commercially toward the forests of Lebanon and Cilicia to obtain wood for their fleets and a hundred other uses. The need for base metals attracted Greek merchants to the territory of the Etruscans, which still contains gigantic slag heaps left by the iron producers. There is some disagreement about the relative importance of the bulk and luxury trades in explaining the rise of Genoa and Venice to commercial prominence in the Middle Ages, but it is clear that their own capacity to grow could not have been sustained without regular food supplies from Sicily, Sardinia, Crete, and even the Crimea.

Timber for ship construction could not be found everywhere. Dalmatia and Istria served the Venetians as a local source of timber. Access to regular supplies of wood also permitted the emergence of shipbuilding industries, notably along the Ligurian Coast near Genoa and in the heart of Venice at the famous Arsenal, where mass production of galleys was possible by the fifteenth century. Other products closely associated with the Mediterranean, including citrus fruits, artichokes, watermelon, and most importantly cotton, silk, and sugar, arrived only in the Middle Ages as a result of the Islamic conquests in the seventh and eighth centuries. Arriving in Muslim Spain and Sicily, they soon became regular fare further afield. By 1500 silk industries were active in Milan, Genoa, and Tuscany, and Malta was one of the better-known sources of cotton in the fifteenth century.

The role of island societies changed over time. Whereas in prehistoric Greece the islands, not just Crete, but smaller islands such as Santorini-Thera, were apparently major political centers, the political conglomerations of later centuries tended to be based on the mainland, with the exception of the Norman kingdom of Sicily in the twelfth century (which also possessed large mainland territories). Sardinia under the prehistoric rulers of the Nuraghi (castles that appear to have controlled tiny statelets) was a flourishing center of culture with advanced metal technology, a leader in the western Mediterranean in a manner it would never again become. Some islands served as bridges between cultures. Malta was a prehistoric cult center for the peoples of the central Mediterranean. Later, as part of the medieval kingdom of Sicily, it became a conservative society, for it still preserves the Arabic language of its Muslim conquerors even though the population has been Christian since the thirteenth century.

Islands were colonized and exploited by mainlanders, a process already visible in ancient Sicily and Sardinia, where Phoenicians, Greeks, and later Romans took charge of the plentiful agricultural resources of the islands. In the earliest phases this colonization took the shape of city foundations, so Syracuse was an offshoot of Corinth though free to conduct its own affairs. On the opposite mainland, Carthage was an offshoot of Tyre, controlling the Sicilian Straits and enabling the Phoenicians to make their way freely between the east and west Mediterranean. Such daughter cities were also a feature of the medieval Mediterranean. Pera-Galata developed as a Genoese twin of Constantinople, receiving immeasurably greater commercial income in the fourteenth century than the Byzantine capital. Ciudad de Mallorca (modern Palma) was a second Barcelona, repopulated by Catalans and Provençals after they seized the city from the Muslims in 1229.

More commonly, when trading in territory owned by a competing power (Byzantium or Islam), medieval merchants set up colonies within the existing city, organized around *fonduks*, warehouses that also served as inns, chapels, and administrative centers. Thirteenth-century Tunis gave large areas to the Genoese, Pisan, and Catalan *fonduks*. In the crusader kingdom of Jerusalem, Acre (modern Akko, Israel) was partly divided among Genoese, Pisan, and Venetians.

Following the collapse of the Roman Empire, the Mediterranean underwent a commercial recession, but the coming of Islam and the resurgence of Byzantium made it once again into a vigorous center of exchanges by 900 CE. One way this can be traced is in the development of commercial law. The Rhodian Sea Law, practiced in Constantinople, provided a widely used code whereby commercial cases could be adjudicated, for example, disputes between captains and passengers. Similar legal codes emerged in the western Mediterranean during the period of Catalan commercial preeminence (c. 1250–c. 1500). The law code entitled Consulate of the Sea was printed in Barcelona in 1494 but incorporates much older material. Throughout the Catalan world commercial law courts functioned in the elegant palaces called *llotjas*, which still survive in Palma, Valencia, and elsewhere.

The Mediterranean was not a closed system. The Black Sea was an important source of goods transshipped through Constantinople and Pera and gave medieval Mediterranean merchants (particularly the Genoese) access to both grain supplies and the trade routes that stretched across Asia as far as the courts of the Mongol rulers. At the other end the increased navigation between the Atlantic and the Mediterranean after the end of the thirteenth century opened supplies of English wool to Italian cloth producers and brought Italian capital to Lisbon, Seville, and ultimately the other side of the Atlantic.

Shipping design was influenced by the North European models as well, and Mediterranean imitations of the "cog" became a common sight after about 1300. After 1400 Atlantic shipping became noticeable in the Mediterranean.

Valencia was supplied with fish from the Basque provinces, Portuguese sailors reached Sicily, even England sought to create a Levant trade of its own in the mid-fifteenth century, and Naples riposted by sending vessels to England. The presence of outsiders, to whom the Dutch have to be added after about 1600, had major effects on the economy of the region and may help explain the stagnation of Italian trade and industry in the seventeenth century, a period that even in Venice saw a retreat back to the land. But some older centers, such as Marseille and Dubrovnik, flourished anew.

This integration of the Mediterranean into the wider world was taken a stage further when the Suez Canal opened in the late nineteenth century. The cumbersome route around Africa to India could be abandoned, and Indian Ocean goods could reach the Mediterranean by way of the Red Sea. However, the new masters of the trade routes and political arrangements were the British and the French. Britain, with its bases in Egypt, Cyprus, Malta, and Gibraltar, was particularly well placed to benefit, though the collapse of the Turkish Ottoman Empire brought both powers influence in Syria and Palestine as well after World War I.

The other great change in the twentieth century was the rise of mass tourism. A new relationship developed between Mediterranean Europe and northern Europe. Great swaths of Mediterranean Spain consisted of hotels, apartments, and restaurants. Loss of tourists (as in Egypt and Israel following terrorist violence) could cripple local economies. Yet ease of travel affected fruit and vegetables as well as humans. Out-of-season fruits and flowers, particularly from Israel and Spain, were all the more attractive to those who had tasted them in situ on their exotic holidays. The asparagus and artichoke achieved their final victories.

BIBLIOGRAPHY

Braudel, Fernand. *The Mediterranean and the Mediterranean World in the Age of Philip II*. Translated by S. Reynolds, 2 vols. London, 1973.
Grove, Alfred T., and Oliver Rackham. *The Nature of Mediterranean Europe*. New Haven, 2001.
Horden, Peregrine, and Nicolas Purcell. *The Corrupting Sea: A Study of Mediterranean History*. Oxford, 2000.
Watson, Andrew M. *Agricultural Innovation in the Early Islamic World*. Cambridge, 1983.

DAVID ABULAFIA

MELLON FAMILY. Between 1870 and 1920, three generations of this family of American finance capitalists funded diverse businesses centered in Pittsburgh. By the 1930s, the Mellons were among the wealthiest U.S. families, along with the Fords, the Rockefellers, and the du Ponts.

Born in Ireland, family patriarch Thomas Mellon (1813–1908) grew up on a farm in western Pennsylvania. Eschewing agriculture, he moved to nearby Pittsburgh in 1832, earned a law degree, and was elected county judge in 1859. Savings from his practice were invested in local real estate and mortgages, and earned particularly large returns after the city's Great Fire of 1845. Four of his sons survived to adulthood: Thomas (1844–1899), James (1846–1934), Andrew (1855–1937), and Richard (1858–1933). Between 1864 and 1872, he lent his sons funds to enter the coal, lumber, and construction businesses in the Pittsburgh area; this was the first indication that the Mellon family would make its mark by investing in vertically integrated local businesses.

In 1870, Judge Mellon founded T. Mellon & Sons, a private bank and the foundation of the family's financial empire. Pittsburgh had a burgeoning coal and steel industry, and Mellon's loans to local entrepreneurs were highly profitable. An early customer, Henry Clay Frick, received a $100,000 loan to purchase local coal fields and build coke ovens. Frick merged with Andrew Carnegie's steel firm (another early Mellon customer) in 1882. In 1899, Frick co-founded Union Steel with the Mellons; this was merged two years later into J. P. Morgan's United States Steel Corporation.

Andrew joined his father's bank in 1874, rising to its presidency in 1882. (In 1902, T. Mellon & Sons received a national bank charter and became a subsidiary of Union Trust, organized in 1889 by Andrew Mellon and Henry Clay Frick.) By 1890, Judge Mellon turned over control of the family's property—totaling $2.5 million—to Andrew. In partnership with brother Richard, Andrew continued his father's focus on lending to local businessmen. The brothers behaved like other contemporary finance capitalists such as J. P Morgan: lend, but also acquire a stake in your borrower's business; but the Mellons were distinguished by a commitment to diverse, vertically integrated industries. They invested in everything from oil to steel, pipelines, tankers, and railroad cars, as well as service stations that sold refined gasoline.

Andrew Mellon's first major investment came in 1890. Charles Hall, inventor of a process for refining aluminum, formed the Pittsburgh Reduction Company to manufacture the metal. Needing capital, Hall approached T. Mellon & Sons. Andrew opened a line of credit and purchased company stock; and, by 1894, the Mellons owned over 12 percent of the company. Patent rights and tariff walls created monopoly profits in aluminum, which the Mellons multiplied by investing in companies whose output were linked to aluminum production, such as mineral deposits, hydroelectric power from Niagara Falls, and rolling mills. By the mid-1920s, the Mellon family owned more that one-third of the company, renamed Alcoa (the Aluminum Company of America).

Other Pittsburgh-area entrepreneurs used Mellon's money and management. When Edward G. Acheson created the new abrasive Carborundum, the Mellons' bank provided funds for a manufacturing plant near the Niagara hydroelectricity source, in 1895. As a "bonus" for the loan, the Mellon's acquired company stock. James Mellon's son William (1868–1949) invested bank funds in a network of electric streetcar lines in Pittsburgh. The cars were designed by local inventor George Westinghouse and the electricity to run them came from coal-fired plants owned by the Mellon's. In 1900, Mellon money helped launch the careers of two local engineers, Charles D. Marshall and Howard D. McClintic. The McClintic-Marshall Construction Company, with the Mellons as majority stockholders, produced structural steel for projects ranging from the Golden Gate Bridge to the Panama Canal locks. McClintic-Marshall used raw steel produced by Mellons' Union Steel Company.

With his uncles' backing in the early 1890s, William developed oil wells, a refinery, and pipelines in southwestern Pennsylvania. He sold the company (at great profit) to Rockefeller's Standard Oil in 1895, but was back in the business in 1901 with the discovery of the Spindletop gusher in Texas. A Pittsburgh-area company, J. M. Guffey, owned the claim but lacked development capital. To avoid association with Standard Oil, Guffey sought funds from the Mellons. T. Mellon & Sons bought $2.5 million of the company's bonds, and Andrew and Richard purchased 13 percent of its stock. In 1902, the brothers sent William to Texas to oversee the firm; he soon expanded into new oil wells in Indian Territory (now Oklahoma), and reorganized the business as Gulf Oil in 1907.

The Mellon family's most important asset, Gulf Oil, grew to be one of the world's largest oil producers, opening wells in countries such as Mexico and Kuwait and tapping American offshore deposits through underwater drilling. Once again, the Mellons magnified their profits by investing in associated enterprises, including refineries, pipelines, tanker fleets, and gasoline service stations. (They opened the nation's first in service station Pittsburgh in 1913.)

World War I proved very profitable for the Mellons as the federal government contracted for railroad cars (produced by Standard Steel Car, for which the Mellons were chief financiers) and aluminum. The family was enriched by another new technology: the Koppers coal-to-coke ovens, which recovered by-products of coal distillation such as natural gas and toluol (used to produce TNT). The Mellons linked their one-third share in Koppers to ownership of coal fields and utilities networks designed to distribute the natural gas to homes for heating and lighting.

By 1920, their fortune exceeded $2 billion. Although the family was little known outside Pittsburgh, Andrew Mellon was named President Warren G. Harding's secretary of the treasury. He held this position in the Coolidge and Hoover administrations and achieved a number of objectives: reducing the national debt, restructuring foreign debt to the United States, and decreasing corporate and personal income tax rates, particularly for the wealthy. "The Mellon Plan" for taxes rested on a notion that, in the 1980s, came to be known as "supply side economics." Mellon considered high tax rates counterproductive: they reduced revenues by forcing the wealthy into tax-exempt assets such as municipal bonds that he deemed far less beneficial to the economy than direct investment in industry.

Some called Andrew Mellon the greatest secretary of the treasury since Alexander Hamilton, but others blamed his policies for unequal distribution of income in the 1920s and, ultimately, the stock market crash of 1929. His image was further tarnished by prosecution for underpayment of federal taxes, but now he is best known for funding the National Gallery of Art and Carnegie Mellon University.

BIBLIOGRAPHY

Clark, James A., and Michael T. Halbouty. *Spindletop*. New York, 1952.

Cowles, Alfred. *The True Story of Aluminum*. Chicago, 1958.

Denton, Frank Richard. *The Mellons of Pittsburgh*. New York, 1948.

Hersh, Burton. *The Mellon Family: A Fortune in History*. New York, 1978.

Koskoff, David E. *The Mellons: The Chronicle of America's Richest Family*. New York, 1978.

Love, Phillip H. *Andrew W. Mellon: The Man and His Work*. Baltimore, 1929.

Mellon, Thomas. *Thomas Mellon and His Times*. Pittsburgh, 1994.

Mellon, William Larimer, with Boyden Sparkes. *Judge Mellon's Sons*. Privately printed. 1948.

O'Connor, Harvey. *Mellon's Millions*. New York, 1933.

KERRY A. ODELL

MERCANTILISM. The term *mercantilism* refers to both economic doctrines and commercial policies that advocate governmental intervention in economic activity as necessary to the best interests of the nation-state. The term *mercantile system* appeared as early as the writings of

Count Mirabeau, a French physiocrat, but was institutionalized by Adam Smith, an ardent opponent of mercantilism. Mercantilism per se was brought into wide use by the German Historical School.

The Mercantilists and Their Doctrines. The mercantilists were a miscellaneous aggregation of European writers, officials, merchants, and policy makers, most of them active in England between 1600 and 1750. Among the British writers, Thomas Mun (1571–1641) and Sir Josiah Child (1630–1699) were merchants affiliated with the East India Company. Others included Charles Davenant, John Locke, Edward Misselden, Sir William Petty, John Pollexfen, and the Dutch physician Bernard de Mandeville. The best-known French mercantilist is Jean Baptiste Colbert (Louis XIV's finance minister, whose interventionist policy was termed Colbertism). Other important figures included the German cameralist Johann Joachim Becher and the Italian Antonio Serra.

A monistic interpretation of mercantilism is erroneous. Over time, mercantilist doctrine shifted; writers did not develop a unified position, yet common dogma, assumptions, and assertions run through all mercantilist writings. The main convictions on which mercantilist doctrine is based are the following: (1) People can improve upon nature through commerce and technology, and these are critical to the wealth and power of a state. In addition, secondary production and commerce are more important to the wealth of nations than the fruits of nature, that is, agriculture. (2) People pursue their own interests without concern for the effect on the nation-state. Individual welfare is not the same as the welfare of the national economy, and economic policy should foster the latter over the former. (3) There is no preestablished harmony in the world; Adam Smith's "invisible hand" does not exist. (4) Power and plenty are the essential elements of the welfare of a nation. Although plenty is an absolute concept, power is a concept relative to other nations: the increase of one country's power necessarily means the relative decrease of that of another.

These convictions led the mercantilists to perceive intervention as necessary and beneficial to the well-being of the nation-state, as developed in the three central themes of their writings: trade theory, monetary theory, and a general concept of society.

Trade theory. The balance of trade doctrine, which affirms that a given country's prosperity is best achieved by an increase in its stores of precious metal, is the main element of the mercantilist system. An inflow of precious metals in a country without access to gold and silver mines can be achieved only by a favorable balance of trade. A balance of trade surplus is achieved by enacting trade restriction policies that promote the export and restrict the import of goods. Some mercantilists were concerned with individual trade balances with specific countries, whereas

others, Mun most famously, insisted that only aggregate balances were of importance.

Monetary theory. The monetary aspect of mercantilist doctrine focuses on the reasons why an increase in money is an important national objective. There was a diversity of opinions among the mercantilists regarding the effects of money on the economy. The simplest and most naive approach to understanding this desire for monetary accumulation was bullionism, a belief that conferred upon precious metals a "store of wealth" function by identifying wealth with money. Bullionism gradually disappeared, since most mercantilist literature made it clear that wealth consists of a given country's production of goods rather than its stock of precious metals. Mercantilists contended that an increase in precious metals is important because money, through its circulation function, has an effect on output and wealth through two main channels: (1) An increase in money reduces interest rates, in turn leading to an increase in output. (2) Money is a factor of production equivalent to capital; an increase in money will therefore stimulate production and employment.

The mercantilists' monetary doctrine is also related to noneconomic arguments: (1) An inflow of money may increase revenues to the monarch. In this sense, mercantilism has some connection with cameralism, which above all promotes increasing revenues to the prince. (2) Money is the sinews of war, as expressed by Colbert: "Trade is the source of public finance, and public finance is the vital nerve of war."

General concepts of society. Mercantilism also focused on general concepts of society shaped by the will to stimulate production and increase the competitive power of the nation, going beyond the strict theory of trade and money. Mercantilists commonly held that, first, development of manufactured goods is important. Mercantilists focused more on production than on consumption and favored interventionism that would promote the industrial sector. Rebutting the mercantilist focus on production, Smith wrote, "Consumption is the sole end and purpose of all production." After 1750, there was a clear evolution of ideas featuring a greater concern for the position of the consumer.

Second, mercantilists stressed that an increase in population is beneficial to the economy, because where land is ample and inhabitants are few, there is poverty. The reasons for this effect are diverse. Focusing on the production side, an increase in population can lead, through an excess demand for goods, to invention and industrialization. Focusing on the labor market, population increase can lead to lower wages, which some mercantilists thought would improve trade, whereas others believed that lower wages would be an impetus for workers to work more. However, views regarding the benefits of low wages were not unanimous. Mercantilists were aware that in comparing England to the Netherlands, the country with higher wages was nonetheless the richest. Some of the mercantilists also noted that higher wages can lead to a higher standard of living and higher worker efficiency. An increase in population was also noted for its noneconomic effects, chief among them an increase in the nation's overall power, as the mercantilists believed that there was a certain relationship between a nation's population and its power.

Third, mercantilists maintained that savings and thrift should be promoted among the elite. Although some mercantilist writers deemed spending on luxuries by the rich as beneficial, most opposed the consumption of luxuries.

Fourth, according to mercantilists, frugality should be encouraged among the poor, and idleness discouraged. The mercantilists favored child labor as a means to decrease idleness, as well as reducing poverty, by increasing family income. Some mercantilists also opposed attempts to train workers for more qualified work as a means to keeping wages low, the social effect of which would likewise be less idleness.

Finally, mercantilists viewed colonialism as an efficient policy, because colonies serve as a protected market for export and a supplier of raw materials.

Historiography of Mercantilism. Depending on the inclination for or against protectionism, one either ridicules the mercantilists' lack of a perfect system (and their sometimes erroneous logic) or lauds the modernity of their arguments. The two principal groups that discussed the mercantilist doctrine were the classical economists and the German Historical School. For the classical economists in particular, and all liberals in general, mercantilism is portrayed in a negative light.

One line of criticism claimed that mercantilist views were incoherent and mired in confusion, and that mercantilism was little better than nonsense, because mercantilist theory was based on the premise that national wealth can be measured by the quantity of precious metals in a given nation's possession. As noted above, although bullionism was mentioned by the early mercantilist writers, it was not the foundation of most of the mercantilists' commercial policy, and indeed it disappeared in later writings.

Adam Smith's criticism of mercantilism stemmed from his dedication to the consumption side of the economy, which led him to the conclusion that trade could benefit all. In contrast, mercantilism viewed trade as a zero-sum game, where one country necessarily profits at the expense of another, since mercantilism's focus went beyond consumption. Smith's second criticism of mercantilism was that mercantilist policies did not emerge from a national goal, but rather from the interest of merchants and manufacturers in retaining their monopolies—in other words, Smith viewed mercantilism as a rent-seeking doctrine.

From a theoretical point of view, the weak link in mercantilist doctrine is that the mercantilists were unaware of the price-specie-flow mechanism later developed by David Hume. The price-specie-flow mechanism contended that an increase in money in the long run leads to higher prices, leading in turn to less competitiveness, resulting in a decrease in net exports, finally causing money to flow back out.

In contrast to this liberal, antimercantilist view, the German Historical School, which did not view the economy as separate from politics, regarded mercantilism as a coherent system centered on the nation-state conducting economic policies for the purpose of achieving power and national unity.

Gustav Schmoller emphasized that the aim of mercantilist policies was to secure national unity and develop a powerful centralist state, or what he termed "state making." Reaching these goals demanded the development of the economic interests of the nation. In other words, the mercantile system was necessary for replacing local policy with that of the nation-state.

William Cunningham, a Scottish clergyman who criticized the liberal political economy of England, asserted that mercantilism was primarily a system that unduly mobilized economic policy into the service of power. The paradigm that links power to trade policy was the need for accumulation of bullion, because a stock of bullion with which to purchase ammunition and hire mercenaries at short notice was necessary for waging war. In this context, because attaining power was clearly a relative matter vis-à-vis other countries, the mercantilists perceived trade as a zero-sum game.

Mercantilism (1931/1955), Eli Heckscher's classic historical study, paints mercantilism as an economic policy necessary for the adaptation of the medieval institutions of European society to new economic and social conditions. He emphasized that the centerpiece of mercantilist doctrine was the employment of economic forces in increasing the power and the unification of the state. However, Heckscher maintained that mercantilism's ultimate end was the pursuit of power only, and that unification was merely an interim goal.

Jacob Viner (1937) objected to Heckscher's view, maintaining that wealth and power were twin aims of mercantilism. For Viner, plenty and power were equal in their importance as means to national security.

John Maynard Keynes also examined the mercantile system and criticized Smith for ridiculing it. Keynes argued that mercantilist doctrine should be understood in the light of its goals of increasing employment and stimulating economic activity.

Mercantilist Practices and Their Effects on the Economy. Mercantilist policies in Europe were mainly adopted during the sixteenth to the eighteenth centuries by French and English policy makers, but were also implemented in Spain, Sweden, and Denmark. Not all interventionist and protectionist policies are mercantilist in their essence. To be considered mercantilist, policies must have the nation at their center, and either promote the hoarding of precious metal by promoting export and hampering imports or promote intervention to encourage the manufacture of goods. Legislation intended to prevent the export of machines and tools, as well as the emigration of skilled workers, was also mercantilist in spirit.

Protectionist policies predated the mercantilist era, but these typically created the opposite effect; that is, they created obstacles to exports and facilitated imports in order to retain goods in the country. However, as early as the fifteenth century, some policies were mercantilist, such as the Corn Laws, which date back to 1436.

In Britain, the important mercantilist measures were the Cloth Act of 1552, which regulated the types of cloth manufactured; the Statute of Artificers in 1563, which decreased the power of guilds and regulated wages; the Navigation Acts of 1651, enacted by Oliver Cromwell, which allowed trade with the colonies to be carried out only on British ships with the aim of developing the shipping industry; the Calico Act of 1721, which prohibited imports of calico from India; and the prohibition on exporting machines of 1774. In France, Colbert implemented some protectionist measures in the form of the tariffs of 1668, but mostly enforced regulations and intervention in the manufacture of goods.

Did mercantilist policies work? The English Navigation Acts are usually regarded as a successful strategic move that contributed to the development of the shipping industry, but there is less of a consensus concerning most mercantilist trade policy. Liberals traditionally have believed that mercantilism was superfluous to the development of England and France, and more specifically, that the development of the cotton industry—which played a central role in the Industrial Revolution—owed nothing to legislative protection and therefore to mercantilism. A contrary assessment was made by Paul Bairoch (1993, 2000), who stressed the important role of mercantilism in early modern industrialization and economic development and asserted that mercantilism was a catalyst of the Industrial Revolution.

Mercantilism, vilified by some and revered by others, has at the essence of its commercial and regulative policies the political goal of national sovereignty and the welfare of the nation-state. Although free trade is cosmopolitan in its focus, mercantilism is nation-based. It is a doctrine that views not only the welfare of the individual but also the power of the nation-state relative to other nations. The debate between mercantilism and free trade centered on the place of the nation-state and *raison d'état* relative to the place of the individual. This debate has evolved—because the concept of the nation-state is currently considered passé—making way for an economic debate on managed trade versus free trade.

BIBLIOGRAPHY

Bairoch, P. *Economics and World History: Myths and Paradoxes.* Chicago, 1993.
Child, Josaiah. *A New Discourse of Trade.* London, 1693.
Coats, A. W. "In Defence of Heckscher and the Idea of Mercantilism." *Scandinavian Economic History Review* 5.2 (1957).
Cole, Charles W. *Colbert and a Century of French Mercantilism.* New York, 1939; reprint, Hamden, Conn., 1964.
Coleman, Donald C., ed. *Revisions in Mercantilism.* London, 1969.
Cunningham, William. *The Growth of English Industry and Commerce.* New York, 1968.
Heckscher, Eli F. *Mercantilism.* 2 vols. London, 1931; reprint, 1955.
Irwin, Douglas A. "Mercantilism as Strategic Trade Policy: The Anglo-Dutch Rivalry for the East India Trade." *Journal of Political Economy* 99 (1991), 1296–1314.
Johnson, Edgar A. J. *Predecessors of Adam Smith: The Growth of British Economic Thought.* New York, 1937.
Judges, A. V. "The Idea of a Mercantile State." In *Revisions in Mercantilism*, edited by D. C. Coleman. London, 1939; reprint, 1969.
Mandeville, Bernard. *The Fable of the Bees* (1705). Oxford, 1924.
Mun, Thomas. *England's Treasure by Forraign Trade* (1664). Oxford, 1937.
Schmoller, Gustav. *The Mercantile System and Its Historical Significance* (1884). New York, 1967.
Schumpeter, Joseph A. *History of Economic Analysis.* New York, 1954.
Viner, J. *Studies in the Theory of International Trade.* New York, 1937.
Wilson, Charles. "Treasure and Trade Balances: The Mercantilist Problem." *Economic History Review* 2 (1949).

ELISE S. BREZIS

MERCED. During the medieval reconquest, Christian warriors fought to receive *merced* from their victorious kings. When King Alfonso VI (1065–1109) banished the Cid from Castile, the Cid sought to regain the king's favor by giving him Muslim booty, including one hundred harnessed horses. Through these gifts captured in marauding raids against Muslim cities, the Cid attained Alfonso's *merced* of reinstatement as his vassal. In these examples, *merced* resembled Cicero's definitions of *merces* as favor, reward, and bribe.

Medieval Spanish kings believed that, by granting *mercedes*, they fulfilled their obligations as the fount of justice. In his most famous law code, *Las siete partidas*, King Alfonso X (1221–1284) claimed that kings tempered the severity of the law through royal *mercedes* of right of appeal, confirmation of wills, dispensations from compulsory military service, and tax exemptions. In his law code for cities, the *Fuero real*, Alfonso additionally listed pardons and legitimations as *mercedes*. In practice, *merced* provided equity by suspending the law in specific cases when strict interpretation would result in harm to petitioners.

The founder of the Trastámara dynasty, Enrique II (1369–1379), having seized the throne from the legitimate ruler, transformed the economic foundations of Castilian society by rewarding his supporters with a new type of *merced*, the *mayorazgo*, estates comprised of one or more towns carved out of the royal patrimony. The *mayorazgo* differed from other types of private property in being exempt from Spanish inheritance law, which required that the parental estate be partitioned equitably among all children of a legitimate marriage.

The last Trastámara monarchs, King Fernando and Queen Isabel (1474–1516), granted *mercedes* for enterprises that drove Spain's expansion into the New World: business and conquest contracts, joint-stock company charters, mining rights, and export privileges. They empowered a subcommittee of the Royal Council, the *Cámara de Castilla*, to administer the growing volume of *mercedes*.

Charles I (1517–1555), the first of the Habsburg rulers in Spain, formed an administrative meritocracy of lawyers and ecclesiastics by making them dependent on his *merced* of compensation, comprised of promotions, benefices, magistracies, and clientage favors. Charles did not sell offices, but he rewarded loyalists the *merced* of an income only after they had provided years of service. He granted a new and historically important *merced* to the *Cortes* (parliament), the right to address petitions and grievances before discussing subsidy amounts. While earlier monarchs alienated villages from disorderly cities and disloyal nobles for political reasons, the Habsburgs programmatically granted the *merced* of township to hundreds of villages in exchange for huge cash "services." In the seventeenth century, the Habsburgs did not follow Charles's policy of providing *merced* to men who labored for the crown, but rather they converted royal government into a patronage system based on bidding.

The Bourbons (1700 to present) continued to grant *merced* in the same patterns but with diminished resources. The new constitutional Spain of the early nineteenth century, financially devastated by damage to its economic infrastructure suffered during the Napoleonic invasion, abolished *mayorazgos* and seigneurial jurisdiction and began a half century of converting municipal commons, church lands, and seigneurial estates into national property. *Merced* as an economic instrument ended when the king no longer owned the government or its income as private property.

BIBLIOGRAPHY

Clavero, Bartolomé. *Mayorazgo: Propiedad feudal en Castilla, 1369–1836*. Madrid, 1974.

Dios, Salustiano de. *Gracia, merced y patronazgo real: La Cámara de Castilla entre 1474–1530*. Madrid, 1993.

Escudero, José Antonio. *Curso de historia del derecho: Fuentes e instituciones político-administrativas*. 2d ed. Madrid, 1995.

Guilarte, Alfonso María. *El régimen señorial en el siglo XVI*. 2d ed. Valladolid, Spain, 1987.

Nader, Helen. *Liberty in Absolutist Spain: The Habsburg Sale of Towns, 1516–1700*. Baltimore, 1990.

AURELIO ESPINOSA

MERCHANT GUILDS. Merchant guilds, or hanses as they were also called, are in their strictest sense a peculiarly Western form of merchant community, distinguished not just by the functions they typically perform but also by the terms of association. In Europe, merchant guilds emerged in the High Middle Ages, when commerce was being superimposed on a feudal landscape, and when commercial classes were disrupting traditional social hierarchies. They prospered for several centuries until superseded by both statelike authorities and other kinds of merchant organizations. Outside Europe, analogous institutions existed although in many such places ties of kin (or birth) and sometimes religion, rather than social function alone, typically formed the basis of merchant associations. In some regions, China in particular, the state was positioned very differently with respect to commerce and merchant culture. As a result, the merchant communities of India, China, and the Middle East—which in both premodern and modern times managed complex commercial networks and often provided their members the same kinds of protections and privileges—were not precisely identical to either the Western hanse or the various other kinds of merchant associations that developed in Europe. Nevertheless, given the occasionally marked similarities between certain non-Western and Western merchant associations—hanses being only one of the latter—it is useful to consider them together, for the comparison reveals a great deal about the respective commercial cultures.

European hanses or merchant guilds originally were voluntary associations of traveling merchants providing mutual aid in the form of military protection during long-distance voyages. They arose in the political vacuum created by the fragmented political landscape of the day, when no local authority had the capacity or the will to protect and govern long-distance trade, or even to regulate the entrepôts of long-distance trade routes. Hanses thus quickly assumed increasingly political functions as they negotiated the uneasy terrain through which their members had to pass as they journeyed from place to place. For example, they secured transit rights or brokered agreements to standardize and limit tolls and other fees demanded by territorial sovereigns. Early in their history, hanses also became vehicles for securing and maintaining collective trade privileges, often acquiring for their members monopolies over supply or distribution of particular goods and, in some cases, winning control of all import or export trade in a given locality.

Although hanses pursued so varying a range of economic activities that none was precisely identical to another, overall the hanse was a limited kind of economic organization. Hanses did not provide insurance *per se*, they were not banks or credit organizations (except that their members might stand as guarantors for one another), and they never formed business partnerships in the manner of the Italian *commenda, compania,* or *societas.* They were distinct from craft guilds, and often the enemy of craft guilds, so opposed were the fundamental economic interests of merchants on the one hand and producers on the other. In this regard, merchant guilds should be distinguished from the large number of so-called craft guilds that were dominated by merchant-craftsmen, including many men who had altogether abandoned production for commerce. These guilds—the London greater livery companies, for example—often came to represent merchant interests almost exclusively and as such sought to dominate markets and govern trade practices rather as the merchant guilds did; but their focus on control of local markets and retail as well as wholesale trade (rather than trade routes) and their overlapping with the craft guild has led most scholars to treat them separately.

Hanses were a characteristically northern European institution, for it was in this region of dispersed political authority that commercial associations could assume overtly political functions. Although some merchant guilds in southern cities (scholars have often so labeled the *Arti di Calimala* and *Arti di Lana* in Florence, for example) acquired monopoly and management rights over certain branches of commerce, the earliest and best-known hanses are northern. Indeed, one scholar has argued that Venice knew no merchant guilds because the city itself was, in effect, a merchant guild, that is, a civic body run by and for long-distance merchants and providing its members the military, technological, and legal infrastructure necessary for long-distance trade (Frederic C. Lane, *Venice: A Maritime Republic*, Baltimore, 1973).

Merchant guilds apparently existed as early as the tenth or eleventh century CE, but it is not until the twelfth century that surviving records reveal much about their functions or composition. Certain German hanses are mentioned during this period, as are several in England—in York, Ipswich, and Leicester, for example. From this period there is also evidence of the Hanse of London, a body of Flemish merchants from the major cloth-producing towns in Flanders who traveled to England to purchase the high-quality wool needed to make luxury woolens. Despite its apparent importance—or the importance of the trade it

managed and of the merchants involved in it—this hanse's activities and powers are obscure, and scholars are not even sure how long it functioned. The most extensive evidence from this early period comes, instead, from a smaller hanse in the region, the merchant guild of the city of Saint Omer, which published a "customal" or set of regulations sometime between 1083 and 1127. The provisions concerning economic matters treat tolls and transit rights, mutual protection during travel, the procedures by which members could offer surety on behalf of other members, and, above all, the exclusivity of its benefits, that is, the denial of protection or privileges to nonmembers.

The customal of Saint Omer also exposes the terms on which the guild was established, revealing its particular constitutional principles and its sociocultural character. It is these features that most clearly distinguish the European merchant guild from other merchant organizations, in Europe and elsewhere. The guild at Saint Omer was a voluntary organization, open to all merchants in the city except clerics and warriors (by definition, it was closed to foreign merchants), and each member was positioned as the equal of all others—equally eligible for office, equally subject to its rules of conduct, equally entitled to aid and protection, equally granted the trade privileges accruing to membership. Although scholars have shown that merchant guilds were not so egalitarian as their formal structure implied, for wealth and birth played major roles in establishing leadership and determining policy, hanses were both open and nonhierarchical to a degree not imaginable in other kinds of merchant associations, such as the family firm turned commercial empire (for example, the Medici organization), the joint-stock company, or even looser kin-based networks. In this respect, merchant guilds were much closer to craft guilds, for as "guilds" they were fraternal organizations with, as many scholars have argued, deep roots in Latin Christian culture, especially its ideal of fellowship and solidarity. Merchant guilds were thus social and religious as well as economic organizations. Many seem to have begun as drinking and social clubs reserved for wholesale merchants, the *Richerzeche* of medieval Cologne being one of the best known. They were also devotional and charitable societies of a sort, often with their own patron saints, altars, and feast days; and all set aside part of their revenues (taken from dues) for gifts to those members who had fallen on hard times or to their families, and frequently to the poor of their communities.

Some merchant guilds had long, well-institutionalized histories, even coming to function as quasi-public authorities. Late-medieval Paris, for example, had a hanse, also called *les marchands de l'eau*, an association that controlled trade in goods imported via the city's waterways. Initially, this meant exclusive rights to trade in commodities such as fish and wine brought in on the Seine (or to tax

MERCHANT GUILD. *The Sampling Officials of the Drapers' Guild.* Painting (1662) by Rembrandt van Rijn. (Rijksmuseum, Amsterdam)

foreign merchants granted such rights); but the Parisian hanse was in certain periods able to extend its authority to cover transshipment of such goods throughout the city (and beyond) and to regulate weights, measures, market rules, and so on. In effect, the hanse for a time became a secondary government of the city, with its own courts and administrators, and even its own *prévot*, who was just barely subordinate to the king's own *prévot* or governor of Paris.

The best-known version of such institutionalization was the Hanseatic League. It was not a hanse as such but a loose union of various hanses that had long been established throughout the Baltic, northern Europe, and the Rhineland, the first apparently being in Visby on the island of Gotland. Between 1356 and 1370 (Treaty of Stalsund), about two centuries after their beginnings, these hanses were organized by leading towns of the region into the league, under the de facto leadership of Lübeck. It had four principal branches, in London, Cologne, Bruges, and Novgorod, where members established resident colonies or "nations." In the London Stalhof, for example, merchants of the Hanse resided, often along with their families, intermarrying, sharing business information, socializing, and worshiping—all with the principal objective of acquiring and preserving the political clout necessary for nurturing economic interests. The league survived into the seventeenth century, even at times organizing military actions against competitors in order to protect trade rights;

but by the mid-sixteenth century it was clear that the league had outlived its usefulness since brutal competition from English, Dutch, and other merchants had encroached upon its markets.

Merchant communities operating throughout the Middle East, South Asia, and China during the long and rich commercial histories of these regions resemble the European hanse in many respects. None, however, seems to have been formed outside the ties of kinship as were the European hanses; and in many places religion or ethnicity served as the basis of merchant community, factors that played little role among the members of Western Christian culture (except that hanses were local in origin, and thus embodied local culture). Some merchant associations were ethnically defined, such as the Armenians, who, dominating trade in much of the early modern Middle East, were bound by well-developed traditions of solidarity and mutual trust entirely like those nurtured by the European guild. Muslim communities in the Indian Ocean, many of which formed resident "nations" analogous to the Hanse nation at London took a leading role in medieval trade. In precolonial India, the Banjaras, nomadic people in the north who were linked by ties of kinship, emerged as the major purveyors of salt and grain through vast expanses, providing exactly the kind of protection, shared information, and mutual aid to their fellow herder-traders that the first medieval hanse merchants granted one another.

Recent studies of India on the eve of British colonization have emphasized the complexity and the richness of that society's commercial infrastructure, documenting the degree to which merchants exchanged information and technology, openly competed for business, and cooperated in protecting trade routes, all reminiscent of late-medieval European commercial culture. The *bania*, for example, a merchant/shopkeeper caste group with eighty-four subcastes, displayed a strong sense of group solidarity and provided mutual help, even among subcastes, while developing sophisticated commercial techniques such as brokerage, deposit banking, bills of exchange, and insurance. Between about 1500 and 1700, to cite another example, the Ganges valley saw the development of various ascetic sects, self-regulating bodies that both protected and governed trade, in many ways recalling the activities of European guilds and other merchant associations during the same period. Thus, the evidence does not support Max Weber's famous claim that occupational specialization based on caste so fragmented Indian artisan and merchant populations that no independent, self-conscious merchant class could emerge and thus no ethic of civic fraternization that transcended birth (Max Weber, *The City*, translated and edited by D. Martindale and G. Neuwirth, New York, 1958). Nevertheless, because merchant communities in India were built predominantly through caste networks, not outside them, and because the family firm was the fundamental social unit of trade networks, it is impossible to argue that the European merchant guild was exactly replicated in the subcontinent.

In China, with an equally complex commercial history, some merchant associations behaved as did many of the Western hanses; but here too differences in political and social infrastructure prevented the emergence of precisely comparable organizations. In Confucian society, merchants stood at the bottom of a social order dominated by literati, who were challenged only by military classes in some periods. During the thirteenth and fourteenth centuries, however, merchant communities were established, for example, in South Fujian (the Hokkiens), especially in the port of Quanzhou. The community sent sojourners throughout the South China Sea area, including what is now Vietnam, Cambodia, Somalia, and Java. During the Ming dynasty (1368–1644 CE), however, overseas travel and private commerce were forbidden to all Chinese; so these communities became sorts of outlaws, forbidden to return home and compelled to organize themselves abroad as nations reminiscent of the western. They survived into the colonial period, when Spanish, Portuguese, and Dutch merchants entered the arena; but, without the support of their government, they were unable to compete with these new communities of traders. The modern period witnessed other examples of guildlike organizations. What Western-

ers labeled the great guild of Newchwang regulated banking and market trading in that port city; the Swatow guild, a quasi-military organization, enacted and enforced rules concerning trade and served as guardian of the interests of its members. Probably the best-known guild of this period was in Canton, which, between 1757 and 1842, was the staple for trade between China and Western nations. There thirteen firms, commonly called the Co-hungs, managed that trade, rather like the English Staplers had done in Calais from the late fourteenth into the sixteenth century (1363–1558). This guild existed, however, at the sufferance of a highly bureaucratized state and served to contain and govern trade in the interests of that state, not—as in the Western case—in lieu of or in cooperation with the state.

Seen as an association of long-distance traders organized to provide mutual protection and secure trading privileges, merchant guilds can be regarded as an essential feature of commercial life where statelike institutions did not provide these services or chose to delegate them, and where the risks of long-distance trade made monopolies or similar privileges practical. Everywhere they emerged, however, they took different forms, depending in particular on the social position of indigenous trade and traders. The classic Western hanse, with its emphasis on fellowship, mutual aid, and voluntarism and its relative political autonomy, seems to have been unique to that region; elsewhere merchant communities were more deeply embedded in kinship networks that precluded such principles of association and were sometimes entirely subordinate to the state. However, the Western hanse was a relatively short-lived form of association, barely surviving the Middle Ages; for its economic functions were limited, and the trade privileges it existed to preserve were easily undermined by merchant groups better adapted to early-modern commercial culture.

BIBLIOGRAPHY

Bayly, C. A. *Rulers, Townsmen, and Bazaars: North Indian Society in the Age of British Expansion, 1770–1870*. Oxford, 1993.

Black, Antony. *Guilds and Civil Society in European Political Thought from the Twelfth Century to the Present*. London, 1984.

Brandt, A. von. "Die Hanse als mittelalterliche Wirtschafts-organisation—Entstehen, Daseinsformen, Aufgaben" In A. von Brandt et al., *Die Deutsche Hanse als Mittler zwischen Ost und West* (Wissenschaftliche Abhandlungen der Arbeitsgemeinschaft für Forschung des Landes Nordrhein-Westfalen 27), pp. 9–38. Cologne and Opladen, 1963.

The Cambridge Economic History of Europe, vol. 2, edited by M. Postan and E. E. Rich, pp. 223–243. Cambridge, 1952.

The Cambridge Economic History of Europe, vol. 3, edited by M. Postan, E. E. Rich, and Edward Miller. pp. 11–118. Cambridge, 1963.

Dollinger, P. *The German Hansa*. London, 1964.

Gungwu, Wang. "Merchants without Empire: the Hokkien Sojourning Communities." In *The Rise of Merchant Empires: Long-Distance Trade in the Early Modern World, 1350–1750*, edited by James D. Tracey, pp. 400–423. Cambridge, 1990.

Habib, Irfan. "Merchant Communities in Precolonial India." In *The Rise of Merchant Empires: Long-Distance Trade in the Early Modern World, 1350–1750*, edited by James D. Tracey, pp. 371–400. Cambridge, 1990.

Lloyd, T. H. *England and the German Hanse, 1157–1611*. Cambridge, 1991.

Mauro, Frédéric. "Merchant Communities, 1350–1750." In *The Rise of Merchant Empires: Long-Distance Trade in the Early Modern World, 1350–1750*, edited by James D. Tracey, pp. 255–287. Cambridge, 1990.

Morse, Hosea Ballou. *The Gilds of China*. 1909. Reprint. Taipei, 1966.

MARTHA HOWELL

MERGERS. *See* Integration, *subentry on* Horizontal Integration.

METALLURGIC INDUSTRY *[This entry contains three subentries, a historical overview and discussions of technological change and industrial organization and markets.]*

Historical Overview

The progress of the modern world is intimately linked to the use of metals and the development of metallurgy. It is hard to think of any human activity that is in no way connected to the use of metals. Throughout history warfare has been a leading sector in metal demands, from swords and guns to modern battleships and tanks, but now civilian sources of demand predominate. People live and work in buildings erected on steel frames, or at least kept together with iron nails; eat with steel cutlery; and travel in cars made of iron and steel or on trains running on steel rails. Iron is by far the most important metal, but people's lives depend on other metals as well; copper, for instance, is an important component in electricity transmission, and airplanes are constructed of aluminum. Gold and silver might have lost much of their historical role as means of exchange in the form of coins, but are still important in jewelry and other kinds of ornamental work.

Reflecting this importance, metals and metallurgy have figured prominently in much economic-history writing. David Landes pointed to the link between the modern industrial world and the use of metals, stating that the Industrial Revolution was a process whereby the use of organic materials was replaced by the use of metals. Other important links between metals and economic development include those between the inflow of silver from the Spanish colonies and the price revolution, as well as between the beginning of metal using and the Neolithic revolution.

Early History. Almost ten thousand years ago, copper, together with gold, was the first metal handled. Excavations in present-day Turkey have shown signs of copper smelting from about 7000 to 6000 BCE. In the following millennia the use of copper gradually spread, or appeared as an independent discovery; from its origins in southwest Asia, by about 4000 BCE it had reached southeast Europe, and two thousand years later it was found in many places in Europe. Its eastward diffusion occurred at a similar pace; between 3000 and 2500 BCE copper was used in China, and from the same time scholars also can date the beginning of a copper age in India. Such early employment of metals used copper in a relatively pure form, but fairly soon the copper alloy bronze (with about 10 percent tin added to the copper) substituted for pure copper. The development of bronze, which had the advantage of both being harder than copper and easier to cast, might have occurred because many copper deposits also included tin. Bronze began to be used from 3000 to 2500 BCE in the Near East and then spread both in an eastward and a westward direction. Bronze's crucial role in human development is seen in the name of the period from about 3000 to 1000 BCE (differing between different locations), which is normally called the Bronze Age.

The use of iron also originated in the eastern Mediterranean, apparently in the second millennium BCE, although it was not until around 1000 BCE that it had an impact. In the last millennium BCE, iron making spread in the Old World, in Asia, and to Europe and Africa; but bronze remained the essential metal for most everyday purposes, and not until at least a few centuries into that millennium can historians speak of an Iron Age in most places. Initially iron was made according to the direct method, wrought iron being produced directly by smelting iron ore in a furnace. China was an exception to this pattern, as blast furnaces were used early on, producing cast iron wares.

The expansion of the Roman Empire meant that iron making around the Mediterranean took off. Iron was needed for military purposes in the buildup of the empire, with swords as the principal weapon, but the Romans also used iron wares, such as nails and beams, in construction. The creation of the empire not only led to expanded demand; it also meant a spread of iron-making techniques throughout Europe. This last process was then accelerated by the breakup of the empire and the migration of iron-making groups wandering around Europe.

The Roman period was not only one in which the use of iron in Europe and around the Mediterranean expanded; it also was a time in which production and use of metals rose generally. Copper was in demand, as copper alloys such as bronze and brass (copper mixed with zinc, or a calamine ore) were used by the Romans, as were lead and silver. Most of the demand for nonferrous metals stemmed from a rise in coinage. Silver was used for high-value coins, whereas brass was the content in less valued coins for everyday use. Lead, which had a much older history originating in what is now Turkey, was used by the Romans for water-related engineering, such as pipes and cisterns. The production of these nonferrous metals, as well as the different alloys, was complicated by the fact that they were sometimes extracted from the same mine and refined in processes related to one and another. Silver was seen as a by-product of lead production and vice versa, and zinc ore could also be found in relation to lead.

Iron. During the last millennium iron has been the most important metal, as it can be made in a variety of different ways, shapes, and forms (steel is one form of iron), with many different uses. A Swedish eighteenth-century metallurgist, Sven Rinman, wrote that no other metal could, without affecting its inner structure, be made with so many "differences" as iron. During the last millennium, three instances of important change can be observed: the development of the blast furnace in the medieval period, the introduction of mineral coal during the Industrial Revolution, and the development of modern steel processes in the late nineteenth century.

Wrought iron, the kind of iron used in Europe as opposed to China, where cast iron was preferred, was traditionally made directly from the ore, in charcoal-fired bloomeries. It was mainly consumed locally, with only smaller volumes being sold in distant markets. This system ended in medieval times with the introduction of blast furnaces and the so-called indirect method. One early example is the Swedish furnace Lapphyttan, which dates from the twelfth century. Pig iron, made in a blast furnace, was not malleable and had to be further treated in a forge before it could be brought to market.

European iron production started to rise, as did the trade in iron. Sweden became a leading producer, and the Hanseatic League shipped large volumes from Stockholm; whereas Basque iron, still produced in bloomeries, found its way to the British market. Another important producer was the Low Countries around Liège, where wrought iron was also fabricated into metal goods such as weapons and nails. Production in this area expanded with the rising power of the Dutch economy. Iron and iron commodities were brought from Liège, and from the seventeenth century on also from Sweden, to Amsterdam for use in the shipping industry or for export throughout the world.

Toward the end of the seventeenth century, the center of the European iron market moved from the Dutch Republic to Britain, as did economic power more generally. British iron production was insufficient to supply the rising demand from a growing metalworking industry as well as an expanding empire. As a result, British home-produced iron was augmented by rising volumes of foreign iron. Swedish iron was added to Basque iron, and from the mid-eighteenth century on, these supplies were augmented by growing volumes from Russia. Foreign iron was also reexported, and Swedish iron found its way, on board slave

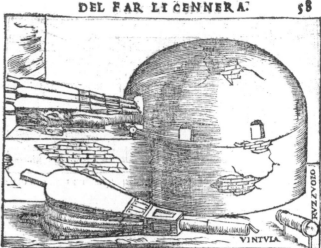

METALLURGIC INDUSTRY. German cupeling furnace with a brick dome and a cupeling hearth with iron hood, both used to separate metals from ores. Illustration from *De la pirotechnia*, by Vannocio Biringuccio, 1540, p. 58. (Prints and Photographs Division, Library of Congress)

ships, to the African coast where it was added to African-produced iron. The East India Company was another important reexporter of iron. European iron was used in Asia, along with Asian iron, in the production of nails.

From its position at the center of the world market, Britain took the next technological step in iron making: using mineral coal as a fuel. Coke smelting was introduced by Abraham Darby in the early eighteenth century, and Henry Cort perfected the refining of pig iron with his puddling and rolling technique toward the end of the eighteenth century. As a result, British iron production soared; and after the spread of the new technology to continental Europe and North America, so did world production. British production increased more than tenfold in a few decades from the end of the eighteenth century to the mid-nineteenth century, and world production followed. With this new technology and global trading patterns that gravitated, around the British economy, the important role of iron in the development of the modern society was firmly established. The nineteenth century cemented it further with the expansion of railway networks all over the world. British ironworks, especially large Welsh ironworks such as the Dowlais, exported rails worldwide, and were soon followed by iron producers from Belgium, Germany, and the United States.

Wrought iron was a soft material not suitable for use when hardness or sharpness was needed. In such cases, steel was the solution. However, steel, which was an alloy made from wrought iron, was an expensive material. A number of different production processes could be used, but the most common was the cementation method, producing blister steel. From the second half of the eighteenth century on, Sheffield became the steel center of the world, with the largest concentration of cementation furnaces. It was also there that Benjamin Huntsman invented the crucible production method, making crucible steel around the middle of the eighteenth century. It was not until the second half of the nineteenth century that cheap steel could be produced. Henry Bessemer invented the method bearing his name in the 1850s, and the open-hearth method, invented by Wilhelm Siemens and Pierre Martin, followed in the 1860s.

Some scholars have seen the diffusion of the modern steel processes as the time when the iron industry fully became adapted to an industrial way of production. Steelworks, especially in the United States, grew in size and also merged into gigantic enterprises with employment measured in the tens of thousands. During the twentieth century the rate of technological change accelerated, and steel was made by many different processes. The use of electricity was tried shortly before the turn of the twentieth century, and it soon became commonplace. The production of iron and steel also grew at an enormous rate. At the turn of the twenty-first century more than 800 million tons of steel were being produced annually wordwide, four times as high as in 1950. The second half of the twentieth century also saw a radically altered geography of iron and steel production. In 1950 western Europe and the United States still dominated world production, with the Soviet Union an important newcomer. In 2000 China was the world's leading steel producer, with Japan in second place.

Nonferrous Metals. Of the nonferrous metals, copper always has been the most important, and to some extent the development of copper production and trade bears some resemblance to that of iron production and trade. One strik-ing similarity is the role of military demand, with bronze cannons an essential part of early-modern warfare. Copper continued to be needed in brass making and remained important for coinage. In the fifteenth and sixteenth centuries copper chiefly was produced in central Europe, for example, in Hungary, the Tyrol, and the Harz, from ore that also contained some silver. The central market was initially Antwerp, but later Hamburg took over, and the main consuming locations were Aachen, with its brass industry, and Portugal, where copper was traded with Africa.

In the seventeenth century the European copper trade was dominated by the Falun mine in Sweden. More than half of Europe's production, slightly below three thousand tons, originated in Sweden. During this period Hamburg gradually lost its central position to Amsterdam, which was linked not only to European sources of copper but, from the 1620s on, also with Japanese copper. Dutch East India ships brought copper back from Batavia as ballast. During this period, brassworks were established near Amsterdam. As with iron, copper trade left the Dutch republic from the end of the seventeenth century for Britain, and, again as with iron, the introduction of mineral coal and a large imperial market were an essential part of this move. Copper ore mined in Cornwall, where tin was also mined, was shipped to south Wales, where it was smelted with coal. Slave ships from Bristol and Liverpool once again provided a main artery out to the world market. Brass manufacturing and the toy trade in Birmingham proved to be another important market for British copper production in the eighteenth century, as well as, from the end of the century on, the sheathing of ships. Around 1800, some eight thousand tons of copper was produced in Britain, more than twice as much as in the rest of Europe.

During the nineteenth century demand for copper expanded, in a development related to its property of conducting electricity. Copper became a suitable material for telegraph, telephone, and electricity networks. New deposits of copper ore were discovered outside Europe, and today the main mines are found in Chile, North America, Russia, and Central Africa. Shortly before the turn of the millennium, total annual copper production was about nine million tons.

Even though iron, steel, and copper have dominated the consumption of metals ever since they began to be used, other metals have remained an essential part of metal making. Tin, which initially was used in bronze making, is today an important part of the steel industry, used as a coating material. From the eighteenth century on, it has been used for protecting rolled iron sheets from roasting in the making of tin plates; and from the nineteenth century on, it has played an important role in the food industry as a plating for steel cans used as food containers. Zinc, which initially, in the form of calamine ore, was used in brass making, is today also an important coating material for steel.

Lead has developed more independently than tin and zinc although lead was used, together with tin, in the making of pewter. From the end of the nineteenth century on, lead also played an important role in development of the modern society. It could be used to store electric energy, in the form of batteries, and a large share of the lead now produced is used in making batteries. Also lead was used in the twentieth century as a gasoline additive.

Gold and silver differ from iron and copper, as well as most other metals, in that they have been of great economic importance throughout history, even though they have seldom played a major role in industrial production. Instead they have served as means of circulation, in the form of coins, and as standards of value. These precious metals have also served as signs of power and prestige, often in the form of commodities made by skilled artisans.

The reason for gold's importance is its limited supply, as well as the ease of shaping it. Around 1500, before the opening of the Atlantic economy, world gold production was about five tons annually. Three hundred years later production had risen to about fifteen tons per year. In the next two hundred years, production rose substantially. After 1848, and the discovery of gold in California, forty tons of gold was produced annually; and after the opening of the deposits in southern Africa in the later years of the nineteenth century, a more than tenfold increase occurred. A century later, production amounts to about two thousand tons. South Africa remains the most important producer in the world with about a third of total production, with Russia, the United States, and Australia as other important gold producers. Of the present production of gold, the largest share is used for jewelry; but measured in shares of the total stock of gold, as much as a third is stored around the world as gold reserves.

Unlike gold, silver has to some extent been used for productive purposes in the modern society. It has become an important part of the photographic industry, where it is used in making films. Before the mid-nineteenth century, however, silver was used for the same purposes as gold—for coins, jewelry, and ornamental work. The production and the consumption of silver have risen over time with the expansion of the global economy, with silver coins often more important for everyday transactions than gold coins. With Europe's colonization of southern America, this rise expanded dramatically. Large volumes of American silver were shipped over the Atlantic to Europe, and even further to Asia. Cádiz became an important trading center for silver destined for Asia. The large influx of silver into Europe in the early-modern period resulted in rapidly rising prices, in the process known as the price revolution. North America and South America are still the main sources of silver.

If gold and silver gradually have lost their role as means of exchange, they have also lost their former dominant position as the sole metals used for ornamentation and objects of desire. Especially from the eighteenth century on, a practice started, particularly in Britain, in which precious metals were imitated by cheaper substitutes. In the Birmingham toy trade and in Sheffield, cheap jewelry and other ornamental commodities were produced by using plating techniques or new metal alloys such as ormolu.

BIBLIOGRAPHY

Ashton, T. S. *Iron and Steel in the Industrial Revolution.* Manchester, 1924.

Bakewell, Peter. "Mining in Colonial Spanish America." In *The Cambridge History of Latin America*, vol. 2, *Colonial Latin America*, edited by Leslie Bethell. Cambridge, 1984.

Berg, Maxine, and Helen Clifford, eds. *Consumers and Luxury: Consumer Culture in Europe, 1650–1850.* Manchester, 1999.

Birch, Alan. *The Economic History of the British Iron and Steel Industry, 1784–1879.* London, 1967.

Evans, Chris, Owen Jackson, and Göran Rydén. "Baltic Iron and the British Iron Industry in the Eighteenth Century." *Economic History Review* 4 (2002), 642–665.

Florén, Anders. *Vallonskt järn: Industriell utveckling i de södra Nederländerna före industrialiseringen.* Uppsala, 1998.

Hildebrand, Karl Gustaf. *Swedish Iron in the Seventeenth and Eighteenth Centuries: Export Industry before the Industrialization.* Stockholm, 1992.

Hyde, Charles, H. *Technological Change and the British Iron Industry, 1700–1870.* Princeton, 1977.

Kellenbenz, Hermann, ed. *Schwerpunkte der Eisengewinnung und Eisenverarbeitung in Europa, 1500–1650.* Cologne, 1974.

Lindroth, Sten. *Gruvbrytning och kopparhantering vid Stora Kopparberget intill 1800-talets början.* Uppsala, 1955.

Magnusson, Gert. "Bergsmän, arbetare, bönder, gruvor, hyttor och oxar: Kring den äldsta industrialiseringen i Sverige." *Daedalus* (1997).

Nef, John U. "Mining and Metallurgy in Medieval Civilisation." In *The Cambridge Economic History of Europe*, vol. 2, *Trade and Industry in the Middle Ages*, edited by M. M. Postan and Edwards Miller. Cambridge, 1987.

Tylecott, R. F. *A History of Metallurgy.* London, 1992.

Westermann, Ekkehard. "Copper Production, Trade and Use in Europe from the End of the Fifteenth Century to the End of the Eighteenth Century." In *Copper as Canvas: Two Centuries of Masterpiece Paintings on Copper, 1575–1775*, pp. 117–130. New York, 1999.

Wengenroth, Ulrich. *Enterprise and Technology: The German and British Steel Industries.* Cambridge, 1994.

GÖRAN RYDÉN

Technological Change

From a beginning in southern Turkey as early as 8500 BCE, artisans worldwide learned to fashion useful metal objects by heating and hammering native copper and iron meteorites they found on the earth's surface. This was the only metallurgical technique people in North America and Australia used before colonial times; elsewhere artisans learned to smelt metal from ore. Because ores give no visual clues that they can be transformed into metal, archaeologists view the discovery of smelting as a discontinuity in humankind's technological achievements. They trace copper smelting to 6500 BCE at sites in southeast Turkey, and find successively later dates outward from southwest Asia, as for Spain (2000 BCE), India (2500 BCE), and China (1500 BCE). Artisans in Anatolia learned to smelt iron—inherently more difficult than making copper—by 2000 BCE. Again, later dates are found at greater distances from this origin. Archaeologists initially interpreted the radiance of these dates as evidence of diffusion of smelting knowledge, but now increasingly find evidence for its independent invention.

Smelting. While individual artisans could smelt lead, copper, or iron, and make bronze, smelting on a scale large enough to supply metal beyond immediate local needs was an industrial activity. It required numerous participants with diverse skills. Smelting processes are labor intensive, and application of mechanical power further enhanced their industrial character. Innovation, organization of work with division of labor, and the use of mechanical power characterize industrial metallurgy.

People in India and China organized industrial production of metals before anyone did in the West. Artisans smelted copper throughout India by 1400 BCE. Slag deposits in Tonglüshan show that Chinese artisans had made one hundred thousand tons of copper by 750 BCE. Scholars now believe that smelting wrought iron by the bloomery (direct) technique was an independent invention in India and in China, making this metal widely available by 800 BCE. The Chinese took their iron metallurgy along a unique course with their adoption of the blast furnace to make cast iron beginning about 400 BCE. They further industrialized this technique in 31 CE with water power to pump the air blast. The Chinese mass-produced cast-iron tools; Indian artisans specialized in massive forged products, such as the famous Delhi pillar. This 7.2-meter-high iron column, made about 300 CE and notable for its corrosion resistance, contains hundreds of individual iron blooms forged into a solid mass.

Indian artisans made two unique contributions to industrial metallurgy in medieval times: they smelted more than a million tons of zinc by the retort process near Zawar. In eastern India they produced wootz, a high-carbon cast steel made by fusion in crucibles, on a large scale. Smiths in the Middle East forged wootz steel from India into the famous Damascus sword blades.

Next to East Asia, early metallurgy throve best around the eastern Mediterranean. Egyptians obtained copper from smelters working at their Timna outpost (now in Israel) and iron from Meroe, Sudan, where output attained 150 kilograms per day. Extraction of silver from lead ores at Laurion from 600 to 250 BCE, which supplied the wealth of Athens, was on such a scale that lead-bearing dust from Laurion is found today buried in the Greenland ice cap.

While the Romans contributed little to metallurgical technique, they ramped up the scale of production: artisans at La Montagne (France) made iron at the rate of five tons per day.

Metallurgy in northern Europe remained modest compared with the accomplishments in India and China until the thirteenth century CE, when entrepreneurs in Sweden, and soon after in Germany, built water-powered blast furnaces. Europeans were not then burdened with the centralized, bureaucratic control that had stifled innovation in China. Their climate and geology gave them numerous, reliable rivers on which water power could be developed with modest capital. They had abundant forest resources for fuel and convenient ore deposits. Through the following centuries, military needs stimulated European innovation and production, as in the manufacture of cannon, while colonial expansion enlarged the resource base and opened opportunities for new processing methods, such as the techniques of silver smelting the Spanish brought to Peru in the sixteenth century. Vannocio Biringuccio's *De la pirotechnia* (1540), Georgius Agricola's *De re metallica* (1556), and Lazarus Ercker's *Treatise on Ores and Assaying* (1580) explained metallurgical operations in practical terms, and encouraged capitalists to invest in mining and smelting enterprises. Openness, free exchange of information, and vigorous capitalism set early modern European metallurgy apart from practice elsewhere.

Europeans made a big step toward metallurgical industrialization in the sixteenth century with their integrated ironworks. They used the indirect process with a blast furnace to make pig iron that they could either fashion into cast products, such as pots or cannon, or convert to wrought iron at the adjacent finery forge. The indirect method recovered more of the iron in the ore used (at a cost of somewhat higher fuel consumption), and enabled ironmasters to shift their product mix as demand changed, an important advantage at works dependent on military orders. Both French and English colonists set up integrated ironworks in North America to take advantage of the continent's abundant fuel resources. Two of these, the Saugus works in Massachusetts (1640) and the Forges of Saint Maurice in Quebec (1741), are now national monuments.

Making Steel. While artisans could use iron of indifferent quality for things like nails, they used steel (because of its high cost) for critical purposes that demanded high quality, such as edge weapons and body armor. Except for Indian cast steel that reached them by way of the Middle East, Europeans got along with steely iron made in bloomery forges through the sixteenth century. By 1600, artisans in Prague, and some years later in Nuremberg, were making blister steel by the cementation process. (Carbon diffused into iron bars that were packed in charcoal and held at red heat for a week or more. The gas released as the metal was converted to steel formed blisters.) English artisans adopted the cementation process in 1614, thereby laying the foundation for the dominant position that Sheffield steel would hold in world markets into the twentieth century.

Because blister steel retained the inclusions of the slag present in the wrought iron from which it was made, small and delicate parts, such as clock springs, made from it were liable to break. Sheffield resident and clockmaker Benjamin Huntsman solved this problem around 1740 by melting blister steel in crucibles so as to free it of inclusions. Indians made their wootz cast steel in handful-size crucibles; Huntsman and his Sheffield colleagues increased the ingot size a hundredfold with their clay crucibles and coal-fired furnaces. They soon established a worldwide reputation for the superior quality of their steel.

Using Mineral Coal. Competing demands for wood for shipbuilding and other purposes raised the cost of fuel at European ironworks by the late sixteenth century, particularly in southern England, and led ironmasters to search for ways to use mineral coal in place of charcoal. Between 1622 and 1638, Dud Dudley made iron, probably of indifferent quality, in a blast furnace at Himley, Staffordshire, with mineral coal. Abram Darby achieved reliable production with a furnace at Coalbrookdale in 1709 by first coking his coal so as to reduce its sulfur content. Darby's technique, coupled with more powerful blowing engines powered by steam rather than falling water, removed existing resource and technical constraints on large-scale pig iron production. Darby cast cylinders for the Boulton and Watt engines, some of which subsequently powered additional blast furnaces, making a powerful stimulus to further industrial growth. The famous 1777 Iron Bridge at Coalbrookdale stands today as a symbol of this industrial advance. James B. Neilson's 1828 addition of stoves to preheat the air pumped into blast furnaces completed the innovations that brought the iron smelting into its modern form.

Darby's innovation left the second component of the integrated ironworks, the conversion of high-carbon pig to low-carbon wrought iron, still dependent on charcoal fuel. Sulfur contaminated wrought iron made in contact with mineral coal. John Wood solved this problem in 1761 with his potting and stamping process: he used clay pots to protect the iron from contact with coal. Henry Cort's puddling process eliminated the need for the pots. In 1781, Cort perfected Peter Onions's idea of using a reverberatory furnace, in which the firebox is separate from the hearth holding the iron. Cort also introduced grooved rolls to shape the iron balls made in the puddling furnace. Three decades of additions and improvement by Richard Crawshay, Samuel Rogers, and Joseph Hall opened the way to production of wrought iron on a scale that could sustain nineteenth-century railways, engineering works, and iron shipbuilding.

Next to iron, copper was the most important industrial metal. European artisans, primarily in Germany, smelted copper with the techniques that had been described by Agricola in 1556. They used a dozen or more successive steps of oxidation and reduction that consumed much fuel. In the 1690s, the availability of cheap coal induced entrepreneurs to erect copper smelters works in Swansea, Wales, where they gradually modified the German technique so that two reverberatory furnaces and seven steps sufficed. Adoption of copper sheathing for the hulls of wooden ships in the eighteenth century dramatically expanded the demand for Welsh copper. For nearly a hundred and fifty years, works in Swansea smelted ores imported from Germany, Cornwall, and eventually from South America and the United States, to make most of the world's copper.

Brass, an alloy of copper and zinc, had been widely used in India and China, which lacked sources of tin to make bronze, and by the Romans, who made brass by the cementation process in which zinc ore was reduced in the presence of molten copper. Cementation could at most get 29 percent zinc into copper. When William Champion of Bristol, England, initiated smelting of metallic zinc in the West in 1738, he could make brass with any desired composition. In 1807, Abbé Dony at Liège improved Champion's vertical retort zinc-smelting method into the horizontal retort technique used worldwide until the mid-twentieth century. Champion and Dony made zinc and brass available for industrial use.

New Methods. With new methods of making wrought and pig iron, copper, and zinc in quantity with mineral coal fuel at hand by the early nineteenth century, only steel remained tied to small-scale, batch production. Henry Bessemer's success with his pneumatic converter in 1856, combined with Robert Mushet's demonstration of the importance of manganese additions, enabled Bessemer to initiate tonnage steel production in Sheffield in 1864. A year later, Alexander Lyman Holley transferred the Bessemer process to America with the first commercial converter plant in Troy, New York. Over the next decade, Holley supervised construction of converter plants at the principal works in the United States. Meanwhile, William Siemens in England and Emile and Pierre Martin in France demonstrated how to make large batches of steel in open-hearth furnaces. The open-hearth process allowed closer control of composition and quality than the Bessemer converter did, and gradually superseded the pneumatic process.

Through 1870, Americans had adapted European metallurgical techniques to their particular markets and resources. In the 1880s, however, they made major innovations in copper and aluminum smelting on their own.

METALLURGIC INDUSTRY. Molten steel is poured from an electric furnace into a ladle, Allegheny-Ludlum steel plant, Brackenridge, Pennsylvania, 1942. (Alfred T. Palmer/Office of War Information Photograph Collection/Library of Congress)

Welsh secrecy and the complexities of their procedures frustrated American copper smelters. In 1880, Pierre Manhês and Paul David working in Vaucluse, France, had successfully applied the principle of the Bessemer converter to the final stage of copper smelting, in which copper sulfide prepared in reverberatory furnaces was converted to copper metal with an air blast. Franklin Farrel licensed the French process, modified it, and had it in large-scale production in Butte, Montana, by 1884. By making the converter in the shape of a horizontal cylinder and adopting a basic lining, William Pierce and E. A. C. Smith at the Baltimore Copper Smelting and Rolling Company in 1908 dramatically improved converter productivity. Pierce-Smith converters remain primary equipment at copper smelters worldwide into the twenty-first century.

Lighter Metals. Independently and almost simultaneously, in 1886 Charles Hall in the United States and Paul Héroult in France found how to make aluminum by electrolysis of alumina dissolved in molten cryolite (a sodium-aluminum fluoride). Hall began his experiments while a student at Oberlin College in Ohio, aided by his chemistry professor, Frank Jewett. Like Hall, Héroult also became fascinated with a desire to make aluminum while he was a student, and both succeeded at the age of twenty-three. In

the United States, the Pittsburgh Reduction Works (later Alcoa) began commercial aluminum production in 1888. This, when combined with Alfred Wilm's perfection of the age-hardening technique for making the high-strength alloy known as Dualumin in 1911, ushered in the age of light metals.

Much of America's industrial prowess at the beginning of the twentieth century depended on machines that cut metal into finished products with steel tools. Rapid tool wear limited production capacity. In the 1870s, Robert Mushet discovered that steels containing up to 10 percent tungsten had remarkable cutting capacity. The full potential of Mushet steel remained unrecognized until the 1890s, when Frederick Taylor (of scientific management fame) and Maunsel White found a heat treatment that dramatically increased the life of tungsten-steel tools in trials they carried out at the Bethlehem Steel Company. With this information at hand, Sheffield steelmakers then developed tungsten-chromium-vanadium high-speed steel (so named because of its ability to cut at high speeds) by 1908. Existing machine tools lacked the power and rigidity to use high-speed steel tools to their full capacity. The new steel triggered massive redesigns in the machine tool industry.

Iron-chromium alloys attracted investigators in Germany, England, France, and the United States in the late nineteenth century. About 1910, Philipp Monnartz in Germany discovered their corrosion resistance. By 1912, Elwood Haynes in the United States and Henry Brearley in England had developed iron-chromium stainless steel alloys for cutlery. They avoided the threat of patent litigation by a pooling arrangement in 1916. Next, researchers at the Krupp laboratories in Essen showed that with nickel additions, stainless steel could be easily rolled into large sheets, opening the way for its architectural use. Sheffield metallurgists also developed the iron-silicon alloy that dramatically improved the efficiency of the transformers needed for high-voltage transmission lines.

Historians typically associate metallurgical innovations with particular inventors, such as Darby, Cort, Siemens, or Bessemer. Closer examination shows the hands of others in these innovations: Bessemer would never have gotten pneumatic steel into production without the aid of Percy, Mushet, and Göransson. By the dawn of the twentieth century, metallurgical innovation depended on numerous individuals, often backed by the facilities of a research laboratory. Americans followed the European lead in 1928, when the United States Steel Company set up its laboratory for fundamental research. Research metallurgists focused on developing new alloys properties until the late twentieth century. Then rising public concern forced researchers to deal with the environmental degradation caused by mines, mills, and smelters. Besides designing new alloys, metallurgical researchers began to devise ways to reduce energy consumption, control emissions, and remediate polluted mine, mill, and smelter sites.

BIBLIOGRAPHY

Aitchison, Leslie. *A History of Metals.* London, 1960.
Alexander, William, and Arthur Street. *Metals in the Service of Man.* 10th ed. Harmondsworth, U.K., 1994.
Barraclough, K. C. *Steelmaking, 1850–1900.* London, 1990.
Craddock, Paul T. *Early Metal Mining and Production.* Washington, D.C., 1995.
Day, Joan, and R. F. Tylecote. *The Industrial Revolution in Metals.* London, 1991.
Gordon, Robert B. *American Iron, 1607–1900.* Baltimore, 1996.
McHugh, Jeanne. *Alexander Holley and the Makers of Steel.* Baltimore, 1980.
Misa, Thomas. *A Nation of Steel.* Baltimore, 1995.
Tylecote, R. F. *A History of Metallurgy.* 2d ed. London, 1991.

ROBERT B. GORDON

Industrial Organization and Markets

Ever since the English historian Arnold Toynbee (1852–1883) included the notion of an Industrial Revolution within the scientific study of history in the 1880s, it has been common to analyze economic development in terms of discontinuities. In spite of more recent discussions centered around such notions as proto-industrialization and views of a more slow and gradual development, the coming of the industrial era is still seen as a more-or-less dramatic break with the past in such areas as technology, organization, and markets. The textile industries have been the linchpin of these discussions, with such features as mechanical spinning, the factory system, and a market for cheap factory-made cloth. The Industrial Revolution has been seen as the development from a flexible putting-out structure centered around a capitalist investing in variable capital, such as raw materials and stocks, to the technologically sophisticated factory system based around a centralized production unit owned jointly by a group of capitalists/industrialists.

As an opposite of this development, the metallurgic industries have been portrayed in terms of continuity. With regard to the iron industry, the most important of the metallurgic industries, technology has been at the forefront of this argument. Since the early medieval period and the development of the blast furnace, the industry has been structured around centralized production units, requiring large outlays in fixed capital, and therefore also of several capitalists acting in concert. The dominance of wage labor has also been stressed. New research has, however, revealed that it is not possible to draw such a sharp dividing line between the experiences of the metallurgic industries and the textile trades. Instead, it has been shown that the former did develop along lines previously thought of as belonging only to the latter trades.

Centralized and Decentralized Production Units. The dawn of a modern metallurgic industry can be dated to the early medieval period, the European development of the blast furnace, and the subsequent rise of the so-called indirect method of ironmaking. Blast furnaces had by then existed in China for about a thousand years, but only for the making of cast iron. The development in Europe did take another, and radically different, path. Lapphyttan, in Sweden, is so far the oldest dated European blast furnace, and it was used from the end of the twelfth century. From the same period, we can also date the gradual step from bog ore to rock ore in Sweden, and the subsequent development of a new organization of production and market participation.

In Sweden, the links between ironmaking and the ownership of mines were crucial. The free peasantry of the areas of Sweden rich in such minerals as iron and copper became the owners of mines, and it was also they who produced the metals. In ironmaking, whole villages collectively owned mines and erected furnaces in which pig iron was produced, using charcoal made in the adjacent forests. This pig iron was further treated in forges to so-called "osmund iron," which was sold to German merchants in the trading towns on the Swedish coast. A large share of this iron was exported on behalf of the Hanseatic League. In Lübeck and Gdańsk, whole quarters of these towns were occupied by forgemen and blacksmiths with their workshops. This iron was further refined and shaped into tools and other commodities for a wider market.

The Swedish metallurgic industry was a clear example of a decentralized structure based on freeholding peasants making the metals. Similar patterns were found in the Low Countries and Spain, for example. In continental Europe, a different structure of centralized production sites prevailed, at least within the nonferrous industry. On the one hand, we have a development in which the expanding state took a firmer grip over mining and metallurgical expansion—one such feature was to claim mines as a regale—and on the other hand, there is the growing size of the enterprises and the linked development of technology. This resulted in the large copper and silver mines with adjacent smelting works that were being developed in Saxony, the Harz, Bohemia, and other places. They were run by large capitalists like the Fuggers and were worked by wage laborers.

Large centralized production units owned by capitalists and worked by wage laborers pointed toward the future, but much in early-modern metallurgic development also remained close to the medieval roots, and the outcome was a mixture of centralized and decentralized production units. The period shows a more varied social structure of metal making as well as a spatial expansion of the marketing of metals. The Swedish industry bridged many of the differing social organizations of production of the period. The foundation of ironmaking, as well as copper and silver production, remained the metal-making peasants with their ore extraction and smelting procedures in hundreds of peasant-owned smelting furnaces in central Sweden, but the subsequent processes of turning the raw metals into commodities for a wider market was gradually removed from their hands. Within ironmaking, the peasants were forced to sell their pig iron to large ironworks owned by capitalistic ironmasters and worked by wage laborers, at fixed prices. A similar development occurred in copper making but with much being sold to state-controlled copper works. Much of Swedish iron and copper was sold on the international market by important merchants acting on a global scale. This changing structure should be seen in relation to a steep rise in both Swedish iron and copper production from the late sixteenth century.

In central Europe, and foremost in Russia, the development of centralized production units expanded during the early modern period, with the rise of Absolutist Monarchies and state promotion of iron production. In Russia, this development can be dated from 1701 and the founding of the Neviansk Ironworks. This was a first step by Peter the Great (1672–1725), in an attempt to transform the vast woodlands and mineral-rich area of the Urals. Serf labor was the key in this task, and the outcome was the making of many large ironworks estates inhabited by thousands of serfs. They did not just cut wood or mine ore, but they also performed skilled work as furnace and forge workers. During the eighteenth century, private landowners, such as the powerful Demidoff family, were given a large share of Russia's iron production, without changing the basic structure of the industry within the feudal system.

It is likely that Peter the Great set this process in motion as a means to enhance the Russian armament industry, but soon these works supplied other demands, internal as well as external. In the eighteenth century, Russian serf workers produced an iron that was exported to Great Britain, the most demanding iron-consuming society of the age, where it competed with Swedish iron. These ironworks also began producing metalwares for the Russian market. Rolling and slitting mills were soon erected along the streams next to the furnaces and forges. From the end of the eighteenth century, copper, gold, and platinum were discovered in the area, and the works then became a kind of centralized multimetal production site based on serf labor.

If forced labor was used in Russian metal production, the situation was even worse on the other side of the Atlantic. In both North and South America, slave labor was used as the founding principle of the metallurgic industry. In the British Colonies in the north, slaves were used in the production of iron for both internal consumption and exportation to Great Britain. It was, however, in Latin America that the use of slave labor really took root, especially in the goldfields, where black slaves were used as the main source of labor. In silver production in the Spanish colonies, black slaves were in a small minority, and the organization rested instead on Indians, who were forced to leave their homes and move to the mines and work. During a period of six to twelve months, they lived at the production sites before they were allowed to go back home.

The British experience was an all-together different one. Landholdings remained in the hands of the aristocracy and so did ownership of mines, sites for smelting, and other works. In contrast to the situation on continental Europe, industrialists rented land on which they extracted ore or coal and constructed smelting works. In ironmaking, this division between landholding and industrial activities began in the sixteenth century, with the emergence of professional ironmasters and skilled independent artisans. The deployment of independent artisans could be seen as a step toward a capitalist way of organizing production. But for centuries, this development was brought to a kind of standstill as British ironmasters subcontracted production as well as paying the workers a piece rate, a procedure that lasted at least until the mid-nineteenth century. These ironmasters were in that sense not industrialists but rather merchant capitalists organizing production along market lines. The British iron industry retained a decentralized structure with many small furnaces and forges spread over the whole country, each employing about ten workers. They were owned by a small number of ironmasters loosely connected in partnerships among which iron was bought and sold.

Another radically different feature of the British metallurgic industries, at least the iron industry and possibly along similar lines to the situation in the Low Countries, was its relationship to the market. If iron production in the early modern period foremost was based upon local or regional markets, with Sweden and Russia as exceptions to this by producing for export, the British economy was exceptional in that it demanded much more iron than it could produce. Bar iron, home produced or imported, was consumed in a rising metalware production. In such expanding towns as Birmingham and Sheffield, iron was forged into a widening variety of metal goods. In the Birmingham toy trade, many items made combined iron with copper, brass, and steel. In the rapidly expanding British economy, metals were also demanded for construction purposes. It can be established that at least a quarter of the total volume of iron being transmitted through the British market was turned into nails, and iron was also used in shipbuilding. Copper was also much sought after in the shipyards, as sheathing was needed if the ships were to survive the tropical seas.

Changing Technology. With the gradual introduction of coal into all sections of the British metallurgic industries, the decentralized structure was lost, as spatial reorganization took place in favor of the coalfields. South Wales became the home of copper smelting as well as ironmaking. In the former case, copper from Cornwall was shipped to the Swansea area, while the iron industry's new center became Merthyr Tydfil, where four of the largest ironworks in the world were located. The Dowlais ironworks, the largest of them all, was typical. From a very modest start with only one blast furnace being erected in 1758, it grew slowly in the eighteenth century. From the beginning of the new century and with the development of puddling, which was done at its neighbouring Cyfarthfa works, the rise of the Dowlais ironworks was more rapid. It was mainly in relation to the expansion of the railway system and the supply of iron rails that the Merthyr works should be seen. Initially, Welsh iron was sold to British railway firms, but gradually an even larger share was exported, first to Europe and later to supply global demand. In the 1860s, the workforce at Dowlais numbered more than eight thousand people.

The growth of an iron industry using mineral coal was a British development, but it was not long before the novelty was exported to continental Europe. The Belgian iron industry was the first to be transformed along lines that previously took place in Great Britain. A decentralized iron industry became concentrated to the coal basins of Liège and Charleroi. It was especially in the former region that the new centralized industry took root. The British entrepreneur John Cockerill (1790–1840), who started his career by making machines for the cotton industry, created in the 1820s, in Seraing outside Liège, an industrial complex consisting of coal pits, coke-fired blast furnaces, puddling furnaces, and rolling mills as well as mechanical workshops employing two thousand workers.

Coke-smelting and puddling took longer to be established in Germany and France, but after mid-century, coal became the main fuel there as well. The change was faster in bar ironmaking, as both French and German ironmasters used imported coke-smelted pig iron from Great Britain. This process was supported by the tariff policy of both these countries. Around 1900, coal technology reigned in Europe, with only Sweden of the main European iron producers remaining tied to charcoal. The development in the United States took a while to get started, and until the mid-century, large volumes of iron were imported from Great Britain. At the same time, charcoal-made iron still dominated internal production. This changed dramatically in the second half of the century, with a fast rise of production in conjunction with a swift replacement of charcoal for coal. In the 1880s, U.S. pig iron production surpassed British production.

Even though coal technology spread to many ironmaking regions in the industrialized world and became a kind of "industrial standard" in the third quarter of the nineteenth century, the period has in a technical sense been seen as the time for the introduction of cheap steel. Ironmaking can in a technical sense be divided into three parts: pig-iron making in blast furnaces, refining to wrought iron in forges, and shaping of the metals in mills. During the nineteenth century, productivity rose in the first and last of these parts; coke smelting meant a rapidly rising production per furnace, and steam engines and technical development within mill technology meant a similar rise in the output of bar iron and rails. In spite of the use of coal in bar ironmaking, puddling remained the main obstacle to a more rational organization of ironmaking, as the output of each puddling furnace remained determined on the skill and strength of the puddlers. The development of the Bessemer, Thomas, and open-hearth methods solved this problem.

Even though these methods had their origin in the development of the British iron industry, they came to be production technologies that were used more efficiently by

METALLURGIC INDUSTRY. One end of Hull-Rust-Mahoning, the largest open pit iron mine in the world, Hibbing, Minnesota, 1941. (John Vachon/Prints and Photographs Division, Library of Congress)

Germans and Americans in their endeavor to surpass the British industry. As with puddling, the development of new steel methods, especially the Bessemer methods, were connected to the construction of a global railway network. Contrary to puddling, earlier in the century this development worked to the advantage of the Germans and the Americans as their home markets were far from being stagnant and were also protected by high tariffs.

Cartels and Mergers. One complicating feature in relation to the introduction of the steel processes was the depressed state of the world economy in the decades after the mid-1870s, and, as a result, the much tougher competitive market situation. The combined effect of substantial outlays in new technology and a competitive market gradually led to attempts within the industry to both amalgamate and to form cartels in order to better control the market and price development. In Germany, a cartel already was formed in the late 1870s between Bessemer producers, and in the next decade, an international cartel was formed between steel producers from Germany, Austria, Belgium, and Great Britain. On the other side of the Atlantic, the

situation was different, with companies more inclined to merge instead of forming cartels. In 1900, the United States Steel Corporation was founded as the world's largest steel company, based on the former Carnegie Steel Company and Federal Steel Company. A few years later, the Bethlehem Steel Corporation was founded. Together, these two giants dominated steel production in America. In Germany, this situation was mirrored after the turn of the century by the dominant Krupp and Thyssen companies, with a combined employment of close to one hundred thousand men at the outbreak of World War I.

Markets. The metallurgic industries had always acted on an international market. Metal had been transported between regions and countries and to some extent also between continents; but from the later nineteenth century, it is possible to talk about a globalization in a much more dense way. Metallurgic production spread around the world, with rising production in America creating new structure from the late nineteenth century and Soviet made iron and steel doing likewise from the interwar period. After World War II, the spectacular rise in Asia once again restructured world metal production. A result of this development became a more integrated world market with many competitors, instead of a structure with fewer production sites and a distribution net all over the world. Another important feature is the separation of mines from the location of smelting sites. In the rise of steel production in Europe, much iron ore came from northern Spain and northern Sweden; and in more recent years, the bulk of iron ore is distributed from Australia and Brazil. In copper production, much ore has been produced in Chile and the Republic of the Congo.

The introduction of coal technology in ironmaking created large centralized works, employing in many cases many thousands of workers, but the new steelworks outgrew the ironworks. Gigantic works in Pennsylvania employed tens of thousands of workers, and even larger were the steelworks founded in the Soviet Union. The enormous size created a problem with coordination and control. The Carnegie Company was a pioneer in developing the means to control production flows and workers.

The structure that was formed in metallurgic industries around 1900 in the Western world seems to have remained intact until the late 1960s. The same companies still dominated world production, with Japanese companies being the only major "intruders" into the market. In recent decades, this has changed, and a breakup of some of these great concerns has been visible. In the European steel industry, one trend has been to split companies along production lines and to form new companies based on a much smaller set of commodities. These new companies often have production sites in many places throughout Europe. Another trend, visible in America, is a development toward a more diversified structure within the corporations. The United States Steel Company, from 1986 the USX Corporation, is now involved in the oil and gas industry as well as the chemical industry.

BIBLIOGRAPHY

Ågren, Maria, ed. *Iron-Making Societies: Early Industrial Development in Sweden and Russia, 1600–1900.* Oxford, 1998.

Bakewell, Peter. "Mining in Colonial Spanish America." In *The Cambridge History of Latin America,* vol. 2, *Colonial Latin America,* edited by Lesile Bethell, pp. 105–151. Cambridge, 1984.

Berg, Maxine. "Factories, Workshops, and Industrial Organization." In *The Economic History of Britain since 1700,* vol. 1, *1700–1860,* edited by Roderick Floud and Donald McCloskey, pp. 123–150. 2d ed. Cambridge, 1994.

Birch, Alan. *The Economic History of the British Iron and Steel Industry, 1784–1879.* London, 1967.

Chandler, Alfred D. *The Visible Hand: The Managerial Revolution in American Business.* Cambridge, Mass., 1977.

Evans, Chris, and Göran Rydén. "British Ironmasters in the Eighteenth Century," In. *Europäische Montanregion Harz,* edited by H-J. Gerhard, K. H. Kaufhold and E. Westermann, pp. 81–92. Göttingen, 2001.

Florén, Anders. *Vallonskt järn: Industriell utveckling i de södra Nederländerna före industrialiseringen.* Uppsala, 1998.

Fremdling, Rainer. *Technologischer Wandel und internationaler Handel im 18. und 19. Jahrhundernt: Die Eisenindustrien in Grossbritannien, Belgien, Frankreich, und Deutschland.* Berlin, 1986.

Hildebrand, Karl-Gustaf. *Swedish Iron in the Seventeenth and Eighteenth Centuries: Export Industry before the Industrialization.* Stockholm, 1992.

Kellenbenz, Hermann ed. *Schwerpunkte der Eisengewinnung und Eisenverarbeitung in Europa, 1500–1650.* Cologne, 1974.

Kellenbenz, Hermann, ed. *Schwerpunkte der Kupferproduktion und des Kupferhandels in Europa 1500–1650.* Cologne, 1977.

Lindroth, Sten. *Gruvbrytning och kopparhantering vid Stora Kopparberget intill 1800–talets början.* Del I–II. Uppsala, 1955.

Magnusson, Gert. "Bergsmän, arbetare, bönder, gruvor, hyttor och oxar: Kring den äldsta industrialiseringen i Sverige." In *Svenskt järn under 2500 år. Från gruvpigor och smedsdrängar till operatörer,* edited by J-E Pettersson. *Daedalus,* 1997.

Nef, John U. "Mining and Metallurgy in Medieval Civilisation." In *The Cambridge Economic History of Europe,* vol. 2, *Trade and Industry in the Middle Ages,* edited by M. M. Postan and Edwards Miller. 2d ed. Cambridge, 1987.

Temin, Peter. *Iron and Steel in Nineteenth-Century America.* Cambridge, Mass., 1964.

Tylecote, R. F. *A History of Metallurgy.* London, 1992.

Westermann, Ekkehard. "Copper Production, Trade, and Use in Europe from the End of the Fifteenth Century to the End of the Eighteenth Century." In *Copper as Canvas: Two Centuries of Masterpiece Paintings on Copper, 1575–1775,* pp. 117–130. New York, 1999.

Wengenroth, Ulrich. *Enterprise and Technology: The German and British Steel Industries.* Cambridge, 1994.

GÖRAN RYDÉN

MEXICO. The economic history of post-conquest Mexico can be divided, somewhat arbitrarily, into six distinct periods. In the first, from the Spanish Conquest in 1519 to 1630, the indigenous population declined by more than 90 percent but productivity increased. In the second period, from 1630 to 1810, per capita output probably fluctuated around a level comparable to that of the thirteen British North American colonies in the early eighteenth century. Upswings occurred due to occasional bursts of activity associated with short-lived bonanzas in the colony's main export industry, silver mining; but the long-term trend was flat. The third period began with the outbreak of the independence wars (1810–1821), which provoked a sharp decline in per capita income led by the collapse of silver mining and external trade, from which the economy did not fully recover until after 1880. Elite political strife, peasant rebellions, and foreign invasions interrupted each short-lived upswing until a military coup brought Porfirio Díaz to power in 1877.

The fourth era in Mexican economic history, conventionally called the "Porfiriato" after President Díaz, coincided with the onset of sustained economic growth from the 1870s until the outbreak of the Mexican Revolution in 1911. In this era, political stability and institutional reform, combined with the development of an extensive railroad network and foreign direct investment, led to rapid, export-led economic growth. The fifth period extends from 1911 until 1982. The economy had just managed to recover from the Revolution (1911–1917) in the 1920s, when the Great Depression provoked a shift toward state-led import-substitution industrialization (ISI) that came to be viewed as part of the Revolution's legitimating legacy. This strategy produced high rates of economic growth from the 1930s until the financial and economic crisis of 1982.

The sixth and final era began with the 1982 crisis and the decisive shift in 1985–1986 to a market-oriented economic strategy that culminated with the signing of the North American Free Trade Agreement (NAFTA) with Canada and the United States. This treaty went into effect on 1 January 1994. Despite its promise, rates of economic growth achieved in this era averaged well below those of the Porfiriato and ISI periods.

The Conquest Era, 1521–1630. The Aztec (also called *Mexica*) capital city of Tenochtitlán fell to an invading army of Spanish adventurers and indigenous allies led by Hernán Cortés on 13 August 1521. The Spaniards called their new colony Nueva España (New Spain). Spanish rule lasted until Mexico became independent in 1821.

Rapid and profound demographic and economic changes followed the Conquest. A pre-Columbian population estimated variously at between 10 and 30 million fell to barely 1.1 million by 1605 as a result of introduction of European diseases for which the native population had no natural immunities. Abuse, forced labor, malnutrition, and social disruption contributed to the high mortality rates in the virgin soil epidemics that took four to five generations to run their course. Demographic recovery at rates of less than 1 percent in the seventeenth and eighteenth centuries raised the total population of the colony to nearly 6 million in 1810 (see Table 1).

The Spanish conquerors introduced European plants, animals, technology, and economic organization. The indigenous side of this "Colombian Exchange" included corn (maize) and beans (*frijoles*), staples of the indigenous diet, as well as cacao (for chocolate), cochineal (red dye) and indigo (blue dye), tomatoes, peanuts, pumpkins, and many varieties of hot peppers (*chiles*). The Europeans brought wheat and other grains, bananas, sugar cane, melons, onions, grapes, and orchard crops as well as a variety of domesticated ungulates (hoofed animals), including sheep, cattle, horses, donkeys, pigs, and goats. Initially, these animals contributed to undermining the indigenous economy as ungulate irruptions in several areas devastated native agriculture. However, many indigenous communities eventually acquired animals for production and transportation as well as for food.

By the end of the sixteenth century, the remaining indigenous population probably had a more productive agriculture and a more varied diet than before the Conquest. As the population fell, those who survived abandoned marginal lands or converted them to pasture. Land grants to Spanish immigrants led to the creation of private haciendas and ranchos and accelerated the introduction of new plants and animals as well as iron tools and implements.

The chief value of New Spain to the mother country, however, came from silver production. The indigenous population produced small quantities of precious metals from surface and placer mines. In the 1530s, the Spaniards introduced deep-shaft silver mining at Sultepec and Zumpango near Mexico City and at Taxco to the south. The major strikes, however, occurred in the north at Zacatecas (1546) and Guanajuato (1550). The mines used a mixed labor force of indigenous forced laborers, free wageworkers, and (later in the century) African slaves. Productivity increased with the introduction in the mid-1550s of the

TABLE 1. *Population and Per Capita GDP of Mexico, 1519–1999*

Year	Population (millions)	Growth rate of population	Per Capita GDP (international dollars of 1990)	Growth rate of per capita GDP	Total percent change in per capita GDP between dates
1519	10 to 30		500–600		
1605	1.1	(2.0) to (3.1)	755	0.2–0.4	20–34
1700	2.6	0.9	755	0	0
1800	6.0	0.8	755	0	0
1820	6.2	0.3	566	−1.4	−25
1845	7.5	0.9	592	0.2	5
1860	8.0	0.4	535	−0.7	10
1867	8.5	0.7	535	0	0
1877	9.7	1.3	642	1.9	17
1900	13.6	1.5	1,157	2.6	80
1910	15.2	1.1	1,435	2.2	19
1940	19.7	0.9	1,556	0.3	8
1980	69.7	3.2	5,254	3.1	238
1992	89.6	2.2	5,112	−0.2	−3
1999	95.8	0.9	5,817	1.6	14

(1) Population based on INEGI (1985).

(2) The estimate of GDP per capita 1519 is pure speculation; it assumes that 400 1990 international dollars would represent a bare subsistence.

(3) 1630 and 1700 GDP per capita estimates are set equal to 1800 to embody the assumption that per capita GDP did not change much in the colonial era. (See Coatsworth, 1988.)

(4) The 1800, 1845, 1860, and 1877 GDP per capita figures are based on Coatsworth (1978, 1989). They are converted to 1990 international dollars following Maddison (1994, 1995). Maddison's 1994 estimates extrapolated INEGI (1985) figures to construct estimates for 1820, 1850, 1870, and 1877. However, the INEGI figures are merely Coatsworth's 1978 estimates, which he first published in 1970 dollars, converted by INEGI to pesos of 1970 at the 1970 exchange rate of 26.5 pesos to the dollar. To covert INEGI's GDP figures from 1970 pesos to 1990 international dollars, Maddison divided them by 2.5. His estimates are thus those of Coatsworth multiplied by 26.5 and then divided by 2.5; this is the same as Coatsworth's figures multiplied by 10.6. I have preferred to use Coatsworth's 1989 estimates of Mexican GDP in pesos of 1900. These figures are converted to 1990 international dollars using the ratio of 1910 GDP per capita estimates by Coatsworth in 1900 pesos to Maddison in 1990 international dollars (13.6).

(5) For 1820 GDP per capita, I set aside Maddison's extrapolation in favor of a figure that reflects the substantial decline in economic activity known to have occurred during the independence wars between 1810 and 1820. The figure in the table assumes that per capita income fell by one-fourth, probably an upper limit, though contemporary estimates run up to one-third.

(6) The 1900, 1910, 1940, 1980, and 1992 GDP per capita estimates are from Maddison (1995).

(7) The 1999 estimate is from the INEGI Web page converted to 1990 dollars using the ratio applied by Maddison for 1992.

"amalgamation" process, which used small amounts of mercury to refine ore too poor in silver content to be refined by traditional smelting. The Spanish crown retained ownership of all subsoil mineral resources and levied a tax of 20 percent on gross output, the royal "fifth," later dropped under certain conditions to a royal "tenth."

To subordinate and exploit the indigenous population, the Spaniards experimented with a variety of institutional arrangements. The Spanish Law of the Indies assigned differing rights, privileges, obligations, and taxes to the colony's diverse ethnic strata or "castes." Indigenous villages received communal lands in mortmain, which made alienation and sale illegal and thus restrained, but did not eliminate, usurpation and theft. Indians could not bear arms, ride horses, dress like Europeans, move from their villages without permission, or aspire to certain occupations and offices. Indians were usually exempt from sales and excise taxes, but paid a *tributo* (head tax) not levied on others. Africans, mestizos (people of mixed European and indigenous ancestry), and others of mixed ancestry received a mixture of privileges and exclusions. Europeans stood at the top of the hierarchy.

Initially, the crown issued grants of *encomienda* to leading conquerors, "entrusting" them with responsibility for conversion and control of indigenous peoples in specified villages and areas. *Encomenderos* demanded personal service and collected tribute payments in kind or labor, using native lords as go-betweens. Faced with high mortality rates, similar to those that had virtually wiped out the entire indigenous population of the Caribbean by 1520, the crown formally abolished Indian slavery and personal service with the "New Laws," issued in 1542, but simultaneously encouraged the use of African slaves. The same legislation sought to abolish the *encomienda*, but this provision was temporarily withdrawn. The crown had already begun creating royal *encomiendas*, assigning indigenous villages to direct supervision by royal officials. By the 1570s, most private *encomiendas* had been abolished or abandoned in central Mexico, where population decline had made them far less valuable than before. After experimenting with government-managed labor drafts called *repartimientos de indios* for Spanish employers, the system was abandoned in stages between 1599 and 1630 in favor of a free-labor market distorted by caste distinctions.

Colonial Stagnation, 1630–1821. The slow recovery of the indigenous population after about 1630 coincided with a period of stagnation in government revenues, trade, and mining output. In per capita terms, the era period from 1630 to 1690 probably witnessed a substantial decline in the sectors dominated by the enterprise of Spaniards and creoles (Spaniards born in the colony). The period from 1690 to 1810, though usually treated as a distinct era of growth and prosperity, is now viewed as a century in which GDP did not grow faster than the population. Substantial advances in mining output occurred from the 1690s into the 1720s, but the rise in silver production over the entire century barely exceeded population growth. After 1750, interregional migration accelerated, particularly from the depressed Puebla-Tlaxcala area to the grain estates, mining centers, and artisan industries of the Bajío, north and west of Mexico City. This movement pushed cattle and sheep raising northward. Woolen textile production fell, however, displaced by cotton substitutes increasingly smuggled in from Britain.

In the second half of the eighteenth century, the Spanish government initiated a series of administrative and economic policy reforms, especially during the reign of King Charles (Carlos) III (1759–1788). Collectively known as the "Bourbon Reforms," the policy changes sought to centralize power, tighten administration, raise taxes, increase trade, and promote mining production. The reforms had mixed economic effects. Mining production benefited from lower prices charged by the royal monopolies that supplied mercury and blasting powder as well as from tax exemptions and the creation of a mining Tribunal (1776) and an engineering academy (1792). Trade increased when ships were allowed to sail without waiting for the annual fleets (1740), new ports in Spain and the colonies opened to trade (1764–1778), and the monopoly of the Mexico City Merchant Guild (*Consulado*) on all foreign trade transactions ended (1778). Other measures lowered some export taxes and encouraged trade between the colonies, but the fundamental commercial monopoly that required all foreign trade to be carried in Spanish ships through Spanish ports remained in place. In addition, administrative and fiscal reforms increased burdens on other sectors of the economy by raising excise and sales taxes, collecting the *tributo* more efficiently, imposing new government monopolies on the production and sale of tobacco as well as other products, and issuing new and cumbersome regulations to reduce contraband. The net effect of the Bourbon Reforms was probably small and possibly even negative. With GDP per capita stagnant over the eighteenth century, Mexico's economy fell from rough parity with the thirteen British North American colonies to approximately 44 percent of U.S. GDP in 1800.

Independence to Restored Republic, 1821–1876. A legacy of inefficient economic organization compounded by political instability blocked Mexican economic growth at independence. Many of the colonial regulations and restrictions on economic activity disappeared in 1821, including caste-based limits on occupational mobility and officeholding as well as the prohibition on direct trade with countries other than Spain. However, many colonial institutions and practices continued until the Liberal Revolution in the 1850s, while political risks increased dramatically. Between 1821 and 1867, thirty-three individuals served as Mexico's chief of state, some of whom returned to office several times. There were more than fifty changes of administration, many of them violent and nearly all unconstitutional. During the same years, Mexico experienced fourteen large-scale indigenous and peasant revolts and at least sixty local rural rebellions.

Instability bankrupted successive administrations and made it impossible for Mexico to make regular payments on its external public debt after defaulting in 1827. A short-lived conservative-inspired development bank, the Banco de Avío, used customs revenues to finance the importation of modern textile and other machinery in the 1830s, but the revenues were soon diverted to military expenditures, and most of the new enterprises failed. Instability also made the country vulnerable to foreign aggression. Mexico experienced three major foreign invasions (Spain in 1829, the United States in 1846–1848, and France in 1863–1867). Most disastrous for the country was the U.S. invasion that forced Mexico to cede half of its national territory. The California Gold Rush in the United States began only a few months after California ceased to be a part of Mexico.

The Liberal Revolution, called *La reforma*, brought Benito Juárez to power from 1855 to 1872 and resulted in a new Constitution of 1857 that separated church and state; outlawed the archaic privileges (called *fueros*) of Catholic priests and military officers, which had exempted them from the jurisdiction of ordinary civil and criminal courts; abolished the inalienability of property (mortmain) and ordered the privatization of the landholdings of indigenous villages, municipal governments, and the church; and established a federal system of government with strict limitations on the taxing powers of the national government. When the church refused to sell its properties and supported Conservative revolts, the Liberal regime confiscated church lands and urban properties and sold them at auction. In 1864, Mexican conservatives allied to the church invited Austrian archduke Maximilian of Habsburg to become "emperor" of Mexico, backed by a French of expeditionary force sent by Napoleon III. In 1867, Napoleon withdrew his forces, and the Liberals under Juárez restored the republic. By this time Mexican GDP per capita had fallen well below late colonial levels.

The Porfiriato, 1876–1911. Mexico's first modern spurt of sustained economic growth occurred during the Porfiriato. Population grew from 9.7 to 15.2 million (1.3 percent per annum). GDP per capita rose 2.5 percent per year. The end of civil and international strife, along with the reform legislation of the Liberal Revolution and succeeding governments, encouraged both domestic and foreign investment. The new legislation included a complete revision of the tariff code as well as new commercial and mining codes in the 1880s.

High transportation costs, which had inhibited regional specialization and kept much of Mexico's land and mineral resources isolated from profitable exploitation, were finally overcome with the building of an extensive railroad network. Though the Mexican government first granted a concession for railway construction in 1837, the first major line, running between Mexico City and Veracruz, was not inaugurated until 1873. A period of rapid construction began in 1880, when the government approved concessions for two trunk lines to run from Mexico City to the U.S. border. Other lines followed until the rail network reached a total of 19,205 kilometers (11,934 miles) on the eve of the Revolution in 1910. Recognizing the importance of efficient rail service and fearing acquisition of Mexican rail companies by unscrupulous U.S. "financiers," the government decided to "Mexicanize" the major companies. Between 1903 and 1908, the government purchased a controlling interest in all the major companies and created a new enterprise, the National Railways of Mexico (Ferrocarriles Nacionales de México), to run the system.

Primary product exports fueled Mexico's economic growth during the Porfirian era, though domestic agriculture and manufacturing also grew substantially. Exports grew 7.6 percent per annum from 1878 to 1910 as the export portfolio diversified. Silver exports fell from 76.3 percent of total exports in 1877–1878 to 28.8 percent in 1910–1911, as the price of silver fell by more than half. Since Mexico maintained a silver-based monetary system until the Monetary Reform of 1905, progressive devaluation may have initially stimulated exports. Meanwhile, export production of industrial metals, such as copper, lead, and zinc, increased rapidly to supply external, mainly U.S., demand. When the U.S. McKinley Tariff of 1890 raised duties on ore imported to the United States but kept rates on processed metals low, U.S., European, and Mexican companies heavily invested in the creation of a modern smelting industry. Mexico also became a major oil producer by 1910, with the discovery of large deposits in the Tehuantepec region and along the Gulf Coast north of the port of Veracruz.

While mineral ores, metals, and petroleum never amounted to less than half of all exports during the Porfiriato, agricultural exports also boomed. The demand for henequen fiber, native to Yucatán and produced nowhere else in the world, skyrocketed when it went into use as binder twine in McCormick reapers on farms throughout the United States. Mexico also exported chickpeas from Sonora, coffee from Tabasco and Chiapas, vanilla from Veracruz state, and cattle and hides from the northern states along the U.S. border in this era.

Demographic and economic growth stimulated both domestic and foreign direct investment in industry. Domestic light manufacturing (textiles, beer, paper, shoes, food processing) modernized with a national market now accessible by rail. The production of cotton and other industrial crops grew rapidly, while domestic food production kept pace with population.

Despite the material progress between 1867 and 1910, Mexican social conditions did not improve and may even have worsened significantly for many. Life expectancy at birth in the late Porfiriato was estimated at 29.5 years, the infant mortality rate stood more than 280 per 1,000 live births, and illiteracy remained high at 78 percent. Inequality in the distribution of income as well as assets probably increased. Modernization and economic growth provoked widespread concentration of landownership. Church and public lands passed to wealthy bidders while indigenous villagers were forced to privatize communal plots, making them vulnerable to usurpation. Railroads connected once-isolated crop and cattle lands to distant markets and made them worth taking. Landless villagers poured into the market for unskilled labor, just as economic growth increased demand and salaries for skilled and educated employees. With tax revenues to the central government running at less than 5 percent of GDP, the Díaz government had few resources to devote to social questions.

Revolution and Institutionalization, 1911–1982. The Mexican Revolution marked a watershed in Mexico's economic history. As many as one million inhabitants may have died in civil warfare between 1911 and 1916, while another half million or more fled the country. Contending armies wreaked havoc on the railroads, seizing locomotives and rolling stock for troop transportation while blowing up track and bridges to deny their use to enemies. Insecurity in the countryside increased as peasant militias and military commanders seized haciendas. Successive governments sought to enlist urban workers' support by backing strikes and enforcing wage agreements. Global demand for Mexican exports, especially oil and metals, skyrocketed during World War I but collapsed in the 1919 recession. The economy began to recover in the 1920s, but growth declined again due in part to renewed civil strife, including a widespread peasant revolt called the Cristero War (1926–1929) linked to church-state conflicts. Mexico had just surpassed prerevolutionary levels of per capita GDP when the Great Depression struck.

Pressures for political, social, and economic change, encouraged during the presidential administration of Lázaro Cárdenas (1934–1940), led to massive agrarian reform and government support for union organizing. Between 1935 and 1940, the Cárdenas government expropriated and redistributed eighteen million hectares of land, amounting to a third of the country's arable farmland. In 1938, when foreign-owned petroleum companies refused to obey an order of the Mexican Supreme Court upholding an official arbitration decision that favored oil workers and their union, the Cárdenas government expropriated the companies and created Petroleos Mexicanos (PEMEX), a state-owned company, to take over production and distribution. A retaliatory embargo by the United States and Great Britain ended quickly as World War II broke out and Mexico's oil and mineral resources became vital to the Allied war effort.

The depression reduced Mexico's capacity to import, while government policies tended to cushion the fall in consumer demand among lower- and middle-income people. Mexican industry experienced a quick recovery from the depression and substantial growth in manufacturing output, but since the country lacked the capacity to import capital goods, this growth was achieved by making more intensive use of existing plants and equipment. During World War II, this trend continued and intensified, as the economy responded to huge increases in demand for war-related metals and other products. Bottlenecks grew in transportation, smelting, and other industries. Output rose but productivity declined. Wartime inflation reversed the wage gains achieved in the 1930s but favored some farmers, including those newly endowed with land titles. In 1942, the United States and Mexico cooperated to create a large-scale guest-worker program that permitted some three hundred thousand Mexican workers to perform agricultural labor and eventually other jobs in the United States to make up for wartime labor shortages. This *bracero* (laborer) program lasted until the U.S. government closed it down in 1964, by which time more than four million Mexicans had participated.

After 1940, the government's strategy shifted from reform and redistribution to investment and productivity growth. The governing party was renamed the Partido de la Revolución Institucional (PRI) in 1946 to emphasize this change of direction. The political capital accumulated in the Cárdenas era and the high rates of economic growth actually achieved during the postwar decades legitimated the regime and contributed to stability. Labor peace was assured by collaboration between the government and the leaders of the Confederación de Trabajadores de México (CTM), the largest union federation officially incorporated into the PRI beginning in 1938. An explicit strategy of import-substitution industrialization (ISI) adopted during the administration of President Miguel Alemán Valdés from 1946 to 1952 required an environment that protected domestic manufacturers and welcomed (but for political reasons also strictly regulated) foreign direct investment. Government development banks like Nacional Financiera (NAFINSA) provided loans and other assistance to many domestically owned industries. After a sharp devaluation in 1954, Mexican authorities pegged the peso to the U.S. dollar and worked successfully to keep inflation low; this policy of "stabilizing development" continued until U.S.

MEXICO. Metal refinery in Chihuahua, 1987. (© Kal Muller/Woodfin Camp and Associates, New York)

macroeconomic policy itself became unstable in the early 1970s.

Over the four decades from 1940 to 1980, Mexican per capita GDP grew at an annual average rate of 3.2 percent. This post–World War II "miracle" coincided with high rates of population growth due mainly to falling mortality rates. Manufacturing and services grew faster than the economy as a whole. Agricultural production kept pace with population growth until the 1970s. The ISI strategy also succeeded in reducing the country's "dependence" on exports and foreign investment. From 1940 to 1976, exports fell from 11.6 to 3.8 percent of GDP. Mexico's share of world trade also fell dramatically.

Internal pressures combined with external shocks to undermine Mexico's ISI strategy in the 1970s. The U.S. decision to float the dollar in 1971, the 1973–1974 oil price shock, and U.S. "stagflation" created dilemmas for Mexican policymakers. Political worries following the repression of a nationwide prodemocracy student movement in 1968 pushed Mexican authorities to deepen the country's commitment to protectionism, public ownership, and centralized regulation of economic activity. Balance of payments and fiscal constraints made these policies unsustainable. President Luis Echevarría Alvarez (1970–1976) was forced to devalue the peso and sharply reduce spending in the last year of his administration.

The discovery of vast new oil reserves in the states of Tabasco and Chiapas and in the Gulf of Mexico, announced in 1976, restored the government's shaky credit and allowed the new administration of José López Portillo (1976–1982) to borrow heavily from international commercial banks, both to finance petroleum development and to cover fiscal deficits. In 1976, Mexico was a net importer of petroleum products. By 1980, oil exports amounted to more than U.S. $6 billion, more than 70 percent of total exports. Awash in petrodollars and commercial loans to government and the private sector, Mexico experienced a brief episode of Dutch disease. With the peso overvalued by as much as 30 percent, nonoil export producers lost markets and declined sharply.

A severe financial and economic crisis hit Mexico when the oil boom ended during 1981 and 1982. The crisis originated not in Mexico but in the United States, where U.S. authorities began driving up interest rates to control inflation. This caused a rapid increase in Mexico's debt burden and then, as a deep recession hit the United States, a rapid fall in oil prices. With debt payments spiraling upward and oil revenues down sharply, Mexico was forced in September 1982 to announce that it could not meet payments on its external debt, much of it now in short-term instruments that were payable in full in less than 180 days. The peso collapsed, the government nationalized the banking system, and though Mexico eventually met its debt payments with loans from international agencies and the United States, the economy sank into a deep and prolonged recession provoked by sharp cuts in spending and increased taxes.

The Free Trade Era, from 1982 into the Twenty-first Century. After failing in efforts to revive the economy without abandoning ISI and the prevailing state-directed economic strategy, the new administration of President Miguel de la Madrid Hurtado (1982–1988) abruptly abandoned it in favor of a new strategy based on freer trade, deregulation, and privatization. In 1985 to 1986, Mexico joined the General Agreement on Trade and Tariffs (GATT), dropped tariff rates on a wide range of imports, and began dismantling a long list of nontariff regulatory barriers to foreign imports. These policies were carried further under succeeding presidents, Carlos Salinas de Gortari (1988 to 1994), Ernesto Zedillo Ponce de León (1994–2000), and Vicente Fox Quesada (2000–). The economic policy changes enacted by the Salinas administration were especially dramatic and decisive. The government lowered tariffs even further and eliminated most other nontariff barriers, did away with a wide range of regulations and restrictions on foreign direct investment, renegotiated the external debt on more favorable terms, privatized several hundred state-owned companies, and in 1993 signed the North American Free Trade Agreement (NAFTA) with the United States and Canada.

The effects of Mexico's new economic strategy varied across sectors of the economy. Inefficient producers deprived of tariff and other protections quickly succumbed to foreign competition, though grain farmers and commercial banks got a temporary reprieve when NAFTA negotiators agreed to delay the full effects of external competition for especially weak sectors of the Mexican economy for up to fifteen years. Small and medium manufacturers of consumer products were especially hard hit. New foreign direct investment concentrated in sectors privatized by the government, such as telecommunications, airlines, steel, and truck manufacturing, and in sectors producing for the U.S. market, such as automobiles and auto parts. Assembly plants using imported components to produce export products (called *maquiladoras*) expanded rapidly after NAFTA and spread out from the northern states to other regions of the country. Mexican exports rose from 8.2 percent of GDP in 1980 to 28.1 percent in 1999. By this time, petroleum exports had declined to 7.2 percent of total exports. GDP growth, however, remained disappointing. In 1999, Mexican GDP per capita was only 10.7 percent above the level it had reached in 1980.

At the end of the twentieth century, Mexico's economy had resumed growing steadily, though still at rates below those of the 1950s and 1960s. Economic integration with the United States reached unprecedented levels as the full impact of NAFTA took hold. Slower population growth—down to 1.6 percent per year at the end of the twentieth century—promised lower dependency, lower unemployment rates, and higher savings. The cumulative effects of welfare improvements during the twentieth century were also evident. Life expectancy rose to more than seventy years, the infant mortality rate had dropped to about thirty per one thousand live births, and the illiteracy rate was down to 10 percent. Nonetheless, Mexico continued to lag in efforts to address poverty, low educational attainment, and a wide range of chronic public health problems, including rural malnutrition as well as urban air and water pollution.

BIBLIOGRAPHY

Bazdresch, Carlos, and Santiago Levy. "Populism and Economic Policy in Mexico, 1970–1982." In *The Macroeconomics of Populism in Latin America*, edited by Rudiger Dornbusch and Sebastian Edwards, pp. 223–262. Chicago, 1991.

Cárdenas, Enrique. "A Macroeconomic Interpretation of Nineteenth-Century Mexico." In *How Latin America Fell Behind: Essays on the Economic Histories of Brazil and Mexico, 1800–1914*, edited by Stephen Haber, pp. 65–92. Stanford, Calif., 1997.

Coatsworth, John H. "Obstacles to Economic Growth in Nineteenth-Century Mexico." *American Historical Review* 83.1 (1978), 80–100.

Coatsworth, John H. "La historiografía económica de México." *Revista de Historia Económica* 6.2 (1988), 277–291.

Coatsworth, John H. "The Decline of the Mexican Economy, 1800–1860." In *La formación de las economías latinoamericanas y los intereses económicos europeos en la época de Simón Bolívar*, edited by Reinhart Liehr, pp. 25–53. Berlin, 1989.

Gibson, Charles. *The Aztecs under Spanish Rule: A History of the Valley of Mexico, 1519–1810*. Stanford, Calif., 1964.

Haber, Stephen. *Industry and Underdevelopment: The Industrialization of Mexico, 1890–1940*. Stanford, Calif., 1989.

Hofman, Andre, and Nanno Mulder. "The Comparative Productivity Performance of Brazil and Mexico, 1950–1994." In *Latin America and the World Economy since 1800*, edited by John H. Coatsworth and Alan M. Taylor, pp. 85–109. Cambridge, 1998.

INEGI (Instituto Nacional de Estadística, Geografía e Informática). *Estadísticas históricas de México*. 2 vols. Mexico City, 1985.

Lustig, Nora. *Mexico: The Remaking of an Economy*. Washington, D.C., 1992.

Maddison, Angus. "Explaining the Economic Convergence of Nations, 1820–1989." In *Convergence of Productivity: Cross National Studies and Historical Evidence*, edited by W. J. Baumol, R. R. Nelson, and E. N. Wolff, pp. 20–61. Oxford, 1994.

Maddison, Angus. *Explaining the Economic Performance of Nations: Essays in Time and Space*. Aldershot, U.K., 1995.

Maddison, Angus. *Monitoring the World Economy, 1820–1992*. Paris, 1995.

Marichal, Carlos. "Obstacles to the Development of Capital Markets in Nineteenth-Century Mexico." In *How Latin America Fell Behind: Essays on the Economic Histories of Brazil and Mexico, 1800–1914*, edited by Stephen Haber, pp. 118–145. Stanford, Calif., 1997.

Potash, Robert. *Mexican Government and Industrial Development in the Early Republic: The Banco de Avío*. Amherst, Mass., 1983.

Reynolds, Clark. *The Mexican Economy: Twentieth-Century Structure and Growth*. New Haven, 1970.

Salvucci, Richard J. *Textiles and Capitalism in Mexico: An Economic History of the Obrajes, 1539–1840*. Princeton, 1987.

JOHN H. COATSWORTH

MEXICO CITY. The greater Mexico City Metropolitan Area (MCMA), covering 4,918 square kilometers, contained a total population of 16.8 million people in 1995, second in the world only to Tokyo. Of that number, 8.6 million lived in

MEXICO CITY. Rush hour at a subway station, 1985. (© Stephanie Maze/Woodfin Camp and Associates, New York)

the Federal District (Distrito Federal), which includes all of Mexico City proper, and 8.3 million lived in thirty four contiguous municipalities in the State of Mexico. The MCMA thus represented 18.4 percent of Mexico's 1995 total population of 91.2 million. The MCMA produces roughly 20 percent of the nation's manufactured goods. Its inhabitants earn more than 30 percent of the national income.

Originally called Tenochtitlán, Mexico was founded in 1325 by a band of Nahuá-speaking "Mexica" or Aztecs, warrior nomads from the far north employed at the time as mercenaries by various city-states in the Valley of Mexico. The Aztecs chose a swampy island in salty Lake Texcoco avoided by others and built a large city connected to the lakeshore by causeways. By 1519, on the eve of the Spanish conquest, the city had become the capital of a large empire and grown to between 100,000 and 300,000 inhabitants. The Aztec rulers brought in fresh water on aqueducts, produced crops on raised fields or *chinampas* (sometimes erroneously called "floating gardens"), and took fish and algae from Lake Texcoco and two adjacent freshwater lakes. Ecological stress and periodic food shortages were recorded prior to the conquest.

From 1519 until 1821, Mexico City served as the capital of the Spanish viceroyalty of New Spain. The Spaniards introduced European diseases, allowed Aztec sanitation practices to lapse, and forced indigenous residents to work on tearing down and rebuilding the city. After several floods, the colonial government decided to drain all three of the lakes in the valley. Forced labor on huge drainage canals fur-

ther elevated mortality rates, destroyed most of the preconquest *chinampas*, irreparably damaged the fragile ecology of the basin, and made the city more vulnerable to earthquake damage. The population fell to a low of 30,000 before recovering to approximately 100,000 to 130,000 on the eve of the wars of independence (1810–1821).

In addition to its role as the seat of civil and ecclesiastical governance and home to the colony's economic elite, the city also served as New Spain's main commercial entrepôt, linking the silver mines of the north to Veracruz, the colony's main port on the Gulf of Mexico. The city's artisan and manufacturing establishments concentrated mainly on food processing, cotton and woolen textiles, pottery making, tanning and leather goods, and construction materials. The largest industrial employer in the late eighteenth century was the government-owned tobacco factory, with more than 600 workers. The government also owned and operated a gunpowder factory and a large mint, both royal monopolies.

Swelled by refugees during the wars of independence, Mexico City's population rose to more than 150,000 by 1821, but stagnated at about 200,000 from the 1830s to the 1870s. Though per-capita income in Mexico fell in this period of civil strife and foreign intervention, Mexican entrepreneurs established a series of modern cotton mills and other manufacturing operations beginning in the late 1840s. By 1865, a city census claimed 377 "factories," of which 58 produced cotton and woolen thread. Most of the others consisted of large workshops for producing light consumer goods from candles and matches to cookies and shirts.

The city's population resumed growing during the era of President Porfirio Díaz (1876–1911). In 1910, on the eve of the Mexican Revolution (1910–1917), the country's third census put the city's population at 471,066 and that of the Federal District (which still included a number of separate towns and villages) at 720,753. Mexico City became the hub of a national railroad network built in this era. The city's industrial base modernized and expanded, especially in textiles, cement, brewing, paper, food processing, and other consumer goods.

During the revolution, Mexico City's population swelled with refugees, but the city kept growing even after the fighting ended in 1917. Population growth accelerated over the next three decades as mortality rates fell and industrial and service employment rose. The Federal District benefited disproportionately from the expansion of government agencies, the development of service industries, and the import-substitution industrialization (ISI) that began in the 1930s and took off in the 1950s. The growth of population in the MCMA reached a peak of 6.6 percent per year in that decade as the national baby boom coincided with massive rural to urban migration. High rates of population growth continued through the 1970s. By 1980, the MCMA reached 14.3 million inhabitants, 20.6 percent of the nation's population, and produced more than 40 percent of GDP.

As Mexico City grew, urban problems accumulated. Air pollution from motor vehicles, industries, leaking propane cooking gas tanks (natural gas is not piped to most homes), and dried excrement from open sewage canals reached alarming proportions in the 1990s. Crime rates also peaked in the late 1990s. The economic crisis of the 1980s reduced migration into the city, and as the government ended protection for domestic manufacturing, industrial employment shifted toward the northern states closer to the United States. Together with declining birthrates, these factors helped to reduce MCMA population growth to a low of 0.2 percent per annum in the 1980s, followed by a modest recovery to just under 2 percent in the 1990s.

BIBLIOGRAPHY

Davis, Diane. *Urban Leviathan: Mexico City in the Twentieth Century.* Philadelphia, 1994.

Iliades, Carlos. "Composición de la fuerza de trabajo y de las unidades productivas en la ciudad de México, 1788–1873," In *La ciudad de México en la primera mitad del siglo XIX*, edited by Regina Hernández Franyuti, vol. 2, pp. 250–278. Mexico, 1994.

Kandell, Jonathan. *La Capital: The Biography of Mexico City.* New York, 1988.

Pezzoli, Keith. *Human Settlements and Planning for Ecological Sustainability: The Case of Mexico City.* Cambridge, 1988.

JOHN H. COATSWORTH

MIDDLEMAN MINORITIES. Homogeneous trading networks (HTN) or trade diasporas have been ubiquitous in economies where the legal framework for the protection of property rights and enforcement of contracts were not well developed. Historian Philip Curtin (1984) provided numerous examples of HTNs: Jewish trade networks in medieval Europe, Armenian trade networks, Chinese trade networks in Southeast Asia, and so on. Take the case study of the Chinese merchants in Southeast Asia (Landa, 1978). In the 1960s and 1970s, the middlemen involved in the marketing of smallholders' rubber were composed of a tightly knit, ethnically homogeneous middleman group (EHMG)—the Hokkien-Chinese traders linked by ties of kinship, clanship, locality, and dialect/ethnicity. Embedded within the EHMG was the Confucian code of ethics of mutual aid and reciprocity. Confucian ethics in traditional Chinese society prescribe differences in the degree of obligation for mutual aid/reciprocity among various categories of kin. An individual's obligation and loyalty is first and foremost to his own family. It is then extended to kinsmen of the lineage, and finally to one's own clan (Yang, 1957; Levy, Jr., 1968). The overseas Chinese adapted Confucian cultural values, designed for the kinship group in traditional China, to the environment of a multiethnic Chinese society, itself embedded within a larger multiethnic society composed of Europeans, Chinese, and indigenous populations. The overseas Chinese community organized themselves along five major dialect/ethnic mutual aid ("pang") groups: Hokkien, Teochew, Cantonese, Hakka, and Hiananese. The Chinese dialect/ethnic boundary defines the (Confucian) limits of mutual aid and cooperation for members of the group, that is, an ethnic/dialect community is typically the constituency for its mutual aid associations, and for the formation of particularistic economic relationships with various cooperating partners (e.g., partners or employees of a firm, trading partners, etc.).

In a number of my published articles, (1981, reprinted in 1994, chapter 5; 1988; 2000) I have developed an economic theory of the EHMG and of entrepreneurial success of these middleman minority ethnic groups, with specific reference to Chinese merchants in Southeast Asia. My theory draws on the concepts of "infrastructure" in development economics, "institution" and "transaction costs" in the New Institutional Economics (NIE), and "biology of morality" (Alexander, 1987) in evolutionary biology. Of the various components of infrastructure discussed in development economics—law and order, transportation facilities, banking and credit institutions, education, and public health—the most fundamental is the legal infrastructure or the institutional framework of a market economy (Wharton, 1967; Parsons, 1967). The concept of institution is defined in the NIE (Eggersson, 1990, 19 chapter 1, Landa, 1994, chapter 1) as the rules of the game in a society—both formal rules (e.g., contract law, the constitution) and informal rules (codes of ethics, morality, etc.)—that constrain human behavior. The major function of institutions is to introduce social order by reducing uncertainty—by generating greater predictability of human behavior—hence economizing on transaction costs of coordinating recurrent human interactions. Transaction costs, a concept introduced by R. H. Coase (1937), refers to the costs of exchange, such as the enforcement of contracts, and the search for information of prices and the reputation of potential trading partners. In less-developed countries, such as those in Southeast Asia in the 1960s and 1970s, where infrastructure is not well developed, entrepreneurs must perform gap-filling roles by forming clublike organizational arrangements to provide themselves with infrastructure essential for entrepreneurship. The EHMG is precisely such an informal clublike economic organization for the provision of infrastructure for members of the trading group. Within the EHMG are located functional equivalents of several components of infrastructure provided by formal institutions in well-developed economies:

1. The Confucian code of ethics, embedded in the EHMG, promotes mutual trust among Hokkien merchants via reputational effects, backed up by social sanctions (e.g., gossip and ostracism from the group); it is the functional equivalent of modern contract law which, by reducing the risks of breach of contract, economizes on the transaction costs of private protection of contracts (Landa, 1981, reprinted in 1994, chapter 5).
2. The informal social networks and the formal mutual aid associations embedded within the wider dialect/ethnic group provide Chinese middlemen with the functional equivalent of credit-rating institutions.
3. The informal credit networks within the EHMG, made possible by the underlying collective trust of members, provide the function equivalent of banks and financial institutions for the supply of capital that economize on the opportunity costs of holding cash.
4. The flexibility of creditor-debtor roles among the Chinese embedded in the EHMG provide a built-in insurance for reducing risks of bankruptcy.

The EHMG can also be considered an informal organization for economizing on information costs in a less-developed economy in the following ways: (1) Individual traders can quickly acquire information on the trustworthiness/creditworthiness of a potential trading partner by cognitively classifying all potential trading partners into seven categories based on kinship/social distance and inferring from kinship/social distance the degree of trustworthiness of a potential trading partner; and (2) by sorting all potential trading partners into their respective categories by looking for symbols of kinship identity or group/ethnic identity, such as clan names, language, dress, ritual practices, and racial characteristics of a potential trading partner (Landa, 1981; Carr and Landa, 1983). This individual decision making based on a categorization/classificatory system is a fast and efficient system of information acquisition in an underdeveloped economy where information is scarce and costly to obtain.

The Chinese middleman economy is a clublike, private-ordering type of governance structure operating within a country's informal sector (Landa, 1988) in which members, through in-group mutual aid and cooperation, provide themselves with infrastructure/club goods essential for middleman entrepreneurship. This in-group cooperation gave the Chinese middleman group a competitive advantage vis-à-vis other ethnic groups to appropriate the role of middleman in Southeast Asia. Seen in this perspective, the role of Confucian ethics has a biological basis. Biologist Richard Alexander (1987, p. 1) speaking of the "biology of moral systems" says: "the concepts of moral and ethical arise because of the conflict of interest, and that—at least up to now—moral systems have been designed to assist group members and explicitly not to assist the members of other competing groups." Central to Alexander's perspective is his emphasis on intergroup competition and the conflict of interest between groups that promotes intragroup competition. It is this in-group cooperation among Chinese middlemen, which excluded the indigenous population from middleman roles, that is at the economic root of the envy of Chinese by the indigenous population. This has historically led to episodes of interethnic conflict and violence in the multiracial societies of Southeast Asia. This also prompted indigenous governments, emerging from colonial rule, to adopt discriminatory policies against the Chinese in Southeast Asia. The policy implication for promoting interethnic harmony in racially diverse economies with foreign ethnic minority groups dominating merchant roles is for the state to play an important role in creating a well-developed infrastructure, including the legal-institutional infrastructure of a market economy (Landa, 1978, 1981, 2000). The theory of EHMG, developed for Chinese merchants, can be generalized to other ethnic merchant groups (Carr and Landa, 1983).

[*See also* Commercial and Trade Diasporas.]

BIBLIOGRAPHY

Alexander, Richard D. 1987. *The Biology of Moral Systems*. Hawthorne, N.Y., 1987.

Carr, Jack, and Janet T. Landa. "The Economics of Symbols, Clan Names, and Religion." *Journal of Legal Studies* 12.1 (1983), 135–156.

Coase, R. H. "The Nature of the Firm." *Economica* 4 (November 1937), 386–405. Reprinted in *Readings in Price Theory*, edited by G. J. Stigler and K. E. Boulding. Chicago, 1952.

Curtin, Philip D. *Cross-Cultural Trade in World History*. Cambridge, 1984.

Eggertsson, Thrainn. *Economic Behavior and Institutions*. Cambridge, 1990.

Landa, Janet T. "The Economics of the Ethnically Homogeneous Chinese Middleman Group: A Property Rights-Public Choice Approach." Ph.D. diss., Virginia Polytechnic Institute and State University, 1978.

Landa, Janet T. "A Theory of the Ethnically Homogeneous Chinese Middleman Group: An Institutional Alternative to Contract Law." *Journal of Legal Studies* 10.2 (June 1981), 349–362.

Landa, Janet T. "Underground Economies: Generic or Sui Generis? In *Beyond the Informal Sector: Including the Excluded in Developing Countries*, edited by Jerry Jenkins, pp. 75–103. San Francisco, 1988.

Landa, Janet T. *Trust, Ethnicity, and Identity: Beyond the New Institutional Economics of Ethnic Trading Networks, Contract Law, and Gift-Exchange*. Ann Arbor, 1994.

Landa, Janet T. "The Law and Bioeconomics of Ethnic Cooperation and Conflict: A Theory of Chinese Merchant Success." *Journal of Bioeconomics* 1.3 (2000), pp. 269–284.

Levy, Jr., Marion J. *The Family Revolution in Modern China*. New York, 1968.

Parsons, Kenneth H. "Comment." In *Agricultural Development and Economic Growth*, edited by Herman M. Southworth and Bruce H. Johnston, pp. 143–146. Ithaca, N.Y., 1967.

Wharton, Clifton R. "The Infrastructure for Agricultural Growth." In *Agricultural Development and Economic Growth*, edited by Herman M. Southworth and Bruce F. H. Johnston, pp. 107–142. Ithaca, N.Y., 1967.

Yang, Lien-Sheng. "The Concept of 'Pao' as a Basis for Social Relations in China." In *Chinese Thought and Institutions*, edited by John K. Fairbanks, pp. 291–309. Chicago, 1957.

JANET T. LANDA

MIGRATION. *See* Internal Migration *and* International Migration.

MILL, JOHN STUART (1806–1873), English philosopher and economist.

John Stuart Mill was not only one of the most important economists of the nineteenth century, but also a philosopher, politician, utilitarian, philosophical radical, advocate of liberalism, and supporter of women's rights.

Born in 1806 to James Mill (1773–1836) and his wife Harriet, John Mill was a child prodigy. He began to learn Greek at age three, read Plato at seven, and began Latin at eight. Except for a year spent in France, he was educated at home by his father. He spent his whole childhood in study, and had no time for either toys or playmates. At age seventeen he joined his father as an employee of the East India Company, where he worked six hours a day writing dispatches. The same year he was arrested for distributing pamphlets on birth control. For about five months during the winter of 1826–1827, Mill suffered from a fit of depression, which he called in his *Autobiography* "a crisis in my mental history." He recovered by reading Wordsworth, and resolved to add emotions to his rationality. Mill continued to work at the East India Company, and was eventually

JOHN STUART MILL. Portrait by George Frederick Watts (1817–1904). (Prints and Photographs Division, Library of Congress)

promoted to and held the rank of chief examiner, until the company was dissolved in 1858. Mill frequently wrote for periodicals, and from 1834 to 1840 was editor of the *London and Westminster Review*, the voice of the short-lived Philosophical Radical party.

In 1830 Mill fell in love with Harriet Taylor, who was unfortunately already married to John Taylor. Harriet fell in love with Mill, but refused to leave her husband or to be unfaithful to him. Their "scandalous" but chaste relationship continued for almost two decades. In 1849 John Taylor died, and in 1851 Mill married Harriet. Harriet's intellectual influence was profound; most of Mill's writings were really joint productions with Harriet.

After Harriet's death in 1858, Mill lived and collaborated with his stepdaughter Helen Taylor. Mill was elected to the House of Commons in 1865 and served until 1868; and in 1867 he became the first member of parliament to suggest that women be given the right to vote. He died in 1873.

Mill's most important book is probably *On Liberty*, in which he suggests that an individual's freedom of choice should be limited only when those choices would harm others. Using an economic metaphor to support free speech, Mill argues that all ideas should be allowed to compete in the marketplace of ideas, where competition will ensure that only the best ideas survive.

Mill's *Principles of Political Economy*, published in 1848, was a popular textbook; it went through 32 editions in 50 years. In economic theory, Mill was a link between Ricardo and Malthus. He learned Ricardian economics from his father, but modified many of Ricardo's theories. After Malthus and Ricardo gave economics the title "the dismal science," Mill provided a more optimistic economics. Mill noted that although production is constrained by the laws of nature, the distribution of income is a choice made by society. Since economic institutions are not fixed by nature, they can be changed for the better. Mill thought that society could improve by moving toward socialism. However, he considered the specific plans put forward by socialists to be either impractical or inconsistent with individual freedom. Mill was more critical of the utopian socialists in the first edition of his *Principles*, but, under Harriet's influence, became less critical in later editions. Mill feared population growth, but he believed that people could limit fertility enough to allow for improved living standards.

BIBLIOGRAPHY

SELECTED WORKS BY MILL
A System of Logic (1843).
Principles of Political Economy (1848).
On Liberty (1859).
Utilitarianism (1863).
The Subjection of Women (1869).
Autobiography (1873).

WORKS ABOUT MILL
Hayek, Friedrich A. von. *John Stuart Mill and Harriet Taylor: Their Correspondence and Subsequent Marriage.* London, 1951.
Packe, Michael St. John. *The Life of John Stuart Mill.* London, 1954.
Schumpeter, Joseph. *History of Economic Analysis*, pt. 3. New York, 1954.

JOYCE BURNETTE

MINIFUNDIA. The term *minifundia* refers to farms that are small, usually both in absolute terms and in relation to larger farms in the same agrarian system (the haciendas or latifundia). Depending on the agrarian structure in question, these small farms may be predominantly run by owner-operators, tenants who pay rent in money, sharecroppers, or persons who are granted rights to a small plot as part of an arrangement in which they provide labor services to the landowner on whose farm they live and work.

These alternative arrangements cover a spectrum defined in terms of the degree and manner of control over the labor force exercised by the rich and powerful. Where that control is weak or negligible, large farms will be unimportant and the system will be made up of independent owner-operated small farms, as in parts of the United States and some other industrial countries, including Japan since its postwar agrarian reform, Taiwan, and Korea. Such family farm systems, to achieve rising productivity, require that public policy provide the infrastructure, the research and development, and so forth, needed to generate growth. When it is not present, their productivity often languishes, as in the case of Haiti after its land reform, parts of Russia after the Emancipation Act of 1861, and, allegedly, Mexico's *ejidos* after the early-twentieth-century revolution in that country. When it is provided, these farms have shown much capacity to achieve productivity growth.

In low-productivity systems most farms are both small (since traditional technologies have no significant economies of scale) and owner-operated (or the equivalent). An agriculture productive enough to generate a surplus above the subsistence needs of the workers paves the way for a rentier class, which then needs access to labor services on favorable terms in order to maximize its benefits. A practice like sharecropping on small operating units may be preferable to slavery or paid labor from the largeholder's perspective because it provides a better incentive to high labor productivity. In some cases the smallholder has enough land to use all of his family's labor supply; in others his plot may be just big enough to produce some items for home consumption, with the rest of his labor supplied to the largeholder's farm.

In most agricultural systems the bulk of employment is found on small farm units even if, as is often the case, most of the land is found in large ones. Frequently a high share of output comes from the smaller units because their land is more productive. Through their contribution to agricultural employment, the small farms can be thought of as deterring the unrest or uprising that might otherwise result from large numbers of people having no source of gainful employment. In many countries the small family farms have produced most of the staple food crops, both for the agricultural population itself and for the rising urban population, while larger farms produce the export crops.

[*See* Land Reform and Confiscations.]

BIBLIOGRAPHY
Pearse, Andrew. *The Latin American Peasant.* London, 1975.

R. ALBERT BERRY

MINING [*This entry contains four subentries, a historical overview and discussions of technological change; industrial organization, the environment, and pollution; and work safety regulation.*]

Historical Overview

In ancient times, mining was highly labor intensive, and diminishing returns were the rule. Late Paleolithic and Neolithic humans mined for flint in shallow pits or panned for gold in streams. Their tools were constructed out of wood, stone, and animal bone. Below ground, miners employed fires to loosen rock, and they transported ores in sacks or baskets. Because early humans lacked the tools to work at even moderate depths, they mined deposits close to the surface. Production was generally sufficient, however, because surface deposits were relatively abundant and metallurgy was in its infancy.

The world has consumed ever greater amounts and kinds of minerals since these modest beginnings. Moreover, mining itself has radically changed. Mines are now thousands of feet deep or wide, and most of the work once done by human labor is now performed by machine. Nonetheless, the basic obstacles to mining have not changed. Those obstacles are of three kinds: (1) solving such important technical problems in mining as ventilation, flooding, cave-ins, transporting ores, and breaking rock; (2) creating institutions that safeguard costly investments in mines; and (3) securing an adequate labor force. Satisfying the growing demand for minerals has thus largely depended on overcoming these obstacles. The civilizations and nations that were able to surmount them used the world's mineral abundance to their advantage: their economies grew faster and they enjoyed higher standards of living.

Mining from Ancient Times to the Early Middle Ages. The world's first center of mining and metallurgy was the regions adjoining Mesopotamia in the fourth millennium BCE. Upland tribes in Asia Minor, Armenia, Elam (present-day southwest Iran), the Caucasus, and Persia worked deposits of gold, silver, tin, and copper and supplied the metallurgically skilled Sumerians with these metals, which were used for decorative arts, to manufacture agricultural implements and weaponry, and for trade. Archaeological evidence suggests mining in these regions peaked between 2400 and 2000 BCE and from 1500 to 1200 BCE.

In ancient Egypt and China, mining assumed even greater importance. Mining technology was still primitive, yet both civilizations overcame significant technical obstacles. Egypt produced large amounts of gold, copper, and quarried stone—mostly by brute force of labor. Gold was mined from the Eastern and Nubian deserts as early as 3100 BCE to satisfy the extravagant consumption of the pharaohs and to trade for such valuable goods as tin and coniferous woods produced outside of the kingdom. Both slaves and free laborers worked in the mines, and thousands in the pharaohs' service died from over-exertion, malnutrition, and disease.

On the other hand, China mined large amounts of copper from the middle of the second millennium BCE as the remnants of the Thung-ling and Thung-lu Shan mines show. Later, with the discovery of ways to produce malleable cast iron and hardened steel around the third century BCE, the Chinese began to mine iron ore in great quantities. This, in turn, spurred the world's first large-scale mining of coal a century later. Chinese miners were renowned for their clever methods of timbering underground tunnels and shafts, which prevented cave-ins and allowed mines to reach great depths.

The scale and scope of mining expanded in the city-states and kingdoms of the Aegean, where metals of several kinds were intensively mined. Indeed, Hellenistic history demonstrates that mining stimulated trade, enriched whole populations, and provided the means for defense. Beginning in the sixth century BCE, the Greeks mined the rich deposits of silver, lead, zinc, and iron found at Laurion on the Attican peninsula. Laurion's yields of silver, for example, enabled Athens to pay dividends to its citizens, to mint coins, and to finance a navy that defeated the Persian Xerxes at the straits of Salamis in 480 BCE, saving the city from conquest. Laurion's mines were fairly sophisticated: they were deep (more than three hundred feet in some instances) and for the most part well ventilated. Greek miners employed iron tools.

Rome conquered much of the European and Mediterranean world to gain control of the regions' mineral wealth, but the Romans were not gifted miners and did not contribute appreciably to the growth of mining technology. Rome's single contribution, historians agree, was its water wheel, which raised water from the deep, flooded Rio Tinto mines in Spain. Nonetheless, mining in Europe flourished under Roman rule as never before. Essentially, Rome's strategy was to bring distant lands under its control, to employ native labor and technology, and to tax mine production. This strategy was successful in Great Britain, Gaul, the Balkans, Cyprus, and Spain. Great Britain, for example, was rich in the base metals tin, lead, iron, and copper, and mines in Mendip Hills, Shrewsbury, and Derbyshire became important sources of lead and tin for the construction of Roman pipes, roofs, and pewterware.

Across Europe, the disintegration of the Roman Empire had deleterious consequences for mining, as it did for industry and trade generally. Making mines profitable required the protection of property rights, and without such protections, mines fell into disuse. Moreover, ores often needed to be transported great distances. But roads were allowed to deteriorate and general lawlessness to prevail, making overland transportation costly. Thus, highly productive mines, such as those at Rio Tinto in Spain, were abandoned. Where mining was practiced, it was done on a smaller scale and at shallower depths than before. The supply of precious and nonprecious metals dwindled, generating shortages of currency and inputs for crafts and manufacture and contributing to the secular decline of trade in western Europe.

Mining between 500 and 1450 CE. After the collapse of the Roman Empire, European mining experienced a prolonged depression punctuated by brief upturns. Under the rule of Charlemagne (r. 768–814 CE), for example, there was a resurgence. Defunct mines around Rothausberg, Schemnitz, and Kremintz (near where the present-day borders of Hungary, Slovakia, and Austria meet) were temporarily reopened. Also, in 1170 rich silver deposits were discovered at Freiberg, inaugurating Europe's most prosperous era of mining since Roman rule. A great, albeit temporary, increase in the supply of precious metals and the growth of trade ensued.

By the fourteenth century, copper mining in Sweden and lead mining in England were flourishing. And on the coattails of the iron industry, coal was mined in large quantities for the first time in Mons, Liège, and northern England. But these examples were exceptions more than the rule. Old patterns were hard to break, and, generally speaking, mining stagnated. Slow population growth in central Europe during the fourteenth and fifteenth centuries prolonged and worsened the depression. Even had demand for precious metals not fallen off, it is unlikely Europe would have sustained increases in output. New deposits would be discovered, but diminishing returns quickly set in as miners exhausted their shallower parts. Best practice techniques of mining still had not surpassed those of Roman times.

While Europe was hobbled by technological and institutional shortcomings, China experienced a mining boom. During the Northern Song Dynasty (960–1126 CE), China mined unprecedented quantities of coal and iron as industry and technology rapidly progressed. Iron mining had to keep pace with the growing demand for minted coins, weapons, armor, agricultural implements, salt pans, and nails. It is estimated that by the end of the eleventh century, China was producing between 75,000 and 150,000 tons of iron per year two and a half to five times the level of output in England and Wales in 1640 (Hartwell, 1962). Also, production of coal took off as charcoal and wood for iron furnaces and forges, nonferrous industry, and home heating became evermore scarce and expensive. The consequence of this boom was that mining ranked second only to agriculture. During this period, Chinese mining methods exhibited a definite labor-using bias. For tasks employing drafts animals in Europe—that is, in hoisting, hauling, and draining—China often employed men, women, and children. Neither is there much evidence that gunpowder was widely used in mining, despite China's advanced knowledge of explosives. After 1500, Chinese mining technology clearly lagged behind that of Europe.

Productivity Growth in European Mining, 1450–1700 CE. In European mining, the period from 1450 to 1530 marked an important turning point. For the first time, productivity growth did not peter out. Technological change, although slow, was significant, sustained, and

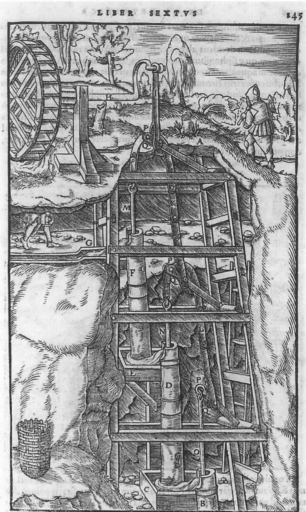

MINING. Cutaway view of large vertical mine shaft, with machinery powered by water wheel. Illustration from Georgius Agricola's *De re metallica*, 1556, book 6, p. 145. (Prints and Photographs Division, Library of Congress)

widely diffused. What changed was that engineering was brought to bear on mechanical problems in mining for the first time, and Europe's best thinkers devoted themselves more and more to studying physical and mechanical phenomena. Their efforts resulted in significant advances in harnessing water and animal power for draining mines and transporting materials, for example.

Moreover, the Saxons—skilled and ingenious miners—spread best-practice techniques—the use of gunpowder for blasting, to name one—across Europe as they colonized new lands. Georg Bauer's (1494–1555, also known as Agricola) and Lazarus Ercker's (1530–1594) influential treatises on mining and metallurgy were evidence of the growth of engineering knowledge; they cataloged best-practice mining techniques of the fifteenth and sixteenth centuries and were widely read across Europe. This renaissance was accompanied by rapid increases in mine output. Silver production in central Europe, for instance, increased as much as five times during these decades (Nef, 1964).

By the 1500s, European mining had once again lapsed into depression, but the cause was no longer technological. Instead, foreign competition and backward institutions slowed mining down. Discoveries of gold and silver in the New World—the Potosí mines of Bolivia, for instance—added to the supply of precious metals and made many European mines unprofitable. Moreover, archaic laws over property rights and the consolidation of control over lands by European lords and princes further retarded mining.

Great Britain largely escaped these pressures, however. It did not concentrate on the mining of gold and silver; it had a comparatively efficient system of property rights; its deposits had never been as intensively mined as those on continental Europe; there was cheap supply of labor in the form of independent miner-farmers; and compared with the continent, warfare was infrequent (Burt, 1995). Great Britain was thus uniquely prepared for a rapid expansion of its mining industry. Growth in demand for coal for industry and home heating and for such nonferrous metals as lead, tin, and copper for use in warfare, construction, and shipbuilding led the way. Thus, output of British lead, for example, which had been 500 to 600 tons in the 1560s, stood at 12,500 tons by the 1630s. As output increased, the business organization of mining operations changed. Semijoint shock companies, professional management, and a paid labor force emerged.

Mining and the Industrial Revolution, c. 1700–c. 1900 CE. Technological change and the rise of industry during the Industrial Revolution caused mining to boom. The demand for minerals of all kinds increased, and mining became vastly more efficient. In Europe and the United States, the demand for minerals was closely tied to technological developments in metalworking, construction, manufacturing, and transportation. For example, Henry Cort's (1740–1800) puddling and rolling process and Abraham Darby's (1678?–1717) coke-fired furnace lowered the cost of producing wrought iron and increased the demand for both iron ore and coal. At the same time, technological change was making it possible to recover minerals ever more cheaply.

Among the most important eighteenth-century innovations were Thomas Newcomen's (1663–1729) and James Watt's (1736–1819) steam engines for draining and ventilating mines and hoisting and lowering materials and

men. Also, gunpowder for blasting rock, although known in Great Britain before the seventeenth century, became widely practiced during the eighteenth century and greatly reduced the need for physical labor (Burt, 1991). During the nineteenth century, mine safety improved with Humphrey Davy's (1778–1829) safety lamp. There were now many fewer deadly mine explosions. In the late nineteenth and early twentieth centuries, mechanical coal cutters and loaders, borers, and drills based on pneumatic, electrical, and diesel power replaced the pick and shovel.

Mines supplied many raw materials for Great Britain's industrial revolution. British mines supplied coal, iron, tin, lead, and copper to the burgeoning manufacturing sector that included large iron and textile manufacturers, as well as smaller brickmakers, brewers, and tin smelters. Mines also supplied coal for home heating and production. Before 1800, British production of ferrous, nonferrous metals (lead, tin, and copper), and coal increased apace. But thereafter, output of nonferrous metals declined as cheaper sources of supply became available abroad. Meanwhile, the production of coal and iron continued to rise throughout the nineteenth century, although coal did so at a much greater rate.

As mining increased, the industry accounted for an ever greater share of British income and employment. Altogether, mining and quarrying constituted 3.5 percent of national income by mid-nineteenth century, 60 percent of which came from coal, 10 percent from iron, and 12.5 percent from tin, copper, and lead. Coal mines employed 220,000 people, eight times the number in iron mines. Mining income and employment continued to rise until World War I because of international demand for British coal. By 1907, British coal production, which exceeded 225 million tons, accounted for 90 percent of mining and quarrying income, and the mining sector as a whole now constituted 5.5 percent of national income. The British workforce employed in mining and quarrying—again the majority of which was employed in coal mines—had increased from 400,000 in 1841 (3.1 percent) to 1.2 million (6 percent) in 1911.

Although the world demanded ever greater amounts of metals and fuels for industry, precious stones and metals were still in great demand. Diamonds and other precious stones had long been the preserve of India, but the discoveries of diamonds near Hopetown and Dutoitspan between 1867 and 1872 quickly transformed South Africa into the world's leading producer. At first, South African mines were small, ownership of claims was widely dispersed, and diamond mining itself was highly labor intensive. But the scale of activity increased once the diamond colossus De Beers won control over South Africa's richest mines in 1890 and brought needed capital and modern technology.

Meanwhile, South Africa was also emerging as the world's dominant producer of gold. Strikes in the Yukon, United States, and Australia had attracted thousands of placer miners to the world's frontiers and added significantly to global stocks of gold, but discoveries of gold at Witwatersrand in the Transvaal in 1886 produced the largest bounty yet. The Transvaal deposits were deep below ground, however, and thus required heavy machinery to be mined. Steam engines for hoisting, mechanical drills for breaking rock, stamp mills for the crushing of rocks, and the invention of the cyanide process for extracting gold from ore in 1899 made mining possible and immensely productive. Despite their use of modern technology, South African mines depended heavily on African laborers, who often worked under unsafe and discriminatory conditions.

During the late nineteenth and early twentieth centuries, British mining went into relative decline because cheaper sources of supply emerged abroad. Australia, Europe, and the United States increased production of industrial metals and fuels. For example, the coal fields of the Ruhr, Saar, and Upper Silesia were mined and fueled much of European industrial growth. By 1912, Germany was producing 172 million tons of coal, third only to the United States and Great Britain. Also, Australia mined large quantities of lead and silver at Broken Hill from the 1880s onward. Nonetheless, new discoveries of anthracite coal in Pennsylvania, iron in Minnesota's Mesabi Range, and copper in Nevada and Utah best exemplified the world's newfound mineral abundance. The United States, more than any other nation, ended Great Britain's dominance.

The expansion of mining in the United States was extraordinary. Production of iron ore, for example, increased from 3.8 million tons in 1870 to 67.6 million tons in 1920. During that same period, output of bituminous and Pennsylvania anthracite coal increased more than sixteenfold from 40.3 million tons to 658.2 million tons. By 1913, the United States was the world's leading producer of copper (56 percent of the world's output), coal (39 percent), molybdenum (38 percent), bauxite (36 percent), iron ore (36 percent), silver (30 percent), and tungsten (17 percent), not to mention natural gas (95 percent) and petroleum (65 percent).

Mining's share of national income grew from 1.5 percent in 1870 to 3.6 percent in 1920. This remarkable growth stemmed from strong demand in the domestic and foreign manufacturing, transportation, communications, and electric industries. It was also due to productivity-increasing innovations in mining technology. American-invented technologies such as strip- and open-pit mining, introduced by the engineers Daniel C. Jackling (1869–1956) and Robert C. Gemmell, made it possible for economies of scale to be achieved and for mining to be made economical in instances it never would have been before.

With large-scale steam-, electric-, and diesel-powered shovels and trucks to strip away overburden, ores of less than 1 percent concentration could now be profitably mined.

Gavin Wright (1990) has argued that the United States owes its industrial leadership at the turn of the twentieth century to the exploitation of its rich, nonreproducible natural resources. Analysis of the factor content of imports and exports shows that the United States had a comparative advantage in producing natural resource-intensive goods. This advantage reflected not just resource abundance, but contemporary technological leadership in mining, the emergence of a cadre of geologists and mining engineers, and the favorable economic climate for the development of natural resources, that is, well-established property rights, an extensive transportation network, and a free-trade area. Circumstantial evidence also supports Wright's hypothesis: technological change was often natural-resource biased; energy-intensive continuous-process and mass-production methods were common; consumer products, such as the automobile, were tailored to the resource-rich environment; and such American manufacturing giants as U.S. Steel had cheap and abundant sources of ores and fuels for production.

The basis for America's industrial leadership rested not on natural resource abundance *per se*, but rather on superior mineral exploration and development. Indeed, analysis of trade after 1945 shows that the United States was no longer resource abundant relative to the rest of the world (Wright, 1990). The developing world has explored its lands more thoroughly, discovered reserves, and increased production of minerals. The consequence has been a major reorientation in sources of supply. For example, the countries of Asia and the Pacific now produce 64 percent of the world's barite, 80 percent of its tungsten, 70 percent of its refined tin, and 86 percent of its refined zinc. China alone produces 77 percent of world's tungsten. Chile, Mexico, and Peru now account for 39 percent of the world's copper, and Brazil, Guyana, Jamaica, Suriname, and Venezuela supply 29 percent of the world's bauxite.

[*See also* Gold and Silver Industry *and* Salt and Salt Making.]

BIBLIOGRAPHY

Burt, Roger. "Lead Production in England and Wales, 1700–1770." *European History Review* 22.2 (1969), 249–268.

Burt, Roger. "The International Diffusion of Technology in the Early Modern Period: The Case of the British Non-Ferrous Mining Industry." *European History Review* 44.2 (1991), 249–271.

Burt, Roger. "The Transformation of the Non-ferrous Metals Industries in the Seventeenth and Eighteenth Centuries." *Economic History Review* 48.1 (1995), 23–45.

Burt, Roger. "The Extractive Industries." In *The Cambridge Economic History of Britain*, edited by Roderick Floud and Paul Johnson. Cambridge, forthcoming 2003.

Chandler, Alfred D. "Anthracite Coal Production and the Beginnings of the Industrial Revolution in the United States." *Business History Review* 46.2 (1972), 141–181.

Craddock, Paul T. *Early Metal Mining and Production.* Washington, D.C., 1995.

Davisson, William I., and James E. Harper. *European Economic History*, vol. 1, *The Ancient World.* New York, 1972.

Deane, Phyllis, and W. A. Cole. *British Economic Growth, 1688–1959.* Cambridge, 1964.

Dodd, Don, and Wynelle Dodd. *Historical Statistics of the United States, 1790–1970.* Tuscaloosa, 1976.

Golas, Peter J. *Science and Civilisation in China: Mining*, vol. 5, part 13. Cambridge, 1999.

Gordon, Robert B. *American Iron, 1607–1900.* Baltimore, 1996.

Hartwell, Robert. "A Revolution in the Chinese Iron and Coal Industries during the Northern Sung." *Journal of Asian Studies* 21 (1962), 153–162.

Healy, J. F. *Mining and Metallurgy in the Greek and Roman World.* London, 1978.

Mokyr, Joel. *The Lever of Riches.* New York, 1990.

Nef, John U. *The Conquest of the Material World.* Chicago, 1964.

Pollard, Sidney. "A New Estimate of British Coal Production, 1750–1850." *Economic History Review* 33.2 (1980), 212–235.

Temple, John. *Mining: An International History.* London, 1972.

Wilson, Arthur J. *The Living Rock: The Story of Metals since Earliest Times and Their Impact on Developing Civilization.* Cambridge, 1994.

Wright, Gavin. "The Origins of American Industrial Success, 1879–1940." *American Economic Review* 80.4 (1990), 651–668.

United States Geologic Survey. *Mineral Industry Surveys.* 1999.

JAMES I. STEWART

Technological Change

Mining has undergone extraordinary change since prehistoric man first began to dig for flint and pigments. The bulk of this change, however, has proceeded not at a steady pace throughout history, but by leaps and bounds in the last 250 years since the Industrial Revolution (c. 1700–1900). Among the most important developments in mining since the Industrial Revolution are the substitution of inanimate for animate forms of power (steam and electrical power for human and animal power), the substitution of capital for labor, the application of geological science to the discovery and recovery of valuable minerals, economies of scale, and the introduction of modern methods of management to mining activity.

Today, commercial mining is a high-volume, capital-intensive, and tightly coordinated activity that encompasses a wide range of basic methods from underground cut-and-fill and block-caving mining to open-pit mining and quarrying. In underground coal mines, for example, multipurpose machines—continuous miners—cut and load coal into cars or onto conveyor belts—work done with pick and shovel just one hundred years ago. And prospecting for minerals is now a science employing satellite imagery and modern chemistry and geology, whereas for millenniums past it was a matter of fortuity. The practical effects of these innovations have been to lower production costs, raise the productivity of labor, open up reserves that were previously uneconomical to recover, and make mining a safer, although not always a more environmentally friendly, activity.

Mining from Ancient Times to 1700 CE. For most of human history, mining was neither capital intensive nor so widely practiced. Early miners employed simple labor-intensive technologies: They dug shallow pits and mined flint with picks fashioned from ox or horse bones and deer antlers and horns. During the Neolithic period (c. 6000–2500 BCE), stone mining was intensively practiced in some places, and some basic technological advances made. In modern-day Belgium and Holland, for example, remains exist of flint mines having galleries of more than five hundred meters in length and shafts sunk to depths of ten meters. Archaeologists believe these sites date to 3000 BCE.

With the discovery of metals and basic advances in metallurgy, mining for metals displaced mining for flint. Surface and underground deposits of gold, silver, copper, and tin were mined for the production of agricultural implements, weaponry, coins, and crafts. While copper was mined in Asia Minor, Armenia, and Elam and sold to the Sumerians as early as 3500 BCE, not much is known about how these mines operated. More is known about the Egyptians (c. 3400–300 BCE), who were prolific miners of copper and gold and employed armies of slaves in their mines. The Egyptians made some notable technical advances. At the Timna Valley copper mines (c. 1000 BCE), German archaeologists in the 1970s uncovered a complex of shafts and tunnels that displayed technically advanced systems of ventilation, roof support, and illumination. The Egyptians performed their most remarkable feats in stone quarrying, however. They cut obelisks weighing more than 1 million kilograms (1,100 tons) and unwieldy limestone blocks from stone.

China, although isolated for much of its history, must be mentioned. The Chinese are best known for their ingenious methods of timbering. Timbers supported excavations, minimized the frequency of cave-ins, and permitted mine shafts to be wider and to reach greater depths. The copper mines of Thung-lü Shan in the first millennium BCE, which reached depths of more than fifty meters, demonstrate China's mastery in this regard. China was also metallurgically advanced; it was fashioning steel and malleable cast-iron mining tools by the third century.

Greek civilization (c. 1900–150 BCE) made some noteworthy advances in mining, especially in mine design and layout. At the lead and silver mines at Laurion near Athens, the best examples of Hellenistic mining technology, the Greeks sank shafts to more than one hundred meters and rigged pulley systems to haul materials up and down. They also cut extensive systems of shafts, galleries, pillars, and stalls—many constructed in regular proportions. The galleries were cut in pairs to serve as in- and outroads. Also, crosscuts connected shafts and galleries to maximize the flow of air through the mines, and fires were employed to aid ventilation further. In mine drainage, the Greeks improved upon existing technology with Archimedean screws, revolving spiral tubes that lifted water. Wrought-iron tools with wooden handles replaced the bronze implements of the Egyptians.

The Romans, successors to the Greeks, made little technological progress in mining, but they did spread best-practice methods across the Empire. Their one technological feat was to improve the draining of mines, building on their knowledge of water control. Roman mines employed a number of technologies toward this end, including adits or inclined drainage tunnels, chains of pots machines, and the Archimedean screw, but their real contribution was the water wheel. At the Rio Tinto mines in southwestern Spain, a succession of wheels, turned by humans on treadmills, raised water thirty meters from below ground. The effect of this Roman ingenuity was to render previously flooded mines workable, a significant achievement, considering the universality of flooding. The Romans also did much to elevate mining to a semiskilled profession. Although slavery was practiced throughout the Empire, the Romans often substituted skilled artificers for unskilled slaves.

Between 500 and 1400 CE, there were no fundamental advances in mining technology in Europe. This was a period of sustained depression in mining interrupted only by brief bursts of activity. The absence of major technological change meant that miners encountered diminishing returns: rich new deposits would be discovered, but only their shallowest parts could be exploited. In contrast, China's mining industry experienced a boom. China used ever greater amounts of labor in mines to meet the increasing demand for iron, copper, and coal. Despite China's pioneering work in explosives (c. 1000 CE), Chinese miners rarely employed gunpowder, a potentially major labor-saving technology. The poor quality of gunpowder was most likely the cause (Golas, 1999).

Only in the fifteenth century did mining techniques and methods of Europeans surpass the Romans' in sophistication (Nef, 1964). Many technologies of Classical Antiquity were improved upon. Mine shafts became deeper as better ways of ventilating them were devised. Thus, Georgius Agricola's (1494–1555) De re metallica (1556), an influential and widely read treatise on mining technology, describes mines at Kuttenberg as deep as four hundred meters. Also, mines were now ventilated by man-powered revolving fans and bellows. In hauling, equipment and ore had been lifted and lowered in wooden or animal-skin buckets connected to windlasses. The payload was limited by the lack of friction in the system and the strength of men to do the lifting. Geared wheels and animal power were introduced to solve this problem. Miners also developed elaborate systems for transmitting water power via rods and wheels from river valleys below to the mines above. Most importantly, the Saxons, Europe's most talented miners at this time, spread a labor-saving innovation across Europe during the sixteen and seventeenth centuries: gunpowder for the purposes of blasting rock. With regard to Great Britain, Burt (1991) challenges this view.

The Industrial Revolution and Afterwards: 1700 CE to the Present. Despite better means of ventilating and draining mines and hauling materials, miners were still extremely limited in their ability to exploit mineral deposits. The scale of operations remained small and mining was still highly labor intensive, even in Great Britain, the leading producer of minerals during the sixteenth and seventeenth centuries (Burt, 1991). Greater exploitation depended upon locating rich new deposits and reaching greater depths, which, in turn, depended on improvements in ventilation, vertical haulage, and drainage. The English geologist William Smith (1769–1839) did much to elevate prospecting to a science by systematically mapping the geology of England and Wales. But real productivity gains would have to await the substitution of capital for labor in the drilling, boring, and movement of ore underground. Technologies based on steam and electric power developed during the Industrial Revolution supplied the means of accomplishing most of these ends. Sometimes these technologies were developed for other purposes and applied to mining. In other instances, the growth in demand for already-existing and new metals became an important impetus for technological change.

The introduction of steam power had an immediate impact on mine drainage and hauling by vastly increasing the volume of water that could be removed from mines, the weight of materials that could be hoisted up and down, and the speed with which those materials could be moved. Indeed, Thomas Newcomen's (1663–1729) steam engine found its first successful commercial application in the coal mines near Wolverhampton in 1712. By 1778, there were seventy such machines at work in the tin mines at Cornwall. Although Newcomen's invention was adopted by other European nations and the American colonies, it was notoriously inefficient. James Watt's (1736–1819) more efficient double-acting steam engine soon displaced Newcomen's engines. Forty-five were in operation by 1798 at Cornwall and 321 in Great Britain and Ireland. Overall, there were 828 steam engines of all kinds in coal mines and 209 in copper and lead mines by 1800.

Mining had always been labor-intensive work, and it was not until the introduction of compressed air and

MINING. Boy shovelling coal while man operates a punching machine that drills into coal, Laura Mine, Red Star, West Virginia, 1908. (Lewis W. Hine/National Child Labor Committee Collection/Prints and Photographs Division, Library of Congress)

electricity in the late nineteenth and early twentieth centuries that ancient tools—the pick, shovel, hand-powered borer, and wedge—were replaced by their power driven analogues—mechanical borers, drills, and loaders. Holes for blasting rock, for example, were drilled by hand until the steam-powered boring machine—first conceived but not commercially introduced by the Cornish engineer Richard Trevithick (1771–1833) in 1813—was made practicable by later inventors. Even where hand-held tools were used, however, they were of higher quality by the 1800s than those of centuries earlier once steel had replaced wrought iron. And by the twentieth century, drill bits were constructed out of even harder metals like tungsten carbide.

The development of pneumatic and electric power during the late nineteenth and early twentieth centuries revolutionized mining operations below ground. Once power could be generated above ground and delivered efficiently to where it was needed below, inanimate power replaced human power and mining productivity increased apace. First, the French engineer Germain Sommeiller (1815–1871) improved upon the mechanical drill by powering it with compressed air instead of steam. Nonetheless, pneumatic technology was in its early stages and the adoption of Sommeiller's invention was limited at first. Still, his invention heralded a new wave of innovation, speeded along by developments in electric power.

By the beginning of the twentieth century, a new generation of coal-cutting machines, called longwall cutters—so-called for the long coal faces they worked at great depths—emerged. These machines were safe, efficient, reliable, and required less maintenance than older vintages. The combination of longwall cutters and conveyors became standard in European coal mines and is known as "conventional" machine mining. By 1930, another significant advancement had been made: the Meco-Moore cutter-loader. This was a cutting machine and loader, thus obviating the need for miners to undertake the laborious work of shoveling coal onto conveyors. This invention was subsequently improved during World War II with the development of the AB-Meco-Moore cutter-loader, which was capable of simultaneously cutting and loading.

Machines like these substantially changed how mining was carried out below ground. For example, the amount of British coal cut by machine increased from 1.5 percent in 1900 to 80 percent in 1950. Americans developed similar multipurpose machines, suited only to their shallower coal deposits. Whereas the Europeans used long-wall cutting methods for deep coal mining, Americans adapted machinery to their board and pillar methods. Not to be forgotten, the development of hydraulic roof supports—necessary to prevent cave-ins—increased the rate at which coal faces and thus cutting could proceed. These twentieth century innovations meant that labor productivity in

American coal mines increased substantially from three tons of coal per worker per day in 1900 to fourteen tons by 1960.

Underground transportation also improved. Because coal deposits generally lie in horizontal beds, extensive networks of tunnels had to be dug from the main shafts to the coal faces, forcing miners to transport coal long distances underground in some cases. At the start of the Industrial Revolution, women and children often performed this function with wicker baskets fitted on wooden sleds. But by the late eighteenth century, ponies were employed underground, to be superseded quickly by wheeled trams. Eventually, trolleys were placed on rails and pulled by horses or moved by self-acting inclines. In 1812, George Stephenson (1781–1848) introduced steam power for underground hauling. And in 1902, British engineers produced the first practicable coal-face conveyor, thus saving much labor in the maintenance of roads and transport of materials.

As mines became deeper, ensuring adequate ventilation and illumination became serious obstacles. Not only was oxygen depleted at great depths (a condition known as black-damp), but poisonous and explosive gases often accumulated to dangerous levels (conditions known as after-damp and fire-damp, respectively), especially in coal mines. From the end of the eighteenth century through the nineteenth century, mine safety became a major concern as gas explosions killed hundreds of miners. In 1860, a gas explosion killed 145 miners at the Risca mine at Newport, and 178 died in 1867 at the Ferndale colliery in Rhondda Valley. From this time forward, engineers paid close attention to ventilation; they applied basic principles of thermodynamics and systems of shafts, tunnels, and doors to guide the flow of air. Yet another strategy was to ventilate the mines mechanically with fans and blowers. The first mechanical air pump was used at the Hebburn colliery in 1807, and after 1830 fans were widely used.

Illuminating mines was still another technological hurdle, both because there was the need for better sources of light below ground and because it was flame from coal miners' lamps that often sparked fatal explosions. Thus, while engineers worked on improving ventilation, there was a parallel effort to devise a safer and more effective ways of illuminating mines. A number of failed efforts were made at first, including phosphorescence from decaying fish, mirrors, and flint and steel mills. The problem was not solved until the Sunderland Society for Preventing Accidents in Coal Mines enlisted the help of the English chemist Humphrey Davy (1778–1829). In 1815, Davy invented the safety lamp, which enclosed the flame of the miner's candle in metal gauze instead of glass, an invention that survived into the twentieth century. Still, the lamp was neither 100 percent safe nor wholly effective at first. A number of improvements had to be made before Davy's original invention could be said to be both.

Technological advances discussed so far were significant, but the most important innovation of the twentieth century was open-cast or strip mining. In this kind of mining, heavy machines remove overburden to expose underlying ores. This method requires bulldozers and cranes with shovels capable of lifting huge loads. Shovels or bulldozers powered by internal combustion engines have replaced those powered by steam and electricity over the twentieth century. The U.S. Steel Corporation was one of the first to employ strip mining in Minnesota's iron ore Mesabi Range early in the twentieth century. The advantage of surface mining was that it made the recovery of low-grade deposits economical. In 1899, engineers Daniel C. Jackling (1869–1956) and Robert C. Gemmell showed that ores as low as 2 percent grade could be profitably mined by open-pit methods, provided mining was conducted on a large enough scale. By 1913, the Bingham copper mine in Utah, for which they developed their plan, had a capacity of forty-five hundred tons of ore per day, whereas a five hundred-ton mill had been considered large by the day's standards. By 1960, open-cast mining accounted for one-third of all U.S. coal production, and it is estimated that today two-thirds of all U.S. mining is done by strip- or open-pit methods.

BIBLIOGRAPHY

Bromehead, C. N. "Mining and Quarrying." In *A History of Technology*, edited by Charles Singer, et al., vol. 1, pp. 558–571. Oxford, 1954.

Bromehead, C. N. "Mining and Quarrying to the Seventeenth Century." In *A History of Technology*, edited by Charles Singer, et al., vol. 2, pp. 1–40. Oxford, 1956.

Bryan, Sir Andrew. "Coal-Mining." In *A History of Technology*, edited by Trevor I. Williams, vol. 6, pp. 359–375. Oxford, 1978.

Burt, Roger. "The International Diffusion of Technology in the Early Modern Period: The Case of the British Non-Ferrous Mining Industry." *European History Review* 44.2 (1991), 249–271.

Burt, Roger. "The Transformation of the Non-Ferrous Metals Industries in the Seventeenth and Eighteenth Centuries." *Economic History Review* 48.1 (1995), 23–45.

Craddock, Paul T. *Early Metal Mining and Production*. Washington, D.C., 1995.

Deane, Phyllis, and W. A. Cole. *British Economic Growth*. Cambridge, 1964.

Healy, John F. *Mining and Metallurgy in the Greek and Roman World*. London, 1978.

Golas, Peter J. *Science and Civilisation in China: Mining*, vol. 5, part 13. Cambridge, 1999.

McDivitt, James F., and Gerald Manners. *Minerals and Men*. Baltimore, 1974.

Mokyr, Joel. *The Lever of Riches*. New York, 1990.

Nef, John U. "Coal Mining and Utilization." In *A History of Technology*, edited by Charles Singer, et al., vol. 3, pp. 72–88. New York, 1957.

Nef, John U. *The Conquest of the Material World*. Chicago, 1964.

Peterson, D. J., et al., *New Forces at Work in Mining: Industry Views of Critical Technology*. Santa Monica, Calif., 2001.

Ritson, J. A. S. "Metal and Coal Mining, 1750–1875." In *A History of Technology*, edited by Charles Singer, et al., vol. 4, pp. 64–98. New York, 1958.

Rosenberg, Nathan. "Technology." In *Encyclopedia of American Economic History*, edited by Glenn Porter, pp. 294–308. New York, 1980.

Temple, John. "Metal Mining." In *A History of Technology*, edited by Trevor I. Williams, vol. 6, pp. 410–426. Oxford, 1978.

Temple, John. *Mining: An International History*. London, 1972.

Weisgerber, G., and E. Pernicka. "Ore Mining in Prehistoric Europe." In *Prehistoric Gold in Europe: Mines, Metallurgy, and Manufacture*, edited by Giulio Morteani and Jeremy P. Northover, pp. 159–182. Dordecht, 1995.

Williams, Trevor I. *A Short History of Twentieth Century Technology*. Oxford, 1982.

Wilson, A. J. *The Living Rock*. Cambridge, 1996.

JAMES I. STEWART

Industrial Organization, the Environment, and Pollution

The modern mining industry owes its origins to the energy requirements of the early industrialization process with particular reference to the burning of coal, coke, and lignite as the principal mineral fuels. Subsequently, the development of the manufacturing industry greatly expanded the range of minerals used in the production process. Prior to 1850, the raw material requirements of industry in terms of minerals were limited to iron, copper, lead, and zinc with the use of silver and gold confined to ornamental and monetary purposes. In the final quarter of the nineteenth century, however, the onset of the "second industrial revolution" led to a considerable expansion in the production of mineral raw materials. Between 1880 and 1913, production of copper ores doubled every thirteen years; iron ore, phosphates, zinc, and coal every fifteen to seventeen years; and lead and tin every twenty years. By the 1920s, the range of nonfuel raw materials had expanded considerably to include bauxite, chromite, manganese, molybdenum, nickel, and titanium. This diversification in production was prompted by advances in science and technology and also by demand-side forces in favor of improved product specification. Thus, molybdenum became an essential requirement for the manufacture of harder steel alloys: chromite ore began to be used as a refractory in furnace linings, while aluminum, and to a lesser extent, magnesium, found essential uses where lightness was a desirable quality, as in the manufacture of aircraft. The impressive supply-side response elicited by the expansion in demand continued well into the twentieth century. In 1860, the world output of coal was approximately 135 million tons; by 1900, it was in excess of 700 million tons and had reached 1,700 million tons by 1955. Iron ore production, which stood at 40 million tons in 1880, had doubled by 1898 and doubled again by 1930. Nickel ore production, negligible until the 1880s, had reached 10,000 short tons

per annum by 1900, 20,000 tons in 1910, and 100,000 tons by 1939. Improved techniques in scientific exploration were accompanied by greater capital intensity in mining, extraction, and refining processes. This, in turn, enhanced commercial supply by facilitating the use of relatively low-grade ores hitherto uneconomical to exploit. This was exemplified in the application of the flotation process of concentrating ores after 1900, leading to substantial increases in the output of lead, zinc, and copper.

The expansion of mineral production led to immense changes in the sources of supply and also in the relationship between mineral producers and consumers in the industrialized world. Between 1850 and 1914, the development of mechanical transportation was a necessary prerequisite for the expansion of trade, and hence the international distribution of industry, but so too was the proximity of coal and iron ore resources. In this setting, the scope for mineral discovery and production was greatest in dual economies where modern industrialization was already underway but where there were substantial virgin lands awaiting exploitation. In the decades before 1914, the United States was ideally placed in these respects. With the aid of inward investment from western Europe, considerable mineral reserves were opened up, particularly in the western states where mineral output rose to the point of national self-sufficiency and ultimately to the generation of a thriving export trade. The North American experience was replicated in Russia, albeit less impressively, at least until the post-1945 phase of Soviet industrialization. Elsewhere, the main impetus to mineral production was located in the peripheral regions of white settlement, where capital and technical expertise could be attracted from metropolitan financial centers, notably the City of London. Australia, Canada, and South Africa were the principal beneficiaries in this respect, although Brazil, too, was subject to substantial inward flows of capital and entrepreneurship directed at the exploitation of iron ore deposits. Other mineral sources were located in relatively inaccessible parts of the world, at least in terms of their relationship with the international economy. New Caledonia, for example, was the source of the first commercially viable source of nickel, beginning in the 1870s. Tin mining was inaugurated in Malaya by Chinese immigrants, but large-scale exploitation had to await the arrival of European enterprise in the 1890s. By 1939, when Malaya produced one-third of world output, 70 percent of domestic production was accounted for by European mining companies.

The industrialization process, with its burgeoning demand for metallic and nonmetallic minerals, was facilitated greatly by the changing scale of mining operations. The shift from selective to mass mining resulted not only in a quantum leap in productive capacity, but also facilitated the exploitation of progressively lower-grade ores, thereby extending the commercial life of numerous ore deposits. Coincidentally, mass mining came to be inextricably linked with large-scale smelting operations, as in the case of copper and other metals. Since it was uneconomical to transport ores containing much less than 1 percent of copper, it made sense to smelt such ores at the mine itself. Mass mining could also entail radical changes in mining methods in favor of open-pit operations at the expense of shaft mining. The increasing capital intensity of mining, together with the dispersed location of mineral ore deposits and the long gestation period following the initial investment to the point of sale, had major consequences for the organization and structure of mining enterprise. In the British case, investment in the international primary sector in the later-nineteenth century was dominated by freestanding companies, a form of multinational enterprise where London-based "brass plate" head offices administered overseas production facilities. An early example of the type was the Saint John d'el Rey Mining Company, formed in 1830 to open up the Brazilian goldfields. By 1913, the company operated the deepest mine in the world and employed twenty-five hundred workers in its Brazilian operations. But even before 1914, larger and more diversified multinational companies had begun to develop. An excellent illustration is provided by the Rio Tinto Company (later RTZ), founded in 1873 to exploit copper ore deposits in Spain. By the late 1940s, the company was heavily dependent on its shareholdings in the northern Rhodesian copper belt, although the process of building a chain of largely autonomous companies to develop mineral production in aluminium, uranium, lead, zinc, tin, iron ore, and coal began in the early 1960s.

In the interwar period, British-owned mineral companies underwent considerable consolidation in the face of commercial depression and surplus capacity. A good example is provided by the London Tin Corporation: by 1930 it had absorbed more than twenty British companies active in the Malayan tin industry, accounting for one-third of total production. The Corporation then embarked on an ambitious program of acquisitions in Thailand, Myanmar (formerly Burma), and Nigeria, where it controlled half of that country's tin production. In the United States, early mining enterprises were invariably inaugurated by individual prospectors who staked claims based on mineral outcroppings. Since intensive exploration was precluded by funding limits and the absence of collateral, successful exploitation was dependent on access to venture capital, whereby the owner of the claim received a share of the net income but lost control of the property. The origins of numerous large mining companies can be traced back to the acquisition of claims in this way. For the exploitation of extensive mineral deposits, such as the open-pit porphyry ore bodies in Utah, Arizona, and New Mexico, the necessary large-scale enterprise was funded by Eastern investors and the owners of successful gold and silver mines.

American multinational mining companies on the RTZ model began to appear before 1900. While some companies remained committed to a single metal at the mining stage, others diversified into a range of minerals and the subsequent production stages of smelting and semifabrication. By 1939, most American multinationals had diversified their mineral production to include coal and petroleum, while a small minority had ventured into manufacturing. Good examples of diversification strategies are provided by the Kennecott Copper Company and the American Smelting and Refining Company (ASARCO). The Kennecott Company, formed before 1914 by the merger of several copper mines in the western United States, Alaska, and Chile, was able to expand its activities with financial aid from the Guggenheim Brothers and J. P. Morgan and Company. As a fully integrated copper enterprise, Kennecott engaged in a strategy of diversification after World War I, acquiring interests in coal, lead, zinc, silver, iron ore, and other minerals. In 1929, it entered the fabricating business by purchasing the Chase Brass and Copper Company. This was followed by the acquisition of an electrical communication wire and cable manufacturing company. In contrast to Kennecott, ASARCO was founded in 1899 as a processor of metals mined by other companies, with an initial focus on lead. In 1922, however, it diversified into copper mining by forming the Northern Peru Mining and Smelting Company. This was followed by the acquisition of mining interests in Canada, Mexico, and Australia. After 1950, ASARCO emerged as one of the world's leading copper producers, owning some of the largest mines in the industry.

The Special Case of Coal Mining. In many ways, the most crucial raw material germane to the industrialization process was coal, insofar as it alleviated a threatened scarcity of fuel in the early eighteenth century and was simultaneously applied to the smelting and manufacturing of iron. In addition, its direct use in the generation of steam power revolutionized industrial and transportation processes from the 1780s onward. In this context, coal was not only the backbone of modern industrialization at the level of national economies, it also made a decisive contribution to the development of an increasingly integrated international economy via the innovation of the ocean-going steamship. In 1865, world output of coal amounted to 182 million tons. Great Britain accounted for half of the total, with double the output of both the United States and Germany, the next largest producers. By 1900, world production had increased more than fourfold, with the United States as the leading producer, a position that was maintained until the 1970s. In the same period, German production increased sixfold while British output more than doubled. In the first two decades of the twentieth century, world output doubled, with an additional increase of one-third between 1920 and 1950. During these years, the USSR emerged as a major producer and was joined by China after 1950. Taking Great Britain, the United States and Germany as the dominant producers up to World War II, there were revealing contrasts and comparisons in terms of business and market structures. In both Great Britain and the United States, coal mining was a heavily fragmented industry. In the former, 75 percent of the labor force in 1924 was employed in 1,385 mines operated by the 467 colliery undertakings employing more than 500 men each. In the American bituminous industry, there were 9,331 active mines in 1923; and in 1929, the 17 largest undertakings produced only 20 percent of total output, with the next 70 largest firms responsible for another 23 percent. Fragmentation on this scale led to intense competition, and in circumstances of trade depression, to surplus productive capacity. This invariably was accompanied by attacks on wages, given their high proportion of the total cost of production.

Both industries were subject to severe industrial unrest in the later 1920s, leading to substantial wage cuts. The persistence of trade depression, however, prompted the search for less painful means of restoring profitability, focusing on the stabilization of the market. In Great Britain, attempts to form voluntary marketing schemes were followed by statutory legislation in 1930 for compulsory cartelization on an individual coal field basis. Successively modified and refined, the cartel system proved to be successful in stabilizing prices even to the extent of permitting modest wage increases in the later 1930s. It also provided the structural framework for state control of the industry after 1939, thereby helping to pave the way for public ownership in 1947. The American industry replicated British experience to the extent that effective cartelization was the product of government enforcement. During the 1930s, there were several unsuccessful attempts to restrain competition via legislative means. Under the Guffey-Snyder Act of 1935, a National Bituminous Coal Commission was established to enforce fair competition and also to set minimum-price schedules. Challenged in the courts and declared unconstitutional, the 1935 Act was followed by further legislation in 1937 that reestablished the Commission within the legal requirements set by the Supreme Court. In 1940, effective cartelization was finally achieved under the auspices of the Department of the Interior.

The organization of the German coal-mining industry provides revealing contrasts to British and American experience since cartelization had already reached an advanced form by 1914. The movement toward the restraint of trade was propelled by investment banks determined to limit their liabilities in the face of trade recession and by "ruinous competition" in the form of cutthroat price reductions. In addition, cartel agreements could be enforced in the courts. The cartel movement was all-pervasive in German industry from the 1870s onward, although it was the raw material–producing sector that pioneered this particular organizational form. The most striking development was the formation in 1893 of the Rhine-Westphalian Coal Syndicate, accounting for 86 percent of the output of coal in the Ruhr district and 50 percent of total German output. The syndicate was a superior form of cartel insofar as it supplemented the regulation of output and prices with centralized sales and marketing. The Ruhr Syndicate was held up as a model of cartel organization and the form diffused rapidly throughout the industrial economy in general. By 1914, the entire German coal industry had been cartelized within large regional syndicates. In the Ruhr, one significant effect of cartelization was to encourage concentration as larger firms bought up and closed smaller mines in order to acquire their output quotas. This process accelerated after 1900 so that of sixty-six collieries allocated quotas of less than 1 percent at the inception of the syndicate, more than two-thirds had disappeared from the membership list by 1914. Heavily concentrated and subject to cartelization, the German coal industry was far better placed than its British and American counterparts to withstand the turbulent market conditions of the interwar period.

Mining and the Environment. The mining process in general can be defined in several stages: exploration, extraction, movement, concentration, smelting, and refining. All these stages give rise to environmental damage in the form of air, soil, and water pollution, leading to adverse effects on health and property. In the nineteenth century, most mining operations were conducted beneath the surface in order to extract relatively high-grade minerals. During the twentieth century, however, the gradual degradation of ore quality led to the expansion of open pit or surface mining, resulting in enhanced surface waste and dumping, which, in turn, produced extensive environmental pollution. After 1970, the control of pollution became an increasingly contentious political and economic issue, both in developed and developing economies. In addition, there was increasing concern about the depletion rate of nonrenewable resources. In the face of these concerns, economists developed a body of economic theory designed to address the social costs of mineral exploitation. In this respect, the key concept is externalities, that is, the costs of pollution are largely external costs, insofar as they are borne by society as a whole and minimally, if at all, by the polluter. Thus, to the extent that the social costs of pollution exceed the private costs, free market economies will be afflicted by an overproduction of pollution. Thus, it was argued that pollution should be prevented or regulated by governments to the point where the benefits to be derived from enhanced measures of pollution control exceed the costs of the additional controls. In formal economic terms, if marginal benefits exceed marginal costs, then more resources should be devoted to pollution control. Conversely, if marginal costs exceed marginal benefits, then fewer resources should be allocated to pollution control. In the former case, the agenda for government action was defined in terms of regulatory frameworks and/or taxation of the polluter. Controlling pollution to the point of complete prohibition is extremely costly. On the reasonable assumption that antipollution equipment is expensive to install and maintain, the cost to society of controlling pollution is the opportunity cost in terms of the other goods and services foregone. In this light, there is an optimal level of pollution where an additional amount of control produces a marginal benefit equal to its marginal cost. If the benefit exceeds cost, then extra spending on pollution control can be justified. Conversely, if costs exceed benefits, less should be spent on controls.

An alternative method of dealing with pollution is to levy taxes with the rate varying with the degree of pollution, thereby providing financial incentives for firms and industries to apply effective controls. At the level of the individual firm, it would pay to reduce pollution to the point at which the marginal cost of reduction is equal to the tax, while for the wider society, the level of taxation should be set at the point where the marginal benefit of eliminating another unit of pollution is equal to the marginal cost of elimination. Although economists were generally agreed that the taxation of pollution was commendable in terms of the incentive effect, actual levels of taxation proved difficult to set in view of the critical problem of calculating the extent of the social benefit to be derived from reducing, or eliminating, the various kinds of pollution. Certainly, few governments after 1970 devised antipollution policies on the basis of "making the polluter pay," preferring instead to control pollution by imposing regulatory frameworks.

One of the main justifications for the regulation of pollution is the absence of clearly defined property rights. A mining enterprise may choose to dispose of waste materials into a river because there is no obvious encroachment on private property. On the other hand, it would not choose to deposit waste in a farmer's field if only to avoid the risk of prosecution. Thus, in the absence of clearly defined property rights, there is a divergence between private and social costs insofar as the polluter views the river as a free dumping ground, while the pollution affects not only the farmer but the community at large. Assigned and enforceable property rights, however, hold out the prospect of equalizing private and social costs in order to produce a socially optimum level of pollution. In the case of a farmer subject

to water pollution arising from mining activities, ownership of the relevant stretch of river would result in the social cost of pollution being transformed into a private cost to the mine owner. Conversely, if ownership of the river was vested in the mine owner, then the farmer would be prepared to pay the polluter to reduce or eliminate the volume of waste. The establishment and enforcement of property rights may be a way of internalizing externalities, but their effectiveness as a form of pollution control is inevitably limited by the high transaction costs resulting from attempts to enforce an agreement on many participants.

In the developed industrial economies, the period from 1970 onward was marked by the introduction of increasingly complex environmental controls and regulation of mining activities in the form of mining laws, agreements between governments and mining corporations, and general environmental laws applicable to all industries. For example, in the United States, the Resource Conservation and Recovery Act provides for the regulation of waste accumulation as well as the setting of standards for treatment and disposal, while the 1980 Comprehensive Environmental Response Compensation and Liability Act sets out regulatory procedures for the removal of old disposal sites according to the "polluter pays" principle. Mining laws and agreements, moreover, became increasingly stringent in addressing environmental concerns, not least in terms of the requirement for comprehensive environmental impact assessments as a precondition for the issue of licenses for exploration and exploitation. Historically, developing economies have lagged behind in these respects, but from the 1980s onward both multinational and state-owned mining corporations have been subject to environmental regulation and control. This has been the product both of domestic concerns and also the increasing awareness of international development agencies, such as the World Bank, the Inter-American Development Bank, and the Asian Development Bank, of the environmental consequences of the mining ventures that they support.

BIBLIOGRAPHY

Auty, Richard M., and Raymond F. Mikesell. *Sustainable Development in Mineral Economies*. Oxford, 1998.

Dempsey, Stanley, and James E. Fell, Jr. *Mining the Summit: Colorado's Ten Mile District, 1860–1960*. Norman, Okla., 1986.

Dore, Elizabeth. *The Peruvian Mining Industry: Growth, Stagnation, and Crisis*. Boulder, Colo., 1988.

Eakin, Marshall C. *British Enterprise in Brazil: The St. John d'el Rey Mining Company and the Morro Velho Gold Mine, 1830–1960*. Durham, N.C., and London, 1989.

Fell, James E., Jr. *Oils and Metals: The Rocky Mountain Smelting Industry*. Lincoln, Nebr., 1980.

Fisher, Anthony C. *Resource and Environmental Economics*. Cambridge, 1981.

Furobotn, Erik, and Svetozar Pejovich. "Property Rights and Economic Theory: A Survey of Recent Literature." *Journal of Economic Literature* 10.1 (1972), 1137–1162.

Harvey, Charles E. *The Rio Tinto Company: An Economic History of a Leading International Mining Concern, 1873–1954*. Penzance, U.K., 1981.

Johnson, James P. *The Politics of Soft Coal: The Bituminous Industry from World War I through the New Deal*. Urbana, Ill., 1979.

Jones, Geoffrey. *British Multinationals: Origins, Aims, and Performance*. Aldershot, U.K., 1986.

Mikesell, Raymond F., and John W. Whitney. *The World Mining Industry: Investment Strategy and Public Policy*. Winchester, Mass., 1987.

Moran, Theodore H. *Multinational Corporations and the Politics of Dependence: Copper in Chile*. Princeton, 1974.

Navin, Thomas R. *Copper Mining and Management*. Tucson, Ariz., 1978.

Pounds, N., and W. N. Parker. *Coal and Steel in Western Europe*. London, 1957.

Schmitz, Christopher. "The Rise of Big Business in the World Copper Industry." *Economic History Review* 39.3 (1986), 392–410.

Supple, Barry. *The History of the British Coal Industry*, vol. 4, *1913–1946: The Political Economy of Decline*. Oxford, 1987.

Van Rensburg, W. C. J., and S. Bambrick. *The Economics of the World's Mineral Industries*. Johannesburg, 1978.

MAURICE KIRBY

Work Safety Regulation

The expansion of manufacturing promoted the expansion of industries involved in the extraction of minerals from the earth. These minerals—coal, iron ore, copper, tin, zinc, silver, and gold—played a critical part in economic expansion. More recently, the demand for bauxite and uranium has added to the range of mining activities around the world.

For most of the nineteenth and twentieth centuries, coal extraction dominated the mining sector in terms of proven reserves, tonnage extracted, and workers employed. It had a particular significance in the industrialization of Europe of the nineteenth century, a significance that was replicated in the twentieth century in the United States, the Soviet Union, China, and South Africa.

The coal extraction industry has tended to exemplify the problems faced in mining in general, and many aspects of mining regulation derived from the experience of the coal industry. In its early, nonmechanized phases, coal mining was associated with high levels of death and damage to the work force.

The Nature of Mining. Mining activities are most often conducted away from major urban centers and have often been shaped by practices that draw upon rural traditions and relationships. In the United Kingdom, bonded labor existed in the mining industry until it was outlawed by legislation in 1872. Slave and bonded labor existed in U.S. mines in much of the nineteenth century. The huge expansion of mining in the central Siberian region of the Soviet Union in the 1930s was achieved through the use of forced labor. More recently, the Turkish mining industry has been developed through the use of forced labor.

Turkey's National Protection Law of 1940 required the unemployed and males over sixteen who had miners in their family to become miners. Gold and coal mining in South Africa has relied on migrant workers who enter into contracts that bind them to the companies and their living and working regimes.

The most common and productive form of mineral extraction involves deep mining through the use of underground tunnels. Minerals normally are deposited in seams within the strata of the earth. These seams commonly run in parallel with one another and with the earth's surface. These seams are entered though vertical shafts. Miners enter the mine through cages that drop them to the level of the seam, where they then walk or are transported along tunnels to the face of the seam where mining is under way.

Some mineral seams that run close to the surface of the earth have been extracted through surface forms of mining known as open-cast, open-cut, or strip mining. The depth, extent, and scale of surface mining operations increased significantly as a result of technological developments in the last three decades of the twentieth century. Major coal and iron ore extraction in Brazil, Colombia, Australia, Russia, and the United States is now conducted though this method of mining, which is often regulated quite differently from underground mining.

Mining Hazards. Deep mining is most often associated with harsh labor conditions. It has become commonly understood to involve dirty, difficult, and dangerous work. Coal miners who went on strike in the Soviet Union in 1989 listed soap as one of their demands, drawing attention to the lack of after-work washing facilities. More significant have been the ways in which mining operations can threaten the safety of miners. Machinery accidents, cave-ins, gas explosions, suffocation from gas buildups, and sudden flooding of underground work areas are all hazards associated with deep mining.

Major incidents involving a large loss of life are almost always associated with explosions or flooding. Such incidents have been reduced in Europe and the United States through the introduction of detailed mining regulations.

Mining has also been associated with occupational diseases caused by working underground in often hazardous conditions. Most common are diseases of the lungs (pneumoconiosis and silicosis) associated with the inhalation of mineral dust. In acute cases, these diseases can be fatal.

Examples of Mining Accidents. The history of mining is filled with examples of serious injury and loss of life. Historical documentation is generally incomplete. In the United Kingdom, accurate data on deaths exist only from 1851. These reveal that until the introduction of state ownership in 1947, the death toll in the British coal mines typically reached 1,000 miners or more each year. Using the 1918 official statistics, Frank Hodges calculated that one

British miner was killed every six minutes and one was seriously injured every three minutes.

The worst mining disasters have been associated with explosions. In West Stanley in County Durham, 168 men and boys were killed in an explosion in 1909; at Senghennydd in South Wales, 384 miners were killed in October 1913, and 265 were killed at Gresford in North Wales in 1934. In 1951, another explosion killed eighty-three men at the colliery in Easington, County Durham, in northeastern of England.

Mining disasters can affect entire local communities as well. In October 1966, a coal tip overlooking the village of Aberfan in South Wales avalanched down the mountainside, engulfing a school and killing 116 children and 28 adults.

In the United States, data collected by the Mines Safety and Health Administration show that 92 percent of fatalities in U.S. mines in the twentieth century occurred in coal mines. The pattern of these fatalities (as in the United Kingdom) showed a marked decline in the last half of the century. From 1900 to 1910, the death toll in U.S. coal mines exceeded 2,000 a year. The worst incident happened at the Fairmount Coal Company's mine in Monongah, West Virginia, in 1907, when 362 men and boys were killed. In 1968, in Farmington, West Virginia (less than a mile from Monongah), an explosion and resulting fire killed seventy-eight miners.

History of Regulation. Historically, large-scale mining disasters have provided the impetus for state regulation and reform of mining practices, especially in Europe and the United States.

Early in the nineteenth century, the perils faced by coal miners in northern England gave rise to considerable public concern. A series of accidents in 1837 and 1838 led to the formation of a committee in South Shields, which recommended the compulsory registration of mines, a system of government inspection, and the exclusion of women and children from work underground. The Royal Commission on the employment of children in the mines reported in 1842 and gave further voice to these concerns. That year saw the enactment of the Mines Act, which outlawed the employment of women, girls, and boys under the age of ten in underground mines. It also established, for the first time, a limited system of inspection.

The system of inspection was tightened in 1850 in an act that obliged employers to notify the Home Office immediately of any fatality. These early attempts at regulating the industry made clear the hazardous nature of conditions underground and the extent of the injury inflicted upon the work force. These developments provided support for the miners' trade union in its demands for further controls.

The Mines Regulation Act of 1872 established a framework that was to direct the administration of safety regulation in U.K. mines for the next fifty years. These principles were developed and given greater force with subsequent legislation. The primary principles involved the requirement that mine managers hold a certificate of competency, the requirement for inspection and the involvement of workers' representatives in this process, restriction on hours worked, and an updating of the general rules of mining, especially with regard to ventilation.

These principles were developed and driven forward by repeated mining disasters and by the work of the Mines Inspectorate, whose annual reports provided detailed recommendations for further regulation. These arrangements were extended to the welfare and health of coal miners. Efforts to improve mining safety continued in the twentieth century. The Miners Welfare Commission in 1939 called for heavy investment in pit-head baths and safety research. Safety efforts culminated with the coal industry's nationalization in 1946. The National Coal Board (NCB) took formal responsibility for safety and the medical examination of miners through the Pneumoconiosis Supervision Scheme. Much reduced in size, the NCB was privatized in 1993, and all safety arrangements were retained.

In the United States, although there were strong objections to federal involvement in economic activity, the Monongah disaster in 1907 prompted Congress to toughen the regulation of the mines. By 1910, the increase in death and accidents led the federal government to establish a Bureau of Mines to conduct research into mine safety. In spite of petitioning from miners' trade unions, the level of regulation remained weaker in the United States than in Europe.

Things changed in the 1960s, when the explosion at Farmington finally made clear that the industry required more elaborate federal regulation. In 1969, the Federal Coal Mine Health and Safety Act was enacted. The act provided for four mandatory inspections each year for underground mines and two for surface mines, mandatory fines and criminal penalties for knowing and willful violations, the removal of exemptions from inspection for "nongassy" mines, greater powers for inspectors, powers for miners to request federal inspections, heightened safety and health standards, and compensation for mines who contracted pneumoconiosis.

The Mine Enforcement and Safety Administration was created out of the Bureau of Mines in 1973. This was the first federal agency with the sole purpose of ensuring that all mines in the United States were organized as safe working environments. The Federal Mine Safety and Health Act of 1977 gave the agency (now called the Mine Safety and Health Administration) greater enforcement authority regarding miner training and fire regulations.

Both the United Kingdom and the United States have seen considerable improvement in mining safety. However, concern remains over miner health, which has been described as "the largest, most unacceptable, and unnecessary problem the industry faces."

Current Issues. Technological developments and tougher regulations allied with regimes of inspection and training have been effective in the European Union and the United States. However, in other parts of world, conditions for miners have possibly worsened. In 1995 the International Labor Organization's Coal Mines Committee reported that at least 11,000 deaths and 1 million serious accidents occurred in coal mining worldwide each year. It identified "overexertion" as a major cause. This is certainly the case in China, whose 5.4 million miners now account for more than half of all mining deaths worldwide each year. The mines of the former Soviet Union have become increasingly unsafe, especially in Ukraine. Lacking investment, established safety regimes have not been enforced in the face of production demands. Consequently, 3,700 miners have been killed since 1991, with 80 workers dying in an explosion at the Barakov mine in 2000.

BIBLIOGRAPHY

Albury, D. and J. Schwartz. *Partial Progress: The Politics of Science and Technology*. London, 1982.

Ashworth, W. *The History of British Coal*, vol. 5, *1946–1982: The Nationalised Industries*. Oxford, 1986.

Bergman, D. M. *Death on the Job: Occupational Health and Safety Struggles in the United States*. New York, 1978.

Braithwaite, J. *To Punish or Persuade: Enforcement of Coal Mining Safety*. Albany, N.Y., 1985.

Dawson, S., P. Willman, M. Bamford, and A. Clinton. *Safety at Work: The Limits of Self Regulation*. Cambridge, 1988.

Elling, R. *The Struggle for Workers' Health: A Study in Six Industrialized Countries*. Farmingdale, N.Y., 1986.

Hutchins, B. L., and A. Harrison. *A History of Factory Legislation*. Reprint, London, 1996.

Nichols, T. *The Sociology of Industrial Injury: Employment and Work Relations in Context Series*. London, 1997.

HUW BEYNON

MINTS. *See* Money and Coinage.

MIXED FARMING. Within farming there are two sectors of production—arable and pastoral. Arable agriculture is concerned with the production of crops; this could be food (wheat, barley, potatoes) or raw materials (flax, oil seeds). Pastoral agriculture is concerned with the production of animals; this again could be food (beef, pork, milk, butter) or raw materials (hides, bones, wool). If a farm specializes in one or other type of output, then it is said to be either an arable farm or a pastoral farm. But if a single farm produces both types of output, then it is known as a mixed farm, and the farmer is engaged in mixed farming.

Farms in the industrialized world usually specialize in either arable or pastoral production, but this is a phenomenon of the post–World War II era. Until then mixed farming was the normal pattern of production, particularly in Europe. This is because the production processes for arable and pastoral farming were interdependent, and it was difficult to undertake one form of activity without the other. What were the sources of this production interdependence?

First, arable production requires motive power for many tasks. Plowing is one of the most important and energy-intensive tasks, and it needs to be accomplished quickly (when the weather is optimal for sowing seed) and effectively (with even depth and distribution of furrows). Oxen, horses, and mules are much superior to human labor for pulling a plow, so arable farms almost always found it expedient to keep animals, even if their requirement for motive power was limited to a short period in the agricultural year. Given that the demand for animal power might be limited to a few weeks of the year, it was often desirable to combine the power services of the animal with other services, such as meat or milk production. Hence a farm that was engaged primarily in arable production might keep some cows that could be used for both plowing and milking (O'Brien and Keyder, 1978).

Second, arable production requires fertilizer to restore soil fertility. In the absence of fertilizer, successive crops remove nutrients from the soil, and yields decline to a low level. Before the advent of chemical fertilizers in the late nineteenth century, the primary form of fertilizer was animal dung. Hence arable farms needed a reliable source of animal dung, and this was most easily achieved by keeping animals and producing pastoral output in addition to crops (Overton, 1996).

Third, pastoral production required fodder for the animals. The main source of fodder was grass from pasture land, but this was supplemented by grass and vegetables from the arable sector. Up to the eighteenth century humans and animals competed for land resources. A piece of land could not be used to produce food for humans and animals simultaneously, and hence a common complaint was that the number of animals in existence was limiting the food available for people. However, this constraint was eased from 1700 onward because new types of crops were introduced, particularly turnips and clover. These crops replaced fallow land in the crop rotation. But they could be eaten only by animals (this is particularly true for clover). So if arable farmers wanted to increase their output by replacing unremunerative fallow with a profitable crop such as clover, then they had to start keeping animals to eat the new crops. That is, they had to engage in mixed farming.

As shown, the primary reason to adopt mixed farming was production interdependence. There are several other important advantages of the system. Some of these advantages are also important motivations for employing crop rotation and are discussed in detail in that section. First, mixed farming enables the farmer to use inputs more effectively, notably by spreading his or her labor demand over different types of workers in the local population (many pastoral production tasks, such as milking, were undertaken by women, whereas most arable production tasks were undertaken by men). Second, mixed farming provides insurance against weather and price shocks. The arable output of the farm may be reduced by crop failure, but the pastoral output is likely to be largely unaffected. Conversely, if the pastoral output is reduced by an epizootic, the arable sector is likely to be largely unaffected. Third, mixed farming is an adaptable system, and the farmer can quickly alter the mix of arable and pastoral outputs in response to price changes. For example, if the price of grain is low but the price if meat is high, then the farmer can turn his or her grain into meat by feeding it to his or her animals and fattening them up.

Mixed farming tended to occur in sedentary farming systems such as characterized large parts of Europe and Asia from antiquity onward. Persistent tilling of the soil leads to low soil fertility; this has to be countered by intensive seedbed preparation (that is, more plowing) and intensive use of fertilizers (that is, dung). Both of these activities required animals and hence a move to mixed farming. This is particularly true of western Europe, where high population densities induced high levels of output per acre to feed the local populations. The apogee of this system is observed in northwestern Europe in the eighteenth and nineteenth centuries. Britain pursued intensive forms of mixed farming, in which almost every product and byproduct was used to its maximum. This was associated with Norfolk four-course crop rotation. Half of the arable land was devoted to high-value grains (wheat and barley); the straw left over from the wheat and barley harvest was fed to cattle. The other half of the land was devoted to turnips and clover, which was used to feed cattle and sheep through the winter. The sheep produced wool and mutton; the cattle produced beef, milk, cheese, and hides. Cheese production used the cream from the milk; the skimmed milk was then fed to pigs to fatten them for pork production. All the animals produced dung, which was used to maximize the yields of the wheat and barley crops. The clover crop fixed nitrogen directly from the air and thereby raised wheat and barley yields in addition to providing animal fodder. Nothing was wasted (Shiel, 1991).

Mixed farming was largely absent from the Americas, Africa, Australia, and large parts of Asia. Slash and burn agriculture, which was practiced in large areas of the Americas, relies on natural regeneration of soil fertility and little soil preparation. With little need for draft animals or manure, it was almost exclusively an arable system. Conversely, nomadic herding, which characterized large areas of northern Asia, relied on huge natural grasslands to provide animal feed. The nomads had no need to plow and no need to increase soil fertility because they grew no crops. Instead of keeping cattle (which were well-adapted for plowing but required higher-quality grass), the nomads kept sheep or goats. They did not use the animal dung for fertilizer—instead they burned it as fuel.

But which way did causation run in this pattern of development? Is it the case that these societies did not develop mixed farming because they did not need intensive forms of production (because their population densities were relatively low)? Or is it the case that their population densities had to be low because they could not move to an intensive agricultural production system? It has been argued that outside of Europe and Asia there were no animals that would have been suitable for domestication as draft animals (Diamond, 1997). This would virtually preclude any move to a mixed farming system and would necessitate low population densities.

Complicating this picture is the weak development if not the total absence of interdependent mixed farming systems in the densely populated parts of Asia. There wet-paddy rice cultivation made a minimal use of draft animals and substituted for animal dung with all manner of other fertilizers. Human labor substituted for animals in the provision of both draft power and fertilizer.

Mixed farming largely died out after World War II, certainly in western Europe. By definition mixed farming prevents specialization in either pastoral or arable production. This means that pastoral production has to take place in geographical areas that are not well suited to growing grass, and arable production has to take place in areas that are not well suited to growing crops. The mixed farming strategy was optimal time the benefits of interdependence outweighed the costs of lack of specialization. But technological change has broken the interdependence between arable and pastoral production. For example, the advent of cheap chemical fertilizers made it more efficient to purchase chemical fertilizer than to keep animals on an arable farm for their dung. And the advent of artificial feedstuffs made it more efficient to purchase feedstuffs from a factory than to grow turnips and clover on a pastoral farm to provide winter fodder. The consequence is much greater regional specialization in production. For example, in Britain the wet western areas are largely devoted to cattle and sheep production, while the drier eastern areas are largely devoted to grain production.

BIBLIOGRAPHY

Diamond, Jared. *Guns, Germs, and Steel*. London, 1997.
O'Brien, Patrick, and Caglar Keyder. *Industrialisation in Britain and France: Two Paths to the Twentieth Century*. Chichester, U.K., 1978.

Overton, Mark. *The Agricultural Revolution*. Cambridge, 1996.

Shiel, Robert S. "Improving Soil Fertility in the Pre-Fertilizer Era." In *Land, Labour, and Livestock: Historical Studies in European Agricultural Productivity*, edited by Bruce M. S. Campbell and Mark Overton pp. 51–77. Manchester, 1991.

Slicher van Bath, B. H. *The Agrarian History of Western Europe, 500–1850*. New York, 1963.

LIAM BRUNT

MONASTERIES. Saint Anthony of Egypt (251–356), the first Christian monk, withdrew from the world to live as a hermit at the age of twenty. The eremitical way of life was practiced in the Eastern Church from that time until 1500 (the term of this article) and in the Western Church from the fourth century. From an early date some hermits chose to live in groups or congregations while remaining essentially solitaries. In the cenobitic way of life, by contrast, monks were committed to a life of obedience to their abbot within a community, and this life, also, is recorded in both the East and the West from the fourth century. In the Eastern Church eremitical and cenobitic forms of monasticism coexisted in a fruitful tension. In the Western Church cenobitic monasticism was dominant from the ninth century, and the Rule of Saint Benedict of Nursia (c. 480–c. 550) was widely accepted as normative. Here, hermits were often under pressure to enter an existing ecclesiastical structure. With the notable exception of the Carthusian Order, founded by Saint Bruno (c. 1032–1101), the new orders that revitalized monasticism in the West in the eleventh and twelfth centuries were cenobitic, though often with a difference. The Cistercians practiced a degree of asceticism unknown among the older Benedictines, and the Augustinian and Premonstratensian canons performed a monastic office but also exercised the cure of souls outside the monastery.

The differences between eremitical and cenobitic forms of monastic life were crucially important for the economy of the regions where each or either took root. Hermits needed food, clothing, and shelter, and if, like the Camaldoli of Arezzo, in Italy, founded by Saint Romuald of Ravenna (c. 950–1027), or like the Carthusians, they lived in congregations, their needs were the greater, since even a rudimentary common life required buildings in addition to the hermitages of the individual monk or nun. These needs were, even so, small in comparison with those of cenobitic monks and nuns, who inhabited more elaborate buildings, supported more dependents, adopted a less frugal way of life than hermits, and, in the West, often practiced charity on a scale that itself needed funding. Only landed endowments, given by founders and benefactors, could ensure for monasteries of this kind the stability they needed, and because they lacked these on an adequate scale many monasteries had only a transient existence.

The total extent of land owned by monasteries was, even so, very large. The Domesday Survey (1086) suggests that nearly 15 percent of the landed wealth of England was then in monastic hands. By 1150 the comparable figure may well have been 25 percent, and an estimate of this order of magnitude is realistic for Western Europe as a whole. In addition, the Augustinian and Premonstratensian canons acquired a great deal of tithe income, which had been deflected from parish churches to serve their needs. The Cistercians were sometimes guilty of exaggerating the deserted aspect of the lands they colonized. But many of their foundations were indeed on the edge of the existing cultivated area, and as vigorous colonists of wastelands for pastoral husbandry they left an indelible mark on the landscape wherever they settled.

In the thirteenth and fourteenth centuries, both lay and ecclesiastical landowners in England normally exploited their demesnes, or home farms, directly and not through lessees, as commonly happened elsewhere. At the beginning and end of the fourteenth century, conventual demesnes here—that is, the demesnes whose income was assigned to the monastic community and not to the abbot of the monastery in question—were less actively involved than the demesnes of other kinds of landowners in commercial agriculture; they were more often exploited with household needs in mind.

But this conclusion applies to arable demesnes and not to the pastoral demesnes that regionally were no less extensive. In the early fourteenth century, the Cistercians in England were among the greatest producers of wool then in existence for the export market. In general, it is hard to discern a distinctively monastic pattern of estates administration, either in England or in the many parts of Europe where monks, in common with other landowners, lived mainly on the rents of their tenants.

The Cistercian grange, a compact estate consisting largely of a home farm, was unlike not only the typical manor in lay hands but also the typical Benedictine manor. As an economic unit, a monastic estate had more in common with other ecclesiastical or lay estates of similar size than with other monastic estates, whatever their size. Capital resources, for example, depended more on the size of the estate in question than on the order in the Church—monastic, episcopal, or lay—to which the owner belonged. Although it has often been suggested that the status of monasteries as perpetual corporations enabled them to take a distinctively long-term view of economic problems, the proposition is hard, if not impossible, to prove.

"Give to the poor" was an imperative for all monks, but how this command was fulfilled varied with time and place. In Byzantium, where many monasteries were situated in large towns but did not occupy a dominant position there, institutional forms of monastic charity seem to have

MONASTERY. Monks of the Carthusian Order, Chartreuse, France, 1982. Founded in 1084, the monastery is among the oldest religious communities in Western Christianity. (© Adam Woolfitt/Woodfin Camp and Associates, New York)

been rare. For most of this period in western Europe, the typical town was small, and many small and not so small towns were dominated by a single monastery. Thus in the ninth century, the Frankish town of Centula-Saint Riquier, which may have had as many as seven thousand inhabitants, was dominated by the monastery of Centula-Saint Riquier. Among the poor for whom the abbot of Saint Riquier provided daily were 150 widows and sixty clerics; and the abbey maintained a school. These practices remind us that even at this early date monastic charity was not entirely indiscriminate, but included an element of careful choice.

In the predominantly rural economies of the West, monastic charity, administered to poor pilgrims and travelers in hostelries situated within the monastery, and to casual poor and local poor at the almonry gate, assumed great importance. Moreover, from the ninth century on, the cult of Purgatory ensured that monks had more than the leftovers of their own meals to distribute in these institutions, for it became the common practice to mark the anniversary of a benefactor's death with a distribution of a portion of food and drink to the poor. At the great monastery of Cluny, in Burgundy, founded in the tenth century and having many benefactors, it became necessary in the mid-twelfth century to restrict the number of daily portions to fifty, so heavy had the burden on monastic resources become in the meantime.

The growth of population, which gathered momentum in the late eleventh century and the early twelfth century, meant that the need for alms, especially in towns, now constantly exceeded the supply. Under these circumstances monastic almsgiving, whether in cash or in kind, became more discriminating than previously, and more systematic. Resident almsmen and women—who were, no doubt, chosen carefully—and support for hospitals are typical features of this period. These trends grew even stronger in the fourteenth century, when a general decline in population resulted in a widespread scarcity of labor, and fears grew that indiscriminate almsgiving might tempt able-bodied poor to decline work for wages. During this period, many monks, and perhaps nuns too, received regular wages or pocket money, and it is possible that some of this money was devoted to private almsgiving. The extent and character of monastic charity remain to a large extent elusive in the fourteenth and fifteenth centuries, as in earlier periods. But it seems clear that the importance of monasteries in relation to that of other relief agencies, and especially in relation to that of guilds and confraternities, both of which were part religious, part secular, institutions, declined.

BIBLIOGRAPHY

Bryer, Anthony A. M. "The Late Byzantine Monastery in Town and Countryside." In *The Church in Town and Countryside*, vol. 16 of *Studies in Church History*, edited by Derek Baker, pp. 219–241. Oxford, 1979.

Campbell, Bruce M. S. *English Seignioral Agriculture, 1250–1450*. Cambridge, 2000.

Harvey, Barbara F. *Living and Dying in England, 1100–1540: The Monastic Experience*. Oxford, 1993.

Henderson, John S. *Piety and Charity in Late Medieval Florence*. Oxford, 1994.

Knowles, David. *Christian Monastcism*. London, 1969.

McKitterick, Rosamond D. "Town and Monastery in the Carolingian Period." In *The Church in Town and Countryside*, vol. 16 of *Studies in Church History*, edited by Derek Baker, pp. 93–102. Oxford, 1979.

Pullan, Brian S. *Rich and Poor in Renaissance Venice*: *The Social Institutions of a Catholic State to 1620*. Oxford, 1971.

Southern, Richard W. *Western Society and the Church in the Middle Ages*. Harmondsworth, 1970.

BARBARA HARVEY

MONETARY POLICY. *See* Stabilization Policies.

MONETARY STANDARDS. A monetary standard refers to the set of monetary arrangements and institutions governing the supply of money. It differs from the term *monetary regime*, defined as a set of monetary arrangements and institutions accompanied by a set of expectations by the public with respect to policymaker actions and by policymakers about the public's reaction to their actions.

There are two distinguishable aspects of monetary standards/regimes: domestic and international. The domestic aspect refers to the institutional arrangements and policy actions of monetary authorities. The international aspect relates to monetary arrangements between nations. The two basic types of monetary arrangements are fixed and flexible exchange rates, along with a number of intermediate variants, including adjustable pegs and managed floats.

Historically, the two types of monetary standards/regimes are those based on convertibility of all forms of money into currency, generally specie, and those based on fiat. The former prevailed until the 1930s, although the Bretton Woods system from 1944 to 1971 embodied an indirect link to gold; the latter has held sway ever since.

The Theory of Specie Standards as Domestic Standard. The specie standards adopted as far back as ancient times are types of commodity money standards, which have generally been based on silver, gold, or bimetallism (gold and silver coins circulating at a fixed ratio of their weights). However, other commodities, such as bronze, copper, or cowrie shells have also been used.

Under a specie standard such as the gold standard, the monetary authority defines the weight of gold coins or else fixes the price of an ounce of gold in terms of the national currency or money-of-account. By being willing to buy and sell gold freely at the mint price, the authority maintains the fixed price. Ownership or use of gold is unrestricted.

The Theory of Specie Standards as International Standards. The international specie standard evolved from domestic standards with the common fixing of the specie price by different nations. Unlike later arrangements, the classical gold standard, which prevailed from 1880 to 1914, was not the result of an international agreement but was driven largely by market forces.

Under the classical gold standard fixed-exchange-rate system, the world's monetary gold stock was distributed according to the member nations' demand for money and use of substitutes for gold. Disturbances to the balance of payments were automatically equilibrated by the price-specie flow mechanism (as elaborated by David Hume [1711–1776]). Under that mechanism, arbitrage in gold kept the price levels of various nations in line with each other.

Central banks also played an important role in the international gold standard by varying their discount rates and using other tools of monetary policy, thereby speeding up adjustment to balance-of-payments disequilibria.

The Specie Standard as a Rule. One of the most important features of the specie standard was that it embodied a monetary rule or commitment mechanism that constrained the actions of the monetary authorities. To the classical economists, it was preferable for monetary authorities to follow rules rather than to subject monetary policy to the discretion of well-meaning officials. Now a rule serves to bind policy actions over time. This view of such policy rules, in contrast to the earlier tradition that stressed both impersonality and automaticity, stems from the recent literature on the time inconsistency of optimal government policy.

In terms of the modern perspectives of Kydland and Prescott (1977) and Barro and Gordon (1983), the rule served as a commitment mechanism to prevent governments from setting policies sequentially in a time-inconsistent manner. According to this approach, adherence to the fixed price of gold was the commitment that prevented governments from creating surprise fiduciary money issues in order to capture seigniorage revenue, or from defaulting on outstanding debt (Bordo and Kydland, 1996). On this basis, adherence to the specie standard rule before 1914 enabled many countries to avoid the problems of high inflation and stagflation that troubled the late twentieth century.

The specie standard rule in the century before World War I can also be interpreted as a contingent rule, or a rule with escape clauses (Grossman and Van Huyck, 1988; Bordo and Kydland, 1996). The monetary authority maintained the standard—kept the price of the currency in terms of specie fixed, except in the event of a well-understood emergency, such as a major war. In wartime, it might suspend specie convertibility and issue paper money to finance its expenditures, and it could sell debt issues in terms of the nominal value of its undepreciated paper. The rule was contingent in the sense that the public understood that the suspension would last for only the duration of the wartime emergency plus some period of postwar adjustment, and that afterwards the government would adopt the deflationary policies necessary to resume payments at the original parity.

Observing such a rule would allow the government to smooth its revenue from different sources of finance: taxation, borrowing, and seigniorage (Lucas and Stokey, 1983; Mankiw, 1987). That is, in wartime, present taxes on labor effort reduced output when it was needed most, but relying on future taxes or borrowing was optimal. At the same time, positive collection costs might also make it optimal to use the inflation tax as a substitute for conventional taxes (Bordo and Vegh, 2002). A temporary suspension of convertibility then allowed the government to use the optimal mix of the three sources of finance.

The basic specie standard rule is a domestic rule, enforced by the reputation of the specie standard itself, that is, by the historical evolution of specie as money. An alternative commitment mechanism was to guarantee gold convertibility in the constitution, as was the case in Sweden before 1914 (Jonung, 1984).

Although the specie standard rule originally evolved as a domestic commitment mechanism, its enduring fame is as an international rule: namely, maintenance of specie convertibility to the established par. Maintenance of a fixed price of gold by its adherents in turn ensured fixed exchange rates. The fixed price of domestic currency in terms of specie served as a nominal anchor under the international monetary system.

Fiat Money Standards. Although a specie standard such as the gold standard has the desirable properties of automaticity, of providing a credible commitment mechanism, and of producing long-term price level and exchange rate stability, it also has defects that argue the case for a fiat standard. These include swings in the world price level because of the vagaries of the gold standard (gold demand and supply shocks); the high resource costs of basing the monetary system on specie; inadequate supplies of precious metals to prevent long-run deflation; the international transmission of the business cycle and financial crises via the fixed-exchange rates of the specie standard; and the tendency to violate the rules of the game and to ignore the need for cooperation.

The case for a fiat money standard is that it could in theory provide a stable money supply, growing at a rate sufficient to match the long-run growth of output without deflation and with minimal resource costs (Friedman, 1960).

Moreover, under a fiat regime, monetary and fiscal policy can be used to offset shocks to the real economy and smooth the business cycle. Similarly, fiat money and a floating exchange rate can insulate the domestic economy from foreign real shocks. Finally, the issue of fiat money can serve as an inflation tax on the real purchasing power of money balances to provide tax revenue during emergencies.

To achieve many of these positive attributes of a fiat money standard, the monetary authority needs a credible commitment mechanism to renounce any resort to sustained money issues over the amount required to match long-run real growth. In the nineteenth-century environment in which adherence to the specie standard reigned supreme, the issue of paper money by a government was tolerated only during temporary wartime emergencies, such as during the suspension period in England during the Napoleonic wars. Permanent paper money issue was anathema because of the belief that it would lead to permanent and growing inflation; and one well-documented example is that of the British "paper pound" inflation from 1797 to 1815. As a result, the basic trust between the public and the government embodied in specie coins eroded.

This view gradually changed in the twentieth century. World War I led to a breakdown of the classical gold standard and to high or hyperinflation in the belligerent countries. The high real costs of the disinflation required to restore gold convertibility at the original parity produced severe economic and social problems in many postwar western countries. Groups harmed by the deflation that gold standard adherence imposed gained political power. They laid the groundwork for the case for managed money and the end of the gold standard (Eichengreen, 1992; Polanyi, 1944). However, the transition from specie to a fiat standard that would match the price level stability that had been achieved by the specie standard took most of the twentieth century to achieve.

Monetary Standards from Specie Standards to Fiat Money: Bimetallism and the Gold Standard. The use of precious metals (gold, silver, copper) as money can be traced back to ancient Lydia. These metals were adopted as money because of their desirable properties (durability, recognizability, storability, portability, divisibility, and easy standardization). Earlier commodity money systems were bimetallic—gold was used for high-value transactions, silver for low-value ones. The bimetallic ratio (the ratio of the mint price of gold relative to the mint price of silver) was set close to the market ratio to ensure that both metals circulated. Otherwise, the overvalued metal would drive the undervalued metal out of circulation, in accordance with Gresham's Law.

The problems that plagued early bimetallic systems were periodic shortages of smaller silver coins and a deterioration in quality (Glassman and Redish, 1988; Redish, 2000; Sargent and Velde, 2002). They were dealt with by debasement and alteration of the bimetallic ratio.

England ultimately solved the problem of devising an efficient commodity money standard (Redish, 2000) by shifting to a monometallic gold standard with token silver coins early in the nineteenth century, a transformation made possible by technical improvements in coin production. Another problem facing commodity systems in the premodern era was the tendency of monarchs to debase the currency to obtain revenue in wartime. The development of efficient tax systems and the use of standardized coins ended the practice (Bordo, 1986).

Although the gold standard operated relatively smoothly for close to four decades, the episode was punctuated by periodic financial crises. In most cases, when faced with both an internal and external drain, the Bank of England and other European central banks followed Bagehot's rule of lending freely but at a penalty rate. On several occasions (e.g., 1890 and 1907) even the Bank of England's adherence to convertibility was put to the test and, according to Eichengreen (1992), cooperation with the Banque de France and other central banks was required to save its adherence. Whether this was the case is a moot point: the cooperation that did occur was episodic, ad hoc, and not an integral part of the operation of the gold standard. Of greater importance is that during periods of financial crises, private capital flows aided the Bank of England.

By 1914, the gold standard had evolved de facto into a gold exchange standard. In addition to substituting other national fiduciary moneys for gold to economize on scarce gold reserves, many countries held convertible foreign exchange (mainly deposits in London) as international reserves. Thus, the system evolved into a massive pyramid of credit built upon a narrow base of gold. The possibility of a confidence crisis, triggering a collapse of the system increased as the gold reserves of the center diminished (Triffin, 1960). The advent of World War I triggered the collapse. The belligerents scrambled to convert their outstanding foreign liabilities into gold. Although the gold standard was reinstated in two variants later in the twentieth century it could never be restored to its original structure.

Interwar Gold Exchange Standard. The gold standard was reinstated after World War I as a gold exchange standard. Great Britain and other countries, alarmed by the postwar experience of inflation and exchange-rate instability, were eager to return to the halcyon days of gold convertibility before the war. The system reestablished in 1925 was an attempt to restore the old regime but to economize on gold in the face of a perceived gold shortage. Based on principles developed at the Genoa conference in 1922, members were encouraged to adopt central bank statutes that substituted foreign exchange for gold reserves and discouraged gold holdings by the private sector. The new system lasted only six years, crumbling after Great Britain's departure from gold in September 1931. The system failed because of several fatal flaws in its structure and because it did not embody a credible commitment mechanism.

The fatal flaws included the adjustment problem (asymmetric adjustment between deficit countries such as Great Britain and such surplus countries as France and the United States); the failure by countries to follow the rules of the gold standard game (e.g., both the United States and France sterilized gold flows); the liquidity problem (inadequate gold supplies, the wholesale substitution of key currencies for gold as international reserves, leading to a convertibility crisis); and the confidence problem (leading to sudden shifts among key currencies and between key currencies and gold) (Bordo, 1993; Eichengreen, 1990).

The commitment mechanism of the interwar gold standard was much weaker than that of the classical gold standard. Because monetary policy was politicized in many countries, the commitment to convertibility was not believed. Hence, invoking the contingency clause and altering parity would have led to destabilizing capital flows. Moreover, central bank cooperation was limited. The system collapsed in the face of the shocks of the Great Depression.

Bretton Woods. The Bretton Woods system was the last specie-related standard. It was a variant of the gold standard in the sense that the United States (the most important commercial power) defined its parity in terms of gold, and all other members defined their parities in terms of dollars. The Articles of Agreement, signed at Bretton Woods, New Hampshire, in 1944, represented a compromise between American and British plans. It combined the flexibility and freedom for policymakers of a floating rate system, which the British team wanted, with nominal stability of the gold standard rule, emphasized by the United States. The system established a pegged exchange rate system, but members could alter their parities in the face of fundamental disequilibrium. Members were encouraged to use domestic stabilization policies to offset temporary disturbances, and they were protected from speculative attack by capital controls. The International Monetary Fund (IMF) was created to provide temporary liquidity assistance and to oversee the operation of the system.

Although based on the principle of convertibility, the Bretton Woods system differed from the classical gold standard in a number of fundamental ways. First, it was an arrangement mandated by an international agreement between governments, whereas the gold standard evolved informally from private arrangements. Second, domestic policy autonomy was encouraged even at the expense of convertibility, in sharp contrast to the gold standard, for which convertibility was key. Third, capital movements were suppressed by controls. It became an asymmetric system, with the United States rather than Great Britain as the central country.

The flaws of the Bretton Woods system echoed those of the gold exchange standard. Adjustment was inadequate, prices were downwardly inflexible, and declining output was countered by expansionary financial policy. Under the rules, the pegged exchange rate could be altered, but rarely was in practice because of fear of speculative attacks, reflecting market beliefs that governments would not pursue the policies necessary to maintain convertibility (Eichengreen, 1992). Hence, the system was propped up by capital controls in its early years and by G-10 and IMF lending in the later years. The liquidity problem echoed that of the interwar gold exchange standard. As a substitute for scarce gold, the system relied increasingly on U.S. dollars generated by persistent U.S. payments deficits. The French resented the resulting asymmetry between the United States and the rest of the world. The Bretton Woods confidence problem was manifest in the risk of a run on U.S. gold reserves as outstanding dollar liabilities increased relative to gold reserves.

The Bretton Woods system collapsed between 1968 and 1971. The United States broke the implicit rules of the dollar standard by not maintaining price stability. The rest of the world did not want to absorb additional dollars that would lead to inflation. Surplus countries (especially Germany) were reluctant to revalue.

Another important source of strain on the system was the unworkability of the adjustable peg under increasing capital mobility. Speculation against a fixed parity could not be stopped by either traditional policies or international rescue packages. The Americans' hands were forced by rumors of British and French decisions in the summer of 1971 to convert dollars into gold. The impasse was ended when President Richard Nixon closed the gold window on 15 August 1971.

The Managed Float and the Fiat Standard. As a reaction to the flaws of Bretton Woods, the world turned to generalized floating exchange rates in March 1973. Though the early years of the floating exchange rates were often characterized as a dirty float, whereby monetary authorities extensively intervened to affect both the levels and volatility of exchange rates, by the 1990s it evolved into a system where exchange market intervention occurred primarily with the intention of smoothing fluctuations.

The advent of generalized floating in 1973 allowed each country more flexibility to conduct independent monetary policy. In the 1970s, inflation accelerated as advanced countries attempted to use monetary policy to maintain full employment. However, monetary policy could be used to target the level of unemployment only at the expense of accelerating inflation (Friedman, 1968; Phelps, 1968). In addition, the United States and other countries used expansionary monetary policy to accommodate oil price shocks in 1973 and 1979. The high inflation rates that ensued led to a determined effort by monetary authorities in the United States, the United Kingdom, and other countries to disinflate.

The 1980s witnessed renewed emphasis by central banks on low inflation as their primary (if not sole) objective. Although no formal monetary rule has been established, a number of countries have granted their central banks independence from the fiscal authority and have also instituted mandates for low inflation or price stability.

In some respects, for the United States and other major countries there appears to be a return to a rule like the convertibility principle and the fixed nominal anchor of a specie standard.

The European Monetary Union (EMU). Within the context of the worldwide shift toward a floating exchange rate regime, the majority of European countries have opted for a monetary union. The EMU has many attributes of the classical gold standard, including perfectly fixed exchange rates (one national currency) and the free mobility of goods, capital, and labor. It differs significantly, however, in that it is based on a fiat standard. The euro is issued and controlled by the European Central Bank. The actions of the independent ECB are constrained by a mandate for low inflation, which its founders hoped would serve as the type of credible nominal anchor that gave long-run price stability to the classical gold standard.

[*See also* Exchange Rates; Gold Standard, *and* Gresham's Law.]

BIBLIOGRAPHY

Barro, R. J., and D. B. Gordon. "Rules, Discretion, and Reputation in a Model of Monetary Policy." *Journal of Monetary Economics* 12 (1983), 101–121.

Bordo, Michael D. "Money, Deflation, and Seignorage in the Fifteenth Century: A Review Essay." *Journal of Monetary Economics* 12 (1986).

Bordo, Michael D. "The Bretton Woods International Monetary System." In *A Retrospective on the Bretton Woods System: Lessons for International Monetary Reform*, edited by M. D. Bordo and B. Eichengreen. Chicago, 1993.

Bordo, Michael D., and Finn Kydland. "The Gold Standard as a Commitment Mechanism." In *Economic Perspectives on the Classical Gold Standard*, edited by Tamin Bayoumi, Barry Eichengreen, and Mark Taylor. Cambridge, 1996.

Bordo, Michael D., and Hugh Rockoff. "The Gold Standard as a 'Good Housekeeping Seal of Approval.'" *Journal of Economic History* 56.2 (June 1996), 389–428.

Bordo, Michael D., and Carlos Vegh. "If Only Alexander Hamilton Had Been Argentinean: A Comparison of the Early Monetary Experiences of Argentina and the United States." *Journal of Monetary Economics* (March 2002).

Eichengreen, Barry. *Elusive Stability*. New York, 1990.

Eichengreen, Barry. *Golden Fetters: The Gold Standard and the Great Depression, 1919–1939*. New York, 1992.

Ford, A. G. *The Gold Standard 1880–1914: Britain and Argentina*. Oxford, 1962.

Friedman, Milton, *A Program of Monetary Stability*. New York, 1960.

Glassman, D., and Angela Redish. "Currency Depreciation in Early Modern England and France." *Explorations in Economic History* 25 (1988), 75–97.

Grossman, Herschel J., and John B.Van Huyck. "Sovereign Debt as a Contingent Claim: Excusable Default, Repudiation, and Reputation." *American Economic Review* 78 (1988), 1088–1097.

Kydland, F. E., and E. C. Prescott, "Rules Rather than Discretion: The Inconsistency of Optimal Plans." *Journal of Political Economy* 85 (1977), 473–491.

Lucas, Robert E. Jr., and Nancy L. Stokey. "Optimal Fiscal and Monetary Policy in an Economy without Capital." *Journal of Monetary Economics* 12 (1983), 55–93.

Mankiw, Gregory N. "The Optimal Collection of Seigniorage: Theory and Evidence." *Journal of Monetary Economics* 20 (1987), 327–342.

Polanyi, Karl. *The Great Transformation*. New York, 1944.

Redish, Angela. "The Evolution of the Gold Standard in England." *Journal of Economic History* 50 (1990), 789–806.

Redish, Angela. *Bimetallism: An Economic and Historical Analysis*. Cambridge, 2000.

Sargent, Thomas, and François Velde. *The Big Problem of Small Change*. Princeton, 2002.

Triffin, Robert. *Gold and the Dollar Crisis*. New Haven, 1960.

Michael D. Bordo

MONEY AND COINAGE *[This entry contains three subentries, an overview and discussions of money and coinage before and after 1750.]*

General Overview

The classic definition of money is functional: money is a medium of exchange, a store of value, a unit of account, and thus also a standard of deferred payment. Of these functions, the medium-of-exchange function is key. Economist Robert Clower defined the role of money by stating that, in a monetary economy, "money buys goods and goods buy money but goods don't buy goods." However, for individuals to trade goods for money, they must expect that the value of the money will remain stable; so a medium of exchange must also be a store of value. In addition, moneys typically have been denominated in the unit of account of the economy, enhancing their convenience as a payments medium.

Within this definition there are a variety of types of money, and a few more definitions are useful. Commodity money refers to a money valued according to the nonmonetary value of its components. Coins of pure gold or cattle are examples of this. At the other extreme, fiat money is "intrinsically useless and inconvertible," such as notes issued by central banks in many countries today. In between these poles lies convertible money, sometimes called fiduciary or credit money, whose issuer commits to convert the money into another asset, typically either government-issued fiat money (e.g., checkable bank deposits) or commodity money (e.g., bank notes under a gold standard).

In the absence of a medium of exchange, trade between two parties is restricted, in the extreme case, to those who share a "double coincidence of wants." By expanding trading opportunities, monetization—the increased use of money—permits increased specialization in an economy. Economists typically emphasize the improved efficiency of trade through the elimination of the need for barter as the rationale for introduction and expansion of the use of money, whereas historians and numismatists emphasize the use of money by rulers to control both their society and the economy of the state.

Historically, the use of units of account preceded the use of money as a medium of exchange. There are Babylonian records from the eighteenth and nineteenth centuries BCE mandating payments in weights of silver. The first media of exchange were naturally occurring commodities (famous examples include cowrie shells and precious metals) that traded by weight or count. These media, however, were superseded by coined money, issued by a state or a ruler who gave the coins an official value in the local unit of account. Ideally, the homogeneity of coins enabled them to trade by tale, that is, by count, rather than being weighed for each transaction; and the punch or the stamp on the coin suggested that the state stood behind it. However, history presents many examples of the state's taking advantage of this by debasing its coins (reducing the percentage of silver or gold in a coin, or its weight), thereby promoting the rise of money changers, who specialized in valuing coins (as well as in exchanging foreign for domestic coins).

Over time, the high resource cost of commodity money led to a substitution of convertible bank notes (i.e., convertible into coin) for coin as a medium of exchange. Banks could issue notes and keep only a small reserve (i.e., engage in fractional-reserve banking) to meet withdrawals, and thus could acquire interest revenue by lending out the remainder. The downside of this arrangement was that note holders had to be confident that the note could not be counterfeit and that the bank would be able to redeem the notes in coin on demand. In addition, the banks would hold deposits for their customers, who could make payments by drawing a check on their account. Again the bank could profit from lending out the deposit, but customers would worry that their deposit was indeed redeemable.

Coinage was, almost always and everywhere, a state prerogative; and although the introduction of bank notes changed the role of the state, it did not preclude it. In

MONEY AND COINAGE. The insignia of the post of the count of the holy largesse, an official of the Roman Empire, as depicted in the *Notitia Dignitatum*, showing coins, buckels, and other precious-metal ornaments that could be used for payment, c. 400. (The Bodelian Library, University of Oxford)

China, paper money privately issued in the eleventh century was soon banned by the state, which issued its own notes. In Europe the first banks, the Stockholm Bank (1656) and the Bank of England (1694), received state charters in return for financial benefits to the government.

In the nineteenth and twentieth centuries, central banks, motivated by the desire to create a sound and uniform national currency and also to acquire the expected profits, took over the issue of bank notes, maintaining the promise to convert them into either gold or notes of other central banks that were in turn convertible into gold on demand. However, by the late twentieth century those promises had been removed, and most countries issued fiat moneys, that is, money issued by a state without any promise to convert it into something else, and—unlike commodity money—intrinsically useless. However, the medium of exchange for most transactions is not these notes but checks written on deposit accounts held in private banks, accounts that now promise to pay central-bank money on demand.

Monetary systems have operated at a variety of levels, from local retail transactions, typically of low value, to very large-value international transactions; and the medium of exchange has differed by level, with local transactions conducted in the local currency, whether regional or national, and international transactions conducted in relatively few currencies. These international currencies typically have been those renowned for their stability and issued by states that were net lenders: in medieval Europe, gold coins of the Italian city-states; in early modern Europe, Dutch bank money; in the nineteenth and early twentieth centuries, sterling (British pounds); and in the later twentieth century U.S. dollars (and to a lesser extent, German marks and Japanese yen).

A fundamental characteristic of money is that it is limited in supply; for if there is a demand for money and a limited supply, the money will have positive value. Early moneys made of precious metals in coin or bullion satisfied the scarcity requirement; that is, gold and silver were valuable because they were rare, and they were prized for their non-monetary qualities. The price level in an economy in which money-of-account was based on silver reflected the relative price of silver as determined by its supply and the demand for it. If the supply of silver rose (for example, in Europe after the inflow of silver from the Americas in the sixteenth century), then its price would fall, or equivalently the silver-based prices of goods would rise.

However, because moneys typically were valued in the unit of account, at values determined by the government (ruler, king, etc.), the government could affect the price level by altering the value of the money. In medieval Europe, princes at times reduced the silver content of coins, or, in the case of gold coins or large-denomination silver coins, raised their unit-of-account value; and both of these actions usually had the consequence of raising the price level (if not proportionately) by creating more money, that is, as valued in unit of account, though not as measured by the weight of silver. Under today's fiat-money standards, the government or the central bank directly controls the amount of fiat money issued and—because banks relate the amount of their deposit accounts to the stock of fiat money—the price level.

Monetary authorities historically manipulated coinage or money because it yielded financial gains, both direct and indirect. In the medieval and early modern periods, direct revenues came from making more coins from a given weight of metal or from taking more seignorage per coin. In the modern period, "printing money" has the same effect. These actions also generate indirect gains as the resulting inflation reduces the real value of debts. Such behavior was most likely to occur when the monetary authority desperately needed revenue, which in turn was most likely during (expensive) wars. Thus, wars have been associated with inflation since the emergence of money.

At the beginning of the twenty-first century, the world of money is adjusting to rapid globalization and technological change. In particular, there are experiments with electronic cash, which might eliminate the need for bank notes and even bank checking accounts. The diversity of national currencies is falling, as European countries form a monetary union, based on the Euro, and some South American countries "dollarize" by adopting the U.S. dollar as their currency.

BIBLIOGRAPHY

Davies, Glyn. *A History of Money from Ancient Times to the Present Day.* Cardiff, 1994.

Spufford, Peter. *Money and Its Use in Medieval Europe.* Cambridge, 1988.

Williams, Jonathan, ed. *Money: A History.* New York, 1997.

ANGELA REDISH

Money and Coinage before 1750

The earliest written records of money are from the law codes of Mesopotamia (such as Hammurabi's code) dating from the nineteenth century BCE. In these codes, fines are stated in weights of silver, and ideal prices for certain goods are similarly listed in silver equivalents. Silver was not only a unit of account but a medium of exchange: archaeologists have found silver ingots and thin wires of silver that they believe were used as a means of payment. In the precoinage period, the silver would have been weighed on a balance to ascertain the amount paid. Early Egyptian records (thirteenth to eleventh centuries BCE) show similar use of gold as a unit of account and a medium of exchange, as it was more plentiful than silver in Egypt. Archaeologists have suggested that cowrie shells were used as a medium of exchange in China from 1600 to 1000 BCE (and continued to be used in Africa and India at a much later date).

The use of coinage emerged independently in the West and in China. In the seventh century BCE in Turkey—then called Lydia—coins were produced from electrum, a naturally occurring amalgam of gold and silver. The details of this issue are unclear. Who issued the coins: the state or private individuals? What was their role? How were they valued, given that their manufacture was uneven (because of variation in both size and composition)? However, within two centuries, Greek states were producing coins of pure gold and silver with modern characteristics. The coins were issued by the state; they functioned as a medium of exchange; they traded at "official values" in the unit of account. Historians' knowledge of the first Chinese coins is also vague. In the late seventh and early sixth cen-

turies BCE the Zhou state began the issue of coins, which were in the shape of spades; in the states of Qi (Shandong) and Yan (Hebei), coins in the shape of knives were issued. These coins were cast in bronze and were from five to twenty centimeters in length. Although they had the shape of daily instruments, they were clearly intended purely for monetary use and circulated widely in China for more than three centuries.

The Chinese Monetary System. In the third century BCE the Qin dynasty established a standardized coinage across China. The spade and the knife coins were abolished, and a new *banliang* coinage was introduced. These circular coins with a square hole remained typical of Chinese and Chinese-derivative coinage until the nineteenth century. The coins were named by their weight (*banliang* meaning a half ounce or approximately twenty grams) and were cast in bronze. Gold coins were minted on occasion, but their use was very limited. Although they still were called *banliang*, the weight of the coins declined over time, and coin issues became less standardized as the Qin empire decayed.

The next phase of Chinese coinage was the *wuzhu* coins (again named after their weight—five grains), issued by the Han dynasty from about 118 BCE. These two were cast bronze coins, circular with a square hole, and again as the dynasty lost control over the continent, the coinage became less standardized. With the establishment of the Tang dynasty in the early seventh century, a new coinage was introduced. The Tang ended the tradition of naming a coin by its (initial) weight and introduced the Kaiyuan *tongbao*, which was also again a circular cast bronze coin with a hole in its center. The Kaiyuan became the model for Asian coinages (e.g., Japanese and Korean) until as late as the nineteenth century. The value of one coin was very low, and so the medium of exchange became strings of one hundred and later one thousand coins. Strings then became a unit of account, and in this world, debasement occurred through the ruler's issue of short strings of only seven hundred cash. For larger-value payments, this "cash" (the name for these coins) economy was supplemented by the use of silk and silver as a means of payment.

The Song dynasty (900–1200 CE) introduced dramatic changes to this complex monetary system. Uniform coinage was reintroduced throughout the empire, and by the mid-eleventh century, bronze coins reigned supreme. Monetization was encouraged by transmuting in-kind payments to monetary payments, and the use of silk declined while the use of silver in ingots (sycee) expanded, particularly in the twelfth century.

But the innovation for which the Song are best known is the introduction of paper money. The use of paper money began in the tenth century in Sichuan province as receipts issued by merchants for coins that they held on deposit, perhaps to reduce the costs of interregional payments that had to be made in heavy, and often uneven, bronze (in Sichuan, iron) coins. The state took over the issue of paper and banned the issue of private notes in 1024. The Song issues (and those of the southern Song, at least in the period 1171–1240) circulated concurrently with "cash" and depreciated only mildly.

The conquering Mongols (1276–1367) banned the use of Song paper, and redeemed it at a 50:1 ratio. They mandated the use of their own paper money, which was convertible into silver, until the early fourteenth century. Von Glahn suggests that, under the Song, paper money supplemented "cash," the primary money. In contrast, under the Yuan (Mongols), paper was the primary money, supplemented by bronze. In part, this reflected the fact that, the Song paper money was restricted to relatively high denominations, whereas the Yuan issued both large and small denominations. In the 1350s, the dying days of Mongol rule in China, the printing presses were used to finance deficits, and hyperinflation ensued.

In 1375, the Ming emperors (1360–1644) prohibited the use of gold and silver coins and returned to the issue of paper money. Unlike the earlier issues, this money depreciated steadily from the beginning of the fifteenth century, and issue ceased in 1428. In part the depreciation is attributed to extensive counterfeiting, which met with less severe punishment than that handed out by the Mongols. After this, the monetary system comprised the bronze "cash" and silver ingots (debatably called a regime of parallel bimetallism). Silver became more prominent, both in response to increased supplies—from the New World (see below)—and in response to government decisions to make payments and accept receipts in silver. The unit of account was a tael (about forty grams) of silver. Williams states that under the Ming 90 percent of government salaries were paid in silver.

The Qing (1644–1911) continued the policies of the Ming. The currency revolved around bronze coins issued by the state and silver ingots (sycee). (There was a small and brief issue of paper money, in 1651–1661). The silver ingots were privately produced, and each silversmith put his mark on the ingot to commit to its weight and fineness. South America was the source of much of the silver, and in coastal regions silver dollars circulated although in the interior they were more likely to be melted down into ingots before circulating.

The Western Monetary System. From the sixth century to the first century BCE, the Greek city-states issued silver coins in standardized denominations, of which the tetradrachm (approximately twelve grams) was the most popular. The use of coin expanded across society, reflecting both demand (the growing commercialization of the society) and supply (the access to silver mines). Coins were inscribed with the city's name or emblem, which was expected to stand as a guarantee of the quality of the coinage and to deter counterfeiting. In addition to the relatively high-value silver coins, the Greeks also struck bronze coins in lower denominations.

Roman coinage developed from that of Greece. Early Rome used bronze ingots as money, but in 212 BCE a monetary reform introduced the bronze as and the silver denarius, weighing approximately four grams and valued at ten asses (raised to a value of sixteen asses in 140 BCE). Literary evidence, including that drawn from the Bible, suggests that the use of coinage became commonplace in Roman society, and in the societies that Rome conquered. This coinage, like that of Greece, was issued in the name of the city, and supervised by the magistrates of the Roman republic. However, after the transition from republic to empire, the emperor himself issued the coinage. The major change in the monetary system was the introduction, and soon dominance, of a gold coinage, with the aureus valued at twenty-five denarii. Williams reports that during the third and fourth centuries CE, "hundreds of millions of coins were struck," with the majority of the value being in gold aureii.

The quality of the coinage did not survive the empire. By 260 CE the fineness of the silver coin had fallen to below 10 percent, the bronze coinage had ceased, and even the gold coinage was issued in debased metal. In the late third century, Aurelius guaranteed the content of the silver coin to be at least 5 percent silver and Diocletian responded by allowing a flexible exchange rate between the gold and silver coinages, with the result that gold traded essentially as bullion. Shortly before the empire was divided into western and eastern components at the end of the fourth century, Constantine introduced a gold solidus (4.5 grams of pure gold) that became the major coin of the Byzantine Empire. In Britain, Spufford suggests that no coin circulated between 435 CE and the mid-sixth century, when local issues of silver pennies began.

Although European coinage was limited over the next several centuries, Islamic coinage expanded, drawing on both Greek and Roman/Byzantine traditions. The principal coins were the gold dinar, which evolved from the solidus, and the silver dirham, which evolved from the Greek drachma. The relative value and the scarcity of the coins varied with the extent of the empires and the bounty of the mines. Gold came predominantly and steadily from Africa, but silver was more erratic in supply (essentially no silver was coined in the century to 1171 CE) and came both from trade and domestic mines.

From the eighth century to the twelfth century, European money systems were based on the penny, a silver coin weighing from one to two grams, depending on the issuer. In 799, Charlemagne consolidated the coinage of pennies in the Holy Roman Empire, requiring that all pennies be minted from dies that he produced and be of approximately 1.7 grams of virtually pure silver. The coins were hammered; that is, they were made by hammering this metal flat into a roughly circular disk, then putting the disk onto a lower die, on which the obverse impression was raised, and then putting the other die on the disk, hammering in the impression.

Although the penny (denier, denarius) was the only coin produced in Europe until the twelfth century, a unit of account developed that called a dozen pennies a sol (shilling, solidus, and so on) based upon the Greco-Roman system of counting with a base of twelve and the Gallic-Celtic system of counting with a base of twenty (e.g., *quatre-vingts* = 80). Thus a contract might state that two pounds four shillings had to be paid, but the payment would in fact be made with 528 pennies.

Although the penny remained the sole type of coin in the West until the eleventh century, even the minimal uniformity introduced by Charlemagne soon disappeared. The dispersion of political power led to the dispersion of minting rights, so that mints that had produced for the emperor began producing on their own account. Ownership of the mint implied the ability to earn profits. In the first instance, the mint owner would buy, say, a pound (*livre*) of silver, and produce about 590 pennies with it, but would only pay say 580 pence for the metal. The difference would go toward the cost of minting (brassage) and the minter's own profit (seigniorage). Although Charlemagne seems to have had only a minimal profit goal, his successors were much more interested in generating seigniorage from the mint. They could do this by either paying less for a given weight of metal or making the metal into more pennies. The latter was the chosen route, and over the next few centuries, the weight and the fineness of the pennies declined, if at different paces at different mints.

The breakdown of the empire had been accompanied by dispersion of minting rights, whereas the gradual rise of state power led to the consolidation of these rights, and by the early thirteenth century the mint was under the control of the state in most of western Europe. At the same time, the inconvenience of using only pennies for trade became more noticeable as trade expanded. The increased commercial activity that began in the Italian cities in the eleventh century finally led to the introduction of higher-value coins. The first change was the introduction of large silver coins of high fineness—variously called the *gros*, the groat, *grossi*—and worth approximately thirty times as much as pennies. The introduction of these coins created a problem that would be amplified by the introduction of gold coins a century later, and which has become known as Gresham's law: bad money drives out good.

The monetary authorities gave the new coins ratings in terms of the unit of account, which was effectively in terms of the existing pennies/denarii. This created difficulties if the relative values of the new and old coins diverged. If one grosso was valued at thirty denarii, and the denarii began to lose silver content, the relative value of the grosso would rise to, say, thirty-two denarii. Then traders would no longer be indifferent to paying a contract in grosso (at thirty denarii) or denarii, but would pay in denarii (unless they were given a premium for payment in grossi). In any event, the authorities typically responded—with a lag—by raising the value of the grossi.

The introduction of the large silver coins did not resolve the need for a medium of exchange for large transactions, and in the mid-thirteenth century Florence began minting a gold coin (the florin, in 1254), an action quickly followed by Genoa (the genoin, in 1254) and Venice (the ducat, in 1284) and more slowly by other European mints. The Italian coins became the international currency for the next few centuries; and although the states reduced the weight and fineness (hence the value) of their silver coins, the gold coins remained stable.

In a monetary economy the price level depends on the relative supply and demand for money. As European economies monetized, the demand for silver and gold rose more rapidly than did their supply, thus tending to cause prices to fall. This tendency was offset in the fourteenth century by the impact of the Black Death, but economic and demographic recovery again began to put pressure on the supply of money.

In the mid-fifteenth century, new supplies of silver were found in Europe; but most of them were not readily accessible from the surface, and most were mixed with copper, a major problem that was soon resolved by two technological innovations: water-powered drainage pumps to permit deeper mine shafts and the Seiger process of smelting such ores with lead to liberate the silver. That in turn produced a veritable silver-mining boom in central Europe, from around 1460 to about 1530, increasing silver outputs more than fivefold. When that boom peaked, the Spanish were discovering and soon exploiting even greater supplies of silver in the Americas (Peru, Bolivia, and Mexico); but not until the 1560s did American imports match European production. The New World silver and gold were direct gains to Spain, but a combination of military expenditures and balance-of-payments flows quickly dispersed the bullion not only across Europe but also to Asia. In Europe the result, from both sources of the new silver, was a steady, generally sixfold increase in nominal prices from the early sixteenth century to the mid-seventeenth century, an era known as the Price Revolution (ca. 1520–ca. 1640).

The increase in supplies of precious metals was one significant monetary change in this early-modern era; a

COINAGE. Scene from a stained-glass window depicting a stage in the process of minting, Konstanz, Germany, circa 1624. (Constance Rosgartenmuseum, Konstanz, Germany)

second was an improvement in coining methods. The technology of hammering coins remained largely unchanged from the earliest days of coinage until the seventeenth century. The result was that coins made on disks were not perfectly round, and often were made with imperfectly placed dies. Such commonplace irregularities promoted and facilitated the common crime of clipping—that is, cutting bits of metal from the coin's edge, without distorting its appearance, and then melting down and selling the clipped silver as bullion. Although today this may seem rather petty, historically it often disrupted the monetary system. An (admittedly extreme) example of the scale of clipping is the state of the hammered coinage in England in 1695: Lowndes estimated that these coins on average weighed half their "official" weight. Of course, the average reflected the fact that the full-weight coins were more likely to have been used for foreign trade than those that were clipped—a result predicted by Gresham's law.

The key minting innovation was the use of screw presses to manufacture the coins, both to roll out the flans and to stamp the dies. The result was a far more uniform coin, which contemporaries stated was almost never seen to be clipped. In both France and England, milling was introduced in the mid-seventeenth century. In France the hammered coinage was recalled (demonetized) when the new coinage was introduced; but in England it was not, a situation that led there to the recoinage of 1696 (i.e., the occasion of Lowndes's inquiry).

The millennium lasting to 1750 was the age of coin in Europe, and paper money was very much in an experimental (and a not very successful) phase. Credit for the first issue of paper money is usually given to John Palmstruch,

who founded the Stockholm Bank in 1656. Sweden used not gold or silver for its coinage but copper, partly to increase the demand for and therefore the price of its large domestic supply of copper. This was a particularly inconvenient coinage, so much so that it promoted initiatives to reduce the need to transport and trade in copper coin. In 1661, the Stockholm Bank received the right to issue notes, which were convertible into coin, but whose widespread use reduced the need for payments to be made in coin. The bank operated as a fractional reserve bank; that is, it kept a reserve for redeeming notes while lending out the rest of the money on deposit. However, by 1667, the Stockholm Bank had "overlent" and thus became bankrupt.

The Bank of England (established in 1694) and the Bank of Scotland (1695) began issuing notes in the late-seventeenth century. As in Sweden, the notes were convertible into coin on demand, and the banks kept a reserve to meet redemption demand and lent out the remainder of the funds; and the notes were for relatively large denominations. Again, like the Stockholm Bank, the Bank of England had considerable government involvement; that is, the government allowed the bank to operate if it received a share of the profits (directly or indirectly).

The paper money issues of John Law are the best-known French experiments. In 1719 he established the Banque Generale, which was authorized to issue notes. All was well until, during that same year, Law merged the bank with his Mississippi Company and the Compagnie des Indes. Shares in the merged company could be bought with *billets d'état* (small-denomination government bonds). Although the playing-card currency issued in New France in

1685 was probably the first paper currency issued in North America, it was quickly redeemed and was a relatively transient experiment. Paper currency issues in the British North American colonies began in 1690 when Massachusetts issued circulating bills of credit. The notes were made legal tender, and their value was supported by the promise to receive them in taxes. Between 1690 and 1776, all thirteen colonies experimented with paper money. Some issued notes backed by mortgage loans, and others notes backed by taxes. Although possibly beneficial on the fiscal side, the experience was a mixed success with respect to inflation; some colonies issued limited amounts of notes, which then circulated at parity with the silver coinage (e.g., Pennsylvania), whereas others issued increasing numbers of notes (e.g., Rhode Island), typically to finance wartime expenditures, which generated a premium on the silver coinage.

A Final Comment. The history of most monetary systems derives from Chinese or Western traditions, or a meld of both, but these two traditions evolved separately and in very different ways. In China, the unit of account and the predominant coins, were bronze; for much of Western history, coins of gold and silver dominated. In China, silver supplemented the bronze coinage as a means of payment, but in the form of privately produced ingots that traded as bullion, that is, at market prices. Paper money was widely used in China in the twelfth to fourteenth centuries CE, but then fell into disuse as inflation and counterfeiting created serious disruptions to the system. In contrast, the use of paper money emerged much later in the West, beginning only in the eighteenth century. The reasons for these differences in monetary forms have not been explored. Was it happenstance? Was it a result of very different political institutions, or perhaps differences in the structure of the economy? The answers will shed light on the nature of money and its role in the economy.

BIBLIOGRAPHY

Davies, Glyn. *A History of Money from Ancient Times to the Present Day.* Cardiff, 1994.

Grierson, Philip. *Origins of Money.* London, 1977.

Williams, Jonathan, ed. *Money: A History.* New York, 1997.

WORKS ON CHINA

Chen, Chaunan, Pin-Tsun Chang, and Shikuan Chen. "The Sung and Ming Paper Monies: Currency Competition and Currency Bubbles." *Journal of Macroeconomics* 17.2 (1995), 273–288.

Xinwei, Peng. *A Monetary History of China.* Translated by E. H. Kaplan. Bellingham, Wash., 1994.

Von Glahn, R. *Fountain of Fortune: Money and Monetary Policy in China, 1000–1700.* Los Angeles, 1996.

WORKS ON EUROPE

Bloch, Marc. *Esquisse d'une histoire monetaire de l'Europe.* Paris, 1954.

Cipolla, Carlo. *Money, Prices and Civilization in the Mediterranean World.* Princeton, 1956.

Spufford, Peter. *Money and Its Use in Medieval Europe.* Cambridge, 1988.

Wee, Herman van der. "Monetary, Credit and Banking Systems." In *Cambridge Economic History of Europe*, vol. 5, edited by E. E. Rich and C. Wilson. Cambridge, 1977.

ANGELA REDISH

Money and Coinage after 1750

The striking aspect of money and coinage after 1750 is how money divorced itself from coinage. Today, coinage represents a small percentage of the monetary base (central bank liabilities). Coins are today pure tokens whose physical composition and method of production are irrelevant to their nature and value: they are just like notes, but printed on metal instead of paper. At the start of the period, however, coins were not only a quantitatively dominant part of money (three-quarters of the monetary base worldwide as late as 1913), they defined money. This article will sketch the broad outlines of that process.

Coinage. Differences and changes in coinage can be seen in four areas: structure of denominations, technology changes, development of token value, and establishment of standards.

Denominations. Around 1750, the structure of coinage was essentially the same as it was in the Middle Ages throughout most of Europe and its colonies. It had three components. The first comprised gold coins. The medieval florins, sequins, and ducats of Italy (3.5 grams) had been replaced in the mid-seventeenth century by larger coins such as the Spanish pistole or double escudo (6.7 grams), the French Louis (6.7 and later 7.6 grams), and the English guinea (8.4 grams). These coins, worth several weeks' wages in the eighteenth century, were used for large transactions. The second component consisted of silver coins. The mainstay in most countries was a large silver coin of around 25 grams (variously called thaler, *écu, real de ocho,* and crown) and its subdivisions. Such a coin would pay several days' wages. The last component comprised the small change. It was made of copper, either pure or alloyed with silver (it is then called billon), and the coins were the penny, kreutzer, maravedi, and their multiples.

This structure, in its material aspect (metals used and size of coins), remained essentially intact until the early twentieth century, the only notable change being the replacement of copper with bronze or nickel in the nineteenth century. The changes that took place were in the relation between this material structure, on one hand, and the economic and legal role played by its components, on the other. These changes were effected by an alteration in monetary policy, that is, in the way governments produced and treated coinage. This alteration, in turn, was predicated on technological changes.

Technology. The major technological change in coin production was the adaptation of the steam engine to the minting press as a source of power by Matthew Boulton in the 1790s. Boulton adapted the steam engine to drive a traditional screw press. The German Dietrich Uhlhorn adopted a radically different approach and designed in 1817 a system to convert the rotating movement coming from the engine into a precise up-down movement of the die striking the coin. Uhlhorn's machine, or a variant developed in France by Pierre-Antoine Thonnelier, quickly became the dominant minting press. The late eighteenth century also saw engineers in France (Jean-Pierre Droz and Paul Gengembre) make improvements to die manufacturing, engraving the edges of coins, and automated handling of coins. By 1850, mints were producing coins as good in quality as those of today, although not as efficiently. The late-twentieth-century's innovations were mainly in finding ways of using cheaper metals while still deterring counterfeiting.

The upshot of these technological improvements was to make government-produced coins harder to sweat and clip, and also harder to counterfeit, at least without substantial and conspicuous investment. This made the government an effective monopolist in the provision of monetary objects.

Token coinage. Traditionally, small coins had formed the basis of the accounting system. Large coins were rated in terms of small coins, either by the market or by the authorities, and the rates fluctuated over time. Units of account, in terms of which prices and contracts were denominated, could be based on large or small coins. In most cases, the basic unit was based on small coins; for example, the pound represented 240 pennies (between 800 and 1971).

Increasingly, governments saw it as their role to assign and maintain stable values of larger coins in terms of smaller coins, and to provide a monetary system in which large and small coins represented fixed fractions or multiples of a single unit of value. This concept of monetary policy stood in sharp contrast to the hitherto discretionary exercise of the sovereign's power to define the content of coins and alter it at will.

To reach this goal, governments turned smaller denominations into tokens whose value did not depend on their intrinsic content, but was derived either from their artificial scarcity (the government minting them on its own account) or their convertibility into larger coins. This was possible because, having become a monopolist in the provision of coinage, the government could fix the price or the quantity.

Standards. The result of this process was to transfer the basis of the accounting system from the small coin (now a token) to the silver coin, the gold coin, or both. Depending on which coin became the new basis, countries ended up on a silver standard, a gold standard, or a bimetallic standard. As of 1820, only Britain, producing 5 percent of world output, was on the gold standard. Many countries still used a unit defined by a fixed quantity of silver, which had been the monetary metal par excellence since the Middle Ages. Gold was not used for monetary purposes in some countries (e.g., China and India). When it was used, the value of gold coins in terms of the silver coinage was either free or fixed at an official price.

The choice of a standard can, at first sight, be reduced to the choice of a numeraire in standard price theory. One good (silver or gold) is chosen so that its price is normalized to 1. All other prices in the economy are expressed in ounces or grams of that good. In such a view, bimetallism is an attempt to use two goods concurrently as numeraire, something the government cannot achieve unless it is somehow able to fix the relative price of the two goods. If that relative price is determined by existing supplies and the technology to increase them, it is beyond the government's control. In practice, bimetallism must collapse to a gold or a silver standard, depending on which metal is cheaper.

Another view distinguishes a metal in its monetary uses and its nonmonetary uses as distinct goods. The prices of a metal in the two uses are tied together by melting and free minting. But the price of metal in nonmonetary use relative to other goods depends on the quantity in that use, not the total quantity. Shifting metal from one use to the other changes that price, so that a wide range of relative prices between gold and silver is achievable for given quantities of the metals. If a significant group of countries settles on some official price of gold in terms of silver coinage, quantities will adjust from one use to the other so that the relative price matches the official price. This appears to be the case in the first half of the nineteenth century, when France maintained a 15.5 ratio (a silver franc contained 15.5 times as much metal as a gold franc), and the world price of gold in terms of silver remained remarkably close to that number. Even this view concedes that the range of possible prices is constrained by the relative availability of the two metals.

Starting in 1850, gold discoveries in California and improvements in extraction techniques changed this availability. The continued viability of bimetallism became a subject of debate, and for the rest of the century monetary affairs were dominated by the "battle of the standards," decisively won by gold in 1873 when the United States, Germany, France, and others abandoned the free coinage of silver. By 1913, over 80 percent of world output was produced in countries on the gold standard, a fact that reflects both the increasing economic dominance of countries on a gold standard and the progressive adoption of the gold standard by other countries.

The implementation of the gold standard, as far as coinage was concerned, consisted of making silver coins into convertible tokens. As the world price of silver dropped in 1873, when reduced demand for monetary silver made nonmonetary silver suddenly abundant, the intrinsic value of the silver coinage in formerly bimetallic countries fell, making them instantaneously token. All that remained was for the central banks and treasuries to adopt a more or less official policy of exchanging the silver coinage for gold on demand. This development had taken place in Great Britain in the 1830s, and the practice was adopted in the United States, Great Britain, and France in the 1880s. The structure of coinage had thus evolved from the medieval triad of gold, silver, and billon, into a gold coin surrounded by subsidiary coins of silver and bronze.

From Commodity to Fiat Money. Fiat money is money that is neither intrinsically valuable nor a claim to anything intrinsically valuable. In theory, the distinction is to some extent arbitrary. If an object fulfills a monetary purpose, it has by the very fact additional value above and beyond its intrinsic content. Indeed, monopoly producers of coinage (e.g., sovereigns) were able to appropriate that value by charging a seigniorage fee for the service of turning metal into money. The relative importance of intrinsic content as a component of the total value of the monetary object, and therefore the degree to which that object is fiat money, can vary considerably.

Chronology. Our period can be divided by the watershed of 1914. Before then, experiments with fiat (mainly unbacked paper) currency are more the exception than the rule; the reverse holds after.

The possibility that money could be made of base materials had been recognized and exploited before, for example, in Ming China. In western Europe, early examples were siege monies, arising when the authorities in a besieged town, cut off from their sources of funds, issued tokens to pay the troops with a promise of redemption if the siege was lifted. The card money of 1690s colonial Quebec is a variant, as may have been the paper monies issued by the colonies of New England. After the seventeenth century, however, the scale changes from that of a besieged town to that of a warring (or bankrupt) nation.

A spectacular experiment was carried out in France from 1718 to 1720 by the Scotsman John Law, a gambler, projector, and economic theorist who won the confidence of French authorities. His scheme involved a note-issuing bank and a privileged trading company, which jointly took over most of the state's fiscal activities and converted the national debt into a mixture of unbacked notes (which completely replaced metallic currency) and overvalued shares. Law's scheme failed, but the eighteenth century saw more experiments. Sweden, having pioneered the use of banknotes in the 1660s, was on an unbacked banknote standard from 1745 to 1776, and Russia's state-issued currency was inconvertible from 1786. Various paper currencies were in use in the British colonies of America, and the

American Continental Congress financed the Revolutionary War with an ill-fated paper continental from 1775 to 1781. The long and very costly European war that lasted from 1792 to 1815 saw belligerents turn to fiat money for extended periods of time. In 1790, the French issued a currency, the assignat, initially backed by nationalized land holdings. The exigencies of war caused the currency soon to exceed its official backing, and it ended in hyperinflation in 1796. When metal flowed back to France to resume its monetary role, the Bank of England suffered drains on its reserves of gold and was forced to suspend the convertibility of its notes in 1797. The suspension was temporary, but the needs of war finance extended it until 1819. Its possible consequences on prices were the subject of a famous debate called the "Bullion Controversy." Other belligerents, such as Austria and Russia, also relied on paper money to a large extent. By the time peace returned to Europe, most countries had direct experience with paper money.

The French and British episodes starkly illustrated the possible outcomes of an unbacked currency: whereas the assignats became worthless in a few years, the notes of the Bank of England were ultimately redeemed in gold at face value. The British experiment defined the gold standard as a "contingent rule," in the phrase of Bordo and Kydland. Paper money circulates alongside metal and remains convertible into metal at a fixed rate. In times of emergency, the government suspends convertibility but implicitly promises to redeem the notes, then expands issue and finance deficits. Once the emergency is over, the government makes good on its promise, if it can. (The notes issued by the Confederate States of America were explicitly contingent on the ratification of a peace treaty with the United States of America.) The nineteenth century witnessed repeated occurrences of such temporary suspensions: in 1848, when a wave of revolutions swept through Europe, state banks in France and Italy suspended the convertibility of their notes. Serious distrust for this discretion remained: the terms of the monetary union of Vienna of 1857, between the sundry German states and Austria, prohibited members from issuing inconvertible legal tender currencies.

Countries were more or less adept at redeeming their notes: Austria worked assiduously toward a resumption of convertibility, only to have this goal postponed by yet another war (1800, 1848, 1859, 1866). A distinction has been made between core countries more closely adhering to the gold standard, except for rare and well-defined emergencies, and periphery countries (southern and eastern Europe, Latin America), which were more likely to suspend convertibility for extended periods of time for a broader set of reasons.

When war broke out in 1914, belligerents, but also some neutral countries, followed what was by then standard procedure and went off the gold standard, that is,

COINAGE. Coins rolling off the quarter press at the United States Mint, Philadelphia, Pennsylvania. (Courtesy of the United States Treasury Department)

suspended (explicitly or practically) the full convertibility of their central banks' liabilities. The costs of the war proved unprecedented, and the return to convertibility at prewar parity was rarely achieved: the United Kingdom did so in 1925; the United States had never completely abandoned the standard, although it had restricted gold export from 1917 to 1919. The defeated countries did not achieve full resumption, and even some of the victors, such as France, returned to convertibility at less than the prewar parity.

The interwar period saw efforts, both individual and collective, at building an international system of currencies ultimately convertible into gold or into other currencies convertible into gold. The "gold exchange standard" was established by 1927, just in time for the Great Depression to force the same countries to suspend or reduce convertibility, starting with the United Kingdom in 1931. After World War II, another gold exchange standard was formally established at a conference in Bretton Woods in 1944. In this system, the U.S. dollar was convertible into gold for non-U.S. residents, and other central banks acted in foreign exchange markets to keep their own currencies close to a fixed (but potentially adjustable) parity. The full implementation (from the full return of western European currencies to convertibility) lasted only thirteen years, from 1958 until President Nixon ended the convertibility of the U.S. dollar into gold in 1971.

Since 1971, no currency is explicitly tied to the price of a commodity, or to anything that economists might see as determined by fundamentals (technology and preferences). Instead, a variety of regimes prevails. At one extreme, some currencies are tied to other currencies, by formal arrangements such as currency boards in which the domestic monetary base is fully backed by foreign exchange, or by a conventional peg. The distinction is akin to that between 100 percent reserve and fractional reserve banking. Examples of currency boards include Hong Kong from 1983, Argentina from 1991 to 2001, Estonia from 1992, Lithuania from 1994, Bulgaria and Bosnia from 1997, and a few Caribbean islands. Examples of conventional pegs since Bretton Woods include the European monetary system from 1977 to 1999. At the other extreme, currencies are tied to nothing at all. That is the case in particular of the major world currencies: the U.S. dollar, the Japanese yen, and the European euro. There is an assortment of exchange rates ("dirty floats," "crawling pegs") between these two extremes.

Whether or not currencies are formally tied to an external anchor, and how the conduct of monetary policy ultimately relies on government discretion, because any promise made or any rule announced can and has been ignored or altered, if the government has an incentive to do so. Governments with strong incentives to use large-scale fiat money creation end up erasing the value their currency has above its intrinsic content. In the case of paper money, they drive the price level to something close to infinity. Hyperinflations multiplied in the twentieth century. War-ravaged nations after the two world wars provided two series of examples, the most notorious being Germany's inflation of 1922–1923, the most spectacular being Hungary's inflation of 1946. Latin American and African countries in the 1970s and 1980s and formerly Communist countries in the 1990s also experienced severe hyperinflation.

This historical sketch brings out three major themes: the causal role of war finance in the emergence of fiat money, the instrumental role of central banks and the changes they underwent as a result, and the growing understanding of the money supply as a policy instrument. All three themes in turn play up the increasingly forceful role of governments in monetary matters.

War finance. As the preceding discussion makes clear, the development of paper money was driven in large part by the exigencies of war finance. Siege money had illustrated the ability of fiat money to provide emergency funding, carrying with it lessons (enunciated as early as the thirteenth century) about the value of a credible promise. In the nineteenth century, war finance was the allowable contingency under which the gold standard could be suspended by "orthodox" governments. In the twentieth century, war finance receded in importance, even if it was World War I that destroyed the gold standard and produced the first great hyperinflations. In recent years, countries at peace have also proven capable of generating substantial inflation. As government spending has grown considerably, wars have ceased to be the main source of major fiscal shocks.

Central banks. Central banks generally started as private corporations engaged in the common business of banking, which involved the issue of convertible notes. What made them distinctive was a privileged relationship with the state, instituted for the benefit of the state as well as that of the bank's shareholders. The central bank might serve as the state's bank and handle its monies. More importantly, it was assigned some role in helping the state borrow, either by lending directly or by marketing the state's bonds. The attraction of a central bank for the state was its ability to monetize debt, that is, quickly and cheaply to marshal resources for the state in times of need. Of course, the issue of unconvertible currency for fiscal reasons did not require a central bank; the United States issued the so-called "greenback" between 1861 and 1865 without one.

Over the course of the nineteenth century, central banks became increasingly defined by their holding either a complete monopoly on or a considerable advantage in note issue. Examples include the Netherlands Bank in 1814, the Austrian National Bank in 1816, the Bank of England in 1844, and the Bank of France in 1848, and the German Imperial Bank in 1875. They were frequently given a preeminent position in their countries' banking sectors in other respects, and other roles accrued to them over the course of time. One was as linchpin in the payments system. Another was as a regulator of liquidity in times of exchange rate, financial, or commercial crisis. The Federal Reserve System in the United States was in fact created in 1913 to fulfill these roles. Because the central banks were able quickly to issue notes that were widely accepted, and because they could be freed from the obligation to maintain convertibility by government fiat, the role of lender of last resort naturally devolved to them. In such instances, they were called upon to lend to the private sector rather than to the public sector.

Monetary Policy. Monetary policy changed considerably over this period. In the days of multiple denominations, monetary policy reduced to the choice by government of two parameters for each denomination: the metal content of the coin and the purchase price of the metal. Implementation of the gold standard made the choice moot for all but the gold coin, for which the two parameters became one (when seigniorage is zero or close to it, the purchase price is the inverse of the coin content). The sole remaining parameter was therefore the gold content of the coin or currency (7.32 grams per pound sterling, 1.50 grams per U.S. dollar, 0.29 grams per French franc, 0.32 grams per German mark, etc.).

True, the growing role of central banks gave them additional responsibilities. In terms of monetary policy, however, the main concern was to maintain the stability of a system in which the price level was fundamentally connected to the relative value of gold. The banks took actions to facilitate the mechanics of that connection, and they did not see their discounting and lending activities as obstacles or diversions from it.

World War I effectively severed that connection, although it took several decades for governments to abandon their attempts at maintaining a semblance of it. In the course of the war, governments generated a large number of implicit promises, and redeeming them required raising enough resources through taxation. But dissatisfaction with the operation of the gold standard had been brewing for some time, and it surfaced in the works of Knut Wicksell, Alfred Marshall, and Irving Fisher. Monetary policy used to be about the best way to tie the currency to an external anchor. But the movements induced by the anchor itself (inflations and deflations caused by the uneven rate of gold extraction relative to world growth) led policymakers to think that they could do better. Fisher, who considered price stability to be the ultimate goal, proposed frequently varying the parameter (the gold content of the dollar) to offset variations in the relative price of gold. He later proposed to anchor the dollar to a quantity of paper, and to manage that quantity so as to achieve price stability.

Why does price stability, or more generally, the path of prices, matter? The traditional concern was partly one of equity (the redistributive effects of price variations on pre-existing nominal contracts) and partly one of efficiency (the dislocation of economic activity created by uncertainty in prices). As it became clearer that money had effects on real economic activity, the notion that such effects could be exploited rather than avoided gained prominence, particularly in the aftermath of the Great Depression and the relative success of countries that abandoned the gold standard early on. An exploitable trade-off between inflation and unemployment became a cornerstone of policy. The existence of the trade-off remains embedded in much economic thinking, even if misgivings have grown over the extent to which it can be exploited.

It took seventy-seven years from the first shots of World War I to the closure of the American gold window, which suggests a pronounced reluctance on the part of policy-makers to completely forgo the discipline of the gold standard. Countries that do not or cannot rely on another currency (via some exchange rate regime) to peg the value of their own currency have had to reconcile the potentially conflicting aims of price stability and output stabilization, and in so doing to rely only on their own management of the currency. The proper balance of rules and discretion in that management remains an open question.

[*See also* Bretton Woods System; Exchange Rates; Gold Standard; Monetary Standards; *and* War Finance.]

BIBLIOGRAPHY

Bordo, Michael D. *The Gold Standard and Related Regimes: Collected Essays.* Cambridge, 1999.

Cooper, Denis R. *The Art and Craft of Coinmaking: A History of Minting Technology.* London, 1988.

Eichengreen, Barry. *Golden Fetters.* New York, 1992.

Redish, Angela. *Bimetallism: An Economic and Historical Analysis.* Cambridge, 2000.

Sargent, Thomas J., and François R. Velde. *The Big Problem of Small Change.* Princeton, 2001.

FRANÇOIS R. VELDE

MONEY-CHANGING [*This entry contains two subentries, on money changing in the ancient world and early Middle Ages and from the Middle Ages to the present.*]

Ancient World and Early Middle Ages

To study currency exchange in antiquity, it is important to distinguish between the quite different roles assigned to money-changers in the monetary systems of the Greek and Roman worlds. The Greek period was characterized by a large number of mints, each producing a distinct type of coin. These mints adopted regional weight standards at the outset (the alloy used seems to have been more or less similar). In contrast, during the Roman period, the Republic and then the Empire succeeded in imposing a homogenization of weights and later in making the entire monetary system uniform; thus the money-changer's role and function was substantially different.

Money-changers' functions in the ancient world are difficult to separate from those of lenders and bankers. This conflation of roles may go back to archaic societies that lacked currency; for example, during the early Babylonian period, temples (or the royal palace or wealthy private individuals) made loans in kind or in precious metals; lending and exchanging money for metals or goods were thus part of a single operation. In the same period, in second-millenium Egypt, the development of commerce produced a class of people who both lent and exchanged money. While we have a fair amount of documentation regarding bankers, information about currency exchange is scarce.

Money-Changing in Ancient Greece. In the Greek world, the development of monetary systems based on several different weight standards made it necessary to develop systems for exchanging coinage: each city-state (or nation-state) allowed only its own currency in its territory.

Here again, exchange was one aspect of a banker's function. The way Greek money-changers operated and their economic importance remains largely unknown. However, the homogeneity of the treasuries, both in continental Greece and in the colonies, suggests that exchange, melting down, and reminting coins were highly important activities in that they had to do with the economic identity of the city-state. Monetary diversity was rapidly understood as an obstacle to the economic development of hegemonic cities. Between the fifth and the second centuries BCE, the accounts of city-states were generally kept in a single accounting unit in order to get beyond the diversity of types and standards. The contributions of Athens's allies, presented and stored in a variety of currencies, were accounted for in terms of Athenian coinage. Finally, probably around 449 or 446 BCE, Athens imposed the Athenian standard and weights on its allies by decree.

Owing to the diversity of standards and coins, the Greek cities needed a large number of money-changers. Between 343 and 333 BCE, Olbia adopted commercial rules, imposing a fixed exchange rate within the city. Such customs and rules as these presupposed a system of currency exchange. The Greek cities imposed the fixed rate of their own coinages, but the storehouses of the city-states and temples kept the various types of coins without melting them down (this was the case of the stores in Delos). Surviving texts (for example Plutarch, *Lysander,* 16), and treasuries show that some coins (like those of Athens) circulated everywhere and that accounts were kept in Athenian currency (because of the decree). In the Roman period, the Greek cities, which had maintained the diversity of their mints, continued to need a large number of money-changers. Currency exchange was thus at the heart of the economic life of cities, but we have very little information about it.

Money-Changing in the Roman Empire. The Roman Empire was characterized both by a powerful inclination to centralize and by a homogenization of monetary practices. Rome imposed its monetary system and standards on conquered peoples and on allies. Accounts relating to money-changers are very rare in Rome. While a number of texts describe the activity of lenders and bankers, the exchange of money is known only through a single literary allusion (Seneca, *Apocolocyntosis* 9, 63). Despite this paucity of references, a number of elements, such as inscriptions, a few graffiti, and allusions in private texts, allow us to conceive of the importance of the role of the *kollubistikai trapezai* (in the east) and of the *nummularii* (in the west). In Italy, during the second century BCE, the trade of *nummularius* began to be clearly distinguishable from that of *argentarius*. The *nummularius* specialized in operations having to do with money itself, while the *argentarius* worked with account books.

The expansion of Rome's territory brought with it an increased need for currency exchange. Banks and money-changers were widespread throughout Roman Egypt, as in the rest of the Empire. Such money-handlers as the *publicani* (tax collectors), who funneled sums from Rome to local governors and who were in charge of transfers of money toward Rome as well as of mints, used money-changers, but we can say nothing specific about the latters' role.

The penury of texts and documents is a result of the homogeneous monetary system set up by the Roman Empire. Currency exchange took place only at borders between monetary zones. The scarcity of Latin lapidary inscriptions is explained by the fact that the *nummularii* in the west chiefly exchanged divisionary coins (like Augustus's grandfather; see Suetonius, *Augustus*, 4, 4), whereas the traditional monetary diversity of the Eastern world required the presence of a very large number of money-changers. The Latin term (*permutatio*) that we find in Cicero alludes more to a transfer of funds than to an exchange operation. Currency exchange that might have been part of a transfer is not explicitly described.

The crisis of the third century swept away the money-handling professions. Money-changers must have survived the monetary crisis and continued to exchange the weak new currencies while the *argentarii* disappeared (there is no further mention of them in Rome after 260). Bankers disappeared throughout the Empire. Under Lucius Aurelian (c. 215–275), the Romans' revolt is said to have been led by monetary officials, but we do not know whether the latter were employees of the treasury or money-changers unhappy with Aurelian's reforms or both. At all events, an allusion from the *Histoire Auguste* (38) demonstrates the importance of the money-related trades.

The efforts that were undertaken at the end of the third century by Aurelian and pursued by Diocletian (r. 284–305) and Constantine (r. 306–337) to reconstruct the monetary system led to the establishment of a monetary system integrating the former eastern and western parts of the Empire. The system was based on a gold coin (the solidus) whose weight, established by Constantine, did not change for several centuries, whereas the weight and alloys of silver and bronze coins varied frequently.

The monetary and fiscal system adopted the solidus as a base unit for assessments of value, debts, and taxes. Money-changers thus converted divisionary currencies into gold and vice versa. The conversion might involve the divisionary coinages themselves, or even conversions of wheat or silver metal. In many cases, landowners were charged with collecting taxes from their peasant farmers. Recourse to a money-changer was thus not a necessity. This system of *autopragia* is mentioned in the Theodosian Code (*Codex Theodosianus*) as early as 366; it allowed villages or landowners to organize the collection of taxes on their own lands.

The fourth century saw the appearance of *collectarii* (*zygostates* in Greek), charged with buying and selling solidi. A law of 23 April 363 (*Codex Theodosianus* XII 7.2), instituted the function of *collectarius* in each city: this official's charge included verifying the weights and alloys of coins presented by the populace. The gaps between the official sale or purchase prices levied by the *collectarii* on the one hand and commercial rates on the other were the source of Symmachus's complaint (Symmachus, *Relationes* 29).

Thus the role of money-changers evolved during the Late Empire: the homogenization of the monetary system throughout the Empire had made exchanges among the various zones unnecessary. The predominance of gold in the economic system had increased the money-changers' economic importance, since taxes henceforth had to be paid in gold. In the fifth century, a "money-changers' guild" existed in Rome (*Codex Theodosianus* XVI 4.5).

The fifth-century invasions that broke the Empire into several blocs brought an end to its political unity. The establishment of new political entities led to the production of new coinages, often in gold, but of varying types, weights, and alloys. Was the role of money-changers modified during the sixth century? If we consider the lasting homogeneity of the monetary stock in the various states and the importance of the coinages produced in mints along the frontiers, we have to acknowledge that foreign currencies must have been exchanged and melted down. Here again, we have no literary testimony whatsoever. The economic role of currency exchange is thus not very well known. Its importance seems to be somewhat limited, except during the Late Empire.

The Church Fathers mentioned money-changers on a number of occasions, especially in comparisons: the good Christian ought to be pure as good money. A soul, like a coin, could be weighed (St. John Chrysostom, *In principium actorum*, 4), its sound could be heard (*Palladii dialogus de vita s. Joannis Chrysostomi*, 4), and Saint Augustine compared the weighing of souls to that of coins (*Sermon* 330, 3). Christians ought to act like money-changers: they should take all that is true gold and reject all that is false (Cyril of Jerusalem, *Catechetical Lectures*, 6.36). If we compare the pure soul of the Christian to the pure gold of coins, the role of the money-changer becomes determining. Many texts compare falsified money to the soul of the heretic.

By extension, the Fathers compared the *nummularii* to Christians who spread the Gospel (for example, Gregory the Great, *Homiliae in Evangelia*, 9.14). However, money-changers who made speculative investments were criticized (Basil, *Regulae brevius tractatae*, 254). It is true that their behavior resembled that of usurers.

We have access to a small number of archaeological objects related to the money-changer's trade: some ivory money-bag labels bearing a proper name and the term *nummularius*. We also have quite a number of scales or assay balances destined to verify the weight of a single coin (most often, the silver denarius or the Late Empire solidus). Monetary weights corresponding principally to the solidus were common.

[*See also* Fairs, *subentry on* European Fairs; Pawnbroking and Personal Loan Markets; *and* Usury.]

BIBLIOGRAPHY

Andreau, Jean. *Banking and Business in the Roman World*. Translated by Janet Lloyd. Cambridge, 1999.

Bogaert, Raymond. "Changeurs et banquiers chez les pères de l'église." *Ancient Society* 4 (1973), 269–270.

Bogaert, Raymond. "Les Kollubistikai Trapezai dans l'Égypte gréco-romaine." *Anagennesis: A Papyrological Journal* 3.1 (1983), 21–64.

Depeyrot, Georges. *Histoire de la monnaie, des origines au 18ᵉ siècle*. 3 vols. Wetteren, Belgium, 1995–1996.

Lewis, David Malcolm. "The Athenian Coinage Decree." In *Coinage and Administration in the Athenian and Persian Empires: The Ninth Oxford Symposium on Coinage and Monetary History*, edited by Ian Carradice, pp 53–63. Oxford, 1987.

Mattingly, Harold. "The Athenian Coinage Decree." *Historia* 10 (1961), 148–188.

Thompson, Wesley E. "A View of Athenian Banking." *Museum Helveticum* 36 (1979), 224–241.

Vera, Domenico. "I *nummularii* di Roma e la politica monetaria nel IV secolo d.c. (per una interpretazione du Simmaco, *Relatio* 29)." *Atti della accademia delle scienze di Torino* 108 (1974), 201–250.

Vera, Domenico. *Commento storico alle Relationes di Quinto Aurelio Simmaco : Introduzione, commento, testo, traduzione, appendice sul libro X, 1–2, indici*, pp. 220–232. Pisa, Italy, 1981.

GEORGES DEPEYROT
Translated from French by Catherine Porter

Middle Ages to the Present

Few rulers in the medieval and modern periods sought to restrict the circulation of coinage in their realm to the products of their own mint, and even fewer succeeded. The outstanding exception was England, where from the thirteenth through the sixteenth centuries the Royal Exchanger took all foreign specie to the mint to be transformed into English coins. The Calais Staple and then London goldsmiths eventually took over this function, but England remained an area of unified monetary circulation. In the rest of Europe, and in its colonies of the modern period, a wide variety of coinage circulated legally, and buyers frequently had to have their own coins exchanged to those required by the seller, usually in the domestic coinage, silver or gold. This could be done at the state mint or, more commonly, with private money-changers.

Mints were operated by governmental authorities (though in the Middle Ages these could be ecclesiastic and even monastic), whose interest in coins derived chiefly from the amount of seigniorage (profit) that they could derive from their manufacture. To encourage the delivery of bullion to their mints, and occasionally to benefit the working of their local markets and the activities of their merchants and manufacturers, rulers sometimes enacted minting policies that encouraged individuals to bring foreign, outdated, counterfeit, and underweight coins to the mint for exchange. In the interest of providing ample and sound currency to their realms, governments at times eschewed their own seigniorage and, extraordinarily, even subsidized the labor costs of minting (brassage) by returning coined gold or silver on a weight-for-weight basis to those who brought designated coinages to their mint.

For the most part, however, money-changing was in the hands of private individuals working in local marketplaces, sometimes licensed by the state or controlled by autonomous guilds. Changers often acted as an intermediary between merchants and mint, offering newly minted coins in the marketplace in exchange for an agio fee. Changers frequently engaged in other financial activities, chiefly moneylending, pawnbroking, deposit banking, and paper transfer of credit; they also often operated mints on a contractual basis. Since these activities tended to leave fuller documentation than money-changing and were tied in with more evolved economic activities, they have received more extensive attention in the literature. They are dealt with in other articles in this encyclopedia; here we will

MONEY CHANGING. *The Money Changer,* painting by Marco dell' Avogadro from *Codex Sphaere,* fifteenth century. (Biblioteca Estense, Modena, Italy/Scala/Art Resource, NY)

examine the actual process of the changing of one coin for another, commonly called manual exchange.

Exchange could operate vertically, between various coins of the same minting authority, or horizontally, between coins of different minting regimes. Coinages in the later medieval and modern period generally fell into three categories—gold, white (more than half silver), and black (billon or copper)—and vertical exchange rates even among coins of the same mint issued in the same period often varied with market conditions. Exchange could also involve furnishing coins in return for precious metal in the form of bullion, ingots, or plate, although most medieval principalities forbade commerce in bullion, requiring that such metal be sold to the mint. Exchange rates among coinages reflected to some extent the relationship of the value of their constituent metals; in particular, relative values of gold and white coinages moved in response to changes in the bimetallic ratio. Black coins usually had a high level of surplus value over their intrinsic worth (to account for the higher cost of the copper and labor in minting them), and their value depended as much on the expectation of future exchange back to gold or silver coinage as

on their intrinsic metallic contents, though a suspected debasement was almost a guarantee of a loss in value even for such quasi-fiduciary coinages. Supply and demand also played a part in coin values, fueled by the arbitrage practiced by merchants and travelers who sought to profit from reported discrepancies in the relative prices of metals or demand for particular coins in different markets.

The first requirement for the money-changer was to identify the coins offered to him in exchange for ones in his stock. Medieval and modern coins usually could be identified from their legends (inscriptions) and types (imagery) at least in terms of their mint and general period of issuance. In the case of coins that had undergone mutations of standard, such as a series of debasements, small details in the punctuation of the legends or types (privy marks) could be key to distinguishing issues with different intrinsic and hence market values. Minters sometimes struck and distributed nonmonetary versions of new issues in base metal for reference by potential users (*pieforts*); and after the introduction of printing, illustrated tariffs from official or private sources were helpful in identifying issues. Black money was often too small or too poorly struck to allow ready identification, but such coinages seldom traveled far from their mint, so changers would be able to recognize from experience most with which they came into contact.

An important skill in money-changing was the recognition of counterfeits. Comparison with struck samples, either *pieforts* or actual coins of known authenticity, was the best basis for identifying coins of forgers' mints or imitative coins from other state mints. Many medieval and modern coins were struck from dies manufactured with punches containing individual letters or elements of the image; though a coin issue might use hundreds of individual dies, these would all have been made from the same set of official punches, whose identification would be diagnostic in the recognition of counterfeits. Nevertheless, in various periods counterfeits could makeup a significant part, and even the majority, of the coinage in circulation, and their recognition could save the money-changer not only loss of profit but also of capital. In many instances, money-changers were charged by the state with eliminating counterfeits from circulation, often by cutting or marking them so they could not circulate or by bringing them to the mint.

The determination of the intrinsic value of a coin, the fineness and weight of the metals in it, was an important corollary to the recognition of the issue on the basis of appearance. Coin lists in medieval merchant manuals and printed tariffs often supplied information on the fineness to be expected in certain coinages. But since so much of the value of coins depended on their intrinsic value, it was incumbent on the money-changer to verify the quality of individual coins encountered. The fineness of gold alloys could be determined relatively easily and fairly precisely with a touchstone. In this procedure, the edge of the coin was rubbed against a slate, and the resulting mark was compared for color against a set of needles of graduated fineness of gold alloys. The graduation could be as tight as one-eighth of a carat (of which twenty-four designated pure gold), so that in theory distinctions in alloy could be as precise as 0.52 percent. Silver alloys could not be tested with the touchstone; the only practical way to determine the fineness of a silver coin was to melt it down, separate the elements using the cupellation process, and weigh the remaining silver. This was obviously not possible in the case of small numbers of coins, but such an assay was sometimes done in the case of an unfamiliar issue of suspected standard; the findings from the sacrificed samples would be applied to other coins of identical appearance. In the case of most silver-based coins, white and black, the fineness could be inferred only on the basis of the recognition of examples as genuine and the inference of their alloy on the basis of ordinances, coin lists, and tariffs.

The determination of weight was much more straightforward. Until the milling of coin edges became standard in the eighteenth century, even coins of a known standard were weighed to guard against the shearing of metal from their edges, that is, by clipping. Coins could be weighed in mass with a balance either by counting the number of examples in a given weight (*al marco*) or by weighing a specific number (*al pezzo*). Coins could also be weighed individually using a balance beam (*trebuchet*) or steelyard set to rise if the specimen was lighter than the allowed tolerance (*remède*) and fall if it was heavier. Individual brass weights marked with the image and value of major trade coins were in the tool kits of most money-changers of the early modern era.

Once a coin was identified in terms of issue, authenticity, alloy, and weight, it was up to the money-changer to decide how many coins of another issue to give for it or how much of a commission to charge for changing it into a standard coinage or a credit voucher in a money of account. This would of course depend to a great extent on competition among money-changers and the potential for the money-changer to use the new coin in arbitrage exchanges for added profit. Before the era of daily listings in newspapers, information on the relative values of metals and specific coins was transmitted through private letters, especially those of the factors of the major international banks and merchant companies. The actual fee charged for manual exchange was sometimes set by the state and was seldom more than one or two percent of the value of the coins involved.

[*See also* Fairs, *subentry on* European Fairs; Gresham's Law; Pawnbroking and Personal Loan Markets; *and* Usury.]

BIBLIOGRAPHY

There are no comprehensive studies on money changing in the medieval and modern period or monographs on such activity in a particular time or place. Most works that treat the topic do so in the context of the extension of the activities of money changers into the banking functions of taking of deposits, offering of credit, and writing and redeeming instruments of exchange. The following books are among the most useful in discerning the actual process of the manual exchange of coins.

Braudel, Fernand. *Civilization and Capitalism, 15th–18th Century*, vol. 2, *The Wheels of Commerce*. Translated by Siân Reynolds. New York, 1982. Originally published as *Civilisation matérielle, économie et capitalisme: XVᵉ-XVIIIᵉ siècle*, vol. 2, *Les jeux de l'échange*. Paris, 1979. The best overall view of the role of coinages of various types in the economy of the early modern world.

The Dawn of Modern Banking. New Haven, 1979. Selected papers delivered at a conference held at UCLA 23–25 Sept. 1977. See especially the introductory essay by Robert S. Lopez (pp. 1–23), and those on Lucca by Thomas W. Blomquist (pp. 53–75) and the Islamic world by Abraham L. Udovich (pp. 255–73).

De la Roncière, Charles. *Un changeur florentin du Trecento: Lippo di Fede del Sega (1285 env.–1363 env.)*. Paris, 1973. The best study of a single money-changer, though more in terms of his banking activities than actual money-changing.

De Roover, Raymond. *Money, Banking, and Credit in Mediaeval Bruges*. Cambridge, Mass., 1948. Gives much information on the social and economic background of money-changers, as well as their exchange and banking activities.

De Roover, Raymond. *The Rise and Decline of the Medici Bank, 1397–1494*. Cambridge, Mass., 1963.

Grierson, Philip. *Numismatics*. Oxford, 1975.

Grierson, Philip. *Later Medieval Numismatics (11th–16th Centuries): Selected Studies*. London, 1979.

Lane, Frederic C., and Mueller, Reinhold C. *Money and Banking in Medieval and Renaissance Venice*, vol. 1, *Coins and Moneys of Account*. Baltimore, 1985.

Mueller, Reinhold C. *Money and Banking in Medieval and Renaissance Venice*, vol. 2, *The Venetian Money Market; Banks, Panics, and the Public Debt, 1200–1500*. Baltimore, 1997. Treats far more than specifically the Venetian case.

Spufford, Peter. *Handbook of Medieval Exchange*. London, 1986. Tabular listings of the values of later medieval European coinages, preceded by an ample introduction.

Spufford, Peter. *Money and Its Use in Medieval Europe*. Cambridge, 1988.

ALAN M. STAHL

MONGOLIA. *See* Central Asia.